Now in its Secon

*The Complete Guide*

# CALIFORNIA HIKING

## 1995-96 Edition

## by Tom Stienstra &
## Michael Hodgson

ISBN 0-935701-93-1

Foghorn
Press
BOOKS BUILDING COMMUNITY™

*The Complete Guide*

# CALIFORNIA HIKING

## by Tom Stienstra & Michael Hodgson

## 1995-96 Edition

Foghorn Press

BOOKS BUILDING COMMUNITY™

# CREDITS

Managing Editor—*Ann-Marie Brown*

Editors—*Howard Rabinowitz, Julianne Boyajian*

Research Editors—*Robyn Schlueter, Debi Cordes*

Maps—*Michele Thomas*

Graphics—*Kirk McInroy*

Cover Photo—*All-Stock Photo*

Tom and Michael have shared many hikes and much information in the course of doing this book. Ultimately, Tom was responsible for the San Francisco Bay Area and Northern California (chapters A to E, except for D4 and E4), and Michael was responsible for Lake Tahoe, Yosemite and Southern California (chapters F to J, and D4 and E4).

Foghorn Press is committed to preservation of the environment. All Foghorn Press outdoors titles are printed on the California standard for recycled paper, which is 50% recycled paper and 10% post-consumer waste.

Dear Hikers,

We're pleased to present to you the completely revised and updated second edition of *California Hiking,* a compendium of 1,000 hikes around the glorious Golden State, exhaustively researched by Tom Stienstra and Michael Hodgson. If you're new to hiking in California, we hope this guide gives you the impetus to set off on the trail. Experienced hikers should find dozens of challenging and little-known trails off the beaten path.

While our information is as current as possible, changes to fees, facilities, roads and trails sometimes are made after we go to press. Earthquakes, fires, rainstorms and other natural phenomena can radically change the condition of hiking trails and wilderness areas. Please be certain to call the agencies listed under "who to contact" for each trail for updated information.

Please remember to exercise caution in the outdoors. While many of the hikes in this book are easy strolls on developed park lands, others are difficult treks that require crossing potentially rapid and turbulent streams, scrambling off-trail, navigating steep mountain ridges, climbing on boulders and in caves, and other activities that require no small amount of wilderness expertise. No one should undertake any of the hikes described in this book without recognizing and personally assuming the associated risks. While our difficulty ratings may serve as a general guide, you alone are responsible for determining your own level of fitness and ability to partake in the hikes described in these pages.

We welcome your comments and suggestions about *California Hiking.* Please mail in the enclosed postcard or write to us at: Foghorn Press, 555 DeHaro Street #220, San Francisco, CA 94107.

Like you, we love the outdoors. Please enjoy and protect it.

*Ann-Marie Brown*
*Managing Editor*

# TABLE OF CONTENTS

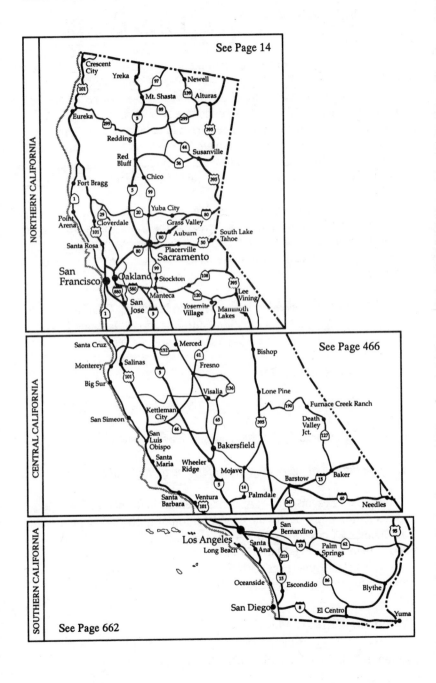

NORTHERN CALIFORNIA

See Page 14

Crescent City
Yreka
97
Newell
Mt. Shasta
199
Alturas
101
89
Eureka
299
5
299
395
Redding
44
Susanville
Red Bluff
36
395
Chico
Fort Bragg
5
99
1
Yuba City
80
29
20
Point Arena
Cloverdale
Grass Valley
80
Auburn
50
South Lake Tahoe
Santa Rosa
80
Placerville
101
Sacramento
99
San Francisco
Oakland
Stockton
108
395
880
580
Manteca
120
Lee Vining
San Jose
5
Yosemite Village
Mammoth Lakes
1

CENTRAL CALIFORNIA

See Page 466

Santa Cruz
Merced
152
Bishop
Monterey
Salinas
41
Fresno
101
5
Big Sur
Visalia
136
Lone Pine
San Simeon
Kettleman City
65
190
Furnace Creek Ranch
46
395
Death Valley Jct.
127
San Luis Obispo
Bakersfield
Santa Maria
Wheeler Ridge
Mojave
Barstow
15
Baker
5
14
San Simeon
Santa Barbara
Ventura
Palmdale
247
40
Needles
101

SOUTHERN CALIFORNIA

San Bernardino
95
Los Angeles
Santa Ana
62
10
Palm Springs
Long Beach
215
Oceanside
15
Escondido
86
Blythe
San Diego
8
El Centro
Yuma
See Page 662

# HOW TO USE THIS BOOK

You can search for the perfect hike in two ways:

1) If you know the name of the trail you'd like to hike, or the name of the surrounding geographical area (town name, national or state forest name, national or state park name, lake or river name, etc.), use the index beginning on page 812 to locate it, and turn to the corresponding page. If you are looking for a specific trail name, you'll find that all trails are listed in the index in capital letters.

2) If you'd like to hike in a particular part of the state and want to find out what trails are available there, use the California state map on page 12 or in the back of this book. Find the map area you'd like to hike in (such as E1 for the San Francisco Bay Area or H3 for Santa Barbara), then turn to the corresponding pages in the book.

This book is conveniently divided into Northern, Central and Southern California sections. Within these sections, the book is divided further into map areas to allow for greater detail.

Northern California, pages 13-464 (maps AØ-E5)

Central California, pages 465-660 (maps F1-H8)

Southern California, pages 661-811 (maps I2-J8)

•*See the bottom of every page for reference to corresponding maps.*

The San Francisco Bay Area has been divided even further into four smaller maps, due to the concentration of trails in that area. All of Chapter E1 covers the Bay Area (pages 258-393), but look for separate maps for the Marin County area (pages 258-303), the San Francisco Peninsula (pages 304-327), the East Bay (pages 328-357) and the South Bay (pages 358-393).

## What the Ratings Mean

Every hiking trail in this book is designated with an overall rating of 1 through 10, and a difficulty rating of 1 through 5.

## OVERALL RATING

🏔1 🏔2 🏔3 🏔4 🏔5 🏔6 🏔7 🏔8 🏔9 🏔10

Poor ............................................... Fair ...................................... Great

## DIFFICULTY RATING

👢1 👢2 👢3 👢4 👢5

A Stroll ..................................... Moderate ......................... A Butt-Kicker!

The overall rating is based largely on scenic beauty, but also takes into account factors such as how crowded the trail is and whether or not the noise of nearby civilization intrudes on the hike.

The difficulty rating is based on the steepness of the trail and the level of backcountry skills required to traverse it. A flat, open trail that is clearly marked would be rated a #1 boot, while a cross-country scramble with huge elevation gains would be rated a #5 boot.

## Hiking the Pacific Crest Trail, the John Muir Trail and the Tahoe Rim Trail

This book is actually two books in one. Not only does it provide you with 1,000 individual out-and-back or loop hikes, but it also details the entire Pacific Crest Trail in California—all 1,700 miles of it, from the Mexico border to Oregon. The 211-mile John Muir Trail, which overlaps with the Pacific Crest Trail, is also described, as is the 70-mile Tahoe Rim Trail. These hikes are split into sections throughout the book and are organized according to where their major trailheads are located. They can be easily identified on the maps and in the chapters as they are referred to by their initials—PCT, JMT and TRT. The JMT is broken into four sections in this book and can be found in chapters E4 and F5. The TRT is found completely in chapter D4.

The PCT is broken into 48 sections in this book and can be found in chapters A1, B1, B2, B3, C3, D3, D4, E4, F5, G5, H4, H5, I5, I6 and J6. As the PCT is usually hiked from south to north, you will find the last section, PCT-48, in chapter A1 and the first section, PCT-1, in chapter J6. In each chapter that the PCT appears, the segments are grouped together at the end of the chapter, so you can plan to hike individual segments or, if you're very ambitious, the entire length of the state.

## About Trail Names, Distances and Times

Each trail in this book has been given a number, a name and a listing for mileage and approximate time required. The trail's number allows you to find it easily on the chapter map. The trail name is either the actual name of the trail (listed on signposts and maps) or is a name the authors have given to a series of connected trails or a loop trail they suggest. In these cases, the trail name is the name of the major destination or focal point of the trail. All mileages and approximate times are for round-trip travel, unless specifically noted as one-way. In the case of one-way hikes, a car shuttle is advised.

## Note to Wheelchair Users

For each trail, we have designated a list of "user groups," and under this designation, we have tried to list as much information about wheelchair facilities and access as possible. You will note that we alternately use the words "wheelchair facilities" and "wheelchair access," and that often a trail will be designated as "partially wheelchair accessible." As everyone's definition of wheelchair accessible or wheelchair facilities seems to vary, please call ahead to the agency listed under "who to contact" for the trail to make sure that your particular needs will be met.

## About Maps

For every trail in *California Hiking,* we provide you with map names for USGS (United States Geologic Survey) topographic maps. Please note that you cannot order USGS topographic maps from the Forest Service; these maps can only be obtained from USGS. To order maps or to request a California Catalog of Topographic and Other Published Maps, write to:

Western Distribution Branch
U.S. Geologic Survey
Box 25286, Federal Center
Denver, CO 80225

Each map listed is a 7.5-minute size map. Maps costs $2.50 each. For orders of less than $10, the USGS charges a $1 handling fee.

A private company called Map Link also carries a complete selection of USGS topographic maps for California. While the maps cost a bit more than ordering them directly, Map Link provides a good option if the USGS is out of stock. To reach Map Link, phone (805) 965-4402 or write to: Map Link, 25 East Mason Street, Santa Barbara, CA 93101.

Many major sporting goods stores also carry USGS maps, but the selection is often limited to a relatively narrow geographic area.

# INTRODUCTION

Many of our friends were horror-stricken when they first heard we were writing this book. After all, wouldn't it mean that all their secret, favorite trails would be revealed to all? Well, it turns out that now our friends are elated instead. Like so many people, they are discovering it is difficult to imagine how many wondrous hikes are available in the state of California.

With that in mind, we hope *California Hiking 1995-96* will quickly become your hiking bible, a guide to California's 1,000 best hikes, including hundreds of little-known spots in all regions of the state.

It features 350 hikes within 90 minutes driving time of both San Francisco and Los Angeles, along with an additional 650 sprinkled across the state, including California's most remote areas. The hikes detail the most beautiful regions across 20 million acres of national forest, 18.5 million acres of land managed by the Bureau of Land Management, 100 state parks, 53 federal wilderness areas, 12 national parks, and dozens of regional and county parks.

The book also features a hiker-friendly format and easy-to-use map grid system. It assures that any reader will be able to find the location of a quality hike in virtually any area in less than 10 seconds. Each listing includes snapshot ratings for trail beauty and difficulty, as well as the estimated length and time required for each walk. In addition, precise, easy-to-follow directions to each trailhead are provided, along with any special trail rules, information about permits, maps and phone contacts, and a detailed description of each hike. There are 60 detailed maps and a 30-page index for cross-referencing.

We've included a wide variety of hikes, ranging from as short as 10-minute walks to lookouts and waterfalls, to week-long trips into remote wildlands. We've also included every section of the Pacific Crest Trail in California, covering more than 1,700 trail miles. Many of the featured hikes range in length from one to three hours, perfect for most people looking for an afternoon of peace.

The outdoors is good for the soul, and hiking can cleanse the body and mind. Our best advice is to go for it—and don't be surprised if we see you on the trail.

*—Tom Stienstra & Michael Hodgson*

# Chapter Reference Map



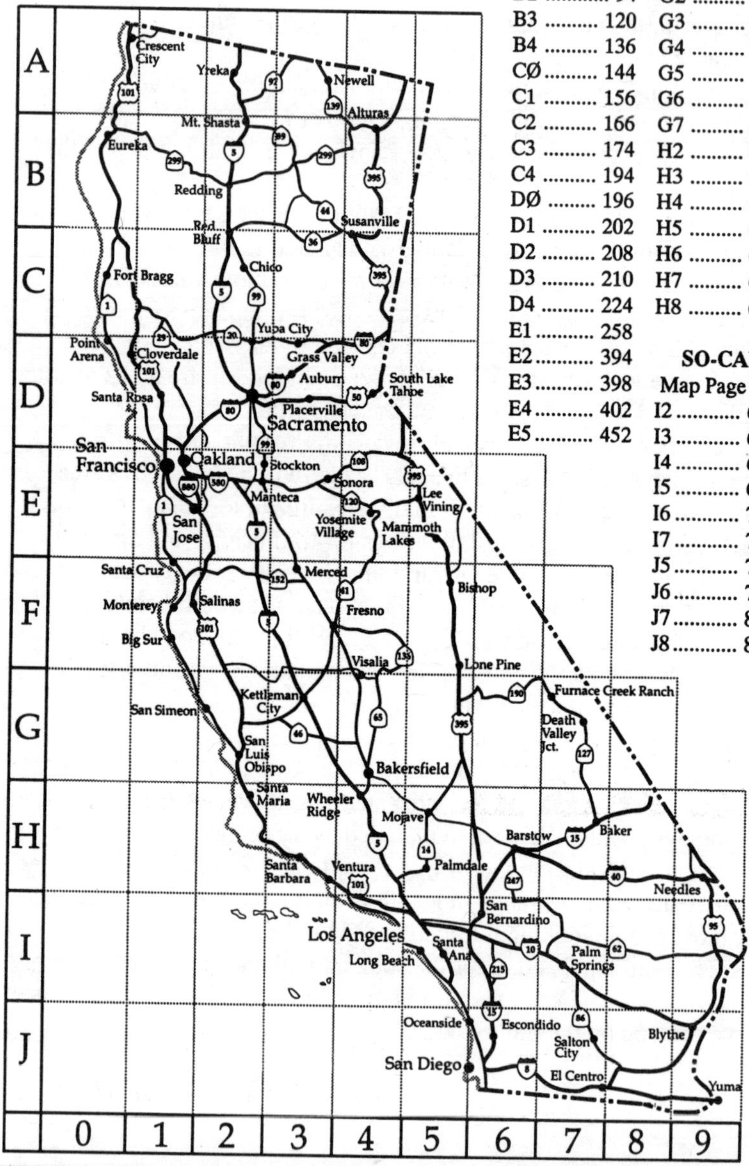

# NORTHERN AREA HIKING TRAILS

### OVERALL RATING

1 2 3 4 5 6 7 8 9 10

Poor...................................................Fair.................................................Great

### DIFFICULTY RATING

1 2 3 4 5

A Stroll........................................Moderate.........................A Butt-Kicker!

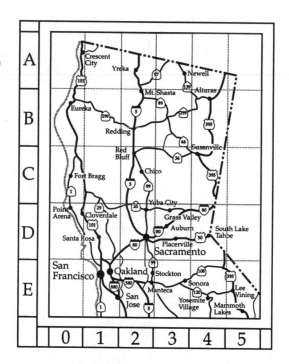

**Map AØ** ....................................... (20 trails)
Featuring: Del Norte County coast, Smith River National Recreation Area, Jedediah Smith Redwoods State Park, Del Norte Redwoods State Park, Redwood National Park, Prairie Creek Redwoods State Park.

**Map A1** .............. (3 PCT sections, 22 trails)
Featuring: Smith River National Recreation Area, Siskiyou Wilderness, Marble Mountain Wilderness, Russian Wilderness, Etna Summit, Seiad Valley, Rogue Wilderness, Klamath National Forest, Siskiyou Mountains.

**Map A2** ........................................ (5 trails)
Featuring: Klamath River, Klamath National Forest, Yreka.

**Map A3** ........................................ (9 trails)
Featuring: Lava Beds National Monument, Klamath Wildlife Refuge, Modoc National Forest, Medicine Lake.

**Map A4** ........................................ (3 trails)
Featuring: Modoc National Forest, Goose Lake.

**Map BØ** ...................................... (14 trails)
Featuring: Patrick's Point State Park, Eureka, Trinidad Head, Samoa Peninsula, Humboldt Bay, Arcata Redwood Park, Humboldt Redwoods State Park, King Range National Conservation Area.

**Map B1** .............. (2 PCT sections, 19 trails)
Featuring: Six Rivers National Forest, Trinity Alps Wilderness, Russian Wilderness, Trinity Lake, Ruth Lake.

**Map B2** .............. (3 PCT sections, 31 trails)
Featuring: Shasta-Trinity National Forest, Mt. Shasta, Trinity Alps Wilderness, Lake Siskiyou, Castle Crags State Park, McCloud River, Shasta Lake, Redding, Whiskeytown Lake National Recreation Area, Shasta State Historic Park, Scott Mountain.

**Map B3** .............. (3 PCT sections, 19 trails)
Featuring: Modoc National Forest, McArthur-Burney Falls State Park, Lake Britton, Lassen National Forest, Thousand Lakes Wilderness, Lassen Volcanic National Park, Butte Lake, Caribou Wilderness.

**Map B4** ........................................ (8 trails)
Featuring: South Warner Wilderness, Blue Lake, Modoc National Forest.

**Map CØ** ...................................... (15 trails)
Featuring: Richardson Grove State Park, Benbow Lake State Recreation Area, Sinkyone Wilderness State Park, Fort Bragg, MacKerricher State Park, Russian Gulch State Park, Jackson State Forest, Van Damme State Park, Hendy Woods State Park, Cow Mountain Recreation Area.

**Map C1** ........................................ (14 trails)
Featuring: Yolla Bolly Wilderness, Snow Mountain Wilderness, Mendocino National Forest.

**Map C2** .......................................... (9 trails)
Featuring: Tehama Wildlife Area, Ishi Wilderness, Black Butte Reservoir, Chico.

**Map C3** .............. (6 PCT sections, 24 trails)
Featuring: Lassen Volcanic National Park, Lake Almanor, Lassen National Forest, Caribou Wilderness, Plumas National Forest, Lake Oroville, Tahoe National Forest, Plumas-Eureka State Park, Smith Lake, Silver Lake, Bucks Lake Wilderness, Sierra City, Packer Lake, Gold Lakes Basin, Sardine Lake, Fowler Creek, Little Grass Valley Reservoir, Humboldt Summit.

**Map C4** ........................................... (1 trail)
Featuring: Tahoe National Forest.

**Map DØ** ......................................... (8 trails)
Featuring: Mendocino coast, Manchester State Beach Park, Gualala Point Regional Park, Stillwater Cove Regional Park, Lake Sonoma, Salt Point State Park, Austin Creek State Recreation Area, Bodega Bay.

**Map D1** .......................................... (7 trails)
Featuring: Robert Louis Stevenson State Park, Lake Berryessa, Spring Lake Regional Park, Santa Rosa, Bothe-Napa State Park, Sugarloaf Ridge State Park, Jack London State Park.

**Map D2** ........................................... (1 trail)
Featuring: American River, Sacramento.

**Map D3** ................ (1 PCT section, 20 trails)
Featuring: Bullards Bar Reservoir, Tahoe National Forest, Emigrant Gap, Nevada City, Carr Lake, Donner, American River, Sugar Pine Reservoir, French Meadows Reservoir, Granite Chief Wilderness, Hell Hole Reservoir, Mokelumne Wilderness.

**Map D4** .............. (5 PCT sections, 42 trails)
Featuring: Donner Pass, Donner Summit, Donner Lake, Lake Tahoe, Granite Chief Wilderness, Alpine Meadows, Desolation Wilderness, Emerald Bay, D. L. Bliss State Park, Mokelumne Wilderness, Carson Pass, Echo Summit, Big Meadows, Dagget Pass, Spooner Summit, Brockway Summit, Ebbetts Pass, Carson Pass, Echo Lake.

**Map E1-Marin** ........................... (63 trails)
Featuring: Point Reyes National Seashore, Tomales Bay State Park, Samuel P. Taylor State Park, Alpine Lake Dam, Lagunitas Lake, Mt. Tamalpais State Park, Muir Woods National Monument, Stinson Beach, San Francisco Bay, Golden Gate Bridge, China Camp State Park, Angel Island State Park.

**Map E1-S. F. Peninsula** .............. (34 trails)
Featuring: San Francisco, Linda Mar Bay, San Pedro Beach, San Pedro County Park, McNee Ranch State Park, Coyote Point County Park, Crystal Springs Reservoir, Half Moon Bay, Purisima Creek Redwoods Open Space Preserve, Skyline Ridge, Huddart Park, Wunderlich Park, San Francisco Bay Wildlife Refuge.

**Map E1-East Bay** ........................ (44 trails)
Featuring: Napa River, Point Pinole, Wildcat Canyon Regional Park, Tilden Regional Park, Inspiration Point, Robert Sibley Volcanic Regional Preserve, San Pablo Reservoir, Carquinez Strait, Briones Regional Park, San Leandro Reservoir, Contra Loma Regional Park, Crown Memorial State Beach, Huckleberry Regional Preserve, Redwood Regional Park, Anthony Chabot Regional Park, Las Trampas Regional Wilderness, Mt. Diablo State Park, Morgan Territory Regional Park, Coyote Hills Regional Park, Pleasanton Ridge Regional Park, Dumbarton Bridge, San Francisco Bay National Wildlife Refuge, Alameda Creek, Mission Peak Regional Preserve, Sunol Regional Wilderness.

**Map E1-South Bay** ..................... (53 trails)
Featuring: Pigeon Point Lighthouse, Butano State Park, Portola State Park, Castle Rock State Park, Big Basin Redwoods State Park, Waddell Creek, Vasona Lake County Park, Lexington Reservoir, Año Nuevo State Reserve, Loch Lomond Park, Henry Cowell Redwoods State Park, Calero Reservoir County Park, Coyote-Hellyer County Park, Anderson Lake County Park, Henry Coe State Park, Coyote Lake County Park, Mt. Madonna County Park.

**Map E2** .......................................... (2 trails)
Featuring: Del Valle Regional Park, Del Valle Reservoir, Sunol Regional Park, Ohlone Regional Park, Livermore, Rose Peak, Mission Peak, Murietta Falls.

**Map E3** .......................................... (2 trails)
Featuring: Calaveras Big Trees State Park.

**Map E4** .... (3 PCT, 2 JMT sections, 60 trails)
Featuring: Stanislaus National Forest, Ebbetts Pass, Sonora Pass, Yosemite National Park, Tuolumne Meadows, Hetch Hetchy Reservoir.

**Map E5** .......................................... (20 trails)
Featuring: Toiyabe National Forest, Hoover Wilderness, Inyo National Forest, Ansel Adams Wilderness, Mono Lake Tufa State Reserve, Grant Lake, June Lake, Mammoth Lakes, John Muir Wilderness, Devil's Postpile National Monument.

# MAP A∅

20 TRAILS
PAGES 16-29

NOR-CAL MAP ....................... see page 14
adjoining maps
NORTH ............................... no map
EAST (A1) ............................ see page 30
SOUTH (B∅) ....................... see page 68
WEST ................................. no map

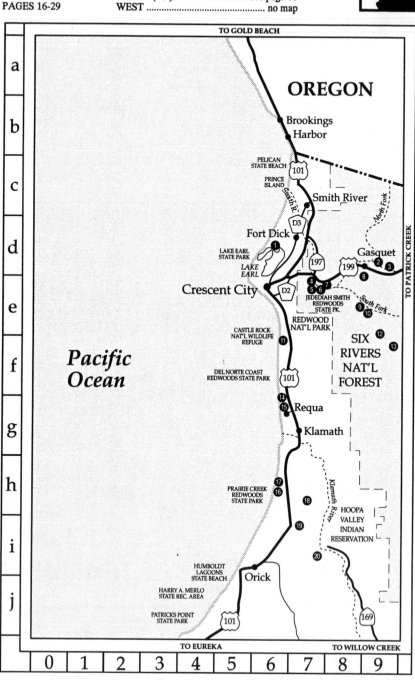

**Map AØ featuring:** Del Norte County coast, Crescent City, Smith River National Recreation Area, Jedediah Smith Redwoods State Park, Del Norte Redwoods State Park, Redwood National Park, Prairie Creek Redwoods State Park, Klamath

## 1. PELICAN BAY SAND DUNES    2.5 mi/1.0 hr

*Reference:* **On Del Norte County coast north of Crescent City; map AØ, grid d6.**

*User groups:* Hikers, dogs and horses. No wheelchair facilities.

*Permits:* No permits are required. Parking and access are free.

*Directions:* From Crescent City, drive nine miles north on US 101 and turn west on Lake Earl Drive (County Road D3). Drive 1.5 miles southwest, then turn west on Morehead Road and continue to Lower Lake Road. Turn right and drive a short distance north, then turn west on Kellogg Road and proceed to the parking lot at the end of the road.

*Maps:* For a free brochure and map, write to Del Norte County Parks at the address below. To obtain a topographic map of the area, ask for Crescent City and Smith River from the USGS.

*Who to contact:* Del Norte County Parks, 840 Ninth Street, Crescent City, CA 95531; (707) 464-7230.

*Trail notes:* The Pelican Bay Sand Dunes seem to sweep on forever, spanning more than 10 miles from the edge of Lake Earl on south along the Pacific Ocean, reaching nearly all the way to Crescent City. After parking and heading south on the beachfront, you can walk for five minutes or five hours—take your pick. Either way, you get a walk where you feel like a solitary speck among the enormous backdrop of untouched sand dunes and ocean. Only rarely will you see other people. The area is known by several names, including Fort Dick Beach, Kellogg Beach and Pelican Bay Sand Dunes, but by any name, it is a good place to escape. It is just wide-open beach for miles.

## 2. STONEY CREEK TRAIL    1.6 mi/0.75 hrs

*Reference:* **In Smith River National Recreation Area northeast of Crescent City; map AØ, grid d9.**

*User groups:* Hikers and dogs. No mountain bikes or horses are allowed. No wheelchair facilities.

*Permits:* No permits are required. Parking and access are free.

*Directions:* From Crescent City, drive north on US 101 for five miles, then turn east on US 199 and drive 17 miles to Gasquet. Turn left on Middle Fork/ Gasquet Road and travel about 100 feet, then turn right on North Bank Road and travel one mile. Turn right on Stoney Creek Road and continue a short distance to the trailhead.

*Maps:* For a free brochure and hiking guide, write to Smith River National Recreation Area at the address below. For a map of Six Rivers National Forest, send $3 to USDA-Forest Service, 630 Sansome Street, San Francisco, CA 94111. To obtain a topographic map of the area, ask for Shelly Creek Ridge from the USGS.

*Who to contact:* Smith River National Recreation Area, P.O. Box 228, Gasquet, CA 95543; (707) 457-3131.

*Trail notes:* This easy walk in an unblemished river setting will take you to the mouth of Stoney Creek, right where it pours into the North Fork Smith River. It's the kind of special place where you just sit and listen to the flow of moving water as it gurgles and pops its way over stones smoothed by years of river flows. The hike is easy, with a few ups and downs, as it follows a bluff adjacent to the North Fork Smith, a designated Wild and Scenic River, then is routed right out to the mouth of Stoney Creek. You're surrounded by woods and water.

---

# 3. ELK CAMP RIDGE TRAIL    19.0 mi/1.0 day

*Reference:* In Smith River National Recreation Area northeast of Crescent City; map AØ, grid d9.

*User groups:* Hikers, mountain bikes, dogs and horses. No wheelchair facilities.

*Permits:* No permits are required. Parking and access are free.

*Directions:* From Crescent City, drive north on US 101 for five miles, then turn east on US 199 and drive 17 miles to Gasquet. Turn left on Middle Fork/Gasquet Road and travel 100 feet, then bear right as the road forks. Continue one-half mile, then turn right on Old Gasquet Toll Road. Drive 2.3 miles, then turn left at the sign for the trailhead. Continue one mile to the trailhead. The last mile is very steep and rough.

*Maps:* For a free brochure and hiking guide, write to Smith River National Recreation Area at the address below. For a map of Six Rivers National Forest, send $3 to USDA-Forest Service, 630 Sansome Street, San Francisco, CA 94111. To obtain topographic maps of the area, ask for Gasquet, High Plateau Mountain and Shelly Creek Ridge from the USGS.

*Who to contact:* Smith River National Recreation Area, P.O. Box 228, Gasquet, CA 95543; (707) 457-3131.

*Trail notes:* This trail is like a walk through history. It was originally part of a pack trail between Crescent City and the gold mines in southern Oregon, and the memories of the old days can shadow your hike much of the way. The trailhead is at 1,200 feet, but the route climbs right up to the ridge, reaching over 3,000 feet. On the ridge, there are excellent views of surrounding peaks (Preston Peak is the big one) and the Smith River Canyon. You may also notice that much of the vegetation along the trail is stunted, a result of the high mineral content in serpentine rocks. The trail keeps climbing and ends at 3,400 feet.

*Special note:* Since most of the route traces a ridgeline, there are no suitable camping areas. Hence, most people do not try to reach the end of the trail.

---

# 4. STOUT GROVE TRAIL    0.5 mi/0.5 hr

*Reference:* In Jedediah Smith Redwoods State Park northeast of Crescent City; map AØ, grid e7.

*User groups:* Hikers only. No mountain bikes, dogs or horses are allowed. The trail is **wheelchair accessible**; for those who want closer vehicular access, phone the park at (707) 458-3310 to receive the key to the gate.

*Permits:* No permits are required. Parking and access are free.

*Directions:* From Crescent City, drive about five miles north on US 101, then turn east on US 199. Drive about 10 miles (past the formal entrance to Jedediah Smith Redwoods State Park) to Hiouchi. Just past Hiouchi, turn right on South Fork Road and cross two bridges. At a junction, turn right on Howland Hill Road and drive about two miles to a small parking area and signed trailhead.

**Maps:** For a free trail map, write to Jedediah Smith Redwoods State Park at the address below. To obtain a topographic map of the area, ask for Hiouchi from the USGS.

**Who to contact:** Write to Jedediah Smith Redwoods State Park at 1375 Elk Valley Road, Crescent City, CA 95531; (707) 458-3310, (707) 464-9533 or (707) 445-6547.

**Trail notes:** Visiting giant, old redwood trees can affect people for a long time. That is the attraction here, to see the Stout Tree, the largest redwood in Jedediah Smith State Park. It is so old that it can make your stay on Earth seem mighty brief. The trail is wide and level, a 20-minute walk that takes an easy course to the Stout Grove, and then on to the Stout Tree. Most people take longer than 20 minutes, of course, because they're not used to seeing anything this size, and they take their time absorbing the surroundings. The trail makes a great sidetrip for campers at Jedediah Smith State Park, yet it gets missed by many because it is not directly accessible from the campground.

## 5. BOY SCOUT TREE TRAIL    2.8 mi/2.0 hrs

**Reference:** In Jedediah Smith Redwoods State Park northeast of Crescent City; map AØ, grid e7.

**User groups:** Hikers only. No mountain bikes, dogs or horses are allowed. No wheelchair facilities.

**Permits:** No permits are required. Parking and access are free.

**Directions:** From Crescent City, drive about five miles north on US 101, then turn east on US 199. Drive about 10 miles (past the formal entrance to Jedediah Smith Redwoods State Park) to Hiouchi. Just past Hiouchi, turn right on South Fork Road, and cross two bridges. At a junction, turn right on Howland Hill Road and drive about five miles to a small parking area and signed trailhead on the right side of the road.

**Maps:** For a free trail map, write to Jedediah Smith Redwoods State Park at the address below. To obtain a topographic map of the area, ask for Hiouchi from the USGS.

**Who to contact:** Jedediah Smith Redwoods State Park, 1375 Elk Valley Road, Crescent City, CA 95531; (707) 458-3310, (707) 464-9533 or (707) 445-6547.

**Trail notes:** This is the kind of place where a nature lover can find religion—it is that beautiful. The trail is a soft dirt path, often sprinkled with redwood needles, that allows visitors to penetrate deep into an old-growth redwood forest, complete with a giant fern understory and high-limbed canopy. The centerpiece is the Boy Scout Tree, the largest tree in the forest here, but what you will remember the most is the pristine serenity of a forest of old redwoods. It is an easy hike—you just walk into the forest, then a few hours later, walk out. Those two hours in between can change how you feel about the world.

# 6. MILL CREEK TRAIL 4.5 mi/2.25 hrs

*Reference:* In Jedediah Smith Redwoods State Park northeast of Crescent City; map AØ, grid e7.

*User groups:* Hikers only. No mountain bikes, dogs or horses are allowed. No wheelchair facilities.

*Permits:* No permits are required. Parking and access are free.

*Directions:* From Crescent City, drive about five miles north on US 101, then turn east on US 199. Drive about 10 miles (past the formal entrance to Jedediah Smith Redwoods State Park) to Hiouchi. Just past Hiouchi, turn right on South Fork Road, and cross two bridges. At a junction, turn right on Howland Hill Road and drive about five miles to a small parking area and signed trailhead on the left side of the road.

*Maps:* For a free trail map, write to Jedediah Smith Redwoods State Park at the address below. To obtain a topographic map of the area, ask for Hiouchi from the USGS.

*Who to contact:* Jedediah Smith Redwoods State Park, 1375 Elk Valley Road, Crescent City, CA 95531; (707) 458-3310, (707) 464-9533 or (707) 445-6547.

*Trail notes:* Woods and water make a great mix for hikers and campers, and that is exactly what you get at Jedediah Smith State Park. This park is one of California's most popular, complete with giant redwoods, a campground and, of course, the Smith River, which cuts a path right through the center of it. This trail provides a taste of both big redwoods and big water. It is an easy walk, skirting the river bluff for much of the route, sometimes overlooking the river, other times taking a short cutout through the forest. Note that the trailhead for the Mill Creek Trail is not at the Jedediah Smith Park Campground, so you need not pay an entrance fee at the park kiosk in order to take this hike.

# 7. CRAIG'S CREEK TRAIL 7.4 mi/4.25 hrs

*Reference:* In Smith River National Recreation Area northeast of Crescent City; map AØ, grid e7.

*User groups:* Hikers, mountain bikes and dogs. No horses are allowed. No wheelchair facilities.

*Permits:* No permits are required. Parking and access are free.

*Directions:* From Crescent City, drive north on US 101 for five miles, then turn east on US 199 and drive 10 miles. Just past Hiouchi, turn right on South Fork Road and drive approximately one-third of a mile. Park in the boat launch facility area.

*Maps:* For a free brochure and hiking guide, write to Smith River National Recreation Area at the address below. For a map of Six Rivers National Forest, send $3 to USDA-Forest Service, 630 Sansome Street, San Francisco, CA 94111. To obtain a topographic map of the area, ask for Hiouchi from the USGS.

*Who to contact:* Smith River National Recreation Area, P.O. Box 228, Gasquet, CA 95543; (707) 457-3131.

*Trail notes:* An old miners' pack route, vintage 1800s style, has been converted into this hiking trail. It starts along the South Fork Smith River, then loops up the slopes of Craig's Creek Mountain, then back down to the river, ending where Craig's Creek enters the South Fork. In the process, it rises above the river and passes through forest, including old-growth redwoods and Douglas fir. Because of the contour of the mountain, the hike includes a good climb but then descends. The starting and ending elevations are the same, 200 feet. The climb keeps many visitors away, and most of the time you can have the entire trail to yourself. The South Fork Smith is very pretty here, a clear, free-flowing stream that drains a huge expanse of the Siskiyou Wilderness.

---

## 8. FRENCH HILL TRAIL          5.4 mi/3.25 hrs

*Reference:* In Smith River National Recreation Area northeast of Crescent City; map AØ, grid e8.

*User groups:* Hikers, mountain bikes, dogs and horses. No wheelchair facilities.

*Permits:* No permits are required. Parking and access are free.

*Directions:* From Crescent City, drive north on US 101 for five miles, then turn east and drive 17 miles to Gasquet. Park at the Gasquet Ranger Station. The trail is located directly across the highway.

*Maps:* For a free brochure and hiking guide, write to Smith River National Recreation Area at the address below. For a map of Six Rivers National Forest, send $3 to USDA-Forest Service, 630 Sansome Street, San Francisco, CA 94111. To obtain a topographic map of the area, ask for Gasquet from the USGS.

*Who to contact:* Smith River National Recreation Area, P.O. Box 228, Gasquet, CA 95543; (707) 457-3131.

*Trail notes:* This trail was created originally as a route to transport supplies to build the Camp Six fire lookout station. Well, the lookout has been retired, but they left a high-tech automatic rain gauge in its place. In 1983, this rain gauge documented the most rain ever recorded in the continental U.S. for one season, 257 inches. In the dry season (there really is one up here, believe it or not), the hike to this spot provides a 1,600-foot climb, from a trailhead elevation of 400 feet to the lookout summit of 2,000 feet. It passes through old-growth Douglas fir and sugar pines, a forest that has thrived on getting so much moisture.

---

## 9. McCLENDON FORD TRAIL          2.0 mi/1.5 hr

*Reference:* In Smith River National Recreation Area east of Crescent City; map AØ, grid e8.

*User groups:* Hikers and dogs. No mountain bikes or horses are allowed. No wheelchair facilities.

*Permits:* No permits are required. Parking and access are free.

*Directions:* From Crescent City, drive north on US 101 for five miles, then turn east on US 199 and drive 10 miles. Just past Hiouchi, turn right on South Fork Road and drive 14 miles, then turn right on an unsigned road junction. Travel three miles to a sign indicating the trailhead, then turn left and continue two miles.

*Maps:* For a free brochure and hiking guide, write to Smith River National Recreation Area at the address below. For a map of Six Rivers National Forest, send $3 to USDA-Forest Service, 630 Sansome Street, San Francisco, CA 94111. To obtain a topographic map of the area, ask for Ship

Mountain from the USGS.

**Who to contact:** Smith River National Recreation Area, P.O. Box 228, Gasquet, CA 95543; (707) 457-3131.

**Trail notes:** This is a perfect trail for a hot summer day, complete with a swimming hole. It is an easy hike through a large forest of Douglas fir. The trail crosses Horse Creek, a small tributary, and then is routed out to a pretty beach on the South Fork Smith River. Starting elevation is 1,000 feet, and ending elevation is 200 feet. Get the idea? Right, this trail follows an easy descent down to the river, and takes about 45 minutes to get there. The swimming hole on the river is secluded, out of the way of most vacationers, and most often you have the place completely to yourself. Note: This is also the trailhead for the South Kelsey Trail.

## 10. GUNBARREL TRAIL          2.4 mi/1.75 hrs

**Reference:** In Smith River National Recreation Area east of Crescent City; map AØ, grid e8.

**User groups:** Hikers and dogs. No mountain bikes or horses are allowed. No wheelchair facilities.

**Permits:** No permits are required. Parking and access are free.

**Directions:** From Crescent City, turn east on US 199 and drive 27 miles. Turn right on Little Jones Creek Road and drive south 9.6 miles. When the road forks, proceed straight ahead on Forest Service Road 16N02 and drive 4.8 miles, then turn left on Forest Service Road 16N18 and drive three miles. Bear left on Forest Service Road 15N34 and continue 1.2 miles. Park at the end of the road. The trailhead is on the left.

**Maps:** For a free brochure and hiking guide, write to Smith River National Recreation Area at the address below. For a map of Six Rivers National Forest, send $3 to USDA-Forest Service, 630 Sansome Street, San Francisco, CA 94111. To obtain a topographic map of the area, ask for Ship Mountain from the USGS.

**Who to contact:** Write to Smith River National Recreation Area at P.O. Box 228, Gasquet, CA 95543; (707) 457-3131.

**Trail notes:** Now just a minute, here. Do you really want to try this hike? If so, get your ambitions in clear focus, and if you like what you see, then go for it, because your reward will be complete peace and solitude. But it comes with a price—a terrible, long and circuitous drive to reach the trailhead, two hours from the Gasquet Ranger Station. Then the hike itself demands a steep climb on the return trip, a 1,200-foot elevation gain over little more than a mile. This trail starts at a ridgeline at 2,500 feet, then dives down the canyon all the way to the South Fork Smith River, where it junctions with the South Kelsey Trail. The return is the killer, a terrible climb, and that is why few people make this round-trip. If you want solitude, a better bet is just hiking in for 15 or 20 minutes, picking a log to sit on, and after communing with the trees for a while, heading back to the starting point.

# 11. COASTAL TRAIL

**14 mi/8.0 hrs**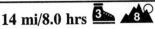

## (Last Chance Section)

*Reference:* in Del Norte Redwoods State Park south of Crescent City; map AØ, grid f6.

*User groups:* Hikers only. No mountain bikes, dogs or horses are allowed. No wheelchair facilities.

*Permits:* No permits are required. Parking and access are free.

*Directions:* From Crescent City, drive south on US 101 and drive approximately 2.5 miles. At milepost 23.03, turn west on Enderts Beach Road and drive 2.5 miles to the trailhead at the end of the road.

*Maps:* For a trail guide, send $1.50 to Redwood National Park Headquarters at the address below. To obtain a topographic map of the area, ask for Sister Rocks from the USGS.

*Who to contact:* Redwood National Park Headquarters, 1111 Second Street, Crescent City, CA 95531; (707) 464-6101 or (707) 445-6547.

*Trail notes:* You get a little bit of heaven and a little bit of hell on this hike. It is one of the feature trips on the Del Norte coast, coursing through a virgin forest and meadows with beautiful wildflowers (in the spring), granting great coastal views in several spots. The trail starts along the coast, then veers up sharply into dense old-growth. That's the heaven. The hell starts when you start the climb, a gain of 1,400 feet, difficult and steep. It doesn't stop there. Ever wonder why the trees are so big? You're likely to find out that it's because they are dripping with moisture, with heavy rain in the winter and ponderous fog in summer. There's more. Wood ticks flourish here, and it is a good idea to wear your socks outside the legs of your pants, to keep the ticks off your legs and also to make them easily visible should they climb aboard for the ride. Like many coastal hikes, hitting good weather is the key.

---

# 12. SOUTH KELSEY TRAIL   **32.2 mi/3.0 days**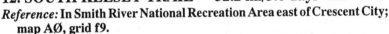

*Reference:* In Smith River National Recreation Area east of Crescent City; map AØ, grid f9.

*User groups:* Hikers, dogs and horses. No mountain bikes are allowed. No wheelchair facilities.

*Permits:* No permits are required. Parking and access are free.

*Directions:* From Crescent City, drive north on US 101 for five miles, then turn east on US 199 and drive 10 miles. Just past Hiouchi, turn right on South Fork Road and drive 14 miles, then turn right on an unsigned road junction. Travel three miles to a sign indicating the trailhead, then turn left and continue two miles.

*Maps:* For a free brochure and hiking guide, write to Smith River National Recreation Area at the address below. For a map of Six Rivers National Forest, send $3 to USDA-Forest Service, 630 Sansome Street, San Francisco, CA 94111. To obtain a topographic map of the area, ask for Summit Valley from the USGS.

*Who to contact:* Smith River National Recreation Area, P.O. Box 228, Gasquet, CA 95543; (707) 457-3131.

*Trail notes:* Back before cars, trains and planes, the Kelsey Trail spanned 200 miles from Crescent City eastward to Fort Jones near Yreka. In the mid-

1800s, it was built by Chinese laborers as a mule train route. Today it has a different purpose, with different sections providing excellent backpacking circuits. The trailhead is near Horse Creek on the South Fork Smith River at a 1,200-foot elevation. The trail initially drops down along the South Fork and continues south for seven miles, then rises up above the river, climbing all the way for six miles to Baldy Peak. There are spectacular views here. Another 3.1 miles will get you to your destination, Harrington Lake in Klamath National Forest, set at 5,775 feet. With so much "up" going in, take heart that at least the return trip will be mainly downhill. The trailhead also provides access to the McClendon Ford Trail. Other maintained sections of the Kelsey Trail are noted in the Marble Mountain Wilderness (see chapter A1).

## 13. SUMMIT VALLEY TRAIL  16.2 mi/2.0 days

*Reference:* In Smith River National Recreation Area east of Crescent City; map AØ, grid f9.

*User groups:* Hikers, dogs and horses. No mountain bikes are allowed. No wheelchair facilities.

*Permits:* No permits are required. Parking and access are free.

*Directions:* From Crescent City, drive north on US 101 for five miles, then turn east on US 199 and drive 10 miles. Just past Hiouchi, turn right on South Fork Road and drive 14 miles, then turn right on Forest Road 15. Travel 15 miles to the trailhead on the left. Park on the side of the road.

*Maps:* For a free brochure and hiking guide, write to Smith River National Recreation Area at the address below. For a map of Six Rivers National Forest, send $3 to USDA-Forest Service, 630 Sansome Street, San Francisco, CA 94111. To obtain a topographic map of the area, ask for Summit Valley from the USGS.

*Who to contact:* Smith River National Recreation Area, P.O. Box 228, Gasquet, CA 95543; (707) 457-3131.

*Trail notes:* This hike is best taken in the early summer, when the wildflowers are blooming, the Smith River is running with fresh, ample flows, and the temperatures are not too warm. The latter becomes a factor on the return trip, a killer climb. The trailhead is set on a ridge at 4,600 feet, with the first mile of the hike on an old jeep road. It travels through meadows, and this is where the wildflowers are so spectacular in the spring. But then the trail drops, plunging down into a canyon, landing you along the South Fork Smith River at Elkhorn Bar, an 1,160-foot elevation. Here it junctions with the South Kelsey Trail; there are a few primitive campsites along the river. Well, when it comes to hiking, what goes down must come up, and you got it, the return trip is a death march, a 3,500-foot climb over the span of eight miles. Your car waiting at the trailhead never looked so good. This trip can be lengthened easily by junctioning with the South Kelsey Trail.

## 14. YUROK LOOP  1.0 mi/0.5 hr

*Reference:* In Redwood National Park south of Crescent City; map AØ, grid g6.

*User groups:* Hikers only. No dogs, mountain bikes or horses are allowed. **Partial wheelchair access** is available.

*Permits:* No permits are required. Parking and access are free.

*Directions:* From Crescent City, drive south on US 101 for approximately 14 miles. Turn right at the sign for the Lagoon Creek Parking Area. Park there; the trailhead is adjacent.

*Maps:* For a trail guide, send $1.50 to Redwood National Park Headquarters at the address below. To obtain a topographic map of the area, ask for Requa from the USGS.

*Who to contact:* Redwood National Park Headquarters, 1111 Second Street, Crescent City, CA 95531; (707) 464-6101.

*Trail notes:* For such a short, easy walk, the Yurok Loop offers many benefits for visitors. This is an easy loop that heads west into forest, then descends to circle the Lagoon Creek Pond. The pond is stocked with trout, which attracts herons and egrets, who join the beavers, otters and waterfowl. Keep a good lookout for them. The loop hike returns to the parking area. Because the walk is so easy, it gets a lot of use during the summer vacation season by tourists from all over the world who want to see what a redwood tree looks like. In the offseason, however, the trail is seldom used. The Hidden Beach section of the Coastal Trail junctions with this trail.

---

## 15. COASTAL TRAIL
### (Hidden Beach Section)

8.0 mi/5.0 hrs

*Reference:* **In Redwood National Park south of Crescent City; map AØ, grid g6.**

*User groups:* Hikers only. No dogs, mountain bikes or horses are allowed. **Partial wheelchair access** is available.

*Permits:* No permits are required. Parking and access are free.

*Directions:* From Eureka, drive north on US 101 for about 60 miles to the Klamath River. Turn west on Requa Road and drive 2.5 miles to the Klamath Overlook. The trailhead is at the south end of the parking area.

*Maps:* For a trail guide, send $1.50 to Redwood National Park Headquarters at the address below. To obtain a topographic map of the area, ask for Requa from the USGS.

*Who to contact:* Redwood National Park Headquarters, 1111 Second Street, Crescent City, CA 95531; (707) 488-3461 or (707) 464-6101.

*Trail notes:* This section of the Coastal Trail can be quite crowded by North Coast standards, and providing you don't mind the company, it is a great hike. It follows along coastal bluffs and rocky cliffs, with sweeping views of the ocean, and ultimately, of Hidden Beach. In late winter, the trailhead at Klamath Overlook is an excellent place to spot migrating whales (scan for their spouts), and is **wheelchair accessible.** Not all is flawless, however. For one thing, don't even think about hiking off the trail, because poison oak is all over the place. For another, fog often drops down and covers everything. So much for the views.

## 16. COASTAL TRAIL 5.4 mi/3.0 hrs
### (Fern Canyon/Ossagon Section)

*Reference:* In Prairie Creek Redwoods State Park south of Klamath; map AØ, grid h6.

*User groups:* Hikers and mountain bikes. No dogs or horses are allowed. No wheelchair facilities.

*Permits:* No permits are required. There is a state park day-use fee of $5 per vehicle.

*Directions:* From Eureka, drive north on US 101 for 41 miles to Orick. Continue north for three miles to Davison Road. Turn west on Davison Road and drive eight miles to the Fern Canyon Trail. The access road is quite bumpy and holey, and no trailers or motor homes are permitted.

*Maps:* Trail maps are available at the park visitor center for a nominal charge. A free state parks guide can be obtained by calling (707) 445-6547. To obtain a topographic image of the area, ask for Fern Canyon from the USGS.

*Who to contact:* Prairie Creek Redwoods State Park, 600-A West Clark Street, Eureka, CA 95502; (707) 488-2171, (707) 488-3461 or (707) 445-6547.

*Trail notes:* Be forewarned: This trail is part of a popular 20-mile bicycle loop in Prairie Creek Redwoods State Park, and not all the riders are as ethical as they should be. In fact, this trail was once the favorite hike of Rosemary O'Neil, a faithful reader, until she got plowed over. "I was enjoying myself, walking up a hill, when this young guy on a bike came flying over the top and ran over me," she wrote us. "Then an instant later, he was gone. It isn't fair at all, and I'll never go back." Too bad the park hasn't resolved this kind of crap, because it is otherwise a great hike, with a good chance of seeing Roosevelt elk (Prairie Creek Park is loaded with them), and easy access to a huge, spotless beach (not a single piece of litter), Fern Canyon (see next trip), and a dense forest (quiet and pretty). The fog and rain, common in this area, can be downers. Try to hit the weather right.

## 17. FERN CANYON LOOP TRAIL 0.8 mi/0.5 hr

*Reference:* In Prairie Creek Redwoods State Park south of Klamath; map AØ, grid h6.

*User groups:* Hikers only. No dogs, mountain bikes or horses allowed. No wheelchair facilities.

*Permits:* No permits are required. There is a state park day-use fee of $5 per vehicle.

*Directions:* From Eureka, drive north on US 101 for 41 miles to Orick. Continue north for three miles to Davison Road. Turn west on Davison Road and drive eight miles to the Fern Canyon Trail. The access road is quite bumpy and holey, and no trailers or motor homes are permitted.

*Maps:* Trail maps are available at the park visitor center for a nominal charge. A free state parks guide can be obtained by calling (707) 445-6547. To obtain a topographic image of the area, ask for Fern Canyon from the USGS.

*Who to contact:* Prairie Creek Redwoods State Park, 600-A West Clark Street, Eureka, CA 95502; (707) 488-2171, (707) 488-3461 or (707) 445-6547.

*Trail notes:* The Fern Canyon Loop might just be the most inspiring short hike in California. When you walk along the bottom of Fern Canyon, you will be surrounded on each side by 50-foot-high walls covered with giant ferns, a dramatic setting that isn't duplicated anywhere in the state. There is also a small waterfall which adds to the beauty, pouring in through a chasm in the wall in the canyon, gushing into Home Creek. But it is Home Creek, which runs through the bottom of the canyon, that can cause the one serious problem here. In winter, this creek can flood, making the trail impassable. Although bridges are provided from May through September, always wear waterproof footwear because you often have to hop back and forth across the stream in order to reach the back of the canyon. At the end of the canyon, turn left and climb up the trail to the canyon rim, and then continue through the forest back to the trailhead. A bonus is the adjacent beach, wide-open and spanning for miles. Note that this trail is well known and recommended by many, so it can get a lot of use during the summer months.

## 18. LOST MAN CREEK TRAIL    2.0 mi/1.0 hr

*Reference:* In Redwood National Park south of Klamath; map AØ, grid h7.
*User groups:* Hikers only. No dogs, mountain bikes or horses are allowed. The trail is **partially wheelchair accessible**.
*Permits:* No permits are required. Parking and access are free.
*Directions:* From Eureka, drive north on US 101 for 41 miles to Orick. Continue north for 3.5 miles, just past Davison Road, to Lost Man Creek Road. Turn right and drive to the parking area and trailhead. Trailers and motor homes are prohibited from Lost Man Creek Road.
*Maps:* For a trail guide, send $1.50 to Redwood National Park Headquarters at the address below. To obtain a topographic map of the area, ask for Orick from the USGS.
*Who to contact:* Write to Redwood National Park Headquarters at 1111 Second Street, Crescent City, CA 95531; (707) 488-3461 or (707) 464-6101.
*Trail notes:* Lost Man Creek is very pretty, with many rock pools and surrounded by lush vegetation. It is also a destination that is easy to reach. The trail heads southeast, climbing moderately then nearly leveling out along the creek. Bring your camera, because it is rare to reach such a natural, pristine setting with such a short walk. While the two-mile roundtrip is as far as most hikers take it, the trail actually continues on for 10 miles, all the way back down to Bald Hills Road. It is so steep that you will be howling like a lone wolf baying at the moon. Almost nobody but deranged souls makes the 20-mile roundtrip.

## 19. REDWOOD CREEK TRAIL    17.0 mi/1 day

*Reference:* In Redwood National Park south of Klamath; map AØ, grid i7.
*User groups:* Hikers only. No dogs, mountain bikes or horses are allowed. No wheelchair facilities.
*Permits:* No permits are required. Parking and access are free.
*Directions:* From Eureka, drive north on US 101 for 41 miles to Orick. About a quarter-mile north of Orick, turn right on Bald Hills Road. Drive a half-mile to the parking area.
*Maps:* For a trail guide, send $1.50 to Redwood National Park Headquarters at the address below. To obtain a topographic map of the area, ask for Orick from the USGS.

***Who to contact:*** Write to Redwood National Park Headquarters at 1111 Second Street, Crescent City, CA 95531; (707) 488-3461 or (707) 464-6101.

***Trail notes:*** The Redwood Creek Trail has become a feature hike in Redwood National Park. Though most visitors cut the trip short, it still provides exceptional beauty even in short pieces. The trail is routed along Redwood Creek, a pretty stream that flows out to sea near Orick. As you hike into the interior, you will notice the diversity of the forest, with spruce, alder, redwoods and maples, and lush fern beds in some areas. Stay on the trail because stinging nettle are also abundant here. The stream attracts a diversity in wildlife, with ducks, herons and hawks the most common sightings, and ruffed grouse and eagles occasionally seen. In the summer, the first mile or two of the trail can be quite crowded, but just keep on going. The farther you go, the less people you will see. Note that during the winter, the creek can flood the trail in some areas, making it impassable.

---

## 20. TALL TREES TRAIL     2.5 mi/1.5 hrs

***Reference:*** In Redwood National Park south of Klamath; map AØ, grid i7.

***User groups:*** Hikers only. No dogs, mountain bikes or horses are allowed. No wheelchair facilities.

***Permits:*** A permit is required if you want to drive to the trailhead; a limited number of cars are allowed per day. Permits are free and can be obtained at the Redwood Information Center. In the summer months, it is advisable to arrive as early as possible; permits usually run out by 10 a.m. Trailhead parking is free. A shuttle service is also available, see "Directions" below.

***Directions:*** From Eureka, drive north on US 101 for 40 miles. About one mile before reaching Orick, stop at the Redwood Information Center. (Here you secure a permit number, which is actually a gate combination number you will need.) Continue north on US 101 through Orick. About a quarter-mile north of Orick, turn right on Bald Hills Road (look for the "Tall Tree Access" sign) and drive seven miles to a locked gate. Open the gate, drive through, close and lock the gate, then drive six miles down the gravel road to the trailhead. No motor homes or trailers are permitted. Note: From Memorial Day through Labor Day, a shuttle bus service is available from the Redwood Information Center. However, it runs a maximum of twice per day, and its viability as a service is reviewed each year by the Park Service. A $7 donation is requested for shuttle service.

***Maps:*** For a trail guide, send $1.50 to Redwood National Park Headquarters at the address below. To obtain a topographic map of the area, ask for Orick from the USGS.

***Who to contact:*** Write to Redwood National Park Headquarters at 1111 Second Street, Crescent City, CA 95531; (707) 488-3461 or (707) 464-6101.

***Trail notes:*** This hike is routed into a grove of redwoods that has cathedral-like beauty, tall and ancient, with the trail shaded and surrounded by a lush fern understory. Your mission here is to reach Tall Trees Grove, home of the park's tallest tree, 367 feet high and an estimated 600 years old. Hey, some say this is the tallest tree in the world, but that claim usually sets off a debate. In the summer, the Tall Trees Trail is extremely popular, with visitors from all over America arriving to see the giant old-growth redwoods. The hike to the grove is just over a mile, and if you want to extend the adventure, you can return on the Redwood Creek Trail, or head off on the Emerald Ridge Loop.

*Special note:* One word of caution: Although there are typically high numbers of people on this trail, resist the urge to trek off-trail. There's a lot of poison oak that is sure to get you if you do.

# MAP A1

3 PCT SECTIONS
22 TRAILS
PAGES 30-49

NOR-CAL MAP ....................... see page 14
adjoining maps
NORTH ............................................. no map
EAST (A2) ................................. see page 50
SOUTH (B1) ............................... see page 78
WEST (AØ) ............................... see page 16

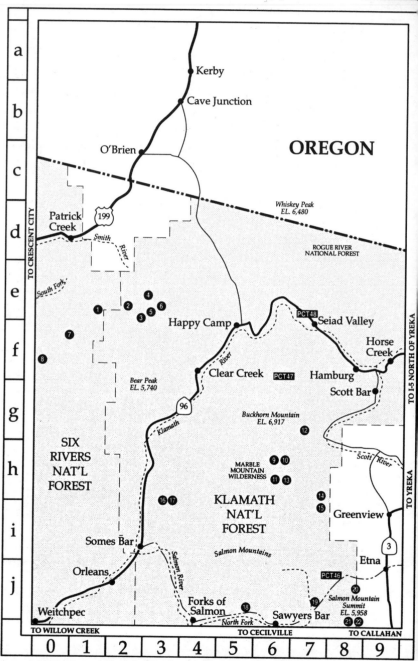

**Map A1 featuring:** Smith River National Recreation Area, Siskiyou Wilderness, Marble Mountain Wilderness, Somes Bar, Sawyers Bar, Etna, Russian Wilderness, Etna Summit, Seiad Valley, Rogue Wilderness, Klamath National Forest, Happy Camp, Siskiyou Mountains

## 1. DOE FLAT TRAIL  3.0 mi/1.5 hrs

*Reference:* In Smith River National Recreation Area east of Crescent City; map A1, grid e1.

*User groups:* Hikers only. No dogs, mountain bikes or horses are allowed. No wheelchair facilities.

*Permits:* A permit is required only for hikers planning to camp in the wilderness. Contact Smith River National Recreation Area to obtain a free permit. Parking and access are free.

*Directions:* From Crescent City, drive north on US 101 for five miles, then turn east on US 199 and drive 27 miles. Turn right on Little Jones Creek Road and drive south 9.6 miles. When the road forks, bear sharply left on Forest Service Road 16N02 and drive 3.5 miles to the trailhead at the end of the road.

*Maps:* For a free brochure and hiking guide, write to Smith River National Recreation Area at the address below. For a map of Klamath National Forest, send $3 to USDA-Forest Service, 630 Sansome Street, San Francisco, CA 94111. To obtain a topographic map of the area, ask for Devil's Punchbowl from the USGS.

*Who to contact:* Smith River National Recreation Area, P.O. Box 228, Gasquet, CA 95543; (707) 457-3131.

*Trail notes:* Doe Flat is the best backpacking jump-off point for the Siskiyou Wilderness, and as long as you know that, you will have all the motivation you need for the trip. There are several excellent destinations from Doe Flat, including Buck Lake, Clear Creek and Wilderness Falls; all are detailed in the following trips. But hiking to Doe Flat is hardly inspirational. It's a 1.5-mile jaunt on a closed road to get there, leaving Bear Basin and topping Siskiyou Pass, then cruising down to the Doe Flat Camp. The trail follows an old mining road along Doe Creek to an old mine site, reaching a good camping area at Doe Flat. The area is well wooded, including some huge Jeffrey pines and cedars. For late arrivals, a bonus is that there is a small primitive camping area at the trailhead, including three campsites and a vault toilet.

## 2. BUCK LAKE TRAIL  4.5 mi/2.5 hrs

*Reference:* In Siskiyou Wilderness east of Crescent City; map A1, grid e2.

*User groups:* Hikers only. No dogs, mountain bikes or horses are allowed. No wheelchair facilities.

*Permits:* A permit is required only for hikers planning to camp in the wilderness. Contact Smith River National Recreation Area to obtain a free permit. Parking and access are free.

*Directions:* From Crescent City, drive north on US 101 for five miles, then turn east on US 199 and drive 27 miles. Turn right on Little Jones Creek Road and drive south 9.6 miles. When the road forks, bear sharply left on Forest Service Road 16N02 and drive 3.5 miles to the trailhead at the end of the road. Hike east on Doe Flat Trail for one mile to reach the Buck Lake Trail.

*Maps:* For a free brochure and hiking guide, write to Smith River National Recreation Area at the address below. For a map of Klamath National Forest, send $3 to USDA-Forest Service, 630 Sansome Street, San Francisco, CA 94111. To obtain a topographic map of the area, ask for Devil's Punchbowl from the USGS.

*Who to contact:* Smith River National Recreation Area, P.O. Box 228, Gasquet, CA 95543; (707) 457-3131.

*Trail notes:* It was Memorial Day weekend the first time we saw Buck Lake, the opening day of trout season, and there were so many rising brook trout that all the dimples on the lake surface looked like rain drops. Buck Lake is in the heart of a wilderness forest setting at a 4,300-foot elevation, a little, crystal-pure lake surrounded by old-growth firs. From Doe Flat, it is an easy three-quarter-mile hike. There are plenty of deer and bear in the area, and the brook trout are abundant at the lake, but alas, small. From Doe Flat to Buck Lake, you will cross through beautiful meadows and forest, including Douglas fir, white fir and red fir, along with some maples. In the fall, the changing colors of the maples adds a pretty touch to the trip.

---

## 3. DEVIL'S PUNCHBOWL     13.0 mi/2.0 days

*Reference:* In Siskiyou Wilderness east of Crescent City; map A1, grid e2.

*User groups:* Hikers only. No dogs, mountain bikes or horses are allowed. No wheelchair facilities.

*Permits:* A permit is required only for hikers planning to camp in the wilderness. Contact Smith River National Recreation Area to obtain a free permit. Parking and access are free.

*Directions:* From Crescent City, drive north on US 101 for five miles, then turn east on US 199 and drive 27 miles. Turn right on Little Jones Creek Road and drive south 9.6 miles. When the road forks, bear sharply left on Forest Service Road 16N02 and drive 3.5 miles to the trailhead at the end of the road. Follow the Doe Flat Trail for three miles to reach the trailhead.

*Maps:* For a free brochure and hiking guide, write to Smith River National Recreation Area at the address below. For a map of Klamath National Forest, send $3 to USDA-Forest Service, 630 Sansome Street, San Francisco, CA 94111. To obtain a topographic map of the area, ask for Devil's Punchbowl from the USGS.

*Who to contact:* Smith River National Recreation Area, P.O. Box 228, Gasquet, CA 95543; (707) 457-3131.

*Trail notes:* You'll be wondering if you're afflicted with a hex or a charm when you take the trip to Devil's Punchbowl. The hex? The trail includes a climb with about a hundred switchbacks, an endless up, up and up, that'll have you wheezing like a donkey low on hay. The charm? The sight of the lake first coming into view will enchant you. It's small but pristine, set in a mountain granite bowl, framed by an imposing back wall, a shrine. To make this trip, you start by hiking past Doe Flat, continuing a short way along Doe Creek, then turning right, crossing the creek, and starting the endless switchbacks up the mountain. Note that at times the sign marking the Devil's Punchbowl Trail gets stolen, so keep alert for the trail turnoff along Doe Creek. When you finally top the ridge, the route crosses Devil's Creek and leaves the forest behind, crossing bare granite domes, the trail marked only by small stacks of rocks. This place is something of a legend, but is visited only by those willing to pay the price of the terrible climb to reach it.

*Special note:* The entire region surrounding Devil's Punchbowl consists of sheets of bare granite. The few campsites here consist of small flat sleeping spaces on rock. There is no firewood available so bring a backpacking stove for cooking. Bring Zip-Loc bags in order to carry out all refuse, including human waste.

---

## 4. YOUNG'S VALLEY TRAIL    4.0 mi/2.0 hrs

*Reference:* In Siskiyou Wilderness east of Crescent City; map A1, grid e3.

*User groups:* Hikers and horses. No dogs or mountain bikes are allowed. No wheelchair facilities.

*Permits:* A permit is required only for hikers planning to camp in the wilderness. Contact Smith River National Recreation Area to obtain a free permit. Parking and access are free.

*Directions:* From Crescent City, drive north on US 101 for five miles, then turn east on US 199 and drive 32 miles. Turn right on Forest Service Road 18N07 and drive approximately five miles. Continue on 18N07 as it veers right and twists its way about 10 miles past Sanger Lake and beyond to the end of the road and the trailhead. The last three miles are very rough.

*Maps:* For a free brochure and hiking guide, write to Smith River National Recreation Area at the address below. For a map of Klamath National Forest, send $3 to USDA-Forest Service, 630 Sansome Street, San Francisco, CA 94111. To obtain a topographic map of the area, ask for Devil's Punchbowl from the USGS.

*Who to contact:* Smith River National Recreation Area, P.O. Box 228, Gasquet, CA 95543; (707) 457-3131.

*Trail notes:* The two-mile trip from Young's Valley down Clear Creek to Young's Meadow is one of the greatest and easiest trips in Northern California. Young's Meadow, set at a 4,500-foot elevation, is very pretty and makes an excellent picnic site as well as a campsite. It is set on the western slope of Preston Peak. It's an easy walk in, too, a gradual 600-foot descent as you hike down along Clear Creek, and yet this trail doesn't get a lot of traffic. In addition, the ambitious can take this trip further, much further. It is a great first leg to a multi-day trip, ultimately heading either farther down Clear Creek to Wilderness Falls, an awesome setting (see the following trail), or to Rattlesnake Meadows on the slopes of Preston Peak, a short but rugged climb.

---

## 5. WILDERNESS FALLS    14.0 mi/2.0 days

*Reference:* In Siskiyou Wilderness east of Crescent City; map A1, grid e3.

*User groups:* Hikers only. No dogs, mountain bikes or horses are allowed. No wheelchair facilities.

*Permits:* A permit is required only for hikers planning to camp in the wilderness. Contact Klamath National Forest to obtain a free wilderness permit.

Parking and access are free.

*Directions:* From Crescent City, drive north on US 101 for five miles, then turn east on US 199 and drive 32 miles. Turn right on Forest Service Road 18N07 and drive approximately five miles. Continue on 18N07 as it veers right and twists its way about 10 miles past Sanger Lake and beyond to the end of the road and the trailhead. The last three miles are very rough.

*Maps:* For a map of Klamath National Forest, send $3 to USDA-Forest Service, 630 Sansome Street, San Francisco, CA 94111. To obtain a topographic map of the area, ask for Devil's Punchbowl from the USGS.

*Who to contact:* Klamath National Forest, Happy Camp Ranger District, P.O. Box 377, Happy Camp, CA 96039; (916) 493-2243. Smith River National Recreation Area, P.O. Box 228, Gasquet, CA 95543; (907) 457-3131.

*Trail notes:* Wilderness Falls is one of the great secrets of northwestern California, a true hidden jewel, dramatic and pure, and not only untouched, but largely unseen. It is a bubbling tower of water created by Clear Creek, first crashing down about 50 feet into a boulder, then pounding its way down into a foaming pool 100 feet across. Our recommended route is to start on the Clear Creek National Recreation Trail out of Young's Valley (see previous trail). Follow the Clear Creek Trail for about seven miles to the waterfall. There is an excellent campsite about a quarter mile upstream from the falls. It is an easy hike to the waterfall, but the trip back is up all the way, and is best started very early in the morning, when the temperature is the coolest.

---

# 6. PRESTON PEAK     12 mi/2.0 days

*Reference:* **In Siskiyou Wilderness east of Crescent City; map A1, grid e3.**

*User groups:* Hikers only. No dogs, mountain bikes or horses are allowed. No wheelchair facilities.

*Permits:* A permit is required only for hikers planning to camp in the wilderness. Contact Klamath National Forest to obtain a free wilderness permit. Parking and access are free.

*Directions:* From Crescent City, drive north on US 101 for five miles, then turn east on US 199 and drive 32 miles. Turn right on Forest Service Road 18N07 and drive approximately five miles. Continue on 18N07 as it veers right and twists its way about 10 miles past Sanger Lake and beyond to the end of the road and the trailhead. The last three miles are very rough.

*Maps:* For a map of Klamath National Forest, send $3 to USDA-Forest Service, 630 Sansome Street, San Francisco, CA 94111. A special map of the Marble Mountain Wilderness can also be purchased for $6. To obtain a topographic map of the area, ask for Devil's Punchbowl from the USGS.

*Who to contact:* Klamath National Forest, Happy Camp Ranger District, P.O. Box 377, Happy Camp, CA 96039; (916) 493-2243.

*Trail notes:* Only mountaineers need sign up for this trip. The last mile to reach the summit of Preston Peak is steep, rough and primitive, and with no marked trail, you must have the ability to scramble cross-country and recognize a dangerous spot when you see it. That done, you will gain the top, 7,309 feet, by far the highest spot in the region, with wondrous surrounding views. Even Mt. Shasta way off to the southeast comes clearly into view, along with the famous peaks in the Trinity Alps and Marble Mountain Wilderness. The most common route to climb Preston Peak is to hike the Young's Valley Trail to Young's Meadow (an easy two miles), head down the Clear Creek Trail (another easy mile), then turn east on the Rattlesnake Meadow Trail (about two miles, very steep, rough and primitive). At the end of the Rattlesnake Meadow Trail, hikers must go cross-country for another mile or so to Preston Peak. The last mile is a scramble.

*Special note:* Always stay off this mountain in wet weather because the route is very slippery, and always avoid routes that cross through loose shale, which can be extremely dangerous.

---

# 7. ISLAND LAKE TRAIL     10.4 mi/2.0 days

*Reference:* In Smith River National Recreation Area east of Crescent City; map A1, grid f0.

*User groups:* Hikers only. No dogs, mountain bikes or horses are allowed. No wheelchair facilities.

*Permits:* A permit is required only for hikers planning to camp in the wilderness. Contact Smith River National Recreation Area to obtain a free permit. Parking and access are free.

*Directions:* From Crescent City, drive north on US 101 for five miles, then turn east on US 199 and drive 27 miles. Turn right on Little Jones Creek Road and drive south 9.6 miles. When the road forks, continue straight on Forest Service Road 16N02 and drive 2.5 miles, then turn left on Forest Service Road 16N28 and proceed two miles west to the trailhead at the end of the road. Note: Forest Service Road 16N28 is very rough and often impassable in the rainy season; phone the Smith River National Recreation Area before planning a trip.

*Maps:* For a free brochure and hiking guide, write to Smith River National Recreation Area at the address below. For a map of Klamath National Forest, send $3 to USDA-Forest Service, 630 Sansome Street, San Francisco, CA 94111. To obtain a topographic map of the area, ask for Devil's Punchbowl from the USGS.

*Who to contact:* Smith River National Recreation Area, P.O. Box 228, Gasquet, CA 95543; (707) 457-3131.

*Trail notes:* Island Lake is a mountain bowl framed by the back wall of Jedediah Mountain, a wild, primitive area where endangered spotted owls are more common than hikers. The trailhead is at Little Bear Basin, and after making the quick walk past a clear-cut down to Elk Creek, you will enter the untouched Siskiyou Wilderness. Enjoy the stream, because the hike that follows is anything but enjoyable. The trail is routed along a mountain spine, climbing up, up and up for more than four miles. It finally tops a ridge and turns around a bend, where little Island Lake comes into view. The climb can seem endless. There is an excellent camp at the lake, set in trees near the lake's shore. The trout are eager to bite, but most are very small brook trout— all dinkers. A great afternoon sidetrip is to hike the rim around the lake, most easily done in a counter-clockwise direction, claiming the top of Jedediah Mountain, a perfect picnic site and a great lookout.

## 8. BALDY PEAK TRAIL 10.4 mi/2.0 days

*Reference:* In Siskiyou Wilderness east of Crescent City; map A1, grid f0.

*User groups:* Hikers only. No dogs, mountain bikes or horses are allowed. No wheelchair facilities.

*Permits:* A permit is required only for hikers planning to camp in the wilderness. Contact Smith River National Recreation Area to obtain a free permit. Parking and access are free.

*Directions:* This trailhead can be reached only by hiking the Gunbarrel Trail (see Chapter AØ). From Crescent City, drive north on US 101 for five miles, then turn east on US 199 and drive 27 miles. Turn right on Little Jones Creek Road and drive south 9.6 miles. When the road forks, proceed straight ahead on Forest Service Road 16N02 and drive 4.8 miles, then turn left on Forest Service Road 16N18 and drive three miles. Bear left on Forest Service Road 15N34 and continue 1.2 miles. Park at the end of the road. The trailhead is on the left. Hike the Gunbarrel Trail for 1.2 miles to reach the Baldy Peak section of the South Kelsey Trail.

*Maps:* For a free brochure and hiking guide, write to Smith River National Recreation Area at the address below. For a map of Klamath National Forest, send $3 to USDA-Forest Service, 630 Sansome Street, San Francisco, CA 94111. To obtain a topographic map of the area, ask for Prescott Mountain from the USGS.

*Who to contact:* Smith River National Recreation Area, P.O. Box 228, Gasquet, CA 95543; (707) 457-3131.

*Trail notes:* The route to Baldy Peak is actually a section of the South Kelsey Trail (see Chapter AØ), the historic route that once spanned from Crescent City east all the way through the Marble Mountain Wilderness to Fort Jones. This section of it is an excellent trip, and if you get caught in the rain, a bonus is that the Bear Wallow Shelter (not much more than a roof) is available just beyond the summit. The trip starts on the Gunbarrel Trail (see Chapter AØ), which extends for 1.25 miles to the junction with the Kelsey Trail. From there, it is four miles to Baldy Peak at 5,775 feet. The views are outstanding, especially Preston Peak (at 7,309 feet) to the north, the most impressive feature in this unpeopled landscape. An option for those with plenty of time and endurance is to continue east on the Kelsey Trail, which extends about 12 miles further to Red Hill (5,642 feet), Bear Peak (5,740 feet) and nearby Bear Lake. The latter has an excellent campsite.

## 9. PARADISE LAKE TRAIL 4.0 mi/2.75 hrs

*Reference:* In Marble Mountain Wilderness west of Yreka; map A1, grid h6.

*User groups:* Hikers, dogs and horses. No mountain bikes are allowed. No wheelchair facilities.

*Permits:* A campfire permit is required only for hikers planning to camp in the wilderness. Contact Klamath National Forest to obtain a free permit. Parking and access are free.

*Directions:* From Interstate 5 at Yreka, take the Highway 3/Fort Jones exit and drive 16.5 miles to Fort Jones. Turn right on Scott River Road and drive 18 miles to the turnoff for Indian Scotty Campground. Turn left and cross the concrete bridge, then bear left and drive about five miles on Forest Service

Road 43N45. Turn right on an unmarked Forest Service Road and follow the signs indicating the Paradise Lake Trailhead for approximately six miles. The trailhead is at the wilderness border.

*Maps:* A trail information sheet can be obtained by contacting the Scott River Ranger District at the address below. For a map of Klamath National Forest, send $3 to USDA-Forest Service, 630 Sansome Street, San Francisco, CA 94111. A map of the Marble Mountain Wilderness can also be purchased for $3. To obtain topographic maps of the area, ask for Scott Bar and Marble Mountain from the USGS.

*Who to contact:* Klamath National Forest, Scott River Ranger District, 11263 North Highway 3, Fort Jones, CA 96032; (916) 468-5351.

*Trail notes:* Paradise Lake, set at a 5,920-foot elevation, is the easiest to reach of the 79 lakes in the Marble Mountain Wilderness. It's a short enough hike for a day trip, and pretty enough with good lakeside campgrounds to turn your trip into an overnighter. There are also some excellent sidetrips, including climbing Kings Castle (see next trail), which tops the mountain rim on the back side of the lake. From the trailhead at 4,880 feet, the route quickly enters a designated wilderness, then climbs for nearly two miles, steeply in some areas, and switches back and forth through an old, untouched forest. It then emerges from the trees and rises to a saddle, and on the other side is Paradise Lake, sitting in a mountain pocket, emerald-green and peaceful. It is a mostly shallow lake with few trout, but it does have one deep area. Because it is only a two-hour hike to reach the lake, there are usually campers here all summer long. When we visited, there was a strange religious ceremony of some kind going on in which about 50 people had hiked in, formed a circle and started chanting. We climbed Kings Castle to get well out of earshot and reclaim our own sense of peace.

---

# 10. KINGS CASTLE TRAIL    5.5 mi/5.0 hrs

*Reference:* In Marble Mountain Wilderness west of Yreka; map A1, grid h6.

*User groups:* Hikers, dogs and horses. No mountain bikes are allowed. No wheelchair facilities. (Dog and horses not advised because of the rough terrain.)

*Permits:* A campfire permit is required only for hikers planning to camp in the wilderness. Contact Klamath National Forest to obtain a free permit. Parking and access are free.

*Directions:* From Interstate 5 at Yreka, take the Highway 3/Fort Jones exit and drive 16.5 miles to Fort Jones. Turn right on Scott River Road and drive 18 miles to the turnoff for Indian Scotty Campground. Turn left and cross the concrete bridge, then bear left and drive about five miles on Forest Service Road 43N45. Turn right on an unmarked Forest Service Road and follow the signs indicating the Paradise Lake Trailhead for approximately six miles. The trailhead is at the wilderness border. Hike 1.9 miles to Paradise Lake, then bear right and continue another half-mile to Kings Castle.

*Maps:* A trail information sheet can be obtained by contacting the Scott River Ranger District at the address below. For a map of Klamath National Forest, send $3 to USDA-Forest Service, 630 Sansome Street, San Francisco, CA 94111. A map of the Marble Mountain Wilderness can also be purchased for $3. To obtain topographic maps of the area, ask for Scott Bar and Marble

Mountain from the USGS.

**Who to contact:** Klamath National Forest, Scott River Ranger District, 11263 North Highway 3, Fort Jones, CA 96032; (916) 468-5351.

**Trail notes:** Kings Castle is the imposing perch that sits on the back side of Paradise Lake, a half-mile climb that tops out at the summit at 7,405 feet. It is a great hike with unforgettable views, looking down at little Paradise Lake as well as far beyond to Northern California's most famous mountain peaks. From the trailhead of Paradise Lake Trail, you make the 1,040-foot climb up to Paradise Lake. From there, the trail crosses the lake's inlet on the left side, then laterals across the side wall toward the peak, eventually switching back and forth to gain the rim behind the lake. The trail then loops and climbs the back side of Kings Castle, a special trip every step of the way, a climb of 2,525 feet from the trailhead. On our first visit here, we missed the trail and wound up scrambling cross-country style for hours right up to the face of Kings Castle. When we finally gained the summit, we looked at each other, smiling, silently congratulating ourselves for being such rugged mountaineers. Right then, two Girl Scouts suddenly arrived from the other side, cheerful and bouncy, scarcely breathing hard. "How'd you get up here?" I asked. "We just took the trail," one of them answered. We just stood there. There's a trail? What trail?

---

# 11. MARBLE MOUNTAIN RIM   16 mi/2.0 days

**Reference:** In Marble Mountain Wilderness west of Yreka; map A1, grid h6.

**User groups:** Hikers, dogs and horses. No mountain bikes are allowed. No wheelchair facilities. (Dogs and horses not advised because of the rough terrain.)

**Permits:** A campfire permit is required only for hikers planning to camp in the wilderness. Contact Klamath National Forest to obtain a free permit. Parking and access are free.

**Directions:** From Interstate 5 at Yreka, take the Highway 3/Fort Jones exit and drive 16.5 miles to Fort Jones. Turn right on Scott River Road and drive 18 miles to the turnoff for Indian Scotty Campground. Turn left and cross the concrete bridge, then bear left and drive about five miles on Forest Service Road 43N45. Look for the sign indicating the Lovers Camp Trailhead. Continue two miles to the trailhead.

**Maps:** A trail information sheet can be obtained by contacting the Scott River Ranger District at the address below. For a map of Klamath National Forest, send $3 to USDA-Forest Service, 630 Sansome Street, San Francisco, CA 94111. A map of the Marble Mountain Wilderness can also be purchased for $3. To obtain a topographic map of the area, ask for Marble Mountain from the USGS.

**Who to contact:** Klamath National Forest, Scott River Ranger District, 11263 North Highway 3, Fort Jones, CA 96032; (916) 468-5351.

**Trail notes:** Marble isn't usually thought of as a precious stone, but it is gemlike for hikers on this trail. With Marble Valley nearby, climbing the Marble Mountain Rim can make for a perfect weekend trip and can easily be extended into a longer one. The trailhead at Lovers Camp is probably the most popular in the entire wilderness, especially for packers going by horse (corrals are available at the trailhead). The route heads up Canyon Creek, a moderate climb, then intersects with the Pacific Crest Trail at Marble Valley. This area is very scenic, with lots of deer and wild orchids. Turn right and the trail crosses Marble Mountain itself, and once you've arrived, a sidetrip to the Marble Rim is mandatory. The views are stunning, sweeping in both directions, with steep drop-offs adding to the quiet drama.

## 12. KELSEY CREEK TRAIL    18.0 mi/2.0 days

*Reference:* In Marble Mountain Wilderness west of Yreka; map A1, grid h6.

*User groups:* Hikers, dogs and horses. No mountain bikes are allowed. No wheelchair facilities.

*Permits:* A campfire permit is required only for hikers planning to camp in the wilderness. Contact Klamath National Forest to obtain a free permit. Parking and access are free.

*Directions:* From Interstate 5 at Yreka, take the Highway 3/Fort Jones exit and drive 16.5 miles to Fort Jones. Turn right on Scott River Road and drive 20 miles to the Kelsey Creek Bridge, cross it, then turn left and follow the road for one mile to the trailhead.

*Maps:* A trail information sheet can be obtained by contacting the Scott River Ranger District at the address below. For a map of Klamath National Forest, send $3 to USDA-Forest Service, 630 Sansome Street, San Francisco, CA 94111. A map of the Marble Mountain Wilderness can also be purchased for $3. To obtain topographic maps of the area, ask for Scott Bar and Grider Valley from the USGS.

*Who to contact:* Klamath National Forest, Scott River Ranger District, 11263 North Highway 3, Fort Jones, CA 96032; (916) 468-5351.

*Trail notes:* The Kelsey Trail offers many miles of beautiful streamside travel, with the Paradise Lake Basin as the intended destination for most hikers on this route. The trailhead is set near the confluence of Kelsey Creek and the Scott River, and from there, the trail follows upstream on Kelsey Creek. Wildflowers are abundant in the meadows. In three miles, you will reach Maple Falls, the prettiest waterfall in the region. The trail continues up the canyon, finally rising to intersect with the Pacific Crest Trail just below Red Rock. From this junction, you have many options. The closest lake is secluded Bear Lake, a pretty spot but alas with some tules and mosquitoes. To reach it from the junction requires a short but steep drop down into the basin to the immediate west.

## 13. SKY HIGH LAKES    9.0 mi/2.0 days

*Reference:* In Marble Mountain Wilderness west of Yreka; map A1, grid h6.

*User groups:* Hikers, dogs and horses. No mountain bikes are allowed. No wheelchair facilities.

*Permits:* A campfire permit is required only for hikers planning to camp in the wilderness. Contact Klamath National Forest to obtain a free permit. Parking and access are free.

*Directions:* From Interstate 5 at Yreka, take the Highway 3/Fort Jones exit and drive 16.5 miles to Fort Jones. Turn right on Scott River Road and drive 18 miles to the turnoff for Indian Scotty Campground. Turn left and cross the concrete bridge, then bear left and drive about five miles on Forest Service Road 43N45. Look for the sign indicating the Lovers Camp Trailhead.

Continue two miles to the Lovers Camp Trailhead.

**Maps:** A trail information sheet can be obtained by contacting the Scott River Ranger District at the address below. For a map of Klamath National Forest, send $3 to USDA-Forest Service, 630 Sansome Street, San Francisco, CA 94111. A map of the Marble Mountain Wilderness can also be purchased for $3. To obtain a topographic map of the area, ask for Marble Mountain from the USGS.

**Who to contact:** Klamath National Forest, Scott River Ranger District, 11263 North Highway 3, Fort Jones, CA 96032; (916) 468-5351.

**Trail notes:** The Sky High Lakes make for a great, easy overnighter, four miles each day, or an inspired one-day in-and-outer. The trip starts at Lovers Camp, one of two trails at this trailhead (the other leads to Marble Mountain). For this trip, take the trail out of Lovers Camp on the left, which follows along Red Rock Creek in the Red Rock Valley. Near the crest, you will reach Shadow Lake, the first of a half dozen lakes that are sprinkled about the basin. Lower Sky High Lake and Frying Pan Lake are our favorites for swimming and fishing. The trail hooks up with the Pacific Crest Trail at each end of the Sky High Lakes, making a loop trip possible. The trip can also easily be extended for a week or longer in either direction on the Pacific Crest Trail, with many lakeside camps available along the way.

---

# 14. BIG MEADOWS TRAILHEAD

6.5 mi/4.5 hrs

**Reference:** In Marble Mountain Wilderness west of Yreka; map A1, grid h7.

**User groups:** Hikers, dogs and horses. No mountain bikes are allowed. No wheelchair facilities.

**Permits:** A campfire permit is required only for hikers planning to camp in the wilderness. Contact Klamath National Forest to obtain a free permit. Parking and access are free.

**Directions:** From Interstate 5 at Yreka, take the Highway 3/Fort Jones exit and drive 16.5 miles to Fort Jones. Turn right on Scott River Road and drive seven miles, then turn left on Quartz Valley Road and drive about five miles to the sign for Shackleford Trailhead. Turn right and follow the road for about one mile to the first bridge. Continue until you see a gate. From here the roads are completely unmarked; follow the roads with the heaviest tread for about seven miles until you reach the trailhead.

**Maps:** A trail information sheet can be obtained by contacting the Scott River Ranger District at the address below. For a map of Klamath National Forest, send $3 to USDA-Forest Service, 630 Sansome Street, San Francisco, CA 94111. A map of the Marble Mountain Wilderness can also be purchased for $3. To obtain a topographic map of the area, ask for Boulder Peak from the USGS.

**Who to contact:** Klamath National Forest, Scott River Ranger District, 11263 North Highway 3, Fort Jones, CA 96032; (916) 468-5351.

**Trail notes:** The Marble Mountain Wilderness gets a lot of use, but this trailhead has always been obscure, unsigned and difficult to find. Your reward for the search is having the closest route to the scenic Wrights Lakes. It is only a three-mile trip to Lower Wright Lake, set in a mountain basin beneath Boulder Peak, 8,299 feet. The trail starts by routing through Big Meadows, which would be a place of great beauty if cattle weren't always giving the area a pounding. Watch the trail for meadow muffins. From Big Meadows, the trail becomes quite challenging, but in short order you will arrive at Upper Wright Lake and soon thereafter, Lower Wright Lake, by far the bigger of the two. It is a pretty camp with good fishing and swimming opportunities.

## 15. SHACKLEFORD CREEK TRAIL

13.0 mi/2.0 days

*Reference:* In Marble Mountain Wilderness west of Yreka; map A1, grid h7.

*User groups:* Hikers, dogs and horses. No mountain bikes are allowed. No wheelchair facilities.

*Permits:* A campfire permit is required only for hikers planning to camp in the wilderness. Contact Klamath National Forest to obtain a free permit. Parking and access are free.

*Directions:* From Interstate 5 at Yreka, take the Highway 3/Fort Jones exit and drive 16.5 miles to Fort Jones. Turn right on Scott River Road and drive seven miles, then turn left on Quartz Valley Road and drive about five miles to the sign for Shackleford Trailhead. Turn right and proceed to the trailhead at the end of the road.

*Maps:* A trail information sheet can be obtained by contacting the Scott River Ranger District at the address below. For a map of Klamath National Forest, send $3 to USDA-Forest Service, 630 Sansome Street, San Francisco, CA 94111. A map of the Marble Mountain Wilderness can also be purchased for $3. To obtain a topographic map of the area, ask for Boulder Peak from the USGS.

*Who to contact:* Klamath National Forest, Scott River Ranger District, 11263 North Highway 3, Fort Jones, CA 96032; (916) 468-5351.

*Trail notes:* Campbell, Cliff and Summit Lakes are three of the prettiest lakes in the Marble Mountain Wilderness. The ease of reaching them on the Shackleford Trail (only 5.5 miles to Campbell Lake) makes them a popular destination all summer long. The trail is routed up Shackleford Creek to a basin set just below the Pacific Crest Trail. Here you will find a series of small mountain lakes. In addition to these three largest lakes, there are also little Gem, Jewel and Angel Lakes. Visiting all of them can make for a great day of adventuring. A bonus is that the trip can be extended by hiking up the rim to the Pacific Crest Trail, then turning right and marching three miles to the Sky High Lakes.

## 16. HAYPRESS MEADOWS TRAILHEAD

20.0 mi/2.0 days

*Reference:* **In Marble Mountain Wilderness near Somes Bar; map A1, grid i3.**

*User groups:* Hikers, dogs and horses. No mountain bikes are allowed. No wheelchair facilities.

*Permits:* A campfire permit is required only for hikers planning to camp in the wilderness. Contact Klamath National Forest to obtain a free permit. Parking and access are free.

*Directions:* From Interstate 5 at Yreka, take the Highway 3/Fort Jones exit and drive 28 miles to Etna. Turn west on Sawyers Bar Road and drive approximately 35 miles to Forks of Salmon. Turn west on Salmon River Road and drive about 20 miles to a sign indicating Camp 3 and Wilderness Trails (located a quarter mile east of Somes Bar). Turn left and drive eight miles to the trailhead at Camp 4.

*Maps:* A trail information sheet can be obtained by contacting the Ukonom Ranger District at the address below. For a map of Klamath National Forest, send $3 to USDA-Forest Service, 630 Sansome Street, San Francisco, CA 94111. A map of the Marble Mountain Wilderness can also be purchased for $3. To obtain a topographic map of the area, ask for Somes Bar from the USGS.

*Who to contact:* Klamath National Forest, Ukonom Ranger District, P.O. Drawer 140, Orleans, CA 95556; (916) 627-3291.

*Trail notes:* If it is possible to love something to death, then One Mile Lake and the Cuddihy Lakes basin are in for such a fate. This area is perfect for backpacking, with beauty, lookouts and good trail access, but heavy use may force the Forest Service to close it off to overnight use. If you go, plan on no more than one night in this area before moving on, and don't plan on having the place to yourself. After parking at the trailhead at 4,500 feet, the first two miles of trail lead up and across a fir-covered slope of a small peak (a little butt-kicker of a climb), then the trail descends into Haypress Meadows, a major junction. Turn right and head up Sandy Ridge, a long, steady climb, and plan to top the ridge and then camp at Monument Lake, Meteor Lake, One Mile Lake or Cuddihy Lakes. The view from Sandy Ridge is a sweeping lookout of the Marble Mountains to the east and the Siskiyous to the west, with mountain-top glimpses of Mt. Shasta and the Marble Rim. Bears are very common at the Cuddihys.

---

## 17. SPIRIT LAKE TRAIL 34.0 mi/4.0 days

*Reference:* **In Marble Mountain Wilderness near Somes Bar; map A1, grid i3.**

*User groups:* Hikers, dogs and horses. No mountain bikes are allowed. No wheelchair facilities.

*Permits:* A campfire permit is required for hikers planning to camp in the wilderness. Contact Klamath National Forest to obtain a free permit. Parking and access are free.

*Directions:* From Interstate 5 at Yreka, take the Highway 3/Fort Jones exit and drive 28 miles to Etna. Turn west on Sawyers Bar Road and drive approximately 35 miles to Forks of Salmon. Turn west on Salmon River Road and drive about 20 miles to a sign indicating Camp 3 and Wilderness Trails (located a quarter mile east of Somes Bar). Turn left and drive eight miles to the trailhead at Camp 4.

*Maps:* A trail information sheet can be obtained by contacting the Scott River Ranger District at the address below. For a map of Klamath National Forest, send $3 to USDA-Forest Service, 630 Sansome Street, San Francisco, CA 94111. A map of the Marble Mountain Wilderness can also be purchased for $3. To obtain topographic maps of the area, ask for Somes Bar and Marble Mountain from the USGS.

*Who to contact:* Klamath National Forest, Scott River Ranger District, 11263

North Highway 3, Fort Jones, CA 96032; (916) 468-5351.

*Trail notes:* We've hiked to hundreds and hundreds of mountain lakes, and Spirit Lake is one of the prettiest we've ever seen. It sits at the bottom of a mountain bowl, completely encircled by old-growth trees, with a few campsites set at lakeside. The abundance of wildlife can be remarkable. The far side of the lake is a major deer migration route, an osprey makes regular trips to pluck trout out of the lake for dinner, and the fishing is quite good, especially early in the summer. Spirit Lake can be the feature destination for a week-long backpack loop, heading out on the Haypress Meadow Trail, up to Sandy Ridge, and then out to the lake, about 17 miles one-way. Most hikers will stop for the night at One Mile or the Cuddihy Lakes on the way out, and that is why those two areas get so much use. Spirit Lake is best visited during the first week of June, when the nights are still cold, the people are few, and the area abounds with fish and deer.

---

# 18. LITTLE NORTH FORK TRAILHEAD

16 mi/2.0 days

*Reference:* **In Marble Mountain Wilderness near Sawyers Bar; map A1, grid j5.**

*User groups:* Hikers, dogs and horses. No mountain bikes are allowed. No wheelchair facilities.

*Permits:* A campfire permit is required for hikers planning to camp in the wilderness. Contact Klamath National Forest to obtain a free permit. Parking and access are free.

*Directions:* From Interstate 5 at Yreka, take the Highway 3/Fort Jones exit and drive 28 miles to Etna. Turn west on Sawyers Bar Road and drive approximately 20 miles to the town of Sawyers Bar. Continue west on the same road for 3.5 miles to Little North Fork Campground. The trailhead is adjacent to the campground.

*Maps:* A trail information sheet can be obtained by contacting the Salmon River Ranger District at the address below. For a map of Klamath National Forest, send $3 to USDA-Forest Service, 630 Sansome Street, San Francisco, CA 94111. A map of the Marble Mountain Wilderness can also be purchased for $3. To obtain a topographic map of the area, ask for Sawyers Bar from the USGS.

*Who to contact:* Klamath National Forest, Salmon River Ranger District, P.O. Box 280, Etna, CA 96027; (916) 467-5757.

*Trail notes:* Your destination options? There are many: Chimney Rock, Clear Lake, Lily Lake and Chimney Rock Lake. This makes for an excellent trip, providing you don't mind the long grind of a climb to reach the lakes. Like a lot of trails on the edge of the wilderness, this one starts with a long climb out of a river canyon. From the Little North Fork Trailhead (a free Forest Service camp is available here), you start by climbing out toward Chimney Rock, grunting out a rise of about 4,000 feet as you depart the river lowlands and gain access to the Marble Mountain Wilderness. It is about an eight-mile trip to Clear Lake, a good first day's destination. While you can simply return the next day, most people will take several days to venture deeper into the wilderness, with 13 lakes and 20 miles of stream in the Abbotts Upper Cabin Area and English Peak area.

## 19. MULE BRIDGE TRAILHEAD

**28.0 mi/3.0 days**

*Reference:* In Marble Mountain Wilderness west of Etna; map A1, grid j7.

*User groups:* Hikers, dogs and horses. No mountain bikes are allowed. No wheelchair facilities.

*Permits:* Contact Klamath National Forest to obtain a free permit.

*Directions:* From Interstate 5 at Yreka, take the Highway 3/Fort Jones exit and drive 28 miles to Etna. Turn west on Etna-Somes Bar Road (Main Street in town) and drive 21 miles to Idlewild Campground. As you enter the campground, take the left fork in the road and continue two miles to the trailhead.

*Maps:* A trail information sheet can be obtained by contacting the Salmon River Ranger District at the address below. For a map of Klamath National Forest, send $3 to USDA-Forest Service, 630 Sansome Street, San Francisco, CA 94111. A map of the Marble Mountain Wilderness can also be purchased for $3. To obtain a topographic map of the area, ask for Sawyers Bar from the USGS.

*Who to contact:* Klamath National Forest, Salmon River Ranger District, P.O. Box 280, Etna, CA 96027; (916) 467-5757.

*Trail notes:* The trailhead at Idlewild Campground is set alongside the Salmon River, and once you've tightened your backpack, get ready for a long, endless climb up the river drainage. The trail follows along the Salmon River all the way up to its headwaters near the Pacific Crest Trail, gaining about 3,500 feet in the process. Plan on climbing for nearly 14 or 15 miles up along the river until you start reaching the higher country with many lakeside camps, as well as the Pacific Crest Trail. The prettiest glacial-formed lakes in this area are Shelly Lake (14 miles), Osprey Lake (14 miles) and Bug Lake (14 miles), with good campsites available at Cabin Gulch (12 miles, 6,000 feet), Grants Meadow (14 miles, 6,200 feet) and Shelly Meadows (15 miles, 6,300 feet).

## 20. TAYLOR LAKE TRAIL

**1.0 mi/0.5 hrs**

*Reference:* From Etna Summit into Russian Wilderness west of Etna; map A1, grid j8.

*User groups:* Hikers, dogs, horses and **wheelchairs**. No mountain bikes are allowed.

*Permits:* A campfire permit is required only for hikers planning to camp in the wilderness. Contact Klamath National Forest to obtain a free permit. Parking and access are free.

*Directions:* From Interstate 5 at Yreka, take the Highway 3/Fort Jones exit and drive 28 miles to Etna. Turn west on Etna-Somes Bar Road (Main Street in town) and drive 10.25 miles. Turn left on a signed access road just past Etna Summit and continue to the trailhead.

*Maps:* A trail information sheet can be obtained by contacting the Salmon River Ranger District at the address below. For a map of Klamath National Forest, send $3 to USDA-Forest Service, 630 Sansome Street, San Francisco, CA 94111. A map of the Marble Mountain Wilderness can also be purchased for $3. To obtain a topographic map of the area, ask for Eaton Peak from the USGS.

**Who to contact:** Klamath National Forest, Salmon River Ranger District, P.O. Box 280, Etna, CA 96027; (916) 467-5757.

**Trail notes:** Taylor Lake is proof that wilderness-like lakes can be accessible by a wheelchair. The trail is hard-packed dirt and **wheelchair accessible**, though wheelchairs with wide wheels are recommended. For those with boots instead of wheels, it's about a 10-minute walk to Taylor Lake, a long, narrow lake set on the northern end of the Russian Wilderness. Trout fishing is often very good here, and the walk is short enough so you can bring along a small raft or float tube. For a sidetrip option, the Pacific Crest Trail runs just above (east) of the lake, although the most direct access in the area for the PCT is at nearby Etna Summit. The only downer here is that occasionally the Forest Service permits cows to graze, and they stomp the grass at the far end of the lake and occasionally even walk in the shallows.

---

## 21. BIG BLUE LAKE       6.0 mi/4.5 hrs

**Reference:** In Russian Wilderness west of Etna; map A1, grid j8.

**User groups:** Hikers only. No dogs, horses or mountain bikes are allowed. No wheelchair facilities.

**Permits:** A campfire permit is required only for hikers planning to camp in the wilderness. Contact Klamath National Forest to obtain a free permit. Parking and access are free.

**Directions:** From Interstate 5 at Yreka, take the Highway 3/Fort Jones exit and drive 28 miles to Etna. Turn west on Etna-Somes Bar Road (Main Street in town) and drive 20 miles. Just before the Salmon River Bridge, turn left on Forest Service Road 40N54 and continue eight miles to the Music Creek Trailhead.

**Maps:** A trail information sheet can be obtained by contacting the Salmon River Ranger District at the address below. For a map of Klamath National Forest, send $3 to USDA-Forest Service, 630 Sansome Street, San Francisco, CA 94111. A map of the Marble Mountain Wilderness can also be purchased for $3. To obtain a topographic map of the area, ask for Sawyers Bar from the USGS.

**Who to contact:** Klamath National Forest, Salmon River Ranger District, P.O. Box 280, Etna, CA 96027; (916) 467-5757.

**Trail notes:** There are no trails to Big Blue Lake, and right off, that stops most people from even considering the trip. But if you are willing to scramble a bit, both up along a ridgeline and then down into a granite mountain bowl, your reward is a gorgeous lake, one of the prettiest in Northern California. There are just two camps at the lake, one mosquito-infested site along the northern shore, and another secluded, bugless camp near the outlet, with the lake just out of view. After parking at the Music Creek Trailhead, you start the trip by hiking up a moderate grade, climbing about a mile and junctioning with the Pacific Crest Trail. Turn left and hike on the PCT for less than a mile, climbing as you go. When you reach a saddle in the mountain, do not continue down the other side on the trail, but instead turn left and leave the trail, traversing across the mountain slope to Big Blue. After about an hour, you will arrive at the rim above the lake. From here you can drop down, and by following the tree line and scrambling across huge granite boulders, you can work your way down to the lake's shore. This last scramble is most easily accomplished in a counterclockwise direction in the mountain bowl around the lake. It's a bit tricky, but it's a do-able scamper for mountaineers in excellent physical condition.

## 22. STATUE LAKE 6.0 mi/4.0 hrs

*Reference:* **In Russian Wilderness west of Etna; map A1, grid j8.**

*User groups:* Hikers only. No dogs, horses or mountain bikes are allowed. No wheelchair facilities.

*Permits:* A campfire permit is required only for hikers planning to camp in the wilderness. Contact Klamath National Forest to obtain a free permit. Parking and access are free.

*Directions:* From Interstate 5 at Yreka, take the Highway 3/Fort Jones exit and drive 28 miles to Etna. Turn west on Etna-Somes Bar Road (Main Street in town) and drive 20 miles. Just before the Salmon River Bridge, turn left on Forest Service Road 40N54 and continue eight miles to the Music Creek Trailhead.

*Maps:* A trail information sheet can be obtained by contacting the Salmon River Ranger District at the address below. For a map of Klamath National Forest, send $3 to USDA-Forest Service, 630 Sansome Street, San Francisco, CA 94111. A map of the Marble Mountain Wilderness can also be purchased for $3. To obtain a topographic map of the area, ask for Sawyers Bar from the USGS.

*Who to contact:* Klamath National Forest, Salmon River Ranger District, P.O. Box 280, Etna, CA 96027; (916) 467-5757.

*Trail notes:* Statue Lake earned its name from the one-of-a-kind granite sculptures that frame the back wall of the lake. When you first arrive at the small lake, it is a wondrous yet solemn sight, one of nature's mountain temples. Some of the granite outcrops look like fingers that have been sculpted with a giant chisel. There is a small, primitive campsite on a granite bluff, from which you can often see small brook trout rising to feed. After parking at the Music Creek Trailhead, you start the trip by hiking up a moderate grade, climbing about a mile, and junctioning with the Pacific Crest Trail. Turn right and hike on the PCT for about 1.5 miles, an easy walk in the forest. When you reach a small spring creek, stop and fill up your canteens, then leave the trail and head uphill. It's about a 30-minute hike cross-country to the lake, the last 10 minutes over a large field of boulders.

# PACIFIC CREST TRAIL
## GENERAL INFORMATION
**92.0 mi. one way/8.0 days**

*Reference:* **Trail sections extend from Etna Summit north through the Marble Mountains to Seiad Valley on Highway 96, then onward to Rogue Wilderness in southern Oregon.**

*User groups:* Hikers, horses and dogs. No mountain bikes are allowed. No wheelchair access.

*Permits:* A campfire/wilderness permit is required for all hikers camping along this section of trail. For day use, a permit is not required.

*Maps:* The Klamath National Forest map provides a good overall view of the trail in this section. A map of the Marble Mountain Wilderness is also available. Send $3 for each to USDA-Forest Service, 630 Sansome Street, San Francisco, CA 94111. To obtain topographic maps, see each trail section for specific maps.

*Who to contact:* Klamath National Forest, Scott River Ranger District, 11263 North Highway 3, Fort Jones, CA 96032; (916) 468-5351.

*Trail notes:* This section of the Pacific Crest Trail includes some of its most and least popular sections in Northern California. The Etna Trailhead is an excellent jumpoff, once you get past the first few miles of dry, often hot terrain, heading directly into the Marble Mountain Wilderness, crossing through Marble Valley, past Marble Mountain itself, then onward past Paradise Lake to the northern sections of the wilderness. Most of the trail here is above tree line, with outstanding lookouts at several points, including a great vista from Marble Rim. As you head north, the trail becomes less and less traveled, eventually leaving the Marbles and descending along Grider Creek to the Klamath River town of Seiad Valley. From here, the trail is routed 34 miles north into Oregon. That section of the trail starts with a steep five-mile climb to Upper Devil's Peak, which keeps most day hikers off the route.

# PCT-46
## ETNA SUMMIT to GRIDER CREEK
**49.0 mi. one way/4.0 days**

*Reference:* **From Etna Summit north into Marble Mountain Wilderness west of Etna; map A1, grid j8.**

*User groups:* Hikers, dogs and horses. No mountain bikes are allowed. No wheelchair facilities.

*Permits:* A campfire permit is required only for hikers planning to camp in the wilderness. Contact Klamath National Forest to obtain a free permit. Parking and access are free.

*Directions:* From Interstate 5 at Yreka, take the Highway 3/Fort Jones exit and drive 28 miles to Etna. Turn west on Etna-Somes Bar Road (Main Street in town) and drive 10.5 miles to Etna Summit. The parking area is on the right.

*Maps:* A trail information sheet can be obtained by contacting the Salmon River Ranger District at the address below. For a map of Klamath National Forest, send $3 to USDA-Forest Service, 630 Sansome Street, San Francisco, CA 94111. A map of the Marble Mountain Wilderness can also be purchased for $3. To obtain a topographic image of the area, ask for Eaton Peak from the USGS.

*Who to contact:* Klamath National Forest, Salmon River Ranger District, P.O. Box 280, Etna, CA 96027; (916) 467-5757.

*Trail notes:* The Etna Summit is one of the major access points for the Pacific Crest Trail in Northern California. There is a good, safe parking area (good views from here, too), and at an elevation of 5,492 feet, you don't have to start your hike with a wicked climb, like what is demanded at so many other wilderness trailheads. From Etna Summit, the trail starts by crossing rugged, dry country which is best dealt with in the morning, reaching Shelly Lake about eight miles in. There's a campground at Shelly Meadows, a good first-night stopover. From there, an excellent second-day destination is the Marble Valley, about another 10 miles north, camping in the Sky High Lakes Basin. The next 20 miles of trail cross through and out of the Marble Mountains. In the process, you will pass Marble Mountain (a sidetrip to Marble Rim is mandatory), Paradise Lake and Kings Castle; many visitors will make camp at Paradise Lake. From there, the trail follows Big Ridge to Buckhorn Mountain (6,908 feet), goes past Huckleberry Mountain (6,303 feet) and then drops down to the headwaters of Grider Creek, the next major trailhead access point.

---

## PCT-47                7.0 mi. one way/1.0 day
## GRIDER CREEK to SEIAD VALLEY

*Reference:* **In Klamath National Forest, southeast of Happy Camp to Grider Creek Trailhead; map A1, grid f6.**

*User groups:* Hikers, dogs and horses. No mountain bikes are allowed. No wheelchair facilities.

*Permits:* No permits are required. Parking and access are free.

*Directions:* From Interstate 5 north of Yreka, turn west on Highway 96 and drive approximately 57 miles to Happy Camp. Turn south on Forest Service Road 70001 and drive about four miles, then turn east on Forest Service Road 45N19 and follow it to the trailhead at the end of the road.

*Maps:* A trail information sheet can be obtained by contacting the Scott River Ranger District at the address below. For a map of Klamath National Forest, send $3 to USDA-Forest Service, 630 Sansome Street, San Francisco, CA 94111. To obtain a topographic map of the area, ask for Seiad Valley from the USGS.

*Who to contact:* Klamath National Forest, Scott River Ranger District, 11263 North Highway 3, Fort Jones, CA 96032; (916) 468-5351.

*Trail notes:* The Pacific Crest Trail provides a good access point at the headwaters of Grider Creek, though most hikers use it in order to head south into the Marble Mountain Wilderness, not north. Heading north, it is about a 12-mile trip to the town of Seiad Valley on Highway 96, an excellent place for PCT hikers to pick up a food stash and dump garbage. The trail here follows Grider Creek, an easy descent northward as the stream pours toward the Klamath River. A good Forest Service campground (Grider Creek Camp) is available about three miles before reaching Seiad Valley.

# PCT-48      36.0 mi. one way/3.0 days
## SEIAD VALLEY to OREGON BORDER

*Reference:* **In Klamath National Forest, from Seiad Valley to Siskiyou Mountains; map A1, grid e7.**

*User groups:* Hikers, dogs and horses. No mountain bikes are allowed. No wheelchair facilities.

*Permits:* No permits are required. Parking and access are free.

*Directions:* From Interstate 5 north of Yreka, turn west on Highway 96 and drive approximately 40 miles to the town of Seiad Valley. Continue one mile west on Highway 96. The trailhead is on the north side. Parking is minimal; park across the highway.

*Maps:* A trail information sheet can be obtained by contacting the Oak Knoll Ranger District at the address below. For a map of Klamath National Forest, send $3 to USDA-Forest Service, 630 Sansome Street, San Francisco, CA 94111. To obtain a topographic map of the area, ask for Seiad Valley from the USGS.

*Who to contact:* Klamath National Forest, Oak Knoll Ranger District, 22541 Highway 96, Klamath River, CA 96050; (916) 465-2241.

*Trail notes:* Not many people hike this section of the Pacific Crest Trail, the northernmost segment in California. But it's a great chunk of trail, whether for a day hike or for the whole duration, all the way to Wards Fork Gap on the edge of the Rogue Wilderness in southern Oregon. For an excellent day hike, head up from the trailhead to the junction of the Boundary National Recreation Trail, a seven-mile trip one way. The first five miles are a steep climb out of the Klamath River Valley, rising to Upper Devil's Peak, elevation 6,040 feet.

# MAP A2

NOR-CAL MAP ........................ see page 14
adjoining maps
NORTH ...................................... no map
EAST (A3) ............................. see page 56
SOUTH (B2) ........................... see page 94
WEST (A1).............................. see page 30

5 TRAILS
PAGES 50-55

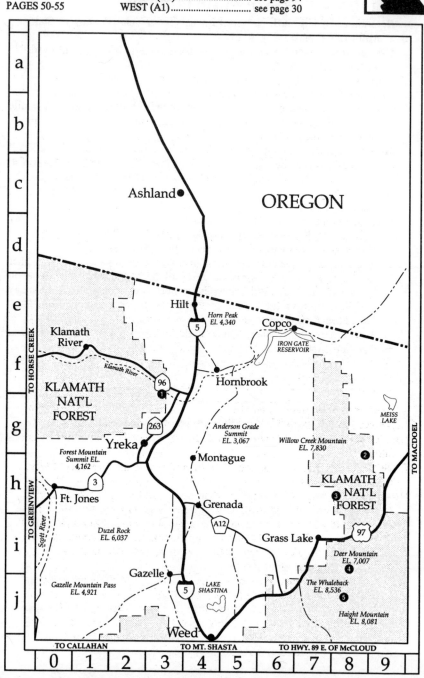

OREGON

Ashland

Hilt
Horn Peak
EL. 4,340
Copco

IRON GATE
RESERVOIR

Klamath
River

Klamath River

Hornbrook

KLAMATH
NAT'L
FOREST

MEISS
LAKE

Anderson Grade
Summit
EL. 3,067

Willow Creek Mountain
EL. 7,830

Yreka

Forest Mountain
Summit EL.
4,162

Montague

KLAMATH
NAT'L
FOREST

Ft. Jones

Duzel Rock
EL. 6,037

Grenada

A12

Grass Lake

Deer Mountain
EL. 7,007

Gazelle

Gazelle Mountain Pass
EL. 4,921

LAKE
SHASTINA

The Whaleback
EL. 8,536

Haight Mountain
EL. 8,081

Weed

TO HORSE CREEK

TO GREENVIEW

Scott River

TO MACDOEL

TO CALLAHAN       TO MT. SHASTA       TO HWY. 89 E. OF McCLOUD

| 0 | 1 | 2 | 3 | 4 | 5 | 6 | 7 | 8 | 9 |

**Map A2 featuring:** Klamath River, Klamath National Forest, Yreka

## 1. TREE OF HEAVEN TRAIL    3.5 mi/2.0 hrs

*Reference:* **On Klamath River in Klamath National Forest northwest of Yreka; map A2, grid f3.**

*User groups:* Hikers, dogs, mountain bikes and horses. No wheelchair facilities.

*Permits:* No permits are required. Parking and access are free.

*Directions:* From Yreka, drive 10 miles north on Interstate 5 to the Highway 96 exit. Turn west on Highway 96 and drive about five miles. Look for the Tree of Heaven Campground on the left. The trailhead is at the west end of the campground.

*Maps:* A trail guide can be obtained by contacting the Oak Knoll Ranger District at the address below. For a map of Klamath National Forest, send $3 to USDA-Forest Service, 630 Sansome Street, San Francisco, CA 94111. To obtain a topographic map of the area, ask for Badger Mountain from the USGS.

*Who to contact:* Klamath National Forest, Oak Knoll Ranger District, 22541 Highway 96, Klamath River, CA 96050; (916) 465-2241.

*Trail notes:* The trail out of the Tree of Heaven Campground is one of the best streamside trails anywhere along the Klamath River. It heads downstream along the Klamath, a level path that sometimes probes through heavy vegetation, and other times offers direct river access. The fall is an excellent time for berry picking. The trail ends at a good fishing access spot, though the fishing is poor during the prime camping/hiking/vacation season. Salmon start arriving in September in this area, steelhead in November and December. The Tree of Heaven river access is also a good take-out point for rafters and drift boaters after making the all-day run down from Iron Canyon Dam.

## 2. JUANITA LAKE TRAIL    1.75 mi/1.0 hrs

*Reference:* **In Klamath National Forest east of Yreka; map A2, grid g8.**

*User groups:* Hikers, **wheelchairs**, dogs and mountain bikes. No horses are allowed.

*Permits:* No permits are required. Parking and access are free except when camping.

*Directions:* From Interstate 5 at Weed, take the Weed/College of the Siskiyous exit and drive north through town to the Highway 97 turnoff. Drive approximately 35 miles northeast, then turn left on Ball Mountain Road and drive two miles. Turn right at the sign for Juanita Lake and continue about three miles to the lake, following the signs all the way. The trailhead is near the boat dock at the campground.

*Maps:* A trail guide can be obtained by contacting the Goosenest Ranger District at the address below. For a map of Klamath National Forest, send $3 to USDA-Forest Service, 630 Sansome Street, San Francisco, CA 94111. To obtain a topographic image of the area, ask for Panther Rock from the USGS.

*Who to contact:* Klamath National Forest, Goosenest Ranger District, 37805 Highway 97, Macdoel, CA 96058; (916) 398-4391.

*Trail notes:* Not many people know about Juanita Lake, even many Siskiyou County residents, but when they find out, taking this easy loop trail around the lake is usually one of their preferred options. The lake is set in a mixed conifer forest, though few trees here are large, and wildlife in the area includes osprey and bald eagles. In the last hour of light during summer, both osprey and eagles occasionally make a fishing trip at the lake. Juanita Lake is a small lake that provides lakeside camping and fishing for brook trout— it's stocked with 2,000 per year. The small fishing piers are **wheelchair accessible**, a nice touch. A good sidetrip is driving on the Forest Service Road up to Ball Mountain, located about two miles southwest of the lake, for great views of Mt. Shasta from the 7,786-foot summit.

---

## 3. GOOSENEST     4.0 mi/2.75 hrs

*Reference:* In Klamath National Forest north of Mt. Shasta; map A2, grid h7.
*User groups:* Hikers, dogs, mountain bikes and horses. No wheelchair facilities.
*Permits:* No permits are required. Parking and access are free.
*Directions:* From Interstate 5 at Weed, take the Weed/College of the Siskiyous exit and drive north through town to the Highway 97 turnoff. Turn right on Highway 97 and drive about 25 miles northeast. About three-quarters of a mile past the Tennant turnoff, turn left on Forest Service Road 46N10 and drive about seven miles to a junction of dirt roads. Here, turn left on County Road 7K007 and drive one mile, then turn left again on Forest Service Road 45N22 and drive six miles. Turn right on Forest Service Road 45N72Y and drive 2.5 miles to the trailhead at the base of the mountain.
*Maps:* A trail guide can be obtained by contacting the Goosenest Ranger District at the address below. For a map of Klamath National Forest, send $3 to USDA-Forest Service, 630 Sansome Street, San Francisco, CA 94111. To obtain a topographic map of the area, ask for Grass Lake from the USGS.
*Who to contact:* Klamath National Forest, Goosenest Ranger District, 37805 Highway 97, Macdoel, CA 96058; (916) 398-4391.
*Trail notes:* This is a short, steep trail that peaks out at the top of Goosenest at a 8,280-foot elevation. The surrounding views are extraordinary, especially looking south at Mt. Shasta. But looking east is also memorable, toward the high prairie country around Meiss Lake and the Butte Valley Wildlife Area, as well as to the west of the little Shasta Valley. Despite the great views, the trail gets very little use, even in the summer months. Most local residents are not aware that the trailhead access is located fairly near the top of the mountain. The surrounding forest is primarily hemlock and red fir. While mountain bikes are permitted, they are not recommended; you are likely to walk them most of the way.

---

## 4. DEER MOUNTAIN     4.0 mi/2.25 hrs

*Reference:* In Klamath National Forest north of Mt. Shasta; map A2, grid i8.
*User groups:* Hikers, dogs, mountain bikes and horses. No wheelchair facilities.
*Permits:* No permits are required. Parking and access are free.
*Directions:* From Interstate 5 at Weed, take the Weed/College of the Siskiyous exit and drive north through town to the Highway 97 turnoff. Turn right on Highway 97 and drive approximately 15 miles. Turn right on Deer Mountain Road and drive four miles to Deer Mountain Snowmobile Park. Turn right

on Forest Service Road 44N23 and drive about two miles. There is no designated trailhead; park off the road and hike cross-country to the mountain top. Forest Service Road 43N69 loops around the base of the mountain; you may also hike from anywhere along that road.

*Maps:* A trail guide can be obtained by contacting the Goosenest Ranger District at the address below. For a map of Klamath National Forest, send $3 to USDA-Forest Service, 630 Sansome Street, San Francisco, CA 94111. To obtain a topographic image of the area, ask for The Whaleback from the USGS.

*Who to contact:* Klamath National Forest, Goosenest Ranger District, 37805 Highway 97, Macdoel, CA 96058; (916) 398-4391.

*Trail notes:* Deer Mountain is the second of a line of small peaks set on the north side of Mt. Shasta that extend all the way to the Medicine Lake wildlands. Looking north from Shasta, the first peak is the Whaleback, at a 8,528-foot elevation, and the second is Deer Mountain, at 7,006 feet. Starting elevation at the parking area is 6,200 feet, so you have an 800-foot climb to gain the summit. The trail is routed through forest consisting of various pines and firs. This route gets very little use, even though it is easy to reach and the destination is a mountain top. Most out-of-towners visiting this area are attracted to the trails on Mt. Shasta instead, and most locals just plain overlook it.

---

# 5. THE WHALEBACK      3.0 mi/2.5 hrs

*Reference:* **In Klamath National Forest north of Mt. Shasta; map A2, grid i8.**

*User groups:* Hikers, dogs, mountain bikes and horses. No wheelchair facilities.

*Permits:* No permits are required. Parking and access are free.

*Directions:* From Interstate 5 at Weed, take the Weed/College of the Siskiyous exit and drive north through town to the Highway 97 turnoff. Turn right on Highway 97 and drive approximately 15 miles, then turn right on Deer Mountain Road and drive four miles to Deer Mountain Snowmobile Park. Continue three miles east on Forest Service Road 19, then turn right on Forest Service Road 42N24 and drive three miles to a gate. Park and hike in. There is no designated trail; you must hike cross-country from the road. The peak is approximately 1.5 miles from the gate.

*Maps:* A trail guide can be obtained by contacting the Goosenest Ranger District at the address below. For a map of Klamath National Forest, send $3 to USDA-Forest Service, 630 Sansome Street, San Francisco, CA 94111. To obtain a topographic image of the area, ask for The Whaleback from the USGS.

*Who to contact:* Klamath National Forest, Goosenest Ranger District, 37805 Highway 97, Macdoel, CA 96058; (916) 398-4391.

*Trail notes:* When you pass Mt. Shasta driving north on Interstate 5, you will see this large hump-like mountain that sits directly north of Shasta. It looks like a huge volcanic bump that was born when Shasta was active. This is the Whaleback, 8,528 feet high, providing an excellent hike with a surprise reward at the top. That surprise is a large crater. The Whaleback Summit is actually a volcanic cindercone with a collapsed center. This interesting geology, along with the unsurpassed view of Mt. Shasta to the south, makes this a first-rate hike. Yet almost nobody tries it, most likely because they don't realize how near you can drive to the top, or because there is no formal trail. After parking at the gate, you just hike cross-country style up to the rim. It's a scramble only in a few places, a 1.5-mile hike. In the process, you will climb 1,100 feet, from a starting elevation of 7,400 feet to Whaleback Rim.

## LEAVE NO TRACE TIPS

### Plan ahead and prepare

• Learn about the regulations and issues that apply to the area you are visiting.

• Avoid heavy-use areas.

• Obtain all maps and permits.

• Bring extra garbage bags to pack out any refuse you come across.

# MAP A3

NOR-CAL MAP ........................ see page 14
adjoining maps
NORTH ................................... no map
EAST (A4) ............................. see page 64
SOUTH (B3) .......................... see page 120
WEST (A2) ............................. see page 50

9 TRAILS
PAGES 56-63

**Map A3 featuring:** Lava Beds National Monument, Klamath Wildlife Refuge, Modoc National Forest, Medicine Lake

## 1. CAPTAIN JACKS STRONGHOLD
1.5 mi/1.5 hrs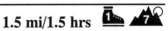

*Reference:* **In Lava Beds National Monument south of Klamath Wildlife Refuge; map A3, grid h4.**

*User groups:* Hikers only. No dogs, mountain bikes or horses are allowed. The trail is **partially wheelchair accessible**.

*Permits:* No permits are required. A $4 park entrance fee is charged for each car.

*Directions:* From Interstate 5 at Redding, turn east on Highway 299 and drive 133 miles to Canby. Turn north on Highway 139 and drive 20 miles, then turn west on Lava Beds National Monument Road and follow the signs to the park entrance. Continue about 3.5 miles to the visitor center, then proceed north another 10 miles on Hill Road, then turn east and continue to the trailhead at Captain Jacks Stronghold.

*Maps:* A free brochure is available by contacting Lava Beds National Monument at the address below. To obtain a topographic map of the area, ask for Captain Jacks Stronghold from the USGS.

*Who to contact:* Lava Beds National Monument, P.O. Box 867, Tulelake, CA 96134; (916) 667-2282 or (916) 667-2231.

*Trail notes:* Captain Jack was a Modoc warrior who fought U.S. troops attempting to relocate Native Americans off their historical lands and onto a reservation. Eventually in 1873, Captain Jack was captured and hanged, and this site was later named for him. Captain Jacks Stronghold provides a good introduction to the Lava Beds National Monument, an easy walk across volcanic fields, with lots of trenches, dips and rocks. From this trailhead, there are actually two loop trails available, including a shorter route that is just a half-mile long. The general terrain is level, with a trailhead elevation of 4,047 feet and a high point of 4,080 feet, but when you hike it, you will find that the trail is anything but flat. Note that during the winter, this is an outstanding area to see mule deer. Many of the famous photographs of big bucks in California were taken in this area. The wildlife viewing is best at the onset of winter, after the first inch or two of snow has fallen. In addition, a good sidetrip is nearby to Tule Lake, a favorite wintering area for waterfowl and bald eagles.

## 2. WHITNEY BUTTE TRAIL
6.8 mi/4.0 hrs

*Reference:* **In Lava Beds National Monument south of Klamath Wildlife Refuge; map A3, grid i4.**

*User groups:* Hikers and horses. No dogs or mountain bikes are allowed. No wheelchair facilities.

*Permits:* No permits are required. A $4 park entrance fee is charged for each car.

*Directions:* From Interstate 5 at Redding, turn east on Highway 299 and drive 133 miles to Canby. Turn north on Highway 139 and drive 20 miles, then turn west on Lava Beds National Monument Road and follow the signs to the park entrance. Continue about 3.5 miles to the visitor center, then proceed another two miles north on Hill Road to the turnoff for Merrill Cave. The trailhead is at the end of the road.

*Maps:* A free brochure is available by contacting Lava Beds National Monument at the address below. To obtain a topographic map of the area, ask for Schonchin Butte from USGS.

*Who to contact:* Lava Beds National Monument, P.O. Box 867, Tulelake, CA 96134; (916) 667-2282 or (916) 667-2231.

*Trail notes:* The Whitney Butte Trail is one of three wilderness trails in Lava Beds National Monument, and for many, it is the best of the lot. From the trailhead at Merrill Cave, set at 4,880 feet, the trail heads west for 3.4 miles, skirting the northern flank of Whitney Butte (5,004 feet). The trail ends at the edge of the Callahan Lava Flow, a massive flow on the park's southwest boundary. This area bears a surprising resemblance to the surface of the moon, and skilled photographers who know how to use sunlight to their advantage can take black-and-white pictures that will fool most people.

---

## 3. THOMAS WRIGHT TRAIL     2.2 mi/1.0 hr

*Reference:* **In Lava Beds National Monument south of Klamath Wildlife Refuge; map A3, grid i4.**

*User groups:* Hikers only. No dogs, mountain bikes or horses are allowed. No wheelchair facilities.

*Permits:* No permits are required. A $4 park entrance fee is charged for each car.

*Directions:* From Interstate 5 at Redding, turn east on Highway 299 and drive 133 miles to Canby. Turn north on Highway 139 and drive 20 miles, then turn west on Lava Beds National Monument Road and follow the signs to the park entrance. Continue about 3.5 miles to the visitor center, then proceed another five miles to the trailhead on the right.

*Maps:* A free brochure is available by contacting Lava Beds National Monument at the address below. To obtain a topographic image of the area, ask for Captain Jacks Stronghold from the USGS.

*Who to contact:* Lava Beds National Monument, P.O. Box 867, Tulelake, CA 96134; (916) 667-2282 or (916) 667-2231.

*Trail notes:* If you sense ghosts shadowing your footsteps, well, it won't be the first time. Some say this area is haunted by the ghosts of Modoc Indians, who fought troops in several violent battles for custody of the land. While the Modoc warriors eventually lost that war, some say they actually won in the long run, since their spirits haunt modern-day visitors. At the end of the trail, there are interpretive signs that explain the Thomas-Wright battlefield site. From here, an excellent sidetrip is continuing off-trail, clambering up to the Hardin Butte, a 130-foot climb. It sits on the western edge of the huge Schonchin Lava Flow.

---

## 4. SCHONCHIN BUTTE TRAIL     1.5 mi/1.0 hr

*Reference:* **In Lava Beds National Monument south of Klamath Wildlife Refuge; map A3, grid i4.**

*User groups:* Hikers only. No dogs, mountain bikes or horses are allowed. No wheelchair facilities.

*Permits:* No permits are required. A $4 park entrance fee is charged for each car.

*Directions:* From Interstate 5 at Redding, turn east on Highway 299 and drive

133 miles to Canby. Turn north on Highway 139 and drive 20 miles, then turn west on Lava Beds National Monument Road and follow the signs to the park entrance. Continue about 3.5 miles to the visitor center, then proceed another 2.5 miles north on Hill Road. Turn right at the sign for Schonchin Butte and drive approximately one mile on an unpaved road to the trailhead.

*Maps:* A free brochure is available by contacting Lava Beds National Monument at the address below. To obtain a topographic map of the area, ask for Schonchin Butte from the USGS.

*Who to contact:* Lava Beds National Monument, P.O. Box 867, Tulelake, CA 96134; (916) 667-2282 or (916) 667-2231.

*Trail notes:* This is a short hike, but for many it's a butt-kicker. A portion of it is quite steep, steep enough to get most folks wheezing like old coal-powered locomotives. That's true even though the trail climbs just 250 feet, from a trailhead elevation of 5,000 feet to the lookout at 5,253 feet. Schonchin Butte has an old fire lookout, and of course, the views are spectacular, especially of the Schonchin Lava Flow to the northeast. Because of the close proximity to the visitor center, as well as the short distance involved, many visitors make the tromp to the top.

---

# 5. MEDICINE LAKE LOOP    4.5 mi/2.5 hrs

*Reference:* **In Modoc National Forest northeast of Mt. Shasta; map A3, grid j2.**

*User groups:* Hikers, dogs, mountain bikes and horses. No wheelchair facilities.

*Permits:* No permits are required. Parking and access are free unless you're camping.

*Directions:* From Redding, turn north on Interstate 5 and drive 56 miles. Take the McCloud-Reno exit and travel 29 miles east on Highway 89 to Bartle. Just past Bartle, turn northeast on Powder Hill Road (Forest Service Road 49) and drive 31 miles to Medicine Lake Road. Continue on Medicine Lake Road to the lake.

*Maps:* A free brochure on the Medicine Lake Highlands is available by contacting the Double Head Ranger District at the address below. For a map of Modoc National Forest, send $3 to USDA-Forest Service, 630 Sansome Street, San Francisco, CA 94111. To obtain a topographic map of the area, ask for Medicine Lake from the USGS.

*Who to contact:* Modoc National Forest, Double Head Ranger District, P.O. Box 369, Tulelake, CA 96134; (916) 667-2246.

*Trail notes:* When you stand on the shore of Medicine Lake, it might be difficult to believe that this was once the center of a volcano. The old crater is now filled with water and circled by conifers, and the lake is clear and crisp. It is set at 6,700 feet, a unique and popular destination for camping, boating and fishing. At some point in their stay, most campers will take a morning or afternoon to walk around the lake. While there is no specific trail, the route is clear enough. There is a sense of timeless history here. Although its geology is comparable to Crater Lake in Oregon, Medicine Lake is neither as deep nor as blue. But a bonus here is the good shorefishing for large brook trout, often in the 12- to 14-inch class, buoyed by the largest stocks of trout of any lake in the region (30,000 per year). There are also many excellent nearby sidetrips, including ice caves (along the access road on the way in), a great mountain-top lookout from Little Mt. Hoffman just west of the lake, and nearby little Bullseye and Blanche lakes.

---

# 6. MEDICINE LAKE GLASS FLOW
**2.0 mi/2.0 hrs**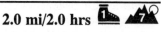

*Reference:* In Modoc National Forest north of Medicine Lake; map A3, grid j3.

*User groups:* Hikers and dogs. The terrain is not suitable for mountain bikes or horses. No wheelchair facilities.

*Permits:* No permits are required. Parking and access are free.

*Directions:* From Redding, turn north on Interstate 5 and drive 56 miles. Take the McCloud-Reno exit and travel 29 miles east on Highway 89 to Bartle. Just past Bartle, turn northeast on Powder Hill Road (Forest Service Road 49) and drive approximately 33.5 miles (2.5 miles past the Medicine Lake turnoff). The glass flow is located just off the road on the left; park and go in.

*Maps:* A free brochure on the Medicine Lake Highlands is available by contacting the Double Head Ranger District at the address below. For a map of Modoc National Forest, send $3 to USDA-Forest Service, 630 Sansome Street, San Francisco, CA 94111. To obtain a topographic map of the area, ask for Medicine Lake from the USGS.

*Who to contact:* Modoc National Forest, Double Head Ranger District, P.O. Box 369, Tulelake, CA 96134; (916) 667-2246.

*Trail notes:* The Medicine Lake Glass Flow covers 570 acres but has no designated trails. You can explore in any direction you wish, investigating the ancient, dull, stony-gray dacite, which runs 50 to 150 feet deep. This is part of the Medicine Lake Highlands, located just a mile north of Medicine Lake, where "rocks that float and mountains of glass" (poetic description from Forest Service geologists) resemble the surface of the moon. That is why this area was selected by the Manned Spacecraft Center in 1965 for study by astronauts preparing for the first manned trip to the moon. Most people will just poke around for an hour or two, take a few pictures, and leave saying they've never seen anything like it.

---

# 7. LITTLE MT. HOFFMAN
**0.25 mi/0.25 hr**

*Reference:* In Modoc National Forest north of Medicine Lake; map A3, grid j3.

*User groups:* Hikers, dogs, mountain bikes and horses. No wheelchair facilities.

*Permits:* No permits are required. Parking and access are free.

*Directions:* From Redding, turn north on Interstate 5 and drive 56 miles. Take the McCloud-Reno exit and travel 29 miles east on Highway 89 to Bartle. Just past Bartle, turn northeast on Powder Hill Road (Forest Service Road 49) and drive 31 miles to Medicine Lake Road. Turn left and continue to Headquarters Campground on the west side of the lake. You can park and hike in from here. In the summer, the road to the summit is accessible by car.

*Maps:* A free brochure on the Medicine Lake Highlands is available by contacting the Double Head Ranger District at the address below. For a map of Modoc National Forest, send $3 to USDA-Forest Service, 630 Sansome Street, San Francisco, CA 94111. To obtain a topographic map of the area, ask for Medicine Lake from the USGS.

*Who to contact:* Modoc National Forest, Double Head Ranger District, P.O. Box 369, Tulelake, CA 96134; (916) 667-2246.

*Trail notes:* Mt. Hoffman, at a 7,309-foot elevation, is one of the great spots to take pictures in Northern California. Looking north, you get a sweeping view of the Lava Beds National Monument and beyond to Mt. McLaughlin in Oregon. To the east is Big Glass Mountain and to the south is Lassen Peak. To the west, of course, is Mt. Shasta, the most dramatic photo opportunity available here. The summit is easy to reach in the summer with a road going eight miles right to the top; from there you can walk around the summit, enjoying the views in all directions. There is an old Forest Service lookout station here that is used only rarely during thunderstorms, from which spotters will scan for lightning strikes and the start of forest fires. This is one of the few places where you get world-class views without a difficult hike.

---

## 8. GLASS MOUNTAIN 2.5 mi/1.5 hrs

*Reference:* In Modoc National Forest east of Medicine Lake; map A3, grid j3.

*User groups:* Hikers and dogs. The terrain is not suitable for mountain bikes or horses. No wheelchair facilities.

*Permits:* No permits are required. Parking and access are free.

*Directions:* From Redding, turn north on Interstate 5 and drive 56 miles. Take the McCloud-Reno exit and travel 29 miles east on Highway 89 to Bartle. Just past Bartle, turn northeast on Powder Hill Road (Forest Service Road 49) and drive approximately 29 miles. Turn right on Forest Service Road 97 and drive about six miles, then turn north on Forest Service Road 43N99 and continue to the southern border of Glass Mountain.

*Maps:* A free brochure on the Medicine Lake Highlands is available by contacting the Double Head Ranger District at the address below. For a map of Modoc National Forest, send $3 to USDA-Forest Service, 630 Sansome Street, San Francisco, CA 94111. To obtain a topographic map of the area, ask for Medicine Lake from the USGS.

*Who to contact:* Modoc National Forest, Double Head Ranger District, P.O. Box 369, Tulelake, CA 96134; (916) 667-2246.

*Trail notes:* Glass Mountain is one of the most unusual settings in the Medicine Lake Highlands, a glass flow that covers 4,210 acres. It was created when glassy dacite and rhyolitic obsidian flowed from the same volcanic vent without mixing, creating a present-day phenomenon that exhibits no modification from weather, erosion or vegetation. There are no designated trails on Glass Mountain, so visitors just wander about, inspecting the geologic curiosities as they go. Take care to stay clear of the obsidian, which can have arrowhead-sharp edges and be quite slippery. Don't walk on it and don't handle it. Instead, stay on the gray-colored dacite.

---

## 9. TIMBER MOUNTAIN 0.5 mi/1.0 hr

*Reference:* In Modoc National Forest near Highway 139 California border check station; map A3, grid j6.

*User groups:* Hikers, dogs, mountain bikes and horses. The lookout is **partially wheelchair accessible**, but the trails are not.

*Permits:* No permits are required. Parking and access are free.

*Directions:* From Interstate 5 at Redding, turn east on Highway 299 and drive

133 miles to Canby. Turn north on Highway 139 and drive 20 miles, then turn west on Forest Service Road 97 and drive about a mile. Turn south on County Road 97A and drive 1.5 miles, then continue south on Forest Service Road 44N19 and continue for about three miles to the base of the mountain. The road continues to the summit, where there is a Forest Service lookout.

*Maps:* For a map of Modoc National Forest, send $3 to USDA-Forest Service, 630 Sansome Street, San Francisco, CA 94111. To obtain a topographic map of the area, ask for Perez from the USGS.

*Who to contact:* Modoc National Forest, Double Head Ranger District, P.O. Box 369, Tulelake, CA 96134; (916) 667-2246.

*Trail notes:* When it comes to seeing wildlife, timing is everything. You can make this trip to Timber Mountain in the summer and wonder how it ever earned such a high rating in this book. After all, from the lookout at 5,086 feet, the view is quite nice of the high Modoc plateau country, but hey, a 9? Make this trip in December and you will see why. In three hours, we saw about 400 deer, including dozens of big mule deer bucks with giant racks. What happens, you see, is that when the cold weather starts (long after the deer season has ended), the herd migrates out of Oregon and arrives in this area for winter. In turn, what you do is make the drive to the summit, park near the Forest Service lookout, then prepare for some fun. You creep to the summit rim, then peer over the side and down the mountain slope, scanning with binoculars. Small groups of 10 to 15 deer seem to be everywhere. That is how you spend your time here, creeping to the edge, peering over the tops of rocks, spotting and stalking, maybe taking a few photographs with a telephoto lens. It can be the best place to see deer in California.

## LEAVE NO TRACE TIPS

### Keep the wilderness wild

• Let nature's sound prevail. Avoid loud voices and noises.

• Leave radios and tape players at home.
At drive-in camping sites, never open car doors with music playing.

• Careful guidance is necessary when choosing any games to bring for children. Most toys, especially any kind of gun toys with which children simulate shooting at each other, should not be allowed on a camping trip.

• Control pets at all times, or leave them with a sitter at home.

• Treat natural heritage with respect. Leave plants,
rocks and historical artifacts where you find them.

# MAP A4

NOR-CAL MAP ....................... see page 14
adjoining maps
NORTH ........................................... no map
EAST ............................................... no map
SOUTH (B4) .......................... see page 136
WEST (A3) .............................. see page 56

3 TRAILS
PAGES 64-67

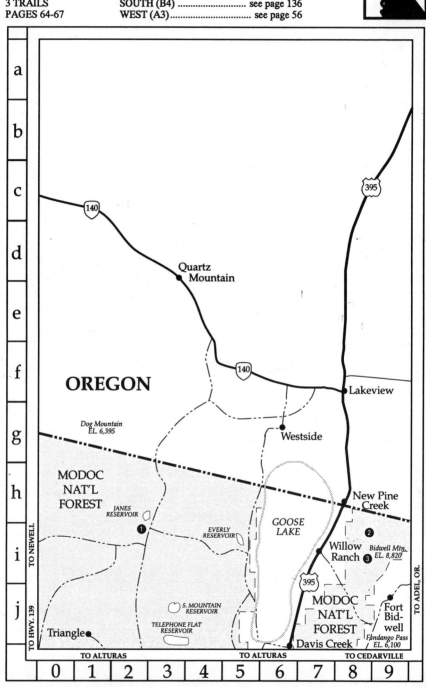

## Map A4 featuring: Modoc National Forest, Goose Lake

# 1. JANES RESERVOIR     1.0 mi/0.75 hr

*Reference:* **In Modoc National Forest north of Alturas; map A4, grid i2.**

*User groups:* Hikers, dogs, mountain bikes and horses. No wheelchair facilities.

*Permits:* No permits are required. Parking and access are free.

*Directions:* From Interstate 5 at Redding, turn east on Highway 299 and drive 146 miles to Alturas. Turn north on US 395 and travel about 20 miles to the "town" of Davis Creek. Turn left on Westside Road and drive 12 miles, then turn west on South Main Road and travel 14.5 miles. Turn south on Crowder Flat Road and proceed a half mile to Janes Reservoir.

*Maps:* For a map of Modoc National Forest, send $3 to USDA-Forest Service, 630 Sansome Street, San Francisco, CA 94111. To obtain a topographic image of the area, ask for South Mountain from the USGS.

*Who to contact:* Modoc National Forest, Devil's Garden Ranger District, P.O. Box 5, Canby, CA 96015; (916) 233-4611.

*Trail notes:* A dirt road leads from the southwest corner of Janes Reservoir to Huffman Butte, about a two-mile drive (if your car can't handle the road, you can hike it). The best strategy is to park at the base of the butte, then make the easy climb to the top of it. The reward is a nice view of the lake and the surrounding stark terrain. This is sagebrush country, the high plateau land of Modoc country. You are likely to see cattle, possibly wild mustangs, and with the number of wetlands in the area, good numbers of waterfowl, particularly Canada geese. However, you are unlikely to see people. Even though it is very remote for a drive-to area, a bonus is that there are a number of sidetrips possible to other lakes. The best are the Alphabet lakes (C Reservoir has the best trout fishing) and Big Sage Reservoir on Crowder Flat Road.

# 2. LILY LAKE to CAVE LAKE     0.5 mi/0.5 hr

*Reference:* **In Modoc National Forest east of Goose Lake; map A4, grid i8.**

*User groups:* Hikers, dogs, mountain bikes and horses. No wheelchair facilities.

*Permits:* No permits are required. Parking and access are free.

*Directions:* From Interstate 5 at Redding, turn east on Highway 299 and drive 146 miles to Alturas. Turn north on US 395 and drive 40 miles to the town of New Pine Creek (on the Oregon/California border). Turn left on Forest Service Road 2 and drive 5.5 miles east to the lake.

*Maps:* For a map of Modoc National Forest, send $3 to USDA-Forest Service, 630 Sansome Street, San Francisco, CA 94111. To obtain a topographic image of the area, ask for Mt. Bidwell from the USGS.

*Who to contact:* Modoc National Forest, Warner Mountain Ranger District, P.O. Box 220, Cedarville, CA 96104; (916) 279-6116.

*Trail notes:* While there are no designated trails, the quarter-mile walk from the campground at Lily Lake over to Cave Lake is an easy and rewarding trip. The surroundings at Lily Lake are quite beautiful, mostly forest with few humans around, and pretty little flowers blooming in the lily pads along the shallow eastern shore of the lake. As you walk to Cave Lake, the surroundings quickly change. This lake is also small, but with a barren shoreline, the trees placed well back from the water. There's a great contrast between the two lakes. A bonus is decent fishing for rainbow trout at Lily Lake and brook trout at Cave Lake. A good sidetrip is making the short walk over to the headwaters of Pine Creek, a small but pretty stream that is overlooked by most visitors.

## 3. HI GRADE NATIONAL RECREATION TRAIL

1.1 mi/0.5 hr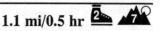

*Reference:* **In Modoc National Forest east of Goose Lake; map A4, grid i8.**

*User groups:* Hikers, dogs, mountain bikes and horses. No wheelchair facilities.

*Permits:* No permits are required. Parking and access are free.

*Directions:* From Interstate 5 at Redding, turn east on Highway 299 and drive 146 miles to Alturas. Turn north on US 395 and drive approximately 36 miles. Turn right on Forest Service Road 9 and drive 4.5 miles. At the Buck Creek Ranger Station, turn left on Forest Service Road 47N72 and drive about six miles to the trailhead. Four-wheel-drive vehicles are required.

*Maps:* For a map of Modoc National Forest, send $3 to USDA-Forest Service, 630 Sansome Street, San Francisco, CA 94111. To obtain topographic images of the area, ask for Mt. Bidwell and Willow Ranch from the USGS.

*Who to contact:* Modoc National Forest, Warner Mountain Ranger District, P.O. Box 220, Cedarville, CA 96104; (916) 279-6116.

*Trail notes:* This trail is actually 5.5 miles long, but only 1.1 miles are specifically designed for hiking. The rest is a designated four-wheel-drive trail, one of the only national four-wheel-drive trails in the state. Of course, you can still hike all of it, but it is better to use four-wheeling to get out there, then hike the final mile to get way out there. As you go, watch for signs of old, abandoned mining operations, because gold was discovered here. They never found enough to cause any outpouring of goldminers, though, and the result is a very sparsely populated county, with this area being abandoned completely. The surrounding habitat is a mix of high desert and timber, though the trees tend to be small. A good sidetrip from the nearby Buck Creek Ranger Station is to Fandango Pass, with good views to the east of Surprise Valley and the Nevada mountains. This is where a group of immigrants arrived, topped the ridge, looked west and saw Goose Lake, and shouted, "Ah ha, the Pacific Ocean! We have arrived!" So they started dancing the Fandango, but alas, got massacred by marauding Indians. That's how the mountain pass got its name.

## LEAVE NO TRACE TIPS

### Respect other users

• Horseback riders have priority over hikers. Step to the downhill side of the trail and talk softly when encountering horseback riders.

• Hikers and horseback riders have priority over mountain bikers. When mountain bikers encounter other users, even on wide trails, they should pass at an extremely slow speed. On very narrow trails, they should dismount and get off to the side, so the hiker or horseback rider can pass without having their trip disrupted.

• Mountain bikes are not permitted on most single-track trails and are expressly prohibited on all portions of the Pacific Crest Trail, in designated wilderness areas and on most state park trails. Mountain bikers breaking these rules should be confronted, told to dismount and walk their bikes until they reach a legal area.

• It is illegal for horseback riders to break off branches that may lay in the path of wilderness trails.

• Horseback riders on overnight trips are prohibited from camping in many areas, and are usually required to keep stock animals in specific areas where they can do no damage to the landscape.

# MAP BØ

14 TRAILS
PAGES 68-77

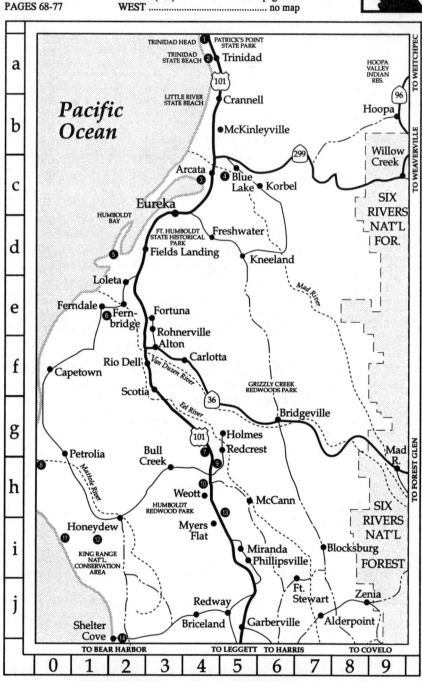

**Map BØ featuring:** Patrick's Point State Park, Eureka, Trinidad Head, Samoa Peninsula, Arcata, Humboldt Bay, Arcata Redwood Park, Ferndale, Humboldt Redwoods State Park, King Range National Conservation Area, Shelter Cove

## 1. RIM LOOP TRAIL    3.0 mi/2.5 hrs

*Reference:* **At Patrick's Point State Park north of Eureka; map BØ, grid a4.**

*User groups:* Hikers only. No dogs, mountain bikes or horses are allowed. **Partial wheelchair access** is available.

*Permits:* No permits are required. A state park day-use fee of $5 per car is charged.

*Directions:* From Eureka, turn north on US 101 and drive approximately 25 miles to Trinidad and the Patrick's Point State Park signed turnoff. Follow the signs to the entrance station, then proceed to the Agate Beach parking area.

*Maps:* For a park map and brochure, send a self-addressed stamped envelope and a check or money order for 75 cents to Patrick's Point State Park at the address below. To obtain a topographic map of the area, ask for Trinidad from the USGS.

*Who to contact:* Patrick's Point State Park, 41250 Patrick's Point Drive, Trinidad, CA 95570; (707) 677-3570 or (707) 445-6547.

*Trail notes:* Patrick's Point State Park is set on a coastal headland that is lush with ferns, spruce and wildflowers, and bordered by the Pacific where you can go tidepool hopping or whale watching. That means you get the best of two different worlds. This trail is the best way to visit them. At times it tunnels through thick vegetation, at other times it opens up to sweeping ocean views. A bonus is that along the way, there are several spur tails that provide access to many feature areas, including Mussel Rocks, Wedding Rock, Agate Beach, Lookout Rock, Abalone Point and Palmer's Point. The views are sensational at all of these spots. The spur trails, while short (they add just 1.5 miles to the hike), will make this a two- to three-hour trip, because you just won't want to rush through it. The only downers are the fog and the heavy out-of-state tourist traffic, both common during the summer.

*Special note:* The best **wheelchair accessible** section of the Rim Trail is from Wedding Rock to Patrick's Point, and visitors must park at the Wedding Rock parking area to access it.

## 2. TSURAI LOOP    1.5 mi/1.0 hr

*Reference:* **On Trinidad Head on the Humboldt coast north of Eureka; map BØ, grid a4.**

*User groups:* Hikers only. No dogs, mountain bikes or horses are allowed. No wheelchair facilities.

*Permits:* No permits are required. Parking and access are free.

*Directions:* From Eureka, turn north on US 101 and drive approximately 22 miles to Trinidad. Turn left on Main Street and drive to Trinity Street. Turn left and continue to the end of the road. Turn right on Edwards Street and continue to the parking area.

*Maps:* For free maps and brochures, write to the Trinidad Chamber of Commerce at P.O. Box 356, Trinidad, CA 95570; (707) 677-3448. To obtain a topographic map of the area, ask for Trinidad from the USGS.

*Who to contact:* For general information, write to Axel Lindgren at P.O. Box 62, Trinidad, CA 95570; (707) 677-3473.

*Trail notes:* The Tsurai Loop is a great, easy walk with coastal views, unique terrain and a nearby restaurant. The views are of the rocky Trinidad harbor and coast, with benches available along the way to sit and watch for the "puff-of-smoke" spouts on the ocean surface from migrating whales. The terrain includes the 300-foot miniature mountain at Trinidad Head, the pretty beachfront to the north of the Head area, and the Trinidad Pier. The restaurant? It's called Seascape, and you can get a crab omelette for breakfast there that'll have your mouth watering every time you start driving north of Eureka on Highway 101. In the summer, the trail is quite popular among tourists because of the striking nature of Trinidad Head.

---

# 3. SANCTUARY TRAIL 2.0 mi/1.0 hr

*Reference:* **In Arcata Marsh and Wildlife Sanctuary on the northern edge of Humboldt Bay; map BØ, grid c4.**

*User groups:* Hikers and dogs. No mountain bikes or horses are allowed. No wheelchair facilities.

*Permits:* No permits are required. Parking and access are free.

*Directions:* From Eureka, turn north on US 101 and drive to Arcata. Take the Samoa Boulevard exit and drive west on Samoa Boulevard to I Street. Turn south and continue to the parking area.

*Maps:* For a free, detailed trail map, contact the City of Arcata at the address below, ask for the Marsh and Wildlife Sanctuary Trail map. To obtain a topographic map of the area, ask for Arcata South from the USGS.

*Who to contact:* City of Arcata, Environmental Services Department, 736 F Street, Arcata, CA 95521; (707) 822-5953.

*Trail notes:* The Arcata Marsh is the most popular birdwatching area in Northern California, and it is best explored by walking the Sanctuary Trail. The trail is short, flat and routed for perfect viewing possibilities. The setting is unique, with the coast, saltwater bay, brackish water marsh, pond, foothills and streams all nearby. That means an outstanding variety of species are attracted here, with sightings often including belted kingfishers, ospreys, peregrine falcons, black phoebes, and song and savannah sparrows. In other words, birds from nearly all habitat types are represented. That is why the Audubon Society gives guided tours regularly here, and why most visitors give the area great respect by keeping the noise level down.

---

# 4. REDWOOD LOOP 6.2 mi/3.0 hrs

*Reference:* **In Arcata Redwood Park in Arcata foothills; map BØ, grid c5.**

*User groups:* Hikers, dogs, mountain bikes and horses. Certain sections of the trail are off-limits to horses and mountain bikes; check the trail map for details. No wheelchair facilities.

*Permits:* No permits are required. Parking and access are free.

*Directions:* From Eureka, turn north on US 101 and drive to Arcata. Take the 14th Street exit and drive about one mile east on 14th Street into the parking area at the end of the road. Look for the "Redwood Park Trails" sign. Bikers and equestrians should use the Meadow Trailhead, located where 14th Street enters the park.

*Maps:* For a free, detailed trail map, contact the City of Arcata at the address below, ask for the Community Forest Trail map. To obtain topographic maps of the area, ask for Arcata North and Arcata South from the USGS.

*Who to contact:* City of Arcata, Environmental Services Department, 736 F Street, Arcata, CA 95521; (707) 822-5953.

*Trail notes:* The Arcata Redwoods provide a respite for students at nearby Humboldt State or locals who want to wander among a beautiful second-growth forest. There is a network of trails available in the park, about 10 miles in all, and this loop is devised by connecting several of them. For newcomers, a map is an absolute necessity. Start at the sign noting Redwood Park Trail (mountain bikes are not allowed at this trailhead), and take the Nature Trail, routing past many huge stumps, a small creek, and a forest of redwoods and spruce. The complete route features a 1,200-foot elevation gain and then loss, a steep trail both on the way up as well as on the way down. This gradient keeps many off the trail, including mountain bikers.

---

# 5. TABLE BLUFF COUNTY PARK

9.0 mi/1.0 day

*Reference:* **On Humboldt Coast on the southern edge of Humboldt Bay south of Eureka; map BØ, grid d2.**

*User groups:* Hikers and dogs. No mountain bikes or horses are allowed. No wheelchair facilities.

*Permits:* No permits are required. Parking and access are free.

*Directions:* From Eureka, turn south on US 101 and drive 7.5 miles to the Hookton Road exit. Turn west and drive about five miles to Table Bluff County Park. Continue three-tenths of a mile and park at the base of Table Bluff.

*Maps:* A free brochure can be obtained by contacting Humboldt County Parks at the address below. To obtain a topographic map of the area, ask for Tyee City from the USGS.

*Who to contact:* Humboldt County Parks Department, 1106 Second Street, Eureka, CA 95501; (707) 445-7652.

*Trail notes:* Don't get spooked at the listed nine miles of trail. Actually, you can walk as little or as much as you desire. The nine-mile length is the maximum roundtrip distance, but there is no developed trail. You can simply take the short trail to the Table Bluff Lighthouse, a great lookout, or you can meander south on the sand dunes, best walked at low tides near the water line, where the sand is firmest. The route continues south along a sand spit, with the Pacific Ocean on one side and the Eel River Lagoon on the other. It extends to the Eel River Wildlife Area and all the way to the mouth of the Eel River. Very few people make the entire trip. One reason is that the north wind is common here in the afternoon, and on the trip back, it will be in your face.

---

# 6. DOUBLE LOOP

2.2 mi/2.0 hrs

*Reference:* **In Russ City Park in Ferndale south of Eureka; map BØ, grid e2.**

*User groups:* Hikers and dogs. No mountain bikes or horses are allowed. No

wheelchair facilities.

*Permits:* No permits are required. Parking and access are free.

*Directions:* From Eureka, turn south on US 101 and drive about 11 miles. Take the Ferndale exit, cross Fernbridge, and drive five miles west through town. Turn left on Ocean Street and continue three-quarters of a mile to the park.

*Maps:* A free map and brochure can be obtained by contacting the City of Ferndale at the address below. To obtain a topographic map of the area, ask for Ferndale from the USGS.

*Who to contact:* City of Ferndale, P.O. Box 238, Ferndale, CA 95536; (707) 786-4224.

*Trail notes:* Russ City Park is Humboldt County's backyard wilderness. It covers just 105 acres, but has been retained in its primitive state for wildlife, birds and hikers. The trail is called "Double Loop" because it is set in the shape of a figure eight, which is quite rare. It includes a climb up Lytel Ridge, passing Francis Creek, with sections routed amid heavy fern beds and large firs and offering views of a small pond and the Eel River flood plain. While the trip is relatively short and easy enough, the terrain is steep in spots and the trail is challenging, complete with switchbacks. Heavy fog or rain can make it slippery here. Since it is a city park, Russ Park is little known by outsiders and can provide quiet, secluded hiking.

---

# 7. 5 ALLENS' TRAIL          1.5 mi/1.5 hrs

*Reference:* **In Humboldt Redwoods State Park south of Eureka; map BØ, grid g4.**

*User groups:* Hikers only. No dogs, mountain bikes or horses are allowed. No wheelchair facilities.

*Permits:* No permits are required. Parking and access are free.

*Directions:* Northbound on US 101, take the Founders Tree/Rockefeller Forest exit and follow the signs for 1.5 miles to the trailhead. Southbound on US 101, take the second Redcrest exit. Turn south and follow the signs for four miles to the trailhead.

*Maps:* A map and trail guide can be obtain by sending a self-addressed, stamped envelope and a check or money order for $1 to Humboldt Redwoods State Park at the address below. To obtain a topographic map of the area, ask for Weott from the USGS.

*Who to contact:* Humboldt Redwoods State Park, P.O. Box 100, Weott, CA 95571; (707) 946-2409 or (707) 445-6547.

*Trail notes:* The 5 Allens' Trail will provide a lasting impression of Humboldt Redwoods State Park for one reason: It's a butt-kicker. Ah, but it is also very short, and that is the lure. It is well worth the effort in exchange for quiet wonders. From the trailhead near the Eel River, you walk through a tunnel under the highway, then start the climb. Up, up and up it goes, climbing 1,200 feet over the course of just three-quarters of a mile. In the process, it passes through a forest of mixed conifers, the tree canopy providing needed shade in the summer. Even though the trail is quite short, few people make it to the end. But if you want a quiet, peaceful spot, and are willing to pay to get it, you will find it at the end. A great sidetrip from the trailhead is to hike north instead, for the short walk along the Eel River to High Rock, one of the better shoreline fishing spots for steelhead during the winter fish migrations.

## 8. LOST COAST TRAIL    25 mi. one way/2 days

*Reference:* On Humboldt Coast south of Eureka in King Range National Conservation Area; map BØ, grid h0.

*User groups:* Hikers, dogs and horses. No mountain bikes are allowed. No wheelchair facilities.

*Permits:* No day-use permits are required. A campfire permit is required if you wish to stay overnight. A free permit can be obtained at any BLM office or state fire department.

*Directions:* From Eureka, turn south on US 101 and drive approximately 59 miles to Redway. Take the South Fork-Honeydew exit and turn west on Wilder Ridge Road. Drive 23 miles to Honeydew, turn right on Mattole Road and drive 14 miles to Lighthouse Road. Turn left and follow the road to its end. The trailhead is just past Mattole Campground.

*Maps:* A free map and brochure can be obtained by contacting the Bureau of Land Management at the address below. Specify the King Range Conservation Area map. To obtain topographic maps of the area, ask for Petrolia, Cooskie Creek, Shubrick Peak and Shelter Cove from the USGS.

*Who to contact:* Bureau of Land Management, Arcata Resource Area, 1125 16th Street, Room 219, Arcata, CA 95521; (707) 822-7648.

*Trail notes:* The Lost Coast and the people who live here seem to be in a different orbit than the rest of California, and that is exactly why people like to make this visit. It is called the "Lost Coast" because of the way nature has isolated the area, shielded on all sides by natural boundaries. For a first visit, a great day hike is to take the abandoned jeep trail from the campground at Lighthouse Road and head south three miles to the Punta Gorda Light Tower. That will provide a glimpse of the greatness here, and probably inspire you to take the Lost Coast Trail, one of California's greatest weekend trips. The trail spans 25 miles from the mouth of the Mattole River south to Shelter Cove, set primarily on bluffs and beach. In the process it traces some of California's most remote portions of coastline. With two vehicles, one parked at each end of the trail, you can set up your own shuttle, then hike the trail one way. It is better done from north to south, because of winds out of the north; you want them at your back, not in your face. Firm-fitting, waterproof boots with good gripping soles are a necessity—firm-fitting because some of the walking is in soft sand, which can have your ankles screaming for a solid trail; waterproof because there are several small creek crossings; good-gripping because some scrambling over wet boulders is required.

*Special note:* Some parts of the Coastal Trail are impassable during high tides.

---

## 9. FOUNDERS GROVE NATURE TRAIL    0.5 mi/0.5 hr

*Reference:* In Humboldt Redwoods State Park south of Eureka; map BØ, grid h4.

*User groups:* Hikers only. No dogs, mountain bikes or horses are allowed. No wheelchair facilities, but the trail is **accessible to wheelchairs,** though a bit uneven.

*Permits:* No permits are required. Parking and access are free.

*Directions:* From Garberville, turn north on US 101 and drive approximately 20 miles. Take the Founder Tree/Rockefeller Forest exit to the Avenue of the Giants. Continue 100 yards across the Avenue of the Giants to the Founders Grove Parking Area/Trailhead.

*Maps:* A map and trail guide can be obtain by sending a self-addressed, stamped envelope and a check or money order for $1 to Humboldt Redwoods State Park at the address below. To obtain a topographic map of the area, ask for Weott from the USGS.

*Who to contact:* Humboldt Redwoods State Park, P.O. Box 100, Weott, CA 95571; (707) 946-2409 or (707) 445-6547.

*Trail notes:* Humboldt Redwoods State Park has nearly 100 miles of trails, but it is the little half-mile Founders Grove Nature Trail that provides the shortest and most easily-accessible walk in the park. This trail also gives you the quickest payoff. That is why it is the most popular trail in Humboldt Redwoods. The trail is easy to reach, only a minute or two from Highway 101. At the trailhead, you will find a small box containing brochures that describe each element of the self-guided nature trail. Your destination is the Dyerville Giant, the tallest tree in the park, but all the while you will be surrounded by old-growth redwoods, a great reward for such a small physical investment. Howie and Ethel and anyone else can park their Winnebago, and then in minutes be walking among giant trees.

---

# 10. BULL CREEK FLATS     9.0 mi/5.25 hrs

*Reference:* **In Humboldt Redwoods State Park south of Eureka; map BØ, grid h4.**

*User groups:* Hikers only. No dogs, mountain bikes or horses are allowed. No wheelchair facilities.

*Permits:* No permits are required. Parking and access are free.

*Directions:* From Garberville, turn north on US 101 and drive approximately 20 miles. Take the Founder Tree/Rockefeller Forest exit and drive 1.3 miles on Mattole Road to the trailhead.

*Maps:* A map and trail guide can be obtain by sending a self-addressed, stamped envelope and a check or money order for $1 to Humboldt Redwoods State Park at the address below. To obtain a topographic map of the area, ask for Weott from the USGS.

*Who to contact:* Humboldt Redwoods State Park, P.O. Box 100, Weott, CA 95571; (707) 946-2409 or (707) 445-6547.

*Trail notes:* This trail offers a classic streamside walk, complete with giant redwoods and a babbling brook. The trailhead is at Bull Creek Flats (a short walk to the Federation Grove), then heads west along Bull Creek, an easy but steady grade as you hike upstream. All the while you are surrounded by forest, both redwoods and fir in a variety of mixes. The feature of the route is the Big Tree Area, a distance of four miles. There are many redwoods here that range five to ten feet in diameter, as well as the Flat Iron Tree, a huge leaning redwood that grew in strange dimensions in order to support itself. On the broad side, the Flat Iron Tree measures more than 15 feet. After the trail passes the Big Tree Area, it is routed to the mouth of Albee Creek, ending at Mattole Road. The trailhead at Albee Creek at Mattole Road provides a shorter hike to the Big Tree Area, about a mile to the Flat Iron Tree.

## 11. SPANISH RIDGE TRAIL    6.0 mi/3.5 hrs

*Reference:* In King Range National Conservation Area south of Eureka; map BØ, grid i1.

*User groups:* Hikers, dogs and horses. No mountain bikes are allowed. No wheelchair facilities.

*Permits:* No permits are required. Parking and access are free.

*Directions:* From Eureka, turn south on US 101 and drive approximately 59 miles to Redway. Take the South Fork-Honeydew exit and turn west on Wilder Ridge Road. Drive approximately 21.5 miles, then turn west on Smith-Etter Road (Note: This road is very rough and primitive. It is closed from November 1 to March 31). Drive eight miles to Telegraph Ridge Road, then turn northwest and continue 1.5 miles to the trailhead on the left.

*Maps:* A free map and brochure can be obtained by contacting the Bureau of Land Management at the address below ask for the King Range Conservation Area map. To obtain topographic maps of the area, ask for Cooskie Creek and Shubrick Peak from the USGS.

*Who to contact:* Bureau of Land Management, Arcata Resource Area, 1125 16th Street, Room 219, Arcata, CA 95521; (707) 822-7648.

*Trail notes:* In just three fast miles of walking downhill, you can get access to some of the most remote sections of the California coast on this trail. Alas, there's a catch, and with this trail it comes on the return trip. What goes down, as all hikers know, must later go up. From the Spanish Ridge Trailhead, the trail descends 2,000 feet in three miles en route to the coast. Know what that means? Right. Going back, it climbs 2,000 feet in three miles, and unless you can get a helicopter ride back, you're looking at some serious grunt work. But it's worth it. The King Range is very rugged, primitive and unpeopled. It's a wild area where hikers are only temporary visitors. Considering that bumpy access road and the 2,000-foot climb on the return trip, it is rare to see other people here.

## 12. KING CREST TRAIL    10 mi/6.5 hrs

*Reference:* In King Range National Conservation Area south of Eureka; map BØ, grid i1.

*User groups:* Hikers, dogs, mountain bikes and horses. No wheelchair facilities.

*Permits:* No permits are required. Parking and access are free.

*Directions:* From Eureka, turn south on US 101 and drive approximately 59 miles to Redway. Take the South Fork-Honeydew exit and turn west on Wilder Ridge Road. Drive approximately 21.5 miles, then turn west on Smith-Etter Road. (Note: This is a primitive dirt road and is closed from November 1 to March 31.) Drive six miles to the trailhead.

*Maps:* A free map and brochure can be obtained by contacting the Bureau of Land Management at the address below ask for the King Range Conservation Area map. To obtain a topographic map of the area, ask for Shubrick Peak from the USGS.

*Who to contact:* Bureau of Land Management, Arcata Resource Area, 1125 16th Street, Room 219, Arcata, CA 95521; (707) 822-7648.

*Trail notes:* King's Peak is one of the most prized destinations in the King Range. At 4,087 feet, it is the highest point on the Northern California coast, and from it, you get a view that can make you feel like you are perched on top of the world. The ocean seems to stretch on forever to the west, and on a perfect day, you can make out the top of Mt. Lassen to the east behind the ridgeline of the Yolla Bolly Wilderness. To reach King's Peak requires a five-mile hike from the trailhead on Smith-Etter Road, and in the process you climb some 2,200 feet in elevation. It is absolutely mandatory to pick a clear day to make the trip, since paying the price of the climb is buffered by the sweeping views. It is also essential to have a good map and a double canteen water supply, because trail signs are poor and water supplies at trail camps are from dubious sources. The entire King Crest Trail extends 16 miles one-way, starting from the trailhead listed in this hike to King Crest; then it descends 10.5 miles to the beach. That makes a one-way overnight trip an ideal alternative, having placed a shuttle vehicle at trail's end.

---

# 13. WILLIAMS GROVE TRAIL   3.5 mi/2.0 hrs

*Reference:* **In Humboldt Redwoods State Park south of Eureka; map BØ, grid h5.**

*User groups:* Hikers only. No dogs, mountain bikes or horses are allowed. No wheelchair facilities.

*Permits:* No permits are required. Parking and access are free.

*Directions:* From Garberville, turn north on US 101 drive to the Myers Flat exit. Turn right on Avenue of the Giants and drive about one mile north to the Williams Grove parking area, or to the Hidden Springs Campground (reservations advised).

*Maps:* A map and trail guide can be obtain by sending a self-addressed, stamped envelope and a check or money order for $1 to Humboldt Redwoods State Park at the address below. To obtain topographic maps of the area, ask for Weott and Myers Flat from the USGS.

*Who to contact:* Humboldt Redwoods State Park, P.O. Box 100, Weott, CA 95571; (707) 946-2409 or (707) 445-6547.

*Trail notes:* This trail makes an ideal, easy trip for campers staying at the Hidden Springs Campground in Humboldt Redwoods State Park. The camp itself is set in forest just above a big bend in the South Fork Eel River, with the trailhead on the southwest side of the camp. The trail is routed nearly flat out of camp, then turns right and laterals adjacent to the highway. It's easy walking all the way amid redwoods both young and old. Then the trail crosses under the highway and over the river on a bridge (only in summer) to Williams Grove, which has a picnic area and restrooms available. Williams Grove Picnic Area can also be reached by car, and then used as a trailhead to hike this route in reverse.

---

# 14. CHEMISE MOUNTAIN TRAIL 3.0 mi/2.0 hrs

*Reference:* **In King Range National Conservation Area south of Shelter Cove; map BØ, grid j2.**

*User groups:* Hikers, dogs and horses. No mountain bikes are allowed. No wheelchair facilities.

*Permits:* No day-use permits are required. A campfire permit is required if you wish to stay overnight. A free permit can be obtained at any BLM office or state fire department.

***Directions:*** From Eureka, turn south on US 101 and drive approximately 60 miles to Garberville. Turn west on Briceland Road and drive about 12 miles, then turn left on Shelter Cove Road and drive five miles. Turn left on Chemise Mountain Road and continue a quarter of a mile to the trailhead. You can also go another mile up the road to Wailaki Campground and start there.

***Maps:*** A free map and brochure can be obtained by contacting the Bureau of Land Management at the address below ask for the King Range Conservation Area map. To obtain a topographic map of the area, ask for Shelter Cove from the USGS.

***Who to contact:*** Bureau of Land Management, Arcata Resource Area, 1125 16th Street, Room 219, Arcata, CA 95521; (707) 822-7648.

***Trail notes:*** Most visitors to the King Range yearn to climb King's Peak, but just can't gather the time, initiative or energy for such a demanding excursion. The Chemise Mountain Trail largely solves that problem. It has many of the qualities of the King Crest Trail, including a great view, yet without many of the demands, especially the time required. It is only a 1.5-mile climb from the Wailaki Recreation Site to Chemise Mountain, starting from a trailhead elevation of 2,000 feet to the summit at 2,598 feet. So even though the climb is steep, the end of the tunnel is always in sight. So are the great views. The ridgeline of the Yolla Bolly Wilderness is the eastern horizon, a sweeping expanse of ocean is off to the west, and to the south is a deep canyon and several remote coastal ridges. Much of the vegetation near the summit is rather boring brush, but with great views of a primitive area, it doesn't seem to matter. Especially way out here, where it can seem like there isn't another person in the world.

# MAP B1

NOR-CAL MAP ...................... see page 14
adjoining maps
NORTH (A1) ........................... see page 30
EAST (B2) .............................. see page 94
SOUTH (C1) .......................... see page 156
WEST (BØ) ............................ see page 68

**2 PCT SECTIONS**
**19 TRAILS**
**PAGES 78-93**

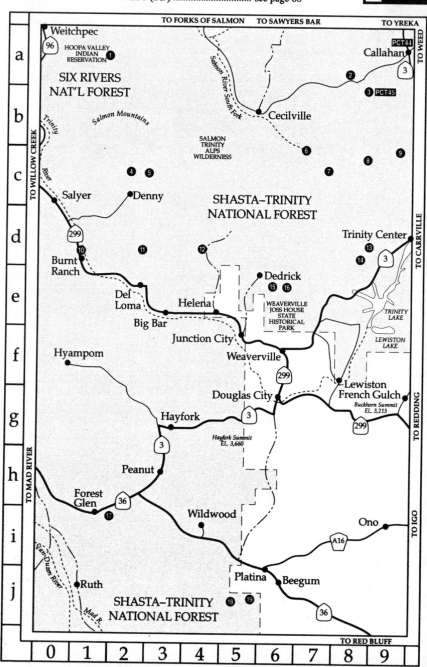

**Map B1 featuring:** Six Rivers National Forest, Trinity Alps Wilderness, Hoopa, Russian Wilderness, Callahan, Cecilville, Trinity Lake, Trinity River's Big Bar, Junction City, Trinity Center, Weaverville, Ruth Lake

## 1. HORSE RIDGE NATIONAL RECREATION TRAIL    13.0 mi. one way/2.0 days

*Reference:* **In Six Rivers National Forest on western edge of Trinity Alps Wilderness east of Hoopa; map B1, grid a1.**

*User groups:* Hikers, dogs and horses. No mountain bikes are allowed. No wheelchair facilities.

*Permits:* A wilderness permit is required for hikers planning on camping. Parking and access are free.

*Directions:* From Arcata, turn east on Highway 299 and drive to Willow Creek. Turn north on Highway 96 and drive about 10 miles into Hoopa Valley to Big Hill Lookout Road. Turn east on Big Hill Lookout Road and drive 11 miles to the Six Rivers National Forest border. The road becomes Forest Service Road 18N01; follow it for eight miles to the trailhead.

*Maps:* For a map of Six Rivers National Forest, send $3 to USDA-Forest Service, 630 Sansome Street, San Francisco, CA 94111. To obtain topographic maps of the area, ask for Tish Tang Point and Trinity Mountain from the USGS.

*Who to contact:* Six Rivers National Forest, Lower Trinity Ranger District, P.O. Box 68, Willow Creek, CA 95573; (916) 629-2118.

*Trail notes:* This is one of the lesser-known National Recreation Trails in the western U.S., but it has many excellent features, and alas, a few negative ones as well. While it can be hiked from one end to the other in a weekend, leaving a shuttle vehicle at both trailheads, our suggestion is to make the six-mile trip to Mill Creek Lakes, set in the least explored western sector of the Salmon Mountains/Trinity Alps. This is a good overnighter and will provide you with a feel for the area. From the trailhead at 4,800 feet, the grades are gradual with relatively easy elevation climbs and descents, and the trail is well wooded for the entire route. If you want to add to your trip, you can extend it southward on the Horse Ridge National Recreation Trail. It peaks out at Trinity Summit, at about 5,800 feet, where there is an historic cabin. Other hikers are rare in this area, and most of the time you will feel as if you have the entire universe to yourself.

*Special note:* Water is scarce along the trail, but cattle are not. That means that whatever water you find, do not drink it without treating it first with the best water filtration system you can afford.

## 2. RUSSIAN LAKE TRAIL    7.0 mi/2.0 days

*Reference:* **In Russian Wilderness west of Callahan; map B1, grid a8.**

*User groups:* Hikers, dogs and horses. Mountain bikes are allowed only outside of the wilderness border. No wheelchair facilities.

*Permits:* A wilderness permit is required for hikers planning to camp. Parking and access are free.

*Directions:* From Redding, drive north on Interstate 5 for 70 miles. Just past Weed, take the Edgewood exit. At the stop sign, turn left and drive through the underpass to another stop sign. Turn right on old Highway 99 and drive about six miles to Gazelle. At Gazelle, turn left on Gazelle-Callahan Road and drive about 20 miles to Callahan. From Callahan on Highway 3, turn west on County Road 402 (Cecilville Road) and drive 17 miles to Trail Creek Campground. The trail heads north out of the campground.

*Maps:* For a map of Klamath National Forest or the Trinity Alps Wilderness, send $3 to USDA-Forest Service, 630 Sansome Street, San Francisco, CA 94111. To obtain topographic images of the area, ask for Deadman Peak and Eaton Peak from the USGS.

*Who to contact:* Klamath National Forest, Scott River Ranger District, 11263 North Highway 3, Fort Jones, CA 96032; (916) 468-5351.

*Trail notes:* The Russian Wilderness is a place so pristine, yet so small, that it just can't handle many visitors. Luckily, very few make the trip. If you go, walk softly and treat the area with fragile care. This trail involves a steep climb and drop, then a short cross-country jaunt, and those two factors keep most visitors away. You start at the Trail Creek Campground, set on Cecilville-Callahan Road, and for the first 1.5 miles, the trail heads steeply up on an old fire lane. A few mountain bikers like walking up this portion, then ripping back downhill to the campground. As you near the crest, you will junction with the Pacific Crest Trail; turn left, then just five minutes later, you will turn again on the trail that is routed down to Syphon Lake, Russian Lake, Waterdog Lake and Lower Russian Lake. The last quarter-mile to Russian Lake, the feature lake in the basin, is off-trail. Many years ago, our friend Paul Wertz filled some 10-gallon milk cans with water and juvenile golden trout, and with a donkey hauling those milk cans, tromped in all the way to this basin and stocked these lakes with those baby golden trout. If you catch one of their progeny, consider what Paul went through to get these fish here, and you may feel a glowing satisfaction by releasing the fish, rather than killing it.

---

# 3. LONG GULCH TRAIL    4.5 mi/3.25 hrs

*Reference:* **In Trinity Alps Wilderness west of Callahan; map B1, grid b8.**

*User groups:* Hikers, dogs and horses. No mountain bikes are allowed. No wheelchair facilities.

*Permits:* A wilderness permit is required for hikers planning to camp. Parking and access are free.

*Directions:* From Redding, drive north on Interstate 5 for 70 miles. Just past Weed, take the Edgewood exit. At the stop sign, turn left and drive through the underpass to another stop sign. Turn right on old Highway 99 and drive about six miles to Gazelle. At Gazelle, turn left on Gazelle-Callahan Road and drive about 20 miles to Callahan. From Callahan on Highway 3, turn west on County Road 402 (Cecilville Road) and drive 11 miles. Turn left on Forest Service Road 39N08 and drive 1.5 miles to the trailhead.

*Maps:* For a map of Klamath National Forest or the Trinity Alps Wilderness, send $3 to USDA-Forest Service, 630 Sansome Street, San Francisco, CA 94111. To obtain topographic images of the area, ask for Deadman Peak and Billys Peak from the USGS.

*Who to contact:* Klamath National Forest, Scott River Ranger District, 11263 North Highway 3, Fort Jones, CA 96032; (916) 468-5351.

*Trail notes:* The Long Gulch Trail rises along Long Gulch Creek, steeply at times, but in just 2.25 miles arrives at Long Gulch Lake. That makes it close enough to go in and out in a day, or better yet, you can make it a good weekend overnighter without tremendous strain. The lake is round and pretty, set northeast of Deadman Peak (7,741 feet) in the Trinity Alps Wilderness. It is stocked by airplane every year with small trout, a nice bonus. Another bonus is how simple it is to extend your trip either to other mountain lakes, or beyond deep into the Trinity Alps Wilderness. Trail Gulch Lake is just another three miles from Long Gulch Lake, a good sidetrip. If you choose to extend into the Trinity Alps instead, the trail is routed along North Fork Coffee Creek to Kickapoo Waterfall, about nine miles from Long Gulch Lake.

## 4. NEW RIVER TRAILHEAD 18.0 mi/2.0 days

*Reference:* In Trinity Alps Wilderness east of Willow Creek; map B1, grid c2.

*User groups:* Hikers, dogs and horses. No mountain bikes are allowed. No wheelchair facilities.

*Permits:* A wilderness permit is required for hikers planning to camp. Parking and access are free.

*Directions:* From Weaverville, drive west on Highway 299 and drive approximately 32 miles. Turn north on County Road 402 (Denny Road) and drive about 17 miles, then turn left on Forest Service Road 7N15 and continue four miles north to the trailhead parking area.

*Maps:* For a map of Shasta-Trinity National Forest or the Trinity Alps Wilderness, send $3 to USDA-Forest Service, 630 Sansome Street, San Francisco, CA 94111. To obtain topographic maps of the area, ask for Jim Jam Ridge, Dees Peak and Trinity Mountain from the USGS.

*Who to contact:* Shasta-Trinity National Forest, Big Bar Ranger District, Star Route 1, P.O. Box 10, Big Bar, CA 96010; (916) 623-6106.

*Trail notes:* Most backpackers in the Trinity Alps Wilderness like high mountain lakes, but here is a trail that features small streams. The highlights are the headwaters of the New River, a tributary to the Trinity River, and Mary Blane Meadow. Because this is a river trail, not a lake trail, it gets far less use than other routes in the region. The trail starts right along the New River, then immediately begins climbing, with Megram Cabin the first landmark you come to, about a mile in. In another mile, you will arrive at a fork in the trail; bear right. Here the trail is routed along Slide Creek, a well-wooded section, and after two miles, you will arrive again at a fork, and again you will stay to the right. The trail will pass Robbers Roost Mine, Emmons Cabin, the Old Denny Cabin Site, and will reach Mary Blane Meadow, a distance of about nine miles from the trailhead. It is set below Mary Blane Mountain, and to the north, Dees Peak. The whole region here is cut with small streams in crevices and canyons.

## 5. EAST FORK LOOP 20.0 mi/3.0 days

*Reference:* In Trinity Alps Wilderness east of Willow Creek; map B1, grid c3.

*User groups:* Hikers, dogs and horses. No mountain bikes are allowed. No

wheelchair facilities.

**Permits:** A wilderness permit is required for hikers planning to camp. Parking and access are free.

**Directions:** From Weaverville, turn west on Highway 299 and drive approximately 32 miles. Turn north on County Road 402 (Denny Road) and drive about 20 miles to the trailhead parking area.

**Maps:** For a map of Shasta-Trinity National Forest or the Trinity Alps Wilderness, send $3 to USDA-Forest Service, 630 Sansome Street, San Francisco, CA 94111. To obtain a topographic map of the area, ask for Jim Jam Ridge from the USGS.

**Who to contact:** Shasta-Trinity National Forest, Big Bar Ranger District, Star Route 1, P.O. Box 10, Big Bar, CA 96010; (916) 623-6106.

**Trail notes:** The East Fork Trailhead provides access to one of the more primitive, less-traveled regions of the Trinity Alps Wilderness. It is an area known for streams and forests in its lower reaches and bare limestone ridges in its higher reaches. The trip starts at the East Fork Trailhead, adjacent to the East Fork New River. It climbs along this vibrant watershed and after two miles, turns right along Pony Creek. In the next six miles, which include quite steep sections, the trail climbs to Limestone Ridge near little Rattlesnake Lake. At Limestone Ridge, you turn right on the New River Divide Trail and head south for six miles, passing Cabin Peak at 6,870 feet and arriving at White Creek Lake. To complete the loop, turn right on the trail at White Creek Lake and start the trip back, descending most of the way. The trail goes past Jakes Upper Camp and Jakes Lower Camp before linking up again with the East Fork Trail for the short jog back to the parking area.

---

# 6. LITTLE SOUTH FORK LAKE TRAIL

13.0 mi/2.0 days

**Reference:** In Trinity Alps Wilderness near Cecilville; map B1, grid c7.

**User groups:** Hikers only. No dogs, horses or mountain bikes are allowed. No wheelchair facilities.

**Permits:** A wilderness permit is required for hikers planning to camp. Parking and access are free.

**Directions:** From Redding, drive north on Interstate 5 for 70 miles. Just past Weed, take the Edgewood exit. At the stop sign, turn left and drive through the underpass to another stop sign. Turn right on old Highway 99 and drive about six miles to Gazelle. At Gazelle, turn left on Gazelle-Callahan Road and drive about 20 miles to Callahan. From Callahan on Highway 3, turn west on Cecilville Road and drive approximately 28 miles. Turn south on Caribou Road (across from East Fork Campground) and drive about six miles to the Summerville Trailhead.

**Maps:** For a map of Klamath National Forest or the Trinity Alps Wilderness, send $3 to USDA-Forest Service, 630 Sansome Street, San Francisco, CA 94111. To obtain a topographic map of the area, ask for Thompson Peak from the USGS.

**Who to contact:** Klamath National Forest, Salmon River Ranger District, P.O. Box 280, Etna, CA 96027; (916) 467-5757.

**Trail notes:** You have to be a little bit crazy to try this trip, and that's why we signed up. There's just no easy way to reach Little South Fork Lake, its two idyllic campsites, excellent swimming and large trout. This route is largely off-trail and requires getting around a big waterfall, but there is no better way in (see special note); we've tried them all. From the Summerville Trailhead, the trip starts out easy enough, with four miles of good trail, first along the Salmon River, then veering to the right along Little South Fork Creek. The trail dead-ends into Little South Fork Creek (a faint route on the other side climbs through brush and up the canyon, and is to be avoided). From here, you're on your own, heading upstream, off the trail. We found the best strategy is to lateral across the slope on the right side of the stream, even though this is where Tom got chased and stung by a horde of bees on one trip. It is steep and difficult. After leaving the trail, it is about 1.25 miles to a beautiful waterfall, divine and pristine; we named it Crystal Falls. To get around the waterfall, loop to the right; if you go to the left, you will add several dreadful hours to the trip. Guess how we know? Heh heh. It's another 1.25 miles to the lake, very slow going all the way, scrambling up and across the wooded slope, seemingly going on forever at the pace of a snail, before you suddenly emerge from the forest on to granite plates. Ahead is the lake, beautifully set in a rock bowl, framed by a high back wall. There are excellent campgrounds at each end of the lake.

*Special note:* We hiked into this lake once from Caribou Lakes by climbing the Sawtooth Ridge, the entire route being off-trail, a slippery and dangerous proposition while carrying full packs. On another trip from Caribou Lakes, we dropped down into Little South Fork Canyon, losing thousands of feet in altitude and in the process getting caught in a brush field like bugs in a spider web. Neither route is recommended.

---

## 7. CARIBOU LAKES TRAIL    18.0 mi/2.0 days

*Reference:* In Trinity Alps Wilderness northwest of Trinity Lake; map B1, grid c8.

*User groups:* Hikers, dogs and horses. No mountain bikes are allowed. No wheelchair facilities.

*Permits:* A wilderness permit is required for hikers planning to camp. Parking and access are free.

*Directions:* From Weaverville, drive north on Highway 3 past Trinity Lake. At the Coffee Creek Ranger Station, turn west on County Road 104 (Coffee Creek Road) and drive 17 miles to the trailhead at the end of the road.

*Maps:* For a map of Klamath National Forest or the Trinity Alps Wilderness, send $3 to USDA-Forest Service, 630 Sansome Street, San Francisco, CA 94111. To obtain a topographic image of the area, ask for Caribou Lakes from the USGS.

*Who to contact:* Klamath National Forest, Salmon River Ranger District, P.O. Box 280, Etna, CA 96027; (916) 467-5757.

*Trail notes:* The Caribou Lakes Basin provides the classic Trinity Alps scene: three high mountain lakes, beautiful and serene, with the back wall of the Sawtooth Ridge casting a monumental backdrop on one side, and on the other side, a drop-off and great views of a series of mountain peaks and ridgelines. Sunsets are absolutely remarkable when viewed from here. Because it is a nine-mile hike to the Caribou Lakes Basin, this makes an excellent first-day's destination for backpackers exploring this section of the

Trinity Alps Wilderness. The trail starts at the bottom of the Salmon River, however, and like all trails that start at the bottom of canyons, it means you start the trip with a terrible climb that never seems to end. Plan on drinking a full canteen of water, then be certain not to miss the natural spring that is available near the crest, just off to the right. After reaching the crest, the trail travels counterclockwise around the mountain, then drops into the Caribou Lakes Basin. Ignore your urge to stop at the first lake, because the best campsites, swimming and views are from Caribou Lake, the last and largest lake you'll reach in this circuit.

---

## 8. UNION LAKE TRAIL    12.0 mi/2.0 days

*Reference:* **In Trinity Alps Wilderness northwest of Trinity Lake; map B1, grid c8.**

*User groups:* Hikers, dogs and horses. No mountain bikes are allowed. No wheelchair facilities.

*Permits:* A wilderness permit is required for hikers planning to camp. Parking and access are free.

*Directions:* From Weaverville, drive north on Highway 3 past Trinity Lake. At the Coffee Creek Ranger Station, turn west on County Road 104 (Coffee Creek Road) and drive approximately 10 miles to the trailhead on the left.

*Maps:* For a map of Shasta-Trinity National Forest or the Trinity Alps Wilderness, send $3 to USDA-Forest Service, 630 Sansome Street, San Francisco, CA 94111. To obtain a topographic image of the area, ask for Caribou Lakes from the USGS.

*Who to contact:* Shasta-Trinity National Forest, Weaverville Ranger District, P.O. Box T, Weaverville, CA 96093; (916) 623-2121.

*Trail notes:* Union Lake sits in a granite basin below Red Rock Mountain. The hike in and out is a good weekend affair, but most visitors are backpackers who are using the camp at the lake as a first-day's destination for a multi-day trip. Of the trailheads on Coffee Creek Road, this one is often overlooked. The trail starts near an old sawmill along Coffee Creek, is routed south (to the left), and in less than a mile, starts the climb adjacent to Union Creek (on your right). Like most hikes that start at a streambed, you pay for your pleasure, going up, not down. After about two miles, the trail crosses Union Creek, and continues on for a few miles, now with the stream on your left. You will pass a trail junction for Bullards Basin, and about a half-mile later, turn right on the cutoff trail to Union Lake.

---

## 9. BOULDER LAKE TRAIL    12.0 mi/2.0 days

*Reference:* **In Trinity Alps Wilderness northwest of Trinity Lake; map B1, grid c9.**

*User groups:* Hikers, dogs and horses. No mountain bikes are allowed. No wheelchair facilities.

*Permits:* A wilderness permit is required for hikers planning to camp. Parking and access are free.

*Directions:* From Weaverville, drive north on Highway 3 past Trinity Lake. At the Coffee Creek Ranger Station, turn west on County Road 104 (Coffee Creek Road) and drive approximately 6.5 miles to Goldfield Campground and the trailhead parking area.

*Maps:* For a map of Shasta-Trinity National Forest or the Trinity Alps Wilderness, send $3 to USDA-Forest Service, 630 Sansome Street, San Francisco, CA 94111. To obtain a topographic image of the area, ask for Ycatapom Peak from the USGS.

*Who to contact:* Shasta-Trinity National Forest, Weaverville Ranger District, P.O. Box T, Weaverville, CA 96093; (916) 623-2121.

*Trail notes:* The hike to Boulder Lake and back makes for a nice weekend backpack trip. Yet many hikers bypass this trailhead in favor of the nearby prestigious Caribou Lakes Trail, so your odds of finding solitude are better here. Out of the Goldfield Campground there are two trails, each routed to Union Lake. Our choice is to take the trail that runs adjacent to Boulder Creek, a long steady grade to be sure, but one where the nearby cold flows of water have a way of keeping you mentally refreshed. As you near Sugar Pine Butte at 8,033 feet, the trail turns sharply to the left, loops in a clockwise direction around a butte, and then connects with the short cutoff trail that leads to Boulder Lake. If there are campers at the lake already, nearby Little Boulder Lake, about a half-hour walk beyond, provides a backup option.

---

# 10. BURNT RANCH FALLS    0.5 mi/0.5 hr

*Reference:* **In Shasta-Trinity National Forest on Highway 299 east of Willow Creek; map B1, grid d1.**

*User groups:* Hikers, dogs, mountain bikes and horses. Mountain bikes and horses are not advised. No wheelchair facilities.

*Permits:* No permits are required. Parking and access are free.

*Directions:* From Weaverville, drive west on Highway 299 to Burnt Ranch. From Burnt Ranch, drive a half mile west on Highway 299 to the trailhead at Burnt Ranch Campground.

*Maps:* For a map of Shasta-Trinity National Forest, send $3 to USDA-Forest Service, 630 Sansome Street, San Francisco, CA 94111. To obtain a topographic map of the area, ask for Ironside Mountain from the USGS.

*Who to contact:* Shasta-Trinity National Forest, Big Bar Ranger District, Star Route 1, P.O. Box 10, Big Bar, CA 96010; (916) 623-6106.

*Trail notes:* Burnt Ranch Falls is not a spectacular cascade of water like other more famous waterfalls, but it is the center of a very pretty, easy-to-reach scene on the Trinity River. It is a small but wide waterfall, comprised of about 10 feet of rock that in low water conditions creates a natural barrier for migrating salmon and steelhead. Thus, the highlight comes when river flows come up a bit in the fall, and you can watch salmon and steelhead jump and sail through the air to get over and past the falls. The trail is short and easy, about a quarter-mile jaunt down from the Burnt Ranch Campground. When you arrive at the river, you will find a rocky area where you can walk out a short ways, then watch the fish jump. It is set in an area along Highway 299 that has a magnificent natural landscape. Looking up from the river, the Trinity canyon walls look like they ascend into the sky. Unlike most waterfalls, Burnt Ranch Falls is a far less compelling scene at high water. During high, turbid flows, it becomes much more difficult for visitors to see fish jumping past the falls.

## 11. NEW RIVER DIVIDE TRAIL 30.0 mi/3 days

*Reference:* In Trinity Alps Wilderness north of Trinity River's Big Bar; map B1, grid d3.

*User groups:* Hikers, dogs and horses. No mountain bikes are allowed. No wheelchair facilities.

*Permits:* A wilderness permit is required for hikers planning to camp. Parking and access are free.

*Directions:* From Weaverville, drive west on Highway 299 past Big Bar. Turn north on Forest Service Road 4 and follow the signs to the Green Mountain parking area.

*Maps:* For a map of Shasta-Trinity National Forest or the Trinity Alps Wilderness, send $3 to USDA-Forest Service, 630 Sansome Street, San Francisco, CA 94111. To obtain a topographic map of the area, ask for Del Loma from the USGS.

*Who to contact:* Shasta-Trinity National Forest, Big Bar Ranger District, Star Route 1, P.O. Box 10, Big Bar, CA 96010; (916) 623-6106.

*Trail notes:* The New River Divide Trail provides access to the Limestone Ridge of the Trinity Alps, taking a ridgeline route most of the way to get you there. This is an area known for lookouts from mountain rims, the headwaters of many small feeder streams and few people. There are few lakes in the area, however. The trip starts at the Green Mountain Trailhead at a 5,052-foot elevation, and in the first three miles, the route skirts around the southern flank of Brushy Mountain, past Panther Camp, Stove Camp and along the eastern flank of Green Mountain. As the trail climbs up toward the Limestone Ridge, you will note that you are perched on a "divide," where the streams on each side of you pour into different watersheds. Eventually, the trail rises all the way to Cabin Peak at 6,870 feet and beyond to little Rattlesnake Lake, a one-way distance of about 15 miles.

## 12. HOBO GULCH TRAIL 40.0 mi/5 days

*Reference:* In Trinity Alps Wilderness north of Junction City; map B1, grid d4.

*User groups:* Hikers, dogs and horses. No mountain bikes are allowed. No wheelchair facilities.

*Permits:* A wilderness permit is required for hikers planning to camp. Parking and access are free.

*Directions:* From Weaverville, drive west on Highway 299 and drive 13 miles to Helena. Turn north on Hobo Gulch Road and continue 20 miles to the Hobo Gulch Trailhead, located at Hobo Gulch Campground.

*Maps:* For a map of Shasta-Trinity National Forest or the Trinity Alps Wilderness, send $3 to USDA-Forest Service, 630 Sansome Street, San Francisco, CA 94111. To obtain a topographic map of the area, ask for Thurston Peaks from the USGS.

*Who to contact:* Shasta-Trinity National Forest, Big Bar Ranger District, Star Route 1, P.O. Box 10, Big Bar, CA 96010; (916) 623-6106.

*Trail notes:* The Hobo Gulch Campground makes for an appealing trailhead because it is set quite deep in the national forest along Backbone Ridge. That means a lot of miles, 20 of them from Highway 299, are taken care of by car instead of on foot. However, this trailhead isn't used that much because it doesn't provide short access to any lakes. It is about 20 rough miles to the nearest feature lake destination, Grizzly Lake. So instead of camping along lakes, here you camp along pretty streams and flats. The trail starts by heading straight north about five miles along the North Fork Trinity River to Rattlesnake Camp, then another three miles past the old Morrison Cabin and on to Pfeiffer Flat. Here the North Fork Trinity is joined by Grizzly Creek, and makes an attractive and unique backpacking destination. From Pfeiffer Flat, the trail follows along Grizzly Creek, rising high toward the Trinity Sawtooth Ridge, a long, tiring pull to beautiful Grizzly Meadows and then to Grizzly Lake, the final mile a scramble over bare rock. Grizzly Lake is a gorgeous high mountain lake, similar to many set in the glacial-carved bowls here. It is located below Thompson Peak at 8,663 feet, the most impressive peak in the Trinity Alps. By climbing the lake bowl in a clockwise direction, it is an exciting scramble to the top of Thompson Peak.

---

## 13. GRANITE LAKE TRAIL   11.0 mi/2.0 days

*Reference:* **In Trinity Alps Wilderness west of Trinity Center; map B1, grid d8.**

*User groups:* Hikers, dogs and horses. No mountain bikes are allowed. No wheelchair facilities.

*Permits:* A wilderness permit is required for hikers planning to camp. Parking and access are free.

*Directions:* From Weaverville, drive north on Highway 3 to Trinity Center. At Swift Creek Road, turn west and follow the signs to the parking area at the wilderness border.

*Maps:* For a map of Shasta-Trinity National Forest or the Trinity Alps Wilderness, send $3 to USDA-Forest Service, 630 Sansome Street, San Francisco, CA 94111. To obtain topographic maps of the area, ask for Covington Mill and Trinity Center from the USGS.

*Who to contact:* Shasta-Trinity National Forest, Weaverville Ranger District, P.O. Box T, Weaverville, CA 96093; (916) 623-2121.

*Trail notes:* When many hikers scan wilderness maps, they often search for trails that are routed a short distance to a beautiful lake for a first night's camp. That is exactly what you get at Granite Lake, but although the trip in is only about five miles, it is anything but easy. From the trailhead, the trip starts simply enough, tracing along the right side of Swift Creek. Don't be fooled. Just beyond the confluence of Swift Creek and Granite Creek, you must cross the stream to the left and then pick up the Granite Lake Trail. This trail runs along the right side of Granite Creek for four miles, in which the last mile includes a very steep section that will have you wondering why you ever thought this was going to be such a short, easy trip. Finally you will rise to Gibson Meadow, and just beyond, Granite Lake, a gorgeous sight below Gibson Peak. For a nature-built mountain water lake, it is a fair size, with good swimming in the day and trout fishing in the evening.

## 14. EAST FORK TRAILHEAD   14.0 mi/2.0 days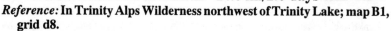

*Reference:* In Trinity Alps Wilderness northwest of Trinity Lake; map B1, grid d8.

*User groups:* Hikers, dogs and horses. No mountain bikes are allowed. No wheelchair facilities.

*Permits:* A wilderness permit is required for hikers planning to camp. Parking and access are free.

*Directions:* From Weaverville, drive north on Highway 3 to Covington Mill. Turn west on a signed Forest Service Road and continue for 2.5 miles to the trailhead.

*Maps:* For a map of Shasta-Trinity National Forest or the Trinity Alps Wilderness, send $3 to USDA-Forest Service, 630 Sansome Street, San Francisco, CA 94111. To obtain a topographic map of the area, ask for Covington Mill from the USGS.

*Who to contact:* Shasta-Trinity National Forest, Weaverville Ranger District, P.O. Box T, Weaverville, CA 96093; (916) 623-2121.

*Trail notes:* Your mission, should you choose to accept it, is the 6.5-mile hike to the west side of Gibson Peak, where Deer Lake, Summit Lake, Luella Lake, Diamond Lake and Siligo Peak can provide days of easy and fun sidetrip destinations. From the trailhead, the trip starts by tracing along the East Fork Stuart Fork, a feeder creek to Trinity Lake. After two miles, you will arrive at a fork in the trail. Take the right fork (the left fork is routed to Bowerman Meadows and little Lake Anna), which climbs further along the stream, then traces past the southern flank of Gibson Peak. At times the trail is steep in this area, but finally you will pass Gibson Peak and Siligo Peak will come into view. The trail also junctions with a loop trail that circles Siligo Peak, and in the process, provides easy access to four high mountain lakes. Summit Lake is the favorite.

## 15. STUART FORK TRAILHEAD           25.0 mi/4.0 days

*Reference:* In Trinity Alps Wilderness northwest of Trinity Lake; map B1, grid e6.

*User groups:* Hikers, dogs and horses. No mountain bikes are allowed. No wheelchair facilities.

*Permits:* A wilderness permit is required for hikers planning to camp. Parking and access are free.

*Directions:* From Weaverville on Highway 299, turn north on Highway 3 and drive 17 miles to Trinity Lake. Turn west on Trinity Alps Road and drive 2.5 miles to the trailhead, located at Bridge Camp.

*Maps:* For a map of Shasta-Trinity National Forest or the Trinity Alps Wilderness, send $3 to USDA-Forest Service, 630 Sansome Street, San Francisco, CA 94111. To obtain a topographic map of the area, ask for Covington Mill from the USGS.

*Who to contact:* Shasta-Trinity National Forest, Weaverville Ranger District, P.O. Box T, Weaverville, CA 96093; (916) 623-2121.

*Trail notes:* Don't say we didn't warn you; the trail didn't get rated a #5 boot for difficulty for nothing. This is an endless climb, very steep at times, particularly as you near the Sawtooth Ridge, spanning nearly 12 miles to Emerald Lake. But after arriving and resting up for a night, the ecstasy follows. Emerald Lake is one of three lakes set in line in a canyon below the Sawtooth Ridge, the others being Sapphire and Mirror. The surroundings are stark and prehistoric looking, and the lakes are gem-like, blue and clear, with big rainbow trout and water that is perfect for refreshing swims. The trail continues a mile past Emerald Lake to Sapphire Lake, and from there, it is an off-trail scramble, often jumping across big boulders, climbing another mile to reach Mirror Lake. The entire scene is surreal.

*Special note:* On the way in to Emerald Lake, many hikers will notice a cutoff trail to the right, then see by their trail maps that it crosses the Sawtooth Ridge and empties into the acclaimed Caribou Lakes Basin. It appears a short, easy trip, but in reality it involves a terrible climb with more than 100 switchbacks.

---

## 16. CANYON CREEK TRAILHEAD

14.0 mi/2.0 days

*Reference:* In Trinity Alps Wilderness north of Weaverville; map B1, grid e6.
*User groups:* Hikers, dogs and horses. No mountain bikes are allowed. No wheelchair facilities.
*Permits:* A wilderness permit is required for hikers planning to camp. Parking and access are free.
*Directions:* From Weaverville, turn west on Highway 299 and drive eight miles to Junction City. Turn north on Canyon Creek Road and drive 16 miles to the trailhead at the end of the road.
*Maps:* For a map of Shasta-Trinity National Forest or the Trinity Alps Wilderness, send $3 to USDA-Forest Service, 630 Sansome Street, San Francisco, CA 94111. To obtain a topographic map of the area, ask for Dedrick from the USGS.
*Who to contact:* Shasta-Trinity National Forest, Weaverville Ranger District, P.O. Box T, Weaverville, CA 96093; (916) 623-2121.
*Trail notes:* This is the kind of place where wilderness lovers can find religion. The destination is Canyon Creek Lakes, set high in a mountain canyon, framed by Sawtooth Mountain to the east and a series of high granite rims to the north. The route in is no mystery, heading straight upstream along Canyon Creek, almost due north, climbing all the way. The trail jumps the stream a few times, then after about 3.5 miles, skirts around Canyon Creek Falls. A mile later you cross Upper Canyon Creek Meadows, and shortly later, now largely above tree line, cross Stonehouse Gulch and reach the first of two lakes. The trail skirts past the left side of the first of the Canyon Creek Lakes, then arrives at the head of the larger of the two. They are like jewels set in the bottom of a gray, stark, high mountain canyon, and once you've seen them, you'll have their picture branded permanently in your mind.

---

## 17. SOUTH FORK NATIONAL TRAIL

20.0 mi/2.0 days

*Reference:* In Shasta-Trinity National Forest east of Ruth Lake on Highway 36; map B1, grid i2.
*User groups:* Hikers and dogs. No mountain bikes or horses are allowed. No wheelchair facilities.

*Permits:* No permits are required. Parking and access are free.

*Directions:* From Redding, drive west on Highway 299 for 43 miles to Douglas City. Turn left (south) on Highway 3 and drive about 25 miles to Hayfork. From Hayfork, continue southwest on Highway 3 and drive 10 miles to Highway 36. Turn west and drive 10 miles to the turnoff for Hell Gate Campground on the left. Continue on Forest Service Road 1S26 to the trailhead.

*Maps:* For a map of Shasta-Trinity National Forest, send $3 to USDA-Forest Service, 630 Sansome Street, San Francisco, CA 94111. To obtain a topographic map of the area, ask for Forest Glen from the USGS.

*Who to contact:* Shasta-Trinity National Forest, Hayfork Ranger District, P.O. Box 159, Hayfork, CA 96041; (916) 628-5227.

*Trail notes:* This is an obscure trail for people who like walking along a stream in virtual oblivion. It is routed along the South Fork Trinity River, heading south toward the Yolla Bolly Wilderness. There are no lakes anywhere near the trail, and for the most part, the trail just meanders along, with that stream nearby providing a constant point of reference. Even the trailhead is remote and obscure, a short drive out of the Hell Gate Campground. Immediately, the trail picks up the stream, and in less than an hour, you will feel as if you have discovered your own private little universe. The temperatures can really smoke out here in the summer, and the stream is your savior. How far might you go? For many, an hour in and an hour out is plenty. You can keep going to Jacques Place, an unrenowned abandoned camp about 10 miles away one-way, or even beyond another five miles to the trail's end at Double Cabin Site, where you can leave a shuttle car and make this a one-way trip.

---

# 18. NORTH FORK BEEGUM TRAILHEAD    10.0 mi/2.0 days

*Reference:* **In Shasta-Trinity National Forest west of Red Bluff; map B1, grid j5.**

*User groups:* Hikers, dogs, horses and mountain bikes. No wheelchair facilities.

*Permits:* No permits are required. Parking and access are free.

*Directions:* From Interstate 5 at Red Bluff, turn west on Highway 36 and drive approximately 45 miles to the Yolla Bolly Ranger Station (west of Platina). Turn south on Stuart Gap Road and drive about eight miles to the trailhead at North Fork Beegum Campground.

*Maps:* For a map of Shasta-Trinity National Forest, send $3 to USDA-Forest Service, 630 Sansome Street, San Francisco, CA 94111. To obtain a topographic map of the area, ask for Pony Buck Peak from the USGS.

*Who to contact:* Shasta-Trinity National Forest, Yolla Bolly Ranger District, HC01, P.O. Box 450, Platina, CA 96076; (916) 352-4211.

*Trail notes:* You want to be by yourself? This region of California gets only a scant number of visitors. While it lacks the high mountains, the sweeping views and lakeside campsites, there is another benefit here that has become far more difficult to find in California: absolute peace and quiet. You get it here. The trail starts out of the North Fork Beegum Campground and is routed south along Beegum Creek for the first few miles. Much of this is quite rocky and difficult, but hey, you wanted to be alone, right? It then rises up to Pole Corral Gap, set at 4,360 feet, adjacent to Little Red Mountain. For most visitors, this is far enough. If you want to turn this into a one-way hike with a shuttle, the route continues down another seven miles to Pattymocus Butte, where there is an old Forest Service lookout station, accessible by vehicle.

*Special note:* A portion of the trail on this route runs across posted private property, the Seeliger Ranch. So stay on the trail. Got it?

---

# 19. BASIN GULCH TRAILHEAD 3.0 mi/2.0 hrs

*Reference:* In Shasta-Trinity National Forest west of Red Bluff; map B1, grid j5.

*User groups:* Hikers, dogs, horses and mountain bikes. No wheelchair facilities.

*Permits:* No permits are required. Parking and access are free.

*Directions:* From Interstate 5 at Red Bluff, turn west on Highway 36 and drive approximately 45 miles to the Yolla Bolly Ranger Station (west of Platina). Turn south on Stuart Gap Road and drive three miles to the trailhead at Basin Gulch Campground.

*Maps:* For a map of Shasta-Trinity National Forest, send $3 to USDA-Forest Service, 630 Sansome Street, San Francisco, CA 94111. To obtain a topographic map of the area, ask for Map File No. 01914/Pony Buck Peak from the USGS.

*Who to contact:* Shasta-Trinity National Forest, Yolla Bolly Ranger District, HC01, P.O. Box 450, Platina, CA 96076; (916) 352-4211.

*Trail notes:* Your destination on this hike is Noble Ridge. In a relatively short time, this trail leaves any resemblance of civilization far behind. That is the attraction, and it is provided with only a short day hike. From the trailhead at Basin Gulch Campground, a 2,772-foot elevation, the trail loops in a half circle, climbing as it goes, reaching the ridge in just 1.5 miles. At a 3,200-foot elevation, making the climb here is punishment enough, and after a picnic lunch, hikers often return back to the camp. But the determined few can go onward, hiking along Noble Ridge all the way for another four miles to a survey marker that marks the ridgetop at 3,933 feet. The trail ends at a Forest Service Road (only three miles from Platina), allowing for a possible one-way hike with a shuttle.

# PACIFIC CREST TRAIL

## GENERAL INFORMATION

**21.0 mi. one way/2-3 days**

*Reference:* Trail sections extend from Scott Mountain east of Callahan to the border of the Russian Wilderness.

*User groups:* Hikers, dogs and horses. No mountain bikes are allowed. No wheelchair facilities.

*Permits:* A wilderness permit is required for certain portions of the trail; see specific sections for details. Parking and access are free.

*Maps:* For an overall view of the trail route in this chapter, send $3 for each map ordered to USDA-Forest Service, 630 Sansome Street, San Francisco, CA 94111. Ask for the Shasta-Trinity National Forest map and the Klamath National Forest map. Information on topographic maps for particular sections of the trail is provided under each specific trail section below from the USGS.

*Who to contact:* Information for the managing national forest is listed separately for each section below.

*Trail notes:* This segment of the Pacific Crest Trail does not travel north to south, but rather is routed east to west. Because it only skirts the northern edge of the Trinity Alps Wilderness, it gets less use than many of the lake-destination trails in the wilderness to the south. Regardless, this route features many excellent, short sidetrips to small mountain lakes in both the Trinity Alps and the Russian Wilderness. That makes it attractive to both weekend hikers as well as those on longer expeditions.

---

## PCT-44

**18.0 mi. one way/2.0 days**

## SCOTT MOUNTAIN to CECILVILLE ROAD

*Reference:* From Highway 3 at Scott Mountain Campground to Cecilville Road near northern border of Trinity Alps Wilderness; map B1, grid a9.

*User groups:* Hikers, dogs and horses. No mountain bikes are allowed. No wheelchair facilities.

*Permits:* A wilderness permit is required for camping in the Trinity Alps Wilderness. Contact the Weaverville Ranger District at the address below for information.

*Directions:* From Callahan, drive south on Highway 3 and drive about seven miles to the trailhead at Scott Mountain Campground.

*Maps:* To obtain topographic images of the area, ask for Scott Mountain, Tangle Blue Lake, Billys Peak and Deadman Peak from the USGS.

*Who to contact:* Shasta-Trinity National Forest, Weaverville Ranger District, P.O. Box T, Weaverville, CA 96093; (916) 623-2121.

*Trail notes:* Short hikes on spur trails to a number of wilderness lakes are the highlight of this section of the Pacific Crest Trail. From the camp at Scott Mountain, the trail is routed west for five miles, where the first of a series of lakes are situated within a half-mile of the trail. They include Upper Boulder Lake, East Boulder Lake, Mid Boulder Lake and Telephone Lake, all quite pretty and easy to reach from the main trail. After hiking past Eagle Peak, set at 7,789-foot elevation, you will pass additional short cutoffs that are routed to West Boulder Lake, Mavis Lake and Fox Creek Lake. One of these is usually selected for a camp, before dropping elevation to the South Fork Scott River, then crossing and heading north into the Russian Wilderness.

---

## PCT-45       3.0 mi. one way/1.0 day
## CECILVILLE ROAD to RUSSIAN WILDERNESS

*Reference:* **From Cecilville Road west of Callahan to southern border of Russian Wilderness; map B1, grid a8.**

*User groups:* Hikers, dogs and horses. No mountain bikes are allowed. No wheelchair facilities.

*Permits:* No permits are required for this section. Parking and access are free.

*Directions:* From Callahan on Highway 3, turn west on Cecilville Road and drive 11.5 miles to the Cecilville Summit. Parking is limited here; a larger parking area is located just past Cecilville Summit at the Carter Meadows Trailhead.

*Maps:* To obtain topographic images of the area, ask for Deadman Peak and Eaton Peak from the USGS.

*Who to contact:* Klamath National Forest, Scott River Ranger District, 11263 North Highway 3, Callahan, CA 96032; (916) 468-5351.

*Trail notes:* From the bottom of the canyon at the North Fork Scott River, you start the long, steady climb up to the southern border of the Russian Wilderness. From the trailhead, a good sidetrip (to the south) is the short trip to Hidden Lake or South Fork Lakes. For those venturing onward on the PCT, you are entering a complex habitat that includes the headwaters of the Scott, Salmon and Trinity rivers, along with the beautiful scenery that diversity brings with it. This section of the trail is rarely used, with less than 1,000 people a year estimated to hike here. Most of them use this as a jump-off spot, heading north into the Russian Wilderness.

*Special note:* For those driving to this trailhead, parking at Carter Meadows is recommended. While this will add about a quarter-mile to your hike, there is water and a vault toilet available there.

*PCT CONTINUATION:* To continue hiking along the Pacific Crest Trail, see Chapter A1, pages 47-49.

# MAP B2

NOR-CAL MAP ...................... see page 14
adjoining maps
NORTH (A2) ........................... see page 50
EAST (B3) .............................. see page 120
SOUTH (C2) ........................... see page 166
WEST (B1) .............................. see page 78

3 PCT SECTIONS
31 TRAILS
PAGES 94-119

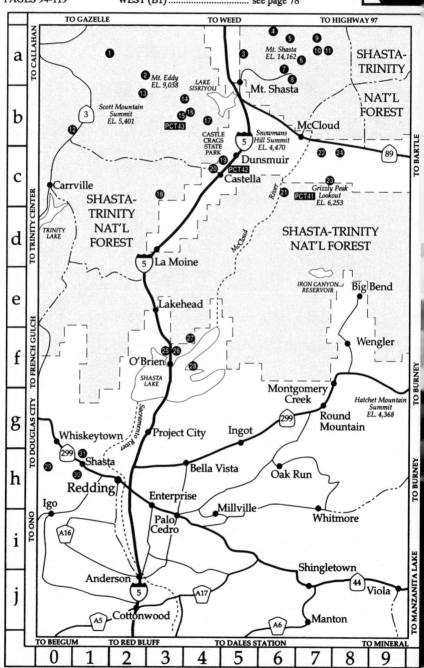

**Map B2 featuring:** Shasta-Trinity National Forest, Mt. Shasta, Trinity Alps Wilderness, Lake Siskiyou, Castle Crags State Park, McCloud River, McCloud, Shasta Lake, Redding, Whiskeytown Lake National Recreation Area, Shasta State Historic Park, Scott Mountain

## 1. KANGAROO LAKE TRAILHEAD     3.0 mi/2.25 hrs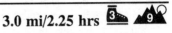

*Reference:* **In Shasta-Trinity National Forest east of Callahan; map B2, grid a2.**

*User groups:* Hikers, **wheelchairs**, dogs, mountain bikes and horses.

*Permits:* No permits are required. Parking and access are free.

*Directions:* From Interstate 5 north of Mt. Shasta, take the Edgewood exit, then turn left and drive a short distance to old Highway 99. Turn right, and drive about six miles to Gazelle. Turn left on Gazelle-Callahan Road and drive over the summit. Continue down the other side of the mountain about five miles, then turn left on Rail Creek Road and drive about five miles. The road deadends at the parking area for Kangaroo Lake. The trail starts to the right of the campground.

*Maps:* A trail guide can be obtained by contacting Klamath National Forest at the address below. For a map of Klamath National Forest, send $3 to USDA-Forest Service, 630 Sansome Street, San Francisco, CA 94111. To obtain a topographic map of the area, ask for Scott Mountain from the USGS.

*Who to contact:* Klamath National Forest, Scott River Ranger District, 11263 North Highway 3, Fort Jones, CA 96032; (916) 468-5351.

*Trail notes:* A remote paved road leads right to Kangaroo Lake, set at 6,050 feet, providing one of the most easily accessible pristine mountain lakes with a campground, **wheelchair accessible** fishing and a great trailhead. From the campground, the trail rises up steeply and connects with the Pacific Crest Trail, then climbs to the ridge above Kangaroo Lake. At the ridge, you can make the easy scramble off the trail to Cory Peak at 7,737 feet for a 360-degree view—it's a great picnic site. All of Northern California's prominent mountain peaks are in view here, and immediately below you to the west is Kangaroo Lake, which looks like a large sapphire. The lake is only 21 acres, but often produces large brook trout, most of them 12 to 14 inches. Backpackers can extend this trip eastward four miles on the Pacific Crest Trail past Robbers Meadow to Bull Lake.

## 2. DEADFALL LAKES TRAIL     5.0 mi/3.0 hrs 

*Reference:* **In Shasta-Trinity National Forest west of Mt. Shasta; map B2, grid a2.**

*User groups:* Hikers, dogs and horses. No mountain bikes are allowed. No wheelchair facilities.

*Permits:* No permits are required. Parking and access are free.

*Directions:* From Interstate 5 north of Weed, take the Edgewood exit and turn west on Forest Road 17. Drive about 13 miles to the Deadfall Lakes parking area, well-signed and on the left side of the road on a mountain saddle.

*Maps:* For a map of Shasta-Trinity National Forest, send $3 to USDA-Forest Service, 630 Sansome Street, San Francisco, CA 94111. To obtain a topographic map of the area, ask for Mount Eddy from the USGS.

*Who to contact:* Shasta-Trinity National Forest, Mt. Shasta Ranger District, 204 West Alma, Mt. Shasta, CA 96067; (916) 926-4511.

*Trail notes:* The sight of Middle Deadfall Lake is always a happy shock to newcomers. Here, secreted away on the west side of Mt. Eddy, are three wilderness lakes, the prize being Middle Deadfall. At 25 acres, it is far larger than you might expect and far prettier as well. Because the parking area and trailhead are at ridgeline, the hike in is much easier to this lake than to other wilderness lakes, an excellent day hike. The trail is routed through a mixed conifer forest, with views provided off to the west, and it's a gentle rising grade most of the way. As you near the lake, you will have to cross a stream, a no-wading, rock-hopping prospect, cross a meadow and then suddenly below you is Middle Deadfall Lake at 7,300 feet, one of the prizes along the Pacific Crest Trail. The best and most secluded campsite here is around to the back side of the lake. There are two other lakes nearby, Upper Deadfall at 7,800 feet, tiny and rarely visited, and Lower Deadfall at 7,150 feet, five acres and overlooked in the shadow of its nearby big brother. You should also note that a great sidetrip for campers at Middle Deadfall Lake is making the 3.5-mile hike to the top of Mt. Eddy at 9,025 feet, a 1,700-foot climb. It is one of Northern California's greatest lookouts, with no better view anywhere of the western slopes of Mt. Shasta.

---

# 3. BLACK BUTTE TRAIL        5.0 mi/3.5 hrs

*Reference:* In Shasta-Trinity National Forest between Interstate 5 and Mt. Shasta; map B2, grid a5.

*User groups:* Hikers and dogs. No horses or mountain bikes are allowed. No wheelchair facilities.

*Permits:* No permits are required. Parking and access are free.

*Directions:* From Interstate 5 at Mt. Shasta, take the Central Mt. Shasta exit and turn east on Lake Street. Follow Lake Street through town; once out of town it becomes Everitt Memorial Highway. From the last stop sign, follow the highway for two miles, then turn left at the Penny Pines sign. Continue on the dirt road for 2.5 miles. When the road crosses the overhead powerline, bear left on another dirt road and proceed another half-mile to the trailhead. Parking is very limited; be sure to park off the road.

*Maps:* A trail information sheet is available by contacting the Mt. Shasta Ranger District at the address below. For a map of Shasta-Trinity National Forest, send $3 to USDA-Forest Service, 630 Sansome Street, San Francisco, CA 94111. To obtain a topographic map of the area, ask for City of Mt. Shasta from the USGS.

*Who to contact:* Shasta-Trinity National Forest, Mt. Shasta Ranger District, 204 West Alma, Mt. Shasta, CA 96067; (916) 926-4511.

*Trail notes:* Anybody who has cruised Interstate 5 north to Oregon and gawked in astonishment at Mt. Shasta has inevitably seen Black Butte right alongside the highway. That's right, it's that conical-shaped, barren cindercone set between the highway and Mt. Shasta, and it can pique a traveler's curiosity. The trail is routed right to the top and can answer all of your questions. But you may not like all the answers. Over the course of 2.5 miles, you will climb 1,845 feet, much of it steep, most of it rocky, and in the summer, all of it hot and dry. There is no shade anywhere. There are only two rewards. One is claiming the summit, at 6,325 feet, where there is the foundation of an old Forest Service lookout and great 360-degree views. The other reward is that it is an excellent warm-up for people who are planning to climb Mt. Shasta. That is, providing you don't need a week to recover.

# 4. BOLAM CREEK TRAILHEAD 3.4 mi/2.5 hrs

*Reference:* **On the northwest slope of Mt. Shasta; map B2, grid a6.**

*User groups:* Hikers only. No dogs, horses or mountain bikes are allowed. No wheelchair facilities.

*Permits:* You must obtain a free wilderness permit from Shasta-Trinity National Forest to enter Mt. Shasta Wilderness. Parking and access are free.

*Directions:* From Interstate 5 at Weed, take the College of the Siskiyous exit and drive north through Weed about 1 mile. Turn north on US 97 and drive approximately 11 miles, then turn right on Bolam Logging Road (Forest Service Road 43N21) and continue to the trailhead at the end of the road.

*Maps:* A trail map of the Mt. Shasta Wilderness can be purchased for $6 from the Mt. Shasta Ranger District at the address below. For a map of Shasta-Trinity National Forest, send $3 to USDA-Forest Service, 630 Sansome Street, San Francisco, CA 94111. To obtain a topographic map of the area, ask for Mount Shasta from the USGS.

*Who to contact:* Shasta-Trinity National Forest, Mt. Shasta Ranger District, 204 West Alma, Mt. Shasta, CA 96067; (916) 926-4511.

*Trail notes:* Mt. Shasta, 14,162 feet tall, is the most prominent landmark in Northern California, and it is well-known for its outstanding summit routes on its southern slopes. What is less known, however, is that there are four trailheads set on Shasta's northern and eastern foothills that grant hikers choice day walks and mountaineers a starting point for difficult climbs over glaciers to the top. Those forgotten four trailheads are at Bolam Creek, North Gate, Brewer Creek and Watkins Glacier. The Bolam Creek Trailhead is at about 5,600 feet, and from it, the trail heads uphill, for the most part tracing a gulch, the headwaters of a small stream. The trail crosses the creek a few times on the way, all easy crossings on a moderate-grade, surrounded primarily by old, gnarled Shasta red firs. The trail spans 1.6 miles to a fork at 6,400 feet, and for day hikers, the best bet is turning right, climbing partially up the treeless slope for a lookout and picnic site.

*Special note:* If you turn left at the fork instead, you will venture through forest, then up through another barren stream drainage. The trail ends, and mountaineers will have to pass both Coquette Falls, and then near the peak, the Bolam Glacier, in order to make the summit. Safety gear and expert climbing skills are required.

# 5. NORTH GATE TRAILHEAD  4.0 mi/2.75 hrs

*Reference:* **On north slope of Mt. Shasta; map B2, grid a6.**

*User groups:* Hikers only. No dogs, horses or mountain bikes are allowed. No wheelchair facilities.

*Permits:* You must obtain a free wilderness permit from Shasta-Trinity National

Forest to enter Mt. Shasta Wilderness. Parking and access are free.

*Directions:* From Interstate 5 at Weed, take the College of the Siskiyous exit and drive north through town. Turn north on US 97 and drive approximately 13.5 miles, then turn right on Military Pass Road and drive approximately five miles. Turn right on Forest Service Road 42N16 and drive about three miles, then turn right on Forest Service Road 42N7A and continue to the parking area at the end of the road.

*Maps:* A trail map of the Mt. Shasta Wilderness can be purchased for $6 from the Mt. Shasta Ranger District at the address below. For a map of Shasta-Trinity National Forest, send $3 to USDA-Forest Service, 630 Sansome Street, San Francisco, CA 94111. To obtain a topographic map of the area, ask for Mount Shasta from the USGS.

*Who to contact:* Shasta-Trinity National Forest, Mt. Shasta Ranger District, 204 West Alma, Mt. Shasta, CA 96067; (916) 926-4511.

*Trail notes:* The North Gate Trailhead, set at about 7,000 feet, is one of Mt. Shasta's most obscure and least used trails. It sits on the north flank of Shasta, just below a mountain mound called North Gate. The route skirts around this mound, following a small stream uphill for 1.6 miles, then as you go further, the trail deteriorates and disappears as you near tree line at 8,400 foot elevation. From here, most day hikers will climb up another 400 feet to the source of the creek, a small spring, and have lunch and enjoy the view to the north.

*Special note:* Mountain climbers who use this route to climb to the Shasta summit will discover the going is quite easy at first after leaving tree line. The trip then becomes very steep, difficult and dangerous, whether crossing Bolam or Hotlum Glacier. This route is for experienced mountain climbers only, who are aware of the extreme risks of crossing steep, sheer glaciers.

---

# 6. SAND FLAT TRAILHEAD    3.4 mi/2.75 hrs

*Reference:* On the southern slope of Mt. Shasta; map B2, grid a6.

*User groups:* Hikers only. No dogs, horses or mountain bikes are allowed. No wheelchair facilities.

*Permits:* You must obtain a free wilderness permit from Shasta-Trinity National Forest to enter Mt. Shasta Wilderness. Parking and access are free.

*Directions:* From Interstate 5 at Mt. Shasta, take the Central Mt. Shasta exit and turn east on Lake Street. Follow Lake Street through town; once out of town it becomes Everitt Memorial Highway. From the last stop sign, follow the highway for 9.5 miles. Turn left at the sign for Sand Flat and follow the road to the trailhead at the end.

*Maps:* A trail map of the Mt. Shasta Wilderness can be purchased for $6 from the Mt. Shasta Ranger District at the address below. For a map of Shasta-Trinity National Forest, send $3 to USDA-Forest Service, 630 Sansome Street, San Francisco, CA 94111. To obtain a topographic map of the area, ask for Mount Shasta from the USGS.

*Who to contact:* Shasta-Trinity National Forest, Mt. Shasta Ranger District, 204 West Alma, Mt. Shasta, CA 96067; (916) 926-4511.

*Trail notes:* The hike from Sand Flat to Horse Camp, a distance of 1.7 miles, will give you a good taste of the Mt. Shasta experience, and you're likely to savor the flavors. Many who make this day hike are often compelled to return to make the climb all the way to the top. We were! Sand Flat provides a good shaded parking area to start from at a 6,800-foot elevation. The trail immediately takes off uphill, gradually at first, and then becomes quite steep. At 7,360 feet, it intersects with the Bunny Flat Trail, and then continues rising through forest. Along the way, there are amazing examples of how avalanches have knocked down entire sections of forest in this area. When you reach Horse Camp at 7,800 feet, nearing timber line, you will find many rewards. The first is spring water flowing continuously out of a piped fountain near the Sierra Hut, perhaps the best tasting water in the world. The second is the foreboding view of Red Banks, which forms the mountain rim above Horse Camp. The third is the opportunity to hike up a short ways above tree line for the sweeping views to the south of Castle Crags and Lake Siskiyou. After taking the first steps on the Summit Trail, you will likely yearn to keep going all the way to the very top of this magic mountain. If you wish to hike the Summit Trail, see the following hike out of Bunny Flat Trailhead.

---

# 7. SHASTA SUMMIT TRAIL    13.6 mi/1.5 days

***Reference:*** **At Bunny Flat Trailhead on the southern slope of Mt. Shasta; map B2, grid a6.**

***User groups:*** Hikers only. No dogs, horses or mountain bikes are allowed. No wheelchair facilities.

***Permits:*** You must obtain a free wilderness permit from Shasta-Trinity National Forest to enter Mt. Shasta Wilderness. Parking and access are free.

***Directions:*** From Interstate 5 at Mt. Shasta, take the Central Mt. Shasta exit and turn east on Lake Street. Follow Lake Street through town; once out of town it becomes Everitt Memorial Highway. From the last stop sign, follow the highway for 10.5 miles to the Bunny Flat parking area and trailhead.

***Maps:*** A trail map of the Mt. Shasta Wilderness can be purchased for $6 from the Mt. Shasta Ranger District at the address below. For a map of Shasta-Trinity National Forest, send $3 to USDA-Forest Service, 630 Sansome Street, San Francisco, CA 94111. To obtain a topographic map of the area, ask for Mount Shasta from the USGS.

***Who to contact:*** Shasta-Trinity National Forest, Mt. Shasta Ranger District, 204 West Alma, Mt. Shasta, CA 96067; (916) 926-4511. A 24-hour climbing report is available by phoning (916) 926-5555. Ice axes and crampons are available for rent at Fifth Season in Mt. Shasta at (916) 926-3606. If you'd like to climb Mt. Shasta with an experienced guide, call Michael Zanger at Shasta Mountain Guides at (916) 926-3117.

***Trail notes:*** The hike to the top of Mt. Shasta is a great challenge, an ascent of 7,000 feet over ice, snow and rock while trying to suck what little oxygen you can out of the thin air. It may be the greatest adventure in the West that most people have an honest chance of achieving. While there are dangers, from tumbling boulders (see special note) to bad weather (which stops half the people who try the climb), hikers in good condition who start the trip very early and have the proper equipment can make it all the way to the top and back in a day. Early? You should depart from Bunny Flat by 3:30 a.m., or hike in a day early, set up a base camp at Horse Camp (tree line), and start no later than 4:30 a.m. Equipment? A daypack with warm clothes, a windbreaker, two canteens of water (refill at Red Bank), food, and an ice ax and crampons are mandatory. The trip starts out of Bunny Flat at 6,900 feet, leads through a forest of Shasta red firs, climbs up to where the trail intersects with the route out of Sand Flat, then turns right and rises to Horse Camp, at 7,800-foot elevation, a distance of 1.8 miles. After filling your canteens at the spring, you start the Summit Trail, your first steps made across a series of large stones called "Olberman's Causeway." From here, the trail quickly rises above timber line, then shortly later, becomes a faint path. Often, this is where the snow and ice starts, and you must stop and strap your crampons on your boots. The walking is easy with crampons, the metal spikes poking holes into the ice surface. The trail climbs up Avalanche Gulch, and some people stop to make trail camps at a flat spot called Helen Lake at 10,440 feet. Some hikers not acclimated to high altitudes will begin experiencing some dizziness, but there is no relief in sight. At this point, the hike gets steeper, about a 35-degree slope, and many give up before reaching Red Banks, a huge red volcanic outcrop at about 12,500 feet. At Red Banks, you will need your ice ax, pulling your way through a narrow and steep rock/ice chute, where a slip is certain without crampons. When you emerge atop Red Bank, you are nearly 13,000 feet high, at the foot of a glacier field and Misery Hill, named because it is a long, slow climb, and many mistake it for being the peak. Once atop Misery Hill, though, you will see the true Shasta Summit, a massive pinnacle of lava which seems to jut straight up into the air. With a final push, you follow the trail, grabbing rocks to help pull you up, sucking the thin air, and with a few last steps, you will be on top. On clear days, you can see hundreds of miles in all directions, and at 14,162 feet, the sky is a deeper cobalt blue than you will have ever imagined. On top, you will sign your name in a logbook in an old rusted metal box, then take in the grand wonders surrounding you. It is a remarkable trip, one we plan on making every year for as long as our bodies can take it.

*Special note, Part I:* It is an absolute must to make an early start. In the hot summer months, towering cumulus clouds sometimes form on Mt. Shasta during the afternoon, and by then you will want to be making the trip down, since a thunder and lightning storm is possible.

*Special note, Part II:* The biggest danger and largest number of injuries on Mt. Shasta come not from falling, but from being hit by tumbling boulders. In fact, our research assistant, Robyn Schlueter, was struck in the foot by a boulder in her first attempt at climbing Shasta. She was hit so hard that it knocked her hiking boot off, breaking her foot and requiring an emergency helicopter airlift out for medical treatment. Always keep a good distance between your hiking partners, do not hike in a vertical line, and if a rock comes bouncing down, always shout, "Rock! Rock!" By the way, Robyn returned to Mt. Shasta the following two years and made it to the top on both trips.

*Special note, Part III:* The mountain is best hiked when it still has a good coating of snow and ice, which allows for excellent footing with crampons. When the snow and ice melts off in late fall, tromping through the small volcanic rocks is like slogging in mushy sand.

*Special note, Part IV:* Drink lots of water. In high altitudes, dehydration is a common problem and can result in early exhaustion and extreme vulnerability to mountain sickness.

# 8. PANTHER MEADOWS 2.8 mi/1.75 hrs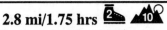

*Reference:* **On the southern slope of Mt. Shasta; map B2, grid a6.**

*User groups:* Hikers only. No dogs, horses or mountain bikes are allowed. No wheelchair facilities.

*Permits:* You must obtain a free wilderness permit from Shasta-Trinity National Forest to enter Mt. Shasta Wilderness. Parking and access are free.

*Directions:* From Interstate 5 at Mt. Shasta, take the Central Mt. Shasta exit and turn east on Lake Street. Follow Lake Street through town; once out of town it becomes Everitt Memorial Highway. From the last stop sign, follow the highway for 15.5 miles to the parking area on the right side of the road.

*Maps:* A trail map of the Mt. Shasta Wilderness can be purchased for $6 from the Mt. Shasta Ranger District at the address below. For a map of Shasta-Trinity National Forest, send $3 to USDA-Forest Service, 630 Sansome Street, San Francisco, CA 94111. To obtain a topographic map of the area, ask for Mount Shasta from the USGS.

*Who to contact:* Shasta-Trinity National Forest, Mt. Shasta Ranger District, 204 West Alma, Mt. Shasta, CA 96067; (916) 926-4511.

*Trail notes:* Panther Meadows is considered a sacred Native American site, and even those who are unaware of it seem to intuitively realize this is a special place and find themselves walking softly and talking quietly when visiting. The trail is easy to reach, located just off to the right of the wide, paved, two-laner Everitt Memorial Highway. This hike is a short one, from Panther Meadows to Gray Butte and back. From the parking area, the trail starts by heading east past meadow and forest, and after six-tenths of a mile, turns right and begins a steady climb for eight-tenths of a mile to the top of Gray Butte at 8,108 feet. It is a perfect lookout to the south, with Castle Crags, Mt. Lassen and the dropoff in the Sacramento Valley all prominent.

# 9. BREWER CREEK TRAILHEAD 4.2 mi/3.0 hrs

*Reference:* **On the northeast slope of Mt. Shasta; map B2, grid a7.**

*User groups:* Hikers only. No dogs, horses or mountain bikes are allowed. No wheelchair facilities.

*Permits:* You must obtain a free wilderness permit from Shasta-Trinity National Forest to enter Mt. Shasta Wilderness. Parking and access are free.

*Directions:* From Interstate 5 south of Mt. Shasta, take the McCloud-Reno exit and turn east on Highway 89. Drive 12 miles to McCloud, then continue eight miles further on Highway 89 and turn north on Military Pass Road (Forest Road 19). Drive 16 miles, then turn west on Brewer Creek Road (Forest Service Road 42N02) and drive about three miles. Turn left on Forest Service Road 42N10 and continue to the parking area. The route is signed.

*Maps:* A trail map of the Mt. Shasta Wilderness can be purchased for $6 from the Mt. Shasta Ranger District at the address below. For a map of Shasta-Trinity National Forest, send $3 to USDA-Forest Service, 630 Sansome Street, San Francisco, CA 94111. To obtain a topographic map of the area, ask for Mount Shasta from the USGS.

*Who to contact:* Shasta-Trinity National Forest, Mt. Shasta Ranger District, 204 West Alma, Mt. Shasta, CA 96067; (916) 926-4511.

*Trail notes:* It is so quiet here that you can practically hear the wildflowers bloom. We've hiked the north slope of Shasta out of the Brewer Creek Trailhead several times and have never seen another person. The trip is a perfect day hike. The trailhead is set near Brewer Creek (7,200 feet), hence the name, and after a short walk through a section of forest that was selectively logged many years ago, you will enter the Shasta Wilderness and be surrounded by old-growth firs, many quite scraggly from enduring harsh winters and the short growing season. Here the trail gets more steep, a steady climb up through forest, gradual switchbacks as it goes. When you near tree line at 7,700 feet, the trail turns to the left and begins to lateral across the mountain. It is 2.1 miles to timber line from the trailhead, and most people hike to this point, then turn back. However, you can add an easy mile or two by climbing a wide, volcanic slope with good footing all the way and rising to 9,500 feet. It is great for a picnic site, providing great views to the north, and also perhaps inspiring dreams of the day when you'll next climb all the way to the top of Shasta.

*Special note:* Mountaineers who try to climb Shasta from this trailhead have only one good route from where the trail meets tree line, and that is to the right up and over Hotlum Glacier. This route is extremely difficult, very steep and dangerous.

---

# 10. WATKINS GLACIER TRAILHEAD

4.0 mi/2.75 hrs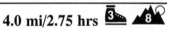

*Reference:* **On the southeast slope of Mt. Shasta; map B2, grid a7.**

*User groups:* Hikers only. No dogs, horses or mountain bikes are allowed. No wheelchair facilities.

*Permits:* You must obtain a free wilderness permit from Shasta-Trinity National Forest to enter Mt. Shasta Wilderness. Parking and access are free.

*Directions:* From Interstate 5 south of Mt. Shasta, take the McCloud-Reno exit and turn east on Highway 89. Drive 12 miles to McCloud, then continue another eight miles east on Highway 89 to Military Pass Road. Turn north and drive about six miles, then turn left on Forest Service Road 41N14. Follow it to Forest Service Road 41N15, then turn right and drive about two miles. Turn left on Forest Service Road 41N61 and drive about 1.5 miles, then turn left on Forest Service Road 41N61A and continue to the parking area at the end of the road.

*Maps:* A trail map of the Mt. Shasta Wilderness can be purchased for $6 from the Mt. Shasta Ranger District at the address below. For a map of Shasta-Trinity National Forest, send $3 to USDA-Forest Service, 630 Sansome Street, San Francisco, CA 94111. To obtain a topographic map of the area, ask for Mount Shasta from the USGS.

*Who to contact:* Shasta-Trinity National Forest, Mt. Shasta Ranger District, 204 West Alma, Mt. Shasta, CA 96067; (916) 926-4511.

*Trail notes:* The Watkins Glacier Trail is one of the least traveled hikes on Mt. Shasta. It features a trek along one of Shasta's ridgelines, climbing steadily from 6,400 feet up to just past tree line at 8,240 feet. Here the trail seems to disappear, but hikers can go onward, hiking another half mile or so without a problem across a hard volcanic gravel field until meeting the glacier fields. Then suddenly, the mountain slope gets very steep, with the Watkins Glacier at 10,000 feet, one of the most sheer slopes that mountaineers consider as a viable route to the top. Of course, most hikers should look at the glacier and try to *picture* the climbing route, but never in their right mind should they actually attempt it. At least not without the assistance of an experienced master, such as Shasta mountaineer Michael Zanger.

## 11. OLD SKI BOWL TRAILHEAD
2.5 mi/2.0 hrs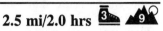

*Reference:* **On the southern slope of Mt. Shasta; map B2, grid a7.**
*User groups:* Hikers only. No dogs, horses or mountain bikes are allowed. No wheelchair facilities.
*Permits:* You must obtain a free wilderness permit from Shasta-Trinity National Forest to enter Mt. Shasta Wilderness. Parking and access are free.
*Directions:* From Interstate 5 at Mt. Shasta, take the Central Mt. Shasta exit and turn east on Lake Street. Follow Lake Street through town; once out of town it becomes Everitt Memorial Highway. From the last stop sign, follow the highway for 16 miles to the parking area at the end.
*Maps:* A trail map of the Mt. Shasta Wilderness can be purchased for $6 from the Mt. Shasta Ranger District at the address below. For a map of Shasta-Trinity National Forest, send $3 to USDA-Forest Service, 630 Sansome Street, San Francisco, CA 94111. To obtain a topographic map of the area, ask for Mount Shasta from the USGS.
*Who to contact:* Shasta-Trinity National Forest, Mt. Shasta Ranger District, 204 West Alma, Mt. Shasta, CA 96067; (916) 926-4511.
*Trail notes:* One of the truly great hikes on Mt. Shasta is climbing from the Old Ski Bowl lodge site up to Green Butte. At 7,800 feet, it is the highest drive-to trailhead on Mt. Shasta, set just above timber line. That means the entire route is across a volcanic slope, with great views every step of the way and a unique destination as well. Green Butte, a huge rock outcrop set at 9,193 feet is a perfect perch. At the parking area, there is an obvious trail (though it's unsigned) that leads up toward Green Butte, which is also clearly obvious just a mile away. But while the trip is short in distance, it is very steep, with a 1,300-foot elevation gain. Along the way, a great bonus is a natural spring set about halfway up the butte; be sure to find it and fill your canteen with this sweet tasting spring water. While Green Butte is the destination of most visitors here, the hiking route continues to 9,600 feet before disintegrating in the lava rubble and snow. The "Old Ski Bowl" is one of the legendary spots on Shasta. It was here that a developer desecrated Shasta wildlands by building a ski area above tree line. Well, nature gives and nature takes back. With no trees to hold snow in place, the old mountain wiped out the ski lifts with an avalanche, and again, Shasta is untouched, rising like a diamond in a field of coal.

## 12. BIG BEAR LAKE TRAIL
8.0 mi/2.0 days

*Reference:* In Trinity Alps Wilderness south of Callahan; map B2, grid b1.
*User groups:* Hikers, dogs and horses. No mountain bikes are allowed. No wheelchair facilities.
*Permits:* A wilderness permit is required for hikers planning to camp in the wilderness. Parking and access are free.

*Directions:* From Callahan, drive south on Highway 3 and drive about 13 miles to the turnoff for the Bear Creek Parking Area. Turn right and continue to the trailhead.

*Maps:* For a map of Shasta-Trinity National Forest, send $3 to USDA-Forest Service, 630 Sansome Street, San Francisco, CA 94111. To obtain a topographic map of the area, ask for Reference Code Tangle Blue Lake from the USGS.

*Who to contact:* Shasta-Trinity National Forest, Weaverville Ranger District, P.O. Box T, Weaverville, CA 96093; (916) 623-2121.

*Trail notes:* Searching for the ideal hike to introduce a youngster to the wilderness or a great day hike for aspiring mountaineers? This might just be it, a four-mile hike up to Big Bear Lake, a large, beautiful lake by wilderness standards. It has an overnight camp, so you can go back down the next day. If there is a negative to this trip, it is this: The trail ends at the lake, so if the lakeside campsites are already taken when you arrive, you're out of luck for a quality place to camp for the night. The trailhead is easy to reach, just off Highway 3 north of Trinity Lake. The route is simple but not easy. It follows Bear Creek for the entire route, with one stream crossing but climbing all the way. Once you reach the lake, a bonus is the sidetrip to Little Bear Lake, which takes about a mile of scrambling cross-country style to reach.

---

# 13. TOAD LAKE TRAIL    1.5 mi/2.0 days 🥾 ⛰️8

*Reference:* In Shasta-Trinity National Forest west of Mt. Shasta; map B2, grid b2.

*User groups:* Hikers, dogs, horses and mountain bikes. No wheelchair facilities.

*Permits:* No permits are required. Parking and access are free.

*Directions:* From Interstate 5 at Mt. Shasta, take the Central Mount Shasta exit and drive 16.5 miles west on W.A. Barr Road (Forest Road 26). Just past the concrete bridge, turn right and drive a short distance, then turn left on Morgan Meadow Road and continue for 10 miles to the parking area. The road is very rough; four-wheel-drive vehicles are recommended.

*Maps:* For a map of Shasta-Trinity National Forest, send $3 to USDA-Forest Service, 630 Sansome Street, San Francisco, CA 94111. To obtain a topographic map of the area, ask for Mount Eddy from the USGS.

*Who to contact:* Shasta-Trinity National Forest, Mt. Shasta Ranger District, 204 West Alma, Mt. Shasta, CA 96067; (916) 926-4511.

*Trail notes:* What? How is this possible? Are we suffering from some rare form of mental illness? While the latter might be true, that is not why a 1.5-mile roundtrip hike, rating only a #1 boot in difficulty, is projected as a two-day trip. The reason is because the drive to the trailhead is interminable, the road winding and twisting its way up the slopes of Mt. Eddy, and no one should go up and back in a day. Keep your tongue in your mouth, because the ride is so jarring that you might bite the end of it when you hit a big pothole. But once parked, you will immediately notice the perfect calm, and then with a 15-minute walk to the lake at a 6,950-foot elevation, you will be furnished with a picture-perfect lakeside campsite. The lake covers 23 acres, provides excellent swimming, fair fishing for small trout and excellent sidetrips. The best is the three-quarter-mile hike to Porcupine Lake, taking the trail that is routed behind the lake up to the Pacific Crest Trail, walking south for a quarter-mile on the PCT, and then turning right on the short cutoff to Porcupine. It is one of the most idyllic settings in the Trinity Divide country.

---

## 14. SISSON-CALLAHAN    17.0 mi/2.0 days

*Reference:* **In Shasta-Trinity National Forest near Lake Siskiyou west of Mt. Shasta; map B2, grid b3.**

*User groups:* Hikers, dogs and horses. No mountain bikes are allowed. No wheelchair facilities.

*Permits:* No permits are required. Parking and access are free.

*Directions:* From Interstate 5 at Mt. Shasta, take the Central Mt. Shasta exit and turn west on W.A. Barr Road. Drive 2.5 miles past the Lake Siskiyou turnoff and turn right on a forest access road and drive one-half mile to the trailhead.

*Maps:* For a map of Shasta-Trinity National Forest, send $3 to USDA-Forest Service, 630 Sansome Street, San Francisco, CA 94111. To obtain topographic maps of the area, ask for City of Mount Shasta and Mount Eddy from the USGS.

*Who to contact:* Shasta-Trinity National Forest, Mt. Shasta Ranger District, 204 West Alma, Mt. Shasta, CA 96067; (916) 926-4511.

*Trail notes:* The Sisson-Callahan Trail is something of a legend in the Mt. Shasta area, long ago being a well-known, well-traveled route up to Mt. Eddy and Deadfall Lakes. But with a much easier route now available from the Deadfall Lakes Trailhead, this trail is often passed over. Why? The route is long, steep and hot, climbing 5,000 feet to the top of Mt. Eddy at 9,025 feet, then nine miles to Deadfall Lakes for the nearest first-class campground. In addition, the great scenic beauty doesn't start until you have climbed several thousand feet, and by then, you will care more about how much water is left in your canteen than about the incredible sweeping view of Mt. Shasta to the east. Alas, even worse are the killer switchbacks you will have to traverse to reach the Eddy ridge. All in all, this is a genuine booger-country, butt-kicker of a trail.

---

## 15. SEVEN LAKES BASIN    5.0 mi/3.25 hrs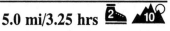
## TRAILHEAD

*Reference:* **In Shasta-Trinity National Forest west of Mt. Shasta; map B2, grid b3.**

*User groups:* Hikers, dogs, horses and mountain bikes. No wheelchair access.

*Permits:* No permits are required. Parking and access are free.

*Directions:* From Interstate 5 at Mt. Shasta, take the Central Mount Shasta exit and drive about 16 miles west on W.A. Barr Road (Forest Road 26) past the Gumboot Lake turnoff. At 2.5 miles past the Gumboot Lake turnoff, park at the Gumboot Saddle/PCT parking area.

*Maps:* For a map of Shasta-Trinity National Forest, send $3 to USDA-Forest Service, 630 Sansome Street, San Francisco, CA 94111. To obtain a topographic map of the area, ask for Mumbo Basin from the USGS.

*Who to contact:* Shasta-Trinity National Forest, Mt. Shasta Ranger District, 204 West Alma, Mt. Shasta, CA 96067; (916) 926-4511.

*Trail notes:* More than half a dozen little untouched lakes highlight the Seven Lakes Basin, one of the prettiest areas of the Trinity Divide. It offers great day hikes, yet is often overlooked by visitors more fascinated by nearby Mt.

Shasta to the east. The Seven Lakes Basin has all the qualities of a true wilderness, yet it is easy to reach and easy to hike. The key is starting at the right trailhead, not right at Gumboot Lake but above at the parking area adjacent to the Pacific Crest Trail. From there, you hike on the PCT southward, arriving at the Seven Lakes Basin in only 2.5 miles. Here you will find little lakes sprinkled all around the high granite country: Upper Seven (at 6,300 feet), Lower Seven (at 6,200 feet), Helen (at 6,700 feet), Mumbo (at 6,100 feet) and several others. You can also hike further on the PCT for another mile to Echo Lake (at 5,900 feet), one of the largest, prettiest lakes in the area, set just below Boulder Peak.

## 16. GUMBOOT LAKE TRAILHEAD

1.5 mi/1.5 hrs

*Reference:* In Shasta-Trinity National Forest west of Mt. Shasta; map B2, grid b3.

*User groups:* Hikers only. No dogs, horses and mountain bikes are allowed. No wheelchair facilities.

*Permits:* No permits are required. Parking and access are free.

*Directions:* From Interstate 5 at Mt. Shasta, take the Central Mount Shasta exit and drive about 16 miles west on W.A. Barr Road (Forest Road 26). Turn left on the Gumboot Lake access road and continue to the trailhead.

*Maps:* For a map of Shasta-Trinity National Forest, send $3 to USDA-Forest Service, 630 Sansome Street, San Francisco, CA 94111. To obtain a topographic map of the area, ask for Mumbo Basin from the USGS.

*Who to contact:* Shasta-Trinity National Forest, Mt. Shasta Ranger District, 204 West Alma, Mt. Shasta, CA 96067; (916) 926-4511.

*Trail notes:* If you always have to have a trail to hike on, well, this trip is not for you. But if you don't mind a little cross-country scramble to a mountain rim, then a short cutoff to a peak for spectacular views of Gumboot Lake and beyond of Mt. Shasta, then sign up for this hike. You start at Gumboot Lake at 6,050 feet, a pretty lake with good trout fishing. Circle the lake on the right side, where there is a good trail. At the back of the lake, break off the trail to the right and start climbing the slope, heading up towards the ridge that circles the back of the lake. A little less than halfway to the top, you will pass Little Gumboot Lake, then scramble your way to the ridge, where you will intersect with the Pacific Crest Trail. Head to the left for a short distance, then again break off the trail, heading on the mountain spine toward the peak that towers over Gumboot Lake, with Mt. Shasta off to the east the backdrop. This peak is your destination. The world may not be perfect, but from this lookout, it comes close.

## 17. LITTLE CASTLE LAKE

3.0 mi/2.25 hrs

*Reference:* In Shasta-Trinity National Forest west of Mt. Shasta; map B2, grid b4.

*User groups:* Hikers and dogs. Not suitable for horses or mountain bikes. No wheelchair facilities.

*Permits:* A wilderness permit is required to enter the Castle Crags Wilderness. Parking and access are free.

*Directions:* From Interstate 5 at Mt. Shasta, take the Central Mt. Shasta exit.

Turn west on W.A. Barr Road and proceed over Box Canyon Dam at Lake Siskiyou, then one mile later, to Castle Lake Road. Turn left and proceed to the parking area at Castle Lake.

*Maps:* For a map of Shasta-Trinity National Forest, send $3 to USDA-Forest Service, 630 Sansome Street, San Francisco, CA 94111. A map of Castle Crags Wilderness can also be purchased for $6. To obtain a topographic map of the area, ask for City of Mount Shasta from the USGS.

*Who to contact:* Shasta-Trinity National Forest, Mt. Shasta Ranger District, 204 West Alma, Mt. Shasta, CA 96067; (916) 926-4511.

*Trail notes:* The tale of Castle Lake (set at a 5,450-foot elevation) is that the water is like none other in the world. People will jump into the lake for complete renewal. When you first touch it, the water is so cold that it is like being initiated into the Arctic Polar Bear Club, but the purported rejuvenating qualities of the water are such that few even care. The trailhead is at the left side of the lake, just across the outlet stream. From there, the trail rises up along the slope just left of the lake, and below you, Castle Lake is a pretty sight, set in a rock bowl with a high back wall. The trail rises up to a saddle at 5,900 feet, then drops down the other side into a little mountain pocket. In that pocket is Little Castle Lake, set at 5,600 feet. After reaching the lake, scramble up the back side of it for a view of Mt. Shasta. A great sidetrip is to Heart Lake, a little lake set at 6,050 feet, located a short scramble off the trail, leading uphill from where the Little Castle Lake Trail crosses the mountain saddle. The best drive-to spot anywhere for photographs of Mt. Shasta is on Castle Lake Road, a turnout about a half-mile downhill from the Castle Lake parking area.

---

# 18. TAMARACK LAKE TRAILHEAD
**5.0 mi/4.0 hrs**

*Reference:* **In Shasta-Trinity National Forest southwest of Mt. Shasta; map B2, grid c3.**

*User groups:* Hikers and dogs. Not suitable for horses and mountain bikes. No wheelchair facilities.

*Permits:* No permits are required. Parking and access are free.

*Directions:* From Interstate 5 south of Mt. Shasta, take the Castle Crags State Park exit and turn west on Forest Road 25. Drive about 12 miles, then turn left on Forest Service Road 38N17 and follow it to the trailhead. This road is extremely rough, the last mile passable only to four-wheel-drive vehicles with large tires and a high clearance. A primitive parking area is available on the right side for other vehicles just prior to this bad section of road..

*Maps:* For a map of Shasta-Trinity National Forest, send $3 to USDA-Forest Service, 630 Sansome Street, San Francisco, CA 94111. To obtain a topographic map of the area, ask for Chicken Hawk Hill from the USGS.

*Who to contact:* Shasta-Trinity National Forest, Mt. Shasta Ranger District, 204 West Alma, Mt. Shasta, CA 96067; (916) 926-4511.

*Trail notes:* This is sacred country for John Reginato, who at 75 knows the outback of Northern California better than any soul who has ever lived. It is Tamarack Lake that is his favorite spot, set high in the Trinity Divide at 5,900 feet. John plans on having his ashes scattered here. It's easy to see why—Tamarack Lake is a beautiful alpine lake that is a place of remarkable serenity. If you can pull yourself away from it, there is a rugged, cross-country route to the north that approaches the summit of Grey Rocks, a series of dark, craggy peaks. The route is steep and difficult, but the view of Castle Crags, Mt. Shasta, the ridges of the Trinity Divide and the Sacramento River Canyon will have you thanking a higher power for the privilege of breathing the air here.

---

# 19. ROOT CREEK TRAIL    2.5 mi/1.75 hrs

*Reference:* **In Castle Crags State Park south of Mt. Shasta; map B2, grid c4.**

*User groups:* Hikers only. No dogs, horses or mountain bikes are allowed. No wheelchair facilities.

*Permits:* No permits are required. A $5 state park entrance fee is charged for each vehicle.

*Directions:* From Interstate 5 south of Mt. Shasta, take the Castle Crags State Park exit. Turn west and follow the signs to the park entrance. Just past the kiosk, bear right and follow the road to its end at the parking area for Vista Point.

*Maps:* A free trail map can be obtained by contacting Castle Crags State Park at the address below. To obtain a topographic map of the area, ask for Dunsmuir from the USGS.

*Who to contact:* Castle Crags State Park, P.O. Box 80, Castella, CA 96017; (916) 235-2684.

*Trail notes:* Castle Crags State Park features a series of huge, ancient granite spires that tower over the Sacramento River canyon, the kind of sight that can take your breath away the first time you see it while cruising north on Interstate 5. That sight inspires a lot of people to take one of the hikes at the park, and while most don't have the time, energy or body conditioning to complete the Crags Trail, the Root Creek Trail is a good second choice. From the parking area, walk back down the road about 40 yards to reach the signed trailhead at 2,500 feet. Take the Kettlebelly Trail for a quarter mile, then turn right on Root Creek Trail. From here the route traces up the Kettlebelly Ridge, passing through a thick, cool forest. Suddenly, the trail breaks out above the trees, then deadends at the foot of a granite wall below Castle Dome. Below you is the Sacramento River canyon, plunging at your feet. On windless days, if you listen close, you can just make out the sound of passing traffic on the highway—so close, yet truly in a different world.

---

# 20. CRAGS TRAIL    6.1 mi/4.0 hrs

*Reference:* **In Castle Crags State Park south of Mt. Shasta; map B2, grid c4.**

*User groups:* Hikers only. No dogs, horses or mountain bikes are allowed. No wheelchair facilities.

*Permits:* No permits are required. A $5 state park entrance fee is charged for each vehicle.

*Directions:* From Interstate 5 south of Mt. Shasta, take the Castle Crags State Park exit. Turn west and follow the signs to the park entrance. Just past the kiosk, bear right and follow the road to the parking area adjacent to Vista Point.

*Maps:* A free trail map can be obtained by contacting Castle Crags State Park at the address below. To obtain a topographic map of the area, ask for

Dunsmuir from the USGS.

***Who to contact:*** Castle Crags State Park, P.O. Box 80, Castella, CA 96017; (916) 235-2684 or (916) 538-2200.

***Trail notes:*** From Vista Point in Castle Crags State Park, you can gaze up at the wondrous crags and spot Castle Dome at 4,966 feet, the leading spire on the crags ridge. This is a high, rounded, missile-shaped piece of rock, and yes, this is your destination on the Crags Trail. It is an arduous climb, constantly gaining elevation. The trailhead is well signed, located about 40 yards down the road from the parking area at elevation 2,500 feet. You will start by taking the Kettlebelly/Crags Trail for a quarter mile, then taking off on the Crags Trail when you reach a triangular junction. Here the trail rises through a thick forest, climbing steeply at times, and eventually turns to the right, emerging from the forest and winding through the lower Crags. Once above tree line, the views get better with each rising step. In spring, snow and ice fields are common up this high. An excellent picnic spot is at Indian Springs at 3,600 feet, and many hikers get no further than this point. But the trail goes onward, always climbing, then getting quite steep before finally reaching a saddle at the foot of Castle Dome, where a few trees have somehow gained toeholds. When you set foot on this divine perch, gazing north at Mt. Shasta, it will be a moment you will prize forever.

# 21. McCLOUD NATURE TRAIL   4.5 mi/2.5 hrs

***Reference:*** At Ah-Di-Na Campground on McCloud River south of McCloud; map B2, grid c6.

***User groups:*** Hikers only. No dogs, horses or mountain bikes are allowed. No wheelchair facilities.

***Permits:*** No permits are required. Parking and access are free.

***Directions:*** From Interstate 5 south of Mt. Shasta, take the McCloud-Reno exit and turn east on Highway 89. Drive 12 miles to McCloud, then turn right on Squaw Valley Road and drive about 11 miles to McCloud Reservoir. Turn right at the boat launch and proceed on the road along the lake's shoreline. At a steep left turn at a lake cove, turn right at the sign for Ah-Di-Na Campground and proceed another seven miles on the dirt road, past Ah-Di-Na Campground (on your left) to the road's end at The Nature Conservancy boundary.

***Maps:*** For a map of Shasta-Trinity National Forest, send $3 to USDA-Forest Service, 630 Sansome Street, San Francisco, CA 94111. To obtain a topographic map of the area, ask for Lake McCloud from the USGS.

***Who to contact:*** Shasta-Trinity National Forest, McCloud Ranger District, P.O. Box 1620, McCloud, CA 96057; (916) 964-2184.

***Trail notes:*** Have you ever yearned for a place where old trees are left standing, deer and bobcat roam without fear, and where a crystal-perfect river flows free in an untouched canyon? The McCloud River Preserve is such a place, and because it is managed by The Nature Conservancy, it will always remain that way. That is the attraction here. While the lower McCloud River is best known for its flyfishing for trout, there is an excellent hiking trail that runs aside the river, spanning more than two miles from the parking area on downstream. It is an easy yet beautiful walk among woods and water and it is well worth it to hike out to the end, where the river plunges into a series of deep holes and gorges. The trout can be a lot more difficult to catch at the McCloud River than you often hear. The best technique is using weighted nymphs with a strike indicator, being equipped with chest waders and a wading staff for the very slippery river bottom. Please remember that removing anything from this preserve, even a leaf or a stone, is not permitted.

## 22. LOWER McCLOUD FALLS   0.25 mi/0.5 hr

*Reference:* In Shasta-Trinity National Forest east of McCloud; map B2, grid c7.

*User groups:* Hikers, **wheelchairs** and dogs. Not suitable for horses or mountain bikes.

*Permits:* No permits are required. Parking and access are free.

*Directions:* From Interstate 5 south of Mt. Shasta, take the McCloud-Reno exit and turn east on Highway 89. Drive 12 miles to McCloud, then continue another five miles east on Highway 89. At the sign for Fowler's Camp, turn right and follow the signs to Lower Falls.

*Maps:* For a map of Shasta-Trinity National Forest, send $3 to USDA-Forest Service, 630 Sansome Street, San Francisco, CA 94111. To obtain a topographic map of the area, ask for Lake McCloud from the USGS.

*Who to contact:* Shasta-Trinity National Forest, McCloud Ranger District, P.O. Box 1620, McCloud, CA 96057; (916) 964-2184.

*Trail notes:* The Lower McCloud Falls may not be the most majestic waterfall in California, but there may be none better for swimming. On hot summer days, youngsters will jump off the granite rim, then fly through the air for about 15 feet and land in the waterfall's pool like cannon balls. You can drive right to the Lower Falls. After parking, there are two routes upstream. The better of the two is to rock hop your way right along the river for 10 or 15 minutes, then pick a nice little spot to sit and watch the water go by. The more common trail is the paved walkway that is routed from Lower Falls to Fowler's Camp. Lower Falls is a chute-like waterfall, in which a chute of water pours into a large pool, surrounded by a granite rim. A ladder is available for swimmers and jumpers.

## 23. GRIZZLY PEAK   0.25 mi/0.25 hr

*Reference:* In Shasta-Trinity National Forest southeast of Mt. Shasta; map B2, grid c7.

*User groups:* Hikers and dogs. Horses and mountain bikes are not advised. No wheelchair facilities.

*Permits:* No permits are required. Parking and access are free.

*Directions:* From Interstate 5 south of Mt. Shasta, take the McCloud-Reno exit and turn east on Highway 89. Drive 12 miles to McCloud, then turn right on Squaw Valley Road and drive about 11 miles to McCloud Reservoir. Keep to the right at the boat ramp, then drive around the lake and over the dam, then turn right at the Forest Service road, continuing into the national forest. A mile past Hawkins Creek, turn left at the signed intersection and drive to its end at Grizzly Peak. The road is long, bumpy and steep in places, and four-wheel-drive vehicles with good clearance are recommended.

*Maps:* For a map of Shasta-Trinity National Forest, send $3 to USDA-Forest

Service, 630 Sansome Street, San Francisco, CA 94111. To obtain a topographic map of the area, ask for Grizzly Peak from the USGS.

*Who to contact:* Shasta-Trinity National Forest, McCloud Ranger District, P.O. Box 1620, McCloud, CA 96057; (916) 964-2184.

*Trail notes:* Grizzly Peak at 6,252 feet provides a sweeping view to the west of the McCloud Flats, a sea of conifers and beyond to the eastern facing slopes of Mt. Shasta at 14,162 feet. To get here, it is a long, dusty, bumpy and circuitous drive past Brushy Butte, Mica Gulch and finally to Grizzly Peak. You will find a forest fire lookout station here, a perfect spot to scan hundreds of thousands of acres of forest. The walk is a short one, about a 15-minute traipse to the peak, the trail routed through low-lying brush. Lightning rods are set up here, and if you look below you to the east, you will spot a little-used segment of the Pacific Crest Trail. On our visit, Tom was just one step from the peak when he heard a strange buzzing sound, looked down, and saw that he was about to plant his size-12 boot right atop a five-foot rattlesnake. Held up just in time! A moment later, while explaining the importance of staying calm in rattlesnake country, a small lizard scurried across the trail, and Tom started suddenly, as if he'd been poked with a cattle prod. Calm? Yeah, surrre.

---

# 24. MIDDLE FALLS TRAIL        0.5 mi/0.5 hr

*Reference:* **At Fowler's Camp in Shasta-Trinity National Forest east of McCloud; map B2, grid c8.**

*User groups:* Hikers and dogs. Horses and mountain bikes are not allowed. No wheelchair facilities.

*Permits:* No permits are required. Parking and access are free.

*Directions:* From Interstate 5 south of Mt. Shasta, take the McCloud-Reno exit and turn east on Highway 89. Drive 12 miles to McCloud, then continue another five miles east on Highway 89. At the sign for Fowler's Camp, turn right and enter the campground. At the "Y" stay to the left, drive through the campground and park adjacent to the restroom. The trailhead is directly across the road.

*Maps:* For a map of Shasta-Trinity National Forest, send $3 to USDA-Forest Service, 630 Sansome Street, San Francisco, CA 94111. To obtain a topographic map of the area, ask for McCloud from the USGS.

*Who to contact:* Shasta-Trinity National Forest, McCloud Ranger District, P.O. Box 1620, McCloud, CA 96057; (916) 964-2184.

*Trail notes:* The Middle Falls of the McCloud River is one of the prettiest waterfalls in Northern California, a wide and tall cascade of water that pours over a 75-foot cliff and then falls into a deep pool in a rock bowl. The hike is easy, a 10- to 15-minute walk on a trail that skirts the left side of the McCloud River. You will round a bend, probably hear the waterfall before you see it, and then suddenly, there it is, this wide sheet of falling water. It's something like a miniature Niagara Falls. On summer weekends, teenagers will climb to the rim above the falls, then plunge 100 feet into the pool like human missiles. It's a dangerous venture that we do not recommend. Only in recent years has the Middle Falls become known. That is because the surrounding land was owned by Champion, a lumber company, who never saw fit to build a trail. But the Forest Service obtained this area in a land swap

with Champion, then built the trail in 1989, providing a perfect hike out of
Fowler's Camp.

# 25. WATERS GULCH OVERLOOK
3.0 mi/1.5 hrs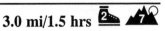

*Reference:* At Packers Bay on Shasta Lake north of Redding; map B2, grid f3.

*User groups:* Hikers and dogs. Not suitable for horses or mountain bikes. No
wheelchair facilities.

*Permits:* No permits are required. Parking and access are free.

*Directions:* From Interstate 5 at Redding, drive north to Shasta Lake and take
the Packers Bay exit. Drive southwest on Packers Bay Road to the trailhead,
located one-quarter of a mile before the boat ramp.

*Maps:* A detailed trail map can be obtained by contacting Earthwalk Press, 2239
Union Street, Eureka, CA 95501; (800) 828-MAPS. For a map of Shasta-
Trinity National Forest, send $3 to USDA-Forest Service, 630 Sansome
Street, San Francisco, CA 94111. To obtain a topographic map of the area,
ask for O'Brien from the USGS.

*Who to contact:* Shasta-Trinity National Forest, Shasta Lake Ranger District,
14221 Holiday Road, Mountain Gate, CA 96003; (916) 275-1587.

*Trail notes:* Shasta Lake is so big, the biggest reservoir in California, that it can
be difficult to know where to start in your mission to explore it. A good
answer is right here on the Waters Gulch Loop. It connects to the Overlook
Trail, an eight-tenths of a mile cutoff that climbs atop a small mountain and
furnishes a view of the main lake. The trailhead is at Packers Bay, easily
accessible off Interstate 5. The trail heads west across a peninsula, then turns
right at Water's Gulch, a cove on the main Sacramento River arm of the lake.
While there are many drive-to areas where you can get lake views, here you
can get a little seclusion as well.

# 26. BAILEY COVE LOOP TRAIL 2.8 mi/1.5 hrs

*Reference:* On the McCloud arm of Shasta Lake north of Redding; map B2,
grid f3.

*User groups:* Hikers, dogs and mountain bikes. No horses are allowed. No
wheelchair facilities.

*Permits:* No permits are required. Parking and access are free.

*Directions:* From Interstate 5 north of Redding, take the Shasta Caverns exit
and follow the signs to Bailey Cove Boat Ramp and Picnic Area.

*Maps:* A detailed trail map can be obtained by contacting Earthwalk Press, 2239
Union Street, Eureka, CA 95501; (800) 828-MAPS. For a map of Shasta-
Trinity National Forest, send $3 to USDA-Forest Service, 630 Sansome
Street, San Francisco, CA 94111. To obtain a topographic map of the area,
ask for O'Brien from the USGS.

*Who to contact:* Shasta-Trinity National Forest, Shasta Lake Ranger District,
14221 Holiday Road, Mountain Gate, CA 96003; (916) 275-1587.

*Trail notes:* Our favorite part of Shasta Lake is the McCloud arm, where the
mountain canyon features limestone formations and the lake's clear emerald
waters. This trail provides a great view of these phenomena, as well as a
close-to-the-water loop hike on one of the lake's featured peninsulas. From
the trailhead, start by hiking on the left fork, which will take you out along

Bailey Cove. As you continue, the loop trail continues in a clockwise direction, first along the McCloud arm of the lake, then back to the parking area along John's Creek Inlet. When you reach the mouth of Bailey Cove, stop and enjoy the view. Directly across the lake are the limestone formations, featuring North Gray Rocks at a 3,114-foot elevation, and topped by Horse Mountain at 4,025 feet. The famous Shasta Caverns are located just below North Gray Rocks.

---

## 27. HIRZ BAY TRAIL    3.2 mi/1.75 hrs

*Reference:* On the McCloud arm of Shasta Lake north of Redding; map B2, grid f4.

*User groups:* Hikers, dogs and mountain bikes. No horses are allowed. No wheelchair facilities.

*Permits:* No permits are required. Parking and access are free.

*Directions:* From Interstate 5 north of Redding, take Gilman Road exit and follow Gilman Road east to Hirz Bay Campground.

*Maps:* A detailed trail map can be obtained by contacting Earthwalk Press, 2239 Union Street, Eureka, CA 95501; (800) 828-MAPS. For a map of Shasta-Trinity National Forest, send $3 to USDA-Forest Service, 630 Sansome Street, San Francisco, CA 94111. To obtain a topographic map of the area, ask for O'Brien from the USGS.

*Who to contact:* Shasta-Trinity National Forest, Shasta Lake Ranger District, 14221 Holiday Road, Mountain Gate, CA 96003; (916) 275-1587.

*Trail notes:* Most people discover this trail by accident, usually while camping either at Hirz Bay Group Camp or the tiny two-site Dekkas Rock Camp. That is because this trail links those two campsites, routed along the west side of the beautiful McCloud arm of Shasta Lake. The trail traces the shoreline of the lake, in and out along small coves and creek inlets. Straight across the lake are pretty views of the deep coves at Campbell Creek and Dekkas Creek, unique limestone outcrops, and Minnesota Mountain at 4,293 feet.

---

## 28. GREENS CREEK    12.0 mi/7.0 hrs
## BOAT-IN TRAIL

*Reference:* On McCloud arm of Shasta Lake north of Redding; map B2, grid f4.

*User groups:* Hikers and dogs. Horses and mountain bikes are not allowed. No wheelchair facilities.

*Permits:* No permits are required. Parking and access are free.

*Directions:* This trail can be accessed only by boat. Boat ramps are located to the north at Hirz Bay Campground (see directions for Hirz Bay Trail) or to the south at Lakeview Marina Resort (off Shasta Caverns Road). The trailhead is at Greens Creek Boat-in Camp on the east side of the McCloud River arm.

*Maps:* A detailed trail map can be obtained by contacting Earthwalk Press, 2239 Union Street, Eureka, CA 95501; (800) 828-MAPS. For a map of Shasta-Trinity National Forest, send $3 to USDA-Forest Service, 630 Sansome Street, San Francisco, CA 94111. To obtain a topographic map of the area, ask for O'Brien from the USGS.

*Who to contact:* Shasta-Trinity National Forest, Shasta Lake Ranger District,

14221 Holiday Road, Mountain Gate, CA 96003; (916) 275-1587.

*Trail notes:* Let's get a few things straight from the start: 1) Almost no one hikes this entire trail. 2) Almost no one hikes part of this trail. 3) Almost no one even knows about this trail. Why? Because even with two million people estimated to visit Shasta Lake every year, the only way to access this trail is from an obscure boat-in campsite at Greens Creek on the east side of the McCloud arm of the lake. At the back of the cove at Greens Creek, you will find a small Forest Service billboard, posted with recreation guide sheets, and behind it is the campground and trailhead. The trip is easily shortened, and usually is, because there are many fascinating sidetrips on the steep climb up toward a saddle between Town Mountain at 4,325 feet and Horse Mountain at 4,025 feet. The trail enters an oak/madrone forest that is interspersed with limestone formations. The latter are worth exploring, and if you spend enough time hiking and investigating, you may find some small caves, a highlight of the trip. Most people are inspired to hike just high enough to get a good clear view of the lake below, but not much farther.

---

## 29. DAVIS GULCH TRAIL    6.0 mi/3.5 hrs  

*Reference:* **At Whiskeytown Lake National Recreation Area west of Redding; map B2, grid h0.**

*User groups:* Hikers, dogs and horses. No mountain bikes are allowed. No wheelchair facilities.

*Permits:* A free permit is required for hikers planning to camp in the backcountry. Parking and access are free.

*Directions:* From Interstate 5 at Redding, turn west on Highway 299 and drive seven miles. At the Whiskeytown Visitor Center, turn left on J.F. Kennedy Memorial Drive and follow the signs to Brandy Creek Picnic Area.

*Maps:* For a detailed trail map, contact Whiskeytown National Recreation Area at the address below. To obtain a topographic map of the area, ask for Igo from the USGS.

*Who to contact:* Whiskeytown National Recreation Area, P.O. Box 188, Whiskeytown, CA 96095; (916) 241-6584.

*Trail notes:* The Davis Gulch Trail is Whiskeytown Lake's best hike, an easy, meandering route along the southwest end of the lake. It starts out of the Brandy Creek Picnic Area at 1,300 feet and climbs up to 1,650 feet, a moderate climb on a wide, flat footpath. Most of the trees are oaks or madrones, and as you go, there are many good views of Whiskeytown Lake. The trail spans three miles and deadends at an information billboard along an access road. That means with two vehicles, it is possible to turn this into a one-way hike, and better yet, hike the whole route downhill—ending at the Brandy Creek Picnic Area instead of starting there.

---

## 30. SHASTA MINE    2.5 mi/1.75 hrs  
##     LOOP TRAIL

*Reference:* **At Whiskeytown Lake National Recreation Area west of Redding; map B2, grid h1.**

*User groups:* Hikers, dogs, horses and mountain bikes. No wheelchair facilities.

*Permits:* A free permit is required for hikers planning to camp in the backcountry. Parking and access are free.

*Directions:* From Interstate 5 at Redding, turn west on Highway 299 and drive seven miles. At the Whiskeytown Visitor Center, turn left on J.F. Kennedy Memorial Drive and proceed 2.8 miles to the trailhead on the left.

*Maps:* For a detailed trail map, contact Whiskeytown National Recreation Area at the address below. To obtain a topographic map of the area, ask for Igo from the USGS.

*Who to contact:* Whiskeytown National Recreation Area, P.O. Box 188, Whiskeytown, CA 96095; (916) 241-6584.

*Trail notes:* Just south of Whiskeytown Lake is the old Shasta Mine, hidden in a cavern near a fork of Clear Creek, a piece of history that is overlooked by many visitors. But yes, gold fever struck here as well as in many other areas of California, and that affliction is well chronicled on this hike. The trail itself provides an easy loop hike, with a trailhead elevation of 1,129 feet, and very shallow trail gradients. The route includes crossing a small fork of Clear Creek and heading along Orofino Gulch. Many visitors will hike straight to the old Shasta Mine and back, rather than hiking the entire loop trail.

---

# 31. RUINS TRAIL     0.5 mi/0.25 hr

*Reference:* At Shasta State Historic Park west of Redding; map B2, grid h1.

*User groups:* Hikers and dogs. No mountain bikes or horses are allowed. No wheelchair facilities.

*Permits:* No permits are required. Parking and access are free.

*Directions:* From Interstate 5 at Redding, turn west on Highway 299 and drive six miles. Turn right at the sign for Shasta State Historic Park. The trail begins off Main Street at the Charter Oak Hotel.

*Maps:* A map and brochure can be obtained by sending $1 to Shasta State Historic Park at the address below. To obtain a topographic map of the area, ask for Redding from the USGS.

*Who to contact:* Shasta State Historic Park, P.O. Box 2430, Shasta, CA 90687; (916) 244-1848.

*Trail notes:* This trail is like a short walk through history, bringing the town of Shasta back to life the way it was when gold rush excitement swept the area in 1850. It is not a hike and it is not in the wilderness; rather it is a self-guided interpretive walk through an old gold rush town. It is advisable to buy the cheap Tour Guide, which explains numbered exhibits along the walk. The walk is routed past the old courthouse, hotel, butcher shop, pioneer barn and cemetery, all maintained in their 1850 condition. By the way, many people get the town of Shasta confused with the city of Mt. Shasta. The latter is the town nestled at the foot of Northern California's highest mountain. The town of Shasta, on the other hand, is this abandoned gold rush town in the foothills west of Redding.

# PACIFIC CREST TRAIL
**90.0 mi. one way/8-9 days**

## GENERAL INFORMATION

*Reference:* **Trail sections extend from Ash Camp at McCloud River south of McCloud Reservoir to Highway 3 at Scott Mountain.**

*User groups:* Hikers, dogs and horses. No mountain bikes are allowed. No wheelchair facilities.

*Permits:* Wilderness permits may be required in certain sections. Parking fees may also apply. See specific listings for details.

*Directions:* See individual listings for specific trailhead directions.

*Maps:* For an overall view of the route in this chapter, send $3 to USDA-Forest Service, 630 Sansome Street, San Francisco, CA 94111, ask for Shasta-Trinity National Forest. A map of Castle Crags Wilderness can also be purchased for $6. Topographic maps for particular sections of the trail are provided under each trail listing below.

*Who to contact:* Shasta-Trinity National Forest; see each listing for the managing ranger district.

*Trail notes:* This section of the Pacific Crest Trail traverses some of the most diverse and dynamic country in Northern California. It includes the lush and vibrant McCloud River and Sacramento River, where the trail drops as low as 2,000 feet, and it climbs to the Trinity Divide Ridge and its dozens of small, untouched lakes. A short sidetrip is available to the top of Mt. Eddy, a 9,025-foot elevation. The trail also runs right beneath Castle Crags, a series of sculpted granite spires, a setting that can astonish newcomers.

---

## PCT-41
**30.0 mi. one way/2.0 days**

## ASH CAMP to CASTLE CRAGS WILDERNESS

*Reference:* **From Ash Camp on McCloud River west into Castle Crags State Park; map B2, grid c7.**

*User groups:* Hikers, dogs and horses. No mountain bikes are allowed. No wheelchair facilities.

*Permits:* Wilderness permits are required only in Castle Crags Wilderness. Parking and access are free.

*Directions:* From Interstate 5 south of Mt. Shasta, take the McCloud-Reno exit and turn east on Highway 89. Drive 12 miles to McCloud, then turn right on Squaw Valley Road and drive about 14 miles, past McCloud Reservoir, to the trailhead at Ash Camp.

*Maps:* To obtain topographic maps of the area, ask for Shoeinhorse Mountain, Yellowjacket Mountain and Dunsmuir from the USGS.

*Who to contact:* Shasta-Trinity National Forest, McCloud Ranger District, P.O. Box 1620, McCloud, CA 96057; (916) 964-2184.

*Trail notes:* Of the hundreds of rivers along the Pacific Crest Trail, it is the McCloud River that often seems most vibrant with life. This segment of the PCT starts right alongside the McCloud River at Ash Camp, set at about 3,000 feet. It is then routed downstream along the McCloud for 2.5 miles, one of the most prized sections of trail in this region. At Ah-Di-Na Camp, the trail starts to rise, eventually turning up Squaw Valley Creek and climbing beyond to top Girard Ridge at 4,500 feet. When you top the ridge, Mt. Shasta, Black Butte and Castle Crags suddenly pop into view. After traversing the ridge for a few miles, the trail suddenly drops and cascades down to the Sacramento River Canyon. Your toes will be jamming into your boots as you head downhill. At the river, you might stop to soak your feet before picking up and heading west into Castle Crags State Park.

## PCT-42                      25.0 mi. one way/2.0 days
## CASTLE CRAGS to MUMBO BASIN

*Reference:* From Castle Crags State Park west into Shasta-Trinity National Forest; map B2, grid c5.

*User groups:* Hikers and horses. No dogs are allowed on trails in Castle Crags State Park. No mountain bikes are allowed. No wheelchair facilities.

*Permits:* A permit is required to enter the Castle Crags Wilderness. Parking fee at Castle Crags State Park is $4. There is no fee if you park outside and walk in.

*Directions:* From Interstate 5 south of Mt. Shasta, take the Castle Crags State Park exit and drive west to the park entrance. Just past the kiosk is a special parking area for PCT hikers.

*Maps:* To obtain topographic maps of the area, ask for Dunsmuir, Seven Lakes Basin and Mumbo Basin from the USGS.

*Who to contact:* Castle Crags State Park, P.O. Box 80, Castella, CA 96017; (916) 235-2684.

*Trail notes:* This is a key juncture for the PCT, where the trail climbs out of a river canyon and back to high ridgelines. It is in a classic region, the Trinity Divide, known for sculpted lakes in granite and sweeping views of Mt. Shasta. From the Sacramento River at Castle Crags, at a 2,000-foot elevation, the trail laterals up the north side of Castle Creek Canyon, rising just below the base of the awesome Crags, then finally hitting the rim at the back side of Castle Ridge. It follows the rim in a half-circle to the west, to the Seven Lakes Basin and beyond to the Mumbo Basin and the Gumboot Lake Trailhead. The final five miles of this segment pass by a dozen pristine mountain lakes. The biggest is Echo Lake at 5,900 feet, set just below Boulder Peak, and the highest is Helen Lake at 6,700 feet, requiring a half-mile sidetrip.

## PCT-43                      35.0 mi. one way/4.0 days
## MUMBO BASIN to SCOTT MOUNTAIN

*Reference:* In Shasta-Trinity National Forest, from Gumboot Trailhead to Scott Mountain; map B2, grid b3.

*User groups:* Hikers, dogs and horses. No mountain bikes are allowed. No wheelchair facilities.

*Permits:* No permits are required. Parking and access are free.

*Directions:* From Interstate 5 at Mt. Shasta, take the Central Mount Shasta exit and drive about 16 miles west on W.A. Barr Road (Forest Road 26) to the Gumboot Lake turnoff. Continue west on Road 26 for about 2.5 miles to the Gumboot Saddle/PCT parking area.

*Maps:* To obtain a topographic map of the area, ask for Mumbo Basin, South China Mountain and Scott Mountain from the USGS.

*Who to contact:* Shasta-Trinity National Forest, McCloud Ranger District, P.O. Box 1620, McCloud, CA 96057; (916) 964-2184.

*Trail notes:* The PCT starts at a popular trailhead but quickly jumps northward into remote, beautiful country. Most hikers using this trailhead head south into the Seven Lakes Basin, but PCT hikers, forging northward, have other wonders awaiting. The first, only a mile up the trail, is the view below to the left of Picayune Lake, pretty and secluded. The trail heads on, passing little Porcupine Lake, an idyllic setting which requires a quarter-mile sidetrip, and then over the rim and down to Deadfall Lakes, an excellent camping spot. From the ridge, an irresistible sidetrip is the one-mile trek to the top of Mt. Eddy, 9,025 feet, with its incomparable view of Mt. Shasta. From Deadfall Lakes, the trail continues down, rounds the headwaters of the Trinity River, then climbs back up Chilcoot Pass and Bull Lake. From here, it's a 10-mile pull to Scott Mountain Summit Trailhead.

*PCT CONTINUATION:* To continue hiking along the Pacific Crest Trail, see Chapter B1, pages 92-93.

## LEAVE NO TRACE TIPS

**Travel lightly**

• Visit the backcountry in small groups.

• Below tree line, always stay on designated trails.

• Do not cut across switchbacks.

• When traveling cross-country where no trails are available, follow animal trails or spread out with your group so no new routes are created.

• Read your map and orient yourself with landmarks, a compass and altimeter. Avoid marking trails with rock cairns, tree scars or ribbons.

# MAP B3

NOR-CAL MAP ...................... see page 14
adjoining maps
NORTH (A3) ........................... see page 56
EAST (B4) ............................... see page 136
SOUTH (C3) ........................... see page 174
WEST (B2) ............................... see page 94

3 PCT SECTIONS
19 TRAILS
PAGES 120-135

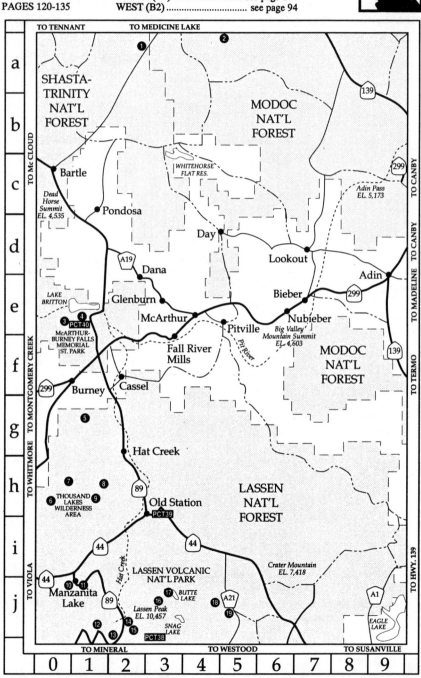

TO TENNANT
TO MEDICINE LAKE

a

SHASTA-
TRINITY
NAT'L
FOREST

MODOC
NAT'L
FOREST

b

TO Mc CLOUD

139

Bartle

WHITEHORSE
FLAT RES.

299

TO CANBY

c

Dead
Horse
Summit
EL. 4,535

Pondosa

Adin Pass
EL. 5,173

Day

d

A19

Dana

Lookout

Adin

TO CANBY

LAKE
BRITTON

Glenburn

Bieber

TO MADELINE

e

PCT40

McArthur

Pitville

Nubieber

299

McARTHUR-
BURNEY FALLS
MEMORIAL
ST. PARK

Fall River
Mills

Big Valley
Mountain Summit
EL. 4,603

MODOC
NAT'L
FOREST

TO TERMO

f

299

Burney

Cassel

Pit River

139

TO MONTGOMERY CREEK

g

TO WHITMORE

Hat Creek

h

7

8

89

Old Station

LASSEN
NAT'L
FOREST

6

THOUSAND
LAKES
WILDERNESS
AREA

9

PCT39

i

44

44

TO VIOLA

Hat Creek

Crater Mountain
EL. 7,418

TO HWY. 139

j

44

10

11

LASSEN VOLCANIC
NAT'L PARK

17

BUTTE
LAKE

A21

A1

Manzanita
Lake

89

16

18

EAGLE
LAKE

12

Lassen Peak
EL. 10,457

14

19

13

15

SNAG
LAKE

PCT38

TO MINERAL
TO WESTOOD
TO SUSANVILLE

0  1  2  3  4  5  6  7  8  9

**Map B3 featuring:** Modoc National Forest, McArthur-Burney Falls State Park, Burney, Lake Britton, Lassen National Forest, Thousand Lakes Wilderness, Lassen Volcanic National Park, Butte Lake, Caribou Wilderness

## 1. ICE CAVES TRAIL　　0.25 mi/0.5 hr　

*Reference:* **In Modoc National Forest south of Medicine Lake; map B3, grid a2.**

*User groups:* Hikers and dogs. The terrain is not suitable for mountain bikes or horses. No wheelchair facilities.

*Permits:* No permits are required. Parking and access are free.

*Directions:* From Redding, turn north on Interstate 5 and drive 56 miles. Take the McCloud-Reno exit and travel 29 miles east on Highway 89 to Bartle. Just past Bartle, turn northeast on Powder Hill Road (Forest Service Road 49) and drive approximately 21 miles to the ice caves. They are just off the road on the west side.

*Maps:* For a map of Modoc National Forest, send $3 to USDA-Forest Service, 630 Sansome Street, San Francisco, CA 94111. To obtain a topographic map of the area, ask for Medicine Lake from the USGS.

*Who to contact:* Modoc National Forest, Double Head Ranger District, P.O. Box 818, Tulelake, CA 96134; (916) 667-2246.

*Trail notes:* The Ice Caves are for people who are curious about the volcanic formations of the Medicine Lake area, yet who don't necessarily want to sign up for an expedition to explore them. That is because the Ice Caves are located just off the road, requiring only a short walk to reach them. What you will find here is a series of strange-looking caves, mostly shallow gouges in the volcanic rocks except for one that is deep and wide, a hollowed out grotto in a lava flow. Call it our imagination, but on our visit here we sensed the presence of old spirits, perhaps the ghosts of the Modoc Indians that used this area. Perhaps not. Regardless, it felt strange and uncomfortable and we caught the first train out of Dodge.

## 2. BURNT LAVA FLOW　　2.5 mi/1.5 hrs　

*Reference:* **In Modoc National Forest south of Medicine Lake; map B3, grid a5.**

*User groups:* Hikers and dogs. The terrain is not suitable for mountain bikes or horses. No wheelchair facilities.

*Permits:* No permits are required. Parking and access are free.

*Directions:* From Redding, turn north on Interstate 5 and drive 56 miles. Take the McCloud-Reno exit and travel 29 miles east on Highway 89 to Bartle. Just past Bartle, turn northeast on Powder Hill Road (Forest Service Road 49) and drive approximately 24 miles. Turn east on Forest Service Road 42N25 and proceed to the Burnt Lava Flow Geologic Area.

*Maps:* For a map of Modoc National Forest, send $3 to USDA-Forest Service, 630 Sansome Street, San Francisco, CA 94111. To obtain a topographic map of the area, ask for Porcupine Butte from the USGS.

*Who to contact:* Modoc National Forest, Double Head Ranger District, P.O.

Box 818, Tulelake, CA 96134; (916) 667-2246.

*Trail notes:* When you walk across the Burnt Lava Flow, a land of "rocks that float and mountains of glass," it may seem like you are exploring some prehistoric area that resembles the moon. But get this: This lava formation is only about 200 years old, the youngest flow in the Medicine Lake Highlands. It is located south of Glass Mountain, covering some 8,760 acres, yet with little "islands" of forests amid the bare, jet-black lava flow. When we took an aerial survey of the area, the Burnt Lava Flow was one of the most fascinating portions of the entire region. On foot, it is even stranger. There is no trail, so you just pick your direction, with most visitors going from tree island to tree island. There are a few weird spots where the ground can be like quicksand when it's dry and like wet concrete when it's wet. Just walk around those spots, staying on the hard, black lava flow.

---

## 3. BURNEY FALLS TRAIL          1.0 mi/0.5 hr

*Reference:* In McArthur-Burney Falls State Park north of Burney; map B3, grid e1.

*User groups:* Hikers only. No dogs, horses or mountain bikes are allowed. There is paved **wheelchair access** at the falls overlook point at the beginning of the trail.

*Permits:* No permits are required. A $5 state park day-use fee is charged for each vehicle.

*Directions:* From Interstate 5 at Redding, turn east on Highway 299 and drive 50 miles to Burney. Continue five miles east on Highway 299, then turn north on Highway 89 and drive 5.8 miles to the state park entrance. Park at the main lot and follow the signs to the trailhead.

*Maps:* A trail guide can be obtained by contacting the state park at the address below. To obtain a topographic map of the area, ask for Burney Falls from the USGS.

*Who to contact:* McArthur-Burney Falls State Park, 24898 Highway 89, Burney, CA 96013; (916) 335-2777 or (916) 538-2200.

*Trail notes:* Visitors from across the West are attracted to this state park to see Burney Falls. It is spectacular, 129 feet high, wide and cascading. The waterfall plunges over a cliff in two pieces, split at the rim by a small bluff where two trees have managed toeholds, although the river flows over the top of them during high water from the spring snowmelt. From the park entrance station, it is about a 50-foot walk to a rocky overlook, a perfect spot for photographs of the waterfall. It is here where the Burney Falls Trail starts, an easy one-mile loop around the waterfall and back. It is a self-guided nature trail, but rather than having to carry a brochure with you along the trail, you can just read the small, attractive signs that explain the feature sites. It is possible to walk quite close to the bottom of the waterfall, but expect a residual spray from the pounding water.

---

## 4. RIM TRAIL          3.0 mi/1.75 hrs

*Reference:* At Lake Britton at McArthur-Burney Falls State Park north of Burney; map B3, grid e1.

*User groups:* Hikers only. No dogs, horses or mountain bikes are allowed. No wheelchair facilities.

*Permits:* No permits are required. A $5 state park day-use fee is charged per vehicle.

*Directions:* From Interstate 5 at Redding, turn east on Highway 299 and drive 50 miles to Burney. Continue five miles east on Highway 299, then turn north on Highway 89 and drive 5.8 miles to the state park entrance. The trailhead is just opposite Campground No. 12.

*Maps:* A trail guide can be obtained by contacting the state park at the address below. To obtain a topographic map of the area, ask for Burney Falls from the USGS.

*Who to contact:* McArthur-Burney Falls State Park, 24898 Highway 89, Burney, CA 96013; (916) 335-2777 or (916) 538-2200.

*Trail notes:* The Rim Trail provides an ideal hike for campers at Burney Falls State Park. The trail starts at the campground, then is routed to the rim of Lake Britton, a distance of 1.5 miles. It is an easy walk and pretty too, routed first through forest, then emerging with a good lookout of the lake. An easy sidetrip is down to the beach. This lake is set in a gorge, and the water seems to have special qualities, sometimes shimmering with effervescence. The fishing is good too, especially for crappie, but with bass, bluegill and trout plentiful as well. This is a rare combination for a mountain lake.

---

# 5. BURNEY MOUNTAIN SUMMIT

**0.25 mi/0.25 hr**

*Reference:* **In Lassen National Forest south of Burney; map B3, grid g1.**

*User groups:* Hikers, dogs, horses and mountain bikes. No wheelchair facilities.

*Permits:* No permits are required. Parking and access are free.

*Directions:* From Interstate 5 at Redding, turn east on Highway 299 and drive 50 miles to Burney. Continue five more miles east, then turn south on Highway 89 and drive 10.5 miles. Turn west on Forest Service Road 34N19 and drive 10 miles, then turn right on Forest Service Road 34N23 and continue four miles to the mountain summit. In the winter, the Summit access road is blocked with a locked gate, where you can park and then hike to the top.

*Maps:* For a map of Lassen National Forest, send $3 to USDA-Forest Service, 630 Sansome Street, San Francisco, CA 94111. To obtain topographic maps of the area, ask for Burney Mountain West and Burney Mountain East from the USGS.

*Who to contact:* Lassen National Forest, Hat Creek Ranger District, P.O. Box 220, Falls River Mills, CA 96028; (916) 336-5521.

*Trail notes:* The view is just so good from the top of Burney Mountain (at 7,863 feet) that we had to include this trip in the book. The "hike" consists of just moseying around the summit, gazing off in all directions. However, if you show up in the winter when the access road is gated, it is a four-mile hike up the road to the top of the mountain. Almost nobody makes that trip. Burney Mountain often gets lost in the shadow of its big brothers, Mt. Lassen and Mt. Shasta, but of the three, the view just might be best from Burney. That's because sighting Lassen or Shasta makes for impressive panoramas in both directions, a view that just can't be duplicated.

## 6. MAGEE TRAILHEAD 10.0 mi/2.0 days

*Reference:* **On the southwest boundary of Thousand Lakes Wilderness north of Lassen National Park; map B3, grid h0.**

*User groups:* Hikers and horses. No dogs or mountain bikes are allowed. No wheelchair facilities.

*Permits:* No permits are required. Parking and access are free.

*Directions:* From Interstate 5 at Redding, turn east on Highway 299 and drive 50 miles to Burney. Continue five more miles east, then turn south on Highway 89 and drive 31 miles. Turn right on Forest Service Road 16 and drive 9.5 miles, then turn right on Forest Service Road 32N48 and continue to the parking area at the end of the road.

*Maps:* For a map of Lassen National Forest, send $3 to USDA-Forest Service, 630 Sansome Street, San Francisco, CA 94111. To obtain topographic maps of the area, ask for Thousand Lakes Valley and Jacks Backbone from the USGS.

*Who to contact:* Lassen National Forest, Hat Creek Ranger District, P.O. Box 220, Falls River Mills, CA 96028; (916) 336-5521.

*Trail notes:* The Thousand Lakes Wilderness is a tiny, overlooked wilderness, but it is excellent for short hikes, either for a day or a weekend. The hike to Magee Lake and back is a great weekender. From the trailhead at 6,120 feet, you head east for 2.5 miles, then turn north toward Magee Peak, climbing all the way. The trail skirts the eastern slope of that mountain, and a possibility here is bushwhacking a quarter of a mile off the trail to the summit at 8,550 feet. After topping Magee Peak, you will descend for about two miles to Magee Lake. For overnighters, a mandatory sidetrip is to Everett Lake, which is located less than a quarter mile to the northeast.

## 7. CYPRESS TRAILHEAD 6.0 mi/3.75 hrs

*Reference:* **On the north boundary of Thousand Lakes Wilderness north of Lassen National Park; map B3, grid h0.**

*User groups:* Hikers and horses. No dogs or mountain bikes are allowed. No wheelchair facilities.

*Permits:* No permits are required. Parking and access are free.

*Directions:* From Interstate 5 at Redding, turn east on Highway 299 and drive 50 miles to Burney. Continue five more miles east, then turn south on Highway 89 and drive 10.5 miles. Turn west on Forest Service Road 34N19 and drive seven miles, then turn south on Forest Service Road 34N60 and continue two miles to the parking area.

*Maps:* For a map of Lassen National Forest, send $3 to USDA-Forest Service, 630 Sansome Street, San Francisco, CA 94111. To obtain topographic maps of the area, ask for Thousand Lakes Valley and Jacks Backbone from the USGS.

*Who to contact:* Lassen National Forest, Hat Creek Ranger District, P.O. Box 220, Falls River Mills, CA 96028; (916) 336-5521.

*Trail notes:* You like lakes? You came to the right place. The Cypress Trailhead at 5,400 feet is the number one starting point for the Thousand Lakes Wilderness, with many small lakes sprinkled about in a radius of just two miles. After taking off down the trail, you will hike for three miles before coming to Eiler Lake, the largest lake in this region. It is set just below Eiler Butte. Since the hike is only a six-mile roundtrip, it is a viable day hike. But since a network of trails here connect to other lakes, an option is to keep on going for an overnighter. From the south side of Eiler Lake, the trail loops deeper into the wilderness in a clockwise arc. In the process, it passes near several other lakes, including Box Lake and Barrett Lake. Both of these provide good fishing for small trout.

---

## 8. TAMARACK TRAILHEAD    6.0 mi/3.5 hrs

*Reference:* **On the east boundary of Thousand Lakes Wilderness north of Lassen National Park; map B3, grid h1.**

*User groups:* Hikers and horses. No dogs or mountain bikes are allowed. No wheelchair facilities.

*Permits:* No permits are required. Parking and access are free.

*Directions:* From Interstate 5 at Redding, turn east on Highway 299 and drive 50 miles to Burney. Continue five more miles east, then turn south on Highway 89 and drive 14 miles. Turn west on Forest Service Road 33N25 and drive five miles, then turn right on Forest Service Road 33N23Y and proceed to the parking area at the end of the road.

*Maps:* For a map of Lassen National Forest, send $3 to USDA-Forest Service, 630 Sansome Street, San Francisco, CA 94111. To obtain topographic maps of the area, ask for Thousand Lakes Valley and Jacks Backbone from the USGS.

*Who to contact:* Lassen National Forest, Hat Creek Ranger District, P.O. Box 220, Falls River Mills, CA 96028; (916) 336-5521.

*Trail notes:* From the Tamarack Trailhead, your first destination is Barrett Lake, a three-mile hike. From here a variety of activities are available. Have a picnic, swim or fish and then return, or if you have backpacking gear, head onward to several other wilderness lakes. The trailhead elevation is 5,200 feet, and from here, the trail is routed into the northwestern interior of the Thousand Lakes Wilderness. After two miles you will reach a fork in the trail; turn left (south), which will lead you to Barrett Lake in just another mile of hiking. Note that there is a complex trail network in this area with many junctions, creating a situation in which backpackers can invent their own multi-day route. From here, other attractive destinations include Durbin Lake, a half mile to the south, and Everett and Magee Lakes, another 2.5 miles away.

---

## 9. BUNCHGRASS TRAILHEAD 8.0 mi/2.0 days

*Reference:* **On the south boundary of Thousand Lakes Wilderness north of Lassen Volcanic National Park, map B3, grid h1.**

*User groups:* Hikers, dogs, horses and mountain bikes. No wheelchair facilities.

*Permits:* No permits are required. Parking and access are free.

*Directions:* From Interstate 5 at Redding, turn east on Highway 299 and drive 50 miles to Burney. Continue five more miles east, then turn south on Highway 89 and drive 31 miles. Turn right on Forest Service Road 16 and drive six miles, then turn right on Forest Service Road 32N45 and proceed to the parking area at the end of the road.

*Maps:* For a map of Lassen National Forest, send $3 to USDA-Forest Service,

630 Sansome Street, San Francisco, CA 94111. To obtain topographic maps of the area, ask for Thousand Lakes Valley and Jacks Backbone from the USGS.

**Who to contact:** Lassen National Forest, Hat Creek Ranger District, P.O. Box 220, Falls River Mills, CA 96028; (916) 336-5521.

**Trail notes:** This trailhead is obscure and difficult to reach, and because of that, few visitors choose this as a jumpoff spot for their treks. The destination is Durbin Lake, a four-mile hike one way, making for an easy weekend backpack trip. The trailhead elevation is 5,680 feet, and from there it's a fair walk in, a little up and down, and if you're not in shape, you'll know it well before you reach the lake. You will find not only Durbin Lake, but beyond it, Hall Butte at 7,187 feet. A sidetrip option is to hike out on the trail for three miles, skirting the western side of Hall Butte, then bushwhacking off-trail for a half mile to reach the top.

---

# 10. MANZANITA LAKE TRAIL     1.5 mi/1.0 hr

**Reference: At the western entrance to Lassen Volcanic National Park on Highway 44; map B3, grid j1.**

**User groups:** Hikers only. No horses, dogs or mountain bikes are allowed. No wheelchair facilities.

**Permits:** A wilderness permit is required for hikers planning to camp in the backcountry. A $5 national park day-use fee is charged for each vehicle.

**Directions:** From Interstate 5 at Redding, turn east on Highway 44 and drive 46 miles to the park entrance. The trailhead is at Manzanita Lake just past the visitor center.

**Maps:** Trail maps are available for $3.95. To order a map, contact Loomis Museum, c/o Lassen Volcanic National Park at the address below. For a map of Lassen National Forest, send $3 to USDA-Forest Service, 630 Sansome Street, San Francisco, CA 94111. To obtain a topographic map of the area, ask for Manzanita Lake from the USGS.

**Who to contact:** Lassen Volcanic National Park, P.O. Box 100, Mineral, CA 96063; (916) 595-4444.

**Trail notes:** There is no prettier lake in Lassen Park that you can reach by car than Manzanita Lake. That is why the campground here is considered such a perfect destination for many. It is the largest camp in the park, 179 sites, and it is easy to reach, located just beyond the entrance station at the western boundary of the park. The trail simply traces around the shoreline of this pretty lake at a 5,950-foot elevation, easily accessible from either the parking area just beyond the entrance station or from the campground. A good sidetrip is across the road to Reflection Lake, a small and also very pretty lake, which adds about a half mile to the trip.

---

# 11. NOBLES EMIGRANT     10.0 mi/1.0 day
# TRAIL

**Reference: From Manzanita Lake Trailhead in Lassen Volcanic National Park east of Red Bluff; map B3, grid j1.**

**User groups:** Hikers only. No horses, dogs or mountain bikes are allowed. No wheelchair facilities.

**Permits:** A wilderness permit is required for hikers planning to camp in the backcountry. A $5 national park day-use fee is charged for each vehicle.

*Directions:* From Interstate 5 at Redding, turn east on Highway 44 and drive 46 miles to the park entrance. The trailhead is across the road from Manzanita Lake, just past the visitor center.

*Maps:* Trail maps are available for $3.95. To order a map, contact Loomis Museum, c/o Lassen Volcanic National Park at the address below. For a map of Lassen National Forest, send $3 to USDA-Forest Service, 630 Sansome Street, San Francisco, CA 94111. To obtain a topographic map of the area, ask for Manzanita Lake from the USGS.

*Who to contact:* Lassen Volcanic National Park, P.O. Box 100, Mineral, CA 96063; (916) 595-4444.

*Trail notes:* The most difficult part of this hike are the first two steps. Why? Because the trailhead is set near the park entrance amid a number of small roads and a maintenance area, and despite a trail sign, many visitors can't find it and give up. It's worth the search, because it is a great day hike for campers staying at Manzanita Lake. It is an easy, moderate grade, routed first through an old forest, with towering firs, cedars and Jeffrey pines. About 2.5 miles in, however, you will arrive at Lassen's strange "Dwarf Forest." You are not only surrounded by stunted trees, but you also get views of Chaos Crags, a jumble of pinkish rocks that is what is left of an old broken-down volcano. Many visitors will hike to this point, then turn around and return to the campground. The trail follows part of an historical route, originally a portion of the California Trail, an east-west route used by immigrants in the 1850s. There is no water available on the trail, so be sure to have at least one filled canteen per hiker. Because of the moderate slope, in the winter months this trail makes for an outstanding cross-country ski route.

---

## 12. LASSEN PEAK TRAIL    4.8 mi/3.5 hrs

*Reference:* **In Lassen Volcanic National Park east of Red Bluff; map B3, grid j1.**

*User groups:* Hikers only. No horses, dogs or mountain bikes are allowed. No wheelchair facilities.

*Permits:* A wilderness permit is required for hikers planning to camp in the backcountry. A $5 national park day-use fee is charged for each vehicle.

*Directions:* From Interstate 5 at Red Bluff, turn east on Highway 36 and drive 47 miles. Turn north on Highway 89 and travel 4.5 miles to the park entrance. Continue 7.5 miles to the parking area and trailhead on the left.

*Maps:* Trail maps are available for $3.95. To order a map, contact Loomis Museum, c/o Lassen Volcanic National Park at the address below. For a map of Lassen National Forest, send $3 to USDA-Forest Service, 630 Sansome Street, San Francisco, CA 94111. To obtain a topographic map of the area, ask for Lassen Peak from the USGS.

*Who to contact:* Lassen Volcanic National Park, P.O. Box 100, Mineral, CA 96063; (916) 595-4444.

*Trail notes:* The peak of Mt. Lassen at 10,457 feet is a huge volcanic flume with hardened lava flows, craters, outcrops and extraordinary views in all directions. Exploring Lassen Peak has become such a popular hike, perhaps the best introduction to mountain climbing a hiker could ask for, that the National Park Service may enforce a trail quota in the future. The climb to the top is a 2.5-mile zig-zag of a hike on a hard, flat trail, climbing just over 2,000 feet in the process. The trailhead at 8,400 feet is adjacent to a large parking area set at the base of the summit along Highway 89, which means that many visitors can spontaneously decide to try the climb. Our suggestion is to plan it instead, starting early, at least by 7:30 a.m. (when the temperature is still cool). Bring a lunch and a canteen or two of water. In the morning, with the air still cool, it is about a two-hour walk to the top, a 15-percent grade most of the way. The views are superb, with Mt. Shasta 100 miles north appearing close enough to reach out and grab. To the east are hundreds of miles of forests and lakes, and to the west, the land drops off to several small volcanic cones and the northern Sacramento Valley.

*Special note:* Winds are common at Lassen Summit, especially on summer afternoons. Hikers should stash a windbreaker in their daypacks.

---

## 13. SHADOW LAKE TRAIL          1.6 mi/1.0 hr

*Reference:* **In Lassen Volcanic National Park east of Red Bluff; map B3, grid j2.**

*User groups:* Hikers only. No horses, dogs or mountain bikes are allowed. No wheelchair facilities.

*Permits:* A wilderness permit is required for hikers planning to camp in the backcountry. A $5 national park day-use fee is charged for each vehicle.

*Directions:* From Interstate 5 at Red Bluff, turn east on Highway 36 and drive 47 miles. Turn north on Highway 89 and travel 4.5 miles to the park entrance. Continue 9.5 miles to the trailhead on the left.

*Maps:* Trail maps are available for $3.95. To order a map, contact Loomis Museum, c/o Lassen Volcanic National Park at the address below. For a map of Lassen National Forest, send $3 to USDA-Forest Service, 630 Sansome Street, San Francisco, CA 94111. To obtain a topographic map of the area, ask for Reading Peak from the USGS.

*Who to contact:* Lassen Volcanic National Park, P.O. Box 100, Mineral, CA 96063; (916) 595-4444.

*Trail notes:* A hike of less than a mile on this trail will bring you past little Terrace Lake, and then shortly later, to Shadow Lake. It is rare that one can reach such a pretty lake surrounded by wildlands in such a short distance. The trail involves a short, steep climb to reach Terrace Lake, and then a quarter-mile juncture to skirt the southeast shoreline of Shadow Lake (at least five times the size of Terrace Lake). The lakes are set just north of Reading Peak, which reaches 8,701 feet. The trailhead is at 8,000 feet, and because of the altitude, some hikers may experience some shortness of breath and dizziness when making the climb up to the lakes.

---

## 14. SUMMIT LAKE LOOP          0.5 mi/0.5 hr

*Reference:* **In Lassen Volcanic National Park east of Red Bluff; map B3, grid j2.**

*User groups:* Hikers. Horses are allowed, but there are many rules governing their use, including a required special permit. No dogs or mountain bikes are allowed. No wheelchair facilities.

*Permits:* A wilderness permit is required for hikers planning to camp in the backcountry. A $5 national park day-use fee is charged for each vehicle.

Horses require a special permit.

*Directions:* From Interstate 5 at Redding, turn east on Highway 44 and drive 46 miles to the park entrance. Continue southeast on Highway 89 for 12 miles to the trailhead at Summit Lake.

*Maps:* Trail maps are available for $3.95. To order a map, contact Loomis Museum, c/o Lassen Volcanic National Park at the address below. For a map of Lassen National Forest, send $3 to USDA-Forest Service, 630 Sansome Street, San Francisco, CA 94111. To obtain a topographic map of the area, ask for Reading Peak from the USGS.

*Who to contact:* Lassen Volcanic National Park, P.O. Box 100, Mineral, CA 96063; (916) 595-4444.

*Trail notes:* Summit Lake at 7,000 feet is a beautiful spot where deer visit almost every summer evening. There are nearby campgrounds on both sides of the lake (north and south), set in conifers with a pretty meadow just south of the lake along Kings Creek. This hike is a simple walk around Summit Lake, best taken at dusk when the changing evening colors will reflect a variety of tints across the lake surface. Though no lakes in Lassen Park are stocked with trout and the fishing is typically poor, you may still see a rising trout or two. The best place to see wildlife, especially deer, is in the meadow adjacent to Kings Creek, the lake's outlet stream.

---

## 15. SUMMIT LAKE TRAILHEAD 8.0 mi/5.5 hrs

*Reference:* In Lassen Volcanic National Park east of Red Bluff; map B3, grid j2.

*User groups:* Hikers. Horses are allowed, but there are many rules governing their use, including a required special permit. No dogs or mountain bikes are allowed. No wheelchair facilities.

*Permits:* A wilderness permit is required for hikers planning to camp in the backcountry and for equestrians. A $5 national park day-use fee is charged for each vehicle. Horses require a special permit.

*Directions:* From Interstate 5 at Redding, turn east on Highway 44 and drive 46 miles to the park entrance. Continue southeast on Highway 89 for 12 miles to the trailhead at Summit Lake.

*Maps:* Trail maps are available for $3.95. To order a map, contact Loomis Museum, c/o Lassen Volcanic National Park at the address below. For a map of Lassen National Forest, send $3 to USDA-Forest Service, 630 Sansome Street, San Francisco, CA 94111. To obtain a topographic map of the area, ask for Reading Peak from the USGS.

*Who to contact:* Lassen Volcanic National Park, P.O. Box 100, Mineral, CA 96063; (916) 595-4444.

*Trail notes:* You get it all on this hike to Lower Twin Lake: beautiful lakes, forest, meadows and wildflowers, all of it a prime testimonial of the beauty of the Lassen Wilderness. It makes an outstanding day hike for campers staying at the Summit Lake Campground, or an easy overnighter for backpackers. The trail starts on the north side of Summit Lake, rising 500 feet in the first mile. If you can make it past this climb, you've got it made. You will arrive at Echo Lake in just another mile, and then to Upper Twin and Lower Twin in the next two miles, dropping 500 feet on your way. It is all very pretty, a great bonus for Summit Lake campers.

*Special note:* No campfires are permitted in Lassen Park.

## 16. CINDER CONE TRAIL 4.0 mi/3.0 hrs

*Reference:* **From Butte Lake Trailhead in Lassen Volcanic National Park; map B3, grid j3.**

*User groups:* Hikers. Horses are allowed, but there are many rules governing their use, including a required special permit. No dogs or mountain bikes are allowed. No wheelchair facilities.

*Permits:* A wilderness permit is required for hikers planning to camp in the backcountry. A $5 national park day-use fee is charged for each vehicle. Horses require a special permit.

*Directions:* From Interstate 5 at Redding, turn east on Highway 44 and drive 60 miles. At the town of Old Station, continue east on Highway 44 for 10.5 miles. Turn south on Road 18 and continue seven miles to the trailhead at Butte Lake.

*Maps:* Trail maps are available for $3.95. To order a map, contact Loomis Museum, c/o Lassen Volcanic National Park at the address below. For a map of Lassen National Forest, send $3 to USDA-Forest Service, 630 Sansome Street, San Francisco, CA 94111. To obtain a topographic map of the area, ask for Prospect Peak from the USGS.

*Who to contact:* Lassen Volcanic National Park, P.O. Box 100, Mineral, CA 96063; (916) 595-4444.

*Trail notes:* Huge chunks of Lassen Park are overlooked by visitors simply because their access is not off the park's main roadway, Highway 89. Butte Lake and the Cinder Cone Trail are such areas, set in the northeastern corner of the park. When you first arrive by car, you will find a large, attractive lake, Butte Lake, quite a surprise for newcomers. At the northwest corner of the lake, you will find the trailhead for the Nobles Emigrant Trail/Cinder Cone Trail, elevation 6,100 feet. The trail starts out easy, heading southwest through forest. But don't be fooled. After 1.5 miles, you will reach the Cinder Cone cutoff, and there everything suddenly changes. The last half-mile rises to the top of the Cinder Cone, a short but very intense climb of 800 feet to the summit at 6,907 feet. The views are unforgettable, especially south to the Painted Dunes and Fantastic Lava Beds, a classic volcanic landscape.

## 17. PROSPECT PEAK TRAIL 6.6 mi/4.5 hrs

*Reference:* **At Butte Lake in Lassen Volcanic National Park; map B3, grid j3.**

*User groups:* Hikers. Horses are allowed, but there are many rules governing their use, including a required special permit. No dogs or mountain bikes are allowed. No wheelchair facilities.

*Permits:* A wilderness permit is required for hikers planning to camp in the backcountry. A $5 national park day-use fee is charged for each vehicle. Horses require a special permit.

*Directions:* From Interstate 5 at Redding, turn east on Highway 44 and drive 60 miles. At the town of Old Station, continue east on Highway 44 for 10.5 miles. Turn south on Road 18 and continue seven miles to the Nobles Emigrant Trailhead at the lake. Hike about a half mile, then turn north toward Prospect Peak.

*Maps:* Trail maps are available for $3.95. To order a map, contact Loomis Museum, c/o Lassen Volcanic National Park at the address below. For a map of Lassen National Forest, send $3 to USDA-Forest Service, 630 Sansome Street, San Francisco, CA 94111. To obtain a topographic map of the area, ask for Prospect Peak from the USGS.

*Who to contact:* Lassen Volcanic National Park at P.O. Box 100, Mineral, CA 96063; (916) 595-4444.

*Trail notes:* To hike to the top of most mountains requires a long, grinding climb, and alas, it is no different to gain the summit of Prospect Peak. Your reward will be some of the best views in Lassen Park, and a trail that gets little use compared to the others in the park. The trailhead (Nobles Emigrant Trail) at elevation 6,100 feet is adjacent to Butte Lake, and after less than a half-mile, you will turn right at the junction with the Prospect Peak Trail. The trail immediately starts to climb, and get used to it, because there will be no respite for several hours. It climbs more than 2,200 feet over the course of just 3.3 miles, finally topping the summit at 8,338 feet. From here you can see most of the prominent peaks in the park, including Mt. Lassen, Mt. Hoffman and Crater Butte, along with thousands and thousands of acres of national forest to the north. This trip makes a perfect hike in the early spring because the snowmelt occurs earlier here than in the rest of the park, so the climb can be made when the air is still cool. If you wait until summer, you will discover this a dry, forsaken place.

---

## 18. CONE LAKE TRAILHEAD    4.0 mi/2.5 hrs

*Reference:* **On the northern boundary of the Caribou Wilderness east of Lassen Volcanic National Park; map B3, grid j4.**

*User groups:* Hikers only. No horses, dogs or mountain bikes are allowed. No wheelchair facilities.

*Permits:* No permits are required. Parking and access are free.

*Directions:* From Interstate 5 at Redding, turn east on Highway 44 and drive 60 miles. At the town of Old Station, continue east on Highway 44 for 30 miles. At the Bogard Work Station, turn right on Forest Service Road 10 and drive five miles, then turn right on Forest Service Road 32N09 and continue 1.5 miles to the Cone Lake Trailhead.

*Maps:* For a map of Lassen National Forest, send $3 to USDA-Forest Service, 630 Sansome Street, San Francisco, CA 94111. To obtain a topographic map of the area, ask for Bogard Buttes from the USGS.

*Who to contact:* Lassen National Forest, Hat Creek Ranger District, P.O. Box 220, Falls River Mills, CA 96028; (916) 336-5521.

*Trail notes:* The prize destination on this hike is Triangle Lake, a pretty spot set in the northern Caribou Wilderness near Black Butte. It is an excellent day hike. The trailhead is located at tiny Cone Lake, just outside the wilderness. From here, you hike for nearly a mile before passing the wilderness boundary, which is clearly marked. At that point, you sense the change in features, the land becoming wild and untouched, a striking contrast. You head a mile south, arriving at Triangle Lake, a pretty spot that provides good fishing during the evening for pan-size trout. If you want more, you can get more, heading onward from the lake. Here, the trail forks. The right fork is routed right into Lassen Volcanic National Park, a distance of only 1.5 miles, from which you can access Widow Lake (a Lassen Wilderness Permit is required). The left fork, on the other hand, leads to Twin Lakes over the course of just a half-mile hike.

# 19. CARIBOU LAKE TRAILHEAD

**12.0 mi/2.0 days**

*Reference:* **On the eastern boundary of the Caribou Wilderness east of Lassen Volcanic National Park; map B3, grid j5.**

*User groups:* Hikers only. No horses, dogs or mountain bikes are allowed. No wheelchair facilities.

*Permits:* No permits are required. Parking and access are free.

*Directions:* From Interstate 5 at Red Bluff, turn east on Highway 36 and drive 83 miles to the town of Westwood (located east of Lake Almanor). Turn north on County Road A21 and drive 12.5 miles, then turn left on Silver Lake Road and continue past Silver Lake to the trailhead parking area at Caribou Lake.

*Maps:* For a map of Lassen National Forest, send $3 to USDA-Forest Service, 630 Sansome Street, San Francisco, CA 94111. To obtain a topographic map of the area, ask for Red Cinder from the USGS.

*Who to contact:* Lassen National Forest, Hat Creek Ranger District, P.O. Box 220, Falls River Mills, CA 96028; (916) 336-5521.

*Trail notes:* The Caribou Lakes Trailhead provides a hiking trip that is a parade past mountain lakes. Rarely are there this many wilderness lakes so close to a trailhead. This trip starts at Caribou Lake, heading west, and in no time, you start passing all kinds of tiny lakes. The first one, Cowboy Lake, is only a quarter-mile down the trail. In another 15 minutes, you will come to Jewel Lake. This procession of lakes never seems to stop—Eleanor Lake is next, then after turning left at the fork (two miles in), you pass Black Lake, North and South Divide Lakes, and further on, Long Lake. Long Lake should be your destination, six miles from the trailhead, a great two-day backpack adventure. The Caribou Wilderness is quite small, just nine miles from top to bottom, and only five miles across, with elevations ranging from 5,000 to 7,000 feet. This trip will provide a visit to the best of it.

# PACIFIC CREST TRAIL      114.0 mi. one way/9.0 days
## GENERAL INFORMATION

*Reference:* **Trail sections extend from Lassen Volcanic National Park north to Shasta-Trinity National Forest west of McArthur-Burney Falls State Park.**

*User groups:* Hikers, dogs (except in Burney Falls State Park) and horses. No mountain bikes are allowed.

*Permits:* Permits may be required in certain sections; see individual listings below. Contact the national forest or national park office for information on combined permits for multiple-permit areas.

*Directions:* See individual listings for specific directions to each trailhead.

*Maps:* For an overall view of the trail route in this chapter, send $3 for each map ordered to USDA-Forest Service, 630 Sansome Street, San Francisco, CA 94111. Ask for Lassen National Forest and Shasta-Trinity National Forest. For a trail map of the section in Lassen Volcanic National Park, contact Loomis Museum, c/o Lassen Volcanic National Park, P.O. Box 100, Mineral, CA 96063; (916) 595-4444. The map is $3.95 plus tax.

*Trail notes:* You get a little bit of bliss, a little bit of paradise, then a big load of bull pucky on the 114-mile segment of the Pacific Crest Trail that crosses through this chapter's map. The bliss is in Lassen Volcanic National Park, where the trail passes by high mountain lakes circled with conifers, then goes by a strange but compelling volcanic area. The paradise comes at Burney Falls, a 129-foot waterfall that is a portrait of serenity, along with nearby Lake Britton. Then it is off to no man's land, and here you will be swearing your way up to Grizzly Peak in a place where water and breezes are rare, and where an endless climb through brushy terrain will have you wondering why you are doing this. It gets worse when you can scarcely follow the trail because of logging roads, brush and zero trail maintenance.

---

## PCT-38      32.0 mi. one way/3.0 days
## LASSEN NATIONAL PARK to HIGHWAY 44

*Reference:* From Warner Valley Campground in Lassen Volcanic National Park to Highway 44; map B3, grid j3.

*User groups:* Hikers, dogs and horses. No mountain bikes are allowed. No wheelchair facilities.

*Permits:* A wilderness permit is required for hikers planning to camp in the Lassen Volcanic National Park backcountry and for equestrians. You may not camp with horses in the national park's backcountry. A corral is available by reservation for overnighters. A national park entrance fee is charged: $5 per vehicle or $3 per hiker.

*Directions:* From Interstate 5 at Red Bluff, turn east on Highway 36 and drive 70 miles to the town of Chester. Turn north on Warner Valley Road (improved dirt) and proceed 16 miles to the campground.

*Maps:* To obtain topographic maps of the route, ask for Reading Peak, West Prospect Peak and Old Station from the USGS.

*Who to contact:* Lassen Volcanic National Park, P.O. Box 100, Mineral, CA 96063; (916) 595-4444, and Lassen National Forest, Hat Creek Ranger

District, P.O. Box 220, Falls River Mills, CA 96028; (916) 336-5521.

*Trail notes:* Every step is a pleasure in Lassen National Park, starting from the wooded Warner Valley (at 5,680 feet) at Springs Creek and then heading north into the park's most remote terrain. The trail is routed across Grassy Swale, past Swan Lake and on to Lower Twin Lake (seven miles in), a pretty body of water circled by conifers. From here, the trail heads north, skirting the western flank of Fairfield Peak (7,272 feet) and then onward, turning west past Soap Lake and Badger Flat, then out past the park's boundary. As you hike toward Highway 44, you will be lateraling across Badger Mountain (6,973 feet) to your right, with the Hat Creek drainage off to your immediate left. In this latter stretch of trail, you will cross no major lakes or streams (plan your water well), but just forge on through the national forest, mostly second-growth, crossing a few roads along the way. In the spring, wildflowers are exceptional on the Hat Creek rim. A small, primitive Forest Service campground is located on the trail about 10 miles north of the border of Lassen National Park.

---

## PCT-39      40.0 mi. one way/3.0 days
## HWY 44 to McARTHUR-BURNEY FALLS STATE PARK

*Reference:* **From Highway 44 parking area north to McArthur-Burney Falls State Park; map B3, grid h3.**

*User groups:* Hikers, dogs (except in the state park) and horses. No mountain bikes are allowed. No wheelchair facilities.

*Permits:* No permits are required. A state park entrance fee is charged: $5 per vehicle or $2 per hiker.

*Directions:* From Interstate 5 at Redding, turn east on Highway 44 and drive 60 miles. At the town of Old Station, continue east on Highway 44 for 2.5 miles to the trailhead parking area on the left.

*Maps:* To obtain topographic maps of the route, ask for Old Station, Murken Bench, Hogback Ridge, Cassel, Dana and Burney Falls from the USGS.

*Who to contact:* Lassen National Forest, Hat Creek Ranger District, P.O. Box 220, Falls River Mills, CA 96028; (916) 336-5521.

*Trail notes:* The features of this segment of the Pacific Crest Trail are Hat Creek, Baum Lake, Crystal Lake and the spectacular Burney Falls. From the trailhead at Highway 44, the stream is routed through the wooded watershed of Hat Creek, then to a long, shadeless section that will have you counting the drops of water in your canteen. After departing from Hat Creek, the PCT heads past Baum Lake and Crystal Lake, the latter being 27 miles in from the trailhead. You cross Highway 299, and from there, it is an eight-mile romp to Burney Falls State Park and its breathtaking 129-foot waterfall.

---

## PCT-40      52.0 mi. one way/4.0 days
## McARTHUR-BURNEY FALLS PARK to ASH CAMP

*Reference:* **From McArthur-Burney Falls State Park west into Ash Camp into Shasta-Trinity National Forest; map B3, grid e1.**

*User groups:* Hikers, dogs (except in the state park) and horses. No mountain bikes are allowed. No wheelchair facilities.

*Permits:* No permits are required. A state park entrance fee is charged: $5 per vehicle or $2 per hiker.

*Directions:* From Interstate 5 at Redding, turn east on Highway 299 and drive 50 miles to Burney. Continue five miles east on Highway 299, then turn north on Highway 89 and drive 5.8 miles to the state park entrance. Follow the signs to the trailhead.

*Maps:* To obtain topographic maps of the route, ask for Burney Falls, Skunk Ridge and Grizzly Peak from the USGS.

*Who to contact:* McArthur-Burney Falls State Park, 24898 Highway 89, Burney, CA 96013; (916) 335-2777.

*Trail notes:* It may be difficult to leave the woods, waters and aura of Burney Falls, but off you go, facing dry country and some of Northern California's least-used portions of the Pacific Crest Trail. From Burney Falls, the PCT heads west, touching the Pit River Arm of Lake Britton, and then forward into Lassen National Forest, crossing into Shasta-Trinity National Forest and up to Grizzly Peak. Much of this route is across exposed slopes, dry and hot, where the trail has deteriorated in many spots due to the encroachment of brush and zero trail maintenance by the Forest Service. Knowing you are smack between the lush beauty of Burney Falls (behind you) and the McCloud River (ahead of you) can make dealing with the present brush-infested landscape a frustrating encounter. Always fill your canteens with water wherever you find it, and don't hesitate to make a camp if, late in the day, you find even a small flat spot with water nearby. After the dry, beastly climb near Grizzly Peak, most hikers will want to make a lightning-fast descent down to the eden of the McCloud River at Ash Camp. But hold your horses. As long as you've come this far, make the short sidetrip to Grizzly Peak, and while you are looking at the incredible view of Mount Shasta and the McCloud flats, congratulate yourself for completing such a terrible hike.

*PCT CONTINUATION:* To continue hiking along the Pacific Crest Trail, see Chapter B2, pages 116-118.

NOR-CAL MAP ........................ see page 14
adjoining maps
NORTH (A4) ............................. see page 64
EAST ............................................... no map
SOUTH (C4) ........................... see page 194
WEST (B3) ............................... see page 120

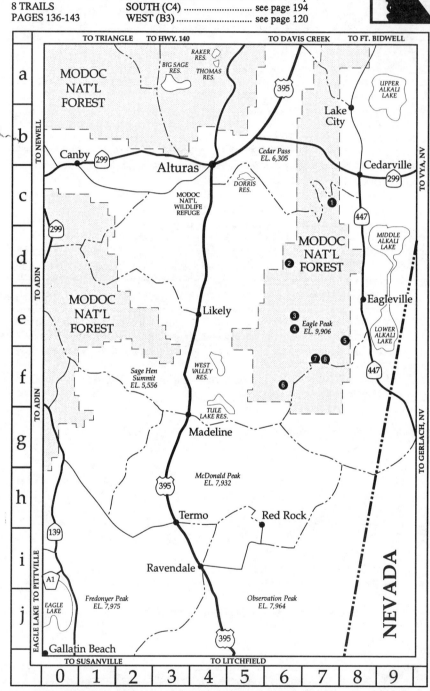

## Map B4 featuring: South Warner Wilderness, Alturas, Blue Lake, Modoc National Forest

## 1. PEPPERDINE TRAILHEAD 12.0 mi/2.0 days

*Reference:* On the northern boundary of South Warner Wilderness east of Alturas; map B4, grid c7.

*User groups:* Hikers, dogs and horses. No mountain bikes are allowed. No wheelchair facilities.

*Permits:* A wilderness permit is required for hikers planning to camp. Parking and access are free.

*Directions:* From the south end of Alturas, turn east on County Road 56 and drive 13 miles to the Modoc National Forest boundary. Continue west for six miles on Parker Creek Road, then turn south at the sign for Pepperdine Campground and continue to the trailhead.

*Maps:* For a map of the South Warner Wilderness, send $3 to USDA-Forest Service, 630 Sansome Street, San Francisco, CA 94111. To obtain a topographic map of the area, ask for Warren Peak from the USGS.

*Who to contact:* Modoc National Forest, Warner Mountain Ranger District, P.O. Box 220, Cedarville, CA 96104; (916) 279-6116.

*Trail notes:* The six-mile trip on the Summit Trail to Patterson Lake is the most popular hike in the South Warner Wilderness. That still doesn't mean you'll run into other people or horses, because the Warners are a remote, lonely place rarely visited by hikers from the Bay Area, Sacramento or Los Angeles. Patterson Lake is set in a rock basin at 9,000 feet, just below Warren Peak (9,718 feet), the highest lake in the wilderness and the highlight destination for most visitors. The Pepperdine Trailhead at 6,900 feet is located just beyond Porter Reservoir, where a primitive campground and a horse corral are available. The hike is a sustained climb, gaining 2,100 feet in elevation, passing to the right of Squaw Peak (8,646 feet) and then tiny Cottonwood Lake. From Squaw Peak looking east, it will seem as if you are looking across hundreds of miles of a stark, uninhabited landscape.

## 2. PINE CREEK TRAILHEAD    4.0 mi/3.0 hrs

*Reference:* On the northwestern boundary of South Warner Wilderness east of Alturas; map B4, grid d6.

*User groups:* Hikers, dogs and horses. No mountain bikes are allowed. No wheelchair facilities.

*Permits:* A wilderness permit is required for hikers planning to camp. Parking and access are free.

*Directions:* From the south end of Alturas, turn east on County Road 56 and drive six miles to the Modoc National Forest boundary. Turn south on West Warner Road and drive about 10 miles to the sign for the Pine Creek Trailhead. Turn east and continue 1.75 miles to the parking area.

*Maps:* For a map of the South Warner Wilderness, send $3 to USDA-Forest Service, 630 Sansome Street, San Francisco, CA 94111. To obtain a topographic map of the area, ask for Eagle Peak from the USGS.

*Who to contact:* Modoc National Forest, Warner Mountain Ranger District, P.O. Box 220, Cedarville, CA 96104; (916) 279-6116.

*Trail notes:* Modoc County is the least populated and least-known region of California, with only 15,000 residents sprinkled across a huge area. Yet there are many outstanding adventures available here, including one of the truly great short hikes available anywhere. And here it is, the Pine Creek Trail, which provides a magnificent yet short traipse into one of the most attractive areas of the South Warner Wilderness. The trail starts along the South Fork of Pine Creek, about 6,800 feet in elevation, then heads straight east into the wilderness, climbing up the lush west-facing slopes. In the course of two miles, the trail rises up 1,000 feet to the Pine Creek Basin. Along the trail are several small lakes, the largest being the two set right along the trail as you enter the basin. Above you is a granite-faced rim, stark and with few trees, where the headwaters of eight small creeks start from springs, then pour down the mountain, join and flow into Pine Creek Lake.

---

# 3. SOUP SPRING TRAILHEAD     3.0 mi/2.0 hrs

*Reference:* On the western boundary of South Warner Wilderness east of Alturas; map B4, grid e6.

*User groups:* Hikers, dogs and horses. No mountain bikes are allowed. No wheelchair facilities.

*Permits:* A wilderness permit is required for hikers planning to camp. Parking and access are free.

*Directions:* From the south end of Alturas, turn east on County Road 56 and drive six miles to the Modoc National Forest boundary. Turn south on West Warner Road and drive about 13 miles to the sign for Soup Springs Campground. Turn east and drive to the parking area at the end of the road.

*Maps:* For a map of the South Warner Wilderness, send $3 to USDA-Forest Service, 630 Sansome Street, San Francisco, CA 94111. To obtain a topographic map of the area, ask for Eagle Peak from the USGS.

*Who to contact:* Modoc National Forest, Warner Mountain Ranger District, P.O. Box 220, Cedarville, CA 96104; (916) 279-6116.

*Trail notes:* Mill Creek is a small, pristine trout stream that brings the lonely Warner Mountains to life. It is a short hike to get here, up a hill, over it and then down heading into a valley. In this valley floor you will find Mill Creek, only a 1.5-mile walk out of the Soup Spring Trailhead. Mill Creek is a great spot for a picnic lunch or a high-finesse fishing trip. The trout are extremely sensitive, so anything clumsy, like letting your shadow hit the water or clanking your boots on the shore, will spook them off the bite. The trout are small, dark and chunky, unlike any seen elsewhere. Note: Some hikers use the Soup Spring Trail as a way of climbing up near the Warner Rim and intersecting with the Summit Trail, the feature hike in the South Warner Wilderness. That makes sense, with a free, primitive campground and corral at the trailhead, and then a four-mile romp uphill to the Summit Trail junction. It includes a 1,000-foot climb on the way, with the trail routed up the Slide Creek Canyon over the last two miles of trail.

## 4. MILL CREEK FALLS TRAILHEAD
**0.5 mi/0.5 hr**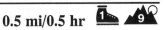

*Reference:* **On the southwestern boundary of South Warner Wilderness east of Alturas; map B4, grid e6.**

*User groups:* Hikers and dogs. No horses or mountain bikes are allowed. No wheelchair facilities.

*Permits:* A wilderness permit is required for hikers planning to camp. Parking and access are free.

*Directions:* From Alturas, turn south on US 395 and drive 18.5 miles to Likely. Turn east on Jess Valley Road and drive nine miles. When the road forks, bear left and drive 2.5 miles, then turn right and continue two miles to the trailhead.

*Maps:* For a map of the South Warner Wilderness, send $3 to USDA-Forest Service, 630 Sansome Street, San Francisco, CA 94111. To obtain a topographic map of the area, ask for Eagle Peak from the USGS.

*Who to contact:* Modoc National Forest, Warner Mountain Ranger District, P.O. Box 220, Cedarville, CA 96104; (916) 279-6116.

*Trail notes:* The short, easy walk from the Mill Creek Falls Trailhead to Clear Lake will lead you to one of the prettiest spots in Modoc County. The trail skirts along the right side of the lake, a pretty high mountain water set at 6,000 feet. Of the lakes and streams in the Warners, it is Clear Lake that has the largest fish, big brown and rainbow trout ranging over 10 pounds. There just aren't that many of them. Backpackers can head onward from Clear Lake on the Poison Flat Trail, but expect a very steep howler of a climb before intersecting with the Mill Creek Trail.

## 5. EMERSON TRAILHEAD
**7.0 mi/2.0 days**

*Reference:* **On the eastern boundary of South Warner Wilderness east of Alturas; map B4, grid e8.**

*User groups:* Hikers, dogs and horses. No mountain bikes are allowed. No wheelchair facilities.

*Permits:* A wilderness permit is required for hikers planning to camp. Parking and access are free.

*Directions:* From Alturas, turn east on Highway 299 and drive 22 miles to Cedarville, then turn south on County Road 1 and travel 16 miles to Eagleville. Continue another 1.5 miles south on County Road 1, then turn right on Emerson Road and proceed three miles to the trailhead. Emerson Road is very steep and can be slippery when wet.

*Maps:* For a map of the South Warner Wilderness, send $3 to USDA-Forest Service, 630 Sansome Street, San Francisco, CA 94111. To obtain a topographic map of the area, ask for Emerson Peak from the USGS.

*Who to contact:* Modoc National Forest, Warner Mountain Ranger District, P.O. Box 220, Cedarville, CA 96104; (916) 279-6116.

*Trail notes:* Don't be yelpin' about the dreadful climb up to North Emerson Lake, because we're warning you right here, loud and clear, that it qualifies as a first-class booger-country butt-kicker. If you choose to go anyway, well, you asked for it. The trail climbs 2,000 feet in 3.5 miles, but much of that is in a hellish half-mile stretch that'll have you howling for relief. Your reward is little North Emerson Lake, set at 7,800 feet in a rock bowl with a high sheer back wall, a wonderland-like setting. The trailhead is the most remote of those providing access to the Warners, located on the east side of the mountain rim near stark, dry country. A primitive campground is available here at the trailhead. Out of camp, take the North Emerson Trail. And while you're at it, get yourself in the right frame of mind to cheerfully accept that you will be getting your butt kicked. North Emerson Lake is worth every step.

---

# 6. BLUE LAKE LOOP   2.4 mi/1.25 hrs

*Reference:* **At Blue Lake in Modoc National Forest southeast of Alturas; map B4, grid f6.**

*User groups:* Hikers and dogs. No horses or mountain bikes are allowed. No wheelchair facilities.

*Permits:* A wilderness permit is required for hikers planning to camp. Parking and access are free.

*Directions:* From Alturas, turn south on US 395 and drive 18.5 miles to Likely. Turn east on Jess Valley Road and drive nine miles. When the road forks, bear right and travel seven miles on Blue Lake Road. Turn right at the sign for Blue Lake and continue to the parking area.

*Maps:* For a map of Modoc National Forest, send $3 to USDA-Forest Service, 630 Sansome Street, San Francisco, CA 94111. To obtain a topographic map of the area, ask for Jess Valley from the USGS.

*Who to contact:* Modoc National Forest, Warner Mountain Ranger District, P.O. Box 220, Cedarville, CA 96104; (916) 279-6116.

*Trail notes:* Blue Lake is a pretty spot, shaped like an egg and rimmed with trees, one of the prettiest lakes you can reach by driving. That makes the easy 2.4-mile loop hike around the lake very special, taking the Blue Lake Loop National Trail. With a campground at the lake, this trail makes a good sidetrip for overnight visitors. In addition, there is a fishing pier and **wheelchair accessible** restroom available. A bonus is that there are some huge trout in this lake, brown trout in the 10-pound class, and they provide quite a treasure hunt amid good numbers of foot-long rainbow trout.

---

# 7. EAST CREEK LOOP   15.0 mi/2.0 days

*Reference:* **On the southern boundary of South Warner Wilderness east of Alturas; map B4, grid f7.**

*User groups:* Hikers, dogs and horses. No mountain bikes are allowed. No wheelchair facilities.

*Permits:* A wilderness permit is required for hikers planning to camp. Parking and access are free.

*Directions:* From Alturas, turn south on US 395 and drive 18.5 miles to Likely. Turn east on Jess Valley Road and drive until you reach South Warner Road. Turn south and drive southeast, heading toward Patterson Campground. Turn left at the East Creek Trailhead access road and drive a short distance to the parking area.

*Maps:* For a map of the South Warner Wilderness, send $3 to USDA-Forest Service, 630 Sansome Street, San Francisco, CA 94111. To obtain a topographic map of the area, ask for Emerson Peak from the USGS.

*Who to contact:* Modoc National Forest, Warner Mountain Ranger District, P.O. Box 220, Cedarville, CA 96104; (916) 279-6116.

*Trail notes:* The East Creek Loop is our favorite loop hike in the Warner Mountains. It can be completed in a weekend, not including driving time, and provides a capsule look at the amazing contrasts of the Warners. It includes small, pristine streams as well as high barren mountain rims. The East Creek Trail, elevation 7,100 feet, is routed 5.5 miles north into the wilderness. Just before the junction with the Poison Flat Trail, there is a spring located on the left side of the trail; don't miss it! You will need the water for the upcoming climb. Turn right at the junction with the Poison Flat Trail, then make the 800-foot climb above tree line, then turn right again on the Summit Trail. The loop is completed by taking the Summit Trail back south, crossing high, stark country, most of it over 8,000 feet in elevation. In the last two miles, the trail drops sharply, losing 1,000 feet on the way to Patterson Campground, the end of the loop trail. To reach the parking area at East Creek Trailhead requires a half-mile walk on the Forest Service Road.

---

# 8. SUMMIT TRAIL 45.0 mi/4.0 days

*Reference:* **On the southern boundary of South Warner Wilderness east of Alturas; map B4, grid f7.**

*User groups:* Hikers. Horses are allowed, but there are many rules governing their use, including a required special permit. No dogs or mountain bikes are allowed. No wheelchair facilities.

*Permits:* A wilderness permit is required for hikers planning to camp. Parking and access are free. Special permit required for horses.

*Directions:* From Alturas, turn south on US 395 and drive 18.5 miles to Likely. Turn east on Jess Valley Road and drive until you reach South Warner Road. Turn south and drive southeast to Patterson Campground. The trailhead is at the camp.

*Maps:* For a map of the South Warner Wilderness, send $3 to USDA-Forest Service, 630 Sansome Street, San Francisco, CA 94111. To obtain a topographic map of the area, ask for Emerson Peak from the USGS.

*Who to contact:* Modoc National Forest, Warner Mountain Ranger District, P.O. Box 220, Cedarville, CA 96104; (916) 279-6116.

*Trail notes:* The Warner Mountains have a mystique about them, a charm cultivated by the thoughts of hikers who dream of an area where the landscape is remote and untouched and the trails are empty. That is why the Summit Loop is the backpacking trek that most hikers yearn to take some day. However, only rarely do they get around to it. For most, the Warners are just too remote, too far away, and the trip requires too much time. If you are one of the lucky few to get here, you will find this hike traverses both sides of the Warner ridge, providing an intimate look at a diverse place. The west side of the Warner Mountains is a habitat filled with small pine trees, meadows and the headwaters of many small streams. The east side, however, is stark and rugged, with great long-distance lookouts to the east across high desert and miles of sagebrush and juniper. You will start the trip at the Patterson Camp Trailhead, elevation 7,200 feet, and from there, the trail climbs quickly, rising to 8,200 feet in two miles, accessing high, barren country. Great views abound from here as you head north. To reach the north end of the wilderness, you take the turn at the Owl Creek Trail and hike to Linderman Lake, set at the foot of Devils Knob (8,776 feet), and beyond past Squaw Peak (8,646 feet). To return you will make the hairpin left turn at the Summit Trail, and walk back on the mostly lush western slopes of the Warners. Highlights on the return loop include Patterson Lake (9,000 feet), the headwaters of Mill Creek and North Fork East Creek, and many beautiful and fragile meadows. The trail ends at the East Creek parking area, a half-mile walk from the Patterson Camp Trailhead. Savor every moment of this trip—it is one of the greatest little-known hiking trips anywhere in America.

## Leave No Trace Tips

### Camp with care

- Choose a pre-existing, legal site. Restrict activities to areas where vegetation is compacted or absent.

- Camp at least 75 steps (200 feet) from lakes, streams and trails.

- Always choose sites that will not be damaged by your stay.

- Preserve the feeling of solitude by selecting camps that are out of view when possible.

- Do not construct structures or furniture or dig trenches.

# MAP CØ

**15 TRAILS**
**PAGES 144-155**

NOR-CAL MAP ........................ see page 14
adjoining maps
NORTH (BØ) ........................... see page 68
EAST (C1) ............................... see page 156
SOUTH (DØ) .......................... see page 196
WEST ...................................... no map

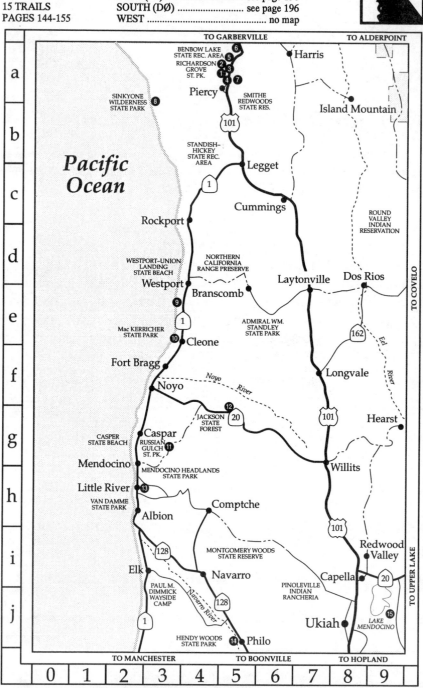

TO GARBERVILLE    TO ALDERPOINT

**a**

BENBOW LAKE STATE REC. AREA ⑥ ⑤
RICHARDSON GROVE ST. PK. ② ① ③
④ ⑦
Harris
Piercy
SMITHE REDWOODS STATE RES.
Island Mountain

SINKYONE WILDERNESS STATE PARK ⑧

**101**

**b**

*Pacific Ocean*

STANDISH–HICKEY STATE REC. AREA

Legget

**1**

**c**

Cummings
ROUND VALLEY INDIAN RESERVATION

Rockport

**d**

WESTPORT–UNION LANDING STATE BEACH
NORTHERN CALIFORNIA RANGE PRESERVE
Laytonville
Dos Rios

Westport
Branscomb
⑨

**e**

MacKERRICHER STATE PARK
ADMIRAL WM. STANDLEY STATE PARK
**162**

**1**
⑩ Cleone
Fort Bragg

Longvale

**f**

Noyo
*Noyo River*
⑫
**20**
JACKSON STATE FOREST
**101**
Hearst

**g**

CASPER STATE BEACH
Caspar
RUSSIAN GULCH ST. PK. ⑪
Mendocino
MENDOCINO HEADLANDS STATE PARK
Willits

**h**

Little River ⑬
VAN DAMME STATE PARK
Comptche
Albion
**101**

**i**

**128**
MONTGOMERY WOODS STATE RESERVE
Redwood Valley
Elk
PAUL M. DIMMICK WAYSIDE CAMP
Navarro
PINOLEVILLE INDIAN RANCHERIA
Capella
**20**

**j**

**1**
*Navarro River*
**128**
Ukiah
LAKE MENDOCINO ⑮
HENDY WOODS STATE PARK
⑭ Philo

TO MANCHESTER    TO BOONVILLE    TO HOPLAND

TO COVELO
TO UPPER LAKE

| 0 | 1 | 2 | 3 | 4 | 5 | 6 | 7 | 8 | 9 |

**Map CØ featuring:** Richardson Grove State Park, Benbow Lake State Recreation Area, Sinkyone Wilderness State Park, Fort Bragg, MacKerricher State Park, Russian Gulch State Park, Jackson State Forest, Van Damme State Park, Hendy Woods State Park, Cow Mountain Recreation Area, Ukiah

## 1. LOOKOUT POINT LOOP TRAIL

1.7 mi/1.0 hr

*Reference:* In Richardson Grove State Park south of Garberville; map CØ, grid a5.

*User groups:* Hikers only. No dogs, horses or mountain bikes are allowed. No wheelchair facilities.

*Permits:* No permits are required. A $5 state park entrance fee is charged for each vehicle.

*Directions:* From Garberville, drive south on US 101 and drive approximately nine miles to the park entrance. Follow the signs to the Redwood Day-Use Parking Area. Access to the trailhead is at the parking area and also out of Madrone Campground and Hartsook Inn.

*Maps:* For a trail guide and brochure, send $1 to Richardson Grove State Park at the address below. To obtain a topographic map of the area, ask for Garberville from the USGS.

*Who to contact:* Richardson Grove State Park, 1600 US Highway 101, Suite 8, Garberville, CA 95542; (707) 247-3318 or (707) 445-6547.

*Trail notes:* Big woods. Big water. That is what the Lookout Point Loop Trail supplies, with a tour through giant redwoods culminating at the canyon rim over the South Fork Eel River. Giant redwoods approaching 300 feet tall and an estimated 1,000 years old are the highlight of Richardson Grove, while younger redwoods, fir and tan oak fill out the forest. The trail passes through forest and rises to Lookout Point, where there is an excellent view of the South Fork. You can also see the Oak Flat Campground from here. As an undammed, free-flowing river, the South Fork Eel River can appear a small trickle in late summer or a howling torrent during peak flows in winter. When looking down from Lookout Point during summer, it may seem hard to imagine how high the Eel has risen in high water years. In 1955, 1963 and 1986, the river actually flooded its banks and wiped out several camp-grounds in the state park. This is an easy and popular hike, both for daytime park visitors, overnighters at Madrone Camp, or people staying at Hartsook Inn. From the latter, there is a half-mile spur trail that is connected to the Lookout Point Loop Trail.

## 2. DURPHY CREEK LOOP

4.5 mi/3.0 hrs

*Reference:* In Richardson Grove State Park south of Garberville; map CØ, grid a5.

*User groups:* Hikers only. No dogs, horses or mountain bikes are allowed. No wheelchair facilities.

*Permits:* No permits are required. A $5 state park entrance fee is charged for each vehicle.

*Directions:* From Garberville, drive south on US 101 and drive approximately nine miles to the park entrance. Follow the signs to the Redwood Day-Use Parking Area. The trailhead is at the parking area.

*Maps:* For a trail guide and brochure, send $1 to Richardson Grove State Park at the address below. To obtain a topographic map of the area, ask for Garberville from the USGS.

*Who to contact:* Richardson Grove State Park, 1600 US Highway 101, Suite 8, Garberville, CA 95542; (707) 247-3318 or (707) 445-6547.

*Trail notes:* Be ready for a good climb, have a full canteen of water, and note: No whiners allowed. Why? Because this loop trail is the most challenging hike in Richardson Grove State Park. It starts easily enough, routed right along the left side of Durphy Creek, a tolerant grade. But when the trail turns left and starts to climb up the canyon, all tolerance is forgotten. The trail climbs 800 feet in less than half a mile, with a short cutoff to Tan Oak Springs, then onward to the ridge at 1,400 feet. On the way back down, the route descends through a dense forest of tan oaks and is quite steep in the last half mile, including some switchbacks. To complete the loop, turn left at the Lookout Point Trail and hike back towards the park office.

*Special note:* Restrooms and water are available at the trailhead.

---

## 3. REDWOOD EXHIBIT TRAIL 0.25 mi/0.25 hr

*Reference:* In Richardson Grove State Park south of Garberville; map CØ, grid a5.

*User groups:* Hikers only. No dogs, horses or mountain bikes are allowed. No wheelchair facilities.

*Permits:* No permits are required. A $5 state park entrance fee is charged for each vehicle.

*Directions:* From Garberville, drive south on US Highway 101 and drive approximately nine miles to the park entrance. Follow the signs to the Redwood Day-Use Parking Area. The trailhead is at the parking area.

*Maps:* For a trail guide and brochure, send $1 to Richardson Grove State Park at the address below. To obtain a topographic map of the area, ask for Garberville from the USGS.

*Who to contact:* Richardson Grove State Park, 1600 US Highway 101, Suite 8, Garberville, CA 95542; (707) 247-3318 or (707) 445-6547.

*Trail notes:* Highway 101 cuts a swath right through the center of Richardson Grove State Park, and even the long-distance freeway burners slow down to 25 miles per hour to gawk at the giant redwoods. Some even park. If that includes you, the Redwood Exhibit Trail furnishes a short, easy stroll amid many of the park's largest and oldest trees. The actual exhibit trail is only a quarter mile, but it is possible to continue on, linking up with the Lookout Point Trail. After walking among those old giant redwoods, you may notice you don't drive quite so fast on the highway anymore.

---

## 4. SETTLERS LOOP TRAIL 0.7 mi/0.5 hr

*Reference:* In Richardson Grove State Park south of Garberville; map CØ, grid a5.

*User groups:* Hikers only. No dogs, horses or mountain bikes are allowed. No wheelchair facilities.

*Permits:* No permits are required. A $5 state park entrance fee is charged for each vehicle.

*Directions:* From Garberville, drive south on US Highway 101 and drive approximately nine miles to the park entrance. Follow the signs to the visitors center. The trailhead is adjacent to the parking lot.

*Maps:* For a trail guide and brochure, send $1 to Richardson Grove State Park at the address below. To obtain a topographic map of the area, ask for Garberville from the USGS.

*Who to contact:* Richardson Grove State Park, 1600 US Highway 101, Suite 8, Garberville, CA 95542; (707) 247-3318 or (707) 445-6547.

*Trail notes:* The Settlers Loop Trail is the most popular hike for campers staying at the Oak Flat Campground, the largest camp in Richardson Grove State Park. The trail is short and simple, set on the east side of the South Fork Eel River, and features an easy walk through Settler's Meadow. If you want to extend the hike, the Settlers Loop Trail intersects with the southern end of the Toumey Trail. From this intersection, the Toumey Trail (see hike number 7 this chapter) climbs 250 feet over the course of about a half mile to reach Panorama Point. From here, there is a sweeping view of Richardson Grove's giant redwoods, well worth the short climb.

---

## 5. WOODLAND'S LOOP TRAIL    1.6 mi/1.0 hr

*Reference:* In Richardson Grove State Park south of Garberville; map CØ, grid a5.

*User groups:* Hikers only. No dogs, horses or mountain bikes are allowed. No wheelchair facilities.

*Permits:* No permits are required. A $5 state park entrance fee is charged for each vehicle.

*Directions:* From Garberville, drive south on US Highway 101 and drive approximately nine miles to the park entrance. The trailhead is accessible from the parking lot, just inside the entrance.

*Maps:* For a trail guide and brochure, send $1 to Richardson Grove State Park at the address below. To obtain a topographic map of the area, ask for Garberville from the USGS.

*Who to contact:* Richardson Grove State Park, 1600 US Highway 101, Suite 8, Garberville, CA 95542; (707) 247-3318 or (707) 445-6547.

*Trail notes:* You want easy? You get easy. You want forest? You get forest. You want a campground trailhead? You get a campground trailhead. The Woodland's Loop does all that and more, an easy, pretty trail that starts at the Huckleberry Campground. The trail crosses North Creek, then is routed through both redwoods and tan oaks, dense at times. It also includes a gentle uphill portion, rising about 250 feet. The trail and camp are set on the west side of US 101, and with the South Fork Eel River on the east side of the highway, there is no direct river access from this trail or the nearby campground.

---

## 6. PIONEER MEADOW LOOP    3.5 mi/2.5 hrs

*Reference:* In Benbow Lake State Recreation Area south of Garberville; map CO, grid a5.

*User groups:* Hikers only. No dogs, horses or mountain bikes are allowed. No

wheelchair facilities.

*Permits:* No permits are required. A $5 state park entrance fee is charged for each vehicle.

*Directions:* From Garberville, drive two miles south on US Highway 101 to the Benbow exit. Follow the signs to the campground; the trailhead is at campground number 73.

*Maps:* A map and brochure can be obtained by contacting Benbow Lake State Recreation Area at the address below. To obtain a topographic map of the area, ask for Garberville from the USGS.

*Who to contact:* Benbow Lake State Recreation Area, c/o Richardson Grove State Park, 1600 US Highway 101, Suite 8, Garberville, CA 95542; (707) 923-3238 or (707) 445-6547.

*Trail notes:* You can scan map after map and never find Benbow Lake. Not because it doesn't exist, but rather because it doesn't exist most of the year. You see, Benbow Lake is a seasonal lake, created each summer only by a temporary dam on the Eel River. When the Eel is dammed, Benbow Lake becomes a popular recreation site for sunbathing, swimming, non-power boating and camping. Hiking is also a viable alternative, especially on this loop trail. You start on the Pratt Mill Trail near Campground No. 73 at elevation 400 feet, and can create a 3.5-mile loop by connecting to the Pioneer Trail. This route features some river frontage, a sprinkling of giant redwoods, a meadow and a portion of trail along Benbow Lake. There is also the option of taking the Ridge Trail cutoff, a one-mile spur that climbs another 250 feet to an excellent 1,000-foot lookout, with views of the Eel River drainage.

---

# 7. TOUMEY GROVE TRAIL    3.8 mi/2.75 hrs

*Reference:* In Richardson Grove State Park south of Garberville; map CØ, grid a5.

*User groups:* Hikers only. No dogs, horses or mountain bikes are allowed. No wheelchair facilities.

*Permits:* No permits are required. A $5 state park entrance fee is charged for each vehicle.

*Directions:* From Garberville, drive south on US Highway 101 and drive approximately nine miles to the park entrance. Follow the signs to Oak Flat Campground, or to the parking area near the Summer Bridge. The trailheads are at both locations. This trail can only be accessed in the summer months.

*Maps:* For a trail guide and brochure, send $1 to Richardson Grove State Park at the address below. To obtain a topographic map of the area, ask for Garberville from the USGS.

*Who to contact:* Richardson Grove State Park, 1600 US Highway 101, Suite 8, Garberville, CA 95542; (707) 247-3318 or (707) 445-6547.

*Trail notes:* The Toumey Trail is one of Richardson Grove State Park's feature summer hikes. It includes walking over the South Fork Eel River on "Summer Bridge" (a temporary, seasonal span), through a majestic stand of old redwoods, up to Kauffman Springs, and beyond to the Panorama Point Lookout. The trail can be accessed at two spots, either at the north end near a parking area at Summer Bridge, or at the south end at Oak Flat Campground (see Settlers Loop Trail, hike number 4 in this chapter). If you are not camping at Oak Flat, we suggest starting this hike at the parking area near the Summer Bridge. From here, the trail crosses the river and enters the redwoods; take your time and enjoy the surroundings. The trail climbs 300 feet, rising quickly with a few switchbacks, then arrives at Panorama Point, with excellent views of the Eel River Canyon and Richardson Grove Redwoods. Many hikers simply return from this point, but the trail can be extended another mile down to the Oak Flat Campground.

*Special note:* This trail can only be accessed in the summer months.

---

# 8. LOST COAST TRAIL     16.7 mi. one way/2.0 days

*Reference:* In Sinkyone Wilderness State Park south to Usal Campground on Mendocino coast; map CØ, grid b3.

*User groups:* Hikers. Horses are allowed only on the section of trail between Orchard Camp and Wheeler Camp. No wheelchair facilities. No dogs or mountain bikes are allowed.

*Permits:* No permits are required. Parking and access are free unless you plan to camp.

*Directions:* From US Highway 101 north of Garberville, take the Redway exit and turn west on Briceland Road. Drive 36 miles to the park and continue to the visitor center, past Needle Rock Barn, and park at Orchard Camp. Be aware that the access road is unpaved, may close unexpectedly in the winter, and four-wheel-drive vehicles are often required in wet weather. There are no signs pointing the way to the park.

*Maps:* A trail map and brochure can be obtained by sending $1 to Sinkyone Wilderness State Park at the address below. To obtain a topographic map of the area, ask for Bear Harbor from the USGS.

*Who to contact:* Sinkyone Wilderness State Park, P.O. Box 245, Whitethorn, CA 95489; (707) 986-7711 or (707) 445-6547.

*Trail notes:* The remote and rugged wilderness that once symbolized the Northern California coast is now protected forever in Sinkyone Wilderness State Park. Not many folks hike it, or even know how to get here. There are no directional signs along roads, no highways leading here, and the park is virtually never promoted. The few people that do visit will find a primitive, steep and unforgiving terrain that provides a rare coastal wilderness experience. The best way to get it is on the Lost Coast Trail, best hiked north to south to keep the north winds out of your face. From the northern trailhead at Orchard Camp, we advise you to split your trip in two by camping at Little Jackass Creek Camp. That will make your first day's hike 10.2 miles, the second 6.5 miles. Here is a more detailed breakdown. Day 1: From the trailhead at Orchard Camp, the trail starts out flat and pleasant, arcing around Bear Harbor Cove. From here, the trail climbs 800 feet and then back down, in the process passing through a redwood grove and also breaking out for sweeping coastal views. Enjoy them, because the hike gets more difficult, including a steep climb up, over and down a mountain, finally descending into Little Jackass Creek Camp, set aside a small stream. Day 2: The closeout of a two-day hike should always be as enjoyable as possible, and so it is here, with divine views in many spots along the 6.5-mile route. Alas, there is usually payment for views, and that payment comes in several rugged climbs in the park's most remote sections. After climbing to nearly 1,000 feet, the trail ends with an 800-foot downgrade over the last mile, descending to the Usal Campground parking area.

*Special note:* At the northern boundary of the Sinkyone Wilderness, this trail heads north into the King Range National Conservation Area, where it is routed for another 30 miles to the mouth of the Mattole River. See Chapter BØ.

---

## 9. BRUHEL POINT TIDEPOOLS   1.2 mi/1.0 hr

*Reference:* **On Mendocino coast north of Fort Bragg; map CØ, grid e3.**
*User groups:* Hikers and dogs. Not suitable for mountain bikes or horses. No wheelchair facilities.
*Permits:* No permits are required. Parking and access are free.
*Directions:* From Westport, drive south on US Highway 1 to the Vista Point exit. Park at the turnout off the exit ramp. The tidepools are a short walk from the parking lot.
*Maps:* To obtain a topographic map of the area, ask for Inglenook from the USGS.
*Who to contact:* CalTrans, P.O. Box 3700, Eureka, CA 95502; (707) 445-6423.
*Trail notes:* Some of the best tidepools on the Pacific Coast can be found in Mendocino, and one of the best of the best is here, located just south of Bruhel Point. When you first arrive, you will find a roadside vista point (no overnight parking), restrooms and a beach access trail. This is your calling. The trail is routed north toward Bruhel Point, much of it along the edge of ocean bluffs. We do not recommend freelancing a descent down the bluff, but rather urge you take only the cut-off trails, which lead to the best tidepool areas. Time your trip during a low tide, or better yet, a minus low tide. That is when the ocean pulls back, leaving a series of holes and cuts in a rock basin that remain filled with water and provides perfect habitat and viewing areas for all kinds of tiny marine life.

---

## 10. LAKE CLEONE TRAIL   1.0 mi/0.5 hr

*Reference:* **In MacKerricher State Park on Mendocino coast north of Fort Bragg; map CO, grid e3.**
*User groups:* Hikers only. No dogs, horses or mountain bikes are allowed. Trail is **partially wheelchair accessible**. Horse trails are available elsewhere in the park.
*Permits:* No permits are required. Parking and access are free.
*Directions:* From Fort Bragg, drive north on US Highway 1 for three miles to the park entrance. Turn left and drive to the parking area beside the lake. The trailhead is on the east side of the parking lot.
*Maps:* For a brochure and trail map, send $1 to MacKerricher State Park at the address below. To obtain a topographic map of the area, ask for Inglenook from the USGS.
*Who to contact:* MacKerricher State Park, P.O. Box 440, Mendocino, CA 95460; (707) 937-5804 or (707) 865-2391.
*Trail notes:* Somehow the politicians haven't found out about MacKerricher State Park, one of the last remaining state parks where day-use access is free. When they do, they will probably jack up the price. Considering what awaits

visitors, the bargain is all the more surprising. The centerpiece at MacKerricher is a rare and beautiful coastal lake, Lake Cleone, which provides low-impact boating, fishing and a good trail all the way around it. The lake always seems to be full to the brim, is bordered to the west by some sturdy cypress trees and beyond by the Pacific Ocean, and to the east by a pretty marsh. The trail around the lake can be accessed from two campgrounds, Cleone Camp and Surfwood Camp. The lake is stocked with trout twice per month during the summer season by the Department of Fish and Game.

*Special note:* On the south side of the lake, a **wheelchair-accessible** trail runs under Highway 1 through an underpass and beyond to an excellent seal watching area.

---

## 11. FALLS LOOP TRAIL          7.0 mi/4.0 hrs

*Reference:* **In Russian Gulch State Park on Mendocino coast south of Fort Bragg; map CØ, grid g3.**

*User groups:* Hikers only. No mountain bikes, dogs or horses are allowed. However, a paved trail for bicycles and **wheelchairs** is routed 2.5 miles to the trailhead of the Falls Loop Trail.

*Permits:* No permits are required. A $5 state park entrance fee is charged for each vehicle.

*Directions:* From Fort Bragg, drive south on Highway 1 for six miles to the Russian Gulch State Park entrance. Turn left and follow the signs to the trailhead.

*Maps:* For a brochure and trail map, send $1 to Russian Gulch State Park at the address below. To obtain a topographic map of the area, ask for Mendocino from the USGS.

*Who to contact:* Russian Gulch State Park, P.O. Box 440, Mendocino, CA 95460; (707) 937-5804 or (707) 445-6547.

*Trail notes:* A 35-foot waterfall secluded in deep forest makes this walk one of the prettiest on the Mendocino coast. The fall pounds into a rock basin, spraying mist over visitors, welcome after a good hike on a hot summer day. It's not exactly a secret either, getting heavy use, particularly during the vacation season. The route is simple, taking the North Trail for 2.5 miles out to its junction with the Falls Loop Trail. At this junction, turn left and you will hike less than a mile to reach the falls. The entire trip has little elevation gain, an easy walk out to the Falls Loop Trail, then a 200-foot gain to the waterfall. As you go, you will delve deeper and deeper into forest, and though a lot of the old-growth was taken long ago, much is still divine. Note: A paved trail (gated) runs 2.5 miles along Russian Gulch Creek to the junction of the Falls Loop Trail, meaning mountain bikers can make the trip to the falls with only a one-mile hike—ride to the Falls Loop Trail Junction, park and walk one mile from there.

---

## 12. CHAMBERLAIN CREEK          0.5 mi/0.5 hr
## WATERFALL TRAIL

*Reference:* **In Jackson State Forest east of Fort Bragg; map CØ, grid g5.**

*User groups:* Hikers and dogs. No horses or mountain bikes are allowed. No wheelchair facilities.

*Permits:* No permits are required. Parking and access are free.

*Directions:* From Fort Bragg, drive south on Highway 1 to the turnoff for Highway 20. Turn east on Highway 20 and drive 17 miles. Turn left on Road 200, just past the Chamberlain Creek Bridge, drive 1.2 miles and then bear left as the road forks. Continue for about three more miles. Park on the side of the road and follow the hand railing down a steep slope to access the trail.

*Maps:* For a free trail map, contact Jackson State Forest at the address below. To obtain a topographic map of the area, ask for Northspur from the USGS.

*Who to contact:* Jackson State Forest, 802 North Main Street, Fort Bragg, CA 95437; (707) 964-5674.

*Trail notes:* Hidden in Jackson State Forest is a 50-foot waterfall set in a canyon framed by redwoods, the kind of place where explorers can get religion. The trail is short, yet steep, secluded and beautiful, set back off an old dirt logging road. This access road, by the way, can get muddy in the winter and can be impassable for two-wheel drive vehicles. After parking, you will find the trail is routed down the canyon to the stream, starting with a series of steps, with a railing to keep you out of trouble if the steps are wet and slippery. Despite the beauty of the area and the popularity of the Mendocino coast, Jackson State Forest is typically overlooked by most visitors to the area. For many years, we too were guilty, avoiding the area since we knew logging was still permitted here. It was our loss.

---

## 13. FERN CANYON TRAIL      8.1 mi/5.0 hrs

*Reference:* **In Van Damme State Park on Mendocino coast south of Mendocino; map CØ, grid h2.**

*User groups:* Hikers only. No dogs or horses are allowed. The first 2.3 miles of the trail is designed for **wheelchair** and mountain bike use.

*Permits:* No permits are required. A $5 state park entrance fee is charged for each vehicle.

*Directions:* From Mendocino, drive south on Highway 1 for 2.5 miles to the park entrance. Turn left and follow the signs to the trailhead. For campers, start near Campground 26.

*Maps:* For a brochure and trail map, send $1 to Van Damme State Park at the address below. To obtain a topographic map of the area, ask for Mendocino from the USGS.

*Who to contact:* Van Damme State Park, P.O. Box 440, Mendocino, CA 95460; (707) 937-5804 or (707) 445-6547.

*Trail notes:* If only this trail were lesser known…yes, then it would be just about perfect. But alas, that is far from the case. It is heavily used in summer, and even in winter, there always seem to be at least a few people out exploring here. That makes sense since the Fern Canyon Trail in Van Damme State Park is one of the prettiest trails in Mendocino. The trail starts by heading up the Little River, crossing back and forth many times across the stream on small bridges. Here you are at the bottom of the canyon, set amid redwoods and a remarkable fern understory. After 2.3 miles, the trail connects to a 3.5-mile loop. At this point, many people simply return to park headquarters. However, if you want to leave much of the crowd behind, we suggest heading onward on the loop trail up the Little River. The route then climbs up the canyon wall and loops back down on an old logging road, routing hikers back down to the Fern Canyon Trail.

*Special note:* Do not get this "Fern Canyon Trail" confused with the "Fern Canyon Trail" on the Humboldt County coast, which is detailed in Chapter AØ.

---

## 14. BIG HENDY GROVE TRAIL   1.0 mi/0.5 hr

*Reference:* **In Hendy Woods State Park in Mendocino Forest; map CØ, grid j5.**

*User groups:* Hikers and **wheelchairs** (for 0.25 miles). No dogs, horses or mountain bikes are allowed.

*Permits:* No permits are required. A $5 state park entrance fee is charged for each vehicle.

*Directions:* From Mendocino, drive south on Highway 1 for approximately 16 miles to Elk. Turn east on Greenwood Road and continue to the park entrance. This road is narrow and winding. A slightly more developed, alternate route from Mendocino is to take Highway 128 east to Greenwood Road, then turn right and continue to the park entrance. If approaching from US 101, turn west on Highway 253 (south of Ukiah) and drive to Highway 128, then continue northwest to Greenwood Road. Turn left and continue to the park. Follow the signs to Big Hendy Grove.

*Maps:* For a brochure and trail map, send $1 to Hendy Woods State Park at the address below. To obtain a topographic map of the area, ask for Philo from the USGS.

*Who to contact:* Hendy Woods State Park, P.O. Box 440, Mendocino, CA 95460; (707) 937-5804 or (707) 445-6547.

*Trail notes:* This easy and short walk through an ancient redwood forest can have visitors to Hendy Woods smiling for days. Hendy Woods is located in the redwood-filled canyon of the Navarro River, which flows to the sea on the Mendocino coast. While the park covers 845 acres, it is the two old-growth redwood groves that are most compelling. The groves are called Little Hendy (20 acres) and Big Hendy (80 acres). At the latter is a half-mile Discovery Trail and an additional quarter-mile trail (**wheelchair accessible**). Both loops can be linked to make a hike that is about a mile long. You will be walking among towering redwoods, moss-covered stumps, and a sprinkling of giant fallen trees, all set amid ferns, sorrel and occasional trillium.

---

## 15. GLEN EDEN TRAIL   8.0 mi/5.0 hrs

*Reference:* **In Cow Mountain Recreation Area east of Ukiah; map CØ, grid j9.**

*User groups:* Hikers, horses and mountain bikes. No wheelchair facilities.

*Permits:* No permits are required. Parking and access are free.

*Directions:* From Ukiah, turn east on Talmage Road. Follow it to West Side Road, then turn right. Drive about a quarter mile, then turn left at the sign for Cow Mountain. Drive up Mill Creek Road for approximately three miles. You will pass two ponds; after you pass the second pond, turn left at the sign for North Cow Mountain and follow the road for about four miles to the trailhead, located near the Willow Creek day-use area.

*Maps:* For a free trail map of the Cow Mountain area, contact the BLM at the address below. To obtain a topographic map of the area, ask for Cow Mountain from the USGS.

**Who to contact:** Bureau of Land Management, Ukiah District Office, 555 Leslie Street, Ukiah, CA 95482; (707) 468-4000.

**Trail notes:** This trail will have you sweating like Charles Manson's cellmate. The Glen Eden Trail is not only difficult to find (follow our directions precisely), but has several steep sections, and is typically quite hot. The chaparral-covered slopes are peppered with pine and oak, with many miles of trails and fire roads. But it is extremely rare to see other hikers, no off-road vehicles are allowed (unlike the southern portion of the Cow Mountain Recreation Area). In addition, the views of Clear Lake and the Mayacmas Range are outstanding. Start the trip by hiking up the Mayacmas Trail, which traces first Willow Creek and then Mill Creek. In little over a mile, you will junction with the Glen Eden Trail. Turn right and climb out—the trail eventually crosses Mendo Rock Road (another trailhead possibility) and continues up to a series of great overlooks of Clear Lake. To return, retrace your route.

## Leave No Trace Tips

### Campfires

• Fire use can scar the backcountry. If a fire ring is not available, use a lightweight stove for cooking.

• Where fires are permitted, use exisiting fire rings, away from large rocks or overhangs.

• Do not char rocks by building new rings.

• Gather sticks from the ground that are no larger than the diameter of your wrist.

• Do not snap branches of live, dead or downed trees, which can cause personal injury and also scar the natural setting.

• Put the fire "dead out" and make sure it is cold before departing. Remove all trash from the fire ring.

• Remember that some forest fires can be started by a campfire that appears to be out. Hot embers burning deep in the pit can cause tree roots to catch on fire and burn underground. If you ever see smoke rising from the ground, seemingly from nowhere, dig down and put the fire out.

# MAP C1

NOR-CAL MAP ....................... see page 14
adjoining maps
NORTH (B1) ........................... see page 78
EAST (C2) ............................. see page 166
SOUTH (D1) .......................... see page 202
WEST (CØ) ............................ see page 144

14 TRAILS
PAGES 156-165

TO RUTH

TO BEEGUM

36

a

② ③ ④⑤

①

YOLLA
BOLLY
MIDDLE EEL
WILDERNESS

TO ZENIA

Harvey Peak
EL. 7,361

b

⑥

⑧

c

⑦

Castle Peak
EL. 6,258

MENDOCINO
NAT'L
FOREST

TO RED BLUFF

ROUND
VALLEY
INDIAN
RES.

Ball Rock
EL. 6,660

Flournoy

TO CORNING

d

Covelo

Mendocino Pass
EL. 5,000

Paskenta

TO DOS RIOS

e

Black
Butte
EL. 7,448

162

Newville

32

TO ORLAND

BLACK
BUTTE
LAKE

f

Mt. Sanhedrin
EL. 6,183

MENDOCINO
NAT'L
FOREST

Alder
Springs

g

Eel River

Elk Creek

Fruto

STONY
GORGE
RES.

162

h

LAKE
PILLSBURY

⑨ ⑩ ⑪

⑫

TO WILLOW

Potter
Valley

i

Fouts
Springs

⑭

⑬

Stonyford

EAST
PARK
RES.

TO CALPELLA

20

j

COW
MOUNTAIN
REC. AREA

29

Upper Lake

Bartlett
Springs

Lodoga

Sites

TO MAXWELL

TO LAKEPORT

TO NICE

TO HOUGH SPRINGS

TO HWY. 20

0  1  2  3  4  5  6  7  8  9

**Map C1 featuring:** Yolla Bolly Wilderness, Snow Mountain Wilderness, Mendocino National Forest

## 1. WATERSPOUT LOOP     17.0 mi/2.0 days

*Reference:* **On western boundary of Yolla Bolly Wilderness west of Red Bluff; map C1, grid a2.**

*User groups:* Hikers, dogs and horses. No mountain bikes are allowed. No wheelchair facilities.

*Permits:* A campfire permit is required for hikers planning to camp. Parking and access are free.

*Directions:* From Interstate 5 at Red Bluff, turn west on Highway 36 and drive approximately 50 miles to the Harrison Gulch Ranger Station. Continue 8.5 miles east on Highway 36, then turn south on Forest Service Road 30 (Wildwood-Mad River Road). Drive approximately 24 miles, then turn south on Forest Service Road 27N02 and continue to the Waterspout Trailhead on the left.

*Maps:* For a map of Mendocino National Forest, send $3 to USDA-Forest Service, 630 Sansome Street, San Francisco, CA 94111. To obtain a topographic map of the area, ask for Yolla Bolly from the USGS.

*Who to contact:* Mendocino National Forest, Corning Ranger District, P.O. Box 1019, Corning, CA 96021; (916) 824-5196.

*Trail notes:* The Yolla Bolly Wilderness is known for providing little-traveled routes to an intricate series of small streams, including the headwaters of different forks of the Eel River and Trinity River. That is the appeal of this loop trail, which traces the headwaters of the North Fork of the Middle Fork Eel, then loops back on Buck Ridge. There are no lakes along the route, but then again, there are usually no people either. The trail starts at the remote Waterspout Trailhead, named for a spring located along the access road about a mile from the parking area. Within a mile, the trail crosses the stream, then is routed along it southward for seven miles. The nearby Morrison Trail camp is a good spot to overnight. From there you can loop back by turning left at Wrights Valley, then turn left again a mile later, hiking Buck Ridge and the Yellowjacket Trail back to Waterspout.

## 2. CEDAR BASIN TRAIL     6.0 mi/3.75 hrs

*Reference:* **On northern boundary of Yolla Bolly Wilderness west of Red Bluff; map C1, grid a3.**

*User groups:* Hikers, dogs and horses. No mountain bikes are allowed. No wheelchair facilities.

*Permits:* A campfire permit is required for hikers planning to camp. Parking and access are free.

*Directions:* From Interstate 5 at Red Bluff, turn west on Highway 36 and drive approximately 50 miles to the Harrison Gulch Ranger Station. Continue 8.5 miles east on Highway 36, then turn south on Forest Service Road 30 (Wildwood-Mad River Road). Drive approximately 18 miles, then turn left on Forest Service Road 28N40. Continue for five miles, then turn left on Forest Service Road 27N17 and proceed two miles to the West Loop Gap

Trailhead at the end of the road. Look closely; the trailhead can be difficult to find.

*Maps:* For a map of Shasta-Trinity National Forest, send $3 to USDA-Forest Service, 630 Sansome Street, San Francisco, CA 94111. To obtain a topographic map of the area, ask for North Yolla Bolly from the USGS.

*Who to contact:* Shasta-Trinity National Forest, Yolla Bolly Ranger District, Platina, CA 96076; (916) 352-4211.

*Trail notes:* The little-known West Loop Gap Trailhead is the jumpoff spot for an excellent day hike to Cedar Basin and back, giving hikers the chance to explore the headwaters of the South Fork Trinity River. The trip in to Cedar Basin is three miles, starting at a 6,000-foot elevation. At Cedar Basin, you will find four different small streams, all of which join and form the South Fork Trinity. This basin is set below the North Yolla Bolly Mountains (to the immediate north), which top out at 7,863 feet. A network of other trails in the area intersects at Fisher Ridge, a mile out of Cedar Basin, providing the chance to extend your trip for many days. However, note that the only dependable water sources in this area are at river crossings.

---

# 3. BLACK ROCK LAKE TRAIL   4.5 mi/3.0 hrs

*Reference:* **On northern boundary of Yolla Bolly Wilderness west of Red Bluff; map C1, grid a3.**

*User groups:* Hikers, dogs and horses. No mountain bikes are allowed. No wheelchair facilities.

*Permits:* A campfire permit is required for hikers planning to camp. Parking and access are free.

*Directions:* From Interstate 5 at Red Bluff, turn west on Highway 36 and drive approximately 50 miles to the Harrison Gulch Ranger Station. Continue 8.5 miles east on Highway 36, then turn south on Forest Service Road 30 (Wildwood-Mad River Road). Drive approximately six miles, then turn east on Forest Service Road 35 and continue to the Stuart Gap Trailhead.

*Maps:* For a map of Shasta-Trinity National Forest, send $3 to USDA-Forest Service, 630 Sansome Street, San Francisco, CA 94111. To obtain a topographic map of the area, ask for North Yolla Bolly from the USGS.

*Who to contact:* Shasta-Trinity National Forest, Yolla Bolly Ranger District, Platina, CA 96076; (916) 352-4211.

*Trail notes:* The 2.25-mile hike from the Stuart Gap Trailhead to Black Rock Lake is one of the best day hikes in the Yolla Bolly Wilderness. The trailhead is at the northern tip of the wilderness at 5,600 feet, where you hike about a mile along the northwestern flank of North Yolla Bolly Mountain (7,863 feet) toward Pettyjohn Basin. You then turn right and tromp another 1.25 miles to the lake, with the trail contouring through open stands of pine and fir and some small meadows. It is a small lake, set just below Black Rock Mountain (7,755 feet), ideal for swimming, but only rarely has it ever been stocked with trout. There are many other excellent day hikes from this trailhead, including to Yolla Bolly Lake (which has trout), Black Rock Mountain (great views), North Yolla Bolly Mountain (great views) and Cedar Basin (several creeks). Any of these make for classic days, remote and quiet. The trailhead can also be used as a jumpoff spot for a hike straight south on the Pettyjohn Trail into the wilderness interior.

# 4. TOMHEAD SADDLE LOOP 15.0 mi/2.0 days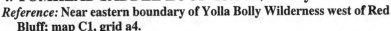

*Reference:* **Near eastern boundary of Yolla Bolly Wilderness west of Red Bluff; map C1, grid a4.**

*User groups:* Hikers, dogs and horses. No mountain bikes are allowed. No wheelchair facilities.

*Permits:* A campfire permit is required for hikers planning to camp. Parking and access are free.

*Directions:* From Interstate 5 at Red Bluff, turn west on Highway 36 and drive approximately 13 miles. Turn left (south) on Cannon Road and proceed about five miles to Pettyjohn Road. Turn west on Pettyjohn Road to Saddle Camp, then turn south on Forest Service Road 27N06 and proceed three miles to the parking area at Tomhead Saddle Campground.

*Maps:* For a map of Shasta-Trinity National Forest, send $3 to USDA-Forest Service, 630 Sansome Street, San Francisco, CA 94111. To obtain a topographic map of the area, ask for North Yolla Bolly from the USGS.

*Who to contact:* Shasta-Trinity National Forest, Yolla Bolly Ranger District, Platina, CA 96076; (916) 352-4211.

*Trail notes:* Why is it that many backpacking trips that have treacherous sections often start out easy, often leading hikers into a misplaced sense of calm? While we do not know the answer to that, we do know that this is a trail that does exactly that. From the trailhead at Tomhead Saddle, 5,500 feet, take the Humboldt Trail west toward East Low Gap. It seems an easy walk, with little elevation gain or loss. "What, me worry?" Well, you turn left on the Sanford Ridge Trail, eventually dropping down into Burnt Camp, an eight-mile first day. But get this: No water is available anywhere along the route. If your canteen is dry, Burnt Camp will seem like Eden, set along the South Fork of Cottonwood Creek. All seems right again. But it isn't, at least not if you don't like slippery stream crossings. The second day, hiking out from Burnt Camp, you will take the Cottonwood Trail to Hawk Camp, then take the Syd Cabin Ridge Trail back to the parking area at Tomhead Saddle. This includes five stream crossings, some of them across slick bedrock. We were thinking of making a video of people crossing the river, then selling it as the "Yolla Bolly Guide To Ballet."

# 5. SYD CABIN RIDGE TRAIL 8.0 miles/2.0 days

*Reference:* **On eastern boundary of Yolla Bolly Wilderness west of Red Bluff; map C1, grid a4.**

*User groups:* Hikers, dogs and horses. No mountain bikes are allowed. No wheelchair facilities.

*Permits:* A campfire permit is required for hikers planning to camp. Parking and access are free.

*Directions:* From Interstate 5 at Red Bluff, turn west on Highway 36 and drive approximately 13 miles. Turn left (south) on Cannon Road and proceed about five miles to Pettyjohn Road. Turn west on Pettyjohn Road to Saddle Camp, then turn south on Forest Service Road 27N06 and proceed three miles to the parking area at Tomhead Saddle Campground.

*Maps:* For a map of Shasta-Trinity National Forest, send $3 to USDA-Forest Service, 630 Sansome Street, San Francisco, CA 94111. To obtain a topographic map of the area, ask for North Yolla Bolly from the USGS.

***Who to contact:*** Shasta-Trinity National Forest, Yolla Bolly Ranger District, Platina, CA 96076; (916) 352-4211.

***Trail notes:*** Not many people hike into the Yolla Bolly Wilderness, set up a camp, then hike back out the next day. But here is a chance to do exactly that. The trailhead is at the Tomhead Saddle, located just west of Tomhead Mountain, elevation 6,757 feet. From here you hike past Tomhead Spring on the Syd Cabin Ridge Trail, then drop down into Hawk Camp. This trail camp is set just below the confluence of three feeder streams, an ideal spot to overnight. If you plan on extending your trip for several days into the wilderness, a network of trails intersects just beyond Hawk Camp, but note that a stream crossing is required.

## 6. IDES COVE NATIONAL RECREATION TRAIL

8.0 mi/5.0 hrs

***Reference:*** **On southeastern boundary of Yolla Bolly Wilderness west of Red Bluff; map C1, grid b4.**

***User groups:*** Hikers, dogs and horses. No mountain bikes are allowed. No wheelchair facilities.

***Permits:*** A campfire permit is required for hikers planning to camp. Parking and access are free.

***Directions:*** From Red Bluff, turn west on County Road 356 (Forest Route 22) and drive approximately 41 miles. Then turn right on a signed access road and continue to the Ides Cove Trailhead.

***Maps:*** For a map of Mendocino National Forest, send $3 to USDA-Forest Service, 630 Sansome Street, San Francisco, CA 94111. To obtain a topographic map of the area, ask for South Yolla Bolly from the USGS.

***Who to contact:*** Mendocino National Forest, Corning Ranger District, P.O. Box 1019, Corning, CA 96021; (916) 824-5196.

***Trail notes:*** At 8,092 feet, the South Yolla Bolly Mountain is the highest point in this wilderness. The Ides Cove National Recreation Trail skirts this mountain as part of one of the top one-day loop trails available in the Yolla Bollys, and a bonus is that a shorter loop hike (3.5 miles) is also convenient here. Another bonus is that a free campground with horse facilities is available at the trailhead. Despite that, the trail gets only light use. From the Ides Cove Trailhead, the trail drops down to the headwaters of Slide Creek, then is routed out to the foot of Harvey Peak at 7,361 feet, the halfway point, a good spot for lunch. The trail then turns sharply and is routed back along the flank of the South Yolla Bolly Mountains. It passes both Long Lake and Square Lake, tiny water holes, but both are stocked with brook trout.

## 7. WRIGHTS VALLEY TRAIL

8.0 mi/4.5 hrs

***Reference:*** **On southern boundary of Yolla Bolly Wilderness west of Red Bluff; map C1, grid c2.**

***User groups:*** Hikers, dogs and horses. No mountain bikes are allowed. No wheelchair facilities.

***Permits:*** A campfire permit is required for hikers planning to camp. Parking and access are free.

***Directions:*** From Willits, drive north on US Highway 101 for 13 miles to

Longvale. Turn east on Highway 162 and drive to Covelo. Continue east on Highway 162 for 13 miles to the Eel River Bridge. Turn left (north) at the bridge onto Forest Service Road M1 and drive approximately 24 miles. Turn left onto Forest Service Road 25N15C and continue to the Rock Cabin Trailhead.

*Maps:* For a map of Mendocino National Forest, send $3 to USDA-Forest Service, 630 Sansome Street, San Francisco, CA 94111. To obtain a topographic map of the area, ask for South Yolla Bolly from the USGS.

*Who to contact:* Mendocino National Forest, Covelo Ranger District, 78150 Covelo Road, Covelo, CA 95428; (707) 983-6118.

*Trail notes:* The Rock Creek Trail extends north into the Yolla Bolly Wilderness, up, over, then down a short ridge before it pours into Wrights Valley. It's about a four-mile trip one way. Here you will find the headwaters of the Middle Fork of the Eel River, one of the prettiest streams in the wilderness. The trail is well marked and includes two creek crossings. While the Yolla Bollys provide few lakes, the Middle Fork awaits you, providing some of the best trout fishing in the region.

*Special note:* Map-gazing hikers will likely notice a small lake, Henthorne Lake, that is set just 2.5 miles from the Rock Cabin Trailhead, complete with two wilderness cabins. Resist the urge to visit. This is private property, a nature reserve for some lucky soul. Hikers are often tempted to hike in via a very faint cowboy trail (with a river crossing) and camp here illegally. The Forest Service hopes to purchase this parcel and complete the wilderness.

---

# 8. SOLDIER RIDGE TRAIL    8.0 mi/2.0 days

*Reference:* **On southern boundary of Yolla Bolly Wilderness west of Red Bluff; map C1, grid c3.**

*User groups:* Hikers, dogs and horses. No mountain bikes are allowed. No wheelchair facilities.

*Permits:* A campfire permit is required for hikers planning to camp. Parking and access are free.

*Directions:* From Willits, drive north on US 101 for 13 miles to Longvale. Turn east on Highway 162 and drive to Covelo. Continue east on Highway 162 for 13 miles to the Eel River Bridge. Turn left (north) at the bridge and drive approximately 27 miles on Forest Service Road M1 to the trailhead at the end of the road.

*Maps:* For a map of Mendocino National Forest, send $3 to USDA-Forest Service, 630 Sansome Street, San Francisco, CA 94111. To obtain a topographic map of the area, ask for South Yolla Bolly from the USGS.

*Who to contact:* Mendocino National Forest, Covelo Ranger District, 78150 Covelo Road, Covelo, CA 95428; (707) 983-6118.

*Trail notes:* This is a mighty short walk as backpack trips go, just 3.5 miles to Kingsley Lake. But the rugged climb on the Soldier Ridge Trail to get there, along with the charm of this little lake, will compel you to stay overnight anyway. Actually, it's a long drive in the middle of nowhere just to reach the trailhead, and then when you get there, you'll face a testing 3.5-mile climb up the spine of Soldier Ridge toward the Yolla Bolly Crest. At the crest are three mountains lined in a row, Sugarloaf Mountain (elevation 7,367 feet), Solomon Peak (7,581 feet) and Hammerhorn Mountain (7,567 feet). The trail crosses through a saddle between Sugarloaf Mountain and Solomon Peak, then drops down to little Kingsley Lake, created from the headwaters of Thomas Creek. All is quiet and peaceful here.

## 9. SNOW MOUNTAIN LOOP    11.0 mi/1.0 day

*Reference:* **On northwestern boundary of Snow Mountain Wilderness in Mendocino National Forest; map C1, grid h4.**

*User groups:* Hikers, dogs and horses. No mountain bikes are allowed. No wheelchair facilities.

*Permits:* A campfire permit is required for hikers planning to camp. Parking and access are free.

*Directions:* From Willows on Interstate 5, turn west on Highway 162 and drive to the town of Elk Creek. Turn west on Ivory Mill Road and continue to the Ivory Mill Station. Turn south on Forest Service Road M3 and proceed to the West Crockett Trailhead.

*Maps:* For a map of Mendocino National Forest, send $3 to USDA-Forest Service, 630 Sansome Street, San Francisco, CA 94111. To obtain a topographic map of the area, ask for Crockett Peak and St. John Mountain from the USGS.

*Who to contact:* Mendocino National Forest, Stonyford Ranger District, 5080 Lagoda-Stonyford Road, Stonyford, CA 95979; (916) 963-3128.

*Trail notes:* Almost nobody knows about the Snow Mountain Wilderness, and far fewer know about this excellent loop trail that traverses the region's most treasured areas. Snow Mountain itself is a double-peaked mountain, that big ridge that is located about midway between Interstate 5 at Willows and US 101 at Willits. This trail starts at the northern boundary of the wilderness at the West Crockett Trailhead (just west of Crockett Peak), crosses the headwaters of Stony Creek (the last water for four miles) and then is routed along the North Ridge Trail toward Snow Mountain. It climbs much of the way, reaching a small loop that is set between East Snow Mountain (7,056 feet) and West Snow Mountain (7,038 feet). To get back on a loop, you take the Milk Ranch Trail, which drops down from Snow Mountain and traces along the Middle Fork of Stony Creek for much of the route back to the parking area. Much of this area can be quite dry and hot in peak summer, especially on the North Ridge. Two notes: Rattlesnakes are common; and hikers should always be certain to carry a lot of water here—twice as much as usual.

## 10. UPPER NYE TRAILHEAD    4.0 mi/2.5 hrs

*Reference:* **On northern boundary of Snow Mountain Wilderness in Mendocino National Forest; map C1, grid h4.**

*User groups:* Hikers, dogs and horses. No mountain bikes are allowed. No wheelchair facilities.

*Permits:* A campfire permit is required for hikers planning to camp. Parking and access are free.

*Directions:* From Willows on Interstate 5, turn west on Highway 162 and drive 21 miles to the town of Elk Creek. Turn west on Ivory Mill Road and drive about 10 miles to the Ivory Mill Station. Turn south on Forest Service Road M3 and proceed 17 miles to the trailhead.

*Maps:* For a map of Mendocino National Forest, send $3 to USDA-Forest Service, 630 Sansome Street, San Francisco, CA 94111. To obtain a topographic map of the area, ask for Crockett Peak and St. John Mountain from the USGS.

*Who to contact:* Mendocino National Forest, Stonyford Ranger District, 5080 Lagoda-Stonyford Road, Stonyford, CA 95979; (916) 963-3128.

*Trail notes:* Much of Mendocino National Forest has been logged, with large patch cuts that in many cases have been slow to regrow. But the Snow Mountain Wilderness is like a little protected island amid the devastation, and this trail furnishes a short hike to one of its least visited, quiet streamside settings. You start at the Upper Nye Trailhead (the primitive Waters Camp is a quarter mile away), then hike the eastern slopes of the Snow Mountain Ridge down to Bear Wallow Creek. It's a two-mile hike, with one steep section. The creek is quite small, a lovely spot to lean against a tree and watch the water run by for a while. Be forewarned that temperatures get quite warm in this region in the summer, particularly so on the hikes on the east facing slopes, such as this one.

---

# 11. WINDY POINT TRAILHEAD

**3.25 mi/1.75 hrs**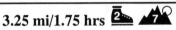

*Reference:* **On northern boundary of Snow Mountain Wilderness in Mendocino National Forest; map C1, grid h5.**

*User groups:* Hikers, dogs and horses. No mountain bikes are allowed. No wheelchair facilities.

*Permits:* A campfire permit is required for hikers planning to camp. Parking and access are free.

*Directions:* From Willows on Interstate 5, turn west on Highway 162 and drive 21 miles to the town of Elk Creek. Turn west on Ivory Mill Road and continue 10 miles to the Ivory Mill Station. Turn south on Forest Service Road M3 and proceed 16 miles to the trailhead.

*Maps:* For a map of Mendocino National Forest, send $3 to USDA-Forest Service, 630 Sansome Street, San Francisco, CA 94111. To obtain a topographic map of the area, ask for Crockett Peak and St. John Mountain from the USGS.

*Who to contact:* Mendocino National Forest, Stonyford Ranger District, 5080 Lagoda-Stonyford Road, Stonyford, CA 95979; (916) 963-3128.

*Trail notes:* Every wilderness has secret spots, and so it is here in the Snow Mountain Wilderness. On a hot summer day, when every drop of water is counted as if it were liquid gold, you will find a simple paradise on this short walk to the headwaters of a tiny fork of Bear Wallow Creek. The hike starts at Windy Point, the most northern trailhead in the Snow Mountains. The trail heads straight east on the Bear Wallow Trail for a little more than a mile across very dry country. About 1.5 miles in, start looking for a spur trail on the right side, and when you see it, take it. This spur drops a short distance down to the source of the North Fork of Bear Wallow Creek, a true secret little spot. If you think there are too many people in the world, just come here and look around.

## 12. BEAR WALLOW TRAILHEAD

4.0 mi/2.5 hrs

*Reference:* **On eastern boundary of Snow Mountain Wilderness in Mendocino National Forest; map C1, grid h5.**

*User groups:* Hikers, dogs and horses. No mountain bikes are allowed. No wheelchair facilities.

*Permits:* A campfire permit is required for hikers planning to camp. Parking and access are free.

*Directions:* From Willows on Interstate 5, turn west on Highway 162 and drive to the town of Elk Creek. Turn south and continue to Stonyford. Turn west on Fouts Springs Road and drive about eight miles, then turn north on Forest Service Road 18N06 and continue to the parking area.

*Maps:* For a map of Mendocino National Forest, send $3 to USDA-Forest Service, 630 Sansome Street, San Francisco, CA 94111. To obtain a topographic map of the area, ask for Fouts Springs from the USGS.

*Who to contact:* Mendocino National Forest, Stonyford Ranger District, 5080 Lagoda-Stonyford Road, Stonyford, CA 95979; (916) 963-3128.

*Trail notes:* Whoa, it can get hot out here. In summer, an early start for a hike is mandatory, particularly out here on the east-facing slopes of the Snow Mountain Wilderness. Your destination is a pretty section of Bear Wallow Creek, a small feeder stream to the Stony Fork of Stony Creek. The hike starts at the Bear Wallow Trailhead. From here, the Bear Wallow Trail is routed north for two miles, and at that point, start looking for a trail junction on the left side. Don't miss it. Turn left and take the quarter-mile traipse down to Bear Wallow Creek, a pretty spot, and a decent destination for a day's walk. If you miss the turn, the Bear Wallow Trail continues all the way to Windy Point Trailhead, and with no water available, you'll be wondering how the heck did you ever get out here. "Beam me up, Scotty."

## 13. BOX SPRING LOOP

10.0 mi/1.0 day

*Reference:* **On southwestern boundary of Snow Mountain Wilderness in Mendocino National Forest; map C1, grid i4.**

*User groups:* Hikers, dogs and horses. No mountain bikes are allowed. No wheelchair facilities.

*Permits:* A campfire permit is required for hikers planning to camp. Parking and access are free.

*Directions:* From Willows on Interstate 5, turn west on Highway 162 and drive to the town of Elk Creek. Turn south and continue to Stonyford. Turn west on Fouts Springs Road and drive approximately 32 miles, then turn north on a signed access road and continue to the parking area at the end of the road at the Summit Spring Trailhead.

*Maps:* For a map of Mendocino National Forest, send $3 to USDA-Forest Service, 630 Sansome Street, San Francisco, CA 94111. To obtain a topographic map of the area, ask for Fouts Springs from the USGS.

*Who to contact:* Mendocino National Forest, Stonyford Ranger District, 5080 Lagoda-Stonyford Road, Stonyford, CA 95979; (916) 963-3128.

*Trail notes:* This is not a trail for the indifferent. Do you yearn for the passion of the mountain experience? Do you crave the zest of life when you have a bad case of dry-mouth and discover a mountain spring? Is the price of a climb worth it for the mountaintop payoff? You need to answer yes, yes and yes to be ready for this loop hike. It includes two killer climbs, a wonderful little spring along the trail, and the ascent of West Snow Mountain, 7,038 feet. Still interested? Then read on. The trail starts at the Summit Spring Trailhead, and in the first mile, includes a no-fun clamber up to High Rock. At the trail junction here, you turn right on the Box Spring Loop Trail, and hike past the headwaters of Trout Creek to Box Spring, located just to the right of the trail near another trail junction. In hot weather, typically all summer, this spot is paradise. Turn left and make the three-mile climb up West Snow Mountain, sweating it out every step of the way. Enjoy this victory for a while before dropping back down for the final three miles back to the trailhead and parking area. This is an excellent loop hike, one that furnishes several rewards, but will make you earn every one of them.

---

# 14. TROUT CREEK TRAILHEAD

5.0 mi/3.0 hrs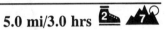

**Reference:** On southeastern boundary of Snow Mountain Wilderness in Mendocino National Forest; map C1, grid i5.

**User groups:** Hikers, dogs and horses. No mountain bikes are allowed. No wheelchair facilities.

**Permits:** A campfire permit is required for hikers planning to camp. Parking and access are free.

**Directions:** From Willows on Interstate 5, turn west on Highway 162 and drive to the town of Elk Creek. Turn south and continue to Stonyford. Turn west on Fouts Springs Road and drive approximately eight miles, then turn west on a signed access road and continue to the parking area at the end of the road.

**Maps:** For a map of Mendocino National Forest, send $3 to USDA-Forest Service, 630 Sansome Street, San Francisco, CA 94111. To obtain a topographic map of the area, ask for Fouts Springs from the USGS.

**Who to contact:** Mendocino National Forest, Stonyford Ranger District, 5080 Lagoda-Stonyford Road, Stonyford, CA 95979; (916) 963-3128.

**Trail notes:** Almost every hike has a chance for both the exceptional as well as the dreadful. The Trout Trail is the best example of that in the Snow Mountain Wilderness. In this case, the exceptional is the destination, Trout Creek, a pretty brook. The dreadful is what might be waiting to keep you company, and we don't mean people. From the trailhead, you will start the hike by dropping down to Trout Creek, crossing it, then climbing up the southern slope of the watershed and hiking out to Rattlesnake Glades. Here the trail drops back down to Trout Creek, your destination. Wait a minute now, what was the name of that glade? Right, Rattlesnake Glades. Get the hint? This is rattlesnake country, and while you may not see any on your walk, if you wait long enough, you can be sure that you will. Try to be a good person and do not step on Mr. or Mrs. Rattlesnake. They don't like that.

# MAP C2

NOR-CAL MAP ........................ see page 14
adjoining maps
NORTH (B2) ............................ see page 94
EAST (C3) ............................... see page 174
SOUTH (D2) ........................... see page 208
WEST (C1) .............................. see page 156

9 TRAILS
PAGES 166-173

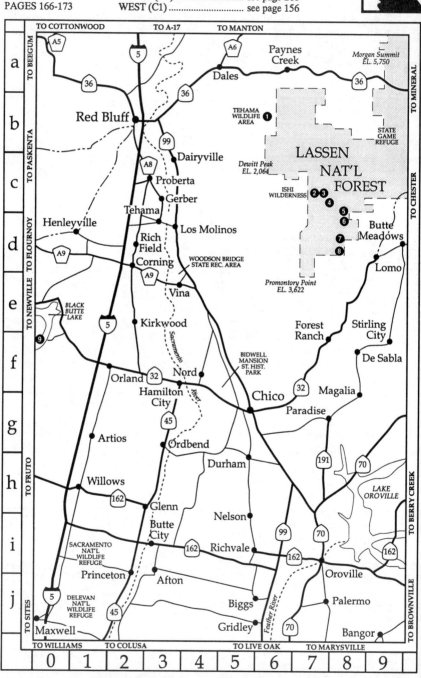

**Map C2 featuring:** Tehama Wildlife Area, Red Bluff, Ishi Wilderness, Black Butte Reservoir, Chico

## 1. McCLURE TRAIL   9.0 mi/1.0 day

*Reference:* **In Tehama Wildlife Area east of Red Bluff; map C2, grid b6.**
*User groups:* Hikers, dogs and mountain bikes. No wheelchair facilities.
*Permits:* No permits are required. Parking and access are free.
*Directions:* From Interstate 5 at Red Bluff, turn east on Highway 36 and drive 20 miles to the town of Paynes Creek. Turn south on Plum Creek Road and drive to Ishi Conservation Camp. Continue about 2.5 miles south to High Trestle Road and follow it to Hogsback Road. Park across from the intersection of High Trestle and Hogsback roads and walk about a quarter of a mile on the dirt road to the trailhead. Access to this area is closed to the public from December 1 through the first Saturday in April. Access is also restricted for a short period during deer season in late September.
*Maps:* For a free map, contact Tehama Wildlife Area at the address below. To obtain a topographic map of the area, ask for Dewitt Peak from the USGS.
*Who to contact:* Department of Fish and Game, Tehama Wildlife Area, P.O. Box 188, Paynes Creek, CA 96075; (916) 597-2201.
*Trail notes:* At first glance the Tehama Wildlife Area might just appear to be rolling oak woodlands, nothing special. Look again. This is a habitat managed expressly for wildlife, and it includes a beautiful stream, abundant vegetation and plenty of animals. This trail accesses the best of it, heading down a steep canyon to Antelope Creek, buffered by riparian vegetation. Wild pigs roam the canyons, deer are rampant in late fall (typically migrating in after the hunting season is over), and there are also lots of squirrels, hawks and alas, rattlesnakes. In late winter and spring, the canyons and hillsides come alive in green, and all wildlife seems to prosper. They better when they have the chance, because the heat here can seem unbearable in summer. The deer herd, hammered by drought at the beginning of the 1990s, is on a big rebound here.

## 2. TABLE MOUNTAIN TRAIL   3.2 mi/2.5 hrs

*Reference:* **In Ishi Wilderness east of Red Bluff; map C2, grid c7.**
*User groups:* Hikers, dogs and horses. No mountain bikes are allowed. No wheelchair facilities.
*Permits:* A campfire permit is required for hikers planning to camp. Parking and access are free.
*Directions:* From Interstate 5 at Red Bluff, turn east on Highway 36 and drive to the town of Paynes Creek. Turn south on Little Giant Mill Road (Road 202) and travel approximately seven miles until you reach an intersection. Turn south at Ponderosa Way and drive about 10 miles, then turn west on Forest Service Road 28N57 and follow the Peligreen Jeep Trail for six miles to the trailhead. The last five miles of road are suitable for four-wheel-drive vehicles only.
*Maps:* For a free trail map, contact the Almanor Ranger District at the address below. To obtain a topographic map of the area, ask for Panther Spring and Butte Meadows from the USGS.

*Who to contact:* Lassen National Forest, Almanor Ranger District, P.O. Box 767, Chester, CA 96020; (916) 258-2141.

*Trail notes:* This trail may be short, but it is anything but sweet. Except, that is, from the top of Table Mountain, elevation 2,380 feet, where you are supplied with a sweeping view of the Sacramento Valley and the surrounding land of Ishi. This is where Ishi, the last survivor of the Yahi Yana Indian tribe, escaped from a band of white settlers who exterminated the rest of the Yahis. Before being killed off, they had lived here for 3,000 years. The trail starts from the northwest corner of the wilderness at the Table Mountain Trailhead, and then is routed 1.6 miles to the summit. It is very steep and challenging, and most hikers will be wheezing like worn-out donkeys before making the top. Because of the hot summers, it absolutely critical to either start the trip very early in the morning or time it during cool weather.

---

# 3. RANCHERIA TRAIL     4.0 mi/2.75 hrs

*Reference:* **In Ishi Wilderness east of Red Bluff; map C2, grid c7.**

*User groups:* Hikers, dogs and horses. No mountain bikes are allowed. No wheelchair facilities.

*Permits:* A campfire permit is required for hikers planning to camp. Parking and access are free.

*Directions:* From Interstate 5 at Red Bluff, turn east on Highway 36 and drive to the town of Paynes Creek. Turn south on Little Giant Mill Road (Road 202) and travel approximately seven miles until you reach an intersection. Turn south at Ponderosa Way and drive about 10 miles. Then turn west on Forest Service Road 28N57 and follow the Peligreen Jeep Trail for two miles to the Rancheria Trailhead. The last two miles of road are suitable for four-wheel-drive vehicles only.

*Maps:* For a free trail map, contact the Almanor Ranger District at the address below. To obtain a topographic map of the area, ask for Panther Spring and Butte Meadows from the USGS.

*Who to contact:* Lassen National Forest, Almanor Ranger District, P.O. Box 767, Chester, CA 96020; (916) 258-2141.

*Trail notes:* On a map, the Rancheria Trailhead looks like the closest and easiest trailhead to reach into the Ishi Wilderness from Red Bluff. And what the heck, the trail looks pretty short, too. But when you go there, a completely different picture will come in focus. First off, the trailhead access road is quite rough, impassable for most cars, and that is just a prelude to what lies ahead. The trail starts by following an old jeep road, then leaves the road at a fence line off to the right. If it's hot, which is typical here most of the year, you'll already be reaching for your canteen. The trail then drops like a cannonball for a thousand feet into the Mill Creek Canyon, a surprising and awesome habitat, with some of the prettiest areas of the Ishi. Too bad you can't enjoy them more, because shadowing your every move is the knowledge that you have to climb back out of that canyon, likely during the hottest part of the day. By the time you reach your car, your butt will be thoroughly kicked.

## 4. LOWER MILL CREEK    13.0 mi/1.0 day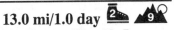

*Reference:* **In Ishi Wilderness east of Red Bluff; map C2, grid c7.**

*User groups:* Hikers, dogs and horses. No mountain bikes are allowed. No wheelchair facilities.

*Permits:* A campfire permit is required for hikers planning to camp. Parking and access are free.

*Directions:* From Interstate 5 at Red Bluff, turn east on Highway 36 and drive to the town of Paynes Creek. Turn south on Little Giant Mill Road (Road 202) and travel approximately seven miles until you reach an intersection. Turn south at Ponderosa Way and drive about 17 miles to the Mill Creek Trailhead.

*Maps:* For a free trail map, contact the Almanor Ranger District at the address below. To obtain a topographic map of the area, ask for Panther Spring and Butte Meadows from the USGS.

*Who to contact:* Lassen National Forest, Almanor Ranger District, P.O. Box 767, Chester, CA 96020; (916) 258-2141.

*Trail notes:* If you only have time for one trail in the Ishi Wilderness, the Mill Creek Trail is the one to pick. That goes whether you want to invest just an hour or have planned a full day, because any length of trip can be a joy here. The trail simply parallels the creek for 6.5 miles to its headwaters at Papes Place, with magnificent scenery and many good fishing and swimming holes along the way. This is a dramatic canyon, and as you stand along the stream the walls can seem to ascend into heaven. It's a land shaped by thousands of years of wind and water. Note: Directly across from the trailhead on Ponderosa Way is another trailhead, this one for a route that follows Upper Mill Creek into Lassen National Forest. While not as spectacular as Lower Mill Creek, it provides a viable option for hiking, fishing and swimming.

## 5. LASSEN TRAIL    12.6 mi/1.0 day

*Reference:* **In Ishi Wilderness east of Red Bluff; map C2, grid c8.**

*User groups:* Hikers, dogs and horses. No mountain bikes are allowed. No wheelchair facilities.

*Permits:* A campfire permit is required for hikers planning to camp. Parking and access are free.

*Directions:* From Interstate 5 at Red Bluff, turn east on Highway 36 and drive to the town of Paynes Creek. Turn south on Little Giant Mill Road (Road 202) and travel approximately seven miles until you reach an intersection. Turn south at Ponderosa Way and drive about 24 miles to the Lassen Trailhead.

*Maps:* For a free trail map, contact the Almanor Ranger District at the address below. To obtain a topographic map of the area, ask for Panther Spring and Butte Meadows from the USGS.

*Who to contact:* Lassen National Forest, Almanor Ranger District, P.O. Box 767, Chester, CA 96020; (916) 258-2141.

*Trail notes:* In the gold rush days, the miners built this trail as part of a link between Deer Creek to the south and Mill Creek to the north. It is the only north/south trail in the Ishi Wilderness, crossing the volcanic tablelands to the gold fields. Be warned that the ridge is dry, often hot, and no water is available, so don't even dream of making this hike without a full canteen. What's worse is that the trip fools a lot of visitors, starting out very easy for the first 3.2 miles, heading along an old abandoned road. Easy, eh? It then changes moods, and believe us, so will you. The trail descends to Boat Gunwale Creek, weaving through some nasty hillside brush. After crossing the creek, the trail deteriorates, virtually disappearing at times. The persistent and adept few will find the trail (or a resemblance of one) is routed all the way to the Mill Creek Canyon, although it is easy to get confused on the way there. Most folks, however, will not have to worry about finding the trail to Mill Creek Canyon. They will have turned around long before that juncture, heading straight back to their car.

---

## 6. MOAK TRAIL · · · 14.0 mi/2.0 days

*Reference:* **In Ishi Wilderness east of Red Bluff; map C2, grid d8.**

*User groups:* Hikers, dogs and horses. No mountain bikes are allowed. No wheelchair facilities.

*Permits:* A campfire permit is required for hikers planning to camp. Parking and access are free.

*Directions:* From Interstate 5 at Red Bluff, turn east on Highway 36 and drive to the town of Paynes Creek. Turn south on Little Giant Mill Road (Road 202) and travel approximately seven miles until you reach an intersection. Turn south at Ponderosa Way and drive about 26 miles to the Moak Trailhead.

*Maps:* For a free trail map, contact the Almanor Ranger District at the address below. To obtain a topographic map of the area, ask for Panther Spring and Butte Meadows from the USGS.

*Who to contact:* Lassen National Forest, Almanor Ranger District, P.O. Box 767, Chester, CA 96020; (916) 258-2141.

*Trail notes:* Hit it right in the spring, and the Moak Trail is likely the best overnight hike in California's foothill country. Hit it wrong in the summer and you will wonder what you did to deserve such a terrible fate. In the spring, the foothill country is loaded with wildflowers and tall, fresh grass, and the views of the Sacramento Valley are spectacular. The trail includes a poke-and-probe section over a lava rock boulder field, and there are good trail camps at Deep Hole (2,800 feet) and Drennan. It is an excellent weekend trip, including a loop route by linking the Moak Trail with the Buena Vista Trail, most of it easy walking. Alas, try this trip in the summer or fall and you'll need to have your gray matter examined at Red Bluff General. No wildflowers, no shade, 100-degree temperatures, and as for water, yer dreamin'.

---

## 7. DEER CREEK TRAIL · · · 14.0 mi/1.0 day

*Reference:* **In Ishi Wilderness east of Red Bluff; map C2, grid d8.**

*User groups:* Hikers, dogs and horses. No mountain bikes are allowed. No wheelchair facilities.

*Permits:* A campfire permit is required for hikers planning to camp. Parking and access are free.

*Directions:* From Interstate 5 at Red Bluff, turn east on Highway 36 and drive to the town of Paynes Creek. Turn south on Little Giant Mill Road (Road

202) and travel approximately seven miles until you reach an intersection. Turn south at Ponderosa Way and drive about 32 miles to the Deer Creek Trailhead.

**Maps:** For a free trail map, contact the Almanor Ranger District at the address below. To obtain a topographic map of the area, ask for Panther Spring and Butte Meadows from the USGS.

**Who to contact:** Lassen National Forest, Almanor Ranger District, P.O. Box 767, Chester, CA 96020; (916) 258-2141.

**Trail notes:** It is no accident that the Deer Creek Trail is the most popular hike in the Ishi Wilderness. You are not only rewarded with striking surroundings, but it is a pleasurable romp even if you cut the trip short to just an hour or two. That is because the trail runs midway up naked slopes, offering spectacular views of Deer Creek Canyon's basaltic cliffs, spires, and of the stream below. The trailhead is at the southeast border of the wilderness, and right from the start, it is routed along the north shore of Deer Creek. Iron Mountain at 3,274 feet is located to the immediate north. The trail is directed along the stream into the wilderness interior, skirting past the northern edge of what is called the Graham Pinery—a dense island of ponderosa pine growing on a mountain terrace. A bonus is good trout fishing in Deer Creek, birdwatching for hawks, eagles and falcons at the rock cliffs, and a large variety of wildlife, including rattlesnakes (here's your warning), wild pigs, and lots of squirrels and quail.

---

## 8. DEVIL'S DEN TRAIL          9.0 mi/1.0 day

**Reference:** In Ishi Wilderness east of Red Bluff; map C2, grid d8.

**User groups:** Hikers, dogs and horses. No mountain bikes are allowed. No wheelchair facilities.

**Permits:** A campfire permit is required for hikers planning to camp. Parking and access are free.

**Directions:** From Interstate 5 at Red Bluff, turn east on Highway 36 and drive to the town of Paynes Creek. Turn south on Little Giant Mill Road (Road 202) and travel approximately seven miles until you reach an intersection. Turn south at Ponderosa Way and drive about 32.5 miles to the Devil's Den Trailhead, just south of the Deer Creek Trailhead.

**Maps:** For a free trail map, contact the Almanor Ranger District at the address below. To obtain a topographic map of the area, ask for Panther Spring and Butte Meadows from the USGS.

**Who to contact:** Lassen National Forest, Almanor Ranger District, P.O. Box 767, Chester, CA 96020; (916) 258-2141.

**Trail notes:** The Devil's Den Trailhead is less than a half mile from the Deer Creek Trailhead, but there the similarity ends. This trail includes a rough climb, beastly in summer, with no water available over the stretch where you will need it most. The main attraction here is that the trail is routed through a series of habitat zones over the course of the first 3.5 miles, providing a series of striking contrasts. The trail starts easy, routed along Deer Creek for the first mile. Enjoy yourself because what follows is not exactly a picnic. The trail turns left, climbing up Little Pine Creek all the way to the ridge top, with the last mile on an old, abandoned road, hot and chunky. In the process, the vegetation changes from riparian along the creek, to woodland on the slopes, then chaparral on the ridge. In addition, an island of conifers, the Graham Pinery, is available for viewing with a quarter-mile sidetrip.

## 9. BIG OAK TRAIL        1.0 mi/0.5 hr

*Reference:* **At the head of Black Butte Reservoir west of Chico; map C2, grid f0.**

*User groups:* Hikers and dogs. No horses or mountain bikes are allowed. No wheelchair facilities.

*Permits:* No permits are required. Parking and access are free.

*Directions:* From Interstate 5 at Orland, take the Black Butte Lake exit. Drive 10 miles west on Newville Road, then turn left on Road 206. Follow it to Road 200A and continue to the trailhead.

*Maps:* A free brochure is available by contacting the U.S. Corps of Engineers at the address below. To obtain a topographic map of the area, ask for Julian Rocks from the USGS.

*Who to contact:* U.S. Corps of Engineers, Black Butte Lake, 19225 Newville Road, Orland, CA 95963; (916) 865-4781.

*Trail notes:* The Army Corps of Engineers has really screwed up some of California's once-great riverside habitat with massive rip-rap projects, but here they actually did something right: They protected Stony Creek by doing nothing but building a trail (of course, they had to build a dam here first). The route, an easy jaunt, follows the Stony Creek drainage above the head of Black Butte Reservoir. The riparian habitat here is in a protected state, providing an excellent area to see wildlife and birds. It has recently become part of California's Watchable Wildlife system. Alas, this hike is not without problems. First is the weather, which is close to intolerable in the summer, a real temperature tantrum, and that's when most people have time to visit the area. Second is that during the prime times, spring and fall, it seems just about everybody camping at the lake gets around to walking this trail (hey, you can't blame them), so you can expect to run into folks. The best time for hiking is at dusk, when wildlife viewing is at its best.

## LEAVE NO TRACE TIPS

### Sanitation

If no refuse facility is available:

• Deposit human waste in "cat holes" dug six to eight inches deep. Cover and disguise the cat hole when finished.

• Deposit human waste at least 75 paces (200 feet) from any water source or camp.

• Use toilet paper sparingly. When finished, carefully burn it in the cat hole, then bury it.

• If no appropriate burial locations are available, such as in popular wilderness camps above tree line in hard granite settings— Devil's Punchbowl in the Siskiyou Wilderness is such an example— then all human refuse should be double-bagged and packed out.

• At boat-in campsites, chemical toilets are required. Chemical toilets can also solve the problem of larger groups camping or long stays at one location where no facilities are available.

• To wash dishes or your body, carry water away from the source and use small amounts of biodegradable soap. Scatter dishwater after all food particles have been removed.

• Scour your campsites for even the tiniest piece of trash and any other evidence of your stay. Pack out all the trash you can, even if it's not yours. Finding cigarette butts, for instance, provides special irritation for most campers. Pick them up and discard them properly.

• Never litter. Never. Or you become the enemy of all others.

**6 PCT SECTIONS**
**24 TRAILS**
**PAGES 174-193**

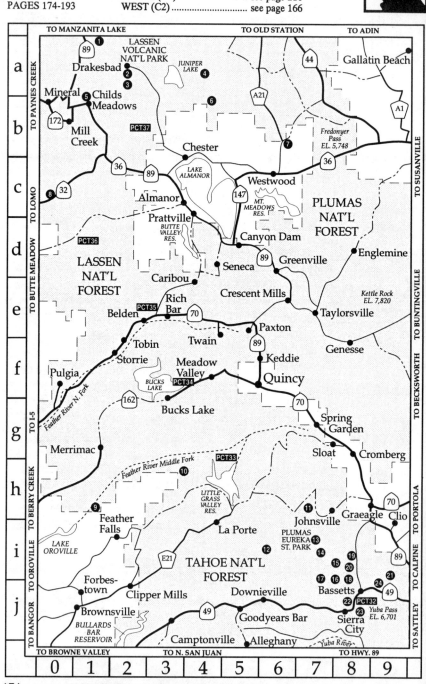

**Map C3 featuring:** Lassen Volcanic National Park, Drakesbad, Lake Almanor, Lassen National Forest, Caribou Wilderness, Plumas National Forest, Lake Oroville, Plumas-Eureka State Park, Quincy, Downieville, Tahoe National Forest, Smith Lake, Silver Lake, Bucks Lake Wilderness, Sierra City, Packer Lake, Gold Lakes Basin, Sardine Lake, Fowler Creek, Little Grass Valley Reservoir, Humboldt Summit

## 1. BUMPASS HELL TRAIL        6.0 mi/3.0 hrs

*Reference:* **In Lassen Volcanic National Park east of Red Bluff; map C3, grid a1.**

*User groups:* Hikers only. No dogs, horses or mountain bikes are allowed. No wheelchair facilities.

*Permits:* A wilderness permit is required for hikers planning to camp in the backcountry. A $5 national park day-use fee is charged for each vehicle.

*Directions:* From Interstate 5 at Red Bluff, turn east on Highway 36 and drive 47 miles. Turn north on Highway 89 and travel 4.5 miles to the park entrance. Continue 6.25 miles to the trailhead on the right.

*Maps:* Trail maps are available for $3.95. To order a map, contact Loomis Museum, c/o Lassen Volcanic National Park at the address below. To obtain a topographic map of the area, ask for Lassen Peak from the USGS.

*Who to contact:* Lassen Volcanic National Park, P.O. Box 100, Mineral, CA 96063; (916) 595-4444.

*Trail notes:* Bumpass Hell is like a walk into the land of perdition, complete with steam vents, boiling mud pots and hot springs. It is all set amid volcanic rock, prehistoric looking and a bit creepy, as if at any moment a dinosaur will come around the bend and start eating tourists. The trip to Bumpass Hell is the most popular hike in the park, and it makes sense because it is not only the park's largest thermal area, but an excellent morning walk. The trail starts with a gradual 500-foot climb over the first mile, then descends 250 feet into the thermal area. It sits in a pocket just below Bumpass Mountain (8,753 feet), with a self-guiding leaflet available that explains the area. There are typically large numbers of tourists at Bumpass Hell, but you can get beyond them by extending your trip to Cold Boiling Lake, another 3.5 miles (one-way), which includes two steep portions of trail.

## 2. DEVIL'S KITCHEN TRAIL        4.4 mi/2.5 hrs

*Reference:* **At Drakesbad in Lassen Volcanic National Park; map C3, grid a2.**

*User groups:* Hikers only. No dogs, horses or mountain bikes are allowed. No wheelchair facilities.

*Permits:* A wilderness permit is required for hikers planning to camp in the backcountry. A $5 national park day-use fee is charged for each vehicle.

*Directions:* From Chester on Highway 36, turn north on Warner Valley Road and drive 16.5 miles to the trailhead, located about a half mile past Warner Valley Campground.

*Maps:* Trail maps are available for $3.95. To order a map, contact Loomis

Museum, c/o Lassen Volcanic National Park at the address below. To obtain a topographic map of the area, ask for Reading Peak from the USGS.

*Who to contact:* Lassen Volcanic National Park, P.O. Box 100, Mineral, CA 96063; (916) 595-4444.

*Trail notes:* Drakesbad is the undiscovered Lassen, beautiful, wild and remote. It gets missed by nearly everybody because its access is obscure and circuitous out of Chester. In other words, there is no way to get here when entering from either of the main park entrances. But those who make it here will find a quiet paradise, along with this easy trip to Devil's Kitchen, a unique geologic thermal area. The trail is an easy hike, heading west above Hot Springs Creek. After two miles, it drops down into this barren pocket of steaming vents and boiling pots, where you will immediately see why it was tagged as Devil's Kitchen. A great sidetrip is available here, but few people know about it. From Devil's Kitchen, if you walk just a quarter-mile upstream on Hot Springs Creek, you'll discover a delightful little waterfall.

---

## 3. DRAKE LAKE TRAIL     4.5 mi/2.75 hrs

*Reference:* At Drakesbad in Lassen Volcanic National Park; map C3, grid a2.

*User groups:* Hikers only. No dogs, horses or mountain bikes are allowed. No wheelchair facilities.

*Permits:* A wilderness permit is required for hikers planning to camp in the backcountry. A $5 national park day-use fee is charged for each vehicle.

*Directions:* From Chester on Highway 36, turn north on Warner Valley Road and drive 16.5 miles to the trailhead, located about a half mile past Warner Valley Campground.

*Maps:* Trail maps are available for $3.95. To order a map, contact Loomis Museum, c/o Lassen Volcanic National Park at the address below. To obtain a topographic map of the area, ask for Reading Peak from the USGS.

*Who to contact:* Lassen Volcanic National Park, P.O. Box 100, Mineral, CA 96063; (916) 595-4444.

*Trail notes:* Drake Lake is one of our favorite spots in Lassen Park, a beautiful alpine lake where deer are more plentiful than people. It sits in a remote forested pocket, very secluded and pristine, and is just difficult enough of a climb that many take a pass on the trip. From the trailhead at Drakesbad, at about 5,700 feet, it's nearly an 800-foot climb over the course of two miles to Drake Lake (6,482 feet). Midway up the grade, it gets quite steep and stays that way for nearly 45 minutes. The lake is the payoff, emerald green and circled by firs. After you catch your breath, you may feel like jumping in and cooling off, particularly if it's a hot summer day. Well, we've got news for you. In early summer the water is still ice cold, and just when you realize that, a battalion of mosquitoes will show up and start feasting on all your bare, sumptuous flesh. Then what? Jump in and freeze your buns? Stand there and get devoured? Heck no, you'll have your clothes back on in record time.

---

## 4. JUNIPER LAKE LOOP     12.0 mi/2.0 days

*Reference:* In Lassen Volcanic National Park north of Lake Almanor; map C3, grid a4.

*User groups:* Hikers only. No dogs, horses or mountain bikes are allowed. No wheelchair facilities.

*Permits:* A wilderness permit is required for hikers planning to camp in the backcountry. A $5 national park day-use fee is charged for each vehicle.

*Directions:* From Chester on Highway 36, turn north on Juniper Lake Road and drive 11 miles to the trailhead near the ranger station. The access road is quite rough, trailers and motor homes are not recommended.

*Maps:* Trail maps are available for $3.95. To order a map, contact Loomis Museum, c/o Lassen Volcanic National Park at the address below. To obtain a topographic map of the area, ask for Mount Harkness from the USGS.

*Who to contact:* Lassen Volcanic National Park, P.O. Box 100, Mineral, CA 96063; (916) 595-4444.

*Trail notes:* The Juniper Lake Loop explores Lassen Park's least known yet most beautiful back country, with nine lakes, many lookouts and pretty trail camps along this 12-mile route. It starts at the trailhead adjacent to the Juniper Lake Ranger Station, a long bumpy ride out of Chester just to get there. If you arrive late, a campground is available at the lake, elevation 6,792 feet. At the north end of Juniper Lake, the trail heads straight north, and though it has plenty of up and down, along with a pretty level stretch through Cameron Meadow, it is mostly down, descending 800 feet to Snag Lake, elevation 6,076 feet. Here the trail turns left and climbs 600 feet in less than a mile, topping a ridge and then pouring out to Rainbow Lake, a mile later to Lower Twin Lake (6,537 feet), and in another mile, Swan Lake (6,628 feet). Any of these can make for a good trail camp. The second day, you loop back, skirt the south flank of Crater Butte (7,267 feet), head past Horseshoe Lake and then to the starting point. Alas, this trip is not flawless. The fishing is poor, mosquitoes are rampant in the early summer, and nights are very cold in the fall. Note: From the north end of Juniper Lake, a great sidetrip is the half-mile, 400-foot climb to Inspiration Point, which provides a memorable view of Lassen Park's backcountry.

# 5. SPENCER MEADOW TRAIL 10.0 mi/1.0 day

*Reference:* **In Lassen National Forest just south of Lassen National Park; map C3, grid b0.**

*User groups:* Hikers, dogs, horses and mountain bikes. No wheelchair facilities.

*Permits:* No permits are required. Parking and access are free.

*Directions:* From Interstate 5 at Red Bluff, turn east on Highway 36 and drive 43 miles to Mineral. Continue east on Highway 36 for about seven miles to the trailhead parking area on the left.

*Maps:* For a map of Lassen National Forest, send $3 to USDA-Forest Service, 630 Sansome Street, San Francisco, CA 94111. To obtain a topographic map of the area, ask for Childs Meadows from the USGS.

*Who to contact:* Lassen National Forest, Almanor Ranger District, P.O. Box 767, Chester, CA 96020; (916) 258-2141.

*Trail notes:* Spencer Meadow is a pastoral scene, a high mountain meadow on the southern flank of Lassen. It is here that explorers can discover an effervescent spring pouring forth, the source of Mill Creek, the creation of the headwaters of a Sacramento River tributary. Hiking access is easy, with the trailhead located at a parking area just off Highway 36. From here you hike straight north toward Lassen on the Spencer Meadow Trail. Over the course of five miles, the trail passes a small spring (about halfway in, look for the faint spur trail on the left), then tiny Patricia Lake (on the right, hidden), and finally Spencer Meadow and the Mill Creek Spring. An insider's note is that there is a trailhead closer to Spencer Meadow on Forest Service Road 29N40, but reaching it involves a long, rough, complicated drive on back roads.

## 6. INDIAN MEADOW TRAIL   6.0 mi/2.0 days

*Reference:* **On the southern boundary of the Caribou Wilderness north of Lake Almanor; map C3, grid b4.**
*User groups:* Hikers, dogs and horses. No mountain bikes are allowed. No wheelchair facilities.
*Permits:* No permits are required. Parking and access are free.
*Directions:* From Chester, drive five miles east on Highway 36 and turn north on Forest Service Road 10. Drive approximately 9.5 miles, then turn left on Forest Service Road 30N25 and continue to the trailhead.
*Maps:* For a map of Lassen National Forest, send $3 to USDA-Forest Service, 630 Sansome Street, San Francisco, CA 94111. To obtain a topographic map of the area, ask for Childs Meadows from the USGS.
*Who to contact:* Lassen National Forest, Almanor Ranger District, P.O. Box 767, Chester, CA 96020; (916) 258-2141.
*Trail notes:* Hidden between South Caribou Mountain and Black Cinder Rock is a little alpine pocket where dozens of small alpine lakes are sprinkled about the southern Caribou Wilderness. It is a slice of paradise that some hikers call the "Hiking Lakes." The trail out of Indian Meadow is a loop route that crosses right through these lakes, including the area's larger and most divine settings, Beauty Lake, Long Lake, Posey Lake and Evelyn Lake. While the trip can be made in a day, you likely won't feel like leaving, and we recommend planning an easy overnight backpacking trip. Another bonus of an overnight trip is that you can take the side trip up to Hidden Lakes, a series of several small but pretty waters, set just below South Caribou Mountain. After arriving at the trailhead at Indian Meadow, the trip starts easily enough, crossing Hay Meadow. In another mile, you will reach Beauty Lake, the first of five major lakes on this loop hike. They are all good for swimming, although a bit cold, and Beauty and Posey have the best trout fishing. Note that although the Caribou Wilderness abuts Lassen Park, it is often overlooked in the big park's shadow. That is to your benefit, as long as you know about this trail.

## 7. BIZZ JOHNSON   25 mi. one way/3.0 days

*Reference:* **In Lassen National Forest west of Susanville; map C3, grid b6.**
*User groups:* Hikers, dogs, horses and mountain bikes. No wheelchair facilities.
*Permits:* No permits are required. Parking and access are free.
*Directions:* From Westwood on Highway 36, turn north on County Road A21 and drive four miles to the trailhead parking area.
*Maps:* For a free brochure, contact the Bureau of Land Management at the address below. For a map of Lassen National Forest, send $3 to USDA-Forest Service, 630 Sansome Street, San Francisco, CA 94111. To obtain topographic maps of the area, ask for Westwood East, Fredonyer Pass and Susanville from the USGS.

*Who to contact:* Lassen National Forest, Eagle Lake Ranger District, 55 South Sacramento Street, Susanville, CA 96130; (916) 257-2151, or Bureau of Land Management, Eagle Lake Resource Area, 2545 Riverside Drive, Susanville, CA 96130; (916) 257-5381.

*Trail notes:* In the 1960s, when Shasta legend John Reginato heard that Southern Pacific was going to abandon a rail line between Westwood and Susanville, he urged that it be converted to a hiking trail. The idea struck home, and the Bureau of Land Management worked with the U.S. Forest Service to develop and refine it. Now in the 1990s, this trail is one of the true multiple-use routes in Northern California where there is plenty of room for hikers, mountain bikers and horseback riders. In the winter, it makes a great trip on cross-country skis or on a snowmobile, with many trailheads providing different access points. The route traces the old Fernley and Lassen railroad line. It follows the Susan River Canyon for most of the trail, features beautiful views in many areas, and also passes through two old railroad tunnels. Yet it is raw and primitive. You will not cross any developed areas. Guess they had it right when they built that first railroad line.

---

# 8. DEER CREEK TRAIL          8.0 mi/1.0 day

*Reference:* **In Lassen National Forest along Highway 32 west of Lake Almanor; map C3, grid c0.**

*User groups:* Hikers, dogs and horses. Mountain bikes are not advised. No wheelchair facilities.

*Permits:* No permits are required. Parking and access are free.

*Directions:* From Chester, drive 12 miles west on Highway 36. Turn south on Highway 32 and continue approximately 12 miles to the parking area on the right.

*Maps:* For a map of Lassen National Forest, send $3 to USDA-Forest Service, 630 Sansome Street, San Francisco, CA 94111. To obtain a topographic map of the area, ask for Onion Butte from the USGS.

*Who to contact:* Lassen National Forest, Almanor Ranger District, P.O. Box 767, Chester, CA 96020; (916) 258-2141.

*Trail notes:* The Deer Creek Trail has all the ingredients to make it ideal for a trout angler: A pretty stream running right alongside the trail, good access throughout, and fish—often plenty of them in the summer months. From the parking area, the trail is routed downstream along the river for about 10 miles, but rarely does anybody ever walk all the way to the end. Instead they take their time, fishing along the way, maybe stopping a bit to enjoy a pretty waterfall about a mile from the trailhead. In the summer, Deer Creek is cold and clear, tumbling its way over rocks and into pools, seemingly with trout in every one. It is no accident. This river is stocked nearly every week, and in the course of a year those stocks total more than 50,000 rainbow trout and 6,000 brook trout. While access is good off Highway 32, note that it is a narrow two-laner with many low-speed turns, and that driving up from Chico with a trailer or in a motor home is not advised.

## 9. FEATHER FALLS NATIONAL TRAIL

**8.0 mi/6.0 hrs**

*Reference:* **In Plumas National Forest east of Lake Oroville; map C3, grid h2.**

*User groups:* Hikers and dogs. No horses or mountain bikes are allowed. No wheelchair facilities.

*Permits:* No permits are required. Parking and access are free.

*Directions:* From Oroville, take Highway 162 east and drive about 10 miles to Forbestown Road. Take Forbestown Road east six miles to Lumpkin Road. Turn left on Lumpkin Road and proceed eight miles to the small town of Feather Falls. Just beyond town limits, turn north at the sign for Feather Falls and proceed to the parking area at the end of the road.

*Maps:* For a map of Plumas National Forest, send $3 to USDA-Forest Service, 630 Sansome Street, San Francisco, CA 94111. To obtain a topographic map of the area, ask for Brush Creek from the USGS.

*Who to contact:* Plumas National Forest, LaPorte Ranger District, P.O. Drawer 369, Challenge, CA 95925; (916) 675-2462.

*Trail notes:* Few things worth remembering come easy, and so it is at Feather Falls. It's heaven to look at, hell to reach. At 640 feet, it is the sixth tallest waterfall in America, free-falling in a silver band of water into a granite canyon, the kind of sight that can leave you feeling refreshed for weeks. It's a good thing, because you will likely feel like a dry sponge by the time you get there. The trail climbs 2,500 feet over a four-mile span, very steep in parts. Add in hot weather, typical here in the summer, and you're looking at payback time if you're not physically fit. Even so, this is by far the most popular trail in the region, and gets heavy use in the summer. Be sure to get an early start so the climb is made in cool weather, bring plenty of water to keep your body hydrated, and keep plugging away. Feather Falls is worth the trip.

## 10. HARTMAN BAR NATIONAL TRAIL

**4.0 mi/3.0 hrs**

*Reference:* **In Plumas National Forest east of Lake Oroville; map C3, grid h3.**

*User groups:* Hikers and dogs. No horses or mountain bikes are allowed. No wheelchair facilities.

*Permits:* No permits are required. Parking and access are free.

*Directions:* From LaPorte, drive east on Quincy-LaPorte Road and drive 1.5 miles, then turn north on Little Grass Valley Road and drive to Black Rock Campground. Turn left on Forest Service Road 94 and travel to Forest Service Road 22N42Y, turn right and continue to the parking area at the end of the road.

*Maps:* For a map of Plumas National Forest, send $3 to USDA-Forest Service, 630 Sansome Street, San Francisco, CA 94111. To obtain topographic maps of the area, ask for Cascade and Haskins Valley from the USGS.

*Who to contact:* Plumas National Forest, LaPorte Ranger District, P.O. Drawer 369, Challenge, CA 95925; (916) 675-2462.

*Trail notes:* Hikers often pay for their pleasure, and this hike involves two installments. The trail descends from the Hartman Ridge down the canyon to Hartman Bar on the Middle Fork Feather River. Going down will have your toes jamming into your boots, and the trip back can have your heart firing off like cannon shots. But awaiting is the Middle Fork Feather, one of the prettiest streams you have ever seen, and with some of the best trout fishing as well. In fact, of the hundreds of trout streams in California, the Middle Fork Feather is clearly in the top five. In addition, the world's tallest Ponderosa pine is along the trail. If you don't like to fish, but would rather explore further, a footbridge crosses the stream and climbs up the other side of the canyon, meeting Catrell Creek in half a mile. If you want to split the trip in two, the primitive Dan Beebe Camp is available along the river.

## 11. EUREKA PEAK LOOP    3.0 mi/2.0 hrs

*Reference:* In Plumas-Eureka State Park south of Quincy; map C3, grid h7.

*User groups:* Hikers only. No dogs, horses or mountain bikes are allowed. No wheelchair facilities.

*Permits:* No permits are required. Parking and access are free.

*Directions:* From the junction of Highways 70 and 89 near Blairsden, turn south on Highway 89. Drive a short distance, then turn west on County Road A14 (Graeagle-Johnsville Road) and proceed to the park entrance. The trailhead is located at the north end of Eureka Lake.

*Maps:* For a trail map, send 75 cents to Plumas-Eureka State Park at the address below. To obtain a topographic map of the area, ask for Johnsville from the USGS.

*Who to contact:* Plumas-Eureka State Park, 310 Johnsville Road, Blairsden, CA 96103; (916) 836-2380 or (916) 525-7232.

*Trail notes:* From Eureka Peak, elevation 7,447 feet, you get a panorama of the southern Sierra Nevada. That includes all the peaks of the Gold Lakes Basin, with Mt. Elwell (7,812 feet) most prominent to the south, and Plumas Forest to the north and west, crowned by Blue Nose Mountain (7,290 feet), Stafford Mountain (7,019 feet) and Beartrap Mountain (7,232 feet). It is the view that compels people to make the climb, a serious three-mile loop, with the first half being a grunt to the top. The trailhead starts at Eureka Lake, elevation 6,300 feet, the feature destination for most visitors to the state park. Many people start this trail by accident, having seen the trailhead sign while visiting the lake. That is a mistake. The trip should be planned, bringing plenty of water and snacks with you to enjoy from the summit.

## 12. CHIMNEY ROCK TRAIL    2.0 mi/1.25 hrs

*Reference:* North of Downieville in Tahoe National Forest; map C3, grid i6.

*User groups:* Hikers, dogs and horses. Mountain bikes are not advised. No wheelchair facilities.

*Permits:* No permits are required. Parking and access are free.

*Directions:* From Downieville, drive west on Highway 49 for two-tenths of a mile to Saddleback Road, a dirt road. Drive eight miles north to a five-way intersection. Proceed straight through onto Road 25-23-1. Drive three-tenths of a mile until you come to a Y intersection. Go straight through for one mile to another intersection, and go straight through again. Continue for one mile, then bear right on Road 25-23-1-2 (look for the "Dead End" sign). Continue about a half mile to an intersection and head straight through. After about 100 yards, bear left on an obscure road (Poker Flat Trail) and continue for one mile to a turnout at the base of Bunker Hill. Park here and hike in six-tenths of a mile to the trailhead. The total mileage from Downieville is 13 miles. Note: Sections of the road are quite rough.

*Maps:* For a map of Tahoe National Forest, send $3 to USDA-Forest Service, 630 Sansome Street, San Francisco, CA 94111. To obtain a topographic map of the area, ask for Mt. Fillmore from the USGS.

*Who to contact:* Tahoe National Forest, Downieville Ranger District, 15924 Highway 49, Camptonville, CA 95922; (916) 288-3231.

*Trail notes:* Chimney Rock is a huge volcanic cone that is 12 feet in diameter at its base, then rises nearly straight up for 25 feet. There are great views from the top, well worth the trip. Yet because the route to the trailhead is so complicated, few either know of Chimney Rock or get around to making the trip. From the trailhead at 6,400 feet, it's a 400-foot climb over the course of a mile to reach it. While enjoying the perch atop Chimney Rock, you may choose to extend your trip or just make the easy descent back to the trailhead. The trip can be lengthened into an eight-mile loop. To do so, from Chimney Rock, take the trail eastward. It descends at first, the rises again around Needle Point and Rattlesnake Peak. For explorers, additional sidetrips into beautiful Empire Creek Canyon are possible when you intersect with the Empire Creek Trail.

---

# 13. UPPER JAMISON TRAIL    8.2 mi/2.0 days

*Reference:* **In Plumas-Eureka State Park on the northern boundary of Gold Lakes Basin, south of Quincy; map C3, grid i7.**

*User groups:* Hikers only. No dogs, horses or mountain bikes are allowed. No wheelchair facilities.

*Permits:* No permits are required. Parking and access are free.

*Directions:* From the junction of Highways 70 and 89 near Blairsden, turn south on Highway 89. Drive a short distance, then turn west on County Road A14 (Graeagle-Johnsville Road) and proceed to the park entrance. At the museum, turn left on Johnsville-LaPorte Road and continue to the trailhead at Upper Jamison Campground.

*Maps:* For a trail map, send 75 cents to Plumas-Eureka State Park at the address below. To obtain a topographic map of the area, ask for Johnsville from the USGS.

*Who to contact:* Plumas-Eureka State Park, 310 Johnsville Road, Blairsden, CA 96103; (916) 836-2380 or (916) 525-7232.

*Trail notes:* There is no reason to rush your way through this trail, which passes Grass Lake, Jamison Lake and Rock Lake, but rather take your time at it, stopping to enjoy the lakes along the way. Or take our suggestion and turn it into an overnight backpacking trip. The trail provides a glimpse of the beauty of the northern section of Lakes Basin Recreation Area, a country of beautiful alpine lakes and beveled granite mountains. From the trailhead near the parking area for Upper Jamison Campground, start the trip by taking the Grass Lake Trail. It follows along Little Jamison Creek, rising two miles to Grass Lake, with the trail skirting along the east side of the lake. For many on a day hike, this is far enough. However, we urge you to forge onward. It's another two miles to Jamison Lake, with the trail climbing more steeply, then crossing the creek twice before arriving at the outlet of Jamison Lake.

Another quarter mile will route you over to Rock Lake, a pretty sight below Mt. Elwell, elevation 7,812 feet. Good trail camps are available at Rock Lake, Jamison Lake and Grass Lake.

## 14. MOUNT ELWELL TRAIL    6.0 mi/3.5 hrs

*Reference:* **At Smith Lake in Gold Lakes Basin south of Quincy; map C3, grid i7.**

*User groups:* Hikers, dogs and horses. Mountain bikes are not allowed. No wheelchair facilities.

*Permits:* No permits are required. Parking and access are free.

*Directions:* From the junction of Highways 70 and 89 near Blairsden, turn south on Highway 89 and drive about three miles. Turn west on Forest Service Road 24 (Gold Lake Highway) and drive until you see the sign for Gray Eagle Lodge. Turn right and continue to the trailhead.

*Maps:* For a map of Plumas National Forest, send $3 to USDA-Forest Service, 630 Sansome Street, San Francisco, CA 94111. To obtain a topographic map of the area, ask for Gold Lake from the USGS.

*Who to contact:* Plumas National Forest, Beckwourth Ranger District, P.O. Box 7, Blairsden, CA 96103; (916) 836-2575.

*Trail notes:* From atop Mt. Elwell, 7,812 feet, you are surrounded by the Gold Lakes Basin, a wildland filled with alpine lakes and granite mountains. You'll find yourself dreaming of the days when you might visit them. This trail is a good way to start. It begins at Smith Lake at 6,700 feet on the Smith Lake-Gray Eagle Lodge Trail and climbs all the way, 1,100 feet over the course of three miles, to the top of Mt. Elwell. It makes a great day trip for folks staying at the Gray Eagle Lodge at Smith Lake. Though few go onward from Mt. Elwell, the trip can be extended simply enough. The trail continues past Mt. Elwell, descending 0.75 miles to the Long Lake Trail junction, then another three-quarters of a mile to a four-wheel-drive route.

## 15. LAKES BASIN TRAILHEAD   5.6 mi/3.0 hrs

*Reference:* **At Silver Lake on the eastern border of Bucks Lake Wilderness north of Sierra City; map C3, grid i7.**

*User groups:* Hikers, dogs and horses. Mountain bikes are not allowed. No wheelchair facilities.

*Permits:* No permits are required. Parking and access are free.

*Directions:* From the junction of Highways 70 and 89 near Blairsden, turn south on Highway 89 and drive about three miles. Turn west on Forest Service Road 24 (Gold Lake Highway) and drive until you see the sign for the Lakes Basin Trailhead.

*Maps:* For a map of Plumas National Forest, send $3 to USDA-Forest Service, 630 Sansome Street, San Francisco, CA 94111. To obtain a topographic map of the area, ask for Gold Lake from the USGS.

*Who to contact:* Plumas National Forest, Beckwourth Ranger District, P.O. Box 7, Blairsden, CA 96103; (916) 836-2575.

*Trail notes:* Long Lake is one of the celestial settings in the heaven-like Gold Lakes Basin. It is the feature destination on this hike, a good tromp that includes some steep rocky portions. The trailhead is at the Lakes Basin Campground at 6,300 feet. From here, the trail is clear and well-maintained, but requires a huff and a puff, marching 2.3 miles. Here you will see the turnoff for a spur trail that is routed one-half mile to Long Lake, and one mile to little Silver Lake. Long Lake is always a surprise to newcomers, much larger than most high-country lakes, and very pretty. The trail skirts along the southeast shoreline.

*Special note:* No camping is permitted at either Long Lake or Silver Lake.

## 16. BUTCHER RANCH TRAIL    8.0 mi/5.0 hrs

*Reference:* **West of Packer Lake in Tahoe National Forest; map C3, grid i7.**
*User groups:* Hikers, dogs and horses. Mountain bikes are not allowed. No wheelchair facilities.
*Permits:* No permits are required. Parking and access are free.
*Directions:* From Sierra City, drive five miles east on Highway 49, then turn north on Gold Lake Highway at Bassetts. Drive 1.4 miles, then turn left and cross the Salmon Creek Bridge. Drive three-tenths of a mile and turn right on Packer Lake Road. Continue 2.5 miles to Packer Lake. The road forks here; take the left fork (Packer Saddle Road) and drive 2.1 miles. Turn left at the sign for Sierra Buttes Lookout. Drive a half mile and bear right, continue another half mile to a sign indicating Butcher Ranch, take the right fork and drive seven-tenths of a mile to a sign directing you to the trailhead. Note: The road is quite steep and is recommended for high-clearance or four-wheel-drive vehicles only. Passenger cars can park at the sign for the trailhead and hike in a half mile to the trailhead.
*Maps:* For a map of Tahoe National Forest, send $3 to USDA-Forest Service, 630 Sansome Street, San Francisco, CA 94111. To obtain a topographic map of the area, ask for Sierra City from the USGS.
*Who to contact:* Tahoe National Forest, Downieville Ranger District, 15924 Highway 49, Camptonville, CA 95922; (916) 288-3231.
*Trail notes:* This is a hike for those who yearn for a mountain canyon paradise where wildflowers are abundant, fishing is good, and a sidetrip will take you to a pristine stream with gorgeous deep pools. The Butcher Ranch Trail furnishes all of that and more, and getting there isn't even too difficult. It's the getting back that will wear you out, but hey, we'll get to that. The trailhead is obscure and hard to reach, and that keeps many people away. When you start hiking, you may wonder why we rated it a 9 for difficulty. After all, the trail follows the contour of Butcher Creek for 1.5 miles to the confluence of Butcher Ranch and Pauley Creeks. You then parallel Pauley Creek, with its deep and beautiful pools. On the way down, you will drop nearly 2,000 feet in elevation over the course of four miles; try not to laugh on your way down. Because what goes down must come up, and on the return, you will be wondering why you ever talked yourself into this trip.

## 17. PAULEY CREEK TRAIL    15.0 mi/2.0 days

*Reference:* **West of Packer Lake in Tahoe National Forest; map C3, grid i7.**
*User groups:* Hikers, dogs and horses. Mountain bikes are not allowed. No wheelchair facilities.
*Permits:* No permits are required. Parking and access are free.
*Directions:* From Sierra City, drive five miles east on Highway 49 and turn north on Gold Lake Highway at Bassetts. Drive 1.4 miles, then turn left and

cross the Salmon Creek Bridge. Drive three-tenths of a mile and turn right on Packer Lake Road. Continue for 2.5 miles to Packer Lake. The road forks here; take the left fork (Packer Saddle Road) and drive 2.1 miles. Turn left at the sign for Sierra Buttes Lookout. Drive a half mile and bear right, continue another half mile to a sign indicating Butcher Ranch. Take the right fork and drive seven-tenths of a mile to a sign directing you to the trailhead. Note: The road is quite steep and is recommended for high-clearance or four-wheel-drive vehicles only. Passenger cars can park at the trailhead sign and hike in a half mile to the Butcher Creek Trailhead. To reach to Pauley Creek Trail, you must hike 1.5 miles west on the Butcher Creek Trail to its intersection with Pauley Creek.

*Maps:* For a map of Tahoe National Forest, send $3 to USDA-Forest Service, 630 Sansome Street, San Francisco, CA 94111. To obtain topographic maps of the area, ask for Downieville, Sierra City and Gold Lake from the USGS.

*Who to contact:* Tahoe National Forest, Downieville Ranger District, 15924 Highway 49, Camptonville, CA 95922; (916) 288-3231.

*Trail notes:* It is extremely rare when a sidetrip hike is awarded with its own separate mention, but the Pauley Creek Trail is one of those rare places that deserves a detailed listing. This is a side trip from the Butcher Ranch Trail, hike number 16. By extending that walk on the Pauley Creek Trail, you will enter a land where there are streamside trail camps, spectacular wildflower blooms in early summer, and excellent trout fishing. Wildlife is also abundant in this watershed. The trailhead is difficult to reach and the return hike out of the canyon back to the trailhead involves a 2,000-foot climb. So much for the rough stuff. It is beautiful all along the stream and rare to see other people. Out here you can feel as if you have entered a time machine—explore a wild land as if it was 200 years ago.

---

# 18. DEER LAKE TRAIL          5.0 mi/3.5 hrs

*Reference:* West of Packer Lake in Tahoe National Forest; map C3, grid i8.

*User groups:* Hikers, dogs and horses. No mountain bikes are allowed. No wheelchair facilities.

*Permits:* No permits are required. Parking and access are free.

*Directions:* From Sierra City, drive five miles east on Highway 49 and turn north on Gold Lake Highway at Bassetts. Drive 1.4 miles and turn left and cross the Salmon Creek Bridge. Drive three-tenths of a mile, then turn right on Packer Lake Road. Continue two miles to the trailhead. Parking is available in the Packsaddle camping area just opposite the trailhead.

*Maps:* For a map of Tahoe National Forest, send $3 to USDA-Forest Service, 630 Sansome Street, San Francisco, CA 94111. To obtain a topographic map of the area, ask for Sierra City from the USGS.

*Who to contact:* Tahoe National Forest, Downieville Ranger District, 15924 Highway 49, Camptonville, CA 95922; (916) 288-3231.

*Trail notes:* Most lakes are green, but Deer Lake is the deepest azure blue you can imagine, and with the spectacular Sierra Buttes in the background, it is easy to understand why this trip is so popular. And popular it is, with this trail getting some of the heaviest use of any in this section of Tahoe National Forest. It's a 2.5-mile hike to the lake, in the process climbing 1,000 feet, topping out at 7,110 feet. From the trailhead, you will climb up through a basin and receive a sweeping view of the massive Sierra Buttes and the surrounding forested slopes. As you head on, you will cross a signed spur trail, a quarter-mile route to Grass Lake. It is well worth the short detour; approach quietly because deer are common here. Then it is onward, over the ridge and down to Deer Lake. On warm evenings, the brook trout can leave countless circles while feeding on surface insects. This hike has it all, and alas, that is why it often includes other people.

## 19. FRAZIER FALLS TRAIL  1.0 mi/1.0 hr

*Reference:* **In Bucks Lake Wilderness north of Sierra City; map C3, grid i8.**
*User groups:* Hikers, dogs and horses. Mountain bikes are not allowed. No wheelchair facilities.
*Permits:* No permits are required. Parking and access are free.
*Directions:* From the junction of Highways 70 and 89 near Blairsden, turn south on Highway 89 and drive about three miles. Turn west on Forest Service Road 24 (Gold Lake Highway) and drive until you see the sign for Frazier Falls. Turn left and continue to the end of the road.
*Maps:* For a map of Plumas National Forest, send $3 to USDA-Forest Service, 630 Sansome Street, San Francisco, CA 94111. To obtain a topographic map of the area, ask for Gold Lake from the USGS.
*Who to contact:* Plumas National Forest, Beckwourth Ranger District, P.O. Box 7, Blairsden, CA 96103; (916) 836-2575.
*Trail notes:* Frazier Falls is a 100-foot, silver-tasseled waterfall that tumbles out of a chute into a rocky basin where refracted light through the water droplets can make it all seem blessed. And maybe it is. The trail is a breeze, a half-mile romp on a gentle route that leads to the scenic overlook of the falls. The best time to visit is early summer, when snowmelt from the high country is peaking, filling Frazier Falls like a huge fountain. In addition, wildflower blooms along the trail in early summer add a splash of all colors, with violet lupine the most abundant. The road to the trailhead is paved all the way, the hike is easy, the falls are beautiful, and as you might expect, thousands of people make the trip every summer.

## 20. GOLD LAKE TRAILHEAD  1.4 mi/1.0 hr

*Reference:* **On southern boundary of Gold Lakes Basin north of Sierra City; map C3, grid i8.**
*User groups:* Hikers, dogs and horses. Mountain bikes are not allowed. No wheelchair facilities.
*Permits:* No permits are required. Parking and access are free.
*Directions:* From the junction of Highways 70 and 89 near Blairsden, turn south on Highway 89 and drive about three miles. Turn west on Forest Service Road 24 (Gold Lake Highway) and drive until you see the sign for Frazier Falls. Turn left and continue to the end of the road.
*Maps:* For a map of Plumas National Forest, send $3 to USDA-Forest Service, 630 Sansome Street, San Francisco, CA 94111. To obtain a topographic map of the area, ask for Gold Lake from the USGS.
*Who to contact:* Plumas National Forest, Beckwourth Ranger District, P.O. Box 7, Blairsden, CA 96103; (916) 836-2575.
*Trail notes:* The 0.7-mile hike to Big Bear Lake is an easy, popular and pretty

walk, most commonly taken by visitors staying at Gold Lake Lodge. The trailhead is located alongside the parking lot at the lodge; the trail is actually a closed road, good for horseback riding. It is routed west to Big Bear Lake, the first in a series of beautiful alpine lakes in the Gold Lakes Basin. While most day-users return after a picnic at Big Bear Lake, the trip can easily be extended, either west to Round Lake, or north to Long Lake or Silver Lake. Most of this country is in the 6,000 to 7,000-foot elevation range, high granite country filled with alpine lakes.

## 21. HASKELL PEAK TRAIL     3.0 mi/2.0 hrs

*Reference:* **North of Highway 49 in Tahoe National Forest; map C3, grid i9.**
*User groups:* Hikers, dogs and horses. Mountain bikes are not allowed. No wheelchair facilities.
*Permits:* No permits are required. Parking and access are free.
*Directions:* From Sierra City, drive five miles east on Highway 49, then turn north on Gold Lake Highway at Bassetts. Drive 3.7 miles, then turn right on Forest Service Road 9 (Haskell Peak Road) and drive 8.4 miles. The trailhead is on the left; parking is available on either side of the road.
*Maps:* For a map of Tahoe National Forest, send $3 to USDA-Forest Service, 630 Sansome Street, San Francisco, CA 94111. To obtain a topographic map of the area, ask for Clio from the USGS.
*Who to contact:* Tahoe National Forest, Downieville Ranger District, 15924 Highway 49, Camptonville, CA 95922; (916) 288-3231.
*Trail notes:* Haskell Peak is one of the great yet unknown lookouts. On clear days you can see many mountains both nearby and distant, including Mt. Shasta and Mt. Lassen in Northern California, Mt. Rose in Nevada, and the closer Sierra Buttes. To get this view requires a 1,100-foot climb over the course of 1.5 miles, topping out at the 8,107-foot summit. The trail climbs through heavy forest for the first mile, a decent, steady grade. It then flattens and reaches an open area where Haskell Peak comes into view. From here, it is only a quarter-mile but very steep climb to the top. You will discover that Haskell Peak is the flume of an old volcano, and has many unusual volcanic rock formations. You will also discover that just about nobody knows about this great hike.

## 22. SIERRA BUTTES TRAIL     5.0 mi/3.5 hrs

*Reference:* **At Sardine Lake in Tahoe National Forest; map C3, grid j8.**
*User groups:* Hikers only. No dogs, horses or mountain bikes are allowed. No wheelchair access.
*Permits:* No permits are required. Parking and access are free.
*Directions:* From Sierra City, drive five miles east on Highway 49 and turn north on Gold Lake Highway. Drive 1.5 miles, then turn left at the signed access road for Sardine Lake. Drive about two miles until the road deadends at the lodge/restaurant on the shore of Sardine Lake. The trail starts as a jeep road, located immediately behind the small parking area.
*Maps:* For a map of Tahoe National Forest, send $3 to USDA-Forest Service, 630 Sansome Street, San Francisco, CA 94111. To obtain a topographic map of the area, ask for Sierra City from the USGS.
*Who to contact:* Tahoe National Forest, Downieville Ranger District, 15924

Highway 49, Camptonville, CA 95922; (916) 288-3231.

*Trail notes:* The Sierra Buttes Lookout Station, 8,587 feet high and with a railed stairway to the top, provides a destination for one of California's best day hikes and greatest viewpoints. The trip starts at Sardine Lake, a true jewel at 6,000 feet in elevation—small, blue and perfect—with the Buttes providing a postcard-like backdrop. You start by hiking on an old jeep road, which loops around the lake to the right, then becomes a trail and climbs through a series of switchbacks to 6,700 feet. You loop around the mountain bowl that frames Sardine Lake in a counter-clockwise direction, passing Tamarack Lakes, and then climbing some 1,500 feet to reach the top. The trail traces the rim to the lookout, and is capped by a stairway with 176 steps that seem to project into wide open space. Climbing it is an astounding sensation, almost like climbing the cable at Half Dome. The lookout itself also juts out into space, and it can seem quite eery as you scan miles and miles of Sierra mountain country, from Mt. Lassen in the north all the way to the Tahoe Rim to the south. Stand here one time and you will never forget it the rest of your life.

---

## 23. HAYPRESS CREEK TRAIL    6.0 mi/1.0 day

*Reference:* **East of Sierra City in Tahoe National Forest; map C3, grid j8.**
*User groups:* Hikers, dogs and horses. No mountain bikes are allowed. No wheelchair facilities.
*Permits:* No permits are required. Parking and access are free.
*Directions:* At the eastern end of Sierra City, turn off Highway 49 onto Wild Plum Road at the sign for Wild Plum Campground. Drive one mile to the Wild Plum Trailhead parking area. Walk through Wild Plum Campground and follow the trail to an intersection a quarter mile past a bridge over Haypress Creek. The trail is to the right.
*Maps:* For a map of Tahoe National Forest, send $3 to USDA-Forest Service, 630 Sansome Street, San Francisco, CA 94111. To obtain a topographic map of the area, ask for Haypress Valley from the USGS.
*Who to contact:* Tahoe National Forest, Downieville Ranger District, 15924 Highway 49, Camptonville, CA 95922; (916) 288-3231.
*Trail notes:* A canyon with a hidden stream and a waterfall that is surrounded by old-growth red fir make this a wonderful day hike for the properly inspired. Why properly inspired? Because the trail climbs from 4,400 feet up Haypress Creek to 5,840 feet, a 1,440-foot rise over just three miles. The trail starts out almost flat for the first half mile, then crosses over Haypress Creek on a footbridge. There is an excellent view of the Sierra Buttes in this area. Then you continue on the Haypress Creek Trail, rising past a rocky area and into forest, and alas, passing some logging activity where the trail turns to road for a short spell. Don't despair. The trail soon enters an old-growth forest, contouring along Haypress Canyon, and passes by a lovely waterfall. This hike makes for a great day hike with a picnic, and trail use is typically quite light.

---

## 24. CHAPMAN CREEK TRAIL    3.0 mi/2.0 hrs

*Reference:* **East of Sierra City in Tahoe National Forest; map C3, grid j9.**
*User groups:* Hikers, dogs, horses and mountain bikes. No wheelchair facilities.

**Permits:** No permits are required. Parking and access are free.

**Directions:** From Sierra City, drive eight miles east on Highway 49 to Chapman Creek Campground. The trailhead and a parking area are located at the north end of the campground.

**Maps:** For a map of Tahoe National Forest, send $3 to USDA-Forest Service, 630 Sansome Street, San Francisco, CA 94111. To obtain a topographic map of the area, ask for Sierra City from the USGS.

**Who to contact:** Tahoe National Forest, Downieville Ranger District, 15924 Highway 49, Camptonville, CA 95922; (916) 288-3231.

**Trail notes:** Chapman Creek is a babbling brook where one might walk along, perhaps stopping for a picnic, to fish a little, or to do absolutely nothing. That's right, nothing. It's that kind of place. The trailhead, elevation 5,840 feet, is set at a campground, providing easy access. Outside of campers, few others know of it. The trail winds easily along the contours of Chapman Creek under the canopy of a dense forest, rising gently along the way. It climbs to 6,400 feet, a rise of 560 feet in a span of 1.5 miles. The river is the lifeblood for a variety of birds and wildlife, but few visitors make the trip for that reason. Rather they come to stroll and let their minds wander and be free.

# PACIFIC CREST TRAIL
## GENERAL INFORMATION
**161.0 mi. one way/2.0 wks**

*Reference:* **Trail sections extend from the northern border of Tahoe National Forest (Yuba River) to Lassen Volcanic National Park.**

*User groups:* Hikers, dogs and horses. No mountain bikes are allowed. No wheelchair facilities.

*Permits:* Fire permits may be required in some backcountry areas. See individual listings below.

*Directions:* Directions to specific trailheads are given below.

*Maps:* For national forest maps, send $3 for each map ordered to USDA-Forest Service, 630 Sansome Street, San Francisco, CA 94111. For an overview of the trail route in this chapter, ask for Plumas and Lassen national forests. Information on specific topographic maps is given below.

*Trail notes:* If you plan on hiking only one section of the Pacific Crest Trail in this region, then make your selection with care. Highlights here include the Sierra Buttes, Gold Lakes Basin, Bucks Lake Wilderness and Middle Fork Feather River, all world-class settings. But there are lowlights as well, including terrible chunks of trail through dry, hot country where there are too many rattlesnakes to take lightly. Much of the country ranges 5,000 to 7,000 feet in elevation, yet drops as low as 2,310 feet at Belden on the North Fork Feather River and 3,180 feet on the Middle Fork Feather. That means you will face long slow climbs and descents as you hike in and out of river canyons.

---

## PCT-32
## YUBA RIVER to FOWLER CREEK
**51.0 mi. one way/4.0 days**

*Reference:* **In Tahoe National Forest, off Highway 49 east of Sierra City; map C3, grid j8.**

*User groups:* Hikers, dogs and horses. No mountain bikes are allowed. No wheelchair access.

*Permits:* No permits are required. Parking and access are free.

*Directions:* From Sierra City, travel northeast on Highway 49 for two-tenths of a mile to the Pacific Crest Trail access point.

*Maps:* To obtain topographic maps of the area, ask for Haypress Valley, Sierra City, Mt. Fillmore and Onion Valley from the USGS.

*Who to contact:* Tahoe National Forest, Downieville Ranger District, Star Route, Box 1, Camptonville, CA 95922; (916) 288-3231.

*Trail notes:* Pristine alpine lakes and high mountain lookouts highlight this section of the Pacific Crest Trail. While just as beautiful as the section of trail south near Tahoe, this stretch gets far less use. It starts at the Yuba River, and in the first two miles, climbs an endless series of switchbacks up the back side of the Sierra Buttes, a terrible climb with a great reward. Note that the spur trail up to the Sierra Buttes Fire Lookout is an additional 1,400-foot climb, but furnishes one of the top lookouts in California. The trail then heads north, skirting past the western border of the Gold Lakes Basin, where a dozen high alpine lakes make for easy side trips and camps. With some terrible switchbacks, the PCT passes Mt. Gibraltar (7,343 feet), Stafford Mountain (7,019 feet), Mt. Etna (7,163 feet) and flanks below Pilot Peak (7,457 feet).

It then drops down the western slope, eventually descending to the Fowler Creek Trailhead.

---

## PCT-33      26.0 mi. one way/3.0 days
## FOWLER CREEK to BUCKS SUMMIT

*Reference:* **At Fowler Creek north of Little Grass Valley Reservoir in Plumas National Forest; map C3, grid h5.**

*User groups:* Hikers, dogs and horses. No mountain bikes are allowed. No wheelchair access.

*Permits:* No permits are required. Parking and access are free.

*Directions:* From LaPorte, turn east on Quincy-LaPorte Road and drive 1.5 miles, then turn north on Little Grass Valley Road and drive to Black Rock Campground. Bear left on Forest Service Road 94 and drive to Forest Service Road 22N65Y. Turn right and continue to the parking area.

*Maps:* To obtain topographic maps of the area, ask for Onion Valley, Dogwood Peak and Bucks Lake from the USGS.

*Who to contact:* Plumas National Forest, LaPorte Ranger District, P.O. Drawer 369, 10087 LaPorte Road, Challenge, CA 95925; (916) 675-2462.

*Trail notes:* Most PCT hikers will want to sprint through this section of trail. From Fowler Creek, it passes through Plumas National Forest country until reaching the southern border of the Bucks Lake Wilderness. It starts quite nicely, dropping down to the Middle Fork Feather River (3,180 feet), a great trout stream, where an excellent footbridge gets you across a gorge. Enjoy it, because the rest of this route won't exactly have you writing postcards over the euphoria. It climbs out from the Middle Fork Feather to Lookout Rock, elevation 6,955 feet, a long, dry pull, then drops down to Bucks Creek. Most of this region is dry, rattlesnake country, so watch your step, and time your water stops.

---

## PCT-34      20.0 mi. one way/2.0 days
## BUCKS SUMMIT to FEATHER RIVER

*Reference:* **At Bucks Summit Trailhead at the southern boundary of Bucks Lake Wilderness west of Quincy; map C3, grid f3.**

*User groups:* Hikers, dogs and horses. No mountain bikes are allowed. No wheelchair access.

*Permits:* A fire permit is required if you want to camp in Bucks Lake Wilderness. Parking and access are free.

*Directions:* From Quincy, turn west on Bucks Lake Road and drive approximately 11 miles to the trailhead, located at Bucks Summit.

*Maps:* To obtain a topographic map of the area, ask for Bucks Lake from the USGS.

*Who to contact:* Plumas National Forest, Quincy Ranger District, 3696 Highway 70, Quincy, CA 95971; (916) 283-0555.

*Trail notes:* From Bucks Summit to Belden is 20 miles, all of it on the Pacific Crest Trail through the Bucks Lake Wilderness. In the process, the trail passes across a granitic-based alpine area, where forest is interspersed with glacial-smoothed rock peaks. The trailhead is at Bucks Summit, elevation 5,531 feet, and from here the route generally follows the ridgeline for many miles, climbing to the southern flank of Mt. Pleasant, 6,924 feet. Along the way, a short spur trail to little Rock Lake provides a good sidetrip. The trail heads past Three Lakes, where another spur trail provides another option, this one to Kellogg Lake. From here, the trail begins descending, then drops very sharply to the North Fork Feather River at Belden, all the way down to 2,310 feet. Your big toes will be sore for days from jamming into the front of your boots.

---

## PCT-35       26.0 mi. one way/2.0 days
## FEATHER RIVER to HUMBOLDT SUMMIT

*Reference:* At Belden Trailhead on Highway 70 in Plumas National Forest; map C3, grid e2.

*User groups:* Hikers, dogs and horses. No mountain bikes are allowed. No wheelchair facilities.

*Permits:* No permits are required. Parking and access are free.

*Directions:* From Quincy, turn west on Highway 70 and drive approximately 26 miles to the trailhead, located at the roadside rest area at Belden.

*Maps:* To obtain topographic maps of the area, ask for Belden and Humboldt Peak from the USGS.

*Who to contact:* Plumas National Forest, Quincy Ranger District, 3696 Highway 70, Quincy, CA 95971; (916) 283-0555.

*Trail notes:* The trail is not only rough from Belden to Humboldt Summit, but it is not especially pretty, especially compared to the nearby wilderness. The climb is a mighty dry slice of life. From the North Fork Feather River at Belden, elevation 2,310 feet, the PCT climbs 4,777 feet over the course of this two-day thumper to Humboldt Summit at 7,087 feet. There are no lakes along this trail, only a few small waterholes requiring short sidetrips. Instead, the prettiest sections are along streams, the first being Chips Creek, which runs adjacent to the trail for eight miles, then later a short crossing over the headwaters of Willow Creek. Some hikers might prefer to take three days instead of two to traverse this section, but with Lassen Park looming ahead, you will find yourself putting in long days to get through this area.

---

## PCT-36       28.0 mi. one way/2.0 days
## HUMBOLDT SUMMIT to DOMINO SPRING

*Reference:* At Humboldt Summit in Lassen National Forest southwest of Lake Almanor; map C3, grid d1.

*User groups:* Hikers, dogs and horses. No mountain bikes are allowed. No wheelchair facilities.

*Permits:* No permits are required. Parking and access are free.

*Directions:* From Chester, turn west on Highway 36 and drive two miles to the junction with Highway 89. Turn south on Highway 89 and drive four miles. Then turn right on County Road 308 (Humboldt Road) and travel 15 miles to the trailhead parking area.

*Maps:* To obtain topographic maps of the area, ask for Humboldt Peak and Stover Mountain from the USGS.

*Who to contact:* Lassen National Forest, Almanor Ranger District, P.O. Box 767, Chester, CA 96020; (916) 258-2141.

*Trail notes:* The idea of back-to-back 14-mile days to get through this chunk of trail may not appeal to many hikers, especially while carrying full-weight expedition packs. But that is standard for most hikers on this stretch of PCT, with little here to tarry for and with Lassen Park beckoning ahead. The trail starts just below Humboldt Peak at 7,087 feet and heads north along the ridge line, for the most part, past Butt Mountain (7,866 feet) and down to Soldier Meadows. A spring and stream make this a delightful stop before crossing Highway 36, forging onward another three miles to the Stove Springs Campground. The trail then skirts around the western flank of North Stove Mountain and drops down to Domino Springs, where another campground is available.

---

## PCT-37       11.0 mi. one way/1.0 day
## DOMINO SPRING to LASSEN VOLCANIC NAT. PARK

*Reference:* **At Domino Spring Trailhead in Lassen National Forest west of Lake Almanor; map C3, grid b2.**

*User groups:* Hikers, dogs and horses. No mountain bikes are allowed. No wheelchair facilities.

*Permits:* No permits are required. Parking and access are free.

*Directions:* From Chester on Highway 36, turn north on Warner Valley Road (County Road 312) and drive about six miles. Turn left on Old Red Bluff Road (County Road 311) and continue three miles to the parking area at Domino Springs.

*Maps:* To obtain a topographic map of the area, ask for Stover Mountain from the USGS.

*Who to contact:* Lassen National Forest, Almanor Ranger District, P.O. Box 767, Chester, CA 96020; (916) 258-2141.

*Trail notes:* With each passing step, the scenery gets better and better. Finally you leave dry, hot forest country and enter Lassen Park at Warren Valley. All the suffering seems over and only paradise awaits. From Domino Springs, the Pacific Crest Trail is routed straight north through Lassen Forest. The Little North Fork of the North Fork Feather is located a quarter-mile to the west and is a good sidetrip, both for swimming and fishing for large brown trout. As you enter Lassen Park, you will pass Little Willow Lake, and in two miles, arrive at Boiling Springs Lake and the Warner Valley Campground. This is a good layover spot, with the sidetrip to Devil's Kitchen recommended.

**PCT CONTINUATION:** To continue hiking along the Pacific Crest Trail, see Chapter B3, pages 133-135.

# MAP C4

NOR-CAL MAP ....................... see page 14
adjoining maps
NORTH (B4) .......................... see page 136
EAST .................................. no map
SOUTH (D4) ......................... see page 224
WEST (C3) ........................... see page 174

1 TRAIL
PAGES 194-195

TO ARDIN — TO RAVENDALE

TO WESTWOOD

TO GALLATIN BEACH

**a**

Shinn Peaks
EL. 7,274

BISCAR
WILDLIFE
AREA

**b**

139

36

Susanville

395

A27

Litchfield

Hot Springs Peaks
EL. 7,680

**c**

Johnstonville

395

Standish

A3

Wendel

Janesville

Buntingville

Thompson
Peak
EL. 7,795

**d**

ANTELOPE
LAKE

**e**

Milford

PLUMAS
NAT'L
FOREST

A25

Herlong

A26

**f**

TO GENESEE

Dixie Mountain
EL. 8,323

DIXIE MOUNTAIN
GAME REFUGE

Doyle

**g**

DAVIS
LAKE

FRENCHMAN
LAKE

FRENCHMAN
RES. REC. AREA

Constantia

395

**h**

TO GRAEAGLE

Portola

Beckworth

A15

70

Chilcoot

**i**

Vinton

A23

Beckworth Pass
EL. 5,212

Hallelujah Jct.

NEVADA

Calpine

Loyalton

49

**j**

TO BASSETTS

Sattley

Sierraville ❶

89

TAHOE
NAT'L
FOREST

395

TO HOBART MILLS — TO RENO, NV

0 1 2 3 4 5 6 7 8 9

## 1. BOTANICAL TRAIL          1.0 mi/0.5 hr

*Reference:* **In Tahoe National Forest; map C4, grid j1.**

*User groups:* Hikers, dogs and horses (but dogs and horses not recommended). No mountain bikes allowed. No wheelchair facilities.

*Permits:* No permits required. Parking and access are free for day use. Reservations are available and a fee is required for camping.

*Directions:* From Sierraville, drive 4.5 miles southeast on Highway 89 to Cottonwood Creek Campground on your left.

*Maps:* For a map of Tahoe National Forest, send $3 to USDA-Forest Service, 630 Sansome Street, San Francisco, CA 94111.

*Who to contact:* Call the Sierraville Ranger District at (916) 994-3401 or write Tahoe National Forest, Highway 49 and Coyote Street, Nevada City, CA 95959.

*Trail notes:* The Botanical Trail is a half-mile nature trail that follows along little Cottonwood Creek. The trailhead is at the Cottonwood Creek Campground, set at 5,800 feet in the Sierra Nevada. The trail leads out of camp, with a brochure available at the trailhead. The brochure has listings that correspond to numbered posts along the trail, which explain a variety of plants and trees unique to the area. This is a short, easy trip along a refreshing stream with a little botany lesson along the way. A good sidetrip is to Campbell Hot Springs, located a very short drive west of Sierraville off Highway 49.

# MAP DØ

NOR-CAL MAP ...................... see page 14
adjoining maps
NORTH (CØ) ......................... see page 144
EAST (D1) ........................... see page 202
SOUTH .................................. no map
WEST .................................... no map

8 TRAILS
PAGES 196-201

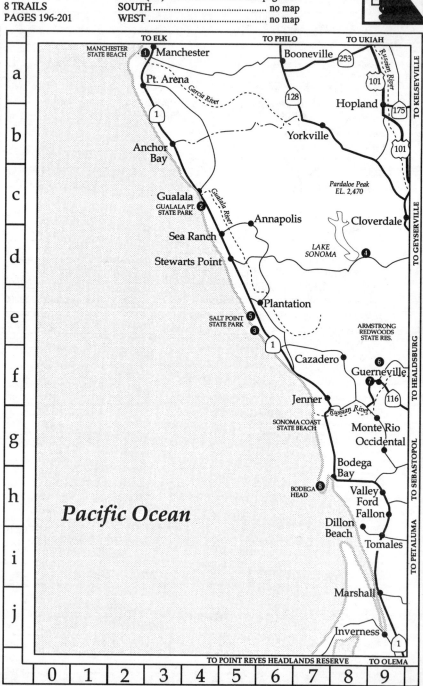

Pacific Ocean

TO ELK · Manchester
MANCHESTER STATE BEACH
TO PHILO
Booneville · 253
TO UKIAH
Russian River
Pt. Arena
Garcia River
128
101
TO KELSEYVILLE
1
Hopland
175
Yorkville
101
TO GEYSERVILLE
Anchor Bay
Gualala River
Pardaloe Peak EL. 2,470
Gualala
GUALALA PT. STATE PARK
Annapolis
Cloverdale
Sea Ranch
LAKE SONOMA
Stewarts Point
Plantation
SALT POINT STATE PARK
ARMSTRONG REDWOODS STATE RES.
1
TO HEALDSBURG
Cazadero
Guerneville
116
Jenner
Russian River
Monte Rio
Occidental
SONOMA COAST STATE BEACH
TO SEBASTOPOL
Bodega Bay
BODEGA HEAD
Valley Ford
Fallon
Dillon Beach
TO PETALUMA
Tomales
Marshall
Inverness
1
TO POINT REYES HEADLANDS RESERVE
TO OLEMA

a b c d e f g h i j

0 1 2 3 4 5 6 7 8 9

**Map DØ featuring:** Mendocino coast, Manchester State Beach Park, Gualala Point Regional Park, Stillwater Cove Regional Park, Healdsburg, Lake Sonoma, Salt Point State Park, Austin Creek State Recreation Area, Guerneville, Bodega Bay

## 1. ALDER CREEK TRAIL    4.0 mi/1.75 hrs

*Reference:* **In Manchester State Beach Park on Mendocino coast north of Point Arena; map DØ, grid a2.**

*User groups:* Hikers and horses. Dogs are not allowed. Terrain not suitable for mountain bikes. No wheelchair facilities.

*Permits:* No permits are required. A $5 state park day-use fee is charged for each vehicle.

*Directions:* From Point Arena, drive north on Highway 1 to Kinney Lane. Turn left and drive a short distance to the park entrance.

*Maps:* For a brochure and trail map, send $1 to Manchester Beach State Park at the address below. To obtain a topographic map of the area, ask for Point Arena from the USGS.

*Who to contact:* Manchester Beach State Park, P.O. Box 440, Mendocino, CA 95460; (707) 937-5804 or (707) 865-2391.

*Trail notes:* Manchester State Beach has two moods, one sweet, one foul. In late winter and fall, radiant sunbeams set the Mendocino coast aglow, making for flawless beach walks. But in summer, the coast here can turn wrathful, with winds powering out of the north. It can feel like your head could blow off if it wasn't attached by the neck. The hike here starts adjacent to park headquarters and is routed past Lake Davis to the beach, continuing north along the beach to the mouth of Alder Creek. This is an attractive coastal lagoon, known for attracting many species of birds, including whistling swans. It is also the area where the San Andreas Fault heads off from land into the sea.

## 2. HEADLANDS LOOP    1.5 mi/0.75 hr

*Reference:* **In Gualala Point Regional Park on Mendocino coast; map DØ, grid c4.**

*User groups:* Hikers and dogs. No horses are allowed. One trail is paved for **wheelchairs** and mountain bikes.

*Permits:* No permits are required. There is a $3 parking fee.

*Directions:* From Gualala, drive south on Highway 1 for a quarter mile (over the Gualala River) and turn west into the park entrance. Continue to the visitor's center.

*Maps:* To obtain a topographic map of the area, ask for Gualala from the USGS.

*Who to contact:* Gualala Point Regional Park, P.O. Box 95, Gualala, CA 95445; (707) 785-2377.

*Trail notes:* The Headlands to Beach Loop is an easy and short walk that furnishes coastal views, a lookout of the Gualala River, and includes a route amidst giant coastal cypress trees. From the visitor center, the trail is routed along the Gualala River, then turns and loops to the left. Here you can take the short cutoff trail that leads to the beach. On the way back, the trail traces along the ocean bluffs for a short spell, and with it comes the coastal views, Then the trail turns inland and returns to the visitor center. Bonuses here include excellent whale watching during the winter and good wildflower blooms on the grassy hillsides in spring.

---

## 3. STOCKOFF CREEK LOOP    1.25 mi/0.75 hr

*Reference:* **In Stillwater Cove Regional Park north of Jenner; map DØ, grid e5.**

*User groups:* Hikers and dogs. No horses or mountain bikes are allowed. No wheelchair facilities.

*Permits:* No permits are required. A $3 day-use fee is charged for each vehicle.

*Directions:* From Jenner, drive north on Highway 1 and drive 16 miles to the park entrance.

*Maps:* For a free brochure, contact Sonoma County Regional Parks at the address below. To obtain a topographic map of the area, ask for Plantation from the USGS.

*Who to contact:* Stillwater Cove Regional Park, 2300 County Center Drive, Suite 120, Building A, Santa Rosa, CA 95403; (707) 847-3245.

*Trail notes:* Highway 1 is one the top tourist drives in America, and that is why the coastal state parks get such heavy use in the summer months. This little regional park, however, is sometimes overlooked by out-of-state traffic. The trailhead is located at the day-use parking lot, and after starting the walk, almost immediately you will enter a surprising forest comprised of firs and redwoods. You then come to the Loop Trail junction, where you turn right. The trail is  routed along the creek, crosses a few bridges, then eventually rises above the watershed and loops back through forest to the parking area. It is an easy, pretty and secluded loop hike. A bonus is visiting Stillwater Cove, which requires crossing Highway 1 and then dropping down to the beach, which has a dramatic rock-strewn shore.

---

## 4. SOUTH LAKE TRAILHEAD    5.0 mi/2.5 hrs

*Reference:* **At Lake Sonoma northwest of Healdsburg; map DØ, grid d8.**

*User groups:* Hikers and dogs. No horses or mountain bikes are allowed. No wheelchair facilities.

*Permits:* No permits are required. Parking and access are free.

*Directions:* From Santa Rosa, drive 12 miles north on US Highway 101 to the town of Healdsburg. Take the Dry Creek Road exit and turn left. Drive 11 miles to the lake. The trailhead is located at the south end of the lake.

*Maps:* For a free map, contact U.S. Corps of Engineers at the address below. To obtain a topographic map of the area, ask for Warm Springs Dam from the USGS.

*Who to contact:* U.S. Corps of Engineers, Lake Sonoma, 3333 Skaggs Springs Road, Geyserville, CA 95441; (707) 433-9483.

*Trail notes:* Lake Sonoma is one of the best examples in California where the government folks have done something right. They not only built this lake, but added a superb boat ramp, marina and campgrounds (some boat-in) and started a good bass fishery. They also cut 43 miles of trail, enough to spend days traipsing around the hills. The South Lake Trailhead is the best starting point, though the short trail at Vista Point has the best views (and most wind in the spring, heat in the summer). From the trailhead, the route traces along the lake, enters and exits a series of small groves, and extends along the lake's fingers. When you've had enough, just turn back. Many trails bisect the route and extend into more remote surrounding country, allowing ambitious hikers to create longer adventures. This area gets very hot in the summer. Most of the habitat is oak grasslands, and rarely you may see wild pigs, deer or rattlesnakes.

---

## 5. STUMP BEACH TRAIL     3.5 mi/1.5 hrs

*Reference:* **In Salt Point State Park north of Jenner; map DØ, grid e5.**

*User groups:* Hikers. Dogs, horses and mountain bikes are allowed on selected trails. One trail (Gerstle Cove) in the park is paved for **wheelchairs.**

*Permits:* No permits are required. A $5 state park day-use fee is charged per vehicle.

*Directions:* From Jenner, drive north on Highway 1 for 20 miles to the park entrance. Turn right and continue to the entrance kiosk. The trailhead is at the Salt Point parking area.

*Maps:* For a trail map, send 50 cents to Salt Point State Park at the address below. To obtain a topographic map of the area, ask for Plantation from the USGS.

*Who to contact:* Salt Point State Park, 25050 Coast Highway 1, Jenner, CA 95450; (707) 847-3221 or (707) 865-2391.

*Trail notes:* The dramatic, rocky shoreline of Salt Point State Park is memorable to anyone who has seen it. This trail provides the best look at it, including some simply awesome views from a 400-foot high ocean bluff. The trailhead is at the parking area set near the tip of Salt Point, and from there, you hike north, over Warren Creek, a seasonal stream, and then across the bluffs. You can practically feel the crashing of ocean breakers below you, the spray rocketing skyward. The trail eventually winds around and down to Stump Beach Cove, a pretty sandy beach where the calm waters are in sharp contrast to the nearby mauling ocean breakers. Salt Point State Park is known for excellent sport abalone diving in season, and also for providing one of the few marine reserves (Gerstle Cove) where no form of marine life may be taken or disturbed.

---

## 6. GILLIAM CREEK LOOP     8.9 mi/1.0 day

*Reference:* **In Austin Creek State Recreation Area north of Guerneville; map DØ, grid f9.**

*User groups:* Hikers and horses. No dogs or mountain bikes are allowed. No wheelchair facilities.

*Permits:* No permits are required. A $5 state park day-use fee is charged for each vehicle.

*Directions:* From Santa Rosa on US 101, take the Guerneville-Highway 116 exit. Turn west and continue to Guerneville, then turn north on Armstrong Woods Road. Drive 2.5 miles to the Armstrong Redwoods State Park entrance. The trailhead is about 2.5 miles past the entrance.

*Maps:* For a trail map, send 50 cents to Austin Creek State Recreation Area at the address below. To obtain a topographic map of the area, ask for Guerneville from the USGS.

**Who to contact:** Austin Creek State Recreation Area, 17000 Armstrong Redwoods Road, Guerneville, CA 95446; (707) 869-2015 or (707) 865-2391.

**Trail notes:** The rolling hills, open forests and streamside riparian habitat in Austin Creek Recreation Area can seem a million miles distant from the redwood forests of Armstrong Redwoods. Yet the two parks are actually coupled, forming 5,000 acres of contiguous parkland. While most tourists are walking around the redwoods at Armstrong, this trail offers a quieter and more ambitious alternative. From the trailhead at 1,100 feet, you contour across the slope, then drop down to the headwaters of Stonehouse Creek at 400 feet. The trail then follows along the stream, past the confluence with Gilliam Creek, extending 3.7 miles into the back country, all the way down to a 200-foot elevation. At the confluence of Austin Creek, you turn right and hike deeper into wild, hilly country along the stream, then return on the loop on the East Austin Creek Trail. The final two miles retraces your steps, climbing 700 feet in the process. At this point, you may ask, "Are we having fun yet?"

## 7. EAST RIDGE TRAIL      6.8 mi/1.0 day

**Reference:** In Armstrong Redwoods State Reserve north of Guerneville; map DØ, grid f9.

**User groups:** Hikers and horses. No dogs or mountain bikes are allowed. No wheelchair facilities.

**Permits:** No permits are required. A $5 state park day-use fee is charged for each vehicle.

**Directions:** From Santa Rosa on US 101, take the Guerneville-Highway 116 exit. Turn west and continue to Guerneville, then turn north on Armstrong Woods Road. Drive 2.5 miles to the Armstrong Redwoods State Park entrance. The trailhead is adjacent to the visitor's center.

**Maps:** For a trail map, send 50 cents to Austin Creek State Recreation Area at the address below. To obtain a topographic map of the area, ask for Guerneville from the USGS.

**Who to contact:** Armstrong Redwoods State Reserve, 17000 Armstrong Redwoods Road, Guerneville, CA 95446; (707) 869-2015 or (707) 865-2391.

**Trail notes:** It is almost obligatory to hike either the Discovery Trail or Armstrong Nature Trail in Armstrong Redwoods, both very short and beautiful strolls through the park's grove of huge redwoods. But after that taste, your appetite will likely be whetted for something more inspiring. The East Ridge Trail provides it, rising 1,400 feet over the course of 3.4 miles, at times providing lookouts below into a sea of redwood tops. The trailhead is at a 200-foot elevation, adjacent to Fife Creek. The route climbs gradually at first, then in the first half mile rises to cross the headwaters of Fife Creek, elevation 600 feet. Your climb has only just begun, and if you're already running out of gas, you'd best head back. That is because the trail continues on, climbing all the way, contouring its way up towards McCray Mountain (1,940 feet), topping out at a service road at 1,600 feet.

# 8. BODEGA HEAD LOOP        1.5 mi/1.0 hr

*Reference:* **On the Sonoma coast west of Bodega Bay; map DØ, grid h7.**

*User groups:* Hikers only. No horses, dogs or mountain bikes are allowed. No wheelchair facilities.

*Permits:* No permits are required. Parking and access are free.

*Directions:* From Highway 101 at Petaluma, take the East Washington exit. Take Bodega Avenue west through Petaluma and drive for 26 miles to Bodega Bay (the road will turn into Highway 1). At the town of Bodega Bay, turn left on East Shore Road and drive less than a half mile. At the stop sign, turn west on Bay Flat Road and continue around Bodega Bay, the road turns into West Side Road. Continue past Spud Point Marina to Bodega Head Parking Area.

*Maps:* For a brochure, send 80 cents to SOS, P.O. Box 221, Duncan Mills, CA 95430.

*Who to contact:* For a free travel packet, write to Bodega Bay Chamber of Commerce, P.O. Box 146, Bodega Bay, CA 94923, or call (707) 875-3422. You can also contact Sonoma Coast State Beach, P.O. Box 123, Duncan Mills, CA 95430; (707) 875-3483.

*Trail notes:* A short loop hike at Bodega Head will provide an introduction to one of California's great coastal areas. The trail starts at the east parking lot, and in just 1.5 miles, will take you into a wonderland, with views of cliffs, untouched beaches, and southward to the sea and beyond. A sidetrip is also available on this hike, a short tromp on a spur trail up to the tip-top of Bodega Head for 360-degree views. Rarely does the ocean seem so vast as it does from here. In spring and early summer, the wind can really howl. In late summer, fall or late winter, Bodega Bay gets its warmest and often wind-free weather of the year.

# MAP D1

NOR-CAL MAP ........................ see page 14
adjoining maps
NORTH (C1) ........................... see page 156
EAST (D2) .............................. see page 208
SOUTH (E1) ........................... see page 258
WEST (DØ) ............................ see page 196

7 TRAILS
PAGES 202-207

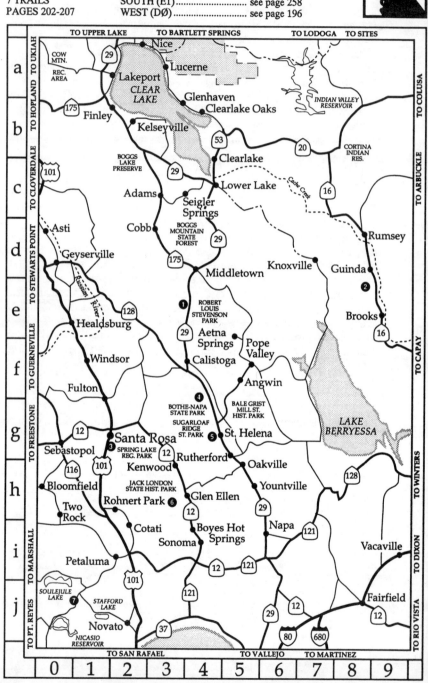

TO UPPER LAKE   TO BARTLETT SPRINGS        TO LODOGA   TO SITES

**a**
TO HOPLAND    TO UKIAH
COW MTN. REC. AREA
29  Nice
Lucerne
Lakeport  *CLEAR LAKE*
INDIAN VALLEY RESERVOIR
TO COLUSA

**b**
175  Finley
Glenhaven
Clearlake Oaks
Kelseyville
53
20
CORTINA INDIAN RES.

**c**
TO CLOVERDALE
101
BOGGS LAKE PRESERVE
29  Clearlake
Lower Lake
*Cache Creek*
16
TO ARBUCKLE
Adams
Seigler Springs

**d**
TO STEWARTS POINT
Asti
Geyserville
Cobb
BOGGS MOUNTAIN STATE FOREST
29
175  Middletown
Knoxville
Rumsey
Guinda

**e**
*Russian River*
128
Healdsburg
❶
ROBERT LOUIS STEVENSON PARK
29  Aetna Springs
Pope Valley
❷
Brooks
16
TO CAPAY

**f**
TO GUERNEVILLE
Windsor
Fulton
Calistoga
Angwin

**g**
TO FREESTONE
12
Sebastopol
❸
Santa Rosa
SPRING LAKE REG. PARK
❹
BOTHE-NAPA STATE PARK
SUGARLOAF RIDGE ST. PARK
❺
BALE GRIST MILL ST. HIST. PARK
St. Helena
*LAKE BERRYESSA*
TO WINTERS

**h**
116
Bloomfield
Two Rock
12  Kenwood
Rutherford
Oakville
128
JACK LONDON STATE HIST. PARK
Rohnert Park ❻
Glen Ellen
12
Yountville
29
Napa
121

**i**
TO MARSHALL
Cotati
Sonoma
Boyes Hot Springs
12
121
Vacaville
Petaluma
101

**j**
TO PT. REYES
*SOULEJULE LAKE* ❼
STAFFORD LAKE
101
121
121
*NICASIO RESERVOIR*
Novato
37
29  12
80  680
Fairfield
12
TO DIXON
TO RIO VISTA

TO SAN RAFAEL    TO VALLEJO   TO MARTINEZ

0  1  2  3  4  5  6  7  8  9

**Map D1 featuring:** Robert Louis Stevenson State Park, Calistoga, Lake Berryessa, Spring Lake Regional Park, Santa Rosa, Bothe-Napa State Park, Sugarloaf Ridge State Park, Sonoma, Jack London State Park, Petaluma

---

## 1. MOUNT ST. HELENA TRAIL 10.0 mi/4.5 hrs

*Reference:* **In Robert Louis Stevenson State Park north of Calistoga; map D1, grid e3.**

*User groups:* Hikers only. No dogs, horses or mountain bikes are allowed. No wheelchair facilities. Mountain bikes are allowed on a nearby fire road, one-quarter mile north on Highway 29.

*Permits:* No permits are required. Parking and access are free.

*Directions:* From Calistoga, drive approximately eight miles north on Highway 29 to the signed trailhead.

*Maps:* To obtain a topographic map of the area, ask for Mount St. Helena from the USGS.

*Who to contact:* Robert Louis Stevenson State Park, c/o Bothe-Napa Valley State Park, 3801 St. Helena Highway North, Calistoga, CA 94515; (707) 942-4575 or (707) 938-1519.

*Trail notes:* Mount St. Helena is Sonoma County's highest mountain, the peak that strikes such a memorable silhouette when viewed from the Bay Area. This trail climbs to the summit at 4,343 feet, requiring an ascent of 2,068 feet over the course of five miles. The route follows a moderate grade for the most part, then rises above the forest and includes two very steep sections, one at the very end of your climb. In the summer, the hike can be pure hell, since much of the trail is actually an abandoned road with little shade, there is no water anywhere along the route, and the heat commonly blazes in the 90s and 100s out here. Most visitors make the trip when temperatures are more tolerable, of course. The mountain is most often visited in the winter, when the summit is commonly flecked with snow from passing storms, quite a treat for most folks in the area. In fact, when the snow level drops to 3,500 feet, the entire mountain top can get a good pasting of a foot of snow. In spring, north winds clear the air. Visibility is best at this time, with remarkable views in all directions. No matter when you hike, be certain to bring plenty of water, a daypack with high-energy food, a windbreaker and a change of shirts (so you won't be making the return downhill trip with a cold, wet shirt).

---

## 2. BLUE RIDGE TRAIL 16.0 mi/1.0 day

*Reference:* **North of Lake Berryessa; map D1, grid e8.**

*User groups:* Hikers, dogs, horses and mountain bikes. No wheelchair facilities. While horses and mountain bikes are allowed, they are not recommended because of the steep, rocky terrain.

*Permits:* No permits are required. Parking and access are free.

*Directions:* From Interstate 5 at Woodland, turn west on Highway 16 and drive about 30 miles. At Lower Yolo County Park, turn left onto a gravel road and look for a concrete bridge. Park in the unpaved area near Cache Creek.

Follow the dirt road through a meadow to the trailhead. In the winter, the dirt road is blocked by a locked gate; park instead at Lower Yolo County Park and walk down to the trailhead.

*Maps:* For a free primitive trail map, contact the BLM at the address below. To obtain a topographic map of the area, ask for Guinda from the USGS.

*Who to contact:* Bureau of Land Management, Clear Lake Resource Area, 2550 North State Street, Ukiah, CA 95482; (707) 468-4000.

*Trail notes:* There are relatively few trails on BLM land in Northern California, but all of them are special in one way or the other. Unfortunately, usually it's the other. The Blue Ridge Trail, for instance, includes a stretch with a 2,000-foot elevation gain in just three miles, and many pieces of trail that are very steep, rocky and dry. The trail follows the ridge for eight miles (most folks don't last anywhere near that long), and you'd better be as fit as a Tibetan sherpa to try it. But hey, in spring this can be a sensational hike, with wildflowers ablaze and bushes and trees in full bloom. You will see songbirds, swallows, falcons and eagles flitting, hovering and soaring. There are also a good share of lizards and rattlesnakes. The views are exceptional in all directions, with the Sutter Buttes and Snow Mountain most prominent, but with even Shasta and Lassen in view on clear days. In fact, the area has just about everything; everything that is, except water. You either bring at least two or three quarts per person, or you surrender, swearing never to hike here again.

---

# 3. SPRING LAKE TRAIL    2.0 mi/1.0 hr 🥾 ⛰️

*Reference:* In Spring Lake Regional Park in eastern Santa Rosa; map D1, grid g2.

*User groups:* Hikers and dogs. Horses are allowed only on designated trails. The park has 2.3 miles of trail that are paved for **wheelchair** and bicycle use.

*Permits:* No permits are required. There is a $3 parking fee.

*Directions:* From US Highway 101 in Santa Rosa, drive east on Highway 12 until it becomes Hoen Avenue. Turn left on Newanga Avenue and drive to the park entrance. The various trailheads are well marked and easily accessible from the parking area.

*Maps:* For a detailed trail map, send 25 cents to Spring Lake Park at the address below. To obtain a topographic map of the area, ask for Santa Rosa from the USGS.

*Who to contact:* Spring Lake Regional Park, 5390 Montgomery Drive, Santa Rosa, CA 95409; (707) 539-8082.

*Trail notes:* Spring Lake is Santa Rosa's backyard fishing hole, a popular place for trout fishing, an evening picnic or a short hike. For newcomers, we suggest the walk along the west shore of Spring Lake to the west dam, then turning left and heading into adjoining Howard Park to Ralphine Lake. It's an easy, enjoyable stroll, nothing serious. The lake is stocked with trout in winter and spring and provides a fair warm water fishery in the summer. Non-powered boating keeps things fun and quiet. For children, pony rides are quite popular. Robyn Schlueter, our research editor, remembers those pony rides fondly. "My grandmother used to take me here when I was little."

## 4. COYOTE PEAK LOOP    5.0 mi/3.0 hrs

*Reference:* **In Bothe-Napa State Park south of Calistoga; map D1, grid g4.**

*User groups:* Hikers. Horses and mountain bikes are allowed on fire roads. No dogs are allowed. No wheelchair facilities.

*Permits:* No permits are required. A $5 state park fee is charged per vehicle.

*Directions:* From the town of St. Helena, drive five miles north on Highway 128/29, past Bale Grist Mill State Park, to the park entrance on the left side of the road. The trailhead is just past the Ritchey Creek Campground turnoff, near the picnic area. There is parking for about six cars near the trailhead.

*Maps:* For a brochure and trail map, send 75 cents to Bothe-Napa Valley State Park at the address below. To obtain a topographic map of the area, ask for Calistoga from the USGS.

*Who to contact:* Bothe-Napa Valley State Park, 3801 St. Helena Highway North, Calistoga, CA 94515; (707) 942-4575 or (707) 938-1519.

*Trail notes:* Who ever heard of redwoods in the Napa Valley? Who ever heard of a mountain peak there, too? Only those who also know of Bothe-Napa State Park, which is like an island of wildlands in a sea of winery tourist traffic. Bothe-Napa has some of the most easterly stands of coastal redwoods, Douglas fir and an excellent lookout from Coyote Peak, all quite a surprise for newcomers. The best way to see it is on the Coyote Peak/ Redwood Trail Loop, starting just past the Ritchey Creek Campground turnoff, near the picnic area. You take the Ritchey Trail for a half-mile, then veer left on the Redwood Trail. Here you are surrounded by some of the park's highest stands of redwoods. The trail continues along Ritchey Creek for a quarter mile, then connects to the Coyote Peak Trail. Take the Coyote Peak Trail, which rises quickly, skirting the northern flank of Coyote Peak. (A short spur trail will take you all the way to the top, 1,170 feet.) Then the trail drops down the other side of the hill and intersects with the South Fork Trail, which heads all the way back down to Ritchey Creek. Note that temperatures can be extremely hot in the summer, as high as 105 degrees.

---

## 5. BALD MOUNTAIN LOOP    8.2 mi/1.0 day

*Reference:* **In Sugarloaf Ridge State Park north of Sonoma; map D1, grid g4.**

*User groups:* Hikers, horses and mountain bikes. Check for special trail restrictions on mountain bikes. No dogs are allowed. No wheelchair facilities.

*Permits:* No permits are required. A $5 state park day-use fee is charged for each vehicle.

*Directions:* From US Highway 101 at Santa Rosa, turn east on Highway 12 and continue to Adobe Canyon Road. Turn left and proceed to the main entrance.

*Maps:* For a trail map and brochure, send 75 cents to Sugarloaf Ridge State Park at the address below. To obtain a topographic map of the area, ask for Kenwood from the USGS.

*Who to contact:* Sugarloaf Ridge State Park, 2605 Adobe Canyon Road, Kenwood, CA 95452; (707) 833-5712 or (707) 938-1519.

*Trail notes:* Bald Mountain, elevation 2,729 feet, overlooks the Napa Valley with Mount St. Helena set to the north. On clear days from the summit, you can see portions of the San Francisco Bay Area, and then be thankful you are here instead of there. The old mountain is the centerpiece of Sugarloaf Ridge

State Park, a 2,700-acre park featuring redwoods in Sonoma Creek watershed, open meadows peppered with oaks on the hilltops, and some chaparral on ridges. The Bald Mountain Loop is the most ambitious hike in the park, an 8.2-mile trek that starts at the parking lot, then is routed in a loop by taking the Bald Mountain, Gray Meadow, Brushy Peaks and Meadow trails. Many less demanding hikes are available in the park, but this route will give you the best sense of the park's wildest lands. It is best hiked in the spring, when the air is still cool, the hills are green and wildflowers are in bloom. There is an extra bonus as well: When Sonoma Creek is flowing well, there is a beautiful 25-foot waterfall located downstream from the campground.

---

## 6. LAKE TRAIL      1.5 mi/0.75 hr  

*Reference:* **In Jack London State Park north of Sonoma; map D1, grid h3.**
*User groups:* Hikers. Horses and mountain bikes are allowed on selected trails. No dogs are allowed. No wheelchair facilities.
*Permits:* No permits are required. A $5 state park day-use fee is charged for each vehicle.
*Directions:* From US Highway 101 at Santa Rosa, turn east on Highway 12 and travel to Kenwood. Turn right on Warm Springs Road and continue to Arnold Drive. Turn right and drive a short distance. Then turn right on London Ranch Road and proceed to the park entrance.
*Maps:* For a trail map and brochure, send $1 to Jack London State Historic Park at the address below. To obtain a topographic map of the area, ask for Glen Ellen from the USGS.
*Who to contact:* Jack London State Historic Park, 2400 London Ranch Road, Glen Ellen, CA 95442; (707) 938-5216 or (707) 938-1519.
*Trail notes:* You will likely feel the shadow of the ghost of Jack London as you walk in his steps on the Lake Trail. It was here that Jack London created his dreams as one of America's true great writers and philosophers. It was also here that those dreams were shattered, first from a devastating fire that devoured his ranch home, then from an illness at age 40 from which he could not recover. Most visitors start the trip by touring London's cottage, winery ruins, barns and a distillery. Yearning for more, the Lake Trail easily provides it, a short walk to a small pond, which served as a favorite recreation area for London and his guests. The trail circles it, then returns back to the parking area. However, this short trip alone does not do justice to the passion London had for the Sonoma mountains. From the lake, you can extend your trip on the Mountain Trail, a steep, four-mile, 1,800-foot climb to the Sonoma Mountain summit at 2,363 feet. Note that the actual summit is outside park boundaries, and that you will come to a gate on the fire road/trail when you cross into private property. Always check with park rangers for access status prior to making the summit climb.

---

## 7. SOULEJULE LAKE TRAIL      1.5 mi/0.75 hr  

*Reference:* **In Sonoma County southwest of Petaluma; map D1, grid j0.**
*User groups:* Hikers and dogs. Horses and mountain bikes are not advised. No wheelchair facilities.
*Permits:* No permits are required. Parking and access are free.
*Directions:* From US Highway 101 at Novato, take the San Marin exit and

continue west to Novato Boulevard. Turn right and drive nine miles. Turn right again on Petaluma-Point Reyes Road and drive a quarter mile, then turn left on Wilson Hill Road. Drive three miles northwest, then turn left on Marshall-Petaluma Road and continue for five miles to the signed turnoff on the left. Park at the base of the dam.

*Maps:* To obtain a topographic map of the area, ask for Hicks Mountain from the USGS.

*Who to contact:* Marin Municipal Water District, 220 Mellen Avenue, Corte Madera, CA 94925; (415) 924-4600.

*Trail notes:* How do you pronounce Soulejule? Probably not the right way, but when you make this easy hike to this secluded lake, then start catching the bass here, you won't care much. Soulejule is a little-known, hike-in lake in northern Marin. You can drive to the base of the dam, then make the short hike to the lake's edge. As you walk around the lake, stop now and then and make a cast, using either a white Crappie Killer or a one-inch floating Rapala. It's a great way to spend a spring evening, walking a little, fishing a little, maybe catching a little, with small bass and crappie cooperating during the winter-to-summer transition. By the way, how do you pronounce Soulejule? Like this: Soo-La-Hoo-Lee. Just like it looks.

# MAP D2

NOR-CAL MAP ....................... see page 14
adjoining maps
NORTH (C2) ........................... see page 166
EAST (D3) ............................. see page 210
SOUTH (E2) .......................... see page 394
WEST (D1) ............................ see page 202

1 TRAIL
PAGES 208-209

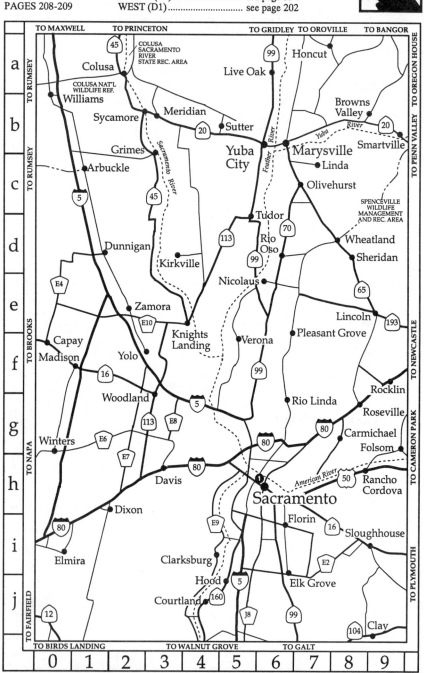

# 1. AMERICAN RIVER 23.0 mi. one way/1.0 day  PARKWAY

*Reference:* **Along American River from Sacramento to Rancho Cordova; map D2, grid h6.**

*User groups:* Hikers, dogs, horses and mountain bikes. Note restrictions for mountain bikes and hikers in trail note below. Wheelchairs are not allowed on the actual trail, but **wheelchair accessible** restrooms, fishing areas and picnic grounds are available along the way.

*Permits:* No permits are required. Each county park charges a $4 fee for each vehicle.

*Directions:* The trail begins at Discovery Park in Sacramento. From Interstate 5, take the Richards Boulevard exit and head west to Jiboom Street. Turn north and follow the road into the park. But note, the trail's prettiest access point is Goethe Park in Rancho Cordova. To get to Goethe Park, head east on US Highway 50 and take the Bradshaw North exit. Follow Bradshaw to Folsom and turn east. Continue to Rod Braudy Drive and turn north. Follow the road into the park.

*Maps:* For a free map of the trail, contact the County Parks Department at the address below. To obtain topographic maps of the area, ask for Sacramento East, Carmichael, Citrus Heights and Folsom from the USGS.

*Who to contact:* County of Sacramento, Parks and Recreation Division, Park Ranger Section 4040, Bradshaw Road, Sacramento, CA 95827: (916) 366-2061.

*Trail notes:* The American River Parkway is an idea that sounded good in concept, but works even better in practice. The idea was to create a route along the American River, linking Sacramento all the way upstream past Rancho Cordova and Fair Oaks. The result was this multiple-use trail that runs 23 miles from Discovery Park in Sacramento all way up to Folsom. There are actually two separate, parallel trails, one paved for bicyclists only and a dirt trail for horses. Walkers and joggers should stay off the paved portion and instead use the shoulder of the bike trail or the horse trail. Virtually no one hikes the entire trail, of course, but most people enjoy short sections of it, usually on evening walks, jogs or rides. Spring and fall are the prettiest times along the American River. In spring, the adjacent trees and grass have greened up, the river is rolling fresh, and by May, schools of shad are swimming upstream. In fall, the river is lit by the bright colors of trees turning color. In summer, 100-degree afternoon temperatures keep trail use low during the day, but when evening shade emerges, so do joggers and walkers.

# MAP D3

NOR-CAL MAP ...................... see page 14
adjoining maps
NORTH (C3) .......................... see page 174
EAST (D4) ............................. see page 224
SOUTH (E3) .......................... see page 398
WEST (D2) ............................. see page 208

1 PCT SECTION
20 TRAILS
PAGES 210-223

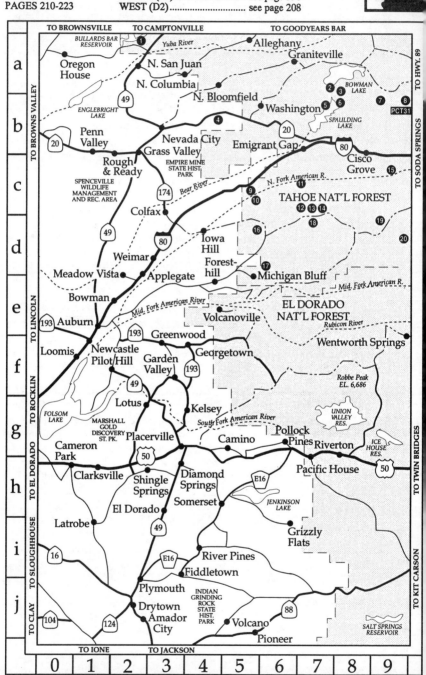

**Map D3 featuring:** Bullards Bar Reservoir, Tahoe National Forest, Emigrant Gap, Nevada City, Carr Lake, Donner, North Fork American River, Foresthill, American River, Cisco Grove, Sugar Pine Reservoir, French Meadows Reservoir, Granite Chief Wilderness, Hell Hole Reservoir, South Fork American River, Mokelumne Wilderness

## 1. BULLARDS BAR TRAIL     7.0 mi/1.0 day

*Reference:* **On Bullards Bar Reservoir in Tahoe National Forest; map D3, grid a1.**

*User groups:* Hikers, dogs, horses and mountain bikes. No wheelchair facilities.

*Permits:* No permits are required. Parking and access are free.

*Directions:* From Nevada City, drive north on Highway 49 to Marysville Road (south of Camptonville). Turn left and follow the signs to the Dark Day Picnic Area/Boat Ramp turnoff. Turn right and continue for a half mile. Take the left fork to the picnic area and the trailhead.

*Maps:* For a map of Tahoe National Forest, send $3 to USDA-Forest Service, 630 Sansome Street, San Francisco, CA 94111. To obtain topographic maps of the area, ask for Camptonville and Challenge from the USGS.

*Who to contact:* Tahoe National Forest, Downieville Ranger District, 15924 Highway 49, Camptonville, CA 95922; (916) 288-3231.

*Trail notes:* Don't get spooked at the seven-mile trail length, because most folks just saunter along for a few miles, maybe take a dunk in the lake or cast out a fishing line and sit a spell, then turn back. You see, this is a trail that traces along the shoreline of Bullards Bar Reservoir. The trailhead is at the Dark Day Picnic Area, and from there, the trail is routed west, contouring along the lake's shore. There are many good spots for fishing or swimming. It is nearly flat, ranging between 2,243 feet and 2,250 feet in elevation, with a sprinkling of huge ponderosa pines and Douglas firs. A heck of a lot of folks take a walk here, one of the heavier-used trails in this county.

## 2. LINDSEY LAKES TRAIL     7.0 mi/3.75 hrs

*Reference:* **In Tahoe National Forest north of Emigrant Gap; map D3, grid a7.**

*User groups:* Hikers, dogs and horses. Mountain bikes are not advised. No wheelchair facilities.

*Permits:* No permits are required. Parking and access are free.

*Directions:* From Auburn, drive east on Interstate 80 for four miles, past Emigrant Gap. Take the Highway 20 exit and head west, driving about five miles to Bowman Lake Road (Forest Service Road 18). Turn right and drive north until you see a sign that says "Lindsey Lake, Feely Lake, Carr Lake." Turn right and follow the signs to the parking area for Lindsey Lake. The road can be extremely rough; four-wheel-drive vehicles are advised.

*Maps:* For a map of Tahoe National Forest, send $3 to USDA-Forest Service, 630 Sansome Street, San Francisco, CA 94111. To obtain topographic maps of the area, ask for English Mountain and Graniteville from the USGS.

*Who to contact:* Tahoe National Forest, Nevada City Ranger District, P.O. Box

6003, Nevada City, CA 95959; (916) 265-4531.

*Trail notes:* The Grouse Lakes area is a classic Sierra basin in the 6,000-foot range, and the feature hike is the Lindsey Lakes Trail. This is a 3.5-mile trail that deadends after climbing past the three Lindsey Lakes, and also has a great sidetrip option. The trailhead is at Lower Lindsey Lake at 6,160 feet. It is routed up to the other Lindsey Lakes, a short trail but quite steep in a few places, topping out at 6,400 feet. It gets medium use, provides good swimming holes with cold water, and poor fishing. The best fishing in this basin is at nearby Culbertson Lake, where there is a great sidetrip, hiking out to Rock Lakes and up to Bullpen Lake. The latter is one of the few lakes anywhere that has been stocked with Arctic grayling. Another sidetrip from the Lindsey Lake Trail is the Crooked Lakes Trail. See hike number 3 in this chapter.

---

## 3. CROOKED LAKES TRAIL    6.0 mi/3.5 hrs

*Reference:* In Tahoe National Forest north of Emigrant Gap; map D3, grid a7.
*User groups:* Hikers, dogs and horses. Mountain bikes are not advised. No wheelchair facilities.
*Permits:* No permits are required. Parking and access are free.
*Directions:* From Auburn, drive east on Interstate 80 for four miles, past Emigrant Gap. Take the Highway 20 exit and head west, driving about five miles to Bowman Lake Road (Forest Service Road 18). Turn right and drive north until you see a sign that says "Lindsey Lake, Feely Lake, Carr Lake." Turn right and follow the signs to the parking area. Take the Lindsey Lake Trail to the junction with the Crooked Lakes Trail. The road can be extremely rough; four-wheel-drive vehicles are advised.
*Maps:* For a map of Tahoe National Forest, send $3 to USDA-Forest Service, 630 Sansome Street, San Francisco, CA 94111. To obtain a topographic map of the area, ask for English Mountain from the USGS.
*Who to contact:* Tahoe National Forest, Nevada City Ranger District, P.O. Box 6003, Nevada City, CA 95959; (916) 265-4531.
*Trail notes:* A lot of folks hike on the Lindsey Lakes Trail (hike number 2 in this chapter), and why not? It's pretty and short. But you can avoid many of those people with a little extra effort, starting your trip on the Lindsey Lakes Trail, then taking the turnoff for the Crooked Lakes Trail. In the course of 2.25 miles, the trail climbs up to the most scenic lakes in the Grouse Lakes area. Your destination is Upper Rock Lake, a small lake set in a pristine high Sierra habitat. From the trailhead, it is a 700-foot climb, topping out at 6,880 feet. The trip can be extended from Upper Rock Lake by heading south, in the process passing Penner Lake, Crooked Lakes and Island Lake.

---

## 4. PIONEER TRAIL    24.0 mi/2.0 days

*Reference:* East of Nevada City, adjacent to Highway 20 in Tahoe National Forest; map D3, grid b4.
*User groups:* Hikers, dogs and horses. No mountain bikes are allowed. No wheelchair facilities.
*Permits:* No permits are required. Parking and access are free.
*Directions:* From Nevada City, turn east on Highway 20 and drive seven miles

to the trailhead across from Lone Grave. If the parking lot there is full, more parking and trail access are available at Skillman Flat, Upper Burlington Ridge and Omega Rest Area, all located to the east off of Highway 20.

*Maps:* For a map of Tahoe National Forest, send $3 to USDA-Forest Service, 630 Sansome Street, San Francisco, CA 94111. To obtain a topographic map of the area, ask for Washington from the USGS.

*Who to contact:* Tahoe National Forest, Nevada City Ranger District, P.O. Box 6003, Nevada City, CA 95959; (916) 265-4531.

*Trail notes:* Hiking the Pioneer Trail is like taking a history lesson where you trace the route of the first wagon road opened by emigrants and gold seekers in 1850. There are three campgrounds along the route for backpackers, and although you can hike it, the trail is better suited for mountain biking. The trailhead is at Lone Grave, 3,500 feet, and from there heads east 12 miles to Bear Valley, gaining 2,000 feet in the process. You will pass Central House (once a stagecoach stop), White Cloud (the site of the largest mill on the West Coast), Skillman Flat (site of a burned-down mill), and Omega Overlook (site of a huge hydraulic gold mining operation). From the Omega Overlook, you also get dramatic views of granite cliffs and the Yuba River. The amount of use on this trail is increasing, particularly by mountain bikers making the one-way trip downhill from Bear Valley to Lone Grave. If you meet others, always demonstrate the utmost courtesy—bikers should always get off and walk when passing hikers.

---

# 5. ROUND LAKE TRAIL    4.5 mi/3.0 hrs

*Reference:* At Carr Lake in Tahoe National Forest north of Emigrant Gap; map D3, grid b7.

*User groups:* Hikers, dogs and horses. Mountain bikes are not advised. No wheelchair facilities.

*Permits:* No permits are required. Parking and access are free.

*Directions:* From Auburn, drive east on Interstate 80 for four miles, past Emigrant Gap. Take the Highway 20 exit and head west, driving about five miles to Bowman Lake Road (Forest Service Road 18). Turn right and drive north until you see a sign that says "Lindsey Lake, Feely Lake, Carr Lake." Turn right and follow the signs to the Carr Lake parking area, then continue on foot to the trailhead at Feely Lake. The road can be extremely rough; four-wheel-drive vehicles are advised.

*Maps:* For a map of Tahoe National Forest, send $3 to USDA-Forest Service, 630 Sansome Street, San Francisco, CA 94111. To obtain topographic maps of the area, ask for English Mountain and Graniteville from the USGS.

*Who to contact:* Tahoe National Forest, Nevada City Ranger District, P.O. Box 6003, Nevada City, CA 95959; (916) 265-4531.

*Trail notes:* The Round Lake Trail accesses a series of beautiful high Sierra Lakes, including Island Lake, Long Lake, Round Lake and Milk Lake. That is why it gets heavy use, despite it being a demanding hike, at times quite steep. The trailhead is at Feely Lake, 6,720 feet, and the trail heads east, climbing first to Island Lake. The lake gets its name from the little rocky islands that are sprinkled about; there are several good campgrounds here. Forging on, the trail passes Long Lake and Round Lake, then arrives at Milk Lake. The latter is a deep cobalt blue, as blue as Tahoe and Hell Hole, and has campsites near the east and west ends. If they are full, there is another camp on Grouse Ridge, a short, steep hike just south of the lake.

## 6. GROUSE RIDGE TRAIL 16.2 mi/2.0 days

*Reference:* **In Tahoe National Forest north of Emigrant Gap; map D3, grid b8.**

*User groups:* Hikers, dogs, horses and mountain bikes. No wheelchair facilities.

*Permits:* No permits are required. Parking and access are free.

*Directions:* From Auburn, drive east on Interstate 80 for four miles, past Emigrant Gap. Take the Highway 20 exit and head west, driving about five miles to Bowman Lake Road (Forest Service Road 18). Turn right and continue north to Graniteville Road, then turn right and drive for three miles. Turn right on Faucherie Lake Road and continue for a quarter mile to the Sawmill Lake Trailhead. The road can be extremely rough; four-wheel-drive vehicles are advised.

*Maps:* For a map of Tahoe National Forest, send $3 to USDA-Forest Service, 630 Sansome Street, San Francisco, CA 94111. To obtain topographic maps of the area, ask for Cisco Grove and English Mountain from the USGS.

*Who to contact:* Tahoe National Forest, Nevada City Ranger District, P.O. Box 6003, Nevada City, CA 95959; (916) 265-4531.

*Trail notes:* The Grouse Ridge Trail weaves up and down from a mountain crest, connecting Sawmill Lake (to the north) to the Eagle Lakes, a one-way distance of 8.25 miles. But the beauty of this trail is that along the way, there are a number of short sidetrips you can take to make quick hits at a half dozen lakes. The elevations span from 6,160 feet to 6,400 feet, with the ups and downs in short yet serious spurts. From Sawmill Lake, you will climb up a timbered slope, and at the ridge come to a turnoff to Rock Lake (worth the visit). You then pass Shotgun Lake (actually a wet meadow), and then onward to Middle Lake, Crooked Lakes and Milk Lake. The views are divine much of the way.

*Special note:* At Sawmill Lake, the trail crosses the spillway of the dam. In spring and early summer, this may be impassable due to high water spilling into Canyon Creek.

## 7. BEYERS LAKES TRAIL 12.5 mi/2.0 days

*Reference:* **In Tahoe National Forest northwest of Donner; map D3, grid b8.**

*User groups:* Hikers, dogs and horses. Mountain bikes are not advised. No wheelchair facilities.

*Permits:* No permits are required. Parking and access are free.

*Directions:* From Auburn, drive east on Interstate 80 for four miles, past Emigrant Gap. Take the Highway 20 exit and head west, driving about five miles to Bowman Lake Road (Forest Service Road 18). Turn right and drive for 19 miles, then turn right on Meadow Lake Road and continue about six miles to the trailhead at Meadow Lake. The road can be extremely rough; four-wheel-drive vehicles are advised.

*Maps:* For a map of Tahoe National Forest, send $3 to USDA-Forest Service, 630 Sansome Street, San Francisco, CA 94111. To obtain topographic maps of the area, ask for Cisco Grove and English Mountain from the USGS.

*Who to contact:* Tahoe National Forest, Nevada City Ranger District, P.O. Box

6003, Nevada City, CA 95959; (916) 265-4531.

*Trail notes:* Beautiful Baltimore Lake and the Beyers Lakes are your destinations on this trail, where you get excellent camping, fishing and swimming (if you don't mind freezing your buns off). It is an excellent two-day backpacking trip. The trailhead is at Meadow Lake at 5,500 feet, set below Hartley Butte (7,457 feet). From here the trail heads southwest on a rough old four-wheel-drive route to Baltimore Lake, which lies in a timbered basin, a divine setting. The evening trout bite is good here, and there are also lakeside campsites. The trail leaves Baltimore Lake and climbs over a mountain saddle at 7,140 feet, then descends into the Beyers Lakes Basin. This is another pristine panorama, with a group of four lakes nestled in granite, bordered by a sprinkling of fir trees.

---

## 8. MOUNT LOLA TRAIL    19.0 mi/2 to 3 days

*Reference:* **In Tahoe National Forest northwest of Donner; map D3, grid b9.**

*User groups:* Hikers, dogs and horses. Mountain bikes are not advised. No wheelchair facilities.

*Permits:* No permits are required. Parking and access are free.

*Directions:* From Auburn, drive east on Interstate 80 for four miles, past Emigrant Gap. Take the Highway 20 exit and head west, driving about five miles to Bowman Lake Road (Forest Service Road 18). Turn right and drive 19 miles, then turn right on Meadow Lake Road and continue past Meadow Lake to the trailhead, located at White Rock Lake. The road can be extremely rough; four-wheel-drive vehicles are advised.

*Maps:* For a map of Tahoe National Forest, send $3 to USDA-Forest Service, 630 Sansome Street, San Francisco, CA 94111. To obtain topographic maps of the area, ask for Independence Lake and Webber Peak from the USGS.

*Who contact:* Tahoe National Forest, Sierraville Ranger District, P.O. Box 95, Highway 89, Sierraville, CA 96126; (916) 994-3401.

*Trail notes:* Mt. Lola is the highest peak in the Tahoe National Forest. It rises up 9,148 feet, and the climb up on this trail will have you wailing "Low-lah," just like the song, because this hike requires something of a fixed rhythm to make it to the top. It involves a 2,500-foot climb, at times quite steep and seemingly endless, but if you are fit, the payoff is right up there with the best in the business. The trail follows along Cold Stream (decent evening trout fishing) to its headwaters, much of the trail passing through thick forest and beautiful open meadows, then rises sharply above tree line to the summit. The views are breathtaking of the Sierra Divide, a lookout you will never forget. The celebration continues as you walk down the back side of Lola, following a switch-backed trail down to White Rock Lake, a one-way distance of 9.5 miles from the trailhead.

---

## 9. EUCHRE BAR TRAIL    6.0 mi/3.5 hrs

*Reference:* **On North Fork American River near Baxter; map D3, grid c5.**

*User groups:* Hikers, dogs and horses. Mountain bikes are not advised. No wheelchair facilities.

*Permits:* No permits are required. Parking and access are free.

*Directions:* From Interstate 80 east of Auburn, take the Alta exit. Turn right on Morton, then turn left on Casa Loma. Follow Casa Loma until you see the

Rawhide Mine sign, then turn right. Follow the road three-quarters of a mile past the second railroad crossing to a parking area. The trailhead is one-tenth of a mile beyond the parking area.

*Maps:* For a map of Tahoe National Forest, send $3 to USDA-Forest Service, 630 Sansome Street, San Francisco, CA 94111. To obtain topographic maps of the area, ask for Dutch Flat and Westville from the USGS.

*Who to contact:* Tahoe National Forest, Foresthill Ranger District, 22830 Foresthill Road, Foresthill, CA 95631; (916) 478-6254.

*Trail notes:* A river runs through almost every Sierra gulch and canyon, yet if that river cannot be seen from a road, many people don't have a clue that it exists. So it is with this portion of the North Fork American River, with access provided on the Euchre Bar Trail. From the trailhead, the route winds steeply down to the river to Euchre Bar, where you will find a suspension footbridge that crosses the river. From here the trail is routed upstream along the river for 2.4 miles, an excellent piece of stream for fishing, camping, gold panning and swimming in cold water. If you want a lesson in pain, you can continue on the trail for another five miles. It climbs the old Dorer Ranch Road, passing mining ruins and abandoned equipment from the Gold Rush era, climbing 2,000 feet in dry, dusty country.

---

## 10. ITALIAN BAR TRAIL     4.5 mi/3.5 hrs

*Reference:* **Near North Fork American River in Tahoe National Forest; map D3, grid c5.**

*User groups:* Hikers, dogs and horses. Mountain bikes are not advised. No wheelchair facilities.

*Permits:* No permits are required. Parking and access are free.

*Directions:* From Interstate 80 at Auburn, turn east on Foresthill Road and drive 16 miles to the town of Foresthill. Continue northeast on Foresthill Road for 13 miles to Forest Service Road 66 (Humbug Ridge Road), then turn left and drive three miles north to the trailhead.

*Maps:* For a map of Tahoe National Forest, send $3 to USDA-Forest Service, 630 Sansome Street, San Francisco, CA 94111. To obtain a topographic map of the area, ask for Westville from the USGS.

*Who to contact:* Tahoe National Forest, Foresthill Ranger District, 22830 Foresthill Road, Foresthill, CA 95631; (916) 478-6254.

*Trail notes:* Miners from the 1850s were like goats, and they knew the most direct route between two points was a straight line. As a result, this old route that miners used to reach the North Fork American River is almost straight down going in, then straight up coming out, with a 3,000-foot elevation change over the course of 2.25 miles. It's about as fun as looking for a tiny gold nugget lost on the beach. Heading down from the trailhead at 5,400 feet, switchbacks help little. The trail ends at the river, and from here you must scramble and rockhop along the river banks. You will end up with a secluded spot where all seems perfect. It will seem that way until you start the hike back, a 3,000-foot climb, when you will wonder why you ever talked yourself into this hike.

# 11. AMERICAN RIVER    21.4 mi/2.0 days

*Reference:* **On North Fork American River east of Foresthill; map D3, grid c6.**

*User groups:* Hikers, dogs and horses. Mountain bikes are not advised. No wheelchair facilities.

*Permits:* No permits are required. Parking and access are free.

*Directions:* From Interstate 80 at Auburn, turn east on Foresthill Road and drive 16 miles to the town of Foresthill. Continue northeast on Foresthill Road for 15 miles to the Mumford Trailhead on the left side of the road.

*Maps:* For a map of Tahoe National Forest, send $3 to USDA-Forest Service, 630 Sansome Street, San Francisco, CA 94111. To obtain a topographic map of the area, ask for Duncan Peak from the USGS.

*Who to contact:* Tahoe National Forest, Foresthill Ranger District, 22830 Foresthill Road, Foresthill, CA 95631; (916) 478-6254.

*Trail notes:* A 90-minute hike from the Mumford Trailhead (see hike number 12) will route you down into a steep canyon and alongside the beautiful and remote North Fork American River. Here you turn right and take the American River Trail upstream. This is what you came for, with the trail heading upstream along a pristine section of river, a steady, easy grade. You will pass old mining sites and abandoned cabins, at times dense vegetation, at other times pretty river views. This trail makes for a great getaway, with good exploring and trout fishing. Alas, nothing is perfect, and neither is this hike. It has three foibles: 1) It crosses two creeks, Tadpole and New York, which are difficult, dangerous fords when running high during the snowmelt period in spring and early-summer; 2) A mile upriver of Tadpole Creek, and then again at New York Creek, the trail runs adjacent to private property— take notice on your map, and stay on the trail here; 3) The hike back out of the canyon to your parked car is a terrible grunt, from 2,640 feet along the river to 5,360 feet, a climb of 2,720 feet in 3.25 miles.

# 12. MUMFORD BAR TRAIL    6.5 mi/1.0 day

*Reference:* **Near American River in Tahoe National Forest; map D3, grid c6.**

*User groups:* Hikers, dogs and horses. Mountain bikes are not advised. No wheelchair facilities.

*Permits:* No permits are required. Parking and access are free.

*Directions:* From Interstate 80 at Auburn, turn east on Foresthill Road and drive 16 miles to the town of Foresthill. Continue northeast on Foresthill Road for 15 miles to the Mumford Trailhead on the left side of the road.

*Maps:* For a map of Tahoe National Forest, send $3 to USDA-Forest Service, 630 Sansome Street, San Francisco, CA 94111. To obtain topographic maps of the area, ask for Duncan Peak and Westville from the USGS.

*Who to contact:* Tahoe National Forest, Foresthill Ranger District, 22830 Foresthill Road, Foresthill, CA 95631; (916) 478-6254.

*Trail notes:* You have to be part mountain goat and part idiot to want do this hike. Guess how we know? The hike is almost straight down to the North Fork American River for over 3.25 miles, and you know what that means, right? Right, it's almost straight up coming back. From the trailhead at 5,360 feet, the first mile of trail follows an old four-wheel-drive route that deteriorates and then drops down to the river canyon at 2,640 feet. Here the river is designated as Wild and Scenic. It's quite pretty, with good canyon views and fishing spots. You can extend your walk by taking the American River Trail (see hike number 11) and staying overnight, which is our recommendation. Otherwise you will have to climb back out of the canyon on the same day, and even most mountain goats would not choose to do that.

---

# 13. BEACROFT TRAIL 4.5 mi/1.0 day

*Reference:* **Near American River in Tahoe National Forest; map D3, grid c7.**

*User groups:* Hikers, dogs and horses. Mountain bikes are not advised. No wheelchair facilities.

*Permits:* No permits are required. Parking and access are free.

*Directions:* From Interstate 80 at Auburn, turn east on Foresthill Road and drive 16 miles to the town of Foresthill. Continue northeast on Foresthill Road for 19 miles to the trailhead, located one mile past Secret House Campground.

*Maps:* For a map of Tahoe National Forest, send $3 to USDA-Forest Service, 630 Sansome Street, San Francisco, CA 94111. To obtain a topographic map of the area, ask for Duncan Peak from the USGS.

*Who to contact:* Tahoe National Forest, Foresthill Ranger District, 22830 Foresthill Road, Foresthill, CA 95631; (916) 478-6254.

*Trail notes:* The Beacroft Trail is the "no-option" option to hiking down to the North Fork American River. The trailhead is located four miles beyond the Mumford Trailhead, and after having reviewed the steep descent and climb required for that hike, you might want to look elsewhere for an easier route down. So there's the Beacroft Trail option. Yet it isn't much of one, requiring an even more hellacious effort, dropping 3,240 feet in only 2.25 miles. The trip back will have you howling. How can such a short trail be so steep? Ask the goldminers who built the darn thing, who apparently did not have an abundance of useful gray matter between their ears, or much gold to carry on the return trip, either. When you reach the river, you can turn left on the American River Trail, which traces some of the most beautiful, accessible portions of this stream. Alas, even here you face an obstacle. Within the first mile, you have to cross New York Creek, a difficult (and sometimes dangerous) ford when full of snowmelt in early summer.

---

# 14. SAILOR FLAT TRAIL 6.5 mi/1.0 day

*Reference:* **Near American River in Tahoe National Forest; map D3, grid c7.**

*User groups:* Hikers, dogs and horses. Mountain bikes are not advised. No wheelchair facilities.

*Permits:* No permits are required. Parking and access are free.

*Directions:* From Interstate 80 at Auburn, turn east on Foresthill Road and drive 16 miles to the town of Foresthill. Continue northeast on Foresthill Road for 25 miles to Sailor Flat Road. Turn left and continue one mile north to the trailhead.

*Maps:* For a map of Tahoe National Forest, send $3 to USDA-Forest Service, 630 Sansome Street, San Francisco, CA 94111. To obtain topographic maps of the area, ask for Royal Gorge and Duncan Peak from the USGS.

*Who to contact:* Tahoe National Forest, Foresthill Ranger District, 22830 Foresthill Road, Foresthill, CA 95631; (916) 478-6254.

*Trail notes:* Of the series of trailheads on Foresthill Road that provide access to the North Fork American River, this is the one most distant, most remote, and alas, most difficult. The Sailor Flat Trailhead is at the end of the road, out in the middle of nowhere at 6,400 feet, yet there are remains of an old, long-abandoned gold stamp mill still standing nearby. The hike starts out easily enough, with the first 1.5 miles following an old mining road, where hikers will not confront anything serious. Don't be fooled. The trail then becomes much steeper, with switchback after switchback taking you down into the canyon. When you reach the river at 3,360 feet, you will have dropped 3,040 feet in only 3.25 miles. You can explore further by turning left on the American River Trail, which traces the most beautiful sections of this river, heading downstream past meadows, canyon views and good spots for fishing and goldpanning. Note: With a shuttle vehicle and a partner, you can create an excellent one-way hike here covering 15.6 miles. From the Sailor Flat Trailhead, hike down to the American River Trail, turn left, hike along the river to Mumford Bar, turn left and hike out to Foresthill Road (see hike numbers 11 and 12 in this chapter).

---

## 15. LOCH LEVEN LAKES    7.0 mi/1.0 day

*Reference:* South of Cisco Grove in Tahoe National Forest; map D3, grid c9.
*User groups:* Hikers, dogs and horses. Mountain bikes are not advised. No wheelchair facilities.
*Permits:* No permits are required. Parking and access are free.
*Directions:* From Sacramento, take Interstate 80 eastbound and take the Big Bend exit. Or take Interstate 80 westbound and take the Rainbow Road exit. Follow the signs to the Big Bend Visitor Center, which is located adjacent to the highway. The parking area and trailhead are about a quarter mile east of the visitor center.
*Maps:* For a map of Tahoe National Forest, send $3 to USDA-Forest Service, 630 Sansome Street, San Francisco, CA 94111. To obtain a topographic map of the area, ask for Cisco Grove from the USGS.
*Who to contact:* Tahoe National Forest, Nevada City Ranger District, P.O. Box 6003, Nevada City, CA 95959; (916) 265-4531.
*Trail notes:* Most people would like to know what heaven is like, but aren't real willing to sign up for the trip. The 3.5-mile hike to Loch Leven Lakes furnishes an answer, because after all, heaven should look something like this. You get vistas of ridges and valleys, high alpine meadows, and glaciated mountain terrain with a series of pristine lakes. With the trailhead so easily accessible off Interstate 80, the trail has become well known and gets heavy use. The trail starts at 5,680 feet, then works its way upward on a moderate grade to the southwest. Granite outcroppings are numerous and huge boulders (deposited by receding glaciers) are found sprinkled among Jeffrey and lodgepole pine. The trail crosses a creek and railroad tracks, climbs through a cool forest, then tops the summit and winds its way down to Lower Loch Leven Lake. Many people stop here, content with the surroundings. But you can forge on for another mile, circling Middle Loch Leven Lake, then head east up to High Loch Leven Lake at 6,800 feet. Fishing is good during the evening bite, and there are backcountry campgrounds at each lake.

# 16. GREEN VALLEY TRAIL 4.5 mi/1.0 day

*Reference:* **On North Fork American River near Sugar Pine Reservoir; map D3, grid d5.**

*User groups:* Hikers, dogs and horses. Mountain bikes are not advised. No wheelchair facilities.

*Permits:* No permits are required. Parking and access are free.

*Directions:* From Interstate 80 at Auburn, turn east on Foresthill Road and drive 16 miles to the town of Foresthill. Continue northeast on Foresthill Road for about seven miles, then turn left on Forest Service Road 10 and follow it for five miles until you cross the Sugar Pine Dam. Continue one mile past the dam, then turn north on Elliot Ranch Road and proceed three miles to the trailhead.

*Maps:* For a map of Tahoe National Forest, send $3 to USDA-Forest Service, 630 Sansome Street, San Francisco, CA 94111. To obtain a topographic map of the area, ask for Dutch Flat from the USGS.

*Who to contact:* Tahoe National Forest, Foresthill Ranger District, 22830 Foresthill Road, Foresthill, CA 95631; (916) 288-3231.

*Trail notes:* It's amazing what people will go through to create a space that feels like their own. You have a chance to do that on the Green Valley Trail, finding an idyllic spot along the North Fork American River. But the price is steep, and the return trip will put you through more punishment than is typically handed out at Folsom Prison. The trip starts at a little-known trailhead, elevation 4,080 feet, near Sugar Pine Reservoir. From here, the Green Valley Trail is steep and often rocky, dropping 2,240 feet in 2.25 miles before reaching the North Fork American. We do not advise planning on extending your trip. It is possible to continue downriver for a short way, or cross the river (good luck) and hike upstream into Green Valley. However, these sections of trail are in very poor condition, and on the upstream route, cross private property whose owners don't take kindly to visitors.

# 17. MICHIGAN BLUFF TRAIL 4.0 mi/2.5 hrs

*Reference:* **In Tahoe National Forest east of Foresthill; map D3, grid d5.**

*User groups:* Hikers, dogs, horses and mountain bikes. No wheelchair facilities.

*Permits:* No permits are required. Parking and access are free.

*Directions:* From Interstate 80 at Auburn, turn east on Foresthill Road and drive 16 miles to the town of Foresthill. Continue northeast on Foresthill Road and follow the signs to Michigan Bluff. The trailhead is located about a quarter mile east of Michigan Bluff.

*Maps:* For a map of Tahoe National Forest, send $3 to USDA-Forest Service, 630 Sansome Street, San Francisco, CA 94111. To obtain a topographic map of the area, ask for Michigan Bluff from the USGS.

*Who to contact:* Tahoe National Forest, Foresthill Ranger District, 22830 Foresthill Road, Foresthill, CA 95631; (916) 288-3231.

*Trail notes:* If only the Forest Service would ban motorcycles, or "dirt bikes" as they're called, from this trail, this hike would be just about perfect. While it is rare to run into dirt bikes here, they are legal and it is only a matter of time until word circulates about this route. The attraction is beautiful Eldorado Canyon, with good fishing and camping along Eldorado Creek. The trailhead is at 3,520 feet, and from here the trail quickly drops into the canyon, with switchbacks leading to a footbridge over Eldorado Creek, a distance of about two miles. The trip can be extended by crossing the bridge, then hiking up the other side of the canyon, offering scenic views of rugged topography.

## 18. FOREST VIEW TRAIL   1.5 mi/0.75 hr

*Reference:* **In Tahoe National Forest east of Foresthill; map D3, grid d7.**
*User groups:* Hikers and dogs. No horses or mountain bikes are allowed. No wheelchair facilities.
*Permits:* No permits are required. Parking and access are free.
*Directions:* From Interstate 80 at Auburn, turn east on Foresthill Road and drive 16 miles to the town of Foresthill. Turn east on Mosquito Ridge Road and drive 27 miles to the trailhead.
*Maps:* Free interpretive brochures are available at the trailhead. For a map of Tahoe National Forest, send $3 to USDA-Forest Service, 630 Sansome Street, San Francisco, CA 94111. To obtain a topographic map of the area, ask for Greek Store from the USGS.
*Who to contact:* Tahoe National Forest, Foresthill Ranger District, 22830 Foresthill Road, Foresthill, CA 95631; (916) 288-3231.
*Trail notes:* The world's largest trees, the Giant Sequoia, attract many visitors on this easy, well-maintained interpretive trail. It is set at 5,200 feet on Mosquito Ridge Road, which provides many views of the area's wild and superb landscape. The trail meanders through a virgin old-growth forest, with half a dozen truly monster-sized trees, the northernmost grove of Giant Sequoias in California. On the Big Trees Interpretive Trail, there are 16 numbered stops in one-half mile that coincide with numbered text in a brochure available at the trailhead. The entire 1.5-mile loop extends to the Forest View Trail. Despite the long drive to the trailhead on Mosquito Ridge, this trail gets quite a bit of use.

## 19. McGUIRE TRAIL   7.8 mi/4.0 hrs

*Reference:* **At French Meadows Reservoir in Tahoe National Forest; map D3, grid d8.**
*User groups:* Hikers, dogs, horses and mountain bikes. No wheelchair facilities.
*Permits:* No permits are required. Parking and access are free.
*Directions:* From Interstate 80 at Auburn, turn east on Foresthill Road and drive 16 miles to the town of Foresthill. Turn east on Mosquito Ridge Road and drive 36 miles to the French Meadows Reservoir Dam. Cross the dam and continue east, skirting the south side of the lake. At the northeast end of the lake, turn left and follow the signs to McGuire Boat Ramp.
*Maps:* For a map of Tahoe National Forest, send $3 to USDA-Forest Service, 630 Sansome Street, San Francisco, CA 94111. To obtain a topographic map of the area, ask for Bunker Hill from the USGS.
*Who to contact:* Tahoe National Forest, Foresthill Ranger District, 22830 Foresthill Road, Foresthill, CA 95631; (916) 288-3231.
*Trail notes:* The McGuire Trail has become a favorite sidetrip for families visiting or camping at French Meadows Reservoir at 5,290 feet. The trail follows along the north shore of the lake, poking in and out of timber, then follows an easy grade to the top of Red Star Ridge, 5,600 feet. There are good

views of the lake below. It's a good-size lake, covering nearly 2,000 acres when full, and is stocked with more than 30,000 trout each year, joining a population of resident brown trout and holdovers from stocks of rainbow trout in previous years. One problem here is lake drawdowns are common in late summer, exposing lots of stumps and boulders, creating a navigational hazard for boaters.

## 20. HELLHOLE TRAIL    13.0 mi/2.0 days

*Reference:* **In Granite Chief Wilderness east of Hell Hole Reservoir; map D3, grid d9.**

*User groups:* Hikers, dogs and horses. No mountain bikes. No wheelchair facilities.

*Permits:* A campfire permit is required for hikers planning to camp in the wilderness. Parking and access are free.

*Directions:* From Interstate 80 in Truckee, turn south on Highway 89 and drive to Tahoe City. Continue south on Highway 89 for four more miles to Caspian Picnic Area. Turn west on Blackwood Canyon Road and drive 2.3 miles, then cross the creek and continue another 4.8 miles to Barker Pass. The pavement ends here, but continue another 2.3 miles down the road to the Powderhorn Trailhead. Park here. Walk on the Powderhorn Trail for four miles to Diamond Crossing, where the Hellhole Trail intersects.

*Maps:* For a map of Tahoe National Forest, send $3 to USDA-Forest Service, 630 Sansome Street, San Francisco, CA 94111. To obtain a topographic map of the area, ask for Wentworth Springs from the USGS.

*Who to contact:* Tahoe National Forest, Truckee Ranger District, P.O. Box 399, Truckee, CA 95734; (916) 587-3558.

*Trail notes:* Do you yearn for a challenging trek in a very remote high mountain wilderness setting? Then this is it. It's way out there in booger country, requires wilderness skills and worst of all, a difficult stream crossing and traversing a landslide. Sound fun? Who said it was fun? The Powderhorn Trailhead is a remote trailhead, set at 6,400 feet on the edge of a boundary to the Granite Chief Wilderness. From here you hike four miles down to Diamond Crossing (fording Powderhorn Creek), where you will intersect with the Hellhole Trail. Here you turn left, and shortly later, will have to cross Five Lakes Creek, a difficult and sometimes dangerous encounter, especially during snowmelt. If you make it, you will then descend to Little Buckskin Creeks (two more fords, these a lot easier) and into Steamboat Canyon. About one-half mile down the trail from Steamboat Canyon is a slippery landslide that demands extreme caution. The trail drops down toward the Rubicon River and the awesome Hell Hole Reservoir. Few hikers traverse this trail, mainly those who are not concerned about living long, healthy lives.

*Special note:* The stream crossings required on this route can be life-threatening during periods of high snowmelt and runoff.

# PACIFIC CREST TRAIL (PCT)

## PCT-31        38.0 mi. one way/3.0 days
## DONNER PASS to YUBA RIVER

*Reference:* **From Highway 80 to Highway 49 in Tahoe National Forest; map D3, grid b9.**

*User groups:* Hikers, dogs and horses. No mountain bikes are allowed. No wheelchair facilities.

*Permits:* No permits are required for this section of Pacific Crest Trail. Parking and access are free.

*Directions:* From Auburn, drive east on Interstate 80 to Boreal/Donner Summit. Take the exit for the Donner Summit Picnic Area. The trailhead is located at the picnic area.

*Maps:* For a map of Tahoe National Forest, send $3 to USDA-Forest Service, 630 Sansome Street, San Francisco, CA 94111. To obtain topographic maps of the area, ask for Norden, Soda Springs, Webber, Haypress Valley and English Mountain from the USGS.

*Who to contact:* Tahoe National Forest, Truckee Ranger District, 10342 Highway 89, North Truckee, CA 96161; (916) 587-3558, or Tahoe National Forest, Sierraville Ranger District, P.O. Box 95, Highway 89, Sierraville, CA 96126; (916) 994-3401.

*Trail notes:* This is not one of the glamour sections of the Pacific Crest Trail, but it is hardly a stinker either. For the most part, it follows a crest connecting a series of small mountain tops, then drops down to Jackson Meadow Reservoir and beyond to Highway 49. The first part of the trail offers a series of good views, so many that some PCT hikers may take them for granted after a while. Here the trail is routed past Castle Peak (elevation 9,103 feet), Basin Peak (9,015 feet) and Lacey Mountain (8,214 feet). This makes an ambitious first day, perhaps stopping first at Paradise Lake or White Rock Lake. As the trail drops to Jackson Meadow Reservoir, the views end, but in time, the lake comes into view, quite pretty, surrounded by firs. The PCT then skirts past the east side of Jackson Meadow Reservoir, passes several drive-to campgrounds, heads through Bear Valley (this isn't *the* Bear Valley) and then drops down steeply to Milton Creek and beyond four miles to Loves Falls at Highway 49.

*PCT CONTINUATION:* To continue hiking along the Pacific Crest Trail, see Chapter C3, pages 190-193.

# MAP D4

5 TRT SECTIONS
5 PCT SECTIONS
37 TRAILS
PAGES 224-257

NOR-CAL MAP ........................ see page 14
adjoining maps
NORTH (C4) ........................... see page 194
EAST ....................................... no map
SOUTH (E4) ........................... see page 402
WEST (D3) ............................. see page 210

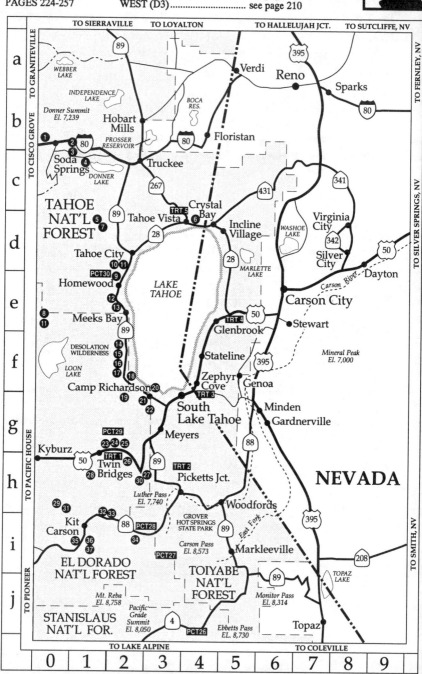

**Map D4 featuring:** Truckee, Donner Pass, Donner Summit, Donner Lake, Squaw Valley Ski Resort, Lake Tahoe, Tahoe City, Incline Village, Granite Chief Wilderness, Alpine Meadows, Desolation Wilderness, Emerald Bay, South Lake Tahoe, D. L. Bliss State Park, Kyburz, Mokelumne Wilderness, Carson Pass, Echo Summit, Big Meadows, Dagget Pass, Spooner Summit, Brockway Summit, Ebbetts Pass, Carson Pass, Echo Lake

## 1. LOWER LOLA MONTEZ LAKE    6.0 mi/2.5 hrs

*Reference:* **West of Truckee and Donner Pass and just north of Interstate 80; map D4, grid b0.**

*User groups:* Hikers, horses, dogs and mountain bikes. No wheelchair facilities.

*Permits:* Campfire permits are required for open fires or camp stoves. Parking and access are free.

*Directions:* From Truckee, drive west on Interstate 80 to the Soda Springs Norden exit. Do not cross back over the freeway, but stay on the unsigned paved road (east) for approximately three-tenths of a mile to the parking area for the trail.

*Maps:* Send $3 to the USDA-Forest Service, 630 Sansome Street, San Francisco, CA 94111 and ask for the Tahoe National Forest map. For a topographic map, ask for Soda Springs from the USGS.

*Who to contact:* Tahoe National Forest, Truckee Ranger District, 10342 Highway 89, North Truckee, CA 96161; (916) 587-3558.

*Trail notes:* Hike for approximately a quarter of a mile to a road which will lead across Lower Castle Creek. Use extreme caution when crossing this creek during high water, especially during spring snowmelt. Following the creek ford, hike for another quarter mile to the trail which will climb for a short way until meeting up with yet another road. Follow this road for approximately one mile under a pleasant forest canopy to the road's end and a quiet meadow. The trail resumes at the meadow and continues on to Lower Lola Montez Lake. There is excellent camping around the lake and fairly decent fishing. Much of the land surrounding the trail to the lake crosses private property. Please tread lightly and quietly, respecting the rights of the landowners.

## 2. GLACIER MEADOW LOOP    0.5 mi/0.5 hr

*Reference:* **West of Truckee and east of Sacramento at Donner Summit; map D4, grid b1.**

*User groups:* Hikers, horses and dogs. No mountain bikes are allowed. No wheelchair facilities.

*Permits:* No permits are required. Parking and access are free.

*Directions:* Drive west on Interstate 80 from Truckee and exit at Castle Peak Area/Boreal Ridge—just west of the Donner Summit roadside rest area. The sign for the Pacific Crest Trailhead is what you are looking for, and it is located on the south side of the highway. Follow the directions on the sign for four-tenths of a mile to the PCT Trailhead parking. Although the Glacier Meadows Loop Trail is accessible from the rest area, unattended parking is not permitted.

*Maps:* Send $3 to the USDA-Forest Service, 630 Sansome Street, San Francisco, CA 94111 and ask for the Tahoe National Forest map. For a topographic map, ask for Norden from the USGS.

*Who to contact:* Tahoe National Forest, Truckee Ranger District, 10342 Highway 89, North Truckee, CA 96161; (916) 587-3558.

*Trail notes:* This trail is a great leg stretcher if you are heading to or from Lake Tahoe and you need a sanity break. The self-guided nature trail is a short and pleasant stroll along a path with interpretive signs that explain how glacial action carved and polished the local region. Water and restrooms are available at the trailhead.

---

## 3. WARREN LAKE          12.0 mi/2.0 days

*Reference:* West of Truckee and just north of Donner Pass on Interstate 80; map D4, grid c1.

*User groups:* Hikers, horses, dogs and mountain bikes (mountain bikes must stay off the Pacific Crest Trail). No wheelchair access.

*Permits:* Campfire permits are required and may be obtained from the Truckee Ranger District Office, address listed below. Parking and access are free.

*Directions:* Drive west on Interstate 80 from Truckee and exit at Castle Peak Area/Boreal Ridge—just west of the Donner Summit roadside rest area. The sign for the Pacific Crest Trailhead is located on the south side of the highway. Follow the directions on the sign for a quarter of a mile to the PCT Trailhead parking. Although the trail is accessible from the Donner Pass rest area, unattended parking is not permitted. Parking is not allowed in the Cal Trans parking lot.

*Maps:* Send $3 to the USDA-Forest Service, 630 Sansome Street, San Francisco, CA 94111 and ask for the Tahoe National Forest map. For topographic maps, ask for Norden and Independence from the USGS.

*Who to contact:* Tahoe National Forest, Truckee Ranger District, 10342 Highway 89, North Truckee, CA 96161; (916) 587-3558.

*Trail notes:* This is a two-thumbs-up overnight opportunity that offers an almost amazing amount of solitude and peace despite its easy access to hundreds of thousands of people and the Interstate. From the PCT trailhead, hike on the PCT access trail to the Summit Lake Trail turnoff (just beyond the freeway underpass). Wildflowers are outstanding from spring until summer in the meadow you will hike through just before reaching Summit Lake. Just past the Summit Lake turnoff, the trail climbs pleasantly through lodgepole pine, red fir and mountain hemlock forest to an 8,570 foot saddle with glorious views. From the saddle, the trail will descend into the valley along the northeastern slopes of Castle and Basin Peaks. Expect numerous stream crossings along the way, especially during the snowmelt. Pack your fishing rod because there is good fishing for eastern brook and rainbow trout in both Summit and Warren lakes. Water and restrooms are available at the trailhead.

## 4. LOCH LEVEN LAKES          6.0 mi/3.0 hrs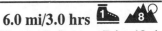

*Reference:* **South of Interstate 80 and west of Donner Lake; map D4, grid c1.**

*User groups:* Hikers, horses, dogs and mountain bikes (mountain bikes must stay off the Pacific Crest Trail). No wheelchair access.

*Permits:* No permits are required. Parking and access are free.

*Directions:* From Interstate 80, west of Truckee and Donner Lake, take the Big Bend exit. Look for the sign "Private Road, Public Trail" located across from the Big Bend Ranger Station, west of the Rainbow Tavern.

*Maps:* Send $3 to the USDA-Forest Service, 630 Sansome Street, San Francisco, CA 94111 and ask for the Tahoe National Forest map. For topographic maps, ask for Emerald Bay and Echo Lake from the USGS.

*Who to contact:* Tahoe National Forest, Truckee Ranger District, 10342 Highway 89, North Truckee, CA 96161; (916) 587-3558.

*Trail notes:* This is an outstanding sanity-restoration hike if you must head for Sacramento or the Bay Area at the day's end. Three beautiful glacial tarns make up the Loch Leven Lakes. A well-graded trail accesses the first lake after a two-mile climb and then continues on, reaching the two other lakes within the next mile. All three island-dotted lakes are outstanding for swimming—brrrr, bring warm clothes to change into.

## 5. SHIRLEY LAKE          5.0 mi/3.0 hrs

*Reference:* **Squaw Valley Ski Resort, near Lake Tahoe; map D4, grid d1.**

*User groups:* Hikers and dogs. No horses or mountain bikes are allowed. No wheelchair facilities.

*Permits:* No permits are required. Parking and access are free.

*Directions:* From Tahoe City on the north shore of Lake Tahoe, drive on Highway 89 north towards Truckee. The Squaw Valley Ski Resort exit will appear on the left after approximately six miles. Turn into the resort and park in the lot near the tram building at the end of Squaw Peak Road. The Shirley Lake Trail begins next to the tram building.

*Maps:* Send $3 to the USDA-Forest Service, 630 Sansome Street, San Francisco, CA 94111 and ask for the Lake Tahoe Basin Management Unit map. For a topographic map of the area, ask for Tahoe City from the USGS.

*Who to contact:* Tahoe Truckee Ranger District, 10342 Highway 89, North Truckee, CA 96161; (916) 587-3558.

*Trail notes:* There are two ways to go at this hike, one from the bottom up and the other from the top down. The mileage and estimated hiking time listed above assumes that you will begin next to the tram building and elect to hike up, following Squaw Creek past gorgeous waterfalls (in the spring) and giant boulders to Shirley Lake (the lake dries up by July or August). It is possible to ride the tram up ($10 for adults; $5 for children under 12) and hike down, but this will add a mile or two and another hour of travel time to the mix. If you are hiking from the tram building up, keep Squaw Creek and the tramway to your left at all times. The trail may diverge and disappear periodically, but as long as you are near the creek, you are on the right track. When hiking down, keep the creek to your right. The creek does dry up completely by August, sometimes by July, and it becomes easier to actually boulder-hop directly up the creek bed. If the creek is dry, we would recommend that you limit your exploration to the lower reaches of the creek, turning back when the going gets steep. This option will give you a round-trip of between two to three miles, depending on how far you push it.

## 6. STATELINE TRAIL          0.5 mi/0.5 hr

*Reference:* **East of Tahoe City and west of Incline Village on the north shore of Lake Tahoe; map D4, grid d4.**

*User groups:* Hikers, dogs and horses. No mountain bikes are allowed. No wheelchair facilities.

*Permits:* No permits are required. Parking and access are free.

*Directions:* From Tahoe City, drive east on State Highway 28 to Crystal Bay. Old Biltmore Casino is the landmark. Turn right on Lake Shore Avenue and then left on Forest Service Road 1601. Drive uphill to the lookout parking lot on the hill. The trail begins and ends at the parking lot.

*Maps:* Send $3 to the USDA-Forest Service, 630 Sansome Street, San Francisco, CA 94111 and ask for the Lake Tahoe Basin Management Unit map. For a topographic map, ask for Kings Beach from the USGS.

*Who to contact:* Lake Tahoe Basin Management Unit, 870 Emerald Bay Road, Suite 1, South Lake Tahoe, CA 96150; (916) 573-2600.

*Trail notes:* If you need a fresh-air respite after the stresses of the road or gambling losses, head to the overlook. The short self-guided interpretive trail offers super views of Lake Tahoe below and the north shore area. This trail is outstanding in the early spring when snow still blankets the peaks surrounding the lake.

## 7. FIVE LAKES TRAIL          4.5 mi/2.5 hrs

*Reference:* **In the Granite Chief Wilderness, west of Tahoe City and south of Truckee; map D4, grid d1.**

*User groups:* Hikers, dogs and horses. No mountain bikes are allowed. No wheelchair facilities.

*Permits:* No day-use permits are needed. Permits are required for overnight camping in the Granite Chief Wilderness and may be obtained from the Lake Tahoe Basin Management Unit, (916) 573-2600. Parking and access are free.

*Directions:* From Interstate 80, just west of Truckee, take the South Lake Tahoe exit and drive on Highway 89 south for approximately 9.5 miles to Alpine Meadows Road. Turn west and drive 2.1 miles up Alpine Meadows Road to a parking area for the Five Lakes Trail located on the right. There is limited parking.

*Maps:* Send $3 to the USDA-Forest Service, 630 Sansome Street, San Francisco, CA 94111 and ask for the Lake Tahoe Basin Management Unit map. For topographic maps of the area, ask for Granite Chief and Tahoe City from the USGS.

*Who to contact:* Tahoe Truckee Ranger District, 10342 Highway 89, North Truckee, CA 96161; (916) 587-3558.

*Trail notes:* This is an ideal family destination, providing you don't choose to head out on a summer weekend when the parking area and trail are frustratingly congested. The Forest Service does not advise camping at Five Lakes due to its heavy visitation. Still, for a day trip, especially on a weekday or in late spring or early fall, the jaunt is well worth it, simply for the joy of picnicking among wildflowers or casting a fishing line on tranquil waters. Hike on the Five Lakes Trail towards the Pacific Crest Trail. Your route will climb steeply through meadows full of wildflowers and then up a rocky track overlooking Alpine Meadow's ski area. The climbing levels out to a moderate ascent after a mile or so and shortly enters the Granite Chief Wilderness and blessed shade.

## 8. McGUIRE TRAIL (WESTERN STATES TRAIL)

8.0 mi/4.0 hrs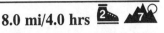

*Reference:* **East of Auburn, south of Donner Pass and west of Lake Tahoe; map D4, grid e0.**

*User groups:* Hikers, horses, dogs and mountain bikes. No wheelchair access.

*Permits:* No permits are required. Parking and access are free.

*Directions:* From Foresthill, east of Auburn, drive east on Mosquito Ridge Road 96 to French Meadows Reservoir. Drive to the east end of the reservoir and then turn left to the McGuire Boat Ramp. The trailhead is located at the boat ramp.

*Maps:* Send $3 to the USDA-Forest Service, 630 Sansome Street, San Francisco, CA 94111 and ask for the Tahoe National Forest map. For a topographic map of the area, ask for Bunker Hill from the USGS.

*Who to contact:* Foresthill Ranger District, 22830 Foresthill Road, Foresthill, CA 95631; (916) 367-2224.

*Trail notes:* This is an outstanding trail for the entire family to enjoy. The hike will take you on a scenic route along the north shore of French Meadows Reservoir, through timber and then up to the top of Red Star Ridge. The French Meadows Reservoir is located at 5,300 feet and is a good base of operations for fishing, swimming, hiking and even canoeing. It's a popular spot in the summer, so expect to share the reservoir and the trail with other humans.

## 9. WARD CREEK TRAIL

3.2 mi/1.5 hrs

*Reference:* **South of Tahoe City and west of Highway 89; map D4, grid d2.**

*User groups:* Hikers, horses, dogs and mountain bikes. No wheelchair facilities.

*Permits:* No permits are required.

*Directions:* From Tahoe City, drive south on Highway 89 for two miles to Pineland Drive. Turn right on Pineland and then in approximately one-half mile, turn left onto Twin Peaks Drive. Twin Peaks becomes Ward Creek Boulevard. Stay on Ward Creek, passing the turnoff on the right for Paige Meadow and taking Forest Service Road 15N02 on the left. Park in the limited roadside parking.

*Maps:* Send $3 to the USDA-Forest Service, 630 Sansome Street, San Francisco, CA 94111 and ask for the Lake Tahoe Basin Management Unit map. For topographic maps of the area, ask for Homewood and Tahoe City from the USGS.

*Who to contact:* Lake Tahoe Basin Management Unit, 870 Emerald Bay Road, Suite 1, South Lake Tahoe, CA 96150; (916) 573-2600.

*Trail notes:* Ward Creek offers an excellent picnic destination for families or couples seeking a little peace and solitude amid picturesque meadows dotted with springtime wildflowers. From the parking area, the trail (actually a logging road) follows a rolling route for just over 1.5 miles to Ward Creek. During the spring, the runoff may be a little high, making crossing the creek a very wet proposition at best, dangerous at worst. Caution is the better part of valor here. In the late summer, the creek will have subsided, allowing for easy crossing. Unnamed trails criss-cross the meadows and along the banks of the creek, begging for casual exploration. When you are ready, retrace your steps back to the road and your car.

---

## 10. PAIGE MEADOW  3.0 mi/1.0 hr

*Reference:* **South of Tahoe City and west of Highway 89; map D4, grid d2.**
*User groups:* Hikers, horses, dogs and mountain bikes. No wheelchair facilities.
*Permits:* No permits are required. Parking and access are free.
*Directions:* From Tahoe City, drive south on Highway 89. Turn right onto Fountain Avenue, which is north of William Kent Campground. Turn right on Pine Avenue, then left on Park Height Drive. Turn right on Big Pine Drive and then left on Silvertip. The trailhead is signed.
*Maps:* Send $3 to the USDA-Forest Service, 630 Sansome Street, San Francisco, CA 94111 and ask for the Lake Tahoe Basin Management Unit map. For topographic maps of the area, ask for Homewood and Tahoe City from the USGS.
*Who to contact:* Lake Tahoe Basin Management Unit, 870 Emerald Bay Road, Suite 1, South Lake Tahoe, CA 96150; (916) 573-2600.
*Trail notes:* If you like wildflowers, then this will be a favorite hike, especially in the spring. Bring along your camera and wildflower identification books. This trail is easy to follow and fairly level, making it an ideal trek for the entire family.

---

## 11. BEAR PEN  13.0 mi/1.0 day

*Reference:* **Southwest of Tahoe City and west of Lake Tahoe; map D4, grid d2.**
*User groups:* Hikers, horses and dogs. No mountain bikes are allowed.
*Permits:* A campfire permit is required for all campfire and stove use. Day-use permits are not required. Parking and access are free.
*Directions:* From Tahoe City, drive south on State Highway 89 for 4.2 miles to the Caspian Picnic Area. Turn west on Blackwood Canyon Road and drive approximately 7.1 miles until the pavement ends. From here, it is another 2.3 miles on dirt to a parking area and the trailhead for Powderhorn Creek, Diamond Crossing and Bear Pen.
*Maps:* Send $3 to the USDA-Forest Service, 630 Sansome Street, San Francisco, CA 94111 and ask for the Tahoe National Forest map. For topographic maps, ask for Wentworth Springs and Homewood from the USGS.
*Who to contact:* Tahoe National Forest, Truckee Ranger District, 10342 Highway 89, North Truckee, CA 96161; (916) 587-3558.
*Trail notes:* The trail to Bear Pen, which is a small meadow at the end of a canyon, offers plenty of solitude through gorgeous stands of Jeffrey pine and outstanding wildflower displays—lupine, mule ears and pennyroyal to name a few. The trail lies within the Granite Chief Wilderness. Hike up the Powderhorn Trail to Diamond Crossing and then bear right on the trail to Bear Pen. The first mile or so of the trail crisscrosses a logging road through

private land before entering the wilderness—respect the landowner's privacy. Powderhorn Creek can be a challenge to cross at high water. Late spring, summer and fall are ideal for hiking. The rest of the time, enjoy the terrain on skis or snowshoes.

---

# 12. SUGAR PINE POINT NATURE TRAILS

1.6 mi/1.0 hr

*Reference:* **South of Tahoe City on Highway 89; map D4, grid e2.**

*User groups:* Hikers. Mountain bikes are allowed designated trails. No horses or dogs are allowed. **Limited wheelchair access** on a short designated trail.

*Permits:* No permits required, but a $5 day-use fee is charged by Sugar Pine Point State Park.

*Directions:* From Tahoe City, drive south on Highway 89 for approximately 10 miles to the signed entrance to Sugar Pine Point State Park.

*Maps:* For a map/brochure of Sugar Pine Point State Park (50 cents in summer only), contact the park at (916) 525-7982. Send $3 to the USDA-Forest Service, 630 Sansome Street, San Francisco, CA 94111 and ask for the Lake Tahoe Basin Management Unit map. For a topographic map, ask for Kings Beach from the USGS. In the winter, a schedule of guided cross-country ski trips may be received by sending a self-addressed and stamped envelope to the park at the address listed below.

*Who to contact:* Sugar Pine Point State Park, P.O. Box D, Tahoma, CA 96142; (916) 525-7982, or the Sierra District at (916) 525-7232.

*Trail notes:* Sugar Pine Point State Park is the largest of the Lake Tahoe-area state parks, and it is also the only one of the state parks that keeps its campground open year-round. Winter snows bring cross-country skiing enthusiasts here to enjoy the several miles of maintained trail. During the warmer months, you can hike the several nature trails; one is the half-mile long (each way) Rod Beaudry Trail and the other is a 1.25-mile trek that winds through sugar pines and the Edwin Z'Berg Natural Preserve. The nature trails, as well as the natural history museum and walking tours of the Ehrman Mansion, create a pleasant afternoon rambling escape, suitable for all ages. The Rod Beaudry Trail is paved and **wheelchair-accessible** with some assistance. The trail begins to the left of the main road, just past the water tower and Nature Center. After crossing a bridge over General Creek behind the mansion and approximately one-quarter mile from the start, the trail junctions with the nature trail winding through the Edwin Z'Berg Natural Preserve. Head to the right on the unpaved treadway to enter the preserve, or stay to the left on the paved route and finish the out-and-back Rod Beaudry trek. Please secure all your food—bears are becoming a nuisance here.

---

# 13. GENERAL CREEK LOOP TRAIL

6.5 mi/3.0 hrs

*Reference:* **South of Tahoe City on Highway 89; map D4, grid e2.**

*User groups:* Hikers, mountain bikes and dogs. No horses are allowed. There is limited **wheelchair access.**

*Permits:* A $5 day-use fee is charged by Sugar Pine Point State Park. This trail enters the heavily visited Desolation Wilderness. Permits are required for overnight stays and may be obtained from the Lake Tahoe Basin Management Unit, (916) 573-2600. Day hikers must register by using the self-service permit register located at the trailhead. Group sizes are limited to 15—please keep yours much smaller if possible.

**Directions:** From Tahoe City, drive south on Highway 89 for approximately 10 miles to the signed entrance to Sugar Pine Point State Park. Parking for the General Creek Trailhead is located at the General Creek Campground. Ask at the entrance station exactly where to park.

**Maps:** For a map/brochure of Sugar Pine Point State Park (50 cents), contact the park at (916) 525-7982. Send $3 to the USDA-Forest Service, 630 Sansome Street, San Francisco, CA 94111 and ask for the Lake Tahoe Basin Management Unit map. For topographic maps of the area, ask for Kings Beach, Homewood and Rockbound Valley from the USGS. Tom Harrison Cartography also publishes an excellent map of the area. Call (415) 456-7940 and ask for the Desolation Wilderness map. The cost is $5.95 plus tax and shipping.

**Who to contact:** Sugar Pine Point State Park, P.O. Box D, Tahoma, CA 96142; (916) 525-7982.

**Trail notes:** For the more adventurous visitor to Sugar Pine State Park, head up from the General Creek Campground along General Creek towards Lost and Duck Lakes, located within the Desolation Wilderness. You won't be going all the way into the wilderness (unless you have overnight aspirations). Instead, from the parking area, the trail leads for several miles along the north side of General Creek, through wet and somewhat lush terrain, especially in the spring. Wildflowers are super. At a wooden bridge and trail junction, bear left (going straight takes you towards the Desolation Wilderness) across a bridge and then head right, now on the south side of General Creek. You soon leave the forest and head into open terrain that is much drier and sunnier than the first half of the hike. Hike back toward the campground, turning left at another wooden bridge and then right, retracing the first half-mile back to the parking area. You can use this trail to access the Desolation Wilderness and it is a good entry point since it sees relatively light use. Be sure to have the necessary permits before crossing the boundary. Remember that mountain bikes are not allowed within the wilderness.

---

## 14. MEEKS BAY TRAIL           8.0 mi/5.0 hrs

**Reference:** In the Desolation Wilderness and west of South Lake Tahoe; map D4, grid f2.

**User groups:** Hikers, dogs and horses. No mountain bikes are allowed. No wheelchair facilities.

**Permits:** This trail enters the heavily visited Desolation Wilderness. Permits are required for overnight stays and may be obtained from the Lake Tahoe Basin Management Unit, (916) 573-2600. From June 15 to Labor Day, permits are issued per day on a quota system. Reservations are accepted 90 days in advance. Day-hikers must register by using the self-service permit register located at the trailhead. Group sizes are limited to 15—please keep yours much smaller if possible. Dogs must be leashed at all times. Parking and access are free.

*Directions:* From South Lake Tahoe, head north on Highway 89 approximately 17 miles to the Meeks Bay Resort. Across the highway, look for a green Forest Service gate and the trail sign. Be sure to park legally and clear of the highway. Parking is allowed only in the dirt parking area.

*Maps:* Send $3 to the USDA-Forest Service, 630 Sansome Street, San Francisco, CA 94111 and ask for the Lake Tahoe Basin Management Unit map. For topographic maps, ask for Homewood and Rockbound Valley from the USGS. Tom Harrison Cartography also publishes an excellent map of the area. Call (415) 456-7940 and ask for the Desolation Wilderness map. The cost is $5.95 plus tax and shipping.

*Who to contact:* Lake Tahoe Basin Management Unit, 870 Emerald Bay Road, Suite 1, South Lake Tahoe, CA 96150; (916) 573-2600.

*Trail notes:* The Tahoe/Yosemite Trail is a very popular access point leading to a wonderful and refreshing chain of lakes: Genevieve (4.6 miles), Crag (4.9 miles), Hidden (5.7 miles), Shadow (5.9 miles), Stony Ridge (6.3 miles) and Rubicon (8.1 miles). Once you're in the backcountry, the lakes will beckon you to pitch a tent and stay a while. If your map and compass skills are up to snuff, you can wander aimlessly and gloriously for hours in any direction you choose. The trail up to the lakes parallels Meeks Creek, whose tumbling presence is a constant reminder of the power of water. Pack along your fly rod for this hike, as we've seen 10-inch trout just waiting in line for a fly to ripple Rubicon's glassy surface. Campfires are not allowed so bring your pack stove.

---

## 15. RUBICON TRAIL      9.0 mi/3.0 hrs

*Reference:* North of Emerald Bay in South Lake Tahoe; map D4, grid f2.

*User groups:* Hikers only. No mountain bikes, dogs or horses are allowed. **Limited wheelchair access.**

*Permits:* A $5 day-use fee is charged for entry into D. L. Bliss State Park. No hiking permit is required.

*Directions:* From South Lake Tahoe, drive north on State Highway 89 to D. L. Bliss State Park. The Rubicon Trailhead begins at the lakeshore directly at the termination of Lester Beach Road.

*Maps:* Send $3 to the USDA-Forest Service, 630 Sansome Street, San Francisco, CA 94111 and ask for the Lake Tahoe Basin Management Unit map. For topographic maps, ask for Meeks Bay and Emerald Bay from the USGS.

*Who to contact:* D. L. Bliss State Park, P.O. Box 266, Tahoma, CA 96142; (916) 525-7277.

*Trail notes:* This is an incredibly beautiful trail that skirts the shore of Lake Tahoe, affording wonderful views into the deep blue waters below. In the spring, when the peaks are still capped in snow, the deep blue waters of Lake Tahoe contrast spectacularly with the deep greens of the trees and the brilliant whites of the snowy peaks. Columbine, leopard lily, lupine and yellow monkey flower carpet the way in early spring. This trail makes a very scenic ski or snowshoe trip too, when the snow is covering the earth. Don't forget your camera on this trail—no matter what time of year. A word of warning: Expect lots of company on weekends, especially during the crowded summer months of July and August. Your best bet for solitude is midweek and offseason. Another note of interest: In a public taste testing, the waters from the Rubicon River came in number one! Even with all the good taste, however, never drink the water without treating it or, to preserve taste, filtering it.

# 16. BALANCING ROCKS NATURE TRAIL

0.6 mi/1.0 hr

*Reference:* **In D. L. Bliss State Park, west of Lake Tahoe; map D4, grid f2.**

*User groups:* Hikers only. No dogs, horses or mountain bikes are allowed. No wheelchair facilities.

*Permits:* No permits are required. There is a $5 day-use fee charged by the state park. The fee allows access to Sugar Pine Point State Park, also.

*Directions:* From South Lake Tahoe, drive north on State Highway 89 to D. L. Bliss State Park. The trailhead is located inside the park.

*Maps:* A state park map is available from the address listed below for 50 cents. Ask for the D. L. Bliss/Emerald Bay State Parks map. For topographic maps, ask for Meeks Bay and Emerald Bay from the USGS.

*Who to contact:* D. L. Bliss State Park, P.O. Box 266, Tahoma, CA 96142; (916) 525-7277.

*Trail notes:* This is a very beautiful and flat interpretive trail through a lakeside forest. Interpretive signs and a park brochure offer information about how the plants interact with the craggy rocks of the area and produce soil. The interpretive brochure may be picked up from a holder at the trailhead. You are asked to return the brochure when finished. The trail's namesake, top-heavy Balancing Rock, is the primary attraction. For some reason, erosion has eaten away the rock beneath it more quickly than in the surrounding granite, leaving the rock precariously perched. Rangers indicate that it won't take too much more shaking from the next major earthquake or two to send the natural monument tumbling—we wonder what they'll name the trail then? Spring, summer or fall are snow-free. In the winter, bring your snowshoes or Nordic skis.

# 17. EAGLE FALLS TRAIL

10.0 mi/5.0 hrs

*Reference:* **In the Desolation Wilderness and west of South Lake Tahoe; map D4, grid f2.**

*User groups:* Hikers and dogs. No mountain bikes or horses are allowed. No wheelchair facilities.

*Permits:* This trail enters the heavily visited Desolation Wilderness. Permits are required for overnight stays and may be obtained from the Lake Tahoe Basin Management Unit, (916) 573-2600. Day hikers must register by using the self-service permit register located at the trailhead. Group sizes are limited to 15—please keep yours much smaller if possible. Dogs must be leashed at all times. Parking and access are free.

*Directions:* From South Lake Tahoe, head approximately eight miles north on Highway 89 to the Eagle Falls Picnic Area, located on the southwestern shore of Emerald Bay. There is limited parking at the trailhead with additional spaces available alongside the highway on the dirt pullout. Be sure to park legally and clear of the highway.

*Maps:* Send $3 to the USDA-Forest Service, 630 Sansome Street, San Francisco, CA 94111 and ask for the Lake Tahoe Basin Management Unit map.

For topographic maps, ask for Emerald Bay and Rockbound Valley from the USGS. Tom Harrison Cartography also publishes an excellent map of the area. Call (415) 456-7940 and ask for the Desolation Wilderness map. The cost is $5.95 plus tax and shipping.

*Who to contact:* Lake Tahoe Basin Management Unit, 870 Emerald Bay Road, Suite 1, South Lake Tahoe, CA 96150; (916) 573-2600.

*Trail notes:* This is a very popular and at times very congested trail that guides the hiker through gorgeous alpine terrain. You will enjoy some superb views of Lake Tahoe along the route. The trail will climb past Eagle Falls, Eagle Lake, and then the Velma Lakes Basin before joining the Pacific Crest Trail near Dicks Lake. Turn around any time you get fatigued, or hike in and camp near the Velma Lakes for a wonderfully relaxing overnight excursion. We recommend turning this into a three-day overnight trip, taking one full day to explore the Velma Lakes area. A great day hike is up the backside of Dicks Peak (9,974 feet) for a top-of-the-world view. Remember to treat any water before drinking it. Although the trail passes near numerous lakes and a number of streams, it is advisable to carry two quarts of water at all times for trail sipping—it can get very hot and dusty in places. If you are seeking a short day hike, plan on heading only to Eagle Falls, six-tenths of a mile roundtrip, from the parking area and across a steel girder bridge.

# 18. CASCADE FALLS                1.5 mi/1.0 hr 

*Reference:* **Near Emerald Bay, southwest end of Lake Tahoe; map D4, grid f2.**

*User groups:* Hikers, dogs and horses. No mountain bikes. No wheelchair facilities.

*Permits:* No permits are required.

*Directions:* From South Lake Tahoe, drive north on State Highway 89 to the Bayview Campground near Emerald Bay. The trail begins at the upper parking lot, which is reached by driving through the campground. Parking is limited. If the upper lot is full, you can possibly find parking on the other side of Highway 89 at Inspiration Point. Keep in mind that the parking lots fill up quickly—it is best to begin your trip early in the morning.

*Maps:* Send $3 to the USDA-Forest Service, 630 Sansome Street, San Francisco, CA 94111 and ask for the Lake Tahoe Basin Management Unit Map. For topographic maps, ask for Emerald Bay and Echo Lake.

*Who to contact:* Lake Tahoe Basin Management Unit, 870 Emerald Bay Road, Suite 1, South Lake Tahoe, CA 96150; (916) 573-2600.

*Trail notes:* This hike is a short but sweet one. The views are excellent and the spring wildflowers are stunning. If that isn't enough, the Cascade Falls offer an awesome display of billowing spray and froth as they tumble down granite walls into the southern end of Cascade Lake. At the trailhead and the first trail junction, bear left, away from the trail leading to Granite Lake, and then head right at the second junction, climbing quickly to trail junction number three. Head left and onto a rocky overlook. After approximately one-half mile of hiking, the trail climbs up toward the falls and a series of granite slabs. Footing can be quite treacherous if these are wet—step carefully. Although the path disappears on the granite and frequent attempts at marking the route with cairns get destroyed, follow your ears to the roar of the falls and you will not go wrong. Do not approach the falls too closely. Retrace your steps when ready. Dogs must be leashed at all times. Late spring, summer and early fall are usually snow-free. Although the scenery is superb and the trail elevation gain and loss is not too difficult, the route is narrow and the area near the falls itself is quite steep and hazardous. Under no circumstances would we advise bringing small children up here unless they are closely supervised.

---

## 19. MT. TALLAC TRAIL 10.0 mi/8.0 hrs

*Reference:* **In the Desolation Wilderness and west of South Lake Tahoe; map D4, grid g2.**

*User groups:* Hikers, dogs and horses. No mountain bikes are allowed. No wheelchair facilities.

*Permits:* This trail enters the heavily visited Desolation Wilderness. Permits are required for overnight stays and may be obtained from the Lake Tahoe Basin Management Unit, (916) 573-2600. Day hikers must register by using the self-service permit register located at the trailhead. Group sizes are limited to 15—please keep yours much smaller if possible. Dogs must be leashed at all times. Parking and access are free.

*Directions:* From South Lake Tahoe, drive north on State Highway 89 for approximately 3.5 miles to the Mt. Tallac Trailhead sign, located directly across from the main entrance to Baldwin Beach. Follow the dirt road (suitable for all vehicles) to the trailhead parking.

*Maps:* Send $3 to the USDA-Forest Service, 630 Sansome Street, San Francisco, CA 94111 and ask for the Lake Tahoe Basin Management Unit map. For a topographic map, ask for Emerald Bay from the USGS. Tom Harrison Cartography also publishes an excellent map of the area. Call (415) 456-7940 and ask for the Desolation Wilderness map. The cost is $5.95 plus tax and shipping.

*Who to contact:* Lake Tahoe Basin Management Unit, 870 Emerald Bay Road, Suite 1, South Lake Tahoe, CA 96150; (916) 573-2600.

*Trail notes:* This hike takes you up, high above Fallen Leaf Lake, past the tiny, yet pretty lakes, Cathedral and Floating Island, and then to the peak of Mt. Tallac at 9,735 feet. From the vantage point of Mt. Tallac, one of the tallest peaks in the Desolation Wilderness, the hiker is afforded a stunning view. From Mt. Tallac, you can continue on and connect with Lake Gilmore and the Pacific Crest Trail, just over a 1.5 miles away. Several campsites along the way are outstanding, despite their proximity to Lake Tahoe. Cathedral Lake is perhaps the best, with good swimming to be found along the south shore. A short scramble up the talus jungle offers good views of the Tahoe area. From Cathedral Lake, it is a challenging 2.4-mile hike up almost 2,000 feet to Mt. Tallac—but the panoramic view is worth every drop of sweat!

*Special note:* Keep in mind that since the peak is so exposed, it is no place to be during a storm, especially a lightening storm. If clouds threaten, seek lower ground immediately.

## 20. TALLAC HISTORIC SITE

**1.3 mi. one way/1.0 hr**

*Reference:* **Just west of South Lake Tahoe and east of the Forest Service Center along the shore of Lake Tahoe; map D4, grid f3.**

*User groups:* Hikers, dogs and **wheelchairs.** No mountain bikes or horses are allowed.

*Permits:* No permits are required. Parking and access are free.

*Directions:* Drive just west of South Lake Tahoe on State Highway 89 and turn north toward the Kiva Picnic Area. You have a choice of two parking lots: the one at Kiva which fills up rapidly in the summer and the one at the Forest Service Center.

*Maps:* Send $3 to the USDA-Forest Service, 630 Sansome Street, San Francisco, CA 94111 and ask for the Lake Tahoe Basin Management Unit map. For a topographic map, ask for Emerald Bay from the USGS.

*Who to contact:* Lake Tahoe Basin Management Unit, 870 Emerald Bay Road, Suite 1, South Lake Tahoe, CA 96150; (916) 573-2600.

*Trail notes:* This is a short but very pleasant historic stroll affording a peek into the lives and personalities of turn-of-the-century Tahoe landowners through their houses. Interpretive signs and exhibits provide extra insights. We would recommend partaking of the guided walks through the homesteads and grounds. Either way, by yourself or on a guided walk, be sure to take in the arboretum and the Baldwin-McGonagle House, the latter contains super exhibits on the Washo Indians that used to reside in the area.

## 21. GLEN ALPINE TRAIL LOOP

**12.25 mi/2.0 days**

*Reference:* **In the Desolation Wilderness Area west of South Lake Tahoe; map D4, grid g2.**

*User groups:* Hikers, horses and dogs. No mountain bikes are allowed. No wheelchair facilities.

*Permits:* Both day-use and camping permits are required. Day-use permits may be obtained at the self-registration board located at the trailhead. Overnight permits may be obtained by calling the Lake Tahoe Basin Management Unit at (916) 573-2600. Campfires are not allowed at any time—backpacking stoves only! Group sizes are limited to 15, but it is recommended that you strive to keep yours much smaller. Parking and access are free.

*Directions:* From South Lake Tahoe, drive north on State Highway 89 for three miles to Fallen Leaf Road. Turn left (south) on Fallen Leaf Road and follow it (use caution because it is narrow and often congested), past Fallen Leaf Lake to the designated trailhead parking at Lily Lake.

*Maps:* Send $3 to the USDA-Forest Service, 630 Sansome Street, San Francisco, CA 94111 and ask for the Lake Tahoe Basin Management Unit map. For topographic maps, ask for Emerald Bay and Echo Lake from the USGS. Tom Harrison Cartography also publishes an excellent map of the area. Call (415) 456-7940 and ask for the Desolation Wilderness map. The cost is $5.95 plus tax and shipping.

*Who to contact:* Lake Tahoe Basin Management Unit, 870 Emerald Bay Road, Suite 1, South Lake Tahoe, CA 96150; (916) 573-2600.

*Trail notes:* Lake Aloha is probably one of the most scenic and most popular destinations within the Desolation Wilderness, but by accessing it via its northeastern shore, you will leave a vast majority of the crowds behind—unless you insist on visiting during a peak holiday weekend such as July 4th. The loop will also give you an outstanding opportunity to hike on a section of the famed Pacific Crest Trail. Beginning at Lily Lake, hike up the dirt road to the beginning of the Glen Alpine Trail. Follow this past the Grass Lakes and Glen Alpine Springs turnoffs and up to the PCT cutoff to Susie Lake. Follow the PCT south past Susie Lake and Heather Lake to Lake Aloha. Continue south on the PCT along the shore, past the Lake Margery and Lake Lucille cutoff to Haypress Meadow. Just past Haypress, leave the PCT and turn west on the trail back to Fallen Leaf Lake past the Triangle Lake and Echo Peak cutoffs. The beauty of this loop trip is the myriad of options you have to take wonderful sidetrips to enjoy views or tranquil solitude away from the maddening crowds that sometimes congregate on the lakes' shores. It is also possible to return via the Mt. Tallac Trail. If you choose the Mt. Tallac option, take the Fallen Leaf turnoff once at Cathedral Lake for a return to Fallen Leaf Lake. It is then a two-mile hike along the shore and back up the road to Lily Lake where you left your car.

---

## 22. ANGORA LAKES TRAIL     1.0 mi/1.0 hr

*Reference:* **South of Desolation Wilderness and west of Lake Tahoe; map D4, grid g3.**

*User groups:* Hikers, dogs, horses and mountain bikes. No wheelchair facilities.

*Permits:* No permits are required. Dogs must be leashed at all times. Parking and access are free.

*Directions:* From South Lake Tahoe, drive north on State Highway 89 for approximately three miles to Fallen Leaf Road. Turn left at the first paved road (no name) and drive to Forest Service Road 12N14. Turn right and drive past Angora Lookout to the road's end. The trailhead is located at the road's end.

*Maps:* Send $3 to the USDA-Forest Service, 630 Sansome Street, San Francisco, CA 94111 and ask for the Lake Tahoe Basin Management Unit map. For topographic maps, ask for Emerald Bay and Echo Lake from the USGS.

*Who to contact:* Lake Tahoe Basin Management Unit, 870 Emerald Bay Road, Suite 1, South Lake Tahoe, CA 96150; (916) 573-2600.

*Trail notes:* This is a scenic and easy hike. Angora Lakes are actually two lakes and are framed nicely by cliffs, creating a dramatic backdrop for photo buffs. That's the good news. The detraction is that this area is very crowded on weekends, especially during the summer. Plan your trip during a weekday if possible—although even then you may encounter youth groups from nearby camps and day programs. Still, the hike is pleasant enough along a smooth trail with only moderate elevation gain—approximately 200 feet. Swimming and fishing (for cutthroat trout) are allowed. Although it looks tempting, do not dive from the cliffs—they are dangerous and people have been seriously injured. There is a small resort at Angora Lakes where refreshments may be purchased. Keep a sharp eye out for mountain bikes and vehicles, which can sneak up on you. Dogs must be leashed at all times and are not allowed at the upper lake. Spring, summer and fall are snow-free. In the winter, bring your snowshoes or nordic skis.

# 23. HORSETAIL FALLS TRAIL   4.0 mi/2.0 hrs

*Reference:* West of South Lake Tahoe at the south border of the Desolation Wilderness; map D4, grid g2.

*User groups:* Hikers and dogs (but dogs are not recommended). No horses or mountain bikes are allowed. No wheelchair facilities.

*Permits:* This trail enters the heavily visited Desolation Wilderness. Permits are required for overnight stays and may be obtained from the Lake Tahoe Basin Management Unit, (916) 573-2600. Day-hikers must register by using the self-service permit register located at the trailhead. Group sizes are limited to 15—please keep yours much smaller if possible. Dogs must be leashed at all times. Parking and access are free.

*Directions:* From the Highway 49 junction in Placerville, drive five miles east up Highway 50 to the Eldorado National Forest Information Center. If you haven't already gotten a permit, do so now. From here, continue driving another 35 miles or so to Strawberry. Approximately 1.75 miles past Strawberry is Twin Bridges. The parking for the trailhead is located just past the bridge, crossing Pyramid Creek outside of town and left off the highway. Parking is limited. For drivers heading west from Lake Tahoe, if you hit Twin Bridges, you have driven approximately a quarter of a mile too far.

*Maps:* Send $3 to the USDA-Forest Service, 630 Sansome Street, San Francisco, CA 94111 and ask for the Eldorado National Forest map. For topographic maps, ask for Echo Lake and Pyramid Peak from the USGS. Tom Harrison Cartography also publishes an excellent map of the area. Call (415) 456-7940 and ask for the Desolation Wilderness map. The cost is $5.95 plus tax and shipping.

*Who to contact:* Information Center, Eldorado National Forest, 3070 Camino Heights Drive, Camino, CA 95709; (916) 644-6048.

*Trail notes:* This trail is very difficult to follow, and there is serious doubt as to whether there is, in fact, a trail at all in places. Still, it is the quickest and most direct access into the Desolation Wilderness, and the rewards are spectacular, rugged scenery and relative solitude since most casual hikers do not attempt this trek. The trail begins easily enough following Pyramid Creek, but steepens dramatically as it nears the base of Horsetail Falls at one mile. Approximately a quarter of a mile past the Desolation Wilderness boundary is a vantage point where you can enjoy the views and ponder whether or not you wish to continue. If you are feeling exhausted or inexperienced, turn back now! From here on up, it gets tough and slippery, even under the best conditions. The route crosses the steep and polished bedrock and then heads up and up and, Oh God!, up some more over talus toward Avalanche Lake. One half of the 1,300 feet you will gain is earned in the last 750 yards. Ouch.

*Special note:* As much as we love this hike, we caution you that it is for very experienced hikers only and most certainly only in good weather. Don't even think about trying this hike in rainy or snowy conditions, no matter how experienced you are. People have died here, slipping from the slick, ice-polished granite slabs into the falls hundreds of feet below. If the weather turns sour, head back to the car. The mountain will always be there tomorrow; make sure you can say the same.

# 24. LAKE OF THE WOODS    10.5 mi/5.0 hrs

*Reference:* **West of South Lake Tahoe and east of Placerville off Highway 50; map D4, grid g2.**

*User groups:* Hikers and dogs. No mountain bikes or horses are allowed. No wheelchair facilities.

*Permits:* Both day-use and camping permits are required. Day-use permits may be obtained at the registration area located near the dock at Echo Lake Resort. Overnight permits may be obtained from the Eldorado National Forest Information Center at (916) 644-6048. Campfires are not allowed at any time—backpacking stoves only! Group sizes are limited to 15, but it is recommended that you strive to keep yours much smaller.

*Directions:* From the junction of Highway 50 and Highway 89 in South Lake Tahoe, drive south on Highway 50 for approximately 9.8 miles to a sign on the right (west) side of the highway indicating Echo Lake and Echo Lake Road. Turn right and drive six-tenths of a mile to a junction and bear left, driving one more mile to a parking area above Echo Lake Resort. Hikers and overnighters must use the upper lot since the resort limits parking in the lower lot to two hours maximum.

*Maps:* Send $3 to the USDA-Forest Service, 630 Sansome Street, San Francisco, CA 94111 and ask for the Eldorado National Forest map. For a topographic map ask for Echo Lake from the USGS.

*Who to contact:* Information Center, Eldorado National Forest, 3070 Camino Heights Drive, Camino, CA 95709; (916) 644-6048.

*Trail notes:* Although the Echo Lake Trailhead can be extremely crowded due to its accessibility and close proximity to several gorgeous lakes ideal for swimming and picnicking, you will leave the majority of the public behind by the time you reach Lake of the Woods. The lake itself is large and easily accommodates numerous visitors without seeming as if you are shoulder-to-shoulder with thousands of weekend warriors seeking a good time. Camping is good around the lake and this is an ideal destination for families. If you want to cut some hiking time and distance off the hike, you can partake of the popular water taxi service that will take you by boat from Echo Lake Resort to the boat dock at Upper Echo Lake. The taxi option will shave approximately five miles off your total distance. There is a phone at the taxi's western terminus which you can use to call the resort to get a ride back. Assuming you are going to hike it all the way, cross over the dam on the right near the dock and follow the trail that leads northeast above the lake. Views to Lake Tahoe and then Ralston Peak and Pyramid Peak are memorable. Climb along the route that basically parallels the shoreline of Echo and Upper Echo lakes. You will pass a trail to the left that drops steeply to the water taxi dock at Upper Echo Lake. For those using the taxi, it is a steep and breathless scramble up 100 feet or so to join the main trail. Before long you will arrive at a trail junction just before the Desolation Wilderness boundary. At the junction, continue straight on the main trail leading to Tamarack Lake. Approximately four miles from the start (1.4 miles from the taxi boat dock at Upper Echo Lake) you will arrive at another junction with a trail leading left to Tamarack Lake. Keep climbing, now steeply to another junction where you will bear left, skirting Haypress Meadows and arriving at the north shore of Lake of the Woods. The west side of the lake is the most popular as it features warmer water (more sun throughout the day) and the best campsites. Always be sure to set up camp at least 100 feet away from the lake shore.

## 25. RALSTON PEAK      3.0 mi/1.0 hr

*Reference:* **West of South Lake Tahoe and east of Placerville off Highway 50; map D4, grid g2.**

*User groups:* Hikers, dogs and horses. No mountain bikes are allowed. No wheelchair facilities.

*Permits:* This trail enters the heavily visited Desolation Wilderness. Permits are required for overnight stays and may be obtained from the Eldorado National Forest Information Center at (916) 644-6048. Day hikers must register by using the self-service permit register located at the trailhead. Group sizes are limited to 15—please keep yours much smaller if possible. Dogs must be leashed at all times. Parking and access are free.

*Directions:* From Placerville, drive east on Highway 50 for approximately 48 miles to Camp Sacramento. Park at the trailhead parking on the north side of the highway, directly across from Camp Sacramento. The road at the east end of the parking area leads you about 200 yards to the trailhead.

*Maps:* Send $3 to the USDA-Forest Service, 630 Sansome Street, San Francisco, CA 94111 and ask for the Eldorado National Forest map. For a topographic map, ask for Echo Lake from the USGS. Tom Harrison Cartography also publishes an excellent map of the area. Call (415) 456-7940 and ask for the Desolation Wilderness map. The cost is $5.95 plus tax and shipping.

*Who to contact:* Information Center, Eldorado National Forest, 3070 Camino Heights Drive, Camino, CA 95709; (916) 644-6048.

*Trail notes:* The first mile of this trail begins easily enough, but once it enters the Desolation Wilderness, the trail begins to climb steeply, heading to the top of Mt. Ralston at 9,235 feet (an elevation gain of approximately 2,640 feet.) The views from the peak are magnificent, once you catch your breath. If the weather is clear, you will see surrounding peaks and lakes, as well as azure blue Lake Tahoe at your feet. Pack plenty of water!

## 26. EMIGRANT LAKE      9.5 mi/5.0 hrs

*Reference:* **South of Lake Tahoe; map D4, grid i2.**

*User groups:* Hikers, horses and dogs. No mountain bikes are allowed. No wheelchair facilities.

*Permits:* No day-use permits are required. Permits are required for campfires and stoves—obtain them from the Eldorado National Forest Information Center, (916) 644-6048.

*Directions:* From State Highway 88 at the Highway 89/88 junction south of Lake Tahoe, drive to Carson Pass. Continue driving approximately five miles west of the pass to the trailhead parking area signed for Caples Lake, which is located on the south side of the highway near Caples Lake Dam.

*Maps:* Send $3 to the USDA-Forest Service, 630 Sansome Street, San Francisco, CA 94111 and ask for the Eldorado National Forest map. For a topographic map, ask for Caples Lake from the USGS.

*Who to contact:* Information Center, Eldorado National Forest, 3070 Camino Heights Drive, Camino, CA 95709; (916) 644-6048.

*Trail notes:* This is an excellent overnight trip for the entire family or for those seeking to initiate a first-time backpacker. Picnickers will enjoy the relatively effortless jaunt as well. From the trailhead sign, the trail contours for approximately 2.5 miles alongside the south shore of Caples Lake. The treadway passes through several tiny yet picturesque groves of aspen, particularly colorful in the fall. At Emigrant Creek, the trail veers south along the creek and toward Emigrant Lake. The trail begins to climb gently for approximately one mile to a trail junction. Head left and cross Emigrant Creek within the first half-mile. The crossing can be a wet one early in the season. Three-quarters of a mile further on finds you at Emigrant Lake, a deep, granite-ringed body of water. Campsites are few, but good.

---

## 27. HAWLEY GRADE      3.0 mi/1.5 hrs
## NATIONAL RECREATION TRAIL

*Reference:* **South of Lake Tahoe; map D4, grid h3.**

*User groups:* Hikers, mountain bikes, horses and dogs. **Wheelchair access is limited.**

*Permits:* No permits are needed. Parking and access are free.

*Directions:* From South Lake Tahoe, drive south on Highway 50, through the town of Meyers. Approximately 13 miles past Meyers, turn left on Upper Truckee Road and follow it south for about four miles to the Bridge summer homes. Look for the "Hawley Grade" sign and a boulder-blocked end of the road designating the beginning of the trail. Park at the turnout just before the trailhead.

*Maps:* Send $3 to the USDA-Forest Service, 630 Sansome Street, San Francisco, CA 94111 and ask for the Lake Tahoe Basin Management Unit map. For a topographic map, ask for Echo Lake from the USGS. Wilderness Press prints a good map of the area on waterproof paper. Call (800) 443-7227 and ask for Fallen Leaf Lake. The cost is $4 plus tax.

*Who to contact:* Lake Tahoe Basin Management Unit, 870 Emerald Bay Road, Suite 1, South Lake Tahoe, CA 96150; (916) 573-2600.

*Trail notes:* Hawley Grade was the first wagon road to be built across the central Sierra and was once, although only briefly, a vital link in the trans-Sierra route to Sacramento. Now not much more than a trail through the alders, bushes and wildflower, Hawley Grade is a pleasant enough out-and-back hike. The nearby Truckee River tumbles over boulders. Views of Lake Tahoe to the north may be enjoyed during parts of the hike. However, Highway 50 will begin to become an audible irritant, enough so that once reaching the highway at mile 1.5, you will be immediately encouraged to perform an about-face and return to the silence and peace you just left.

---

## 28. CODY LAKE      1.0 mi/1.0 hr

*Reference:* **South of Highway 50 and east of Placerville; map D4, grid h1.**

*User groups:* Hikers, horses and dogs. No mountain bikes are allowed. No wheelchair facilities.

*Permits:* No permits are required. Parking and access are free.

*Directions:* From Placerville, drive east on US Highway 50 to 42 Mile Picnic Area located near Strawberry Lodge. Turn south on Packsaddle Pass Road and drive five miles towards the Scout Camp. Turn left at the Cody Lake sign and continue driving 1.25 miles to the parking area on the right. The signed trailhead is located on the left side of the road across from the parking area.

*Maps:* Send $3 to the USDA-Forest Service, 630 Sansome Street, San Francisco, CA 94111 and ask for the Eldorado National Forest map. For a topographic map, ask for Tragedy Spring from the USGS.

*Who to contact:* Information Center, Eldorado National Forest, 3070 Camino Heights Drive, Camino, CA 95709; (916) 644-6048.

*Trail notes:* This is a very easy yet scenic trail to the glacier-formed Cody Lake. The lake itself is tucked into a rocky shelf part way up the side of a canyon draining into Cody Creek. Few people make the short pilgrimage so don't be surprised if you have this pretty little jewel all to yourself. This is a perfect picnic hike.

---

## 29. BUCK PASTURE  6.0 mi/3.0 hrs

*Reference:* **South of Kyburz on Highway 50; map D4, grid h0.**

*User groups:* Hikers, horses and dogs. No mountain bikes are allowed. No wheelchair facilities.

*Permits:* No permits are required. Parking and access are free.

*Directions:* From US Highway 50 at Kyburz, take Silver Fork Road for approximately seven miles to Cody Meadows Road. Turn left and drive on Cody Meadows for about five miles to Negro Flat. At Negro Flat, turn right on a four-wheel-drive road and follow it for approximately two more miles to the trailhead.

*Maps:* Send $3 to the USDA-Forest Service, 630 Sansome Street, San Francisco, CA 94111 and ask for the Eldorado National Forest map. For topographic maps, ask for Tragedy Spring and Caples Lake from the USGS.

*Who to contact:* Information Center, Eldorado National Forest, 3070 Camino Heights Drive, Camino, CA 95709; (916) 644-6048.

*Trail notes:* This is an easy out-and-back hike that takes you along a good path to Buck Pasture, then up and along the scenic north ridge of Caples Creek valley. The trail is hikable in the summer and early fall. During the rest of the year, explore the area on snowshoes or cross-country skis—but you'll have to begin your trek much further down, as the road is closed seasonally by snow.

---

## 30. DARDANELLES LAKE  8 mi/6.0 hrs

*Reference:* **South of South Lake Tahoe and northwest of Hope Valley off Highway 89; map D4, grid h4.**

*User groups:* Hikers, dogs and horses. No mountain bikes are allowed. No wheelchair facilities.

*Permits:* Day-use permits are not required. Overnight camping permits are required. Contact the Tahoe Basin Management Unit at (916) 573-2600.

*Directions:* From the junction of Highway 50 and Highway 89 in South Lake Tahoe, drive south on Highway 50 / 89 to its split (in 4.8 miles) at Meyers. Stay on Highway 89 for 5.5 miles to the Big Meadows Trailhead located on the right side of the highway. There is a parking area located on the left side of the road approximately 100 yards beyond the trailhead sign.

*Maps:* Send $3 to the USDA-Forest Service, 630 Sansome Street, San Francisco, CA 94111 and ask for the Lake Tahoe Basin Management Unit map. For topographic maps ask for Echo Lake and Freel Peak from the USGS.

*Who to contact:* Lake Tahoe Basin Management Unit, 870 Emerald Bay Road, Suite 1, South Lake Tahoe, CA 96150; (916) 573-2600.

*Trail notes:* This hike is a moderately difficult trek through wildflower speckled meadows, over several mountain streams and up to a rock-rimmed lake just begging for swimmers. From the trailhead, climb up and towards Big Meadow, across a wooden bridge and then, at one-half mile, into the meadow itself. Hike through the meadow, enjoying the wildflowers to its southern end, and then begin climbing on a well-worn trail through the forest. At a saddle, the trail descends rapidly to a junction. Heading left will guide you to Round Lake (one-half mile distant), worth a peek if you have the time and inclination. Or you can stay right and follow the trail alongside a creek to another trail junction. Bear left, crossing a narrow stream, and head west through a pleasant grove of aspen. After a mile or so of gentle walking, the trail begins to climb abruptly through boulders and granite slabs. Keep a sharp eye out for the rock cairns marking the route. The trail heads back into the forest briefly before dumping you out onto the lake's eastern edge. Campsites ring the lake. Please be sure to camp at least 100 feet away from the shore. Fishing is good for trout. The water is warm (relatively speaking), so enjoy a good splash. Head back the way you came.

---

## 31. OLD SILVER LAKE    6.0 mi/4.0 hrs

*Reference:* **East of Highway 50 and the town of Kyburz; map D4, grid h1.**

*User groups:* Hikers, horses and dogs. No mountain bikes are allowed. No wheelchair facilities.

*Permits:* No permits are required. Parking and access are free.

*Directions:* From US Highway 50 at Kyburz, drive on Silver Fork Road for 10 miles. Shortly after passing Silver Fork Campground, and just before crossing over the Fitz Ranch Bridge, turn left on a four-wheel-drive dirt road and drive approximately one-quarter of a mile to the Caples Creek Trailhead. Hike on the Caples Creek Trail to the Old Silver Lake Trail which begins just past Jake Schneiders Meadow.

*Maps:* Send $3 to the USDA-Forest Service, 630 Sansome Street, San Francisco, CA 94111 and ask for the Eldorado National Forest map. For topographic maps ask for Tragedy Spring and Caples Lake from the USGS.

*Who to contact:* Information Center, Eldorado National Forest, 3070 Camino Heights Drive, Camino, CA 95709; (916) 644-6048.

*Trail notes:* This is a scenic and somewhat strenuous hike, climbing up from Caples Creek through mixed virgin pine and fir. There is no bridge to cross Caples Creek, so use caution and be prepared to get at least your feet wet. Another side hike, beginning at the same trailhead, leads to Government Meadows. Stay on the Caples Creek Trail, ignoring the intersections with the Silver Fork Trail and Old Silver Lake. This trail section will take you on a scenic little jaunt around several pleasant and peaceful meadows. The Government Meadows detour will add approximately two miles to the overall journey.

## 32. LAKE MARGARET      4.0 mi/3.0 hrs

*Reference:* In the Mokelumne Wilderness, south of Lake Tahoe and east of Highway 88; map D4, grid i1.

*User groups:* Hikers, horses, dogs and mountain bikes. There are no wheelchair facilities.

*Permits:* No day-use permits are required. A campfire permit is required for campfires and stoves being used outside of developed campgrounds. Permits may be obtained from the Eldorado National Forest Information Center, (916) 644-6048. Parking and access are free.

*Directions:* From State Highway 88 at the Highway 89/88 junction south of Lake Tahoe, drive to Carson Pass. From Carson Pass on Highway 88, drive west to just past Caples Lake. The trailhead parking is located on the north side of the highway, two-tenths of a mile west of Caples Lake and one-half mile east of Kirkwood Inn and the turnoff for the Kirkwood Ski Area. The trailhead is signed and located at the west end of the parking area.

*Maps:* Send $3 to the USDA-Forest Service, 630 Sansome Street, San Francisco, CA 94111 and ask for the Eldorado National Forest map. For a topographic map, ask for Caples Lake from the USGS.

*Who to contact:* Information Center, Eldorado National Forest, 3070 Camino Heights Drive, Camino, CA 95709; (916) 644-6048.

*Trail notes:* This is the perfect escape for those who desire a quick nature fix with minimal sweat equity. The trail itself is relatively level and extremely easy, passing near the lush Caples Creek and through stunning wildflower displays—especially in the spring. Fall color lovers will thrill to the golden leaves of aspen lining a pretty section of trail approximately two miles from the trailhead. The trail dead-ends, after a short climb following cairns over granite slabs at scenic Lake Margaret. The lake is deep and granite-rimmed, ideal for swimming (brrrr) and picnicking. Two campsites are available on the east shore and two more along the west shore. Due to the out-and-back nature of this route, as well as the attraction of water and wildflowers, this trail does see heavy use on weekends—tread lightly please.

## 33. LITTLE ROUND TOP      5.0 mi/3.0 hrs

*Reference:* North of the Mokelumne Wilderness, south of Lake Tahoe and north of Highway 88; map D4, grid i2.

*User groups:* Hikers, horses, dogs and mountain bikes. No wheelchair facilities.

*Permits:* No day-use permits required. A campfire permit is required for campfires and stoves. Permits may be obtained from the Eldorado National Forest Information Center, (916) 644-6048. Parking and access are free.

*Directions:* From State Highway 88 at the Highway 89/88 junction south of Lake Tahoe, drive to Carson Pass. From Carson Pass on Highway 88, drive west a short distance and then turn north at the CalTrans maintenance station near Caples Lake. Continue for two miles up Schneiders Cow Camp Road to Schneiders Cow Camp. Although this is where you will park, the trailhead begins a half mile further down the four-wheel-drive road.

*Maps:* Send $3 to the USDA-Forest Service, 630 Sansome Street, San Francisco, CA 94111 and ask for the Eldorado National Forest map. For topographic maps, ask for Caples Lake and Echo Lake from the USGS.

**Who to contact:** Information Center, Eldorado National Forest, 3070 Camino Heights Drive, Camino, CA 95709; (916) 644-6048.

**Trail notes:** The trail wanders upward through lodgepole and whitebark towards a junction with the Pacific Crest Trail. Here, the main path ends, but it is worth the extra effort to wander cross-country a short distance to "bag" the nearby peak of Little Round Top (9,500 feet). Keep in mind that although mountain bikes are allowed on the trail, mountain bikes are not allowed on the PCT itself. If you do ride your mountain bike, leave it behind for the peak-bagging attempt as mountain bikes are meant for trail use only, not cross-country travel.

---

## 34. ROUND TOP PEAK AND ROUND TOP LAKE    7.5 mi/5.0 hrs

**Reference:** South of Lake Tahoe; map D4, grid i2.

**User groups:** Hikers, horses and dogs. Mountain bikes are not allowed. No wheelchair facilities.

**Permits:** Day-use permits are not required. Permits are required for campfires and stoves—obtain them from the Eldorado National Forest Information Center; (916) 644-6048.

**Directions:** From State Highway 88 at the Highway 89/88 junction south of Lake Tahoe, drive to Carson Pass. Continue driving 1.7 miles west of the pass to the turnoff for Woods Lake Campground on the left (south). Turn left and drive 1.5 miles to the campground. Park in the day-use picnic area to the left of the entrance.

**Maps:** Send $3 to the USDA-Forest Service, 630 Sansome Street, San Francisco, CA 94111 and ask for the Eldorado National Forest map. For topographic maps, ask for Carson Pass and Caples Lake from the USGS.

**Who to contact:** Information Center, Eldorado National Forest, 3070 Camino Heights Drive, Camino, CA 95709; (916) 644-6048.

**Trail notes:** This trail leads you past scenic Winnemucca Lake and to Round Top Lake, both suitable camping or daydreaming spots. Begin hiking at the trailhead signed for Winnemucca Lake. The climbing is gentle and forested for the first mile. Once you break out of the trees and onto the ridgeline, the views become wonderful. One-half mile after leaving the trees, you will arrive at a trail junction and Winnemucca Lake. Round Top looms above. If you are only after a quick swim and a picnic, hang out here and then retrace your steps. Otherwise, continue right at the trail junction toward Round Top Lake one mile further on (9,500 feet in elevation). If you have the energy, scramble a steep one-half mile or so up Round Top Peak (elevation 10,380 feet), to the east of the trail near Round Top Lake. The views from the summit of the surrounding Mokelumne Wilderness and the distant Desolation Wilderness are memorable. Pack warm clothing no matter what time of year. Summer and fall are usually snow-free. Any other time of the year, plan on either snowshoeing or skiing in. Avoid this area on holidays as it is often crowded.

## 35. SHEALOR LAKE          3.0 mi/3.0 hrs

*Reference:* **North of Highway 88, west of Carson Pass and south of Lake Tahoe; map D4, grid i1.**

*User groups:* Hikers, horses, dogs and mountain bikes. No wheelchair access.

*Permits:* No day-use permits are required. A campfire permit is required for campfires and stoves used outside of developed campgrounds. Permits may be obtained from the Eldorado National Forest Information Center, (916) 644-6048. Parking and access are free.

*Directions:* From State Highway 88 at the Highway 89/88 junction south of Lake Tahoe, drive to Carson Pass. From Carson Pass on Highway 88, drive west to just past Silver Lake. The trailhead is located on the west side of Highway 88 between Kay's Resort and the Plasse turnoff.

*Maps:* Send $3 to the USDA-Forest Service, 630 Sansome Street, San Francisco, CA 94111 and ask for the Eldorado National Forest map. For a topographic map, ask for Tragedy Spring from the USGS.

*Who to contact:* Information Center, Eldorado National Forest, 3070 Camino Heights Drive, Camino, CA 95709; (916) 644-6048.

*Trail notes:* From the trailhead, the trail climbs steeply and steadily over granite slabs and through open forest for approximately three-quarters of a mile before dropping abruptly down to Shealor Lake. You will definitely earn your right to the beautiful scenery with sweat equity.

## 36. HIDDEN LAKE          6.0 mi/3.0 hrs

*Reference:* **South of Lake Tahoe and west of the Mokelumne Wilderness Area; map D4, grid i1.**

*User groups:* Hikers, horses and dogs. No mountain bikes are allowed. No wheelchair facilities.

*Permits:* Campfire permits are required for stoves and campfires. Parking and access are free.

*Directions:* From State Highway 88 at the Highway 89/88 junction south of Lake Tahoe, drive to Carson Pass. From Carson Pass on Highway 88, drive west to Silver Lake. At the north end of the lake, near the spillway, turn east at the sign and road for Kit Carson Lodge. The trailhead parking is located on the east side of the lake near the north entrance to the Campfire Girls Camp.

*Maps:* Send $3 to the USDA-Forest Service, 630 Sansome Street, San Francisco, CA 94111 and ask for the Eldorado National Forest map. For a topographic map, ask for Caples Lake from the USGS.

*Who to contact:* Information Center, Eldorado National Forest, 3070 Camino Heights Drive, Camino, CA 95709; (916) 644-6048.

*Trail notes:* This is an easy and scenic hike past Granite Lake (one mile each way) to Hidden Lake. For a loop journey, continue past Hidden Lake to the Off-Highway-Vehicle Trail and turn right (west) towards the Stockton Muni Camp. At the camp, turn right (north) and walk back to Silver Lake, and then continue on the trail skirting the east shore until you arrive back at the parking area and your car.

## 37. COLE CREEK LAKES 5.0 mi/2.5 hrs

*Reference:* **In the Mokelumne Wilderness south of Lake Tahoe and east of Highway 88; map D4, grid i1.**

*User groups:* Hikers, horses and dogs. No mountain bikes are allowed. No wheelchair facilities.

*Permits:* No day-use permits required. A wilderness permit is required, and a campfire permit is required for campfires and stoves. Permits may be obtained from the Eldorado National Forest Information Center, (916) 644-6048. Parking and access are free.

*Directions:* From State Highway 88 at the Highway 89/88 junction south of Lake Tahoe, drive to Carson Pass. From Carson Pass on Highway 88, drive west past Silver Lake. Turn southeast onto the four-wheel-drive road that is directly across from the Tragedy Spring Picnic Area. Drive past the Plasse Lookout and find the trailhead near the old Plasse Trading Post site. This road may be closed due to snow or other conditions—check with the Eldorado National Forest Information Center before heading out.

*Maps:* Send $3 to the USDA-Forest Service, 630 Sansome Street, San Francisco, CA 94111 and ask for the Eldorado National Forest map. For a topographic map, ask for Mokelumne Peak from the USGS.

*Who to contact:* Information Center, Eldorado National Forest, 3070 Camino Heights Drive, Camino, CA 95709; (916) 644-6048.

*Trail notes:* This is a relatively easy hike leading to a cluster of lakes. The lakes are tucked in among the trees, high in the mountains, and almost seem to be begging for someone to cast a fishing line upon their mirrored surfaces. Note: If the gate on the road leading from the picnic area is closed, you can still hike in, but it will add seven miles to your round-trip total.

---

## TAHOE RIM TRAIL (TRT) 70.0 mi/7.0 days
## GENERAL INFORMATION

*Reference:* **Surrounding the perimeter of Lake Tahoe, beginning at Echo Summit and heading north above the eastern shore to Tahoe Summit.** The PCT trail route is the designated route along the western ridges.

*User groups:* Hikers, horses and dogs. Limited mountain bike access. **Wheelchair access planned in limited sections.**

*Permits:* No permits needed for day use except where the trail passes through wilderness areas. Overnight camping permits required. Contact the Lake Tahoe Basin Management Unit at (916) 573-2600. Parking and access are free.

*Directions:* The trail is accessed at multiple points around Lake Tahoe. Specific trail access directions are provided below under each particular trail section heading.

*Maps:* For a very general map, contact the Tahoe Rim Trail Organization at the address and phone listed below. Topographic maps for particular sections of trail are provided under each specific trail section heading listed below. For an overall view of the trail route, send $3 to the USDA-Forest Service, 630 Sansome Street, San Francisco, CA 94111 and ask for the Lake Tahoe Basin Management Unit map.

*Who to contact:* General trail and volunteer information available through the

Tahoe Rim Trail Organization, P.O. Box 11551, South Lake Tahoe, CA 96158; (916) 577-0676. Camping and permit information available from the Lake Tahoe Basin Management Unit, 870 Emerald Bay Road, Suite 1, South Lake Tahoe, CA 96150; (916) 573-2600.

*Trail notes:* Imagine a trail that winds completely around one of the most spectacular lakes in the western United States and the highest and largest alpine lake in North America. The goal of the Tahoe Rim Trail Organization is to provide a 150-mile trail that will allow you an opportunity to experience six counties, three national forests and two states in a 12-day time period— or in sections as your heart desires. The trail is not complete by any means, and its construction relies entirely on volunteer workers. At present, about 70 miles of trail is completed in various sections as described below.

---

## TRT-1                       0.1 mi. one way/0.25 hr
## ECHO SUMMIT to PACIFIC CREST TRAIL

*Reference:* **From Echo Summit to the Pacific Crest Trail; map D4, grid h2.**

*User groups:* Hikers, horses and dogs. No mountain bikes are allowed. No wheelchair facilities.

*Permits:* No day-use permits are needed. A campfire permit is required. Parking and access are free.

*Directions:* Located 14 miles west of the summit on the south side of Highway 50. From South Lake Tahoe, drive south on Highway 50. Turn off of Highway 50 on the old Echo Summit Ski Area Road (look for a Snow Park sign) and park in the spaces provided for the trail along the left side of the road a few hundred yards in.

*Maps:* For a topographic map, ask for Emerald Bay from the USGS.

*Trail notes:* This is the trailhead for the Pacific Crest National Scenic Trail, which makes up the western leg of the Tahoe Rim Trail (TRT). Basically, this is an unattractive section of trail that provides ready access to the PCT/ Tahoe Rim Trail section.

---

## TRT-2                    22.4 mi. one way/2.0 days
## BIG MEADOWS (LUTHER PASS) to KINGSBURY GRADE

*Reference:* **From Big Meadows (Luther Pass) to Kingsbury Grade; map D4, grid h4.**

*User groups:* Hikers, horses, dogs and mountain bikes. No wheelchair facilities.

*Permits:* No day-use permits are needed. A campfire permit is required. Parking and access are free.

*Directions:* The Big Meadows Trailhead is located just off Highway 89, 5.5 miles southeast of the Highway 50/89 junction in Meyers (south of South Lake Tahoe) and 5.9 miles northwest of the Highway 89/88 junction in Hope Valley.

*Maps:* For topographic maps, ask for Emerald Bay and South Lake Tahoe from the USGS.

*Trail notes:* Parking, restrooms and a horse staging area are available. A car shuttle is required. The trail passes by Star Lake, the ideal place to overnight, and then near Monument Peak. Do not camp within 100 feet of the lake's shore. Outstanding views of the Carson Valley may be enjoyed along the way. Leave one car at Kingsbury Grade Trailhead (see directions that follow under TRT-3). From the Big Meadows Trailhead, the trail climbs gently for two miles through aspen and fir, arriving at a junction with one trail leading right to Grass Lake. Stay left on the main trail and hike northeast, climbing more steeply now with views to the south of Luther Pass, Pickett Peak and Hawkins Peak. Continue along, now on a more rocky and loose path leading past Freel Meadows and then to a saddle overlooking Hell Hole Canyon and Lake Tahoe, six miles from the trailhead. Continue climbing steeply to another trail junction at Armstrong Pass, seven miles from the trailhead. Keep hiking straight on the main path where the trail contours around Freel Peak, climbing and descending only moderately until it meets up with the western shore of peaceful Star Lake, approximately 12.8 miles from Big Meadows. Enjoy the rest and scenery. From Star Lake, the trail contours along at around 9,000 feet for approximately five miles to Monument Pass. The views are stunning! From the pass, drop your pack and take a quick half-mile round-trip jaunt up to the 10,067-foot summit of Monument Peak. Back at the pass, the trail drops steeply down via a series of switchbacks into Mott Canyon. Signs of civilization become more evident now as the trail meets up with roads and chair lifts. The climb out of Mott Canyon is mind-bending—take it slowly. The saving grace are the views to the south of the dramatic face of Freel Peak. Cross a ski slope or two once out of the canyon and then descend gently down to the Heavenly Valley ski resort and parking—9.4 miles from Star Lake.

---

## TRT-3                    12.0 mi. one way/2.0 days
## KINGSBURY GRADE to SPOONER SUMMIT

*Reference:* **From Kingsbury Grade to Spooner Summit; map D4, grid g4.**
*User groups:* Hikers, horses and dogs. No mountain bikes are allowed. No wheelchair facilities.
*Permits:* No day-use permits are needed. A campfire permit is required. Parking and access are free.
*Directions:* From Highway 50 north of South Lake Tahoe, drive to the top of Kingsbury Grade (Highway 207) and turn north onto North Benjamin. This street changes into Andria Drive from which point you will drive approximately two more miles to the end of Andria. A bulletin board is located on the west side of the road and designates the trailhead. Parking is limited.
*Maps:* For topographic maps, ask for South Lake Tahoe in California and Glenbrook in Nevada from the USGS.
*Trail notes:* Parking is available. This trailhead is located near Heavenly Valley Ski Area. A car shuttle is required. Leave one car at Spooner Summit (see directions that follow under TRT-4). It is possible to do this hike in one day with a shuttle as long as you get an early start. Some of the climbing is strenuous. Water is not reliable in the summer, so pack all that you will need. Camping is allowed. From the parking area, head north on the trail, climbing steeply for approximately 1.5 miles until reaching an elevation of 8,250 and excellent views of Lake Tahoe and the surrounding terrain. The trail continues climbing, more gently now, up to a summit with an elevation of 8,900 feet, approximately five miles from the trailhead. The trail follows an undulating route along the ridgeline, crossing and recrossing Forest Service

Road 14N32 several times. The views north to Mount Rose and west towards the Desolation Wilderness are unbelievable. Keep hiking, passing just below and to the west of Genoa Peak at eight miles. A quick sidetrip to the summit is worthwhile as the panoramic scenery from the 9,150-foot peak is memorable. To the north you can see Mount Rose and Rifle Peak. To the northwest, take in the Granite Chief Wilderness. To the west, gaze at the Desolation Wilderness and the shimmering beauty of the Tahoe Basin. From Genoa Peak, keep hiking north, arriving at South Camp Peak in just under two miles. From here, the route begins to descend, leaving the ridgeline as it contours and winds its way toward Spooner Summit. Several excellent rocky viewpoints along the way offer scenic overlooks with Washoe Valley spreading to the east and Lake Tahoe glimmering to the west. Descending quickly and into the forest, the trail switchbacks down to Spooner Summit and the parking area, approximately 5.5 miles from South Camp Peak.

*Special note:* The road crossing at Spooner Summit is hazardous—use extreme caution when attempting to cross busy Highway 50.

---

# TRT-4                    13.0 mi. one way/2.0 days
# SPOONER SUMMIT to TUNNEL CREEK ROAD

*Reference:* **From Spooner Summit to Tunnel Creek Road; map D4, grid e5.**

*User groups:* Hikers, horses and dogs. No mountain bikes are allowed. No wheelchair access.

*Permits:* No day-use permits are needed. A campfire permit is required. Parking and access are free.

*Directions:* North of South Lake Tahoe and south of Incline Village on Highway 50 just past the Highway 50 and Highway 28 interchange. The Spooner Summit Trailhead is on a dirt parking pull-off located at the Spooner Summit sign.

*Maps:* For a topographic map, ask for Marlette Lake in Nevada from the USGS.

*Trail notes:* This is one of Michael's favorite TRT sections because of the vistas (thoughtfully signed, rather like a Kodak Photo Spot) and loop possibilities with Spooner Lake Trail and North Canyon Road alongside Canyon Creek. Those with families will enjoy the opportunity to hike in partway on gentle trails, set up a picnic and then return easily to the car. Parking is available. Restrooms are available at the Spooner Summit Rest Area. Do not leave your car unattended at the Rest Area—use the designated dirt pullout for trailhead access only. The trail passes through Lake Tahoe Nevada State Park. From the trailhead, begin climbing gently along a sandy pathway up and above Spooner Lake, which will soon become visible through the trees to the west. At a trail junction, stay right, crossing a road, and begin climbing a bit more steeply, although nothing that will cause the heart to beat overtime. In just under two miles of hiking, arrive at the first vista point with a spur trail leading to the overlook. Take in Lake Tahoe, Genoa Peak and Carson Valley before returning to the main trail and continuing north. Within one-quarter mile, pass another vista point and then one-half mile further on, yet another. Getting your fill of vistas yet? Three miles from the trailhead you will hike through old-growth red fir forest, a rarity in these parts. At four miles you will arrive at a trail junction and a decision. Backpackers will head left and down to the campground. Those wanting to opt for an eight-mile loop back to

Spooner Summit will also head left and down to North Canyon Road for a return to the trailhead and Spooner Summit. Keep hiking straight if you are staying on the TRT. Pass another spur road branching left at 5.5 miles and leading down to North Canyon Road (offering a just-over-11-mile-loop option). Keep straight on the TRT to the junction with a trail leading right and up to the summit of Snow Valley Peak. They should have named this "Gale Peak" because the winds up here are unbelievable. Dress warmly. If it is windy on the trail, you may want to reconsider climbing to the 9,214-foot summit unless you enjoy getting wind-blasted. Take a peek at the trees, all leaning dramatically to the east, if you doubt the wind's power. Staying on the TRT, keep hiking north along a spectacular ridgeline route to Tunnel Creek Road, approximately eight miles away.

---

# TRT-5    18.5 mi. one way/2.0 days
# BROCKWAY SUMMIT to TAHOE CITY

*Reference:* **From Brockway Summit to Tahoe City; map D4, grid d4.**

*User groups:* Hikers, horses and dogs. Limited mountain bike access. No wheelchair facilities.

*Permits:* No day-use permits are needed. A campfire permit is required. Parking and access are free.

*Directions:* The Brockway Summit Trailhead may be accessed off Highway 267, north of Kings Beach and Highway 28. The trailhead is located at a large dirt turnout, 14 miles south of the summit on the northwest side and just north of the "Leaving Lake Tahoe Forest" sign. The Tahoe City Trailhead is located at the west end of Tahoe City, 18 miles north from Highway 89 on Fairway Drive across from the Fairway Community Center. Parking is available.

*Maps:* For topographic maps, ask for Kings Beach and Tahoe City from the USGS.

*Trail notes:* A Tahoe Rim Trail bulletin board, set back from the road approximately 100 yards, marks the beginning of the northbound section of trail at Tahoe City. Mountain bikes are only allowed between Painted Rock and Watson Lake. From Brockway Summit to Watson Lake, the distance is approximately seven miles, with wonderful views overlooking Lake Tahoe. Vehicles can and do drive to Watson Lake because of the easy access from the parking area to Lava Cliffs (a three-mile round trip), where the views warrant picnicking quietly while gazing at the awesome scenery. Camping is good on the west shore of Watson Lake, or if you prefer to leave most of humanity behind, further down the trail towards Tahoe City. Away from the lake and Watson Creek, the camping is dry, so pack all the water you will need. From the Lava Cliffs down to Tahoe City, the trail winds 10 miles through pine-scented forest with nothing but the sound of wind through the branches to soothe your soul.

# PACIFIC CREST TRAIL     98.6 mi. one way/10.0 days
## GENERAL INFORMATION

*Reference:* **Trail sections extend from Highway 4 near Ebbetts Pass to trailhead parking near Donner Pass.**

*User groups:* Hikers, horses and dogs (except in national parks). No mountain bikes are allowed. No wheelchair facilities.

*Permits:* A backcountry permit is required for traveling through various wilderness and special-use areas that the trail traverses. In addition, a campfire permit is required for the use of portable camp stoves or the building of campfires (where permitted). To make it simple, you can contact the national forest, BLM or national park office at your point of entry for a combined permit that is good for traveling through multiple-permit areas during your dates of travel.

*Maps:* For an overall view of the trail route in this section, send $3 for each map ordered to the USDA-Forest Service, 630 Sansome Street, San Francisco, CA 94111, ask for the Lake Tahoe Basin Management Unit map, the Tahoe National Forest map, the Eldorado National Forest map and the Stanislaus National Forest map. Topographic maps for particular sections of the trail are provided under each specific trail section heading listed below.

*Who to contact:* Contact either the national forest, BLM or national park office at your trailhead—see specific trailheads and corresponding agencies listed within each section.

*Trail notes:* Trail elevations within this section range from 7,000 feet to over 10,000 feet. Although the lower reaches of the PCT are open from mid-June to mid-October, several high passes within the region may remain snow-covered until mid-July, making hiking difficult. Snow-covered passes are impossible to navigate with pack stock and horses. For this reason, the highest usage period for the most heavily traveled section of the California PCT occurs during the month of August.

---

# PCT-26     12.0 mi. one way/1.0 day
## EBBETTS PASS to BLUE LAKES ROAD

*Reference:* **From Highway 4 near Ebbetts Pass north to Blue Lakes Road south of Carson Pass and Highway 88; map D4, grid j4.**

*User groups:* Hikers, horses and dogs. No mountain bikes are allowed. No wheelchair facilities.

*Permits:* A backcountry permit is required for traveling through various wilderness and special-use areas that the trail traverses. In addition, a campfire permit is required for the use of portable camp stoves or the building of campfires (where permitted). To make it simple, you can contact the national forest, BLM or national park office at your point of entry for a combined permit that is good for traveling through multiple-permit areas during your dates of travel.

*Directions:* For the Ebbetts Pass Trailhead—From Angels Camp, head east on Highway 4 to Ebbetts Pass. For the Blue Lakes Road Trailhead—From the Highway 88/89 interchange at Hope Valley, head west on Highway 88 to Blue Lakes Road and turn left. Stay on Blue Lakes Road to the trailhead parking, just before reaching Blue Lakes.

*Maps:* For topographic maps, ask for Ebbetts Pass, Pacific Valley and Carson Pass from the USGS.

*Who to contact:* Information Center, Eldorado National Forest, 3070 Camino Heights Drive, Camino, CA 95709; (916) 644-6048.

*Trail notes:* As you depart Ebbetts Pass, you will cross a series of fantastic volcanic formations in the Mokelumne Wilderness. The country here may look stark from a distance, but it is loaded with tiny wildflowers. The trail is quite good—a lot of hikers make great time in this area—but the lack of available water can become a concern. We suggest tanking up when you get the chance, such as at Eagle Creek below Reynolds Peak (9,690 feet). The Mokelumne Wilderness is a relative breeze, and you will find yourself approaching civilization at a series of small lakes in Tahoe National Forest. The trail rises up a stark, wind-blown, sandy ridge, with excellent views of the Blue Lakes, but again, no water for several miles until you drop down near Lost Lake. You will actually cross several roads on this stretch of trail, and maybe even see a car—a moment of irony for long-distance PCT hikers.

---

## PCT-27      12.0 mi. one way/1.0 day 4 9
## BLUE LAKES ROAD to CARSON PASS

*Reference:* **From Blue Lakes Road north to Carson Pass and Highway 88; map D4, grid i3.**

*User groups:* Hikers, horses and dogs. No mountain bikes are allowed. No wheelchair access.

*Permits:* A backcountry permit is required for traveling through various wilderness and special-use areas that the trail traverses. In addition, a campfire permit is required for the use of portable camp stoves or the building of campfires (where permitted). To make it simple, you can contact the national forest, BLM or national park office at your point of entry for a combined permit that is good for traveling through multiple-permit areas during your dates of travel.

*Directions:* For the Blue Lakes Road Trailhead—From the Highway 88/89 interchange at Hope Valley, head west on Highway 88 to Blue Lakes Road and turn left. Stay on Blue Lakes Road for 11 miles to the trailhead parking, just before reaching Blue Lakes. For the Carson Pass Trailhead—From the Highway 88/89 interchange at Hope Valley, head west on Highway 88 to Carson Pass.

*Maps:* For topographic maps, ask for Pacific Valley and Carson Pass from the USGS.

*Who to contact:* Information Center, Eldorado National Forest, 3070 Camino Heights Drive, Camino, CA 95709; (916) 644-6048.

*Trail notes:* Many hikers underestimate the climb over Elephant Back to reach Carson Pass. After all, on a map it doesn't look like much, and from a distance, as you size it up, it looks easy enough. Wrong! It's a long, grueling pull. The trip out of Blue Lakes starts easily, with a dirt road often in view and adding a bit of early angst to the affair. As you go, you keep wondering when the climb will start. Well, eventually it does, and alas, it takes a couple of hours, enough to kick the butt of anybody who is not in shape. Guess how we know? After topping the Elephant Back, the route drops down to Carson Pass at a rest stop, where you will likely meet humanity, but believe it or not, no water. Conserve yours if you plan on going onward, because it takes another hour of hiking before you will reach the next trickle.

---

## PCT-28           15.8 mi. one way/1.2 days
## CARSON PASS to ECHO LAKE RESORT

*Reference:* **From Carson Pass at Highway 88 north to Echo Lake near Highway 50, just south of Lake Tahoe; map D4, grid i3.**

*User groups:* Hikers, horses and dogs. No mountain bikes are allowed. No wheelchair facilities.

*Permits:* A backcountry permit is required for traveling through various wilderness and special-use areas that the trail traverses. In addition, a campfire permit is required for the use of portable camp stoves or the building of campfires (where permitted). To make it simple, you can contact the national forest, BLM or national park office at your point of entry for a combined permit that is good for traveling through multiple-permit areas during your dates of travel.

*Directions:* For the Carson Pass Trailhead—From the Highway 88/89 interchange at Hope Valley, head west on Highway 88 to Carson Pass. For the Echo Lake Resort Trailhead—Take Highway 50 west from Lake Tahoe to Echo Lake and Echo Summit.

*Maps:* For topographic maps, ask for Carson Pass, Caples Lake and Echo Lake from the USGS.

*Who to contact:* Information Center, Eldorado National Forest, 3070 Camino Heights Drive, Camino, CA 95709; (916) 644-6048. Or contact the Lake Tahoe Basin Management Unit, 870 Emerald Bay Road, Suite 1, South Lake Tahoe, CA 96150; (916) 573-2600.

*Trail notes:* When you have hiked on the Pacific Crest Trail for weeks, the first glimpse of Lake Tahoe in the distance can seem like a privileged view into heaven. From Ebbetts Pass, the view is just a few miles distant. You start by hiking over a short mountain rim (nice view to the west of Caples Lake), then dropping into the headwaters of the Truckee River. After making the rim, as you gaze northward, Lake Tahoe suddenly comes into view. It is like having a divine vision. In addition, finally there is water available, with several small creeks you can pump liquid from as you walk into the Truckee headwaters. At the same time, you will be greeted by a beautiful high meadow surrounded by a light forest. All seems right with the world again. With Echo Lake Resort within one-day's hiking time, you will be amazed at how inspired you can get on this section of trail. It is very pretty, weaving in and out of lush canyons, along creeks, and eventually to beautiful and tiny Showers Lake. Here the trail seems to drop off to Never-Never Land, descending very quickly and steeply in the march toward Tahoe. Contentment reigns. When you reach Little Norway, however, reality sets in. Cars are everywhere. The trail suddenly grinds down amid cabins and vacation property. There is one last hill to climb, then the PCT drops quickly to the parking lot for Echo Lake.

Almost nobody hiking the PCT immediately heads north into Desolation Wilderness from here. Virtually everyone stops for at least a day, gets cleaned up, re-supplied and fed by something other than a Power Bar. But after a day, the trail calls again. If you hear it, well, you just have to answer it.

# PCT-29     32.3 mi. one way/3.0 days
## ECHO LAKE RESORT to BARKER PASS

*Reference:* **From Echo Lake near Highway 50 and south of Lake Tahoe to Forest Route 3 near Barker Pass northwest of Emerald Bay; map D4, grid g2.**

*User groups:* **Hikers, horses and dogs. No mountain bikes are allowed. No wheelchair facilities.**

*Permits:* **A backcountry permit is required for traveling through various wilderness and special-use areas that the trail traverses. In addition, a campfire permit is required for the use of portable camp stoves or the building of campfires (where permitted). To make it simple, you can contact the national forest, BLM or national park office at your point of entry for a combined permit that is good for traveling through multiple-permit areas during your dates of travel.**

*Directions:* **For the Echo Lake Resort Trailhead—Take Highway 50 south from Lake Tahoe to Echo Lake and Echo Summit. For the Barker Pass Trailhead—From Tahoe Pines on Highway 89, head north for a half mile to the Kaspian Picnic Grounds and then bear left (west) for seven miles on Forest Service Road 15N03.**

*Maps:* **For topographic maps, ask for Echo Lake, Emerald Bay and Rockbound Valley from the USGS.**

*Who to contact:* **Lake Tahoe Basin Management Unit, 870 Emerald Bay Road, Suite 1, South Lake Tahoe, CA 96150; (916) 573-2600.**

*Trail notes:* **As this section of trail passes through the Desolation Wilderness, up and into the Granite Chief Wilderness area, you will be sharing the trail with more people than almost any other section of the PCT. Why? Because of the incredibly beautiful granite domes and proliferation of deep blue lakes, all within easy access from Lake Tahoe and nearby Highway 50. From the dam at Echo Lake, the trail climbs through pines, past Upper Echo Lake, and then continues up and north toward Triangle Lake. Keep hiking toward Haypress Meadows, past Lake Margery and then alongside the eastern shore of Lake Aloha. There is a designated camping area near the northeastern shore, just as the trail veers east and toward Heather Lake. Keep on truckin' past Susie Lake and the Gilmore and Dicks lakes—an up-and-down proposition that will make you feel the burn in your thighs and lungs. There are good campsites near Gilmore Lake. If you are so inclined, and the weather cooperates, pack along enough water for an overnight at Dicks Lake, elevation 9,380 feet. It is windswept, but there is enough shelter from stubby trees to provide a decent windbreak, and the sunrise/sunset combination from this vantage point is spectacular. After dropping down from the pass to Dicks Lake, keep hiking past Upper and Middle Velma lakes and to the west of Phipps Peak. The trail skirts the ridgeline, keeping the higher knobs to the east as it gradually descends toward Richardson Lake, just beyond the Desolation Wilderness boundary. Stock up on water because you will be camping near Barker Pass, a dry camp located near the edge of the Granite Chief Wilderness.**

# PCT-30     31.4 mi. one way/3.0 days
## BARKER PASS to DONNER PASS

*Reference:* **From Forest Route 3 near Barker Pass northwest of Emerald Bay north to the trailhead parking near Interstate 80 and old Highway 40 at Donner Pass; map D4, grid e1.**

*User groups:* Hikers, horses and dogs. No mountain bikes are allowed. No wheelchair facilities.

*Permits:* A backcountry permit is required for traveling through various wilderness and special-use areas that the trail traverses. In addition, a campfire permit is required for the use of portable camp stoves or the building of campfires (where permitted). To make it simple, you can contact the national forest, BLM or national park office at your point of entry for a combined permit that is good for traveling through multiple-permit areas during your dates of travel.

*Directions:* For the Barker Pass Trailhead—From Tahoe Pines on Highway 89, head north for a half mile to the Kaspian Picnic Grounds and then bear left (west) for seven miles on Forest Service Road 15N03. For the Donner Pass Trailhead—Drive west on Interstate 80 from Truckee and exit at Castle Peak Area Boreal Ridge—just west of the Donner Summit roadside rest area. The sign for the Pacific Crest Trailhead is what you are looking for, and it is located on the south side of the highway.

*Maps:* For topographic maps, ask for Emerald Bay, Rockbound Valley, Homewood, Tahoe City, Granite Chief and Norden from the USGS.

*Who to contact:* Tahoe National Forest, Truckee Ranger District, 10342 Highway 89, North Truckee, CA 96161; (916) 587-3558. Or contact the Lake Tahoe Basin Management Unit, 870 Emerald Bay Road, Suite 1, South Lake Tahoe, CA 96150; (916) 573-2600.

*Trail notes:* Cinch down your boots, because this section of PCT is an up-and-down roller coaster ride. Views from the tops of both Twin Peaks (located just northeast of the trail after entering the Granite Chief Wilderness) and Tinker Knob are outstanding. From Barker Pass up and past Twin Peaks and then on to Ward Peak, the terrain is volcanic and loose—watch your steps. From Ward Peak, the trail switchbacks steeply down to Five Lakes and Five Lakes Creek (where there is good camping), and then continues up and down all the way to Donner Pass. The wildflower displays along the open and brushy slopes, and in meadows dotting the edge of streams and lakes, are very colorful. Along the way you will pass near two ski resorts—Alpine Meadows and Squaw Valley. Expect crowds on weekends around Squaw, since hikers often use the tram there to gain elevation and then spend their day wandering around the ridges.

*PCT CONTINUATION:* To continue hiking along the Pacific Crest Trail, see Chapter D3, page 223.

# MAP E1

NOR-CAL MAP ........................ see page 14
adjoining maps
NORTH (D1) ............................ see page 202
EAST (E2) ............................... see page 394
SOUTH (F1) ............................. see page 468
WEST ..................................... no map

194 TRAILS
PAGES 258-393

For Marin area hikes, please see Map E1-Marin on opposite page.

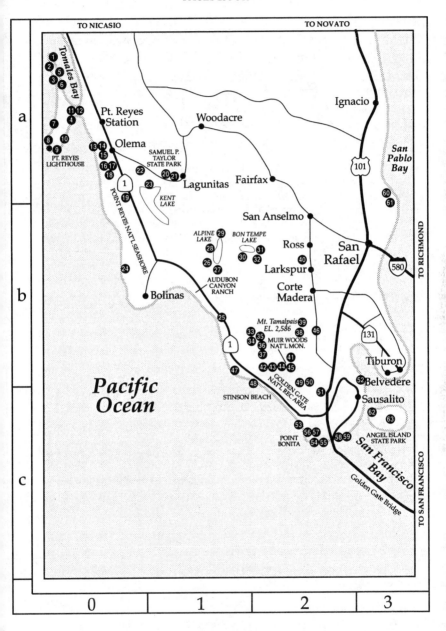

## Map E1-Marin featuring: Point Reyes National Seashore, Tomales Bay State Park, Limantour Beach, Samuel P. Taylor State Park, San Rafael, Mt. Tamalpais, Alpine Lake Dam, Lagunitas Lake, Mt. Tamalpais State Park, Muir Woods National Monument, Stinson Beach, Marin Headlands, San Francisco Bay, Golden Gate Bridge, China Camp State Park, Angel Island State Park

## 1. TOMALES POINT TRAIL      6.0 mi/3.5 hrs

*Reference:* **In Point Reyes National Seashore in northwest Marin County; map E1-Marin, grid a0.**

*User groups:* Hikers and horses (Note: It is a violation of federal law to herd, chase or otherwise harass the elk). No mountain bikes or dogs are allowed. Pierce Ranch is accessible to **wheelchairs**, the Tomales Point Trail is not.

*Permits:* No permits are required. Parking and access are free.

*Directions:* From San Francisco, drive north on US Highway 101 to San Rafael and take the Sir Francis Drake Boulevard exit. Turn west on Sir Francis Drake Boulevard and drive about 20 miles to the town of Olema. Turn right on Highway 1 and drive a very short distance. Then turn left at Sir Francis Drake Highway and drive north for 8.2 miles to Pierce Ranch Road. Turn right and drive 9.5 miles to Pierce Ranch parking area and the trailhead.

*Maps:* For a free map of Point Reyes National Seashore, write to Superintendent, Point Reyes National Seashore, Point Reyes, CA 94956. To obtain a topographic map of area, ask for Tomales from the USGS.

*Who to contact:* Call Point Reyes National Seashore at (415) 663-1092, or write them at the address listed above.

*Trail notes:* Imagine meeting up with an elk that stands five feet at the shoulder, with antlers practically poking holes in the clouds...that's the chance you have on this trail, the best hike in California to see wildlife. Often the elk are quite close to the parking area, and in the evening, they usually congregate near a watering area set in a valley about three miles in. We have seen as many as 75 elk on one trip, and on another, 13 elk, six deer, three rabbits and a fox, all in just two hours. The trail has a flat walking surface and easy grades, with the Pacific Ocean to your west and Tomales Bay to your east, beautiful sights. Many off-trail sidetrips are possible by following elk trails through the low brush. A bonus opportunity is to continue your trip for an extra mile all the way to Tomales Point. The only negative is the occasional poor hiking weather, when wind and fog envelop the area.

## 2. McCLURES BEACH TRAIL      1.0 mi/0.5 hr

*Reference:* **In Point Reyes National Seashore in northwest Marin County; map E1-Marin, grid a0.**

*User groups:* Hikers only. No mountain bikes, dogs or horses are allowed. No wheelchair access.

*Permits:* No permits are required. Parking and access are free.

*Directions:* From San Francisco, drive north on US 101 to San Rafael and take the Sir Francis Drake Boulevard exit. Turn west on Sir Francis Drake

Boulevard and drive about 20 miles to the town of Olema. Turn right on Highway 1 and drive a very short distance. Then turn left at Sir Francis Drake Highway and drive north for 8.2 miles to Pierce Ranch Road. Turn right and drive 9.5 miles to Pierce Ranch, then turn left and drive a half mile to the parking area and trailhead.

*Maps:* For a free map of Point Reyes National Seashore, write to Superintendent, Point Reyes National Seashore, Point Reyes, CA 94956. To obtain a topographic map of area, ask for Tomales from the USGS.

*Who to contact:* Call Point Reyes National Seashore at (415) 663-1092, or write them at the address listed above.

*Trail notes:* In the divine panorama of Point Reyes, McClures Beach is one easy-to-reach spot that is often overlooked. It sits in the shadow of nearby Pierce Ranch and its 200-strong elk herd, and most visitors never take the quarter-mile drive to road's end, except perhaps to use the restrooms and telephone there. But an easy, half-mile walk will lead you to McClures Beach, with tidepools to the south and beachfront to the north. This area is always best visited during minus low tides so you can survey the tidepool life. All matter of tiny marine creatures can be viewed playing their war games. Also during low tides, beachcombing along McClures and Driftwood Beach (to the immediate north) can unveil unusual finds. One other thing: The sunsets from this beach can be spectacular, especially during fall and early winter, when skies can look like a scene out of *The Ten Commandments.*

---

## 3. ABBOTTS LAGOON TRAIL　3.2 mi/1.5 hrs

*Reference:* **In Point Reyes National Seashore in northwest Marin County; map E1-Marin, grid a0.**

*User groups:* Hikers and mountain bikes (first mile only, do not cross bridge). No dogs or horses are allowed. **Wheelchair accessible** with assistance.

*Permits:* No permits are required. Parking and access are free.

*Directions:* From San Francisco, drive north on US 101 to San Rafael and take the Sir Francis Drake Boulevard exit. Turn west on Sir Francis Drake Boulevard and drive about 20 miles to the town of Olema. Turn right on Highway 1, and drive a very short distance, then turn left at Sir Francis Drake Highway and drive north for 8.2 miles to Pierce Point Road. Turn right and drive 4.4 miles to a small parking area with restrooms. The trailhead is on the left side of the road.

*Maps:* For a free map of Point Reyes National Seashore, write to Superintendent, Point Reyes National Seashore, Point Reyes, CA 94956. To obtain a topographic map of area, ask for Drake's Bay from the USGS.

*Who to contact:* Call Point Reyes National Seashore at (415) 663-1092, or write them at the address listed above.

*Trail notes:* A short ridge keeps Abbotts Lagoon out of sight of park visitors driving up and down nearby Pierce Point Road. That is what keeps it secluded, despite the trail providing such an easy walk with such excellent results. In fact, the trail surface is called "soil cement," and it is **wheelchair accessible** about halfway to the ocean bluff. From the trailhead (look for the restrooms), you climb that low ridge, and just like that, below you is Abbotts Lagoon, and beyond, the Pacific Ocean. The lagoon is an ideal place for beginning canoeing or kayaking, providing you don't mind the portage. Birdwatching is often good here, because there is a rare mix of waterfowl that require freshwater and seabirds migrating along the coast. If you walk past the lagoon, the distance from the trailhead is 1.6 miles to Point Reyes Beach, where there are miles and miles of sand dunes and untouched waterfront both to the north and south.

---

# 4. ESTERO TRAIL          8.8 mi/4.0 hrs

*Reference:* **In Point Reyes National Seashore in northwest Marin County; map E1-Marin, grid a0.**

*User groups:* Hikers, horses and mountain bikes (restricted at Drake's Head). No dogs are permitted. The first two miles is **wheelchair accessible**.

*Permits:* No permits are required. Parking and access are free.

*Directions:* From San Francisco, drive north on US 101 to San Rafael and take the Sir Francis Drake Boulevard exit. Turn west on Sir Francis Drake Boulevard and drive about 20 miles to the town of Olema. Turn right on Highway 1 and drive a short distance. Then turn left at Sir Francis Drake Highway and drive north for 7.4 miles. Turn left and drive one mile to the parking area for Estero Trailhead.

*Maps:* For a free map of Point Reyes National Seashore, write to Superintendent, Point Reyes National Seashore, Point Reyes, CA 94956. To obtain a topographic map of area, ask for Drake's Bay from the USGS.

*Who to contact:* Call Point Reyes National Seashore at (415) 663-1092, or write them at the address listed above.

*Trail notes:* The Estero Trail crosses a valley, parallels a bay, is routed up a ridge and then down to the waterfront where there awaits a perfect, quiet spot for a picnic lunch. That route makes it an ideal hike for newcomers to the Point Reyes National Seashore, providing glimpses of a variety of settings. In addition, the roundtrip is long enough for a workout, yet it is quite pleasant with no gut-wrencher climbs. From the parking area, you walk 2.4 miles, then turn left at the signed junction. The compensation for climbing Drake's Head is a view of Drake's Estero, an outstanding kayaking location; from the turnoff, the walk is just six-tenths of a mile to the ridge. From there, you turn right and walk 1.4 miles to the waterfront, set on the edge of Estero de Limantour. This is a beautiful spot, and we suggest you get an early start so you can enjoy it, and not worry about rushing the 4.4-mile return trip to beat darkness.

---

# 5. MARSHALL BEACH TRAIL   2.4 mi/1.25 hrs

*Reference:* **In Point Reyes National Seashore in northwest Marin County; map E1-Marin, grid a0.**

*User groups:* Hikers, mountain bikes and horses. No dogs are allowed. No wheelchair access.

*Permits:* No permits are required. Parking and access are free.

*Directions:* From San Francisco, drive north on US 101 to San Rafael and take the Sir Francis Drake Boulevard exit. Turn west on Sir Francis Drake Boulevard and drive about 20 miles to the town of Olema. Turn right on Highway 1 and drive a short distance. Then turn left (north) at Sir Francis Drake Highway and drive for 8.2 miles to Pierce Ranch Road. Turn right and

drive 1.3 miles to just past the access road to Tomales Bay State Park. Turn
right and drive 2.6 miles to the parking area for the Marshall Beach Trail.

*Maps:* For a free map of Point Reyes National Seashore, write to Superintendent, Point Reyes National Seashore, Point Reyes, CA 94956. To obtain a
topographic map of area, ask for Tomales from the USGS.

*Who to contact:* Call Point Reyes National Seashore at (415) 663-1092, or write
them at the address listed above.

*Trail notes:* The most secluded beach in Marin County? This might just qualify.
Marshall Beach is set on the demure waters of Tomales Bay, a pretty spot
sheltered from north winds by Inverness Ridge. The trailhead is overlooked
because there are no signs leading you to it, until you reach the trailhead
itself. In addition, it is overshadowed by Tomales Bay State Park, which you
must drive past (many don't) in order to reach it. The hike is 1.2 miles one-
way, taking an elliptical route down into a gulch to a protected cove that helps
shelter the beach. It's the kind of place where you can just sit and watch the
water lap gently at the shore, and somehow, that is plenty.

---

# 6. JOHNSTONE TRAIL     8.0 mi/4.0 hrs

*Reference:* In Tomales Bay State Park in northwest Marin County; map
E1-Marin, grid a0.

*User groups:* Hikers only. No horses, mountain bikes or dogs are allowed. The
park headquarters is **wheelchair accessible**, the trail is not.

*Permits:* A state park day-use fee is charged at the entrance station.

*Directions:* From San Francisco, drive north on US 101 to San Rafael and take
the Sir Francis Drake Boulevard exit. Turn west on Sir Francis Drake
Boulevard and drive about 20 miles to the town of Olema. Turn right on
Highway 1 and drive a short distance. Then turn left at Sir Francis Drake
Highway and drive north for 8.2 miles to Pierce Ranch Road. Turn right and
drive 1.2 miles, then turn right again on the access road for Tomales Bay
State Park and drive 1.5 miles to the parking area and trailhead.

*Maps:* A small map/brochure is available for a fee at the entrance station to
Tomales Bay State Park, Star Route, Inverness, CA 94937. To obtain a
topographic map of the area, ask for Tomales from the USGS.

*Who to contact:* Call Tomales Bay State Park at (415) 669-1140 or (415) 456-
1286.

*Trail notes:* The centerpiece hike of Tomales Bay State Park is the Johnstone
Trail, ranging from Hearts Desire Beach to Shell Beach, a four-mile trip one-
way. In the process, you will pass through a procession of different habitats,
including beaches, forests, meadows and fields. The highlight is the gentle
waterfront of Tomales Bay, protected from north winds by Inverness Ridge
at Point Reyes. When viewed from the ridge, the bay appears cobalt blue,
beautiful and soft, unlike most saltwater bays which look green and harsh.
Up close, its docile nature makes it perfect for wading, waterplay, hand-
launching small boats, or during low tides, clamming (be certain to have a
fishing license). A good sidetrip off the Johnstone Trail is to take the Jepson
Trail cutoff, which provides quick access to a dramatic grove of craggy,
virgin Bishop pine. In the spring, wildflower blooms can be spectacular.

# 7. SOUTH BEACH TRAIL    0.1 mi/0.25 hr

*Reference:* In Point Reyes National Seashore in northwest Marin County; map E1-Marin, grid a0.

*User groups:* Hikers, horses and leashed dogs. No mountain bikes allowed. No wheelchair access.

*Permits:* No permits are required. Parking and access are free.

*Directions:* From San Francisco, drive north on US 101 to San Rafael and take the Sir Francis Drake Boulevard exit. Turn west on Sir Francis Drake Boulevard and drive about 20 miles to the town of Olema. Turn right on Highway 1 and drive a short distance. Then turn left at Sir Francis Drake Highway and drive north for 13.6 miles. Turn right and drive to the parking lot for South Beach.

*Maps:* For a free map of Point Reyes National Seashore, write to Superintendent, Point Reyes National Seashore, Point Reyes, CA 94956. To obtain a topographic map of area, ask for Drake's Bay from the USGS.

*Who to contact:* Call Point Reyes National Seashore at (415) 663-1092, or write to them at the address listed above.

*Trail notes:* If you like untouched miles of beachfront, you came to the right place. The Point Reyes Beach extends for nearly 10 miles, all of it pristine, where the surf rolls on endlessly. The trail provides a short walk to South Beach, located about three miles north of Point Reyes Lighthouse. This is a nice beach picnic site where you can take the dog (leashed, of course) for a beach walk, one of the few places at Point Reyes where dogs are permitted. The best stroll here is south for about a mile to an expanse of sand dunes. It is a wise idea to call ahead for weather conditions; low fog is common here, especially during the summer. A word of warning: Do not swim or body surf here. This stretch of coast is known for its treacherous undertow, the kind that can trap even the strongest swimmers, pulling you under and pushing you out to sea regardless of your attempts to swim back to the beach.

# 8. POINT REYES LIGHTHOUSE   0.8 mi/0.5 hr

*Reference:* In Point Reyes National Seashore in northwest Marin County; map E1-Marin, grid a0.

*User groups:* Hikers and mountain bikes (restricted from the stairs). No dogs or horses. **Partially accessible to wheelchairs.**

*Permits:* No permits are required. Parking and access are free.

*Directions:* From San Francisco, drive north on US 101 to San Rafael and take the Sir Francis Drake Boulevard exit. Turn west on Sir Francis Drake Boulevard and drive about 20 miles to the town of Olema. Turn right on Highway 1 and drive a short distance. Then turn left at Sir Francis Drake Highway and drive north for 18.4 miles. The road dead ends at the parking area for the Point Reyes Lighthouse.

*Maps:* For a free map of Point Reyes National Seashore, write to Superintendent, Point Reyes National Seashore, Point Reyes, CA 94956. To obtain a topographic map of area, ask for Drake's Bay from the USGS.

*Who to contact:* Call Point Reyes National Seashore at (415) 663-1092, or write to them at the address listed above.

*Trail notes:* There may be no better place than here anywhere on land to watch migrating whales. From Point Reyes, you scan the ocean, watching for a whale spout, what appears to be a little puff of smoke on the ocean surface. When you see it, you zoom in closer, perhaps using binoculars, and if you are lucky, might even get a tail salute. The chances are good, with 21,000 gray whales migrating past here every winter on the great whale highway just offshore of Point Reyes. The trail to the lookout is short and paved, and includes a dramatic descent down a railed stairway. On the way back, it requires a modest climb, steep for some, so stop to pant a bit at three rest stops. On clear weekends, particularly in winter, it can be crowded. A fence set on the edge of the cliff keeps visitors from falling overboard, and provides one of the most dramatic coastal lookouts anywhere. Sunsets are unforgettable.

## 9. CHIMNEY ROCK TRAIL 2.8 mi/1.25 hrs

*Reference:* In Point Reyes National Seashore in northwest Marin County; map E1-Marin, grid a0.

*User groups:* Hikers and mountain bikes. No dogs or horses are allowed. The first quarter mile of the trail is **wheelchair accessible**.

*Permits:* No permits are required. Parking and access are free.

*Directions:* From San Francisco, drive north on US 101 to San Rafael and take the Sir Francis Drake Boulevard exit. Turn west on Sir Francis Drake Boulevard and drive about 20 miles to the town of Olema. Turn right on Highway 1, and drive a short distance, then turn left at Sir Francis Drake Highway and drive north for 17.3 miles. Turn left and drive nine-tenths of a mile to the parking lot for the Chimney Rock Trail.

*Maps:* For a free map of Point Reyes National Seashore, write to Superintendent, Point Reyes National Seashore, Point Reyes, CA 94956. To obtain a topographic map of area, ask for Drake's Bay from the USGS.

*Who to contact:* Call Point Reyes National Seashore at (415) 663-1092, or write to them at the address listed above.

*Trail notes:* A lot of visitors miss out on Chimney Rock because of its proximity to the Point Reyes Lighthouse, the feature destination at the park. But the Chimney Rock lookout is easy to reach, about a half-hour hike, and provides a cutoff to a vista that is nearly the equal of the Point Reyes Lighthouse. From the parking area, the trail is routed 1.4 miles to land's end. Chimney Rock, or at least what is supposed to be Chimney Rock, sits just offshore. Just beyond the halfway point to land's end, hikers can take a short cutoff trail that provides a great vista of the Pacific Ocean. During the winter, especially between late December and March, this is a great spot to watch for the spouts of migrating whales. Another bonus on this trail is that on your way back, the last eight-tenths of a mile can be completed on a loop trail, so you don't have to repeat the route you started the trip on. One note: At the end of the trail, where a wooden guard rail keeps you from falling overboard, you will look down at an assortment of coastal rocks, and ask, "So, which one of those suckers is Chimney Rock?" Good question. Like most visitors, we never figured it out.

# 10. SIR FRANCIS DRAKE TRAIL  1.9 mi/1.0 hr

*Reference:* In Point Reyes National Seashore in northwest Marin County; map E1-Marin, grid a0.

*User groups:* Hikers and mountain bikes. No dogs or horses are allowed. No wheelchair access.

*Permits:* No permits are required. Parking and access are free.

*Directions:* From San Francisco, drive north on US 101 to San Rafael and take the Sir Francis Drake Boulevard exit. Turn west on Sir Francis Drake Boulevard and drive about 20 miles to the town of Olema. Turn right on Highway 1 and drive a short distance. Then turn left at Sir Francis Drake Highway and drive north for 13.1 miles. Turn left and drive 1.2 miles to the parking lot at the Kenneth Patrick Visitor Center and the trailhead.

*Maps:* For a free map of Point Reyes National Seashore, write to Superintendent, Point Reyes National Seashore, Point Reyes, CA 94956. To obtain a topographic map of area, ask for Drake's Bay from the USGS.

*Who to contact:* Call Point Reyes National Seashore at (415) 663-1092, or write to them at the address listed above.

*Trail notes:* Hey, this spot is not exactly a secret. In fact, you might as well stand on the Golden Gate Bridge with a megaphone and announce it to the world. At the trailhead, for instance, you will discover a large parking lot and visitor center, complete with exhibits, maps and books (maybe even this one). The trail traces the back of the arcing beaches along Drake's Bay, providing scenic lookouts to the bay's protected waters. The trail continues to the mouth of Drake's Estero, then returns via an inland loop that includes a short climb up, then down, a waterfront bluff. This is one of the more popular hikes at the Point Reyes National Seashore. And why not? It is an easy walk, provides great scenic beauty, and traces three different habitats: beach frontage, the mouth of a lagoon, and hillside bluffs. Just don't expect it to be a secret.

# 11. BUCKLIN TRAIL LOOP   7.1 mi/3.25 hrs

*Reference:* In Point Reyes National Seashore in northwest Marin County; map E1-Marin, grid a0.

*User groups:* Hikers and horses. No mountain bikes or dogs are allowed. No wheelchair access.

*Permits:* No permits are required. Parking and access are free.

*Directions:* From San Francisco, drive north on US 101 to San Rafael and take the Sir Francis Drake Boulevard exit. Turn west on Sir Francis Drake Boulevard and drive about 20 miles to the town of Olema. Turn right on Highway 1 and drive a short distance. Then turn left at Sir Francis Drake Highway and drive north for 6.4 miles. Turn left on Mount Vision Road and drive 3.9 miles to the parking area and the trailhead.

*Maps:* For a free map of Point Reyes National Seashore, write to Superintendent, Point Reyes National Seashore, Point Reyes, CA 94956. To obtain topographic maps of area, ask for Inverness and Drake's Bay from the USGS.

*Who to contact:* Call Point Reyes National Seashore at (415) 663-1092, or write to them at the address listed above.

*Trail notes:* Broad, sweeping views of Drake's Bay and the Pacific Ocean are your compensation for hiking the Bucklin Trail. The trailhead is at the Mt. Vision parking area, elevation 1,240 feet, and the suggested route makes an outstanding loop hike. After parking, the trail is directed along Inverness Ridge for a half-mile. Then turn right at the trail junction, where the Bucklin Trail descends on a wide crest for 2.4 miles to Muddy Hollow Trail. For the best loop hike, turn left at this intersection, hike 0.4 miles, then turn left again at the intersection of Drake's View Trail. Your reward is a short respite through a valley, then a two-mile climb back up to Inverness Ridge, where you turn left, and finish out the hike. Sound good? It is. Just make sure you pick a clear day, and as you gaze across miles and miles of azure blue waters, you will be reminded just how special this planet is. Last time we checked, it was still the best one around.

---

## 12. INVERNESS RIDGE TRAIL   6.2 mi/3.0 hrs

*Reference:* In Point Reyes National Seashore in northwest Marin County; map E1-Marin, grid a0.

*User groups:* Hikers, horses and mountain bikes (not permitted on any spur trails). No dogs are allowed. **Wheelchair accessible** with assistance.

*Permits:* No permits are required. Parking and access are free.

*Directions:* From San Francisco, drive north on US 101 to San Rafael and take the Sir Francis Drake Boulevard exit. Turn west on Sir Francis Drake Boulevard and drive about 20 miles to the town of Olema. Turn right on Highway 1 and drive a short distance. Then turn left at Sir Francis Drake Highway and drive north for 6.4 miles. Turn left on Mount Vision Road and drive 3.9 miles to the parking area and the trailhead.

*Maps:* For a free map of Point Reyes National Seashore, write to Superintendent, Point Reyes National Seashore, Point Reyes, CA 94956. To obtain topographic maps of area, ask for Inverness and Drake's Bay from the USGS.

*Who to contact:* Call Point Reyes National Seashore at (415) 663-1092, or write to them at the address listed above.

*Trail notes:* Inverness Ridge Trail provides open ridgeline views of the Pacific Ocean, quiet paths through forest, and gentle climbs and descents. It starts at the Mt. Vision trailhead, then is routed south along the ridge line, skirting just west of Point Reyes Hill, elevation 1,336 feet. The hike covers 3.1 miles until it hits Limantour Road and the Bayview Trail trailhead. At that point, you can return by reversing your course, or the ambitious can continue on and turn it into a 9.3-mile loop hike. If you like broad views, the Inverness Ridge Trail is a good way to get them. For much of the hike, you are perched along many of the highest points in the Point Reyes National Seashore. What makes this trail great is that you don't need to hike the entire route to get the rewards. Many people just head in a mile or so, sit down and enjoy the views, and then make the easy return.

---

## 13. MUDDY HOLLOW LOOP   7.1 mi/3.25 hrs

*Reference:* In Point Reyes National Seashore at Limantour Beach in northwest Marin County; map E1-Marin, grid a0.

*User groups:* Hikers and horses. No mountain bikes or dogs are permitted.

Muddy Hollow Road is accessible to **wheelchairs** with assistance.

*Permits:* No permits are required. Parking and access are free.

*Directions:* From San Francisco, drive north on US 101 to San Rafael and take the Sir Francis Drake Boulevard exit. Turn west on Sir Francis Drake Boulevard and drive about 20 miles to the town of Olema. Turn right on Highway 1 and drive a very short distance. Then turn left at Sir Francis Drake Highway and drive north for two miles to Limantour Road. Turn left and drive 7.6 miles to Limantour Beach and the trailhead.

*Maps:* For a free map of Point Reyes National Seashore, write to Superintendent, Point Reyes National Seashore, Point Reyes, CA 94956. To obtain a topographic map of area, ask for Drake's Bay from the USGS.

*Who to contact:* Call Point Reyes National Seashore at (415) 663-1092, or write to them at the address listed above.

*Trail notes:* This is one of the greatest coastal loop hikes available anywhere. It is routed through a variety of terrains and settings, but starts and ends right on the beach. The trailhead is at Limantour Beach, and from there, you hike north up Muddy Hollow, a shallow valley that drains rainfall into the Estero de Limantour. After 1.4 miles, turn left on Muddy Hollow "Road" and hike 2.1 miles. Here the trail crosses the coastal hills, climbing to about 300 feet, then dropping into another valley and crossing Glenbrook Creek. Turn left at the Glenbrook/Estero Trail, which will lead you back to the parking area over the course of 3.9 miles. The latter sector traces the shore of the Estero, a serene setting on calm, blue-sky days. From the Limantour parking area, this is also an excellent jump-off spot for canoeing and kayaking. The Estero de Limantour is protected by the narrow Limantour sand spit.

---

# 14. COAST TRAIL     15.0 mi. one way/2.5 days

*Reference:* **In Point Reyes National Seashore in northwest Marin County; map E1-Marin, grid a0.**

*User groups:* Hikers and horses. Mountain bikes are permitted only from the Laguna Trailhead to the Coast Campground and are otherwise prohibited. No dogs are allowed. Partially accessible to **wheelchairs** with assistance.

*Permits:* No permits are required. Parking and access are free.

*Directions:* From San Francisco, drive north on US 101 to San Rafael and take the Sir Francis Drake Boulevard exit. Turn west on Sir Francis Drake Boulevard and drive about 20 miles to the town of Olema. Turn right on Highway 1 and drive a very short distance. Then turn left at Sir Francis Drake Highway and drive north for two miles to Limantour Road. Turn left and drive six miles. Turn left on the access road for the Point Reyes Hostel and drive two-tenths of a mile to the trailhead on the right side of the road.

*Maps:* For a free map of Point Reyes National Seashore, write to Superintendent, Point Reyes National Seashore, Point Reyes, CA 94956. To obtain topographic maps of area, ask for Inverness and Double Point from the USGS.

*Who to contact:* Call Point Reyes National Seashore at (415) 663-1092, or write to them at the address listed above.

*Trail notes:* Of the handful of overnight hiking trips available in the Bay Area, it is the Coast Trail that provides the most extended tour into a land of charm. It is located north of Bolinas on the remote Marin Coast and includes camps at ocean bluffs, great ridge lookouts, coastal lakes, a beach with sculptured rocks and tidepools, and a rare coastal waterfall. The continuous back-country route is 15 miles, long enough for lingering hikers to spend a weekend at it, Friday evening through Sunday, and short enough for the ambitious to tackle in a single day. There are only a few catches: You need a hiking partner who will double as a shuttle driver, that is, you will leave cars at each end of the trail. While camping is free, you will need a reservation through the headquarters of Point Reyes National Seashore, and come planned to do your cooking with a small backpack stove, not a campfire. Tents are also recommended, because the coastal weather is the Bay Area's most unpredictable—clear, calm and warm one day, then suddenly foggy, windy and clammy the next. The best trailhead for the Coast Trail is at the Point Reyes Hostel, so you will be hiking north to south, keeping the wind at your back and out of your face. The first camp, Coast Camp, is an easy 2.8-miler, ideal for reaching on a Friday evening after getting off work. The sound of ocean waves will waft you to sleep. The next day, you will hike south, getting glimpses along the way of Sculptured Beach, magnificent rock stacks and tunnels. There is a 0.2-mile cutoff that drops down to the beach and will allow you to explore the unique geologic formations and tidepools. When you continue on, the Coast Trail eventually turns inland, then drops down a canyon and to Wildcat Camp, set on a bluff overlooking the ocean, finishing a 6.6-mile day (seven miles if you take the cutoff to Sculptured Beach). On Day 3, figure a 5.6-mile closeout, with plenty of sideshows along the way. You will hike past a series of coastal lakes, nearby Wildcat Lake and little Ocean Lake, and also have the opportunity to see Alamere Falls, a pretty waterfall that tumbles to the beach. Then after climbing to a short ridge, you will skirt above Pelican Lake and later, along the northern shore of Bass Lake. The trail then heads up a coastal hill, topping out at 563 feet, then laterals down a canyon and back to ocean bluffs. Following the trail, you turn left, and a mile later, reach the Palomar Trailhead. You will be ready to reach your shuttle car and head for the barn. Providing you have a shuttle partner, it is one of the Bay Area's greatest hikes.

---

## 15. LAGUNA LOOP TRAIL    5.5 mi/2.5 hrs  

*Reference:* **In Point Reyes National Seashore in northwest Marin County; map E1-Marin, grid a0.**

*User groups:* Hikers and horses. Mountain bikes are permitted only from the Laguna Trailhead to the Coast Campground and are otherwise prohibited. No dogs are allowed. No wheelchair access.

*Permits:* No permits are required. Parking and access are free.

*Directions:* From San Francisco, drive north on US 101 to San Rafael and take the Sir Francis Drake Boulevard exit. Turn west on Sir Francis Drake Boulevard and drive about 20 miles to the town of Olema. Turn right on Highway 1 and drive a very short distance. Then turn left at Sir Francis Drake Highway and drive north for two miles to Limantour Road. Turn left and drive six miles. Turn left on the access road for the Point Reyes Hostel and drive two-tenths of a mile past the hostel to the trailhead on the right side of the road.

*Maps:* For a free map of Point Reyes National Seashore, write to Superintendent, Point Reyes National Seashore, Point Reyes, CA 94956. To obtain a topographic map of area, ask for Inverness from the USGS.

***Who to contact:*** Call Point Reyes National Seashore at (415) 663-1092, or write to them at the address listed above.

***Trail notes:*** The trailhead for the Laguna Loop Trail is just two-tenths of a mile down the road from the Point Reyes Hostel, adjacent to the park's Environmental Education Center. From here, the trail points up to Inverness Ridge for 1.8 miles, with great views of Drake's Bay on the way. At the ridge, you turn right and hike seven-tenths of a mile toward Mt. Wittenberg at 1,407 feet, the highest point at Point Reyes National Seashore. On the north flank of Mt. Wittenberg, hikers should turn right on Fire Lane Trail, which provides a loop hike for three miles back to the Laguna Trailhead. This comprises an excellent loop hike that includes a bit of a climb and Pacific lookouts that is short enough to complete easily in a few hours. An option here is adding an overnight camp to your trip. At the Mt. Wittenberg trail junction, if you continue south on the Sky Trail (instead of turning right on the loop trail), in just a half mile you will reach Sky Camp, the easiest to reach of the Point Reyes environmental campsites.

# 16. MOUNT WITTENBERG LOOP 8.6 mi/5.0 hrs

***Reference:*** **In Point Reyes National Seashore near Olema in northwest Marin County; map E1-Marin, grid a0.**

***User groups:*** Hikers and horses. No mountain bikes or dogs are allowed. No wheelchair access.

***Permits:*** No permits are required. Parking and access are free.

***Directions:*** From San Francisco, drive north on US 101 to San Rafael and take the Sir Francis Drake Boulevard exit. Turn west on Sir Francis Drake Boulevard and drive about 20 miles to the town of Olema. Turn right on Highway 1 and drive a very short distance. Then turn left at Sir Francis Drake Highway and drive north for seven-tenths of a mile. Turn left at the "Seashore Information" sign and drive to the parking lot for the park headquarters.

***Maps:*** For a free map of Point Reyes National Seashore, write to Superintendent, Point Reyes National Seashore, Point Reyes, CA 94956. To obtain a topographic map of area, ask for Inverness from the USGS.

***Who to contact:*** Call Point Reyes National Seashore at (415) 663-1092, or write to them at the address listed above.

***Trail notes:*** Of the trails that start at Point Reyes park headquarters, it is Sky Trail/Mt. Wittenberg Trail that gets the least use. Why? Simple, because this sucker goes up, the most direct route (1.7 miles) from park headquarters at elevation 105 feet to Mt. Wittenberg at 1,407 feet. That means there are fewer people here than on the other trails, and that alone is plenty reason to inspire the wise, well-conditioned few to make this trip. At Mt. Wittenberg, the trail turns left and traces Inverness Ridge southward, breaking out of trees as it nears the coast for ocean views. Along the way, you will have the option of turning left and looping back on trails if you desire to cut the trip short. Our suggested day hike is to continue to the Baldy cutoff (another three miles), then complete the loop by returning to park headquarters by taking the Bear Valley Trail, though it can be rather crowded. This route provides the option at the Sky Trail/Baldy Trail junction to make the 1.5-mile trip down to

Kelham Beach. However, it is only for the ambitious. Why? Because this option will require a 1,000-foot climbout on the way back, but hey, you wanted to be alone, right? At the least, just making the climb to Wittenberg and then back down (a 3.4-mile roundtrip), a quick huff and a puff, is worth tightening your boots for.

## 17. BEAR VALLEY TRAIL          8.2 mi/4.0 hrs

*Reference:* **In Point Reyes National Seashore near Olema in northwest Marin County; map E1-Marin, grid a0.**

*User groups:* Hikers, horses (weekdays only) and mountain bikes (first three miles only). No dogs are allowed. The first 1.5 mile is **wheelchair accessible.** The trail to Divide Meadow is **wheelchair accessible** with assistance.

*Permits:* No permits are required. Parking and access is free.

*Directions:* From San Francisco, drive north on US 101 to San Rafael and take the Sir Francis Drake Boulevard exit. Turn west on Sir Francis Drake Boulevard and drive about 20 miles to the town of Olema. Turn right on Highway 1 and drive a very short distance. Then turn left at Sir Francis Drake Highway and drive north for seven-tenths of a mile. Turn left at the "Seashore Information" sign and drive to the parking lot for the park headquarters.

*Maps:* For a free map of Point Reyes National Seashore, write to Superintendent, Point Reyes National Seashore, Point Reyes, CA 94956. To obtain a topographic map of area, ask for Inverness from the USGS.

*Who to contact:* Call Point Reyes National Seashore at (415) 663-1092, or write to them at the address listed above.

*Trail notes:* The Bear Valley Trail has all the ingredients to get rated as a "10," starting with a pretty route through forests, past Divide Meadow to Bear Valley, and down along Coast Creek to the beach to Arch Rock and Sea Tunnel. The views at trail's end are marvelous. So, you ask, why is it rated only a 6? The answer is because the trail is actually a park service road made of compressed rock, and it's a good thing, because it gets a ton of traffic, including bicycles. It's the most heavily used trail in Point Reyes National Seashore. The best element is that it is **wheelchair accessible**, one of the prettiest wheelchair routes in California. Just put it in power drive, with a modest 215-foot climb required from park headquarters to Divide Meadow. Wheelchairs and bikes are permitted to the Glen Camp Trail, 3.2 miles from park headquarters. After that, you hike down the Coast Creek drainage, a 0.7-mile trek down to the beach.

## 18. RIFT ZONE TRAIL 5.2 mi. one way/2.25 hrs

*Reference:* **In Point Reyes National Seashore near Olema in northwest Marin County; map E1-Marin, grid a0.**

*User groups:* Hikers and horses. No mountain bikes or dogs are allowed. No wheelchair access.

*Permits:* No permits are required. Parking and access are free.

*Directions:* From San Francisco, drive north on US 101 to San Rafael and take the Sir Francis Drake Boulevard exit. Turn west on Sir Francis Drake Boulevard and drive about 20 miles to the town of Olema. Turn right on Highway 1 and drive a very short distance. Then turn left at Sir Francis Drake

Highway and drive north for seven-tenths of a mile. Turn left at the "Seashore Information" sign and drive to the parking lot for the park headquarters.

*Maps:* For a free map of Point Reyes National Seashore, write to Superintendent, Point Reyes National Seashore, Point Reyes, CA 94956. To obtain a topographic map of area, ask for Inverness from the USGS.

*Who to contact:* Call Point Reyes National Seashore at (415) 663-1092, or write to them at the address listed above.

*Trail notes:* Some of the best advice we ever got was this: "Don't let school interfere with your education." Well, the Rift Zone Trail provides a lesson from the University of Nature, with one of the world's classic examples of an earthquake fault line, in this case, the San Andreas Fault. The trail starts at park headquarters and is a 5.2-mile one-way hike to the Five Brooks Trailhead, best completed with a shuttle car. Along the way, the hike traces along Olema Creek, where horizontal movement of 21 feet was recorded during the 1906 earthquake. There are many examples of earthquake activity on this trail, including parallel ridges, but the most obvious sign is the clear difference in vegetation types on each side of the earthquake fault. The trail gets heavy use, has no difficult grades, and requires only a few short up-and-downs near its southern junction with the Five Brooks Trailhead.

---

## 19. OLEMA VALLEY   5.3 mi. one way/2.25 hrs

*Reference:* **In Point Reyes National Seashore south of Olema in northwest Marin County; map E1-Marin, grid a0.**

*User groups:* Hikers, horses and mountain bikes. No dogs are allowed. No wheelchair access.

*Permits:* No permits are required. Parking and access are free.

*Directions:* From San Francisco, drive north on US 101 to San Rafael and take the Sir Francis Drake Boulevard exit. Turn west on Sir Francis Drake Boulevard and drive about 20 miles to the town of Olema. Turn left on Highway 1 and drive 3.6 miles to the Five Brooks Trailhead, located on the west side of the road.

*Maps:* For a free map of Point Reyes National Seashore, write to Superintendent, Point Reyes National Seashore, Point Reyes, CA 94956. To obtain a topographic map of area, ask for Bolinas from the USGS.

*Who to contact:* Call Point Reyes National Seashore at (415) 663-1092, or write to them at the address listed above.

*Trail notes:* The phenomenon of two parallel creeks running in opposite directions is the feature of the Olema Valley Trail, which starts at the Five Brooks Trailhead and is routed adjacent to the San Andreas Fault Rift Zone. The curiosity of two earth plates moving in opposite directions create the fault line and the strange marvel of Olema Creek and Pine Gulch Creek. From the trailhead, it is a 1.3-mile walk to the headwaters of Pine Gulch Creek. From there, you can hike southward for four miles, a pretty walk along the creek, before the trail ends at Highway 1. Most hikers turn back long before that, but with a partner and a shuttle car, it makes a great one-way hike, 5.3 miles in all. The trailhead at Five Brooks is at a 180-foot elevation.

## 20. BARNABE TRAIL          5.0 mi/3.5 hrs

*Reference:* **In Samuel P. Taylor State Park west of San Rafael; map E1-Marin, grid a1.**

*User groups:* Hikers, mountain bikes (not permitted on spur trails) and leashed dogs. No horses are allowed. The park headquarters is **wheelchair accessible**, the trail is not.

*Permits:* A $5 state park day-use fee is charged at the entrance station.

*Directions:* From San Francisco, drive north on US 101 to San Rafael and take the Sir Francis Drake Boulevard exit. Turn west on Sir Francis Drake Boulevard and drive about 13 miles to the park entrance.

*Maps:* A small map/brochure is available for a fee at the entrance station to Samuel P. Taylor State Park, P.O. Box 251, Lagunitas, CA 94938. To obtain a topographic map of the area, ask for San Geronimo from the USGS.

*Who to contact:* Phone Samuel P. Taylor State Park at (415) 488-9897, Marin District Headquarters at (415) 456-1286, or write to Samuel P. Taylor State Park at the address listed above.

*Trail notes:* This is the highlight hike at Samuel P. Taylor State Park, a beautiful redwood park set along the primary access road to Point Reyes. The Barnabe Trail is a 2.5-mile route up to Barnabe Peak, 1,466 feet in elevation. The summit is a scenic viewpoint, with Inverness Ridge, Point Reyes and the Pacific Ocean off to the west, miles of sunlit charm. The peak is also a common spot to see hawks and vultures using rising thermals on warm days to float aloft with nary a wingbeat. The landscape of the park changes dramatically during this hike. The canyon bottoms and north-facing slopes are marked by coastal redwoods, cool and shaded. As you climb out of the canyon, a 1,300-foot ascent to the summit, you will rise to open grasslands, always lush and green by spring. Since the trail is a dirt service road, leashed dogs and bicycles are permitted, and all users are urged to share the route with extreme courtesy.

## 21. PIONEER TREE TRAIL     2.0 mi/1.0 hrs

*Reference:* **In Samuel P. Taylor State Park west of San Rafael; map E1-Marin, grid a1.**

*User groups:* Hikers only. No horses, mountain bikes or dogs are allowed. The park headquarters is **wheelchair accessible**, the trail is not.

*Permits:* A $5 state park day-use fee is charged at the entrance station.

*Directions:* From San Francisco, drive north on US 101 to San Rafael and take the Sir Francis Drake Boulevard exit. Turn west on Sir Francis Drake Boulevard and drive about 13 miles to the park entrance.

*Maps:* A small map/brochure is available for a fee at the entrance station to Samuel P. Taylor State Park, P.O. Box 251, Lagunitas, CA 94938. To obtain a topographic map of the area, ask for San Geronimo from the USGS.

*Who to contact:* Phone Samuel P. Taylor State Park at (415) 488-9897, Marin District Headquarters at (415) 456-1286, or write to Samuel P. Taylor State Park at the address listed above.

*Trail notes:* If you like big trees and a simple, quiet walk, the Pioneer Tree Trail in Samuel P. Taylor State Park will provide it. This is a loop trail that circles through the park's feature grove of coastal redwoods, the species that produces the tallest trees in the world. The trailhead is at the south side of Lagunitas Creek at the Redwood Grove Picnic Area, about a quarter mile from park headquarters. From there, you hike up Wildcat Canyon, then traverse across to the Irving Creek drainage, and follow that creek down near its confluence with Lagunitas Creek. The last half mile of the loop trail traces the southern edge of the creek back to the picnic area. It's a pleasant hike on a soft dirt trail, surrounded by the scent of redwoods, and includes a 400-foot climb and drop. Bicycles are prohibited from all but the half-mile service road along Lagunitas Creek in this route.

## 22. BOLINAS RIDGE    10.2 mi. one way/4.5 hrs

*Reference:* In northwest Marin County west of San Rafael; map E1-Marin, grid a1.

*User groups:* Hikers, horses, mountain bikes and leashed dogs. No wheelchair access.

*Permits:* No permits are required. Parking and access are free.

*Directions:* From San Francisco, drive north on US 101 to San Rafael and take the Sir Francis Drake Boulevard exit. Turn west on Sir Francis Drake Boulevard and drive 17.5 miles (or 3.4 miles past the entrance station to Samuel P. Taylor State Park). The trailhead is on the left side of the road. Park along the road.

*Maps:* This trail is included on the free map of Point Reyes National Seashore, write to Superintendent, Point Reyes National Seashore, Point Reyes, CA 94956. To obtain topographic maps of area, ask for ask for Inverness, San Geronimo and Bolinas from the USGS.

*Who to contact:* Phone the Golden Gate National Recreation Area at (415) 663-1092 or (415) 556-0560; or write GGNRA, Fort Mason, Building 201, San Francisco, CA 94123.

*Trail notes:* Spectacular lookouts across miles of foothills as well as an excellent mountain bike route make this a premier trip. It is a perfect one-way trip, with a shuttle car waiting for you at trail's end, or you can simply hike for a while and then turn back when you feel like it. The surrounding landscape is beautiful, with a heavy wooded slope and Kent Lake to the immediate east, Olema Valley and Inverness Ridge to the west, and Bolinas Lagoon and the Pacific Ocean to the south. The trail crosses atop Bolinas Ridge, some of the most remote land in the Golden Gate National Recreation Area. The trailhead near Olema starts with a 700-foot climb in the first 2.5 miles, and many hikers will call it quits at this point, enjoying the view for a while and then turning back for home. The trail keeps climbing, all the way to 1,329 feet in the first four miles, but from that point on, the hike becomes much easier, with only moderate drops and climbs over the last 6.2 miles to trail's end on Bolinas-Fairfax Road. Mountain biking is permitted here, but hikers should fear not, because the trail is not only plenty wide enough to allow it, but has very few hidden turns.

## 23. KENT DAM TRAIL    1.0 mi/0.5 hr

*Reference:* In northwest Marin County west of San Rafael; map E1-Marin, grid a1.

*User groups:* Hikers, mountain bikes and leashed dogs. No horses are allowed.

No wheelchair access. Groups are limited to 19 people.

*Permits:* No permits are required. Parking and access are free.

*Directions:* From San Francisco, drive north on US 101 to San Rafael and take the Sir Francis Drake Boulevard exit. Turn west on Sir Francis Drake Boulevard and drive 12 miles (if you reach Samuel P. Taylor State Park, you have gone too far). Turn left on Peters Dam/Kent Lake Road and drive a half mile to the parking area.

*Maps:* This trail is included on the free map of Point Reyes National Seashore, write to Superintendent, Point Reyes National Seashore, Point Reyes, CA 94956. To obtain topographic maps of area, ask for San Geronimo and Bolinas from the USGS.

*Who to contact:* Phone the Marin Water District at (415) 924-4600, North Marin Water District at (415) 897-4133, or call Western Boat in San Rafael at (415) 454-4177.

*Trail notes:* Most people are astounded the first time they see Kent Lake—they had no idea such a huge lake is secreted away in a Marin canyon. But here it is, nearly four miles long north-to-south, with an additional large arm extending east into Big Carson Creek. One reason the lake remains little known to outsiders is because the parking at the trailhead is quite poor, with just a few spaces along Sir Francis Drake Boulevard. From there you hike on a ranch road along Lagunitas Creek for about a mile, arriving at the east side of Peters Dam. By damming the canyon on Lagunitas Creek, the Marin Water District created this massive lake, and at the same time annihilated the runs of steelhead and silver salmon by de-watering the stream and blocking the migratory path to spawning areas. No water contact is permitted, but quite a few people go swimming here anyway in the summer. Some get caught and cited by occasional patrols by the Marin Water District. Fishing is only fair for bass, and no stocks are ever made by the Department of Fish and Game.

---

# 24. ALAMERE FALLS TRAIL    8.4 mi/4.0 hrs

*Reference:* In Point Reyes National Seashore northwest of Bolinas; map E1-Marin, grid b0.

*User groups:* Hikers and horses. No mountain bikes or dogs are allowed. No wheelchair access.

*Permits:* No permits are required. Parking and access are free.

*Directions:* From San Francisco, drive north on US 101 to San Rafael and take the Sir Francis Drake Boulevard exit. Turn west on Sir Francis Drake Boulevard and drive about 20 miles to the town of Olema. Turn left on Highway 1 and drive 8.9 miles south to Olema-Bolinas Road. Turn right and drive 2.1 miles to Mesa Road. Turn right and drive 5.8 miles to the Palomarin Trailhead.

*Maps:* For a free map of Point Reyes National Seashore, write to Superintendent, Point Reyes National Seashore, Point Reyes, CA 94956. To obtain topographic maps of area, ask for Bolinas and Double Point from the USGS.

*Who to contact:* Call Point Reyes National Seashore at (415) 663-1092, or write to them at the address listed above.

*Trail notes:* Alamere Falls is a surprising waterfall that tumbles down Alamere Creek, over an ocean bluff and then falls 40 feet right down to the beach and into the Pacific Ocean. It is one of the rare ocean bluff waterfalls anywhere. The key for newcomers is that it is best viewed from about a quarter-mile, not from right on top of it, and of course, it is prettiest after winter runs have refilled Alamere Creek. The Palomarin Trailhead is the best starting point, hiking the southern end of the Coast Trail. The trail is routed along the ocean for about a mile, then heads up in the coastal hills to an elevation of about 500 feet, and back down westward two miles to the falls. In the process, you will skirt past the northern end of Bass Lake, and a mile later, along the ridge overlooking larger Pelican Lake. When you near the ocean, an option is to take the 0.4-mile cutoff trail to Double Point, which provides a great ocean lookout as well as a close view of a huge sea rock called Stormy Stack.

---

## 25. AUDUBON CANYON RANCH TRAIL

0.4 mi/0.25 hr

*Reference:* **On Marin coast near Bolinas Lagoon; map E1-Marin, grid b1.**

*User groups:* Hikers only. No horses, mountain bikes or dogs are allowed. No wheelchair access.

*Permits:* Entrance to the ranch is free, but donations are requested. The ranch is open on weekends and holidays only, spring through midsummer.

*Directions:* From San Francisco, drive north on US 101 to San Rafael and take the Sir Francis Drake Boulevard exit. Turn west on Sir Francis Drake Boulevard and drive about 20 miles to the town of Olema. Turn left on Highway 1 and drive south for 10.5 miles, then turn left into Audubon Canyon Ranch.

*Maps:* A small trail map/brochure is available at the ranch headquarters. To obtain a topographic map of area, ask for Bolinas from the USGS.

*Who to contact:* Phone Audubon Canyon Ranch at (415) 868-9244, or write Audubon Canyon Ranch, 4900 Highway 1, Stinson Beach, CA 94970.

*Trail notes:* Here is a little slice of paradise, the premiere place on the Pacific Coast to view herons and egrets, those large, graceful seabirds, as they court, nest, mate and rear their young. However, an important reminder is that Audubon Canyon Ranch is open only on weekends and holidays, 10 a.m. to 4 p.m., spring through midsummer. It is closed the rest of the year. From ranch headquarters, the hike is short but steep, requiring about 20 minutes to reach the canyon overlook. Rest benches are available. From the top, spotting scopes are available that can be used to peer across the valley and zero in on the giant nests in the redwoods. This is a great trip that can be repeated many times, tracking the herons' mating process. The best time is usually in May and June. In May the eggs start hatching, and by June there can be as many as 200 hatchlings in the different nests. They eagerly await breakfast, lunch and dinner, provided when their huge parents return from Bolinas Lagoon and vomit the goodies all over the nest. Hey, what's for dessert?

# 26. ALPINE/KENT LAKE PUMP TRAIL

4.0 mi/1.5 hrs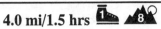

*Reference:* On northwest slopes of Mt. Tamalpais at Alpine Lake Dam, map E1-Marin, grid b1.

*User groups:* Hikers, horses, mountain bikes and leashed dogs. No wheelchair access. Groups are limited to 19 people.

*Permits:* No permits are required. Parking and access are free.

*Directions:* From San Francisco, drive north on US 101 to San Rafael. Take the Sir Francis Drake Boulevard exit and head west into Fairfax. In Fairfax, turn left at the BP gas station, then an immediate right onto Broadway. At the stop sign (within a block), turn left on Bolinas-Fairfax road and head west, continuing along Alpine Lake. Park at the right side of the road near the dam, and look for the gated service road/trailhead.

*Maps:* A hiking/biking map is available from Marin Water District, 220 Nellen, Corte Madera, CA 94925. A detailed hiking map of the area is available for a fee from Olmsted Brothers Map Company, P.O. Box 5351, Berkeley, CA 94705. To obtain a topographic map of area, ask for Bolinas from the USGS.

*Who to contact:* Phone the Marin Water District at (415) 924-4600, North Marin Water District at (415) 897-4133, or write to them at the address listed above.

*Trail notes:* Hiking this trail can feel like you're visiting a chunk of Tennessee wilderness, not a location just five miles from the Marin suburbs. It is quite pretty, tracing the ins-and-outs of Lagunitas Creek amid oak and madrone woodlands. The trail is actually a service road for the pump station between Alpine Dam and the headwaters of Kent Lake, following Lagunitas Creek as it pours northward. The trailhead is located at the north side of Alpine Dam, and after parking, the route takes a gentle grade down along the stream. It's about 1.5 miles to the headwaters of Kent Lake, and in another half-mile, you will begin seeing the main lake. Anywhere throughout this area, you can take a short departure from the trail for an ideal setting for a picnic. Many trails require a great physical investment in return for peace and solitude. Not this one.

# 27. CATARACT FALLS LOOP

6.7 mi/4.0 hrs

*Reference:* On the northwest slopes of Mt. Tamalpais at Alpine Lake Dam, map E1-Marin, grid b1.

*User groups:* Hikers and leashed dogs. No horses or mountain bikes are allowed. No wheelchair access. Groups are limited to 19 people.

*Permits:* No permits are required. Parking and access are free.

*Directions:* From San Francisco, drive north on US 101 to San Rafael. Take the Sir Francis Drake Boulevard exit and head west into Fairfax. In Fairfax, turn left at the BP gas station, then an immediate right onto Broadway. At the stop sign (within a block), turn left on Bolinas-Fairfax Road and head west, continuing along Alpine Lake. Cross the dam and park on the side of the road at the hairpin turn.

*Maps:* A map/brochure of Mt. Tamalpais State Park is available for a small fee at the park visitor center or by mail from Mt. Tamalpais State Park, 801 Panoramic Highway, Mill Valley, CA 94941. A detailed hiking map of the area is available for a fee from Olmsted Brothers Map Company, P.O. Box 5351, Berkeley, CA 94705. To obtain a topographic map of area, ask for Bolinas from the USGS.

*Who to contact:* Phone Mt. Tamalpais State Park at (415) 388-2070, Marin District Headquarters at (415) 456-1286, Marin Water District at (415) 924-4600, or write Mt. Tamalpais State Park at the address listed above.

*Trail notes:* The Cataract Falls are not a single waterfall, but a series of cascades that rush down a beautifully-wooded canyon set in the northwest slopes of Mt. Tamalpais. Ah, but you pay for this one. The hike is quite challenging, er, make that steep, um, make that a real heart-thumper. From the trailhead at the south end of Alpine Lake at elevation 644 feet, it is a 750-foot climb over the span of just a mile to reach the falls at 1,400 feet. That is why many hikers take the easier route from the Laura Dell Trailhead, a 240-foot drop over four-tenths of a mile. But, but, but…if you want more, in this case, you pay more. Our suggested loop hike turns east at the falls, where you hike the High Marsh/Willow Meadow Trail for three miles, crossing a gorgeous wooded section of Mt. Tam, with elevations ranging as high as 1,680 feet. That trail junctions with the Kent Trail, where you turn left and make the one-mile walk down to the shore of Alpine Lake. The last two miles follow along the shore of Alpine Lake, the second prettiest (Loch Lomond is first) of the 44 lakes in the Bay Area. This way you get a classic loop hike that has it all—waterfalls, woods, meadows, views, and the prettiest lake in Marin County, second prettiest in the Bay Area.

---

## 28. LILY GULCH TRAIL     0.6 mi/0.45 hr

*Reference:* **On northwest slopes of Mt. Tamalpais at Alpine Lake Dam, map E1-Marin, grid b1.**

*User groups:* Hikers, horses, mountain bikes and leashed dogs. No wheelchair access. Groups are limited to 19 people.

*Permits:* No permits are required. Parking and access are free.

*Directions:* From San Francisco, drive north on US 101 to San Rafael. Take the Sir Francis Drake Boulevard exit and head west into Fairfax. In Fairfax, turn left at the BP gas station, then an immediate right onto Broadway. At the stop sign (within a block), turn left on Bolinas-Fairfax Road and head west, continuing along Alpine Lake. Park along the road at Alpine Lake's second major cove, Lily Gulch.

*Maps:* A hiking/biking map is available from Marin Water District, 220 Nellen, Corte Madera, CA 94925. A detailed hiking map of the area is available for a fee from Olmsted Brothers Map Company, P.O. Box 5351, Berkeley, CA 94705. To obtain a topographic map of area, ask for Bolinas from the USGS.

*Who to contact:* Marin Water District at (415) 924-4600, or write to them at the address listed above.

*Trail notes:* If you don't have much time, but want to make a quick yet aerobic climb to a Marin landmark, the Lily Gulch Trail to Dutchman's Rock provides that opportunity. The trailhead is very easy to reach, just a pullout on the right side of Bolinas-Fairfax Road, at a very steep bend as the road bends around one of Alpine Lake's arms. The trail is routed up Lily Gulch, which is featured by a winsome creek in the winter, but after just two-tenths of a mile, you turn right on the Dutchman's Rock cutoff trail. It climbs quickly, and in little more than a tenth of a mile, you will reach ol' Dutchman, set at 1,217 feet, one of the highest points (along with Liberty Peak at 1,410 feet to the immediate north) near the north shore of Alpine Lake. In all, it's a climb of more than 500 feet over the course of three-tenths of a mile. Some trails on Mt. Tam can get crowded, but here's one that never is. Why? Most people don't like hiking up.

## 29. PINE MOUNTAIN/ CARSON FALLS

**3.0 mi/1.5 hrs**

*Reference:* On northwest slopes of Mt. Tamalpais west of Fairfax; map E1-Marin, grid b1.

*User groups:* Hikers, horses, mountain bikes and leashed dogs. No wheelchair access. Note: Mountain bikes are allowed on Pine Mountain and Oat Hill roads, but not on the hiking trail down to Carson Falls. Groups are limited to 19 people.

*Permits:* No permits are required. Parking and access are free.

*Directions:* From San Francisco, drive north on US 101 to San Rafael. Take the Sir Francis Drake Boulevard exit and head west into Fairfax. In Fairfax, turn left at the BP gas station, then an immediate right onto Broadway. At the stop sign (within a block), turn left on Bolinas-Fairfax Road and head west up the hill. Continue past the golf course toward Alpine Lake. The parking area is located at the first hairpin turn at Alpine Lake, along the left side of the road. Park and walk across the road to the trailhead.

*Maps:* A hiking/biking map is available from Marin Water District, 220 Nellen, Corte Madera, CA 94925. A detailed hiking map of the area is available for a fee from Olmsted Brothers Map Company, P.O. Box 5351, Berkeley, CA 94705. To obtain a topographic map of area, ask for Bolinas from the USGS.

*Who to contact:* Marin Water District at (415) 924-4600, or write to them at the address listed above.

*Trail notes:* Your destination is Carson Falls, a set of small waterfalls that tumble into granite pools, hidden on the north slopes of Mt. Tamalpais. It's a quiet, divine spot and to reach it is an easy walk across hilly grasslands, often with a hawk or two floating about overhead, then a short jog down a canyon into the Carson Creek drainage. The trailhead (1,078 feet) is adjacent to one of the better parking areas provided on lands administered by the Marin Water District. After parking, you cross Bolinas-Fairfax Road to reach the trailhead, Pine Mountain Road (a water district service road). The road climbs 400 feet over the course of a mile, reaching a junction with Oat Hill Road. You turn left here, hike 0.3 miles, then turn right on the hiking trail that is routed two-tenths of a mile down to Carson Creek and the series of small waterfalls. Of course, they are best seen after a good rain, but there is usually at least a trickle of water into early summer.

## 30. THREE LAKES TRAIL

**5.5 mi/2.5 hrs**

*Reference:* On northwest slopes of Mt. Tamalpais at Lagunitas Lake near San Anselmo; map E1-Marin, grid b1.

*User groups:* Hikers only. No horses, mountain bikes or leashed dogs are allowed. No wheelchair access. Groups are limited to 19 people.

*Permits:* A $3 park day-use fee is charged at the entrance station.

*Directions:* From San Francisco, drive north on US 101 to San Rafael. Take the

Sir Francis Drake Boulevard exit and head west into Fairfax. In Fairfax, turn left at the BP gas station, then an immediate right onto Broadway. At the stop sign (within a block), turn left on Bolinas-Fairfax Road and head west up the hill. Turn left at Sky Oaks Road and drive to the park entrance.

*Maps:* A map/brochure is available for a fee at the park entrance station or by mail from Sky Oaks Ranger Station, P.O. Box 865, Fairfax, CA 94978. A detailed hiking map of the area is available for a fee from Olmsted Brothers Map Company, P.O. Box 5351, Berkeley, CA 94705. To obtain a topographic map of area, ask for San Rafael from the USGS.

*Who to contact:* Phone Sky Oaks Ranger Station at (415) 459-5267, Marin Water District at (415) 924-4600, or write them at the address listed above.

*Trail notes:* This is one of the Bay Area's best loop hikes. There is no signed or officially-named "Three Lakes Trail," but you link a series of trails to route past three lakes. The route starts at Lagunitas Lake and heads west along the shorelines of Bon Tempe and Alpine Lake, then up the mountain (only a 400-foot climb), and back down (east) to Lagunitas. Lakes are the focus of this adventure, and no other hike in the Bay Area connects in such intimate fashion with three of the prettiest. The trailhead, elevation 740 feet, is at Lagunitas Picnic Area, adjacent to Lagunitas Lake, the smallest of the eight lakes in Marin County. Walk west along the Bon Tempe Shadyside Trail, which traces the western shore of Bon Tempe Lake, and beyond that, connect to the Kent Trail, which follows the pristine, southern edge of Alpine Lake for two miles. To make the loop back to Lagunitas, you make a left turn on the Kent Trail (elevation 760 feet) and make a 400-foot climb up Mt. Tamalpais. At the junction with Stocking Trail, turn left and then loop back (with a short jog right on Rocky Ridge Road) to Lagunitas Lake. A map is very helpful, of course, and is provided at the Sky Oaks Ranger Station.

---

## 31. DEER PARK TRAIL    2.0 mi/1.25 hrs

*Reference:* On northwest slopes of Mt. Tamalpais near San Anselmo; map E1-Marin, grid b2.

*User groups:* Hikers only. No horses, mountain bikes or dogs are allowed. No wheelchair access. Groups are limited to 19 people.

*Permits:* No permits are required. Parking and access are free.

*Directions:* From San Francisco, drive north on US 101 to San Rafael. Take the Sir Francis Drake Boulevard exit and head west into Fairfax. In Fairfax, turn left at the BP gas station, then an immediate right onto Broadway. At the stop sign (within a block), turn left on Bolinas-Fairfax Road. Drive a half mile and turn left on Porteous Avenue and drive to Deer County Park.

*Maps:* A hiking/biking map is available from Marin Water District, 220 Nellen, Corte Madera, CA 94925. A detailed hiking map of the area is available for a fee from Olmsted Brothers Map Company, P.O. Box 5351, Berkeley, CA 94705. To obtain a topographic map of area, ask for San Rafael from the USGS.

*Who to contact:* Marin Water District at (415) 924-4600, or write to them at the address listed above.

*Trail notes:* The Deer Park trailhead is quite popular, but by taking the Deer Park Trail rather than the other trail options, you can get peace as well as quite a workout. The latter is because the trail climbs about 350 feet in less than a mile. It's steep—this is a case where you pay for your pleasure. But pleasure you will get. The trail rises on the slopes of Bald Hill, and as you go higher, the views open up around you, and not just of the surrounding countryside; this is a common area to see deer, and wildflower blooms are quite good in the spring. If you want more, you get more, with the opportunity to link up with a spider's web network of other trails in the area.

---

## 32. PHOENIX LAKE TRAIL     2.7 mi/1.5 hrs

*Reference:* **On the north slope of Mt. Tamalpais near Ross; map E1-Marin, grid b2.**

*User groups:* Hikers, horses, mountain bikes (restricted from lake's southern shoreline) and leashed dogs. No wheelchair access. Groups are limited to 19 people.

*Permits:* No permits are required. Parking and access are free.

*Directions:* From San Francisco, drive north on US 101 to Marin, then take the take the Sir Francis Drake Boulevard exit and head west. Turn left on Lagunitas Road and continue for a few miles into Natalie Coffin Greene Park. The lake is a quarter mile from the parking area.

*Maps:* A hiking/biking map is available from Marin Water District, 220 Nellen, Corte Madera, CA 94925. A detailed hiking map of the area is available for a fee from Olmsted Brothers Map Company, P.O. Box 5351, Berkeley, CA 94705. To obtain a topographic map of area, ask for San Rafael from the USGS.

*Who to contact:* Marin Water District at (415) 924-4600, or write to them at the address listed above.

*Trail notes:* Of the eight lakes in Marin County, it is Phoenix that is the least accessible. The parking is not only poor, but the lake can be difficult to find for newcomers, an intolerable situation considering how well-loved the lake is. And loved it is, a little 25-acre jewel that sits in a pocket just west of the town of Ross. From Greene Park, it's an easy 0.2-mile walk to the lake. At the small dam, there are stairs on one side that will route visitors down to a lake trail at water's edge. The trail around the entire lake is 2.3 miles. In the winter, the lake is stocked with trout twice per month, and in the spring, bass fishing can be decent. Like all Marin lakes, no water contact is permitted.

---

## 33. LAURA DELL LOOP     2.5 mi/1.5 hrs

*Reference:* **In Mt. Tamalpais State Park; map E1-Marin, grid b2.**

*User groups:* Hikers and leashed dogs. No horses or mountain bikes are allowed. No wheelchair access.

*Permits:* No permits are required. Parking and access are free.

*Directions:* From San Francisco, take US 101 north into Marin. Take the Stinson Beach exit and drive about four miles to the Panoramic Highway. Turn right and continue up the hill for 5.5 miles to Pantoll Road. Turn right on Pantoll Road and drive about 1.5 miles to the "T" intersection. Turn left on Ridgecrest Road and drive 1.4 miles to the parking area for Laura Dell Trailhead.

*Maps:* A map/brochure of Mt. Tamalpais State Park is available for a small fee at the park visitor center or by mail from Mt. Tamalpais State Park, 801 Panoramic Highway, Mill Valley, CA 94941. A detailed hiking map of the area is available for a fee from Olmsted Brothers Map Company, P.O. Box 5351, Berkeley, CA 94705. To obtain topographic maps of area, ask for Bolinas and San Rafael from the USGS.

**Who to contact:** Phone Mt. Tamalpais State Park at (415) 388-2070, Marin District Headquarters at (415) 456-1286, Marin Water District at (415) 924-4600, or write Mt. Tamalpais State Park at the address listed above.

**Trail notes:** Cataract Falls is the most adored of the waterfalls on Mt. Tamalpais, and the Laura Dell Trailhead provides the easiest route to see them. Instead of the gut-wrencher climb from Alpine Lake (see hike number 27, this chapter), here you start high and glide down to them, then can return via a gentle loop. The trailhead is at 1,640 feet, and from there you start on the Laurel Dell Trail and hike four-tenths of a mile down to the Laurel Dell picnic area. At the edge of the picnic area, pick up the Cataract Falls trail and walk to Cataract Falls at 1,400 feet. When running at full strength, this cascading falls is a truly precious sight, available so close to an urban setting. At the falls, turn right on the High Marsh Trail, hike onward, then turn right at any of the next three trail intersections to return to the Laura Dell Trailhead. Of these three choices, the best return loop trail is the second choice, a short cutoff that will put you within a few hundred yards of the trailhead.

---

## 34. ROCK SPRINGS TRAIL    0.6 mi/0.5 hr

**Reference:** In Mt. Tamalpais State Park; map E1-Marin, grid b2.

**User groups:** Hikers only. No horses, mountain bikes or dogs are allowed. No wheelchair access.

**Permits:** No permits are required. Parking and access are free.

**Directions:** From San Francisco, take US 101 north into Marin. Take the Stinson Beach exit and drive about four miles to the Panoramic Highway. Turn right and continue uphill for 5.5 miles. Turn right on Pantoll Road and drive 1.5 miles, where a parking area is located across from a "T" intersection. This is the Rock Springs Trailhead.

**Maps:** A map/brochure of Mt. Tamalpais State Park is available for a small fee at the park visitor center or by mail from Mt. Tamalpais State Park, 801 Panoramic Highway, Mill Valley, CA 94941. A detailed hiking map of the area is available for a fee from Olmsted Brothers Map Company, P.O. Box 5351, Berkeley, CA 94705. To obtain a topographic map of area, ask for San Rafael from the USGS.

**Who to contact:** Phone Mt. Tamalpais State Park at (415) 388-2070, Marin District Headquarters at (415) 456-1286, Marin Water District at (415) 924-4600, or write Mt. Tamalpais State Park at the address listed above.

**Trail notes:** Five different trails start at Rock Springs, but our favorite here is the shorty to O'Rourke's Bench, where you can have a picnic lunch with an awesome view to the west. On one trip, the coast was socked in with low stratus clouds, yet from this lookout, it looked like a sea of fog. Protruding mountain tops looked like islands. On another day, the sunset was extraordinary from this spot. O'Rourke's Bench is quite easy to reach. After parking at Rock Springs, cross Ridgecrest Boulevard and take the O'Rourke Bench Trail for three-tenths of a mile. After just 10 or 15 minutes, you will come upon this little bench set on a knoll at 2,071 feet. Next to the bench you will find a plaque that reads: "Give me these hills and the friends I love. I ask no other heaven. To our dad O'Rourke, in joyous celebration of his 76th birthday, Feb. 25th, 1927. From the friends to whom he showed this heaven."

---

# 35. BARTH'S RETREAT     2.0 mi/0.45 hr

*Reference:* **In Mt. Tamalpais State Park; map E1-Marin, grid b2.**

*User groups:* Hikers only. No horses, mountain bikes or dogs are allowed. No wheelchair access.

*Permits:* No permits are required. Parking and access are free.

*Directions:* From San Francisco, take US 101 north into Marin. Take the Stinson Beach exit and drive about four miles to the Panoramic Highway. Turn right and continue uphill for 5.5 miles. Turn right on Pantoll Road and drive 1.5 miles. There is parking area located across from a "T" intersection. This is the Rock Springs Trailhead but there is a sign indicating Barth's Retreat.

*Maps:* A map/brochure of Mt. Tamalpais State Park is available for a small fee at the park visitor center or by mail from Mt. Tamalpais State Park, 801 Panoramic Highway, Mill Valley, CA 94941. A detailed hiking map of the area is available for a fee from Olmsted Brothers Map Company, P.O. Box 5351, Berkeley, CA 94705. To obtain a topographic map of area, ask for San Rafael from the USGS.

*Who to contact:* Phone Mt. Tamalpais State Park at (415) 388-2070, Marin District Headquarters at (415) 456-1286, Marin Water District at (415) 924-4600, or write Mt. Tamalpais State Park at the address listed above.

*Trail notes:* Rarely can the features of the land change more quickly than on the hike to Barth's Retreat on Mt. Tamalpais. In just a mile's walk, you cross past a serpentine swale, a small creek with riparian habitat, go through a forest and then arrive at an open area called Barth's Retreat. Barth, by the way, was Emil Barth, a prolific musician/hiker/trail builder who constructed his camp here in the early 1900s. This hike provides a quick glimpse of the diversity Mt. Tam offers, and when linked with the short hike to O'Rourke's Bench, which also starts from Rock Springs, it can feel like you've seen the world in a two-hour time capsule.

---

# 36. MOUNTAIN THEATER     3.0 mi/1.5 hrs

*Reference:* **In Mt. Tamalpais State Park; map E1-Marin, grid b2.**

*User groups:* Hikers only. No horses, mountain bikes or dogs are allowed. No wheelchair access.

*Permits:* No permits are required. Parking and access are free.

*Directions:* From San Francisco, take US 101 north into Marin. Take the Stinson Beach exit and drive about four miles to the Panoramic Highway. Turn right and continue uphill for 5.5 miles. Turn right on Pantoll Road and drive 1.5 miles to the "T" intersection. Turn right and drive a quarter-mile to a parking area on the right side of the road. The Mountain Theater Trailhead is located a short walk from the parking area.

*Maps:* A map/brochure of Mt. Tamalpais State Park is available for a small fee at the park visitor center or by mail from Mt. Tamalpais State Park, 801 Panoramic Highway, Mill Valley, CA 94941. A detailed hiking map of the area is available for a fee from Olmsted Brothers Map Company, P.O. Box 5351, Berkeley, CA 94705. To obtain a topographic map of area, ask for San

Rafael from the USGS.

***Who to contact:*** Phone Mt. Tamalpais State Park at (415) 388-2070, Marin District Headquarters at (415) 456-1286, Marin Water District at (415) 924-4600, or write Mt. Tamalpais State Park at the address listed above.

***Trail notes:*** The roundtrip from Mountain Theater to West Point Inn is one of the classic walks on Mt. Tamalpais—pretty, easy, with landmarks on each end of the hike. The parking area is actually a very short distance from Mountain Theater, Mt. Tam's masterpiece outdoor amphitheater, and you cross right behind it on the Rock Spring Trail en route to West Point Inn. The trail is off-limits to bikes, and is quiet and tranquil, weaving in and out of a hardwood forest, an easy descent most of the way. Over the course of 1.5 miles, you drop 295 feet, from a trailhead elevation of 2,080 feet to trail's end at 1,785 feet. West Point Inn offers great views and a perfect spot for a picnic lunch, and there is often lemonade available inside. A secret here is that there are small cabins (no electricity) available for overnight rental, and for years, we had sworn not to tell anybody about them. Until now, heh, heh, we've kept that promise.

***Special note:*** Much of this trail is on Marin Water District land; see a detailed map. Leashed dogs are permitted here.

---

## 37. BOOTJACK LOOP  6.2 mi/3.0 hrs

***Reference:*** In Mt. Tamalpais State Park; map E1-Marin, grid b2.

***User groups:*** Hikers only. No horses, mountain bikes or dogs are allowed. No wheelchair access.

***Permits:*** No permits are required. A $5 parking fee is charged.

***Directions:*** From San Francisco, take US 101 north into Marin. Take the Stinson Beach exit and drive about four miles to the Panoramic Highway. Turn right and continue uphill for 5.5 miles. Turn left at the parking area. This is the Pantoll Ranger Station and Trailhead.

***Maps:*** A map/brochure of Mt. Tamalpais State Park is available for a small fee at the park visitor center or by mail from Mt. Tamalpais State Park, 801 Panoramic Highway, Mill Valley, CA 94941. A detailed hiking map of the area is available for a fee from Olmsted Brothers Map Company, P.O. Box 5351, Berkeley, CA 94705. To obtain a topographic map of area, ask for San Rafael from the USGS.

***Who to contact:*** Phone Mt. Tamalpais State Park at (415) 388-2070, Marin District Headquarters at (415) 456-1286, Marin Water District at (415) 924-4600, or write Mt. Tamalpais State Park at the address listed above.

***Trail notes:*** Rarely does a hike provide such glimpses of a more dynamic, diverse and delightful habitat than the Bootjack Loop. It crosses a meadow, oak woodlands, some hilly grasslands and submerges deep into redwood forest, then climbs back out, all in the space of 6.2 miles. It includes a steady downgrade, and then on the return trip, a huff-puffer climb, but the redwoods make it worth the grunt. The trail starts at the Pantoll Ranger Station and Trailhead, elevation 1,500 feet, in Mt. Tam State Park. From there, you hike north for 0.4 miles on the Alpine Trail to Van Wyck Meadow, in the process making a descent of 450 feet. From there, you turn right on the Bootjack Trail, taking the trip downhill along a small stream. It leads for 1.3 miles into Muir Woods National Monument, where you turn right on the Ben Johnson Trail and start the steep, climbing return trip. In the next mile, the trail climbs

500 feet, but all the while you are surrounded by one of the Bay Area's richest redwood groves. Many of the trees are gigantic. To complete the loop, you continue up, up and up on the Ben Johnson Trail (to the Stapelveldt Trail) for the final 0.9 miles back to Pantoll Trailhead, a climb of 1,080 feet in all.

---

## 38. EAST PEAK MOUNT TAMALPAIS

0.2 mi/0.25 hrs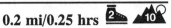

*Reference:* In Mt. Tamalpais State Park; map E1-Marin, grid b2.

*User groups:* Hikers only. No horses or mountain bikes. Leashed dogs are permitted on the paved trail, but not on the mountaintop overlook. No wheelchair access on the trail, but good views are available from the **wheelchair-accessible** parking lot.

*Permits:* No permits are required. A $5 parking fee is charged.

*Directions:* From San Francisco, take US 101 north into Marin. Take the Stinson Beach exit and drive four miles to the Panoramic Highway. Turn right and continue uphill for 5.5 miles to Pantoll Road. Turn right on Pantoll Road and drive about 1.5 miles to the "T" intersection. Turn right on Ridgecrest Road and continue to the East Peak. The road dead ends at the parking area at the base of the summit.

*Maps:* A map/brochure of Mt. Tamalpais State Park is available for a small fee at the park visitor center located adjacent to the parking area or by mail from Mt. Tamalpais State Park, 801 Panoramic Highway, Mill Valley, CA 94941. A detailed hiking map of the area is available for a fee from Olmsted Brothers Map Company, P.O. Box 5351, Berkeley, CA 94705. To obtain a topographic map of area, ask for San Rafael from the USGS.

*Who to contact:* Phone Mt. Tamalpais State Park at (415) 388-2070, Marin District Headquarters at (415) 456-1286, Marin Water District at (415) 924-4600, or write Mt. Tamalpais State Park at the address listed above.

*Trail notes:* There is simply no better place to watch the sun set in the Bay Area than atop Mt. Tam's East Peak. The feeling you get will stay with you for weeks. That is because Mt. Tamalpais is one of the few places that projects a feeling of power, and from its highest point, that power will flow through you. The hike is very short—after all, a parking lot is set at the foot of the summit climb—but quite steep, rising about 330 feet to the top at elevation 2,571 feet. An old lookout station is positioned at the summit, and hikers usually try to find a perch as close as possible to the top. To the east, the Bay looks like the Mediterranean Sea, an azure pool sprinkled with islands, and at night, the lights of the bridges and cities make the Bay Area look almost surreal. But the real magic comes at sunset, particularly on foggy days. That is because the peak is well above the fogline, and when the sun dips into that low stratus to the west, orange light will be refracted for hundreds of miles. See this even one time and you will feel different about what is possible in this world, and perhaps even set new horizons for yourself.

---

## 39. INSPIRATION POINT

2.6 mi/1.0 hrs

*Reference:* In Mt. Tamalpais State Park; map E1-Marin, grid b2.

*User groups:* Hikers, mountain bikes and leashed dogs. No horses are allowed. No wheelchair access on trail, but good views are available from the **wheelchair-accessible** parking lot.

*Permits:* No permits are required. A $5 parking fee is charged.

*Directions:* From San Francisco, take US 101 north into Marin. Take the Stinson Beach exit and drive about four miles to the Panoramic Highway. Turn right and continue uphill for 5.5 miles. Turn right on Pantoll Road and drive 1.5 miles to the "T" intersection. Turn right on Ridgecrest Road and continue to the East Peak. The road dead ends at the parking area at the base of the summit.

*Maps:* A map/brochure of Mt. Tamalpais State Park is available for a small fee at the park visitor center located adjacent to the parking area or by mail from Mt. Tamalpais State Park, 801 Panoramic Highway, Mill Valley, CA 94941. A hiking/biking map is available from Marin Water District, 220 Nellen, Corte Madera, CA 94925. A detailed hiking map of the area is available for a fee from Olmsted Brothers Map Company, P.O. Box 5351, Berkeley, CA 94705. To obtain a topographic map of area, ask for San Rafael from the USGS.

*Who to contact:* Phone Mt. Tamalpais State Park at (415) 388-2070, Marin District Headquarters at (415) 456-1286, Marin Water District at (415) 924-4600.

*Trail notes:* Inspiration Point provides a nearby alternative to East Peak, ideal if you want the same kind of magic that comes at the East Peak (see hike number 38 this chapter), yet without all the people that magic attracts. After parking, instead of heading up to the East Peak, you go the opposite direction and turn right on the fire road, Eldridge Grade. The trail wraps around the northern flank of the East Peak, then makes a hairpin turn to the left around North Knee, set at 2,000 feet. At this point, the Bay comes into view to the east, and you start to understand the attraction. But keep on, because Inspiration Peak awaits just down the road. At the hairpin right turn, take the short but steep cutoff trail on the left and you will quickly reach the top at 2,040 feet. The vista provides miles and miles of charmed views. All seems enchanted.

*Special note:* Much of this trail is on Marin Water District land, where leashed dogs are permitted.

---

## 40. DAWN FALLS          1.4 mi/0.75 hr

*Reference:* **On the eastern slopes of Mt. Tamalpais near Larkspur; map E1-Marin, grid b2.**

*User groups:* Hikers, leashed dogs, mountain bikes and horses (on the adjacent fire road). No wheelchair access. Groups are limited to 19 people.

*Permits:* No permits are required. Parking and access are free.

*Directions:* From San Francisco, drive north on US 101 to Larkspur. Take the Tamalpais Drive exit. Then head west on Tamalpais Drive to Corte Madera Avenue. Turn right and drive about a half mile, then turn left on Madrone Avenue and drive to Valley Way. The trailhead is at the road's end.

*Maps:* A hiking/biking map is available from Marin Water District, 220 Nellen, Corte Madera, CA 94925. A detailed hiking map of the area is available for a fee from Olmsted Brothers Map Company, P.O. Box 5351, Berkeley, CA 94705. To obtain a topographic map of area, ask for San Rafael from the USGS.

*Who to contact:* Marin Water District at (415) 924-4600, or write at them at the address listed above.

*Trail notes:* The Bay Area has many hidden waterfalls, but this one is both easy to reach as well as a beautiful and energizing sight in winter and spring. Dawn Falls is a 25-foot fountain of water, best seen in the early morning when sunlight penetrates the area. Note, however, that in summer and fall, day after day of dry weather reduces it to a trickle, and in the drought years, it can go dry completely. At the trailhead, don't get confused and take the Baltimore Canyon Fire Road, which is far less intimate than the Dawn Falls Trail. The latter probes into a dense woodland, with model riparian habitat on each side of Larkspur Creek near the falls. The Dawn Falls Trail starts as an easy walk, but just when you say, "This is no sweat," wham, it becomes a major sweat, rising nearly 300 feet to Dawn Falls. But not many folks complain about it.

---

## 41. MOUNTAIN HOME TRAIL    2.4 mi/1.0 hr

*Reference:* In Mt. Tamalpais State Park; map E1-Marin, grid b2.

*User groups:* Hikers only. No horses, mountain bikes or dogs are allowed. No wheelchair access.

*Permits:* No permits are required. Parking and access are free.

*Directions:* From San Francisco, take US 101 north into Marin. Take the Stinson Beach exit and drive about four miles to the Panoramic Highway. Turn right and continue to Mountain Home Inn parking area. The trailhead (Panoramic Trail) is on the west side of the road.

*Maps:* A map/brochure of Mt. Tamalpais State Park is available for a small fee at the park visitor center or by mail from Mt. Tamalpais State Park, 801 Panoramic Highway, Mill Valley, CA 94941. A detailed hiking map of the area is available for a fee from Olmsted Brothers Map Company, P.O. Box 5351, Berkeley, CA 94705. To obtain a topographic map of area, ask for San Rafael from the USGS.

*Who to contact:* Phone the Tourist Club at (415) 388-9987, Mt. Tamalpais State Park at (415) 388-2070, Marin District Headquarters at (415) 456-1286, Marin Water District at (415) 924-4600, or write Mt. Tamalpais State Park at the address listed above.

*Trail notes:* You want unique? You get unique: A 1.2-mile hike at Mt. Tamalpais that ends at a great little inn called the Tourist Club, where you can order your favorite elixir to slake your thirst. The trip requires a short hike, steep for one short portion. To reach the Tourist Club, park at the lot at Mountain Home along the Panoramic Highway. From there, take the Panoramic Trail for 0.4 miles (it parallels the Panoramic Highway) to its junction with the Redwood Trail. Then take the Redwood Trail for 0.75 miles. It laterals across the mountain slope, then drops into a pocket where the Tourist Club is perched on a slope. It is a wooden-framed building, where on weekends you not only can get liquid refreshments but can often hear German music being played. Among hiker destinations, there is no other place like it in California.

---

## 42. MATT DAVIS TRAIL 3.2 mi. one way/1.5 hr

*Reference:* On the western slopes of Mt. Tamalpais; map E1-Marin, grid b2.

*User groups:* Hikers only. No horses, mountain bikes or dogs are allowed. No wheelchair access.

*Permits:* No permits are required. A $5 parking fee is charged.

*Directions:* From San Francisco, take US 101 north into Marin. Take the Stinson Beach exit and drive about four miles to the Panoramic Highway. Turn right and continue uphill for 5.5 miles. Turn left at the parking area. This is the Pantoll Ranger Station and Trailhead.

*Maps:* A map/brochure of Mt. Tamalpais State Park is available for a small fee at the park visitor center or by mail from Mt. Tamalpais State Park, 801 Panoramic Highway, Mill Valley, CA 94941. A detailed hiking map of the area is available for a fee from Olmsted Brothers Map Company, P.O. Box 5351, Berkeley, CA 94705. To obtain a topographic map of area, ask for San Rafael from the USGS.

*Who to contact:* Phone Mt. Tamalpais State Park at (415) 388-2070, Marin District Headquarters at (415) 456-1286, Marin Water District at (415) 924-4600, or write Mt. Tamalpais State Park at the address listed above.

*Trail notes:* The 3.2-mile section of the Matt Davis Trail from the Pantoll Trailhead down to Stinson Beach offers dramatic views of the Pacific Ocean. There are many places where you can stop, spread your arms wide and feel like the entire world is in your grasp. It is a great one-way hike— just make sure you hike with a partner and have a shuttle car waiting at trail's end at the Stinson Beach Fire House. After parking at Pantoll, elevation 1,500 feet, cross the road and look for the sign marking the Matt Davis/ Coastal Trail. Soon enough, you will start your descent toward the beach, but first you will enter a lush grove of firs. Here the trail is level for nearly a mile. When you emerge, you will start a steep descent across open grasslands down to Stinson Beach. Only a foggy day can ruin it. Note that the entire Matt Davis Trail is technically nearly double our suggested route, with the trailhead at Mountain Home.

---

# 43. STEEP RAVINE     2.0 mi. one way/1.0 hr

*Reference:* On the western slopes of Mt. Tamalpais; map E1-Marin, grid b2.

*User groups:* Hikers only. No horses, mountain bikes or dogs are allowed. No wheelchair access.

*Permits:* No permits are required. A $5 parking fee is charged.

*Directions:* From San Francisco, take US 101 north into Marin. Take the Stinson Beach exit and drive about four miles to the Panoramic Highway. Turn right and continue uphill for 5.5 miles. Turn left at the parking area. This is the Pantoll Ranger Station and Trailhead.

*Maps:* A map/brochure of Mt. Tamalpais State Park is available for a small fee at the park visitor center or by mail from Mt. Tamalpais State Park, 801 Panoramic Highway, Mill Valley, CA 94941. A detailed hiking map of the area is available for a fee from Olmsted Brothers Map Company, P.O. Box 5351, Berkeley, CA 94705. To obtain a topographic map of area, ask for San Rafael from the USGS.

*Who to contact:* Phone Mt. Tamalpais State Park at (415) 388-2070, Marin District Headquarters at (415) 456-1286, Marin Water District at (415) 924-4600, or write Mt. Tamalpais State Park at the address listed above.

*Trail notes:* Hiking the Steep Ravine Trail is like being baptized by the divine spirit of nature. The trail has remarkable beauty, including cathedral-like redwoods, a lush undergrowth and a pretty stream. From the trailhead at Pantoll, the Steep Ravine Trail descends 1,100 feet in the course of two miles, ending at Highway 1 near Rocky Point. The only catch is that you must have a partner with a shuttle car waiting at trail's end. That done, you've got it made. When looking at a trail map, you might think this trail is just a simple option to the nearby Matt Davis Trail. Wrong. After departing, it doesn't take long heading down hill before you'll be surrounded by redwoods. The trail follows along Webb Creek, with eight creek crossings in all. A trail landmark is the junction with the Dipsea Trail; from here it is one-half mile to the end of the trail. The Steep Ravine Trail is a place where hikers can get their own brand of religion.

## 44. MAIN TRAIL    2.0 mi/1.0 hr

*Reference:* In Muir Woods National Monument near Mill Valley; map E1-Marin, grid b2.

*User groups:* Hikers only. No horses, mountain bikes or dogs (except for seeing-eye dogs) are allowed. The first section of trail is **wheelchair accessible**.

*Permits:* No permits are required. Parking and access are free. Donations for printed materials are requested.

*Directions:* From San Francisco, take US 101 north into Marin. Take the Highway 1 exit, continue to the traffic light and turn left on Shoreline Highway (Highway 1). Continue for a few miles and take the right fork onto Panoramic Highway. Then drive one mile and at the junction take the left lower road, signed Muir Woods. Drive one mile to Muir Woods Parking Area.

*Maps:* A map/brochure is available for a fee at the visitor center, or by mail from Muir Woods National Monument, Mill Valley, CA 94941.

*Who to contact:* Phone Muir Woods at (415) 388-2596, or write them at the address listed above. To obtain a topographic map of area, ask for San Rafael.

*Trail notes:* This might just be the most heavily used trail in the Bay Area, yet not necessarily by Bay Area residents. You see, tourists from all over the world visiting San Francisco have a common sidetrip: After taking an obligatory picture of the Golden Gate Bridge from Vista Point, they drive to Muir Woods to see what a real redwood tree looks like. Soon enough, they are walking on the Main Trail, a paved route set along Redwood Creek, completely encompassed by giant redwoods. The trail is very pretty and an easy walk, but often more like a parade. After about a mile, the trail starts to climb to the left, and just like that, most all the tourists head back to the parking lot. An option is turning this into a loop hike by taking the Hillside Trail up the west side of the canyon, and looping back to the Muir Woods headquarters. The loop trail is three miles and includes a pleasant climb.

## 45. OCEAN VIEW TRAIL    3.0 mi/1.75 hrs
## (PANORAMIC HIGHWAY TRAIL)

*Reference:* In Muir Woods National Monument near Mill Valley; map E1-Marin, grid b2.

*User groups:* Hikers only. No horses, mountain bikes or dogs (except for seeing-eye dogs) are allowed. The first section of the trail is **wheelchair accessible**.

*Permits:* No permits are required. Parking and access are free. Donations for printed materials are requested.

*Directions:* From San Francisco, take US 101 north into Marin. Take the Highway 1 exit, continue to the traffic light and turn left on Shoreline Highway (Highway 1). Continue for a few miles and take the right fork onto Panoramic Highway. From there drive one mile and at the junction, take the left lower road, signed Muir Woods. Drive one mile to Muir Woods Parking Area.

*Maps:* A map/brochure is available for a fee at the visitor center, or by mail at Muir Woods National Monument, Mill Valley, CA 94941. To obtain a topographic map of area, ask for San Rafael from the USGS.

*Who to contact:* Phone Muir Woods at (415) 388-2596, or write them at the address listed above.

*Trail notes:* When you arrive at Muir Woods, are there tour buses shooting people out like popcorn machines? Yes? Then listen up, because the Ocean View Trail provides your best chance of getting away from them. After passing the information stand and starting the paved hike on the valley floor, turn right on the Ocean View Trail. In less than a minute, you will enter a different world. In this world, there is solitude, redwood beauty, and alas, a steep hike. From the valley floor, the trail heads up the east side of the canyon, a steady grade, steep enough to get you puffing in a natural rhythm. It climbs 570 feet in 1.2 miles, rising above the valley where you can look down into a sea of redwoods. To complete the loop, turn left on the Lost Trail, elevation 750 feet, which offers a very step descent over just four-tenths of a mile back down to the valley floor at 300 feet. There you turn left, and return to headquarters on the Fern Creek Trail. A great escape.

*Special note:* While this trail is listed as "Ocean View Trail," most call it "Panoramic Highway Trail." It is listed as both on various maps and signs. Ironically, there is no ocean view.

---

## 46. DIPSEA TRAIL  6.6 mi. one way/3.5 hrs

*Reference:* On Mt. Tamalpais from Mill Valley to Stinson Beach; map E1-Marin, grid b2 and b1.

*User groups:* Hikers only. No horses, mountain bikes or dogs are allowed. No wheelchair access.

*Permits:* No permits required. Parking and access are free.

*Directions:* From San Francisco, take US 101 north into Marin. Take the East Blithedale/Tiburon Boulevard exit, then head east on East Blithedale (it becomes Throckmorton) into Mill Valley. Continue on Throckmorton to Old Mill Park. The trailhead is at the bridge and Old Mill Creek, which leads to the stepped staircase.

*Maps:* The Dipsea Trail crosses several jurisdictions. A map/brochure of Mt. Tamalpais State Park is available for a small fee at the park visitor center, or by mail from Mt. Tamalpais State Park, 801 Panoramic Highway, Mill Valley, CA 94941. A detailed hiking map of the area is available for a fee from Olmsted Brothers Map Company, P.O. Box 5351, Berkeley, CA 94705. To obtain topographic maps of area, ask for San Rafael and Bolinas from the USGS.

*Who to contact:* Phone Mt. Tamalpais State Park at (415) 388-2070, Marin

District Headquarters at (415) 456-1286, Marin Water District at (415) 924-4600, Muir Woods at (415) 388-2596. Write Muir Woods National Monument, Mill Valley, CA 94941. Write Mt. Tamalpais State Park at the address listed above.

*Trail notes:* The Dipsea Trail is a rite of passage for Marin hikers, where you get a glimpse of both heaven and hell in a morning's 6.6-mile lesson. The annual Dipsea Race has turned this trail into something of a legend, as well as a classic love-hate relationship. You love it because it offers the perfect east-to-west crossing of Mt. Tamalpais, from Mill Valley to Stinson Beach, in the process crossing through Muir Woods and making a beautiful descent down to the coast. You hate it because it starts at an infamous set of unending staircase steps, crosses on paved roads, and just when you start to get tired, includes a killer climb up Cardiac Hill. Of course, if you haven't figured it out by now, this is a one-way-only hike, shuttle partner required. The trail starts in Mill Valley on Cascade Way with those hated steps, 671 in all. According to park rangers, those steps spawned the legend that "Marin hikers never die, they just reach the 672nd step." When the trail tops the stairs and reaches pavement, look for the faint arrows, painted on the street to mark the way. They will route you along Sequoia Road, then Walsh Drive, then Bay View, where you cross the Panoramic Highway and finally leave pavement and start the descent into Muir Woods. From there, the trail is well-signed. Noted spots include Cardiac Hill, where you are handed a 480-foot climb in 0.4 miles. In return, you are also presented with phenomenal views of both the Pacific Ocean and San Francisco, as well as the knowledge that almost all of the rest of the trail is down. The final 2.3 miles include a descent across the Marin hills, a visit into lush Steep Ravine Canyon, then a final push across coastal bluffs to the parking area at Stinson Beach. Like we said, it's a rite of passage.

---

## 47. ROCKY POINT TRAIL  0.2 mi/0.25 hr

*Reference:* On Marin coast south of Stinson Beach; map E1-Marin, grid b1.

*User groups:* Hikers and leashed dogs. No horses or mountain bikes are allowed. No wheelchair access.

*Permits:* For day use, parking and access are free. For overnight use, a reservation is required at Steep Ravine Cabins/Environmental Campsites.

*Directions:* From San Francisco, take US 101 north into Marin. Take the Stinson Beach/Highway 1 exit and continue to the coast at Muir Beach Overlook. Then drive north on Highway about four miles to the Rocky Point access road (gated) on the left side of the highway.

*Maps:* A map/brochure of Mt. Tamalpais State Park is available for a small fee at the park visitor center or by mail from Mt. Tamalpais State Park, 801 Panoramic Highway, Mill Valley, CA 94941. A detailed hiking map of the area is available for a fee from Olmsted Brothers Map Company, P.O. Box 5351, Berkeley, CA 94705. To obtain topographic maps of area, ask for Bolinas and Point Bonita from the USGS.

*Who to contact:* Mt. Tamalpais State Park at (415) 388-2070, Marin District Headquarters at (415) 456-1286, or write Mt. Tamalpais State Park at the address listed above.

*Trail notes:* One of the special little secrets in the outdoors is here at Rocky

Point, where primitive cabins set on an ocean bluff are available for overnight rentals. It is one of the most dramatic camp settings on the Pacific Coast, with passing whales, pelicans and murres, freighters and fishing boats. Sunsets can be exceptional. The cabins cost $30 per night, plus a $6.75 reservation fee, and include a wood stove, picnic table and flat wood surface for sleeping. You bring everything else, which should include good walking shoes for this short hike down to the beach. From the cabins, you head back to the Rocky Point access road, turn right, then take the trail down to the cove, a descent of about 80 feet. Another beach trail is available on the north side of Rocky Point down to the southern end of Redrock Beach.

---

## 48. OWL TRAIL          2.0 mi/1.0 hr

*Reference:* **On Marin coast south of Stinson Beach; map E1-Marin, grid c1.**
*User groups:* Hikers only. No horses, mountain bikes or dogs are allowed. The Muir Beach Overlook is **wheelchair accessible**, the Owl Trail is not.
*Permits:* No permit required. Parking and access are free.
*Directions:* From San Francisco, take US 101 north into Marin. Take the Stinson Beach/Highway 1 exit and continue to the coast. Turn left at Muir Beach Overlook and drive a short distance to the parking area.
*Maps:* A map/brochure is available at the Marin Headlands Visitor Center, or by mail from Golden Gate National Recreation Area, Marin Headlands, Building 1056, Fort Cronkite, Sausalito, CA 94965. A detailed hiking map of the area is available for a fee from Olmsted Brothers Map Company, P.O. Box 5351, Berkeley, CA 94705. To obtain a topographic map of area, ask for Point Bonita from the USGS.
*Who to contact:* Phone Marin Headlands Visitor Center at (415) 331-1540, or GGNRA headquarters at (415) 556-0560.
*Trail notes:* According to park rangers, a number of two-foot-tall great horned owls patrol the surrounding area of this trail. While we didn't see any owls, we did see other reasons why this trail is so special. From beginning to end, it offers a pretty setting along the Marin Coast and a very easy walk along the coastal hills. The trailhead is near the Muir Beach Overlook, which alone is worth the trip, with great views of the southern Marin Coast. But don't stop there, like so many visitors, but try the hike northward on the Owl Trail. From the trailhead at 440 feet, the Owl Trail descends 240 feet in 0.9 miles on its northward course to Slide Ranch. There you can make the trip down to the beach, with the opportunity to add an 0.7-mile loop to your trip.

---

## 49. MI-WOK LOOP          3.5 mi/2.0 hrs

*Reference:* **In Marin Headlands near Sausalito; map E1-Marin, grid c2.**
*User groups:* Hikers, horses, mountain bikes (partial access) and leashed dogs. No wheelchair access.
*Permits:* No permit required. Parking and access are free.
*Directions:* From San Francisco, take US 101 north into Marin City. Take the Stinson Beach/Highway 1 exit and head west. After passing under the overpass, turn left on Tennessee Valley Road and continue until it dead ends at the trailhead.
*Maps:* A map/brochure is available at the Marin Headlands Visitor Center, or by mail from Golden Gate National Recreation Area, Marin Headlands,

Building 1056, Fort Cronkite, Sausalito, CA 94965. A detailed hiking map of the area is available for a fee from Olmsted Brothers Map Company, P.O. Box 5351, Berkeley, CA 94705. To obtain a topographic map of area, ask for Point Bonita from the USGS.

*Who to contact:* Phone Marin Headlands Visitor Center at (415) 331-1540, or GGNRA headquarters at (415) 556-0560.

*Trail notes:* The Mi-Wok Loop is a near circular hike that traverses across the pretty grasslands of the Marin Headlands, connecting a number of trails to provide a decent, physical loop hike. There are good views throughout, including those from a great 880-foot lookout to the west at the junction of Ridge Road and the Fox Trail. The hike starts at the Mi-Wok Stables, elevation 200 feet, where you head north on the Mi-Wok Trail, rising as you go, heading into higher country. The trail turns left, then heads west for 0.6 miles, still climbing to the junction of Mi-Wok Trail and Ridge Road. At this point, to make the loop hike, turn left on Ridge Road, where the trail tops out at 1,000 feet. The next mile offers spectacular views of the ocean, a piece of trail where every step can be special. To return back to Mi-Wok Stables, turn left at the Fox Trail and hike 1.1 miles, then left again on the Tennessee Valley Trail (paved), and hike out the last 0.4 miles to the stables. Trail use is typically high on weekends, and that includes mountain bike traffic on Ridge Road.

---

## 50. TENNESSEE VALLEY    4.2 mi/2.0 hrs

*Reference:* **In Marin Headlands near Sausalito; map E1-Marin, grid c2.**

*User groups:* Hikers, horses and mountain bikes. Note: Horses and mountain bikes must take the forked fire road. No dogs are allowed. No wheelchair access.

*Permits:* No permit required. Parking and access are free.

*Directions:* From San Francisco, take US 101 north into Marin City. Take the Stinson Beach/Highway 1 exit and head west. After passing under the overpass, turn left on Tennessee Valley Road and continue until it dead ends at the trailhead.

*Maps:* A map/brochure is available at the Marin Headlands Visitor Center, or by mail from Golden Gate National Recreation Area, Marin Headlands, Building 1056, Fort Cronkite, Sausalito, CA 94965. A detailed hiking map of the area is available for a fee from Olmsted Brothers Map Company, P.O. Box 5351, Berkeley, CA 94705. To obtain a topographic map of area, ask for Point Bonita from the USGS.

*Who to contact:* Phone Marin Headlands Visitor Center at (415) 331-1540, or GGNRA headquarters at (415) 556-0560.

*Trail notes:* This is a very popular, scenic trail in the Marin Headlands that traces Tennessee Valley out to Tennessee Cove and the Pacific Ocean. While the area is not wooded, the views of the Pacific Ocean can be gorgeous and the sunsets memorable. The best trailhead is at Mi-Wok Stables, elevation 200 feet. From there, the first 0.8 miles is paved and is a popular bike route. It turns to gravel for the final 1.1 miles, tracing alongside a pretty lagoon before dropping the final 0.2 miles to Tennessee Cove. With the easy, meandering grade, hard flat surface and ocean views, the trail has become a favorite of family hikers.

## 51. MORNING SUN TRAIL    0.2 mi/0.5 hr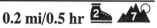

*Reference:* **In Marin Headlands near Sausalito; map E1-Marin, grid c2.**

*User groups:* Hikers only. No horses, mountain bikes or dogs are allowed. No wheelchair access.

*Permits:* No permit required. Parking and access are free.

*Directions:* From San Francisco, take US 101 north into Marin. After passing through the tunnel and driving down the grade, take the Spencer Road exit. Drive a half mile on Spencer Road (on the west side of US 101) to the parking area and trailhead.

*Maps:* A map/brochure is available at the Marin Headlands Visitor Center, or by mail from Golden Gate National Recreation Area, Marin Headlands, Building 1056, Fort Cronkite, Sausalito, CA 94965. A detailed hiking map of the area is available for a fee from Olmsted Brothers Map Company, P.O. Box 5351, Berkeley, CA 94705. To obtain a topographic map of area, ask for San Francisco North from the USGS.

*Who to contact:* Phone Marin Headlands Visitor Center at (415) 331-1540, or GGNRA headquarters at (415) 556-0560.

*Trail notes:* This trail didn't get its name by accident. After the short but steep climb to the junction with the Alta Trail, you will discover this is a magnificent location to watch sunrises, with varying hues of yellows and oranges pouring down from the eastern sky and across San Francisco Bay. It is one of the best places in the Bay Area to watch a sunrise. There is a good parking area at the trailhead, and from there you climb about 400 feet, peaking out at 800 feet at the Alta Junction. A bonus is that from Alta, the trip can easily be extended in either direction, or you can create a pretty 5.2-mile loop trip by linking the Rodeo Valley Trail and Bobcat Trail.

## 52. BICENTENNIAL BIKE PATH 4.5 mi/2.0 hrs

*Reference:* **On the San Francisco Bay shoreline from Sausalito to Corte Madera; map E1-Marin, grid c3.**

*User groups:* Hikers, leashed dogs and mountain bikes. No horses are allowed. The trail is **wheelchair accessible**.

*Permits:* No permit required. Parking and access are free.

*Directions:* From San Francisco head north on US 101. After crossing the Golden Gate Bridge, take the Sausalito exit. Drive on Second Street/ Bridgeway though Sausalito to Harbor Drive and park. The trail starts there.

*Maps:* A detailed hiking map of the area is available for a fee from Olmsted Brothers Map Company, P.O. Box 5351, Berkeley, CA 94705. To obtain a topographic map of area, ask for San Francisco North from the USGS.

*Who to contact:* Richardson Bay Audubon Center, (415) 388-2524.

*Trail notes:* Can folks out for an easy stroll mix in with joggers and bikers on the same path? The Bicentennial Bike Path proves it is possible, primarily because it was designed for it. This is a paved byway that starts in Sausalito and then heads north, tracing the shoreline of Richardson Bay northward into Corte Madera. It is a great nature walk, easy and pleasant. From Sausalito, the route passes beneath the US 101 overpass, then heads toward Bothin Marsh along the edge of Richardson Bay, crossing two exceptional little bridges that provide passage over tidelands. At low tide, there are often hundreds of little sandpipers poking around in the mud, and in the nearby sloughs bordered by pickleweed, you can often spot egrets, night herons, sometimes perhaps a pelican. The Richardson Bay Audubon Center can make a good sidetrip. Bikers can extend the trip all the way to Ross, but have to make a few connections on city streets to do it.

## 53. FORT CRONKITE TRAIL   5.2 mi/2.5 hrs

*Reference:* **In Marin Headlands at the mouth of San Francisco Bay; map E1-Marin, grid c2.**

*User groups:* Hikers, horses, mountain bikes and leashed dogs. Fort Cronkite and the picnic area is **partially wheelchair accessible.**

*Permits:* No permit required. Parking and access are free.

*Directions:* From San Francisco, take US 101 over the Golden Gate Bridge. Take the Alexander Avenue exit and turn left underneath the highway. Then take the wide paved road (Conzelman Road, but there is no sign) to the right, look for the sign that says "Marin Headlands." Continue for one mile, take a right on McCullough Road (the downhill fork) and shortly later turn left on Bunker Road. Drive about 2.5 miles to where the road dead ends at the Fort Cronkite/Rodeo Beach parking lot.

*Maps:* A map/brochure is available at the Marin Headlands Visitor Center, or by mail from Golden Gate National Recreation Area, Marin Headlands, Building 1056, Fort Cronkite, Sausalito, CA 94965. A detailed hiking map of the area is available for a fee from Olmsted Brothers Map Company, P.O. Box 5351, Berkeley, CA 94705. To obtain a topographic map of area, ask for Point Bonita from the USGS.

*Who to contact:* Phone Marin Headlands Visitor Center at (415) 331-1540, or GGNRA headquarters at (415) 556-0560.

*Trail notes:* Fort Cronkite, perched on an ocean bluff above Rodeo Beach, was the "support community" for the Headlands military fortifications in the 1930s and 1940s. From here, a paved pathway extends north up to Wolf Ridge, climbing to a 960-foot summit at what is known as "Hill 88." The land here consists primarily of coastal grasslands, so from the summit you get outstanding views of the Pacific Ocean. It is paved all the way, and there are times when a few bikers will careen downhill, hell-bent for leather, sending hikers scattering for the bushes. Enforcement of the speed limit has helped, as well as peer pressure from more ethical riders. While it is a 5.2-mile roundtrip, you'll do the 2.6-mile return trip at least twice as fast as the journey up.

## 54. LOWER FISHERMAN'S   0.4 mi/0.25 hr
## TRAIL

*Reference:* **In Marin Headlands at the mouth of San Francisco Bay; map E1-Marin, grid c2.**

*User groups:* Hikers only. No horses, mountain bikes or dogs are allowed. No wheelchair access.

*Permits:* No permit required. Parking and access are free.

*Directions:* From San Francisco, take US 101 over the Golden Gate Bridge. Take the Alexander Avenue exit and turn left underneath the highway. Then take the wide paved road (Conzelman, but there is no sign) to the right, look for the sign that says "Marin Headlands." Continue for one mile, take a right on McCullough Road (the downhill fork) and shortly later turn left on Bunker Road. Drive a short distance to Fort Barry. Turn left and drive to the parking area on the left side of the road.

*Maps:* A map/brochure is available at the Marin Headlands Visitor Center, or by mail from Golden Gate National Recreation Area, Marin Headlands, Building 1056, Fort Cronkite, Sausalito, CA 94965. A detailed hiking map of the area is available for a fee from Olmsted Brothers Map Company, P.O. Box 5351, Berkeley, CA 94705. To obtain a topographic map of area, ask for Point Bonita from the USGS.

*Who to contact:* Phone Marin Headlands Visitor Center at (415) 331-1540, or GGNRA headquarters at (415) 556-0560.

*Trail notes:* Bonita Cove offers a delightful beach and sea-level view of the entrance to the Bay and the Golden Gate. If only the weather was better ... summer days are typically cold and foggy here. There is a good parking area at the trailhead. From there, the hike is short with a fair gradient, just 0.2 miles long and dropping about 150 feet in the process. It pours out on to a beach sheltered by nearby Point Bonita. The trail gets its name from the anglers over the years who have used the trail in the summer months to fish for striped bass and halibut. A popular sidetrip from the trailhead is to visit Battery Alexander, which is located just west of the parking area on the north side of Conzelman Road.

## 55. UPPER FISHERMAN'S TRAIL          0.6 mi/0.5 hr 🥾 ⛰️6️⃣

*Reference:* **In Marin Headlands at the mouth of San Francisco Bay; map E1-Marin, grid c2.**

*User groups:* Hikers only. No horses, mountain bikes or dogs are allowed. No wheelchair access.

*Permits:* No permit required. Parking and access are free.

*Directions:* From San Francisco, take US 101 over the Golden Gate Bridge. Take the Alexander Avenue exit and turn left underneath the highway. Then take the wide paved road (Conzelman, but there is no sign) to the right, look for the sign that says "Marin Headlands." Continue for one mile, take a right on McCullough Road (the downhill fork) and shortly later turn left on Bunker Road. Continue a short distance and take the first left to the Upper Fisherman's Parking Area and the trailhead.

*Maps:* A map/brochure is available at the Marin Headlands Visitor Center, or by mail from Golden Gate National Recreation Area, Marin Headlands, Building 1056, Fort Cronkite, Sausalito, CA 94965. A detailed hiking map of the area is available for a fee from Olmsted Brothers Map Company, P.O. Box 5351, Berkeley, CA 94705. To obtain a topographic map of area, ask for Point Bonita from the USGS.

*Who to contact:* Phone Marin Headlands Visitor Center at (415) 331-1540, or GGNRA headquarters at (415) 556-0560.

*Trail notes:* This trail provides an option for reaching Bonita Cove (see hike number 54). While the scenery is not as pretty as the Lower Fisherman's Trail to the nearby west, the fishing is typically far better at this spot. The reason is because the cove here is protected by Point Diablo, where baitfish often congregate during tidal transitions. Those baitfish, typically schools of anchovies, attract striped bass and halibut. From the parking area, the trail requires about a half-mile walk with about a 300-foot elevation change, and you'll know it when you make the return trip up. The best views are out to sea and of the passing ships, while Point Diablo largely blocks the view of the Golden Gate.

## 56. FORT BARRY TRAILHEAD   1.4 mi/0.75 hr

*Reference:* In Marin Headlands near Rodeo Lagoon; map E1-Marin, grid c2.
*User groups:* Hikers, horses and leashed dogs. No mountain bikes are allowed. No wheelchair access.
*Permits:* No permit required. Parking and access are free.
*Directions:* From San Francisco, take US 101 over the Golden Gate Bridge. Take the Alexander Avenue exit and turn left, proceed underneath the highway. Then take the wide paved road (Conzelman, but there is no sign) to the right, look for the sign that says "Marin Headlands." Continue for one mile, take a right on McCullough Road (the downhill fork) and shortly later turn left on Bunker Road. Drive a short distance to Fort Barry.
*Maps:* A map/brochure is available at the Marin Headlands Visitor Center, or by mail from Golden Gate National Recreation Area, Marin Headlands, Building 1056, Fort Cronkite, Sausalito, CA 94965. A detailed hiking map of the area is available for a fee from Olmsted Brothers Map Company, P.O. Box 5351, Berkeley, CA 94705. To obtain a topographic map of area, ask for Point Bonita from the USGS.
*Who to contact:* Phone Marin Headlands Visitor Center at (415) 331-1540, or GGNRA headquarters at (415) 556-0560.
*Trail notes:* Fort Barry was a "nerve center" for military operations in an era long past. It remains a place to calm the nerves of those who are feeling frazzled. After parking and exploring Fort Barry a bit, take the unpaved road/ trail that heads west from the fort. It is routed along the south side of Rodeo Lagoon and out to the bluffs overlooking the ocean, all in just 0.7 miles. It is a great and easy walk, with good views all around on clear days. The fort is set at the foot of Rodeo Valley, and can furnish a living history lesson.

## 57. HAWK HILL   0.1 mi/0.25 hr

*Reference:* In Marin Headlands near Rodeo Lagoon; map E1-Marin, grid c2.
*User groups:* Hikers only. No horses, mountain bikes or leashed dogs are allowed. No wheelchair access.
*Permits:* No permit required. Parking and access are free.
*Directions:* From San Francisco, take US 101 over the Golden Gate Bridge. Take the Alexander Avenue exit and turn left, proceed underneath the highway. Then take the wide paved road (Conzelman, but there is no sign) to the right, look for the sign that says "Marin Headlands." Continue on Conzelman (a left at the fork with McCullough Road) and drive a short distance to the Hawk Hill parking area. Note: The access road (Conzelman) is closed each day at sunset.
*Maps:* A map/brochure is available at the Marin Headlands Visitor Center, or by mail from Golden Gate National Recreation Area, Marin Headlands, Building 1056, Fort Cronkite, Sausalito, CA 94965. A detailed hiking map

of the area is available for a fee from Olmsted Brothers Map Company, P.O. Box 5351, Berkeley, CA 94705. To obtain a topographic map of area, ask for San Francisco North from the USGS.

*Who to contact:* Phone Marin Headlands Visitor Center at (415) 331-1540, or GGNRA headquarters at (415) 556-0560.

*Trail notes:* Awesome views of both raptors and the Golden Gate Bridge make this a choice trip. Each year more than 10,000 hawks fly over the Marin Headlands during the five-month migration season, peaking in September and October, and they are best viewed from this lookout. In addition, there may be no better spot to see the Golden Gate Bridge, with the city skyline providing a backdrop. It is an easy and fun trip, especially for youngsters. You can drive nearly to the top of Hawk Hill, and after parking, you hike up a short distance, equivalent to a few blocks, to reach the lookout summit. As many as 2,800 hawks have been counted on a single day from this spot. The most common raptors seen are the red-tailed hawk, Cooper's hawk, turkey vulture, American kestrel and northern harrier. All you need is a clear October day.

---

## 58. VISTA POINT/FORT BAKER 2.5 mi/1.5 hrs

*Reference:* **In Marin Headlands at the northern foot of Golden Gate Bridge; map E1-Marin, grid c2.**

*User groups:* Hikers, mountain bikes and leashed dogs. No horses are allowed. Vista Point is **wheelchair accessible**, but the trail is not.

*Permits:* No permit required. Parking and access are free.

*Directions:* From San Francisco, take US 101 over the Golden Gate Bridge, get in the right lane and take the Vista Point exit.

*Maps:* A map/brochure is available at the Fort Baker Visitor Center, or by mail from Golden Gate National Recreation Area, Marin Headlands, Building 1056, Fort Cronkite, Sausalito, CA 94965. A detailed hiking map of the area is available for a fee from Olmsted Brothers Map Company, P.O. Box 5351, Berkeley, CA 94705. To obtain a topographic map of area, ask for San Francisco North from the USGS.

*Who to contact:* Phone Marin Headlands Visitor Center at (415) 331-1540, or GGNRA headquarters at (415) 556-0560.

*Trail notes:* Vista Point, the famous lookout from the northern end of the Golden Gate Bridge, is like a mini United Nations. It is where travelers from around the world stop to take their photos. Little do they know that with a short walk, they can get even better views. From the parking area, a paved trail loops under the north foot of the bridge, then works its way back-and-forth, descending down to Fort Baker. There you will find a bay cove, and from the shoreline looking up, the Golden Gate seems even more inspiring. You can stroll along the shoreline and out to the fishing pier, or check out the children's Discovery Museum. A nearby large grassy area makes an excellent picnic site. There are also picnic tables near Lime Point, set below the north end of the bridge. You can also extend the trip out to Yellow Bluff (see hike number 59), for more spectacular views and picnic sites.

## 59. YELLOW BLUFF TRAIL     1.5 mi/1.0 hr

*Reference:* **In Marin Headlands at the northern foot of Golden Gate Bridge; map E1-Marin, grid c2.**

*User groups:* Hikers, mountain bikes and leashed dogs. No horses are allowed. Fort Baker is **wheelchair accessible**, but the trail is not.

*Permits:* No permit required. Parking and access are free.

*Directions:* From San Francisco take US 101 north over the Golden Gate Bridge. Take the Alexander Avenue and stay to the right at the split. Continue a very short distance, then turn left and drive a few hundred yards to a stop sign. Turn right and drive a half mile to the parking area for Fort Baker.

*Maps:* A map/brochure is available at the Fort Baker Visitor Center, or by mail from Golden Gate National Recreation Area, Marin Headlands, Building 1056, Fort Cronkite, Sausalito, CA 94965. A detailed hiking map of the area is available for a fee from Olmsted Brothers Map Company, P.O. Box 5351, Berkeley, CA 94705. To obtain a topographic map of area, ask for San Francisco North from the USGS.

*Who to contact:* Phone Marin Headlands Visitor Center at (415) 331-1540, or GGNRA headquarters at (415) 556-0560.

*Trail notes:* This is a little piece of heaven. From Yellow Bluff, San Francisco looks like the land of Oz, the Golden Gate Bridge like a link to Valhalla. Yellow Bluff, which is the first major land point along the Marin shore east of the Golden Gate, is a stunning lookout across the Bay and the surrounding landmarks. The trail is flat, short and unpublicized, and there are also a few picnic tables in the area. From Fort Baker, walk on the trail that heads east near the shoreline of the Bay. You can turn the trip into a triangular-shaped loop hike by continuing along the shore of the Bay, heading toward Sausalito, then turning left at the trail junction and hiking back to Fort Baker. One of the great features of this area is that it is often sunny, even when the Marin Headlands to the west is buried in fog.

## 60. SHORELINE TRAIL     5.0 mi/2.0 hrs

*Reference:* **In China Camp State Park east of San Rafael; map E1-Marin, grid b3.**

*User groups:* Hikers, horses and mountain bikes. Dogs are not allowed. No wheelchair access.

*Permits:* A $5 state park day-use fee is charged at the entrance station.

*Directions:* From San Francisco, take US 101 north to San Rafael. Take the North San Pedro exit and drive east for three miles to the park entrance.

*Maps:* A small brochure/map is available for a fee at park headquarters, or by mail from State Parks, Marin District Office, 1455A East Francisco Boulevard, San Rafael, CA 94901. To obtain a topographic map of area, ask for San Quentin from the USGS.

*Who to contact:* Phone China Camp State Park at (415) 456-0766, Marin District Headquarters at (415) 456-1286, or write them at the address listed above.

*Trail notes:* The Shoreline Trail is the best introduction to China Camp State Park a hiker could ask for. The trail meanders along the shore of San Pablo

Bay, bordered by an undisturbed hills on one side, the bay's waterfront on the other. It starts at the parking area and is well-signed. The first mile of the trail provides good lookouts across the bay, and the latter half crosses a meadow, then is routed adjacent to tidal areas, marshes and wetlands, home for many species of waterfowl. Because the hike does not include any serious elevation gains or losses, the trip back on the same trail does not include any surprise climbs. An option on the return trip is to take the MiWok Fire Trail, which provides a loop hike back to headquarters with a 300-foot climb and drop.

## 61. BAY VIEW TRAIL 11.5 mi/4.5 hrs

*Reference:* **In China Camp State Park east of San Rafael; map E1-Marin, grid b3.**

*User groups:* Hikers, mountain bikes and horses. No dogs are allowed. No wheelchair access.

*Permits:* A $3 day-use and parking fee is charged at China Camp Village.

*Directions:* From San Francisco, take US 101 north to San Rafael. Take the North San Pedro exit and turn east on North San Pedro. Drive for five miles to China Camp Village.

*Maps:* A small map/brochure is available for a fee at park headquarters, or by mail from State Parks, Marin District Office, 1455A East Francisco Boulevard, San Rafael, CA 94901. For a topographic map, ask for San Quentin from the USGS.

*Who to contact:* Phone China Camp State Park at (415) 456-0766, or Marin District Headquarters at (415) 456-1286, or write them at the address listed above.

*Trail notes:* The Bay View Trail is the most ambitious hike anywhere along the shore of San Pablo Bay. From China Camp Village, start the trip by hiking out on the Shoreline Trail, then link the Peacock Gap Trail to the Bay View Trail to access the park's most remote reaches. The Bay View Trail climbs to about 600 feet, in the process traversing much of the park. The highest point in the park can be visited by taking the Back Ranch Fire Trail to the Ridge Fire Trail, providing a panorama of San Pablo Bay, San Francisco Bay, Mount St. Helena, Mount Diablo, Angel Island and San Francisco. Our recommended return route is to drop down to the Back Ranch Meadows Campground and walk back on the Shoreline Trail.

## 62. PERIMETER ROAD 5.0 mi/2.5 hrs

*Reference:* **In Angel Island State Park in San Francisco Bay; map E1-Marin, grid c3.**

*User groups:* Hikers and mountain bikes (helmets are required for those 17 and under). No dogs (except for seeing-eye dogs) or horses are allowed. The Perimeter Road is accessible to **wheelchairs,** but many portions are too steep.

*Permits:* There is a day-use fee and a ferry boat ticket fee. The cost varies according to your departure point. Ferry ticket fees vary seasonally, but the average price is $5 per person, $1 per bicycle from Tiburon; $8 per person from San Francisco; $10 per person from Vallejo.

*Directions:* Ferry service to Angel Island is available from Tiburon, San

Francisco and Vallejo. *To reach the Tiburon Ferry:* Take US 101 in Marin to Tiburon Boulevard. Head east on Tiburon Boulevard, curving along the Bay's shoreline. Park at one of the pay lots in Tiburon, and then walk a short distance to the Tiburon Ferry. It is well-signed. *To reach the San Francisco Ferry:* Take US 101 to the Marina Boulevard exit near the southern foot of the Golden Gate Bridge. Drive on Marina Boulevard toward Fisherman's Wharf. The ferry departs from Pier 43 1/2. *To reach the Vallejo Ferry:* Take Interstate 80 to US 780. Continue to Curtola Parkway (which becomes Mare Island Way). Drive to 495 Mare Island Way, where free parking is available. The docking area is directly across from the parking lot.

*Maps:* A topographic map/brochure is available for $1 at the park and for $2 through the mail from the Angel Island Association, Box 866, Tiburon, CA 94920. For a detailed topographic map, ask for San Francisco North from the USGS.

*Who to contact:* Angel Island State Park information at (415) 435-1915; Marin State Park District Headquarters at (415) 456-1286. The Tiburon Ferry can be reached at (415) 435-2131. The San Francisco Red & White Fleet can be reached at (800) 229-2784. The Vallejo Blue and Gold Fleet can be reached at (707) 64-FERRY.

*Trail notes:* A hike on the Perimeter Trail around Angel Island provides great views of the bay and a tour amid remnants of a military past, and it is long enough to provide a decent workout. The trail winds past old barracks and abandoned military buildings, climbs through lush eucalyptus forests and across high bluffs, and provides lookouts of San Francisco Bay and its world-class landmarks. When linked with the North Ridge/Sunset Trail (see hike number 63), it is the most scenic hike in the Bay Area. The trail is actually a road, the only downer, but it always inspires. From each lookout you get a completely new look at San Francisco Bay.

---

# 63. NORTH RIDGE/SUNSET TRAIL
## 6.0 mi/3.0 hrs

*Reference:* **In Angel Island State Park in San Francisco Bay; map E1-Marin, grid c3.**

*User groups:* Hikers only. No mountain bikes (they may not even be walked on this trail), dogs (except for seeing-eye dogs) or horses are allowed. No wheelchair access.

*Permits:* There is a day-use fee and a ferry boat ticket fee. The cost varies according to your departure point. Ferry ticket fees vary seasonally, but the average price is $5 per person, $1 per bicycle from Tiburon; $8 per person from San Francisco; $10 per person from Vallejo.

*Directions:* Ferry service to Angel Island is available from Tiburon, San Francisco and Vallejo. *To reach the Tiburon Ferry:* Take US 101 in Marin to Tiburon Boulevard. Head east on Tiburon Boulevard, curving along the Bay's shoreline. Park at one of the pay lots in Tiburon, and then walk a short distance to the Tiburon Ferry. It is well-signed. *To reach the San Francisco Ferry:* Take US 101 to the Marina Boulevard exit near the southern foot of the Golden Gate Bridge. Drive on Marina Boulevard toward Fisherman's Wharf. The ferry departs from Pier 43 1/2. *To reach the Vallejo Ferry:* Take Interstate 80 to US 780. Continue to Curtola Parkway (which becomes Mare

Island Way). Drive to 495 Mare Island Way, where free parking is available. The docking area is directly across from the parking lot.

*Maps:* A topographic map/brochure is available for $1 at the park and for $2 through the mail from the Angel Island Association, Box 866, Tiburon, CA 94920. For a detailed topographic map, ask for San Francisco North from the USGS.

*Who to contact:* Angel Island State Park information at (415) 435-1915; Marin State Park District Headquarters at (415) 456-1286. The Tiburon Ferry can be reached at (415) 435-2131. The San Francisco Red & White Fleet can be reached at (800) 229-2784. The Vallejo Blue and Gold Fleet can be reached at (707) 64-FERRY.

*Trail notes:* When standing on the top of Mt. Livermore, you will be surrounded by dramatic scenery in every direction. That is because at 781 feet, it is the highest point on Angel Island, the virtual center of San Francisco Bay. The views are superb even at night, when the Golden Gate Bridge and the Emerald City are lit in glowing charm. The trail is steep, a 550-foot climb in just a half mile, which will have even the best-conditioned hikers puffing like a locomotive by the time they reach the top. The Summit Trail is actually a cutoff from the Perimeter Trail, and for the ambitious, it is the highlight of a six-mile loop hike on Angel Island.

## LEAVE NO TRACE TIPS

### Plan ahead and prepare

• Learn about the regulations and issues that apply to the area you are visiting.

• Avoid heavy-use areas.

• Obtain all maps and permits.

• Bring extra garbage bags to pack out any refuse you come across.

# MAP E1

NOR-CAL MAP ......................... see page 14
adjoining maps
NORTH (D1) ...................... see page 202
EAST (E2) ......................... see page 394
SOUTH (F1) ...................... see page 468
WEST ............................... no map

**194 TRAILS**
**PAGES 258-393**

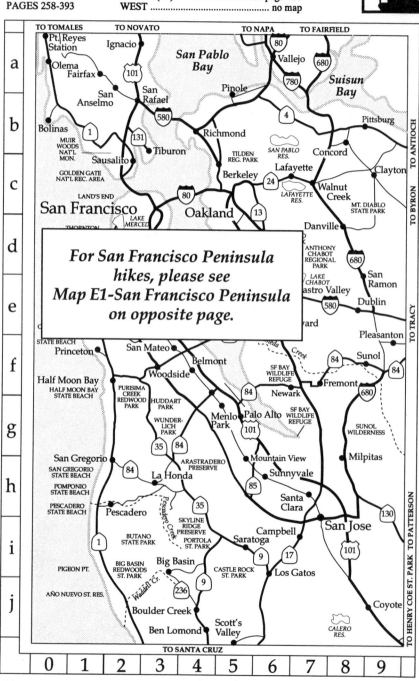

*For San Francisco Peninsula
hikes, please see
Map E1-San Francisco Peninsula
on opposite page.*

# MAP E1-SAN FRANCISCO PENINSULA

## 34 TRAILS
### PAGES 304-327

TO SAN RAFAEL

*Pacific Ocean*

Golden Gate Bridge ⑤

101

LAND'S END ④ ③ ②

San Francisco-Oakland Bay Bridge

① 1

80

**San Francisco**

*LAKE MERCED*

⑥

*San Francisco Bay*

⑦

35

THORNTON STATE BEACH

**Daly City**

82

⑨ ⑩ ⑧ 101

**South San Francisco**

1

⑫

⑬

⑭

**Pacifica**

380

**San Bruno**

**Burlingame**

1

**Millbrae**

*SAN ANDREAS RESERVOIR*

⑪

280

⑯

GRAY WHALE STATE BEACH ⑮ McNEE RANCH STATE PARK

⑱ ⑲

San Mateo Bridge

MONTARA STATE BEACH ⑰

20

92

**San Mateo**

23

**Princeton**

*LOWER CRYSTAL SPRINGS RESERVOIR*

**Woodside**

FITZGERALD MARINE PRESERVE **Miramar**

**Belmont**

PALO ALTO BAYLANDS PRESERVE

Dumbarton Bridge

**Half Moon Bay**

⑳①

280 ㉒

**San Carlos**

HALF MOON BAY STATE BEACH ㉔

PURISIMA CREEK REDWOOD PARK

*UPPER CRYSTAL SPRINGS RESERVOIR*

**Redwood City**

84

㉛

35

㉕ ㉖

**Menlo Park**

㉗

㉜ ㉝

**Sky Londa**

㉘

㉙ 84

101

HUDDART COUNTY PARK ㉚

㉞

TO SAN GREGORIO    TO SARATOGA    TO LA HONDA    TO PALO ALTO

TO OAKLAND

TO HAYWARD

TO FREMONT

| 1 | 2 | 3 | 4 | 5 |

c   d   e   f   g

**Map E1-San Francisco Peninsula featuring:** San Francisco headlands, San Francisco, San Bruno Mountain County Park, Pacifica shoreline, Linda Mar Bay, San Pedro Beach, San Pedro County Park, McNee Ranch State Park, Moss Beach, San Mateo County foothills, Coyote Point County Park, Crystal Springs Reservoir, Woodside foothills, Belmont foothills, Foster City, Half Moon Bay, Purisima Creek Redwoods Open Space Preserve, Skyline Ridge, Huddart Park, Skylonda, Wunderlich Park, Ravenswood, San Francisco Bay Wildlife Refuge

## 1. LANDS END TRAIL   2.5 mi/1.0 hr

*Reference:* **On the San Francisco headlands at the entrance to San Francisco Bay; map E1-San Francisco Peninsula, grid c1.**

*User groups:* Hikers, **wheelchairs**, dogs and mountain bikes (mountain bikes must be walked in narrow sections of the trail). No horses are allowed.

*Permits:* No permits are required. Parking and access are free.

*Directions:* From the Peninsula, take Interstate 280 to Highway 1 in San Bruno. Turn west and drive one mile to Highway 35 (Skyline Boulevard). Turn right onto Highway 35 and drive past Lake Merced, jogging left at the lake, and continue to the Cliff House Restaurant.

From San Francisco, take Geary Boulevard west until it dead ends at the ocean and the Cliff House Restaurant. Parking is available along Geary, Skyline Boulevard and in a dirt lot across from Louis' Restaurant.

*Maps:* For a free map, contact GGNRA at the address below. To obtain a topographic map of the area, ask for San Francisco North from the USGS.

*Who to contact:* Golden Gate National Recreation Area, Fort Mason, Building 201, San Francisco, CA 94123; (415) 556-8371 or (415) 556-0560.

*Trail notes:* In one glance from Lands End, you take in the mouth of the Bay and crashing breakers, with the Golden Gate Bridge and Marin Headlands in the foreground, and the Pacific Ocean, Farallon Islands and Point Reyes in the background. By now you probably have it figured out that this is one of San Francisco's greatest lookouts, and you are right. The trailhead is near the Cliff House Restaurant, where you meander eastward on a dirt trail set near bluffs topped with cypress trees. It is a near-flat, scenic route, tracing the Coastal Trail between Lands End and China Beach, a 2.5-mile roundtrip from the parking area. It is especially popular on Sunday mornings, when a brisk morning walk with the sea breeze in your face can be followed by brunch at one of the two restaurants, the Cliff House or Louis'.

## 2. GOLDEN GATE PROMENADE   3.0 mi/1.25 hrs

*Reference:* **On shore of San Francisco Bay in San Francisco; map E1-San Francisco Peninsula, grid c2.**

*User groups:* Hikers, **wheelchairs**, dogs and mountain bikes. No horses are allowed.

*Permits:* No permits are required. Parking and access are free.

*Directions:* From US 101 at the southern end of the Golden Gate Bridge in San Francisco, take the Marina Boulevard exit. Head southeast toward Fisherman's Wharf. Parking lots are available off Marina Boulevard at Fort Mason, Marina Green, Crissy Field and near the St. Francis Yacht Club.

*Maps:* For a free map, contact GGNRA at the address below. To obtain a topographic map of the area, ask for San Francisco North from the USGS.

*Who to contact:* Golden Gate National Recreation Area, Fort Mason, Building 201, San Francisco, CA 94123; (415) 556-8371 or (415) 556-0560.

*Trail notes:* This is a paved trail along the Bay's shoreline from Marina Green to Fort Point. It is virtually flat and the views are magnificent, with the scenic backdrop of the Golden Gate Bridge, Alcatraz, Tiburon, Sausalito and the Bay. From the parking area at Marina Green, you simply walk on the paved pathway that is routed through Crissy Field, along the Presidio and out to Fort Point, extending to the southern foot of the Golden Gate Bridge. The entire trail is popular for joggers and walkers, especially in the morning. In the afternoon, it can get quite windy. For people looking for a fitness workout, an option here is trying one of the Bay Area's most popular par courses, located at Marina Green. Sidetrips along the route include the old Muni Pier, visiting the Presidio, which runs alongside much of the route, and Fort Point.

---

## 3. GOLDEN GATE BRIDGE    3.0 mi/1.25 hrs

*Reference:* From San Francisco to Marin; map E1-San Francisco Peninsula, grid c2.

*User groups:* Hikers, **wheelchairs**, dogs and mountain bikes (west side of bridge only). No horses are allowed.

*Permits:* No permits are required. Parking and access are free.

*Directions:* From US 101 at the southern end of the Golden Gate Bridge, take the toll plaza parking area exit. There is limited parking directly east of the toll plaza. There is additional parking directly west of the toll plaza at dirt spaces. You must then walk through a short tunnel to reach the foot of the bridge.

*Maps:* For a free map, contact GGNRA at the address below. To obtain a topographic map of the area, ask for San Francisco North from the USGS.

*Who to contact:* Golden Gate National Recreation Area, Fort Mason, Building 201, San Francisco, CA 94123; (415) 556-8371 or (415) 556-0560.

*Trail notes:* This is the number one tourist walk in the world, yet often you discover that relatively few Bay Area residents ever get around to making the trip. The view is incomparable from the center of the Golden Gate Bridge. If you look eastward from the center of the bridge, you see Alcatraz, Angel Island and the Bay framed by the San Francisco waterfront and East Bay hills. Parking is available at either the north end of the bridge at Vista Point, or at the south end of the bridge, just west of the toll station. At the latter, after parking, you walk through a short tunnel that runs under Highway 101, then loops up to the pathway entrance. On weekends, the pathway on the eastern side of the bridge is for walkers only, while the pathway on the western side of the bridge is reserved for bicyclists. From one end to the other, the bridge is 1.22 miles long between spans (it is also 746 feet above the water), but most folks walk halfway out on the bridge and then back to their car, a roundtrip of 1.5 miles.

## 4. COASTAL TRAIL
**2.5 mi/1.0 hr**

*Reference:* **On the San Francisco headlands; map E1-San Francisco Peninsula, grid c2.**

*User groups:* Hikers and **wheelchairs**. Dogs and mountain bikes are allowed but not advised. No horses are allowed.

*Permits:* No permits are required. Parking and access are free.

*Directions:* From US 101 at the southern end of the Golden Gate Bridge, take the toll plaza parking area exit. There is limited parking directly east of the toll plaza. You must then walk through a short tunnel to reach the trailhead. There is additional parking directly west of the toll plaza at dirt spaces near the trailhead.

*Maps:* For a free map, contact GGNRA at the address below. To obtain a topographic map of the area, ask for San Francisco North from the USGS.

*Who to contact:* Golden Gate National Recreation Area, Fort Mason, Building 201, San Francisco, CA 94123; (415) 556-8371 or (415) 556-0560.

*Trail notes:* While Vista Point at the northern foot of the Golden Gate Bridge may be the most popular place to take pictures of the bridge, a lookout from the Coastal Trail provides a more scenic view. This spot is just north of Baker Beach, where the Bay, the bridge and the Marin coast all fit easily into a 35-mm frame, a postcard-like scene. After parking, hike southwest on the Coastal Trail, passing the Fort Scott Overlook, Battery Crosby and Battery Chamberlain en route to the south end of Baker Beach. For photographs, the best strategy is to make the 30-minute walk one way, scanning for picture ideas on the way, and then on the return trip, put those ideas on film. The trail is a soft dirt pathway set in cypress. Don't forget that this is still a big city—hikers should go in pairs or look something like we do, which will scare anyone off. A good sidetrip is down to mile-long Baker Beach for more postcard views of the bridge.

## 5. AGAVE TRAIL
**1.5 mi/1.5 hrs**

*Reference:* **At Alcatraz Island; map E1-San Francisco Peninsula, grid c3.**

*User groups:* Hikers only. No dogs, horses or mountain bikes are allowed. No wheelchair access.

*Permits:* For the ferry boat ride to the island, park day-use fee and audio cassette tour, the fees are $9 for adults, $8 for seniors and $4.50 for children. The trip is available without the audio cassette tour for a few dollars less. Ferry service departs from Pier 41 in San Francisco with the Red & White Fleet on weekends at 9:45 a.m. and every half-hour thereafter until 2:45 p.m., and on weekdays at 9:45 a.m. and every 45 minutes thereafter until 2:45 p.m.

*Directions:* From US 101 heading south into San Francisco, take the Marina Boulevard exit near the southern foot of the Golden Gate Bridge. Drive on Marina Boulevard toward Fisherman's Wharf. Park in a pay lot and walk to Pier 41 at Fisherman's Wharf. The sign for the Red & White Fleet is prominent.

*Maps:* For a free map/brochure, contact the GGNRA at the address below. To obtain a topographic map of the area, ask for San Francisco North from the USGS.

*Who to contact:* Golden Gate National Recreation Area, Fort Mason, Building

201, San Francisco, CA 94123; (415) 556-8371 or (415) 556-0560. The Red & White Fleet can be reached at (415) 546-2628 (recording). Advance tickets can be purchased by credit card (with a reservation fee) by phoning (415) 546-2700.

*Trail notes:* The Agave Trail at Alcatraz, opened in the winter of 1994-1995, is bound to become one of the most popular trails in California. It opens one-third of the island previously closed to visitors, and it provides some of the most breathtaking views of any of the 15,000 miles of hiking trails in the Bay Area. The trip starts with a ferry boat ride with the Red & White Fleet from Pier 41 in San Francisco, and is followed by a park ranger-led tour and personal access to the old Alcatraz prison. Then you gain entrance to what has long been the forbidden zone. The Agave Trail starts at the ferryboat landing, on the east side of Alcatraz, and traces the rim of the island to its southern tip. The trail is quite wide, with a few benches and cement picnic tables situated for sweeping views of both the East Bay and San Francisco. The trail is named "Agave" after the plant, which is common here. From its southern tip, the Agave Trail is routed back to the historic parade ground atop the island, where you'll find some masterpiece sculpture work that includes 110 stone steps. The parade ground is a bird nesting area, so this area will be closed to the public from February to August each year so the birds will not be disturbed. If you visit during a low tide, you can explore further and discover some relatively little-known tidepools at the southwest corner of the island. This part of the island also has an abundance of bird life, including a population of night herons, friendly little fellows. For pure cuteness, they're right up there with chipmunks and baby ducks. The old cellblock is located at the center of the island, with other buildings sprinkled along the eastern shore and northern tip. The ghost of Al Capone is said to still roam here, trying to figure out a way to pay his taxes.

# 6. OCEAN BEACH ESPLANADE 6.0 mi/2.25 hrs

*Reference:* **On the San Francisco coast; map E1-San Francisco Peninsula, grid d1.**

*User groups:* Hikers, dogs and horses. There is **partial wheelchair access.** No mountain bikes allowed.

*Permits:* No permits are required. Parking and access are free.

*Directions:* From the Peninsula, take Interstate 280 to Highway 1 in San Bruno. Turn west and drive one mile to Highway 35 (Skyline Boulevard). Turn right onto Highway 35 and drive five miles, jog left to pass Lake Merced. Parking is on the left side along the beach. From San Francisco, take Geary Boulevard west until it dead ends at the ocean and the Cliff House Restaurant. Turn left onto the Great Highway and drive one mile to the parking area on the right.

*Maps:* For a free map, contact GGNRA at the address below. To obtain a topographic map of the area, ask for San Francisco South from the USGS.

*Who to contact:* Golden Gate National Recreation Area, Fort Mason, Building 201, San Francisco, CA 94123; (415) 556-8371 or (415) 556-0560.

*Trail notes:* Ocean Beach is located along the San Francisco coast's Great Highway and here you will discover a long expanse of beach, a paved jogging trail and miniature parks at Fort Funston and Thornton Beach. The nature of both the trail and the adjacent beach allows visitors to create trips of any length. The beach spans four miles from Seal Rock near the Cliff House south to Fort Funston, and from there, if desired, you can explore further south on the beach all the way past Center Hole to Mussel Rock at the north end of Pacifica. Ocean Beach is a huge expanse of sand that is popular for jogging, especially during low tides when hard-packed sand is uncovered. A paved jogging trail is located just east of the Great Highway.

## 7. FORT FUNSTON SUNSET TRAIL       1.5 mi/0.5 hr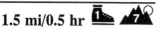

*Reference:* **On San Francisco coast; map E1-San Francisco Peninsula, grid d1.**

*User groups:* Hikers, dogs and horses. No mountain bikes are allowed. There is **partial wheelchair access.**

*Permits:* No permits are required. Parking and access are free.

*Directions:* From the Peninsula, take Interstate 280 to Highway 1 in San Bruno. Turn west and drive one mile to Highway 35 (Skyline Boulevard). Turn right onto Highway 35 and drive five miles, jog left to pass Lake Merced. Parking is on the left side along the beach. From San Francisco, take Geary Boulevard west until it dead ends at the ocean and the Cliff House Restaurant. Turn left onto the Great Highway and drive four miles to the parking area on the right.

*Maps:* For a free map, contact GGNRA at the address below. To obtain a topographic map of the area, ask for San Francisco South from the USGS.

*Who to contact:* Golden Gate National Recreation Area, Fort Mason, Building 201, San Francisco, CA 94123; (415) 556-8371 or (415) 556-0560.

*Trail notes:* Fort Funston is a park set on San Francisco's coastal bluffs, with the ocean on one side, Lake Merced on the other. It is the most popular hang gliding area in the Bay Area, and watching those daredevils is the main attraction. A viewing deck is located adjacent to the parking area. It is also here where the Sunset Trail starts, being routed through coastal bluffs and above the sand dunes north for three-quarters of a mile to the park's border. If there is a problem at this park, it's the weather. If the wind doesn't get you, the fog likely will, especially in the summer. But, but but…don't write it off, because in the fall and winter, the fog clears out and arriving each evening are the kind of sunsets that make your spine tingle. In addition, those hang gliders are worth gawking at, too, especially in the spring when the north winds come up every afternoon. And we'll even tell you a little secret: The beach walk from Fort Funston southward less than a mile to Thornton Beach seems to turn up lots of sand dollars. This is one of the best places in San Francisco to bring a dog.

## 8. SUMMIT LOOP TRAIL       3.1 mi/1.5 hrs

*Reference:* **In San Bruno Mountain County Park near South San Francisco; map E1-San Francisco Peninsula, grid d2.**

*User groups:* Hikers only. No dogs, horses or mountain bikes are allowed. No wheelchair facilities.

*Permits:* No permits are required. There is a $3 entrance fee in the spring and summer.

*Directions:* From US Highway 101 north of South San Francisco, take the Cow Palace exit and continue to Guadalupe Parkway. Turn left and follow

Guadalupe Parkway for approximately two miles to the park.

*Maps:* For a free trail map, contact San Bruno Mountain County Park at the address below. To obtain a topographic map of the area, ask for San Francisco South from the USGS.

*Who to contact:* San Bruno Mountain County Park, 600 Oddstad Boulevard, Pacifica, CA 94044; (415) 355-8289.

*Trail notes:* San Bruno Mountain is a unique island of open space amid the Peninsula's urbanization. It is a landmark in the Bay Area with elevations ranging to 1,314 feet, best known to Peninsula residents as that "big ol' hill" west of Highway 101 near Candlestick Park. Wind and fog can be bigtime downers here. For the inspired, the Summit Loop Trail is the most demanding and rewarding hike in the park. It starts at the parking area on the south side of Guadalupe Canyon Parkway, is routed up past Dairy Ravine, and climbs 725 feet to the Ridge Trail. If you remain inspired, you can connect to the Ridge Trail and climb another 310 feet to the summit. On the return trip, our suggestion is to veer right at the Dairy Ravine Trail, taking the switchback down the canyon, then right again at the Eucalyptus Trail. The latter will send you through a large grove of eucalyptus, then return you to the parking area. With the sidetrip options, you can add 2.5 to 3.5 miles to the hike.

---

## 9. SADDLE TRAIL 2.5 mi/1.25 hrs

*Reference:* In San Bruno Mountain County Park; map E1-San Francisco Peninsula, grid d2.

*User groups:* Hikers only. No dogs, horses or mountain bikes are allowed. No wheelchair facilities.

*Permits:* No permits are required. There is a $3 entrance fee in the spring and summer.

*Directions:* From US Highway 101 north of South San Francisco, take the Cow Palace exit and continue to Guadalupe Parkway. Turn left and follow Guadalupe Parkway for approximately two miles to the park.

*Maps:* For a free trail map, contact San Bruno Mountain County Park at the address below. To obtain a topographic map of the area, ask for San Francisco South from the USGS.

*Who to contact:* San Bruno Mountain County Park, 600 Oddstad Boulevard, Pacifica, CA 94044; (415) 355-8289.

*Trail notes:* Saddle Trail is the feature hike from the parking area/trailhead on the north side of Guadalupe Canyon Parkway. Since San Bruno Mountain Park is split in two by the road, hikers have to decide which half to visit. The north half provides a pair of good loop hikes, the Saddle Trail and the Bog Trail (see hike number 10). Both are easier hikes than the Summit Loop/ Ridge Trail hike on the southern half of the park. From the north parking area, start your trip on the Old Guadalupe Trail, which junctions with the Saddle Trail after a 20-minute walk. From there, take the Saddle Trail, which loops around the northern boundaries of the park, climbing about 150 feet in the process. There are times when the wind can absolutely howl through this area, so pick your hiking days with care. Because most of the habitat is open hillside grasslands, the views of the South Bay are unblocked, spectacular on clear days.

## 10. BOG TRAIL    0.8 mi/0.5 hr

*Reference:* **In San Bruno Mountain County Park; map E1-San Francisco Peninsula, grid d2.**

*User groups:* Hikers only. No dogs, horses or mountain bikes are allowed. No wheelchair facilities.

*Permits:* No permits are required. There is a $3 entrance fee in the spring and summer.

*Directions:* From US Highway 101 north of South San Francisco, take the Cow Palace exit and continue to Guadalupe Parkway. Turn left and follow Guadalupe Parkway for approximately two miles to the park.

*Maps:* For a free trail map, contact San Bruno Mountain County Park at the address below. To obtain a topographic map of the area, ask for San Francisco South from the USGS.

*Who to contact:* San Bruno Mountain County Park, 600 Oddstad Boulevard, Pacifica, CA 94044; (415) 355-8289.

*Trail notes:* Hiking the Bog Trail provides an introduction to San Bruno Mountain County Park, although other trails will be needed if you desire a more passionate experience. The Bog Trail starts at the trailhead on the north side of Guadalupe Canyon Parkway, then is routed along the north flank of the mountain, changing only 30 feet in elevation. The trip can be converted to an easy, short loop hike by linking it with Old Guadalupe Trail, turning right at the trail junction. Most of the surrounding landscape is open hillsides, quite pretty in the spring when the grasslands turn green and are sprinkled with an explosion of wildflowers. This hike is easy, pretty on clear days, and can provide a quick sense of the importance of the open space buffer this park provides for the congested North Peninsula.

---

## 11. ROCKAWAY POINT TRAIL   2.5 mi/1.5 hrs

*Reference:* **On Pacifica shoreline near Linda Mar Bay at San Pedro Beach; map E1-San Francisco Peninsula, grid e1.**

*User groups:* Hikers and dogs. No horses or mountain bikes are allowed. No wheelchair access.

*Permits:* No permits are required. Parking and access are free.

*Directions:* From San Francisco, head south on Interstate 280 to Daly City. Turn south on Highway 1 and drive about five miles into Pacifica. Continue to the southern end of Pacifica and turn right at the parking lot for San Pedro Beach (Linda Mar). The trail starts at the north end of the beach.

*Maps:* To obtain a topographic map of the area, ask for Montara Mountain from the USGS.

*Who to contact:* City of Pacifica, Parks and Recreation Division, 170 Santa Maria Avenue, Pacifica, CA 94044; (415) 738-7380.

*Trail notes:* Sure, you could hike this route to the end and back in a flash. But sometimes, as you will discover here, slow beats fast, because you just plain don't want to miss anything. The trip starts by parking at the Linda Mar Beach parking lot, then hiking the beach northward. The northern end of this beach is a great place to throw sticks for dogs, and also to fish for striped bass in the summer time. At the end of the beach, climb up on the dirt trail that traces around Rockaway Point. Here you will find beautiful views of Linda

Mar Bay, San Pedro Point, Montara Mountain, and of course, the Pacific Ocean. You just kind of meander along, listen to the waves, and let the beauty flow through you. Then, when you feel like it, you turn around and walk the same route back to your car. When you first drive up, don't get spooked if the parking lot seems crowded. Why? Because many of the people here often prefer to spend their time philosophizing about life while looking down into the opening of a beer bottle, rather than taking this walk and experiencing the full fabric of it.

## 12. MILAGRA RIDGE    2.0 mi/0.75 hr

*Reference:* **In Pacifica near Skyline College; map E1-San Francisco Peninsula, grid e2.**

*User groups:* Hikers, **wheelchairs** and mountain bikes (allowed on only one mile of paved trail). No dogs or horses are allowed.

*Permits:* No permits are required. Parking and access are free.

*Directions:* From Interstate 280 in San Bruno, take the Westborough exit and drive west up the hill and across Highway 35 (Skyline Boulevard). Continue to College Avenue and turn right. Drive a very short distance to the end of the road and the trailhead. Limited parking is available.

*Maps:* For a free map, contact GGNRA at the address below. To obtain a topographic map of the area, ask for San Francisco South from the USGS.

*Who to contact:* Golden Gate National Recreation Area, Fort Mason, Building 201, San Francisco, CA 94123; (415) 556-8371 or (415) 556-0560.

*Trail notes:* A mile-long, paved road/trail is routed to the top of Milagra Ridge, offering one of the best kite-flying areas imaginable. Those coastal breezes can almost put a strong kite in orbit; some people even use saltwater fishing rods and reels filled with line to fly their kites. They "play" their kite as if it was a big fish. The parking area to gain access to Milagra Ridge is small and obscure (nobody gets here by accident), but once you park your car, the hike to the top of Milagra Ridge is an easy mile and is **wheelchair accessible** with assistance. The summit was flattened here in the 1950s to accommodate a missile site, now abandoned. Looking westward, visitors will be surprised at the sheer dropoff from the ridge down into Pacifica. Alas, in summer this is one of the foggiest places in the world.

## 13. SWEENEY RIDGE    4.4 mi/2.5 hrs

*Reference:* **On the Peninsula ridgeline in San Bruno; map E1-San Francisco Peninsula, grid e2.**

*User groups:* Hikers and dogs. No horses or mountain bikes are allowed. No wheelchair facilities.

*Permits:* No permits are required. Parking and access are free.

*Directions:* From Interstate 280 in San Bruno, take the Westborough exit and drive west up the hill to Highway 35 (Skyline Boulevard). Turn left onto Highway 35 and drive a short distance to College Drive. Turn right onto College Drive and enter the Skyline College campus on the left. Drive to lot #2. The trailhead is located at the southeast corner of the parking lot.

*Maps:* For a free map, contact GGNRA at the address below. To obtain a topographic map of the area, ask for San Francisco South from the USGS.

*Who to contact:* Golden Gate National Recreation Area, Fort Mason, Building

201, San Francisco, CA 94123; (415) 556-8371 or (415) 556-0560.

*Trail notes:* Hikers usually have to pay dearly to get a 360-degree mountain top view, but at Sweeney Ridge, payment is a 2.2-mile hike from the trailhead at Skyline College. This is the Bay Discovery Site, where Captain Portola was the first of the New World explorers to get a glimpse of what is now San Francisco Bay. You can make the same discovery on the steady grade up to the ridge, for most people requiring about an hour's hiking time, more for some. The route traces through coastal scrub and grassland, topping out at 1,200 feet. On clear days, several of the Bay Area's most impressive mountains are in clear view: Mt. Tamalpais, Mt. Diablo, and nearby Montara Mountain. The views of the South Bay on one side and the Pacific Ocean on the other offer another extraordinary perspective. In the spring, when all is in green, look close and you will discover surprising numbers of wildflowers and their tiny blooms.

---

# 14. MONTARA MOUNTAIN/ SAN PEDRO PARK

7.0 mi/2.5 hrs

*Reference:* **In San Pedro County Park in Pacifica; map E1-San Francisco Peninsula, grid e2.**

*User groups:* Hikers only. No dogs, horses or mountain bikes are allowed. No wheelchair facilities.

*Permits:* No permits are required. There is a $3 entrance fee in the spring and summer.

*Directions:* From San Francisco, take Highway 1 south into Pacifica. Turn east on Linda Mar Boulevard and continue until it deadends at Oddstad Boulevard. Turn right and drive to the park entrance, located about 50 yards on the left.

*Maps:* For a free trail map, contact San Pedro County Park at the address below. To obtain a topographic map of the area, ask for Montara Mountain from the USGS.

*Who to contact:* San Pedro County Park, 600 Oddstad Boulevard, Pacifica, CA 94044; (415) 355-8289.

*Trail notes:* Just 20 minutes south of San Francisco is this secluded trail in San Pedro Valley Park, where visitors are few, the coastal beauty is divine, and hikers can carve out their own personal slice of heaven. The Montara Mountain Trail is the best trail in the park, traversing by the best viewing area for Brooks Falls (read on) and reaching great lookouts of the Pacific Coast. After parking, you walk a short way along the trail in San Pedro Valley, then turn right on the well-signed Montara Mountain Trail. From here, the next mile climbs several hundred feet, and suddenly the waterfall appears in a surprising cascade down a canyon. (Beware of a turnoff that is signed "Brooks Falls Overlook." Last time we were there, someone had hand-written the word "not" underneath, and with good reason. The Overlook Trail doesn't take you to the falls any more—it just leads you back to the parking area. To see the falls, stay on the Montara Mountain Trail, always climbing up the mountain.) The falls are connected in three giant tiers, falling 175 feet in all. They are the least known among the most impressive falls in the Bay Area. One reason they are so little known is because they don't flow year-round. As a tributary to San Pedro Creek, Brooks Creek runs only in late winter and spring, best of course after several days of rain. The hike continues all the way to the North Peak of Montara Mountain at 1,930 feet, 3.5 miles one-way, including a final 1.1-mile push on a fire road to reach the summit. On a clear, spring day, the views are absolutely stunning in all directions, highlighted by the Pacific Ocean and Farallon Islands.

*Special note:* This route can provide the first link in one of the few great one-way hikes (with a shuttle) in the Bay Area. From the top of Montara Mountain, you enter McNee State Park and can hike 3.8 miles to Montara State Beach, descending all the way, with glorious views for the entire route. (See hike number 16, Montara Mountain Trail, McNee Ranch State Park.) So with cars parked at each end of the trail, you can hike 7.3 miles one-way from San Pedro Valley Park, up Montara Mountain and down to Montara State Beach.

---

# 15. SAN PEDRO MOUNTAIN    6.0 mi/2.5 hrs

*Reference:* **In McNee Ranch State Park in Montara; map E1-San Francisco Peninsula, grid e1.**

*User groups:* Hikers and dogs. No horses or mountain bikes are allowed. No wheelchair facilities.

*Permits:* No permits are required. Parking and access are free.

*Directions:* From San Francisco, drive south on Highway 1 for about 17 miles. Pass Pacifica and continue up through Devil's Slide and down to the base of the hill. Look for a small pullout area on the left. There is a small yellow gate with a state park property sign; that is the access point. There is only enough room to accommodate two cars, so if the pullout is full continue south on Highway 1 a short distance and park at the lot for Montara State Beach.

*Maps:* To obtain a topographic map of the area, ask for Montara Mountain from the USGS.

*Who to contact:* California State Parks, Bay Area District, 95 Kelly Avenue, Half Moon Bay, CA 94019; (415) 726-8800.

*Trail notes:* This is an ideal trail for people who like dramatic coastal views, with the route tracing on top of coastal bluffs. Many spots along this trail provide flawless perches for vistas. To get them, take note at the entrance gate, and look for the trail off to the left that is routed up through the hilly grasslands. As you make your first few steps, it doesn't look like much of a trail. But as you continue, rising atop the first crest, you will see how the trail tracks up the spine of the coastal ridgeline, eventually providing a lookout above Gray Whale Cove. From this viewpoint, you may sense some irony: Below you is Highway 1, typically filled with a stream of slow-moving cars wanting to get somewhere else; meanwhile, you are in a place of quiet and serenity, where you are happy to be right where you are. The hike includes a few short climbs across grasslands, and can be converted to a loop hike by turning right at the eventual junction with the Montara Mountain Trail.

---

# 16. MONTARA MOUNTAIN/    7.6 mi/3.75 hrs
# McNEE RANCH

*Reference:* **In McNee Ranch State Park in Montara; map E1-San Francisco Peninsula, grid e1.**

*User groups:* Hikers and dogs. No horses or mountain bikes are allowed. No

wheelchair facilities.

*Permits:* No permits are required. Parking and access are free.

*Directions:* From San Francisco, drive south on Highway 1 for about 17 miles. Pass Pacifica and continue up through Devil's Slide and down to the base of the hill. Look for a small pullout area on the left. There is a small yellow gate with a state park property sign; that is the access point. There is only enough room to accommodate two cars, so if the pullout is full continue south on Highway 1 a short distance and park at the lot for Montara State Beach.

*Maps:* To obtain a topographic map of the area, ask for Montara Mountain from the USGS.

*Who to contact:* California State Parks, Bay Area District, 95 Kelly Avenue, Half Moon Bay, CA 94019; (415) 726-8800.

*Trail notes:* On a clear day from the top of Montara Mountain, the Farallon Islands to the northwest look close enough to reach out and pluck right out of the ocean. To the east, it looks like you could take a giant leap across the Bay and land atop Mt. Diablo. Some 10 miles to the north and south is nothing but mountain wilderness connecting Sweeney Ridge to an off-limits state game preserve. By now, you should be properly inspired for the climb, which for many is a genuine gut-wrencher. From the main access gate to the top is 3.8 miles, a rise of nearly 2,000 feet that includes three killer "ups." From the gate, follow the ranch road up the ridgeline of San Pedro Mountain to the Montara Coastal Range, and at the fork, stay to the right on the dirt road as it climbs and turns. After a 20-minute wheezer of a climb, at a flat spot look for a garbage can on the left side of the trail—a 30-yard cutoff here provides a perch for a dazzling view of the Pacific Coast. After catching your breath, continue on, heading up, up and up, eventually topping out at the summit. Only the radio transmitter on top mars an otherwise pristine setting. All you need for this hike is a clear day, some water and plenty of inspiration.

---

# 17. FITZGERALD MARINE RESERVE

1.0 mi/1.0 hr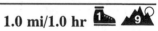

*Reference:* **In Moss Beach; map E1-San Francisco Peninsula, grid f1.**

*User groups:* Hikers only. No dogs, horses or mountain bikes are allowed. No wheelchair facilities.

*Permits:* No permits are required. Parking and access are free.

*Directions:* From San Francisco, take Interstate 280 to Highway 1 in Daly City and continue through Pacifica over Devil's Slide and into Moss Beach. Turn right at the signed turnoff onto California Street. From the Peninsula, take Highway 92 into Half Moon Bay, then head north on Highway 1 for seven miles to Moss Beach. Turn left at the signed turnoff onto California Street.

*Maps:* To obtain a topographic map of the area, ask for Montara Mountain from the USGS.

*Who to contact:* Fitzgerald Marine Reserve, P.O. Box 451, Moss Beach, CA 94038; (415) 728-3584.

*Trail notes:* The closer you look, the better it gets. When you go tidepool hopping, there is nothing more fascinating than discovering the variety of tiny sea life. That is what makes the Fitzgerald Marine Reserve so attractive, a shallow 30-acre reef that provides hundreds and hundreds of tidal pockets every time a minus low tide rolls back the ocean. After parking, it is a short walk down to the tidepools, and from there, you walk on exposed rock, watching the wonders of the tidal waters. Be sure to wear good-gripping boots, and take care not to crush any fragile sea plants as you walk. In the tidepools you will discover hermit crabs, rock crabs, sea anemones, sculpins, starfish, sea snails, and many plants and animals in various colors. An option is to extend your walk south on the beach to the Moss Beach Distillery, a popular watering hole. A few notes: No dogs, no beachcombing, no shell gathering. In other words, OK looky, but no touchy. After all, this is a preserve.

## 18. SAN ANDREAS TRAIL      6.0 mi/2.5 hrs

*Reference:* In San Mateo County foothills south of San Bruno; map E1-San Francisco Peninsula, grid f2.

*User groups:* Hikers and mountain bikes. No dogs or horses are allowed. No wheelchair facilities.

*Permits:* No permits are required. Parking and access are free.

*Directions:* From Interstate 280 in San Bruno, take the Westborough exit and drive west up the hill to the intersection with Highway 35 (Skyline Boulevard). Turn left onto Highway 35 and drive about 2.5 miles to the trailhead entrance on the right. From the south, take Highway 280 to the Millbrae Avenue exit. Head north onto what appears to be a frontage road (Skyline Boulevard) and continue to the parking area on the left.

*Maps:* For a free trail map, contact San Mateo County Parks at the address below. To obtain a topographic map of the area, ask for Montara Mountain from the USGS.

*Who to contact:* San Mateo County Parks, 590 Hamilton Street, Redwood City, CA 94063; (415) 363-4020.

*Trail notes:* The San Andreas Trail overlooks Upper San Andreas Lake, the route winding its way through wooded foothills. Too bad that much of the route is adjacent to Highway 35 (Skyline Boulevard), the only downer. Regardless, it is worth the trip, because to the west are the untouched slopes of Montara Mountain, a game preserve, along with that sparkling lake, both off-limits to the public. The San Andreas Trail starts near the northern end of the lake; a signed trailhead marker is posted on Skyline Boulevard. The trail goes about three miles until the next access point at Hillcrest Boulevard, and from there connects to the Sawyer Camp Trail (see hike number 19). The view of Montara Mountain to the west is particularly enchanting during the summer when rolling fogbanks crest the ridgeline. It's quite a spectacle.

## 19. SAWYER CAMP TRAIL      12.0 mi/5.0 hrs

*Reference:* In San Mateo County foothills south of San Bruno; map E1-San Francisco Peninsula, grid f2.

*User groups:* Hikers and mountain bikes. No dogs or horses are allowed. No wheelchair facilities.

*Permits:* No permits are required. Parking and access are free.

*Directions:* From Interstate 280 in San Bruno, take the Westborough exit and drive west up the hill to the intersection with Highway 35 (Skyline Boulevard). Turn left onto Highway 35 and drive about six miles to the trailhead entrance on the right.

*Maps:* For a free trail map, contact San Mateo County Parks at the address below. To obtain a topographic map of the area, ask for Montara Mountain from the USGS.

*Who to contact:* San Mateo County Parks, 590 Hamilton Street, Redwood City, CA 94063; (415) 363-4020.

*Trail notes:* With the Sawyer Camp Trail you get more of everything that is on the connecting link to the north, the San Andreas Trail. Since the trail is set away from the road, you get more peace. Since it is routed both along a lake and through forest, you get more of nature. But, since much of it is paved, and the route is hardly a secret, you also get more people. In fact, county rangers have had such a problem with speeding bikers on this trail that they often set up radar traps. While the listed one-way mileage is six miles, at any point you can just turn around and go back, cutting the trip as short as you wish. Or better yet, you can bring two vehicles, leaving each one at the two trailheads along Highway 35 (Skyline Boulevard), and make it a one-way trip. From north to south, the hike includes a drop of 400 feet, so if you plan on a return trip, there will be a little huff-and-puff on the way back. A nice touch are park benches set at viewpoints along the lake, where you can often see trout rising and feeding on summer evenings.

---

## 20. COYOTE POINT TRAIL    0.4 mi/0.5 hr

*Reference:* In Coyote Point County Park in San Mateo; map E1-San Francisco Peninsula, grid f3.

*User groups:* Hikers, **wheelchairs** and mountain bikes. No dogs or horses are allowed.

*Permits:* No permits are required. There is a $4 parking fee.

*Directions:* From southbound on US 101, take the Poplar Avenue exit in San Mateo and follow the signs to Coyote Point County Park. From northbound on US 101, take the Dore exit and make an immediate left onto a frontage road, which leads you into the park.

*Maps:* For a free trail map, contact Coyote Point County Park at the address below. To obtain a topographic map of the area, ask for San Mateo from the USGS.

*Who to contact:* Coyote Point County Park, 1701 Coyote Point Drive, San Mateo, CA 94401; (415) 573-2592.

*Trail notes:* It's such a short, flat trail, some hikers may question why they should try it. You'll see on your visit, finding a pretty South Bay lookout, where on a clear day it looks like you could take a running start, jump and glide across the water to the land's edge. You park adjacent to the boat ramp, and from there walk out to land's end at Coyote Point. This is a good fishing area, by the way, for jacksmelt in the spring. From this point, you can scan miles of open water, spotting Mt. Diablo to the east, the San Mateo Bridge to the south, and on clear days, the Bay Bridge to the north. Many are surprised at just how big the South Bay is. An optional sidetrip is to hike north along the bay's shore.

## 21. CRYSTAL SPRINGS TRAIL   6.4 mi/3.0 hrs

*Reference:* **Along Crystal Springs Reservoir in Woodside foothills; map E1-San Francisco Peninsula, grid f3.**

*User groups:* Hikers and mountain bikes. No dogs or horses are allowed. No wheelchair facilities.

*Permits:* No permits are required. Parking and access are free.

*Directions:* From Interstate 280 in San Mateo, take the Highway 92 exit and drive west to Cañada Road/Highway 95. Turn south onto Cañada Road and drive two-tenths of a mile to the parking area on the right side.

*Maps:* For a free trail map, contact San Mateo County Parks at the address below. To obtain a topographic map of the area, ask for San Mateo from the USGS.

*Who to contact:* San Mateo County Parks, 590 Hamilton Street, Redwood City, CA 94063; (415) 363-4020.

*Trail notes:* Crystal Springs is the forbidden paradise of the Bay Area. This trail is as close as the bureaucrats will let you get. Enjoy the view, but don't touch, and don't dare trespass or fish; they'll slam you in the pokey before you know what hit you. After parking, the trail runs on the border of San Francisco watershed land, adjacent to Cañada Road. Beautiful Crystal Springs Reservoir is off to the west, occasionally disappearing behind a hill as you walk south. Deer are commonly seen in this area, a nice bonus. Your destination is the Pulgas Water Temple, a 3.2-mile hike one way, where waters from Hetch Hetchy in Yosemite arrive via canal and thunder into this giant bathtub-like structure, surrounded by Roman pillars and a canopy. At the Pulgas Water Temple, you have the option of continuing for another 4.2 miles to Huddart Park. With a shuttle car, that makes a great one-way hike.

## 22. WATERDOG LAKE TRAIL   4.0 mi/1.75 hrs

*Reference:* **In the Belmont foothills; map E1-San Francisco Peninsula, grid f3.**

*User groups:* Hikers and mountain bikes. No dogs or horses are allowed. No wheelchair facilities.

*Permits:* No permits are required. Parking and access are free.

*Directions:* From Highway 92 in San Mateo, take the Ralston Avenue exit and turn south onto Hallmark Drive. Continue past Benson Way and take the first left and drive 100 feet to the trailhead.

*Maps:* For a trail map contact the City of Belmont Parks at the address below. To obtain a topographic map of the area, ask for San Mateo from the USGS.

*Who to contact:* City of Belmont Parks, 1225 Ralston Avenue, Belmont, CA 94002; (415) 595-7441.

*Trail notes:* The lack of public access to a half-dozen lakes on the Peninsula makes little Waterdog Lake all the more special. Out of the way and often forgotten, the lake was created by damming Belmont Creek in Diablo Canyon, and while not exactly a jewel, it still makes for a unique recreation site. It gets missed because its parking access is so obscure. It takes only 15 minutes to reach the lake, with the trail skirting the northern edge of the lake. Many people stop their walk here, but if you forge on, you will be well compensated. The trail, which is more of a dirt road, rises above the lake and enters John Brooks Memorial Open Space. At the crest of the hill, about a 300-foot climb, there are pretty views of Crystal Springs Reservoir. An option is to extend your trip on the Sheep Camp Trail (a dirt road), which is linked to a gravel road set adjacent to the San Francisco Fish and Game Refuge.

## 23. SAN MATEO PIER      5.0 mi/2.0 hrs

*Reference:* **In South San Francisco Bay in Foster City; map E1-San Francisco Peninsula, grid f4.**

*User groups:* Hikers, **wheelchairs** and mountain bikes. No dogs or horses are allowed.

*Permits:* No permits are required. Parking and access are free.

*Directions:* From US 101 in San Mateo, take the Hillsdale exit east and drive three miles until the road dead ends at the parking lot.

*Maps:* To obtain a topographic map of the area, ask for Redwood Point from the USGS.

*Who to contact:* San Mateo County Parks, 590 Hamilton Street, Redwood City, CA 94063; (415) 363-4020. For detailed information or fishing updates, phone Sun Valley Bait and Tackle at (415) 343-6837.

*Trail notes:* When does a fishing pier make for an excellent hike? When you visit the San Mateo Pier, that's when. This walk provides an unusual adventure, great views, and for people who live nearby, a fresh look at familiar surroundings. This pier used to be the old San Mateo Bridge, but when they built its replacement, they let the old bridge stand from its western footing in Foster City. It extends 2.5 miles into the main channel of the South Bay, and is accessible for free to anyone who wants to visit. Most of the visitors are fishermen who can catch sharks, rays, perch, kingfish, and rarely even sturgeon. Since the pier extends past a mile of tidal flats, there is an abundance of bird life, with dozens of species of seabirds and waterfowl. During minus low tides, the South Bay turns into a weird sight. It becomes miles of mud flats, except for a narrow band of water in its center. By the way, some people call it San Mateo Pier, some call it Foster City Pier, some call it Werder Pier. By any name, it is an unusual hike.

## 24. PILLAR POINT      2.5 mi/1.5 hrs

*Reference:* **In Princeton at Half Moon Bay; map E1-San Francisco Peninsula, grid g1.**

*User groups:* Hikers, dogs and horses (not advised). No mountain bikes are allowed. No wheelchair access.

*Permits:* No permits are required. Parking and access are free.

*Directions:* From the Peninsula, take Interstate 280 south to San Mateo. Turn west on Highway 92 and drive to Half Moon Bay. Turn right onto Highway 1 and drive five miles to Princeton. Turn left at the traffic signal in town, drive about a half mile through Princeton Village and turn left again, going one mile toward a radar station. There is limited parking on the left side of the road. Follow the trail on the west side of the harbor.

*Maps:* To obtain a topographic map of the area, ask for Half Moon Bay from the USGS.

*Who to contact:* There is no managing agency for this area. For general information, phone Huck Finn Sportfishing at (415) 726-7133.

*Trail notes:* This one of the truly great walks along the coast that is overlooked by many visitors and locals alike. It includes a secluded beach with inshore kelp beds and sea lions playing peek-a-boo, and then during low tide, you can walk "around the corner" at Pillar Point and boulder rock-hop your way in wondrous seclusion. Watch your tide book, because the Pillar Point tidal area is under water most of the time. Park at the western side of Princeton Harbor, just below the radar station, then start the trip by walking out along the west side of the harbor. The trail here is on hard-packed dirt above two quiet beaches where grebes, cormorants and pelicans often cavort about. During the evening, the harbor lights are quite pretty here. When you reach the Princeton jetty, turn right and walk along the beach toward Pillar Point; this is where the sea lions often play "Now-you-see-me, now-you-don't." At low tides, continue around Pillar Point and enjoy the rugged beauty, seclusion and ocean views, taking your time as you boulder-hop your way along.

---

## 25. HARKINS FIRE TRAIL 2.0 mi. one way/1.0 hr

*Reference:* **In Purisima Creek Redwoods Open Space Preserve, on Skyline Ridge near San Mateo; map E1-San Francisco Peninsula, grid g2.**

*User groups:* Hikers, horses and mountain bikes. No dogs are allowed. No wheelchair facilities.

*Permits:* No permits are required. Parking and access are free.

*Directions:* From San Francisco, drive south on Interstate 280 for about 15 miles to the Highway 92 cutoff. Head west toward Half Moon Bay, then turn south on Highway 35 (Skyline Boulevard) and drive 4.5 miles to the Whittemore Gulch Trailhead on the right. If you are planning a shuttle trip, drive a second car to Higgins Road Staging Area (see hike number 26).

*Maps:* For a free map, contact the Midpeninsula Regional Open Space District at the address below. A map is also available at the trailhead. To obtain a topographic map of the area, ask for Woodside from the USGS.

*Who to contact:* Midpeninsula Regional Open Space District, 330 Distel Circle, Los Altos, CA 94022; (415) 691-1200.

*Trail notes:* Purisima Creek Redwoods is a magnificent 2,633-acre redwood preserve set on the western slopes of the Santa Cruz Mountains from Skyline Boulevard down to Half Moon Bay. The Harkins Fire Trail is one of the best ways to visit it. Our suggestion is to make it a one-way trip with a shuttle car waiting at trail's end at the Higgins-Purisima parking access. The trail starts at the Whittemore Gulch access on Skyline, elevation 2,000 feet, and descends over 3.2 miles to 400 feet, quite steeply in a series of switchbacks in the last portion of the trail. (To turn this into a loop hike, return via Whittemore Gulch Trail. However, it is a steep, exposed ascent. Rangers have had to provide emergency assistance to unprepared hikers suffering from exhaustion). Before that, however, you are routed through redwoods many people don't realize even exist. For those who want a pristine experience, a good option is to take the Soda Gulch Trail, which junctions after hiking a mile down the Harkins Fire Trail; turn left at the junction. No mountain bikes are allowed on this portion of the trail, which heads past giant trees, redwood sorrel and ferns along creek banks.

## 26. WHITTEMORE GULCH    4.3 mi/3.25 hrs

*Reference:* **In Purisima Creek Redwoods Open Space Preserve, near Half Moon Bay; map E1-San Francisco Peninsula, grid g2.**

*User groups:* Hikers. Horses and mountain bikes are sometimes limited due to wet weather, check with a ranger before your trip. No dogs are allowed. No wheelchair facilities.

*Permits:* No permits are required. Parking and access are free.

*Directions:* From San Francisco, drive south on Interstate 280 for about 15 miles to the Highway 92 cutoff. Head west toward Half Moon Bay. In Half Moon Bay, take Main Street south through town to Higgins Purisima Road. Turn left and drive on the winding road for four miles to the trailhead parking area on the left.

*Maps:* For a free map, contact the Midpeninsula Regional Open Space District at the address below. A map is also available at the trailhead. To obtain a topographic map of the area, ask for Woodside from the USGS.

*Who to contact:* Midpeninsula Regional Open Space District, 330 Distel Circle, Los Altos, CA 94022; (415) 691-1200.

*Trail notes:* Of the three trailheads at Purisima Creek Redwoods, you might expect that this one gets the least use. After all, the elevation is 400 feet, and that means a 1,600-foot climb is required in order to reach Skyline Boulevard, taking any one of three different trails to get there. Well, that's not how it works out. This trailhead is actually quite popular, with most folks making short trips along Purisima Creek and then returning. The Whittemore Gulch Trail, however, offers more of a challenge, especially near the end of the trail. It also offers the return route for a loop hike starting at Skyline Boulevard. The trail starts innocently enough from the Higgins parking area, routed right up Whittemore Gulch, a gentle climb for the first mile. It is even suitable for wheelchairs and strollers. All seems well with the world. Then the bubble pops: In a series of switchbacks, the trail climbs 600 feet in little over a quarter-mile, at about a 10% grade, enough to require the unprepared to stop and let their hearts climb back down out of their throats. After the switchbacks, the trail climbs another 400 feet in a more gracious fashion to reach the Whittemore Gulch Parking Access on Skyline Boulevard. To return, take the Harkins Fire Trail (see hike number 25) back down the grade.

## 27. REDWOOD TRAIL    0.5 mi/0.5 hr

*Reference:* **In Purisima Creek Redwoods Open Space Preserve, on Skyline Ridge near Woodside; map E1-San Francisco Peninsula, grid g2.**

*User groups:* Hikers, **wheelchairs**, horses and mountain bikes. No dogs are allowed.

*Permits:* No permits are required. Parking and access are free.

*Directions:* From San Francisco, drive south on Interstate 280 for about 15 miles to the Highway 92 cutoff. Head west toward Half Moon Bay, then turn south onto Highway 35 (Skyline Boulevard) and drive to the Purisima Creek Parking Area (at mile marker 16.65).

*Maps:* For a free map, contact the Midpeninsula Regional Open Space District at the address below. A map is also available at the trailhead. To obtain a topographic map of the area, ask for Woodside from the USGS.

*Who to contact:* Midpeninsula Regional Open Space District, 330 Distel

Circle, Los Altos, CA 94022; (415) 691-1200.

*Trail notes:* The quarter-mile long Redwood Trail provides an opportunity for anybody to experience the grandeur of redwoods. Anybody? Baby strollers, **wheelchairs,** walkers, or people recovering from poor health can make this walk. It starts at 2,000 feet on Skyline Boulevard and is routed north under a canopy of giant redwoods. At the end of the trail there are picnic tables and a restroom facility available. The return trip is just as easy as the route out. Most people don't really hike this trail, they just kind of mosey along, seeing how it feels to wander and be free among ancient trees.

# 28. HUDDART PARK LOOP HIKE

5.0 mi/3.25 hrs

*Reference:* **In Woodside foothills; map E1-San Francisco Peninsula, grid g3.**

*User groups:* Hikers only. No dogs, horses or mountain bikes are allowed. **Limited wheelchair facilities.**

*Permits:* No permits are required. A $4 entrance fee is charged when the kiosk is attended.

*Directions:* From Interstate 280 in Woodside, take the Woodside Road/ Highway 84 exit and drive west to King's Mountain Road. Turn right and drive two miles to the park entrance.

*Maps:* For a trail map, contact Huddart Park at the address below. To obtain a topographic map of the area, ask for Woodside from the USGS.

*Who to contact:* Huddart Park, 1100 King's Mountain Road, Woodside, CA 94062; (415) 851-1210 or (415) 851-0326. San Mateo County Parks, 590 Hamilton Street, Redwood City, CA 94063; (415) 363-4020.

*Trail notes:* This park is one of the Peninsula's treasures, covering 1,000 acres from the foothills near Woodside on up to Skyline Boulevard. Much of the land is covered by redwoods, a creek runs right through the park, and when you hike high on the east slope, there are occasional views of the South Bay. While there are several short loop trips available here, including the half-mile Redwood Trail, our suggestion is to create a loop hike that circles the park. A map is a necessity, of course. At the Werder Picnic Area, start on the Dean Trail. To make a complete loop, connect to Richard Road's Trail, Summit Springs Trail and Archery Fire Trail, and you will get back to the trailhead. In the process you will get a good overview of the entire park, and discover why this is one of the best hiking parks on the Peninsula. A unique option is taking the Skyline Ridge Trail (see hike number 29) which connects Huddart Park with Wunderlich Park.

*Special note:* The Chickadee Trail at Huddart is **wheelchair-accessible.** Also, horses are allowed on many other trails at Huddart.

# 29. SKYLINE TRAIL

8.0 mi. one way/4.5 hrs

*Reference:* **From Huddart Park to Skylonda, near the Skyline Ridge near Woodside; map E1-San Francisco Peninsula, grid g3.**

*User groups:* Hikers and horses. No dogs or mountain bikes are allowed. No wheelchair facilities.

*Permits:* No permits are required. There is a $4 entrance fee at Huddart Park if the kiosk is attended.

*Directions:* From San Francisco, drive south on Interstate 280 for about 15 miles to the Highway 92 cutoff. Head west toward Half Moon Bay, then turn south on Highway 35 (Skyline Boulevard) and drive 6.5 miles to the trailhead located on the east side of the road. Look for the blue sign marking the Bay Ridge Trail.

*Maps:* For a trail map, contact Huddart Park at the address below. To obtain a topographic map of the area, ask for Woodside from the USGS.

*Who to contact:* Huddart Park, 1100 King's Mountain Road, Woodside, CA 94062; (415) 851-1210 or (415) 851-0326. San Mateo County Parks, 590 Hamilton Street, Redwood City, CA 94063; (415) 363-4020.

*Trail notes:* Great ridgeline views of the South Bay, giant stumps, giant trees and a good, long walk are the highlights of the Skyline Trail. This is the trail that connects Huddart Park with Wunderlich Park, an excellent one-way only walk with a partner. The trip includes a climb of about 700 feet, then a descent of about 1,000 feet, yet for the most part, the route traces right along the Skyline Ridge, amid redwoods and views. It starts at Huddart Park, heading south, and after heading out of the park and crossing Kings Mountain Road, the trail heads up a gradual climb (reconstructed to avoid a steep grade) to the Skyline Ridge, then turns south again. While Skyline Boulevard/Highway 35 is nearby, there are few reminders of that, with the trail routed so it traces ridges and laterals above canyons. Some of the old stumps in this area are huge, and when you start spotting them, look close for the Methuselah Tree. It is the centerpiece of the forest, a surviving colossus that is 15 feet in diameter. When you enter Wunderlich Park, the trail descends sharply in a series of switchbacks, then turns sharply for the last half mile to Skylonda.

---

# 30. MEADOWS LOOP TRAIL     5.5 mi/3.0 hrs

*Reference:* **In Wunderlich Park in the Woodside foothills; map E1-San Francisco Peninsula, grid g3.**

*User groups:* Hikers and horses. No dogs or mountain bikes are allowed. No wheelchair facilities.

*Permits:* No permits are required. Parking and access are free.

*Directions:* From Interstate 280 on the Peninsula in Woodside, take the Woodside/Highway 84 exit. Drive west for 2.5 miles to the park on the right.

*Maps:* For a free map, contact San Mateo County Parks at the address below. To obtain a topographic map of the area, ask for Woodside from the USGS.

*Who to contact:* Contact Wunderlich Park at (415) 851-1210 or (415) 851-7570. San Mateo County Parks, 590 Hamilton Street, Redwood City, CA 94063; (415) 363-4020.

*Trail notes:* Wunderlich Park is one of the best spots on the Peninsula for clearing out the brain cobwebs. The network of trails provide a variety of adventures from short strolls to all-day treks. Take your pick. Ours is the Meadows Loop, which circles much of the park, crossing first through oak woodlands, rising to open grasslands, then past a redwood forest on the way back. This hike includes an elevation gain of nearly a thousand feet, so come ready for it. Make sure you have a trail map, then take this route: Near the park office, look for the signed trailhead, "Alambique Trail," and hike about a half mile. At the junction with the Meadow Trail, turn right, hike a short distance, then turn left on the Meadow Trail and climb up to "The Meadows." This is a perfect picnic site, with rolling hills, grasslands and great views. To complete the loop, forge onward, then turn right at Bear Gulch Trail and take it all the way back, including the switchbacks, to the park entrance.

---

# 31. RAVENSWOOD OPEN SPACE PRESERVE

2.0 mi/0.75 hr

*Reference:* **On the shore of South San Francisco Bay at Ravenswood; map E1-San Francisco Peninsula, grid g5.**

*User groups:* Hikers, mountain bikes and **wheelchairs.** No dogs or horses are allowed.

*Permits:* No permits are required. Parking and access are free.

*Directions:* From US 101 near Palo Alto, take the Willow Road exit (Highway 84) northeast to Newbridge Street. Newbridge becomes Bay Road. Follow Bay Road east to the parking area at its end.

*Maps:* For a free map, contact the Midpeninsula Regional Open Space District at the address below. To obtain a topographic map of the area, ask for Mountain View from the USGS.

*Who to contact:* Midpeninsula Regional Open Space District, 330 Distel Circle, Los Altos, CA 94022; (415) 691-1200.

*Trail notes:* This is a 370-acre parcel rich in marshland habitat, home for a large variety of birds. The first trails became accessible in 1992, along with two excellent observation decks. From the parking area at the end of Bay Road, backtrack by walking across a bridged slough to the trailhead; look for it on the north side of the road. You will immediately come to a fork in the road. You can turn right and walk about 200 feet to an observation deck, with great views of the South Bay and tidal salt marshes. If you go left instead, you will find a hard-surface path that heads north and hooks out toward the Bay to another wood observation deck. This is the primary destination for most visitors.

---

# 32. BAYLANDS CATWALK

0.25 mi/0.5 hr

*Reference:* **On shore of South San Francisco Bay in Palo Alto; map E1-San Francisco Peninsula, grid g5.**

*User groups:* Hikers only. No dogs, horses or mountain bikes are allowed. No wheelchair facilities.

*Permits:* No permits are required. Parking and access are free.

*Directions:* From US 101 in Palo Alto, take the Embarcadero exit east. Drive toward the Bay, jogging left past the airport. Continue past the Yacht Harbor until you reach a sharp right turn. Park at the lot on the right. The nature preserve is on the left.

*Maps:* To obtain a topographic map of the area, ask for Mountain View from the USGS.

*Who to contact:* Palo Alto Baylands Interpretive Center, 1451 Middlefield Road, Palo Alto, CA 94301; (415) 329-2261 or (415) 329-2506.

*Trail notes:* You say, what the heck is the Baylands Catwalk? What it is, you will discover, is an old wooden walkway across tidal marshland that is routed under a series of giant electrical towers. In recent years, the Catwalk has been improved, now with an observation deck set on the edge of South Bay waters.

You start your walk here at the Baylands Interpretive Center, which provides explanatory exhibits of the marshland habitat. From there, you can make the short walk straight east out to the observation deck, about a 10-minute trip. The marsh has an abundant population of birdlife, especially egrets, coots and ducks.

*Special note:* The Catwalk extends north and south across the marsh for a mile, and while this was once a great, easy walk, access is now forbidden and is blocked by a barbed-wire-edged gate.

---

## 33. BAYLANDS TRAIL     4.0 mi/1.5 hrs

*Reference:* **On shore of South San Francisco Bay in Palo Alto; map E1-San Francisco Peninsula, grid g5.**

*User groups:* Hikers, **wheelchairs** and mountain bikes. No dogs or horses are allowed.

*Permits:* No permits are required. Parking and access are free.

*Directions:* From US 101 in Palo Alto, take the Embarcadero East exit. At the second light, across from Ming's Restaurant, turn left onto Geng Street and drive to the end of the road. The trailhead is right behind the grandstand of the Baylands Baseball Park.

*Maps:* To obtain a topographic map of the area, ask for Mountain View the USGS.

*Who to contact:* Palo Alto Baylands Interpretive Center, 1451 Middlefield Road, Palo Alto, CA 94301; (415) 329-2261 or (415) 329-2506.

*Trail notes:* The farther you go, the better it gets. That's how it is on this trail. The Baylands Trail starts without much fanfare, a simple hard-gravel road with an ugly slough on your left, and the Palo Alto golf course on your right. If you keep your eyes looking ahead, often you will see ground squirrels scurrying about, along with an occasional jackrabbit. The trail then reaches a fork. Bikers should turn left, taking the outstanding Baylands bike trail that extends all the way to the Dumbarton Bridge, which has a bike lane, and across the Bay to Fremont. Hikers are better off turning right. Here the trail softens, and the slough becomes the tidal waters of San Francisquito Creek. The pathway continues along and past the golf course, then crosses the departure runway for the Palo Alto Airport, and leads out to land's end where the creek pours into the Bay. This is a classic salt marsh habitat, with lots of birds and wildlife. The views are pretty, the walk is as flat as it gets, and there are always sightings of squirrels, rabbits, egrets, coots or ducks.

---

## 34. SOUTH BAY NATURE TRAIL 2.0 mi/1.0 hr

*Reference:* **In San Francisco Bay Wildlife Refuge near Alviso; map E1-San Francisco Peninsula, grid g5.**

*User groups:* Hikers and mountain bikes. No dogs or horses are allowed. No wheelchair facilities.

*Permits:* No permits are required. Parking and access are free.

*Directions:* From US 101 near Sunnyvale, take Highway 237 east to Zanker Street. Turn left and continue to the parking area at the Environmental Education Center.

*Maps:* To obtain a topographic map of the area, ask for Mountain View the USGS.

***Who to contact:*** San Francisco Bay National Wildlife Refuge, P.O. Box 524, Newark, CA 94560; (510) 792-4275 or (510) 792-0222. Environmental Education Center, (408) 262-2867.

***Trail notes:*** Everybody knows about the San Francisco Bay Wildlife Refuge, right? That's the big nature center located at the eastern foot of the Dumbarton Bridge, right? Very popular, right? Wrong, wrong and wrong. A little-known portion of the San Francisco Bay Wildlife Refuge is set deep in the South Bay marsh near Alviso, and it gets little attention compared to its big brother to the north. Headquarters are at the Environmental Education Center, and from there, you walk on a dirt path set along wild tidal marshland. As you walk northward, you will delve into wilder and wilder habitat, and in the process have a chance to see a dozen species of birds in a matter of minutes. The endangered harvest salt mouse lives in this habitat. Guided nature walks are held regularly on weekend mornings, well worth attending.

NOR-CAL MAP ........................ see page 14
adjoining maps
NORTH (D1) ........................... see page 202
EAST (E2) ............................... see page 394
SOUTH (F1) ............................. see page 468
WEST ....................................... no map

**194 TRAILS**
**PAGES 258-393**

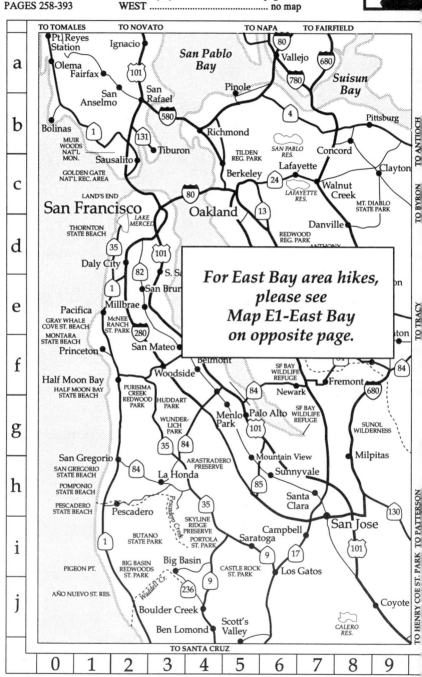

*For East Bay area hikes, please see Map E1-East Bay on opposite page.*

# MAP E1-EAST BAY

44 TRAILS
PAGES 328-357

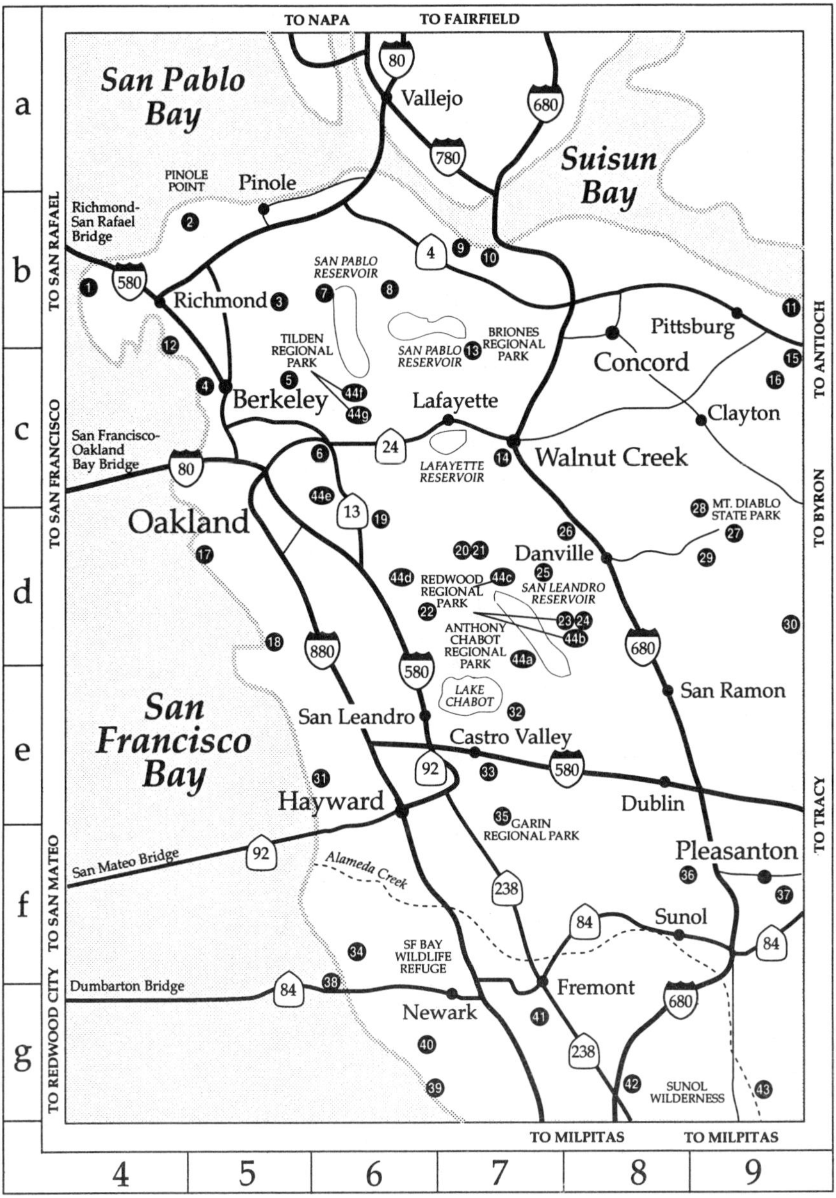
TO NAPA
TO FAIRFIELD
a
b
c
d
e
f
g
4
5
6
7
8
9
TO SAN RAFAEL
TO SAN FRANCISCO
TO SAN MATEO
TO REDWOOD CITY
TO ANTIOCH
TO BYRON
TO TRACY
TO MILPITAS
TO MILPITAS
San Pablo Bay
80
Vallejo
680
780
Suisun Bay
PINOLE POINT
Pinole
Richmond-San Rafael Bridge
2
4
9
10
SAN PABLO RESERVOIR
1
580
Richmond
3
7
8
11
Pittsburg
TILDEN REGIONAL PARK
SAN PABLO RESERVOIR
13
BRIONES REGIONAL PARK
12
Concord
15
16
5
4
Berkeley
44f
44g
Lafayette
Clayton
San Francisco-Oakland Bay Bridge
80
24
6
14
Walnut Creek
LAFAYETTE RESERVOIR
44e
13
19
28
MT. DIABLO STATE PARK
27
Oakland
26
17
20
21
Danville
29
44d
REDWOOD REGIONAL PARK
44c
25
SAN LEANDRO RESERVOIR
22
23
24
44b
30
ANTHONY CHABOT REGIONAL PARK
44a
18
880
580
680
San Ramon
LAKE CHABOT
San Leandro
32
San Francisco Bay
Castro Valley
92
580
33
31
Hayward
Dublin
35
GARIN REGIONAL PARK
92
San Mateo Bridge
Pleasanton
Alameda Creek
238
36
37
84
Sunol
84
34
SF BAY WILDLIFE REFUGE
Dumbarton Bridge
84
38
Fremont
680
Newark
41
40
238
42
39
SUNOL WILDERNESS
43

**Map E1-East Bay featuring:** Vallejo Pier, Napa River, Point Pinole, Wildcat Canyon Regional Park, Tilden Regional Park, Inspiration Point, Robert Sibley Volcanic Regional Preserve, San Pablo Reservoir, Sobrante Regional Preserve, Carquinez Strait, Briones Regional Park, San Leandro Reservoir, Contra Loma Regional Park, Crown Memorial State Beach, Huckleberry Regional Preserve, Redwood Regional Park, Anthony Chabot Regional Park, Las Trampas Regional Wilderness, Mt. Diablo State Park, Diablo Foothills Regional Park, Morgan Territory Regional Park, Coyote Hills Regional Park, Pleasanton Ridge Regional Park, Dumbarton Bridge, San Francisco Bay National Wildlife Refuge, Alameda Creek, Mission Peak Regional Preserve, Sunol Regional Wilderness

## 1. FALSE GUN VISTA POINT     1.0 mi/0.75 hr

*Reference:* **In Miller-Knox Regional Shoreline west of Richmond on the shore of San Francisco Bay; map E1-East Bay, grid b4.**

*User groups:* Hikers and dogs. No horses or mountain bikes are allowed. No wheelchair facilities.

*Permits:* No permits are required. Parking and access are free.

*Directions:* From Interstate 80 southbound in Richmond, take the Cutting Boulevard exit west to Garrard Boulevard. Turn left and drive through the tunnel. The road becomes Dornan Drive; follow Dornan for a half mile to the parking area on the right. From northbound on Interstate 80 in Albany, bear left on Interstate 580 west and take the Cutting Boulevard exit. Turn left on Cutting and proceed as above.

*Maps:* For a free trail map, contact East Bay Regional Parks at the address below and ask for the Miller-Knox Regional Shoreline brochure. To obtain a topographic map of the area, ask for San Quentin from the USGS.

*Who to contact:* East Bay Regional Park District, 2950 Peralta Oaks Court, P.O. Box 5381, Oakland, CA 94605; (510) 635-0135, ext. 2200.

*Trail notes:* A little-known lookout of San Francisco Bay is the highlight of Miller-Knox Regional Shoreline, requiring only a short hike and climb. This parkland covers 260 acres of hill and shoreline property at Point Richmond, and strong afternoon winds in the summer make it an excellent area for kite flying. While most people make the short stroll along Keller Beach, we prefer this hike. From the parking area, it is about a half-mile up Old Country Road and Marine View Trail, with a right turn on the Crest Trail to reach False Gun Vista Point, in the process climbing 300 feet to the lookout (322 feet). On clear days, you get picture-perfect views of San Francisco Bay and its many surrounding landmarks.

## 2. BAY VIEW LOOP          3.0 mi/1.5 hrs

*Reference:* In Point Pinole Regional Shoreline; map E1-East Bay, grid b5.

*User groups:* Hikers, dogs, horses and mountain bikes. The trail is **partially wheelchair accessible.**

*Permits:* No permits are required. A $3 parking fee is charged on weekends only. The shuttle bus ride costs $1 for ages 12 through 61 and 50 cents for seniors or youngsters 6 through 11. Children under six and disabled people ride free.

*Directions:* From Interstate 80 in San Pablo, take the Hilltop exit. Drive west on Hilltop to the intersection with San Pablo Avenue. Turn right on San Pablo Avenue and proceed north for a short distance, then turn left on Richmond Parkway. Proceed a few miles to Giant Highway. Turn right and drive a short distance to the park entrance on your left. It is well-signed. Take the shuttle bus to the Bay.

*Maps:* For a free trail map, contact East Bay Regional Park District at the address below and ask for the Point Pinole Regional Shoreline brochure. To obtain a topographic map of the area, ask for Richmond from the USGS.

*Who to contact:* East Bay Regional Park District, 2950 Peralta Oaks Court, P.O. Box 5381, Oakland, CA 94605; (510) 635-0135, ext. 2200. You may also phone Point Pinole Regional Shoreline directly at (510) 237-6896.

*Trail notes:* On the Bay View Loop, you can walk several miles along the shore of San Pablo Bay without seeing anything but water, passing ships and birds. The reason is because at Point Pinole, cars must stop and park at the entrance station and then you take a shuttle bus to the shoreline. There you will find a nice, long cobble beach, and beautiful views of San Pablo Bay, Marin and Mt. Tamalpais. An excellent fishing pier is also available. The park covers 2,147 acres, and the Bay View Trail is a great loop hike to explore it. From the parking area, it is routed along the shore to Point Pinole, and then back on Woods Trail, which runs through a large grove of eucalyptus.

## 3. SAN PABLO RIDGE LOOP     6.2 mi/3.0 hrs

*Reference:* In Wildcat Canyon Regional Park in the Richmond foothills; map E1-East Bay, grid b5.

*User groups:* Hikers, dogs, horses and mountain bikes. No wheelchair facilities.

*Permits:* No permits are required. Parking and access are free.

*Directions:* From Interstate 80 northbound in Richmond, take the Amador/ Solano exit and drive three blocks on Amador. Turn right on McBryde Avenue and head east. After passing Arlington Boulevard continue straight (the road is now Park Avenue) and bear left through a piped gate to the parking area.

*Maps:* For a free trail map, contact East Bay Regional Parks at the address below and ask for the Wildcat Regional Park brochure. To obtain a topographic map of the area, ask for Richmond from the USGS.

*Who to contact:* East Bay Regional Park District, 2950 Peralta Oaks Court, P.O. Box 5381, Oakland, CA 94605; (510) 635-0135, ext. 2200. You may also phone the Tilden Nature Area at (510) 525-2233.

*Trail notes:* For newcomers to Wildcat Park, it can be hard to believe how quickly you can get to a remote land with great views. But here it is. San

Pablo Ridge rises about a thousand feet high east of Richmond, and it takes a short grunt of a hike to get to the top, but it is well worth the grunting. That is because you get great views off one side of the ridge of San Pablo Reservoir and Briones Lake, and off the other side of San Francisco Bay. Of all the views of San Francisco, this is certainly one of the best. Start at the parking area and hike up the Belgum Trail, turning right at San Pablo Ridge, climbing about 700 feet over the course of 2.5 miles. Once on top, slow down and enjoy the cruise. To return on a loop, turn right on the Mezue Trail, and right again on the Wildcat Creek Trail back to the parking area. The latter traces alongside the prettiest segments of Wildcat Creek.

## 4. BERKELEY PIER　　　　1.2 mi/0.75 hr

*Reference:* **Near Berkeley on the shore of San Francisco Bay; map E1-East Bay, grid b5.**

*User groups:* Hikers and **wheelchairs**. No dogs, horses or mountain bikes are allowed.

*Permits:* No permits are required. Parking and access are free.

*Directions:* From Interstate 80 in Berkeley, take the University Avenue exit and follow the signs to the Berkeley Marina. The pier is at the foot of University Avenue, just past the bait shop and marina.

*Maps:* To obtain a topographic map of the area, ask for Oakland West from the USGS.

*Who to contact:* Berkeley Marina, 201 University Avenue, Berkeley, CA 94701; (510) 644-6376.

*Trail notes:* This historic structure extends 3,000 feet into San Francisco Bay amidst landmarks that people come from around the world to see. It is an easy walk—straight, flat and long—and while most people can make it out to the end of the pier in 20 minutes, there is no reason to hurry. The Golden Gate Bridge is a classic sight from the end of the pier, especially during sunsets, when you will discover why the Gate is so appropriately named. Things look different out here, especially if you bring a loaf of French bread to nibble on and maybe a little of your favorite elixir to wash it down. Fishing success always varies, but the best time is in the early summer, when halibut school on the Berkeley Flats.

## 5. NIMITZ WAY　　　　10.0 mi/4.25 hrs

*Reference:* **In Tilden Regional Park at Inspiration Point in the Berkeley hills; map E1-East Bay, grid c5.**

*User groups:* Hikers, dogs, horses and mountain bikes. The trail is **partially wheelchair accessible**.

*Permits:* No permits are required. Parking and access are free.

*Directions:* From Highway 24 in the East Bay, proceed to just east of the Caldecott Tunnel and take the Fish Ranch Road exit west to Grizzly Peak Boulevard. Turn right, continue up the hill, and turn right again onto South Park Drive. Proceed one mile to Wildcat Canyon Road, bear right and continue to the parking area at Inspiration Point on the left. South Park Drive is sometimes closed in the winter due to newt migrations. An alternate route from Highway 24 is to go through the Caldecott Tunnel and exit at Orinda. Turn left on Camino Pablo. Drive north for about two miles, then turn left on Wildcat Canyon Road. Follow it to Inspiration Point on the right.

*Maps:* For a free trail map, contact East Bay Regional Parks at the address below and ask for the Tilden Regional Park brochure. To obtain a topographic map of the area, ask for Briones Valley from the USGS.

*Who to contact:* East Bay Regional Park District, 2950 Peralta Oaks Court, P.O. Box 5381, Oakland, CA 94605; (510) 635-0135, ext. 2200. You may also phone the Tilden Nature Area at (510) 525-2233.

*Trail notes:* When you first start this trail, you might wonder why we rated it so high. The views? Sure, they're great, sweeping vistas of the East Bay foothills, but hey, the trail is paved, more appropriate for bikes, wheelchairs and joggers than hikers. And so it is for the first four miles of trail, but then suddenly, you will enter a different universe. You pass a gate, the trail turns to dirt, and just like that no one is around as you climb San Pablo Ridge. The views are stunning in all directions, particularly to the east of Briones and San Pablo lakes, and to the west of San Francisco Bay and the city's skyline. Your goal should be to climb at least to Wildcat Peak, elevation 1,250 feet and two miles out, before you turn around and head for home. This is one of the best pieces of the 31-mile East Bay Skyline National Recreation Trail.

---

# 6. ROUND TOP LOOP TRAIL    1.7 mi/1.0 hr

*Reference:* **In Robert Sibley Volcanic Regional Preserve in the Berkeley hills; map E1-East Bay, grid c6.**

*User groups:* Hikers and dogs. The trail is partially accessible to **wheelchairs**, horses and mountain bikes.

*Permits:* No permits are required. Parking and access are free.

*Directions:* From Highway 24 in the East Bay, proceed to just east of the Caldecott Tunnel and take the Fish Ranch Road exit west to Grizzly Peak Boulevard. Turn left and continue to Skyline Boulevard. Then continue straight ahead for another quarter mile to the park entrance and parking area on the left.

*Maps:* For a free trail map, contact East Bay Regional Parks at the address below and ask for the Sibley Volcanic Regional Preserve brochure. To obtain a topographic map of the area, ask for Briones Valley from the USGS.

*Who to contact:* East Bay Regional Park District, 2950 Peralta Oaks Court, P.O. Box 5381, Oakland, CA 94605; (510) 635-0135, ext. 2200.

*Trail notes:* The remains of the Bay Area's long-extinct volcano, Mount Round Top, can be explored at Sibley Preserve. What you actually see is exposed volcanic rock, with your trip assisted by a self-guided tour using a pamphlet available at the trailhead. After the volcano blasted out its lava contents about nine million years ago, the interior of the mountain collapsed into the void left by the outburst, with blocks of volcanic stone scattered everywhere around the flanks of the mountain. A gated road leads to the top, elevation 1,763 feet, but the mountain is best visited on the Round Top Loop Trail. Hike this trail in a clockwise direction so the numbered posts (1 through 9) on the self-guided tour correspond in order with the most interesting volcanic outcrops.

# 7. LAUREL LOOP TRAIL     0.7 mi/0.5 hr

*Reference:* **In Kennedy Grove Regional Park near San Pablo Reservoir in El Sobrante; map E1-East Bay, grid b6.**

*User groups:* Hikers, dogs, horses and mountain bikes. No wheelchair facilities.

*Permits:* No permits are required. There is a $3 parking fee when the kiosk is attended.

*Directions:* From Interstate 80 in Richmond, take the San Pablo Dam Road exit. Turn east and drive through El Sobrante for 3.5 miles to the park entrance on the left. From the entrance, follow the pavement to the northwestern parking lot.

*Maps:* For a free trail map, contact East Bay Regional Parks at the address below. Specify the Kennedy Grove Regional Recreation Area brochure. To obtain a topographic map of the area, ask for Richmond from the USGS.

*Who to contact:* East Bay Regional Park District, 2950 Peralta Oaks Court, P.O. Box 5381, Oakland, CA 94605; (510) 635-0135, ext. 2200. You may also phone the park directly at (510) 223-7840.

*Trail notes:* Kennedy Grove is set at the base of San Pablo Dam where visitors will discover a rich grove of eucalyptus located adjacent to a large lawn/meadow. This loop hike takes hikers through the eucalyptus and then back, skirting the lawn areas. It is best hiked in a clockwise fashion, departing from the trailhead located at the gate at the northeast corner of the parking area. This is the kind of park where people toss frisbees, pass a football, or play a low-key softball game. Hiking is just a side event.

# 8. SOBRANTE RIDGE TRAIL     1.6 mi/1.0 hr

*Reference:* **In Sobrante Ridge Regional Preserve near El Sobrante; map E1-East Bay, grid b6.**

*User groups:* Hikers, dogs, horses and mountain bikes. No wheelchair facilities.

*Permits:* No permits are required. Parking and access are free.

*Directions:* From Interstate 80 in Richmond, take the San Pablo Dam Road exit. Drive east for three miles and turn left on Castro Ranch Road. Drive about one mile until you reach Conestoga Way, then turn left and drive to Carriage Drive. Turn left again, and drive two blocks to Coach Way. Turn right and continue to the park entrance and parking area at the end of the road.

*Maps:* For a free trail map, contact East Bay Regional Parks at the address below and ask for the Sobrante Ridge Regional Preserve brochure. To obtain a topographic map of the area, ask for Briones Valley from the USGS.

*Who to contact:* East Bay Regional Park District, 2950 Peralta Oaks Court, P.O. Box 5381, Oakland, CA 94605; (510) 635-0135, ext. 2200. You may also phone the park directly at (510) 223-7840.

*Trail notes:* Sobrante Ridge Park was the missing link to an East Bay corridor of open space, finally acquired in the mid 1980s. It is wild and scenic, and now protected, assured to remain that way forever. The park covers 277 acres of rolling hills, open ridgeline, and wooded ravines, and this hike provides the best of it. From the trailhead at Coach Drive, take the Sobrante Ridge Trail, which rises in an elliptical half-loop to the left. After seven-tenths of a mile, you will come to the junction of Broken Oaks Trail. Turn left here, and make the short loop (less than a quarter-mile long), then retrace your steps on the Sobrante Ridge Trail. This trail provides an easy yet intimate look at one of the Bay Area's newest parklands.

## 9. FRANKLIN RIDGE LOOP TRAIL
3.1 mi/1.75 hrs

*Reference:* **In Carquinez Strait Regional Shoreline near Martinez; map E1-East Bay, grid b7.**

*User groups:* Hikers, dogs, horses and mountain bikes. No wheelchair facilities.

*Permits:* No permits are required. Parking and access are free.

*Directions:* From Highway 4 in Martinez, take the Alhambra Avenue exit and drive north for two miles toward the Carquinez Strait. Turn left on Escobar Street, drive three blocks and then turn right on Talbart Street. Talbart Street becomes Carquinez Scenic Drive. Follow that for about a half mile to the parking area on the left.

*Maps:* For a free trail map, contact East Bay Regional Parks at the address below and ask for the Carquinez Strait Regional Shoreline brochure. To obtain a topographic map of the area, ask for Benicia from the USGS.

*Who to contact:* East Bay Regional Park District, 2950 Peralta Oaks Court, P.O. Box 5381, Oakland, CA 94605; (510) 635-0135, ext. 2200.

*Trail notes:* This parkland is the gateway to the San Joaquin Delta, set on the hillsides overlooking Martinez. The Franklin Ridge Loop Trail is the best way to see it, rising to 750 feet. From the ridge, there are good views of Mt. Tamalpais on one side, and on the other, Mt. Diablo. From the parking area at the Carquinez Strait East Staging Area, the hike heads south on the California Riding and Hiking Trail toward Franklin Ridge, climbing as it goes, at times quite steeply, then connects to the Franklin Ridge Loop. When you reach the loop, note that this trail is best hiked in a clockwise direction. Most of the park is open, rolling grasslands, but there are some groves of eucalyptus and a few wooded ravines.

## 10. MARTINEZ SHORELINE
2.2 mi/1.0 hr

*Reference:* **In Martinez Regional Shoreline near Martinez; map E1-East Bay, grid b7.**

*User groups:* Hikers, dogs, horses and mountain bikes. The restrooms are wheelchair-accessible, but the trail is not.

*Permits:* No permits are required. Parking and access are free.

*Directions:* From Highway 4 in Martinez, take the Alhambra Avenue exit. Drive north on Alhambra for two miles to Escobar Street and turn right. Continue on Escobar Street for three blocks to Ferry Street and turn left. Drive across the railroad tracks and bear right onto Joe DiMaggio Drive. Turn left on North Coast Street and drive to the parking area next to the fishing pier.

*Maps:* For a free trail map, contact East Bay Regional Parks at the address below and ask for the Martinez Regional Shoreline brochure. To obtain a topographic map of the area, ask for Benicia from the USGS.

*Who to contact:* East Bay Regional Park District, 2950 Peralta Oaks Court, P.O. Box 5381, Oakland, CA 94605; (510) 635-0135, ext. 2200.

*Trail notes:* The Shoreline Trail is the most attractive walk at Martinez

Waterfront Park, a 343-acre parcel that includes marshlands and bay frontage. Start your hike from the parking area located at the foot of the Martinez Fishing Pier, and walk back on North Court Street to the trailhead at Sand Beach. The hike skirts a pond, crosses Arch Bridge (over Alhambra Creek) and runs along the waterfront, past an old schooner hull, to the park's western boundary. It is easy and flat, with the bay on one side, marshlands on the other. It is popular for bicycling, jogging and birdwatching. An option is walking out to the Martinez Pier, a short walk from the parking lot, one of the few piers anywhere where steelhead are caught in the winter in the Bay Area.

## 11. ANTIOCH PIER      0.5 mi/0.5 hr

*Reference:* In Antioch Regional Shoreline near Antioch; map E1-East Bay, grid b9.

*User groups:* Hikers, **wheelchairs**, dogs and bicycles. No horses are allowed.

*Permits:* No permits are required. Parking and access are free.

*Directions:* From Highway 4 in Antioch, take the Wilbur Street exit and turn right on Wilbur. Make an immediate left on Bridgehead Road and continue to the parking area at the end of the road.

*Maps:* For a free trail map, contact East Bay Regional Parks at the address below and ask for the Antioch Regional Shoreline brochure. To obtain a topographic map of the area, ask for Antioch North from the USGS.

*Who to contact:* East Bay Regional Park District, 2950 Peralta Oaks Court, P.O. Box 5381, Oakland, CA 94605; (510) 635-0135, ext. 2200.

*Trail notes:* This is a short but scenic walk along a marshlands and out to the end of a 550-foot fishing pier, one of the best fishing piers in the Bay Area. The parkland encompasses only 7.5 acres, but it is set along the lower San Joaquin River, just upstream from the Antioch Bridge. From the parking lot, the trail is 0.14 miles to the foot of the pier, with a gated, **wheelchair accessible** road on your right and wetlands on your left. The pier extends into the San Joaquin River, right into the pathway of migrating striped bass, sturgeon, and at other times, catfish and even salmon. At the end of the pier, if you catch no fish, you will still catch views of the Antioch Bridge and San Joaquin River at its widest point.

## 12. POINT ISABEL SHORELINE 1.0 mi/0.75 hr

*Reference:* In Point Isabel Regional Shoreline near Berkeley; map E1-East Bay, grid c4.

*User groups:* Hikers and dogs. No horses or mountain bikes are allowed. The restrooms are wheelchair-accessible, but the trail is not.

*Permits:* No permits are required. Parking and access are free.

*Directions:* From Interstate 80 in south Richmond, take the Central Avenue exit and drive west to Isabel Street. Turn right onto Isabel Street and drive to the parking area at the end of the street.

*Maps:* For a free trail map, contact East Bay Regional Parks at the address below and ask for the Point Isabel Regional Shoreline brochure. To obtain a topographic map of the area, ask for Richmond from the USGS.

*Who to contact:* East Bay Regional Park District, 2950 Peralta Oaks Court, P.O. Box 5381, Oakland, CA 94605; (510) 635-0135, ext. 2200.

Foghorn Press
555 De Haro Street, Suite 220
San Francisco, CA 94107

# Get a free copy of Adventure West just for speaking your mind!

Please help us provide you with the best possible books on the outdoors by filling out this card. To thank you for your effort, we'll send you a complimentary issue of **Adventure West Magazine**, America's award-winning guide to fun and discovery in the 13 Western states, plus western Canada and western Mexico.

Name: _____

Address: _____

Phone: ( )

City: _____ State: _____ Zip: _____

Which book did you purchase/receive? _____

Where did you purchase your book? _____

Where did you hear about this book? _____

What other outdoors subjects would you like to see in a book? _____

Comments welcome: _____

## Outdoor and Recreation books from
### For more information call 1-800-FOGHORN

Foghorn Press

BOOKS BUILDING COMMUNITY.

*Trail notes:* Beautiful bayfront views of San Francisco and the Golden Gate attract visitors to the Point Isabel Regional Shoreline. It is located on a shoreline point that extends into San Francisco Bay just north of Golden Gate Fields Racetrack. Here is a 21-acre park that provides an easy shoreline walk, rich birdwatching opportunities and those great views. From the parking area, the trail extends northward along the Bay's shoreline, then east along Hoffman Channel, and ends with a short loop trail along the edge of Hoffman Marsh. The best time to see birds here is in the fall, when year-round residents are joined by migratory species.

---

## 13. BRIONES CREST LOOP    5.6 mi/3.25 hrs

*Reference:* In Briones Regional Park north of Lafayette; map E1-East Bay, grid c7.

*User groups:* Hikers, dogs and horses. Mountain bikes are allowed on all but the last mile of the loop. No wheelchair facilities.

*Permits:* No permits are required. There is a $3 parking fee when the kiosk is attended.

*Directions:* From Interstate 680 north of Pleasant Hill, take Highway 4 west for three miles to the Alhambra Avenue exit. Turn south on Alhambra, drive for a half mile and bear right onto Alhambra Valley Road. Continue for another mile to Reliez Valley Road. Turn left and follow Reliez Valley Road a half mile to the parking area on the right. Look for the trailhead indicating the Alhambra Creek Trail.

*Maps:* For a free trail map, contact East Bay Regional Parks at the address below and ask for the Briones Regional Park brochure. To obtain a topographic map of the area, ask for Briones Valley from the USGS.

*Who to contact:* East Bay Regional Park District, 2950 Peralta Oaks Court, P.O. Box 5381, Oakland, CA 94605; (510) 635-0135, ext. 2200.

*Trail notes:* Briones Regional Park is a 5,700-acre sanctuary of peace set amid several fast-growing East Bay communities. It is one of the best parks for hiking in the East Bay, and this hike is the best of an intricate network of trails in the park. This loop has many trail junctions, and to keep from making a wrong turn, a map is a necessity, of course. From the trailhead, take the Alhambra Creek Trail and Spengler Trail (turn right) to the Briones Crest Trail and turn left. This stretch of trail rises to Briones Peak at 1,483 feet in just 2.5 miles. It is the highest point in the park and grants a panoramic view of the East Bay's rolling hillsides, quiet and tranquil. To complete the loop, turn left on Spengler Trail, then right on Diablo View Trail. The latter is a 1.1-mile section that closes out the hike with great views of the slopes of Mt. Diablo.

---

## 14. LAFAYETTE/    7.75 mi. one way/4.0 hrs
## MORAGA TRAIL

*Reference:* North of San Leandro Reservoir; map E1-East Bay, grid c7.

*User groups:* Hikers, **wheelchairs**, dogs, horses and mountain bikes.

*Permits:* No permits are required. Parking and access are free.

*Directions:* From Highway 24 near Lafayette, take the Pleasant Hill exit south. Turn right on Olympic Boulevard and park at the Olympic Staging Area.

*Maps:* For a free trail map, contact East Bay Regional Parks at the address below and ask for the Lafayette-Moraga Regional Trail brochure. To obtain topographic maps of the area, ask for Walnut Creek and Las Trampas Ridge from the USGS.

**Who to contact:** East Bay Regional Park District, 2950 Peralta Oaks Court, P.O. Box 5381, Oakland, CA 94605; (510) 635-0135, ext. 2200.

**Trail notes:** The Lafayette-Moraga Trail is a 7.75-mile linear park, in other words, the trail is the park, a line from Lafayette to Moraga. Much of it is paved, some of it is compacted soil, and some of it is dirt, making most of it more popular for bikers and joggers than hikers. The hike starts at the Olympic Staging Area in Lafayette, and curls to the left for the first 3.5 miles, eventually heading south along Las Trampas Creek to Bollinger Canyon. At Moraga, the trail passes through downtown Moraga to the Valle Vista Staging Area on Canyon Road. This is the end of the trip for most visitors, but it is possible for hikers (no bicycles or dogs allowed on this part) to continue to the west on land managed by the East Bay Municipal Utility District. Permits are required; phone (510) 287-0469.

## 15. PROSPECT TUNNEL LOOP   4.5 mi/2.5 hrs

**Reference: In Black Diamond Mines Regional Preserve in the Mt. Diablo foothills near Antioch; map E1-East Bay, grid c9.**

**User groups:** Hikers, dogs, horses and mountain bikes. A short portion of the trail is accessible to hikers only. No wheelchair access.

**Permits:** No permits are required. Parking and access are free.

**Directions:** From Highway 4 at Antioch, take the Lone Tree Way exit and drive south to Blue Rock Drive. Turn right, drive to Frederickson Lane, bear right and drive to the gate. There is limited parking on the left. Note: The signs along the way will say "Contra Loma Regional Park," not "Black Diamond Mines." Once past the gate, you will be in Black Diamond Mines Preserve.

**Maps:** For a free trail map, contact East Bay Regional Park at the address below and ask for the Black Diamond Mines Regional Preserve brochure. To obtain a topographic map of the area, ask for Antioch South from the USGS.

**Who to contact:** East Bay Regional Park District, 2950 Peralta Oaks Court, P.O. Box 5381, Oakland, CA 94605; (510) 635-0135, ext. 2200.

**Trail notes:** Bring a flashlight with fresh batteries and you have the chance to explore 200 feet of mountain tunnel, the feature attraction of Black Diamond Mines Regional Preserve. The Prospect Tunnel, driven in the 1860s by miners in search of coal, actually probes 400 feet into the side of Mt. Diablo, and half of that length is now accessible to the public. To reach it is about a 1.5-mile hike from the trailhead, taking the Stewartville Trail from the trailhead off Frederickson Lane. Most of the area is grasslands and foothill country. After exploring the Prospect Tunnel, you can add a loop to this hike. Turn left on the Star Mine Trail, which adds a 1.6-mile loop and passes by a barred tunnel, one of the last active coal mines in the area. The Prospect Tunnel and the Star Mine are two of the most unusual spots in the preserve's 3,700 acres.

# 16. CONTRA LOMA LOOP     1.6 mi/1.0 hr

*Reference:* **In Contra Loma Regional Park near Antioch; map E1-East Bay, grid c9.**

*User groups:* Hikers, **wheelchairs**, dogs, horses and mountain bikes.

*Permits:* No permits are required. A $4 parking fee is charged March through October; $3 from November through February.

*Directions:* From Highway 4 at Antioch, take the Lone Tree Way exit and drive south to Blue Rock Drive. Turn right and follow Blue Rock Drive to Frederickson Lane, bear right and continue to the gate. There is limited parking on the left side of the road. Note: The signs along the way will say "Contra Loma Regional Park." Take a right turn, pass the kiosk and bear left. Drive to the parking lot by the beach.

*Maps:* For a free trail map, contact East Bay Regional Parks at the address below and ask for the Contra Loma Regional Park brochure. To obtain a topographic map of the area, ask for Antioch South from the USGS.

*Who to contact:* East Bay Regional Park District, 2950 Peralta Oaks Court, P.O. Box 5381, Oakland, CA 94605; (510) 635-0135, ext. 2200.

*Trail notes:* Most people go to Contra Loma Regional Park either to fish at Contra Loma Lake, swim and suntan, or picnic. This short loop trail provides an alternative to those activities, tracing along the northwest shore of the lake, then climbing up and over a short hill and looping back to the starting point. From the parking area, start your walk by heading out on the trail to the Cattail Cove Picnic Area. After passing it, the trail turns right and traces along the shore of the lake, passes a fishing pier, and then offers a 10-minute climb up a small hill. To close out the loop glide down the hill. The trail turns left and a mile later returns to the Cattail Cove Picnic Area.

# 17. SHORELINE TRAIL     5.0 mi/2.25 hrs

*Reference:* **At Crown Memorial State Beach, San Francisco Bay shore in Alameda; map E1-East Bay, grid d5.**

*User groups:* Hikers, **wheelchairs**, dogs (on the paved trail only, not the beach) and mountain bikes. No horses are allowed.

*Permits:* No permits are required. There is a parking fee when the entrance kiosk is attended.

*Directions:* From Interstate 580 in Oakland, take Interstate 980 west into Oakland. Take the 12th Street/Alameda exit. Follow the road under Interstate 880 and turn left onto Fifth Street. Proceed to the Oakland/Alameda Tube. At the end of the Tube, you will be on Webster, which dead ends at Central. Turn left on Central, then right on Eighth Street and drive a quarter of a mile to Crown Beach.

*Maps:* For a free trail map, contact East Bay Regional Parks at the address below and ask for the Crown Memorial State Beach brochure. To obtain a topographic map of the area, ask for Oakland West from the USGS.

*Who to contact:* East Bay Regional Park District, 2950 Peralta Oaks Court, P.O. Box 5381, Oakland, CA 94605; (510) 635-0135, ext. 2200.

*Trail notes:* The tide book is your bible at Crown Memorial State Beach, which is set along the shore of San Francisco Bay just south of Crab Cove. High tide is the best time to observe sea birds such as loons, grebes and ducks. Low tides, however, are the best time for observing shorebirds such as sandpipers poking around the exposed mudflats. The trail here is a paved bicycle path, but it is set right along the Bay's shoreline, running 2.5 miles south to an overlook of the Elsie Roemer Bird Sanctuary. The views are also quite good of the Bay. When the wind is down, this is one of the Bay's best swimming areas, and when the wind is up, it's also an excellent area for board sailing.

## 18. ARROWHEAD MARSH  2.0 mi/1.0 hr

*Reference:* **At Martin Luther King Regional Shoreline on San Leandro Bay near Oakland; map E1-East Bay, grid d5.**

*User groups:* Hikers, **wheelchairs** and mountain bikes. No dogs or horses.

*Permits:* No permits are required. Parking and access are free.

*Directions:* From Interstate 880 in Oakland, take the Hegenberger Road exit and follow it towards the airport and Doolittle Drive. Turn right and continue to Swan Way. Turn right again and drive a short distance to the park entrance. Turn left and drive to the parking area at the end of the road.

*Maps:* For a free trail map, contact East Bay Regional Parks at the address below and ask for the Martin Luther King Regional Shoreline brochure. To obtain a topographic map of the area, ask for San Leandro from the USGS.

*Who to contact:* East Bay Regional Park District, 2950 Peralta Oaks Court, P.O. Box 5381, Oakland, CA 94605; (510) 635-0135, ext. 2200.

*Trail notes:* Arrowhead Marsh is one of the best birdwatching areas in the East Bay, with 30 species common here, included several pairs of blue-winged teal. At high tide, this area is also a top spot to see rails, which are typically elusive and more often heard than seen. The marsh is set along San Leandro Bay, with a paved trail skirting the edge off the marsh. From the parking area, the trail is routed one mile out along the Airport Channel, with Arrowhead Marsh on your left. If you want, you can extend your walk across a bridge at San Leandro Creek, then continue along the shore to Garretson Point, adding 1.4 miles roundtrip to your hike. This parkland covers 1,220 acres, including some of the Bay's most valuable remaining wetland habitat.

## 19. HUCKLEBERRY  1.7 mi/1.25 hrs
## LOOP PATH

*Reference:* **In Huckleberry Regional Preserve in the Oakland hills; map E1-East Bay, grid d6.**

*User groups:* Hikers only. No dogs, horses or mountain bikes are allowed. No wheelchair facilities.

*Permits:* No permits are required. Parking and access are free.

*Directions:* From Highway 24 in the East Bay, proceed to just east of the Caldecott Tunnel and take the Fish Ranch Road exit west to Grizzly Peak Boulevard. Bear left and drive on Skyline Boulevard. Continue a short distance past Sibley Volcanic Preserve to the park entrance and parking lot on the left.

*Maps:* For a free trail map, contact East Bay Regional Parks at the address below and ask for the Huckleberry Botanic Regional Preserve brochure. To obtain a topographic map of the area, ask for Oakland East from the USGS.

*Who to contact:* East Bay Regional Park District, 2950 Peralta Oaks Court, P.O. Box 5381, Oakland, CA 94605; (510) 635-0135, ext. 2200.

*Trail notes:* If you know what you're looking for, this is a trip into an ecological wonderland. If you don't, well, it's still a rewarding venture into a tranquil parkland. The only reason people come to Huckleberry is to hike. They don't come to here park, play games or fish. That is because the Huckleberry Loop is routed through a remarkable variety of rare and beautiful plants. From the parking area, follow the path to the left fork, where you will descend steeply through a mature bay forest for a mile. The trail then returns by turning right, and climbing 0.7 miles out of the canyon. This latter section is particularly rich in diverse plant life.

## 20. STREAM TRAIL LOOP    3.5 mi/2.0 hrs

*Reference:* In Redwood Regional Park in the Oakland hills; map E1-East Bay, grid d7.

*User groups:* Hikers, **wheelchairs**, dogs, horses and mountain bikes.

*Permits:* No permits are required. There is a $3 parking fee when the kiosk is attended.

*Directions:* From Highway 24 in the East Bay, proceed to Highway 13 in Oakland and turn south. Drive on Highway 13, turn left on Redwood Road and drive for three miles to the park entrance. Park at the Canyon Meadow Staging Area at the end of the road.

*Maps:* For a free trail map, contact East Bay Regional Parks at the address below and ask for the Redwood Regional Park brochure. To obtain a topographic map of the area, ask for Oakland East from the USGS.

*Who to contact:* East Bay Regional Park District, 2950 Peralta Oaks Court, P.O. Box 5381, Oakland, CA 94605; (510) 635-0135, ext. 2200.

*Trail notes:* Newcomers are often amazed by the beauty of this trail in Redwood Regional Park, and even after the shock wears off, visiting here can still grant you a lasting glow. After all, who ever heard of a redwood forest in Oakland? Or a trout stream? Only visitors to this park, because you get both here. After parking, the best loop route is to hike up the Stream Trail for a quarter-mile, then turn left on the French Trail. You will climb along the western slopes of the redwood canyon, rising to 1,000 feet, and then with the puffing behind you (always hike up when you're fresh), you will turn right on the Fern Trail and shortly later, junction with the Stream Trail. The rest of the route is easy and downhill, as you head back to the park entrance, walking along the pretty Redwood Creek, set in the center of the redwood forest. In late winter and spring, trout swim upstream from San Leandro Reservoir to spawn in this stream (no fishing permitted).

## 21. EAST RIDGE LOOP    4.0 mi/2.5 hrs

*Reference:* In Redwood Regional Park in the Oakland hills; map E1-East Bay, grid d7.

*User groups:* Hikers, dogs and horses. Mountain bikes and **wheelchairs** are permitted on the paved part of the trail.

*Permits:* No permits are required. There is a $3 parking fee when the kiosk is attended.

*Directions:* From Highway 24 in the East Bay, proceed to Highway 13 in Oakland and turn south. Drive on Highway 13, turn left on Redwood Road and drive for three miles to the park entrance. Park at the Canyon Meadow

Staging Area at the end of the road.

*Maps:* For a free trail map, contact East Bay Regional Parks at the address below and ask for the Redwood Regional Park brochure. To obtain a topographic map of the area, ask for Oakland East from the USGS.

*Who to contact:* East Bay Regional Park District, 2950 Peralta Oaks Court, P.O. Box 5381, Oakland, CA 94605; (510) 635-0135, ext. 2200.

*Trail notes:* From atop the East Ridge at 1,100 feet, you look down into a canyon that appears to be filled by a sea of redwoods. Getting that view is quite a treat after a climb of nearly 900 feet from the trailhead. The payback comes when you turn left and loop down into that canyon and waiting for you is Redwood Creek under the cool canopy of a lush forest. This trip is an option to hike number 20 for ambitious hikers and mountain bikers, the latter who are allowed on the East Ridge but barred from the Stream Trail Loop. To take it, from the parking area, turn right on the Canyon Trail, climbing up to the East Ridge in half a mile. Turn left and make the loop by hiking out on the East Ridge, climbing much of the way, then turning left again on Prince Road and returning on the Stream Trail.

---

## 22. GRAHAM TRAIL LOOP        0.75 mi/0.5 hr

*Reference:* In Roberts Regional Recreation Area in the Oakland Hills; map E1-East Bay, grid d7.

*User groups:* Hikers and dogs. No horses or mountain bikes are allowed. The restroom is wheelchair-accessible, but the trail is not.

*Permits:* No permits are required. There is a $3 parking fee on weekends and holidays.

*Directions:* From Highway 24 in the East Bay, drive to Highway 13 in Oakland. Turn south on Highway 13 (follow the signs carefully) and drive three miles to Joaquin Miller Road. Head east on Joaquin Miller Road until you reach Skyline Boulevard. Turn left on Skyline Boulevard and drive approximately one mile to the park entrance on the right.

*Maps:* For a free trail map, contact East Bay Regional Parks at the address below and ask for the Roberts Regional Recreation Area and Redwood Regional Park brochures. To obtain a topographic map of the area, ask for Oakland East from the USGS.

*Who to contact:* East Bay Regional Park District, 2950 Peralta Oaks Court, P.O. Box 5381, Oakland, CA 94605; (510) 635-0135, ext. 2200.

*Trail notes:* Because the entrance to Roberts Regional Recreation Area is set in redwoods, it has proved to be a popular stop for visitors who want to see *Sequoia sempervirens* with minimum effort. If you want to walk only a short distance in the East Bay Area, yet enter a redwood forest, this is the best bet. From the entrance of the parking area, near the swimming pool, take the short trail that is linked to the Graham Trail. Turn right, and you will be routed in a short circle past a restroom to Diablo Vista, then a right turn and back to the parking area. It is short and sweet, just right for many visitors who have no wish for a more challenging encounter.

## 23. GRASS VALLEY LOOP 2.8 mi/1.5 hrs

*Reference:* In Anthony Chabot Regional Park in the Oakland hills; map
  E1-East Bay, grid d7.
*User groups:* Hikers, dogs, horses and mountain bikes. No wheelchair facilities.
*Permits:* No permits are required. Parking and access are free.
*Directions:* From Interstate 580 in Oakland, take the 35th Avenue exit and drive
  east (35th Avenue becomes Redwood Road). Follow Redwood Road, pass
  Skyline Boulevard and continue for three more miles to the Bort Meadow
  Staging Area on the right.
*Maps:* For a free trail map, contact East Bay Regional Parks at the address below
  and ask for the Anthony Chabot Regional Park brochure. To obtain a
  topographic map of the area, ask for Las Trampas Ridge from the USGS.
*Who to contact:* East Bay Regional Park District, 2950 Peralta Oaks Court, P.O.
  Box 5381, Oakland, CA 94605; (510) 635-0135, ext. 2200.
*Trail notes:* A hidden valley in the East Bay hills provides a simple paradise.
  It is called Grass Valley, a meadow that lines a valley floor for more than a
  mile, framed by the rims of miniature mountains on each side. In the spring,
  it glows from various greens from wild grasses, along with wild radish, blue-
  eyed grass and golden poppies. It is quiet and beautiful. The Grass Valley
  Trail is one of the quickest routes to tranquility, starting at the Bort Meadow
  Staging Area, at a trailhead for the East Bay Skyline National Recreation
  Trail. Hike south through Grass Valley and then to Stone Bridge, a distance
  of 1.5 miles. To get back from Stone Bridge, take the Brandon Trail north,
  which is routed along the west side of Grass Valley. To make this a perfect
  day, crown the hike with lunch at Bort Meadow.

## 24. BORT MEADOW 5.4 mi/3.25 hrs

*Reference:* In Chabot Regional Park north of Castro Valley; map E1-East
  Bay, grid d7.
*User groups:* Hikers, dogs, horses and mountain bikes. No wheelchair facilities.
*Permits:* No permits are required. Parking and access are free.
*Directions:* From Interstate 580 in Oakland, take the 35th Avenue exit and drive
  east (35th Avenue becomes Redwood Road). Follow Redwood Road, pass
  Skyline Boulevard and continue for three more miles to the Bort Meadow
  Staging Area on the right.
*Maps:* For a free trail map, contact East Bay Regional Parks at the address below
  and ask for the Anthony Chabot Regional Park brochure. To obtain a
  topographic map of the area, ask for Las Trampas Ridge from the USGS.
*Who to contact:* East Bay Regional Park District, 2950 Peralta Oaks Court, P.O.
  Box 5381, Oakland, CA 94605; (510) 635-0135, ext. 2200.
*Trail notes:* In little over 2.5 miles, this trail crosses through several spectacular
  habitat changes, has good views of a beautiful valley, and enough of a climb
  to get your lungs tootin'. You start at the Bort Meadow Staging Area, a
  trailhead for the East Bay Skyline National Recreation Trail. Head out north
  (to the right) where the trail climbs 300 feet out of Bort Meadow, and at the
  ridge, turn and look south for the great view of Grass Valley, a divine sight
  in the spring months. Note that the trail here climbs across an open face, and
  can be hot and dry on summer afternoons. From the ridge, the trail proceeds

through a hardwood forest with some chaparral, drops 500 feet down into a canyon, crosses Redwood Road and puts you at the entrance to Redwood Regional Park and its redwoods. Just like that, you've seen a wider variety of landscape in a shorter amount of time than on nearly any other trail in the Bay Area.

## 25. ROCKY RIDGE LOOP     4.4 mi/2.5 hrs

*Reference:* In Las Trampas Regional Wilderness south of Moraga; map E1–East Bay, grid d7.

*User groups:* Hikers, dogs and horses. No mountain bikes are allowed. No wheelchair access.

*Permits:* No permits are required. Parking and access are free.

*Directions:* From Interstate 680 in San Ramon, take the Crow Canyon Road exit and head west to Bollinger Canyon Road. Turn north on Bollinger Canyon Road and follow the road for five miles to the parking area.

*Maps:* For a free trail map, contact East Bay Regional Parks at the address below and ask for the Las Trampas Regional Wilderness brochure. To obtain a topographic map of the area, ask for Las Trampas Ridge from the USGS.

*Who to contact:* East Bay Regional Park District, 2950 Peralta Oaks Court, P.O. Box 5381, Oakland, CA 94605; (510) 635-0135, ext. 2200.

*Trail notes:* Rocky Ridge is the prime destination for hikers visiting the 3,800-acre Las Trampas Regional Wilderness. This is a grassy rolling ridge with sandstone outcrops, providing spectacular views both to the east and the west. The outcrops are beautifully sculptured by the wind and colored by many lichen species. You can spend an entire day, if you so desire, just poking around the ridge. To reach Rocky Ridge, start at the staging area at the end of Bollinger Road. From there, take the Rocky Ridge Trail, which starts out with a steep climb, rising about 800 feet over the course of 1.5 miles. Have faith, because once you get that climb behind you, you're atop Rocky Ridge, and the trail eases up. Head south down Rocky Ridge (take the Upper Trail) for a mile, enjoying the views on the way. To hike out the loop, turn left on the Elderberry Trail, which leads two miles downhill to the staging area. Note: A good side adventure is to explore the Wind Caves, hollows in the sandstone outcrops. To reach them from the Upper Trail, turn right on the Sycamore Trail and hike a steep 0.3 miles down to the caves.

## 26. IRON HORSE     15.0 mi. one way/1.0 day
## REGIONAL TRAIL

*Reference:* In the San Ramon Valley from San Ramon to Walnut Creek; map E1–East Bay, grid d8.

*User groups:* Hikers, **wheelchairs**, dogs, horses and mountain bikes.

*Permits:* No permits are required. Parking and access are free.

*Directions:* From Interstate 680 in Danville, take the Rudgear Road exit and park at either the Park and Ride lot (on the east side of the freeway) or the Staging Area (south side).

*Maps:* For a free trail map, contact East Bay Regional Parks at the address below and ask for the Iron Horse Regional Trail brochure. To obtain a topographic map of the area, ask for Las Trampas Ridge from the USGS.

*Who to contact:* East Bay Regional Park District, 2950 Peralta Oaks Court, P.O.

Box 5381, Oakland, CA 94605; (510) 635-0135, ext. 2200.

*Trail notes:* The Iron Horse Regional Trail is a focal point of the national "Rails to Trails" program, where old abandoned rail lines are being converted to hiking trails. When complete, the Iron Horse Trail will span from Shadow Cliffs Lake in Pleasanton northward all the way to Suisun Bay near Martinez. This rail line route was first established in 1890 and abandoned officially in 1976. In only two years, all the railroad tracks were removed, but it is taking quite a bit more time to convert the route to trail. The completed portion starts at Pine Valley Intermediate School in San Ramon and heads about 15 miles north to Walnut Creek. It is often hot and dry here, with little shade (the trail is 75 feet wide) and no water available, but it deserves mention anyway. As trees are planted for shade, piped water becomes available, and the route lengthens, it will become a prominent long-distance trail for jogging, biking, and even walking.

---

# 27. MT. DIABLO SUMMIT LOOP 0.7 mi/0.5 hr

*Reference:* In Mt. Diablo State Park near Danville; map E1-East Bay, grid d9.

*User groups:* Hikers only. No dogs, horses or mountain bikes are allowed. The first half of the trail is designed for **wheelchair use**.

*Permits:* No permits are required. A $5 state park entrance fee is charged for each vehicle.

*Directions:* From Interstate 680 at Danville, take the Diablo Road exit. Follow Diablo Road past Green Valley Road/McCauley Road and continue for 1.5 miles to Mt. Diablo Scenic Boulevard. Turn left (look for the sign that says "Mount Diablo State Park") and proceed toward Mt. Diablo. Note that Mt. Diablo Scenic Boulevard becomes Blackhawk Road. Continue to South Gate Road. Turn left and continue to the Mt. Diablo summit parking area. Park adjacent to the Mt. Diablo Interpretive Center, located in the lower parking area, not in the small parking area at the summit. The trailhead is located opposite the handicapped parking area, the small area between the upper and lower parking lots.

*Maps:* For a trail map and brochure, send $1 to Mount Diablo State Park at the address below. To obtain a topographic map of the area, ask for Diablo from the USGS.

*Who to contact:* Mount Diablo State Park, P.O. Box 250, Diablo, CA 94528; (510) 837-2525 or (415) 726-8800.

*Trail notes:* One of the best lookouts in the world is at the top of Mt. Diablo. No matter how fouled up things get, you can't foul up the view from Mt. Diablo. This loop trail provides a short, easy roundtrip around the top. It is also called the Fire Interpretive Trail, but many call it the Diablo Summit Loop. Since you can drive nearly to the top of the mountain at 3,849 feet, it is the easiest hike in the park, yet also the one with the best views. Looking west, you can see across the Bay to the Golden Gate Bridge (66 miles), the Pacific Ocean, and 25 miles out to sea, the Farallon Islands. Northward, you can see up the Central Valley and spot Mt. Lassen east of Red Bluff (165 miles). To the east, the frosted Sierra crest is often in view, and with binoculars and a perfect day, it is possible to see a piece of Half Dome (135 miles) sticking out from Yosemite Valley. The view from the top of Diablo is said to be second only to that of Mt. Kilimanjaro in terms of the amount of earth surface that is visible from the top.

## 28. GIANT LOOP    8.6 mi/4.75 hrs

*Reference:* In Mt. Diablo State Park near Danville; map E1-East Bay, grid d9.

*User groups:* Hikers and horses. No dogs or mountain bikes are allowed. No wheelchair facilities.

*Permits:* No permits are required. A $5 state park entrance fee is charged for each vehicle.

*Directions:* From Concord, take Clayton Road southeast to the town of Clayton. Turn south on Mitchell Canyon Road and continue to the trailhead at the end of the road.

*Maps:* For a trail map and brochure, send $1 to Mount Diablo State Park at the address below. To obtain a topographic map of the area, ask for Diablo from the USGS.

*Who to contact:* Mount Diablo State Park, P.O. Box 250, Diablo, CA 94528; (510) 837-2525 or (415) 726-8800.

*Trail notes:* This hike can be a demanding test, but it will provide you with a real feel for Mt. Diablo and the least chance of meeting up with other people at Mt. Diablo State Park. The Giant Loop Trail is set on the north side of Mt. Diablo and includes an 1,800-foot climb up to Deer Flat, then a steep descent into Donner Canyon. On the way, you will pass flower-strewn grasslands (spectacular in the spring) and endless views of Northern California. Note that Deer Flat is not only a good spot for lookouts, but it is the most abundant wildlife area in the entire park. In addition, the Giant Loop offers the chance of a great sidetrip to Eagle Peak, elevation 2,369 feet, another of Diablo's best lookouts. Take most of a day and enjoy this one.

---

## 29. CHINA WALL LOOP    3.3 mi/2.0 hrs

*Reference:* **In Diablo Foothills Regional Park on the northwest slopes of Mount Diablo near Danville; map E1-East Bay, grid d9.**

*User groups:* Hikers, dogs, horses and mountain bikes. No wheelchair facilities.

*Permits:* No permits are required. Parking and access are free.

*Directions:* From Interstate 680 northbound in Walnut Creek, take the Ignacio Valley Road exit. Turn right on Ignacio Valley Road and drive to Walnut Avenue, then turn right again and continue to Oak Grove Road. Turn right on Oak Grove Road and then right again on Castle Rock Road. Follow Castle Rock to Borges Ranch Road. The parking area is at the end of Borges Ranch Road. From Interstate 680 southbound, take the North Main Street exit. Drive south on North Main Street to Ignacio Valley Road. Turn left and proceed as above.

*Maps:* For a free trail map, contact East Bay Regional Parks at the address below and ask for the Diablo Foothills Regional Park brochure. To obtain a topographic map of the area, ask for Diablo from the USGS.

*Who to contact:* East Bay Regional Park District, 2950 Peralta Oaks Court, P.O. Box 5381, Oakland, CA 94605; (510) 635-0135, ext. 2200.

*Trail notes:* First of all, let us say that there is no sign at the trailhead denoting "China Wall Loop." We named it that after taking this hike. The China Wall Rock Formation is one of the most fascinating areas on the slopes of giant Mt. Diablo. What you see on this hike is a line of rocks that looks like the Great Wall of China in miniature (well, kind of)—they are prehistoric-looking sandstone formations. In addition, on the hike out, you will get glimpses to the east of Castle Rocks and other prominent sandstone outcrops, which are located just outside the park's boundary. When you look closer, you also have a chance to see golden eagles, hawks and falcons, all of which nest here. To reach China Wall requires only a 1.5-mile hike from the Borges Ranch Trailhead, heading off on the Briones-to-Mt. Diablo Trail. Turn right at the trail junction (Alamo Trail), which runs a half mile along the base of China Wall. To complete the loop hike, turn right again on Hanging Valley Trail and hike back to the parking area.

---

## 30. VOLVON LOOP TRAIL    5.7 mi/3.0 hrs

*Reference:* **In Morgan Territory Regional Park north of Livermore; map E1-East Bay, grid d9.**

*User groups:* The first half of the loop is accessible to hikers, dogs, horses and mountain bikes. The second half is for hikers and dogs only. No wheelchair facilities.

*Permits:* No permits are required. Parking and access are free.

*Directions:* From Interstate 580 in Livermore, take the North Livermore Avenue exit. Drive north to Highland Road and turn left, then drive a short distance and turn right on Morgan Territory Road. Follow Morgan Territory Road to the parking area just past the ridge summit.

*Maps:* For a free trail map, contact East Bay Regional Parks at the address below and ask for the Morgan Territory Regional Preserve brochure. To obtain a topographic map of the area, ask for Tassajara from the USGS.

*Who to contact:* East Bay Regional Park District, 2950 Peralta Oaks Court, P.O. Box 5381, Oakland, CA 94605; (510) 635-0135, ext. 2200.

*Trail notes:* Morgan Territory is located within the traditional homeland of the Volvon, one of five historical Indian nations in the Mt. Diablo area. This trail is the feature hike in the park, and is named after the first people of the area. It is an excellent trip, demanding at times, rising along the park's sandstone hills to a ridgeline with excellent views. From the trailhead (200 feet), take the Volvon Trail, which is routed northward up along the highest point in the park at 1,977 feet. The trail loops around this peak, then returns via the Coyote Trail (hikers only) back down the grade to the starting point. This parkland is most beautiful in the spring, and not just because the hills are greened up, but because one of the best wildflower displays in the Bay Area occurs here.

---

## 31. COGSWELL MARSH LOOP   2.8 mi/1.5 hrs

*Reference:* **At Hayward Regional Shoreline on South San Francisco Bay in Hayward; map E1-East Bay, grid e6.**

*User groups:* Hikers and mountain bikes. No dogs or horses are allowed. No wheelchair facilities.

*Permits:* No permits are required. Parking and access are free.

*Directions:* From Interstate 880 in Hayward, take the West Winton Avenue exit and follow it west toward the Bay and to the entrance and parking area.

*Maps:* For a free trail map, contact East Bay Regional Parks at the address below and ask for the Hayward Regional Shoreline brochure. To obtain a topographic map of the area, ask for San Leandro from the USGS.

*Who to contact:* East Bay Regional Park District, 2950 Peralta Oaks Court, P.O. Box 5381, Oakland, CA 94605; (510) 635-0135, ext. 2200.

*Trail notes:* Cogswell Marsh is the heart of an 800-acre marsh and wetlands, a great place for short nature hikes and identifying many rare birds. It is always a good place to see shorebirds, with the bonus of peregrine falcons typically either hovering over the marsh or perched on a power pylon. As many as 200 white pelicans can be seen here, along with more rare sightings of merlins. From the parking area, the trail starts with a .37-mile hike across landfill, then enters the marshlands, with a loop trail circling the most vital habitat. To keep your feet from getting wet, two short sections are bridged. The loop is best hiked clockwise, so you will be facing the Bay Bridge and San Francisco skyline, an outstanding view, when you walk along the water's edge of the South Bay. Guided weekend nature walks are available here.

---

## 32. SHORELINE LOOP TRAIL 1.75 mi/1.0 hr

*Reference:* In Cull Canyon Regional Park in the Castro Valley foothills; map E1-East Bay, grid e7.

*User groups:* Hikers and dogs. No horses or mountain bikes are allowed. No wheelchair access.

*Permits:* No permits are required. There is a swim fee required to enter the lagoon area (closed in winter). The fee ranges from $1 to $4.

*Directions:* From Interstate 580 eastbound, take the Center Street exit in Castro Valley and drive north to Heyer Avenue. Turn right on Heyer and proceed to Cull Canyon Road, then make a left and continue to the park entrance. From westbound on Interstate 580, take the Castro Valley exit and turn left onto Castro Valley Boulevard. Continue to Crow Canyon Road, turn right and drive a half mile. Turn left on Cull Canyon Road and proceed to the park entrance.

*Maps:* For a free trail map, contact East Bay Regional Parks at the address below and ask for the Cull Canyon Regional Recreation Area brochure. To obtain a topographic map of the area, ask for Hayward from the USGS.

*Who to contact:* East Bay Regional Park District, 2950 Peralta Oaks Court, P.O. Box 5381, Oakland, CA 94605; (510) 635-0135, ext. 2200.

*Trail notes:* Little Cull Canyon Reservoir, set in a canyon and covering just 18 acres, is the backdrop for a picnic area, with this short hike along the lake a popular option for visitors. From the parking area, walk over to the picnic areas, then turn left along the Shoreline Trail. It skirts the western bank of the narrow lake, then loops back along a lagoon. Most of the year, it is a pleasant walk. However, just plain forget it on summer afternoons, when the hot sun brands everything in sight. That is why this park is most famous for its swimming complex, complete with bathhouse and snack bar, not for the hiking, and heaven knows not the fishing.

---

## 33. DON CASTRO LAKE LOOP 1.7 mi/1.0 hr

*Reference:* In Don Castro Regional Park in the Castro Valley foothills; map E1-East Bay, grid e7.

*User groups:* Hikers and dogs. Portions of the trail are paved for bicycle and **wheelchair** use. No horses are allowed.

*Permits:* No permits are required. There is an entrance fee when the kiosk is attended. The fee ranges from $1 to $4.

*Directions:* From Interstate 580 eastbound, take the Center Street exit in Castro Valley and turn right. Drive to Kelly Street and turn left, then drive a short distance and turn left again onto Woodroe and continue to the park entrance. From westbound on Interstate 580, take the Castro Valley exit and drive west on East Castro Valley Boulevard to Grove Way. Turn left and drive to Center Street. Drive a short distance and then turn left again and continue to Kelly Street. Make another left onto Kelly and continue to Woodroe; turn left once again and continue to the park entrance.

*Maps:* For a free trail map, contact East Bay Regional Parks at the address below and ask for the Don Castro Regional Recreation Area brochure. To obtain a topographic map of the area, ask for Hayward from the USGS.

*Who to contact:* East Bay Regional Park District, 2950 Peralta Oaks Court, P.O. Box 5381, Oakland, CA 94605; (510) 635-0135, ext. 2200.

*Trail notes:* Don Castro is a small (23 acres) but pretty lake that attracts swimmers to its lagoon and clear, warm, blue waters. Hiking is typically an afterthought for visitors, who come here primarily to picnic or fish. The trail (actually a road) is routed completely around the small lake, an easy walk or jog in a nice setting. From the parking area, make the short walk along the West Lawn to the dam and start your hike there, circling the lake in a clockwise direction. In the first quarter mile, with the lake on your right, you will pass a fishing pier and the swimming lagoon (on your left). The route continues to the headwaters of the lake at San Lorenzo Creek, crosses the creek, then hems the southern shoreline all the way to the lake's spillway. After climbing a short staircase, you will be back on top, and can hike over the dam and back to the parking area. It's an easy circle.

---

# 34. BAYVIEW TRAIL
3.0 mi/1.5 hrs

*Reference:* **In Coyote Hills Regional Park on the shore of the South Bay near Fremont; map E1-East Bay, grid f6.**

*User groups:* Hikers, dogs, horses and mountain bikes. The trail is paved and technically **wheelchair accessible** but it is quite steep in some sections.

*Permits:* No permits are required. There is a $3 parking fee when the kiosk is attended.

*Directions:* From Highway 84 westbound in Fremont, take the Paseo Padre Parkway exit, turn right (north) and drive to Patterson Ranch Road. Turn left and continue to the parking area. From Highway 84 eastbound on the Peninsula, cross the Dumbarton Bridge and take the Thornton Avenue exit. Turn left, the road becomes Paseo Padre Parkway, and continue north to Patterson Ranch Road. Turn left onto Patterson Ranch Road and continue to the parking area.

*Maps:* For a free trail map, contact East Bay Regional Parks at the address below and ask for the Coyote Hills Regional Park brochure. To obtain a topographic map of the area, ask for Newark from the USGS.

*Who to contact:* East Bay Regional Park District, 2950 Peralta Oaks Court, P.O. Box 5381, Oakland, CA 94605; (510) 635-0135, ext. 2200. You may also phone the park directly at (510) 795-9385.

*Trail notes:* Coyote Hills Regional Park has a rich history that is still visible within its 966 acres. The Shoreline Trail is the favorite here for its excellent views of the South Bay. The park features four Indian shellmounds, which are accumulations of debris from ancient living areas. This walk circles the park, including a 1.5-mile stretch that borders the South Bay and a shorter piece that runs adjacent to a marsh. The park is a wildlife sanctuary, with grassy hills and marshes, providing significant habitat for migrating waterfowl. This loop trail is best hiked in a counterclockwise direction, starting from the main parking area. A great, short sidetrip from the main parking area, by the way, is to take the wooden boardwalk out through the North Marsh.

## 35. HIGH RIDGE LOOP 3.3 mi/2.0 hrs

*Reference:* **In Garin Regional Park in the Hayward foothills; map E1-East Bay, grid f7.**

*User groups:* Hikers, dogs, horses and mountain bikes. No wheelchair facilities.

*Permits:* No permits are required. There is a $3 parking fee when the kiosk is attended.

*Directions:* From Fremont, take Highway 238 (Mission Boulevard) north through Union City to Garin Avenue. Turn right onto Garin Avenue and continue for one mile to the park entrance.

*Maps:* For a free trail map, contact East Bay Regional Parks at the address below and ask for the Garin & Dry Creek Pioneer Regional Parks brochure. To obtain a topographic map of the area, ask for Hayward from the USGS.

*Who to contact:* East Bay Regional Park District, 2950 Peralta Oaks Court, P.O. Box 5381, Oakland, CA 94605; (510) 635-0135, ext. 2200.

*Trail notes:* The hilltops in Garin Park render sweeping views of the East Bay foothills westward to South San Francisco Bay, the number one attraction at this 3,000-acre parkland. The hills span for miles, and in the fall, there are times late in the day when sunbeams will pour through openings between cumulus clouds, creating a divine scene. Of the 20 miles of trails in the park, it is the Ridge Loop Trail that is the best way to see surrounding wildlands, primarily oak grasslands amid rolling foothills. From the parking area (at 380 feet), walk a quarter mile past the picnic areas to Arroyo Flats, then turn left on the High Ridge Trail. In another quarter mile, it will link to the Vista Peak Loop, best hiked in a clockwise direction. You will start climbing, a rise of 550 feet in a mile, topping out at Vista Peak (934 feet), then shortly later, Garin Peak (948 feet). Take your time and enjoy the views.

## 36. RIDGELINE TRAIL 7.0 mi/4.0 hrs

*Reference:* **In Pleasanton Ridge Regional Park west of Pleasanton; map E1-East Bay, grid f9.**

*User groups:* Hikers, dogs, horses and mountain bikes. No wheelchair facilities.

*Permits:* No permits are required. Parking and access are free.

*Directions:* From Interstate 680 in Pleasanton, take the Bernal Road exit west and drive to Foothill Road. Turn left and continue for three miles to the parking area and information center.

*Maps:* For a free trail map, contact East Bay Regional Parks at the address below and ask for the Pleasanton Ridge Regional Park brochure. To obtain a topographic map of the area, ask for Dublin from the USGS.

*Who to contact:* East Bay Regional Park District, 2950 Peralta Oaks Court, P.O.

Box 5381, Oakland, CA 94605; (510) 635-0135, ext. 2200.

*Trail notes:* This park is often overlooked by out-of-towners, but it offers a quiet, natural setting with excellent views from the Ridgeline Trail. Development has purposely been limited in and around Pleasanton Ridge Regional Park in order to retain as natural a feel as possible to the surroundings. They have succeeded, and it is best experienced on this hike. The Ridgeline Trail climbs to elevations of 1,600 feet, with the northern sections giving way to sweeping views, featured by miles of rolling foothills and valleys at the threshold of Mt. Diablo. From the parking area, elevation 300 feet, start the hike on the Oak Tree Trail, which is routed 1.4 miles with a 750 foot climb to the Ridgeline Trail. Turn right and hike two miles along the ridge. You can return on a loop route by turning left on the Thermalito Trail (recommended).

---

## 37. NORTH ARROYO TRAIL     1.3 mi/0.75 hr

*Reference:* **In Shadow Cliffs Regional Recreation Area in Pleasanton; map E1-East Bay, grid f9.**

*User groups:* Hikers and dogs. Portions of the trail are accessible to horses and mountain bikes as well. No wheelchair facilities.

*Permits:* No permits are required. There is a $4 parking fee from March through October; $3 from November through February.

*Directions:* From Interstate 580 in Pleasanton, take Santa Rita Road south. Drive two miles and turn left on Valley Avenue and proceed to Stanley Boulevard. Turn left and drive to the park entrance.

*Maps:* For a free trail map, contact East Bay Regional Parks at the address below and ask for the Shadow Cliffs Regional Recreation Area brochure. To obtain a topographic map of the area, ask for Livermore from the USGS.

*Who to contact:* East Bay Regional Park District, 2950 Peralta Oaks Court, P.O. Box 5381, Oakland, CA 94605; (510) 635-0135, ext. 2200.

*Trail notes:* While you can't walk all the way around Shadow Cliffs Lake, you can explore the Arroyo area, which is a series of smaller ponds. There's no place else like it in the East Bay. From the back of the first parking area, you take a trail over the top of a levee and down to the shore of the first pond. From there, just follow the North Arroyo Trail along the shores of several ponds for about a half mile. For a view of the ponds, make the short climb up the adjacent levee. These ponds are water holes left over from a gravel quarry. The biggest of the ponds, some 80 acres, has been stocked with trout and named Shadow Cliffs Lake, one of the better fishing spots in the East Bay. It is also a good place to swim because the water is often quite clear.

---

## 38. DUMBARTON BRIDGE     4.5 mi/2.5 hrs

*Reference:* **On Dumbarton Bridge from Fremont to East Palo Alto; map E1-East Bay, grid g6.**

*User groups:* Hikers, **wheelchairs**, dogs and mountain bikes. No horses are allowed.

*Permits:* No permits are required. Parking and access are free.

*Directions:* From Redwood City, head east on Highway 84 and cross the Dumbarton Bridge. Take the first exit after the toll plaza, Thornton Avenue. Turn right and drive a quarter mile to Marshland Road. Turn right and drive to the parking area at the eastern foot of the Dumbarton Bridge.

*Maps:* To obtain a topographic map of the area, ask for Newark from the USGS.

*Who to contact:* San Francisco Bay National Wildlife Refuge, P.O. Box 524, Newark, CA 94560; (510) 792-4275 or (510) 792-0222.

*Trail notes:* Let this bridge be a lesson for future bridge designers. When the Dumbarton Bridge was constructed, a biking and hiking path was added along the south side of the roadway, separated from traffic by a cement cordon. That means you can hike to the top of the center span in complete safety for a unique view of the South Bay. This hike is best started from the Fremont side of the bridge, because it is unsafe to leave a car unattended at the western foot of the bridge in East Palo Alto. Note: The bridge trail can be the link for an outstanding bicycle trip. Start at the Alameda Creek Regional Trail in Niles, head over the Dumbarton Bridge, turn left on the Baylands Trail through Palo Alto, then go further south at Charleston Slough on the Baylands Trail to Mountain View Baylands.

## 39. DUMBARTON PIER       1.0 mi/1.0 hr

*Reference:* **In South San Francisco Bay in San Francisco Bay National Wildlife Refuge in Fremont; map E1-East Bay, grid g6.**

*User groups:* Hikers and **wheelchairs**. No dogs, horses or mountain bikes are allowed.

*Permits:* No permits are required. Parking and access are free.

*Directions:* From San Francisco, drive south on US Highway 101 to the Willow Road-Dumbarton exit. Continue east across the Dumbarton Bridge and take the first exit (Thornton Avenue) after the toll plaza. Turn right and drive to Marshlands Road. Turn right again and drive past the San Francisco Bay Wildlife Refuge entrance and visitor center for about three miles, following the signs to Dumbarton Pier.

*Maps:* For a free brochure, contact the refuge at the address below. To obtain a topographic map of the area, ask for Newark from the USGS.

*Who to contact:* San Francisco Bay National Wildlife Refuge, P.O. Box 524, Newark, CA 94560; (510) 792-4275 or (510) 792-0222.

*Trail notes:* Here is an example of the government doing something right. This pier, of course, was once the old Dumbarton Bridge, but when the new high-rise span was built in the 1980s, the roadway extending from Fremont was converted to a fishing pier as part of the San Francisco Bay National Wildlife Refuge. The pier reaches all the way to the channel of the South Bay, a natural migratory pathway for sharks (summer), bat rays (winter), sturgeon (winter), perch (late fall) and jacksmelt (spring). Many seabirds and water-fowl live in this area year round. The easy walk out to the end of the pier also renders pretty sea views of the South Bay's shoreline, and looking north on a clear day, of the San Mateo and Bay bridges.

## 40. TIDELANDS TRAIL       2.5 mi/1.5 hrs

*Reference:* **In San Francisco Bay Wildlife Refuge at the east foot of the Dumbarton Bridge; map E1-East Bay, grid g7.**

*User groups:* Hikers, dogs and mountain bikes. No horses are allowed. There are no wheelchair facilities but the trail can be navigated by most **wheelchair users**.

*Permits:* No permits are required. Parking and access are free.

*Directions:* From San Francisco, drive south on US Highway 101 to the Willow Road-Dumbarton exit. Continue east across the Dumbarton Bridge and take the first exit (Thornton Avenue) after the toll plaza. Turn right and drive a quarter mile to Marshland Road. Turn right and drive a short distance to the visitor center.

*Maps:* For a free brochure, contact the refuge at the address below. To obtain a topographic map of the area, ask for Newark from the USGS.

*Who to contact:* San Francisco Bay National Wildlife Refuge, P.O. Box 524, Newark, CA 94560; (510) 792-4275 or (510) 792-0222.

*Trail notes:* The diversity of bird life can be memorable at the San Francisco Bay Wildlife Refuge, with more than 250 species in a given year using this habitat for food, resting space and nesting sites. In just 15 or 20 minutes, it is not unusual to see a half dozen different species of ducks, an egret, sandpiper, willet, and herons. It is a big refuge, 23,000 acres in all, and the Tidelands Trail pours right through it. It is actually a wide dirt pathway on a levee that is routed amid salt marsh and bay tidewaters. Group nature tours on this trail are offered regularly on weekends. The views of the South Bay, and on clear days, the surrounding foothills, make for a panoramic backdrop. A must is to stop at the headquarters before you head off, which has exhibits and pamphlets that will make your walk more enjoyable.

# 41. ALAMEDA CREEK 11.0 mi. one way/4.5 hrs  REGIONAL TRAIL

*Reference:* On Alameda Creek from Niles to the South Bay; map E1-East Bay, grid g7.

*User groups:* South Trail: Hikers, dogs and mountain bikes. North Trail: Hikers, dogs and horses. No wheelchair facilities.

*Permits:* No permits are required. Parking and access are free.

*Directions:* From Interstate 680 in Fremont, take the Mission Boulevard exit and drive west to Highway 84/Niles Canyon Road. Turn right and make another immediate right on Old Canyon Road. The staging area is on the left.

*Maps:* For a free trail map, contact East Bay Regional Parks at the address below and ask for the Alameda Creek Regional Trail brochure. To obtain a topographic map of the area, ask for Niles from the USGS.

*Who to contact:* East Bay Regional Park District, 2950 Peralta Oaks Court, P.O. Box 5381, Oakland, CA 94605; (510) 635-0135, ext. 2200.

*Trail notes:* An unusual solution to the biker vs. hiker conflict has been discovered here: a double trail. That is, there are two trails, one on each side of Alameda Creek routed from Niles Community Park to the shoreline of the South Bay. The trail on the north bank is designed for horseback riders and hikers. The trail on the South Bank is paved, perfect for bicyclists and joggers. By the way, there are markers at quarter-mile intervals for joggers keeping track of their exact distances. From Niles, the trail routes past Shinn Pond, Alameda Creek Quarries and Coyote Hills Regional Park. For access to Coyote Hills Regional Park and the San Francisco Bay Wildlife Refuge, take the trail on the south side of the creek; there is no direct access to either of those areas on the trail on the north side of Alameda Creek.

## 42. PEAK TRAIL                7.0 mi/5.0 hrs

*Reference:* **In Mission Peak Regional Preserve near Fremont; map E1-East Bay, grid g8.**

*User groups:* Hikers, dogs and horses. No mountain bikes are allowed. No wheelchair facilities.

*Permits:* No permits are required. There is a parking fee charged at the Ohlone College Lot.

*Directions:* From Fremont, take Highway 238 (Mission Boulevard) to the Ohlone College campus. Turn left and park at Lot D or H. Go through the gate at the back of the campus to access the trail.

*Maps:* For a free trail map, contact East Bay Regional Parks at the address below and ask for the Mission Peak Regional Preserve brochure. To obtain a topographic map of the area, ask for Niles from the USGS.

*Who to contact:* East Bay Regional Park District, 2950 Peralta Oaks Court, P.O. Box 5381, Oakland, CA 94605; (510) 635-0135, ext. 2200.

*Trail notes:* You climb from elevation 400 feet at the trailhead to the summit of Mission Peak at 2,517 feet in a span of just 3.5 miles, one of the most intense climbs in the Bay Area. That is why many stay away, far away. But in the spring, it is one of the best hikes around. The grasslands are such a bright green that the hills seem to glow, wildflowers are blooming everywhere, and there are sweeping views of San Francisco, the Santa Cruz Mountains, and on crystal clear days, the Sierra crest to the east. There are two trails up, but the best is starting at the parking lot at Ohlone College, which provides a route less steep than from the other trailhead at the end of Stanford Avenue in Fremont. After parking at Ohlone College, take the Spring Valley Trail, which intersects with the Peak Trail and continues along the northern flank of the mountain up to the summit. A good idea is to bring a spare shirt for this hike, especially in colder months. That's because you will likely sweat through whatever you are wearing on the way up, then when you stop to enjoy the views, get cold and clammy. A spare shirt solves that.

## 43. SUNOL LOOP              4.75 mi/3.5 hrs

*Reference:* **In Sunol Regional Wilderness near Sunol; map E1-East Bay, grid g9.**

*User groups:* Hikers, dogs, horses and mountain bikes. The Indian Joe Creek section of the loop is limited to hikers only. No wheelchair facilities.

*Permits:* No permits are required. Parking and access are free.

*Directions:* From Interstate 680 in the East Bay, take the Calaveras Road exit in Sunol. Turn south on Calaveras and follow it to Geary Road. Turn left on Geary Road and follow it into the park.

*Maps:* For a free trail map, contact East Bay Regional Parks at the address below and ask for the Sunol Regional Wilderness brochure. To obtain a topographic map of the area, ask for La Costa Valley from the USGS.

*Who to contact:* East Bay Regional Park District, 2950 Peralta Oaks Court, P.O. Box 5381, Oakland, CA 94605; (510) 635-0135, ext. 2200.

*Trail notes:* There are hidden places around the Bay Area that make you feel like you have your own secret spots. This is one of those places. Sunol Preserve is a 6,400-acre wilderness and this loop trail crosses past many of the most striking spots: Little Yosemite, a miniature canyon with a pretty stream; Cerro Este, at 1,720 feet, one of the higher points in the park; Cave Rocks, a series of natural, gouged-out rock forms; and Indian Joe Creek, a little brook the runs along the start of the trail. From the parking area, start your loop hike by heading north on Indian Joe Creek Trail, then heading one mile (climbing) to Cave Rocks. Turn right on Rocks Road/Cerro Este Trail and climb up over the summit, then down the other side, all the way to Canyon View Trail. Turn right and return to the parking area. A great option on the Canyon View Trail is to take the short gated cutoff trail that drops down to the floor of Little Yosemite. In the winter, the creek at the bottom of the valley has many tiny pool-and-drop waterfalls.

---

## 44. EAST BAY NATIONAL SKYLINE TRAIL 31.0 mi. one way/3.0 days

*Reference:* **In East Bay Regional Park District, from Chabot Park near Castro Valley to Wildcat Regional Park in the Richmond hills; map E1- East Bay, grids c5, c6, d6, d7.**

*User groups:* Hikers, dogs, horses and mountain bikes. Horses and mountain bikes are restricted in some sections.

*Permits:* No permits are required. A parking fee may be charged at some trailheads.

*Directions:* See individual trailhead listings below for specific directions.

*Maps:* For a brochure and map of the East Bay Skyline National Trail, or individual maps on each regional park, contact East Bay Regional Parks at the address below.

*Who to contact:* East Bay Regional Park District, 2950 Peralta Oaks Court, P.O. Box 5381, Oakland, CA 94605; (510) 635-0135, ext. 2200.

*Trail notes:* A 31-mile trail along the East Bay's skyline offers a unique opportunity for a long-distance hike that can be chopped into many little segments over the course of days or weeks. The trail spans from the Castro Valley foothills northward to the ridgeline behind Richmond, in the process crossing six regional parks that offer a view into the region's prettiest and wildest lands. It is called the East Bay Skyline National Recreation Trail, the Bay Area's longest single continuous trail. We hiked the route south to north in two days, but the trip can be divided into seven sections from the different access points available at parking areas. Bicycles and horses are permitted on the 65 percent of the trail that is wide enough for them. It is a great trip, whether for a weekend or for weeks, taking a little at a time. No permits are needed, leashed dogs are permitted, and access is free. The only drawbacks are the lack of campgrounds along the route, which makes backpacking and overnights impossible, and the lack of piped drinking water. Water is available at only four points over 31 miles of trail, at Lomas Cantadas, Sibley Preserve, Skyline Gate and Bort Meadow. So come prepared with a full canteen (or two) of water per person, along with a hat and sunscreen. Here is a detailed description of the trail, south to north:

## 44a. Proctor Gate to Bort Meadow, Chabot Regional Park

*Directions:* From Interstate 580 in Oakland, take the 35th Avenue exit and drive east. 35th Avenue becomes Redwood Road; follow it, crossing Skyline

Boulevard and Pinehurst Road. Do not turn on Pinehurst; continue on Redwood to the Proctor Gate Staging Area, located on the east border of the park, next to a golf course.

*Trail notes:* The trail starts adjacent to a golf course, is routed up a ridge, then meanders on a ranch road in Chabot Park. At Stonebridge (don't turn left at the trail junction!), the trail leads into Grass Valley and on to Bort Meadows. Distance: 6.5 miles; climbs 600 feet, then drops 320 feet.

## 44b. Bort Meadow to MacDonald Gate, Chabot Regional Park

*Directions:* From Interstate 580 in Oakland, take the 35th Avenue exit and drive east (35th Avenue becomes Redwood Road). Follow Redwood Road, pass Skyline Boulevard and continue for three more miles to the Bort Meadow Staging Area on the right.

*Trail notes:* The 2.7-mile trail climbs steeply out of Bort Meadow, and at the ridge, you should turn and look south for the great view of Grass Valley. This climb is an open exposure, hot and dry in the afternoon, and is best hiked in the early morning. From the ridge, the trail proceeds through a hardwood forest with some chaparral in the mix, drops down into a canyon, crosses Redwood Road and puts you at the entrance to Redwood Regional Park. The trail climbs 300 feet, then drops 500 feet.

## 44c. MacDonald Gate to Skyline Gate, Redwood Regional Park

*Directions:* From Interstate 580 to the west or Interstate 680 to the east, drive to Highway 24. Proceed to Highway 13 and turn south. Continue to Redwood Road and turn left. Continue to the park entrance, then turn south and park at the MacDonald Gate Staging Area.

*Trail notes:* Hikers have two options here, and our preference is to split off at the French Trail in order to hike up the canyon bottom on the Stream Trail, enveloped by redwoods. In addition, bikes are banned from this section of trail. The alternative, a must for bikes, is to take the West Ridge Trail, a steep climb routed to the canyon rim, then dropping to the junction at Skyline Gate. Distance: 5 miles. Elevation change: Via French Trail, drops 200 feet, then climbs 400 feet; via West Ridge, climbs 900 feet, then drops 200 feet.

## 44d. Skyline Gate thru Huckleberry Preserve to Sibley Preserve

*Directions:* From Highway 24 in Oakland, proceed east to Highway 13. Turn south and drive to Joaquin Miller Road, then head east until you hit Skyline Boulevard. Turn left on Skyline and continue to the Skyline Gate Staging Area.

*Trail notes:* This section of trail is a choice hike for nature lovers, with an abundance of bird life and other wildlife, especially in the early morning and late evening. The trail passes through a deciduous woodland habitat, with a short but quite steep climb after entering Huckleberry Preserve. Distance: 3 miles; drops 200 feet, then climbs 480 feet.

## 44e. Sibley Preserve to Lomas Cantadas, Tilden Regional Park

*Directions:* From Interstate 580 to the west or Interstate 680 to the east, drive to Highway 24. Proceed to just east of the Caldecott Tunnel and take the Fish Ranch Road exit west to Grizzly Peak Boulevard. Turn left and continue to Skyline Boulevard. The park entrance and parking area is on the left.

*Trail notes:* This is an unique section of trail that crosses over Caldecott Tunnel, a relatively unpeopled area. The area has many hawks, a nice bonus. Sibley is best-known for its volcanic past, with a sidetrip available of Mt. Round Top, a one-time volcano that blew its top off. No bicycles are permitted. Distance: 3.4 miles; drops 300 feet, then climbs 600 feet.

## 44f. Lomas Cantadas to Inspiration Point, Tilden Regional Park

*Directions:* From Interstate 580 to the west or Interstate 680 to the east, drive to Highway 24. Proceed to just east of the Caldecott Tunnel and take the Fish Ranch Road exit to Grizzly Peak Boulevard. At the stop sign, turn right and continue on Grizzly Peak Boulevard to Lomas Cantadas Road. Turn right, then immediately turn left, following the signs for the Steam Train. Park at the Steam Train Parking Area.

*Trail notes:* This section of trail starts at a major access area off Grizzly Peak Boulevard, with an adjacent sidetrip available to Vollmer Peak, the highest-point on the East Bay Skyline National Trail. The trail is then routed north to Inspiration Point at Wildcat Canyon Road, another well-known access point, losing elevation most of the way. This section of trail has many sweeping views of the East Bay's untouched foothills. Distance: 3 miles; drops 860 feet.

## 44g. Inspiration Point (Tilden) to Wildcat Canyon Regional Park

*Directions:* From Interstate 580 to the west or Interstate 680 to the east, drive to Highway 24. Proceed to just east of the Caldecott Tunnel and take the Fish Ranch Road exit west to Grizzly Peak Boulevard. Turn right, continue up the hill, and turn right on South Park Drive. Proceed one mile to Wildcat Canyon Road, bear right and continue to the parking area at Inspiration Point on the left. Note: South Park Road is sometimes closed in the winter due to newt migrations; an alternate route is as follows: From Highway 24, go through the Caldecott Tunnel and exit at Orinda. Turn left on Camino Pablo. Drive north for about two miles, then turn left on Wildcat Canyon Road. Follow it to Inspiration Point on the right.

*Trail notes:* This last piece of trail starts at the most heavily-used section of the entire route, then crosses its most dramatic and unpeopled area. From Inspiration Point, the trail is actually paved for four miles, ideal for bicycles and **wheelchairs.** Beyond that, the trail turns to dirt and traces San Pablo Ridge, with inspiring views in all directions, before dropping very steeply into Wildcat Canyon Park in the Richmond foothills. Distance: 7.2 miles; drops 800 feet.

NOR-CAL MAP ........................ see page 14
adjoining maps
NORTH (D1) ..................... see page 202
EAST (E2) ........................ see page 394
SOUTH (F1) ...................... see page 468
WEST .............................................. no map

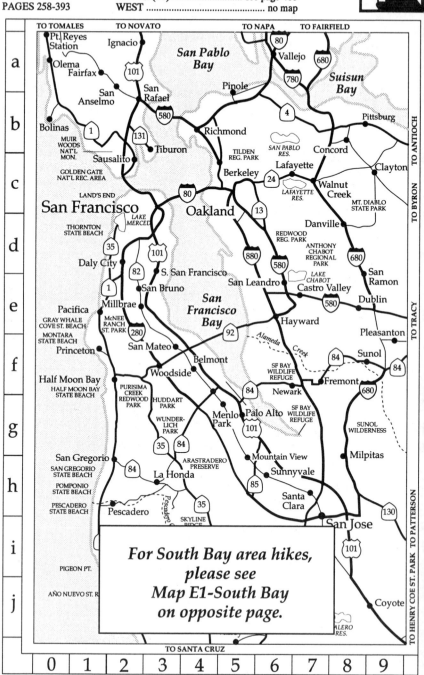

TO TOMALES    TO NOVATO    TO NAPA    TO FAIRFIELD

**a**
Pt. Reyes Station
Ignacio
*San Pablo Bay*
Vallejo
80
680
*Suisun Bay*
Olema
Fairfax
101
San Rafael
Pinole
780
4

**b**
Bolinas
1
San Anselmo
131
580
Richmond
*SAN PABLO RES.*
Concord
Pittsburg
MUIR WOODS NAT'L MON.
Sausalito
Tiburon
*TILDEN REG. PARK*
Lafayette
Clayton

**c**
GOLDEN GATE NAT'L REC. AREA
LAND'S END
80
Berkeley
24
*LAFAYETTE RES.*
Walnut Creek
MT. DIABLO STATE PARK

**d**
San Francisco
*LAKE MERCED*
Oakland
13
Danville
THORNTON STATE BEACH
35
101
REDWOOD REG. PARK
ANTHONY CHABOT REGIONAL PARK

**e**
Daly City
82
S. San Francisco
880
580
680
San Ramon
1
San Bruno
San Leandro
*LAKE CHABOT*
Castro Valley
Dublin
Pacifica
Millbrae
*San Francisco Bay*
580
GRAY WHALE COVE ST. BEACH
McNEE RANCH ST. PARK
280
Hayward
Pleasanton

**f**
MONTARA STATE BEACH
Princeton
San Mateo
Belmont
92
*Alameda Creek*
84
Sunol
84
Half Moon Bay
Woodside
SF BAY WILDLIFE REFUGE
Fremont
680
HALF MOON BAY STATE BEACH
PURISIMA CREEK REDWOOD PARK
HUDDART PARK
84
Newark

**g**
WUNDER-LICH PARK
Menlo Park
Palo Alto
SF BAY WILDLIFE REFUGE
SUNOL WILDERNESS
35
84
101

**h**
San Gregorio
ARASTRADERO PRESERVE
Mountain View
Milpitas
SAN GREGORIO STATE BEACH
84
La Honda
Sunnyvale
POMPONIO STATE BEACH
85
Santa Clara
PESCADERO STATE BEACH
Pescadero
35
SKYLINE RIDGE
San Jose
130

**i**
PIGEON PT.
101

**j**
AÑO NUEVO ST. R
Coyote
*CALERO RES.*

*For South Bay area hikes, please see Map E1-South Bay on opposite page.*

TO SANTA CRUZ

0   1   2   3   4   5   6   7   8   9

TO ANTIOCH
TO BYRON
TO TRACY
TO PATTERSON
TO HENRY COE ST. PARK

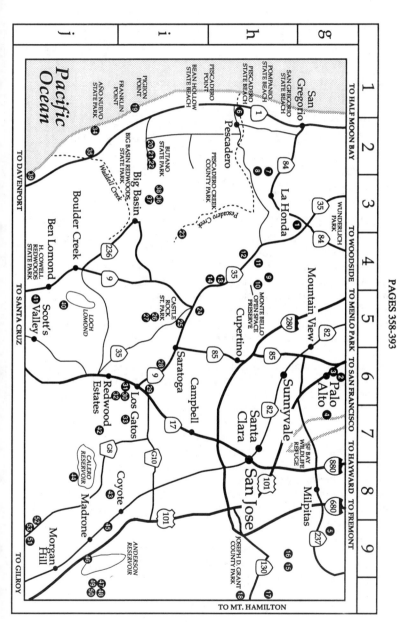

MAP E1-SOUTH BAY
53 TRAILS
PAGES 358-393

**Map E1-South Bay featuring:** Ed R. Levin County Park, Sam McDonald County Park, Memorial Park, Alum Rock City Park, Penitencia Creek County Park, Joseph Grant County Park, Grant Ranch County Park, Pigeon Point Lighthouse, Butano State Park, Portola State Park, Sanborn-Skyline County Park, Castle Rock State Park, Big Basin Redwoods State Park, Waddell Creek, Vasona Lake County Park, Lexington Reservoir, Lexington County Park, Año Nuevo State Reserve, Loch Lomond Park, Henry Cowell Redwoods State Park, Almaden Quicksilver County Park, Santa Teresa County Park, Calero Reservoir County Park, Coyote-Hellyer County Park, Anderson Lake County Park, Henry Coe State Park, Uvas Canyon County Park, Coyote Lake County Park, Mt. Madonna County Park

## 1. WINDY HILL LOOP          8.2 mi/4.5 hrs

*Reference:* **In Windy Hill Open Space Preserve in the Portola Valley foothills; map E1-South Bay, grid g3.**

*User groups:* Hikers and horses. Dogs or mountain bikes are not allowed, except on the Spring Ridge Trail at Windy Hill Open Space Preserve. There are wheelchair facilities in the picnic area adjacent to the parking area.

*Permits:* No permits are required. Parking and access are free.

*Directions:* From Interstate 280 or US 101 on the Peninsula, take Highway 84 west through the mountains to Skyline Boulevard (Highway 35). Turn left on Highway 35 and drive 2.3 miles to the parking area.

*Maps:* For a free trail map and brochure, contact Midpeninsula Open Space District at the address below. To obtain a topographic map of the area, ask for Mindego Hill from the USGS.

*Who to contact:* Midpeninsula Regional Open Space District, 330 Distel Circle, Los Altos, CA 94022; (415) 691-1200.

*Trail notes:* Windy Hill may be known for its north winds on spring afternoons, but it is better known for its remarkable views on any clear day. From the 1,900-foot summit, a grass-covered hilltop west of Portola Valley, hikers can see San Francisco Bay to one side and the Pacific Ocean on the other. If views are all you want, the 0.7-mile Anniversary Trail provides them, routed from the parking area to the summit. If you want more, there is more to get, with an excellent loop hike that drops down into forests, then climbs back out to grasslands. To do it, take the Hamms Gulch Trail, dropping 1,000 feet in elevation, through a remote, pristine, wooded environment. Then loop back on the Razorback Ridge Trail, hiking an extended series of switchbacks to make the return climb. The trail emerges from the woodlands, then turns right on Lost Trail. The last 2.1 miles to the park area offers great views and a refreshing end to a diligent hike.

# 2. CHARLESTON SLOUGH 4.0 mi/1.5 hrs

*Reference:* **In South Bay marshland in Palo Alto; map E1-South Bay, grid g6.**

*User groups:* Hikers and mountains bikes. No dogs or horses are allowed. No wheelchair facilities.

*Permits:* No permits are required. Parking and access are free.

*Directions:* From US 101 in south Palo Alto, take the San Antonio exit and turn east (toward the Bay). After a short distance, turn left onto Bayshore Frontage Road and drive about a mile to Charleston Slough. The parking area is on the right side of the road.

*Maps:* To obtain a topographic map of the area, ask for Mountain View from the USGS.

*Who to contact:* Palo Alto Baylands Interpretive Center, 1451 Middlefield Road, Palo Alto, CA 94301; (415) 329-2506.

*Trail notes:* This trail is actually an old levee road that borders Charleston Slough, providing access to an expanse of wetlands and marsh habitat. It connects to a similar levee road that connects to Shoreline Regional Park in Mountain View, a great bike trip and a good hike. From this trailhead, the best route is to head straight out the levee along Charleston Slough. Within 10 or 15 minutes, with each step you will gain access to an area that has been preserved completely in its native habitat. While from afar the surroundings may appear to be just pickleweed and mud, when you look closer you will begin to see a huge diversity of birds and wildlife that live here, a very rich ecosystem. Way back in the 1950s, striped bass used to enter the mouth of Charleston Slough here and provide some excellent fishing. While the stripers are long gone, still remaining are the quiet times and bird life, making this a favorite place for many visitors.

# 3. SHORELINE REGIONAL PARK 2.0 mi/1.0 hr

*Reference:* **Along South San Francisco Bay in Mountain View; map E1-South Bay, grid g6.**

*User groups:* Hikers and mountain bikes. No horses or dogs are allowed. The trail is **wheelchair accessible**.

*Permits:* No permits are required. Parking and access are free.

*Directions:* From Highway 101 in Mountain View, take Shoreline Boulevard east. Drive on Shoreline Boulevard past the Shoreline Amphitheater to the park entrance station.

*Maps:* To obtain a topographic map of the area, ask for Mountain View from the USGS.

*Who to contact:* Shoreline Regional Park, City of Mountain View, 3070 North Shoreline Boulevard, Mountain View, CA 94043; (415) 903-6392.

*Trail notes:* This is an ideal family destination with a wide variety of activities available, including pleasant walks and bike rides on wide, crushed-gravel byways. There is also a small lake that makes an excellent spot for windsurfing, and many good kite-flying areas on small hills. The best trail at Shoreline Regional Park is routed along the east side of the lake, and then northward on a levee through marshlands. It is quite popular with birdwatchers, with sightings ranging from egrets to LBJs, er, Little Brown Jobs. Near the lake, there is a concession stand that gets a lot of use from the corn dog-and-Coke crowd, which kind of puts everything in perspective.

# 4. SUNNYVALE BAYLANDS 2.0 mi/1.0 hr

*Reference:* On South San Francisco Bay in Sunnyvale; map E1-South Bay, grid g7.

*User groups:* Hikers only. No dogs, horses or mountain bikes are allowed. No wheelchair facilities.

*Permits:* No permits are required. A $3 parking fee is charged.

*Directions:* From Highway 237 in Sunnyvale, take the Lawrence Expressway exit north to Caribbean Drive and follow the signs to the park.

*Maps:* To obtain a topographic map of the area, ask for Mountain View from the USGS. For a free map, write to Sunnyvale Baylands County Park at the address below.

*Who to contact:* Sunnyvale Baylands County Park, c/o Ed R. Levin County Park, 3100 Calaveras Road, Milpitas, CA 95035; (408) 262-6980.

*Trail notes:* The Sunnyvale Baylands County Park really isn't much of a "park" at all, but rather a wildlife preserve surrounded by a levee that provides a good trail for hiking and jogging. It covers 220 acres of South Bay marshland, home for blue herons, great egrets, avocets, black-necked stilts, mallards, pintails and burrowing owls. On nearly every trip you will also see a jackrabbit or two. In fact, these jackrabbits have a way of scaring the bejesus out of you. They hide in the weeds, it seems, until you get close, then suddenly they pop up and take off at warp speed, always a shock. From the parking area adjacent to Highway 237, hike along the levee, turning left as it parallels Calabasis Creek. To your left is a seasonal wetland preserve. The trail continues along the creek, then turns left again and runs alongside Guadalupe Slough. Here to your left is an open water bird preserve.

# 5. MONUMENT PEAK TRAIL 6.5 mi/4.0 hrs

*Reference:* In Ed R. Levin County Park in the Milpitas foothills; map E1-South Bay, grid g9.

*User groups:* Hikers and horses. No dogs or mountain bikes are allowed. No wheelchair facilities.

*Permits:* No permits are required. A $3 day-use fee is charged.

*Directions:* From San Jose, take Interstate 680 north to Milpitas. Take the Calaveras Road East exit and follow Calaveras Road to the park. The trail starts near the northwest end of Sandy Wool Lake.

*Maps:* For a free trail map, contact Ed Levin Park at the address below. To obtain topographic maps of the area, ask for Milpitas and Calaveras Reservoir from the USGS.

*Who to contact:* Ed R. Levin County Park, 3100 Calaveras Road, Milpitas, CA 95035; (408) 262-6980.

*Trail notes:* Monument Peak gets overlooked by many, including regular visitors to Levin Park. Yet at 2,594 feet, the views nearly rival that of Mt. Hamilton, with far-ranging vistas of the Santa Clara Valley. There are several reasons why it is overlooked. Of the 13 trails in the park, it is clearly the longest, steepest and most difficult. Most people do not visit Levin Park for a challenge, but rather to play golf at Spring Valley, to go fishing at Sandy Wool Lake, or just for a picnic. But a challenge this climb offers, and there are two routes up. The Monument Peak Trail is actually a road, and you may run head on into mountain bikers ripping downhill. Our suggestion is to take the Tularcitos/Agua Caliente Trail, which provides a more gentle climb without bikes to contend with. It junctions with the Monument Peak Road near the top, where you turn left for the final push to the summit. With the trailhead at 300 feet at Sandy Wool Lake, figure a 2,300-foot climb over the course of about 3.75 miles.

---

## 6. PESCADERO MARSH    3.0 mi/1.5 hrs

*Reference:* **In Pescadero Marsh south of Pescadero; map E1-South Bay, grid h1.**

*User groups:* Hikers only. No dogs, horses or mountain bikes are allowed. No wheelchair facilities.

*Permits:* No permits are required. Parking and access are free.

*Directions:* From the Peninsula in San Mateo, take Highway 92 west to Half Moon Bay. Turn south onto Highway 1 and drive 18 miles south to Pescadero Marsh. Cross the Pescadero Bridge and park at the dirt area on the left side of the highway at Pescadero Road. The trailhead is at the northeastern end of the Pescadero Bridge from the USGS.

*Maps:* To obtain a topographic map of the area, ask for San Gregorio from the USGS.

*Who to contact:* California State Parks, 95 Kelly Avenue, Half Moon Bay, CA 94019; (415) 726-8800.

*Trail notes:* Here is one of the few remaining natural marsh areas on the entire central California coast, a 600-acre marsh that is home to more than 250 different species of birds. The most spectacular is the blue heron, often nearly four feet tall with a wingspan of seven feet. One of the classic sights of any wetland is watching these huge birds lift off with their labored wing beats. The trail is nearly flat, which makes it an easy walk for almost anyone of any age. It starts just northeast of the Pescadero Bridge on Highway 1, a dirt path that is routed amid pampas grass and bogs, along the edge of wetland habitat. The best route is to take the North Pond Trail to Audubon Marsh, then turn and head east and trace the southern edge of the marsh on the Sequoia Trail along Pescadero Creek. The marsh is bordered by the Pacific Ocean on one side and Pescadero Creek on the other, so the result is a unique setting that can attract birds that live in both saltwater and freshwater environments. Guided nature walks are offered most weekends by volunteers from the Half Moon Bay State Parks Department.

---

## 7. McDONALD LOOP    3.1 mi/1.5 hrs

*Reference:* **In Sam McDonald County Park near La Honda; map E1-South Bay, grid h2.**

*User groups:* Hikers only. No dogs, horses or mountain bikes are allowed. No wheelchair facilities.

*Permits:* No permits are required. A $3 parking fee is charged.

*Directions:* From Interstate 280 on the Peninsula, take the Woodside/Highway 84 exit. Drive up the hill past Skyline Boulevard and on for another 10 miles to La Honda. Turn left on La Honda/Pescadero Road, veer left at the "Y" and drive 1.5 miles to Sam McDonald County Park.

*Maps:* For a free trail map, contact Sam McDonald County Park at the address below. To obtain a topographic map of the area, ask for La Honda from the USGS.

*Who to contact:* Sam McDonald County Park, San Mateo County Park and Recreation Department, 590 Hamilton Street, Redwood City, CA 94063; (415) 879-0238 or (415) 363-4020.

*Trail notes:* Though not a long trail, for many the McDonald Loop is long enough, with a few challenging "ups" always a surprise. The park is best known for its redwoods, complete with the classic fern/sorrel understory. This park covers 1,000 acres, is kept in a primitive state, and its trail network is linked by fire trail to Memorial County Park and Portola State Park. The fire trails, by the way, are among the best mountain bike trails on the Peninsula. This loop hike provides a fine introduction to the area. It is an excellent hike year round, yet in the winter, especially during the week, there are rarely other hikers on the trail. A great sidetrip is to visit the Heritage Grove, which adjoins the park and is accessible on Alpine Road about one mile east of the park. There are several ancient redwoods here, and a short, pleasant walk is available among them.

---

# 8. PESCADERO CREEK TRAIL  6.0 mi/2.5 hrs

*Reference:* **In Memorial Park near La Honda; map E1-South Bay, grid h2.**

*User groups:* Hikers only. No dogs, horses or mountain bikes are allowed. No wheelchair facilities.

*Permits:* No permits are required. A $4 day-use fee is charged.

*Directions:* From Interstate 280 on the Peninsula, take the Woodside/Highway 84 exit. Drive up the hill, pass Skyline Boulevard and continue for another 10 miles to La Honda. Turn left on La Honda/Pescadero Road, veer left at the "Y" and drive six miles to Memorial Park.

*Maps:* For a free trail map, contact Memorial County Park at the address below. To obtain a topographic map of the area, ask for La Honda from the USGS.

*Who to contact:* Memorial County Park, 590 Hamilton Street, Redwood City, CA 94063; (415) 879-0238 or (415) 363-4020.

*Trail notes:* Memorial Park is tucked in a pocket of redwoods between the tiny towns of La Honda and Loma Mar. While there are 50 miles of trails available in the area, one of our favorites is the Iverson Trail that is routed along Pescadero Creek. The creek is quite pretty. In the winter, when the water is clear enough, hikers can sometimes see steelhead preparing to spawn. In the summer, the "little trout" are actually steelhead smolts, trying to grow before swimming out to sea, and no fishing is permitted. A bonus in this area is that there are many excellent fire roads for mountain biking.

---

# 9. SAN ANDREAS FAULT TRAIL  0.6 mi/0.5 hr

*Reference:* **In Los Trancos Open Space in the Palo Alto foothills; map E1-South Bay, grid h4.**

*User groups:* Hikers only. No dogs, horses or mountain bikes are allowed. The trail is not wheelchair accessible, but the parking lot is **wheelchair accessible** and offers a nice view.

*Permits:* No permits are required. Parking and access are free.

*Directions:* From Interstate 280 in Palo Alto, turn west onto Page Mill Road and drive seven twisty miles to the signed parking area on the right. Montebello

Open Space Preserve is directly across the street.

*Maps:* For a free trail map, contact the Midpeninsula Open Space District at the address below. A map and trail guide are also available at the parking area. To obtain a topographic map of the area, ask for Mindego Hill from the USGS.

*Who to contact:* Midpeninsula Regional Open Space District, 330 Distel Court, Los Altos, CA 94022; (415) 691-1200.

*Trail notes:* The air is always fresh and scented with bay leaves and damp woods at Los Trancos Open Space Preserve. While there are only seven miles of trails at Los Trancos, one of the Peninsula's feature hikes, the San Andreas Fault Trail, is found here. This is a self-guided tour of an "earthquake trail," with 13 little numbered signposts along the trail that correspond to explanations in the park brochure. It includes several examples of fault movement. If you don't want a geology lesson, there are good views of the Peninsula from the 2,000-foot ridgeline. Most hikers will connect the San Andreas Fault Trail to the Lost Creek Loop Trail, a pleasant and easy bonus trip that is routed into secluded spots along a pretty creek. With the Montebello Open Space Preserve located on the other side of Page Mill Road, there are nearly 3,000 contiguous acres of public open space here.

---

# 10. STEVENS CREEK NATURE TRAIL

3.5 mi/2.0 hrs

*Reference:* **In Monte Bello Open Space Preserve in Palo Alto foothills; map E1-South Bay, grid h4.**

*User groups:* Hikers, horses and mountain bikes (restricted from some trails). No dogs are allowed. This trail is not open to wheelchairs, but the parking lot and a short trail are **wheelchair-accessible** and offer a nice view.

*Permits:* No permits are required unless you plan to utilize the preserve's Backpack Camp. Phone (415) 691-1200 for information.

*Directions:* From Interstate 280 in Palo Alto, turn west onto Page Mill Road and drive seven twisty miles to the signed parking area on the left. Los Trancos Open Space Preserve is directly across the road.

*Maps:* For a free trail map, contact the Midpeninsula Open Space District at the address below. A map and trail guide are also available at the trailhead. To obtain a topographic map of the area, ask for Mindego Hill from the USGS.

*Who to contact:* Midpeninsula Regional Open Space District, 330 Distel Court, Los Altos, CA 94022; (415) 691-1200.

*Trail notes:* Monte Bello Open Space Preserve encompasses more than 2,700 acres of the most natural and scenic lands on the Peninsula. It includes the 2,800-foot Black Mountain, the headwaters of Stevens Creek, and this pretty nature trail. The trail starts by lateraling across a grasslands bluff, then drops 450 feet into the wooded headwaters of Stevens Creek. As you descend through the forest, you will smell spicy bay leaves, note the cool dampness, and see the moss growing on so many trees. The trail emerges from the forest and is routed back along the San Andreas Fault, where two stark images are forthcoming. On one side, to the west, are dense woodlands. Yet to the east are grasslands and chaparral. This is a product of the differences in soil composition created by fault movement. The nature trail has signed points of interest, with explanations for each in the brochure. There are also longer hikes available in the park, the most ambitious being the 7.6-mile (one-way) Canyon Trail to Saratoga Gap.

## 11. COAL CREEK OPEN SPACE  4.0 mi/2.0 hrs

*Reference:* In Coal Creek Open Space Preserve on the Peninsula's Skyline Ridge; map E1-South Bay, grid h4.

*User groups:* Hikers only. No dogs, horses or mountain bikes are allowed. No wheelchair facilities.

*Permits:* No permits are required. Parking and access are free.

*Directions:* From Highway 280 in Palo Alto, take the Page Mill Road exit and drive west on a winding two-lane road up the mountain to Skyline Boulevard. Turn right onto Skyline Boulevard and drive one mile to the parking area, located on the right at the CalTrans Vista Point.

*Maps:* For a free trail map, contact the Midpeninsula Open Space District at the address below. To obtain a topographic map of the area, ask for Mindego Hill from the USGS.

*Who to contact:* Midpeninsula Regional Open Space District, 330 Distel Circle, Los Altos, CA 94022; (415) 691-1200.

*Trail notes:* Most residents of the Peninsula have never heard of Coal Creek Open Space Preserve, and that makes sense, being one of the lesser-developed parklands in the Bay Area. Yet it is worth the trip, set just east of the Skyline Ridge, covering 490 acres of rolling meadows, open grasslands, and the forested headwaters of two creeks. A bonus is that the parking area is adjacent to the CalTrans Vista Point, one of the best lookouts in the Bay Area. The trails at this park cover only four miles, and hey, actually the trails are old ranch roads. They route across the grasslands past a classic-looking barn and down along a small creek. It is best visited with the intention of a short walk and picnic, with many quiet spots available for the latter.

## 12. BOREL HILL TRAIL  1.4 mi/1.0 hr

*Reference:* In Russian Ridge Open Space Preserve on the Peninsula's Skyline Ridge; map E1-South Bay, grid h4.

*User groups:* Hikers, horses and mountain bikes. No dogs are allowed. A **wheelchair-accessible** trail is available from the parking area to Alpine Pond.

*Permits:* No permits are required. Parking and access are free.

*Directions:* From Interstate 280 in Palo Alto, take the Page Mill Road exit and drive west on a winding two-lane road up the mountain to Skyline Boulevard. Cross Skyline Boulevard and turn right into the parking lot at the northwest corner of the intersection.

*Maps:* For a free trail map, contact the Midpeninsula Open Space District at the address below. A map is also available at the trailhead. To obtain a topographic map of the area, ask for Mindego Hill from the USGS.

*Who to contact:* Midpeninsula Regional Open Space District, 330 Distel Circle, Los Altos, CA 94022; (415) 691-1200.

*Trail notes:* Borel Hill is one of the great lookouts on the San Francisco Peninsula, topping out at 2,572 feet and surrounded by grasslands, so hikers get unblocked, 360-degree views. Yet Borel Hill is not well known, a favorite only to hikers who visit Russian Ridge Open Space Preserve.

Russian Ridge is that big grassy ridge near the intersection of Alpine Road and Skyline Boulevard on the Peninsula's ridgeline above Palo Alto. From the parking area, you hike southeast on the Ridge Trail, climbing about 250 feet over the course of 0.7 miles to reach Borel Hill. It is located just southwest of the trail, the obvious highest spot around, the hilltop with no trees, only grasslands. From the summit, with just a sweeping turn of the head, you can see Monterey Bay one moment, then Mt. Diablo and the South Bay the next, great stuff. There are several other trails at Russian Ridge Preserve, the best being the 2.6-mile (one-way) hike out to Mindego Ridge Trail, which is routed out through an oak woodland forest. A new return loop trail was completed for the 1995 hiking season.

## 13. SKYLINE RIDGE TRAIL    3.0 mi/1.5 hrs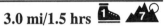

*Reference:* **In Skyline Ridge Open Space Preserve on the Peninsula's Skyline Ridge; map E1-South Bay, grid h4.**

*User groups:* Hikers, horses and mountain bikes. No dogs are allowed. There is a **wheelchair-accessible** trail to Horseshoe Lake.

*Permits:* No permits are required. Parking and access are free.

*Directions:* From Highway 280 in Palo Alto, take the Page Mill Road exit and drive west on a winding two-lane road up the mountain to Skyline Boulevard. Turn left onto Skyline Boulevard and drive eight-tenths of a mile to the main entrance and parking area on the right.

*Maps:* For a free trail map, contact the Midpeninsula Open Space District at the address below. To obtain a topographic map of the area, ask for Mindego Hill from the USGS.

*Who to contact:* Midpeninsula Regional Open Space District, 330 Distel Circle, Los Altos, CA 94022; (415) 691-1200.

*Trail notes:* Most people learn about this park by accident in December, when they come up to the choose-and-cut Christmas Tree Farm on Skyline Boulevard (Highway 35) owned by the Open Space District. They see the parking area for the parkland, maybe a trailhead, and their curiosity starts. At some point, that curiosity should be answered with a hike, and most feel well compensated for the effort. From the parking area on the west side of Skyline, the Ridge Trail is routed around a pretty little farm pond, Horseshoe Lake. From there, the trail is routed into the interior of the park, skirting the flank of the highest mountain in the park at 2,493 feet, and loops back to Skyline Boulevard. You play peek-a-boo here, in and out of woodlands, with occasional views of plunging canyons to the west. A loop hike can be created, but it means going back on a fire road, so most people return to the parking area via the same route.

## 14. LONG RIDGE LOOP    4.6 mi/2.0 hrs

*Reference:* **In Long Ridge Open Space Preserve in Santa Cruz Mountains; map E1-South Bay, grid h4.**

*User groups:* Hikers only. Leashed dogs are permitted only in signed areas. No horses or mountain bikes allowed. No wheelchair facilities.

*Permits:* No permits are required. Parking and access are free.

*Directions:* From Interstate 280 near Santa Clara, turn west onto Saratoga Avenue and drive to Highway 9. Turn west on Highway 9 and continue on a winding road up to the junction with Highway 35 (Skyline Boulevard). Turn north on Skyline Boulevard and drive three miles to the Grizzly Flat parking area on the right.

*Maps:* For a free trail map, contact the Midpeninsula Open Space District at the address below. A map is also available at the trailhead. To obtain a topographic map of the area, ask for Mindego Hill from the USGS.

*Who to contact:* Midpeninsula Regional Open Space District, 330 Distel Circle, Los Altos, CA 94022; (415) 691-1200.

*Trail notes:* When you walk the ridge line here, you are rewarded with gorgeous views of the western slopes of the Santa Cruz Mountains, highlighted by Big Basin and Butano state parks. From the southern part of the park on a clear day, the Pacific Coast comes into view as well. Long Ridge Preserve covers more than 1,000 acres, with a scenic loop hike that peaks out at 2,400 feet, that both climbs the ridge as well as ducks down into pretty, wooded canyons. After departing from the trailhead, you will cross a small creek, then turn right to start the looping hike up Long Ridge. The trail climbs up to Long Ridge Road, then turns and is routed south across the grassy hilltops. At the four-corners trail junction, turn left for the steep switch-backed route down the canyon. At the bottom of the switchbacks, the trail passes the beautiful Jikoji Retreat, a private Zen center set along a surprising little pond, then turns left and loops back to the parking area. This is a pretty oak woodland, with an apple orchard in one area.

---

# 15. EAGLE ROCK LOOP      2.2 mi/1.0 hr

*Reference:* **In Alum Rock City Park in San Jose foothills; map E1-South Bay, grid h9.**

*User groups:* Hikers and mountain bikes. No dogs or horses are allowed. No wheelchair access.

*Permits:* No permits are required. A $3 parking fee is charged.

*Directions:* From Interstate 680 in San Jose, take Alum Rock Avenue east for 3.5 miles to the park entrance.

*Maps:* For a free trail map, contact the Alum Rock Park at the address below. To obtain a topographic map of the area, ask for Calaveras Reservoir from the USGS.

*Who to contact:* Alum Rock City Park, 16240 Alum Rock Avenue, San Jose, CA 95127; (408) 259-5477.

*Trail notes:* At 795 feet, Eagle Rock is pretty short as far as mountains go. But at Alum Rock Park, it's the best perch for a picnic site and view of the Santa Clara Valley. In the winter, after a rain has cleared the air, it becomes a choice spot. For this hike, park at the lot at road's end at the eastern end of the park. That is where you will find a major trailhead, with several routes available. Take the one on the left, the North Rim Trail, to reach Eagle Rock. The hike climbs 300 feet to the canyon rim overlooking the valley cut by Penitencia Creek, then a short (signed) cutoff trail will take you to Eagle Rock. To complete the loop, return to the North Rim Trail and continue on, working your way back down the valley floor. Turn left on the Creek Trail (more like a road), which is routed along Penitencia Creek back to the parking area. There are 13 miles of trails that provide access to the park's 700 acres, but this hike is our favorite here.

## 16. PENITENCIA CREEK    4.0 mi/1.75 hrs

*Reference:* **In Penitencia Creek County Park in east San Jose; map E1-South Bay, grid h9.**

*User groups:* Hikers and mountain bikes. No dogs or horses are allowed. No wheelchair access.

*Permits:* No permits are required. A $3 parking fee is charged.

*Directions:* From Interstate 680 in San Jose, take the Berryessa Road exit east. Turn right onto Capitol Avenue and drive to Penitencia Creek Road. Turn left and continue to the Alum Rock City Park entrance. The trailhead is at the western end of the park.

*Maps:* For a free trail map, contact Penitencia Creek County Park at the address below. To obtain a topographic map of the area, ask for Calaveras Reservoir from the USGS.

*Who to contact:* Penitencia Creek County Park, c/o Ed R. Levin County Park, 3100 Calaveras Road, Milpitas, CA 95035; (408) 262-6980.

*Trail notes:* Hey, to be honest, this isn't much of a trail, more of a bike path, but with the stream alongside, it can make a nice route for a stroll, jog or ride. In addition, there are two bonuses: 1. The park's eastern boundary abuts against Alum Rock City Park, providing access to an additional 13 miles of trails. 2. Near Piedmont Road, behind the fire station, there is an additional 40 acres called "Creek Park" that is linked to this trail and provides an additional loop trail. Penitencia Creek Trail runs for four miles along the stream, adjacent to Penitencia Creek Road, so for joggers making the roundtrip, it makes for an easy eight-miler. Most hikers do about half that, or extend their walks into Creek Park or Alum Rock Park.

## 17. HALLS VALLEY LOOP    5.5 mi/3.0 hrs

*Reference:* **In Joseph Grant County Park in Mt. Hamilton foothills east of San Jose; map E1-South Bay, grid h9.**

*User groups:* Hikers, horses and mountain bikes. No dogs are allowed. No wheelchair facilities.

*Permits:* No permits are required. A $3 entrance fee is charged seven days a week from April to September, and only on weekends and holidays the rest of the year. There is a small, slotted register at the parking area, so you have to pay the do-it-yourself way.

*Directions:* Take US 101 south into San Jose, then turn south onto Interstate 680. Take the Alum Rock Avenue East exit and head east to Mount Hamilton Road. Turn right and drive eight miles to the parking area on the left.

*Maps:* For a free trail map, contact Joseph B. Grant County Park at the address below. To obtain a topographic map of the area, ask for Lick Observatory from the USGS.

*Who to contact:* Joseph B. Grant County Park, 18405 Mt. Hamilton Road, San Jose, CA 95140; (408) 274-6121.

*Trail notes:* Grant Ranch is the Bay Area's great undiscovered wild playland. It covers 9,000 acres in the foothills of Mt. Hamilton, yet gets relatively little use, despite being a perfect setting for hiking and mountain biking. There is plenty of room for both, with 40 miles of hiking trails (horses permitted) and 20 miles of old abandoned ranch roads for mountain biking and hiking. The

Halls Valley Loop provides the best introduction to Grant Ranch. From the parking area along Mt. Hamilton Road, take the main trail/road out past Grant Lake, and at the junction, veer left on the Halls Valley Trail. This skirts Halls Valley to the left, an open landscape of foothills and grasslands, sprinkled with oaks, all quiet and pretty. The trail heads out 2.5 miles, climbing east toward Mt. Hamilton, until it meets the Cañada de Pala Trail. Turn right here, hike up four-tenths of a mile and then turn right again on the Los Huecos Trail to complete the loop. From here, it's a 1.8-mile trip back to the parking area, descending steeply most of the way. Note: There are many great sidetrips on this route. After a rain, one of the best is searching out the little creek at the bottom of Halls Valley, then following it upstream to discover a procession of little waterfalls. For the ambitious, another is climbing 2.2 miles and 500 feet up the ridge (Pala Seca Trail) above Halls Valley to the park's highest point, Antler Point at 2,995 feet, for an overlook of the Santa Clara Valley.

## 18. HOTEL TRAIL 7.0 mi/3.25 hrs

*Reference:* At Grant Ranch County Park in the Mt. Hamilton foothills east of San Jose; map E1-South Bay, grid h9.

*User groups:* Hikers, horses and mountain bikes. No dogs are allowed. No wheelchair facilities.

*Permits:* No permits are required. A $3 entrance fee is charged seven days a week from April to September and only on weekends and holidays the rest of the year. There is a small, slotted register at the parking area, so you have to pay the do-it-yourself way.

*Directions:* Take US 101 south into San Jose, then turn south onto Interstate 680. Take the Alum Rock Avenue East exit and head east to Mount Hamilton Road. Turn right and drive eight miles to the parking area on the left. The Hotel Trail starts on the other side of the road, opposite the parking area.

*Maps:* For a free trail map, contact Joseph B. Grant County Park at the address below. To obtain a topographic map of the area, ask for Lick Observatory from the USGS.

*Who to contact:* Joseph B. Grant County Park, 18405 Mt. Hamilton Road, San Jose, CA 95140; (408) 274-6121.

*Trail notes:* People? What people? The remote habitat around Eagle Lake in Grant Ranch County Park provides visitors with rare tranquility and a good chance to see wildlife. Eagle Lake is set in the most southern reaches of the park's 9,000 acres, the prime destination on the Hotel Trail. After parking at the lot along Mt. Hamilton Road, cross the road and look for the trailhead on the south side of the road. You will find a ranch road (Hotel Trail) that heads southeast, and as you start the hike, scan for wildlife. Wild turkey are commonly seen in this area. As you head deeper into the park's interior, you will be hiking through foothill country, and while bovines are the most common animal encountered (keep your distance from the bulls, of course), there are also herds of wild pigs that are occasionally encountered. Instead of the stereotype of Fearless Hiker Meets Ferocious Boar, these pigs typically sprint off when they see or hear you. The route to Eagle Lake is 3.5 miles, direct, climbing a couple of hundred feet in the process. There are several sidetrip options along the way. The best is turning right on the

Cañada de Pala Trail, and dropping down about a half mile to San Felipe Creek, the prettiest stream in the park.

## 19. WHALER'S COVE     1.0 mi/1.0 hr

*Reference:* **At Pigeon Point Lighthouse on San Mateo County coast, south of Pescadero; map E1-South Bay, grid i1.**

*User groups:* Hikers and dogs. No mountain bikes or horses are allowed. No wheelchair facilities.

*Permits:* No permits are required. Parking and access are free.

*Directions:* From Interstate 280 in San Mateo, turn west onto Highway 92 and drive to Half Moon Bay. Turn south on Highway 1 and drive 23 miles (four miles past the Pescadero turnoff) to Pigeon Point Loop Road. Turn right and drive to the Pigeon Point Lighthouse.

*Maps:* To obtain a topographic map of the area, ask for Pigeon Point from the USGS.

*Who to contact:* There is no managing agency for this area. For general information, phone the Pigeon Point Lighthouse Hostel at (415) 879-0633.

*Trail notes:* This is the best beach we know for finding abalone shells. They come in all sizes, from the massive seven-inchers down to little one-inch shells that make for a perfect necklace, as well as all sizes in between. After parking at Pigeon Point Lighthouse, hike down to the beach directly to the south, a short but steep descent requiring good gripping shoes and some agility. The trail leads to Whaler's Cove, with Shag Rock just offshore and tidal waters in between, a prime abalone ground. During low tide, this is an excellent beach walk, heading south, perhaps playing tag with the light waves. What often occurs is that you start with an eager search for shells, but the tranquility of the ocean will take over, and soon you forget that you are even searching for anything. Right then is when you look down, and lo and behold, there is a beautiful abalone shell. Happens time and time again. By the way, don't get any ideas about abalone diving here. One time a diver got bit in half by a Great White shark in Whaler's Cove, so stay out of the water.

## 20. AÑO NUEVO LOOKOUT     2.75 mi/1.5 hrs

*Reference:* **In Butano State Park near Pescadero; map E1-South Bay, grid i2.**

*User groups:* Hikers only. No dogs, horses or mountain bikes are allowed. No wheelchair facilities.

*Permits:* No permits are required. A $5 state park entrance fee is charged for each vehicle.

*Directions:* From Interstate 280 in San Mateo, turn west on Highway 92 and drive to Half Moon Bay. Turn south onto Highway 1 and drive about 18 miles to the Pescadero turnoff. Turn east on Pescadero Road and drive past the town of Pescadero. Turn right (south) on Cloverdale Road and drive to the signed park entrance on the left. Park at the entrance station.

*Maps:* For a free trail map, contact Butano State Park at the address below. To obtain a topographic map of the area, ask for Franklin Point from the USGS.

*Who to contact:* Butano State Park, P.O. Box 3, Pescadero, CA 94060; (415) 879-2040 or (415) 726-8800.

*Trail notes:* Just pick yourself a clear day, tighten your boots, and this trail will reward you with a good climb and a great view. From the lookout point, Año

Nuevo Island to the south, as well as the Pacific Ocean, seems framed perfectly by conifers. The hike is fairly steep. Park at the entrance station, then start the hike at the trailhead directly to the right. The trail climbs 730 feet in less than a mile to the lookout. We advise continuing on the Año Nuevo Trail, then returning on the Goat Hill Trail to complete the loop. While a short loop, it provides a good climb, a great lookout, then a trip through redwoods for the return descent. And note: Butano is pronounced "Bute-uh-no" and not, we repeat, *not* "Bew-tah-no."

---

## 21. MILL OX LOOP  5.0 mi/2.75 hrs

*Reference:* In Butano State Park near Pescadero; map E1-South Bay, grid i2.

*User groups:* Hikers only. No dogs, horses or mountain bikes are allowed. No wheelchair facilities.

*Permits:* No permits are required. A $5 state park entrance fee is charged for each vehicle.

*Directions:* From Interstate 280 in San Mateo, turn west on Highway 92 and drive to Half Moon Bay. Turn south onto Highway 1 and drive about 18 miles to the Pescadero turnoff. Turn east on Pescadero Road and drive past the town of Pescadero. Turn right (south) on Cloverdale Road and drive to the signed park entrance on the left. The trailhead is a short distance past the entrance station on the left.

*Maps:* For a free trail map, contact Butano State Park at the address below. To obtain a topographic map of the area, ask for Franklin Point from the USGS.

*Who to contact:* Butano State Park, P.O. Box 3, Pescadero, CA 94060; (415) 879-2040 or (415) 726-8800.

*Trail notes:* If you love redwoods and ferns, but also love the sun and warm afternoons, the Mill Ox Loop at Butano State Park provides a perfect option. Why? Because here you get them both in good doses. The trail starts by crossing a small creek in a dense redwood forest, then heads up a very steep grade on switchbacks, emerging at the top of the canyon on the Butano Fire Road. Here you turn right, and get a more gradual climb as you head toward the park's interior. The Fire Road gets plenty of sun, and plenty of shirts come off on the climb en route to 1,138 feet. There are also excellent views of the Pacific Ocean along the way if you turn and look back to the west. When you reach a junction with the Jackson Flats Trail, turn right, and the trail descends quite steeply over a bare rock facing for a quarter-mile, then drops into the Butano Canyon and surrounding redwood forest. The rest of the hike is beautiful and pleasant, a meandering walk past ferns, trillium, redwoods, and rarely in the spring, blooming wild orchids. This is one of our favorites.

---

## 22. BUTANO LOOP  11.0 mi/2.0 days

*Reference:* In Butano State Park near Pescadero; map E1-South Bay, grid i2.

*User groups:* Hikers only. No dogs, horses or mountain bikes are allowed. No wheelchair facilities.

*Permits:* No permits are required. A $5 state park entrance fee is charged for each vehicle.

*Directions:* From Interstate 280 in San Mateo, turn west on Highway 92 and drive to Half Moon Bay. Turn south onto Highway 1 and drive about 18 miles to the Pescadero turnoff. Turn east on Pescadero Road and drive past the town of Pescadero. Turn right (south) on Cloverdale Road and drive to the signed park entrance on the left. The trailhead is a short distance past the entrance station on the left.

*Maps:* For a free trail map, contact Butano State Park at the address below. To obtain a topographic map of the area, ask for Franklin Point from the USGS.

*Who to contact:* Butano State Park, P.O. Box 3, Pescadero, CA 94060; (415) 879-2040 or (415) 726-8800.

*Trail notes:* This is one of the few overnight loop backpack trips in the Bay Area, where you trace the rim of Butano Canyon, complete with a trail camp. But most of the route is on fire roads, and with the advent of mountain bikes, fewer and fewer people are making this trip on foot. Regardless, it can still be routed so almost half of the trip is on trail, not fire road, and provides a mix of redwoods in canyons and sunny lookouts from ridgelines. With our suggested route, the first day is spent primarily in the sun, the second day primarily in the redwoods. Start at the Mill Ox Trailhead (see hike number 21), elevation 200 feet, then hike up the steep grade, turning right on the Butano Fire Road (700 feet). From here, you trace the canyon rim, enjoying views of the redwood-filled valley below and the Pacific Ocean off to the west. The trail climbs steadily, finally reaching 1,713 feet, crossing an old abandoned air strip on the ridgeline, then drops down to the Butano Trail Camp at 1,550 feet, a hike of 5.5 miles for the first day. Reservations are required, of course, and as this is an environmental camp, only lightweight camp stoves are permitted for cooking. On Day Two, you return by turning right on the Olmo Fire Trail, then taking the Doe Ridge/Goat Hill trails back to the starting point. Much of this route laterals and descends into the south side of the Butano Canyon, a soft dirt trail amid redwoods. During the winter, when the Sierra Nevada is entombed in snow and ice, this overnight loop is the perfect alternative backpack.

# 23. SEQUOIA TRAIL     1.0 mi/0.5 hr

*Reference:* **In Portola State Park in Santa Cruz Mountains; map E1-South Bay, grid i4.**

*User groups:* Hikers only. No dogs, horses or mountain bikes are allowed. No wheelchair facilities.

*Permits:* No permits are required. A $5 state park entrance fee is charged for each vehicle.

*Directions:* From Interstate 280 in Palo Alto, take the Page Mill Road exit. Turn west and drive about 10 miles to Highway 35 (Skyline Boulevard). Cross Highway 35 and continue on Alpine Road for four miles. Turn left at the state park road and drive three miles to Portola State Park.

*Maps:* For a park trail map, send a legal-size stamped envelope and 75 cents to Portola State Park at the address below. To obtain a topographic map of the area, ask for Mindego Hill from the USGS.

*Who to contact:* Portola State Park, P.O. Box F, Route 2, La Honda, CA 94020; (415) 948-9098 or (408) 429-2851.

*Trail notes:* The Shell Tree is one of the Peninsula's most unusual and surprising specimens. It is a giant redwood, but a strange-looking creature that has been ravaged by fire yet still lives, now some 17 feet in diameter.

Seeing it is why we suggest hiking the Sequoia Trail, a short, easy loop trail. Even on such a short hike, the surrounding forest, much of it redwood and Douglas fir, can provide a sense of remoteness. If you want more of a workout, the Sequoia Trail is linked to the Summit Trail (across from the group camping area), which ventures to remote land on the eastern border of the park. Portola State Park covers about 1,000 acres, most of it second-growth redwoods, though a few ancient monsters remain. There are 14 miles of trails at the park, but the Iverson Trail connects to Memorial County Park, adding an additional trail network.

## 24. SARATOGA GAP LOOP    9.0 mi/5.0 hrs

*Reference:* **In Saratoga Gap Open Space Preserve on Skyline Ridge in Santa Cruz Mountains; map E1-South Bay, grid i5.**

*User groups:* Hikers, horses and mountain bikes. No dogs are allowed. No wheelchair facilities.

*Permits:* No permits are required. Parking and access are free.

*Directions:* From Interstate 280 near Santa Clara, turn west onto Saratoga Avenue and drive to Highway 9. Drive west on Highway 9 to the junction with Highway 35 (Skyline Boulevard). Look for the CalTrans parking area on the left. The preserve is on the north side of Highway 9, across the road from the parking lot.

*Maps:* For a free trail map, contact the Midpeninsula Regional Open Space District at the address below. A map is also available at the trailhead. To obtain topographic maps of the area, ask for Mindego Hill and Cupertino from the USGS.

*Who to contact:* Midpeninsula Regional Open Space District, 330 Distel Circle, Los Altos, CA 94022; (415) 691-1200.

*Trail notes:* Saratoga Gap serves as a trailhead center for hikers visiting the Peninsula's Skyline Ridge. From here, there are trails leading to five different other parklands, making it possible for hikers to create any length of trip desired. The best is the nine-mile Saratoga Gap Loop. After parking, the trail starts off northward, adjacent to Highway 35 on the Skyline Ridge. After one mile, turn right on Charcoal Road, which is routed down the slope (bikes are permitted on the uphill here!) and into Upper Stevens Creek County Park. The trail descends to the headwaters of Stevens Creek, a quiet, wooded spot. You cross the creek, and shortly later, you reach a trail junction, where you turn left (west) on the Canyon View Trail, then after crossing a small creek, turn left on the Grizzly Flat Trail. That trail climbs back up to Skyline Boulevard, where you cross the road, enter Long Ridge Open Space Preserve, and hike south to where the trail again crosses Skyline Boulevard. Return on the Saratoga Gap Trail to the parking area. The hills here are grassy knobs, sprinkled with oaks and madrones. But the canyons are heavily wooded, with Douglas fir most prominent.

## 25. SUMMIT ROCK LOOP    2.0 mi/1.0 hr

*Reference:* **In Sanborn-Skyline County Park on Skyline Ridge in Santa Cruz Mountains; map E1-South Bay, grid i5.**

*User groups:* Hikers and horses. No dogs or mountain bikes are allowed. No wheelchair facilities.

*Permits:* No permits are required. A $3 day-use fee per vehicle is charged.

*Directions:* From Interstate 280 near Santa Clara, turn west onto Saratoga Avenue and drive to Highway 9. Drive west on Highway 9 to the junction with Highway 35 (Skyline Boulevard). Turn south and drive 2.5 miles to Sanborn-Skyline County Park. The trailhead is located across from Castle Rock State Park on Skyline Boulevard.

*Maps:* For a free trail map, contact the park at the address below. To obtain a topographic map of the area, ask for Castle Rock Ridge from the USGS.

*Who to contact:* Sanborn-Skyline County Park, 16055 Sanborn Road, Saratoga, CA 95070; (408) 867-9959.

*Trail notes:* The Santa Clara Valley never looked so pretty than from Summit Rock, set just east of the Skyline Ridge, the ideal perch for a lookout to the valley below. And getting this view is not difficult on the feature hike at Sanborn-Skyline County Park. The park gets its name since it connects Sanborn Creek with the Skyline Ridge, and between covers some 2,850 acres of mountain terrain. The trailhead for this hike is across Highway 35 from Castle Rock State Park, where hikers start on the Skyline Trail, heading north, adjacent to the road. The Skyline Trail leads right into the Summit Rock Loop, providing easy access to this great lookout. A popular option at the Skyline trailhead is the quarter-mile hike that leads to Indian Rock, for people who like their views to come even easier. Note that park headquarters are not located at this trailhead, but rather are located down off Sanborn Road, where full facilities and other trails are available.

---

# 26. TRAIL CAMP LOOP     5.5 mi/3.0 hrs

*Reference:* **In Castle Rock State Park on Skyline Ridge in Santa Cruz Mountains; map E1-South Bay, grid i5.**

*User groups:* Hikers and horses. No dogs or mountain bikes are allowed. No wheelchair facilities.

*Permits:* No permits are required, but you must self-register at the park entrance. A $3 state park day-use fee is charged.

*Directions:* From Interstate 280 near Santa Clara, turn west on Saratoga Avenue and drive to Highway 9. Drive west on Highway 9 to the junction with Highway 35 (Skyline Boulevard). Turn south and continue 2.5 miles to the entrance to Castle Rock State Park on the right.

*Maps:* For a free brochure, contact Castle Rock State Park at the address below. To obtain a topographic map of the area, ask for Castle Rock Ridge from the USGS.

*Who to contact:* Castle Rock State Park, 15000 Skyline Boulevard, Los Gatos, CA 95030; (408) 867-2952 or (408) 429-2851.

*Trail notes:* Castle Rock State Park is well-known to rock climbers, who practice their art here on both Castle Rock and Goat Rock, both honey-combed sandstone formations. But the park is also very attractive to hikers, a 3,600-acre semi-wilderness park with 32 miles of hiking trails. The park is located on the west side of Skyline Ridge, 3,000 feet in elevation, high enough to be above the smog and also get light snowfall each winter, and also to provide scenic views to the west of Big Basin and Monterey Bay. The Trail Camp Loop provides the best introduction to the park. From the parking lot, take the Saratoga Gap Trail to Trail Camp, a 2.8-mile trip that crosses a rock face, passes a small waterfall, and provides excellent views. To return from

Trail Camp, reverse your direction and then take the Ridge Trail, which passes Goat Rock (a great lookout) and mixed forest in the 2.7 miles en route to the parking area.

# 27. SKYLINE-TO-SEA 38.0 mi. one way/3.0 days  TRAIL

*Reference:* **From Castle Rock State Park via Big Basin to Waddell Creek on the Pacific Coast; map E1-South Bay, grid i5.**

*User groups:* Hikers and horses. No dogs or mountain bikes are allowed. No wheelchair facilities.

*Permits:* No permits are required unless you are camping, but you must self-register at the park entrance. A $3 state park day-use fee is charged. If you plan to camp, the fee is $7 and includes parking.

*Directions:* From Interstate 280 near Santa Clara, turn west on Saratoga Avenue and drive to Highway 9. Drive west on Highway 9 to its junction with Highway 35 (Skyline Boulevard). Turn south and continue 2.5 miles to the entrance to Castle Rock State Park on the right. For a shuttle trip, leave a car at Waddell Creek (see hike number 35 in this chapter).

*Maps:* For a free brochure, contact Castle Rock State Park at the address below. To obtain topographic maps of the area, ask for Castle Rock Ridge and Big Basin from the USGS.

*Who to contact:* Castle Rock State Park, 15000 Skyline Boulevard, Los Gatos, CA 95030; (408) 867-2952. Big Basin Redwoods State Park, 21600 Big Basin Way, Boulder Creek, CA 95006; (408) 338-6132 or (408) 429-2851.

*Trail notes:* What started as a good idea years ago has transformed into one of the most worshipped trails in the Bay Area. The vision was to create a trail that connected Castle Rock State Park on Skyline Ridge to Big Basin and out Waddell Creek to the coast. The result is this 38-mile backpack trip, complete with primitive trail camps, much of it built by volunteers. It is ideal in many ways, including the fact that it is generally downhill, starting at 3,000 feet at Castle Rock and dropping to sea level over the course of the hike. It includes fantastic views, redwood forests, waterfalls and camps. Only in extremely rare conditions will you come across a discarded cigarette butt or a piece of litter; after all, you don't trash what is a piece of heaven. The trail is best hiked in four days, but most do it in three, and it is a must to have a shuttle car waiting at the end of the trail at Waddell Creek on Highway 1. From the trailhead at Castle Rock State Park, hike out to Waterman Gap trail camp (water available) the first day, 9.6 miles. This includes crossing an open rock facing with fantastic views to the west of Big Basin and the coast, where you can envision the route you will be taking. The logical second day is to reach Jay Camp at Big Basin headquarters, a 9.5-mile hike. While this is not exactly a backcountry camping experience, there are restrooms and drinking water. The last day is the grunt, 12 miles out, hiking up and over the Big Basin rim, then down a canyon, passing beautiful 70-foot Berry Creek Falls, crossing Waddell Creek and finishing up at the coast. An excellent option is available if you want to split the last day in two, taking a bonus day by turning right at Berry Creek Falls, then hiking up past Cascade Falls to the Sunset Camp (no piped water), the most remote camp in Big Basin.

## 28. RIDGE TRAIL 6.0 mi/2.75 hrs

*Reference:* In El Sereno Open Space Preserve, Saratoga foothills; map E1-South Bay, grid i6.

*User groups:* Hikers, horses and mountain bikes. No dogs are allowed. No wheelchair facilities.

*Permits:* Phone the Midpeninsula Regional Open Space District at (415) 691-1200 for permit information.

*Directions:* From the intersection of Interstate 280 and Highway 17 in San Jose, turn south onto Highway 17 and drive approximately eight miles to Los Gatos. Continue south about three miles to Montevina Road. Turn right and park at the roadside turnout at the end of the road. There is only space for a few cars.

*Maps:* For a free trail map, contact the Midpeninsula Open Space District at the address below. To obtain a topographic map of the area, ask for Castle Rock Ridge from the USGS.

*Who to contact:* Midpeninsula Regional Open Space District, 330 Distel Court, Los Altos, CA 94022; (415) 691-1200.

*Trail notes:* The El Sereno Open Space is one of the lesser-known parklands in the Bay Area. Why? Because it is not only remote, but there is parking space for only two vehicles. The preserve covers 1,083 acres and is named for Mt. El Sereno, a prominent peak on the adjacent ridge. From the trailhead at the roadside pullout on Montevina Road, hike on the jeep trail, which traces a ridge line. Though it bobs and weaves, you will generally head east, topping a rim and then descending toward Los Gatos, a distance of three miles to the end of the trail. This is where the great views are, best of Lyndon Canyon, Lexington Reservoir and the South Bay. You return via the same trail.

## 29. LAKE VASONA TRAIL 2.0 mi/0.75 hrs

*Reference:* In Vasona Lake County Park near Los Gatos; map E1-South Bay, grid i6.

*User groups:* Hikers and mountain bikes. No dogs or horses are allowed. No wheelchair facilities.

*Permits:* No permits are required. A $3 day-use fee is charged.

*Directions:* From Highway 17 in Los Gatos, take the University Avenue exit to Blossom Hill Road. Turn right and continue to the signed park entrance. Park at the lot nearest to the sailing center.

*Maps:* For a free trail map, contact Vasona Lake County Park at the address below. To obtain a topographic map of the area, ask for Los Gatos from the USGS.

*Who to contact:* Vasona Lake County Park, 298 Garden Hill Drive, Los Gatos, CA 95030; (408) 356-2729.

*Trail notes:* This is the kind of place you would go for a Sunday picnic, maybe play some volleyball or a softball game. Lake Vasona (57 acres) is the centerpiece of a 151-acre park, where rowing and sailing in dinghies is popular. The hike along Lake Vasona is more popular for joggers than walkers, and being paved, gets use by family bicyclists as well. There are a number of places to start your trip, but we suggest parking off Pepper Tree Lane and then hiking from the Vasona Sailing Center. From here you can walk south along the lake as it narrows, cross a small footbridge, then turn left and meander along the lake frontage. The trail continues past Willow Point and ends at the Vasona Dam. The park provides a respite from the nearby mass urbanization and highway.

## 30. ST. JOSEPH'S HILL TRAIL  2.7 mi/1.75 hrs

*Reference:* In St. Joseph's Hill Open Space near Lexington Reservoir; map E1-South Bay, grid i6.

*User groups:* Hikers, leashed dogs and mountain bikes. No horses are allowed. No wheelchair facilities.

*Permits:* No permits are required. Parking and access are free.

*Directions:* From Los Gatos, drive south on Highway 17 approximately four miles to the Alma Bridge Road exit at Lexington Reservoir. The trail starts opposite the boat launching area beyond the dam. Parking is available just east of the dam in Lexington Reservoir County Park.

*Maps:* For a free trail map, contact the Midpeninsula Open Space District at the address below. To obtain a topographic map of the area, ask for Los Gatos from the USGS.

*Who to contact:* Midpeninsula Regional Open Space District, 330 Distel Circle, Los Altos, CA 94022; (415) 691-1200.

*Trail notes:* For most hikers to be willing to hike up, well, there better be considerable compensation awaiting at trail's end. So it is here, a 600-foot climb in the space of 1.5 miles, but in return, you get a perch on top of St. Joseph's Hill, getting views of Lexington Reservoir, the Santa Clara Valley and the adjacent Sierra Azul Mountain Range. The parking area is just east of the dam at elevation 645 feet, and from there, you hike north adjacent to Los Gatos Creek for about a half mile. At the trail junction, turn right and begin the hike up St. Joseph's Hill, with a loop route available near the top. Lexington Reservoir never looked so good.

## 31. LEXINGTON DAM TRAIL   1.0 mi/0.5 hr

*Reference:* In Lexington County Park in Saratoga foothills; map E1-South Bay, grid i6.

*User groups:* Hikers and limited mountain bikes. No dogs or horses are allowed. No wheelchair facilities.

*Permits:* No permits are required. A $3 day-use fee is charged.

*Directions:* From Los Gatos, drive south on Highway 17 to the Alma Bridge Road exit at Lexington Reservoir. Parking is available just east of the dam.

*Maps:* For a free trail map, contact Lexington County Park at the address below. To obtain a topographic map of the area, ask for Los Gatos from the USGS.

*Who to contact:* Lexington County Park, c/o Vasona Lake County Park, 298 Garden Hill Drive, Los Gatos, CA 95030; (408) 356-2729.

*Trail notes:* Lexington Reservoir can be one of the prettiest places in Santa Clara County. It can also be one of the ugliest. The lake might be full one year, then drained down to nothing the next, and after a hot summer look like a dust bowl. Alma Bridge Road circles the lake, and for more ambitious walks, there are several parklands nearby. Park at the lot just east of the dam, then walk across the dam and turn right on the "Pedway." That's as far as many people get—the view of the lake from the dam is what most come for.

But if you keep walking, you will be surprised, with the trail dropping down along Los Gatos Creek. After 1.5 miles, it links to the Los Gatos Creek Trail, and can be taken all the way into town, a popular bike route.

## 32. SIERRA AZUL LOOP  6.1 mi/4.5 hrs

*Reference:* **In Sierra Azul Open Space near Lexington Reservoir; map E1-South Bay, grid i6.**

*User groups:* Hikers, horses and mountain bikes. No dogs are allowed. No wheelchair facilities.

*Permits:* No permits are required. Parking and access are free.

*Directions:* From Los Gatos, take Highway 17 south to the Alma Bridge Road exit at Lexington Reservoir. Turn east and drive 1.5 miles across the dam to the parking area.

*Maps:* For a free trail map, contact the Midpeninsula Open Space District at the address below. To obtain a topographic map of the area, ask for Santa Teresa Hills from the USGS.

*Who to contact:* Midpeninsula Regional Open Space District, 330 Distel Circle, Los Altos, CA 94022; (415) 691-1200.

*Trail notes:* This is the Santa Clara Valley's backyard wilderness park. For many, it is difficult to believe such wild land exists so close to the homes of so many people. The Sierra Azul Loop is a strenuous loop hike that climbs, climbs and climbs as it probes the Sierra Azul Range. At the entrance to Sierra Azul Open Space, the trail rises in the first mile to 1,762 feet at Priest Rock. There the trail nearly levels out for a mile, where you reach the loop junction. Veer to the left, and again the trail starts climbing, and in the next 1.5 miles, it climbs another thousand feet to reach the ridgeline, 2,628 feet in elevation. Turn right at the ridge and enjoy being on top, cruising the next 1.6 miles on the mountain rim. Turn right at the next ridge junction and take the trail back (three miles to the loop junction), enjoying the downhill cruise as you go.

## 33. BALD MOUNTAIN TRAIL  1.0 mi/1.0 hr

*Reference:* **In Sierra Azul Range south of Los Gatos; map E1-South Bay, grid i7.**

*User groups:* Hikers, horses and mountain bikes. No dogs are allowed. No wheelchair facilities.

*Permits:* No permits are required. Parking and access are free.

*Directions:* From San Jose, drive south on the Almaden Expressway to Camden Avenue. Turn west onto Camden Avenue and drive to the intersection with Hicks Road. Turn south and continue to Mt. Umunhum Road. Then turn west and continue to the small (two cars) parking area at district pipe gate SA-7. This is roadside parking only, not a designated parking area.

*Maps:* For a free trail map, contact the Midpeninsula Open Space District at the address below. To obtain a topographic map of the area, ask for Santa Teresa Hills from the USGS.

*Who to contact:* Midpeninsula Regional Open Space District, 330 Distel Court, Los Altos, CA 94022; (415) 691-1200.

*Trail notes:* It's hard to beat being on top of a mountain, especially when it's near Mt. Umunhum, at 3,486 feet, the highest point in the Sierra Azul Range.

From anywhere in the Santa Clara Valley, it is Mt. Umunhum that strikes the most prominent landmark to the western horizon. It's that mountain with the big abandoned radar station on top of it. Alas, the public is not permitted to hike to the top of Mt. Umunhum—a major controversy—but the trip to adjacent Bald Mountain is the next best thing. The trail here is a half-mile route on Mt. Umunhum Road to Bald Mountain, a hilltop knoll with views of the Almaden Valley and across San Jose to Mt. Hamilton, on south to San Benito County. Public access to Mt. Umunhum is prohibited, and the Midpeninsula Regional Open Space District requests a phone call prior to your visit to Bald Mountain. By the way, guess what Umunhum is the Ohlone Indian word for: 1. Eagle? 2. Bear? 3. Hummingbird? The answer: Hummingbird.

## 34. AÑO NUEVO TRAIL  2.5 mi/2.0 hrs

*Reference:* **In Año Nuevo State Reserve on San Mateo County coast south of Pescadero; map E1-South Bay, grid j2.**

*User groups:* Hikers only. No dogs, horses or mountain bikes are allowed. No wheelchair facilities.

*Permits:* From April through November, you must obtain a permit to hike in the Wildlife Protection Area of the park. Permits are available at the park on a first-come, first-served basis. From December through March, access to the park is available only by accompanying a ranger on a scheduled walk. To make a reservation, phone MISTIX at (800) 444-7275. A $4 parking fee is charged. Seal walk tickets are $2 per person.

*Directions:* From Interstate 280 in San Mateo, turn west on Highway 92 to Half Moon Bay. Then drive south on Highway 1 and drive about 30 miles to the park entrance on the right.

*Maps:* For a map and brochure, send 75 cents to Año Nuevo State Reserve at the address below. To obtain a topographic map of the area, ask for Año Nuevo from the USGS.

*Who to contact:* Año Nuevo State Reserve, New Year's Creek Road, Pescadero, CA 94060; (415) 879-2025 or (415) 726-8800.

*Trail notes:* One of the more curious adventures in the Bay Area has become one of the most popular, touring Año Nuevo Reserve to see the giant elephant seals. Yep, this is the place where these giant creatures arrive every winter to fight, mate, give birth, sunbathe and make funny noises. It has become so popular to watch them that reservations are required to join a tour group, typically in December through March. The creatures look like giant slugs, often 2,000 to 3,000 pounds, with even the newborns weighing 75 pounds. The old boars reach nearly 20 feet long and weigh 5,000 pounds. In your tour group, you walk along roped-off trails, winding your way amid the animals. They will appear to have no interest in you at all, and if you keep your distance, that is just how it should be. With a 200mm camera lens, you can get excellent pictures. The best times to visit are in mid-December, when the males battle for harems, and then in late January, when hundreds of pups are born. The rest of the year, this makes a nice, quiet beach walk — hard to believe it's the same place where such a phenomenon takes place in the winter.

## 35. WADDELL CREEK TRAIL    9.0 mi/4.0 hrs

*Reference:* In Big Basin State Park on Santa Cruz County coast south of Año
  Nuevo; map E1-South Bay, grid j2.
*User groups:* Hikers and mountain bikes (not permitted past Waddell Creek
  Bridge). No dogs or horses are allowed. No wheelchair facilities.
*Permits:* No permits are required. A $5 state park entrance fee is charged for
  each vehicle.
*Directions:* From Interstate 280 in San Mateo, turn west onto Highway 92 and
  drive to Half Moon Bay. Turn left (south) on Highway 1 and drive about 30
  miles and pass Año Nuevo State Reserve. Continue south for about three
  miles and look for the signs indicating Big Basin State Park/Rancho del Oso,
  just past the Santa Cruz County line. Park along the left side of Highway 1
  at the entrance to Rancho del Oso.
*Maps:* Contact Big Basin Redwoods State Park for the availability and prices
  of trail maps. To obtain a topographic map of the area, ask for Franklin Point
  from the USGS.
*Who to contact:* Big Basin Redwoods State Park, 21600 Big Basin Way,
  Boulder Creek, CA 95006; (408) 338-6132 or (408) 429-2851.
*Trail notes:* If the only wildlife you see is on the back of quarters, this trail can
  change that, particularly during the last two hours of light on a weekday
  evening. Deer seem to "sprout" out of nowhere at a huge meadow on the
  north side of the trail; rabbits, squirrels and quail often suddenly hip-hop
  around; baby steelhead are growing in Waddell Creek; and ducks and herons
  make year-round homes in the marsh near the coast. The trailhead is located
  on Highway 1 just south of the Santa Cruz County line, starting at the Rancho
  del Oso outpost. The trail, actually a ranch road, starts by skirting a marsh,
  then runs adjacent to Waddell Creek. You can actually turn around at any
  point when you feel like it, of course, but we suggest making the trip all the
  way out to the bridge over Berry Creek. The trail is nearly flat, and has
  become very popular for bike riders on weekends, who typically go too fast
  and keep the wildlife spooked. That's why we suggest hiking during the
  week, when trail users are few and tranquility abounds, a perfect setting for
  an evening wildlife walk.

## 36. REDWOOD LOOP    0.6 mi/0.5 hr

*Reference:* **In Big Basin State Park in Santa Cruz Mountains near Boulder
  Creek; map E1-South Bay, grid i3.**
*User groups:* Hikers only. No dogs, horses or mountain bikes are allowed.
  **Partially wheelchair accessible.**
*Permits:* No permits are required. A $5 state park entrance fee is charged for
  each vehicle.
*Directions:* From the San Francisco Peninsula, take Interstate 280 to Sunny-
  vale/Saratoga Road. Turn south and drive five miles to Saratoga. Turn right
  at Highway 9 and drive up the hill for about seven miles to Skyline Ridge.
  Continue over the other side of Highway 9 about seven more miles to
  Highway 236. Turn right and drive about 10 miles to Big Basin State Park.
  Note: Highway 236 is extremely twisty, motor homes and trailers are not
  advised.

From San Francisco, take Highway 1 south to Santa Cruz. Turn north on Highway 9 and drive approximately 12 miles to Boulder Creek. At the traffic light in town turn left onto Highway 236. Drive about 10 miles on Highway 236 to the Big Basin Park headquarters.

*Maps:* Contact Big Basin Redwoods State Park for availability and prices of trail maps. To obtain a topographic map of the area, ask for Franklin Point from the USGS.

*Who to contact:* Big Basin Redwoods State Park, 21600 Big Basin Way, Boulder Creek, CA 95006; (408) 338-6132 or (408) 429-2851.

*Trail notes:* It is the giant redwoods that attract most people to Big Basin State Park, and it is the Redwood Trail that provides a short, easy, scenic path amid many of the park's largest trees. This trail is paved and gets a lot of use, which keeps the rating down a few notches. There are numbered posts along the way, and with a trail brochure, they provide a self-guided nature walk. The sights include Opal Creek (a pretty stream), the Chimney Tree (which has survived many fires), and several other ancient redwoods. The Santa Clara Tree is 17 feet in diameter and located across Opal Creek at signpost 3; the Father-of-the-Forest is 2,000 years old and is at signpost 8; and Mother-of-the-Forest, the tallest tree in the park at 329 feet, is at signpost 9. Many people take as much as an hour to complete this loop hike. There is no reason to rush.

---

## 37. BERRY CREEK FALLS        12.0 mi/5.5 hrs

*Reference:* In Big Basin State Park in Santa Cruz Mountains near Boulder Creek; map E1-South Bay, grid i3.

*User groups:* Hikers only. No dogs, horses or mountain bikes are allowed. No wheelchair facilities.

*Permits:* No permits are required. A $5 state park entrance fee is charged for each vehicle.

*Directions:* From the San Francisco Peninsula, take Interstate 280 to Sunnyvale/Saratoga Road. Turn south and drive five miles to Saratoga. Turn right at Highway 9 and drive up the hill for about seven miles to Skyline Ridge. Continue over the other side of Highway 9 about seven more miles to Highway 236. Turn right and drive about 10 miles to Big Basin State Park. Note: Highway 236 is extremely twisty, motor homes and trailers are not advised.

From San Francisco, take Highway 1 south to Santa Cruz. Turn north on Highway 9 and drive approximately 12 miles to Boulder Creek. At the traffic light in town turn left onto Highway 236. Drive about 10 miles on Highway 236 to the Big Basin Park headquarters.

*Maps:* Contact Big Basin Redwoods State Park for availability and prices of trail maps. To obtain a topographic map of the area, ask for Franklin Point from the USGS.

*Who to contact:* Big Basin Redwoods State Park, 21600 Big Basin Way, Boulder Creek, CA 95006; (408) 338-6132 or (408) 429-2851.

*Trail notes:* The prettiest sight in the Bay Area might just be Berry Creek Falls, a 70-foot waterfall framed in a canyon, complete with ferns, redwoods and the sound of rushing water. It is our choice as the No. 1 hike in the Bay Area, one that we repeat over and over again. It really helps to get an early start, which makes the entire trip carefree, with no pressure to complete the loop by a certain time. You start at park headquarters, taking the Skyline-to-Sea Trail amid the giant redwoods up to the Big Basin rim, then down the other side, heading west toward to the coast. After topping the rim (at 1,200 feet), the hike descends 600 feet over the course of about four miles to Berry Creek Falls. You round a bend and suddenly, there it is, this divine waterfall. A small bench is set perfectly for viewing while eating a picnic lunch. To return, we recommend going the long way, up the staircase and past the Cascade Falls, both Silver Falls and Golden Falls, then returning on the Sunset Trail. At Silver Falls, it is possible to dunk your head into the streaming water without getting the rest of you wet, a real thrill. The Sunset Trail takes you to the most remote sections of the park, then loops back into redwoods, then back to park headquarters. However, you can trim the hiking time down to about 4.5 hours if you double back on the same trail you came in on. But in such a beautiful place, why cut the experience short?

---

## 38. METEOR TRAIL          5.2 mi/2.5 hrs

*Reference:* **In Big Basin State Park in Santa Cruz Mountains near Boulder Creek; map E1-South Bay, grid i3.**

*User groups:* Hikers only. No dogs, horses or mountain bikes are allowed. No wheelchair facilities.

*Permits:* No permits are required. A $5 state park entrance fee is charged for each vehicle.

*Directions:* From the San Francisco Peninsula, take Interstate 280 to Sunnyvale/Saratoga Road. Turn south and drive five miles to Saratoga. Turn right at Highway 9 and drive up the hill for about seven miles to Skyline Ridge. Continue over the other side of Highway 9 about seven more miles to Highway 236. Turn right and drive about 10 miles to Big Basin State Park. Note: Highway 236 is extremely twisty, motor homes and trailers are not advised.

From San Francisco, take Highway 1 south to Santa Cruz. Turn north on Highway 9 and drive approximately 12 miles to Boulder Creek. At the traffic light in town turn left onto Highway 236. Drive about 10 miles on Highway 236 to the Big Basin Park headquarters.

*Maps:* Contact Big Basin Redwoods State Park for the availability and prices of trail maps. To obtain a topographic map of the area, ask for Franklin Point from the USGS.

*Who to contact:* Big Basin Redwoods State Park, 21600 Big Basin Way, Boulder Creek, CA 95006; (408) 338-6132 or (408) 429-2851.

*Trail notes:* Under the heavy redwood canopy of Big Basin, most hikers don't worry whether it's foggy on the coast or not. But this trail provides a unique reason to worry, with the park's best coastal lookout at trail's end. The Meteor Trail starts at park headquarters on the Skyline-to-Sea Trail, where you head northeast. If you see a sign for Berry Creek Falls, you're going the wrong direction. You hike along Opal Creek for much of the route, a pretty stream in the spring, surrounded by redwoods. Two miles out, you will arrive at the junction of the Meteor Trail, where you turn left and climb 400 feet over the space of a mile to the Middle Ridge Fire Road. From here, the Ocean View Summit (1,600 feet) is only a couple hundred yards off, where you can get a great view to the west of the Waddell Creek watershed and the Pacific

Coast. You return by doubling back. If you visit Big Basin and don't have time for the Berry Creek Falls hike, this is the next best option.

---

# 39. DAVENPORT BEACH    1.0 mi/1.0 hr

*Reference:* **On Santa Cruz County coast north of Santa Cruz; map E1-South Bay, grid j3.**

*User groups:* Hikers, dogs and horses. No mountain bikes are allowed. No wheelchair access.

*Permits:* No permits are required. Parking and access are free.

*Directions:* From the San Francisco Peninsula, take Interstate 280 to Highway 92. Turn west and drive to Half Moon Bay. Then turn south onto Highway 1. Drive past Año Nuevo State Park and continue for another nine miles to Davenport. Park on the right side of the highway at the spacious beach area, one mile north of the high ocean bluff.

*Maps:* To obtain a topographic map of the area, ask for Davenport from the USGS.

*Who to contact:* There is no managing agency for this site.

*Trail notes:* If you have a passion for wide-open ocean frontage, the beach at Davenport provides it. It is made up of pristine, open sand dunes, and often there is nobody around. Except, that is, for the daredevil hang gliders, who use the coastal thermals to float off a cliff at the southern end of the beach and then glide about with apparent comfort. Well, it is a heck of a lot more comforting to stroll along the vast beach, a place of special tranquility. A bonus sidetrip here during the winter is to hike up along the bluffs, one of the best land-based spots to the see the spouts from passing gray whales. Just look for the little "puff of smoke" out to sea.

---

# 40. LOCH LOMOND LOOP    5.0 mi/3.25 hrs

*Reference:* **In Loch Lomond Park in Santa Cruz foothills near Ben Lomond; map E1-South Bay, grid j5.**

*User groups:* Hikers only. No dogs, horses or mountain bikes are allowed. No wheelchair facilities.

*Permits:* No permits are required. A $3 day-use fee is charged. The Loch Lomond Recreation Area is open only from March 1 through September 15. However, rangers are on duty during the winter and will cite trespassers.

*Directions:* From San Jose, turn south on Highway 17, drive to Santa Cruz and take the Mount Hermon Road exit. Drive west on Mount Hermon Road for three miles to Graham Hill Road. Turn left and drive about eight-tenths of a mile, then turn left on Zayante Road and travel five miles to Lompico Road. Turn left and continue five miles to West Drive. Turn left again and drive to Sequoia Road. Turn right and continue into the park.

*Maps:* For a free trail map, contact Loch Lomond Park at the address below. To obtain a topographic map of the area, ask for Felton from the USGS.

*Who to contact:* Loch Lomond County Park, 100 Loch Lomond Way, Felton, CA 95018; (408) 335-7424.

*Trail notes:* There is no prettier lake in the greater Bay Area than Loch Lomond Reservoir, a jewel in the Santa Cruz Mountains, complete with an island and circled by conifers. Its beauty is always a surprise to newcomers, and so is the hiking. Of the 12 miles of hiking trails here, the best trip is the Loch

Lomond Loop. You start east on the Loch Trail, a level path that extends along the lake's shore for 1.5 miles out to Deer Flat. There you turn uphill on the Highland Trail, which climbs and loops to the right up the ridge, a moderate climb. It peaks out at a remote weather station, and with it, you get a great view of the lake below. Bring your camera. To complete the loop, the trail is routed down to the upper picnic area, or you can take the paved road back to the starting point. A bonus at Loch Lomond is good trout fishing, especially in April. Great lake, great views, great hike.

---

## 41. EAGLE CREEK TRAIL    3.0 mi/1.5 hrs

*Reference:* **In Henry Cowell Redwoods State Park near Santa Cruz; map E1-South Bay, grid j5.**

*User groups:* Hikers and horses. No dogs or mountain bikes are allowed. No wheelchair facilities.

*Permits:* No permits are required. A $5 state park entrance fee is charged for each vehicle.

*Directions:* From San Jose, take Highway 17 south, drive to Santa Cruz and take the Mount Hermon Road exit. Drive three miles west on Mount Hermon Road, then turn left on Graham Hill Road and continue south to the park entrance. The trailhead is adjacent to the campground.

*Maps:* For a trail map, send 75 cents to Henry Cowell Park at the address below. To obtain a topographic map of the area, ask for Felton from the USGS.

*Who to contact:* Henry Cowell Redwoods State Park, 101 North Big Trees Road, Felton, CA 95018; (408) 335-4598 or (408) 429-2851.

*Trail notes:* If you visit Henry Cowell Redwoods, there are two places here you just plain can't miss. One of them is the Eagle Creek Trail, which is the most direct route to reach the River Trail and the San Lorenzo River. The other is the Observation Deck (and we'll get to that). The Eagle Creek Trail starts between campsites 82 and 83, then crosses Eagle Creek, then runs adjacent to the stream as it heads toward the San Lorenzo River. Here you are surrounded by redwoods. The trail crosses Pipeline Road and junctions with the River Trail. Many people return at this point. However, a great addition is to hike north on the River Trail along the San Lorenzo River, adding an extra three miles to the trip. Another bonus at this park is the Observation Deck, the highest point in the park with great views of Santa Cruz and Monterey Bay. Reaching it is only a 0.3-mile hike from the campground. Take the Pine Trail, which starts near campsite 49.

---

## 42. MINE HILL LOOP    14.5 mi/7.0 hrs

*Reference:* **In Almaden Quicksilver County Park in San Jose foothills; map E1-South Bay, grid j7.**

*User groups:* Hikers and horses. No dogs or mountain bikes are allowed. No wheelchair access.

*Permits:* No permits are required.

*Directions:* From San Jose, take Highway 85 south to Almaden Expressway. Continue south on Almaden Expressway to Almaden Road. Continue on Almaden Road (through the historic town of New Almaden) to the park entrance on the right.

*Maps:* For a free trail map, contact Almaden Quicksilver County Park at the address below. A trail map is also available at the trailhead. To obtain a topographic map of the area, ask for Santa Teresa Hills from the USGS.

**Who to contact:** Almaden Quicksilver County Park, c/o Calero County Park, 23205 McKean Road, San Jose, CA 95120; (408) 268-3883.

**Trail notes:** You want pleasure? You want pain? You want love? You want hate? This hike provides it. Of the dozen trails at Almaden Quicksilver County Park, this one is the most challenging, and one of the longest single-day hikes at a Bay Area park. Almaden covers 3,600 acres, and with two lakes (Almaden and Guadalupe) and examples of historical mining operations, it is one of the most fascinating. The Mine Hill Trail leads you past remains of the burnt ore dumps along the way. The trail starts at the park entrance about a mile north of Almaden Reservoir, then is routed far into the backcountry, eventually skirting above and past Guadalupe Reservoir to a trail junction, 8.5 miles one-way. To return, turn left on the Guadalupe Trail, which explores even more remote country on the way back, passes Guadalupe Lake's shore, then connects again with the Mine Hill Trail for the last three-quarters of a mile back to the trailhead. Note that some areas adjacent to the Mine Trail are closed to public access because of hazardous residuals remaining from the mercury mines.

---

# 43. COYOTE PEAK LOOP    3.4 mi/2.0 hrs

**Reference:** In Santa Teresa County Park south of San Jose; map E1-South Bay, grid j8.

**User groups:** Hikers and horses. No dogs or mountain bikes are allowed. No wheelchair facilities.

**Permits:** No permits are required.

**Directions:** From US 101 between San Jose and Morgan Hill, take Bernal Road east and proceed to the day-use parking area. Park in the main day-use lot.

**Maps:** For a free trail map, contact Santa Teresa County Park at the address below. To obtain a topographic map of the area, ask for Santa Teresa Hills from the USGS.

**Who to contact:** Santa Teresa County Park, 985 Heller Avenue, San Jose, CA 95111; (408) 225-0225 or Park Administration at (408) 358-3741.

**Trail notes:** It is golfers who best know Santa Teresa County Park, but hikers are discovering the park has some surprise benefits as well. Especially the hike up to Coyote Peak, which provides a surprise lookout of the southern Santa Clara Valley as well as the feature destination in a good loop hike. This park covers 1,688 acres, but the main attractions are the golf course, driving range, bar and restaurant. You can quickly leave development behind, however. Start at the Hidden Springs Trailhead off Bernal Road, hiking south. After one mile, the trail junctions with Coyote Peak Trail, which climbs to the top of Coyote Peak, with a short loop cutoff getting you to the summit. To complete the loop, continue on the Coyote Peak Trail, then take the Ohlone Trail (one mile) back to the parking area. Compared to the manicured greens of the golf course, this trail provides an insight into the park's most primitive and rugged areas, providing a good view for your efforts to get there.

## 44. JUAN CRESPI LOOP     4.8 mi/2.0 hrs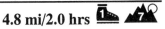

*Reference:* In Calero Reservoir County Park southeast of San Jose; map
    E1-South Bay, grid j8.

*User groups:* Hikers and horses. No dogs or mountain bikes are allowed. No
    wheelchair facilities.

*Permits:* No permits are required.

*Directions:* From San Jose, drive south on US 101 for five miles to Coyote.
    Take the Bernal Road exit west and drive a short distance to the Monterey
    Highway exit. Head south a short way to Bailey Avenue and turn right. Then
    turn left onto McKean Road and continue to the sign for the horse stables.
    Park adjacent to the ranger office.

*Maps:* For a free map, contact Calero Reservoir County Park at the address
    below. To obtain a topographic map of the area, ask for Santa Teresa Hills
    from the USGS.

*Who to contact:* Calero Reservoir County Park at (408) 268-3883 or Parks
    Administration at (408) 358-3741.

*Trail notes:* You'd better know the difference between horse droppings and
    Shinola if you plan to take this hike. Why? Because this is a very popular
    horse trail, and it ain't shoe polish you might step in if you don't watch it. The
    reason people have trouble watching their steps is because of the nice views
    of Calero Reservoir to the north. Start the trip near the entrance gate, and
    follow to the Juan Crespi Trail, turning right toward Calero Reservoir. This
    trail runs along the southern shoreline of the lake for more than a mile before
    making a nearly 180-degree looping left turn. There it becomes the Los
    Cerritos Trail, climbing the ridgeline bordering the southern end of the lake.
    When it tops the ridge, it connects to the Pena Trail. To complete the loop,
    turn left on the Pena Trail, making a descent. A great way to go is to descend
    the Pena Trail, turn right on the Vallecitos Trail, and then left on the Figueroa
    Trail. It adds an extra two miles to the trip, but is well worth it!

## 45. DEL COYOTE NATURE TRAIL 1.2 mi/0.5 hr

*Reference:* In Coyote-Hellyer County Park downstream of Anderson
    Dam, south of San Jose; map E1-South Bay, grid j9.

*User groups:* Hikers only. No dogs, horses or mountain bikes are allowed. No
    wheelchair facilities.

*Permits:* No permits are required. A $3 day-use fee is charged from May to
    October.

*Directions:* From San Jose, drive south on US 101 and take the Hellyer Avenue
    exit. Drive about 300 yards and the park entrance is on the left.

*Maps:* For a free map, contact Coyote-Hellyer County Park at the address
    below. To obtain a topographic map of the area, ask for Morgan Hill from
    the USGS.

*Who to contact:* Coyote-Hellyer County Park, 985 Hellyer Avenue, San Jose,
    CA 95111; (408) 225-0225, or Parks Administration at (408) 358-3741.

*Trail notes:* Thousands and thousands of people roar up and down Highway 101
    south of San Jose with nary a clue of the peaceful little park that sits so
    nearby. It is Coyote Hellyer County Park, just east of the highway, a small,
    shaded stream that is even stocked with rainbow trout in the late spring and

early summer. The hike starts at a picnic area, with the trail just meandering along the stream. The flowing waters come from nearby Anderson Dam, from which steady releases are made well into summer. That is what makes this little park attractive to local residents, a nice little spot for a respite.

---

## 46. SERPENTINE TRAIL     0.8 mi/0.5 hr

*Reference:* **In Anderson Lake County Park near Morgan Hill; map E1-South Bay, grid j9.**

*User groups:* Hikers only. No dogs, horses or mountain bikes are allowed. No wheelchair facilities.

*Permits:* No permits are required. A $3 day-use fee is charged from May to October.

*Directions:* From San Jose, drive south on US 101 to the Cochran Road exit. Take Cochran Road east to the park entrance.

*Maps:* For a free trail map, contact Anderson Lake County Park at the address below. To obtain topographic maps of the area, ask for Mt. Sizer and Morgan Hill from the USGS.

*Who to contact:* Anderson Lake County Park, 1105 Burnett Avenue, Morgan Hill, CA 95037; (408) 779-3634, or Parks Administration at (408) 358-3741.

*Trail notes:* The size of Anderson Lake is always a shocker to newcomers, covering nearly 1,000 acres in a water-filled canyon among the oak woodlands and foothills of the Gavilan Mountains. The Serpentine Trail provides a short walk to the dam overlook, one of the best views at the park. It starts between the Live Oak Group Area and the Toyon Group Area. The trail simply is routed to the northwest corner of the dam. One major problem at Anderson Lake is the fluctuating water levels. This lake needs a lot of water to be filled, and even then, it seems the water managers like to empty the lake almost completely every four or five years. When they do that, you might as well arrange for a trip to the Grand Canyon.

---

## 47. MIDDLE RIDGE LOOP     4.5 mi/3.0 hrs

*Reference:* **In Henry Coe State Park in the Diablo Range east of Morgan Hill; map E1-South Bay, grid j9.**

*User groups:* Hikers, horses and mountain bikes. No dogs are allowed. No wheelchair facilities.

*Permits:* No permits are required unless you plan to camp in the backcountry. A $5 state park day-use fee is charged.

*Directions:* From US 101 at Morgan Hill, take the East Dunne Avenue exit and drive east for 13 slow and twisty miles to the park entrance. From park headquarters, take the Northern Heights Route Trailhead.

*Maps:* For a trail map, send $1.50 to Henry W. Coe State Park at the address below. To obtain topographic maps of the area, ask for Mississippi Creek and Mt. Sizer from the USGS.

*Who to contact:* Henry W. Coe State Park, P.O. Box 846, Morgan Hill, CA 95038; (408) 779-2728 or (209) 826-1196.

*Trail notes:* A good pair of hiking boots is your ticket to the 70,000 acres of wildlands that comprise Coe State Park, a place for someone who wants solitude (and quality fishing) and isn't adverse to rugged hiking to find it. The Middle Ridge Loop is a short day hike that provides a glimpse of the primitive charm of the park, along with some serious ups and downs. From park headquarters, you start by taking the Northern Heights Route over the top of Pine Ridge (elevation 3,000 feet), and then dropping 600 feet down to Little Coyote Creek, then back up past Frog Lake and to Middle Ridge Trail (2,800 feet). This first leg is about two miles, and most visitors will stop along the creek for a reality check and reassess what awaits in this wilderness park. Turn right on the Middle Ridge Trail, hike two miles to the junction with Fish Trail, then turn right again and follow the trail down across Little Coyote Creek. This is one of the prettier sections of this little stream, and really puts a nice capper on the walk. To finish the loop, you have to climb back out of the canyon, over Pine Ridge, and back to the headquarters. This is just enough of a hike to whet your appetite for more challenging routes to the park's interior.

---

## 48. COIT LAKE TRAIL          26.0 mi/2.0 days

*Reference:* In Henry Coe State Park in the Diablo Range east of Morgan Hill; map E1-South Bay, grid j9.

*User groups:* Hikers, horses and mountain bikes. No dogs are allowed. No wheelchair facilities.

*Permits:* No permits are required unless you plan to camp in the backcountry. A $5 state park day-use fee is charged.

*Directions:* From US 101 at Morgan Hill, take the East Dunne Avenue exit and drive east over Morgan Hill and Anderson Lake for 13 miles on the twisty road to the park headquarters. From park headquarters, take the Coit Route Trailhead.

*Maps:* For a trail map, send $1.50 to Henry W. Coe State Park at the address below. To obtain topographic maps of the area, ask for Mississippi Creek and Mt. Sizer from the USGS.

*Who to contact:* Henry W. Coe State Park, P.O. Box 846, Morgan Hill, CA 95038; (408) 779-2728 or (209) 826-1196.

*Trail notes:* There are spring days where you can catch nearly a bass per cast at Coit Lake, just flipping out a one-inch floating Rapala lure. It is often the best pond-style fishing in the greater Bay Area. Unfortunately, that fact inspires many excited people to start hiking off to Coit Lake without first taking a litmus test of the quest they are undertaking. This is a long hike with difficult climbs both ways, particularly if the weather is hot and dry, common out here. Many get busted by the heat before reaching the lake, and return frustrated without making a cast. Heading out on the Coit Route, it's just under a 12-mile trip to reach the lake, and right off, that includes a 1,150-foot drop into China Hole, then a 1,200-foot climb over five miles, much of it through Mahoney Meadow, followed by two easier up-and-downs. Coit Lake is best fished during the last two hours of the evening, but the nearest trail camp is the Pacheco Horse Camp, a mile from Coit Lake, making the first day a 13-miler. The return trip is even tougher because near the end of the trip, when you will be just about worn out, you will have to make that 1,150-foot climb out of China Hole back up to park headquarters, but over the span of only two miles. Add in a hot afternoon, and you'll be ready to surrender when you reach your car.

# 49. MISSISSIPPI LAKE TRAIL 22.0 mi/2.0 days

*Reference:* In Henry Coe State Park in the Diablo Range east of Morgan Hill; map E1-South Bay, grid j9.

*User groups:* Hikers, horses and mountain bikes. No dogs are allowed. No wheelchair facilities.

*Permits:* No permits are required unless you plan to camp in the backcountry. A $5 state park day-use fee is charged.

*Directions:* From US 101 at Morgan Hill, take the East Dunne Avenue exit and drive east over Morgan Hill and Anderson Lake for 13 miles on the twisty road to the park headquarters. From park headquarters, take the Pacheco Route Trailhead.

*Maps:* For a trail map, send $1.50 to Henry W. Coe State Park at the address below. To obtain topographic maps of the area, ask for Mississippi Creek and Mt. Sizer from the USGS.

*Who to contact:* Henry W. Coe State Park, P.O. Box 846, Morgan Hill, CA 95038; (408) 779-2728 or (209) 826-1196.

*Trail notes:* Even though Coe Park was opened to the public in 1981, it already has a few legends, and the most mysterious is Mississippi Lake. This lake is set in the virtual center of the park's 125 square miles, and is the biggest and prettiest lake in the park. But the mystery is not over its scenic beauty, but its ability to create huge trout, with scientists documenting 26-inch wild trout that were only 18 months old. They are all but gone now, with low water in the feeder creek preventing spawning during the 1988-1992 drought, and any trout caught should immediately be released. The legendary huge trout of Mississippi Lake have inspired many to make the trip out, and providing you get a very early start, it is an excellent weekend trip. From park headquarters, you hike out eight miles on the Pacheco Route, and that includes a long drop followed by a killer climb, gaining 1,400 feet over 2.6 miles, from East Fork Coyote Creek over Willow Crest and to the junction with the Interior Route. Turn left on the Interior Route, and the trail becomes a lot easier, and in 3.5 miles, you will be skirting the southern shore of the lake. The nearest trail camp is about a half mile south of the lake, Mississippi Creek Horse Camp.

---

# 50. ROOSTER COMB LOOP   70.0 mi/6.0 days

*Reference:* In Henry Coe State Park in the Diablo Range southeast of San Jose; map E1-South Bay, grid j9.

*User groups:* Hikers, horses and mountain bikes. No dogs are allowed. No wheelchair facilities.

*Permits:* No permits are required unless you plan to camp in the backcountry. A $5 state park day-use fee is charged.

*Directions:* From US 101 at Morgan Hill, take the East Dunne Avenue exit and drive east over Morgan Hill and Anderson Lake for 13 miles on the twisty road to the park headquarters. From park headquarters, take the Pacheco Route Trailhead.

*Maps:* For a trail map, send $1.50 to Henry W. Coe State Park at the address below. To obtain topographic maps of the area, ask for Mississippi Creek and Mt. Sizer from the USGS.

*Who to contact:* Henry W. Coe State Park, P.O. Box 846, Morgan Hill, CA 95038; (408) 779-2728 or (209) 826-1196.

*Trail notes:* "I've always been crazy," Waylon Jennings said, "because it's kept me from going insane." Well, you have to be something of a deranged soul to try this hike. That's why we signed up! It's just plain long, includes seven climbs that'll have you cussing, and explores the park's most remote and arid wildlands, where anything over 10 inches of rain in a year is a flood. Then why do it? This is why: Because no trail on public land in the Bay Area leads to an area more isolated, because Paradise Lake will seem like a mirage after walking 33 miles, and hey, you're a little deranged anyway, right? Highlights of the trip on the way in will include Kelly Lake (about 10.5 miles in), Coit Lake (12 miles in), and in the remote Orestimba drainage, Paradise Lake and Robinson Falls. A spectacular spot is the Rooster Comb, for which the loop is named, a perch that overlooks Orestimba Valley. The only thing simple is the route: You will take the Pacheco Trail (16.7 miles) out to the park's southern boundary, then turn left on the Gill Trail (10.5 miles), then hike the loop on Rooster Comb Trail (10.1 miles), reconnect with the Gill Trail (5 miles), and then head back the way you came. We suggest taking a week to do it, arriving and camping at park headquarters the first night so you can go through your gear and make an early getaway the next morning, and then average 11.6 miles per day for six days. There are several trail camps along the way, and in addition, camping is permitted throughout the wilderness area. If the weather turns hot, this trip can be dangerous to the physically unprepared. And regardless of your physical condition, when you return to your car at park headquarters, you won't feel so crazy anymore.

---

## 51. BLACK ROCK FALLS TRAIL 1.2 mi/1.0 hr

*Reference:* **In Uvas Canyon County Park southwest of Morgan Hill; map E1-South Bay, grid j9.**

*User groups:* Hikers only. No dogs, horses or mountain bikes are allowed. No wheelchair access.

*Permits:* No permits are required.

*Directions:* From San Jose, take US 101 south to the Bernal exit. Make an immediate right to hook up with Monterey Highway. Turn left (south) onto Monterey Highway and drive to Bailey Avenue. Turn right and continue to McKean Road. Turn left onto McKean Road, which turns into Uvas Road. Follow Uvas Road to Croy Road. Turn right and continue to the park entrance, following a narrow road through a small community.

*Maps:* For a free map, contact Uvas Canyon County Park at the address below. To obtain a topographic map of the area, ask for Mt. Madonna from the USGS.

*Who to contact:* Uvas Canyon County Park, 8515 Croy Road, Morgan Hill, CA 95037; (408) 779-9232.

*Trail notes:* A series of small waterfalls is the highlight at Uvas Canyon County Park, waterfalls that are little known to most hikers, including even many nearby residents. But they are here, just a half-hour's walk in, and especially pretty in the spring when Swanson Creek is rushing and the surrounding hillsides are vibrant with life. The trailhead is at the Black Oak Group Picnic Area; look for the well-signed "Nature Trail Loop." The trail is routed up a gentle grade along Swanson Creek, then takes a short jog off to the right to Black Falls. There are several other falls in the area, including Basin Falls and Upper Falls. On the Nature Trail Loop, there is a rest area at Myrtle Flats. While this hike can be easy and fast, most take their time. After all, waterfalls, even small ones, are always something special.

---

# 52. WHITE DEER TRAIL     0.05 mi/0.25 hr

*Reference:* **In Mt. Madonna County Park in Santa Cruz Mountains west of Gilroy; map E1-South Bay, grid j9.**

*User groups:* Hikers and **wheelchairs**. No dogs, horses or mountain bikes are allowed.

*Permits:* No permits are required. A $3 day-use fee is charged.

*Directions:* From San Jose, take US 101 south to Gilroy. Turn west onto Highway 152 and drive 10 miles. Then turn right on Poleline Road and continue to the parking area.

*Maps:* To obtain a topographic map of the area, ask for Mount Madonna from the USGS. For a free trail map, contact Mt. Madonna County Park at the address below.

*Who to contact:* Mt. Madonna County Park, 7850 Poleline Road, Watsonville, CA 95076; (408) 842-2341.

*Trail notes:* The remainders of a rare herd of white deer are the star attraction at Mt. Madonna County Park. These deer are similar to blacktail deer, the most common deer in California, except that they are larger and are white, completely white. They are kept in a pen that is about a 30-foot walk from the parking lot next to headquarters. In late summer, the bucks develop a large set of antlers, quite a sight. The deer are kept penned near headquarters because in the early 1990s, a group of illegals with rifles were killing them off at night, one at a time. Justice was served one night when one of the gunmen shot himself by accident, and was left behind by his fellow culprits. Karma. Only three deer survived the poaching incidents, but two fawns were born in 1994, giving new hope. The "white deer" are actually white Fallow deer, descendents of a pair donated in 1932 by William Randolph Hearst.

---

# 53. BAYVIEW LOOP     2.5 mi/1.75 hrs

*Reference:* **In Mt. Madonna County Park in Santa Cruz Mountains west of Gilroy; map E1-South Bay, grid j9.**

*User groups:* Hikers and horses. No dogs or mountain bikes are allowed. No wheelchair facilities.

*Permits:* No permits are required. A $3 day-use fee is charged.

*Directions:* From San Jose, take US 101 south to Gilroy. Turn west onto Highway 152 and drive 10 miles. Then turn right on Poleline Road and continue to the entrance station. The trailhead is on the left.

*Maps:* To obtain a topographic map of the area, ask for Mount Madonna from the USGS. For a free trail map, contact Mt. Madonna County Park at the address below

*Who to contact:* Mt. Madonna County Park, 7850 Poleline Road, Watsonville, CA 95076; (408) 842-2341.

*Trail notes:* Mt. Madonna Park provides great scenic beauty, good hiking, camping and horseback riding. The park is set around the highest peak in the southern range of the Santa Cruz Mountains, and with 18 miles of hiking trails, the best routes are combinations of different trails. So it is with this triangular loop, starting at the park entrance station at Hecker Pass, elevation 1,270 feet. Take the Bayview Trail and hike north for 1.1 miles, and along the way you can scan west to Monterey Bay. Turn right on the Redwood Trail (it will cross Pole Line Road), and you will walk from those coastal lookouts to forest, the best of both worlds. To complete the loop, take the Redwood/ Rock Springs/Blackhawk/Bayview trails as they junction in sequence. Confused? This park is filled with a spider web of short hikes. By linking them you can customize your adventure. Our suggested loop provides a look at some of the park's prettiest settings.

## MAP E2

NOR-CAL MAP ........................ see page 14
adjoining maps
NORTH (D2) ........................... see page 208
EAST (E3) ............................... see page 398
SOUTH (F2) ........................... see page 476
WEST (E1) .............................. see page 258

2 TRAILS
PAGES 394-397

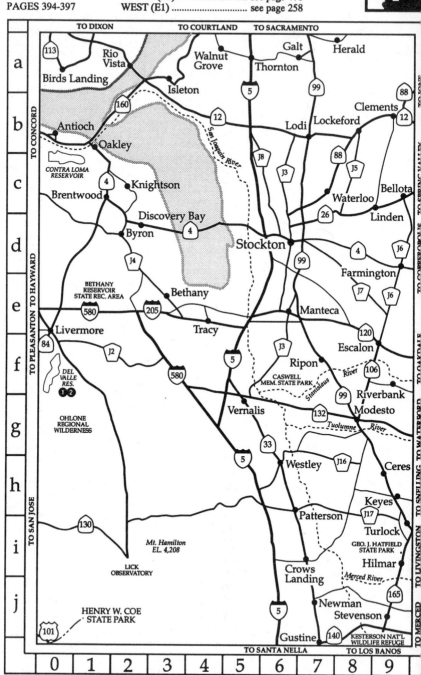

**Map E2 featuring:** Del Valle Regional Park, Del Valle Reservoir, Sunol Regional Park, Ohlone Regional Park, Livermore, Rose Peak, Mission Peak, Murietta Falls

# 1. OHLONE WILDERNESS TRAIL

**28.0 mi. one way/3.0 days**

*Reference:* In Sunol-Ohlone Regional Wilderness; from Del Valle Regional Park south of Livermore to Mission Peak in Fremont; map E2, grid f1.

*User groups:* Hikers, dogs (daytime only) and horses. No mountain bikes are allowed. No wheelchair facilities.

*Permits:* A trail permit/map for the Ohlone Wilderness Trail is required. It costs $2 if you pick it up at the park office or $2.50 if you want to have it mailed to you. To receive your permit by mail, contact East Bay Regional Parks at the address below. A park entrance fee of $4 is charged from March through October, $3 in the offseason.

*Directions to east trailhead:* From eastbound Interstate 580 at Livermore, take the North Livermore Avenue exit. Turn south and travel on North/South Livermore Road (this will turn into Tesla Road) to Mines Road. Turn right and drive about three miles south on Mines Road to Del Valle Road. Turn right and continue for three miles to the entrance to Del Valle Regional Park. Park at the south end of Del Valle Reservoir, which is close to the trailhead.

*Directions to west trailhead:* From Highway 680 at Fremont, take the Mission Boulevard exit near Fremont. Turn east on Stanford Avenue and continue to the parking lot and trailhead at the end of the road.

*Maps:* You will receive a trail map when you purchase your permit. To obtain a topographic map of the area, ask for Mendenhall Springs from the USGS.

*Who to contact:* For information about backcountry camping, phone (510) 562-CAMP. To obtain a wilderness permit/map, send $2.50 to East Bay Regional Parks, 2950 Peralta Oaks Court, P.O. Box 5381, Oakland, CA 94605. For information, phone Regional Park Headquarters at (510) 635-0135, ext. 2200, or Del Valle Regional Park at (510) 373-0332.

*Trail notes:* The East Bay's most unspoiled backcountry lands are accessible to hikers along the spectacular 28-mile Ohlone Trail. The route is set completely in wildlands, starting south of Livermore at Del Valle Regional Park, then cutting a path west to Fremont. In the process, the trail rises through fields of wildflowers, grasslands and oaks and climbs three major summits, Rocky Ridge, Rose Peak (elevation 3,817 feet), and Mission Peak (2,517 feet). It is an ideal three-day backpack trip, with hikers able to make their trail camps at Sunol and Ohlone Regional Parks. That breaks down the trail distances to a 12-mile trip the first day, followed by two days at about eight miles each. Some people close out the final 16 miles in one day. Michael, in a somewhat deranged mood, ran the entire route in one day. Hiking the trail east to west is the only way to fly. That puts the steepest climb right at the beginning when you are fresh, starting at Del Valle Park and climbing Rocky Ridge, an elevation gain of 1,600 feet in 1.5 miles. A great sidetrip here, by the way, is to Murietta Falls (see hike number 2, this chapter). The Ohlone Wilderness Trail traverses the East Bay's wildest country, climbing up and down ridges, the last being Mission Peak. A moment of irony comes when you crest Mission Peak and can actually see your car waiting at the parking lot, yet it is still so far away. This last stretch drops 2,100 feet in 3.5 miles, a terrible toe-jammer that will have your knees and thighs screaming for mercy. Weeks later, though, when your memory banks replay this adventure, it will suddenly seem like "fun."

## 2. MURIETTA FALLS TRAIL   11.0 mi/1.0 day

*Reference:* In Sunol-Ohlone Regional Wilderness; from Del Valle Regional Park south of Livermore to Mission Peak; map E2, grid f1.

*User groups:* Hikers, dogs (daytime only) and horses. No mountain bikes are allowed. No wheelchair facilities.

*Permits:* A trail permit/map for the Ohlone Wilderness Trail is required. It costs $2 if you pick it up at the park office or $2.50 if you want to have it mailed to you. To receive your permit by mail, contact East Bay Regional Parks at the address below. A park entrance fee of $4 is charged from March through October, $3 in the offseason.

*Directions:* From eastbound Interstate 580 at Livermore, take the North Livermore Avenue exit. Turn south and travel on North/South Livermore Road (this will turn into Tesla Road) to Mines Road. Turn right and drive about three miles south on Mines Road to Del Valle Road. Turn right and continue for three miles to the entrance to Del Valle Regional Park. Park at the south end of Del Valle Reservoir, which is close to the trailhead.

*Maps:* You will receive a trail map when you purchase your permit. To obtain a topographic map of the area, ask for Mendenhall Springs from the USGS.

*Who to contact:* East Bay Regional Park, 2950 Perralta Oaks Court, P.O. Box 5381, Oakland, CA 94605; (510) 635-0135, ext. 2200. Del Valle Regional Park; (510) 373-0332.

*Trail notes:* The Bay Area's highest waterfall is little known and only rarely seen. It is hidden away in wilderness in southern Alameda County where few travel. It is Murietta Falls, named after the legendary outlaw of the 1800s, Joaquin Murietta. It is set in the Ohlone Wilderness, where a free-flowing creek runs through a rocky gorge, then plunges 100 feet over a cliff, landing in the rocks below. Upstream, there are an additional series of small pools and cascades, and combined with Murietta Falls, this creates a destination like nothing else in the East Bay. Why do so few people even know about it? It is a buttkicker of a hike to get there, 5.5 miles one-way, most of it up a terribly steep ridge, climbing 1,600 feet in just 1.5 miles, the worst part of the Ohlone Wilderness Trail. It tops out at Rocky Ridge, drops down into Williams Gulch, then climbs again toward even higher Wauhab Ridge. You will reach as high as 3,300 feet in elevation before turning right on the Springboard Trail (signpost 35, not 36). From there, it's one mile to the waterfall. You walk along a ridge about a quarter mile, then turn left on the Greenside Trail, which descends into a valley and to the falls. You can't get a clear view of Murietta Falls from the Greenside Trail. When you reach the creek, leave the trail and work your way carefully downstream. It is a few hundred yards to the top of the falls. An option is to take an unsigned side road/trail off the Greenside Trail, located past the stream. Turn right on this road/trail, which drops in a looping turn down to the floor, providing a better view of the falls. When Murietta Falls first comes into view, it presents an astonishing contrast with the East Bay hills, a grassland/oak habitat where steep cliffs and waterfalls are not expected. But here it is, pouring 100 feet, framed by rapidly greening hills in springtime, a remarkable refuge of tranquility only a few miles from suburbia, concrete and traffic jams. Even in big rain years, the creek is reduced to a trickle by summer, and sometimes even goes dry. In addition, it gets hot out here, really smokin', like 100 degrees come summer. By July, the hills are brown, the waterfall disappears, and only the ghost of Murietta remains to laugh as you struggle up that 1,600-foot climb.

*Special note:* If you want to camp overnight in the wilderness, a trail camp (Stewart's Camp) is available about a half mile from Murietta Falls; reservations are required.

NOR-CAL MAP ........................ see page 14

adjoining maps
NORTH (D3) ........................... see page 210
EAST (E4) .............................. see page 402
SOUTH (F3) ........................... see page 480
WEST (E2) ............................. see page 394

2 TRAILS
PAGES 398-401

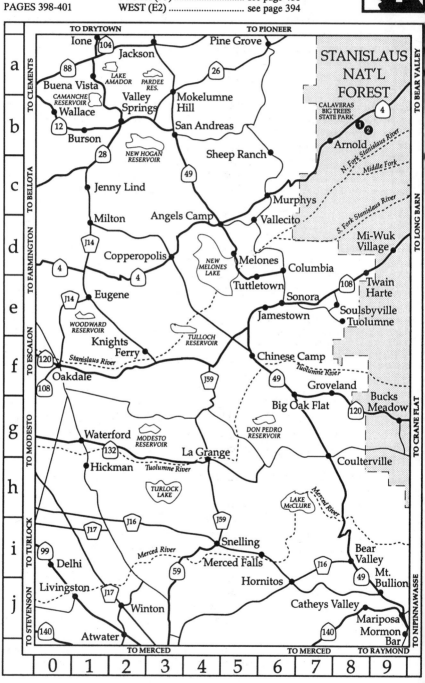

NORTHERN AREA HIKING TRAILS (map page 14)

## 1. NORTH GROVE LOOP 1.0 mi/0.5 hr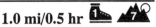

*Reference:* **On Highway 4 northeast of Arnold; map E3, grid b8.**

*User groups:* Hikers and **wheelchairs**. No dogs, horses or mountain bikes are allowed.

*Permits:* No permits are required. There is a $5 state park entrance fee for each vehicle.

*Directions:* From Highway 99 at Stockton, turn east on Highway 4 and drive to the junction of Highways 4 and 49 at Angels Camp. Continue east on Highway 4 for 26 miles to the park, located four miles past Arnold. The trailhead is adjacent to the park entrance.

*Maps:* For a brochure and complete trail map, send $1 to Calaveras Big Trees State Park at the address below. Interpretive brochures are also available at the trailhead for 25 cents. To obtain a topographic map of the area, ask for Dorrington from the USGS.

*Who to contact:* Calaveras Big Trees State Park, P.O. Box 120, Arnold, CA 95223; (209) 795-2334.

*Trail notes:* Even with 150 Giant Sequoias here at Calaveras Big Trees State Park, it is "The Big Stump" that is actually a highlight. You see, the gent who first found this place wanted to prove how big the trees were, so naturally he cut one down, leaving this giant stump behind. Makes perfect sense, just like you'd shoot Bigfoot, right? Surrrrre. Well, Calaveras Big Trees is a very popular state park, and this trail is the most popular walk in the park. Got it? Right. You can expect other people, lots of 'em. The trail is easy and routed among the Giant Sequoias. The sweet fragrance of the massive trees fills the air, something you will never forget. These trees, of course, are known for their tremendous diameters, not height, where it can taken a few dozen people, linking hands, to circle even one.

## 2. SOUTH GROVE LOOP 5.0 mi/3.0 hrs

*Reference:* **On Highway 4 northeast of Arnold; map E3, grid b8.**

*User groups:* Hikers only. No dogs, horses or mountain bikes are allowed. No wheelchair facilities.

*Permits:* No permits are required. There is a $5 state park entrance fee for each vehicle.

*Directions:* From Highway 99 at Stockton, turn east on Highway 4 and drive to the junction of Highways 4 and 49 at Angels Camp. Continue east on Highway 4 for 26 miles to the park, located four miles past Arnold. From the park entrance, head down the parkway for nine miles to the trailhead. Note: The road is closed in winter.

*Maps:* For a brochure and complete trail map, send $1 to Calaveras Big Trees State Park at the address below. To obtain a topographic map of the area, ask for Boards Crossing from the USGS.

*Who to contact:* Calaveras Big Trees State Park, P.O. Box 120, Arnold, CA 95223; (209) 795-2334.

*Trail notes:* The two largest Giant Sequoias in Calaveras Big Trees State Park are on a spur trail of this hike, and that makes it a must-do trip for visitors to the park. But so many tourists are content to just walk the little trail at the North Grove, look at the giant stump, then hit the road. Why rush? As long as you are visiting the park, take the North Grove Loop. The actual loop is 3.5 miles, but the highlight is a spur trail that heads off for three-quarters of a mile to the Agassiz Tree and the Palace Hotel Tree. These are monster-sized. A great photograph is to have a picture of you taken standing at the base of one of these trees; you will look like a Lilliputian in *Gulliver's Travels.*

## LEAVE NO TRACE TIPS

### Keep the wilderness wild

• Let nature's sound prevail. Avoid loud voices and noises.

• Leave radios and tape players at home.
At drive-in camping sites, never open car doors with music playing.

• Careful guidance is necessary when choosing any games to bring for
|children. Most toys, especially any kind of gun toys with which children
simulate shooting at each other, should not be allowed on a camping trip.

• Control pets at all times, or leave them with a sitter at home.

• Treat natural heritage with respect. Leave plants,
rocks and historical artifacts where you find them.

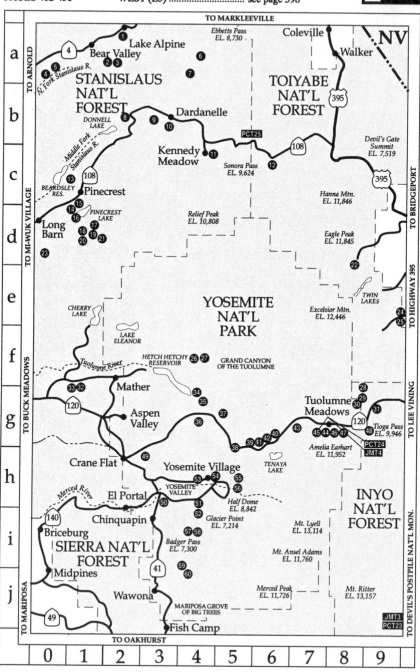

**Map E4 featuring:** Stanislaus National Forest, Ebbetts Pass, Sonora Pass, Pinecrest, Yosemite National Park, Tuolumne Meadows, Hetch Hetchy Reservoir

## 1. INSPIRATION POINT 3.0 mi/1.0 hr

*Reference:* **South of Highway 4, east of Angels Camp and west of Ebbetts Pass; map E4, grid a2.**

*User groups:* Hikers, horses and dogs. No mountain bikes are allowed. No wheelchair facilities.

*Permits:* No day-use permits are required. Wilderness permits are required if you plan on camping. Contact the Calaveras Ranger Station at (209) 795-1381. Parking and access are free.

*Directions:* From the town of Angels Camp, drive northeast for approximately 50 miles on Highway 4 to Lake Alpine. Drive on the east-shore road which heads immediately away from Highway 4 just east of the Chickaree Picnic Ground. Look for the spur road branching east to the Pine Marten Campground, just before the Silver Creek Campground. Park at the Pine Marten Campground.

*Maps:* Send $3 to the USDA-Forest Service, 630 Sansome Street, San Francisco, CA 94111 and ask for the Stanislaus National Forest map. For a topographic map, ask for Spicer Meadow Reservoir from the USGS.

*Who to contact:* Stanislaus National Forest, Calaveras Ranger District, P.O. Box 500, Hathaway Pines, CA 95233; (209) 795-1381.

*Trail notes:* This trail is located within the beautiful Carson-Iceberg Wilderness. From the Pine Marten Campground, hike the Lakeshore Trail to the Inspiration Point Trail junction, a very uninspiring and often crowded half mile. From here on up, the situation improves as the trail heads to the top of Inspiration Point, a barren overlook standing watch over a 360-degree view of the surrounding countryside. Don't forget your camera.

*Special note:* A word of caution: The footing on the slopes before the top are potentially hazardous. Step carefully and watch where your feet are going at all times.

## 2. OSBORNE HILL 2.6 mi/1.5 hrs

*Reference:* **South of Highway 4, east of Angels Camp and west of Ebbetts Pass; map E4, grid a2.**

*User groups:* Hikers, horses, dogs and mountain bikes. No wheelchair access.

*Permits:* No permits are required. Parking and access are free.

*Directions:* From the town of Angels Camp, drive northeast on Highway 4 for approximately 48 miles to Silvertip Campground. The trailhead and parking area (large enough for three to four vehicles) is located approximately one-quarter mile east of the campground.

*Maps:* Send $3 to the USDA-Forest Service, 630 Sansome Street, San Francisco, CA 94111 and ask for the Stanislaus National Forest map. For a topographic map, ask for Tamarack from the USGS.

*Who to contact:* Stanislaus National Forest, Calaveras Ranger District, P.O. Box 500, Hathaway Pines, CA 95233; (209) 795-1381.

*Trail notes:* This is an enjoyable stroll out to Osborne Hill which, at 7,815 feet, offers superb views of the Lake Alpine area. The path continues on to a junction with Emigrant West trail. From the trailhead, begin hiking on a good trail that begins to climb for eight-tenths of a mile up through pine and fir to Osborne Hill (some refer to this as Osborne Point, but the maps call it Osborne Hill, so Osborne Hill it is). From here you can see Dardanelles Cone to the southeast and Lake Alpine to the east. From Osborne Hill, you can keep hiking to the junction with the historic Emigrant Trail, one-half mile away. The meadow in the ridgeline's saddle is a peaceful spot to contemplate for a while, before turning back. This is bear country—be sure to hang all food well away from the tent and maintain a clean camp.

---

## 3. DUCK LAKE 2.5 mi/1.0 hr

*Reference:* South of Highway 4, east of Angels Camp and west of Ebbetts Pass; map E4, grid a2.

*User groups:* Hikers, horses and dogs. No mountain bikes are allowed. No wheelchair access.

*Permits:* No day-use permits are required. Wilderness permits are required if you plan on camping. Contact the Calaveras Ranger District at (209) 795-1381. Parking and access are free.

*Directions:* From the town of Angels Camp, drive northeast on Highway 4 for approximately 50 miles to Lake Alpine. Drive on the east-shore road which heads immediately away from Highway 4 just east of the Chickaree Picnic Ground. Drive past the spur road branching east to the Pine Marten Campground, and continue on to the Silver Valley Campground. Park at the Silver Creek Campground. The trailhead is signed.

*Maps:* Send $3 to the USDA-Forest Service, 630 Sansome Street, San Francisco, CA 94111 and ask for the Stanislaus National Forest map. For a topographic map, ask for Spicer Meadow Reservoir from the USGS.

*Who to contact:* Stanislaus National Forest, Calaveras Ranger District, Highway 4, P.O. Box 500, Hathaway Pines, CA 95233; (209) 795-1381.

*Trail notes:* An easy trail beginning at the Silver Valley Campground, the Duck Lake Trail climbs gradually up a small ridge and then over the crest for a short hike back down to Duck Lake. The fishing is fair here. Anywhere that is as accessible as this is to hikers, campers and fishermen is likely to attract bears—hang all food well away from your tent and maintain a clean camp.

---

## 4. SPICER MEADOW 8.5 mi/5.0 hrs
## RESERVOIR to TWIN LAKES

*Reference:* South of Highway 4, east of Angels Camp, west of Ebbetts Pass and near Spicer Reservoir; map E4, grid a0.

*User groups:* Hikers, horses and dogs. No mountain bikes are allowed. No wheelchair facilities.

*Permits:* No day-use permits are required. Wilderness permits are required if you plan on camping. Contact the Calaveras Ranger District at (209) 795-1381. Parking and access are free.

*Directions:* From the town of Angels Camp, drive northeast for approximately 43 miles on Highway 4 to just past the Big Meadow Campground. Turn right onto Forest Service Road 7N01 and follow it to Forest Service Road 7N75.

Turn right on 7N75 and drive to the Spicer Reservoir Trailhead.

**Maps:** Send $3 to the USDA-Forest Service, 630 Sansome Street, San Francisco, CA 94111 and ask for the Stanislaus National Forest map. For topographic maps, ask for Spicer Meadow Reservoir, Tamarack and Donnell Lake from the USGS.

**Who to contact:** Stanislaus National Forest, Calaveras Ranger District, P.O. Box 500, Hathaway Pines, CA 95233; (209) 795-1381.

**Trail notes:** This trail enters the beautiful Carson-Iceberg Wilderness. Twin Lakes offers an excellent picnic lunch and swimming hole destination for a late summer escape. While swimming in the warm waters is pleasant, forget your fishing rod—the water is too warm to support a fishery. To get to Twin Lakes, cross Highland Creek below the dam and hike back up along the Whitaker Dardanelles towards Clover Meadow and Wheats Meadow. In just under three miles, branch left at the trail junction towards Twin Lakes on the Twin Meadows Trail, heading north. Hike less than one-half mile to arrive at Twin Meadows and the trail's end—more of a gradual disappearance. At Twin Meadows, you must begin to navigate cross-country for just under approximately three-quarter of a mile—staying on the northwest edge of a series of meadows offers you the best chance at hitting the lake dead-on in your first try. There are numerous other small lakes and ponds in the area which can confuse the issue. Don't forget your map and compass! In the spring, especially after the snow has melted, the meadows from the end of the Twin Meadows Trail to Twin Meadows Lake can be very swampy—wet feet are part of the package. During one visit, Michael removed his boots and hiked in Teva sandals with neoprene socks for comfort. There are several stream crossings required on this trail that can be difficult to hazardous during spring snowmelt in June—call the ranger station to check on stream levels before heading out. If in doubt as to your ability to safely cross a stream, don't. The mountains and stream will always be there another day—be sure that you can say the same. Further challenges in the early weeks of June and July are swampy meadows and clouds of mosquitoes. For these reasons, August to September is considered the best time to visit.

---

# 5. SPICER RESERVOIR to SAND FLAT

**10.0 mi/4.0 hrs**

**Reference:** South of Highway 4, east of Angels Camp and west of Ebbetts Pass; map E4, grid a0.

**User groups:** Hikers, horses, dogs and mountain bikes. No wheelchair facilities.

**Permits:** No permits are required. Parking and access are free.

**Directions:** From the town of Angels Camp, drive northeast on Highway 4 for approximately 43 miles. After passing the Big Meadow Campground, turn right onto Forest Service Road 7N01 (Spicer Reservoir Road) and follow it to Forest Service Road 7N75. Turn right on 7N75 and follow it to Spicer Reservoir campground. Take the second left to Sand Flat Trailhead and park in the new parking area. To access the trail from the Stanislaus River and near the Big Meadow Campground, turn off Highway 4 just past the Big Meadow Campground turnoff onto a dirt road signed for Camp Wolfeboro, a Boy Scouts camp. There is limited trailhead parking alongside the road.

**Maps:** Send $3 to the USDA-Forest Service, 630 Sansome Street, San Francisco, CA 94111 and ask for the Stanislaus National Forest map. For topographic maps, ask for Spicer Meadow Reservoir and Tamarack from the USGS.

*Who to contact:* Stanislaus National Forest, Calaveras Ranger District, P.O. Box 500, Hathaway Pines, CA 95233; (209) 795-1381.

*Trail notes:* Mountain bicyclists love this trail for its quick ups and downs, stream crossings and scenery. The elevation gain and loss is never more than several hundred feet. The route heads west from the reservoir through the forest. The treadway will pass through Corral Meadow (the halfway point at approximately five miles) before reaching Sand Flat and the Sand Flat Campground along the Clark Fork of the Stanislaus River. Wildflowers are quite spectacular in June in the open meadows. From Corral Meadow to Sand Flat, the going can get wet during the spring snowmelt. Return the way you came.

---

## 6. BOULDER LAKE          8.0 mi/5.0 hrs

*Reference:* West of Bridgeport and Highway 395 and north of Highway 108 at Sonora Pass; map E4, grid a4.

*User groups:* Hikers, horses and dogs. No mountain bikes are allowed. No wheelchair facilities.

*Permits:* No day-use permits are required. Wilderness permits are required if you plan on camping. Contact the Summit Ranger District at (209) 965-3434. Parking and access are free.

*Directions:* From the town of Sonora, head northeast on Highway 108 toward Sonora Pass, passing through the town of Pinecrest. Three miles west of Dardanelle and approximately five miles east of Niagara Creek Campground, turn north onto Clark Fork Road (Forest Service Road 7N83). Follow 7N83 to its end at Iceberg Meadow and the Clark Fork Meadow trailhead.

*Maps:* Send $3 to the USDA-Forest Service, 630 Sansome Street, San Francisco, CA 94111 and ask for the Stanislaus National Forest map. For a topographic map, ask for Disaster Peak from the USGS.

*Who to contact:* Stanislaus National Forest, Summit Ranger District, 1 Pinecrest Lake Road, Pinecrest, CA 95364; (209) 965-3434.

*Trail notes:* This trail lies within the beautiful Carson-Iceberg Wilderness. Don't forget your map and compass. The last half-mile or so of "trail" to Boulder Lake is sketchy at best. To get to Boulder Lake, hike along the Clark Fork Trail for approximately 2.7 miles to the intersection with the Boulder Lake Trail. Turn north and hike for another 1.3 miles or so to Boulder Lake. Fishing for trout is wonderful along the Clark Fork Stanislaus River and fair in Boulder Lake.

*Special note:* There are several stream crossings required on this trail that can be difficult to hazardous during the spring snowmelt in June. Call the ranger station to check on stream levels before heading out. If in doubt as to your ability to safely cross a stream, don't.

# 7. CLARK FORK TRAIL to SAINT MARY'S PASS

**11.0 mi. one way/7.0 hrs**

*Reference:* West of Bridgeport and Highway 395 and north of Highway 108 at Sonora Pass; map E4, grid a4.

*User groups:* Hikers, horses and dogs. No mountain bikes are allowed. No wheelchair facilities.

*Permits:* No day-use permits are required. Wilderness permits are required if you plan on camping. Contact the Summit Ranger District at (209) 965-3434.

*Directions:* From the town of Sonora, head northeast on Highway 108 toward Sonora Pass, passing through the town of Pinecrest. Three miles west of Dardanelle and approximately five miles east of Niagara Creek Campground, turn north onto Clark Fork Road (Forest Service Road 7N83). Follow 7N83 to its end at Iceberg Meadow and the Clark Fork Meadow trailhead.

For a shuttle trip (a shuttle is recommended if you are trying to turn this into a day-trip), leave one car near the Sonora Pass at the trailhead parking. Use your odometer as the parking area on the north side of the road is not marked and you will drive right past it unless there are several other cars there to remind you. From Sonora Pass, drive northwest for eight-tenths of a mile.

*Maps:* Send $3 to the USDA-Forest Service, 630 Sansome Street, San Francisco, CA 94111 and ask for the Stanislaus National Forest map. For topographic maps, ask for Disaster Peak and, if you are planning on exploring the Clark Fork Meadow area, Sonora Pass and Dardanelles, from the USGS.

*Who to contact:* Stanislaus National Forest, Summit Ranger District, #1 Pinecrest Lake Road, Pinecrest, CA 95364; (209) 965-3434.

*Trail notes:* This trail lies within the beautiful Carson-Iceberg Wilderness. Begin hiking along the Clark Meadow Trail for approximately 2.7 miles to the junction with the Boulder Lake Trail branching off to the left. Continue on the Clark Fork Trail, hiking for another five miles towards Clark Meadow. The trail follows the edge of the canyon above the Clark Fork Stanislaus River for half the way before joining the Clark Fork, sometimes near it, sometimes a distance away, for the remainder of the trek. Campsites are numerous around Clark Meadow. We would recommend camping along the northwestern boundary of the meadow since it is closer to the trail up to Saint Mary's Pass. If it is early in the spring, mosquitoes can be a nightmare. If this is the case, beat a hasty retreat back down the trail from the meadow to the numerous camping sites you passed along the banks and tributaries of the Clark Fork and among the pines. From Clark Meadow, continue another 2.4 steep miles to Saint Mary's Pass, a pass that was used by the 1862-1863 emigrants on their route from Sonora Pass to Clark Fork. That route was abandoned before long in favor of the Deadman Creek route, the current Highway 108. The views from Saint Mary's Pass are definitely worth the huffing and puffing required to get there. The trail is somewhat indistinct, so keep a sharp eye. If Saint Mary's Pass is your only goal, you would be better served to park at the Sonora Pass trailhead mentioned above and hike in from there—a three-mile roundtrip venture with much less effort required.

## 7. DONNELL VISTA 0.3 mi/0.5 hr

*Reference:* **West of Sonora Pass and south of Highway 108 near the town of Pinecrest; map E4, grid b2.**

*User groups:* Hikers and dogs. No mountain bikes or horses are allowed. No wheelchair facilities.

*Permits:* No permits are required. Parking and access are free.

*Directions:* From the town of Sonora, head northeast on Highway 108 toward Sonora Pass, through the town of Pinecrest. Approximately 18 miles east of Pinecrest you will arrive at the signed trailhead and parking area located on the north side of the highway.

*Maps:* Send $3 to the USDA-Forest Service, 630 Sansome Street, San Francisco, CA 94111 and ask for the Stanislaus National Forest map. For a topographic map, ask for Donnell Lake from the USGS.

*Who to contact:* Stanislaus National Forest, Summit Ranger District, 1 Pinecrest Lake Road, Pinecrest, CA 95364; (209) 965-3434.

*Trail notes:* This is an informative walk along a maintained interpretive trail that guides you to a viewpoint at trail's end, offering excellent views of Connell Lake and Dome Rock. Smoking is prohibited on the trail—why would you want to breathe anything but fresh mountain air anyway?

---

## 8. EAGLE CREEK 4.0 mi. one way/2.0 hrs
## TRAIL to DARDANELLE

*Reference:* **West of Sonora Pass and south of Highway 108 near the town of Pinecrest; map E4, grid b3.**

*User groups:* Hikers, dogs, horses and mountain bikes. No wheelchair facilities.

*Permits:* No permits are required. Parking and access are free.

*Directions:* A vehicle shuttle is recommended for this hike, unless you prefer to hike out and back. To get to the trailhead, drive from the town of Sonora northeast on Highway 108 toward Sonora Pass, through the town of Strawberry. East of Strawberry turn right onto Eagle Meadow Road, also known as Forest Service Road 5N01 and signed as the turnoff for Niagara Campground. Follow 5N01 for approximately eight miles to Eagle Meadow and the trailhead. For a one-way trip with a shuttle car, leave one vehicle at Dardanelle Resort, located in the small town of Dardanelle on Highway 108, past Pinecrest and the Eagle Meadow turnoff.

*Maps:* Send $3 to the USDA-Forest Service, 630 Sansome Street, San Francisco, CA 94111 and ask for the Stanislaus National Forest map. For a topographic map, ask for Dardanelle from the USGS.

*Who to contact:* Stanislaus National Forest, Summit Ranger District, 1 Pinecrest Lake Road, Pinecrest, CA 95364; (209) 965-3434.

*Trail notes:* This is a pleasant hike through gorgeous subalpine meadows (resplendent with wildflowers in the spring) and, as the treadway approaches Dardanelle, dense forest which shades nearby Eagle Creek. The trail isn't well-marked. Park at the creek and then hike across to a cabin that is intended for those with cattle permits for the region. The trail begins by the cabin. Turn left and follow the road (north from the cabin). The road soon turns into a trail. Follow the trail through a meadow and then down into the Eagle Creek drainage. The trail will exit at the Bone Spring summer tract homes—follow the road out to the highway and Dardanelle Resort.

## 9. COLUMNS OF THE GIANTS    0.3 mi/0.5 hr

*Reference:* **West of Sonora Pass and south of Highway 108 near the town of Pinecrest; map E4, grid b3.**

*User groups:* Hikers and dogs. No mountain bikes or horses are allowed. No wheelchair facilities.

*Permits:* No permits are required. Parking and access are free.

*Directions:* From the town of Sonora, head northeast on Highway 108 toward Sonora Pass, through the town of Strawberry. Approximately 24 miles east of Strawberry you will arrive at Pigeon Flat Campground. The trailhead and parking area is located next to the campground.

*Maps:* Send $3 to the USDA-Forest Service, 630 Sansome Street, San Francisco, CA 94111 and ask for the Stanislaus National Forest map. For a topographic map, ask for Dardanelle from the USGS.

*Who to contact:* Stanislaus National Forest, Summit Ranger District, 1 Pinecrest Lake Road, Pinecrest, CA 95364; (209) 965-3434.

*Trail notes:* This is an informative walk along a maintained interpretive trail that guides you past two volcanic formations, which cooled at different rates producing fascinating examples of columnar basalt. Be sure to pick up a free interpretive brochure at the trailhead. Smoking is prohibited on the trail.

## 10. KENNEDY LAKE    9.0 mi/4.0 hrs

*Reference:* **West of Sonora Pass and south of Highway 108 near the town of Pinecrest; map E4, grid c4.**

*User groups:* Hikers, dogs and horses. No mountain bikes are allowed. No wheelchair facilities.

*Permits:* No day-use permits are required. Wilderness permits are required if you plan on camping. Contact the Summit Ranger District at (209) 965-3434. Parking and access are free.

*Directions:* From Sonora, drive northeast on Highway 108 toward Sonora Pass through the towns of Pinecrest, Dardanelle and Douglas. Just past the town of Douglas, turn right at the Baker Campground on Kennedy Meadows Road. The trailhead is located at the Kennedy Meadows Resort. Park your vehicle in the designated public parking area (located approximately one mile from Kennedy Meadows) and not in the private lot of the resort.

*Maps:* Send $3 to the USDA-Forest Service, 630 Sansome Street, San Francisco, CA 94111 and ask for the Stanislaus National Forest map. For topographic maps, ask for Pinecrest, Emigrant Lake and Cooper Peak from the USGS. U.S. Forest Service topographic maps, Carson-Iceberg Wilderness and Emigrant Wilderness, are available for $6 each from the Summit Ranger District.

*Who to contact:* Stanislaus National Forest, Summit Ranger District, 1 Pinecrest Lake Road, Pinecrest, CA 95364; (209) 965-3434.

*Trail notes:* This trail enters the Emigrant Wilderness—a fly fishing or angling paradise! Don't even think about leaving your rod at home because most of the lakes are stocked with trout. The trailhead is the Huckleberry Trail, which leads into the Emigrant Basin and Emigrant Lake. It is possible to link a number of trails, creating interesting loops. Two trails described within this book, Burst Rock and Crabtree trails (see hike numbers 19 and 20 in this chapter) can all become part of an excursion into the Emigrant interior. Kennedy Lake lies between Kennedy Peak and Leavitt Peak and, unfortunately for hikers, it is heavily used by horses and pack trips. From the trailhead, hike approximately 2.5 miles up the Huckleberry Trail to the junction with the Kennedy Creek Trail, branching off to the left near the green PG&E maintenance building. The trail is a good one with a bridge crossing the most difficult stream section. From the PG&E building the treadway climbs up-canyon steadily towards Kennedy Peak, sitting like a watchdog above the headwall of the canyon and overlooking picturesque Kennedy Lake. Campsites along the stream below the lake are numerous, with the best located near the confluence of the lake and creek. There is no camping at the lake. Cast your line upon the waters when you are rested and enjoy the fishing for rainbow and brown trout. Head back the way you came.

---

# 11. LEAVITT LAKE      3.2 mi/2.0 hrs

*Reference:* **Just west of Highway 395 and Mono Lake; map E4, grid c6.**

*User groups:* Hikers and horses. No mountain bikes or dogs are allowed. No wheelchair facilities.

*Permits:* No day-use permits are required. Camping permits are required if you plan on camping. Contact the National Park Service at (209) 372-0200 or the Bridgeport Ranger District at (619) 932-7070. Parking and access are free.

*Directions:* From Bridgeport and Highway 395, drive west on Highway 108 for approximately 12 miles to Forest Service Road 077, also signed as the Leavitt Lake Road (approximately five miles east of Sonora Pass). This road is very rough and not recommended for low-slung passenger cars. In approximately 2.9 miles, you will come to a parking area at Leavitt Lake's outlet stream. There are many informal roads that crisscross the area to RV camping sites.

*Maps:* Send $3 to the USDA-Forest Service, 630 Sansome Street, San Francisco, CA 94111 and ask for the Toiyabe National Forest map. For a topographic map, ask for Pickel Meadow from the USGS.

*Who to contact:* Toiyabe National Forest, Bridgeport Ranger District, P.O. Box 595, Bridgeport, CA 93517; (619) 932-7070.

*Trail notes:* The route follows a rugged jeep road that is used occasionally to access remote mining claims that still exist in the area (only those who have mining claims can drive vehicles on this road). Although eyebrows may be raised at the thought of mining claims within the Emigrant Wilderness, it is important to realize that these claims predate the wilderness designation, which is why they are allowed. Still, we are left to ponder the land-use values which appear to stand against everything our modern concept of wilderness implies. The terrain is volcanic and rough, but beautiful. The rewards for shuffling up two steep climbs along the way are panoramic views of the mountains to the south. The Leavitt Lake Trail intersects with the Pacific Crest Trail at its end, providing perhaps the best and most direct access into the heart of the Emigrant Basin. If you are heading into the Basin, pack along a fly rod because the fishing is blue-ribbon caliber. Leavitt Lake itself is well known for trout fishing, which is why it is frequented by RVs and their resident fish-lovers.

## 12. BEARDSLEY TRAIL 0.3 mi/0.5 hr

*Reference:* **West of Sonora Pass and north of Highway 108 near the town of Pinecrest; map E4, grid c1.**

*User groups:* Hikers and dogs. No mountain bikes or horses are allowed. No wheelchair facilities.

*Permits:* No permits are required. Parking and access are free.

*Directions:* From the town of Sonora, head northeast on Highway 108 toward Sonora Pass. Just east of the Pinecrest turnoff, turn left onto Forest Service Road 5N02 (Beardsley Road). Follow 5N02 all the way to Beardsley Lake. The trailhead is located in the day-use area.

*Maps:* Send $3 to the USDA-Forest Service, 630 Sansome Street, San Francisco, CA 94111 and ask for the Stanislaus National Forest map. For a topographic map, ask for Strawberry from the USGS.

*Who to contact:* Stanislaus National Forest, Summit Ranger District, 1 Pinecrest Lake Road, Pinecrest, CA 95364; (209) 965-3434.

*Trail notes:* This is a pleasant leg-stretcher, an informative walk along a maintained interpretive trail that guides you through a pretty forested area adjacent to Beardsley Lake.

## 13. TRAIL OF THE GARGOYLES 1.5 mi/1.0 hr

*Reference:* **West of Sonora Pass and south of Highway 108 near the town of Pinecrest; map E4, grid d1.**

*User groups:* Hikers and dogs. No mountain bikes or horses are allowed. No wheelchair facilities.

*Permits:* No permits are required. Parking and access are free.

*Directions:* From the town of Sonora, head northeast on Highway 108 toward Sonora Pass. After passing through the hamlet of Strawberry, just past the turnoff for Pinecrest, turn right on Herring Creek Road, also known as Forest Service Road 4N12. Drive on 4N12 for approximately six miles to the signed trailhead. The last mile of the road is dirt.

*Maps:* Send $3 to the USDA-Forest Service, 630 Sansome Street, San Francisco, CA 94111 and ask for the Stanislaus National Forest map. For a topographic map, ask for Pinecrest from the USGS.

*Who to contact:* Stanislaus National Forest, Summit Ranger District, 1 Pinecrest Lake Road, Pinecrest, CA 95364; (209) 965-3434.

*Trail notes:* This is an informative walk along a maintained interpretive trail that guides you through a scenic geologic wonder loaded with unique and fascinating volcanic formations. Be sure to pick up a free interpretive brochure at the trailhead.

## 14. WATERHOUSE LAKE 3.0 mi/2.0 hrs

*Reference:* **West of Bridgeport and Highway 395 and south of Highway 108 at Sonora Pass; map E4, grid d1.**

*User groups:* Hikers, horses (day-use only) and dogs. No mountain bikes are allowed. No wheelchair facilities.

*Permits:* No day-use permits are required. Wilderness permits are required if you plan on camping. Contact the Summit Ranger District at (209) 965-3434. Parking and access are free.

*Directions:* From Sonora, drive northeast on Highway 108 past the Pinecrest turnoff and the Summit Ranger Station and through the hamlet of Strawberry. Just after passing through Strawberry, turn right onto Herring Creek Road, also known as Forest Service Road 4N12. Drive past undeveloped Herring Creek Campground and continue for two miles to Forest Service 5N31. Turn right onto 5N31 and drive approximately one-half mile to a large meadow on the right side of the road. At the far end of the meadow is a junction where you will find parking and the trailhead to the left.

*Maps:* Send $3 to the USDA-Forest Service, 630 Sansome Street, San Francisco, CA 94111 and ask for the Stanislaus National Forest map. For a topographic map, ask for Pinecrest from the USGS.

*Who to contact:* Stanislaus National Forest, Summit Ranger District, 1 Pinecrest Lake Road, Pinecrest, CA 95364; (209) 965-3434.

*Trail notes:* This trail enters the Emigrant Wilderness. Follow the treadway along a winding route through red fir forest on the rim of the South Fork Stanislaus River Canyon. From the canyon, the trail disappears, requiring strong navigational skills using a map and compass. The cross-country route is frequently marked by trail ducks (stacked rocks) over the granite slabs leading to Waterhouse Lake, but keep in mind that these route markings are left by other hikers, not rangers—if the hikers were off-route, then so are the ducks. We would recommend that you trust your own compass and map skills. The hike is pleasant enough and the destination is also scenic, although the overall effect is tempered somewhat by the litter that scatters the bottom of Waterhouse Lake. Still, bring along your fishing rod and you will soon overlook the litter—rainbow trout are begging to be caught.

---

## 15. SHADOW OF THE MI-WOK   0.3 mi/0.5 hr

*Reference:* **West of Sonora Pass and south of Highway 108 near the town of Pinecrest; map E4, grid d1.**

*User groups:* Hikers and dogs. No mountain bikes or horses are allowed. No wheelchair facilities.

*Permits:* No permits are required. Parking and access are free.

*Directions:* From the town of Sonora, head northeast on Highway 108 toward Sonora Pass, to the Pinecrest turnoff. Turn right onto Pinecrest Lake Road and park at the Summit Ranger Station on the left. The trail is located across the road from the ranger station.

*Maps:* Send $3 to the USDA-Forest Service, 630 Sansome Street, San Francisco, CA 94111 and ask for the Stanislaus National Forest map. For a topographic map, ask for Pinecrest from the USGS.

*Who to contact:* Stanislaus National Forest, Summit Ranger District, 1 Pinecrest Lake Road, Pinecrest, CA 95364; (209) 965-3434.

*Trail notes:* This is an informative walk along a maintained interpretive trail that describes the Mi-Wok way of life, including their livelihood and history. The Mi-Wok Indians settled in the region around 1000 AD. Smoking is prohibited on the trail.

## 16. COOPER MEADOW  7.0 mi/3.0 hrs

*Reference:* **West of Sonora Pass and south of Highway 108 near the town of Pinecrest; map E4, grid d1.**

*User groups:* Hikers, dogs and horses. No mountain bikes are allowed. No wheelchair facilities.

*Permits:* No day-use permits are required. Wilderness permits are required if you plan on camping. Contact the Summit Ranger District at (209) 965-3434. Parking and access are free.

*Directions:* From Sonora, drive northeast on Highway 108 past the Pinecrest turnoff and the Summit Ranger Station and through the hamlet of Strawberry. Just after passing through Strawberry, turn right onto Herring Creek Road, also known as Forest Service Road 4N12. Stay on 4N12 for four miles to spur road 5N67 and turn right. The Coyote Meadow Trailhead is located on the left after about one mile. At times, the road may be gated—be sure to call ahead to the ranger station to be sure of access.

*Maps:* Send $3 to the USDA-Forest Service, 630 Sansome Street, San Francisco, CA 94111 and ask for the Stanislaus National Forest map. For topographic maps, ask for Dardanelle and Cooper Peak from the USGS.

*Who to contact:* Stanislaus National Forest, Summit Ranger District, 1 Pinecrest Lake Road, Pinecrest, CA 95364; (209) 965-3434.

*Trail notes:* This is an easy jaunt along a heavily used access path into the western Emigrant Basin. The pathway traverses several pretty meadows. The historic cabins and barn at Cooper Meadow and just beyond at Hay Meadow belonged to Cooper Meadow's namesake, Mr. Cooper. At one time, he pastured milking cows in the lush meadows and hauled the dairy products all the way out to Sonora. From Hay Meadow, the trail continues about another three miles up through volcanic terrain to Whitesides Meadow and the trail's terminus at Burst Rock Trail.

## 17. PINECREST LAKE  4.0 mi/2.0 hrs

*Reference:* **West of Bridgeport and Highway 395 and south of Highway 108 near Sonora Pass; map E4, grid d1.**

*User groups:* Hikers and dogs. No mountain bikes or horses are allowed. There is **limited wheelchair access.**

*Permits:* No permits are required. Parking and access are free.

*Directions:* From the town of Sonora, head northeast on Highway 108 toward Sonora Pass, to the Pinecrest turnoff. Turn right onto the Pinecrest Lake Road, driving past the Summit Ranger Station and continuing for one mile to a shopping center. Park here or across the road at the large parking area by the lake.

*Maps:* Send $3 to the USDA-Forest Service, 630 Sansome Street, San Francisco, CA 94111 and ask for the Stanislaus National Forest map. For a topographic map, ask for Pinecrest from the USGS.

*Who to contact:* Stanislaus National Forest, Summit Ranger District, 1 Pinecrest Lake Road, Pinecrest, CA 95364; (209) 965-3434.

*Trail notes:* Designated as a National Recreation Trail, Pinecrest Trail offers a pleasant hike around the scenic shore of Pinecrest Lake that is suitable for the entire family. Pack along your binoculars and bird book because the birdwatching is quite good. Picnic spots abound, especially near the inlet located at the east end of the lake. Remember to pack out everything that you brought in with you. Bicycles are allowed along the paved bike path which goes through the Pinecrest Picnic Area along the shoreline. **Wheelchairs** are also appropriate here. Where the pavement ends and the trail begins, bicycles are not allowed. Add an extra two miles to the journey with an easy and peaceful hike to Catfish Lake, which in reality is a set of shallow ponds surrounded by old-growth forest.

---

# 18. TRAIL OF THE SURVIVORS   0.3 mi/0.5 hr

*Reference:* **West of Sonora Pass and south of Highway 108 near the town of Pinecrest; map E4, grid d1.**

*User groups:* Hikers and dogs. No mountain bikes or horses are allowed. No wheelchair facilities.

*Permits:* No permits are required. Parking and access are free.

*Directions:* From the town of Sonora, head northeast on Highway 108 toward Sonora Pass, to the town of Pinecrest. At Pinecrest, park at the Pinecrest Community Center located just off Dodge Ridge Road.

*Maps:* Send $3 to the USDA-Forest Service, 630 Sansome Street, San Francisco, CA 94111 and ask for the Stanislaus National Forest map. For a topographic map, ask for Pinecrest from the USGS.

*Who to contact:* Stanislaus National Forest, Summit Ranger District, 1 Pinecrest Lake Road, Pinecrest, CA 95364; (209) 965-3434.

*Trail notes:* This is an informative walk along a maintained interpretive trail that describes how the trees struggle for life in a harsh mountain environment. This trail is very easy and suitable for all members of the family. It provides a great introduction to the ecology of the area.

---

# 19. BURST ROCK LOOP        32.5 mi/3.0 days

*Reference:* **West of Sonora Pass and south of Highway 108 near the town of Pinecrest; map E4, grid d1.**

*User groups:* Hikers, dogs and horses. No mountain bikes are allowed. No wheelchair facilities.

*Permits:* No day-use permits are required. Wilderness permits are required if you plan on camping. Contact the Summit Ranger District at (209) 965-3434. Parking and access are free.

*Directions:* From Sonora, drive northeast on Highway 108 through the community of Cold Springs. One-half mile beyond Cold Springs, turn right onto Crabtree Road (4N26)—just before the Pinecrest turnoff and past the turnoff to Dodge Ridge. Drive on Crabtree Road for approximately two miles to Aspen Meadow and Saradella's Pack Station (visual landmark). From Aspen Meadow, the road continues unpaved for about three miles to a junction. Drive straight, now on Forest Service 4N47, for approximately three more miles to Gianelli Cabin which is the trailhead and parking for Burst Rock Trail.

*Maps:* Send $3 to the USDA-Forest Service, 630 Sansome Street, San Francisco, CA 94111 and ask for the Stanislaus National Forest map. For topographic maps, ask for Pinecrest, Emigrant Lake and Cooper Peak from the USGS.

***Who to contact:*** Stanislaus National Forest, Summit Ranger District, 1 Pinecrest Lake Road, Pinecrest, CA 95364; (209) 965-3434.

***Trail notes:*** This trail enters the Emigrant Wilderness, which can provide decent trout fishing at beautiful lakes. From the trailhead, Burst Rock lies a moderate one mile distant thanks to an intelligent trail relocation, which makes the climb much more enjoyable than the steep, mind-bending trek it used to be. Enjoy the incredible views. Burst Rock was named originally Birth Rock as a tribute to the birth of a baby born on the journey of a group of emigrants passing through the region in 1853. If you are seeking a longer overnight escape, continue hiking into the Emigrant Wilderness on the Burst Rock Trail, to the Lake Valley junction, three miles out. Continue on the main trail passing by Whitesides Meadow at 5.8 miles to the junction with the Crabtree Trail at Deer Lake, 11 miles from the trailhead and your first night's camp. Camping at Deer Lake is only allowed in designated sites due to overuse. If there is no room at Deer Lake, retrace your steps up to one of the tarn lakes you passed just before the gentle canyon descent to Deer Lake and camp there. At Crabtree, bear right on the Crabtree Trail and head west towards Piute Meadow, five miles distant, and then on to the Bear Lake Trail junction, approximately 8.5 miles from Deer Lake. Turn right at the Bear Lake Trail and hike one mile to the lake and your second night's camp. The best and most heavily-used camping area is located at the north end of the lake. If your cross-country skills are solid, head north away from Bear Lake navigating cross-country past Granite Lake and Meadow Dam to meet up again with the Burst Rock Trail. Once at Burst Rock, head left or west and retrace your steps back to your car and the parking area. If you don't feel too solid setting out cross-country, then retrace your steps the one mile to the Crabtree Trail. Turn right and continue hiking down the Crabtree Trail for approximately two miles to the Chewing Gum Lake Trail. Hike north up the Chewing Gum Lake Trail approximately six miles to Burst Rock Trail and then head left or west retracing your steps three miles to your car and the parking area.

# 20. CRABTREE TRAIL & BEAR LAKE

**36.0 mi. one-way/5.0 days**

***Reference:*** **West of Sonora Pass and south of Highway 108 near the town of Pinecrest; map E4, grid d1.**

***User groups:*** Hikers, dogs and horses. No mountain bikes are allowed. No wheelchair facilities.

***Permits:*** No day-use permits are required. Wilderness permits are required if you plan on camping. Contact the Summit Ranger District at (209) 965-3434. Parking and access are free.

***Directions:*** From Sonora, drive northeast on Highway 108 through the community of Cold Springs. One-half mile beyond Cold Springs, turn right onto Crabtree Road (4N26)—just before the Pinecrest turnoff and past the turnoff to Dodge Ridge. Drive on Crabtree Road for approximately two miles to Aspen Meadow and Saradella's Pack Station (visual landmark). From Aspen Meadow, the road continues unpaved for about three miles to a junction. Turn right, still on Crabtree Road (4N26) and drive for one mile to the well-marked trailhead and parking area.

*Maps:* Send $3 to the USDA-Forest Service, 630 Sansome Street, San Francisco, CA 94111 and ask for the Stanislaus National Forest map. For topographic maps, ask for Pinecrest, Emigrant Lake and Cooper Peak from the USGS.

*Who to contact:* Stanislaus National Forest, Summit Ranger District, 1 Pinecrest Lake Road, Pinecrest, CA 95364; (209) 965-3434.

*Trail notes:* A car shuttle is recommended for this trail, with the exit point being Burst Rock—see hike number 19 for trip description and parking directions. If you desire a shorter trip, then head to Bear Lake. This is a beautiful and easy two-day trip or long one-day trek. From Bell Creek, hike fifty feet to a trail junction to Chewing Gum Lake. Hike three miles to Camp Lake. At the far end of Camp Lake, head left at a trail junction to Bear Lake. At both Camp Lake and Bear Lake, camping is limited to one-night's stay and camps must be set up within one-quarter mile of the lakes. To begin a longer five-day journey, cross Bell Creek and climb steadily up the Crabtree treadway which soon begins to contour above the Pine Valley. Your path will take you across several streams and open granite ridges—views are wonderful—before dropping you into the heart of the Emigrant Wilderness. Lakes dot the landscape like so many luxurious jewels. Pass by the junction at Deer Lake with the Burst Rock Trail to Whitesides Meadow and then Burst Rock—this will be your exit trail if using a car shuttle—and head on to another trail junction at the east end of Emigrant Lake, where you can camp. To head out, either retrace your steps entirely, choose another trail to create an alternate loop, or head back to the Burst Rock Trail and hike out via Whitesides Meadow and Burst Rock to an awaiting car. No car shuttle possible? Then head back via the Burst Rock Trail toward Burst Rock, but instead of heading all the way to Burst Rock—you will miss out on a stunning view—drop down on the Chewing Gum Lake Trail to Crabtree Camp.

---

# 21. MATTERHORN CANYON  46.0 mi/5.0 days

*Reference:* **In Yosemite National Park, north of Tuolumne Meadows and Tioga Pass Road; map E4, grid e8.**

*User groups:* Hikers and horses. No mountain bikes or dogs are allowed. No wheelchair access.

*Permits:* No day-use permits are required. Wilderness permits are required if you plan on camping. Contact the National Park Service at (209) 372-0200 or the Bridgeport Ranger District at (619) 932-7070.

*Directions:* From Lee Vining, drive north on Highway 395 to Bridgeport. Near the west side of Bridgeport, take the paved Twin Lakes Road south for approximately 13.5 miles to the signed entrance to Mono Village at the west end of upper Twin Lake. Although you will see cars parked outside of the entrance, rangers report that they are not safe there; vehicles do get broken into. Keep your vehicle safe and park for a $5 fee at Mono Village.

*Maps:* Send $3 to the USDA-Forest Service, 630 Sansome Street, San Francisco, CA 94111 and ask for the Toiyabe National Forest map. Tom Harrison Cartography publishes an excellent series of maps of the area. Call (415) 456-7940 and ask for the trail map of the Yosemite High Country, the recreation map of Yosemite National Park, and the map of Yosemite Valley. The cost is $5.95 plus tax and shipping for each map. Trails Illustrated also publishes a super map, Yosemite National Park. The cost is $7.95 and may be ordered by calling (800) 962-1643. For a topographic map, ask for Yosemite Falls from the USGS. A Hoover Wilderness map is available for $3 from the Bridgeport Ranger District; call (619) 932-7070.

**Who to contact:** Public Information Office, National Park Service, P.O. Box 577, Yosemite National Park, CA 95389; (209) 372-0200 or Toiyabe National Forest, Bridgeport Ranger District, P.O. Box 595, Bridgeport, CA 93517; (619) 932-7070.

**Trail notes:** Located entirely within the Hoover Wilderness Area and Yosemite National Park, the Matterhorn Canyon is a 13-mile-long glaciated canyon that is perhaps the most spectacular canyon in all of Yosemite's north country—a polished trough of granite rimmed by snow-capped mountains and dotted with conifer groves. The route begins at Mono Village Resort and heads up the Robinson Creek Trail for about 4.5 miles to the fork to Peeler Lake to the Kerrick Meadow Trail. Head down-canyon along the Rancheria Creek Trail to the Pacific Crest Trail, heading for Seavey Pass and Benson Lake. Stay on the PCT past Rogers Canyon Trail, Volunteer Peak, Smedberg Lake, and through Benson Pass. After Benson Pass, head north into Matterhorn Canyon on the Matterhorn Canyon Trail. Near the end of the canyon, Burro Pass will loom ominously and yet spectacularly before you—endless and legendary switchbacks guide you up and through the pass and then steeply back down. Follow the trail past Crown Point toward the Robinson Creek Trail and then back down Robinson Creek, past Barney Lake to Mono Village Resort and your car.

**Special note:** Bear-proof your camp at all times—this is definitely bear country.

## 22. BOX SPRING TRAIL          6.0 mi/3.0 hrs

**Reference:** North of Yosemite National Park, south of Highway 108 and Sonora Pass; map E4, grid d0.

**User groups:** Hikers, horses and dogs. No mountain bikes are allowed. No wheelchair access.

**Permits:** No day-use permits are required. Wilderness permits are required if you plan on camping. Contact the Mi-Wok Ranger Station at (209) 586-3234. Parking and access are free.

**Directions:** From the town of Sonora, head northeast on Highway 108. Approximately three miles beyond the Mi-Wok Ranger Station, heading east, take the second Long Barn exit off Highway 108 and drive approximately one-tenth of a mile on the Long Barn Road to Forest Service Road 3N01. Turn onto North Fork Road 3N01—signed to North Fork Tuolumne River and Cherry Reservoir. Drive on 3N01 past Hull Creek Campground to Camp Clavey. Shortly after crossing the Clavey River, turn left onto Road 3N16. Stay on Road 3N16 to Road 3N20Y, where you will turn left. Cross Bourland Creek and climb the ridge, through a junction, staying on 3N20Y the entire time. The road will descend above and to the south of Weed Meadow. At an abrupt switchback, where the road turns southwest, park on the pullout at the shoulder. The trail begins 40 feet down the embankment and is marked with a yellow blaze.

**Maps:** Send $3 to the USDA-Forest Service, 630 Sansome Street, San Francisco, CA 94111 and ask for the Stanislaus National Forest map. For topographic maps, ask for Pinecrest, Cherry Lake North, Cooper Peak and Kibbie Lake from the USGS.

**Who to contact:** Stanislaus National Forest, Mi-Wok Ranger District, P.O. Box 100, Mi-Wuk Village, CA 95346; (209) 586-3234.

**Trail notes:** This lightly traveled trail offers good access into the Chain Lakes area (not to be confused with the spectacular Chain of Lakes further east)— a region of unspectacular scenery but decent fishing and enough solitude to warrant an weekend escape. The trail will drop you off at Dutch Lake, the best point from which to explore the surrounding country and other lakes in the chain. Grouse Lake lies another mile away and is a worthwhile destination, as it is a quiet and scenic spot. Rainbow trout fishing is marginal. Mosquitoes abound, so pack plenty of repellent. A good compass and appropriate maps are essential as the tread becomes very vague at times. From the trailhead just below the parking area alongside the road, begin hiking northeast toward a trail junction through pine and fir forest. At the junction, bear right toward the Chain Lakes. Keep hiking, climbing gently, crossing through a number of small meadows to the shore of Dutch Lake. The trail skirts the south shore before meeting up with Chain Lakes Trail, heading south towards Bourland Road. A good campsite may be found near the trail junction. Follow the trail north to arrive at Grouse Lake.

---

## 23. LAKES CANYON  6.4 mi/3.0 hrs

**Reference: Just west of Highway 395 and Mono Lake; map E4, grid e9.**

**User groups:** Hikers and dogs. No horses or mountain bikes are allowed. No wheelchair access.

**Permits:** No day-use permits are required. Camping and fire permits are required if you plan on camping. Contact the Mono Lake Ranger Station at (619) 647-3000. Parking and access are free.

**Directions:** From Lee Vining, drive north on Highway 395, past Mono Lake to Lundy Canyon Road. Turn left on Lundy Canyon Road and follow it almost to Lundy Lake. The trailhead and parking area is located on the east end of Lundy Lake.

**Maps:** Send $3 to the USDA-Forest Service, 630 Sansome Street, San Francisco, CA 94111 and ask for the Inyo National Forest map. For topographic maps, ask for Lundy and Mt. Dana from the USGS.

**Who to contact:** Inyo National Forest, Mono Lake Ranger District, P.O. Box 429, Lee Vining, CA 93541; (619) 647-3000.

**Trail notes:** The Lakes Canyon Trail begins as a mining access road on the east side of Lundy Lake Dam, where only foot travel is permitted beyond the gates. The trail soon enters the Hoover Canyon Wilderness as it climbs on its way to Crystal Lake, following a somewhat steep route up the south side of Lundy Canyon to Lakes Canyon. Although the trail ends at Crystal Lake, an adventurous wanderer will find pleasure in continuing up towards Oneida Lake and the Tioga Crest—outstanding views! Lundy Creek Campground is located near the trailhead and overlooks the lunar-like landscape of nearby Mono Lake.

## 24. 20 LAKES BASIN 10.8 mi/5.0 hrs

*Reference:* **Just west of Highway 395 and Mono Lake; map E4, grid e9.**

*User groups:* Hikers and dogs. No horses or mountain bikes are allowed. No wheelchair access.

*Permits:* No day-use permits are required. Wilderness permits are required if you plan on camping. Contact the Mono Lake Ranger Station at (619) 647-3000. Parking and access are free.

*Directions:* From Lee Vining, drive north on Highway 395, past Mono Lake to Lundy Canyon Road. Turn left on Lundy Canyon Road and follow it to almost past Lundy Lake on a dirt road to the trailhead.

*Maps:* Send $3 to the USDA-Forest Service, 630 Sansome Street, San Francisco, CA 94111 and ask for the Inyo National Forest map. For topographic maps, ask for Dunderberg Peak and Tioga Pass from the USGS.

*Who to contact:* Inyo National Forest, Mono Lake Ranger District, P.O. Box 429, Lee Vining, CA 93541; (619) 647-3000.

*Trail notes:* This trail climbs, almost too steeply at times, through a series of interminable switchbacks, through Lundy Canyon to the 20 Lakes Basin and Lundy Pass. Numerous waterfalls will offer a necessary and pleasant distraction from the burning in your thighs and lungs as you hike. There was once a road that carved its way through the 20 Lakes Basin to a tungsten mine. The mine is now defunct, and the area has been restored to a more natural state, although you will still see tailings and other mining evidence near Steelhead Lake. To get to Steelhead Lake, begin hiking from the trailhead at 8,200 feet, passing by gorgeous falls within the first mile. Keep hiking up and up and, oh god up, to 10,000 feet of elevation and Lake Helen, approximately two miles from the trailhead. The trail gratefully levels out somewhat and continues past Odell Lake at 2.5 miles and then Hummingbird Lake at three miles. At Saddlebag Lake, bear right on the trail rimming the lake and then quickly right again onto the trail leading northwest and away from Saddlebag up towards Steelhead. Steelhead Lake lies approximately 1.5 miles away at 10,270 feet. Pack along your binoculars because the raptor watching is superb—osprey, eagles and hawks soar in the skies above. Take your time during this hike and if you feel light-headed, take a break or turn back—no sense in getting altitude sick over a lake. Open fires are prohibited in the 20 Lakes Basin due to heavy use and depleted wood stock—use your stove only! There are a number of revegetation projects going on in the area. These are signed and you are requested to obey the signs and not travel through the protected areas.

## 25. RANCHERIA MOUNTAIN LOOP 47.45 mi/5.0 days

*Reference:* **East of Groveland on Highway 120 and northeast of Hetch Hetchy Reservoir; map E4, grid f3.**

*User groups:* Hikers and horses. No dogs or mountain bikes are allowed. No wheelchair facilities.

*Permits:* No day-use permits are required. Wilderness permits are required for overnight stays within Yosemite National Park. A $5 day-use fee is good for seven days. For general information, call the National Park Service at (209)

372-0200. To talk to a "live" person, call public affairs at (209) 372-0265.

***Directions:*** From Groveland, drive east on Highway 120/Tioga Pass Road, to just before the Yosemite National Park boundary. Turn north on Evergreen Road and drive to Hetch Hetchy Road. Turn right on Hetch Hetchy Road and drive to the dam and the parking area. Hike across the dam on the Lake Eleanor Road to the Rancheria Falls Trail.

***Maps:*** For topographic maps, ask for Ten Lakes, Piute Mountain, Tiltill Mountain and Hetch Hetchy Reservoir from the USGS. For other maps of Yosemite, see "maps" under hike number 21.

***Who to contact:*** Public Information Office, National Park Service, P.O. Box 577, Yosemite National Park, CA 95389; (209) 372-0200.

***Trail notes:*** For those with strong legs and lungs and a week to test them, this trail is a must! Ups and downs are steep and at times very hot and dry. At every opportunity, you must top off your water bottles. Carpets of wildflowers on the west side of Rancheria Peak will literally astonish even the most jaded wildflower-watcher. A number of views, especially that from Bear Valley Peak, will astound you. Hike the Rancheria Falls Trail to the Rancheria Mountain Trail (5.3 miles). Hike the Rancheria Mountain Trail to a junction with Pleasant Valley Trail (9.9 miles) and then continue straight, now on the Bear Valley Trail. Excellent campsites exist around Bear Valley Lake. Drop into the Kerrick Canyon to the intersection with the Pacific Crest Trail (7.3 miles). Head north and then west on the PCT to the Tilden Canyon Trail (5.6 miles). A camp is located at Wilmer Lake, 1.8 miles past the Tilden junction—retrace your steps to Tilden if you camp here. Hike approximately 12.3 miles through Tiltill Valley (an excellent spot to camp) and to the Rancheria Falls Trail. Hike back on Rancheria Falls to your car at O'Shaughnessy Dam. If you only have time for a day trip, then hike out and back to Rancheria Falls. The 12-mile roundtrip is relatively easy and the falls are beautiful.

***Special note:*** Keep a sharp eye out for bears! Camps around the falls are particularly prone to nocturnal bear visits. Hang all food well away from tents.

---

## 26. JACK MAIN CANYON LOOP

**25.0 mi/3.0 days**

***Reference:*** **East of Groveland on Highway 120 and northeast of Hetch Hetchy Reservoir; map E4, grid f3.**

***User groups:*** Hikers and horses. No dogs or mountain bikes are allowed. No wheelchair facilities.

***Permits:*** No day-use permits are required. Wilderness permits are required for overnight stays within Yosemite National Park. A $5 day-use fee is good for seven days. For general information, call the National Park Service at (209) 372-0200. To talk to a "live" person, call public affairs at (209) 372-0265.

***Directions:*** From Groveland, drive east on Highway 120/Tioga Pass Road, to just before the Yosemite National Park boundary. Turn north on Evergreen Road and drive to Hetch Hetchy Road. Turn right on Hetch Hetchy Road and drive to the dam and the parking area. Hike across the dam on the Lake Eleanor Road and through a tunnel. Stay on the road as it switchbacks uphill to the Laurel Lake Trail on the right. Begin on the Laurel Lake Trail.

*Maps:* For topographic maps, ask for Lake Eleanor, Kibbie Lake and Tiltill Mountain from the USGS. For other maps of Yosemite, see "maps" under hike number 21.

*Who to contact:* Public Information Office, National Park Service, P.O. Box 577, Yosemite National Park, CA 95389; (209) 372-0200.

*Trail notes:* This hike heads through a section of the park which was grazed by the sheep of renegade sheepherders until the 1920s. The namesake of Jack Main Canyon was one of them. Hike approximately three miles to the Laurel Lake turnoff. From here the hike continues to climb gradually up Moraine Ridge, past the junction to Lake Vernon; the views are memorable. If your navigational skills are strong, there is plenty of cross-country wandering opportunity as you traverse the ridges before descending into Jack Main Canyon. Numerous small waterfalls along the way are soothing and invite you to linger. A camp is located at Wilmer Lake, where the trail intersects with the Pacific Crest Trail. From here, head east 1.8 miles to the Tilden junction and head south on the Tilden Canyon Trail. Hike approximately 12.3 miles through Tiltill Valley (an excellent spot to camp) and to the Rancheria Falls Trail. Hike back on Rancheria Falls to your car at O'Shaughnessy Dam. If you only have time for a day hike, then only go so far as Laurel Lake—a great picnic spot. The roundtrip to Laurel is approximately 12 miles.

---

# 27. GARDISKY LAKE        2.0 mi/1.0 hr

*Reference:* **East of Yosemite National Park, west of Lee Vining and Highway 395 and north of Tioga Pass Road; map E4, grid g8.**

*User groups:* Hikers and dogs. No horses or mountain bikes are allowed. No wheelchair facilities.

*Permits:* No day-use permits are required. Wilderness permits are required if you plan on camping. Contact the Mono Lake Ranger District at (619) 647-3000 for more information. Parking and access are free.

*Directions:* From Lee Vining head west on Highway 120/Tioga Pass Road to Saddlebag Lake Road, located just east of Tioga Pass and Tioga Lake. Turn right on Saddlebag Lake Road and follow it for approximately 1.2 miles to the trailhead located on the right side of the road. Tioga Pass Road is closed most winters from November through May.

*Maps:* Send $3 to the USDA-Forest Service, 630 Sansome Street, San Francisco, CA 94111 and ask for the Inyo National Forest map. For topographic maps, ask for Tioga Pass and Mount Dana from the USGS. For other maps of Yosemite, see "maps" under hike number 21.

*Who to contact:* Inyo National Forest, Mono Lake Ranger District, P.O. Box 429, Lee Vining, CA 93541; (619) 647-3000.

*Trail notes:* This is a short, steep but pleasant trail beginning at 9,800 feet and heading up to Gardisky Lake, located in a picturesque subalpine setting at 10,483 feet and just at the base of Tioga Peak. It is also a good spot for a family seeking to introduce adventurous young ones to the joys of wilderness without straying too far from the relative security of a vehicle and nearby civilization. Take your time hiking because the elevation gain is serious. The trail switchbacks up 900 feet to the lake. Be sure to take bearproofing precautions in and around your camp.

## 28. BENNETTVILLE

2.0 mi/1.0 hr

*Reference:* **East of Yosemite National Park, west of Lee Vining and Highway 395 and north of Tioga Pass Road; map E4, grid g8.**

*User groups:* Hikers and dogs. No horses or mountain bikes are allowed. No wheelchair facilities.

*Permits:* No day-use permits are required. Wilderness permits are required if you plan on camping. Contact the Mono Lake Ranger District at (619) 647-3000 for more information.

*Directions:* From Lee Vining head west on Highway 120/Tioga Pass Road to Saddlebag Lake Road and Junction Campground, located just east of Tioga Pass and Tioga Lake. The trailhead is located at Junction campground, just before campsite #1. Tioga Pass Road is closed most winters from November through May.

*Maps:* Send $3 to the USDA-Forest Service, 630 Sansome Street, San Francisco, CA 94111 and ask for the Inyo National Forest map. For a topographic map, ask for Tioga Pass from the USGS. For other maps of Yosemite, see "maps" under hike number 21.

*Who to contact:* Inyo National Forest, Mono Lake Ranger District, P.O. Box 429, Lee Vining, CA 93541; (619) 647-3000.

*Trail notes:* This is a short but enjoyable trail that leads to the abandoned mining towns of Bennettville and Shell Lake. This is yet another trip that is ideal for a family outing, since it remains close to civilization while allowing a taste of wilderness sanctity. From the trailhead, hike north along a well-defined tread toward the historic sites of Bennettville and Shell Lake. The trail is mostly level, gratefully avoiding the steep ups and downs that typify many of the trails in this high-mountain region. Bennettville sprang to life during the gold rush in the late 1800s and served as the Great Sierra Mine headquarters. A road was created to serve the mine and is now known as Tioga Pass Road, although back then it saw very little use as the mine found little valuable silver ore. Of course, this turned out to be good for the future Yosemite Park, and bad for the mining company. From high points around Shell Lake, enjoy the nearby views down into Lee Vining Canyon. The lake is a superb spot for a picnic and, if you are really brave, an ice-cold dip. Head back the way you came when ready.

---

## 29. GLACIER CANYON to DANA LAKE

4.6 mi/5.0 hrs

*Reference:* **Eastern edge of Yosemite National Park, west of Lee Vining and Highway 395 and south of Tioga Pass Road; map E4, grid g8.**

*User groups:* Hikers, dogs and horses. No mountain bikes are allowed. No wheelchair facilities.

*Permits:* No day-use permits are required. Wilderness permits are required if you plan on camping. Contact the Mono Lake Ranger District at (619) 647-3000 for more information. Parking and access are free.

*Directions:* From Lee Vining head west on Highway 120/Tioga Pass Road. The trailhead is located approximately one mile east of Tioga Pass on the west side of Tioga Lake. Tioga Pass Road is closed most winters from November through May.

*Maps:* Send $3 to the USDA-Forest Service, 630 Sansome Street, San Francisco, CA 94111 and ask for the Inyo National Forest map. For topographic maps, ask for Tioga Pass and Mount Dana from the USGS. For other maps of Yosemite, see "maps" under hike number 21.

*Who to contact:* Inyo National Forest, Mono Lake Ranger District, P.O. Box 429, Lee Vining, CA 93541; (619) 647-3000.

*Trail notes:* The trail enters the Ansel Adams Wilderness. The route is not maintained, but is fairly easy to follow for experienced backcountry trekkers, as many utilize the route to ascend Mt. Dana. Your route will lead you up to the headway of Glacier Canyon and the shores of glacier-fed Dana Lake. This area is easily impacted—use only a stove and build no campfires. The back side of 13,053-foot-high Dana Peak looms above the lake. Again, for experienced backcountry travelers, a cross-country route can be carefully picked up to the top and incredible views. From the trailhead, the footpath meanders across subalpine meadows (stick to the trail, please) and around a number of ponds, before climbing steeply up the western ridgeline of Mt. Dana. Although you begin hiking at 10,000 feet, the elevation heading up to 11,100 feet (Dana Lake's elevation) is extreme, so take your time. Drink plenty of water and take numerous rest breaks. At a small meadow, or grassy bench, the pathway ends as the trail wanders up onto rock and rubble. If you wish to "bag" the summit of Mt. Dana, continue climbing straight up to a view that will take your breath away—if the altitude hasn't already. For those seeking Dana Lake, your path heads east, contouring around the mountain's eastern flank and down to the shores of Dana Lake.

*Special note:* You are trekking in a high alpine environment. A hat, mountaineering sunglasses, and good sunscreen are required if you wish to ward off the intense effects of the sun.

---

## 30. TIOGA TARNS      1.0 mi/0.5 hr

*Reference:* **East of Yosemite National Park, west of Lee Vining and Highway 395 and north of Tioga Pass Road; map E4, grid g9.**

*User groups:* Hikers and dogs. No mountain bikes or horses are allowed. No wheelchair facilities.

*Permits:* No permits are required. Overnight camping is not permitted on the Tioga Tarns Trail. Parking and access are free.

*Directions:* From Lee Vining head west on Highway 120/Tioga Pass Road, to Saddlebag Lake Road and Junction Campground, located just east of Tioga Pass and Tioga Lake. The trailhead is located at the campground, just before campsite #1. Tioga Pass Road is closed most winters from November through May.

*Maps:* Send $3 to the USDA-Forest Service, 630 Sansome Street, San Francisco, CA 94111 and ask for the Inyo National Forest map. For a topographic map, ask for Tioga Pass from the USGS. For other maps of Yosemite, see "maps" under hike number 21.

*Who to contact:* Inyo National Forest, Mono Lake Ranger District, P.O. Box 429, Lee Vining, CA 93541; (619) 647-3000.

*Trail notes:* This is an interpretive trail that informs the hiker about the region's natural history and geological features along a signed and scenic treadway. It is an easy introduction to the Yosemite area, suitable for the entire family and all abilities. Also a great leg-stretcher if you only have time for a short break before hitting the road again.

---

# 31. POOPENAUT VALLEY     2.0 mi/4.0 hrs

*Reference:* **East of Groveland on Highway 120 and southwest of Hetch Hetchy Reservoir; map E4, grid g1.**

*User groups:* Hikers only. No dogs, horses or mountain bikes are allowed. No wheelchair facilities.

*Permits:* No permits are required. Overnight camping is not permitted. Parking and access are free.

*Directions:* From Groveland, drive east on Highway 120/Tioga Pass Road, to just before the Yosemite National Park boundary. Turn north on Evergreen Road and drive to Hetch Hetchy Road. Turn right on Hetch Hetchy Road and drive to the Mather Ranger Station. Continue past the ranger station for approximately four miles to a right-hand turn in the road and a small pullout with limited parking spaces (just about enough for two or three vehicles) on the right hand side of the road.

*Maps:* For a topographic map, ask for Lake Eleanor from the USGS. For other maps of Yosemite, see "maps" under hike number 21.

*Who to contact:* Public Information Office, National Park Service, P.O. Box 577, Yosemite National Park, CA 95389; (209) 372-0200.

*Trail notes:* Swimming is not allowed in nearby Hetch Hetchy Reservoir, so if it is a hot summer's day cool-off you seek, then this hike down to the Tuolumne River is your ticket. The trail is steep—you will drop 1,000 feet in one mile (don't forget to leave enough time to trudge back up). The trail itself doesn't actually lead to Poopenaut Valley—that's a short wander upstream to a spacious, flat area. If you hike west from where the trail meets the river, you will find the river cutting through a narrow channel with ridge-top ledges for jumping, located 25 feet or more above the river's surface—Wahoo!

---

# 32. LOOKOUT POINT     3.0 mi/4.0 hrs

*Reference:* **East of Groveland on Highway 120 and southwest of Hetch Hetchy Reservoir; map E4, grid g1.**

*User groups:* Hikers and horses. No dogs or mountain bikes are allowed. No wheelchair facilities.

*Permits:* No day-use permits are required. Wilderness permits are required for overnight stays within Yosemite National Park. A $5 day-use fee is good for seven days. For general information, call the National Park Service at (209) 372-0200. To talk to a "live" person, call public affairs at (209) 372-0265.

*Directions:* From Groveland, drive east on Highway 120/Tioga Pass Road, to just before the Yosemite National Park boundary. Turn north on Evergreen Road and drive to Hetch Hetchy Road. Turn right on Hetch Hetchy Road and drive to the Mather Ranger Station.

*Maps:* For a topographic map ask for Lake Eleanor from the USGS. For other maps of Yosemite, see "maps" under hike number 21.

*Who to contact:* Public Information Office, National Park Service, P.O. Box 577, Yosemite National Park, CA 95389; (209) 372-0200.

*Trail notes:* This is a perfect day hiking opportunity for those who want to view the vast expanse of the Tuolumne Valley without straying too far from their cars into the backcountry. From the Mather Ranger Station, hike approximately two-tenths of a mile to the first junction and make a quick left, heading north through the forest and then up and onto the glaciated granite of Lookout Point.

---

# 33. SMITH PEAK          16.0 mi/2.0 days

*Reference:* **East of Groveland on Highway 120, north of Yosemite Valley and south of Hetch Hetchy Reservoir; map E4, grid g4.**

*User groups:* Hikers and horses. No dogs or mountain bikes are allowed. No wheelchair facilities.

*Permits:* No day-use permits are required. Wilderness permits are required for overnight stays within Yosemite National Park. A $5 day-use fee is good for seven days. For general information, call the National Park Service at (209) 372-0200. To talk to a "live" person, call public affairs at (209) 372-0265.

*Directions:* From Groveland, drive east on Highway 120/Tioga Pass Road, into Yosemite National Park and to Crane Flat. At Crane Flat head east for another 14 miles on Highway 120 to the White Wolf Campground and Lodge turnoff. Drive north on the access road. The trailhead is located at the end of the road beyond the campground. Begin hiking on the Harden Lake Trail. The road to White Wolf is closed seasonally during the fall, winter and early spring. If you wish to access the backcountry during that time, drive east on Highway 120 from Groveland to just before the Yosemite National Park boundary. Turn north on Evergreen Road and drive to Hetch Hetchy Road. Turn right on Hetch Hetchy and drive to the Mather Ranger Station.

*Maps:* For topographic maps, ask for Lake Eleanor and Hetch Hetchy Reservoir from the USGS. For other maps of Yosemite, see "maps" under hike number 21.

*Who to contact:* Public Information Office, National Park Service, P.O. Box 577, Yosemite National Park, CA 95389; (209) 372-0200.

*Trail notes:* From the trailhead at White Wolf and an elevation of 7,200 feet, hike on the Harden Lake Trail for nine-tenths of a mile to Harden Lake and then head west on the White Wolf Mather Trail, climbing and then descending gradually over 5.5 miles to the junction with Smith Peak Trail. There are good campsites to be found here alongside Cottonwood Creek and amid the shade of pine trees at approximately 6,400 feet. If you are camping, set up camp and then head for the summit. Turn right onto the Smith Peak Trail and hike 1.5 miles to the summit at 7,751 feet. The climbing is steep and if you attempt it early in the spring, you may end up hiking across snow patches. From several granite outcroppings on the brush-covered summit, you can gaze down upon Hetch Hetchy Reservoir and into the Grand Canyon of the Tuolumne River. Head back the way you came. If you are attempting this hike from the Mather Ranger Station, keep in mind that you are beginning at around 5,000 feet of elevation, so the hike will be much more strenuous. From the trailhead, hike uphill two-tenths of a mile to a trail junction. Bear left at the junction and then right on the trail leading to Base Line Camp (part of this trail is an old road). Hike approximately two miles to arrive at Base Line. At Base Line, head north and continue climbing gradually 3.8 miles toward Smith Meadow and the intersection with White Wolf Mather Trail and Smith Peak Trail. Head left (north) on Smith Peak, and continue 1.5 miles to the summit. Bears are everywhere—hang your food and keep a clean camp.

*Special note:* The upper reaches of the trail may still be snow covered in early summer—use caution.

---

## 34. WATERWHEEL FALLS via PATE VALLEY   18.0 mi/9.0 hrs

*Reference:* In Yosemite National Park, East of Groveland; map E4, grid g4.

*User groups:* Hikers and horses. No mountain bikes or dogs are allowed. No wheelchair facilities.

*Permits:* No day-use permits are required. Wilderness permits are required if you plan on camping. Parking is free. A $5 day-use fee is good for seven days. For general information, call the National Park Service at (209) 372-0200. To talk to a "live" person, call public affairs at (209) 372-0265.

*Directions:* From Groveland, drive on Highway 120/Tioga Pass Road, into Yosemite National Park and to Crane Flat. At Crane Flat, head east, still on Highway 120 to the White Wolf Campground exit. Turn left towards White Wolf Campground and Lodge. The trailhead is located across the road from the lodge. Tioga Pass Road is usually closed in the winter from November through May.

*Maps:* For topographic maps, ask for Half Dome, El Capitan and Mariposa Grove from the USGS. For other maps of Yosemite, see "maps" under hike number 21.

*Who to contact:* Public Information Office, National Park Service, P.O. Box 577, Yosemite National Park, CA 95389; (209) 372-0200.

*Trail notes:* Begin hiking east towards Luken Lake. At the first junction, head onto the Pate Valley Trail to the left. The trail will guide you along interminable switchbacks as the treadway descends into the Tuolumne Canyon before leveling out and returning to gentler grades as it heads northeast into Pate Valley. If you are so inclined, once you have reached Waterwheel Falls—named for the swirling effect of the falls best experienced during peak runoff in the spring—you can continue hiking another 15 miles or so towards Tuolumne Meadows. A car shuttle, with one vehicle waiting in Tuolumne, would make this a superb one-way weekend jaunt. If you are returning the way you came, back to White Wolf, remember that you now have to hike up the 2,400 feet you just descended—leave plenty of daylight and time for the effort.

---

## 35. YOSEMITE CREEK   17.0 mi/1.0 day

*Reference:* East of Groveland in Yosemite National Park and south of Tioga Pass Road (Highway 120); map E4, grid g4.

*User groups:* Hikers and horses. No dogs or mountain bikes are allowed. No wheelchair facilities.

*Permits:* No day-use permits are required. Wilderness permits are required for overnight stays within Yosemite National Park. A $5 day-use fee is good for seven days. For general information, call the National Park Service at (209) 372-0200. To talk to a "live" person, call public affairs at (209) 372-0265.

*Directions:* From Groveland, drive east on Highway 120/Tioga Pass Road, into

Yosemite National Park and to Crane Flat. At Crane Flat head east for approximately 20 miles on Highway 120/Tioga Pass Road past the White Wolf Campground to the trailhead parking located on both sides of the road. The parking area is immediately before the highway bridge signed Yosemite Creek. Tioga Pass Road is often closed between November and May, so access is seasonal.

*Maps:* For a topographic map, ask for Yosemite Falls from the USGS. For other maps of Yosemite, see "maps" under hike number 21.

*Who to contact:* Public Information Office, National Park Service, P.O. Box 577, Yosemite National Park, CA 95389; (209) 372-0200.

*Trail notes:* If you want to hike to Upper Yosemite Falls without the steep climbing involved when entering from the valley, this is the route. You will experience the dramatic transition from hiking within the rolling terrain of Yosemite Creek to the steep-walled granite sculptures of Yosemite Valley. The Yosemite Creek Trailhead is located on the south side of the highway. Approximately two miles of hiking will find you at the north end of Yosemite Creek Campground. Hike through the campground to the Yosemite Falls Trail and then about 1.75 miles to another junction. Head left and south and continue hiking just over four miles to the brink of Upper Yosemite Falls. Return the way you came or, if you can arrange a car shuttle, keep on hiking down to the valley. Leave the car for the return shuttle at the parking area. Unfortunately, mosquitoes are thick and heavy when the falls are at their best—the months of May and June. During these months, snow patches can make footing tricky, so watch your step.

*Special note:* Bears frequent Yosemite campgrounds and lakeside campsites for obvious reasons—people and the potential of handouts or garbage food. Do not approach or feed bears, ever.

## 36. TEN LAKES BASIN    12.8 mi/2.0 days

*Reference:* **East of Groveland in Yosemite National Park and north of Tioga Pass Road (Highway 120); map E4, grid g5.**

*User groups:* Hikers and horses. No dogs or mountain bikes are allowed. No wheelchair facilities.

*Permits:* No day-use permits are required. Wilderness permits are required for overnight stays within Yosemite National Park. A $5 day-use fee is good for seven days. For general information, call the National Park Service at (209) 372-0200. To talk to a "live" person, call public affairs at (209) 372-0265.

*Directions:* From Groveland, drive east on Highway 120/Tioga Pass Road, into Yosemite National Park and to Crane Flat. At Crane Flat head east for approximately 20 miles on Highway 120/Tioga Pass Road, past the White Wolf Campground to the trailhead parking located on both sides of the road. The parking area is located immediately before the highway bridge signed Yosemite Creek. Tioga Pass Road is often closed between November and May, so access is seasonal.

*Maps:* For topographic maps, ask for Yosemite Falls, Ten Lakes, Falls Ridge and Tenaya Lake from the USGS. For other maps of Yosemite, see "maps" under hike number 21.

*Who to contact:* Public Information Office, National Park Service, P.O. Box 577, Yosemite National Park, CA 95389; (209) 372-0200.

*Trail notes:* The Ten Lakes Trailhead is located on the north side of the road. You will hike on the Ten Lakes Trail the entire way to the first lake and beyond. Just stay on the trail and follow the signs. Late in the summer, the last reliable water prior to reaching the lakes is found at the creekside junction with the White Wolf Trail—tank up here. Michael has hiked here with his 10-year-old daughter with no difficulties, but he does recommend planning a full day for the trip in and trip out when youngsters are along. Youthful minds love the lakes for swimming and all the rocks for clambering around on.

---

## 37. NORTH DOME    10.0 miles / 5.0 hours

*Reference:* **East of Groveland in Yosemite National Park and south of Tioga Pass Road (Highway 120); map E4, grid g5.**

*User groups:* Hikers and horses. No dogs or mountain bikes are allowed. No wheelchair facilities.

*Permits:* No day-use permits are required. Wilderness permits are required for overnight stays within Yosemite National Park. A $5 day-use fee is good for seven days. For general information, call the National Park Service at (209) 372-0200. To talk to a "live" person, call public affairs at (209) 372-0265.

*Directions:* From Groveland, drive east on Highway 120/Tioga Pass Road, into Yosemite National Park and to Crane Flat. At Crane Flat head east on Highway 120/Tioga Pass Road, past the White Wolf Campground and to the Porcupine Flat Campground. From here, continue driving approximately one mile on Highway 120 to a closed road on your right which is signed Porcupine Creek—this used to be the access road for the now closed Porcupine Creek Campground. Park in the designated area. Tioga Pass Road is closed between November and May most years, so access is seasonal.

*Maps:* For a topographic map ask for Yosemite Falls from the USGS. For other maps of Yosemite, see "maps" under hike number 21.

*Who to contact:* Public Information Office, National Park Service, P.O. Box 577, Yosemite National Park, CA 95389; (209) 372-0200.

*Trail notes:* Begin walking south on the abandoned access road down a gentle grade. In approximately one mile beyond the campground, you will encounter a trail junction with Tenaya Lake and Tuolumne Meadows Trail. Continue onward to Indian Rock and North Dome. Take the time for a quick 1.4-mile sidetrip left up the signed branch trail to enjoy a natural arch on the flank side of Indian Rock. Return to the main trail, past a junction with a trail heading right towards Yosemite Falls and up a spur trail to North Dome. Watch your footing on the loose gravel atop this bald, rounded granite summit. From here, you will observe more of Yosemite Valley than from any other vantage point, with the exception of Half Dome. Remember that the return trip is almost all uphill—take your time and be sure you have allotted sufficient water.

---

## 38. MAY LAKE    3.0 mi/3.0 hrs
##     HIGH SIERRA CAMP

*Reference:* **East of Groveland in Yosemite National Park and north of Tioga Pass Road (Highway 120); map E4, grid g6.**

*User groups:* Hikers and horses. No dogs or mountain bikes are allowed. No

wheelchair facilities.

*Permits:* No day-use permits are required. Wilderness permits are required for overnight stays within Yosemite National Park. A $5 day-use fee is good for seven days. For general information, call the National Park Service at (209) 372-0200. To talk to a "live" person, call public affairs at (209) 372-0265.

*Directions:* From Groveland, drive east on Highway 120/Tioga Pass Road, into Yosemite National Park and to Crane Flat. At Crane Flat head east on Highway 120/Tioga Pass Road, past the White Wolf Campground and to the Porcupine Flat Campground. From here, continue driving approximately 3.1 miles on Highway 120 to Old Tioga Pass Road on the left. Head up Old Tioga Pass Road for 1.7 miles to the designated parking area located just before the road is blocked off. Tioga Pass Road is often closed between November and May, so access is seasonal.

*Maps:* For topographic maps, ask for Yosemite Falls and Tenaya Lake from the USGS. For other maps of Yosemite, see "maps" under hike number 21.

*Who to contact:* Public Information Office, National Park Service, P.O. Box 577, Yosemite National Park, CA 95389; (209) 372-0200.

*Trail notes:* The trail to May Lake is a pleasant and easily-followed trek through forest and over granite slabs to the camp. May Lake High Sierra Camp is tough to get reservations for, but that doesn't need to deter the weekend warrior as there is a hiker's camp located just above the lake's south shore. Bring your fishing rod, as there are rainbow and brook trout in the lake. Although fishing is allowed, swimming is not—too bad if the weather is hot. May Lake is a perfect spot to base-camp while you explore the nearby peaks, the most prominent of which is Mt. Hoffman, 10,850 feet high. From the trailhead, begin hiking across a sandy meadow and into the forest where the trail starts to climb. In about one-half mile, the route becomes more rocky and the trees give way to gorgeous vistas looking out over Tenaya Canyon to the east and Half Dome to the south. The Cathedral Range also is visible further in the distance to the east. At 1.25 miles, you will arrive at May Lake. Head left to the backpacker's area or to the right for the May Lake "resort." If you plan on frolicking on the peaks, be sure to pack plenty of sunscreen and wear sunglasses—UV rays are much more intense at high altitude. Do not attempt any peak in the area if a thunderstorm threatens.

---

# 39. POLLY DOME LAKE    12.5 mi/6.0 hrs

*Reference:* **East of Groveland in Yosemite National Park and north of Tioga Pass Road (Highway 120); map E4, grid g6.**

*User groups:* Hikers and horses. No dogs or mountain bikes are allowed. No wheelchair facilities.

*Permits:* No day-use permits are required. Wilderness permits are required for overnight stays within Yosemite National Park. A $5 day-use fee is good for seven days. For general information, call the National Park Service at (209) 372-0200. To talk to a "live" person, call public affairs at (209) 372-0265.

*Directions:* From Groveland, drive east on Highway 120/Tioga Pass Road, into Yosemite National Park and to Crane Flat. At Crane Flat head east on Highway 120/Tioga Pass Road, past the White Wolf Campground and just west of Tuolumne Meadows. Continue driving for approximately one half-mile to a picnic area midway along the lake. The trailhead is located across the road from the picnic area. Tioga Pass Road is closed between November and May most years so access is seasonal.

*Maps:* For topographic maps, ask for Tenaya Lake and Falls Ridge from the USGS. For other maps of Yosemite, see "maps" under hike number 21.

*Who to contact:* Public Information Office, National Park Service, P.O. Box 577, Yosemite National Park, CA 95389; (209) 372-0200.

*Trail notes:* This is the perfect hike for anyone who wants to trek to a readily accessible lake that everyone else isn't also trekking to. The trail is an easy jaunt up to several lakes beneath Polly Dome that are suitable for camping. Keep a sharp eye out for cairns marking the route as it crosses through a rocky area along the way. The last half mile of the hike heads southeast at a trailside pond, just after the rocky section. Your destination is Polly Dome Lake at the base of Polly Dome—it's a can't-miss-it journey. As with any bushwhack, you may get a little scratched and wet (if there is dew or rain on the underbrush), so dress appropriately. Stick to this lake as mosquitoes seem to love the haunts of the upper and smaller lakes.

---

# 40. CLOUDS REST          14.0 mi/7.0 hrs

*Reference:* **East of Groveland in Yosemite National Park and north of Tioga Pass Road (Highway 120); map E4, grid h6.**

*User groups:* Hikers and horses. No dogs or mountain bikes are allowed. No wheelchair facilities.

*Permits:* No day-use permits are required. Wilderness permits are required for overnight stays within Yosemite National Park. A $5 day-use fee is good for seven days. For general information, call the National Park Service at (209) 372-0200. To talk to a "live" person, call public affairs at (209) 372-0265.

*Directions:* From Groveland, drive east on Highway 120/Tioga Pass Road, into Yosemite National Park and to Crane Flat. At Crane Flat head east on Highway 120/Tioga Pass Road, past the White Wolf Campground and just west of Tuolumne Meadows. This road is often closed between November and May, so access is seasonal.

*Maps:* For a topographic map, ask for Tenaya Lake from the USGS. For other maps of Yosemite, see "maps" under hike number 21.

*Who to contact:* Public Information Office, National Park Service, P.O. Box 577, Yosemite National Park, CA 95389; (209) 372-0200.

*Trail notes:* Clouds Rest has all the views offered by Half Dome without the steep drop-offs and hazardous trail conditions that weaken an acrophobic's knees. The trail begins at the parking lot for Sunrise Lakes. Hike toward the lakes. The trail descends pleasantly through the shade of pine trees and across a number of streams before beginning the serious ascent out of Tenaya Canyon. At the trail junction, bear right to Clouds Rest. Views begin after only a short climb. You will pass a somewhat nondescript junction with a horse trail. From here, the hiking trail peters out, but the destination is obvious. Scramble the remaining yards up to the narrow crest and let the view take your breath away. Don't forget your camera or you will be kicking yourself all the way back to the car. We heartily recommend spending a waterless night (pack along a gallon of water if you opt for this camp) on top of Clouds Rest. No fires, please, and pack out every scrap you bring in. Also, take the time to trek off the summit for latrine visits. The top is too fragile to withstand much impact. Your reward for the effort? A sunrise that can't be beaten...anywhere!

## 41. SUNRISE LAKES      7.0 mi/6.0 hrs

**Reference:** East of Groveland in Yosemite National Park and north of Tioga Pass Road (Highway 120); map E4, grid h6.

**User groups:** Hikers and horses. No dogs or mountain bikes are allowed. No wheelchair facilities.

**Permits:** No day-use permits are required. Wilderness permits are required for overnight stays within Yosemite National Park. A $5 day-use fee is good for seven days. For general information, call the National Park Service at (209) 372-0200. To talk to a "live" person, call public affairs at (209) 372-0265.

**Directions:** From Groveland, drive east on Highway 120/Tioga Pass Road, into Yosemite National Park and to Crane Flat. At Crane Flat head east on Highway 120/Tioga Pass Road, past the White Wolf Campground and just west of Tuolumne Meadows. This road is often closed between November and May, so access is seasonal.

**Maps:** For a topographic map, ask for Tenaya Lake from the USGS. For other maps of Yosemite, see "maps" under hike number 21.

**Who to contact:** Public Information Office, National Park Service, P.O. Box 577, Yosemite National Park, CA 95389; (209) 372-0200.

**Trail notes:** The trail to Sunrise Lakes begins at the parking lot and descends pleasantly for approximately two-tenths of a mile through the shade of pine trees to a junction with a trail leading to Tuolumne Meadows. Head right and hike across level ground, across a small stream, before beginning to climb out of Tenaya Canyon at seven-tenths of a mile. Keep climbing on good trail, crossing several streams, with the trail beginning to steepen and the hiking becoming more strenuous at 1.5 miles. Over the next seven-tenths of a mile, the trail switchbacks out of the canyon, offering wonderful views north to Mount Hoffman and down into Tenaya Canyon. The trail levels at approximately 9,160 feet and heads for approximately three-tenths of a mile to a trail junction. At 2.5 miles and the trail junction with the Clouds Rest Trail, turn left and onto the Sunrise Lakes Trail. The tread descends in a northerly direction to lower Sunrise Lake, approximately one mile from the junction and with about 400 feet loss of elevation. Middle Sunrise Lake, just off the trail, is the more remote and quiet of the lake camping areas. Upper Sunrise is the largest and consequently most popular lake. If it is a stunning campsite you seek, and you don't mind the additional hiking over and above the total mileage listed above, then continue on and up past the lakes for 1.5 miles to Sunrise High Sierra Camp and its adjacent backpack camp—the sunrise view from here is inspiring. Return the way you came.

## 42. ELIZABETH LAKE      4.5 mi/3.0 hrs

**Reference:** In Yosemite National Park, west of Lee Vining; map E4, grid g7.

**User groups:** Hikers and horses. No mountain bikes or dogs are allowed. No wheelchair facilities.

**Permits:** No day-use permits are required. A $5 day-use fee is good for seven days. For general information, call the National Park Service at (209) 372-0200. To talk to a "live" person, call public affairs at (209) 372-0265.

*Directions:* From Lee Vining, drive west on Highway 120/Tioga Pass Road, to Tuolumne Meadows and the signed trailhead parking area for Elizabeth Lake located in the group camping area of Tuolumne Meadows Campground.

*Maps:* For a topographic map, ask for Vogelsang from the USGS. For other maps of Yosemite, see "maps" under hike number 21.

*Who to contact:* Public Information Office, National Park Service, P.O. Box 577, Yosemite National Park, CA 95389; (209) 372-0200.

*Trail notes:* Don't forget to pack your camera along on this jaunt because the photo opportunities are everywhere. The shaded trail is an extremely popular day-hike to gem-like Elizabeth Lake—a glimmering Kodak moment if there ever was one. Views abound, including those of the often snow-capped Cathedral Range to the south. Beginning at around 8,700 feet, the trail climbs moderately through pines for approximately one mile before leveling out and reaching pretty Unicorn Creek at 1.5 miles. You will encounter a trail junction at 1.75 miles, but it is an easy decision which way to go—either trail leads to the lake and the distance is about the same. If you want to experience both, why not head in on one and out on the other? Whichever way you choose, you will arrive at Elizabeth Lake at 2.25 miles and 9,480 feet of elevation. This is a day-use area only.

---

## 43. VOGELSANG HIGH SIERRA CAMP

**14.4 mi/2.0 days**

*Reference:* **In Yosemite National Park, west of Lee Vining; map E4, grid g7.**

*User groups:* Hikers and horses. No mountain bikes or dogs are allowed. No wheelchair facilities.

*Permits:* No day-use permits are required. Wilderness permits are required if you plan on camping. A $5 day-use fee is good for seven days. For general information, call the National Park Service at (209) 372-0200. To talk to a "live" person, call public affairs at (209) 372-0265.

*Directions:* From Lee Vining, drive west on Highway 120/Tioga Pass Road, to Tuolumne Meadows and the signed trailhead parking area for the John Muir Trail and Lyell Fork.

*Maps:* For a topographic map, ask for Vogelsang from the USGS. For other maps of Yosemite, see "maps" under hike number 21.

*Who to contact:* Public Information Office, National Park Service, P.O. Box 577, Yosemite National Park, CA 95389; (209) 372-0200.

*Trail notes:* Begin hiking on the John Muir Trail past incredibly scenic meadows and over a number of bridges spanning the Dana Fork of the Tuolumne River, and then up Lyell Canyon to the signed junction with the Rafferty Creek Trail at approximately two miles. Head right and begin the dusty and dry climb up the Rafferty Creek Trail. The Rafferty Creek Trail climbs rapidly up from the meadows of Lyell Canyon amid the lodgepoles and granite slopes of the alpine environment of Cathedral Range, arriving at a trail junction in approximately 4.2 miles. We would recommend beginning your hike early, as this section of the trail can become unbearably hot when the summer sun beats down upon it. At the junction located below Boothe Lake, head left and climb eight-tenths of a mile to Vogelsang. Located near Tuolumne Pass at 10,200 feet, Vogelsang High Sierra Camp tent cabins require advance reservation—months in advance. But don't worry, the nearby backpack campsites are a little less troublesome to reserve. Want to escape the crowds sure to frequent the Vogelsang area? Continue hiking up towards beautiful Evelyn Lake, approximately two miles to the northeast of Vogelsang or granite-bound Ireland Lake, six miles distant. The scenery is stunning, but the mosquitoes fly around the clock here in the early summer. Michael recalls one trip with his wife when his hands disappeared beneath a black cloud of the little buggers while attempting to bear-hang food. He beat a hasty retreat to the tent to recover his sanity. Later trips in the summer are usually free from the hordes. Be sure to bear-proof your campsite.

---

## 44. GAYLOR LAKES          8.0 mi/4.0 hrs

*Reference:* Eastern edge of Yosemite National Park, west of Lee Vining and Highway 395 and north of Tioga Pass Road; map E4, grid g8.

*User groups:* Hikers only. No mountain bikes, horses or dogs are allowed. No wheelchair facilities.

*Permits:* No day-use permits are required. Wilderness permits are required if you plan on camping. A $5 day-use fee is good for seven days. For general information, call the National Park Service at (209) 372-0200. To talk to a "live" person, call public affairs at (209) 372-0265.

*Directions:* Head west from Lee Vining on Highway 120/Tioga Pass Road. Drive to Tioga Pass and the Yosemite National Park boundary. The trailhead for Gaylor Lakes is located on the northwest side of the road at Tioga Pass. The Tioga Pass Road is closed most winters from November through May.

*Maps:* For a topographic map, ask for Tioga Pass from the USGS. For other maps of Yosemite, see "maps" under hike number 21.

*Who to contact:* Public Information Office, National Park Service, P.O. Box 577, Yosemite National Park, CA 95389; (209) 372-0200.

*Trail notes:* The trail climbs moderately with some switchbacks up from the trailhead at 9,300 feet, along a ridge to a saddle located on the south flank of Gaylor Peak at approximately 10,000 feet. From here, approximately three miles from the start, hike on relatively level terrain for another mile among incredible views of wild country and wildflowers amid the high alpine lake setting of Gaylor Lakes. The site of an old mine and the ruins of the Great Sierra Mine cabin can still be seen on the ridge to the north of the lake. If your backcountry skills are strong enough, grab your map and compass and navigate cross-country to nearby Granite Lakes, about one-half mile to the north. Despite the close proximity to the road, Granite Lakes may often be enjoyed without the presence of another human, since there is no official trail leading there.

*Special note:* At no time should you ever attempt to enter any mine shaft that you will see around this area. They are very unstable and highly dangerous. Look, but don't enter. If you are up here with children, keep a close eye on them.

## 45. PARKER PASS to SILVER LAKE
### 21.8 mi. one way/2.0 days

*Reference:* **Eastern edge of Yosemite National Park, west of Lee Vining and Highway 395 and south of Tioga Pass Road; map E4, grid g8.**

*User groups:* Hikers and horses. No mountain bikes or dogs are allowed. No wheelchair facilities.

*Permits:* No day-use permits are required. Wilderness permits are required if you plan on camping. A $5 day-use fee is good for seven days. For general information, call the National Park Service at (209) 372-0200. To talk to a "live" person, call public affairs at (209) 372-0265. Or call the Mono Lake Ranger District at (619) 647-3000.

*Directions:* A car shuttle is required. Leave one vehicle at the Silver Lake Campground trailhead parking, located on a spur road opposite the entrance to the campground. Access the spur road from Highway 395 via the June Lake Loop Road—driving north on June Lake Road the entrance is approximately 8.5 miles from Highway 395. Heading south on June Lake Road the entrance is approximately 7.1 miles. To get to the trailhead located in Yosemite Park, head west from Lee Vining on Highway 120/Tioga Pass Road. Drive over Tioga Pass and drop into Yosemite National Park. The Mono Pass Trailhead is located on the south side of the highway at Dana Meadows, approximately 1.5 miles after passing through the park entrance station. Tioga Pass Road is closed most winters from November through May.

*Maps:* Send $3 to the USDA-Forest Service, 630 Sansome Street, San Francisco, CA 94111 and ask for the Inyo National Forest map. For topographic maps, ask for Tioga Pass, Mount Dana and Koip Peak from the USGS. For other maps of Yosemite, see "maps" under hike number 21.

*Who to contact:* Public Information Office, National Park Service, P.O. Box 577, Yosemite National Park, CA 95389; (209) 372-0200 or Inyo National Forest, Mono Lake Ranger District, P.O. Box 429, Lee Vining, CA 93541; (619) 647-3000.

*Trail notes:* This trail begins in Yosemite and ventures into Inyo National Forest and the Ansel Adams Wilderness. The trek will take you over 11,060-foot Parker Pass and between 12,861-foot Koip Peak and 12,957-foot Kuna Peak before dropping down to Gem Lake and the intersection with Rush Creek Trail, leading to Silver Lake. Thin air and outstanding views along the length of this hike will leave you breathless. Take your time and stop frequently to smell the wildflowers and fresh air—as good an excuse as any to catch your breath! Begin hiking on the Mono Pass Trail at 9,500 feet along an abandoned road through Dana Meadows, which soon crosses several creeks, and then, at one-half mile follows alongside Parker Creek, passing by an historic cabin site. At two miles, pass through a trail junction and keep following alongside Parker Creek to Spillway Lake, four miles from the trailhead. From Spillway, the trail begins to climb in earnest, still alongside Parker Pass Creek and passing a second historic cabin site to a trail junction with the Parker Pass Trail branching off to the right, 4.5 miles from the trailhead and just below Mono Pass. The trail ascends 1.8 miles steeply into Parker Pass. If you are wanting just a day-hike, this is the end and turnaround ·

point. Head back the way you came for just under a 13-mile day. If you are backpacking with car shuttle options, keep on truckin'. The trail traverses for about one mile before beginning a leg-burning, lung-searing climb to around 12,200 feet in less than a mile—thank goodness for switchbacks! The views are outstanding we think, but if truth be told, we were breathing too darn hard to really remember them. We seem to recall Mono Lake looking particularly wonderful. At Koip Pass, the tread begins to head down gradually through a series of switchbacks into the Alger Lakes Basin, approximately six miles from Parker Pass. Camp at any number of suitable and sheltered sites around the lakes. From Alger Lakes, continue hiking towards Gem Lake, approximately 4.5 miles away. Conserve your energy as you make a gradual climb to Gem Pass at 10,500 feet before dropping down more switchbacks through the pines to Gem Lake at 9,052 feet. From Gem Lake, begin hiking on the Rush Creek Trail toward Silver Lake Campground, five miles away.

*Special note:* Don't attempt to trek on this high-altitude trail if thunderstorms threaten.

---

## 46. MONO PASS         8.5 mi/1.0 day

*Reference:* **Eastern edge of Yosemite National Park, west of Lee Vining and Highway 395 and south of Tioga Pass Road; map E4, grid g8.**

*User groups:* Hikers and horses. No mountain bikes or dogs are allowed. No wheelchair facilities.

*Permits:* No day-use permits are required. Wilderness permits are required if you plan on camping. A $5 day-use fee is good for seven days. For general information, call the National Park Service at (209) 372-0200. To talk to a "live" person, call public affairs at (209) 372-0265, or call the Mono Lake Ranger District at (619) 647-3000 for more information.

*Directions:* From Lee Vining, head west on Highway 120/Tioga Pass Road. Drive over Tioga Pass and drop into Yosemite National Park. The Mono Pass Trailhead is located on the south side of the highway at Dana Meadows, approximately 1.5 miles after passing through the park entrance station. Tioga Pass Road is closed most winters from November through May.

*Maps:* Send $3 to the USDA-Forest Service, 630 Sansome Street, San Francisco, CA 94111 and ask for the Inyo National Forest map. For topographic maps, ask for Tioga Pass, Mount Dana and Koip Peak from the USGS. For other maps of Yosemite, see "maps" under hike number 21.

*Who to contact:* Public Information Office, National Park Service, P.O. Box 577, Yosemite National Park, CA 95389; (209) 372-0200 or Inyo National Forest, Mono Lake Ranger District, P.O. Box 429, Lee Vining, CA 93541; (619) 647-3000.

*Trail notes:* This trail begins in Yosemite and ventures ever so slightly into Inyo National Forest and Ansel Adams Wilderness. Although the mileage doesn't amount to much, the climb to 10,600 feet will leave you gasping, as will the numerous ups and downs required to get there. The trail begins on an abandoned road through Dana Meadows, crosses several creeks, and then begins to climb in earnest alongside Parker Pass Creek and past several historic cabin sites. From Mono Pass, the trail descends to Walker Lake— a possible car shuttle parking site if you are so inclined. Most hikers, however, will want to turn around and retrace their steps to the Dana

Meadows parking area. If you seek a little extra mileage in your day, enjoy the quick side hike to Spillway Lake—four miles roundtrip. While camping is allowed in Mono Pass (camp stoves only!), camping is not allowed at Spillway Lake.

*Special note:* Don't attempt the climb into the pass if thunderstorms threaten.

---

## 47. MT. DANA        5.8 mi/5.0 hrs

*Reference:* **Eastern edge of Yosemite National Park, west of Lee Vining and Highway 395 and south of Tioga Pass Road; map E4, grid g9.**

*User groups:* Hikers and horses. No mountain bikes or dogs are allowed. No wheelchair facilities.

*Permits:* No day-use permits are required. Wilderness permits are required if you plan on camping. A $5 day-use fee is good for seven days. For general information, call the National Park Service at (209) 372-0200. To talk to a "live" person, call public affairs at (209) 372-0265, or call the Mono Lake Ranger District at (619) 647-3000 for more information.

*Directions:* From Lee Vining, head west on Highway 120/Tioga Pass Road. Drive to Tioga Pass and to the Yosemite National Park boundary. The trailhead for Mt. Dana is located on the southeast side of the road at Tioga Pass. The Tioga Pass Road is closed most winters from November through May.

*Maps:* Send $3 to the USDA-Forest Service, 630 Sansome Street, San Francisco, CA 94111 and ask for the Inyo National Forest map. For topographic maps, ask for Tioga Pass and Mount Dana from the USGS. For other maps of Yosemite, see "maps" under hike number 21.

*Who to contact:* Public Information Office, National Park Service, P.O. Box 577, Yosemite National Park, CA 95389; (209) 372-0200 or Inyo National Forest, Mono Lake Ranger District, P.O. Box 429, Lee Vining, CA 93541; (619) 647-3000.

*Trail notes:* Take your time climbing to the top of 13,053-foot Mt. Dana, Yosemite's second highest peak. The trail begins at an elevation of 9,950 feet, which means you will gain a mind-bending 3,100 feet or so in just under three miles—whoo-yah! The views from the top are worth all the effort. You will be able to see from Mt. Lyell to Mono Lake. Wildflowers, in season, are an added attraction. Since the peak is so accessible, expect to share the trail with hordes of humanity—all breathlessly seeking the joy of high places. If your backcountry skills are good enough and your loathing of crowds strong enough, we recommend that you seek to make your pilgrimage to the top of Mt. Dana via Dana Lake—see hike number 29.

*Special note:* Don't attempt to trek on this high-altitude trail if thunderstorms threaten.

---

## 48. EL CAPITAN        14.4 mi/1.0 day

*Reference:* **In Yosemite National Park, west of Oakhurst; map E4, grid h3.**

*User groups:* Hikers and horses. No mountain bikes or dogs are allowed. No wheelchair facilities.

*Permits:* No day-use permits are required. Wilderness permits are required if you plan on camping. A $5 day-use fee is good for seven days. For general information, call the National Park Service at (209) 372-0200. To talk to a "live" person, call public affairs at (209) 372-0265.

*Directions:* From Groveland, drive on Highway 120/Tioga Pass Road, into Yosemite National Park and to Crane Flat. At Crane Flat, head east, still on Highway 120, to the turnoff for Tamarack Flat Campground. Turn right and follow the campground access road to an abandoned road at the east end of the campground. Tioga Pass Road is often closed in the winter from November through May.

*Maps:* For topographic maps, ask for Tamarack Flat and El Capitan from the USGS. For other maps of Yosemite, see "maps" under hike number 21.

*Who to contact:* Public Information Office, National Park Service, P.O. Box 577, Yosemite National Park, CA 95389; (209) 372-0200.

*Trail notes:* Don't worry, we're not going to try to lead you on a challenging ascent of the rock face—why climb it when you can walk up anyway? (Only a climber can answer that question.) Assuming that you would rather walk to the top, begin trekking along the abandoned road to Cascade Creek and then along the old road bed to the North Rim Trail. On the North Rim Trail, you will regain every bit of lost elevation via a series of switchbacks through several forest zones. The trail continues to climb, and then climb, and then climb some more to a summit spur trail. The main trail continues on towards Eagle Peak. Take the spur trail to the summit and enjoy the views.

---

# 49. POHONO 21.4 mi/2.0 days

*Reference:* **North of Fresno and east of Merced along the south rim of Yosemite National Park's valley floor; map E4, grid h3.**

*User groups:* Hikers and horses. No dogs or mountain bikes are allowed. No developed wheelchair facilities.

*Permits:* No day-use permits are required. Wilderness permits are required for overnight stays within Yosemite National Park. A $5 day-use fee is good for seven days. For general information, call the National Park Service at (209) 372-0200. To talk to a "live" person, call public affairs at (209) 372-0265. There is no camping allowed below the rim of Yosemite Valley except within established campgrounds.

*Directions:* From Merced just east of Highway 99, follow Highway 140 east to Yosemite National Park. Follow the signs to Yosemite Valley. Once in the valley, turn south on Wawona Road and drive to the Wawona Tunnel. The Pohono Trail begins at the east end of the tunnel. If you can, consider a car shuttle, leaving one car at the hiking parking at Bridalveil Campground—it will shorten the return trip by five miles. To get to Bridalveil Campground, continue driving up Wawona Road past the tunnel to Chinquapin junction and then 7.5 miles up the Glacier Point Road to the campground spur road. Turn right and drive a half mile to the campground entrance and trailhead parking.

*Maps:* For topographic maps, ask for El Capitan and Half Dome from the USGS. For other maps of Yosemite, see "maps" under hike number 21.

*Who to contact:* Public Information Office, National Park Service, P.O. Box 577, Yosemite National Park, CA 95389; (209) 372-0200.

*Trail notes:* Pohono, the Mi-Wok name for Bridalveil Falls, translates literally as "fall of the puffing winds." If you are afraid of heights, forget this hike. From the tunnel trailhead, the Pohono Trail follows the south rim of the

valley, meeting its very edge at several prominent points—Dewey, Crocker
and Taft. The views from each of these is stunning, as the valley floor seems
to drop out literally beneath your feet. The peculiar fissures at Taft Point are
fascinating. In the spring and early summer, the wildflower display borders
on the unbelievable. Once you reach Taft Point, turn around and return the
way you came. If you have arranged a car shuttle, then descend south at a trail
junction past McGurk Meadow to Glacier Point Road, then east to the
campground.

*Special note:* Watch your footing as there are no restraining rails and a slip
would mean a one-way ticket to oblivion. While children would love the
trail, it is not a good one for young minds that wander often and don't pay
close attention to strict guidelines.

---

## 50. NORTH VALLEY FLOOR TRAIL   8.0 mi. one way/4.0 hrs

*Reference:* **North of Fresno and east of Merced on the valley floor of
Yosemite Valley; map E4, grid h4.**

*User groups:* Hikers and horses. No dogs or mountain bikes are allowed. There
are no developed wheelchair facilities, but much of the trail is **wheelchair
accessible,** if you are strong. This is not an official wheelchair trail.

*Permits:* No day-use permits are required. Wilderness permits are required if
you plan on camping. A $5 day-use fee is good for seven days. For general
information, call the National Park Service at (209) 372-0200. To talk to a
"live" person, call public affairs at (209) 372-0265.

*Directions:* From Merced just east of Highway 99, follow Highway 140 east to
Yosemite National Park. Follow the signs to Yosemite Valley. Once in the
valley, turn south on the Wawona Road and drive to the Bridalveil Falls
parking area—the trailhead.

*Maps:* For topographic maps, ask for El Capitan, Yosemite Falls and Half
Dome from the USGS. For other maps of Yosemite, see "maps" under hike
number 21.

*Who to contact:* Public Information Office, National Park Service, P.O. Box
577, Yosemite National Park, CA 95389; (209) 372-0200.

*Trail notes:* From the paved approach to Bridalveil Falls, you will leave the
pavement and head across a creek and up an old road bed to the top of a
moraine with views of Lower Cathedral Rock and El Capitan. More walking
leads to the base of Middle Cathedral Rock. Here the trail joins the road and
passes by a picnic area—a good lunch spot. Just past the picnic spot, at a trail
junction, head north (left) on a trail which leads north to El Capitan Meadow.
You will cross the Merced River and join up with the North Valley Trail.
Head east past El Capitan picnic area, walking between the road and the
river. Views over your shoulder are of Three Brothers. Continue on to Leidig
Meadow and enjoy views of North Dome and Half Dome. The trail crosses
the road again and heads past Sunnyside Campground—frequented by
climbers. Pass by the spur to Lower Fall and glimpse the famed Lost Arrow
Spire above Yosemite Fall. The trail skirts Yosemite Village on the north
side, climbing beneath Castle Cliffs, then crosses Indian Creek before
passing through Church Bowl. From here the trail heads past Ahwahnee
Hotel and the Pines Campground, then crosses Clarks Bridge and the river

before ascending to the gauging station and Happy Isles. Climbers use this trail to access their many climbing routes. Although you will see numerous trails branching off towards the rocks and climbing areas, leave the climbing to the climbers. A number of side trails connect to the South Valley Floor Trail which can be added to the hike to make a pleasant loop.

---

## 51. SOUTH VALLEY 6.5 mi. one way/3.0 hrs  FLOOR TRAIL

*Reference:* **North of Fresno and east of Merced on the valley floor of Yosemite Valley; map E4, grid h4.**

*User groups:* Hikers and horses. No dogs or mountain bikes are allowed. There are no developed wheelchair facilities, but much of the trail is **wheelchair accessible**.

*Permits:* No day-use permits are required. Wilderness permits are required if you plan on camping. A $5 day-use fee is good for seven days. For general information, call the National Park Service at (209) 372-0200. To talk to a "live" person, call public affairs at (209) 372-0265.

*Directions:* From Merced just east of Highway 99, follow Highway 140 east to Yosemite National Park. Follow the signs to Yosemite Valley. Once in the valley, turn south on Wawona Road and drive to the Bridalveil Falls parking area—the trailhead. Take the valley shuttle bus to Happy Isles if you wish to only hike one way or have no intention of connecting with the North Valley Floor Trail for the return.

*Maps:* For topographic maps, ask for El Capitan and Half Dome from the USGS. For other maps of Yosemite, see "maps" under hike number 21.

*Who to contact:* Public Information Office, National Park Service, P.O. Box 577, Yosemite National Park, CA 95389; (209) 372-0200.

*Trail notes:* From the paved approach to Bridalveil Falls, you will leave the pavement and head across a creek and up an old road bed to the top of a moraine with views of Lower Cathedral Rock and El Capitan. More walking leads to the base of Middle Cathedral Rock. Here, the trail joins the road and passes by a good picnic spot. From the picnic area, you will enjoy views of El Capitan, and with a pair of binoculars, you can enjoy watching climbers play on the rock face. From here the trail heads east with views of Taft Point to the south. A large rock slab along the way has mortar holes ground into it from when the Mi-Wok used its surface to grind acorns. Cross over Sentinel Creek and, during the spring melt, enjoy Sentinel Falls. The trail wanders past LeConte Memorial Lodge, named for UC-Berkeley's first geology professor and Yosemite lover Joseph LeConte. Finally, the trail takes you through Curry Camp and on to the marshy ground of Happy Isles. Return the way you came or connect with the North Valley Trail for the journey back. Climbers use this trail to access their many climbing routes. Although you will see numerous trails branching off towards the rocks and climbing areas, leave the climbing to the climbers. A number of side trails connect to the North Valley Floor Trail and can be added to the hike to make a pleasant loop.

## 52. LOWER YOSEMITE FALLS  0.6 mi/1.0 hr

*Reference:* **North of Fresno and east of Merced on the valley floor of Yosemite Valley; map E4, grid h4.**

*User groups:* Hikers, dogs and **wheelchairs (with assistance)**. No mountain bikes or horses are allowed.

*Permits:* No day-use permits are required. Wilderness permits are required if you plan on camping. A $5 day-use fee is good for seven days. For general information, call the National Park Service at (209) 372-0200. To talk to a "live" person, call public affairs at (209) 372-0265.

*Directions:* From Merced just east of Highway 99, follow Highway 140 east to Yosemite National Park. Follow the signs to Yosemite Valley. Park in the Yosemite Falls parking area. If that if full, park in the Valley Visitor Center parking area and walk on the bike path to the Yosemite Falls parking lot— an added half-mile to the hiking distance each way.

*Maps:* For topographic maps, ask for Yosemite Falls and Half Dome from the USGS. For other maps of Yosemite, see "maps" under hike number 21.

*Who to contact:* Public Information Office, National Park Service, P.O. Box 577, Yosemite National Park, CA 95389; (209) 372-0200.

*Trail notes:* The Yosemite Falls Trail is an easy and, at times, extremely crowded walk as the majority of visitors to the valley attempt the pilgrimage to view the water spectacle. The best water show is during the prime runoff months of May and June—the falls are a raging torrent then. In drought years, don't expect much more than a tame trickle. While the paved path to the falls is considered suitable for **wheelchairs**, there are a few challenging spots that may require assistance.

## 53. UPPER YOSEMITE FALLS  6.6 mi/4.0 hrs

*Reference:* **North of Fresno and east of Merced on the valley floor of Yosemite Valley; map E4, grid h4.**

*User groups:* Hikers and horses. No mountain bikes or dogs are allowed. No wheelchair facilities.

*Permits:* No day-use permits are required. Wilderness permits are required if you plan on camping. A $5 day-use fee is good for seven days. For general information, call the National Park Service at (209) 372-0200. To talk to a "live" person, call public affairs at (209) 372-0265.

*Directions:* From Merced just east of Highway 99, follow Highway 140 east to Yosemite National Park. Follow the signs to Yosemite Valley. Park in the westernmost area of the Yosemite Lodge parking lot located in Yosemite Village. The trailhead is located at the northwest corner of the Sunnyside Campground just behind the gas station.

*Maps:* For topographic maps, ask for Yosemite Falls and Half Dome from the USGS. For other maps of Yosemite, see "maps" under hike number 21.

*Who to contact:* Public Information Office, National Park Service, P.O. Box 577, Yosemite National Park, CA 95389; (209) 372-0200.

*Trail notes:* Your feet will be treading on one of the oldest trails in Yosemite National Park. Built between 1873 and 1877, the path was once operated on a toll basis—you paid a fee at the trailhead for the privilege of hiking to the top of the third highest waterfall in the world. Currently, the cost is only the effort and sweat of the hike. On the way up, enjoy the stunning views of Yosemite Valley from Columbia Rock. The best water show from the 2,425-foot cascade is during the prime runoff months of May and June—the falls are a raging torrent then. In drought years, don't expect much more than a tame trickle.

## 54. MIRROR LAKE          13.2 mi/6.0 hrs

*Reference:* **North of Fresno and east of Merced along the south rim of Yosemite National Park's valley floor; map E4, grid h5.**

*User groups:* Hikers and horses. Partial mountain bike and **limited wheelchair access.** No dogs allowed.

*Permits:* No day-use permits are required. Wilderness permits are required for overnight stays within Yosemite National Park. A $5 day-use fee is good for seven days. For general information, call the National Park Service at (209) 372-0200. To talk to a "live" person, call public affairs at (209) 372-0265.

*Directions:* From Merced just east of Highway 99, follow Highway 140 east to Yosemite National Park. Follow the signs to Yosemite Valley. Once in the valley, drive to and through the Pines Campground to the road's end. The trailhead is located at the parking area which is adjacent to the stables and near the shuttle bus stop just across from Clarks Bridge.

*Maps:* For topographic maps, ask for Yosemite Falls and Half Dome from the USGS. For other maps of Yosemite, see "maps" under hike number 21.

*Who to contact:* Public Information Office, National Park Service, P.O. Box 577, Yosemite National Park, CA 95389; (209) 372-0200.

*Trail notes:* Follow the paved trail which climbs ever so gently along the west bank of Tenaya Creek to Mirror Lake, located at the base of Half Dome. The paved portions of this trail to and around Mirror Lake are accessible and very popular with bicycles. They are also suitable for **wheelchairs** with assistance. Once at the lake, you will notice that it really doesn't reflect like a mirror at all. Actually, Mirror Lake is well on its way to becoming a meadow. The lake often dries up by September. To escape the crowds, head upstream from the old parking area (the lake used to be directly accessed by shuttle buses) amid rocky cliffs and enjoy the periodic views of Half Dome. After several more miles of following Tenaya Creek, you will come to a turn-around. The trail back down the east bank of the creek leads to Happy Isles.

## 55. HALF DOME          16.5 mi/8.0 hrs

*Reference:* **North of Fresno and east of Merced along the north rim of Yosemite National Park's valley floor; map E4, grid h5.**

*User groups:* Hikers only. No horses, dogs or mountain bikes are allowed. No wheelchair facilities.

*Permits:* No day-use permits are required. Wilderness permits are required for overnight stays within Yosemite National Park. A $5 day-use fee is good for seven days. For general information, call the National Park Service at (209) 372-0200. To talk to a "live" person, call public affairs at (209) 372-0265.

*Directions:* From Merced just east of Highway 99, follow Highway 140 east to Yosemite National Park. Follow the signs to Yosemite Valley. Once in the valley, drive to the Happy Isles parking area near the Happy Isles shuttle-bus stop in eastern Yosemite Valley.

*Maps:* For topographic maps, ask for Yosemite Falls and Half Dome from the USGS. For other maps of Yosemite, see "maps" under hike number 21.

*Who to contact:* Public Information Office, National Park Service, P.O. Box 577, Yosemite National Park, CA 95389; (209) 372-0200.

*Trail notes:* If you're only able to do one hike in Yosemite Valley, let this be the one. It's not for the faint of heart, the easily winded or those who are afraid of heights. For those who can muster the energy for the journey, the rewards are visually stunning and emotionally stimulating. From Happy Isles, hike on the John Muir Trail past Vernal Falls and Nevada Falls and through Little Yosemite Valley—your campsite for the night if you are planning on a two-day journey. Shortly after leaving the John Muir Trail on the Half Dome Trail you will encounter a short spur trail leading to a spring. This is the last water to the peak and back so tank up! The park has installed a cable trailway (two steel cables about three feet apart) to offer hand-hold security for those who aren't so sure-footed on the slick granite surface. Once at the top, marvel at the enormity of the 8,842 foot peak—it's amazing how level and vast the granite surface is.

*Special note:* Keep in mind that midsummer thunderstorms in the area are common. Plan to be up and off the summit of Half Dome by early afternoon—this means a sunrise start!

---

# 56. CHILNUALNA FALLS from BRIDALVEIL

**14.2 mi/7.0 hrs**

*Reference:* In Yosemite National Park, north of Oakhurst; map E4, grid i4.

*User groups:* Hikers and horses. No mountain bikes or dogs are allowed. No wheelchair facilities.

*Permits:* No day-use permits are required. Wilderness permits are required if you plan on camping. A $5 day-use fee is good for seven days. For general information, call the National Park Service at (209) 372-0200. To talk to a "live" person, call public affairs at (209) 372-0265.

*Directions:* From Oakhurst, drive north on Highway 41 to Yosemite National Park via the Wawona entrance. Upon entering the park, Highway 41 becomes Wawona Road which you will stay on until reaching Glacier Point Road. Turn east on Glacier Point Road and follow it to the trailhead located at Bridalveil Campground.

*Maps:* For topographic maps, ask for Half Dome, El Capitan and Mariposa Grove from the USGS. For other maps of Yosemite, see "maps" under hike number 21.

*Who to contact:* Public Information Office, National Park Service, P.O. Box 577, Yosemite National Park, CA 95389; (209) 372-0200.

*Trail notes:* The trail from Bridalveil Creek Campground to Chilnualna Falls is a scenic and easy walk along gentle grades and through shaded forest. Occasional views are possible by peeking through the trees as the trail winds out near overlooks. Most folks heading to Chilnualna Falls select the much steeper but far shorter eight-mile roundtrip access from Wawona and described later in this chapter. Since climbing 4,000 feet to 7,000 feet in only four miles isn't our favorite option, and crowds can be somewhat annoying, we prefer the longer, more gentle and definitely more peaceful route in from Bridalveil. From the trailhead, hike southeast along Bridalveil Creek passing first one trail junction and then another, leading east (left) to Ostrander Lake, as you pass near Lost Bear Meadow. At 2.5 miles, arrive at another trail junction leading right to Deer Camp and Empire Meadow. Keep straight (left) on the main route heading to another trail junction in 1.4 miles. Left leads east to Chilnualna Lakes. You will bear right towards Chilnualna Falls, arriving at the junction with the Chilnualna Falls Trail in just under three miles. Turn right to access the falls. The falls—a series of wonderful cascades—are awesome, especially when combined with the springtime beauty of numerous wildflowers. A number of suitable and pleasant campsites are located around the trail junctions near Chilnualna Creek.

---

## 57. OSTRANDER LAKE    7.8 mi/5.0 hrs

*Reference:* **In Yosemite National Park, north of Oakhurst; map E4, grid i4.**

*User groups:* Hikers and horses. No mountain bikes or dogs are allowed. No wheelchair facilities.

*Permits:* No day-use permits are required. Wilderness permits are required if you plan on camping. A $5 day-use fee is good for seven days. For general information, call the National Park Service at (209) 372-0200. To talk to a "live" person, call public affairs at (209) 372-0265.

*Directions:* From Oakhurst, drive north on Highway 41 to Yosemite National Park via the Wawona entrance. Upon entering the park, Highway 41 becomes Wawona Road which you will stay on until reaching Glacier Point Road. Turn east on Glacier Point Road and follow it to the trailhead located on the right, approximately 1.3 miles beyond Bridalveil Creek Campground.

*Maps:* For a topographic map, ask for Half Dome from the USGS. For other maps of Yosemite, see "maps" under hike number 21.

*Who to contact:* Public Information Office, National Park Service, P.O. Box 577, Yosemite National Park, CA 95389; (209) 372-0200.

*Trail notes:* Ostrander Lake and the Yosemite Association-managed Ostrander Hut are very popular cross-country ski destinations in the winter. The trail begins on an abandoned road and then winds through past evidence of a forest fire for 1.3 miles to Lost Bear Meadow. You don't actually see the meadow but instead arrive at a trail junction, with the trail to the right heading toward Bridalveil Creek. Stay to the left. From the meadow, the treadway steepens and climbs nearly 1,500 feet before arriving at Ostrander Lake, 3.9 miles from the trailhead. The best camping is at the west end of the lake. This is a very popular destination, so expect crowds if you are visiting during the weekend or peak summer months—don't even think about it on July 4th!

---

## 58. CHILNUALNA LAKES    28.0 mi/4.0 days
## BUENA VISTA PEAK LOOP

*Reference:* **North of Fresno near the southern entrance to Yosemite National Park; map E4, grid i4.**

*User groups:* Hikers and horses. No dogs or mountain bikes are allowed. No wheelchair facilities.

*Permits:* No day-use permits are required. Wilderness permits are required for overnight stays within Yosemite National Park. A $5 day-use fee is good for seven days. For general information, call the National Park Service at (209) 372-0200. To talk to a "live" person, call public affairs at (209) 372-0265.

*Directions:* From Fresno and Highway 99, drive north on Highway 41, past Oakhurst to the south entrance station for Yosemite National Park. Continue north on the Wawona Road to Wawona where you will turn east on Chilnualna Road—the junction is just north of the South Fork Merced River Bridge. Stay on Chilnualna Road for approximately 1.3 miles to "The Redwoods," where the road ends. The trail begins here.

*Maps:* For topographic maps, ask for Mariposa Grove and Wawona from the USGS. For other maps of Yosemite, see "maps" under hike number 21.

*Who to contact:* Public Information Office, National Park Service, P.O. Box 577, Yosemite National Park, CA 95389; (209) 372-0200.

*Trail notes:* See the Chilnualna Falls hike (hike number 59) for information on the falls and the first night's stay. From the falls, continue hiking a zigzag route along the headwaters of Chilnualna Creek to a set of high-altitude lakes—all that remains as evidence of the recent (in geologic time, 10,000 years is recent) recession of glaciers in the area. Approximately 2.5 miles up from the falls you will cross Grouse Lake Creek. At high water, this can be a hazardous 20-foot, slip-and-slide ford across a slick slab of rock— unbuckle your waistbelt and loosen your shoulder straps for this one. Head left and north at the junction just after the crossing towards Turner Meadows for approximately a half mile. At the next junction, head right and east towards Chilnualna Lakes just under five miles away. Buena Vista Peak towers over the lakes—pick your campsite out of sight and sound from others if possible. From the lakes, head up and into the 9,040-foot Buena Vista Pass. At the pass, head south on Buena Vista Trail towards Royal Arch Lake. The next trail junction will take you right and west toward Johnson, Crescent and Grouse lakes. Past Grouse Lake, you will meet up with the Grouse Lake Creek crossing and the return trail to Chilnualna Falls and the parking area. Retrace your steps back to your car.

*Special note:* Bring plenty of mosquito repellent if you explore this region early in the season—mosquitoes are so thick at times, you would swear it was cloudy.

---

## 59. CHILNUALNA FALLS          8.0 mi/4.0 hrs

*Reference:* **North of Fresno near the southern entrance to Yosemite National Park; map E4, grid j4.**

*User groups:* Hikers and horses. No dogs or mountain bikes are allowed. No wheelchair facilities.

*Permits:* No day-use permits are required. Wilderness permits are required for overnight stays within Yosemite National Park. A $5 day-use fee is good for seven days. For general information, call the National Park Service at (209) 372-0200. To talk to a "live" person, call public affairs at (209) 372-0265.

*Directions:* From Fresno and Highway 99, drive north on Highway 41, past Oakhurst to the south entrance station for Yosemite National Park. Continue north on the Wawona Road to Wawona where you will turn east on Chilnualna Road—the junction is just north of the South Fork Merced River Bridge. Stay on Chilnualna Road for approximately 1.3 miles to "The Redwoods," where the road ends. The trail begins here.

*Maps:* For topographic maps, ask for Mariposa Grove and Wawona from the USGS. For other maps of Yosemite, see "maps" under hike number 21.

**Who to contact:** Public Information Office, National Park Service, P.O. Box 577, Yosemite National Park, CA 95389; (209) 372-0200.

**Trail notes:** This somewhat strenuous hike will guide you to one of the tallest waterfalls outside of Yosemite Valley. Chilnualna Falls tumbles hundreds of feet down a narrow chute. Higher up from the falls is yet another 50-foot cascade which can be quite spectacular early in the season during the snow melt. Above the last cascade, the trail switchbacks up to the top of the gorge and a trail junction. One trail leads south towards Bridalveil Campground and the other continues north to Chilnualna Lakes. Just below the main trail and the trail junctions are several pleasant campsites if you wish to spend the night. If you are continuing onward to Chilnualna Lakes, this makes a perfect overnight spot. Bring your swim suit as there are a number of tempting swimming holes with small cascades in the lower reaches of the creek.

**Special note:** Caution: Footing near the fall's brink is loose and hazardous—do not venture too close to the edge!

---

## 60. MARIPOSA GROVE       2.0 mi/1.0 hr

**Reference: North of Fresno, near the southern entrance to Yosemite National Park; map E4, grid j4.**

**User groups:** Hikers and horses. No dogs or mountain bikes are allowed. No wheelchair facilities.

**Permits:** No day-use permits are required. Wilderness permits are required if you plan on camping. A $5 day-use fee is good for seven days. For general information, call the National Park Service at (209) 372-0200. To talk to a "live" person, call public affairs at (209) 372-0265.

**Directions:** From Fresno and Highway 99, drive north on Highway 41 past Oakhurst, to the south entrance station for Yosemite National Park. At the entrance, head east for approximately two miles and park in the Big Trees parking lot.

**Maps:** Pick up the free pamphlet and map entitled "Mariposa Grove by Trail and Tram" available at the information kiosks in the area. Tom Harrison Cartography publishes an excellent series of maps of the area. Call (415) 456-7940 and ask for the *Trail Map of the Yosemite High Country,* the *Recreation Map of Yosemite National Park,* and the *Map of Yosemite Valley.* Cost is $5.95 plus tax and shipping for each map. Trails Illustrated also publishes a super map, Yosemite National Park. The cost is $7.95 and may be ordered by calling (800) 962-1643. For a topographic map, ask for Mariposa Grove from the USGS.

**Who to contact:** Public Information Office, National Park Service, P.O. Box 577, Yosemite National Park, CA 95389; (209) 372-0200.

**Trail notes:** In an area frequented by tour buses and crowds seeking a certain kind of vehicular insular intimacy with the giant sequoia, you are better served to wander from kiosk to kiosk on foot—a much more informative and pleasurable experience. Mariposa Grove is perhaps one of the best and most stunning of the groves of giant sequoia in Yosemite National Park and the sight of the often-photographed Wawona Tunnel Tree (now toppled over from all the human impact and reason enough not to walk through the California Tree, which still stands, tunnel and all). There are a number of trails in the Mariposa Grove area that can be linked to form a wonderful loop trip. Begin hiking at the southwest corner of the parking lot near the information kiosk, on the path signed "Mariposa Grove Foot Trails." One-quarter mile from the trailhead is the Bachelor Tree. At three-quarters of a mile, you will arrive at Grizzly Giant, recognized as one of the largest trees in this grove. At just under one mile, you will hike by California Tree. If you have no more time or wish to move on, then head back the way you came. Otherwise, keep hiking uphill to the upper grove, about two miles distant. If you keep hiking in a long loop, you will pass by the Mariposa Grove Museum, just after the now prone Wawona Tunnel Tree, at 3.5 miles. Just past and right of the museum is a trail leading to the Columbia Tree, listed as the tallest sequoia in this grove at over 295 feet. Pass through several junctions heading for Faithful Couple (two trees merged at the base) at 4.5 miles. Head back towards the California Tree and then return to the parking area for a total roundtrip wander of approximately six to six-and-a-half miles, depending on which trails and sidetrips you choose. The free pamphlet you can get at the kiosk will serve as an excellent guide.

## PACIFIC CREST TRAIL    135.8 mi. one way/14.0 days
## GENERAL INFORMATION

*Reference:* **Trail sections extend from the Agnew Meadows Trailhead north to Ebbetts Pass.**

*User groups:* Hikers, horses and dogs (except in national parks). No mountain bikes allowed. No whelchair facilities.

*Permits:* A wilderness permit is required for traveling through various wilderness and special-use areas that the trail traverses. Contact the national forest, BLM or national park office at your point of entry for a permit that is good for the length of your trip.

*Maps:* For an overall view of the trail route in this section, send $3 for each map ordered to the USDA-Forest Service, 630 Sansome Street, San Francisco, CA 94111. Ask for the Stanislaus National Forest map, Toiyabe National Forest map, Inyo National Forest map and the Sierra National Forest map. Topographic maps for particular sections of trail are provided under each specific trail section heading listed below.

*Who to contact:* Contact either the national forest, BLM or national park office at your trailhead—see specific trailheads and corresponding agencies listed within each section.

*Trail notes:* Trail elevations within this section range from 7,000 feet to over 10,000 feet. Although the lower reaches of the PCT are open from mid-June to mid-October, several high passes within the region may remain snow covered until mid-July, making hiking difficult. Snow-covered passes are impossible to navigate with pack stock and horses.

---

## PCT-23    28.0 mi. one way/3.0 days
## JOHN MUIR TRAIL-3
## AGNEW MEADOWS to TUOLUMNE MEADOWS

*Reference:* **From the Agnew Meadows Trailhead in map E4, grid j9, north to trailhead parking at Tuolumne Meadows on Highway 120.**

*User groups:* Hikers and horses. No dogs or mountain bikes are allowed. No wheelchair facilities.

*Permits:* A wilderness permit is required for traveling through various wilderness and special-use areas that the trail traverses. Contact either the Inyo National Forest at (619) 647-3000 or Wilderness Office of the National Park Service at (209) 372-0200 for a permit that is good for the length of your trip.

*Directions:* From Lee Vining, drive 26 miles south on Highway 395 to Mammoth Junction. Turn west on Highway 203 (Minaret Summit Road) to the town of Mammoth Lakes and drive 14 miles to the Agnew Meadows Campground and the trailhead parking.

*Maps:* For an overall view of the trail route in this section, send $3 for each map ordered to the USDA-Forest Service, 630 Sansome Street, San Francisco, CA 94111, ask for the Inyo National Forest map and the Sierra National Forest map. For topographic maps, ask for Vogelsang Peak, Mount Ritter, Koip Peak and Mammoth Mountain from the USGS.

*Who to contact:* Public Information Office, National Park Service, P.O. Box 577, Yosemite National Park, CA 95389; (209) 372-0200, or Inyo National Forest, Mono Lake Ranger District, P.O. Box 429, Lee Vining, CA 93541;

(619) 647-3000.

*Trail notes:* This section of trail features breathtaking views of the Minarets, many glacial-cut lakes and the wondrous descent into Yosemite. The PCT starts here by leaving Reds Meadows, an excellent place to arrange a food drop (and a chance to eat your first cheeseburger in weeks). The trail heads out into the most beautiful section of Inyo National Forest and the Ansel Adams Wilderness. All in a row, the PCT passes Rosalie Lake, Shadow Lake, Garnet Lake and Thousand Island Lake. If they look like Ansel Adams' pictures in real life, it's because they are. The background setting of Banner and Ritter peaks is among the most spectacular anywhere.

From Thousand Island Lake, the PCT makes a fair climb over Island Pass (10,200 feet), then drops down into the headwaters of Rush Creek, where emerald-green flows swirl over boulders, pouring like a wilderness fountain. From here, it's a decent, steady ascent back above treeline to Donohue Pass (11,056 feet), the southern wilderness border of Yosemite National Park. It was here, while munching a trail lunch, that we saw a huge landslide on the westward canyon wall. A massive amount of rock material fell in just a few seconds—an unforgettable showing of natural forces.

The trail becomes quite blocky at Donohue Pass, and you rock-hop your way down to the headwaters of Lyell Fork, a pretzel-like stream that meanders through the meadows. It pours all the way to Tuolumne Meadows, and following it, the trail is nearly flat for more than four miles. At Tuolumne Meadows, you can resupply, and get yourself another cheeseburger.

To continue on the Pacific Crest Trail, see the listing for PCT-24 (following John Muir Trail-4).

---

# JOHN MUIR TRAIL-4    22 mi. one way /2.0 days
## TUOLUMNE MEADOWS to YOSEMITE VALLEY

*Reference:* **From Tuolumne Meadows Campground in Yosemite, map E4, grid g7, to Happy Isles in Yosemite Valley, map E4, grid h5.**

*User groups:* Hikers and horses. No dogs or mountain bikes are allowed. No wheelchair facilities.

*Permits:* A wilderness permit is required for traveling through various wilderness and special-use areas that the trail traverses. Contact the Wilderness Office of the National Park Service at (209) 372-0200 for a permit that is good for the length of your trip.

*Directions:* From Groveland in the Central Valley foothills, drive east on Highway 120 into Yosemite National Park and continue toward Yosemite Valley. At Crane Flat, turn left on Highway 120 (Tioga Pass Road) and continue for about an hour, driving past Tenaya Lake to the Tuolumne Meadows Campground. There is a signed trailhead parking area for the John Muir Trail here.

*Maps:* For topographic maps, ask for Vogelsang Peak, Half Dome, Yosemite Falls and Tenaya Peak from the USGS. For other maps of Yosemite, see "maps" under hike number 21.

*Who to contact:* Public Information Office, National Park Service, P.O. Box 577, Yosemite National Park, CA 95389; (209) 372-0200.

*Trail notes:* The first glimpses of Yosemite Valley will seem like a privileged view into heaven after having hiked the entire John Muir Trail from Mt.

Whitney. For hikers just intending this one 22-mile section, the rewards can seem just as profound.

The trip starts at Tuolumne Meadows, where backpackers can buy a good, cheap breakfast, obtain wilderness permits, and camp in a special area set aside for JMT hikers. When you take your first steps away from Tuolumne Meadows, resist the urge to rush to the finish line in order to close out a historic expedition. Instead relax and enjoy the downhill glide, always remembering that you are in sacred land.

Compared to the rest of the JMT, this leg will come with far less strain, starting with a 3.1-mile tromp past Cathedral Lakes (requiring a half-mile walk on a signed cutoff trail). If you can time it right, this can make for a great layover camp, with deep, emerald-green water, and Cathedral Peak in the background. At dawn, when there isn't a breath of wind, it can seem like a mountain church.

Beyond Cathedral Lakes, the trail makes a relatively short 500-foot climb over Cathedral Pass, skirts Tresidder Peak, then descends down and through pristine Long Meadow. After passing Sunrise Trail Camp, a decent layover, the trail picks up little Sunrise Creek, and follows it all the way down to Little Yosemite Valley, a popular trail camp. From Cathedral Lakes, it is 14.5 miles to the junction of the Half Dome Trail, another 2.2 miles to Little Yosemite.

For JMT hikers, making the climb to the top of Half Dome is a must, even though it often means putting up with a parade of people, even delays waiting for the line to move at the climbing cable. The Half Dome climb starts with a steep hike for the first mile, followed by steep switchbacks across granite on good trail to the foot of Half Dome's back wall. Here you will find climbing cables to aid your final 300-foot ascent, and as you go, you will discover breathtaking views of Tenaya Canyon. This is considered one of the world's glamour hikes, and while it turns hiking into an act of faith, we have seen eight-year-olds and 70-year-olds make the cable climb. By the way, if you take on Half Dome, be certain to have two canteens of water per person. Adding in the Half Dome sidetrip to the rest of the JMT leg will add a roundtrip of 5.2 miles to your trip.

Because of its proximity to Half Dome, the Little Yosemite Valley Trail Camp is often crowded. From here, though, it is an easy five-mile hike downhill to Yosemite Valley. Again, try not speed through to the end, even though it's an easy tromp downhill all the way. The magic is in the moment.

From Little Yosemite, the JMT is routed along the Merced River. In a mile, you will reach Liberty Cap, and shortly later, Nevada Falls. Then down, down you go, with the trail often turning to giant granite steps, down past Emerald Pool and then to Vernal Falls, another spectacular waterfall.

Since Vernal Falls is just 1.7 miles from the end of the trail, you will start meeting lots of dayhikers coming from the other direction, many gasping for breath as they make the uphill climb out of Yosemite Valley. Many will ask how far you have hiked, some may even want to take your photograph. It may feel a bit inane, but hey, enjoy it. After all, you just finished the John Muir Trail, the greatest hiking trail in the world.

# TUOLUMNE MEADOWS to SONORA PASS

*Reference:* From the trailhead parking at Tuolumne Meadows on Highway 120, map E4, grid g8, north to the Sonora Pass Trailhead.

*User groups:* Hikers and horses. No dogs or mountain bikes are allowed. No wheelchair facilities.

*Permits:* A wilderness permit is required for traveling through various wilderness and special-use areas that the trail traverses. Contact either the Wilderness Office of the National Park Service at (209) 372-0200 or the Stanislaus National Forest at (209) 795-1381 for a permit that is good for the length of your trip.

*Directions:* From Lee Vining, drive west on Highway 120/Tioga Pass Road, to Tuolumne Meadows and the signed trailhead parking area for the John Muir Trail/PCT and Lyell Fork.

*Maps:* For an overall view of the trail route in this section, send $3 for each map ordered to the USDA-Forest Service, 630 Sansome Street, San Francisco, CA 94111, ask for the Stanislaus National Forest map, Toiyabe National Forest map and the Inyo National Forest map. For topographic maps, ask for Pickel Meadow, Tower Peak, Piute Mountain, Matterhorn Peak, Dunderberg Peak, Vogelsang Peak, Tioga Pass, Falls Ridge, Buckeye Ridge and Sonora Pass from the USGS.

*Who to contact:* Public Information Office, National Park Service, P.O. Box 577, Yosemite National Park, CA 95389; (209) 372-0200 or Stanislaus National Forest, Calaveras Ranger Station, P.O. Box 500, Hathaway Pines, CA 95233; (209) 795-1381.

*Trail notes:* Yosemite National Park is well-known for its crowded conditions in the valley, but you can go for days and see almost no one on this section of trail. The beauty of the deep canyons, glacial-cut peaks, untouched meadows and abundant wildlife make it a surreal paradise.

But it is real enough, you can discover. Starting from Tuolumne Meadows, the trail starts out deceptively easily as it follows the Tuolumne River towards the Grand Canyon of the Tuolumne River. It stays easy to Glen Aulin, where you get a great view of Tuolumne Falls, an excellent day-trip from the Tuolumne Meadows drive-in camp. When you cross the bridge here and head up-canyon, you will be leaving most all people behind. In the next three days, you will go up one canyon and down the next, one after another, with breathtaking views and long, demanding climbs. Highlights include Matterhorn Canyon (many deer, trout and views), Benson Lake (the largest white sand beach in the Sierra Nevada), Dorothy Lake (panoramic views to the north), and many beautiful meadows, each like a wilderness church. The one serious negative is the incredible clouds of mosquitoes at the Wilmer Lake area during late spring and early summer.

When you leave Yosemite and enter Toiyabe National Forest, the landscape changes quickly from glacial-cut to volcanic rock, with the trail dropping past several lakes and into a river drainage. Here the trail can be difficult to follow in parts, and in others, your chance of meeting grazing cows is high, particularly by midsummer. It will inspire you to make the long climb up toward Leavitt Pass, set just below 10,800-foot Leavitt Peak, much of it a long, slow, uphill pull, almost all above treeline in gray, stark country. At the pass, the wind whistles by at high speed almost year around, a product of the "venturi effect," in which valley winds are forced through the narrow saddle at the pass, and must speed up to make it through.

The final drop down to Sonora Pass is a one-hour descent that seems to wind all over the mountain, slippery and dangerous when snow-covered. When you reach Highway 108, cross and walk about 100 yards west to a large day-use parking area. The trail picks up again there.

---

# PCT-25        30.8 mi. one way/3.0 days
# SONORA PASS to EBBETTS PASS

*Reference:* **From Highway 108 at Sonora Pass in map E4, grid b5 north to Highway 4 near Ebbetts Pass.**

*User groups:* Hikers, horses and dogs. No mountain bikes are allowed. No wheelchair facilities.

*Permits:* A wilderness permit is required for traveling through various wilderness and special-use areas that the trail traverses. Contact the Stanislaus National Forest at (209) 532-3671 for a permit that is good for the length of your trip.

*Directions:* From Sonora, head east on Highway 108 to the trailhead and parking at Sonora Pass.

*Maps:* For topographic maps, ask for Pickel Meadow, Disaster Peak, Dardanelles Cone and Ebbetts Pass from the USGS.

*Who to contact:* Stanislaus National Forest, 19777 Greenley Road, Sonora, CA 95370; (209) 532-3671.

*Trail notes:* While this section of the Pacific Crest Trail may not have the glamour attraction of the stretch of trail in the southern Sierra, it is just as compelling for those who know it.

From Sonora Pass, you are forced to climb out for a good hour or two, then finally, rise over Wolf Creek Gap (10,300 feet) and then make the easy drop down the Carson Canyon. This is the start of the Carson-Iceberg Wilderness, a giant swath of land that is a rare, unpeopled paradise. The Sierra riparian zones here are lined with flowers, seemingly all kinds and all colors, often in luxuriant beds of greenness.

The PCT climbs out of Carson Canyon, around Boulder Peak, then down and up two more canyons. All the while you keep crossing these little creeks filled with natural gardens. You wind your way across and through these areas, and eventually climb up a ridge, then head down, steeply at times, to Ebbetts Pass. Alas, there is no water here. No problem. A short climb and a half hour later and you can be pumping water, and maybe setting up camp, too, at little Sherrold Lake, not far from the edge of the Mokelumne Wilderness.

*PCT CONTINUATION:* To continue hiking along the Pacific Crest Trail, see Chapter D4, pages 253-257.

NOR-CAL MAP ........................ see page 14
adjoining maps
NORTH ............................................ no map
EAST .............................................. no map
SOUTH (F5) ........................... see page 492
WEST (E4) .............................. see page 402

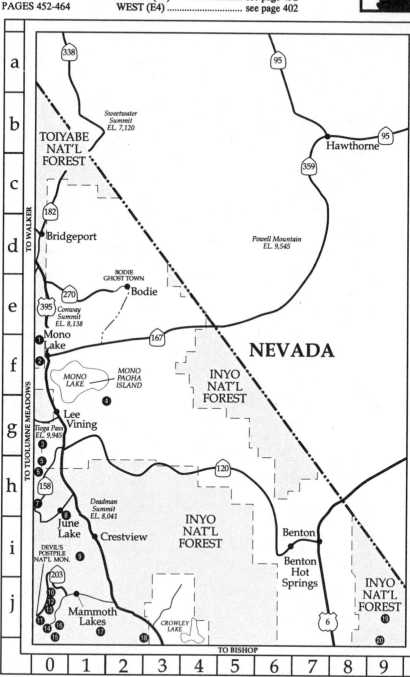

**Map E5 featuring:** Toiyabe National Forest, Bridgeport, Hoover Wilderness, Inyo National Forest, Ansel Adams Wilderness, Lee Vining, Mono Lake Tufa State Reserve, Mono Lake, Grant Lake, June Lake, Mammoth Lakes, John Muir Wilderness, Devil's Postpile National Monument

## 1. VIRGINIA LAKES TRAIL    7.0 mi/2.0 days

*Reference:* In Toiyabe National Forest south of Bridgeport; map E5, grid f0.

*User groups:* Hikers, dogs and horses. No mountain bikes are allowed. No wheelchair facilities.

*Permits:* A wilderness permit is required for hikers planning to camp. Parking and access are free.

*Directions:* From Bridgeport, drive 13.5 miles south on US Highway 395. Turn west on Virginia Lakes Road and drive seven miles to the trailhead at Trumbull Lake Campground.

*Maps:* For a map of Toiyabe National Forest, send $3 to USDA-Forest Service, 630 Sansome Street, San Francisco, CA 94111. To obtain a topographic map of the area, ask for Dunderberg Peak from the USGS.

*Who to contact:* Toiyabe National Forest, Bridgeport Ranger District, P.O. Box 595, Bridgeport, CA 93517; (619) 932-7070.

*Trail notes:* Virginia Lakes are the gateway to a beautiful high-mountain basin where there are eight small alpine lakes within a two-mile circle. The trailhead is at Trumbull Lake Campground, set at 9,600 feet between mountain peaks that poke 12,000-foot-high holes in the sky. From here, you hike west past Blue Lake to Frog Lakes (one mile), then start climbing more seriously, heading up two more miles to Summit Lake. This lake is set just below the Sierra ridge, between Camiaca Peak (11,739 feet) to the north and Excelsior Mountain (12,446 feet) to the south. This makes an ideal first-night camp. If you want a longer trip into even wilder country, you can do it from here. The trail skirts the north end of Summit Lake, then enters one of the most remote sections of Yosemite National Park, dropping into Virginia Canyon along Return Creek.

## 2. LUNDY LAKE TRAILHEAD    6.5 mi/4.0 hrs

*Reference:* In the Hoover Wilderness in Inyo National Forest south of Bridgeport; map E5, grid f0.

*User groups:* Hikers, dogs, horses and mountain bikes (up to the wilderness border). No wheelchair facilities.

*Permits:* A wilderness permit is required for hikers planning to camp. Parking and access are free.

*Directions:* From the junction of Highway 167 and US 395 at Mono Lake, turn west on Lundy Lake Road and drive five miles to Lundy Lake. Continue west two miles past Lundy Lake to the trailhead at the end of the road.

*Maps:* For a map of Inyo National Forest, send $3 to USDA-Forest Service, 630 Sansome Street, San Francisco, CA 94111. To obtain topographic maps of the area, ask for Lundy and Dunderberg Peak from the USGS.

*Who to contact:* Inyo National Forest, Mono Lake Ranger District, P.O. Box

429, Lee Vining, CA 93541; (619) 647-3000.

*Trail notes:* You get a passport into sculpted granite high country, complete with a half dozen gem-like lakes, when you use the Lundy Lake Trailhead as your backpacking jumpoff point. The trailhead is about two miles past Lundy Lake, a long narrow lake set at 7,800 feet. The trail rises along Mill Creek into the Hoover Wilderness, passes two small waterfalls, and then in three miles arrives at Lake Helen. In the next mile you arrive at Odell Lake and little Twin Lake, take your pick. The region has Yosemite-like high-country beauty, yet is set just to the east of the park boundary. The trip can be extended quite easily, creating a great one-way trip with a shuttle. To do it, you cross over the top of Lundy Pass, then drop down past Hummingbird Lake to Saddlebag Lake at 10,087 feet, the highest drive-to lake in California. That makes it a seven-mile trip, one-way.

---

## 3. GIBBS LAKE TRAIL        5.4 mi/3.75 hrs

*Reference:* **On the northern boundary of Ansel Adams Wilderness west of Lee Vining; map E5, grid g0.**

*User groups:* Hikers, dogs, horses and mountain bikes (up to the wilderness border). No wheelchair facilities.

*Permits:* A wilderness permit is required for hikers planning to camp. Parking and access are free.

*Directions:* From Lee Vining, drive about one mile south on US 395, then turn west on Forest Service Road 1N16 (look for the sign indicating Upper Horse Meadow). Drive approximately three miles to the trailhead at the end of the road.

*Maps:* For a map of Inyo National Forest, send $3 to USDA-Forest Service, 630 Sansome Street, San Francisco, CA 94111. To obtain topographic maps of the area, ask for Lee Vining and Mount Dana from the USGS.

*Who to contact:* Inyo National Forest, Mono Lake Ranger District, P.O. Box 429, Lee Vining, CA 93541; (619) 647-3000.

*Trail notes:* The 2.7-mile hike from Upper Horse Meadow to Gibbs Lake is one of the truly great day hikes in California. Since the trailhead is not located at a lake or other attractive destination, nobody gets here by accident. It starts at Upper Horse Meadow, elevation 8,000 feet, and climbs up Gibbs Canyon to Gibbs Lake, 9,530 feet. That figures to a 1,500-foot climb, and except for a half mile of switchbacks at the beginning of the trail, most of the route is a steady grade along Gibbs Creek. It is a pretty spot, backed by bare granite, fronted by conifers. The trail ends at Gibbs Lake, meaning you will not be competing with backpackers arriving from other trails for trail space or a picnic site.

---

## 4. SOUTH TUFA TRAIL        1.0 mi/0.5 hr

*Reference:* **In Mono Lake Tufa State Reserve at the southern end of Mono Lake, east of Lee Vining; map E5, grid g1.**

*User groups:* Hikers, **wheelchairs** and dogs. No horses or mountain bikes are allowed.

*Permits:* No permits are required. Parking and access are free.

*Directions:* From Lee Vining, drive seven miles south on US 395 and then take Highway 120 east for five miles. Turn left at the sign for South Tufa and continue on a dirt road to the parking area.

*Maps:* A free map of the lake is available by contacting the Mono Basin Visitor Center at the address below. To obtain topographic maps of the area, ask for Lee Vining and Mono Mills from the USGS.

*Who to contact:* Mono Lake Tufa State Reserve, P.O. Box 429, Lee Vining, CA 93541; (619) 647-6331 or (619) 525-7232.

*Trail notes:* The strange and remarkable tufa towers, spires and knobs at Mono Lake add to one of the most extraordinary landscapes in California. The place looks like a moonscape, has been called "a landing pad for spaceships," but by anybody's definition, is a peculiar place that compels thousands of people every summer to make this short walk. Mono Lake itself is vast—covering 60 square miles—and is estimated to be over 700,000 years old, one of the oldest lakes in North America. Its alkaline properties create ideal habitat for brine shrimp (ideal feed for birds), and with Paoha Island providing isolation from predators, the Mono Basin has become one of the world's most prolific breeding areas for gulls, grebes, plovers and phalaropes. The actual loop trail is only one mile, but there are several spurs to take that will lead you around for miles. Here you will stroll along the southern shore of the lake, near the South Tufa Area. This is where the strange and gigantic tufa spires sit like old, untouched earth castles.

---

# 5. WALKER LAKE TRAILHEAD 8.2 mi/5.0 hrs

*Reference:* **On the northeastern boundary of Ansel Adams Wilderness southwest of Lee Vining; map E5, grid h0.**

*User groups:* Hikers, dogs, horses and mountain bikes (up to the wilderness border). No wheelchair facilities.

*Permits:* A wilderness permit is required for hikers planning to camp. Parking and access are free.

*Directions:* From Lee Vining, drive south on US Highway 395 for about four miles to Walker Lake Road. Turn west and continue to the trailhead at the east end of the lake.

*Maps:* For a map of Inyo National Forest, send $3 to USDA-Forest Service, 630 Sansome Street, San Francisco, CA 94111. To obtain topographic maps of the area, ask for Mount Dana and Koip Peak from the USGS.

*Who to contact:* Inyo National Forest, Mono Lake Ranger District, P.O. Box 429, Lee Vining, CA 93541; (619) 647-3000.

*Trail notes:* Lower Sardine Lake is a jewel in a high glacial bowl set at 9,888 feet, the kind of lake that made the Ansel Adams Wilderness one of the most treasured places in the world. The hike in is tough and steep, with only one short flat section providing much of a break. The trail starts easy and beautiful, skirting along the northern edge of Walker Lake to its headwaters, Walker Creek. From here, you walk up Bloody Canyon, climbing nearly 2,000 feet in less than two miles. The hike follows Walker Creek, with two stream crossings included in the route up. It can be a real wheezer, a rough go for anyone either out of shape or not acclimated to the altitude. This trail usually opens by mid-June, though that varies each year due to snowpack. An option for backpackers is continuing the hike up and over Mono Pass and into some of Yosemite Park's most remote back country.

## 6. PARKER LAKE TRAIL     4.4 mi/2.5 hrs

*Reference:* **In Ansel Adams Wilderness west of Grant Lake, south of Lee Vining; map E5, grid h0.**

*User groups:* Hikers, dogs and horses. No mountain bikes are allowed. No wheelchair facilities.

*Permits:* A wilderness permit is required for hikers planning to camp. Parking and access are free.

*Directions:* From Lee Vining, drive south on US Highway 395 for about four miles to Highway 158 (June Lake Loop). Turn south and drive 1.5 miles, then turn right on Parker Lake Road and drive two miles. Turn left on Forest Service Road 1S26 and drive one mile until it dead ends at the trailhead at Parker Creek.

*Maps:* For a map of Inyo National Forest, send $3 to USDA-Forest Service, 630 Sansome Street, San Francisco, CA 94111. To obtain topographic maps of the area, ask for Mount Dana and Koip Peak from the USGS.

*Who to contact:* Inyo National Forest, Mono Lake Ranger District, P.O. Box 429, Lee Vining, CA 93541; (619) 647-3000.

*Trail notes:* The High Sierra is known for long killer grades to reach pristine high mountain lakes, but the Parker Lake Trail gives hikers an easy alternative. The trail is not only just 2.2 miles to the lake, but involves an elevation gain of only 300 feet. Yes, there is a God! Though the nearby June Lake Loop gets a lot of vacation traffic, this trailhead is just obscure enough to get missed by most. It sits at 8,000 feet along Parker Creek, then follows the creek upstream, an easy romp for most, arriving at Parker Lake at 8,318 feet. The lake sits surrounded by granite walls to each side. They are impassable, with no trails leading out of the basin, only the one easy route along Parker Creek. It makes for an excellent day trip.

## 7. SILVER LAKE TRAIL     19.2 mi/3.0 days

*Reference:* **On the eastern boundary of Ansel Adams Wilderness west of June Lake; map E5, grid h0.**

*User groups:* Hikers, dogs and horses. No mountain bikes are allowed. No wheelchair facilities.

*Permits:* A wilderness permit is required for hikers planning to camp. Parking and access are free.

*Directions:* From Lee Vining, drive south on US Highway 395 for about 11 miles to June Lake Junction. Turn right on Highway 158 (June Lake Road) and drive six miles to the trailhead at Silver Lake Campground.

*Maps:* For a map of Inyo National Forest, send $3 to USDA-Forest Service, 630 Sansome Street, San Francisco, CA 94111. To obtain topographic maps of the area, ask for June Lake and Koip Peak from the USGS.

*Who to contact:* Inyo National Forest, Mono Lake Ranger District, P.O. Box 429, Lee Vining, CA 93541; (619) 647-3000.

*Trail notes:* Some places will never change until the end of time. People are drawn to them because they provide a sense of permanence that can't be found anywhere else. This is the way it is at the headwaters of Rush Creek, created from drops of melting snow near the Sierra crest at 10,500 feet, then running downhill for miles, into the forest, rolling like a swirling emerald-green fountain. Even a short visit requires a long drive to the trailhead and then a demanding hike with a backpack, in the process contending with a 10-mile climb-out, ice-cold stream crossings, and the possibility of afternoon thunderstorms where lightning bolts and thunderclaps rattle off the canyon rims. The trailhead is at Silver Lake, elevation 7,200 feet. After departing Silver Lake on foot, hikers follow the trail adjacent to Lower Rush Creek upstream towards the Ansel Adams Wilderness. After three miles, you arrive at beautiful Gem Lake at 8,052 feet, and seven miles in, at Waugh Lake at 9,424 feet. Many visitors never get farther than this, camping, swimming and fishing at Gem or Waugh lakes. But it is upstream of Waugh Lake where you can discover the headwaters of Rush Creek, along with the flawless symmetry of the untouched high country. To see it requires climbing 3,300 feet over the course of 9.6 miles. It is one of the prettiest streams anywhere.

---

## 8. YOST LAKE TRAIL    9.5 mi/1.0 day

*Reference:* **On the eastern boundary of Ansel Adams Wilderness at June Lake, map E5, grid i0.**

*User groups:* Hikers, dogs and horses. Mountain bikes are not allowed. No wheelchair facilities.

*Permits:* A campfire permit is required for hikers planning to camp. Parking and access are free.

*Directions:* From Lee Vining, drive south on US Highway 395 for about 11 miles to June Lake Junction. Turn right on Highway 158 (June Lake Road) and drive two miles to the town of June Lake. The trailhead is opposite the June Lake boat ramp.

*Maps:* For a map of Inyo National Forest, send $3 to USDA-Forest Service, 630 Sansome Street, San Francisco, CA 94111. To obtain topographic maps of the area, ask for June Lake and Mammoth Mountain from the USGS.

*Who to contact:* Inyo National Forest, Mono Lake Ranger District, P.O. Box 429, Lee Vining, CA 93541; (619) 647-3000.

*Trail notes:* Yost Lake is a small glacial lake hidden at 9,000 feet on the slopes of June Mountain. Many people have visited the June Lakes area for years without even knowing its existence. But it is up there, truly hidden, and accessible only for those willing to hike to it. From the trailhead (7,800 feet) at June Lake, the trail rises very steeply in the first half mile, climbing nearly 1,000 feet. That will discourage many from going any further; after all, it is 4.75 miles to the lake. Ah, but after that first grunt of a climb, the trail gets much easier, contouring across the slopes of June Mountain. It rises gradually to the headwaters of Yost Creek, then drops into the small basin that guards the lake.

---

## 9. INYO CRATERS    0.75 mi/1.5 hrs

*Reference:* **In Inyo National Forest north of Mammoth; map E5, grid i1.**

*User groups:* Hikers and dogs. The terrain is not suitable for horses or mountain bikes. No wheelchair facilities.

*Permits:* No permits are required. Parking and access are free.

*Directions:* From Lee Vining, drive south on US Highway 395 for about 20 miles to the Mammoth Lakes Scenic Loop (Forest Service Road 3S23). Turn right and drive about three miles, then turn right again on Forest Service

Road 3S30. Follow it to Forest Service Road 3S29, then turn right and continue to the parking area for Inyo Craters Picnic Area.

*Maps:* For a map of Inyo National Forest, send $3 to USDA-Forest Service, 630 Sansome Street, San Francisco, CA 94111. To obtain a topographic map of the area, ask for Mammoth Mountain from the USGS.

*Who to contact:* Inyo National Forest, Mammoth Ranger District, P.O. Box 148, Mammoth Lakes, CA 93546; (619) 934-2505 or (619) 924-5500.

*Trail notes:* The Inyo Craters are a geologic phenomenon that make a great destination for an easy day hike in the Mammoth Lakes area. The craters are phreatic explosion tips, which means that they were created by a steam explosion. When the mountain was a smoldering volcano, melting snow water poured into it, and when that water hit hot magma material, well...kaboom! The hike here is easy and short, less than a half-mile through open forest sprinkled with red fir and Jeffrey pine. In each of the craters is now two tiny ponds, created by the collection of melting snow each spring.

---

# 10. UPPER SODA SPRINGS TRAILHEAD

2.75 mi/2.0 hrs

*Reference:* In Ansel Adams Wilderness west of Mammoth; map E5, grid j0.

*User groups:* Hikers, dogs and horses. No mountain bikes are allowed. No wheelchair facilities.

*Permits:* A wilderness permit is required for hikers planning to camp.

*Directions:* From Lee Vining, drive south on US Highway 395 for 25 miles to Highway 203. Turn west and follow the road to the town of Mammoth Lakes. Continue west on Minaret Summit Road until you see the sign for Upper Soda Springs Campground. Follow the signs to the campground. The trailhead is just west of the camping area. From 7:30 a.m. to 5:30 p.m., access is restricted to shuttle bus from the Mammoth Ski Area, $6 fee. You must take the bus to get in during these times.

*Maps:* For a map of Inyo National Forest, send $3 to USDA-Forest Service, 630 Sansome Street, San Francisco, CA 94111. To obtain a topographic map of the area, ask for Mammoth Mountain from the USGS.

*Who to contact:* Inyo National Forest, Mammoth Ranger District, P.O. Box 148, Mammoth Lakes, CA 93546; (619) 934-2505 or (619) 924-5500.

*Trail notes:* The Upper San Joaquin River is a trout angler's paradise, where we've had days in late June and July catching and releasing 50 to 60 trout. Most of them are little guys, rarely over 10 inches, but they include brook trout, rainbow trout, brown trout, and rarely even golden trout. It is such a contrast from just a mile or two downriver near Devil's Postpile, where a small stretch of river with easy access from campgrounds gets hammered day after day, all summer long. From the Soda Springs Campground, hike on the River Trail upstream along the San Joaquin River, heading out at least a mile or more before fishing. It is a beautiful stream, tumbling over rocks and into pools, with canyon views and lush streamside vegetation. The best technique is to fly fish using a floating line, nine-foot leader, nymphs, and a strike indicator (many of the strikes are very soft). If you want to hike, not fish, it is 6.9 miles from the trailhead to Thousand Island Lake (9,833 feet), a divine spot where boulders dot the surface, creating the appearance of miniature islands. The views of Banner and Ritter peaks, along with the rest of the Minarets, are unsurpassed from here. It is the favorite hike of Scott Greenstein, a Forest Service volunteer we ran into. "In the spring, a new wildflower blooms every week," Scott told us.

## 11. RAINBOW FALLS TRAIL     1.5 mi/1.5 hrs

*Reference:* In Devil's Postpile National Monument west of Mammoth; map E5, grid j0.

*User groups:* Hikers and horses. No mountain bikes or dogs are allowed. No wheelchair facilities.

*Permits:* No permits are required. During summer months, there is a $6 fee for the shuttle bus from 7:30 a.m. to 5:30 p.m.

*Directions:* From US 395, drive to Mammoth Lakes. Turn west on Highway 203 and follow the road through the town of Mammoth Lakes. Continue on Minaret Summit Road to the Mammoth Ski Area. Park here, and on the north side of the parking lot, buy a ticket for the shuttle bus. Take the shuttle bus to Reds Meadows Resort at the end of the road in Devil's Postpile National Monument.

*Maps:* For a map of Inyo National Forest, send $3 to USDA-Forest Service, 630 Sansome Street, San Francisco, CA 94111. To obtain a topographic map of the area, ask for Mammoth Mountain from the USGS.

*Who to contact:* Devil's Postpile National Monument, (619) 934-2289. Inyo National Forest, Mammoth Ranger District, P.O. Box 148, Mammoth Lakes, CA 93546; (619) 934-2505 or (619) 924-5500.

*Trail notes:* Rainbow Falls is an awesome surprise the first time you see it— a tall, wide and often forceful waterfall that inspires as much as it astonishes. It is often overlooked because of nearby Devil's Postpile, the world's best example of columnar rock; the adjacent Ansel Adams Wilderness; and of course, Mammoth Lakes and its dozens of nearby recreation destinations. But this is one of the best short hikes in California. It starts at the Reds Meadows Resort, which is actually more of a headquarters for horseback riders, then the trail is routed south down into a canyon where the Middle Fork San Joaquin River runs. A short cutoff trail at the falls allows hikers to loop down to its base for a classic vantage point. An option is hiking another half-mile downstream, where there is a smaller waterfall. For such a short walk, this trip is a classic.

## 12. MINARET LAKE TRAIL     14.8 mi/2.0 days

*Reference:* In Ansel Adams Wilderness west of Mammoth; map E5, grid j0.

*User groups:* Hikers, dogs and horses. No mountain bikes are allowed. No wheelchair facilities.

*Permits:* A wilderness permit is required for hikers planning to camp.

*Directions:* From Lee Vining, drive south on US Highway 395 for 25 miles to Highway 203. Turn west and follow the road to the town of Mammoth Lakes. Past town, drive 17 miles on Minaret Summit Road to the campground at Devil's Postpile National Monument. The trailhead is just west of the campground. You must hike 1.5 miles on the John Muir Trail to reach the Minaret Lake Trailhead. From 7:30 a.m. to 5:30 p.m., access is restricted to shuttle bus from the Mammoth Ski Area, $6 fee. You must take the bus to get in during these times.

*Maps:* For a map of Inyo National Forest, send $3 to USDA-Forest Service, 630 Sansome Street, San Francisco, CA 94111. To obtain topographic maps of the area, ask for Mammoth Mountain and Mount Ritter from the USGS.

*Who to contact:* Inyo National Forest, Mammoth Ranger District, P.O. Box 148, Mammoth Lakes, CA 93546; (619) 934-2505 or (619) 924-5500.

*Trail notes:* With an early morning start and a fresh head of steam, you can make the 7.4-mile, 1,800-foot climb from Devil's Postpile to Minaret Lake with a good morning effort. What better place might you have a picnic lunch? Perhaps nowhere. It is an enchanting place, with Minaret Lake a real prize, set at 9,793 feet, just below the awesome glacial-carved Minaret Range. From the trailhead, you start the hike by taking the John Muir Trail north, then just beyond Johnston Lake, taking the left fork along Minaret Creek. The trail rises with the creek, and then in the last mile, climbs steeply above tree line, and shortly later, skirts the outlet of Minaret Lake. A high, impassable back wall frames the lake, with the trail circling around the northern shore. You've made it to the kind of place where John Muir got religion.

---

## 13. FERN LAKE LOOP    13.0 mi/2.0 days  

*Reference:* In Ansel Adams Wilderness west of Mammoth; map E5, grid j0.

*User groups:* Hikers, dogs and horses. No mountain bikes are allowed. No wheelchair facilities.

*Permits:* A wilderness permit is required for hikers planning to camp.

*Directions:* From Lee Vining, drive south on US 395 for 25 miles to Highway 203. Turn west and follow the road to the town of Mammoth Lakes. Past town, drive 17 miles on Minaret Summit Road to the campground at Devil's Postpile National Monument. The trailhead is just south of the ranger station. From 7:30 a.m. to 5:30 p.m., access is restricted to shuttle bus from the Mammoth Ski Area, $6 fee. You must take the bus to get in during these times.

*Maps:* For a map of Inyo National Forest, send $3 to USDA-Forest Service, 630 Sansome Street, San Francisco, CA 94111. To obtain topographic maps of the area, ask for Crystal Crag and Cattle Mountain from the USGS.

*Who to contact:* Inyo National Forest, Mammoth Ranger District, P.O. Box 148, Mammoth Lakes, CA 93546; (619) 934-2505 or (619) 924-5500.

*Trail notes:* Fern Lake can make an ambitious one-day trip into and back out of Devil's Postpile, or better, the start of a great 13-mile loop trip. Either way you go, this is an excellent hike, one that has become very popular, sometimes crowded, and that is the only element that can detract. The trip starts at Devil's Postpile, where you hike five miles to Fern Lake, climbing most of the way. Fern Lake is a small lake set in a rock bowl at tree line, below Iron Mountain of the Minarets. From here, the trail contours north across the mountain, poking in and out of sparse forest and bare granite to Beck Cabin (a 1.1-mile sidetrip will take you to Beck Lakes, 9,803 feet). The trip back drops 4.8 miles down to the John Muir Trail, including a very steep half-mile on switchbacks. You turn right and hike the final 1.4 miles back to Devil's Postpile to complete the loop. We strongly advise the sidetrip to Beck Lakes and its celestial mountain scenery, set in a glacial-formed pocket just below the Minarets ridge.

## 14. RED CONE LOOP    6.7 mi/4.0 hrs

*Reference:* **At Horseshoe Lake in Mammoth Lakes; map E5, grid j0.**

*User groups:* Hikers, dogs and horses. No mountain bikes are allowed past the wilderness border. No wheelchair facilities.

*Permits:* A wilderness permit is required for hikers planning to camp. Parking and access are free.

*Directions:* From Lee Vining, drive south on US Highway 395 for 25 miles to Highway 203. Turn west and follow the road to the town of Mammoth Lakes. Turn south on Lake Mary Road and follow it to its end. The trailhead is on the west side of Horseshoe Lake.

*Maps:* For a map of Inyo National Forest, send $3 to USDA-Forest Service, 630 Sansome Street, San Francisco, CA 94111. To obtain a topographic map of the area, ask for Crystal Crag from the USGS.

*Who to contact:* Inyo National Forest, Mammoth Ranger District, P.O. Box 148, Mammoth Lakes, CA 93546; (619) 934-2505 or (619) 924-5500.

*Trail notes:* Horseshoe Lake, elevation 8,900 feet, is at the end of the road of the Mammoth Lakes, an excellent trailhead that makes for a great day hike. The trail is a loop that tops out near Crater Meadow, a beautiful little spot set just below Red Cones, about a five-minute walk off the main trail. This is your destination, where you can have a picnic lunch in virtual peace, then enjoy the walk back down. The contrast is striking: So many people are typically just a short distance down below at Twin Lakes, Lake Mary, Lake Mamie and Lake George, yet you are separated from them by Mammoth Pass, and will be surprised at the relatively few number of people that take this loop hike.

## 15. LAKE GEORGE TRAILHEAD   1.0mi/0.5 hr

*Reference:* **At Lake George in Mammoth Lakes; map E5, grid j0.**

*User groups:* Hikers and dogs. Mountain bikes are not advised. No horses are allowed. No wheelchair facilities.

*Permits:* No permits are required. Parking and access are free.

*Directions:* From Lee Vining, drive south on US Highway 395 for 25 miles to Highway 203. Turn west and follow the road to the town of Mammoth Lakes. Turn south on Lake Mary Road and follow it to Lake Mary. Turn south at Lake Mary and follow the signs to Lake George. The trailhead is at the campground near the northeast shore of the lake.

*Maps:* For a map of Inyo National Forest, send $3 to USDA-Forest Service, 630 Sansome Street, San Francisco, CA 94111. To obtain a topographic map of the area, ask for Crystal Crag from the USGS.

*Who to contact:* Inyo National Forest, Mammoth Ranger District, P.O. Box 148, Mammoth Lakes, CA 93546; (619) 934-2505 or (619) 924-5500.

*Trail notes:* Campers at Lake George will find this easy, short trail provides access to hidden TJ Lake. It's a revelation to many that a pretty alpine lake that is easy to reach is also very secluded. The trail starts at the campground at Lake George, and follows up the inlet stream to TJ Lake. It's about a half mile, an easy grade. Crystal Crag, 10,377 feet, towers above the lake, and adds great natural beauty. The trail skirts along the eastern shoreline of the lake, deadending at the lake's small inlet stream.

## 16. BLUE CRAG LOOP  3.4 mi/1.75 hrs

*Reference:* **At Lake Mary in Mammoth Lakes; map E5, grid j0.**

*User groups:* Hikers, dogs and horses. No mountain bikes are allowed past the wilderness boundary. No wheelchair facilities.

*Permits:* A wilderness permit is required for hikers planning to camp. Parking and access are free.

*Directions:* From Lee Vining, drive south on US Highway 395 for 25 miles to Highway 203. Turn west and follow the road to the town of Mammoth Lakes. Turn south on Lake Mary Road and follow it to Lake Mary. The trailhead is south of Lake Mary, just beyond the Coldwater Campground.

*Maps:* For a map of Inyo National Forest, send $3 to USDA-Forest Service, 630 Sansome Street, San Francisco, CA 94111. To obtain a topographic map of the area, ask for Crystal Crag from the USGS.

*Who to contact:* Inyo National Forest, Mammoth Ranger District, P.O. Box 148, Mammoth Lakes, CA 93546; (619) 934-2505 or (619) 924-5500.

*Trail notes:* The Blue Crag Loop is a scenic loop hike out of the Lake Mary Campground, furnishing access to three small, jewel-like lakes, a pretty meadow, and a close-up view of towering Blue Crag. Nature's artwork is just about perfect here. The trail starts just south of Lake Mary, at the end of the road beyond the Coldwater Campground. You will start the hike by climbing up to Arrowhead Lake (a short spur trail provides shoreline access), then heading up to the base of Blue Crag, overlooking Skelton Lake. To complete the loop, turn right at Blue Crag, pass Gentian Meadow and little Emerald Lake and head back down along Cold Water Creek to the trailhead. It is a short, scenic loop that provides a glimpse of classic high Sierra country, most of it ranging in elevations between 9,000 and 9,700 feet.

## 17. VALENTINE LAKE TRAILHEAD  11.2 mi/1.0 day

*Reference:* **In Inyo National Forest south of Mammoth Lakes; map E5, grid j1.**

*User groups:* Hikers, dogs and horses. No mountain bikes are allowed past the wilderness boundary. No wheelchair facilities.

*Permits:* A wilderness permit is required for hikers planning to camp. Parking and access are free.

*Directions:* From Lee Vining, drive south on US Highway 395 for approximately 27 miles to Sherwin Creek Road (about two miles south of the Mammoth Lakes turnoff). Turn west and drive about 2.5 miles. About one mile before you reach Sherwin Creek Campground, turn left on a spur road and continue a short distance to the trailhead.

*Maps:* For a map of Inyo National Forest, send $3 to USDA-Forest Service, 630 Sansome Street, San Francisco, CA 94111.

*Who to contact:* Inyo National Forest, Mammoth Ranger District, P.O. Box 148, Mammoth Lakes, CA 93546; (619) 934-2505 or (619) 924-5500.

*Trail notes:* The Mammoth Lakes area is a star attraction in the eastern Sierra, but here is little nearby Valentine Lake, not lost but largely forgotten.

Perhaps it is overlooked because the trailhead (7,600 feet) is not at one of the lakes in the Mammoth Lakes Basin or at nearby Devil's Postpile. Or perhaps it is neglected because the climb is such a steep one. Regardless of the reason, a morning's hike, rising 2,100 feet over 5.6 miles, will get you to Valentine Lake at 9,698 feet. Some say the lake is shaped like a teardrop, hence the name Valentine Lake, but when we visited, we thought it was shaped more like a drop of sweat. The hike starts out with a very steep climb, including a half-mile of switchbacks until you hit 8,500 feet. After that, the trail laterals along Sherwin Creek, with two more sets of switchbacks before you reach the lake. The trail ends at the lake's outlet. The lake is surrounded by high mountain walls on three sides, making it impossible to go much further.

---

## 18. CONVICT LAKE TRAIL    15.4 mi/2.0 days

*Reference:* **On the eastern boundary of John Muir Wilderness south of Mammoth; map E5, grid j3.**

*User groups:* Hikers, dogs and mountain bikes. No horses are allowed. No wheelchair access.

*Permits:* No permits are required. Parking and access are free.

*Directions:* From Lee Vining, drive south on US 395 for approximately 31 miles to Convict Lake Road. Turn right and continue to the lake at the end of the road. The trailhead is off a short spur road to the right as you near the lake.

*Maps:* For a map of Inyo National Forest, send $3 to USDA-Forest Service, 630 Sansome Street, San Francisco, CA 94111. To obtain a topographic map of the area, ask for Bloody Mountain from the USGS.

*Who to contact:* Inyo National Forest, Mammoth Ranger District, P.O. Box 148, Mammoth Lakes, CA 93546; (619) 934-2505 or (619) 924-5500.

*Trail notes:* Convict Lake is a mountain shrine, framed by a back wall of bare granite peaks, and the trail that leads from here into the backcountry wilderness is like ascending into heaven. But it's no easy trip. It's not only a long, grueling climb—gaining 3,000 feet in 7.7 miles—but one that includes a tricky and sometimes dangerous stream crossing. The trail starts near Convict Lake (the trailhead is well signed) at 7,621 feet, and skirts along the north shore of the lake, then up through a canyon alongside Convict Creek. About three miles in, you have to ford Convict Creek, which usually requires getting wet, and can be dangerous in the early summer because of high snowmelt. (Many attempts to bridge this crossing have failed, with the bridge always getting washed out by high early-summer flows.) If you get past that crossing, the trail is routed up to a series of large, untouched lakes— Mildred Lake, Lake Dorothy (10,275 feet), Bighorn Lake, Lake Genevieve (10,000 feet), Edith Lake and Cloverleaf Lake. Take your pick. You can spend days exploring this high-mountain paradise.

---

## 19. WHITE MOUNTAIN PEAK TRAIL    7.5 mi/6.0 hrs

*Reference:* **In Inyo National Forest northeast of Bishop; map E5, grid j9.**

*User groups:* Hikers, dogs, horses and mountain bikes. However, dogs, horses and mountain bikes are strongly not advised, due to the extremely high altitudes. No wheelchair access.

*Permits:* No permits are required. Parking and access are free.

*Directions:* From US Highway 395 at Big Pine, take Highway 168 northeast toward Nevada. Drive about 15 miles, then turn left on White Mountain Road. Drive north for 22 miles past Ancient Bristlecone Pine Forest to where the road dead ends at a locked gate. This is the trailhead. Park to the side and be certain not to block the road.

*Maps:* For a map of Inyo National Forest, send $3 to USDA-Forest Service, 630 Sansome Street, San Francisco, CA 94111. To obtain a topographic map of the area, ask for White Mountain Peak from the USGS.

*Who to contact:* Inyo National Forest, White Mountain Ranger Station, 798 North Main Street, Bishop, CA 93514; (619) 873-2500 or (619) 873-2400.

*Trail notes:* White Mountain Peak is the third tallest peak in California, only 249 feet lower than Mt. Whitney (the second-highest peak is Williamson), yet it is little known to hikers outside of the area. The summit is at 14,246 feet, the site of a University of California high-altitude research lab. The hike is a butt-kicker, a climb of 2,600 feet in 7.5 miles at high altitude, following an old Navy-built road to the top. It starts at a locked gate, and follows the road past Mt. Barcroft (13,040 feet), a long grind all the way. The summit constitutes an impressive granite massif with grand views. To the east, you can see a hundred miles into Nevada, and to the west, the Owens Valley and Volcanic Tableland. You'll feel like you're in a different world. When you reach the top, you realize that you are.

---

# 20. METHUSELAH TRAIL    3.0 mi/1.75 hrs

*Reference:* **In Inyo National Forest northeast of Bishop; map E5, grid j9.**

*User groups:* Hikers and leashed dogs. Horses and mountain bikes are not permitted. No wheelchair access.

*Permits:* No permits are required. Parking and access are free.

*Directions:* From US Highway 395 at Big Pine, take Highway 168 northeast toward Nevada. Drive about 15 miles, then turn left on White Mountain Road. Drive north for eight miles past the entrance to the Ancient Bristlecone Pine Forest to the Schulman Grove Picnic Area. Turn right and drive a short distance to the parking area and trailhead.

*Maps:* For a map of Inyo National Forest, send $3 to USDA-Forest Service, 630 Sansome Street, San Francisco, CA 94111. To obtain a topographic map of the area, ask for Westgard Pass the USGS.

*Who to contact:* Inyo National Forest, White Mountain Ranger Station, 798 North Main Street, Bishop, CA 93514; (619) 873-2500 or (619) 873-2400.

*Trail notes:* The Methuselah Tree is the prize of the Ancient Bristlecone Pine Forest. This is the oldest living tree documented in the world, over 4,000 years old. But get this: The rangers won't tell you which one it is, because of the fear that some dimwit will cut it down. So you're left knowing that you have walked among the ancients, but that will have to do. The trail starts at the Schulman Grove Picnic Area, where little birds will sometimes eat right out of your hand. Schulman Grove, elevation 10,100 feet, is the location of the oldest trees in Bristlecone Forest, and they look it. They have been sculpted by centuries of fire, sand, ice and wind, and have the appearance of living driftwood. The trail loops among them, with a few short climbs along the way. It is a short, unusual hike that you will never forget.

# CENTRAL AREA
# HIKING TRAILS

## OVERALL RATING

Poor ................................................ Fair ................................................ Great

## DIFFICULTY RATING

A Stroll ........................................ Moderate .................. A Real Butt-Kicker!

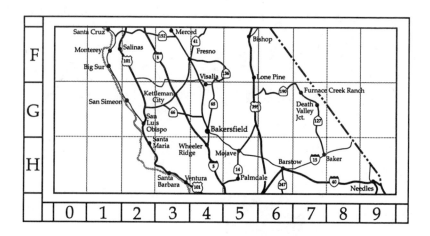

| | | | | | | | | | |
|---|---|---|---|---|---|---|---|---|---|
| 0 | 1 | 2 | 3 | 4 | 5 | 6 | 7 | 8 | 9 |

**Map F1** ...................................... (8 trails)
Featuring: Point Lobos Preserve, Carmel, Pfeiffer Big Sur State Park, Julia Pfeiffer Burns State Park, Los Padres National Forest.

**Map F2** ...................................... (4 trails)
Featuring: Los Banos Wildlife Area, Pinnacles National Monument, Soledad.

**Map F3** ......................................... (1 trail)
Featuring: Merced National Wildlife Refuge.

**Map F4** ...................................... (13 trails)
Featuring: Sierra National Forest, Millerton Lake State Recreation Area, San Joaquin River, Sequoia National Park, Kings Canyon National Park.

**Map F5**...(2 PCT, 2 JMT sections, 65 trails)
Featuring: National Forest, Sequoia National Park, Kings Canyon National Park, Lake Thomas Edison, Mono Hot Springs, Glacier Lodge, Cedar Grove, Mt. Whitney.

**Map F6** ...................................... (2 trails)
Featuring: Death Valley National Park, Saline Valley.

**Map G1** ......................................... (1 trail)
Featuring: Los Padres National Forest.

**Map G2** ...................................... (6 trails)
Featuring: Cambria, Montana de Oro State Park, Lopez Lake.

**Map G3** ......................................... (1 trail)
Featuring: Kreyenhagen Mountain peak, Coalinga Mineral Springs County Park.

**Map G4** ...................................... (3 trails)
Featuring: Sequoia National Park, Kings Canyon National Park, Three Rivers.

**Map G5** .......... (2 PCT sections, 49 trails)
Featuring: Mt. Whitney, Sequoia National Park, Kings Canyon National Park, Golden Trout Wilderness Area, Dome Lands Wilderness Area, Big Meadow, Horse Meadow, Kern River, Walker Pass, Kennedy Meadows.

**Map G6** ...................................... (5 trails)
Featuring: Death Valley National Park, Panamint Range, Searles Lake, Trona Pinnacles.

**Map G7** ...................................... (5 trails)
Featuring: Death Valley National Park.

**Map H2** ...................................... (7 trails)
Featuring: Pismo Beach, Gaviota State Park, Jalama County Park, Oso Flaco Lake.

**Map H3** ...................................... (14 trails)
Featuring: San Joaquin Valley, Carrizo Plain Natural Area, San Rafael Wilderness Area, Los Padres National Forest, Ojai Valley, Painted Rock National Monument.

**Map H4** ......... (2 PCT sections, 10 trails)
Featuring: Los Padres National Forest,
San Fernando Valley, Lake Piru, Castaic
Lake, Bouquet Reservoir, Los Padres
National Forest, Three Points.

**Map H5** ............ (4 PCT sections, 9 trails)
Featuring: Red Rock Canyon State Rec-
reation Area, Antelope Valley Califor-
nia State Poppy Preserve, Butterbredt
Canyon, Angeles National Forest,
Saddleback Butte State Park.

**Map H6** .................................... (3 trails)
Featuring: Mojave Desert, Rainbow
National Natural Landmark.

**Map H7** ...................................... (1 trail)
Featuring: Afton Canyon Natural Area.

**Map H8** .................................... (6 trails)
Featuring: East Mojave National Scenic
Area, Providence Mountains State Rec-
reation Area.

CEN-CAL MAP ...................... see page 466
adjoining maps
NORTH (E1) ......................... see page 258
EAST (F2) ............................. see page 476
SOUTH (G1) ......................... see page 546
WEST ................................... no map

8 TRAILS
PAGES 468-475

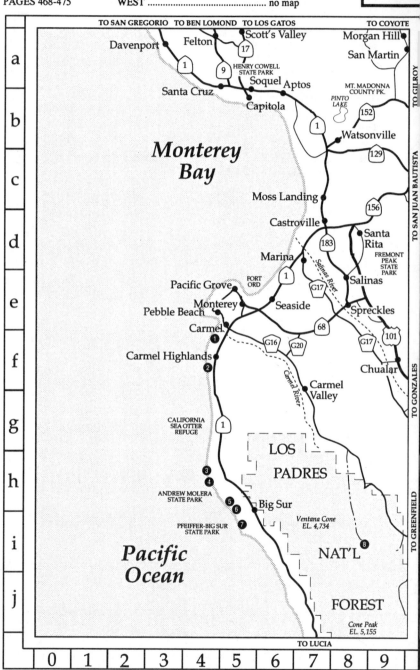

CENTRAL AREA HIKING TRAILS (map page 466)

Map F1 featuring: Point Lobos Preserve, Carmel, Pfeiffer Big Sur State Park, Julia Pfeiffer Burns State Park, Los Padres National Forest

## 1. POINT LOBOS STATE PRESERVE

1.4 mi/1.0 hr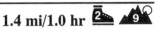

*Reference:* **Point Lobos Preserve, just south of Carmel; map F1, grid f4.**

*User groups:* Hikers only. No mountain bikes, horses or dogs. Parts of some trails are suitable for **wheelchairs**.

*Permits:* No day-use permits are required. Overnight camping is not allowed.

*Directions:* From Carmel, drive four miles south on Highway 1 (135 miles north of San Luis Obispo) to the Point Lobos State Reserve entrance. A $6 day-use fee is charged at the gate. Park at the Sea Lion Point parking area. There are four other parking areas if this one is full.

*Maps:* A park map trail guide is available for 50 cents from the park office—request one before heading out on your hike. For a topographic map, ask for Soberanes Point from the USGS.

*Who to contact:* Point Lobos State Reserve, Route 1, P.O. Box 62, Carmel, CA 93923; (408) 624-4909.

*Trail notes:* There are a number of trails lacing through the park, but we're only going to mention two—after that, your sense of adventure should urge you to explore on your own. Introduce yourself to the park by hiking the Cypress Grove Trail first. This three-quarter-mile trail winds its way through one of only two naturally growing stands of Monterey Cypress trees remaining on earth. Point Lobos State Preserve was originally established to protect these gnarled trees. At the lookouts along the trail, take the time to gaze at nature's curious balance of life—sea otters playing in the surging surf, sea lions basking on the outer rocks, bluff wildflowers clinging to life in chinks of the granite walls, and lace lichen bearding the dead understory limbs. Once back at the parking area, trek over to the Sea Lion Point Trail and follow its three-quarter-mile-long treadway through one of nature's seaside gardens and out to a glorious view. A natural staircase leads to a lower trail and a rock formation known as the Carmelo Formation. Look for hauled-out harbor seals basking in the sun. Barking sea lions hanging out on offshore rocks will entertain you. Keep your distance from the churning display of ocean power. If you wish, the Preserve offers excellent ranger- and docent-led walks and interpretive programs along the trails and down to the tidepools. Schedules are posted at the park's information station or you can call for specific date information.

## 2. GARRAPATA STATE PARK

5.0 mi/2.5 hrs

*Reference:* **Just north of Pfeiffer Big Sur State Park, south of Carmel; map F1, grid f4.**

*User groups:* Hikers only. No mountain bikes, dogs or horses. No wheelchair facilities.

*Permits:* No day-use permits are required for hikes within the state park. At present, the park is designated for day-use only. Parking and access are free.

*Directions:* From Carmel, drive 10 miles south on Highway 1 (129 miles north of San Luis Obispo) to the signs announcing Garrapata State Park. No official park entrance exists at this time. Parking is at turnouts; park at turnouts 13, 14 or 16 on the west side of the highway.

*Maps:* For topographic maps, ask for Point Sur and Soberanes Point from the USGS.

*Who to contact:* Garrapata State Park, c/o Pfeiffer Big Sur State Park, Big Sur, CA 93920; (408) 667-2315.

*Trail notes:* Someone had a sense of humor when they named this park—garrapata is Spanish for "tick." Apparently, the Spanish explorers in 1830 grew so disgusted with the little blood-suckers that they named a creek and canyon in their honor and the state saw fit to extend the recognition to a park name. Despite the unappealing nature of the name, however, this park is anything but—Pacific ocean breakers thunder against the eroding cliffs, sea otters play in the kelp beds, and redwood-shaded canyons slice and wind their way among golden sun-kissed hills. Three trails are worth exploring. The first offers approximately one mile of coastal wandering. From turnout 13, follow the paths that lace west over the bluffs to Soberanes Point and around and up to Whale Peak. During the winter, this peak is an ideal place from which to view migrating California gray whales. Tidepooling along the way is also super, but keep a wary eye out for the odd rogue wave or two. From turnout 14, hike either the three-mile roundtrip Soberanes Canyon Trail, which snakes along beside Soberanes Creek to a grove of redwoods, or the four-mile roundtrip Rocky Ridge Trail which climbs 1,500 feet to spectacular views of Point Sur to the south and the Monterey Peninsula to the north.

---

## 3. POINT SUR LIGHTSTATION 0.5 mi/1.0 hr

*Reference:* **Point Sur State Historic Park, south of Carmel; map F1, grid h5.**

*User groups:* Hikers only. No mountain bikes, horses or dogs are allowed. No wheelchair facilities.

*Permits:* Guided tours that are docent-led are the only way to view the lighthouse. Contact the Point Sur State Historic Park at (408) 625-4419 for more information. They do not accept reservations. Tours are limited in size and fill on a first-come, first-served basis. Rangers advise showing up early. A tour fee is charged—$5 for adults; $3 for ages 13 to 17; $2 for ages 5 to 12. No strollers are permitted on the tour.

*Directions:* From Carmel, drive 20 miles south on Highway 1 to Point Sur State Historic Park.

*Maps:* Send $3 to the USDA-Forest Service, 630 Sansome Street, San Francisco, CA 94111 and ask for the Los Padres National Forest map. For a topographic map, ask for Point Sur from the USGS.

*Who to contact:* California State Parks, Monterey District, 2211 Garden Road, Monterey, CA 93940; (408) 649-2836; or call the park direct at (408) 625-4419.

*Trail notes:* Here's an easy walk along high bluffs overlooking the ocean and through a century-old lighthouse complex that includes the lighthouse, the keeper's house, the barn and the blacksmith's workshop. First pressed into operation in 1889, the lighthouse is still in operation today, although now it is fully automated. The ocean breeze can make this a very chilly walk—be sure to pack along an extra sweater and a wind breaker.

## 4. ANDREW MOLERA STATE PARK/BEACH TRAIL   3.0 mi/2.0 hrs

*Reference:* **Andrew Molera State Park, south of Carmel; map F1, grid h5.**
*User groups:* Hikers only. No mountain bikes, horses or dogs are allowed. No wheelchair facilities.
*Permits:* No day-use permits are required for hikes within the state park; however, a $4 day-use fee is charged at the gate. If you plan on straying into the wilderness area managed by the Forest Service, you will need a visitor's permit. Wilderness permits are needed if you plan on camping overnight in the wilderness area. Contact the Monterey Ranger District at (408) 385-5434 for more information.
*Directions:* From Carmel, drive 21 miles south on Highway 1 to the Andrew Molera State Park entrance.
*Maps:* Park maps are available for 25 cents from the park office—request one before heading out on your hike. Send $3 to the USDA-Forest Service, 630 Sansome Street, San Francisco, CA 94111 and ask for the Los Padres National Forest map. For topographic maps, ask for Point Sur and Big Sur from the USGS.
*Who to contact:* Andrew Molera State Park, Big Sur Station 1, Big Sur, CA 93920; (408) 624-7195.
*Trail notes:* There are over 20 miles of trails that wander through this scenic slice of parkland carved into the bluffs overlooking the ocean and bisected by the Big Sur River. Our little sampler will take you from the trailhead down to the beach via the Beach Trail, along the banks of the Big Sur (just follow the surfers) and then return you on the Creamery Meadow Trail. Wildflowers are quite scenic in the spring. The banks of the Big Sur River are lined with wild berry bushes, but you will have to beat the birds and other scavengers to them. Once you are down at the beach, a short but steep trail leads up to an overlook named Molera Point. In the winter months from January to mid-April, it is possible to watch migrating whales from here—pack along a good pair of binoculars.

## 5. BUZZARDS ROOST TRAIL   3.1 mi/2.0 hrs
*Reference:* **In Pfeiffer Big Sur State Park, south of Carmel; map F1, grid h5.**
*User groups:* Hikers only. No mountain bikes, horses or dogs. No wheelchair facilities.
*Permits:* No day-use permits are required for hikes within the state park, but a $6 day-use fee is charged at the gate. If you plan on straying into the wilderness area managed by the Forest Service, you will need a visitor's permit. Wilderness permits are needed if you plan on camping overnight in the wilderness area. Contact the Monterey Ranger District at (408) 385-5434 for more information.
*Directions:* From Carmel, drive 27 miles south on Highway 1 (112 miles north of San Luis Obispo) to the Pfeiffer Big Sur State Park entrance.
*Maps:* Park maps are available for 25 cents from the park office—request one before heading out on your hike. Send $3 to the USDA-Forest Service, 630

Sansome Street, San Francisco, CA 94111 and ask for the Los Padres National Forest map. For topographic maps, ask for Big Sur and Pfeiffer Point from the USGS.

*Who to contact:* Pfeiffer Big Sur State Park, Big Sur, CA 93920; (408) 667-2315 or Los Padres National Forest, Monterey Ranger District, 406 South Mildred, King City, CA 93930; (408) 385-5434.

*Trail notes:* This is a moderately steep hike that leads along the park's western edge and guides visitors through redwoods and then oak woodlands to the top of Pfeiffer Ridge, where a magnificent and panoramic view of the Pacific Ocean and the Santa Lucia Mountain Range is set before them. The ocean breeze can make this a very chilly walk.

---

# 6. PFEIFFER FALLS 1.7 mi/1.0 hr

*Reference:* **In Pfeiffer Big Sur State Park, south of Carmel; map F1, grid h5.**

*User groups:* Hikers and horses. No mountain bikes or dogs. No wheelchair facilities.

*Permits:* No day-use permits are required for hikes within the state park, but a $6 day-use fee is charged at the gate. If you plan on straying into the wilderness managed by the Forest Service, you will need a visitor's permit. Wilderness permits are needed also if you plan on camping overnight in the wilderness area. Contact the Monterey Ranger District at (408) 385-5434 for more information.

*Directions:* From Carmel, drive 27 miles south on Highway 1 (112 miles north of San Luis Obispo) to the Pfeiffer Big Sur State Park entrance.

*Maps:* Park maps are available for 50 cents from the park office—request one before heading out on your hike. Send $3 to the USDA-Forest Service, 630 Sansome Street, San Francisco, CA 94111 and ask for the Los Padres National Forest map. For topographic maps, ask for Big Sur and Pfeiffer Point from the USGS.

*Who to contact:* Pfeiffer Big Sur State Park, Big Sur, CA 93920; (408) 667-2315 or Los Padres National Forest, Monterey Ranger District, 406 South Mildred, King City, CA 93930; (408) 385-5434.

*Trail notes:* This short stroll along Pfeiffer-Redwood Creek features some of the finest redwood groves in the Big Sur region. Another highlight of the trek is the 60-foot waterfall located at trail's end—truly spectacular during the winter months when water runoff is at its highest.

---

# 7. McWAY CANYON TRAIL 4.0 mi/2.0 hrs

*Reference:* **In Julia Pfeiffer Burns State Park, south of Carmel; map F1, grid i6.**

*User groups:* Hikers and horses. No mountain bikes or dogs. No wheelchair facilities.

*Permits:* No day-use permits are required for hikes within the state park, but a $6 day-use fee is charged at the gate. If you plan on straying into the wilderness area managed by the Forest Service, you will need a visitor's permit. Wilderness permits are needed also, if you plan on camping overnight in the wilderness area. Contact the Monterey Ranger District at (408) 385-5434 for more information.

*Directions:* From Carmel, drive 27 miles south on Highway 1 (112 miles north of San Luis Obispo) to the Pfeiffer Big Sur State Park entrance.

*Maps:* Park maps are available for 50 cents from the park office—request one before heading out on your hike. Send $3 to the USDA-Forest Service, 630 Sansome Street, San Francisco, CA 94111 and ask for the Los Padres National Forest map. For a topographic map, ask for Partington Ridge from the USGS.

*Who to contact:* Julia Pfeiffer Burns State Park, c/o Pfeiffer Big Sur State Park, Big Sur, CA 93920; (408) 667-2315 or Los Padres National Forest, Monterey Ranger District, 406 South Mildred, King City, CA 93930; (408) 385-5434.

*Trail notes:* The McWay Canyon Trail leads into the park's interior and up to 1,800 feet. There are two environmental hike-in campsites that are a good base from which to hang out, watch sunsets and wander around on foot. Permission to use these sites and leave your vehicle overnight in the day-use parking area can be obtained by calling MISTIX at (800) 444-7275. There is no water at the site, so you will need to pack it in. McWay Creek runs year-round and tumbles along the bottom of the canyon of the same name, dumping out into the ocean via a small waterfall. By heading over on the Ewoldsen Trail from the McWay Canyon Trail, you can hook up with the Tan Bark Trail and then head into the Ventana Wilderness. Remember that you will need a wilderness permit to set foot in the wilderness area.

---

## 8. PINE RIDGE TRAIL    23.1 mi/3.0 days

*Reference:* **In Los Padres National Forest, south of Big Sur; map F1, grid i8.**

*User groups:* Hikers, dogs and horses. No mountain bikes allowed. No wheelchair facilities.

*Permits:* No permits are required except during fire season, when a campfire permit is required for stoves or fires. Contact the Monterey Ranger District at (408) 385-5434 for more information.

*Directions:* From Highway 101 in Greenfield, approximately 60 miles north of Paso Robles and 33 miles south of Salinas, drive west on Monterey County Road G-16. Head west for approximately 29 miles to Tassajara Road and turn south. After 1.3 miles, bear left at the junction with Cachagua Road. Drive, much of the way is unpaved, to China Camp, a public campground and the trailhead. Roadside parking is limited. The road can become impassable during wet weather so phone ahead to check conditions.

*Maps:* Send $3 to the USDA-Forest Service, 630 Sansome Street, San Francisco, CA 94111 and ask for the Los Padres National Forest map. For topographic maps, ask for Chews Ridge and Ventana Cones from the USGS.

*Who to contact:* Los Padres National Forest, Monterey Ranger District, 406 South Mildred, King City, CA 93930; (408) 385-5434.

*Trail notes:* This loop trip takes you into the largest wilderness area in the south coast ranges. High valleys, open meadows, pine forests, decent swimming holes and picturesque canyons and waterfalls are on the menu for this trek. The best time to visit is between October and May. Snow can dust the area in winter and the summer can be unbearably hot. Hike the Pine Ridge Trail to Church Creek Divide, then take the Carmel River Trail to Pine Valley Camp, your next point of water. Continue hiking on the Carmel River Trail to the Carmel River Trail junction, still staying on the Carmel River Trail. Numerous river crossings of the Carmel River can become challenging in the winter months during peak runoff—use caution. Plan on spending the night at either Hiding Camp or Buckskin Flat. At Carmel River Camp, the trail joins with the Miller Canyon Trail. Turn onto the Miller Canyon Trail and, depending on your mood, hike out the 9.4 miles to China Camp and your car, or hike to Miller Canyon Camp for the night and then out the next morning.

*Special note:* Since the Miller Canyon Trail is not consistently maintained, and because of the fast growth rate of underbrush as well as possible flooding, we would recommend calling ahead to determine the trail's condition. If the trail is seriously overgrown, it can be difficult to find. Carry two quarts of water with you at all times—water sources are limited. Watch out for poison oak, which appears to absolutely love this climate and soil conditions. Also, this is prime tick country so check yourself and check your friends for ticks—every night and every lunch break.

# Leave No Trace Tips

## Respect other users

- Horseback riders have priority over hikers. Step to the downhill side of the trail and talk softly when encountering horseback riders.

- Hikers and horseback riders have priority over mountain bikers. When mountain bikers encounter other users, even on wide trails, they should pass at an extremely slow speed. On very narrow trails, they should dismount and get off to the side, so the hiker or horseback rider can pass without having their trip disrupted.

- Mountain bikes are not permitted on most single-track trails and are expressly prohibited on all portions of the Pacific Crest Trail, in designated wilderness areas and on most state park trails. Mountain bikers breaking these rules should be confronted, told to dismount and walk their bikes until they reach a legal area.

- It is illegal for horseback riders to break off branches that may lay in the path of wilderness trails.

- Horseback riders on overnight trips are prohibited from camping in many areas, and are usually required to keep stock animals in specific areas where they can do no damage to the landscape.

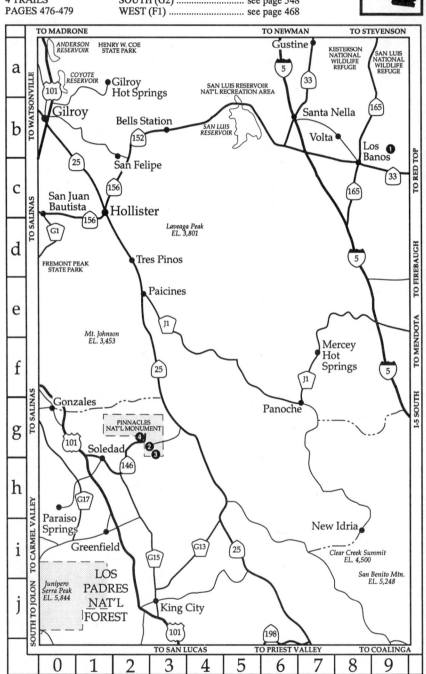

**Map F2 featuring:** Los Banos Wildlife Area, Pinnacles National Monument, Soledad

## 1. GRASSLAND ECOLOGICAL AREA/LOS BANOS WILDLIFE AREA  1.0 mi/1.0 hr

*Reference:* **Near Los Banos; map F2, grid b9.**

*User groups:* Hikers, dogs and mountain bikes (on the roads only). No horses allowed. No wheelchair facilities.

*Permits:* A $2.50 permit is required and may be obtained from the Los Banos Wildlife Area office or by self-registration at the area entrance when waterfowl hunting season is not open (approximately mid-January through September).

*Directions:* From Interstate 5 and Highway 152, east of San Jose, head east on Highway 152 to Los Banos. Turn left onto Mercy Springs Road and drive to Henry Miller Avenue. Turn right onto Henry Miller Avenue and drive to the signed wildlife area entrance.

*Maps:* For topographic maps, ask for Volta and Los Banos from the USGS.

*Who to contact:* Los Banos Wildlife Area, 18110 West Henry Miller Avenue, Los Banos, CA 93635; (209) 826-0463; or Grassland Water District, 22759 South Mercy Springs Road, Los Banos, CA 93635; (209) 826-5188.

*Trail notes:* This is the center of the largest remaining wetland in the state of California. Wildflowers are superb in the spring. Wildlife and waterfowl viewing is best in the fall. Viewing can be restricted during hunting season for obvious reasons. There really aren't formal trails throughout this area, although there is ample opportunity to get out of your car and walk along the dirt roads and levees where permissible—private land and inholdings are everywhere so you must check with either the Los Banos Wildlife Area or the Grassland Water District for specific areas that are currently open. Photography blinds are available by reservation. Map and bird lists are also available. Look for concentrations of white-faced ibis, sandhill cranes, and wintering waterfowl. In the spring, birds of prey frequent the area. Pack along your binoculars for sure. Guided interpretive tours/walks are offered within the Environmental Education Area—call (209) 826-5188. By car, you can drive through the heart of the wetlands on Highway 165, five miles north of Los Banos to Santa Fe Grade, heading northwest towards Gustine. Highway 165 features an auto tour through Kesterson, San Luis and Merced National Wildlife Refuges. You can leave your vehicle in certain areas to stretch your legs. Call (209) 826-3508 for information.

## 2. HIGH PEAK LOOP  5.0 mi/2.5 hrs

*Reference:* **At Pinnacles National Monument, east of Soledad on Highway 101; map F2, grid g3.**

*User groups:* Hikers and limited access for horses. Horses are allowed only on the Bench Trail and old Pinnacles Trail on weekdays from June to September, 8:30 a.m to 5 p.m. No mountain bikes or dogs are allowed. No wheelchair facilities.

*Permits:* Day-use permits are required and are good for one week. The day-use entry fee for the park is $4. There is no backcountry camping allowed.

**Directions:** From Hollister, head south on Highway 25 for 35 miles to Highway 146. Turn right (west) onto Highway 146 at the sign indicating Pinnacles National Monument. Drive approximately 3.5 miles and turn left at a sign indicating the main entrance and visitor's center/picnic area for Pinnacles National Monument.

**Maps:** A trail guide is free with your permit. For a topographic map, ask for North Chalone Peak from the USGS.

**Who to contact:** Pinnacles National Monument, 5000 Highway 146, Paicines, CA 95043; (408) 389-4485.

**Trail notes:** Both maintained and unmaintained wilderness wandering opportunities draw visitors from all over the world—and no wonder. This is a rocky and colorful playground for outdoors enthusiasts of all ages. March and April are perhaps the best times to visit the monument as the wildflowers are in full bloom and a more colorful spectacle would be hard to imagine. Tom calls the Pinnacles "one of the few places where you can stop the world and jump off," if only for an hour or two. The High Peak Loop has no water along the entire path and can get quite hot under a late morning or early afternoon sun—pack along plenty of water and wear a shade hat. From the parking area opposite the visitor's center, begin hiking up the Bear Gulch Trail to the High Peak Trail, forking to the right three-tenths of a mile from the visitors center. The trail winds and climbs through increasingly fascinating rock outcroppings and formations up to Pinnacle Rocks and the jagged crags that make up Scout Peak. From here, the trail heads west, following along the edge of the ridge, winding in and around the crags and, at times, ascends and descends the rock faces themselves via steps cut into the stone with accompanying hand rails provided for safety. Pick up the Condor Gulch Trail and descend gradually back to the parking area and your car.

## 3. BEAR GULCH CAVES TRAIL   2.0 mi/1.0 hr

**Reference:** At Pinnacles National Monument, east of Soledad on Highway 101; map F2, grid g3.

**User groups:** Hikers and limited access to horses. Horses are allowed only on the Bench Trail and old Pinnacles Trail on weekdays from June to September, 8:30 a.m to 5 p.m. No mountain bikes or dogs are allowed. No wheelchair facilities.

**Permits:** Day-use permits are required and are good for one week. The day-use entry fee for the park is $4. There is no backcountry camping allowed.

**Directions:** From Hollister, head south on Highway 25 for 35 miles to Highway 146. Turn right (west) onto Highway 146 at the sign indicating Pinnacles National Monument. Drive approximately 3.5 miles and turn left at a sign indicating the main entrance and visitor's center/picnic area for Pinnacles National Monument.

**Maps:** A trail guide is free with your permit. For a topographic map, ask for North Chalone Peak from the USGS.

**Who to contact:** Pinnacles National Monument, 5000 Highway 146, Paicines, CA 95043; (408) 389-4485.

**Trail notes:** Bear Gulch Caves are subject to closure if there are heavy rains or earthquakes. While this can be disappointing, it beats the heck out of being beaned on the noggin by falling rocks, if you want our opinion. This cave walk is self-guided and requires a flashlight. Children will absolutely love this short walk into the earth's bosom—actually talus caves created from erosion of fallen rocks. The sound of a running stream will keep you company throughout the walk. Once you emerge, head back to the parking area on the Moses Springs Trail or hook up with the High Peak Trail and begin trekking on Michael's favorite walk in these parts, the High Peak Loop (see hike number 2).

---

## 4. THE BALCONIES TRAIL    1.8 mi/1.0 hr

*Reference:* At Pinnacles National Monument, east of Soledad on Highway 101; map F2, grid g2.

*User groups:* Hikers and limited access to horses. Horses are allowed only on the Bench Trail and old Pinnacles Trail on weekdays from June to September, 8:30 a.m to 5 p.m. No mountain bikes or dogs are allowed. No wheelchair facilities.

*Permits:* Day-use permits are required and are good for one week. The day-use entry fee for the park is $4. There is no backcountry camping allowed.

*Directions:* From Highway 101 at Soledad, take Highway 146 (Shirttail Gulch Road) and drive 12 miles to the Chaparral Ranger Station and the west entrance.

*Maps:* A trail guide is free with your permit. For a topographic map, ask for North Chalone Peak from the USGS.

*Who to contact:* Pinnacles National Monument, 5000 Highway 146, Paicines, CA 95043; (408) 389-4485.

*Trail notes:* The Balconies Trail is perhaps the most tame of all the trails in the park and is perfect for families with young children. From the Chaparral Ranger Station and parking area, hike on the Balconies Trail along Chalone Creek to the Balconies Cliffs and Balconies Caves. Be sure to carry flashlights for use in the caves. Caves may be closed at any time and caution should be used, due to low ceilings and slippery rocks.

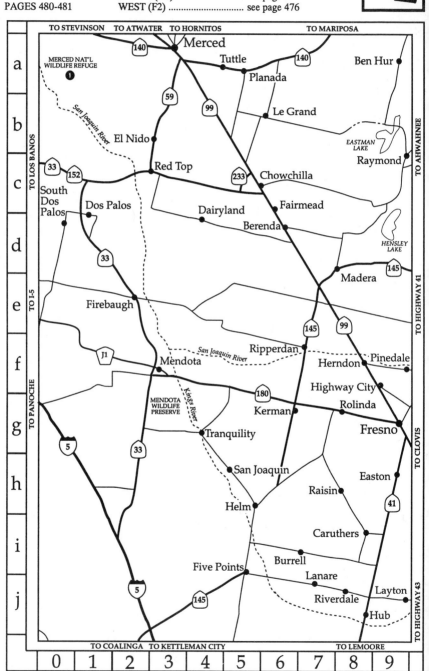

# 1. MERCED NATIONAL   1.0 mi/1.0 hr 🄳 ▲🄳
# WILDLIFE REFUGE/GRASSLAND WETLANDS
# WILDLIFE AREA

*Reference:* **Merced National Wildlife Refuge; map F3, grid a0.**

*User groups:* Hikers, dogs and mountain bikes (on roads only). No horses allowed. No wheelchair facilities.

*Permits:* No permits are needed, but you are required to sign in at the self registration at the area entrance. The area is closed to visiting during shooting days within the hunting season. Hunting season is Wednesday and Saturday mid-October to January—call for specific opening dates. Parking and access are free.

*Directions:* From Interstate 5 and Highway 152, east of San Jose, head east on Highway 152 to Los Banos. Drive through Los Banos to Highway 59. At Highway 59 turn left (north) to Sandy Mush Road, turn left again and follow the signs, driving 7.5 miles to the refuge entrance on the left.

*Maps:* For a topographic map, ask for Sandy Mush from the USGS. A free information and interpretive kit is provided covering three area refuges: Merced, San Luis and Kesterson. Call (209) 826-3508 or write National Wildlife Refuge Complex, P.O. Box 2176, Los Banos, CA 93635.

*Who to contact:* Merced Wildlife Refuge, P.O. Box 2176, Los Banos, CA 93635; (209) 826-3508; or Grassland Water District, (209) 826-5188.

*Trail notes:* This is the center of the largest remaining wetland in the state of California. Wildflowers are superb in the spring. Wildlife and waterfowl viewing is best in the fall. Viewing can be restricted during hunting season for obvious reasons. There really aren't formal trails throughout this area, although there is ample opportunity to get out of your car and walk along the dirt roads and levees where permissible—private land and inholdings are everywhere so you must check with either the Merced National Wildlife Refuge or the Grassland Water District for specific areas that are currently open. Map and bird lists are also available. There is a viewing tower that has been constructed to facilitate bird and wildlife watching in the area. Look for concentrations of white-faced ibis, sandhill cranes, and wintering waterfowl. In the spring, birds of prey frequent the area. Pack along your binoculars for certain. If you like this area, there is much more to be seen. Contact the Grassland Water District for information on guided walks and other wildlife areas within the Water District at (209) 826-5188.

## MAP F4

CEN-CAL MAP ..................... see page 466
adjoining maps
NORTH (E4) ........................ see page 402
EAST (F5) ............................ see page 492
SOUTH (G4) ....................... see page 556
WEST (F3) ........................... see page 480

13 TRAILS
PAGES 482-491

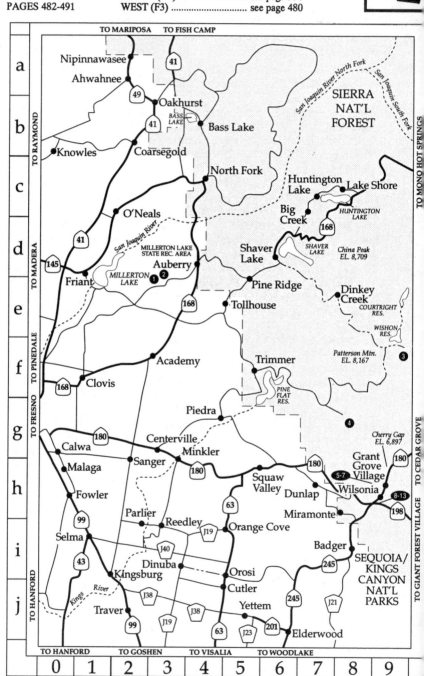

TO MARIPOSA     TO FISH CAMP

**a**
Nipinnawasee
Ahwahnee
41
49
Oakhurst
BASS
LAKE
Bass Lake

San Joaquin River North Fork
San Joaquin South Fork

SIERRA
NAT'L
FOREST

TO RAYMOND

**b**
41
Knowles
Coarsegold

Huntington
Lake     Lake Shore

**c**
North Fork
Big
Creek
168
HUNTINGTON
LAKE

TO MONO HOT SPRINGS

**d**
O'Neals
41
145
San Joaquin River
MILLERTON LAKE
STATE REC. AREA
Auberry
① ②
MILLERTON
LAKE
Friant
Shaver
Lake
SHAVER
LAKE
China Peak
EL. 8,709

TO MADERA

**e**
Pine Ridge
168
Tollhouse
Dinkey
Creek
COURTRIGHT
RES.
WISHON
RES.
③

TO PINEDALE

**f**
Academy
Trimmer
Patterson Mtn.
EL. 8,167
168
Clovis
PINE
FLAT
RES.

TO FRESNO

**g**
Piedra
④
Cherry Gap
EL. 6,897
180
Centerville
Calwa
Minkler
Grant
Grove
Village
180
180

TO CEDAR GROVE

**h**
Malaga
Sanger
180
Squaw
Valley
Dunlap
5-7
Wilsonia
8-13
198
Fowler
63
99
Miramonte

TO GIANT FOREST VILLAGE

**i**
Parlier
Reedley
J19
Orange Cove
Selma
43
J40
Badger
245
SEQUOIA/
KINGS
CANYON
NAT'L
PARKS

TO HANFORD

**j**
Dinuba
Kingsburg
Orosi
Cutler
Yettem
245
J21
Kings River
J38
Traver
99
J19
J38
63
J23
201
Elderwood

TO HANFORD     TO GOSHEN     TO VISALIA     TO WOODLAKE

0   1   2   3   4   5   6   7   8   9

**Map F4 featuring:** Sierra National Forest, Millerton Lake State Recreation Area, San Joaquin River, Sequoia National Park, Kings Canyon National Park, Sequoia National Forest

## 1. SAN JOAQUIN RIVER TRAIL 2.5 mi/1.0 hr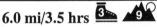

*Reference:* **Near Fresno; map F4, grid d3.**

*User groups:* Hikers, horses, mountain bikes and dogs. No wheelchair facilities.

*Permits:* No permits are required.

*Directions:* From Fresno travel east on Highway 168 to Prather and follow the signs to Auberry. Access the trail via Power House Road to Smalley Road.

*Maps:* For a topographic map of the area, ask for Millerton Lake East from the USGS.

*Who to contact:* Bureau of Land Management, Folsom Resource Area, 63 Natoma Street, Folsom, CA 95630; (916) 985-4474.

*Trail notes:* This 2.5-mile BLM section of the 11-mile trail from the Sierra National Forest to Millerton Lake State Recreation Area offers breathtaking views of the San Joaquin River Gorge. Wildflowers will leave you wide-eyed in the spring. Fishing is considered quite good in Millerton Lake, but not all that great in the San Joaquin River upstream of the lake.

## 2. SQUAW LEAP 6.0 mi/3.5 hrs

*Reference:* **Near Fresno; map F4, grid d3.**

*User groups:* Hikers, horses, mountain bikes and dogs. No wheelchair facilities.

*Permits:* No permits are required.

*Directions:* From Fresno, take travel east on Highway 168 to Prather. Follow the signs to Auberry. Access the trail via Power House Road to Smalley Road.

*Maps:* For a topographic map of the area, ask for Millerton Lake East from the USGS.

*Who to contact:* Bureau of Land Management, Folsom Resource Area, 63 Natoma Street, Folsom, CA 95630; (916) 985-4474.

*Trail notes:* Beginning at the Squaw Creek Campground, a developed and well-marked trail loops up and down the canyon. Nice views of the San Joaquin River Gorge reward the visitor to this region. Wildflowers abound in the spring.

## 3. CROWN VALLEY TRAIL 11.8 mi/6.0 hrs

*Reference:* **In Sierra National Forest, near Sequoia and Kings Canyon national parks; map F4, grid f9.**

*User groups:* Hikers, horses and dogs (outside the national park boundaries). No mountain bikes. No wheelchair facilities.

*Permits:* Day-use permits are not required. Wilderness permits are required for overnight use. For more information, contact the Kings River Ranger District at (209) 855-8321.

*Directions:* From Fresno, and Highway 99, drive north on Highway 41 and then east on Highway 168 to Shaver Lake. At Shaver Lake, turn right onto Dinkey Creek Road. Drive on Dinkey Creek Road for approximately 26

miles to the Courtright/Wishon intersection. Turn right (south) toward Wishon Reservoir and drive approximately 6.5 miles to the signed Crown Valley Trailhead.

*Maps:* Send $3 to the USDA-Forest Service, 630 Sansome Street, San Francisco, CA 94111 and ask for the Sequoia National Forest map. For topographic maps, ask for Rough Spur and Tehipite Dome from the USGS. The Forest Service also publishes a large-sized topographic map titled *John Muir Wilderness and Sequoia/Kings Canyon Wilderness.* The price is $6 and can be ordered from the Forest Service address listed above. Tom Harrison Cartography publishes an excellent map of the area. Call (415) 456-7940 and ask for the recreation map of Sequoia and Kings Canyon national parks. The cost is $5.95 plus tax and shipping. Trails Illustrated also publishes a super map, Sequoia Kings Canyon National Parks. The cost is $7.95 and may be ordered by calling (800) 962-1643.

*Who to contact:* Sierra National Forest, Kings River Ranger District, 34849 Maxon Road, Sanger, CA 93657; (209) 855-8321. In the summer only, you can also contact the Dinkey Creek Ranger Station at (209) 841-3404.

*Trail notes:* This trip is a great one early in the year when the rest of the high country is still buried under snow. Spring is outstanding along the way as the trail passes alongside a pretty stream loaded with wildflowers. We recommend that you don't head out in September and October during deer season as the area is chock full of hunters. From the trailhead, head out on the Crown Valley Trail. Hike as far as you desire, although for a reasonable day trek we would advise going no further than Cabin Creek. This is a good overnight spot, too, for a quick weekender. Expect heavy weekend crowds, as this is a prime access trail into the John Muir Wilderness.

*Special note:* Mosquitoes fly thick and heavy here in the spring, so pack plenty of repellent.

---

# 4. KINGS RIVER    5.0 mi/3.0 hrs
# NATIONAL RECREATION TRAIL

*Reference:* In Sierra National Forest, near Sequoia and Kings Canyon national parks; map F4, grid g8.

*User groups:* Hikers, horses, dogs (outside the national park boundaries) and mountain bikes. No wheelchair facilities.

*Permits:* Day-use permits are not required. Wilderness permits are required for overnight use. For more information, contact the Kings River Ranger District at (209) 855-8321.

*Directions:* From Fresno and Highway 99, take the Belmont Avenue exit and head east on Belmont Avenue. In approximately 15 miles, Belmont becomes Trimmer Springs Road. Drive to Trimmer Springs Road's intersection with Garnet Dyke Road (dirt) and turn right onto Garnet Dyke. (Garnet Dyke is approximately 70 miles from Highway 99.) Drive 13 miles on Garnet Dyke to the trailhead parking.

*Maps:* Send $3 to the USDA-Forest Service, 630 Sansome Street, San Francisco, CA 94111 and ask for the Sequoia National Forest map. For topographic maps, ask for Verplank Ridge and Hume from the USGS. The Forest Service also publishes a large-sized topographic map titled *John Muir Wilderness and Sequoia/Kings Canyon Wilderness.* The price is $6 and can be ordered from the Forest Service address listed above. For other maps of this area, see "maps" under hike number 3.

*Who to contact:* Sierra National Forest, Kings River Ranger District, 34849 Maxon Road, Sanger, CA 93657; (209) 855-8321.

*Trail notes:* Begin hiking along the trail at the trailhead. Pack along your fishing rod because the trout fishing is super. The best time to visit is in the spring when all the dancing poppies are in bloom. The recreation trail follows along the rugged course carved by the Kings River through Kings Canyon. At Garlic Spur, about four miles out, you will be awarded with outstanding views far up the Kings River and of the Windy Cliffs. Wind your way down to Garlic Meadow Creek, five miles from the trailhead, which offers super picnic spots. We would not recommend hiking up Garlic Meadow Creek any distance, as it is choked with underbrush and quite hazardous due to the loose nature of the terrain. When ready, retrace your steps.

*Special note:* Mosquitoes fly thick and heavy here in the spring so pack plenty of repellent. Also, perform tick checks periodically. You will also note that poison oak grows so thickly along the trail that you would think they are cultivating it—stay away from the leaves of three. Finally, we don't recommend hiking this trail in summer—it's too hot!

---

# 5. BOOLE TREE TRAIL      2.0 mi/0.75 hr

*Reference:* **In Kings Canyon National Park; map F4, grid h8.**

*User groups:* Hikers and horses. No mountain bikes or dogs allowed. No wheelchair facilities.

*Permits:* Day-use permits are not required. A $5 entrance fee is collected at Big Stump for Sequoia/Kings Canyon national parks.

*Directions:* From Fresno and Highway 99, drive east on Highway 180 to Grant Grove and the park's Big Stump entrance. From Grant Grove, drive approximately 4.5 miles north on Highway 180 and turn left on Forest Service Road 13S55, clearly signed as Converse Basin/Stump Meadow/ Boole Tree Trail. The parking is located at a wide turnaround area. Park out of the way of other vehicles who may wish to visit.

*Maps:* Send $3 to the USDA-Forest Service, 630 Sansome Street, San Francisco, CA 94111 and ask for the Sequoia National Forest map. For a topographic map, ask for Hume from the USGS. The Forest Service also publishes a large-sized topographic map titled *John Muir Wilderness and Sequoia/Kings Canyon Wilderness*. The price is $6 and can be ordered from the Forest Service address listed above. For other maps of this area, see "maps" under hike number 3.

*Who to contact:* For general information, contact Sequoia and Kings Canyon National Parks, Ash Mountain, Three Rivers, CA 93271; (209) 565-3341. For specific information about Kings Canyon National Park, contact Kings Canyon Visitors Center, Grant Grove, CA 93633; (209) 335-2856. Sequoia National Forest, Hume Lake Ranger District, 35860 East Kings Canyon Road, Dunlap, CA 93621; (209) 338-2251.

*Trail notes:* Ironically, the hike's namesake, Frank Boole, was the one responsible for heading a logging operation that destroyed much of the area around the giant tree that commemorates him—perfect! From the trailhead, hike up to the base of a magnificent Giant Sequoia that dwarfs all the second growth sequoias around it. Although the tree ranks in the top ten for largest in the world, it is not as large as the Forest Service claims. They say it comes in third. When ready, continue hiking on a relatively new section of the trail, completing a pleasant loop trip back to your car.

---

# 6. CABIN CREEK TRAIL     2.0 mi/1.0 hr

*Reference:* **In Sequoia National Forest, near Sequoia and Kings Canyon national parks; map F4, grid h8.**

*User groups:* Hikers and horses. No mountain bikes or dogs allowed. No wheelchair facilities.

*Permits:* Day-use permits are not required. Wilderness permits are required for overnight use. A $5 entrance fee is collected at Big Stump for Sequoia/Kings Canyon national parks.

*Directions:* From Fresno and Highway 99, drive east on Highway 180 to Grant Grove and the park's Big Stump entrance. From Grant Grove, drive approximately 4.5 miles north on Highway 180 and turn left on Forest Service Road 13S55, clearly signed as Converse Basin/Stump Meadow/Boole Tree Trail. The parking is located at a wide turnaround area. Park out of the way of other vehicles who may wish to visit.

*Maps:* Send $3 to the USDA-Forest Service, 630 Sansome Street, San Francisco, CA 94111 and ask for the Sequoia National Forest map. For a topographic map, ask for Hume from the USGS. The Forest Service also publishes a large-sized topographic map titled *John Muir Wilderness and Sequoia/Kings Canyon Wilderness.* The price is $6 and can be ordered from the Forest Service address listed above. For other maps of this area, see "maps" under hike number 3.

*Who to contact:* Sequoia National Forest, Hume Lake Ranger District, 35860 East Kings Canyon Road, Dunlap, CA 93621; (209) 338-2251.

*Trail notes:* Although not marked, the route follows Forest Service Road 13S55 out of the parking area and up along its rugged track to a barbed wire fence. From here, the treadway continues on an old logging skidway to the edge of Cabin Creek Grove—a wonderfully secluded grove of sequoias that managed to escape the logging curse that fell upon the surrounding mountain area. In the grove, trails wander this way and that, but keep your bearings so you don't get turned around—easy to do in here. When ready, retrace your steps.

---

# 7. CHICAGO STUMP TRAIL     0.5 mi/0.5 hr

*Reference:* **In Sequoia National Forest, near Sequoia and Kings Canyon national parks; map F4, grid h8.**

*User groups:* Hikers and horses. No mountain bikes or dogs allowed. No wheelchair facilities.

*Permits:* Day-use permits are not required. A $5 entrance fee is collected at Big Stump for Sequoia/Kings Canyon national parks.

*Directions:* From Fresno and Highway 99, drive east on Highway 180 to Grant Grove and the park's Big Stump entrance. From Grant Grove, drive approximately three miles north on Highway 180 and turn left on Forest Service Road 13S03. Drive for 1.9 miles to a road junction. Head right onto Forest Service Road 13S65 and drive one-tenth of a mile to the signed trailhead for Chicago Stump.

*Maps:* Send $3 to the USDA-Forest Service, 630 Sansome Street, San Francisco, CA 94111 and ask for the Sequoia National Forest map. For a topographic map, ask for Hume from the USGS. The Forest Service also publishes a large-sized topographic map titled *John Muir Wilderness and Sequoia/Kings Canyon Wilderness*. The price is $6 and can be ordered from the Forest Service address listed above. For other maps of this area, see "maps" under hike number 3.

*Who to contact:* Sequoia National Forest, Hume Lake Ranger District, 35860 East Kings Canyon Road, Dunlap, CA 93621; (209) 338-2251.

*Trail notes:* The devastation that rained down upon Converse Basin during the logging heyday is all too evident here. The signed trail leads to fire-blackened Chicago Stump that, until it was cut down so a cross-section could be displayed at the Chicago World's Fair in the late 1800s, was one of the world's largest trees. Wander slowly around the stump's 80-foot perimeter and wonder "what if?" When ready, retrace your steps.

---

## 8. PARK RIDGE TRAIL     5.0 mi/2.5 hr

*Reference:* **In Kings Canyon National Park; map F4, grid h9.**

*User groups:* Hikers and horses. No mountain bikes or dogs allowed. No wheelchair facilities.

*Permits:* Day-use permits are not required. A $5 fee is charged at the park entrance.

*Directions:* From Fresno and Highway 99, drive east on Highway 180 to Grant Grove and the park's Big Stump entrance. From Grant Grove, drive up a signed road indicating Panoramic Point—RVs and cars with trailers are prohibited. The road dead ends at a parking area.

*Maps:* For topographic maps, ask for General Grant Grove and Hume from the USGS. For other maps of this area, see "maps" under hike number 3.

*Who to contact:* For general information, contact Sequoia and Kings Canyon National Parks, Ash Mountain, Three Rivers, CA 93271; (209) 565-3341. For specific information about Kings Canyon National Park, contact Kings Canyon Visitors Center, Grant Grove, CA 93633; (209) 335-2856.

*Trail notes:* Views draw crowds and this trail is no exception. From the parking area, you will hike up the old road to a fire lookout—one of the few lookouts still operating today. From the start, the trail is paved, leading up to Panoramic Point, elevation 7,520 feet. The views from here are expansive and impressive; there are interpretive signs to help you identify the landmarks in Kings Canyon below. The trail continues along the ridge with nifty views to be enjoyed all along the route. At 1.5 miles you will meet up with a fire road. You can head up the fire road to the lookout, but most people prefer to pick up the trail, branching off the road on the other side about 100 feet to the south. Don't head off downridge on the Manzanita or Azalea Trails, which also branch off from this junction. Watch the signs and stay on the Park Ridge Trail, through the forest and back out onto the fire road at about 2.5 miles. Hike the rest of the way, only about a quarter mile, up to the lookout at 7,540 feet. Return the way you came or descend back on the fire road—your pick, but the fire road is a tad shorter.

## 9. HITCHCOCK MEADOW     2.0 mi/1.0 hr

*Reference:* **In Kings Canyon National Park; map F4, grid h9.**

*User groups:* Hikers and horses. No mountain bikes or dogs allowed. No wheelchair facilities.

*Permits:* Day-use permits are not required. Wilderness permits are required for overnight use. A third of the permits are available daily on a first-come, first-served basis. The remainder are available by reservation at least 14 days in advance. For more information, contact the Sequoia and Kings Canyon national parks at (209)335-2856. A $5 park entrance fee is charged.

*Directions:* From Fresno and Highway 99, drive east on Highway 180 to Grant Grove and the park's Big Stump entrance. Continue south approximately one-half mile to the Big Stump parking area.

*Maps:* For topographic maps, ask for General Grant Grove and Hume from the USGS. For other maps of this area, see "maps" under hike number 3.

*Who to contact:* For general information, contact Sequoia and Kings Canyon National Parks, Ash Mountain, Three Rivers, CA 93271; (209) 565-3341. For specific information about Kings Canyon National Park, contact Kings Canyon Visitors Center, Grant Grove, CA 93633; (209) 335-2856.

*Trail notes:* From the trailhead, hike on the Hitchcock Meadow Trail. Your ultimate destination is Viola Falls—a series of pretty cascades that, if the flow is strong enough, become one long torrent of water. The trail is quite pretty, but honestly, the falls are the reason for hiking it. Once at the falls, spend some time kicking back among the ferns, sequoias and dogwoods that grace the stream's edge. Do not try to leave the trail and venture down the canyon as it is steep, slippery, rocky and dangerous. Retrace your steps when ready.

---

## 10. SOUTH BOUNDARY TRAIL    4.0 mi/2.0 hrs

*Reference:* **In Kings Canyon National Park; map F4, grid h9.**

*User groups:* Hikers and horses. No mountain bikes or dogs allowed. No wheelchair facilities.

*Permits:* Day-use permits are not required. Wilderness permits are required for overnight use. A third of the permits are available daily on a first-come, first-served basis. The remainder are available by reservation at least 14 days in advance. For more information, contact the Sequoia and Kings Canyon national parks at (209) 335-2856. A $5 park entrance fee is charged.

*Directions:* From Fresno and Highway 99, drive east on Highway 180 to Grant Grove and the Grant Grove Visitor's Center. The trailhead begins at the Grant Tree parking area.

*Maps:* For topographic maps, ask for General Grant Grove and Hume from the USGS. For other maps of this area, see "maps" under hike number 3.

*Who to contact:* For general information, contact Sequoia and Kings Canyon National Parks, Ash Mountain, Three Rivers, CA 93271; (209) 565-3341. For specific information about Kings Canyon National Park, contact Kings Canyon Visitors Center, Grant Grove, CA 93633; (209) 335-2856.

*Trail notes:* From the trailhead, the official South Boundary Trail skirts a base camp for firefighters and then climbs up through forest for about one mile to the Sunset Trail. If you have the time and energy, a quick sidetrip down the Sunset Trail will take you to Ella Falls—roundtrip one mile. Stay on South Boundary Trail past Viola Falls (see hike number 9). Keep hiking on South Boundary, across Sequoia Creek and then up steeply to a long meadow and the junction with Hitchcock Meadow Trail—about one and three-quarter miles from the start. Hike along the meadow's edge on South Boundary and then begin climbing steeply again to the top of the ridge where the trail will contour, meeting up with Sequoia Creek again approximately two and a quarter miles out. The trail continues on an upward bend up to Highway 180, where it crosses near Sunset Campground (three miles out) to meet up with the pretty Azalea Trail. Turn left (north) and hike back to the parking area.

---

## 11. SUNSET TRAIL    6.0 mi/3.5 hrs

*Reference:* **In Kings Canyon National Park; map F4, grid h9.**

*User groups:* Hikers and horses. No mountain bikes or dogs allowed. No wheelchair facilities.

*Permits:* Day-use permits are not required. Wilderness permits are required for overnight use. A third of the permits are available daily on a first-come, first-served basis. The remainder are available by reservation at least 14 days in advance. For more information, contact the Sequoia and Kings Canyon national parks at . A $5 park entrance fee is charged.

*Directions:* From Fresno and Highway 99, drive east on Highway 180 to Grant Grove and the Grant Grove Visitor's Center. The trailhead begins across the highway from the visitor's center.

*Maps:* For topographic maps, ask for General Grant Grove and Hume from the USGS. For other maps of this area, see "maps" under hike number 3.

*Who to contact:* For general information, contact Sequoia and Kings Canyon National Parks, Ash Mountain, Three Rivers, CA 93271; (209) 565-3341. For specific information about Kings Canyon National Park, contact Kings Canyon Visitors Center, Grant Grove, CA 93633; (209) 335-2856.

*Trail notes:* Waterfalls, beautiful pine trees, and nifty views should be enough to inspire the effort to park the car, fight the often crowded trailhead and then head off into relative solitude. From the trailhead, hike toward the amphitheater and then head off toward Ella Falls, walking past Sunset Campground. You will love the sugarpines you pass by on the first part of the trip. Ella Falls is a wonderful cascade, plunging down 50 feet through a series of granite bowls. Azalea, alder and willow frame the scenery. Further on, the trail passes through a YMCA camp which is private—stay on the trail! After passing through some lush meadows, the trail ends at Grant Tree parking area. Hike through the parking lot and pick up the trail on the east side that leads back to the Grant Grove Visitor's Center.

---

## 12. BIG STUMP TRAIL    1.0 mi/0.5 hr

*Reference:* **In Kings Canyon National Park; map F4, grid h9.**

*User groups:* Hikers and horses. No mountain bikes or dogs allowed. No wheelchair facilities.

*Permits:* Day-use permits are not required. Wilderness permits are required for overnight use. A third of the permits are available daily on a first-come, first-served basis. The remainder are available for reservation at least 14 days in advance. For more information, contact the Sequoia and Kings Canyon National Park at . A $5 park entrance fee is charged.

*Directions:* From Fresno and Highway 99, drive east on Highway 180 to Grant Grove and the park's Big Stump entrance. The trailhead for the Big Stump Trail is located one-half mile beyond the Big Stump entrance station.

*Maps:* For a topographic map, ask for Giant Forest from the USGS. For other maps of this area, see "maps" under hike number 3.

*Who to contact:* For general information, contact Sequoia and Kings Canyon National Parks, Ash Mountain, Three Rivers, CA 93271; (209) 565-3341. For specific information about Kings Canyon National Park, contact Kings Canyon Visitors Center, Grant Grove, CA 93633; (209) 335-2856.

*Trail notes:* Take a walk through a majestic though haunting graveyard of giant sequoia—cut down through indiscriminate logging in the late 1800s. True to national park form, there is even a vending machine at the start of the trail that dispenses an interpretive brochure detailing what you will encounter. Children will love this hike as there are huge stumps to clamber on.

---

# 13. NORTH GROVE LOOP TRAIL 1.5 mi/1.0 hr

*Reference:* In Kings Canyon National Park; map F4, grid h9.

*User groups:* Hikers and horses. No mountain bikes or dogs allowed. No wheelchair facilities.

*Permits:* Day-use permits are not required. Wilderness permits are required for overnight use. A third of the permits are available daily on a first-come, first-served basis. The remainder are available for reservation at least 14 days in advance. For more information, contact the Sequoia and Kings Canyon National Park at . A $5 park entrance fee is charged.

*Directions:* From Fresno and Highway 99, drive east on Highway 180 to Grant Grove and the park's Big Stump entrance. The trailhead begins at the lower end of the General Grant Tree parking area near where the recreational vehicles and tour buses park.

*Maps:* For topographic maps, ask for General Grant Grove and Hume from the USGS. For other maps of this area, see "maps" under hike number 3.

*Who to contact:* For general information, contact Sequoia and Kings Canyon National Parks, Ash Mountain, Three Rivers, CA 93271; (209) 565-3341. For specific information about Kings Canyon National Park, contact Kings Canyon Visitors Center, Grant Grove, CA 93633; (209) 335-2856.

*Trail notes:* This is a pleasant little loop trip that leaves the crowds of the entrance station and tourist attractions behind, allowing you to wander quietly among pines, sequoia and your thoughts. From the RV parking area, hike down the road to a sign indicating the North Grove Loop Trail. Within one-quarter mile, you will bear left (to the west) at a junction. The tread continues descending through old burns and logged areas dating back to the late 1800s, when logging was still a way of life here. About one mile or so from the start, you will arrive at another junction with the Millwood Fire Road. Head south, staying on the North Grove Loop Trail, and begin climbing in earnest. What? You thought this hike was all downhill? Nope. Within one-half mile you arrive at another junction with Sunset Trail. Keep climbing, still on the North Grove Loop and still heading uphill, back to the loop's end and a short jaunt back to the parking area and your car.

## LEAVE NO TRACE TIPS

### Travel lightly

• Visit the backcountry in small groups.

• Below tree line, always stay on designated trails.

• Do not cut across switchbacks.

• When traveling cross-country where no trails are available, follow animal trails or spread out with your group so no new routes are created.

• Read your map and orient yourself with landmarks, a compass and altimeter. Avoid marking trails with rock cairns, tree scars or ribbons.

# MAP F5

2 PCT SECTIONS
2 JMT SECTIONS
65 TRAILS
PAGES 492-541

CEN-CAL MAP ........................ see page 466
adjoining maps
NORTH (E5) ............................ see page 452
EAST (F6) ............................... see page 542
SOUTH (G5) ........................... see page 560
WEST (F4) .............................. see page 482

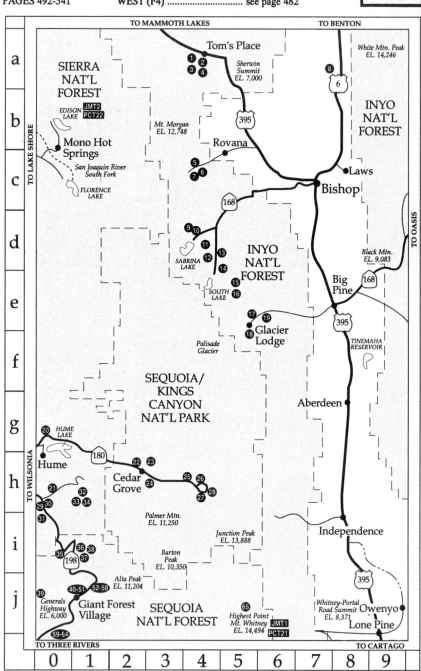

**Map F5 featuring:** Inyo National Forest, Sequoia National Park, Kings Canyon National Park, Lake Thomas Edison, Mono Hot Springs, Glacier Lodge, Cedar Grove, Mt. Whitney

## 1. HILTON LAKES TRAIL     10.5 mi/6.0 hrs

*Reference:* **West of Bishop, Inyo National Forest; map F5, grid a4.**

*User groups:* Hikers, dogs and horses. No mountain bikes allowed. No wheelchair facilities.

*Permits:* Day-use permits are not required. Wilderness permits are required for overnight use year-round. Between March 1 and May 31, advance reservations for quota trails are available by mail, $3 per person. Reservations must be picked up by 8 a.m. or they become available to others on a first-come, first-served basis. Permits are free on a first-come, first-served basis in person on the day of the trip. Arrive early as a strict trail quota is enforced. For more information, contact the White Mountain Ranger Station at (619) 873-2500.

*Directions:* From Bishop, drive north on Highway 395 to Tom's Place. Then drive up Rock Creek Canyon to the Rock Creek Pack Station.

*Maps:* Send $3 to the USDA-Forest Service, 630 Sansome Street, San Francisco, CA 94111 and ask for the Inyo National Forest map. The Forest Service also publishes a large-sized topographic map titled *John Muir Wilderness and Sequoia/Kings Canyon Wilderness*. It can be ordered from the Forest Service at the address listed above for $6. For USGS topographic maps of the area, ask for Mount Abbot, Convict Lake, Tom's Place and Mount Morgan from the USGS.

*Who to contact:* Inyo National Forest, White Mountain Ranger District, 798 North Main Street, Bishop, CA 93514; (619) 873-2500.

*Trail notes:* The Hilton Lakes Trail takes you through a forest of whitebark and lodgepole pine before it enters the peaceful basin of Hilton and Davis Lakes. All the while you are sucking up trail dust and feeling as if the trail is riding the back of a dragon (up and down and up and down and up and—you get the picture). Don't lose sight of the fact that it's the lakes you are coming to see and not the trail. At four miles you will come to a trail junction. Go left to reach Upper Hilton Lake, which contains golden and brook trout. Go right at the trail junction and you will arrive at granite-rimmed Lower Hilton and Davis Lakes, which contain brook and rainbow trout—pack your rod for sure. Also, bring along plenty of insect repellent!

## 2. TAMARACK LAKES TRAIL   11.0 mi/6.0 hrs

*Reference:* **West of Bishop, Inyo National Forest; map F5, grid a4.**

*User groups:* Hikers, dogs and horses. No mountain bikes allowed. No wheelchair facilities.

*Permits:* Day-use permits are not required. Wilderness permits are required for overnight use year-round. Between March 1 and May 31, advance reservations for quota trails are available by mail, $3 per person. Reservations must be picked up by 8 a.m. or they become available to others on a first-come, first-served basis. Permits are free on a first-come, first-served basis in person on the day of the trip. Arrive early as a strict trail quota is enforced. For more information, contact the White Mountain Ranger Station at (619) 873-2500.

*Directions:* From Bishop, drive north on Highway 395 to Tom's Place. Then drive up Rock Creek Canyon to Pine Grove Campground located at the east side of Rock Creek Lake.

*Maps:* Send $3 to the USDA-Forest Service, 630 Sansome Street, San Francisco, CA 94111 and ask for the Inyo National Forest map. The Forest Service also publishes a large-sized topographic map titled *John Muir Wilderness and Sequoia/Kings Canyon Wilderness.* The price is $6 and can be ordered from the Forest Service address listed above. For USGS topographic maps, ask for Mount Abbot, Convict Lake, Tom's Place and Mount Morgan from the USGS.

*Who to contact:* Inyo National Forest, White Mountain Ranger District, 798 North Main Street, Bishop, CA 93514; (619) 873-2500.

*Trail notes:* The Tamarack Lakes Trail begins at the eastern shore of Rock Creek Lake. The trail is steep initially, but soon levels out—hopefully before you do—and begins a moderate climb past the intermediate lakes and up to Tamarack and Buck lakes. Golden trout can be found in Tamarack Lake while brook and Lahonton cutthroat may be pulled from the waters of Dorothy Lake.

---

## 3. LITTLE LAKES VALLEY    9.0 mi/4.5 hrs

*Reference:* **West of Bishop, Inyo National Forest; map F5, grid a4.**

*User groups:* Hikers, dogs and horses. No mountain bikes allowed. No wheelchair facilities.

*Permits:* Day-use permits are not required. Wilderness permits are required for overnight use year-round. Between March 1 and May 31, advance reservations for quota trails are available by mail, $3 per person. Reservations must be picked up by 8 a.m. or they become available to others on a first-come, first-served basis. Permits are free on a first-come, first-served basis in person on the day of the trip. Arrive early as a strict trail quota is enforced. For more information, contact the White Mountain Ranger Station at (619) 873-2500.

*Directions:* From Bishop, drive north on Highway 395 to Tom's Place. Then drive up Rock Creek Canyon to the end of the road at Mosquito Flat. Trailhead parking is located at Mosquito Flat.

*Maps:* Send $3 to the USDA-Forest Service, 630 Sansome Street, San Francisco, CA 94111 and ask for the Inyo National Forest map. The Forest Service also publishes a large-sized topographic map titled *John Muir Wilderness and Sequoia/Kings Canyon Wilderness.* The price is $6 and can be ordered from the Forest Service address listed above. For USGS topographic maps, ask for Mount Abbot, Convict Lake, Tom's Place and Mount Morgan from the USGS.

*Who to contact:* Inyo National Forest, White Mountain Ranger District, 798 North Main Street, Bishop, CA 93514; (619) 873-2500.

*Trail notes:* In Little Lakes Valley, glacial activity becomes vividly evident. Surrounded by 13,000-foot peaks (Mt. Mills, Mt. Dade, Mt. Abbot and Bear Creek Spire), this charming valley has the typical profile of a U-shaped, glacier carved canyon. The lateral moraines that pushed to the sides of the valley by the force and flow of ice are now topped by lakes. The long chain of lakes has become very popular for fishermen and hikers. The Little Lakes Valley Trail begins at the Mosquito Trailhead and continues up and past Lower Morgan Lake, but for the purpose of a good day-hike, we have listed mileage to Lower Morgan Lake as it is a good turnaround point.

## 4. MONO PASS TRAIL 7.0 mi/4.5 hrs

*Reference:* **West of Bishop, Inyo National Forest; map F5, grid a4.**

*User groups:* Hikers, dogs and horses. No mountain bikes allowed. No wheelchair facilities.

*Permits:* Day-use permits are not required. Wilderness permits are required for overnight use year-round. Between March 1 and May 31, advance reservations for quota trails are available by mail, $3 per person. Reservations must be picked up by 8 a.m. or they become available to others on a first-come, first-served basis. Permits are free on a first-come, first-served basis in person on the day of the trip. Arrive early as a strict trail quota is enforced. For more information, contact the White Mountain Ranger Station at (619) 873-2500.

*Directions:* From Bishop, drive north on Highway 395 to Tom's Place. Then drive up Rock Creek Canyon to the end of the road at Mosquito Flat. Trailhead parking is located at Mosquito Flat.

*Maps:* Send $3 to the USDA-Forest Service, 630 Sansome Street, San Francisco, CA 94111 and ask for the Inyo National Forest map. The Forest Service also publishes a large-sized topographic map titled *John Muir Wilderness and Sequoia/Kings Canyon Wilderness*. The price is $6 and can be ordered from the Forest Service address listed above. For USGS topographic maps, ask for Mount Abbot, Convict Lake, Tom's Place and Mount Morgan from the USGS.

*Who to contact:* Inyo National Forest, White Mountain Ranger District, 798 North Main Street, Bishop, CA 93514; (619) 873-2500.

*Trail notes:* Made famous by the William Brewer party who first crossed through here in 1864, Mono Pass is now a great hiking opportunity, but you will pay for the effort in sweat equity. Mono Pass sits at 12,643 feet, 3,000 feet above the trailhead in just over three miles—yowza! Views from Mono Pass—once your eyes uncross and your breathing returns to controllable gasping—are excellent of the Mono Recesses and the Pioneer Basin. The trail is memorable not only for its steepness, but also for its beauty as it ascends up to Ruby Lake where emerald waters shimmer beneath sheer granite walls. The trail begins at the Mosquito Trailhead.

## 5. PINE CREEK TRAIL 23.0 mi/2.0 days
## to LAKE ITALY

*Reference:* **West of Bishop, Inyo National Forest; map F5, grid c4.**

*User groups:* Hikers, dogs and horses. No mountain bikes allowed. No wheelchair facilities.

*Permits:* Day-use permits are not required. Wilderness permits are required for overnight use year-round. Between March 1 and May 31, advance reservations for quota trails are available by mail, $3 per person. Reservations must be picked up by 8 a.m. or they become available to others on a first-come, first-served basis. Permits are free on a first-come, first-served basis in person on the day of the trip. Arrive early as a strict trail quota is enforced. For more information, contact the White Mountain Ranger Station at (619) 873-2500.

*Directions:* From Bishop, take Highway 395 north to Pine Creek Road and turn left. Drive 10 miles to the trailhead parking located near the pack station.

*Maps:* Send $3 to the USDA-Forest Service, 630 Sansome Street, San Francisco, CA 94111 and ask for the Inyo National Forest map. The Forest Service also publishes a large-sized topographic map titled *John Muir Wilderness and Sequoia/Kings Canyon Wilderness*. The price is $6 and can be ordered from the Forest Service address listed above. For USGS topographic maps, ask for Mount Hilgard and Mount Tom from the USGS.

*Who to contact:* Inyo National Forest, White Mountain Ranger District, 798 North Main Street, Bishop, CA 93514; (619) 873-2500.

*Trail notes:* The Pine Creek Trail ascends moderately from the pack station through a forest of Jeffrey pine, juniper, red fir, quaking aspen, and birch trees until it merges with a mining road leading to the Brownstone Mine. Past the mine, the grade steepens as the trail works its way up talus and scree via switchbacks. The trail continues past Lower and Upper Pine Lakes, Honeymoon Lake and then up to Italy Pass (elevation 12,300 feet)—so that's why we are feeling light-headed! Take it slowly. From the pass, enjoy sweeping views of the Owens Valley, the White Mountain Range, the volcanic tablelands and many Sierra peaks. Drop down into the Jumble Lake Basin and then the Lake Italy Basin and Lake Italy—set up camp and rest because you've earned a breather. Once you've recovered, enjoy the scenery. Pack along your fishing rod—brook and golden trout ply the waters.

---

# 6. PINE CREEK TRAIL to MOON LAKE

**20.0 mi/2.0 days**

*Reference:* **West of Bishop, Inyo National Forest; map F5, grid c4.**

*User groups:* Hikers, dogs and horses. No mountain bikes allowed. No wheelchair facilities.

*Permits:* Day-use permits are not required. Wilderness permits are required for overnight use year-round. Between March 1 and May 31, advance reservations for quota trails are available by mail, $3 per person. Reservations must be picked up by 8 a.m. or they become available to others on a first-come, first-served basis. Permits are free on a first-come, first-served basis in person on the day of the trip. Arrive early as a strict trail quota is enforced. For more information, contact the White Mountain Ranger Station at (619) 873-2500.

*Directions:* From Bishop, take Highway 395 north to Pine Creek Road and turn left. Drive 10 miles to the trailhead parking located near the pack station.

*Maps:* Send $3 to the USDA-Forest Service, 630 Sansome Street, San Francisco, CA 94111 and ask for the Inyo National Forest map. The Forest Service also publishes a large-sized topographic map titled *John Muir Wilderness and Sequoia/Kings Canyon Wilderness*. The price is $6 and can be ordered from the Forest Service address listed above. For USGS topographic maps, ask for Mount Hilgard and Mount Tom from the USGS.

*Who to contact:* Inyo National Forest, White Mountain Ranger District, 798 North Main Street, Bishop, CA 93514; (619) 873-2500.

*Trail notes:* The Pine Creek Trail ascends steeply from the pack station through a forest of Jeffrey pine, juniper, red fir, quaking aspen, and birch trees until it merges with a mining road leading to the Brownstone Mine. Past the mine the grade continues climbing steeply as the trail works its way up talus and scree via switchbacks. The trail continues past Lower and Upper Pine Lakes to Honeymoon Lake. Take the left fork of the Pine Creek Pass/Italy Pass towards Pine Creek Pass. Just before the pass, the trail leaves the trees as you climb above timberline and through white granite walls. The pass sits at 11,100 feet so step slowly and keep your pulse rate down. Don't forget to drink plenty of water. From the pass, drop down into French Canyon and then head left on the signed trail indicating Elba and Moon lakes. The trail climbs once again up to Elba Lake and then continues up to Moon Lake which sits at 11,040 feet.

---

# 7. GABLE LAKE TRAIL 8.0 mi/5.0 hrs

*Reference:* **West of Bishop, Inyo National Forest; map F5, grid c4.**

*User groups:* Hikers, dogs and horses. No mountain bikes allowed. No wheelchair facilities.

*Permits:* Day-use permits are not required. Wilderness permits are required for overnight use year-round. Between March 1 and May 31, advance reservations for quota trails are available by mail, $3 per person. Reservations must be picked up by 8 a.m. or they become available to others on a first-come, first-served basis. Permits are free on a first-come, first-served basis in person on the day of the trip. Arrive early as a strict trail quota is enforced. For more information, contact the White Mountain Ranger Station at (619) 873-2500.

*Directions:* From Bishop, take Highway 395 north to Pine Creek Road and turn left. Drive 10 miles to the trailhead parking located near the pack station.

*Maps:* Send $3 to the USDA-Forest Service, 630 Sansome Street, San Francisco, CA 94111 and ask for the Inyo National Forest map. The Forest Service also publishes a large-sized topographic map titled *John Muir Wilderness and Sequoia/Kings Canyon Wilderness*. The price is $6 and can be ordered from the Forest Service address listed above. For a USGS topographic map of the area, ask for Mount Tom from the USGS.

*Who to contact:* Inyo National Forest, White Mountain Ranger District, 798 North Main Street, Bishop, CA 93514; (619) 873-2500.

*Trail notes:* From the pack station, walk through the remains of an old mining operation to find the trailhead. From the trailhead, hike south and up a lightly used, rocky and steep trail to Gable Lakes. The area is rich in mining history, but remember that the policy, enforced by federal law, is look but don't touch.

---

# 8. FISH SLOUGH 1.0 mi/1.0 hr

*Reference:* **North of Bishop and west of Highway 395; map F5, grid a7.**

*User groups:* Hikers. Mountain bikes, leashed dogs and horses are allowed on roads. No wheelchair facilities.

*Permits:* No permits are required.

*Directions:* From Bishop, take Highway 395 north to Highway 6. Go north on Highway 6 for 1.5 miles and turn west onto Five Bridges Road. Drive approximately 2.5 miles to Fish Slough Road, a right turn just after a sand and gravel plant. After approximately 6.5 miles on Fish Slough Road you will come to a fenced pond and Fish Slough.

*Maps:* For topographic maps, ask for Bishop and White Mountain Peak from the USGS.

*Who to contact:* Bureau of Land Management, Bishop Resource Area, 785 North Main Street, Suite E, Bishop, CA 93514; (619) 872-4881.

*Trail notes:* This short wander through a water-fed oasis just off Highway 395 is a great leg-stretcher. Three natural springs flow from volcanic cliffs, creating a slough that has been turned into a cooperatively managed wildlife sanctuary overseen by the BLM, California Department of Fish and Game and Los Angeles Department of Water and Power. Two endangered fish, the Owen's pupfish and the Owen's tui chub may be viewed within the six acres of clear ponds. Other wildlife that can be seen include: yellow-headed blackbird, prairie falcon, green-winged teal, black-crowned night heron, and a multitude of shorebirds, songbirds and waterfowl. This is a self-discovery area with no facilities.

---

# 9. LAMARCK LAKES TRAIL    9.0 mi/4.5 hrs

*Reference:* **West of Bishop, Inyo National Forest; map F5, grid d4.**

*User groups:* Hikers, dogs and horses. No mountain bikes allowed. No wheelchair facilities.

*Permits:* Day-use permits are not required. Wilderness permits are required for overnight use year-round. Between March 1 and May 31, advance reservations for quota trails are available by mail, $3 per person. Reservations must be picked up by 8 a.m. or they become available to others on a first-come, first-served basis. Permits are free on a first-come, first-served basis in person on the day of the trip. Arrive early as a strict trail quota is enforced. For more information, contact the White Mountain Ranger Station at (619) 873-2500.

*Directions:* From Highway 395 in Bishop, turn west onto Line Street (Highway 168 west) and drive for approximately 17 miles to the North Lake turnoff, just before Lake Sabrina. Turn right onto North Lake and park at the trailhead parking located near the pack station. The actual trailhead is located a half mile down the road in the North Lake Campground, but no parking is allowed in the campground unless you are camping there.

*Maps:* Send $3 to the USDA-Forest Service, 630 Sansome Street, San Francisco, CA 94111 and ask for the Inyo National Forest map. The Forest Service also publishes a large-sized topographic map titled *John Muir Wilderness and Sequoia/Kings Canyon Wilderness*. The price is $6 and can be ordered from the Forest Service address listed above. For USGS topographic maps, ask for Mount Thompson and Mount Darwin from the USGS.

*Who to contact:* Inyo National Forest, White Mountain Ranger District, 798 North Main Street, Bishop, CA 93514; (619) 873-2500.

*Trail notes:* Beginning at the campground, Lamarck Lakes Trail wanders across two footbridges and through a grove of aspen trees that are absolutely beautiful in the fall. The trail then continues up through rugged and rocky country among sheer cliffs of granite and rough boulder-strewn slopes. At two miles you will arrive at a junction with the Grass Lake Trail. Stay right and continue climbing (will it ever level out?). From the upper part of the trail, views of Mt. Emerson and the reddish Piute Crags can be seen. At three miles, the trail finally decides to stop punishing you and actually levels out—amazing! At about 3.5 miles, you will come to a spur trail leading to Lower Lamarck Lake. It's deep and begging to be fished, so why argue. Once you have cast about, continue hiking on the main trail up a few switchbacks to Upper Lamarck Lake at 4.5 miles. The lake seems inviting enough, but stick a toe in and you'll soon discover why it looks so clear—nothing warm-blooded could swim in it because it is so cold.

## 10. PIUTE PASS TRAIL    12.0 mi/6.0 hrs

*Reference:* **West of Bishop, Inyo National Forest; map F5, grid d4.**

*User groups:* Hikers, dogs and horses. No mountain bikes allowed. No wheelchair facilities.

*Permits:* Day-use permits are not required. Wilderness permits are required for overnight use year-round. Between March 1 and May 31, advance reservations for quota trails are available by mail, $3 per person. Reservations must be picked up by 8 a.m. or they become available to others on a first-come, first-served basis. Permits are free on a first-come, first-served basis in person on the day of the trip. Arrive early as a strict trail quota is enforced. For more information, contact the White Mountain Ranger Station at (619) 873-2500.

*Directions:* From Highway 395 in Bishop, turn west onto Line Street (Highway 168 west) and drive for approximately 17 miles to the North Lake turnoff just before Lake Sabrina. Turn right onto North Lake and park at the trailhead parking located near the pack station. The actual trailhead is located a half mile down the road in the North Lake Campground, but no parking is allowed in the campground unless you are camping there.

*Maps:* Send $3 to the USDA-Forest Service, 630 Sansome Street, San Francisco, CA 94111 and ask for the Inyo National Forest map. The Forest Service also publishes a large-sized topographic map titled *John Muir Wilderness and Sequoia/Kings Canyon Wilderness*. The price is $6 and can be ordered from the Forest Service address listed above. For USGS topographic maps, ask for Mount Thompson and Mount Darwin from the USGS.

*Who to contact:* Inyo National Forest, White Mountain Ranger District, 798 North Main Street, Bishop, CA 93514; (619) 873-2500.

*Trail notes:* The Piute Pass Trail eases up through a forest of lodgepole pine and quaking aspen and then runs alongside the North Fork of Bishop Creek. Aspen provide outstanding color in the fall and wildflowers (paintbrush, columbine, penstemon) offer spectacular splashes of color in the late spring and early summer. As you enter the high country above Loch Leven, the glaciated canyon is floored with smooth granite and pockmarked with numerous tiny meadows. Watch for yellow-bellied marmots sunning themselves on the rocks. If you camp, watch them raid your pack for food if you don't take proper food storage precautions. This trip climbs up to Piute Pass for superb views from 11,423 feet. If you desire, you can continue on and drop down into the Humphrey's Basin and its innumerable tiny alpine lakes.

## 11. SABRINA BASIN TRAIL 14.0 mi/8.0 hrs

*Reference:* **West of Bishop, Inyo National Forest; map F5, grid d4.**

*User groups:* Hikers, dogs and horses. No mountain bikes allowed. No wheelchair facilities.

*Permits:* Day-use permits are not required. Wilderness permits are required for overnight use year-round. Between March 1 and May 31, advance reservations for quota trails are available by mail, $3 per person. Reservations must be picked up by 8 a.m. or they become available to others on a first-come, first-served basis. Permits are free on a first-come, first-served basis in person on the day of the trip. Arrive early as a strict trail quota is enforced. For more information, contact the White Mountain Ranger Station at (619) 873-2500.

*Directions:* From Highway 395 in Bishop, turn west onto Line Street (Highway 168 west) and drive for approximately 18 miles to Lake Sabrina. Day-use parking is located at the road's end. Overnight parking is located at the turnout near North Lake turnoff.

*Maps:* Send $3 to the USDA-Forest Service, 630 Sansome Street, San Francisco, CA 94111 and ask for the Inyo National Forest map. The Forest Service also publishes a large-sized topographic map titled *John Muir Wilderness and Sequoia/Kings Canyon Wilderness.* The price is $6 and can be ordered from the Forest Service address listed above. For USGS topographic maps, ask for Mount Thompson and Mount Darwin from the USGS.

*Who to contact:* Inyo National Forest, White Mountain Ranger District, 798 North Main Street, Bishop, CA 93514; (619) 873-2500.

*Trail notes:* The Sabrina Basin Trail leads into, yep, you guessed it—a basin. But not just any basin. Rather a basin created from majestic 13,000-foot peaks surrounding a large number of alpine lakes all filled with rainbow, brown and brook trout. Be sure to take the sidetrip on the main trail to Blue Lake, a photographer's paradise. You are sure to burn at least one roll of film as you gaze in wonder at the image of the jagged Thompson Ridge etched sharply in the clear waters of Blue Lake. Add a few clouds and no breeze to the mix and you have a recipe for an 8 x 10 photo hanging on your wall at home. At the Blue Lake junction, head right and up to your choice of picnic or overnight spots at Moonlight, Hungry Packer, Dingleberry, Topsy Turvy or Midnight lakes. Wander off the trail and you will encounter yet more lakes. It is a bejeweled paradise! Past Blue Lake, you can follow rock cairns up to Donkey and Baboon lakes which are situated below the glaciated ramparts of Mount Powell (13,360 feet) and Mount Thompson (13,440 feet).

## 12. SABRINA BASIN TRAIL 6.0 mi/3.0 hrs
## to LAKE GEORGE

*Reference:* **West of Bishop, Inyo National Forest; map F5, grid d4.**

*User groups:* Hikers, dogs and horses. No mountain bikes allowed. No wheelchair facilities.

*Permits:* Day-use permits are not required. Wilderness permits are required for overnight use year-round. Between March 1 and May 31, advance reservations for quota trails are available by mail, $3 per person. Reservations must be picked up by 8 a.m. or they become available to others on a first-come, first-served basis. Permits are free on a first-come, first-served basis in person on the day of the trip. Arrive early as a strict trail quota is enforced. For more information, contact the White Mountain Ranger Station at (619) 873-2500.

**Directions:** From Highway 395 in Bishop, turn west onto Line Street (Highway 168 west) and drive for approximately 18 miles to Lake Sabrina. Day-use parking is located at the road's end. Overnight parking is located at the turnout near North Lake turnoff.

**Maps:** Send $3 to the USDA-Forest Service, 630 Sansome Street, San Francisco, CA 94111 and ask for the Inyo National Forest map. The Forest Service also publishes a large-sized topographic map titled *John Muir Wilderness and Sequoia/Kings Canyon Wilderness*. The price is $6 and can be ordered from the Forest Service address listed above. For USGS topographic maps, ask for Mount Thompson and Mount Darwin from the USGS.

**Who to contact:** Inyo National Forest, White Mountain Ranger District, 798 North Main Street, Bishop, CA 93514; (619) 873-2500.

**Trail notes:** The Tyee Lakes Trail branches steeply off the Sabrina Basin Trail to the left and climbs rapidly up to Lake George and then up and over Table Mountain. If you desire, you can turn this into a one-way hike with a shuttle by leaving one car at South Lake parking for the Tyee Lakes Trail—see hike number 13 for parking and directions. Fishing is good at Lake George for rainbow and brook trout.

---

## 13. TYEE LAKES TRAIL          9.0 mi/4.5 hrs

**Reference:** West of Bishop, Inyo National Forest; map F5, grid d5.

**User groups:** Hikers, dogs and horses. No mountain bikes allowed. No wheelchair facilities.

**Permits:** Day-use permits are not required. Wilderness permits are required for overnight use year-round. Between March 1 and May 31, advance reservations for quota trails are available by mail, $3 per person. Reservations must be picked up by 8 a.m. or they become available to others on a first-come, first-served basis. Permits are free on a first-come, first-served basis in person on the day of the trip. Arrive early as a strict trail quota is enforced. For more information, contact the White Mountain Ranger Station at (619) 873-2500.

**Directions:** From Highway 395 in Bishop, turn west onto Line Street (Highway 168 west) and drive to South Lake Road. Then drive to the end of South Lake Road and the trailhead parking.

**Maps:** Send $3 to the USDA-Forest Service, 630 Sansome Street, San Francisco, CA 94111 and ask for the Inyo National Forest map. The Forest Service also publishes a large-sized topographic map titled *John Muir Wilderness and Sequoia/Kings Canyon Wilderness*. The price is $6 and can be ordered from the Forest Service address listed above. For USGS topographic maps, ask for Mount Thompson and North Palisade from the USGS.

**Who to contact:** Inyo National Forest, White Mountain Ranger District, 798 North Main Street, Bishop, CA 93514; (619) 873-2500.

**Trail notes:** Named for the Native American word for large salmon, the Tyee Lakes Trail is a steep but scenic route into a lakes basin that offers good fishing. The trail becomes somewhat hard to follow over Table Mountain before it drops down to Lake George. From the top of Table Mountain, enjoy the views of Mt. Thompson, Mt. Aggisiz, Mt. Gilbert and the Inconsolable Range. Rainbow and brown trout can be found in these waters so pack along your fishing rod. If you desire, you can turn this into a one-way hike with a shuttle by leaving one car at Sabrina Lake—see hike number 12 for parking and directions.

## 14. GREEN LAKE TRAIL    6.0 mi/3.5 hrs

*Reference:* **West of Bishop, Inyo National Forest; map F5, grid e5.**

*User groups:* Hikers, dogs and horses. No mountain bikes allowed. No wheelchair facilities.

*Permits:* Day-use permits are not required. Wilderness permits are required for overnight use year-round. Between March 1 and May 31, advance reservations for quota trails are available by mail, $3 per person. Reservations must be picked up by 8 a.m. or they become available to others on a first-come, first-served basis. Permits are free on a first-come, first-served basis in person on the day of the trip. Arrive early as a strict trail quota is enforced. For more information, contact the White Mountain Ranger Station at (619) 873-2500.

*Directions:* From Highway 395 in Bishop, turn west onto Line Street (Highway 168 west) and drive to South Lake Road and turn left. Day-use and overnight parking is located at the end of South Lake Road.

*Maps:* Send $3 to the USDA-Forest Service, 630 Sansome Street, San Francisco, CA 94111 and ask for the Inyo National Forest map. The Forest Service also publishes a large-sized topographic map titled *John Muir Wilderness and Sequoia/Kings Canyon Wilderness*. The price is $6 and can be ordered from the Forest Service address listed above. For USGS topographic maps, ask for Mount Thompson and North Palisade from the USGS.

*Who to contact:* Inyo National Forest, White Mountain Ranger District, 798 North Main Street, Bishop, CA 93514; (619) 873-2500.

*Trail notes:* The Green Lake Trail begins at the east end of the parking lot and follows a stock trail (love the smell of that horse manure!) upward through a conifer forest, where it joins with the main trail up to Green Lake. The trail levels off into a lush mountain meadow below Brown Lake. Above this lake, the trail moves upward along a bench where Green Lake lies amidst gnarled, old whitebark pines. Rainbow trout can be found in these waters, so pack along your fishing rod.

## 15. BISHOP PASS TRAIL    11.0 mi/6.0 hrs

*Reference:* **West of Bishop, Inyo National Forest; map F5, grid e5.**

*User groups:* Hikers, dogs and horses. No mountain bikes allowed. No wheelchair facilities.

*Permits:* Day-use permits are not required. Wilderness permits are required for overnight use year-round. Between March 1 and May 31, advance reservations for quota trails are available by mail, $3 per person. Reservations must be picked up by 8 a.m. or they become available to others on a first-come, first-served basis. Permits are free on a first-come, first-served basis in person on the day of the trip. Arrive early as a strict trail quota is enforced. For more information, contact the White Mountain Ranger Station at (619) 873-2500.

***Directions:*** From Highway 395 in Bishop, turn west onto Line Street (Highway 168 west), drive to South Lake Road and turn left. Day-use and overnight parking is located at the road's end.

***Maps:*** Send $3 to the USDA-Forest Service, 630 Sansome Street, San Francisco, CA 94111 and ask for the Inyo National Forest map. The Forest Service also publishes a large-sized topographic map titled *John Muir Wilderness and Sequoia/Kings Canyon Wilderness*. The price is $6 and can be ordered from the Forest Service address listed above. For USGS topographic maps, ask for Mount Thompson and North Palisade from the USGS.

***Who to contact:*** Inyo National Forest, White Mountain Ranger District, 798 North Main Street, Bishop, CA 93514; (619) 873-2500.

***Trail notes:*** The Bishop Pass Trail ascends along the east side of South Lake through a forest of aspen and lodgepole pine and then up to Bishop Pass. The trail offers an excellent opportunity to not only enjoy stunning scenery but to learn about the effects of glacier activity such as glacial cirques, glaciated granite and glacier erratics—all evident from the trail. Majestic views of Hurd Peak, Mt. Thompson and Mt. Goode can be enjoyed from the trail—pack along your camera for sure. If you are seeking a shorter half-day loop trip, branch off the Bishop Pass Trail before reaching Long Lake onto the Chocolate Lakes Trail, which passes along the base of the Inconsolable Range. The trail loops around, rejoining the Bishop Pass Trail at the north end of Long Lake, near Ruwau Lake. If you hike up to Bishop Pass, keep in mind that you are nearly at 12,000 feet so watch your hiking pace and drink plenty of water. Rainbow trout can be found in these waters.

---

# 16. TREASURE LAKES TRAIL    5.6 mi/3.0 hrs  

***Reference:*** **West of Bishop, Inyo National Forest; map F5, grid e5.**

***User groups:*** Hikers, dogs and horses. No mountain bikes allowed. No wheelchair facilities.

***Permits:*** Day-use permits are not required. Wilderness permits are required for overnight use year-round. Between March 1 and May 31, advance reservations for quota trails are available by mail, $3 per person. Reservations must be picked up by 8 a.m. or they become available to others on a first-come, first-served basis. Permits are free on a first-come, first-served basis in person on the day of the trip. Arrive early as a strict trail quota is enforced. For more information, contact the White Mountain Ranger Station at (619) 873-2500.

***Directions:*** From Highway 395 in Bishop, turn west onto Line Street (Highway 168 west) and drive to South Lake Road. Turn left onto South Lake Road. Day-use and overnight parking is located at the road's end.

***Maps:*** Send $3 to the USDA-Forest Service, 630 Sansome Street, San Francisco, CA 94111 and ask for the Inyo National Forest map. The Forest Service also publishes a large-sized topographic map titled *John Muir Wilderness and Sequoia/Kings Canyon Wilderness*. The price is $6 and can be ordered from the Forest Service address listed above. For USGS topographic maps, ask for Mount Thompson and North Palisade from the USGS.

***Who to contact:*** Inyo National Forest, White Mountain Ranger District, 798 North Main Street, Bishop, CA 93514; (619) 873-2500.

*Trail notes:* Beginning at the trailhead, hike up the Bishop Pass Trail for just under a mile to the junction with the Treasure Lakes Trail and head right. After a short climb, the trail drops down over loose rubble, which can be a bit tricky for the unaware. Step lightly and keep concentrating and you'll stay on your feet without any trouble. At 1.5 miles, you will meet and cross the South Fork of Bishop Creek. After following along the creek for a short while, the trail begins to climb and at 2.5 miles crosses the drainage creek for Treasure Lakes. At three miles and after a thigh-burning set of quick switchbacks, you will arrive at Treasure Lakes. The upper and lower lakes are connected by a well-used, though "unofficial" trail. The lakes are located in a gorgeous granite basin surrounded by jagged, high Sierra peaks. Rainbow, brown and golden trout can be found in these waters.

---

## 17. NORTH FORK TRAIL 18.0 mi/9.0 hrs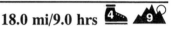
## to PALISADE GLACIER

*Reference:* **West of Bishop, Inyo National Forest; map F5, grid e5.**

*User groups:* Hikers, dogs and horses. No mountain bikes allowed. No wheelchair facilities.

*Permits:* Day-use permits are not required. Wilderness permits are required for overnight use year-round. Between March 1 and May 31, advance reservations for quota trails are available by mail, $3 per person. Reservations must be picked up by 8 a.m. or they become available to others on a first-come, first-served basis. Permits are free on a first-come, first-served basis in person on the day of the trip. Arrive early as a strict trail quota is enforced. For more information, contact the White Mountain Ranger Station at (619) 873-2500.

*Directions:* From Bishop, take Highway 395 south to Big Pine and turn west onto Crocker Street. Drive 10 miles west (up the canyon) to the end of the road. Overnight parking is provided approximately a half mile below the end of the road, in the hikers parking lot. Day-use parking is at the end of the road.

*Maps:* Send $3 to the USDA-Forest Service, 630 Sansome Street, San Francisco, CA 94111 and ask for the Inyo National Forest map. The Forest Service also publishes a large-sized topographic map titled *John Muir Wilderness and Sequoia/Kings Canyon Wilderness.* The price is $6 and can be ordered from the Forest Service address listed above. For USGS topographic maps, ask for Mount Thompson, Coyote Flat, Split Mountain and North Palisade from the USGS. Tom Harrison Cartography also publishes an excellent map of the area. Call (415) 456-7940 and ask for the recreation map of Sequoia and Kings Canyon national parks. The cost is $5.95 plus tax and shipping. Trails Illustrated also publishes a great map, Sequoia/Kings Canyon National Parks. The cost is $7.95 and may be ordered by calling (800) 962-1643.

*Who to contact:* Inyo National Forest, White Mountain Ranger District, 798 North Main Street, Bishop, CA 93514; (619) 873-2500.

*Trail notes:* The North Fork Trail offers access to the Big Pine Lakes and the Palisade Glacier, the largest glacier in the Sierra. Hikers can meander safely along the lower reaches of the glacier, but should not stray onto the upper reaches unless experienced in mountaineering skills on ice and snow. The Palisade Crest, rising above 14,000 feet, contains some of the finest alpine climbing to be found anywhere in California. The main trail heads up through sage, manzanita and Jeffrey pine past Second Falls and along the creek to its headwaters. You will pass by an old stone cabin built years ago by movie actor Lon Chaney. A junction in the trail leads up to Black Lake, which offers superb views of the Palisade Glacier and Crest. We recommend taking this fork to Black Lake as the trail does rejoin the main trail up by Fourth Lake (how's that for an imaginative name?) If you are camping, pick your spot among any of the many lakes in the area, but camp well off the trail and at least 200 feet away from the lake's edge. The trail to Palisade Glacier is located approximately one-half mile above Third Lake (ya gotta love these names) and heads left. The last half mile to the glacier requires boulder-hopping and the trail becomes very obscure. Don't head up here if you are unsure of your balance or your hiking skills. Stay off the glacier's upper slopes unless you have an ice ax, crampons and the requisite skill to use them safely. Head back the way you came.

---

## 18. SOUTH FORK TRAIL     10.0 mi/5.0 hrs

*Reference:* **West of Bishop, Inyo National Forest; map F5, grid f5.**

*User groups:* Hikers, dogs and horses. No mountain bikes allowed. No wheelchair facilities.

*Permits:* Day-use permits are not required. Wilderness permits are required for overnight use year-round. Between March 1 and May 31, advance reservations for quota trails are available by mail, $3 per person. Reservations must be picked up by 8 a.m. or they become available to others on a first-come, first-served basis. Permits are free on a first-come, first-served basis in person on the day of the trip. Arrive early as a strict trail quota is enforced. For more information, contact the White Mountain Ranger Station at (619) 873-2500.

*Directions:* From Bishop, take Highway 395 south to Big Pine and turn west onto Crocker Street. Drive 10 miles west (up the canyon) to the end of the road. Overnight parking is provided approximately a half mile below the end of the road in the hikers parking lot. Day-use parking is at the end of the road.

*Maps:* Send $3 to the USDA-Forest Service, 630 Sansome Street, San Francisco, CA 94111 and ask for the Inyo National Forest map. For topographic maps, ask for Mount Thompson, Coyote Flat, Split Mountain and North Palisade from the USGS. For information on the Forest Service topo map and other maps of the area, see "maps" under hike number 17.

*Who to contact:* Inyo National Forest, White Mountain Ranger District, 798 North Main Street, Bishop, CA 93514; (619) 873-2500.

*Trail notes:* The South Fork Trail is a lightly-used footpath that climbs up beneath the jagged peaks of the Middle Palisade Crest and offers access to the Middle Palisade Glacier. Limber pine grow on the steep slopes below Willow Lake. The trail from Willow Lake to Brainard Lake is very indistinct and marked only by rock cairns. Stay off the glacier unless you have the proper equipment and the knowledge to use it safely.

---

## 19. BARKER CREEK TRAIL     10.0 mi/5.0 hrs

*Reference:* **West of Bishop, Inyo National Forest; map F5, grid e6.**

*User groups:* Hikers, dogs and horses. No mountain bikes allowed. No

wheelchair facilities.

***Permits:*** Day-use permits are not required. Wilderness permits are required for overnight use year-round. Between March 1 and May 31, advance reservations for quota trails are available by mail, $3 per person. Reservations must be picked up by 8 a.m. or they become available to others on a first-come, first-served basis. Permits are free on a first-come, first-served basis in person on the day of the trip. Arrive early as a strict trail quota is enforced. For more information, contact the White Mountain Ranger Station at (619) 873-2500.

***Directions:*** From Bishop, take Highway 395 south to Big Pine and turn west onto Crocker Street. Drive 10 miles west (up the canyon) to the end of the road. Overnight parking is provided approximately a half mile below the end of the road in the hikers parking lot. Day-use parking is at the end of the road.

***Maps:*** Send $3 to the USDA-Forest Service, 630 Sansome Street, San Francisco, CA 94111 and ask for the Inyo National Forest map. For topographic maps, ask for Mount Thompson, Coyote Flat, Split Mountain and North Palisade from the USGS. For information on the Forest Service topo map and other maps of the area, see "maps" under hike number 17.

***Who to contact:*** Inyo National Forest, White Mountain Ranger District, 798 North Main Street, Bishop, CA 93514; (619) 873-2500.

***Trail notes:*** The Baker Creek Trail is lightly used, but don't expect to have it all to yourself. Why? Because you can get near Baker Lake via a four-wheel-drive route from Bishop—why walk when you can drive, right? Right. At any rate, the trail is worth the trek as it offers spectacular views of the Palisade Crest. It takes in the canyons of both forks of Big Pine. The trail begins at a junction off North Fork Trail and heads north, crossing a ridge and then winding through pines. The trail passes Grouse Springs and then climbs to a high point on a gentle ridge, where views of the Middle Palisade and Disappointment Peak tower above the glaciers below. To the north are the rolling and high meadows of Baker Creek and Coyote Flat. Hike as far as you wish and then retrace your steps.

---

# 20. YUCCA POINT TRAIL          2.0 mi/1.5 hrs

***Reference:*** In Sequoia and Kings Canyon national parks; map F5, grid g0.

***User groups:*** Hikers and horses. No mountain bikes or dogs allowed. No wheelchair facilities.

***Permits:*** Day-use permits are not required. Wilderness permits are required for overnight use. Contact the Hume Lake Ranger District at (209) 338-2251 for more information. A $5 entrance fee is collected at Big Stump for Sequoia/Kings Canyon national parks.

***Directions:*** From Fresno and Highway 99, drive east on Highway 180 to Grant Grove and the park's Big Stump entrance. From Grant Grove, drive approximately 14 winding and twisting miles on Highway 80 to the signed Yucca Point Trailhead on the west side of the road. Use caution when turning into the parking area as you are crossing the highway at a blind corner!

***Maps:*** Send $3 to the USDA-Forest Service, 630 Sansome Street, San Francisco, CA 94111 and ask for the Sequoia National Forest map. For topographic maps, ask for Hume and Wren Peak from the USGS. For information on the Forest Service topo map and other maps of the area, see "maps" under hike number 17.

*Who to contact:* Sequoia and Kings Canyon National Parks, Ash Mountain, Three Rivers, CA 93271; (209) 565-3341, or Sequoia National Forest, Hume Lake Ranger District, 35860 East Kings Canyon Road, Dunlap, CA 93621; (209) 338-2251.

*Trail notes:* This trail is primarily used by flyfishing enthusiasts (the wild trout in the river are a challenge and a thrill—catch-and-release only). Regardless, the hike into the Kings River Canyon should prove inspiring for everybody, angler or not. The trail is very hot in the summer, so pack along plenty of water as well as a good sunhat and sunscreen. From the parking area, the trail descends steeply to the river. Going down isn't hard, although your knees will feel the strain. Coming out, though, is an entirely different proposition. Take your time and rest frequently.

---

# 21. EVANS GROVE TRAIL     1.5 mi/0.75 hr

*Reference:* In Sequoia and Kings Canyon national parks; map F5, grid h0.

*User groups:* Hikers and horses. No mountain bikes or dogs allowed. No wheelchair facilities.

*Permits:* Day-use permits are not required. Wilderness permits are required for overnight use. For more information, contact the Hume Lake Ranger District at (209) 338-2251. A $5 entrance fee is collected at Big Stump for Sequoia/Kings Canyon national parks.

*Directions:* A Forest Service map combined with a Tom Harrison Cartography recreation map is a must for negotiating the Forest Service roads to get to the trailhead. From Fresno and Highway 99, drive east on Highway 180 to Grant Grove and the park's Big Stump entrance. From Grant Grove, drive approximately six miles south to the Hume Lake/Quail Flat turnoff. Reset the odometer! Follow the paved, but very narrow route to Weston Meadow and Burton Meadow (Forest Service Road 14S02). At 5.6 miles, turn north toward Kennedy Meadow on Forest Service Road 13S26 (this road can become impassable in heavy rains, check with the Forest Service before heading out). At 12.3 miles, Forest Service Road 13S26 turns into Forest Service Road 13S05. At 15.1 miles, the road comes to an obvious end with a tiny turnaround—park so others can negotiate the tight about-face. The trailhead is signed.

*Maps:* Send $3 to the USDA-Forest Service, 630 Sansome Street, San Francisco, CA 94111 and ask for the Sequoia National Forest map. For a topographic map, ask for Wren Peak from the USGS. For information on the Forest Service topo map and other maps of the area, see "maps" under hike number 17.

*Who to contact:* Sequoia and Kings Canyon National Parks, Ash Mountain, Three Rivers, CA 93271; (209) 565-3341, or Sequoia National Forest, Hume Lake Ranger District, 35860 East Kings Canyon Road, Dunlap, CA 93621; (209) 338-2251.

*Trail notes:* This hike is an easy one and offers wonderful seclusion amid a cathedral-like grove of trees. It is the drive getting there that proves to be a challenge. The trip is dry, so pack along water. The trail wanders through Evans Grove for almost three-quarters of a mile. Stop where you wish and let your mind be free. You will note the end of the grove when the trail descends steeply towards Boulder Creek—you don't want to descend the 3,000 feet, trust us! Good views may be enjoyed by descending a short way if you are so inclined. Don't hike down any further than you are willing to hike back up. When ready, retrace your steps.

## 22. DEER COVE TRAIL     8.0 mi/5.0 hrs

*Reference:* **In Sequoia National Park; map F5, grid h2.**

*User groups:* Hikers and horses. No mountain bikes are allowed. Dogs are allowed in the national forest only. No wheelchair facilities.

*Permits:* Day-use permits are not required. Wilderness permits are required for overnight use. A third of the permits are available daily on a first-come, first-served basis. The remainder are available by reservation at least 14 days in advance. Contact the Sequoia and Kings Canyon National Park at (209) 565-3341 for more information. A $5 entrance fee is charged.

*Directions:* From Fresno and Highway 99, drive east on Highway 180 to Grant Grove and the park's Big Stump entrance. From Grant Grove, drive approximately 28 winding and twisting miles into Kings Canyon, almost to Cedar Grove. About one mile before the Cedar Grove turnoff, locate the signed parking area on the north side of the road.

*Maps:* For a topographic map, ask for Cedar Grove from the USGS. For information on the Forest Service topo map and other maps of the area, see "maps" under hike number 17.

*Who to contact:* Sequoia and Kings Canyon National Parks, Ash Mountain, Three Rivers, CA 93271; (209) 565-3341, or Sequoia National Forest, Hume Lake Ranger District, 35860 East Kings Canyon Road, Dunlap, CA 93621; (209) 338-2251.

*Trail notes:* This trail enters into the gorgeous Monarch Wilderness. The trail can be very hot and dry in the summer, so be sure to carry plenty of water. The trail will lead you past Dear Cove Creek (a good spot for an extended rest break) and up to Wildman Meadow—named by two brothers in the late 1800s, after spending a sleepless night listening to an awful noise they attributed to a wild man. The noise turned out to be an owl. Wildman Meadow is marked by a sign just off the trail and attached to a tree. It makes a good camping spot—though do not camp in the meadow itself. Of course, you will share the meadow with a large stock (read cattle) camp that utilizes the meadow under an agreement with the Forest Service. Head back the way you came.

## 23. CEDAR GROVE OVERLOOK 4.0 mi/2.0 hrs

*Reference:* **In Kings Canyon National Park; map F5, grid h3.**

*User groups:* Hikers and horses. No mountain bikes or dogs allowed. No wheelchair facilities.

*Permits:* Day-use permits are not required. Wilderness permits are required for overnight use. A third of the permits are available daily on a first-come, first-served basis. The remainder are available by reservation at least 14 days in advance. For more information, contact the Sequoia and Kings Canyon national parks at (209) 565-3341. A $5 day-use fee is charged.

*Directions:* From Fresno and Highway 99, drive east on Highway 180 to Grant Grove and the park's Big Stump entrance. From Grant Grove, drive approximately 31 winding and twisting miles into Kings Canyon and Cedar Grove. The trailhead is located just off the village road across the bridge over South Fork Kings River at the pack station parking area.

*Maps:* For a topographic map, ask for Cedar Grove from the USGS. For information on the Forest Service topo map and other maps of the area, see "maps" under hike number 17.

*Who to contact:* For general information, contact Sequoia and Kings Canyon National Parks, Ash Mountain, Three Rivers, CA 93271; (209) 565-3341. For specific information about Kings Canyon National Park, contact Kings Canyon Visitors Center, Grant Grove, CA 93633; (209) 335-2856.

*Trail notes:* Kings Canyon rivals the beauty and grandeur of Yosemite, according to John Muir. True, it doesn't have the huge waterfalls that Yosemite has, but the vertical nature and height of Kings Canyon's ice-polished granite walls are awe-inspiring nonetheless. At the Hotel Creek Trailhead, begin climbing up the canyon wall on the Cedar Grove Overlook Trail. At a fork, head left and onto a knob of granite that offers superb views up and down the canyon. Return the way you came. Pack plenty of water, as there is none on this hot and dry hike.

---

## 24. DON CECIL TRAIL 11.2 mi/6.0 hrs

*Reference:* **In Kings Canyon National Park; map F5, grid h2.**

*User groups:* Hikers and horses. No mountain bikes or dogs allowed. No wheelchair facilities.

*Permits:* Day-use permits are not required. Wilderness permits are required for overnight use. A third of the permits are available daily on a first-come, first-served basis. The remainder are available by reservation at least 14 days in advance. For more information, contact the Sequoia and Kings Canyon national parks at (209) 565-3341. A $5 day-use fee is charged.

*Directions:* From Fresno and Highway 99, drive east on Highway 180 to Grant Grove and the park's Big Stump entrance. From Grant Grove, drive approximately 31 winding and twisting miles into Kings Canyon and Cedar Grove. The trailhead parking is located approximately 200 yards beyond the turnoff to Cedar Grove Village on Highway 180.

*Maps:* For a topographic map, ask for Cedar Grove from the USGS. For information on the Forest Service topo map and other maps of the area, see "maps" under hike number 17.

*Who to contact:* For general information, contact Sequoia and Kings Canyon National Parks, Ash Mountain, Three Rivers, CA 93271; (209) 565-3341. For specific information about Kings Canyon National Park, contact Kings Canyon Visitors Center, Grant Grove, CA 93633; (209) 335-2856.

*Trail notes:* The first mile of this trail out of Cedar Grove is ideal for families, as the path ascends through woods and dense ground cover. Where the trail crosses Sheep Creek is a super spot for a picnic or a place to kick your feet up for awhile and let the sound of water wash your cares away. From here, the trail climbs steeply up to Lookout Peak. From the top you can see parts of the Great Western Divide, all of Cedar Grove and the Monarch Divide. Hike back the way you came. Mosquitoes can be really bothersome in the spring and early summer—wear repellent.

*Reference:* **In Kings Canyon National Park; map F5, grid h4.**

*User groups:* Hikers and horses. No mountain bikes or dogs allowed. No wheelchair facilities.

*Permits:* Day-use permits are not required. Wilderness permits are required for overnight use. A third of the permits are available daily on a first-come, first-served basis. The remainder are available by reservation at least 14 days in advance. For more information, contact the Sequoia and Kings Canyon national parks at (209) 565-3341. A $5 day-use fee is charged.

*Directions:* From Fresno and Highway 99, drive east on Highway 180 to Grant Grove and the park's Big Stump entrance. From Grant Grove, drive approximately 31 winding and twisting miles into Kings Canyon and Cedar Grove. Drive to the end of the road, six miles east of Cedar Grove Village. Park in the first available lot.

*Maps:* For a topographic map, ask for The Sphinx from the USGS. For information on the Forest Service topo map and other maps of the area, see "maps" under hike number 17.

*Who to contact:* For general information, contact Sequoia and Kings Canyon National Parks, Ash Mountain, Three Rivers, CA 93271; (209) 565-3341. For specific information about Kings Canyon National Park, contact Kings Canyon Visitors Center, Grant Grove, CA 93633; (209) 335-2856.

*Trail notes:* Well, it may not have the huge waterfalls of Yosemite, but Kings Canyon has some special falls just the same and Mist Falls is one of them. The falls are best visited in the early spring and summer when the flow of water is high and the falls' watery torrent crashes into the rocks below, creating a mist that coats the upstream side of every rock, plant and tree downstream. Because of the mist, the rocks and area around the falls are extremely slick and hazardous. Stay away from the edge! From the road's end, head east along the South Fork Kings River, crossing Copper Creek and walking on a sandy and then sometimes damp treadway among pine and cedar. At two miles, you will come to a signed junction at Bailey Bridge. Right goes up Bubbs Creek and left (the way we are going) leads up Paradise Valley to Mist Falls. The trail climbs steeply, following alongside the South Fork of the Kings River, winding alternately through shade and sun-dappled open areas. At just under four miles, you will reach the falls. Be very cautious around the falls because, while it is true that this is one of the more spectacular falls in the park, it is also one of the more dangerous. Hikers have been killed here while being overeager to get a better view. Once you have enjoyed the falls, retrace your steps.

**26. BUBBS CREEK LOOP**     4.5 mi/2.0 hrs

*Reference:* **In Kings Canyon National Park; map F5, grid h4.**

*User groups:* Hikers and horses. No mountain bikes or dogs allowed. No wheelchair facilities.

*Permits:* Day-use permits are not required. Wilderness permits are required for overnight use. A third of the permits are available daily on a first-come, first-served basis. The remainder are available by reservation at least 14 days in advance. For more information, contact the Sequoia and Kings Canyon national parks at (209) 565-3341. A $5 day-use fee is charged.

*Directions:* From Fresno and Highway 99, drive east on Highway 180 to Grant Grove and the park's Big Stump entrance. From Grant Grove, drive approximately 31 winding and twisting miles into Kings Canyon and Cedar Grove. Drive to the end of the road, six miles east of Cedar Grove Village. Park in the first available lot.

*Maps:* For a topographic map, ask for The Sphinx from the USGS. For information on the Forest Service topo map and other maps of the area, see "maps" under hike number 17.

*Who to contact:* For general information, contact Sequoia and Kings Canyon National Parks, Ash Mountain, Three Rivers, CA 93271; (209) 565-3341. For specific information about Kings Canyon National Park, contact Kings Canyon Visitors Center, Grant Grove, CA 93633; (209) 335-2856.

*Trail notes:* The Bubbs Creek is a perfect loop trip introduction for the entire family. From the parking area, pick up the trail on the south side and begin hiking through forest on a well-maintained trail. At about one-half mile, you come to a fork. One branch leads to Zumwalt Meadow, but you will head left towards Bubbs Creek. At about 1.5 miles you will pass through an area of downed and topped trees—evidence of the power of an avalanche and the reason a nearby peak was named Avalanche Peak. The next trail junction at about three miles finds the Bubbs Creek Trail heading right and up the Bubbs Creek drainage, but you will go left, across the South Fork Kings River and then left again at another junction with a trail heading right and leading to Mist Falls. The trail you are on leads two miles back to the parking area, only now on the other side of the river.

---

# 27. COPPER CREEK TRAIL 7.0 mi/3.5 hrs  to LOWER TENT MEADOWS

*Reference:* In Kings Canyon National Park; map F5, grid h4.

*User groups:* Hikers and horses. No mountain bikes or dogs are allowed. No wheelchair facilities.

*Permits:* Day-use permits are not required. Wilderness permits are required for overnight use. A third of the permits are available daily on a first-come, first-served basis. The remainder are available by reservation at least 14 days in advance. For more information, contact the Sequoia and Kings Canyon national parks at (209) 565-3341. A $5 day-use fee is charged.

*Directions:* From Fresno and Highway 99, drive east on Highway 180 to Grant Grove and the park's Big Stump entrance. From Grant Grove, drive approximately 31 winding and twisting miles into Kings Canyon and Cedar Grove. Drive to the end of the road, six miles east of Cedar Grove Village. Park in the second lot on the other side of the road's end loop.

*Maps:* For a topographic map, ask for The Sphinx from the USGS. For information on the Forest Service topo map and other maps of the area, see "maps" under hike number 17.

*Who to contact:* For general information, contact Sequoia and Kings Canyon National Parks, Ash Mountain, Three Rivers, CA 93271; (209) 565-3341. For specific information about Kings Canyon National Park, contact Kings Canyon Visitors Center, Grant Grove, CA 93633; (209) 335-2856.

*Trail notes:* See hike number 23 for a description of the Kings Canyon area. The

Copper Creek Trail takes you up through a steep route offering increasingly wonderful over-the-shoulder views of snow-capped peaks and deep canyons. Although the trail continues on, the day-hike section is best ended at Lower Tent Meadow. There are a number of informal campsites here and one established site (complete with a bear-proof food locker). The trail's first mile or so is in the open and quite hot and dry. It's best to attempt it in the early morning. A stand of quaking aspen on the way up is very beautiful, especially in the fall. Take bear precautions at all times, even during a day-hike and especially when camping overnight.

## 28. SPHINX CREEK          10.0 mi/5.0 hrs

*Reference:* **In Kings Canyon National Park; map F5, grid h4.**

*User groups:* Hikers and horses. No mountain bikes or dogs are allowed. No wheelchair facilities.

*Permits:* Day-use permits are not required. Wilderness permits are required for overnight use. A third of the permits are available daily on a first-come, first-served basis. The remainder are available by reservation at least 14 days in advance. For more information, contact the Sequoia and Kings Canyon national parks at (209) 565-3341. A $5 day-use fee is charged.

*Directions:* From Fresno and Highway 99, drive east on Highway 180 to Grant Grove and the park's Big Stump entrance. From Grant Grove, drive approximately 31 winding and twisting miles into Kings Canyon and Cedar Grove. Drive to the end of the road, six miles east of Cedar Grove Village. Park in the first available lot.

*Maps:* For a topographic map, ask for The Sphinx from the USGS. For information on the Forest Service topo map and other maps of the area, see "maps" under hike number 17.

*Who to contact:* For general information, contact Sequoia and Kings Canyon National Parks, Ash Mountain, Three Rivers, CA 93271; (209) 565-3341. For specific information about Kings Canyon National Park, contact Kings Canyon Visitors Center, Grant Grove, CA 93633; (209) 335-2856.

*Trail notes:* From the parking area, pick up the trail on the south side and begin hiking through forest on a well-maintained trail. At about one-half mile you come to a fork. One branch leads to Zumwalt Meadow; you will head left towards Bubbs Creek. At about 1.5 miles you will pass through an area of downed and topped trees—evidence of the power of an avalanche and the reason a nearby peak was named Avalanche Peak. The next trail junction at about three miles finds the Bubbs Creek Trail heading right and up the Bubbs Creek drainage, the direction you will head. The trail crosses and recrosses Bubbs Creek a number of times over bridges and then selects a side and begins to climb in earnest through a series of switchbacks. At four miles or so, the trail levels. Once you reach Sphinx Creek at five miles out, you will arrive at the first legal camping area since leaving the Kings Canyon floor. If you are seeking a short in-and-out weekend overnight, select your spot and hang out. Take adequate bear precautions. Don't forget your fishing rod, as the fishing in Bubbs Creek is quite good. When you are ready, retrace your steps to the canyon floor and your car.

# 29. REDWOOD CANYON LOOP TRIP

6.5 mi/3.5 hrs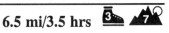

*Reference:* **In Kings Canyon National Park; map F5, grid h0.**

*User groups:* Hikers and horses. No mountain bikes or dogs are allowed. No wheelchair facilities.

*Permits:* Day-use permits are not required. Wilderness permits are required for overnight use. A third of the permits are available daily on a first-come, first-served basis. The remainder are available by reservation at least 14 days in advance. For more information, contact the Sequoia and Kings Canyon national parks at (209) 565-3341. A $5 day-use fee is charged. Camping is not allowed within the Giant Forest itself.

*Directions:* From Fresno and Highway 99, drive east on Highway 180 to Grant Grove and the park's Big Stump entrance. Drive four miles to Quail Flat and then turn right (south) on a dirt road leading to Redwood Saddle. After 1.5 miles, the road divides, take the left fork leading to the parking area/trailhead.

*Maps:* For a topographic map, ask for Lodgepole from the USGS. For information on the Forest Service topo map and other maps of the area, see "maps" under hike number 17.

*Who to contact:* For general information, contact Sequoia and Kings Canyon National Parks, Ash Mountain, Three Rivers, CA 93271; (209) 565-3341. For specific information about Kings Canyon National Park, contact Kings Canyon Visitors Center, Grant Grove, CA 93633; (209) 335-2856.

*Trail notes:* From the trailhead, head into a ravine and to a trail junction. You will bear left, following the trail that is signed for Hart Tree, Fallen Goliath and Redwood Creek. After passing through Hart Meadow at two miles and crossing Buena Vista Creek, the trail heads through a tunnel log (2.7 miles out)—a hollowed-out tree that children love and older folk seem to enjoy as well. At three miles and the junction leading to Hart Tree, stay on the main trail and hike past the Fallen Goliath, a huge downed tree, at 4.5 miles. Past the Fallen Goliath, the track crosses a stream and then reaches a junction. Head right, upstream and back towards the parking area. Hike up the old roadbed to a junction with the trail you hiked in on from the parking area at the beginning and head left and to the parking lot, 6.5 miles from the start.

---

# 30. BUENA VISTA PEAK TRAIL

1.0 mi/0.5 hr

*Reference:* **In Kings Canyon National Park; map F5, grid h0.**

*User groups:* Hikers and horses. No mountain bikes or dogs are allowed. No wheelchair facilities.

*Permits:* Day-use permits are not required. Wilderness permits are required for overnight use. A third of the permits are available daily on a first-come, first-served basis. The remainder are available by reservation at least 14 days in advance. For more information, contact the Sequoia and Kings Canyon national parks at (209) 565-3341. A $5 day-use fee is charged.

*Directions:* From Fresno and Highway 99, drive east on Highway 180 to Grant Grove and the park's Big Stump entrance. From Grant Grove, drive approximately 6.7 miles south on Generals Highway to a small parking area, located on the south side of the highway and signed Buena Vista Peak.

*Maps:* For a topographic map, ask for General Grant Grove from the USGS. For information on the Forest Service topo map and other maps of the area, see "maps" under hike number 17.

*Who to contact:* For general information, contact Sequoia and Kings Canyon National Parks, Ash Mountain, Three Rivers, CA 93271; (209) 565-3341. For specific information about Kings Canyon National Park, contact Kings Canyon Visitors Center, Grant Grove, CA 93633; (209) 335-2856.

*Trail notes:* From the trailhead, hike up to the top of Buena Vista Peak and then retrace your steps. While the peak is close to the highway and you can still hear highway noise on occasion, the view is worth the hike. Do not venture up here if weather threatens—it is no place to be in a lightning storm.

---

## 31. BIG BALDY TRAIL    3.0 mi/1.5 hrs

*Reference:* **In Kings Canyon National Park; map F5, grid i0.**

*User groups:* Hikers and horses. No mountain bikes or dogs are allowed. No wheelchair facilities.

*Permits:* Day-use permits are not required. Wilderness permits are required for overnight use. A third of the permits are available daily on a first-come, first-served basis. The remainder are available by reservation at least 14 days in advance. For more information, contact the Sequoia and Kings Canyon national parks at (209) 565-3341. A $5 day-use fee is charged.

*Directions:* From Fresno and Highway 99, drive east on Highway 180 to Grant Grove and the park's Big Stump entrance. From Grant Grove, drive approximately 6.8 miles south on Generals Highway to a small parking area, located on the south side of the highway and signed Big Baldy Trailhead.

*Maps:* For a topographic map, ask for General Grant Grove from the USGS. For information on the Forest Service topo map and other maps of the area, see "maps" under hike number 17.

*Who to contact:* For general information, contact Sequoia and Kings Canyon National Parks, Ash Mountain, Three Rivers, CA 93271; (209) 565-3341. For specific information about Kings Canyon National Park, contact Kings Canyon Visitors Center, Grant Grove, CA 93633; (209) 335-2856.

*Trail notes:* Plan to head up here on a spring day, preferably after a rainshower the day before has cleared the air, and you will be suitably rewarded with expansive views to the south of Mineral King, to the east of the Great Western Divide, and to the north of the Sierra. On a visit to Montecito Lodge years ago, Michael found this trail is an outstanding cross-country ski tour as well. From the trailhead, hike up through firs for a short way until the trail cover thins, being replaced by bushes. At one mile, you will begin to see the trail's namesake and the summit of your destination. Keep hiking to the top of Big Baldy, elevation 8,209 feet, and then retrace your steps. Do not venture up here if weather threatens—it is no place to be in a lightning storm.

---

## 32. WEAVER LAKE TRAIL    3.5 mi/2.5 hrs

*Reference:* **In Sequoia National Forest; map F5, grid h1.**

*User groups:* Hikers, dogs and horses. No mountain bikes are allowed. No wheelchair facilities.

*Permits:* Day-use permits are not required.

*Directions:* From Fresno and Highway 99, drive east on Highway 180 to Grant

Grove and the park's Big Stump entrance. From Grant Grove, drive approximately 6.9 miles south on Generals Highway to Big Meadows Campground turnoff. Turn left and drive approximately 3.9 miles to Big Meadows Campground. The trailhead parking is located on the south side of the highway next to the ranger station.

*Maps:* Send $3 to the USDA-Forest Service, 630 Sansome Street, San Francisco, CA 94111 and ask for the Sequoia National Forest map. For a topographic map, ask for Muir Grove from the USGS. For information on the Forest Service topo map and other maps of the area, see "maps" under hike number 17.

*Who to contact:* Hume Lake Ranger District, 35860 East Kings Canyon Road, Dunlap, CA 93621; (209) 338-2251.

*Trail notes:* Perhaps you have heard stories that refer to "the old swimmin' hole." Well, if there is a swimming hole in Sequoia National Forest, Weaver Lake would have to be it. The water is clear and relatively warm—no more than two goosebumps per inch of skin. Hey, we're not talking a Jacuzzi, but a wild lake here, OK? From the parking area, hike through the campground, watching carefully not to lose the trail. At the south end of the campground the trail crosses Big Meadow Creek and then begins to climb. At Fox Meadow, you will come to a wooden trail sign and a trail register for you to sign—you are entering the Jennie Lakes Wilderness. Before long, you will come to a trail junction with the Jennie Lakes Trail branching right. You will head left, across the official wilderness boundary and up to a meadow leading to Weaver Lake. If you are looking to turn a camping neophyte onto the pleasures of the outdoors, this is a great place to camp. In July, blueberries ripen on the bushes around the lakes—yummm! Of course, bears think they are tasty too. Bear precautions when camping are an absolute must. No food anywhere near the tent. Fishing is good, but the fish aren't exactly medal winners. Head back the way you came.

---

## 33. JENNIE LAKE TRAIL     12.0 mi/7.0 hrs

*Reference:* **In Sequoia National Forest; map F5, grid i1.**

*User groups:* Hikers, dogs and horses. No mountain bikes are allowed. No wheelchair facilities.

*Permits:* Day-use permits are not required.

*Directions:* From Fresno and Highway 99, drive east on Highway 180 to Grant Grove and the park's Big Stump entrance. From Grant Grove, drive approximately 6.9 miles south on Generals Highway to Big Meadows Campground turnoff. Turn left and drive approximately 3.9 miles to Big Meadows Campground. The trailhead parking is located on the south side of the highway next to the ranger station.

*Maps:* Send $3 to the USDA-Forest Service, 630 Sansome Street, San Francisco, CA 94111 and ask for the Sequoia National Forest map. For a topographic map, ask for Muir Grove from the USGS. For information on the Forest Service topo map and other maps of the area, see "maps" under hike number 17.

*Who to contact:* Hume Lake Ranger District, 35860 East Kings Canyon Road, Dunlap, CA 93621; (209) 338-2251.

*Trail notes:* If you want to experience the most you can from the Jennie Lakes

Wilderness, then head out on this trip which traverses much of the area to the wilderness' namesake, Jennie Lake. Although we have listed this as a day hike in terms of hours, it is much better enjoyed as an overnight. From the parking area, hike through the campground, watching carefully not to lose the trail. At the south end of the campground the trail crosses Big Meadow Creek and then begins to climb. At Fox Meadow, you will come to a wooden trail sign and a trail register for you to sign—you are entering the Jennie Lakes Wilderness. Before long, you will come to a trail junction with the Weaver Lake Trail branching left. Head right, towards Jennie Lake, across the official wilderness boundary and up to Poop Out Pass—yep, you'll be breathing heavy here. From the pass, drop down into the Boulder Creek drainage to Jennie Lake, an emerald green jewel nestled against white granite cliffs. Retrace your steps unless you crave more. If you do, and we are sure you will, then turn this into a three day trek. Camp the first night here, then head out and up to JO Pass. Go left at JO Pass along Profile View Trail to the Weaver Lake Trail. Head left again towards Weaver Lake and spend the second night there. Hike out to the parking area the next day. See hike number 32 for more notes on this area.

---

## 34. MITCHELL PEAK TRAIL    3.0 mi/3.0 hrs

*Reference:* **In Sequoia National Forest; map F5, grid i1.**

*User groups:* Hikers, dogs and horses. No mountain bikes are allowed. No wheelchair facilities.

*Permits:* Day-use permits are not required.

*Directions:* From Fresno and Highway 99, drive east on Highway 180 to Grant Grove and the park's Big Stump entrance. From Grant Grove, drive approximately 6.9 miles south on Generals Highway to Big Meadows Campground turnoff. Turn left and drive approximately 10.4 miles, past Big Meadows Campground and on to Horse Corral Meadow. Then turn south on Forest Service Road 13S12 to Marvin Pass. Drive 2.8 miles to the trailhead parking for Marvin Pass Trail.

*Maps:* Send $3 to the USDA-Forest Service, 630 Sansome Street, San Francisco, CA 94111 and ask for the Sequoia National Forest map. For a topographic map, ask for Mount Stillman from the USGS. For information on the Forest Service topo map and other maps of the area, see "maps" under hike number 17.

*Who to contact:* Hume Lake Ranger District, 35860 East Kings Canyon Road, Dunlap, CA 93621; (209) 338-2251.

*Trail notes:* This quick but strenuous jaunt will take you to the highest point in the Jennie Lakes Wilderness. Register at the trailhead sign-in before heading out. From the trailhead, you climb quickly to Marvin Pass. At the pass, head left (east) toward Roaring River. Still climbing, you will come to another trail junction and you will take the trail signed "Mitchell Peak" to the left (north). At the 10,365-foot summit, you will be able to see for miles. Enjoy the view before retracing your steps back to the car. Don't even think of heading up here if a storm threatens, unless of course you relish the thought of millions of volts of lightning running wild through your body.

## 35. LITTLE BALDY TRAIL    3.6 mi/2.0 hrs

*Reference:* **In Sequoia National Park; map F5, grid i0.**

*User groups:* Hikers and horses. No mountain bikes or dogs are allowed. No wheelchair facilities.

*Permits:* Day-use permits are not required. A $5 day-use fee is charged.

*Directions:* From Visalia and Highway 99, drive east on Highway 198 to the Ash Mountain Sequoia National Park entrance. Drive approximately 17 miles past the entrance to the Giant Forest. Then continue for about another 13.5 miles past Giant Forest Village to a small parking area on the east side of the road in Little Baldy Saddle, approximately 1.5 miles south of the Dorst Campground.

*Maps:* For a topographic map, ask for Giant Forest from the USGS. For information on the Forest Service topo map and other maps of the area, see "maps" under hike number 17.

*Who to contact:* For general information, contact Sequoia and Kings Canyon National Parks, Ash Mountain, Three Rivers, CA 93271; (209) 565-3341. For specific information about Sequoia National Park, contact Sequoia National Park Visitors Center, Three Rivers, CA 93271; (209) 565-3135.

*Trail notes:* Take a hike on the high side, up out of the trees and into the light. The Little Baldy Trail leads up switchbacks to Baldy's ridge and then up to the summit itself at 8,044 feet. Views of Mineral King and the Great Western Divide are stupendous. Don't even think of hiking up here if the weather threatens. Lightning would put a serious damper on your future plans should it hit while you are exposed on the summit top. Retrace your steps back to the parking area when ready.

---

## 36. MUIR GROVE TRAIL    9.2 mi/5.0 hrs

*Reference:* **In Sequoia National Park; map F5, grid i1.**

*User groups:* Hikers and horses. No mountain bikes or dogs are allowed. No wheelchair facilities.

*Permits:* Day-use permits are not required. Wilderness permits are required for overnight use. A third of the permits are available daily on a first-come, first-served basis. The remainder are available by reservation at least 14 days in advance. For more information, contact the Sequoia and Kings Canyon national parks at (209) 565-3341. A $5 day-use fee is charged. Camping is not allowed within the Giant Forest itself.

*Directions:* From Visalia and Highway 99, drive east on Highway 198 to the Ash Mountain Sequoia National Park entrance. Drive approximately 17 miles past the entrance to the Giant Forest and then continue for another 14 miles or so past Giant Forest Village to the Dorst Campground turnoff.

*Maps:* For a topographic map, ask for Muir Grove from the USGS. For information on the Forest Service topo map and other maps of the area, see "maps" under hike number 17.

*Who to contact:* For general information, contact Sequoia and Kings Canyon National Parks, Ash Mountain, Three Rivers, CA 93271; (209) 565-3341. For specific information about Sequoia National Park, contact Sequoia National Park Visitors Center, Three Rivers, CA 93271; (209) 565-3135.

*Trail notes:* While everyone else is gawking at the sequoia groves in Giant

Forest, you will probably be left to gawk in relative solitude at this wonderful little grove of sequoias at the end of Muir Trail. The trailhead is located approximately 50 yards beyond the group campground entrance. The Muir Grove Trail heads out on a easy track, bearing left at a fork and then continuing through a number of flower-sprinkled meadows before climbing up a series of switchbacks to an overlook one mile out. Descend into a ravine drawing tantalizingly near a picturesque stream before climbing back out and arriving at the top of a ridge and the Muir Grove—two miles from the start. Plan a picnic lunch if you really want to fully enjoy the peaceful feeling the grove inspires. Head back the way you came.

## 37. CABIN CREEK TRAIL  2.0 mi/1.0 hr

*Reference:* **In Sequoia National Park; map F5, grid i1.**

*User groups:* Hikers and horses. No mountain bikes or dogs are allowed. No wheelchair facilities.

*Permits:* Day-use permits are not required. Wilderness permits are required for overnight use. A third of the permits are available daily on a first-come, first-served basis. The remainder are available by reservation at least 14 days in advance. For more information, contact the Sequoia and Kings Canyon national parks at (209) 565-3341. A $5 day-use fee is charged. Camping is not allowed within the Giant Forest itself.

*Directions:* From Visalia and Highway 99, drive east on Highway 198 to the Ash Mountain Sequoia National Park entrance. Drive approximately 17 miles past the entrance to the Giant Forest. Then continue for about another 14 miles past Giant Forest Village to the Dorst Campground turnoff. The Cabin Creek Trailhead is located in the group camp area, just north of parking area C.

*Maps:* For a topographic map, ask for Muir Grove from the USGS. For information on the Forest Service topo map and other maps of the area, see "maps" under hike number 17.

*Who to contact:* For general information, contact Sequoia and Kings Canyon National Parks, Ash Mountain, Three Rivers, CA 93271; (209) 565-3341. For specific information about Sequoia National Park, contact Sequoia National Park Visitors Center, Three Rivers, CA 93271; (209) 565-3135.

*Trail notes:* If you are seeking a little exercise on a trail that slices through a pretty section of woods, then this is your hike. It's an out-and-back proposition from Dorst Campground. Begin hiking up Dorst Creek to the Cabin Creek junction. Head right and up alongside Cabin Creek up to the highway. There is a small turnout parking area here if you desire a one-way shuttle trip. If you don't have a car shuttle arranged, turn around and head back the way you came.

## 38. LOST GROVE TRAIL  5.0 mi/3.0 hrs

*Reference:* **In Sequoia National Park; map F5, grid i1.**

*User groups:* Hikers and horses. No mountain bikes or dogs are allowed. No wheelchair facilities.

*Permits:* Day-use permits are not required. Wilderness permits are required for overnight use. A third of the permits are available daily on a first-come, first-served basis. The remainder are available by reservation at least 14 days in advance. For more information, contact the Sequoia and Kings Canyon national parks at (209) 565-3341. A $5 day-use fee is charged. Camping is not allowed within the Giant Forest itself.

**Directions:** From Visalia and Highway 99, drive east on Highway 198 to the Ash Mountain Sequoia National Park entrance. Drive approximately 17 miles past the entrance to the Giant Forest. Then continue for about another 14 miles past Giant Forest Village to the Dorst Campground turnoff. The Lost Grove Trailhead is located in the group camp area, just north of parking area C.

**Maps:** For a topographic map, ask for Muir Grove from the USGS. For information on the Forest Service topo map and other maps of the area, see "maps" under hike number 17.

**Who to contact:** For general information, contact Sequoia and Kings Canyon National Parks, Ash Mountain, Three Rivers, CA 93271; (209) 565-3341. For specific information about Sequoia National Park, contact Sequoia National Park Visitors Center, Three Rivers, CA 93271; (209) 565-3135.

**Trail notes:** This is a good fall hike and a super winter cross-country ski trek, but it isn't exactly peaceful during the summer as the campground is in full swing and the trail is too close to the General's Highway. Still, it is a nice jaunt to a wonderful grove of sequoia. From the trailhead, the hike stays near Dorst Creek—crossing it early on—through a forest of fir. Lupine proliferate in this area so enjoy their color. The trail continues on, through a trail junction and up to the Lost Grove parking area next to the Generals Highway. What, we could have driven here? Yup. Either have a car waiting or retrace your steps.

---

## 39. NORTH FORK TRAIL          4.5 mi/2.0 hrs

**Reference:** In Sequoia National Park; map F5, grid j0.

**User groups:** Hikers and horses. No mountain bikes or dogs are allowed. No wheelchair facilities.

**Permits:** Day-use permits are not required. Wilderness permits are required for overnight use. A third of the permits are available daily on a first-come, first-served basis. The remainder are available by reservation at least 14 days in advance. For more information, contact the Sequoia and Kings Canyon National Park at (209) 565-3341. A $5 entrance fee is charged.

**Directions:** From Visalia and Highway 99, drive east on Highway 198 to Three Rivers. Then head north on North Fork Drive for 10 miles until the road's end. There is a small parking area out of the way of the gates marking the park's boundary. Do not block any gates or driveways.

**Maps:** Send $3 to the USDA-Forest Service, 630 Sansome Street, San Francisco, CA 94111 and ask for the Sequoia National Forest map. For topographic maps, ask for Giant Forest and Shadequarter Mountain from the USGS. For information on the Forest Service topo map and other maps of the area, see "maps" under hike number 17.

**Who to contact:** For general information, contact Sequoia and Kings Canyon National Parks, Ash Mountain, Three Rivers, CA 93271; (209) 565-3341. For specific information about Sequoia National Park, contact Sequoia National Park Visitors Center, Three Rivers, CA 93271; (209) 565-3135.

**Trail notes:** From the parking area continue walking down the fire road to the national park boundary, marked by a white cattle guard and a fence. Keep walking down to Yucca Creek. Fishing is now allowed in the creek, so cast a line in the water. Crossing Yucca Creek you're bound to get your feet wet unless you prefer dancing on culverts. Hike up the creek for a ways to a trail junction. Head left on the North Fork Trail, some distance away from the Kaweah River but still paralleling it more or less. Hike all the way to Burnt Point Creek where there are a number of informal "fishing trails" working their way down to the river—yes, you can fish the Kaweah, just not the Yucca. Head back the way you came.

*Special note:* Watch out for ticks and poison oak. Also, keep a sharp eye out for rattlesnakes.

---

## 40. COLONY MILL ROAD   11.2 mi. one way/5.0 hrs

*Reference:* **In Sequoia National Park; map F5, grid j1.**

*User groups:* Hikers and horses. No mountain bikes or dogs are allowed. No wheelchair facilities.

*Permits:* Day-use permits are not required. Wilderness permits are required for overnight use. A third of the permits are available daily on a first-come, first-served basis. The remainder are available by reservation at least 14 days in advance. For more information, contact the Sequoia and Kings Canyon national parks at (209) 565-3341. A $5 entrance fee is charged.

*Directions:* We recommend doing this hike with a car-shuttle. From Visalia and Highway 99, drive east on Highway 198 to Three Rivers. Then head north on North Fork Drive for 10 miles until the road's end. There is a small parking area out of the way of the gates marking the park's boundary. Leave one car here but do not block the gates. Drive back to Three Rivers and then north on Highway 198 to the Ash Mountain Sequoia National Park entrance. Then continue driving to Crystal Cave Road which branches off to the left just before the Giant Forest. Call the park service ahead of time to be sure that the road is open; it closes for winter and is partially closed Labor Day through September. If the road is open, drive 1.8 miles to Marble Fork Bridge (where you must park if the road is not open) and continue on for 2.5 more miles to an unsigned trailhead for Colony Mill Road. The trailhead is designated by large logs on the left, blocking vehicle access to the trail. If you have the time, continue up the road and take in a walking tour of Crystal Cave—it is worth a peek.

*Maps:* Send $3 to the USDA-Forest Service, 630 Sansome Street, San Francisco, CA 94111 and ask for the Sequoia National Forest map. For topographic maps, ask for Giant Forest and Shadequarter Mountain from the USGS. For information on the Forest Service topo map and other maps of the area, see "maps" under hike number 17.

*Who to contact:* For general information, contact Sequoia and Kings Canyon National Parks, Ash Mountain, Three Rivers, CA 93271; (209) 565-3341. For specific information about Sequoia National Park, contact Sequoia National Park Visitors Center, Three Rivers, CA 93271; (209) 565-3135.

*Trail notes:* You will be hiking down what was once the only way for visitors to get into the park back in 1926. Now it is an almost forgotten corner that you are sure to enjoy. From the trailhead, it is an almost-all-downhill hike.

You will also hike past the now abandoned Colony Mill Ranger Station—no one to watch over here anymore except for the wildlife, and they don't seem to require too much supervision. Keep on hiking along the steep cliffs and canyons all the way out to North Fork Road and your awaiting second car.

---

## 41. MARBLE FORK BRIDGE/SUNSET ROCK TRAIL    3.6 mi. one way/1.5 hrs

*Reference:* **In Sequoia National Park; map F5, grid j1.**

*User groups:* Hikers and horses. No mountain bikes or dogs are allowed. No wheelchair facilities.

*Permits:* Day-use permits are not required. Wilderness permits are required for overnight use. A third of the permits are available daily on a first-come, first-served basis. The remainder are available by reservation at least 14 days in advance. For more information, contact the Sequoia and Kings Canyon national parks at (209) 565-3341. A $5 day-use fee is charged.

*Directions:* We recommend doing this hike with a car-shuttle. From Visalia and Highway 99, drive east on Highway 198 to the Ash Mountain Sequoia National Park entrance and then continue driving to Crystal Cave Road which branches off to the left just before the Giant Forest. Call the park service ahead of time to be sure that the road is open; it closes for winter and is partially closed after Labor Day. If the road is open, drive 1.8 miles to Marble Fork Bridge and then two-tenths of a mile beyond the bridge to a vehicle parking area. If you have the time, continue up the road and take in a walking tour of Crystal Cave—it is worth a peek. Drive back to Generals Highway and then back to Giant Forest Village. The trailhead is located at the east end of the parking lot.

*Maps:* For a topographic map, ask for Giant Forest from the USGS. For information on the Forest Service topo map and other maps of the area, see "maps" under hike number 17.

*Who to contact:* For general information, contact Sequoia and Kings Canyon National Parks, Ash Mountain, Three Rivers, CA 93271; (209) 565-3341. For specific information about Sequoia National Park, contact Sequoia National Park Visitors Center, Three Rivers, CA 93271; (209) 565-3135.

*Trail notes:* Ahhh, the perfect lazy day hike! It's all downhill and there is plenty of fishing to be enjoyed once you get down to the Marble Fork Kaweah River. Begin hiking at the sign that indicates "Sunset Rock / Marble Fork Bridge." At the first trail junction, head up on the paved trail towards Sunset Rock. Sunset Rock offers good views of the Marble Fork of the Kaweah, Ash Peaks Ridge and the Colony Mill Road to the west. From Sunset Rock, the trail drops through pines and cedar and dogwood—ahhh dogwood. Is there a more beautiful tree blossom in the spring and a more rich red leaf in the fall? We don't think so. Once you have reached the Marble Fork Kaweah, you can wander either up or down the river banks on the fisherman's path, but the going is dicey at best—experienced hikers only. One slip could mean disaster by drowning—graphic enough for you?

## 42. MORO ROCK TRAIL     0.25 mi/0.5 hr

*Reference:* **In Sequoia National Park; map F5, grid j1.**

*User groups:* Hikers only. No mountain bikes, dogs or horses are allowed. No wheelchair facilities.

*Permits:* Day-use permits are not required. A $5 entrance fee is charged.

*Directions:* From Visalia and Highway 99, drive east on Highway 198 to the Ash Mountain Sequoia National Park entrance. Then continue to Giant Forest Village and Crescent Meadow Road on the right. Drive on Crescent Meadow to the signed parking area for Moro Rock.

*Maps:* For a topographic map, ask for Giant Forest from the USGS. For information on the Forest Service topo map and other maps of the area, see "maps" under hike number 17.

*Who to contact:* For general information, contact Sequoia and Kings Canyon National Parks, Ash Mountain, Three Rivers, CA 93271; (209) 565-3341. For specific information about Sequoia National Park, contact Sequoia National Park Visitors Center, Three Rivers, CA 93271; (209) 565-3135.

*Trail notes:* No trip to Sequoia is complete unless you have scrambled up Moro Rock stairway. The trip is an informative one with interpretive signs at the beginning and a permanent map mounted up top to help you identify peaks and ranges in view.

*Special note:* Do not even think of climbing up here if weather threatens. The park service reports that people have been struck by lightning on top of Moro and that a few have been killed. Even when dry, the granite steps leading to the top of the rock are steep and slippery. Children must be supervised at all times.

---

## 43. ROUND MEADOW     0.5 mi/0.5 hr
## LOOP TRAIL/TRAIL FOR ALL PEOPLE

*Reference:* **In Sequoia National Park; map F5, grid j1.**

*User groups:* Hikers, horses and **wheelchairs**. No mountain bikes, dogs or horses are allowed.

*Permits:* Day-use permits are not required. A $5 entrance fee is charged.

*Directions:* From Visalia and Highway 99, drive east on Highway 198 to the Ash Mountain Sequoia National Park entrance and then continue to Giant Forest Village. Approximately two-tenths of a mile past Giant Village turn north off the highway at the sign "Round Meadow—Trail For All People." The parking area is **wheelchair accessible**.

*Maps:* Send $3 to the USDA-Forest Service, 630 Sansome Street, San Francisco, CA 94111 and ask for the Sequoia National Forest map. For a topographic map, ask for Giant Forest from the USGS. For information on the Forest Service topo map and other maps of the area, see "maps" under hike number 17.

*Who to contact:* For general information, contact Sequoia and Kings Canyon National Parks, Ash Mountain, Three Rivers, CA 93271; (209) 565-3341. For specific information about Sequoia National Park, contact Sequoia National Park Visitors Center, Three Rivers, CA 93271; (209) 565-3135.

*Trail notes:* Completed in 1989 with private funds, the Trail For All People is indeed that. It is a pretty little nature trail with a gentle grade, winding through the sequoias with interpretive signs along the entire route. It is completely **wheelchair accessible**.

## 44. SUGAR PINE TRAIL   2.0 mi/1.0 hr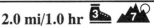

*Reference:* **In Sequoia National Park; map F5, grid j1.**

*User groups:* Hikers only. No mountain bikes, horses or dogs are allowed. No wheelchair facilities.

*Permits:* Day-use permits are not required. A $5 entrance fee is charged.

*Directions:* From Visalia and Highway 99, drive east on Highway 198 to the Ash Mountain Sequoia National Park entrance. Then continue to Giant Forest Village and Crescent Meadow Road on the right. Drive on Crescent Meadow to the signed parking area for Moro Rock.

*Maps:* For topographic maps, ask for Giant Forest and Lodgepole from the USGS. For information on the Forest Service topo map and other maps of the area, see "maps" under hike number 17.

*Who to contact:* For general information, contact Sequoia and Kings Canyon National Parks, Ash Mountain, Three Rivers, CA 93271; (209) 565-3341. For specific information about Sequoia National Park, contact Sequoia National Park Visitors Center, Three Rivers, CA 93271; (209) 565-3135.

*Trail notes:* A walk down the Sugar Pine Trail allows you a peek into a forest's recovery after a forest fire and affords hikers a look at the site of a Native American village. The hike goes by Bobcat Point as well, offering good views off into the distance. From Moro Rock parking area, begin hiking at the signed trailhead located at the southeast end. The trail winds through its namesake, a forest of sugar pine. When you come to a fork in the trail, head either way as the treadway loops around, touching the Crescent Meadow parking area and then heading back to this junction. We recommend heading right or south first as it is the easiest and most interesting way to hike. A Crescent Creek you will notice Native American mortar holes in the rock where they ground acorns for the village. Bobcat Point is along the way too. Once you have looped around and rejoined the junction point, head back the way you came on the first trail section.

## 45. CRESCENT MEADOW   2.0 mi/1.0 hr

*Reference:* **In Sequoia National Park; map F5, grid j1.**

*User groups:* Hikers only. No mountain bikes, horses or dogs are allowed. No wheelchair facilities.

*Permits:* Day-use permits are not required. A $5 entrance fee is charged.

*Directions:* From Visalia and Highway 99, drive east on Highway 198 to the Ash Mountain Sequoia National Park entrance. Then continue to Giant Forest Village and Crescent Meadow Road on the right. Drive on Crescent Meadow past the signed parking area for Moro Rock to the road's end and the Crescent Meadow parking area.

*Maps:* For topographic maps, ask for Giant Forest and Lodgepole from the USGS. For information on the Forest Service topo map and other maps of the area, see "maps" under hike number 17.

*Who to contact:* For general information, contact Sequoia and Kings Canyon National Parks, Ash Mountain, Three Rivers, CA 93271; (209) 565-3341. For specific information about Sequoia National Park, contact Sequoia

National Park Visitors Center, Three Rivers, CA 93271; (209) 565-3135.

*Trail notes:* This is a quick and easy jaunt around one of the more popular trails in this park and you will see why when walking it—good scenery, easy access, a smidgen of history, and interesting things to look at. From the parking area, head off on the signed trail around the south end of Crescent Meadow and then over to Log Meadow. The trail meanders up the west side of Log Meadow and to the east of Crescent Meadow. At Tharp's Log (a log cabin), head left on the Crescent Meadow Trail. Going right is interesting too as it loops around Log Meadow and then ends up back on the Crescent Meadow Trail where you started hiking. Going left takes you past Chimney Tree—a hollowed out sequoia killed by fire. At the next trail junction, head left, still skirting Crescent Meadow back to the parking area.

---

## 46. TRAIL OF THE SEQUOIAS    6.0 mi/3.5 hrs

*Reference:* In Sequoia National Park; map F5, grid j1.

*User groups:* Hikers, horses and **wheelchairs** (on the paved section of Congress Trail). No mountain bikes or dogs are allowed.

*Permits:* Day-use permits are not required. A $5 entrance fee is charged. Camping is not allowed within the Giant Forest itself.

*Directions:* From Visalia and Highway 99, drive east on Highway 198 to the Ash Mountain Sequoia National Park entrance. Drive approximately 17 miles from the entrance to the Giant Forest to the designated parking area for General Sherman Tree, approximately two miles north of Giant Forest Village.

*Maps:* For a topographic map, ask for Giant Forest from the USGS. For information on the Forest Service topo map and other maps of the area, see "maps" under hike number 17.

*Who to contact:* For general information, contact Sequoia and Kings Canyon National Parks, Ash Mountain, Three Rivers, CA 93271; (209) 565-3341. For specific information about Sequoia National Park, contact Sequoia National Park Visitors Center, Three Rivers, CA 93271; (209) 565-3135.

*Trail notes:* Begin your visit and hike in Sequoia by paying homage to the world's largest living thing, the General Sherman Tree (275 feet tall and an estimated weight of 2.8 million pounds). From the parking area, follow the paved Congress Trail loop that begins at General Sherman into a ravine to a junction with the Alta Trail. Head south and uphill on the Trail of the Sequoias—follow the signs to stay on the right path through the trail junctions. The trail heads up and over a ridge, down to Crescent Creek, over to Log Meadow and Tharp's Log (an historic log cabin) and past Crescent Meadow. At Circle Meadow, you can head on the Trail of the Sequoias for a more direct path or head left to Black Arch (a shell of a sequoia), past Cattle Cabin, and to the McKinley Tree and the Congress Trail. Head left and back to the parking area on the last leg of the Congress Trail.

---

## 47. SOLDIERS TRAIL    4.75 mi/3.0 hrs

*Reference:* In Sequoia National Park; map F5, grid j1.

*User groups:* Hikers only. No mountain bikes, horses or dogs are allowed. No wheelchair facilities.

*Permits:* Day-use permits are not required. A $5 entrance fee is charged.

Camping is not allowed within the Giant Forest itself.

*Directions:* From Visalia and Highway 99, drive east on Highway 198 to the Ash Mountain Sequoia National Park entrance. Then continue to Giant Forest Village and Crescent Meadow Road on the right. Drive on Crescent Meadow to the signed parking area for Moro Rock.

*Maps:* For a topographic map, ask for Giant Forest from the USGS. For information on the Forest Service topo map and other maps of the area, see "maps" under hike number 17.

*Who to contact:* For general information, contact Sequoia and Kings Canyon National Parks, Ash Mountain, Three Rivers, CA 93271; (209) 565-3341. For specific information about Sequoia National Park, contact Sequoia National Park Visitors Center, Three Rivers, CA 93271; (209) 565-3135.

*Trail notes:* The Soldiers Trail begins at the northeast end of the parking area. Begin hiking on the treadway. Keep looking for the signs with red lettering and you won't go wrong. This trail is named for the cavalry who used to protect the park in its infancy. The trail heads down to the village where you will bear left and pick up the Moro Rock Trail for the return trip. Be sure to head out on the short spur trail of Moro Rock to Hanging Rock for an outstanding view. Moro Rock Trail ends up back at the Moro Rock parking area. This route is a fun cross-country ski tour in the winter when the paths are snow-covered.

---

# 48. HIGH SIERRA TRAIL 10.0 mi/5.0 hrs

*Reference:* In Sequoia National Park; map F5, grid j1.

*User groups:* Hikers and horses. No mountain bikes or dogs are allowed. No wheelchair facilities.

*Permits:* Day-use permits are not required. Wilderness permits are required for overnight use. A third of the permits are available daily on a first-come, first-served basis. The remainder are available by reservation at least 14 days in advance. For more information, contact the Sequoia and Kings Canyon national parks at (209) 565-3341. A $5 entrance fee is charged. Camping is not allowed within the Giant Forest itself.

*Directions:* From Visalia and Highway 99, drive east on Highway 198 to the Ash Mountain Sequoia National Park entrance. Then continue to Giant Forest Village and Crescent Meadow Road on the right. Drive on Crescent Meadow past the signed parking area for Moro Rock to the road's end and the Crescent Meadow parking area.

*Maps:* For topographic maps, ask for Giant Forest and Lodgepole from the USGS. For information on the Forest Service topo map and other maps of the area, see "maps" under hike number 17.

*Who to contact:* For general information, contact Sequoia and Kings Canyon National Parks, Ash Mountain, Three Rivers, CA 93271; (209) 565-3341. For specific information about Sequoia National Park, contact Sequoia National Park Visitors Center, Three Rivers, CA 93271; (209) 565-3135.

*Trail notes:* The High Sierra Trail is one of the more popular access trails leading into the Sequoia/Kings Canyon National Park's backcountry. Intrepid hikers even put together one way shuttle trips through the Kern Canyon and out to Mt. Whitney on the east side. This area is often bathed in sun by early afternoon. We recommend that whether heading out for a day hike as we describe here, or using the trail for more ambitious aims, start early. Views are super along the way. From the Crescent Meadow parking area, head out on the paved trail to the south, over several bridges and to a trail junction. Head right onto the signed High Sierra Trail. On the way you will pass by Eagle View, the Wolverton Cutoff (a gorgeous trail we describe in hike number 55, this chapter) and then to Panther Creek. We suggest hiking as far as you like on the trail with the Mehrten Meadow/Panther Gap Trail being the furthest you probably should trek for a day-hiking venture. Head back the way you came when ready. If you have a car shuttle, then head back via the Wolverton Cutoff Trail to The General Sherman Tree.

---

# 49. HAZELWOOD NATURE TRAIL

1.0 mi/0.5 hr

**Reference:** In Sequoia National Park; map F5, grid j1.

**User groups:** Hikers only. No mountain bikes, horses or dogs are allowed. No wheelchair facilities.

**Permits:** Day-use permits are not required. A $5 entrance fee is charged. Camping is not allowed within the Giant Forest itself.

**Directions:** From Visalia and Highway 99, drive east on Highway 198 to the Ash Mountain Sequoia National Park entrance. Drive approximately 17 miles from the entrance to the Giant Forest and a small parking area located on the south side of the highway, directly opposite Giant Forest Lodge. The trailhead is signed.

**Maps:** Send $3 to the USDA-Forest Service, 630 Sansome Street, San Francisco, CA 94111 and ask for the Sequoia National Forest map. For a topographic map, ask for Giant Forest from the USGS. For information on the Forest Service topo map and other maps of the area, see "maps" under hike number 17.

**Who to contact:** For general information, contact Sequoia and Kings Canyon National Parks, Ash Mountain, Three Rivers, CA 93271; (209) 565-3341. For specific information about Sequoia National Park, contact Sequoia National Park Visitors Center, Three Rivers, CA 93271; (209) 565-3135.

**Trail notes:** The signed Hazelwood Nature Trail is a perfect introduction to the ecology of the sequoia forest and is completely self-guiding. The trail is well marked and easy to follow through several junctions.

---

# 50. HUCKLEBERRY MEADOW

5.0 mi/2.0 hrs

**Reference:** In Sequoia National Park; map F5, grid j1.

**User groups:** Hikers only. No mountain bikes, horses or dogs allowed. No wheelchair facilities.

**Permits:** Day-use permits are not required. A $5 entrance fee is charged. Camping is not allowed within the Giant Forest itself.

**Directions:** From Visalia and Highway 99, drive east on Highway 198 to the Ash Mountain Sequoia National Park entrance. Drive approximately 17 miles from the entrance to the Giant Forest to a small parking area located on the south side of the highway, directly opposite Giant Forest Lodge. The trailhead is signed.

**Maps:** For a topographic map, ask for Giant Forest from the USGS. For information on the Forest Service topo map and other maps of the area, see "maps" under hike number 17.

***Who to contact:*** For general information, contact Sequoia and Kings Canyon National Parks, Ash Mountain, Three Rivers, CA 93271; (209) 565-3341. For specific information about Sequoia National Park, contact Sequoia National Park Visitors Center, Three Rivers, CA 93271; (209) 565-3135.

***Trail notes:*** In the spring, when the wildflowers are blooming, this trail is a gorgeous one as Huckleberry Meadow becomes a carpet of color at the feet of giants—giant sequoia, that is. Begin hiking on the Hazelwood Nature Trail, leaving it at three-tenths of a mile and a junction where you will stay straight, now on a trail that indicates Bear Hill. Hike past Bear Hill and head right on the Huckleberry Trail fork, leading away from Soldiers Trail and Moro Rock. Hike past Huckleberry Meadow and on to Circle Meadow. Head left at another trail junction, cross Little Deer Creek and head left again at yet another junction, now 2.7 miles out from the trailhead. Hope you have been watching the trail signs or you are going to be one lost puppy. One more time, head left, past bedrock mortars—where Native Americans used to grind acorns for food—and the loop is complete. You are back on the trail you began on, just over three miles from the start. Hike back the way you came on the Hazelwood Nature Trail to the parking area.

---

# 51. CONGRESS TRAIL        2.0 mi/0.5 hr

***Reference:*** **In Sequoia National Park; map F5, grid j1.**

***User groups:*** Hikers and **wheelchairs**. No mountain bikes, horses or dogs are allowed.

***Permits:*** Day-use permits are not required. A $5 entrance fee is charged. Camping is not allowed within the Giant Forest itself.

***Directions:*** From Visalia and Highway 99, drive east on Highway 198 to the Ash Mountain Sequoia National Park entrance. Drive approximately 17 miles from the entrance to the Giant Forest to the designated parking area for General Sherman Tree, approximately two miles north of Giant Forest Village.

***Maps:*** For a topographic map, ask for Giant Forest from the USGS. For information on the Forest Service topo map and other maps of the area, see "maps" under hike number 17.

***Who to contact:*** For general information, contact Sequoia and Kings Canyon National Parks, Ash Mountain, Three Rivers, CA 93271; (209) 565-3341. For specific information about Sequoia National Park, contact Sequoia National Park Visitors Center, Three Rivers, CA 93271; (209) 565-3135.

***Trail notes:*** Sure it's crowded. Yes, the trail is paved, but that makes it accessible to all users. Yes, it feels a bit like "Disneyland in the wild" at times. But if you visit Sequoia and don't pay homage to the world's largest living thing, the General Sherman Tree (275 feet tall and an estimated weight of 2.8 million pounds) then you are really missing out. The tree is majestic, even with crowds, pavement and all. From the parking area, follow the paved Congress Trail loop that begins at General Sherman into a ravine before cutting back to the parking area again.

## 52. LAKES TRAIL
**13.4 mi/7.0 hrs**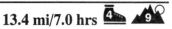

*Reference:* **In Sequoia National Park; map F5, grid j1.**

*User groups:* Hikers and horses. No mountain bikes or dogs are allowed. No wheelchair facilities.

*Permits:* Day-use permits are not required. Wilderness permits are required for overnight use. A third of the permits are available daily on a first-come, first-served basis. The remainder are available by reservation at least 14 days in advance. For more information, contact the Sequoia and Kings Canyon national parks at (209) 565-3341. A $5 entrance fee is charged. Camping is not allowed within the Giant Forest itself.

*Directions:* From Visalia and Highway 99, drive east on Highway 198 to the Ash Mountain Sequoia National Park entrance. Drive approximately 17 miles from the entrance to the Giant Forest and the Wolverton parking area. The trailhead is located to the left of the parking area as you enter from Generals Highway.

*Maps:* For a topographic map, ask for Lodgepole from the USGS. For information on the Forest Service topo map and other maps of the area, see "maps" under hike number 17.

*Who to contact:* For general information, contact Sequoia and Kings Canyon National Parks, Ash Mountain, Three Rivers, CA 93271; (209) 565-3341. For specific information about Sequoia National Park, contact Sequoia National Park Visitors Center, Three Rivers, CA 93271; (209) 565-3135.

*Trail notes:* The scouring action of glaciers centuries ago created little lakes called tarns. The Lakes Trail guides you up to a string of these small tarns which rest in rocky bowls ringed by jagged crags. Heather Lake and Pear Lake are perhaps the most popular of the destinations, although there are other smaller tarns along the way. From the trailhead, avoid the Long Meadow Trail and head east climbing up a moraine ridge. Before long you are hiking above Wolverton Creek and its accompanying wildflowers and tiny meadows. At a junction with a trail leading to Panther Gap, head left towards Heather Lake. You will come to another junction before long and a critical choice. The right is the Hump Trail and it is always open and suitable for everyone—although steep. To the left is our favorite, the Watchtower Trail, which leads along a ledge that was actually dynamited out of the granite, giving you the feeling that at any moment you may drop precipitously into the Tokopah Valley below—it is not for acrophobics! Sometimes the trail may be closed due to snow or avalanche debris. Both trails eventually end up at Heather Lake. Camping is not allowed at Heather Lake, but picnicking certainly is. If you wish to camp, keep on heading up the trail towards Pear Lake, 6.7 miles from the trailhead. If you believe that a throne is everything, then partake of the facilities at Heather Lake. Perched atop the toilet seat you are exposed to the world, literally, but what a view! You'll see what we mean. Head back the way you came when ready.

## 53. MEHRTEN MEADOW
## via PANTHER GAP
**8.0 mi/4.0 hrs**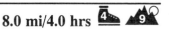

*Reference:* **In Sequoia National Park; map F5, grid j1.**

*User groups:* Hikers and horses. No mountain bikes or dogs are allowed. No

wheelchair facilities.

*Permits:* Day-use permits are not required. Wilderness permits are required for overnight use. A third of the permits are available daily on a first-come, first-served basis. The remainder are available by reservation at least 14 days in advance. For more information, contact the Sequoia and Kings Canyon national parks at (209) 565-3341. A $5 entrance fee is charged. Camping is not allowed within the Giant Forest itself.

*Directions:* From Visalia and Highway 99, drive east on Highway 198 to the Ash Mountain Sequoia National Park entrance. Drive approximately 17 miles from the entrance to the Giant Forest and the Wolverton parking area. The trailhead is located to the left of the parking area as you enter from Generals Highway.

*Maps:* For a topographic map, ask for Lodgepole from the USGS. For information on the Forest Service topo map and other maps of the area, see "maps" under hike number 17.

*Who to contact:* For general information, contact Sequoia and Kings Canyon National Parks, Ash Mountain, Three Rivers, CA 93271; (209) 565-3341. For specific information about Sequoia National Park, contact Sequoia National Park Visitors Center, Three Rivers, CA 93271; (209) 565-3135.

*Trail notes:* From the trailhead, avoid the Long Meadow Trail and head east, climbing up a moraine ridge. Before long you are hiking above Wolverton Creek and its accompanying wildflowers and tiny meadows. At a junction with a trail leading to Panther Gap, head right to Panther Gap. The trail cuts across lush Panther Meadow and reaches Panther Gap in just under a mile. Note the trees broken off 10 to 15 feet up their trunks—evidence of the awesome power of an avalanche. The views from the Gap are stupendous as you peer down upon the Middle Fork Kaweah River far below and the crags of the Great Western Divide far in the distance. At the trail junction, head left. Acrophobics will want no part of this trail, so turn back here. If you choose to continue, be warned that the treadway cuts a narrow ribbon along a ridge with nothing between you and a plummeting fall but the odd tree or two and your sense of balance. At the next junction, head left again to Mehrten Meadow. Several lovely campsites are tucked in along the bank of a stream running through the picturesque meadow—a meadow often peppered with wildflowers in the spring and early summer. Retrace your steps.

---

## 54. TOKOPAH FALLS TRAIL    3.5 mi/2.0 hrs

*Reference:* **In Sequoia National Park; map F5, grid j1.**

*User groups:* Hikers and horses. No mountain bikes or dogs are allowed. No wheelchair facilities.

*Permits:* Day-use permits are not required. A $5 entrance fee is charged. Camping is not allowed within the Giant Forest itself.

*Directions:* From Visalia and Highway 99, drive east on Highway 198 to the Ash Mountain Sequoia National Park entrance. Drive approximately 17 miles from the entrance to the Giant Forest. Then continue for approximately another five miles past Giant Forest Village to the Lodgepole Campground turnoff.

*Maps:* For a topographic map, ask for Lodgepole from the USGS. For information on the Forest Service topo map and other maps of the area, see "maps" under hike number 17.

***Who to contact:*** For general information, contact Sequoia and Kings Canyon National Parks, Ash Mountain, Three Rivers, CA 93271; (209) 565-3341. For specific information about Sequoia National Park, contact Sequoia National Park Visitors Center, Three Rivers, CA 93271; (209) 565-3135.

***Trail notes:*** The Tokopah Trail parallels the boulder-choked river bed of Marble Fork and climbs gradually through a forest of pine, fir and cedar. Plan on hiking to the falls early in the summer when the flow is high and not just another trickle off the towering granite cliffs. The last part of the trail is rather rugged as you clamber over and around rocks to get to a boulder-rimmed bench and designated observation area. The falls are spectacular from where you are and because of the nature of the slippery rocks, you are advised not to attempt closer inspection. According to the park service, a number of intrepid hikers have been killed while seeking a more intimate look at the falls. The trail is an out- and-back affair and begins and ends in the middle of the Lodgepole Campground. Mosquitoes can be really bothersome in the spring and early summer—wear repellent.

---

## 55. WOLVERTON CUTOFF TRAIL

10.0 mi/5.0 hrs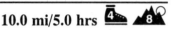

***Reference:*** **In Sequoia National Park; map F5, grid j1.**

***User groups:*** Hikers and horses. No mountain bikes or dogs are allowed. No wheelchair facilities.

***Permits:*** Day-use permits are not required. Wilderness permits are required for overnight use. A third of the permits are available daily on a first-come, first-served basis. The remainder are available by reservation at least 14 days in advance. For more information, contact the Sequoia and Kings Canyon national parks at (209) 565-3341. A $5 entrance fee is charged. Camping is not allowed within the Giant Forest itself.

***Directions:*** From Visalia and Highway 99, drive east on Highway 198 to the Ash Mountain Sequoia National Park entrance. Drive approximately 17 miles from the entrance to the Giant Forest and the designated parking area for General Sherman Tree, approximately two miles north of Giant Forest Village.

***Maps:*** For topographic maps, ask for Giant Forest and Lodgepole from the USGS. For information on the Forest Service topo map and other maps of the area, see "maps" under hike number 17.

***Who to contact:*** For general information, contact Sequoia and Kings Canyon National Parks, Ash Mountain, Three Rivers, CA 93271; (209) 565-3341. For specific information about Sequoia National Park, contact Sequoia National Park Visitors Center, Three Rivers, CA 93271; (209) 565-3135.

***Trail notes:*** Begin your visit and hike in Sequoia by paying homage to the world's largest living thing, the General Sherman Tree (275 feet tall and an estimated weight of 2.8 million pounds). From the parking area, follow the paved Congress Trail loop that begins at General Sherman into a ravine to a junction with the Alta Trail. Head left on to the Alta Trail and proceed to the Wolverton Cutoff Trail and a small meadow. Going left on Wolverton takes you back to Long Meadow and the Wolverton Stables while going right, which you will do, heads around a knoll and uphill, then across

Crescent Creek and up slightly through beautiful stands of sequoia. Sightings of bear and other wildlife are quite common in here so stay quiet and move slowly and alertly. The trail drops quite quickly down a series of switchbacks to meet up with the High Sierra Trail—a drop you don't have to make. Turn around and retrace your steps unless you enjoy hiking down just to hike back up. Keep in mind that this trail is a pack trail used by horses from the Wolverton Corrals, schlepping gear and people up to the High Sierra Trail and camps beyond. Horses have the right of way at all times, so if you hear or see them coming, move off the trail and wait quietly while they pass.

## 56. LONG MEADOW LOOP TRAIL 2.2 mi/1.0 hr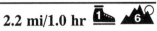

*Reference:* **In Sequoia National Park; map F5, grid j1.**

*User groups:* Hikers and horses. No mountain bikes or dogs are allowed. No wheelchair facilities.

*Permits:* Day-use permits are not required. Wilderness permits are required for overnight use. A third of the permits are available daily on a first-come, first-served basis. The remainder are available by reservation at least 14 days in advance. For more information, contact the Sequoia and Kings Canyon National Park at (209) 565-3341. A $5 day-use fee is charged. Camping is not allowed within the Giant Forest itself.

*Directions:* From Visalia and Highway 99, drive east on Highway 198 to the Ash Mountain Sequoia National Park entrance. Drive approximately 17 miles from the entrance to the Wolverton Road turnoff, approximately three miles past Giant Village. Drive to the Wolverton area parking. The trailhead begins at the southeast end of the parking area at Wolverton Creek.

*Maps:* For topographic maps, ask for Giant Forest and Lodgepole from the USGS. For information on the Forest Service topo map and other maps of the area, see "maps" under hike number 17.

*Who to contact:* For general information, contact Sequoia and Kings Canyon National Parks, Ash Mountain, Three Rivers, CA 93271; (209) 565-3341. For specific information about Sequoia National Park, contact Sequoia National Park Visitors Center, Three Rivers, CA 93271; (209) 565-3135.

*Trail notes:* Keep in mind that this trail is a pack trail used by horses from the Wolverton Corrals, schlepping gear and people up to the High Sierra Trail and camps beyond. Horses have the right-of-way at all times, so if you hear or see them coming, move off the trail and wait quietly while they pass. The trail is an easy one that loops around Long Meadow, part of the way on the Wolverton Cutoff Trail. Much of the trail skirts the edge of the meadow through aspen, fir and pine. At one mile, you will come to a trail junction and a sign indicating Alta Trail. Turn right and head down to Long Meadow through woods to the ski lifts and a footpath leading back to the Wolverton Parking area. This is a great hike for families. Please stick to the trail and refrain from detouring across the meadow—it is a fragile place.

## 57. TWIN LAKES TRAIL 14.5 mi/2.0 days

*Reference:* **In Sequoia National Park; map F5, grid j1.**

*User groups:* Hikers and horses. No mountain bikes or dogs are allowed. No wheelchair facilities.

*Permits:* Day-use permits are not required. Wilderness permits are required for overnight use. A third of the permits are available daily on a first-come, first-served basis. The remainder are available by reservation at least 14 days in advance. For more information, contact the Sequoia and Kings Canyon national parks at (209) 565-3341. A $5 entrance fee is charged. Camping is not allowed within the Giant Forest itself.

*Directions:* From Visalia and Highway 99, drive east on Highway 198 to the Ash Mountain Sequoia National Park entrance. Drive approximately 17 miles from the entrance to the Giant Forest. Then continue for about another five miles past Giant Forest Village to the Lodgepole Campground turnoff on the right. The trailhead is located at the east end of Lodgepole Campground near the bridge spanning the Marble Fork of the Kaweah.

*Maps:* For topographic maps, ask for Lodgepole and Mount Silliman from the USGS. For information on the Forest Service topo map and other maps of the area, see "maps" under hike number 17.

*Who to contact:* For general information, contact Sequoia and Kings Canyon National Parks, Ash Mountain, Three Rivers, CA 93271; (209) 565-3341. For specific information about Sequoia National Park, contact Sequoia National Park Visitors Center, Three Rivers, CA 93271; (209) 565-3135.

*Trail notes:* Tried to hike to Pear Lake but couldn't stomach the swarms of people? You're not alone, which is why we recommend this hike as a more peaceful alternative, although it is a bit more strenuous. The meadows along the way are really wonderful and, if you are quiet enough and no one has preceded you, you may be lucky enough to see bear or deer. An early morning start is best if wildlife viewing is your goal. From the trailhead, the tread climbs steadily up over a ridge and then into deep forest. At about 2.5 miles, the trail reaches Cahoon Meadow, a good spot to take a rest from all the climbing you have been doing. The trail skirts the meadow and starts to climb once more to Cahoon Gap, elevation 8,650 feet. The trail drops down from here to Clover Creek, five miles out, where there are a number of campsites if you wish to cut your journey short—the site is scenic and the fishing is quite good. The trail to Twin Lakes heads right and follows the course of Clover Creek up to Twin Lakes, an outstanding destination. Straight ahead, the trail heads to JO Pass, seven miles away, and the Sunset Meadow trailhead—a one-way hike opportunity if you can con someone into picking you up. "Gee honey, would you like to spend the day driving and sitting around while I hike, fish and have a good time?" If you get a taker, we want to know who they are. Keep in mind that this is bear country so bear-proof your camp—no food or fishy clothing in your tent. Retrace your steps when ready.

---

# 58. ALTA PEAK/     16.0 mi/2.0 days
#    ALTA MEADOW

*Reference:* **In Sequoia National Park; map F5, grid j1.**

*User groups:* Hikers and horses. No mountain bikes or dogs are allowed. No wheelchair facilities.

*Permits:* Day-use permits are not required. Wilderness permits are required for overnight use. A third of the permits are available daily on a first-come, first-served basis. The remainder are available by reservation at least 14 days in advance. For more information, contact the Sequoia and Kings Canyon national parks at (209) 565-3341. A $5 entrance fee is charged. Camping is not allowed within the Giant Forest itself.

*Directions:* From Visalia and Highway 99, drive east on Highway 198 to the Ash Mountain Sequoia National Park entrance. Drive approximately 17 miles from the entrance to the Wolverton Road turnoff, approximately three miles past Giant Village. Drive to the Wolverton area parking. The trailhead begins at the southeast end of the parking area at Wolverton Creek.

*Maps:* For topographic maps, ask for Giant Forest and Lodgepole from the USGS. For information on the Forest Service topo map and other maps of the area, see "maps" under hike number 17.

*Who to contact:* For general information, contact Sequoia and Kings Canyon National Parks, Ash Mountain, Three Rivers, CA 93271; (209) 565-3341. For specific information about Sequoia National Park, contact Sequoia National Park Visitors Center, Three Rivers, CA 93271; (209) 565-3135.

*Trail notes:* Yes, we know the Alta Trail doesn't officially begin at Wolverton and yes, we know that it begins approximately two miles south at Giant Forest. However, why would anyone in their right mind start 1,000 feet lower and two miles further away just so that they can hike a relatively unscenic part of trail along the Generals Highway? That's what we thought and that's why we are beginning our hike at Wolverton. From Wolverton, begin hiking on the Lakes Trail to the Panther Gap Trail. Head right onto Panther Gap Trail, up through the 8,400-foot "gap" to the Alta Trail—ahh there it is. Now, turn left on Alta, hiking past the junction with Seven-Mile Hill Trail and to a junction with the Alta Peak Trail. Here you have a decision to make—to climb or not to climb, that is the question. Sorry. Left and up takes you to Alta Peak at 11,204 feet, 2,000 feet higher than you are now and approximately two miles distant (the views are incredible, but not worth the effort if your breaths are coming in gasps and your muscles are screaming). If you are making this a day-hike and feel doubtful about being able to make it, don't try. You could head straight on to Alta Meadow, a more reasonable destination perhaps, and it still offers over-the-edge views since it is perched on a ridge. Alta Meadow is a good place to camp if you so desire. Head back the way you came when ready.

---

# 59. MARBLE FORK TRAIL to MARBLE FALLS

7.4 mi/6.0 hrs

*Reference:* In Sequoia National Park; map F5, grid j0.

*User groups:* Hikers and horses. No mountain bikes or dogs are allowed. No wheelchair facilities.

*Permits:* Day-use permits are not required. Wilderness permits are required for overnight use. A third of the permits are available daily on a first-come, first-served basis. The remainder are available by reservation at least 14 days in advance. For more information, contact the Sequoia and Kings Canyon national parks at (209) 565-3341. A $5 entrance fee is charged.

*Directions:* From Visalia and Highway 99, drive east on Highway 198 to the Ash Mountain Sequoia National Park entrance. Drive approximately four miles from the entrance to Potwisha Campground and a day-use parking area. The trailhead for Marble Falls begins at Campsite 16.

*Maps:* For a topographic map, ask for Giant Forest from the USGS. For information on the Forest Service topo map and other maps of the area, see "maps" under hike number 17.

*Who to contact:* For general information, contact Sequoia and Kings Canyon National Parks, Ash Mountain, Three Rivers, CA 93271; (209) 565-3341. For specific information about Sequoia National Park, contact Sequoia National Park Visitors Center, Three Rivers, CA 93271; (209) 565-3135.

*Trail notes:* This trail follows the rugged course of the Marble Fork Kaweah River and begins on a dirt road from the campsite. The trail branches out from the road just past a wooden bridge after crossing a concrete water channel. Notice the bands of marble the trail will cross from time to time on the way up to the falls—hence the name Marble Falls and Marble Fork. The falls are actually more a series of pretty cascades frothing their way down-canyon. Once the trail reaches the river's edge, it ends. Unless you are a very experienced backcountry traveler, this is road's end. If you are experienced, watch out for the water which flows fast and furious in the spring as you work your way up the canyon. When ready, head back the way you came.

---

## 60. PICTOGRAPHS LOOP    1.0 mi/0.5 hr

*Reference:* **In Sequoia National Park; map F5, grid j0.**

*User groups:* Hikers and horses. No mountain bikes or dogs are allowed. No wheelchair facilities.

*Permits:* Day-use permits are not required. Wilderness permits are required for overnight use. A third of the permits are available daily on a first-come, first-served basis. The remainder are available by reservation at least 14 days in advance. For more information, contact the Sequoia and Kings Canyon national parks at (209) 565-3341. A $5 entrance fee is charged.

*Directions:* From Visalia and Highway 99, drive east on Highway 198 to the Ash Mountain Sequoia National Park entrance. Drive approximately five miles from the entrance to Hospital Rock picnic area.

*Maps:* Send $3 to the USDA-Forest Service, 630 Sansome Street, San Francisco, CA 94111 and ask for the Sequoia National Forest map. For a topographic map, ask for Giant Forest from the USGS. For information on the Forest Service topo map and other maps of the area, see "maps" under hike number 17.

*Who to contact:* For general information, contact Sequoia and Kings Canyon National Parks, Ash Mountain, Three Rivers, CA 93271; (209) 565-3341. For specific information about Sequoia National Park, contact Sequoia National Park Visitors Center, Three Rivers, CA 93271; (209) 565-3135.

*Trail notes:* This is a quick loop trek around a trail that passes through what was once the sight of a Potwisha Native American village. Bedrock mortars are evident along the way. The trail begins at the Hospital Rock picnic area (Hospital Rock has more pictographs).

---

## 61. PARADISE CREEK TRAIL    4.0 mi/2.0 hrs

*Reference:* **In Sequoia National Park; map F5, grid j0.**

*User groups:* Hikers and horses. No mountain bikes or dogs are allowed. No wheelchair facilities.

*Permits:* Day-use permits are not required. A $5 entrance fee is charged.

*Directions:* From Visalia and Highway 99, drive east on Highway 198 to the Ash Mountain Sequoia National Park entrance. Drive approximately six miles from the entrance to the Hospital Rock picnic area and day-use parking. The trailhead is located a half mile up Generals Highway at Buckeye Flat Campground. No day-use parking is allowed at the campground in the summer and it is closed the rest of the year—how's that for convenience! The trailhead is located next to Campsite 25.

*Maps:* For a topographic map, ask for Giant Forest from the USGS. For information on the Forest Service topo map and other maps of the area, see "maps" under hike number 17.

*Who to contact:* For general information, contact Sequoia and Kings Canyon National Parks, Ash Mountain, Three Rivers, CA 93271; (209) 565-3341. For specific information about Sequoia National Park, contact Sequoia National Park Visitors Center, Three Rivers, CA 93271; (209) 565-3135.

*Trail notes:* This is a pretty trail that wanders through woodlands, occasionally finding its way to picturesque Paradise Creek, crossing it three-quarters of a mile out and then crossing it yet again at one mile. At about two miles, the tread climbs through oak and eventually terminates at a rocky area above Paradise Creek, where you will enjoy kicking back, maybe even partaking in a picnic spread. Head back the way you came.

---

# 62. INDIAN HEAD TRAIL    0.25 mi/0.25 hr

*Reference:* In Sequoia National Park; map F5, grid j0.

*User groups:* Hikers only. No mountain bikes, dogs or horses are allowed. No wheelchair facilities.

*Permits:* Day-use permits are not required. A $5 entrance fee is charged.

*Directions:* From Visalia and Highway 99, drive east on Highway 198 to the Ash Mountain Sequoia National Park entrance. Drive approximately one-tenth of a mile up the highway from the entrance station and look for the parking lot on the right (south) side of the highway. The parking lot is marked by a large carved Indian head. The trail begins at the south end of the lot.

*Maps:* For a topographic map, ask for Giant Forest from the USGS. For information on the Forest Service topo map and other maps of the area, see "maps" under hike number 17.

*Who to contact:* For general information, contact Sequoia and Kings Canyon National Parks, Ash Mountain, Three Rivers, CA 93271; (209) 565-3341. For specific information about Sequoia National Park, contact Sequoia National Park Visitors Center, Three Rivers, CA 93271; (209) 565-3135.

*Trail notes:* Scenery? Hah! It's too crowded to be much of a scenic hike, but the payoff for the short wander is the swimming hole, perfect for a hot summer's day cool-down. There are flat rocks for sunning and a number of pools suitable for splashing and even swimming. Children under supervision should be OK, but not if the flow is fast, which is common in the early spring. Heck, the water's almost too cold then anyway.

---

# 63. ELK CREEK TRAIL    2.0 mi/1.0 hr

*Reference:* In Sequoia National Park; map F5, grid j0.

*User groups:* Hikers only. No mountain bikes, dogs or horses are allowed. No wheelchair facilities.

*Permits:* Day-use permits are not required. Wilderness permits are required for overnight use. A third of the permits are available daily on a first-come, first-served basis. The remainder are available by reservation at least 14 days in advance. For more information, contact the Sequoia and Kings Canyon national parks at (209) 565-3341. A $5 entrance fee is charged.

*Directions:* From Visalia and Highway 99, drive east on Highway 198 to the Ash Mountain Sequoia National Park entrance. Drive approximately 3.6 miles up the highway from the entrance station to a parking area just south of Potwisha Campground, located on the west side of the highway. The trail is unsigned so look carefully for the parking area. If you hit Potwisha, you have gone about two-tenths of a mile too far.

*Maps:* For a topographic map, ask for Giant Forest from the USGS. For information on the Forest Service topo map and other maps of the area, see "maps" under hike number 17.

*Who to contact:* For general information, contact Sequoia and Kings Canyon National Parks, Ash Mountain, Three Rivers, CA 93271; (209) 565-3341. For specific information about Sequoia National Park, contact Sequoia National Park Visitors Center, Three Rivers, CA 93271; (209) 565-3135.

*Trail notes:* If you are seeking out a trail for no other reason than a quick leg stretch and you want to avoid the crowds, the Elk Trail might just be the ticket. It's an out-and-back venture that at its high point offers decent views of Moro Rock and Castle Rocks. Hike until the underbrush becomes too heavy to pass through. Watch out for ticks! This trail is too hot and miserable for summer hiking unless you head out early in the morning, but it is good in the spring and fall.

---

## 64. HOSPITAL ROCK SWIMMING HOLE TRAIL

0.25 mi/0.25 hr

*Reference:* In Sequoia National Park; map F5, grid j0.

*User groups:* Hikers only. No mountain bikes, dogs or horses are allowed. No wheelchair facilities.

*Permits:* Day-use permits are not required. Wilderness permits are required for overnight use. A third of the permits are available daily on a first-come, first-served basis. The remainder are available by reservation at least 14 days in advance. For more information, contact the Sequoia and Kings Canyon national parks at (209) 565-3341. A $5 day-use fee is charged.

*Directions:* From Visalia and Highway 99, drive east on Highway 198 to the Ash Mountain Sequoia National Park entrance. Drive past Potwisha Campground to the Hospital Rock picnic area and parking lot.

*Maps:* For a topographic map, ask for Giant Forest from the USGS. For information on the Forest Service topo map and other maps of the area, see "maps" under hike number 17.

*Who to contact:* For general information, contact Sequoia and Kings Canyon National Parks, Ash Mountain, Three Rivers, CA 93271; (209) 565-3341. For specific information about Sequoia National Park, contact Sequoia National Park Visitors Center, Three Rivers, CA 93271; (209) 565-3135.

*Trail notes:* Yep, we do like swimming holes, if you haven't noticed, and Sequoia National Park has some of the best around. Before you head out on the trail, check out the pictographs at the Park Service Native American exhibit across the highway. Just south of the Native American exhibit is a paved trail that leads down to the Middle Fork Kaweah River, where a number of large swimming holes beckon.

---

## 65. MOUNT WHITNEY          21.0 mi/2.0 days

*Reference:* **Mt. Whitney; map G5, grid a7.**

*User groups:* Hikers and dogs (outside national park boundaries). No mountain bikes or horses are allowed. No wheelchair facilities.

*Permits:* A trailhead quota is in effect from May to October. Permits cost $3 per person and may be requested in advance by mail between March 1 and May 31. Contact the Mount Whitney Ranger District at the address that follows. Wilderness permits are required if you intend on camping. For more information, contact the Mount Whitney Ranger District at (619) 876-6200.

*Directions:* From Lone Pine and Highway 395, head west on Whitney Portal Road for approximately 13 miles to Whitney Portal and the trailhead for the Mt. Whitney Trail.

*Maps:* Send $3 to the USDA-Forest Service, 630 Sansome Street, San Francisco, CA 94111 and ask for the Inyo National Forest map. For topographic maps, ask for Mount Langley and Mount Whitney from the USGS. Tom Harrison Cartography publishes an excellent map of the area. Call (415) 456-7940 and ask for the recreation map of Sequoia and Kings Canyon national parks. The cost is $5.95 plus tax and shipping.

*Who to contact:* Inyo National Forest, Mount Whitney Ranger District, P.O. Box 8, Lone Pine, CA 93545; (619) 876-6200.

*Trail notes:* Mt. Whitney is the highest point in the continental United States at 14,494 feet—need we say more? OK, we will. Alpine country, pretty meadows, unbelievable views, clear skies, clumps of colorful wildflowers, and lots and lots of people—sorry, but it's reality. Everyone wants to climb Whitney. Although some weekend warriors who apparently leave their brains at home in their beer cans attempt to do this hike as a day hike (and they wonder why they feel sick and have a splitting headache? Can you say "altitude sickness"?), we don't recommend it. Hike up part of the way and acclimatize either at Lonepine Lake, 2.8 miles up; Outpost Camp, 3.5 miles up; or Trail Camp, another three miles further up. From the trail crest, turn right and hike up, making the final push to the summit. Trust us, you can't miss it. For more details about climbing Mount Whitney, see PCT-21/John Muir Trail-1 at the end of this chapter.

*Special note:* Pack along plenty of water, sunscreen and a good sunhat. Wear sunglasses for sure. Dress warmly and in layers—even in the summer the peak can get mighty chilly. Don't even try for the summit if weather threatens unless you fancy yourself to be a lightning rod.

# PACIFIC CREST TRAIL　150.0 mi. one way/14.0 days
## GENERAL INFORMATION

*Reference:* **Trail sections extend from the trailhead parking at Whitney Portal north to Agnew Meadows.**

*User groups:* Hikers, horses and dogs (except in national parks). No mountain bikes are allowed. No wheelchair facilities.

*Permits:* A wilderness permit is required for traveling through various wilderness and special-use areas that the trail traverses. Contact the national forest, BLM, or national park office at your point of entry.

*Maps:* For an overall view of the trail route in this section, send $3 for each map to the USDA-Forest Service, 630 Sansome Street, San Francisco, CA 94111, ask for the Inyo National Forest, Sierra National Forest and Sequoia National Forest maps. Topographic maps for particular sections of trail are provided under each specific trail section heading listed below.

*Who to contact:* Contact either the national forest, BLM or national park office at your trailhead—see specific trailheads and corresponding agencies listed within each section.

*Trail notes:* Welcome to the High Sierra, as this section takes you into the heart of it. Bear precautions are at a premium now—no food in the tent and always hang your supplies. Streams may be swollen from the snowmelt and difficult to cross. Snow may still linger in the high passes as late as July. Do not attempt to cross any high angle snowpack or icepack unless you are skilled at handling the situation with an ice ax and crampons. The trail ranges from 7,000 to over 13,000 feet along this portion of the trail.

---

# PCT-21　112.0 mi. one way/11.0 days
## JOHN MUIR TRAIL-1
## WHITNEY PORTAL to LAKE THOMAS EDISON

*Reference:* **From the trailhead parking at Whitney Portal, map F5, grid j6 north to the trailhead parking at Lake Thomas Edison.**

*User groups:* Hikers and horses. No mountain bikes or dogs are allowed. No wheelchair facilities.

*Permits:* A wilderness permit is required for traveling through various wilderness and special-use areas that the trail traverses. Contact the Inyo National Forest District Office at (619) 876-6200.

*Directions:* To the Mt. Whitney Trailhead—From Lone Pine and Highway 395, head west on Whitney Portal Road for approximately 13 miles to Whitney Portal and the trailhead for the Mt. Whitney Trail.

To the Lake Thomas Edison Trailhead—From the town of Shaver Lake, drive north on Highway 168 for approximately 21 miles to the town of Lakeshore. Turn northeast onto Kaiser Pass Road (Forest Service 4S01). Kaiser Pass Road becomes Edison Lake Road at Mono Hot Springs. Drive another five miles north past town to Vermillion Campground and parking for backcountry hikers. The PCT begins near the east end of the lake.

*Maps:* Send $3 for each map ordered to the USDA-Forest Service, 630 Sansome Street, San Francisco, CA 94111 and ask for the Sierra National Forest, Inyo National Forest and Sequoia National Forest maps. For topographic maps, ask for Mt. Whitney, Mount Williamson, Kearsarge Peak, Mount Clarence King, Mount Pinchot, North Palisade, Mount Goddard, Mount Darwin, Mount Henry, Ward Mountain, Florence Lake and Grave-yard Peak.

*Who to contact:* Inyo National Forest, Mount Whitney Ranger District, P.O. Box 8, Lone Pine, CA 93545; (619) 876-6200, or Pine Ridge Ranger District, P.O. Box 300, Shaver Lake, CA 93664; (209) 841-3311. Sequoia National Forest, Cannell Meadow Ranger District, P.O. Box 6, Kernville, CA 93238; (619) 376-3781.

*Trail notes:* You can have a foothold in the sky with every step on the John Muir Trail (and with this section of the PCT). The trail starts at practically the tip-top of North America, Mt. Whitney, and takes you northward across a land of 12,000-foot passes and Ansel Adams-style vistas.

From the trailhead at Whitney Portal, the hike climbs more than 6,100 feet over the course of 10 miles to reach the Whitney summit at 14,494 feet. That includes an ascent over 100 switchbacks (often snow-covered) to top Wotan's Throne and reach Trail Crest (13,560 feet). Here you turn right and take the Summit Trail. In the final stretch to the top, the ridge is cut by huge notch windows in the rock; you look through and the bottom drops out more than 10,000 feet to the little town of Lone Pine below, at 3,800 feet elevation. Finally you make it to the top, and notice how the surrounding giant blocks of rock look as if they were sculpted with a giant hammer and chisel. From here, the entire Western Divide is visible, and to the north are rows of mountain peaks lined up for miles to the horizon. You sign your name in the register (kept in a lightning-proof metal box). You may feel a bit dizzy from the altitude, but know you are someplace very special.

The journey farther north is just as captivating. The route drops into Sequoia National Park, then climbs above treeline for almost a day's worth of hiking as it nears Forester Pass, 13,180 feet. It is not only the highest point on the PCT, but the most dangerous section of trail on the entire route as well. The trail is narrow and steep, cut into a high vertical slab of rock, and is typically icy, with an iced-over snowfield near the top particularly treacher-ous. An ice-ax is an absolute must—a slip here and you could fall thousands of feet.

Once through Forester, the trail heads onward into the John Muir Wilderness along Bubbs Creek, with great wildflowers at nearby Vidette Meadow. Then it is up and over Kearsage Pass (10,710 feet), and after a short drop, you're back climbing again; this time over Glen Pass (11,978 feet), a spectacular, boulder-strewn ridge with great views to the north looking into Kings Canyon National Park. Just two miles from Glen Pass is Rae Lakes, a fantasy spot for camping (one-night limit), with pristine meadows, shore-line campsites, and lots of eager brook trout.

The JMT/PCT then heads through Kings Canyon National Park by following pristine streams much of the way, finally climbing up and over Pinchot Pass (12,130 feet), then back down along the upper Kings River for a long, steady ascent over Mather Pass (12,100 feet). The wonders continue as you hike along Palisade Lakes, then down into LeConte Canyon, followed by an endless climb up to Muir Pass (11,965 feet). In early summer, snowfields are common here, and this can be the most difficult and trying section of the entire PCT, especially if your boots keep postholing through the snow. The country near Muir Pass is stark–nothing but sculpted granite, ice and a few small turquoise lakes—crowned by the stone-made Muir Hut at the pass, where hikers can hide for safety from afternoon thunderstorms and lightning bolts.

The views astound many visitors as you drop into Evolution Valley. It is like a trip to the beginning of time, where all is pure and primary, yet lush and beautiful. You finally leave Kings Canyon National Park, following the headwaters of the San Joaquin River into the Sierra National Forest.

After bottoming out at 7,890 feet, the trail rises steeply in switchback after switchback as it enters the John Muir Wilderness. Finally you top Selden Pass (10,900 feet), take in an incredible view where the rows of surrounding mountain tops look like the Great Pyramids, then make the easy one-mile descent to Marie Lakes, a pretty campsite with excellent trout fishing near the outlet.

The final push on this section of trail is up Bear Mountain, then down a terrible, toe-jamming stretch to Mono Creek. Here you turn left and make the two-mile hike to Edison Lake, an excellent place to have a food stash waiting.

---

## PCT-22       38.0 mi. one way/3.0 days
## JOHN MUIR TRAIL-2
## LAKE THOMAS EDISON to AGNEW MEADOWS

*Reference:* **From Lake Thomas Edison north to Agnew Meadows; map F5, grid b1.**

*User groups:* Hikers, dogs and horses. No mountain bikes are allowed. No wheelchair facilities.

*Permits:* A wilderness permit is required for traveling through various wilderness and special-use areas that the trail traverses. Contact the Inyo National Forest at (619) 934-2505 or the Sierra National Forest at (209) 841-3311.

*Directions:* From Fresno, drive northeast on Highway 168 for approximately 68 miles to the town of Lakeshore at Huntington Lake. Turn northeast onto Kaiser Pass Road (Forest Service 4S01). Kaiser Pass Road becomes Edison Lake Road at Mono Hot Springs. Drive another five miles north past town to Vermillion Campground and the parking area for backcountry hikers. The trail begins near the east end of the lake.

*Maps:* For a map of Inyo National Forest, send $3 to USDA-Forest Service, 630 Sansome Street, San Francisco, CA 94111. To obtain topographic maps of the area, ask for Mammoth Mountain, Crystal Crag, Bloody Mountain, Graveyard Peak, Mount Ritter and Coip Peak.

*Who to contact:* Inyo National Forest, Mammoth Ranger District, P.O. Box 148, Mammoth Lakes, CA 93546; (619) 934-2505. Sierra National Forest, (209) 841-3311.

*Trail notes:* The world is not perfect, but the scene from Silver Pass comes close. At 10,900 feet, you scan a bare, high-granite landscape sprinkled with alpine lakes. Just north of the pass are five small lakes: Chief, Papoose, Warrior, Squaw and Lake of the Lone Indian. This is the highlight on this 38-mile section of the Pacific Crest Trail. The trip starts at Mono Creek, with a good resupply point at Edison Lake (7,650 feet), just two miles away. From the Mono Creek junction, you head north toward Silver Pass, climbing along Silver Pass Creek much of the way. Before you get to Silver Pass, there is a stream crossing that can be dangerous in high runoff conditions. Top Silver Pass at 10,900 feet, and enjoy a five-mile descent and then a quick up to Tully Hole (9,250 feet). Climbing north, you pass Deer Creek, Purple Lake and Lake Virginia. You head up to Red Cones and then make a steady descent toward Devil's Postpile National Monument. A good resupply point is at nearby Red's Meadow Pack Station.

*Special note:* For food drop information, call Vermillion Valley Resort at (209) 855-6558. They are open only in summer and fall.

*PCT CONTINUATION:* To continue hiking along the Pacific Crest Trail or the John Muir Trail, see Chapter E4, pages 447-451.

CEN-CAL MAP ..................... see page 466
adjoining maps
NORTH ........................................ no map
EAST ........................................... no map
SOUTH (G6) ......................... see page 598
WEST (F5) ............................. see page 492

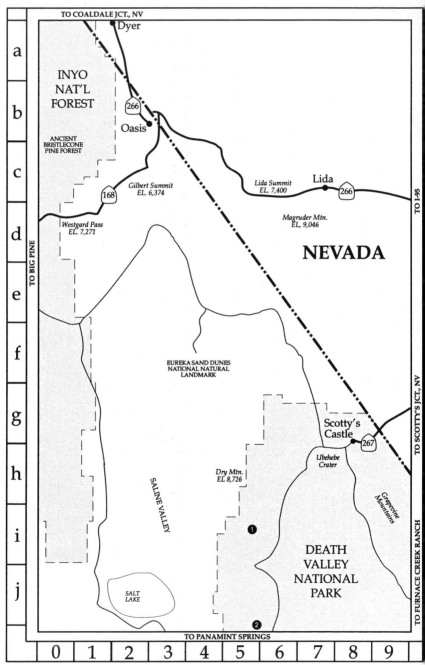

# Map F6 featuring: Inyo National Forest, Death Valley National Park, Saline Valley

## 1. UBEHEBE PEAK TRAIL    5.0 mi/4.0 hrs

*Reference:* **In Death Valley National Park; map F6, grid i5.**

*User groups:* Hikers. Horses are allowed away from developed areas. Leashed dogs are allowed on roads, but not on trails. Mountain bikes are allowed on dirt roads, but not on trails or cross-country. No wheelchair facilities.

*Permits:* No permits are required at this time but filling out the backcountry-use register form located at the visitor's center is highly recommended. Camping is allowed anywhere in the park as long as you are at least five miles from a maintained campground, one mile from a major road, a quarter of a mile from the nearest water source and above sea level. Campfires are not permitted at any time. A $6 entry fee is collected at the Grapevine Entrance Station.

*Directions:* From Highway 395, drive on Highway 190 to Death Valley National Park. Stay on Highway 190 to the Furnace Creek Visitor's Center and check in. From Furnace Creek, drive north on Highway 190 to North Highway and follow the signs to Scotty's Castle and Ubehebe Crater. Just past the Grapevine Entrance Station, turn left onto a paved road toward Ubehebe Crater. At the crater, turn right onto Racetrack Road—a dirt washboard suitable only for high-clearance vehicles. At Teakettle Junction, turn right again and drive approximately 5.6 miles to the Grandstand parking area located on the right, opposite an interpretive sign.

*Maps:* For a topographic map, ask for Ubehebe Peak from the USGS. One of the best overall maps of the area is published by Trails Illustrated and is titled *Death Valley National Monument.* The cost is $7.95 and may be ordered by calling (800) 962-1643.

*Who to contact:* Death Valley National Park, Death Valley, CA 92328; (619) 786-2331.

*Trail notes:* If you are seeking spectacular views of Mt. Whitney, the White Mountains and the Saline Valley, then this is your hike. The trail begins at the parking area and winds a serpentine route up an old mining trail to the summit. The hiking is easy at first, climbing up a gentle slope to the base of a large rock. From here, endless switchbacks will take you up to a saddle just north of Ubehebe Peak. You will see visual evidence and reason for the trail—copper ore. From the saddle and old mine site, the trip continues to the west, skirting the summit of Ubehebe. Your last steps will be a bit of a rock scramble, not too difficult, up a rocky ridge to the 5,678-foot summit of Ubehebe. Return the way you came. Wildflowers in the spring are super. The best time to visit Death Valley is between November and April, although summer months are not out of the question if you like it really hot—like hotter than anywhere else in the United States. No matter when you visit and how short your hike, always carry water with you—one gallon per person per day is the minimum fluid intake for survival. Water does exist in the valley, but it is unreliable so don't count on it no matter what your map may say. Much of the true adventure in Death Valley is found via cross-country travel, but for this you need superb navigational skills. Always check in at the

Furnace Creek Visitor's Center before heading out, to sign the register and inquire about road and trail conditions. Carry survival gear in your car, both for your car and yourself. Know how to cool down an overheated engine and carry plenty of water for the radiator. Don't stick your hands into holes and cracks unless you are trying to get bitten by a rattlesnake or stung by a scorpion. Yes, you should always check your boots before putting them on in the morning and don't be surprised to find a scorpion has cuddled under your sleeping bag while you sleep—they like warmth too.

*Special note:* One last word of wisdom. In the desert, distant objects are always further away than you might think, as the dry air has a tendency to telescope things closer to you—that quick jaunt to a peak on the horizon may turn out to be an all-day epic trip.

---

# 2. COTTONWOOD/      27.0 mi/3.0 days
# MARBLE CANYONS LOOP

*Reference:* **In Death Valley National Park; map F6, grid j5.**

*User groups:* Hikers. Horses are allowed away from developed areas. Leashed dogs are allowed on roads, but not on trails. Mountain bikes are allowed on dirt roads, but not on trails or cross-country. No wheelchair facilities.

*Permits:* No permits are required at this time but filling out the backcountry-use register form located at the visitor's center is highly recommended. Camping is allowed anywhere in the park as long as you are at least five miles from a maintained campground, one mile from a major road and a quarter of a mile from the nearest water source. Campfires are not permitted at any time. A $6 entry fee is collected at the Grapevine Entrance Station.

*Directions:* From Highway 395, drive on Highway 190 to Death Valley National Park. Stay on Highway 190 to the Furnace Creek Visitor's Center and check in. From Furnace Creek, drive north on Highway 190 to Stovepipe Wells and turn right past the campground and towards the airstrip. The road turns to soft sand which is suitable for a high-clearance vehicle, although we recommend a four-wheel-drive vehicle. Drive to the junction with Cottonwood/Marble Canyon Roads and park. The road continues for approximately seven miles down Cottonwood Canyon to the left and two miles down Marble Canyon to the right.

*Maps:* For topographic maps, ask for Sand Flat, East of Sand Flat, Harris Hill and Cottonwood Canyon from the USGS. One of the best overall maps of the area is published by Trails Illustrated and is titled *Death Valley National Monument.* The cost is $7.95 and may be ordered by calling (800) 962-1643.

*Who to contact:* Death Valley National Park, Death Valley, CA 92328; (619) 786-2331.

*Trail notes:* This is an outstanding loop backpack trip that will introduce you to the wonders of backpacking in Death Valley. There are springs along the way, but carry plenty of extra water to be safe. Remember that you cannot camp within a quarter of a mile of any water source—this is to protect the animals. Look for petroglyphs at Marble Canyon's mouth. Our trip begins at the junction where you will head left and begin hiking up the four-wheel-drive road into Cottonwood Canyon. Once the road ends, follow a faint trail and then you are on your own. This trail is not marked at all so be very sure of your navigational skills. Approximately six miles after leaving the road and as you leave the canyon at Cottonwood Springs, you will head right and northeast toward Deadhorse Canyon and then northwest to Marble Canyon. Once in Marble, it is approximately 8.5 miles to the junction and your car. Expert navigational skills are requisite before attempting this trek.

CEN-CAL MAP ..................... see page 466
adjoining maps
NORTH (F1) .......................... see page 468
EAST (G2) ............................. see page 548
SOUTH ................................... no map
WEST ..................................... no map

1 TRAIL
PAGES 546-547

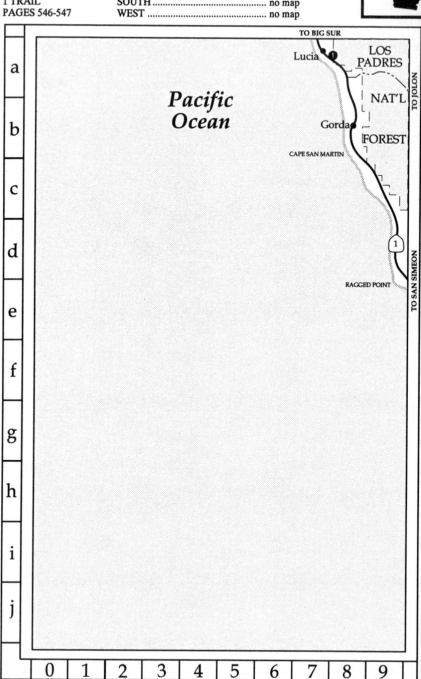

TO BIG SUR

Lucia

LOS PADRES

*Pacific Ocean*

TO JOLON

NAT'L

Gorda

FOREST

CAPE SAN MARTIN

1

RAGGED POINT

TO SAN SIMEON

a b c d e f g h i j

0 1 2 3 4 5 6 7 8 9

# 1. KIRK CREEK TRAIL    10.0 mi/5.0 hrs

*Reference:* In Los Padres National Forest, south of Big Sur; map G1, grid a7.

*User groups:* Hikers, dogs and horses. No mountain bikes are allowed. No wheelchair facilities.

*Permits:* Day-use permits are required and wilderness permits are needed if you plan on camping overnight in the Ventana Wilderness. Contact the Carmel River Station at (408) 659-2612 for more information.

*Directions:* From Big Sur, drive 26 miles south on Highway 1 to the town of Lucia and the signed entrance to the Kirk Creek Campground.

*Maps:* Send $3 to the USDA-Forest Service, 630 Sansome Street, San Francisco, CA 94111 and ask for the Los Padres National Forest map. For a topographic map, ask for Lopez Point from the USGS.

*Who to contact:* Los Padres National Forest, Carmel River Station, 37700 Nathan Road, Carmel Valley, CA 93924; (408) 659-2612 or (408) 385-5434.

*Trail notes:* This loop trip takes you into the Ventana Wilderness, the largest wilderness area in the South Coast Range. The trailhead begins directly opposite the main entrance to Kirk Creek Campground. The trail from Kirk Creek ascends steadily but gradually through open grassland and brush to a pleasant trail camp (Vicente Flat Camp) located under the shade of redwoods at the east end of a large meadow. Ocean views, superb canyon overlooks and the redwood forest are reason enough to lace up your boots and head out for a day or two. If the trek to Vicente Flat isn't enough for you, head northwest for six miles to Goat Camp (excellent ocean views) and then over to Cone Peak (elevation 5,155 feet) and the Cone Peak Parking Area. The Cone Peak Road is dubbed "the steepest climb in North America..." The total distance from Kirk Creek to Cone Peak is 14 miles, one way.

*Special note:* The best time to visit is between October and May. Snow can dust the area in winter. Summer can become unbearably hot. Carry two quarts of water with you at all times—water sources are limited. Watch out for poison oak, which appears to absolutely love the climate and soil conditions.

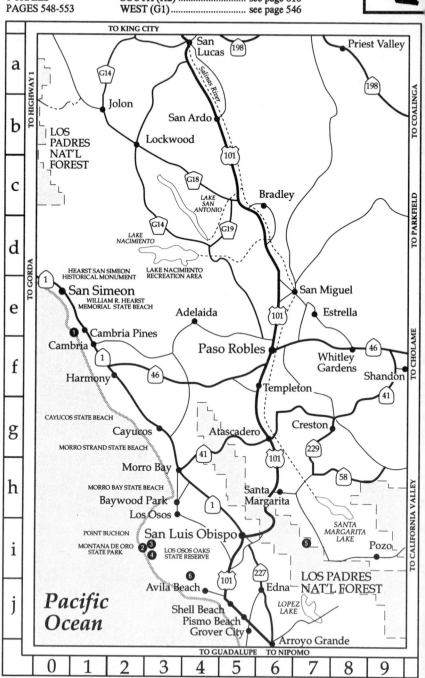

**Map G2 featuring:** Cambria, Montana de Oro State Park, Lopez Lake

## 1. MOONSTONE BEACH TRAIL   1.0 mi/0.5 hr

*Reference:* In Cambria, north of San Luis Obispo on Highway 1; map G2, grid e1.

*User groups:* Hikers and mountain bikes. No dogs or horses are allowed. No wheelchair facilities.

*Permits:* No permits are required

*Directions:* From San Luis Obispo, drive north on Highway 101 to the town of Cambria and then drive 2.5 more miles to Moonstone Beach Drive. Turn left and park at the north end of Moonstone Beach Drive at Vista Point. Moonstone Beach Drive has a north and a south entrance.

*Maps:* For a topographic map, ask for Cambria from the USGS.

*Who to contact:* There is no known contact for this community-maintained beach walk.

*Trail notes:* Moonstone Beach is named for the numerous moonstone agates that have been found there. The hike along the beach isn't particularly long, and you probably won't drive out of your way to trek it. If, however, you find yourself heading up Highway 1 from San Luis Obispo, or heading down past Hearst Castle towards L.A., then by all means, take a brief pit-stop and stretch your legs. You won't be disappointed. Scan the ocean in January and you may spot migrating whales. Numerous trails branching off the main route lead to grassy bluffs—perfect for kicking back and taking in the majesty of the famous California coast.

## 2. BLUFF TRAIL   4.0 mi/1.0 hr

*Reference:* Montana de Oro State Park west of San Luis Obispo; map G2, grid i2.

*User groups:* Hikers and mountain bikes. No horses or dogs are allowed. No wheelchair facilities.

*Permits:* No permits are required

*Directions:* From San Luis Obispo, drive three miles south on Highway 101 to Los Osos/Baywood Park exit. Drive 12 miles west on Los Osos Valley Road. Los Osos Valley Road becomes Pecho Valley Road and enters the state park. The park headquarters and parking is 2.7 miles beyond the entrance sign.

*Maps:* A map for Morro Bay Area State Parks may be obtained from the park headquarters for $1. For a topographic map, ask for Morro Bay South from the USGS.

*Who to contact:* Montana de Oro State Park, Los Osos, CA 93402; (805) 528-0513.

*Trail notes:* This hike affords the visitor super opportunities to enjoy the colorful bluffs and cliffs overlooking Spooner's Cove and Coralina Cove. In the spring, the explosion of color from mustard flower and poppies has inspired many to refer to this park by its English translation—"mountain of gold." Several informal trails leading down to the coves allow for excellent tidepool exploration. Keep your binoculars handy to scan the ocean for harbor seals and the air currents for pelican, albatross and cormorant. Begin hiking at the trailhead near the headquarters on the signed Bluff Trail. Follow the Bluff Trail south as it parallels the coast overlooking first Spooner's Cove, then Coralina and Quarry Cove, reaching a nice overlook above sea caves and near an area called Grotto Rock. Head back the way you came.

---

## 3. ISLAY CREEK/ RIDGE TRAIL LOOP

8.1 mi/4.0 hrs

**Reference:** Montana de Oro State Park west of San Luis Obispo; map G2, grid i3.

**User groups:** Hikers, horses and mountain bikes. No dogs are allowed. No wheelchair facilities.

**Permits:** No permits are required

**Directions:** From San Luis Obispo, drive three miles south on Highway 101 to Los Osos/Baywood Park exit. Drive 12 miles west on Los Osos Valley Road. Los Osos Valley Road becomes Pecho Valley Road and enters the state park. The park headquarters and parking is 2.7 miles beyond the entrance sign. The trailhead for Islay Creek Road lies approximately two-tenths of a mile before reaching the park headquarters—limited parking.

**Maps:** A map for Morro Bay Area State Parks may be obtained from the park headquarters for $1. For a topographic map, ask for Morro Bay South from the USGS.

**Who to contact:** Montana de Oro State Park, Los Osos, CA 93402; (805) 528-0513.

**Trail notes:** Wildflowers are fantastic in the spring and early summer on this hike. So are the views from the Ridge Trail year round—they'll leave you "oohing" and "ahhing." Begin hiking at the trailhead gate for Islay Creek Road. Turn left after three miles onto East Boundary Trail. After five miles or so, you will come to a Y intersection and the Ridge Trail. Turn left on the Ridge Trail past Hazard Peak and continue all the way back to the parking area and your car.

**Special note:** This is prime tick country so check yourself and your friends for ticks every night and every lunch break. Poison oak is also growing in thick bunches along the trails—it's as if they fertilize the darn stuff!

---

## 4. VALENCIA PEAK TRAIL

4.0 mi/2.0 hrs

**Reference:** Montana de Oro State Park west of San Luis Obispo; map G2, grid i3.

**User groups:** Hikers only. No dogs, horses or mountain bikes. No wheelchair facilities.

**Permits:** No permits are required

**Directions:** From San Luis Obispo, drive three miles south on Highway 101 to Los Osos/Baywood Park exit. Drive 12 miles west on Los Osos Valley Road. Los Osos Valley Road becomes Pecho Valley Road and enters the state park. The park headquarters and parking is 2.7 miles beyond the entrance sign.

**Maps:** A map for Morro Bay Area State Parks may be obtained from the park headquarters for $1. For a topographic map, ask for Morro Bay South from the USGS.

**Who to contact:** Montana de Oro State Park, Los Osos, CA 93402; (805) 528-0513.

*Trail notes:* The Valencia Peak Trail begins shortly after leaving park headquarters on Rattlesnake Flats Trail, and proceeds quickly inland, progressively climbing up a series of switchbacks. Fortunately, the profusion of lupine, mustard flower, poppy and Indian paintbrush will keep your mind from focusing on the climb. The trail crosses outcroppings of shale, which are ideal for looking for fossils—look but please don't collect. Once you reach the summit, take a break and enjoy the panorama. On a clear day, you get views of up to 90 miles of coastline in either direction from the summit of Valencia Peak, elevation 1,346 feet. With a topographic map handy, you will be able to pick out Morro Rock, Hollister Peak, Black Mountain and distant Point Sal. Return the way you came.

---

## 5. BIG FALLS CANYON      2.5 mi/1.0 hr

*Reference:* West of San Luis Obispo and north of Santa Maria near Lopez Lake; map G2, grid i7.

*User groups:* Hikers and horses. No dogs or mountain bikes are allowed. No wheelchair facilities.

*Permits:* Wilderness permits for day and overnight use are required. Contact the Santa Lucia Ranger District at (805) 925-9538.

*Directions:* From San Luis Obispo, drive 15 miles south on Highway 101 to Highway 227 and the Lopez Lake exit. Head east on Highway 227 towards Lopez Lake. Approximately one mile after the exit, turn right at a sign indicating Lopez Lake. The road you are on will cross Lopez Lake's dam and then parallel the lake's southern shore. Just before entering the Lopez Lake Recreation Area, turn right onto Hi Mountain Road. In approximately nine-tenths of a mile, turn left onto Upper Lopez Canyon Road and drive 6.4 miles to a sign indicating Lopez Canyon. The pavement will end shortly, although in dry conditions it should be passable by most vehicles. If you are in doubt, park your car and add 3.5 miles to your hike each way. Otherwise, continue driving slowly on the dirt road for 3.5 miles to an unmarked trailhead next to a dry waterfall, located on the western side of the road. Park so that the fire road is not obstructed in any way.

*Maps:* Send $3 to the USDA-Forest Service, 630 Sansome Street, San Francisco, CA 94111 and ask for the Los Padres National Forest map. For a topographic map, ask for Lopez Mountain from the USGS.

*Who to contact:* Santa Lucia Ranger District, 1616 Carlotti Drive, Santa Maria, CA 93454; (805) 925-9538.

*Trail notes:* The Santa Lucia Wilderness lies at the southern end of the Santa Lucia Mountain Range. Few trails lace this rugged area. The Big Falls Canyon Trail is one of the better ones, good for a quick peek of the area. The trail starts out following the Lopez Canyon Creek to the Big Falls Canyon, where the trail winds from one bank to another up Big Falls Canyon Creek. You will pass numerous deep and inviting pools—excellent for taking a cooling dip. In the upper reaches of the canyon, where the stream dries up by midsummer in normal years and the trail disappears into dense thickets of poison oak, turn around—unless you possess a really adventurous spirit.

## 6. PECHO COAST TRAIL 7.0 mi/6.0 hrs

*Reference:* South of Montana De Oro State Park, north of Avila Beach near San Luis Obispo; map G2, grid j3.

*User groups:* Hikers only. No dogs, horses or mountain bikes are allowed. No wheelchair facilities.

*Permits:* This hike is available only with a docent guide from the Nature Conservancy on outings that are reservation-filled only. There are a limited number of hikes led each week. For information and reservations, call (805) 541-8735.

*Directions:* From San Luis Obispo, drive south on Highway 101 to Avila Beach Drive, just north of Pismo Beach, and head towards the coast. Drive on Avila Beach Drive for approximately four miles to the security-gated entrance to Diablo Nuclear Power Plant. Park along Avila Beach Drive where you will meet your Nature Conservancy guide.

*Maps:* For a topographic map, ask for Point San Luis. The Nature Conservancy will provide a free trail brochure upon request when you are making your hike reservation.

*Who to contact:* The Nature Conservancy, Central Coast Preserves, P.O. Box 15810, San Luis Obispo, CA 93406; (805) 541-8735.

*Trail notes:* OK, so the trail begins and ends near a nuclear power plant and all you see at the start is pavement, barbed wire and large gates—relax. Once the trappings of a nuclear zone are left behind, you will be wandering along a pristine section of California coast that has only recently been opened to the public and still sees very few visitors. If you take the time to wander, even if it is in a guided group, you will be rewarded with a walk along steep bluffs, through oak woodland and to the historic Point San Luis Lighthouse. The trail is not difficult at all and, since the walk is docent-led, geared to a snail's pace. This may leave those who have ants in their pants feeling a little fidgety. Along the way, the docent will share incredible volumes of natural history and wonderful stories regarding the local history of the region. At the turnaround point, you will have an opportunity to peer down upon harbor seals and sea otters who frequently bask in the sun along the shoreline. Although the hike is only seven miles roundtrip, it is an all-day affair and not for those in a hurry.

## Leave No Trace Tips

### Camp with care

- Choose a pre-existing, legal site. Restrict activities to areas where vegetation is compacted or absent.

- Camp at least 75 steps (200 feet) from lakes, streams and trails.

- Always choose sites that will not be damaged by your stay.

- Preserve the feeling of solitude by selecting camps that are out of view when possible.

- Do not construct structures or furniture or dig trenches.

**MAP G3**

CEN-CAL MAP ...................... see page 466
adjoining maps
NORTH (F3) ........................... see page 480
EAST (G4) .............................. see page 556
SOUTH (H3) .......................... see page 616
WEST (G2) .............................. see page 548

1 TRAIL
PAGES 554-555

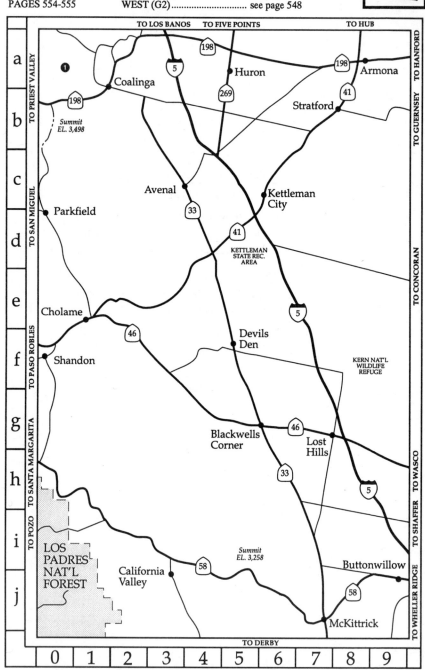

TO LOS BANOS    TO FIVE POINTS    TO HUB

TO PRIEST VALLEY

**①**

198

5

Coalinga

198

Huron

198    Armona

269

TO HANFORD

41

Stratford

TO GUERNSEY

*Summit
EL. 3,498*

TO SAN MIGUEL

Parkfield

Avenal

33

Kettleman
City

41

KETTLEMAN
STATE REC.
AREA

TO CONCORAN

5

TO PASO ROBLES

Cholame

46

Devils
Den

KERN NAT'L
WILDLIFE
REFUGE

Shandon

TO SANTA MARGARITA

46

Blackwells
Corner

Lost
Hills

TO WASCO

33

5

TO SHAFFER

TO POZO

LOS
PADRES
NAT'L
FOREST

*Summit
EL. 3,258*

Buttonwillow

California
Valley

58

58

TO WHEELER RIDGE

McKittrick

TO DERBY

0    1    2    3    4    5    6    7    8    9

**Map G3 featuring:** Kreyenhagen Mountain, Coalinga Mineral Springs County Park

## 1. COALINGA MINERAL SPRING

**4.5 mi/2.0 hrs**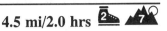

*Reference:* **Near Coalinga west of Interstate 5; map G3, grid a0.**

*User groups:* Hikers, horses, dogs and mountain bikes. No wheelchair facilities.

*Permits:* No permits are required.

*Directions:* From Coalinga, drive 20 miles west on Highway 198 to Coalinga Mineral Springs Road. Turn right (north) and drive four miles to the trailhead parking area at Coalinga Mineral Springs County Park. Camping is available for $3 per night. There is no drinking water.

*Maps:* For a topographic map, ask for Sherman Peak from the USGS.

*Who to contact:* Bureau of Land Management, Hollister Resource Area, 20 Hamilton Court, Hollister, CA 95023; (408) 637-8183.

*Trail notes:* If you are looking for solitude, then this is your spot. Few visit here, yet the hiking is marvelous and quiet along a two-and-a-quarter-mile national recreation trail to Kreyenhagen Mountain peak. The panoramic overlook here offers a bird's-eye view of the shadowy Diablo range. Winter and spring are the best times to visit. The trail is relatively easy to follow although the last mile is quite steep and, if it's hot, likely to wilt your enthusiasm. Always pack plenty of water as there is none available either at the trailhead or along the trail.

CEN-CAL MAP ...................... see page 466
adjoining maps
NORTH (F4) ........................... see page 482
EAST (G5) ............................. see page 560
SOUTH (H4) .......................... see page 628
WEST (G3) ............................. see page 554

3 TRAILS
PAGES 556-559

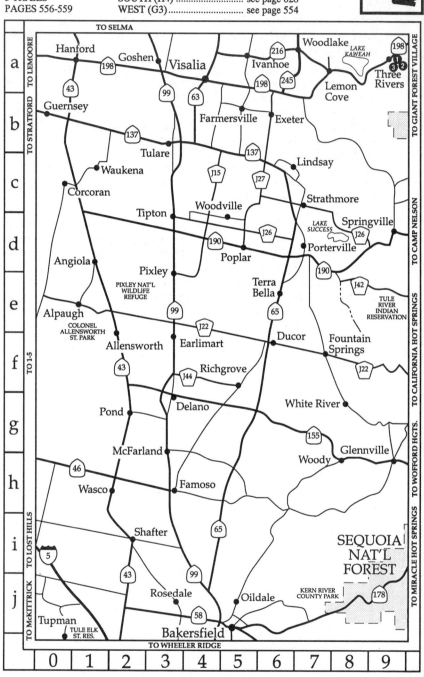

## 1. LOOKOUT POINT FISHERMAN'S TRAIL

1.0 mi/0.5 hr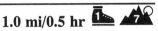

*Reference:* In Kings Canyon National Park; map G4, grid a9.

*User groups:* Hikers and dogs (outside the national park boundaries). No horses or mountain bikes are allowed. No wheelchair facilities.

*Permits:* Day-use permits are not required. Wilderness permits are required for overnight use. For more information, contact the Hume Lake Ranger District at (209) 338-2251. A $5 day-use fee is charged.

*Directions:* From Visalia, head east on Highway 198 to Three Rivers. Continue past Three Rivers for three miles to Mineral King Road. Turn right onto Mineral King Road and drive approximately 10.4 miles east to the Lookout Point Ranger Station. The trailhead is located just east of the sign in front of the station.

*Maps:* Send $3 to the USDA-Forest Service, 630 Sansome Street, San Francisco, CA 94111 and ask for the Sequoia National Forest map. The Forest Service also publishes a large-sized topographic map titled *John Muir Wilderness and Sequoia/Kings Canyon Wilderness*. The price is $6 and can be ordered from the USDA-Forest Service address listed above. For a USGS topographic map, ask for Case Mountain from the USGS. Tom Harrison Cartography publishes an excellent map of the area. Call (415) 456-7940 and ask for the recreation map of Sequoia and Kings Canyon national parks. The cost is $5.95 plus tax and shipping. Trails Illustrated also publishes a super map, Sequoia/Kings Canyon National Parks. The cost is $7.95 and may be ordered by calling (800) 962-1643.

*Who to contact:* For general information, contact Sequoia and Kings Canyon National Parks, Ash Mountain, Three Rivers, CA 93271; (209) 565-3341. For specific information about Kings Canyon National Park, contact Kings Canyon Visitors Center, Grant Grove, CA 93633; (209) 335-2856.

*Trail notes:* This is not an "official" trail anymore, although it once enjoyed a brisk life as part of the old trail system in the park. The trail's namesake, the Lookout Point Ranger Station, was the first adobe building constructed in Sequoia Park back in 1936. The trail was rediscovered and though somewhat overgrown at times, it offers a good route down to the river—a quick route favored by local fishermen. It is rough and steep and not maintained in any way. Only continual use keeps it as clear as it is. There are a number of campsites up and down the river. Use caution crossing the Kaweah during high water.

*Special note:* Watch out for ticks as they love the underbrush you will be crashing through—tick checks are mandatory.

## 2. LADYBUG TRAIL

8.0 mi/4.0 hrs

*Reference:* In Kings Canyon National Park; map G4, grid a9.

*User groups:* Hikers and horses. No mountain bikes or dogs are allowed. No wheelchair facilities.

*Permits:* Day-use permits are not required. Wilderness permits are required for overnight use. For more information, contact the Sequoia and Kings Canyon National Parks at (209) 565-3341. A $5 day-use fee is charged.

*Directions:* From Visalia, head east on Highway 198 to Three Rivers. Turn right onto South Fork Drive and drive 13 miles to the park entrance and South Fork Campground. No entrance or day-use fee is charged at this site. Park at the day-use parking area at the entrance to the campground. The signed trailhead is located on the other side of the campground.

*Maps:* Send $3 to the USDA-Forest Service, 630 Sansome Street, San Francisco, CA 94111 and ask for the Sequoia National Forest map. The Forest Service also publishes a large-sized topographic map titled *John Muir Wilderness and Sequoia/Kings Canyon Wilderness.* The price is $6 and can be ordered from the USDA-Forest Service address listed above. For USGS topographic maps, ask for Dennison Peak and Moses Mountain from the USGS. Tom Harrison Cartography publishes an excellent map of the area. Call (415) 456-7940 and ask for the recreation map of Sequoia and Kings Canyon national parks. The cost is $5.95 plus tax and shipping. Trails Illustrated also publishes a super map, Sequoia/Kings Canyon National Parks. The cost is $7.95 and may be ordered by calling (800) 962-1643.

*Who to contact:* For general information, contact Sequoia and Kings Canyon National Parks, Ash Mountain, Three Rivers, CA 93271; (209) 565-3341. For specific information about Kings Canyon National Park, contact Kings Canyon Visitors Center, Grant Grove, CA 93633; (209) 335-2856.

*Trail notes:* Pack along your swimming suit and your fishing rod on this trek. Add a straw hat to the mix and you just might feel like Huck Finn or Tom Sawyer, whiling away a lazy afternoon. We would recommend that you hike this trail in the spring, early in the day during the summer, or in the fall. The trail leads down to the Kaweah River after crossing a number of streams, and then comes to Ladybug Camp at 1.7 miles. The camp is named for the large number of ladybugs that are found here. From Ladybug Camp, continue on toward Whiskey Log Camp, 2.3 miles distant, through a grassy slope that is covered with wildflowers in the spring. At Cedar Creek, the trail stops being maintained, but it is used heavily and not difficult to follow. If you are good with a map and compass, then head onward to Whiskey Log Camp, still about one mile away. As it is, you will retrace your steps no matter what your final destination.

---

## 3. SOUTH FORK TRAIL  7.2 mi/3.5 hrs

*Reference:* **In Kings Canyon National Park; map G4, grid a9.**

*User groups:* Hikers and horses. No mountain bikes or dogs are allowed. No wheelchair facilities.

*Permits:* Day-use permits are not required. Wilderness permits are required for overnight use. For more information, contact the Sequoia and Kings Canyon National Parks at (209) 565-3341.

*Directions:* From Visalia, head east on Highway 198 to Three Rivers. Turn right onto South Fork Drive and drive 13 miles to the park entrance and South Fork Campground. No entrance or day-use fee is charged at this site. Drive through the campground to the end of the road and the trailhead parking for South Fork Trail on the right.

*Maps:* Send $3 to the USDA-Forest Service, 630 Sansome Street, San Francisco, CA 94111 and ask for the Sequoia National Forest map. The Forest Service also publishes a large-sized topographic map titled *John Muir Wilderness and Sequoia/Kings Canyon Wilderness.* The price is $6 and can be ordered from the USDA-Forest Service address listed above. For USGS topographic maps, ask for Dennison Peak and Moses Mountain from the USGS. Tom Harrison Cartography publishes an excellent map of the area. Call (415) 456-7940 and ask for the recreation map of Sequoia and Kings Canyon national parks. The cost is $5.95 plus tax and shipping. Trails Illustrated also publishes a super map, Sequoia/Kings Canyon National Parks. The cost is $7.95 and may be ordered by calling (800) 962-1643.

*Who to contact:* For general information, contact Sequoia and Kings Canyon National Parks, Ash Mountain, Three Rivers, CA 93271; (209) 565-3341. For specific information about Kings Canyon National Park, contact Kings Canyon Visitors Center, Grant Grove, CA 93633; (209) 335-2856.

*Trail notes:* Known unofficially as the Garfield-Hockett Trail, the South Fork Trail is a steep trek, but for those hikers willing to weather the sweat, the rewards are a number of quaint trail camps (if you wish to spend the night) and a large sequoia grove that is well off the beaten path. From the trailhead, climb up and up and up and up some more—are your legs burning yet? The trail passes through Garfield Grove at 2.9 miles, recognized as one of the largest giant sequoia groves in the park. Keep hiking to Snowslide Canyon, 3.4 miles from the trailhead—named because numerous snow avalanches down its chute keep the lower elevation under snow well after everywhere else has melted off. Just beyond the canyon sits Snowslide Camp at 3.6 miles, which is a pleasant place to spend the night. A nearby creek adds the sounds of a bubbling brook to help set the relaxing mood. Head back the way you came. If you desire a longer trek, you can keep wandering to South Fork Crossing and Meadows at 8.1 miles, Hockett Meadows at 12 miles and finally Mineral King at 24 miles.

2 PCT SECTIONS
49 TRAILS
PAGES 560-597

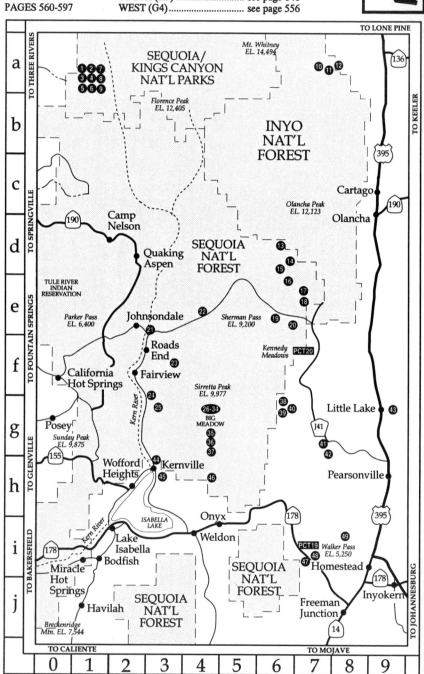

TO LONE PINE

a

SEQUOIA/
KINGS CANYON
NAT'L PARKS

Mt. Whitney
EL. 14,494

136

10  11  12

1  2  7
3  4  8
5  6  9

TO THREE RIVERS

Florence Peak
EL. 12,405

b

INYO
NAT'L
FOREST

TO KEELER

395

c

Cartago

Olancha Peak
EL. 12,123

190

Olancha

TO SPRINGVILLE

190

Camp
Nelson

d

Quaking
Aspen

SEQUOIA
NAT'L
FOREST

13

15  14

16

TULE RIVER
INDIAN
RESERVATION

17

e

18

Parker Pass
EL. 6,400

Johnsondale

22

Sherman Pass
EL. 9,200

19

20

TO FOUNTAIN SPRINGS

21

f

Roads
End

23

Kennedy
Meadows

PCT20

California
Hot Springs

Fairview

24

Sirretta Peak
EL. 9,977

g

Posey

25

26-34
BIG
MEADOW

38

40

39

Little Lake

43

Sunday Peak
EL. 9,875

35

J41

36

37

41

155

Wofford
Heights

44

Kernville

42

Pearsonville

h

45

46

TO GLENVILLE

TO BAKERSFIELD

Onyx

178

395

ISABELLA
LAKE

Weldon

49  Walker Pass
EL. 5,250

i

178

Kern River

Lake
Isabella

Bodfish

PCT19

47  48

Homestead

178

Miracle
Hot
Springs

SEQUOIA
NAT'L
FOREST

Inyokern

TO JOHANNESBURG

j

Havilah

SEQUOIA
NAT'L
FOREST

Freeman
Junction

Breckenridge
Mtn. EL. 7,544

14

TO CALIENTE

TO MOJAVE

0   1   2   3   4   5   6   7   8   9

**Map G5 featuring:** Mt. Whitney, Sequoia National Park, Kings Canyon National Park, Golden Trout Wilderness Area, Dome Lands Wilderness Area, Big Meadow, Horse Meadow, Kern River, Walker Pass, Kennedy Meadows

# 1. COLD SPRINGS NATURE TRAIL

**1.0 mi/0.5 hr**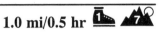

*Reference:* **In Sequoia National Park; map G5, grid a1.**

*User groups:* Hikers and horses. No mountain bikes or dogs allowed. No wheelchair facilities.

*Permits:* Day-use permits are not required. For more information, contact the Sequoia and Kings Canyon National Parks at (209) 565-3341. A $5 day-use fee is charged.

*Directions:* From Visalia, head east on Highway 198 to Three Rivers. Continue past Three Rivers for three miles to Mineral King Road. Turn right onto Mineral King Road and drive approximately 25 miles to Cold Springs Campground.

*Maps:* For a topographic map, ask for Mineral King from the USGS. Tom Harrison Cartography publishes an excellent map of the area. Call (415) 456-7940 and ask for the recreation map of Sequoia and Kings Canyon national parks. The cost is $5.95 plus tax and shipping. Trails Illustrated also publishes a good map, Sequoia/Kings Canyon National Parks. The cost is $7.95 and may be ordered by calling (800) 962-1643.

*Who to contact:* For general information, contact Sequoia and Kings Canyon National Parks, Ash Mountain, Three Rivers, CA 93271; (209) 565-3341. For specific information about Sequoia National Park, contact Sequoia National Park Visitors Center, Three Rivers, CA 93271; (209) 565-3135.

*Trail notes:* This self-guided nature trail begins adjacent to Campsite #6 in the campground. The trail passes through grassy meadows dotted with cottonwood and aspen (giving an incredible color display in the fall) and, in the spring, a wildflower show that inspires "oohs" and "ahhs." Signs along the way help to identify some of the plants that are characteristic to this region.

# 2. CRYSTAL LAKE TRAIL

**10.5 mi/8.0 hrs**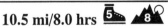

*Reference:* **In Sequoia National Park; map G5, grid a1.**

*User groups:* Hikers and horses. No mountain bikes or dogs are allowed. No wheelchair facilities.

*Permits:* Day-use permits are not required. Wilderness permits are required for overnight use. A third of the permits are available daily on a first-come, first-served basis. The remainder are available by reservation at least 21 days in advance. For more information, contact the Sequoia and Kings Canyon National Parks at (209) 565-3341. A $5 day-use fee is charged.

*Directions:* From Visalia, head east on Highway 198 to Three Rivers. Continue past Three Rivers for three miles to Mineral King Road. Turn right onto Mineral King Road and drive approximately 25 miles to Cold Springs Campground. Continue past the campground to the Monarch Lakes/Sawtooth Pass Trailhead and parking area, located approximately one mile beyond the ranger station.

*Maps:* For a topographic map, ask for Mineral King from the USGS. For more maps of the area, see "maps" under hike number 1.

*Who to contact:* For general information, contact Sequoia and Kings Canyon National Parks, Ash Mountain, Three Rivers, CA 93271; (209) 565-3341. For specific information about Sequoia National Park, contact Sequoia National Park Visitors Center, Three Rivers, CA 93271; (209) 565-3135.

*Trail notes:* We know this sounds bizarre, but the rangers of this area recommend carrying a spare fan belt and radiator hose for your car if you plan on hiking here. Why? Because the marmots have developed quite an appetite for the taste of engine parts with rubber on them. There is no cure, save a slew of spare parts and saying a few mantras to the marmot god. Weird, huh? Anyway, the designers of this trail were miners, more concerned with getting from point A to point B as quickly and directly as possible than they were with comfort. Hence, here we have a trail that literally goes straight up the side of the mountain. "We don't need no stinkin' switchbacks!" they must have said. From the parking area, the trail climbs quickly to a junction where you will head right to Groundhog Meadow. The trail forks again, and again you will go right. After more climbing, the trail junctions again and again, and you head right on a somewhat indistinct track that climbs straight up the rocky slope, past the old Chihuahua Mine and then across a challenging (some would say dangerous) rocky slope with a trail (if you can call it that) clinging to the side. Before long, you will arrive at the outlet to Crystal Lake and stunning views. The lake is often ice-locked until midsummer, so plan accordingly.

---

## 3. EAGLE LAKE TRAIL   7.6 mi/4.5 hrs

*Reference:* **In Sequoia National Park; map G5, grid a1.**

*User groups:* Hikers and horses. No mountain bikes or dogs are allowed. No wheelchair facilities.

*Permits:* Day-use permits are not required. Wilderness permits are required for overnight use. A third of the permits are available daily on a first-come, first-served basis. The remainder are available by reservation at least 14 days in advance. For more information, contact the Sequoia and Kings Canyon National Parks at (209) 565-3341. A $5 day-use fee is charged.

*Directions:* From Visalia, head east on Highway 198 to Three Rivers. Continue past Three Rivers for three miles to Mineral King Road. Turn right onto Mineral King Road and drive approximately 25 miles to Cold Springs Campground. Continue past the campground to the Eagle Crest Parking Area, approximately 1.5 miles east of the ranger station on Mineral King Road.

*Maps:* Send $3 to the USDA-Forest Service, 630 Sansome Street, San Francisco, CA 94111 and ask for the Sequoia National Forest map. For a topographic map, ask for Mineral King from the USGS. For more maps of the area, see "maps" under hike number 1.

*Who to contact:* For general information, contact Sequoia and Kings Canyon National Parks, Ash Mountain, Three Rivers, CA 93271; (209) 565-3341. For specific information about Sequoia National Park, contact Sequoia National Park Visitors Center, Three Rivers, CA 93271; (209) 565-3135.

*Trail notes:* From the trailhead, hike up the trail, past the junction with the track leading to White Chief Canyon and up along Eagle Creek. A huge sinkhole along the way sucks the entire stream into its maw, which explains the dry streambed below. The ground beneath your feet is apparently honeycombed with passages through which the subterranean streams flow, popping out of the mountainside at various points. The trail keeps climbing to the outlet of Eagle Lake, a very popular camping destination because of its dramatic scenery. The jagged crags of Eagle Crest and the gnarled trunks of foxtail pine create a picture-postcard effect. Head back the way you came when ready. See hike number 2 for the strange explanation of why you need to bring extra car parts along for this hike.

## 4. MOSQUITO LAKE TRAIL     7.0 mi/4.5 hrs

*Reference:* **In Sequoia National Park; map G5, grid a1.**

*User groups:* Hikers and horses. No mountain bikes or dogs are allowed. No wheelchair facilities.

*Permits:* Day-use permits are not required. Wilderness permits are required for overnight use. A third of the permits are available daily on a first-come, first-served basis. The remainder are available by reservation at least 14 days in advance. For more information, contact the Sequoia and Kings Canyon National Parks at (209) 565-3341. A $5 day-use fee is charged.

*Directions:* From Visalia, head east on Highway 198 to Three Rivers. Continue past Three Rivers for three miles to Mineral King Road. Turn right onto Mineral King Road and drive approximately 25 miles to Cold Springs Campground. Continue past the campground to the Eagle Crest/Mosquito Lake Parking Area, approximately 1.5 miles east of the ranger station on Mineral King Road.

*Maps:* For a topographic map, ask for Mineral King from the USGS. For more maps of the area, see "maps" under hike number 1.

*Who to contact:* For general information, contact Sequoia and Kings Canyon National Parks, Ash Mountain, Three Rivers, CA 93271; (209) 565-3341. For specific information about Sequoia National Park, contact Sequoia National Park Visitors Center, Three Rivers, CA 93271; (209) 565-3135.

*Trail notes:* Follow the same directions as in hike number 3, heading toward Eagle Lake. Just beyond the sinkholes, go right at a trail junction (left goes to Eagle Lake) and climb up and over a ridge. Drop down into the valley beyond and down to Mosquito Creek. There are a chain of five lakes, but the trail just takes you to the first one, Mosquito Lake. Intrepid explorers and campers will head out and seek the other lakes—especially if they are adventurous anglers. Fishing is good for brook and rainbow trout so don't forget your rod. As the lake's name indicates, mosquitoes can be really bothersome in the spring and early summer—wear repellent. See hike number 2 for the strange explanation of why you need to bring extra car parts along for this hike.

## 5. FAREWELL GAP TRAIL     11.2 mi/7.0 hrs

*Reference:* **In Sequoia National Park; map G5, grid a1.**

*User groups:* Hikers and horses. No mountain bikes or dogs are allowed. No wheelchair facilities.

*Permits:* Day-use permits are not required. Wilderness permits are required for overnight use. A third of the permits are available daily on a first-come, first-served basis. The remainder are available by reservation at least 14 days in advance. For more information, contact the Sequoia and Kings Canyon National Parks at (209) 565-3341. A $5 day-use fee is charged.

*Directions:* From Visalia, head east on Highway 198 to Three Rivers. Continue past Three Rivers for three miles to Mineral King Road. Turn right onto Mineral King Road and drive approximately 25 miles to Cold Springs Campground. Continue past the campground to the Eagle Crest/Mosquito Parking Area, approximately 1.5 miles east of the ranger station on Mineral King Road. The trailhead for Farewell Gap begins at the south end of the Mineral King Pack Station, a short jaunt from the parking area.

*Maps:* For a topographic map, ask for Mineral King from the USGS. For more maps of the area, see "maps" under hike number 1.

*Who to contact:* For general information, contact Sequoia and Kings Canyon National Parks, Ash Mountain, Three Rivers, CA 93271; (209) 565-3341. For specific information about Sequoia National Park, contact Sequoia National Park Visitors Center, Three Rivers, CA 93271; (209) 565-3135.

*Trail notes:* From the trailhead, hike along the East Fork Kaweah River for the first mile or so. It is a pleasant hike alongside aspen and fir trees. The trail crosses both Crystal Creek and Franklin Creek, with the latter being a good picnic spot. From here, the trail begins to climb in earnest. If you have little ones or others not so inclined to traipse up a challenging treadway, this is a good spot to turn around. Further up, you will pass the Franklin Lakes Trail junction on your way up to Farewell Gap, elevation 10,587 feet. Once there, catch your breath and enjoy the expansive views. Head back the way you came.

---

## 6. FRANKLIN LAKES TRAIL   12.0 mi/2.0 days

*Reference:* **In Sequoia National Park; map G5, grid a1.**

*User groups:* Hikers and horses. No mountain bikes or dogs are allowed. No wheelchair facilities.

*Permits:* Day-use permits are not required. Wilderness permits are required for overnight use. A third of the permits are available daily on a first-come, first-served basis. The remainder are available by reservation at least 14 days in advance. For more information, contact the Sequoia and Kings Canyon National Parks at (209) 565-3341. A $5 day-use fee is charged.

*Directions:* From Visalia, head east on Highway 198 to Three Rivers. Continue past Three Rivers for three miles to Mineral King Road. Turn right onto Mineral King Road and drive approximately 25 miles to Cold Springs Campground. Continue past the campground to the Eagle Crest/Mosquito Parking Area, approximately 1.5 miles east of the ranger station on Mineral King Road. The trailhead for Farewell Gap/Franklin Lakes begins at the south end of the Mineral King Pack Station, a short jaunt from the parking area.

*Maps:* For a topographic map, ask for Mineral King from the USGS. For more maps of the area, see "maps" under hike number 1.

*Who to contact:* For general information, contact Sequoia and Kings Canyon National Parks, Ash Mountain, Three Rivers, CA 93271; (209) 565-3341.

For specific information about Sequoia National Park, contact Sequoia National Park Visitors Center, Three Rivers, CA 93271; (209) 565-3135.

*Trail notes:* Follow the directions in hike number 5 to Franklin Creek and continue to climb on the trail from there. Further up, you will encounter the Franklin Lakes Trail junction where you will head left, still climbing past an old mine and up to lower Franklin Lake at 10,300 feet. Yep, that is a concrete dam, but it wasn't built by the Park Service. Instead, it was constructed long ago by a power company who wanted to improve water storage capacity—before this area became a park. Both the upper and lower lakes are in bowls rimmed by foxtail pine—very pretty and inviting. Hang out overnight if you have the time, then head back the way you came.

---

## 7. TIMBER GAP TRAIL    4.0 mi/2.5 hrs

*Reference:* **In Sequoia National Park; map G5, grid a1.**

*User groups:* Hikers and horses. No mountain bikes or dogs are allowed. No wheelchair facilities.

*Permits:* Day-use permits are not required. Wilderness permits are required for overnight use. A third of the permits are available daily on a first-come, first-served basis. The remainder are available by reservation at least 14 days in advance. For more information, contact the Sequoia and Kings Canyon National Parks at (209) 565-3341. A $5 day-use fee is charged.

*Directions:* From Visalia, head east on Highway 198 to Three Rivers. Continue past Three Rivers for three miles to Mineral King Road. Turn right onto Mineral King Road and drive approximately 25 miles to Cold Springs Campground. Continue past the campground to the Sawtooth Parking Area, approximately one mile east of the ranger station on Mineral King Road. The trailhead for Farewell Gap begins at the south end of the Mineral King Pack Station, a short jaunt from the parking area.

*Maps:* For a topographic map, ask for Mineral King from the USGS. For more maps of the area, see "maps" under hike number 1.

*Who to contact:* For general information, contact Sequoia and Kings Canyon National Parks, Ash Mountain, Three Rivers, CA 93271; (209) 565-3341. For specific information about Sequoia National Park, contact Sequoia National Park Visitors Center, Three Rivers, CA 93271; (209) 565-3135.

*Trail notes:* This trail and a little cross-country wandering gives you the opportunity to visit the site of a historic silver mine, not to mention enjoy some nifty views in the process. Hike up the steep treadway from the parking area to the junction with the Monarch Lakes Trail. Bear left and head up to the gap, framed with foxtail pine and red fir. Now comes the cross-country part. Hike east through the trees, maintaining your elevation. Just after leaving the trees you will come upon an old mining road—it's been here unmaintained for over 100 years! Hike in a southeasterly direction now on the old mining road to the site of the Empire Mine Camp and its assorted mining remnants and old chimney. Look up the slope and you may be able to see the mine shaft 1,000 feet above—don't even think about trying to get in it as exploring old mine shafts is dangerous. Retrace your steps to the gap and then return to the parking area.

# 8. MONARCH LAKES TRAIL   10.0 mi/2.0 days

***Reference:*** **In Sequoia National Park; map G5, grid a1.**

***User groups:*** Hikers and horses. No mountain bikes or dogs are allowed. No wheelchair facilities.

***Permits:*** Day-use permits are not required. Wilderness permits are required for overnight use. A third of the permits are available daily on a first-come, first-served basis. The remainder are available by reservation at least 14 days in advance. For more information, contact the Sequoia and Kings Canyon National Parks at (209) 565-3341. A $5 day-use fee is charged.

***Directions:*** From Visalia, head east on Highway 198 to Three Rivers. Continue past Three Rivers for three miles to Mineral King Road. Turn right onto Mineral King Road and drive approximately 25 miles to Cold Springs Campground. Continue past the campground to the Sawtooth Parking Area, approximately one mile east of the ranger station on Mineral King Road. The trailhead for Farewell Gap begins at the south end of the Mineral King Pack Station, a short jaunt from the parking area.

***Maps:*** For a topographic map, ask for Mineral King from the USGS. For more maps of the area, see "maps" under hike number 1.

***Who to contact:*** For general information, contact Sequoia and Kings Canyon National Parks, Ash Mountain, Three Rivers, CA 93271; (209) 565-3341. For specific information about Sequoia National Park, contact Sequoia National Park Visitors Center, Three Rivers, CA 93271; (209) 565-3135.

***Trail notes:*** This trail follows the same route as the Crystal Lake Trail for much of the way, but fortunately it does not experience the same mind-bending climb at the end. Still, it is a tough hike for most and we recommend planning an overnight trip so that you can rest at the lakes and fully enjoy the peaceful ambience. Don't forget your fishing rig as the trout are biting. Hike up from the parking area for one-half mile to the junction with the Timber Gap Trail. Head right toward Monarch Lakes and Crystal Lake. The trail passes through Groundhog Meadow at 1.5 miles—say a few prayers to the groundhog god in the hopes that his subjects are not devouring your vehicle as you hike. See hike number 2 if you're wondering what we mean. Heck, you didn't need that fan belt anyway, now did you? At 3.5 miles and the junction with the Crystal Lake Trail, head left to Lower Monarch Lake. Upper Monarch Lake lies just beyond at five miles and is larger—take your pick. Head back the way you came.

# 9. WHITE CHIEF TRAIL   6.0 mi/4.0 hrs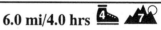

***Reference:*** **In Sequoia National Park; map G5, grid a1.**

***User groups:*** Hikers and horses. No mountain bikes or dogs are allowed. No wheelchair facilities.

***Permits:*** Day-use permits are not required. Wilderness permits are required for overnight use. A third of the permits are available daily on a first-come, first-served basis. The remainder are available by reservation at least 14 days in advance. For more information, contact the Sequoia and Kings Canyon National Parks at (209) 565-3341. A $5 day-use fee is charged.

***Directions:*** From Visalia, head east on Highway 198 to Three Rivers. Continue past Three Rivers for three miles to Mineral King Road. Turn right onto

Mineral King Road and drive approximately 25 miles to Cold Springs Campground. Continue past the campground to the Eagle Crest Parking Area, approximately 1.5 miles east of the ranger station on Mineral King Road.

***Maps:*** For a topographic map, ask for Mineral King from the USGS. For more maps of the area, see "maps" under hike number 1.

***Who to contact:*** For general information, contact Sequoia and Kings Canyon National Parks, Ash Mountain, Three Rivers, CA 93271; (209) 565-3341. For specific information about Sequoia National Park, contact Sequoia National Park Visitors Center, Three Rivers, CA 93271; (209) 565-3135.

***Trail notes:*** Nope, no lakes and no, there isn't a stunning view to reward you either. There are, however, a number of historical sites and an outstanding alpine meadow named White Chief Meadow—worth every step, we say. From the trailhead, hike up the trail leading to Eagle Lake and to the junction with the track leading to White Chief Canyon. Head left toward White Chief. You will pass the ruins of an old cabin that served as a bunkhouse for miners working the rocks at White Chief Mine. The "official" trail ends at the far end of White Chief Meadow, but an informal treadway continues down the canyon for approximately 4.5 miles. If you are adventurous, you may be able to locate several old mining cabins and some marble caverns—don't explore them unless you're experienced and equipped to spelunk. Just above White Chief Meadow you will see the mine shafts, but don't enter them as they are very dangerous and on private property. Did you bring your fishing rod? You'll be kicking yourself if you didn't, because a short cross-country jaunt up the slope to the west of the meadow will bring you to White Chief Lake and some truly amazing fishing. Head back the way you came when ready.

---

# 10. COTTONWOOD LAKES to WHITNEY PORTAL   38.5 mi one-way/5.0 days

***Reference:*** **Mt. Whitney; map G5, grid a7.**

***User groups:*** Hikers only. No mountain bikes, horses or dogs (this trip enters Sequoia National Park) allowed. No wheelchair facilities.

***Permits:*** Day-use permits are not required. Wilderness permits are required if you intend on camping. For more information, contact the Mount Whitney Ranger District at (619) 876-6200. A quota limit is in effect from May to October. Permits, $3 per person, may be requested in advance by mail between March 1 and May 31.

***Directions:*** From Lone Pine and Highway 395, head west on Whitney Portal Road for 3.5 miles and turn left onto Horseshoe Meadow Road. Drive for approximately 20 miles to a sign indicating Cottonwood Lakes. Turn right and drive another mile to the designated parking area. Leave your other car at Whitney Portal. From Lone Pine and Highway 395, head west on Whitney Portal Road for approximately 13 miles to Whitney Portal and the trailhead for the Mt. Whitney Trail.

***Maps:*** Send $3 to the USDA-Forest Service, 630 Sansome Street, San Francisco, CA 94111 and ask for the Inyo National Forest map. For topographic maps, ask for Cirque Peak, Johnson Peak, Mount Whitney and Mount Langley from the USGS. Tom Harrison Cartography publishes an excellent map of the area. Call (415) 456-7940 and ask for the recreation map of

Sequoia and Kings Canyon national parks. The cost is $5.95 plus tax and shipping.

*Who to contact:* Inyo National Forest, Mount Whitney Ranger District, P.O. Box 8, Lone Pine, CA 93545; (619) 876-6200.

*Trail notes:* It's a long one, but every step is magnificent! Alpine lakes, fishing, crystal clear streams, jagged spires, quiet forests, picturesque meadows dotted with wildflowers—sound good? It is. From the trailhead, hike up to Cottonwood Lakes and upper South Fork Lake in the direction of New Army Pass—camp by the lakes near the pass. From the pass, drop down to Rock Creek Lake and into Rock Creek canyon to the intersection with the Pacific Crest Trail. Bear right on the PCT to a crossing of Lower Rock Creek—the fishing is good here. Head up the PCT to the Crabtree Meadow and bear right onto the John Muir Trail and toward the Crabtree Ranger Station, where you will camp. The best camps are beyond the station in one-half mile. Hike up the John Muir Trail to the trail crest at 13,480 feet. You are so close already that if you feel strong enough, you should enjoy the side jaunt (four miles roundtrip) to the Mount Whitney Summit at 14, 494 feet. Continue down to Trail Camp and spend your last night. Hike out to Whitney Portal the following day.

*Special note:* Permits at peak season are hard to come by and must be reserved well in advance. In the lower reaches, bear precautions are necessary. Mosquitoes can be bothersome in the spring. Expect snow in the passes until late June. Wear plenty of sunscreen and sunglasses at higher elevations.

---

# 11. LITTLE COTTONWOOD    10.0 mi/7.0 hrs

*Reference:* Mt. Whitney; map G5, grid a7.

*User groups:* Hikers, horses and dogs (outside national park boundaries). No mountain bikes are allowed. No wheelchair facilities.

*Permits:* Day-use permits are not required. Wilderness permits are required if you intend on camping. For more information, contact the Mount Whitney Ranger District at (619) 876-6200. A quota limit is in effect from May to October. Permits, $3 per person, may be requested in advance by mail between March 1 and May 31.

*Directions:* From Lone Pine and Highway 395, head west on Whitney Portal Road for 3.5 miles and turn left onto Horseshoe Meadow Road. Drive for approximately 18 miles to a parking area on the right, about two miles before the turnoff for Cottonwood Lakes.

*Maps:* Send $3 to the USDA-Forest Service, 630 Sansome Street, San Francisco, CA 94111 and ask for the Inyo National Forest map. For topographic maps, ask for Cirque Peak and Bartlett from the USGS.

*Who to contact:* Inyo National Forest, Mount Whitney Ranger District, P.O. Box 8, Lone Pine, CA 93545; (619) 876-6200.

*Trail notes:* If you want to leave behind the crowds of hikers and backpackers that frequent the Cottonwood Lakes area, then this excursion into a remote and forgotten little valley should do it. The hike cruises alongside a wonderful creek through quiet meadows, shady forests and even offers an occasional between-the-trees view of snow-capped peaks to boot. From the trailhead, climb swiftly up a series of switchbacks and into the Golden Trout Wilderness. Before long, you will be walking alongside Little Cottonwood

Creek, the trail's namesake. At about one-half mile, you will arrive at a spur trail leading to Wonoga Peak. From here the route crosses and recrosses the creek several times as it climbs up the canyon and then beside a meadowy area. There is a suitable place for camping at around three miles, just before the trail leaves the banks of the creek to climb out of the canyon and up onto a ridge. Rock cairns guide the way up to 10,600 feet or so, about 3.5 miles from the trailhead. Enjoy the views of the surrounding mountain peaks and the Cottonwood Basin. The trail drops down a few hundred feet to Golden Trout Camp—leased by a non-profit outdoor educational program—almost 4.5 miles from the trailhead. If you keep hiking, you will soon meet up with the major thoroughfare into the area, Cottonwood Lakes Trail. We prefer to turn around here and retrace our steps. Remember to hike no further than you can hike back out in a day, unless you plan to camp. There are some fairly good campsites along the way.

## 12. WONOGA PEAK SCRAMBLE 2.0 mi/2.0 hrs

*Reference:* **Mt. Whitney; map G5, grid a7.**

*User groups:* Hikers and dogs (outside national park boundaries). No mountain bikes or horses are allowed. No wheelchair facilities.

*Permits:* Day-use permits are not required. Wilderness permits are required if you intend on camping. For more information, contact the Mount Whitney Ranger District at (619) 876-6200. A quota limit is in effect from May to October. Permits, $3 per person, may be requested in advance by mail between March 1 and May 31.

*Directions:* From Lone Pine and Highway 395, head west on Whitney Portal Road for 3.5 miles and turn left onto Horseshoe Meadow Road. Drive for approximately 18 miles to a parking area on the right, about two miles before the turnoff for Cottonwood Lakes.

*Maps:* Send $3 to the USDA-Forest Service, 630 Sansome Street, San Francisco, CA 94111 and ask for the Inyo National Forest map. For topographic maps, ask for Cirque Peak and Bartlett from the USGS.

*Who to contact:* Inyo National Forest, Mount Whitney Ranger District, P.O. Box 8, Lone Pine, CA 93545; (619) 876-6200.

*Trail notes:* Wonoga Peak, at 10,371 feet, sits tantalizingly close to the trailhead and road near Little Cottonwood and Cottonwood Creek Trails and is worth the scramble up an informal trail that winds to the summit. From the top you are afforded sweeping views of the eastern Sierra and the Owens Valley below. From the Little Cottonwood Trail parking area, head north up the drainage on a visible trail and up the canyon, keeping the peak visible before you. Stay to the right and curve around the ridge up to the summit. Return the way you came.

## 13. MANZANITA KNOB TREK    3.5 mi/3.0 hrs

*Reference:*  **In Golden Trout Wilderness Area; map G5, grid d6.**

*User groups:* Hikers, dogs and horses. No mountain bikes are allowed. No wheelchair facilities.

*Permits:* Day-use permits are not required. Wilderness permits are required if you intend on camping. For more information, contact the Mount Whitney Ranger District at (619) 876-6200.

***Directions:*** From the town of Brown on Highway 14, drive north on Highway 14 for four miles to Nine Mile Canyon Road and turn left (west). Drive approximately 35 miles on Nine Mile Canyon Road (it becomes Sherman Pass Road, Forest Service 22S05 at the Sequoia National Forest boundary). Pass Troy Meadows and turn right onto Blackrock Road (Forest Service Road 21S03). Drive to the end of the road and the designated parking area and campground built to serve those heading into the Golden Trout Wilderness.

***Maps:*** Send $3 for each map to the USDA-Forest Service, 630 Sansome Street, San Francisco, CA 94111 and ask for the Golden Trout Wilderness, Sequoia National Forest and the Inyo National Forest maps. For a topographic map, ask for Casa Vieja Meadows from the USGS.

***Who to contact:*** Inyo National Forest, Mount Whitney Ranger District, P.O. Box 8, Lone Pine, CA 93545; (619) 876-6200 or Sequoia National Forest, Cannell Meadow Ranger District, P.O. Box 6, Kernville, CA 93238; (619) 376-3781.

***Trail notes:*** There is no official trail here, but don't let that stop you, especially if you are a classified "peak bagger"—there is a register to be signed here after you get to the top at approximately 8,500 feet. Actually, despite the lack of official trail, there is an abandoned logging road that leads almost to the top of the knob—the last several hundred yards to the boulder-stacked and manzanita-choked (you were wondering about the name?) summit are cross-country along the ridge. From the parking area, head roughly north along the abandoned logging road. At the first junction, go right and at the next, head left and up to the ridge top. Go right, now cross-country, along the ridge to the summit. Sign the register, enjoy the views and head back the way you came.

---

# 14. JORDAN HOT SPRINGS    11.0 mi/2.0 days

***Reference:*** **In Golden Trout Wilderness Area; map G5, grid d6.**

***User groups:*** Hikers, dogs and horses. No mountain bikes are allowed. No wheelchair facilities.

***Permits:*** Day-use permits are not required. Wilderness permits are required if you intend on camping. For more information, contact the Mount Whitney Ranger District at (619) 876-6200.

***Directions:*** From the town of Brown on Highway 14, drive north on Highway 14 for four miles to Nine Mile Canyon Road and turn left (west). Drive approximately 35 miles on Nine Mile Canyon Road (it becomes Sherman Pass Road, Forest Service 22S05 at the Sequoia National Forest boundary). Pass Troy Meadows and turn right onto Blackrock Road (Forest Service Road 21S03). Drive to the end of the road and the designated parking area and campground built to serve those heading into the Golden Trout Wilderness.

***Maps:*** Send $3 for each map to the USDA-Forest Service, 630 Sansome Street, San Francisco, CA 94111 and ask for the Sequoia National Forest and the Inyo National Forest maps. For a topographic map, ask for Casa Vieja Meadows from the USGS.

***Who to contact:*** Inyo National Forest, Mount Whitney Ranger District, P.O. Box 8, Lone Pine, CA 93545; (619) 876-6200 or Sequoia National Forest,

Cannell Meadow Ranger District, P.O. Box 6, Kernville, CA 93238; (619) 376-3781.

*Trail notes:* You will be heading into what used to be a private resort until it was closed by the Forest Service after being included within the wilderness boundaries of the Golden Trout Wilderness. The resort buildings are quite historic, having been here since the early 1900s, and the hike takes you to some hot springs as well. The entire hike is outstanding, in our opinion, as it winds through verdant meadows, alongside a pretty creek, and through patches of wildflowers that are incredible. The route is somewhat steep in places (both up and down) so take your time and preserve your legs and knees. What's the rush anyway? From the trailhead, head north and down on the Black Rock Trail (it starts briefly as the Smith Meadow Trail until it enters the official wilderness boundary). The trail heads to Casa Vieja Meadows approximately 2.5 miles in, where you will encounter (you may have to search a bit as the trail becomes somewhat indistinct) the Jordan Hot Springs Trail heading steeply west. Hike the Jordan Hot Springs Trail for three miles alongside Ninemile Creek to the former resort, located just southwest of the trail via a spur trail. Late spring to early summer is the best time to visit. Holidays can be crowded at the trailhead and overnight entry is regulated via the quota permit system. Bear precautions are necessary if you are camping.

---

# 15. HELLS HOLE TRAIL  23.0 mi/2.0 days

*Reference:* **In Golden Trout Wilderness Area; map G5, grid d6.**

*User groups:* Hikers, dogs and horses. No mountain bikes are allowed. No wheelchair facilities.

*Permits:* Day-use permits are not required. Wilderness permits are required if you intend on camping. For more information, contact the Mount Whitney Ranger District at (619) 876-6200.

*Directions:* From the town of Brown on Highway 14, drive north on Highway 14 for four miles to Nine Mile Canyon Road and turn left (west). Drive approximately 35 miles on Nine Mile Canyon Road (it becomes Sherman Pass Road, Forest Service 22S05 at the Sequoia National Forest boundary). Pass Troy Meadows and turn right onto Blackrock Road (Forest Service Road 21S03) and drive to the end of the road and the designated parking area and campground built to serve those heading into the Golden Trout Wilderness.

*Maps:* Send $3 for each map to the USDA-Forest Service, 630 Sansome Street, San Francisco, CA 94111 and ask for the Sequoia National Forest and the Inyo National Forest maps. For topographic maps, ask for Casa Vieja Meadows and Kern Peak from the USGS.

*Who to contact:* Inyo National Forest, Mount Whitney Ranger District, P.O. Box 8, Lone Pine, CA 93545; (619) 876-6200 or Sequoia National Forest, Cannell Meadow Ranger District, P.O. Box 6, Kernville, CA 93238; (619) 376-3781.

*Trail notes:* Two spectacular waterfalls, some superb fishing, velvety green meadows, a hot spring and a campsite that is almost too perfect to be real— but it is real! From the trailhead, head north and down on the Black Rock Trail (it starts briefly as the Smith Meadow Trail until it enters the official wilderness boundary). The trail heads to Casa Vieja Meadows where you will encounter (you may have to search a bit as the trail becomes somewhat nondistinct) the Jordan Hot Springs Trail heading west. Hike the Jordan Hot Springs Trail alongside Ninemile Creek to a former resort—located just southwest of the trail via a spur trail. After you have enjoyed the hot springs, continue hiking on the Jordan Hot Springs Trail past a trail junction to Sidehill Meadow, and to a trail junction with Lion Trail (Forest Service 33E21) heading south and Hells Hole Trail heading right, still along Ninemile Creek. In a short distance, Ninemile Creek plunges precipitously 80 feet into a granite walled canyon. The roar of the falls is as impressive as the sight is beautiful. After some steep climbing you will come to an overlook via a spur trail to some granite slabs overlooking the Kern River and another magnificent falls cascading down the slabs, shooting a misty spray into the air—really spectacular when the sun's rays refract through the water droplets. Although there are a number of good campsites along the way here, keep hiking to the trail's end at Hells Hole—the campsite nestled among cedars next to a sandy creekside beach is picture-postcard perfect. Head back the way you came when ready. Late spring to early summer is the best time to visit. Holidays can be crowded at the trailhead and overnight entry is regulated via the quota permit system. Bear precautions are necessary if you are camping.

---

## 16. LITTLE HORSE/ BEACH TRAILS LOOP

**10.0 mi/8.0 hrs**

*Reference:* **North of the Dome Lands Wilderness Area; map G5, grid e6.**

*User groups:* Hikers, dogs, horses and mountain bikes. No wheelchair facilities.

*Permits:* Day-use permits are not required. Campfire permits are required if you intend on camping. For more information, contact the Cannell Meadow Ranger District at (619) 376-3781.

*Directions:* From the town of Brown on Highway 14, drive north on Highway 14 for four miles to Nine Mile Canyon Road and turn left (west). Drive approximately 35 miles on Nine Mile Canyon Road (it becomes Sherman Pass Road, Forest Service 22S05 at the Sequoia National Forest boundary). Pass Troy Meadows and turn right onto Beach Meadows Road (Forest Service 21S02). Turn left after approximately four miles onto Forest Service Road 21S19 and then right on Forest Service Road 21S11 to the fire-safe camping area and parking at Beach Meadows.

*Maps:* Send $3 to the USDA-Forest Service, 630 Sansome Street, San Francisco, CA 94111 and ask for the Sequoia National Forest map. For a topographic map, ask for Casa Vieja Meadows from the USGS.

*Who to contact:* Sequoia National Forest, Cannell Meadow Ranger District, P.O. Box 6, Kernville, CA 93238; (619) 376-3781.

*Trail notes:* Despite the periodic interruption from motorized steeds, this hike is a pleasant one, albeit dusty at times thanks to the debris stirred up by motorcycle wheels. The trail connects several luxuriant meadows tucked in among pine forests. From Beach Meadows, head out on the Little Horse Trail (Forest Service 34E02) to Osa Meadows, where you will find the Beach Trail (Forest Service 34E01) for the return at five miles from the start. The hiking is fairly easy with a few ups and downs, but keep in mind that you will share this trek with everyone from mountain bikes to motorcycles. Treat all water well as you are sharing it with cows. Spring is the best time to visit as wildflowers are everywhere. If you are camping, be sure to bear-bag your food.

---

## 17. FISH CREEK TRAIL    10.5 mi/8.0 hrs

*Reference:* **North of the Dome Lands Wilderness Area; map G5, grid e7.**
*User groups:* Hikers, dogs, horses and mountain bikes are allowed. No wheelchair facilities.
*Permits:* Day-use permits are not required. Campfire permits are required if you intend on camping. For more information, contact the Cannell Meadow Ranger District at (619) 376-3781.
*Directions:* From the town of Brown on Highway 14, drive north on Highway 14 for four miles to Nine Mile Canyon Road and turn left (west). Drive approximately 31 miles on Nine Mile Canyon Road (it becomes Sherman Pass Road, Forest Service 22S05 at the Sequoia National Forest boundary) to Troy Meadows and Troy Meadows Campground. The trailhead is at the northwest corner of the meadow.
*Maps:* Send $3 to the USDA-Forest Service, 630 Sansome Street, San Francisco, CA 94111 and ask for the Sequoia National Forest map. For a topographic map, ask for Crag Peak from the USGS.
*Who to contact:* Sequoia National Forest, Cannell Meadow Ranger District, P.O. Box 6, Kernville, CA 93238; (619) 376-3781.
*Trail notes:* If you are like us, you love to wander along streams, sometimes through them, splashing and laughing and getting your feet wet as you explore secluded meadows and pretty forest lands. This is just such a hike. Don't head out unless you enjoy wet feet, because although you are on a trail, it crosses and recrosses Fish Creek so many times that you may as well just be in it. We prefer this trek as an overnight, camping at the halfway point next to Smith Meadow. From Troy Meadow, begin hiking north on the Pack Station Trail (Forest Service 35E07). Just past a narrow little rocky canyon lined with willows, the trail renames itself and becomes Fish Creek Trail (Forest Service 34E33) for the duration of the hike to Smith Meadow. We recommend camping near the south end of the meadow and then exploring the vast grassland or, if you are dayhiking, picnicking at the south end and then heading back the way you came. Spring is the best time to visit as wildflowers are everywhere. Call ahead to see if the creek is passable.

---

## 18. HOOKER TRAIL    6.0 mi/4.0 hrs

*Reference:* **North of the Dome Lands Wilderness Area; map G5, grid e7.**
*User groups:* Hikers, dogs and horses. No mountain bikes are allowed. No wheelchair facilities.
*Permits:* Day-use permits are not required. Campfire permits are required if you intend on camping. For more information, contact the Cannell Meadow Ranger District at (619) 376-3781.
*Directions:* From the town of Brown on Highway 14, drive north on Highway 14 for four miles to Nine Mile Canyon Road and turn left (west). Drive approximately 27 miles on Nine Mile Canyon Road (it becomes Sherman Pass Road, Forest Service 22S05 at the Sequoia National Forest boundary).

Then turn right into a cul-de-sac at the end of a stockman's road, the trailhead for Hooker Trail (Forest Service 35E05) and the Jackass National Recreation Trail (Forest Service 35E13). If you hit Fish Creek Campground, you have gone approximately one mile too far.

*Maps:* Send $3 to the USDA-Forest Service, 630 Sansome Street, San Francisco, CA 94111 and ask for the Sequoia National Forest map. For a topographic map, ask for Crag Peak from the USGS.

*Who to contact:* Sequoia National Forest, Cannell Meadow Ranger District, P.O. Box 6, Kernville, CA 93238; (619) 376-3781.

*Trail notes:* If you love aspens and their dancing leaves, then you will adore this lightly used trail. It leads through a beautiful wooded canyon, through small meadows and up a somewhat steep slope to the magical Hooker Meadow. In the fall, the area is awash in yellow as the aspen turn color before dropping their coats for winter. From the trailhead, hike to Hooker Meadow and then retrace your steps. Spring brings wildflowers to the meadows which add a pleasant touch of color to the green backdrop of lush grass and shimmering leaves.

---

# 19. WOODPECKER MEADOW/ 10.0 mi/8.0 hrs 🏕️ ⛰️8 DARK CANYON TRAILS LOOP

*Reference:* In Dome Lands Wilderness Area; map G5, grid e6.

*User groups:* Hikers, horses and dogs. No mountain bikes are allowed. No wheelchair facilities.

*Permits:* Day-use permits are not required. Campfire permits are required if you intend on camping within the Dome Lands Wilderness Area. For more information, contact the Cannell Meadow Ranger District at (619) 376-3781.

*Directions:* From Kernville, drive north on Sierra Way Road/Kern River Highway to Sherman Pass Road (Forest Service Road 22S05) and turn right. Then drive to the trailhead parking for the Woodpecker Trail (Forest Service 34E08) on the right, 1.5 miles before reaching the Bald Mountain Access Road (Forest Service 22S77) also on the right.

*Maps:* Send $3 to the USDA-Forest Service, 630 Sansome Street, San Francisco, CA 94111 and ask for the Sequoia National Forest map. For topographic maps, ask for Bonita Meadows and Sirretta Peak from the USGS.

*Who to contact:* Sequoia National Forest, Cannell Meadow Ranger District, P.O. Box 6, Kernville, CA 93238; (619) 376-3781.

*Trail notes:* The few who visit here leave justifiably impressed with the scenery and solitude. Those who don't visit, miss out. It is a land of wooded canyons laced with narrow streams. Perhaps best of all, the trip touches Trout Creek, a stream that offers good fishing and demands skinny dipping—love those swimming holes. You can do this trip in one day, as we have listed above, but who would want to? Plan on camping around Trout Creek and really savoring the experience. From the trailhead, hike the Woodpecker Trail to the Rockhouse Basin Trail (Forest Service 35E16) and head right. Hike on this road-turned-trail to Woodpecker Meadow and Trout Creek—explore the meadow and area for great campsites. The Dark Canyon Trail (Forest Service 34E11) branches off to the right at the meadow. Hike the Dark Canyon Trail up to a logging road (unsigned and unnamed) just before reaching Sherman Pass Road. Head right and hike back to the parking area and your car (watch for vehicles on this old jeep route). If you miss the logging road, just hike along the shoulder of Sherman Pass Road to the east (a right turn). This hike is best enjoyed in spring, winter and fall. Summer is too hot.

## 20. BALD MOUNTAIN BOTANICAL TRAIL

0.5 mi/1.0 hr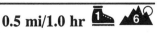

*Reference:* **In Dome Lands Wilderness Area; map G5, grid e6.**

*User groups:* Hikers and dogs. No mountain bikes or horses are allowed. No wheelchair facilities.

*Permits:* Day-use permits are not required. Campfire permits are required if you intend on camping within the Dome Lands Wilderness Area. For more information, contact the Cannell Meadow Ranger District at (619) 376-3781.

*Directions:* From Kernville, drive north on Sierra Way Road/Kern River Highway to Sherman Pass Road (Forest Service Road 22S05) and turn right. Drive to the Bald Mountain Access Road (Forest Service 22S77) heading off to the right. Drive 1.5 miles or so to a locked gate—the trailhead begins here. Park off the road so you are not blocking the gate.

*Maps:* Send $3 to the USDA-Forest Service, 630 Sansome Street, San Francisco, CA 94111 and ask for the Sequoia National Forest map. For a topographic map, ask for Bonita Meadows from the USGS.

*Who to contact:* Sequoia National Forest, Cannell Meadow Ranger District, P.O. Box 6, Kernville, CA 93238; (619) 376-3781.

*Trail notes:* Views from the top of Bald Mountain are some of the best around, sitting sentry over the Dome Lands Wilderness, Southern Sierra and the Golden Trout Wilderness. On a clear day you can see all the way to Mt. Whitney. Views aren't the only reason to trek up here, however. This is also a designated botanical preserve protecting a unique stand of Jeffrey pine, limber pine and red fir all growing together—these are trees normally separated by thousands of feet of elevation. From the gate, hike up the road to the lookout tower on the summit. When ready, retrace your steps. Summer is too hot here—come in spring, winter or fall.

## 21. KERN RIVER TRAIL

7.5 mi/4.0 hrs

*Reference:* **In Dome Lands Wilderness Area; map G5, grid e3.**

*User groups:* Hikers, dogs, horses and mountain bikes. No wheelchair facilities.

*Permits:* Day-use permits are not required. Campfire permits are required if you intend on camping. For more information, contact the Cannell Meadow Ranger District at (619) 376-3781.

*Directions:* From Kernville, drive north on Sierra Way Road/Kern River Highway past Sherman Pass Road (Forest Service Road 22S05) to the Johnsondale Bridge and the designated trailhead parking area on the other side of the bridge.

*Maps:* Send $3 to the USDA-Forest Service, 630 Sansome Street, San Francisco, CA 94111 and ask for the Sequoia National Forest map. For topographic maps, ask for Fairview and Durrwood Creek from the USGS.

*Who to contact:* Sequoia National Forest, Cannell Meadow Ranger District,

P.O. Box 6, Kernville, CA 93238; (619) 376-3781.

*Trail notes:* Perfect at any time of the year, this river hike is especially beautiful in the late spring and early fall. Hike across the old bridge to the trailhead for the Kern River Trail and descend the many steps (58 if we remember correctly, maybe 59?) to the trail. Hike north on the trail alongside the scenic Kern, enjoying the many moods the river has to offer. You may share the river with rafters who are enthusiastically bobbing by. Flyfishers will enjoy this National Wild and Scenic River section since a wild trout program has been implemented. There are a number of campsites along the river if you wish to turn this into an overnighter. Once you reach a point where the trail veers east away from the river, turn around and head back the way you came.

---

# 22. SHERMAN PEAK TRAIL   5.0 mi/3.5 hrs 

*Reference:* **In Dome Lands Wilderness Area; map G5, grid e4.**

*User groups:* Hikers, dogs, horses and mountain bikes. No wheelchair facilities.

*Permits:* Day-use permits are not required. Campfire permits are required if you intend on camping. For more information, contact the Cannell Meadow Ranger District at (619) 376-3781.

*Directions:* From Kernville, drive north on Sierra Way Road/Kern River Highway to Sherman Pass Road (Forest Service Road 22S05) and turn right. Drive to Sherman Pass and the signed vista point. The Sherman Pass Vista Trailhead begins on the other side of the road.

*Maps:* Send $3 to the USDA-Forest Service, 630 Sansome Street, San Francisco, CA 94111 and ask for the Sequoia National Forest map. For topographic maps, ask for Sirretta, Bonita Meadows and Durrwood Creek from the USGS.

*Who to contact:* Sequoia National Forest, Cannell Meadow Ranger District, P.O. Box 6, Kernville, CA 93238; (619) 376-3781.

*Trail notes:* The Sherman Peak Trail provides a hike up to the summit of 9,000-foot Sherman Peak that is suitable for the entire family. You will share the peak with a radio relay tower and other technological paraphernalia, but the view almost makes you forget they are there. Want the same view with a more wild setting? Hike up to the top of Sirretta Peak described in hike number 30, this chapter. This trailhead begins across the road and climbs to the peak via a series of gentle switch backs. Head back the way you came.

---

# 23. PACKSADDLE CAVE TRAIL 5.0 mi/3.5 hrs 

*Reference:* **In Dome Lands Wilderness Area; map G5, grid f3.**

*User groups:* Hikers, horses, dogs and mountain bikes. No wheelchair facilities.

*Permits:* Day-use permits are not required.

*Directions:* From Kernville, drive north on Sierra Way Road/Kern River Highway for 16 miles to Fairview Campground. Just past the campground is a parking area at the Fairview Resort for those who are interested in hiking to Packsaddle Cave. Flint Canyon Trail and Tobias Creek Trail also begin at this parking area.

*Maps:* Send $3 to the USDA-Forest Service, 630 Sansome Street, San Francisco, CA 94111 and ask for the Sequoia National Forest map. For a topographic map, ask for Fairview from the USGS.

*Who to contact:* Sequoia National Forest, Cannell Meadow Ranger District,

P.O. Box 6, Kernville, CA 93238; (619) 376-3781.

*Trail notes:* While Packsaddle Cave no longer sports her jewels (stalagmites and stalactites), as they have all been carted off by vandals, the cave is still impressive enough to warrant a hike. Pack along a flashlight. From the parking area, cross the highway and then head up a jeep road to the trailhead of Packsaddle Trail (Forest Service 33E34). The trail climbs up to the cave through woods and some wild lilac blooms (in spring) and over a number of stream crossings. The views along the trail are pretty, but not overly memorable—you don't really gain enough elevation, and it is the cave you are seeking anyway. At about 1.5 miles, you pass through a saddle and descend to Packsaddle Creek and then begin hiking upstream—passing a small falls and arriving at a junction with the Rincon Trail at just over two miles. Take the spur trail up to Packsaddle Cave. Once you have enjoyed yourself at the cave, head back the way you came.

---

## 24. SALMON CREEK via RINCON TRAIL

3.0 mi/1.5 hrs

*Reference:* **In Dome Lands Wilderness Area; map G5, grid g3.**

*User groups:* Hikers, horses, dogs and mountain bikes. No wheelchair facilities.

*Permits:* Day-use permits are not required. Campfire permits are required if you intend on camping within the Dome Lands Wilderness Area. For more information, contact the Cannell Meadow Ranger District at (619) 376-3781.

*Directions:* From Kernville, drive north on Sierra Way Road/Kern River Highway for 10 miles to Gold Ledge Campground. Just past the campground is Ant Canyon, an unimproved camping area. Park here for the trailhead.

*Maps:* Send $3 to the USDA-Forest Service, 630 Sansome Street, San Francisco, CA 94111 and ask for the Sequoia National Forest map. For a topographic map, ask for Fairview from the USGS.

*Who to contact:* Sequoia National Forest, Cannell Meadow Ranger District, P.O. Box 6, Kernville, CA 93238; (619) 376-3781.

*Trail notes:* Salmon Creek is the destination on this pleasant jaunt, best hiked early in the morning so that you can enjoy a picnic lunch among the spreading oaks on a streamside terrace. From the campground, head east up a dirt road to the South Rincon Motorcycle Path (Forest Service 33E23). The trail zigzags its way up to a ridge and then continues on to a quaint camping/picnic area overlooking the Salmon Creek and, if you squint, offering distant views of Salmon Falls, 20 miles distant. Head back the way you came. This hike is too warm in the summer—hike it spring or fall.

---

## 25. RINCON TRAIL OUT AND BACK

13.5 mi/7.0 hrs

*Reference:* **In Dome Lands Wilderness Area; map G5, grid g3.**

*User groups:* Hikers, horses, dogs and mountain bikes. No wheelchair facilities.

*Permits:* Day-use permits are not required. Campfire permits are required if you intend on camping within the Dome Lands Wilderness Area. For more information, contact the Cannell Meadow Ranger District at (619) 376-3781.

*Directions:* From Kernville, drive north on Sierra Way Road/Kern River

Highway for 10 miles to Gold Ledge Campground. Just past the campground is Ant Canyon, an unimproved camping area. Park here for the trailhead.

**Maps:** Send $3 to the USDA-Forest Service, 630 Sansome Street, San Francisco, CA 94111 and ask for the Sequoia National Forest map. For a topographic map, ask for Fairview from the USGS.

**Who to contact:** Sequoia National Forest, Cannell Meadow Ranger District, P.O. Box 6, Kernville, CA 93238; (619) 376-3781.

**Trail notes:** Wildflowers along the trail in the spring are outstanding. The trail itself follows the ancient Kern Canyon Fault and passes near the Packsaddle Cave (a worthwhile peek even though vandals have literally trashed it). From the campground, head east up a dirt road to the South Rincon Motorcycle Path (Forest Service 33E23). The trail continues north, undulating up and down through several saddles to the Packsaddle Trail. Packsaddle Cave lies two-tenths of a mile to the west. Once you reach the unimproved Rincon Campground, turn around and retrace your steps. This hike is too warm in the summer. Hike it spring or fall. Better yet, head out in the winter when all the nearby peaks have received a dusting of snow—the scene is gorgeous!

---

# 26. BIG MEADOW LOOP TRIP FOR BIKES

10.0 mi/6.0 hrs

**Reference:** In Dome Lands Wilderness Area; map G5, grid g4.

**User groups:** Hikers, mountain bikes, horses and dogs. No wheelchair facilities.

**Permits:** Day-use permits are not required. Campfire permits are required if you intend on camping. For more information, contact the Cannell Meadow Ranger District at (619) 376-3781.

**Directions:** From Kernville, drive north on Sierra Way Road/Kern River Highway to Sherman Pass Road (Forest Service Road 22S05) and turn right. Drive to Cherry Hill Road (Forest Service 22S12) and the signed turnoff on the right for Horse Meadow/Big Meadow. Turn right and drive past Horse Meadow Campground to Big Meadow. Park near the road split that loops around the meadow.

**Maps:** Send $3 to the USDA-Forest Service, 630 Sansome Street, San Francisco, CA 94111 and ask for the Sequoia National Forest map. For topographic maps, ask for Cannell Peak and Sirretta Peak from the USGS.

**Who to contact:** Sequoia National Forest, Cannell Meadow Ranger District, P.O. Box 6, Kernville, CA 93238; (619) 376-3781.

**Trail notes:** What? A biking trail in a hiking book? Well, you can explore this one either way. If you have been craving a good mountain bike journey amid pines and around a glorious meadow with lots of wildlife and wonderful fresh air, this is as good as any. If you wish to overnight, a suitable place to set up a base camp is the Horse Meadow Campground you passed on the way in. Otherwise, there are several good spots around the meadow which are suitable for setting up a primitive base camp. Beyond the obvious loop road around the meadow, there are other forest service roads that branch out which are suitable and enjoyable for exploring. If you are wandering on foot, you can go most anywhere, but remember that on your mountain bike you must stay out of the signed wilderness area. By bike, the loop will take about three hours. In the winter, this loop makes an outstanding cross-country ski opportunity if the road is open to get in. Call the ranger station to inquire. It is best enjoyed in spring, winter and fall. Summer is too hot for hiking or biking.

## 27. DEADWOOD TRAIL 5.0 mi/3.5 hrs

*Reference:* **In Dome Lands Wilderness Area; map G5, grid g4.**

*User groups:* Hikers, horses and dogs. No mountain bikes allowed. No wheelchair facilities.

*Permits:* Day-use permits are not required. Campfire permits are required if you intend on camping. For more information, contact the Cannell Meadow Ranger District at (619) 376-3781.

*Directions:* From Kernville, drive north on Sierra Way Road/Kern River Highway to Sherman Pass Road (Forest Service Road 22S05). Drive to Cherry Hill Road (Forest Service 22S12) and the signed turnoff to the right for Horse Meadow/Big Meadow. Turn right and drive to the Horse Meadow Campground turnoff and Horse Meadow Campground, just before reaching Big Meadow. The trailhead is located at the north end of the campground.

*Maps:* Send $3 to the USDA-Forest Service, 630 Sansome Street, San Francisco, CA 94111 and ask for the Sequoia National Forest map. For a topographic map, ask for Sirretta Peak from the USGS.

*Who to contact:* Sequoia National Forest, Cannell Meadow Ranger District, P.O. Box 6, Kernville, CA 93238; (619) 376-3781.

*Trail notes:* Begin hiking on the Deadwood Trail (Forest Service 34E13) north along a stream, through a pine and fir forest and over Cherry Hill Road at three-quarters of a mile. Continue on rocky Deadwood Trail alongside well-watered and shaded slopes and meadows, past pretty vistas and finally climbing steeply up to the Cannell Trail (Forest Service 33E32), 2.5 miles from the start. Picnicking among the pines at the trail junction is most pleasant. When ready, retrace your steps. The Cannell Trail leads to Sirretta Peak and Trail, two miles away, and then you could take the Sirretta Trail down into Big Meadow, 2.5 miles from the Cannell/Deadwood junction.

## 28. BIG MEADOW 4.5 mi/4.0 hrs
## to HORSE MEADOW TREK

*Reference:* **In Dome Lands Wilderness Area; map G5, grid g4.**

*User groups:* Hikers and dogs. No mountain bikes or horses are allowed. No wheelchair facilities.

*Permits:* Day-use permits are not required. Campfire permits are required if you intend on camping. For more information, contact the Cannell Meadow Ranger District at (619) 376-3781.

*Directions:* From Kernville, drive north on Sierra Way Road/Kern River Highway to Sherman Pass Road (Forest Service Road 22S05) and turn right. Drive to Cherry Hill Road (Forest Service 22S12) and the signed turnoff to the right for Horse Meadow/Big Meadow. Turn right and drive to the Horse Meadow Campground turnoff and Horse Meadow Campground, just before reaching Big Meadow. The trailhead is located at the south end of the campground.

*Maps:* Send $3 to the USDA-Forest Service, 630 Sansome Street, San Francisco, CA 94111 and ask for the Sequoia National Forest map. For a topographic map, ask for Sirretta Peak from the USGS.

*Who to contact:* Sequoia National Forest, Cannell Meadow Ranger District, P.O. Box 6, Kernville, CA 93238; (619) 376-3781.

*Trail notes:* Begin hiking on the unsigned trail, worn alongside this picturesque creek by others who have enjoyed the pleasures of this easy wander. The meadows along the way are often filled with color from wildflowers. In places the trail disappears, but just keep following the creek and you will soon end up at Big Meadows. Wear shoes you don't mind getting wet. Some of the way requires easy rock scrambling. Swimming holes are also wonderful along the way—providing the sun is warm, as the water is not. At Big Meadow, retrace your steps, hike back via the road, or have someone waiting for you to offer a ride back to the campground. Summer is too hot here—come in other seasons.

---

## 29. SALMON CREEK TRAIL    9.0 mi/4.5 hrs

*Reference:* In Dome Lands Wilderness Area; map G5, grid g4.

*User groups:* Hikers and dogs. No mountain bikes or horses are allowed. No wheelchair facilities.

*Permits:* Day-use permits are not required. Campfire permits are required if you intend on camping. For more information, contact the Cannell Meadow Ranger District at (619) 376-3781.

*Directions:* From Kernville, drive north on Sierra Way Road/Kern River Highway to Sherman Pass Road (Forest Service Road 22S05) and turn right. Drive to Cherry Hill Road (Forest Service 22S12) and the signed turnoff to the right for Horse Meadow/Big Meadow. Turn right and drive to the Horse Meadow Campground turnoff and Horse Meadow Campground, just before reaching Big Meadow. The trailhead is located at the northeast end of the campground.

*Maps:* Send $3 to the USDA-Forest Service, 630 Sansome Street, San Francisco, CA 94111 and ask for the Sequoia National Forest map. For topographic maps, ask for Sirretta Peak and Fairview from the USGS.

*Who to contact:* Sequoia National Forest, Cannell Meadow Ranger District, P.O. Box 6, Kernville, CA 93238; (619) 376-3781.

*Trail notes:* Wildflowers, shaded grottos, super swimming holes, good fishing and outstanding scenery await all who trek this path. Your eventual destination is the narrow gap through which Salmon Creek roars (during a good snowmelt year) and plunges several hundred feet to the rocks below. You won't get much of a view of the falls unless you are a skilled rock climber with the appropriate gear and can clamber out and around onto the facing cliff. Still, the magnificence of the water cascading over the edge and the tranquility of the surroundings more than makes up for the lack of a front row seat to the action. From the campground, begin hiking on the Salmon Creek Trail (Forest Service 33E36). Stay on the well-defined trail all the way to the falls. You will pass by Horse Meadow in one mile, wander through a lovely stand of wild lilac and meadow of lupine, and cross and recross Salmon Creek several times. The trail begins to descend about 3.5 miles before making a quick ascent to the top of a rocky ridge with views of the surrounding mountains. Slabs of rock just below the ridge have rock cairns placed on them to guide you (watch your step!) to pools along Salmon Creek. A few hundred yards beyond the pools is the edge of the falls—don't even think of trying to climb down, because it will be a one-way ticket with no return privileges. Retrace your steps when ready.

---

## 30. SIRRETTA PEAK    9.5 mi/6.0 hrs
## via CANNELL AND SIRRETTA TRAILS

*Reference:* **In Dome Lands Wilderness Area; map G5, grid g4.**

*User groups:* Hikers and dogs. No mountain bikes or horses are allowed. No wheelchair facilities.

*Permits:* Day-use permits are not required. Campfire permits are required if you intend on camping. For more information, contact the Cannell Meadow Ranger District at (619) 376-3781.

*Directions:* From Kernville, drive north on Sierra Way Road/Kern River Highway to Sherman Pass Road (Forest Service Road 22S05) and turn right. Drive to Cherry Hill Road (Forest Service 22S12) and to signed turnoff to the right for Horse Meadow/Big Meadow. Turn right and drive past the Horse Meadow Campground turnoff to Big Meadow. At the fork, bear left on Forest Service 23S07 and drive to the parking area located at the north end of the meadow. The trailhead begins here.

*Maps:* Send $3 to the USDA-Forest Service, 630 Sansome Street, San Francisco, CA 94111 and ask for the Sequoia National Forest map. For a topographic map, ask for Sirretta Peak from the USGS.

*Who to contact:* Sequoia National Forest, Cannell Meadow Ranger District, P.O. Box 6, Kernville, CA 93238; (619) 376-3781.

*Trail notes:* This hike takes you up through a wonderful canyon area through one of the few areas where lodgepole pine, white pine, limber pine, Jeffrey pine and foxtail pine are known to grow together. More noteworthy is the fact that this is the southernmost grove of foxtail pine in the Sierra and has been designated as the Twisselman Botanical Area. Over-the-shoulder views of Big Meadow below are stunning. Best of all is the cross-country trek up to Sirretta Peak, a jagged edge of granite reaching to the sky that has been the setting for a number of wilderness weddings and other special moments. Once you are on the peak, take the time to read the summit register (and of course enter your name and witticisms) while admiring the views and burning at least one roll of film. From the parking area, begin hiking north on the Cannell Trail (Forest Service 33E32) up to the junction with the Sirretta Trail (Forest Service 34E12). Head right onto Sirretta and up the ravine to the often windy pass—there is a good picnic spot sheltered from the wind on the lee side of the rocks. From the pass, head north up to the saddle above you (slipping and stumbling up the rocky slope) to the saddle above. At the saddle, head left (southwest) along the ridge to a jumble of boulders. Clamber up the boulders to the summit and stand in awe at the enormity of the view. Retrace your steps when ready. Come in spring or fall. Summer is too hot.

---

## 31. MANTER/WOODPECKER 24.0 mi/3.0 days
## MEADOWS LOOP TRIP

*Reference:* **In Dome Lands Wilderness Area; map G5, grid g4.**

*User groups:* Hikers, dogs and horses. No mountain bikes are allowed. No wheelchair facilities.

*Permits:* Day-use permits are not required. Campfire permits are required if you intend on camping. For more information, contact the Cannell Meadow Ranger District at (619) 376-3781.

*Directions:* From Kernville, drive north on Sierra Way Road/Kern River Highway to Sherman Pass Road (Forest Service Road 22S05) and turn right. Drive to Cherry Hill Road (Forest Service 22S12) and to signed turnoff to the right for Horse Meadow/Big Meadow. Turn right and drive past the Horse Meadow Campground turnoff to Big Meadow. At the fork, bear left on Forest Service 23S07 and drive to the parking area located at the north end of the meadow. The trailhead begins here.

*Maps:* Send $3 to the USDA-Forest Service, 630 Sansome Street, San Francisco, CA 94111 and ask for the Sequoia National Forest map. For a topographic map, ask for Sirretta Peak from the USGS.

*Who to contact:* Sequoia National Forest, Cannell Meadow Ranger District, P.O. Box 6, Kernville, CA 93238; (619) 376-3781.

*Trail notes:* When the rest of the Sierra is still buried under a mantle of snow, this area beckons, but few heed the call. When Michael was a guide, he used to lead regular Memorial Day excursions into the Dome Lands and rarely, if at all, would he see anyone in the Dome Land Wilderness area—even though nearby Big Meadows and the Kern River were packed with recreationists. Grassy meadows, rocky crags, wildflowers, little streamlets, and wildlife are the menu for this outing. From the parking area, hike south along the road beside Big Meadow, past the green buildings of the Big Meadow Cow Camp to the Manter Trailhead on the left. Begin hiking on Manter Trail (Forest Service 34E14). Hike Manter Trail to Manter Meadow and bear left on the Cabin Spur Trail (Forest Service 34E37A) and onto the Woodpecker Trail (Forest Service 34E08) at 4.2 miles. If you get a late start, this is a super place for the first night's camp, with numerous sites to choose from scattered along the trail. Remember to camp well away from the trail and out of sight. Stay on the Woodpecker Trail to the Rockhouse Basin Trail (Forest Service 35E16) where you will head left, approximately 11.5 miles from the trailhead, on to Woodpecker Meadow and Trout Creek—there's good fishing here. There is another nice campsite located here near Dark Canyon Creek, frequented by horse packers. At Woodpecker Meadow, and at about 13 miles, the trail become Sirretta Trail (Forest Service 34E12). Sirretta Trail works its way to near the base of Sirretta Peak and along Little Trout Creek at about 19 miles. There is a good camp here, which is one of Michael's favorites. Head steeply up a series of switchbacks to Sirretta Pass at 9,580 feet and approximately 21 miles from the start. Take a side hike to enjoy Sirretta Peak, (see hike number 30) and then drop down to Cannell Trail (Forest Service 33E32) and return to the parking area and your car.

---

## 32. SOUTH MANTER TRAIL    5.0 mi/3.0 hrs

*Reference:* **In Dome Lands Wilderness Area; map G5, grid g4.**

*User groups:* Hikers, dogs and horses. No mountain bikes are allowed. No wheelchair facilities.

*Permits:* Day-use permits are not required. Campfire permits are required if you intend on camping. For more information, contact the Cannell Meadow Ranger District at (619) 376-3781.

*Directions:* From Kernville, drive north on Sierra Way Road/Kern River Highway to Sherman Pass Road (Forest Service Road 22S05) and turn right. Drive to Cherry Hill Road (Forest Service 22S12) and to signed turnoff to the right for Horse Meadow/Big Meadow. Turn right and drive past the Horse Meadow Campground turnoff to Big Meadow. At the fork, bear left on Forest Service 23S07 and drive to the parking area located at the south end of the meadow next to the South Manter Trailhead (Forest Service 34E37).

*Maps:* Send $3 to the USDA-Forest Service, 630 Sansome Street, San Francisco, CA 94111 and ask for the Sequoia National Forest map. For topographic maps, ask for Cannell Peak and Sirretta Peak from the USGS.

*Who to contact:* Sequoia National Forest, Cannell Meadow Ranger District, P.O. Box 6, Kernville, CA 93238; (619) 376-3781.

*Trail notes:* Manter Meadow is a great destination for a picnic or quick escape outing. It is an emerald green jewel tucked among the jagged peaks and spires of the Dome Lands Wilderness. Wildflowers in the spring are wonderful. From the trailhead, hike on the South Manter Trail (Forest Service 34E37) to Manter Meadow. The trail ends at the cabin. Wander where you will, but don't lose track of where the trail is located as it can sometimes be hard to find if you get too far off the track. Head back the way you came when ready. Mosquitoes can be bothersome in the early spring, depending on the snowmelt. Fall is a good time to visit too, although some days get a little warm and many of the streamlets have dried up. Summer is too darn hot.

---

# 33. TAYLOR DOME SCRAMBLE 4.5 mi/3.0 hrs

*Reference:* **In Dome Lands Wilderness Area; map G5, grid g4.**

*User groups:* Hikers and dogs. No mountain bikes or horses are allowed. No wheelchair facilities.

*Permits:* Day-use permits are not required. Campfire permits are required if you intend on camping. For more information, contact the Cannell Meadow Ranger District at (619) 376-3781.

*Directions:* From Kernville, drive north on Sierra Way Road/Kern River Highway to Sherman Pass Road (Forest Service Road 22S05) and turn right. Drive to Cherry Hill Road (Forest Service 22S12) and to signed turnoff to the right for Horse Meadow/Big Meadow. Turn right and drive past the Horse Meadow Campground turnoff to Big Meadow. At the fork, bear left on Forest Service 23S07 and drive to the parking area located at the south end of the meadow next to the South Manter Trailhead (Forest Service 34E37).

*Maps:* Send $3 to the USDA-Forest Service, 630 Sansome Street, San Francisco, CA 94111 and ask for the Sequoia National Forest map. For topographic maps, ask for Cannell Peak and Sirretta Peak from the USGS.

*Who to contact:* Sequoia National Forest, Cannell Meadow Ranger District, P.O. Box 6, Kernville, CA 93238; (619) 376-3781.

*Trail notes:* From the trailhead at Big Meadow, head off on the South Manter Meadow Trail (Forest Service 34E37) to a south heading connector trail (Forest Service 34E15A) leading to the Big Meadow Trail (Forest Service 34E15). The trail winds, dips and climbs to a boulder-strewn ridge running east to west (or west to east depending on your perspective). The trail continues on to Taylor Meadow, but you are seeking more adventure, yes?

Good, so were we. Head left (east) and up the ridge toward the towering blocks of Taylor Dome, elevation 8,800 feet. The route you follow heads somewhat southeast along the ridge and then up a bare and loose rock flat toward the sheer face of Taylor Dome. Rock climbers revel in its vertical face. You, on the other hand, will probably be satisfied to climb up the slope to the bench just beneath the summit for top-of-the-Dome Lands views. If you are a skilled rock climber, you may wish to pick a route along the ledges and cracks to the summit itself—a worthwhile goal if you have the experience. Head back the way you came when ready.

## 34. WOODPECKER TRAIL          9.0 mi/5.0 hrs

*Reference:* **In Dome Lands Wilderness Area; map G5, grid g4.**

*User groups:* Hikers, dogs, horses and mountain bikes. No wheelchair facilities.

*Permits:* Day-use permits are not required. Campfire permits are required if you intend on camping. For more information, contact the Cannell Meadow Ranger District at (619) 376-3781.

*Directions:* From Kernville, drive north on Sierra Way Road/Kern River Highway to Sherman Pass Road (Forest Service Road 22S05) and turn right. Drive to Cherry Hill Road (Forest Service 22S12) and to signed turnoff to the right for Horse Meadow/Big Meadow. Turn right and drive past the Horse Meadow Campground turnoff to Big Meadow. At the fork, bear left on Forest Service 23S07 and drive to the parking area located at the south end of the meadow next to the South Manter Trailhead (Forest Service 34E37).

*Maps:* Send $3 to the USDA-Forest Service, 630 Sansome Street, San Francisco, CA 94111 and ask for the Sequoia National Forest map. For topographic maps, ask for Cannell Peak and Sirretta Peak from the USGS.

*Who to contact:* Sequoia National Forest, Cannell Meadow Ranger District, P.O. Box 6, Kernville, CA 93238; (619) 376-3781.

*Trail notes:* Wildflowers, streams and gorgeous scenery make for a wonderful trek. Those wishing to turn this into an overnight can find great campsites around the south end of Manter Meadow. From the trailhead, hike on the South Manter Trail (Forest Service 34E37) about three miles to Manter Meadow. At Manter Meadow, head right onto the Woodpecker Trail (Forest Service 34E08) and hike this trail two miles to the cathedral-like spires of Church Dome. Technical climbers come to the dome to play on its spires. Non-climbers can enjoy the dome's summit as there is a trail that leads almost up to the top at 7,833 feet.

*Special note:* Get off the dome if weather threatens. Spring is the best time to visit, although fall isn't bad either. Avoid the area in summer, as it is too hot. If you are camping, be sure to bear-bag your food.

## 35. CANNELL TRAIL          4.5 mi/3.0 hrs
## to CANNELL MEADOW

*Reference:* **In Dome Lands Wilderness Area; map G5, grid g4.**

*User groups:* Hikers, dogs and horses. No mountain bikes are allowed. No wheelchair facilities.

*Permits:* Day-use permits are not required. Campfire permits are required if you intend on camping. For more information, contact the Cannell Meadow Ranger District at (619) 376-3781.

*Directions:* From Kernville, drive north on Sierra Way Road/Kern River Highway to Sherman Pass Road (Forest Service Road 22S05) and turn right. Drive to Cherry Hill Road (Forest Service 22S12) and to signed turnoff to the right for Horse Meadow/Big Meadow. Turn right and drive past the Horse Meadow Campground turnoff to Big Meadow. At the fork, bear right staying on Forest Service 22S12 around the west edge of Big Meadow and to the signed trailhead for Cannell Trail (Forest Service 33E32) located on the right side of the road.

*Maps:* Send $3 to the USDA-Forest Service, 630 Sansome Street, San Francisco, CA 94111 and ask for the Sequoia National Forest map. For a topographic map, ask for Cannell Peak from the USGS.

*Who to contact:* Sequoia National Forest, Cannell Meadow Ranger District, P.O. Box 6, Kernville, CA 93238; (619) 376-3781.

*Trail notes:* This is a pretty day hike along a section of trail that once qualified as a National Scenic Trail, but had that status revoked except for its lower eight miles, since it was crossed in places by logging roads. From the trailhead you will climb up Cannell Trail (Forest Service 33E32) up to a saddle and then down to Forest Service Road 24S56. Head right and hike a short distance on the road to the historic Cannell Meadow Guard Station which looks much as it did when it was built in the early 1900s—with a little renovation, of course. The view from the guard station looks out over the gorgeous green of Cannell Meadow. Head back the way you came.

---

# 36. LITTLE CANNELL TRAIL    3.5 mi/2.0 hrs

*Reference:* **In Dome Lands Wilderness Area; map G5, grid g4.**

*User groups:* Hikers and dogs. Horses are not recommended. No mountain bikes are allowed. No wheelchair facilities.

*Permits:* Day-use permits are not required. Campfire permits are required if you intend on camping. For more information, contact the Cannell Meadow Ranger District at (619) 376-3781.

*Directions:* From Kernville, drive north on Sierra Way Road/Kern River Highway to Sherman Pass Road (Forest Service Road 22S05) and turn right. Drive to Cherry Hill Road (Forest Service 22S12) and to signed turnoff to the right for Horse Meadow/Big Meadow. Turn right and drive past the Horse Meadow Campground turnoff to Big Meadow. At the fork, bear right staying on Forest Service 22S12 around the west edge of Big Meadow and remaining on 22S12 to Long Meadow and a junction with Forest Service Road 24S12 to the right. Turn right and look for the signed trailhead for Little Cannell Trail on the left shortly after the junction.

*Maps:* Send $3 to the USDA-Forest Service, 630 Sansome Street, San Francisco, CA 94111 and ask for the Sequoia National Forest map. For a topographic map, ask for Cannell Peak from the USGS.

*Who to contact:* Sequoia National Forest, Cannell Meadow Ranger District, P.O. Box 6, Kernville, CA 93238; (619) 376-3781.

*Trail notes:* This is a great hike for children and a good one for adults too as it winds its way alongside Fay Creek on a section of trail that was once part of the Pacific Crest Trail. There are a number of excellent picnic spots among the pines on the way. From the trailhead, head downstream to Little Cannell Meadow and a four-wheel-drive route. The meadow is pretty and a good spot to hang out before turning around and retracing your steps back to the parking area.

---

## 37. UPPER DRY LAKE TRAIL    2.5 mi/1.5 hrs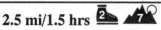

*Reference:* In Dome Lands Wilderness Area; map G5, grid g4.

*User groups:* Hikers, dogs and horses. No mountain bikes are allowed. No wheelchair facilities.

*Permits:* Day-use permits are not required. Campfire permits are required if you intend on camping. For more information, contact the Cannell Meadow Ranger District at (619) 376-3781.

*Directions:* From Kernville, drive north on Sierra Way Road/Kern River Highway to Sherman Pass Road (Forest Service Road 22S05) and turn right. Drive to Cherry Hill Road (Forest Service 22S12) and to signed turnoff to the right for Horse Meadow/Big Meadow. Turn right and drive past the Horse Meadow Campground turnoff to Big Meadow. At the fork, bear right staying on Forest Service Road 22S12 around the west edge of Big Meadow. Stay on Forest Service Road 22S12 past Long Meadow and to the junction with Forest Service Road 24S13. Turn left and drive to Forest Service Road 24S32 leading left and north to Taylor Meadow.

*Maps:* Send $3 to the USDA-Forest Service, 630 Sansome Street, San Francisco, CA 94111 and ask for the Sequoia National Forest map. For a topographic map, ask for Cannell Peak from the USGS.

*Who to contact:* Sequoia National Forest, Cannell Meadow Ranger District, P.O. Box 6, Kernville, CA 93238; (619) 376-3781.

*Trail notes:* Taylor Meadow is a great place to car camp and a perfect base for this dayhike. The trailhead for Upper Dry Lake Trail (Forest Service 34E17) is located at the west end of the meadow near a cattle pen. The trail is an easy jaunt up to a lake that is usually not much more than dry reeds by late summer—hence the name. In the spring, listen to the bullfrogs sing! The meadow-like area around the lake is a good spot for a picnic. Head back the way you came.

---

## 38. STEGOSAURUS FIN    23.0 mi/3.0 days
## LOOP TRIP

*Reference:* In Dome Lands Wilderness Area; map G5, grid g6.

*User groups:* Hikers, dogs and horses. No mountain bikes are allowed. No wheelchair facilities.

*Permits:* Day-use permits are not required. Campfire permits are required if you intend on camping. For more information, contact the Cannell Meadow Ranger District at (619) 376-3781.

*Directions:* From the town of Brown on Highway 14, drive north on Highway 14 for four miles to Nine Mile Canyon Road and turn left (west). Drive 11 miles to the BLM Ranger Station. Turn left on the dirt road opposite the station and drive past the Chimney Peak Campground. Continue down the road for seven miles to the Rockhouse Basin/Dome Lands Wilderness Boundary turnoff on the right. This is a rutted road but suitable for most vehicles if you take it slowly.

*Maps:* Send $3 to the USDA-Forest Service, 630 Sansome Street, San Francisco, CA 94111 and ask for the Sequoia National Forest map. For topographic maps, ask for Rockhouse Basin and Sirretta Peak from the USGS.

*Who to contact:* Sequoia National Forest, Cannell Meadow Ranger District, P.O. Box 6, Kernville, CA 93238; (619) 376-3781.

*Trail notes:* The Dome Lands Wilderness Area is often deserted, even though nearby Big Meadows and the Kern River are packed with recreationists. A neat side hike opportunity exists to the informally named Stegosaurus Fin, to the north of the Dome Lands Wilderness Trail, approximately three miles after leaving Rockhouse Basin. Use your imagination and you will see the "fin", or maybe just a jagged crag. Either way, those with basic rock climbing skills can scramble up the Class III / IV climb to the base of the summit block, but the final 50 feet requires technical skill and climbing gear. The view is super. From the trailhead, head right on the Rockhouse Basin Trail (Forest Service 35E16) and hike to the Dome Lands Trail (Forest Service 35E10). Turn left and hike along the Dome Lands Trail beside Tibbets Creek to a wide sandy flat (good places to camp here), just before the trail veers north away from the creek. Look north to Stegosaurus Fin and hike cross-country to it if you wish. Otherwise, keep hiking on the Dome Lands Trail to the Woodpecker Trail (Forest Service 34E08) and head left (south) to Manter Meadow. Camp here for your second night, lulled to sleep by the sound of owls and trickling water. Next morning, at the meadow's south end, head left on the Manter Creek Trail (Forest Service 35E12) back to Rockhouse Basin. At Rockhouse Meadow and basin, head left onto the Rockhouse Basin Trail (Forest Service 35E16) and back to the parking area and your car. Wildflowers along the hike in the spring are great. This backpack is best done in the spring, although the runoff can be too high—call ahead to be sure the creek can be crossed.

---

# 39. ROCKHOUSE BASIN 3.0 mi/1.5 hrs

*Reference:* **In Dome Lands Wilderness Area; map G5, grid g6.**

*User groups:* Hikers, horses and dogs. No mountain bikes are allowed. No wheelchair facilities.

*Permits:* Day-use permits are not required. Campfire permits are required if you intend on camping within the Dome Lands Wilderness Area. For more information, contact the Cannell Meadow Ranger District at (619) 376-3781.

*Directions:* From the town of Brown on Highway 14, drive north on Highway 14 for four miles to Nine Mile Canyon Road and turn left (west). Drive 11 miles to the BLM Ranger Station. Turn left on the dirt road opposite the station and drive past the Chimney Peak Campground. Continue down the road for seven miles to the Rockhouse Basin/Dome Lands Wilderness Boundary turnoff to the right. This is a rutted road but suitable for most vehicles if you take it slowly.

*Maps:* Send $3 to the USDA-Forest Service, 630 Sansome Street, San Francisco, CA 94111 and ask for the Sequoia National Forest map. For a topographic map, ask for Rockhouse Basin from the USGS.

*Who to contact:* Bureau of Land Management, Ridgecrest Resource Area, 300 South Richmond Road, Ridgecrest, CA 93555; (619) 384-5400 or Sequoia National Forest, Cannell Meadow Ranger District, P.O. Box 6, Kernville, CA 93238; (619) 376-3781.

*Trail notes:* From the trailhead, you immediately enter the Dome Lands Wilderness Area, a region of huge meadows, giant granite domes, tumbling streams and very few people. This quick jaunt doesn't even begin to sample the rich plate the Dome Lands offers, but it will give you a brief sampling of the pleasure of the Kern River and its relaxing environment. Fish, swim, sunbathe (with sunscreen of course) picnic and even camp—it's your choice. Hike several miles on the Rockhouse Basin Trail (Forest Service 35E16) amid the shade of pinyon pine. When you are ready, pack up and head back out. Do watch out for rattlesnakes, who like to bask in the shade of low lying bushes. Summer is to darn hot in here unless you are planning on spending all of your time in the river. Spring is our favorite time because of the wildflowers; fall is nice too.

---

## 40. ROCKHOUSE BASIN      12.0 mi/2.0 days
## to WHITE DOME

*Reference:* **In Dome Lands Wilderness Area; map G5, grid g6.**

*User groups:* Hikers, horses and dogs. No mountain bikes are allowed. No wheelchair facilities.

*Permits:* Day-use permits are not required. Campfire permits are required if you intend on camping within the Dome Lands Wilderness Area. For more information, contact the Cannell Meadow Ranger District at (619) 376-3781.

*Directions:* From the town of Brown on Highway 14, drive north on Highway 14 for four miles to Nine Mile Canyon Road and turn left (west). Drive 11 miles to the BLM Ranger Station. Turn left on the dirt road opposite the station and drive past the Chimney Peak Campground. Then continue down the road for seven miles to the Rockhouse Basin/Dome Lands Wilderness Boundary turnoff to the right. This is a rutted road but suitable for most vehicles if you take it slowly.

*Maps:* Send $3 to the USDA-Forest Service, 630 Sansome Street, San Francisco, CA 94111 and ask for the Sequoia National Forest map. For topographic maps, ask for White Dome and Rockhouse Basin from the USGS.

*Who to contact:* Bureau of Land Management, Ridgecrest Resource Area, 300 South Richmond Road, Ridgecrest, CA 93555; (619) 384-5400 or Sequoia National Forest, Cannell Meadow Ranger District, P.O. Box 6, Kernville, CA 93238; (619) 376-3781.

*Trail notes:* If you liked what you experienced on hike number 39, then this will offer you a chance to hike into the deeper wilderness among domes, spires and pines. The ultimate goal of this trip is the summit of White Dome, with superb views of the Dome Lands beyond the Kern River Canyon below. There is some basic cross-country hiking involved here, so you should possess good navigational skills. From the trailhead, hike on Rockhouse Basin Trail 35E16 to the Manter Creek Trail 35E12 for one quarter mile. Head left onto Manter and work your way across the many channels of the South Fork of the Kern—if you do it without getting your feet wet, we want to know how. The trail soon climbs very steeply to a saddle divide at 4.5 miles. At the saddle, you will head south and up the ridge line toward White Dome and its summit at 7,555 feet, six miles from the start. Once you have played enough around the rocks—and it is addicting—head back the way you came. There are a number of good campsites just off the Manter Trail, past the saddle or on toward the dome. Spring is our favorite time because of the wildflowers. Fall is nice too.

## 41. CHIMNEY CREEK     3.5 mi/2.0 hrs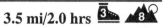

*Reference:* **Pacific Crest Trail, Dome Lands Wilderness Area; map G5, grid g7.**

*User groups:* Hikers, horses and dogs. No mountain bikes are allowed. No wheelchair facilities.

*Permits:* Day-use permits are not required.

*Directions:* From the town of Brown on Highway 14, drive north on Highway 14 for four miles to Nine Mile Canyon Road and turn left (west). Drive 11 miles to the BLM Ranger Station. Turn left on the dirt road opposite the station and drive three miles to the Chimney Peak Campground.

*Maps:* Send $3 to the USDA-Forest Service, 630 Sansome Street, San Francisco, CA 94111 and ask for the Sequoia National Forest map. For a topographic map, ask for Lamont Peak from the USGS.

*Who to contact:* Bureau of Land Management, Ridgecrest Resource Area, 300 South Richmond Road, Ridgecrest, CA 93555; (619) 384-5400.

*Trail notes:* From the campground, the Chimney Creek Trail hops back and forth across narrow Chimney Creek as it works its way between the tall and fissured walls of Chimney Creek Canyon. There are numerous picnic spots along the way—perfect for a romantic hike. There are even wild roses in places along the route. The canyon eventually dumps you out onto the edge of Chimney Meadow, which is privately owned, as indicated by a fence—stay off the meadow!

## 42. LONG VALLEY TRAIL    5.0 mi/2.5 hrs
## to THE KERN

*Reference:* **Pacific Crest Trail, Dome Lands Wilderness Area; map G5, grid g7.**

*User groups:* Hikers and dogs. No horses or mountain bikes are allowed. No wheelchair facilities.

*Permits:* Day-use permits are not required. Campfire permits are required if you intend on camping within the Dome Lands Wilderness Area. For more information, contact the Cannell Meadow Ranger District at (619) 376-3781.

*Directions:* From the town of Brown on Highway 14, drive north on Highway 14 for four miles to Nine Mile Canyon Road and turn left (west). Drive 11 miles to the BLM Ranger Station. Turn left on the dirt road opposite the station and drive 14 miles to the Long Valley Campground.

*Maps:* Send $3 to the USDA-Forest Service, 630 Sansome Street, San Francisco, CA 94111 and ask for the Sequoia National Forest map. For a topographic map, ask for White Dome from the USGS.

*Who to contact:* Bureau of Land Management, Ridgecrest Resource Area, 300 South Richmond Road, Ridgecrest, CA 93555; (619) 384-5400 or Sequoia National Forest, Cannell Meadow Ranger District, P.O. Box 6, Kernville, CA 93238; (619) 376-3781.

*Trail notes:* From the campground, the trail heads steeply west to the Forest

Service boundary and the wilderness boundary where the trail officially becomes Long Valley Trail, Forest Service 36E05. The "trail" follows the Long Valley Creek's course, sometimes on one side, sometimes on the other, all the way to the South Fork of the Kern River. The willows, cottonwoods and wild roses along the way make this a wonderful traipse through the woods—unless you are sweating it out in the summer. Spring is the best time to head out, as the wildflowers are in bloom. Fall ranks a close second. Summer is to be avoided. There are numerous fishing and swimming holes along the way, so don't forget your swimming suit and fishing rod.

## 43. FOSSIL FALLS TRAIL     1.0 mi/0.5 hr

*Reference:* **North of Ridgecrest and east of Highway 395; map G5, grid g9.**
*User groups:* Hikers only. No mountain bikes, dogs or horses are allowed. No wheelchair facilities.
*Permits:* No permits are required.
*Directions:* From Ridgecrest, drive north on Highway 395 approximately 45 miles to Cinder Cone Road. Turn right (east) and drive approximately five miles on Cinder Cone Road. Then head south on unpaved Poleline Road to the signed and designated parking area.
*Maps:* For a topographic map, ask for Little Lake from the USGS.
*Who to contact:* Bureau of Land Management, Ridgecrest Resource Area, 300 South Richmond Road, Ridgecrest, CA 93555; (619) 384-5400.
*Trail notes:* Black lava, sculpted and polished during the Ice Age, creates a series of dry waterfalls here. Native Americans frequented this exceptional site because of the lavish formations created by volcanic activity—activity that provided materials for tool making. On your hike over the lava, you'll see rock rings—remnants of circular huts built by the Paiute Indians. The abundance of obsidian flakes in the area attest to the use of volcanic glass in making knives and other projectiles. Petroglyphs found here are thought to relate to hunting rituals.

## 44. EDISON ROAD     5.5 mi/2.0 hrs

*Reference:* **In Dome Lands Wilderness Area; map G5, grid h3.**
*User groups:* Hikers, horses, dogs and mountain bikes. No wheelchair facilities.
*Permits:* Day-use permits are not required.
*Directions:* From Kernville, drive north on Sierra Way to the Sequoia National Forest boundary. Approximately 1.5 miles beyond the boundary on the right side of the road is a dirt road named Edison. Park you car there.
*Maps:* Send $3 to the USDA-Forest Service, 630 Sansome Street, San Francisco, CA 94111 and ask for the Sequoia National Forest map. For a topographic map, ask for Kernville from the USGS.
*Who to contact:* Sequoia National Forest, Cannell Meadow Ranger District, P.O. Box 6, Kernville, CA 93238; (619) 376-3781.
*Trail notes:* Michael stayed overnight in Kernville a number of years ago and was tipped off to this local "trail" (actually a maintenance road) when inquiring where he might get in a quick run before a river trip began the next morning. "Head up and down the Edison Road," he was told. While the road doesn't have a lot going for it in terms of immediate scenic value, the views on the way up are super, especially in the early morning or early evening, and

the workout is wonderful. Best of all you don't have to worry about traffic while working up a sweat. From the beginning of Edison Road, head up and back the same way, either walking or running. Once at the top, turn around and fly back down.

---

## 45. HARLEY MINE TRAIL    5.5 mi/2.0 days

*Reference:* **In Dome Lands Wilderness Area; map G5, grid h3.**

*User groups:* Hikers, horses and dogs. No mountain bikes are allowed. No wheelchair facilities.

*Permits:* Day-use permits are not required.

*Directions:* From Kernville, drive east up a dirt access road that is opposite Buena Vista. Drive approximately two-tenths of a mile to a flat area suitable for parking.

*Maps:* Send $3 to the USDA-Forest Service, 630 Sansome Street, San Francisco, CA 94111 and ask for the Sequoia National Forest map. For a topographic map, ask for Kernville from the USGS.

*Who to contact:* Sequoia National Forest, Cannell Meadow Ranger District, P.O. Box 6, Kernville, CA 93238; (619) 376-3781.

*Trail notes:* This hike is a beater through dense underbrush, steep slopes and dusty environments. What's the payoff? Finding a register at a mountain summit and then discovering an old chimney that is all that remains of the old Harley Mine buildings. Is it worth it? We're not sure, but we can say we are still picking ticks out of our drawers. If you want sweeping views of Lake Isabella and Kernville below, then we would have to say the sweat and toil is worth every minute—we think. One thing is for certain, you had better be good with a map and compass or you'll never find anything except your shoes. From your car, keep hiking up the road, which soon transforms to a trail that disappears on and off into dense underbrush. A local told us to keep our eyes out for the rock retaining walls that defined the trail's edge when it was maintained—we're still looking for those walls. Once you gain the ridge top, head north (left), now on a somewhat indistinct trail again, to a trail fork. Head left again around a bowl and then onto a ridge—now where did that darn trail go? Lo and behold, you will stumble onto mine relics if you are on the right path and, yep, there's an old chimney. Well, I'll be! From the chimney, head south to the obvious summit of Harley Mountain to record your climb for posterity in the summit register. Think of something pithy to say. Head back the way you came and for gosh sakes, be sure to check for ticks when you get back!

*Special note:* The Kern Valley Society has recently adopted this trail. At the time this book went to press, the mine shafts were not fenced. The Forest Service anticipates they will be fenced in the summer of 1995. The shafts are dangerous, so keep away!

---

## 46. BARTOLAS OVERLOOK    8.0 mi/3.5 hrs

*Reference:* **In Dome Lands Wilderness Area; map G5, grid h4.**

*User groups:* Hikers, dogs, horses and mountain bikes. No wheelchair facilities.

*Permits:* Day-use permits are not required. Campfire permits are required if you intend on camping. For more information, contact the Cannell Meadow Ranger District at (619) 376-3781.

*Directions:* From Kernville, drive north on Sierra Way Road/Kern River Highway to Sherman Pass Road (Forest Service Road 22S05). Drive to Cherry Hill Road (Forest Service 22S12) and to signed turnoff to the right for Horse Meadow/Big Meadow. Turn right and drive past the Horse Meadow Campground turnoff to Big Meadow. At the fork, bear right staying on Forest Service 22S12 around the west edge of Big Meadow and remaining on 22S12 past Long Meadow and to a junction with Forest Service Road 24S13 to the left. Turn left and drive to Forest Service Road 24S14. Turn right on 24S14, drive to the gate and park off the road, take care not to obstruct the gate or road.

*Maps:* Send $3 to the USDA-Forest Service, 630 Sansome Street, San Francisco, CA 94111 and ask for the Sequoia National Forest map. For topographic maps, ask for Cannell Peak and Weldon from the USGS.

*Who to contact:* Sequoia National Forest, Cannell Meadow Ranger District, P.O. Box 6, Kernville, CA 93238; (619) 376-3781.

*Trail notes:* This is a fair hike with a good view at the end. The route is not all that scenic as it follows Forest Service Road 24S14 to its end just before the 7,256-foot summit of Bartolas Peak. Scramble cross-country a short distance to an informal overlook that offers great views not only of the rocky Bartolas summit, but also of the entire area south of the Kern Plateau. Remember, if you are riding a mountain bike—the easiest and quickest way to get here—you must leave it at the road when you hike cross-country into the Dome Lands Wilderness for the last several hundred yards of the trip. Spring is the best time to visit.

---

# 47. WALKER PASS 10.0 mi/6.0 hrs
## to MOUNT JENKINS MEMORIAL

*Reference:* **Walker Pass west of Highway 395; map G5, grid i7.**

*User groups:* Hikers and horses. No dogs or mountain bikes are allowed. No wheelchair facilities.

*Permits:* Day-use permits are not required.

*Directions:* From Highway 14, turn west onto Highway 178 and drive to the Walker Pass Trailhead Campground, built especially for Pacific Crest Trail hikers. The trailhead begins across the highway.

*Maps:* Send $3 to the USDA-Forest Service, 630 Sansome Street, San Francisco, CA 94111 and ask for the Sequoia National Forest map. For a topographic map, ask for Walker Pass from the USGS.

*Who to contact:* Bureau of Land Management, Ridgecrest Resource Area, 300 South Richmond Road, Ridgecrest, CA 93555; (619) 384-5400.

*Trail notes:* Jim Jenkins probably did as much to further the knowledge and documentation of the trails and resources in the Southern Sierra as anyone. He was also extremely active promoting the conservation and protection of the resources in the area. Unfortunately, while returning to his job as a ranger in the Golden Trout Wilderness, he was killed at the young age of 29 by an elderly driver who was reportedly driving erratically, with diminished driving skills and poor vision. Five years later, Mount Jenkins was officially named to honor Jim Jenkins and his contributions to the Southern Sierra. This hike is a mellow trek along the Pacific Crest Trail to Mount Jenkins and the stone memorial constructed to honor him.

## 48. WALKER PASS PCT SOUTH 9.0 mi/5.0 hrs

*Reference:* **Walker Pass west of Highway 395; map G5, grid i7.**

*User groups:* Hikers and horses. No dogs or mountain bikes are allowed. No wheelchair facilities.

*Permits:* Day-use permits are not required. Campfire permits are required for camping. For more information, contact the Cannell Meadow Ranger District at (619) 376-3781.

*Directions:* From Highway 14, turn west onto Highway 178 and drive to the Walker Pass Trailhead Campground, built especially for Pacific Crest Trail hikers. The trailhead begins at the east end of the campground.

*Maps:* Send $3 to the USDA-Forest Service, 630 Sansome Street, San Francisco, CA 94111 and ask for the Sequoia National Forest map. For a topographic map, ask for Walker Pass from the USGS.

*Who to contact:* Sequoia National Forest, Cannell Meadow Ranger District, P.O. Box 6, Kernville, CA 93238; (619) 376-3781.

*Trail notes:* From the campground, hike the PCT south as far as McIvers Spring if you wish, or turn back anytime before then. This trail section into the Keiva Wilderness is a scenic one, especially in the spring when wildflowers carpet the slopes around the throughway. This section is best hiked in the spring and fall—summer can get a tad too warm.

---

## 49. OWENS PEAK 20.0 mi/10.0 hrs

*Reference:* **Walker Pass west of Highway 395; map G5, grid i7**

*User groups:* Hikers only. No horses, dogs, or mountain bikes are allowed. No wheelchair facilities.

*Permits:* No permits are needed.

*Directions:* From Highway 14, turn west onto Highway 178 and drive to the Walker Pass Trailhead Campground, built especially for Pacific Crest Trail hikers. The trailhead begins at the east of the campground.

*Maps:* Send $3 to the USDA-Forest Service, 630 Sansome Street, San Francisco, CA 94111 and ask for the Sequoia National Forest map. For topographic maps, ask for Walker Pass and Owens Peak.

*Who to contact:* Bureau of Land Management, Ridgecrest Resource Area, 300 South Richmond Road, Ridgecrest, CA 93555; (619) 384-5400.

*Trail notes:* From anywhere in Indian Wells Valley, the towering east face of Owens Peak casts a dominant shadow. The 8,453-foot-high peak in the southern Sierra offers strong hikers spectacular vistas of the high Sierra and the western Mojave desert. From the trailhead, hike north on the Pacific Crest Trail for approximately nine miles to the pass at the west end of Indian Wells Canyon. Bear right (northeast) on a rough path that follows the ridgeline for about one mile to the summit. Retrace your steps when ready. The hike has an elevation gain of about 3,200 feet, so expect to be breathing heavily. The spur trail is poorly marked, so you would do well to brush up on your map and compass skills. Carry plenty of water as there is none on the route.

# PACIFIC CREST TRAIL        113.5 mi. one way/11.0 days
## GENERAL INFORMATION

*Reference:* **Trail sections extend from the Walker Pass Trailhead north to Whitney Portal.**

*User groups:* Hikers, horses and dogs (except in national parks). No mountain bikes are allowed. No wheelchair facilities.

*Permits:* A wilderness permit is required for traveling through various wilderness and special-use areas that the trail traverses. Contact the national forest, BLM or national park office at your point of entry for a permit that is good for the length of your trip.

*Maps:* For an overall view of the trail route in this section, send $3 for each map to the USDA-Forest Service, 630 Sansome Street, San Francisco, CA 94111. Ask for the Inyo National Forest and Sequoia National Forest maps. USGS topographic maps for particular sections of the trail are provided under each specific trail section heading listed below.

*Who to contact:* Contact either the national forest, BLM or national park office at your trailhead—see specific trailheads and corresponding agencies listed within each section.

*Trail notes:* Trail elevations within this section range from around 3,800 feet to over 11,500 feet. Welcome to the High Sierra, as this section takes you into the heart of it. Bear precautions are at a premium now—no food in the tent and always hang your supplies. Streams may be swollen from the snowmelt and difficult to cross. Snow may still linger in the high passes as late as July.

*Special note:* Do not attempt to cross any high angle snowpack or icepack unless you are skilled with an ice ax and crampons.

---

# PCT-19        50.0 mi. one way/5.0 days
## WALKER PASS to KENNEDY MEADOWS

*Reference:* **From the Walker Pass Trailhead map G5, grid i7 north to the trailhead parking at Kennedy Meadows.**

*User groups:* Hikers, horses and dogs. No mountain bikes are allowed. No wheelchair facilities.

*Permits:* A wilderness permit is required for traveling through various wilderness and special-use areas that the trail traverses. Contact the Angeles National Forest at (805) 296-9710 for a permit that is good for the length of your trip.

*Directions:* To the Walker Pass Trailhead—From Highway 14 at Vincent, head south on the Angeles Forest Highway (County Road N3) to the Mill Creek Summit and picnic area and the signed Pacific Crest Trail trailhead.

To the Kennedy Meadows Trailhead—From the town of Brown on Highway 14, drive north on Highway 14 for four miles to Nine Mile Canyon Road and turn left (west). Drive on Nine Mile Canyon Road (it becomes Kennedy Meadows Road) to Kennedy Meadows and the signed Pacific Crest Trail trailhead.

*Maps:* For an overall view of the trail route in this section, send $3 for to the USDA-Forest Service, 630 Sansome Street, San Francisco, CA 94111. Ask for the Sequoia National Forest map. For topographic maps, ask for Walker

Pass, Lamont Peak, White Dome, Rockhouse Basin and Crag Peak from the USGS.

***Who to contact:*** Sequoia National Forest, Cannell Meadow Ranger District, P.O. Box 6, Kernville, CA 93238; (619) 376-3781.

***Trail notes:*** Views become extremely panoramic on this section of trail, taking in more and more of the Owens Valley as our trail climbs higher and higher. Campsites become more frequent, too. Drainages in this area are often seeping with water, even in dry years. Views from the top of Spanish Needle, one of the highest peaks in the Southern Sierra, are spectacular. The nearby Kern offers good fishing and the PCT stays somewhat near it as it swings a serpentine route in and out of the Dome Land's eastern boundary. Kennedy Meadows offers the opportunity for refreshments and a nice campground.

---

# PCT-20    63.5 mi. one way/6.0 days
## KENNEDY MEADOWS to WHITNEY PORTAL

***Reference:*** **From the trailhead parking at Kennedy Meadows, map G5, grid f6 north to Mount Whitney.**

***User groups:*** Hikers and horses. No mountain bikes or dogs are allowed. No wheelchair facilities.

***Permits:*** A wilderness permit is required for traveling through various wilderness and special-use areas that the trail traverses. Contact the Angeles National Forest at (805) 296-9710 for a permit that is good for the length of your trip.

***Directions:*** To the Kennedy Meadows Trailhead—From the town of Brown on Highway 14, drive north on Highway 14 for four miles to Nine Mile Canyon Road and turn left (west). Drive on Nine Mile Canyon Road (it becomes Kennedy Meadows Road) to Kennedy Meadows and the signed Pacific Crest Trail trailhead.

   To the Mt. Whitney Trailhead— From Lone Pine and Highway 395, head west on Whitney Portal Road for approximately 13 miles to Whitney Portal and the trailhead for the Mt. Whitney Trail.

***Maps:*** For an overall view of the trail route in this section, send $3 for each map ordered to the USDA-Forest Service, 630 Sansome Street, San Francisco, CA 94111, ask for the Sequoia National Forest and the Inyo National Forest maps. For topographic maps of the area, ask for Crag Peak, Monache Mountain, Templeton Mountain, Cirque Peak, Mount Langley and Mount Whitney from the USGS.

***Who to contact:*** Sequoia National Forest, Cannell Meadow Ranger District, P.O. Box 6, Kernville, CA 93238; (619) 376-3781 or Inyo National Forest, Mount Whitney Ranger District, P.O. Box 8, Lone Pine, CA 93545; (619) 876-6200.

***Trail notes:*** Hang on to your boots, because you are really going to be climbing and your lungs and legs will feel the burn. Fortunately, as you progress deeper and deeper into pristine Sierra wilderness, the views and scenery are so stunning that you almost forget the pain required for the gain. The trek passes through both the Golden Trout and Sierra wildernesses before entering Sequoia National Park and intersecting with the beginning (or end depending on your heading) of the John Muir Trail. Mt. Whitney lies to the east of the trail, and making the short sidetrip is considered mandatory for all

PCT hikers. It is the highest point in the continental U.S., after all. If you want to head out here, you will go east on the Whitney Trail to Whitney Portal, over 12 miles away. Use caution throughout this section as the high passes, exposed ridges and bare peaks are no place to be caught in a lightning storm. Weather can change at any time, so be prepared for the worst and you will experience the best.

*PCT CONTINUATION:* To continue hiking along the Pacific Crest Trail, see Chapter F5, pages 538-541.

## LEAVE NO TRACE TIPS

### Campfires

• Fire use can scar the backcountry. If a fire ring is not available, use a lightweight stove for cooking.

• Where fires are permitted, use exisiting fire rings, away from large rocks or overhangs.

• Do not char rocks by building new rings.

• Gather sticks from the ground that are no larger than the diameter of your wrist.

• Do not snap branches of live, dead or downed trees, which can cause personal injury and also scar the natural setting.

• Put the fire "dead out" and make sure it is cold before departing. Remove all trash from the fire ring.

• Remember that some forest fires can be started by a campfire that appears to be out. Hot embers burning deep in the pit can cause tree roots to catch on fire and burn underground. If you ever see smoke rising from the ground, seemingly from nowhere, dig down and put the fire out.

# MAP G6

CEN-CAL MAP ...................... see page 466
adjoining maps
NORTH (F6) ........................... see page 542
EAST (G7) ............................. see page 604
SOUTH (H6) .......................... see page 650
WEST (G5) ............................. see page 560

5 TRAILS
PAGES 598-603

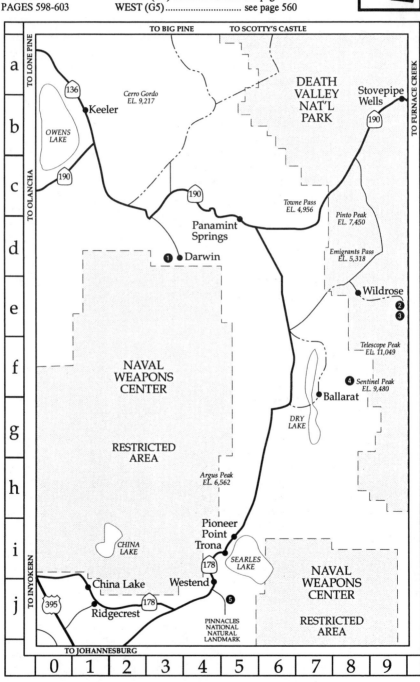

## 1. DARWIN FALLS          1.5 mi/1.0 hr

*Reference:* **Located west of Death Valley National Park; map G6, grid d3.**
*User groups:* Hikers, mountain bikes, horses and dogs. No wheelchair facilities.
*Permits:* No permits are required.
*Directions:* From Olancha on Highway 395, drive east on State Road 190 for
approximately 44 miles. Turn south on Darwin Canyon Road for 2.6 miles
to a dirt road—follow the signs to the designated parking area.
*Maps:* For a topographic map of the area, ask for Darwin from the USGS.
*Who to contact:* Bureau of Land Management, Ridgecrest Resource Area, 300
South Richmond Road, Ridgecrest, CA 93555; (619) 384-5400.
*Trail notes:* Spring is the best time to visit the falls as this is when the canyon
area is teeming with desert wildlife and migrating birds. There is much more
to this area than just the falls, however. The Darwin Plateau rises 4,000 feet
above the valley floor and is cut by deep chasms through volcanic rock faces.
Spring-fed creeks within a number of these canyons create cool and moist
oases from the desert which attract wildlife from all around.

## 2. WILDROSE PEAK TRAIL      8.4 mi/8.0 hrs

*Reference:* **In Death Valley National Park; map G6, grid e9.**
*User groups:* Hikers. Horses are allowed away from developed areas. Leashed
dogs area allowed on roads, but not on trails. Mountain bikes are allowed on
dirt roads, but not on trails or cross-country. No wheelchair facilities.
*Permits:* No permits are required at this time but filling out the backcountry-use
register form located at the visitor's center is highly recommended. Camping
is allowed anywhere in the park as long as you are at least five miles from
a maintained campground, one mile from a major road and a quarter of a mile
from the nearest water source. Campfires are not permitted at any time. A $6
day-use fee is charged.
*Directions:* From Highway 395, drive on Highway 190 to Death Valley
National Park. Stay on Highway 190 to the Furnace Creek Visitor's Center
and check in. From Furnace Creek, head back the way you came on Highway
190 towards Panamint Springs and turn south onto Emigrant Canyon Road.
At the next junction, turn left toward Wildrose Campground and the
Wildrose Ranger Station. The road, paved part way and dirt the rest, leads
to a large turnout on the left for the Charcoal Kilns.
*Maps:* For topographic maps, ask for Emigrant Pass and Wildrose Peak from
the USGS. One of the best overall maps for the area is published by Trails
Illustrated and is titled *Death Valley National Monument.* The cost is $7.95
and may be ordered by calling (800) 962-1643.
*Who to contact:* Death Valley National Park, Death Valley, CA 92328; (619)
786-2331.
*Trail notes:* Being higher in elevation than the surrounding area, Wildrose Peak
actually makes a good summertime destination—it is common for the peak
to be buried under a blanket of snow in the winter. Snow is fitting because
the 9,064-foot-high Wildrose Peak sits in the middle of the Panamint Range,

which is recognized as the wettest range in Death Valley. The trailhead is located at the old kilns, which provided charcoal for processing silver and lead ore in the late 1800s. Views from the top are stunning, especially in the late spring, when nearby Telescope Peak may still be wearing a crown of ice and snow. From the signed trailhead, just northwest of the kilns, begin hiking a traverse above Wildrose Canyon. Before long, you will drop down into a wooded canyon. Approximately one mile from the trailhead, the trail begins to climb out of the canyon, passing a USGS water-level recording device within a quarter mile. From here, the trail narrows and begins to climb in earnest. Just under two miles from the trailhead, you will reach a saddle in the Panamint Range. The trail keeps climbing on a somewhat rocky surface all the way to the broad expanse of Wildrose Peak. The final quarter-mile climbs via a series of intense switchbacks that will leave your head spinning and chest heaving. Once you gather yourself together, however, you will realize the climb was well worth the effort. Your reward is a 360-degree panorama with the best of Death Valley sprawled out beneath your toes. Head back the way you came when ready.

The best time to visit Death Valley is between November and April, although summer months are not out of the question if you like it really hot—like hotter than anywhere else in the United States. No matter when you visit and how short your hike, always carry water with you—one gallon per person per day is the minimum fluid intake for survival. Water does exist in the valley, but it is unreliable, so don't count on it no matter what the map may say. Never camp near a water source in the desert. Wildlife that depend on it will consider you a threat to their survival.

Much of the true adventure in Death Valley is found via cross-country travel, but for this you need superb navigational skills. Always check in at the Furnace Creek Visitor's Center before heading out, to sign the register and inquire about road and trail conditions. Carry survival gear in your car, both for your car and yourself. Know how to cool down an overheated engine and carry plenty of water for the radiator. Don't stick your hands into holes and cracks unless you are trying to get bitten by a rattlesnake or stung by a scorpion. Yes, you should always check your boots before putting them on in the morning, and don't be surprised to find a scorpion has cuddled under your sleeping bag while you sleep—they like warmth too.

*Special note:* One last word of wisdom: In the desert, distant objects are always further away than you might think, as the dry air has a tendency to telescope things closer to you—that quick jaunt to a peak on the horizon may turn out to be an all-day epic trip.

---

# 3. TELESCOPE PEAK TRAIL   14.0 mi/10.0 hrs

*Reference:* **In Death Valley National Park; map G6, grid e9.**

*User groups:* Hikers. Horses are allowed away from developed areas. Leashed dogs are allowed on roads, but not on trails. Mountain bikes are allowed on dirt roads, but not on trails or cross-country. No wheelchair facilities.

*Permits:* No permits are required at this time but filling out the backcountry-use register form located at the visitor's center is highly recommended. Camping is allowed anywhere in the park as long as you are at least five miles from a maintained campground, one mile from a major road and a quarter of a mile from the nearest water source. Campfires are not permitted at any time. A $6 day-use fee is charged.

*Directions:* From Highway 395, drive on Highway 190 to Death Valley National Park. Stay on Highway 190 to the Furnace Creek Visitor's Center and check in. From Furnace Creek, head back the way you came on Highway 190 towards Panamint Springs and turn south onto Emigrant Canyon Road. At the next junction, turn left toward Wildrose Campground and the Wildrose Ranger Station. The road, paved part way and dirt the rest, leads to past the trailhead for Charcoal Kilns and to Mahogany Flat Campground. Park at the campground.

*Maps:* For topographic maps, ask for Jail Canyon and Telescope Peak from the USGS. One of the best overall maps of the area is published by Trails Illustrated and is titled *Death Valley National Monument*. The cost is $7.95 and may be ordered by calling (800) 962-1643.

*Who to contact:* Death Valley National Park, Death Valley, CA 92328; (619) 786-2331.

*Trail notes:* Like Wildrose Peak, Telescope Peak actually makes a good summertime destination—it is common for the peak to be buried under a blanket of snow in the winter. The 11,049-foot-high Telescope Peak sits in the middle of the Panamint Range, the wettest range in Death Valley. The trailhead begins at the campground and winds a steep and narrow route all the way to the bristlecone pine crowned summit. We recommend planning an overnight at or near the summit to enjoy the magic of a changing desert under the spell of a moving sun. Sunrise over the valley and sunset over the Sierra are memorable—if you don't ooh and ahh then maybe your eyes need checking. Plan your hike between May and November. Any other time of the year will require ice axes and crampons, which are a hoot if you have the experience. Little gnats are a pain in the rear, but insect repellent won't help much. The same safety precautions apply here as on the Wildrose Peak Trail, hike number 2 in this chapter.

---

## 4. SURPRISE CANYON     11.0 mi/5.0 hrs

*Reference:* **Panamint Range, southwest of Death Valley National Park; map G6, grid f8.**

*User groups:* Hikers only. No dogs, horses or mountain bikes allowed. No wheelchair facilities.

*Permits:* No permits are required.

*Directions:* Head north out of Trona on the Panamint Valley Road, until you reach the turnoff for Ballarat. Head east at the turnoff to Ballarat. In Ballarat, turn north on Indian Ranch Road and drive approximately two miles to the Surprise Canyon Road (BLM Route P71). Follow Surprise Canyon Road for approximately four miles to Chris Wicht Camp, where you may park your vehicle in the large turnaround. The hike begins in the wash on the north side of the road.

*Maps:* For topographic maps, ask for Wildrose Peak, Emigrant Pass, Panamint, Telescope Peak, Ballarat and Jail Canyon from the USGS.

*Who to contact:* Bureau of Land Management, California Desert District Office, 6221 Box Springs Boulevard, Riverside, CA 92507; (909) 697-5200.

*Trail notes:* Surprise Canyon is an area of outstanding scenic quality and has been designated an Area of Critical Environmental Concern. Telescope Peak sits as a towering monarch over the area at 11,045 feet of elevation. Surrounding terrain is mostly rugged mountains and deeply cut canyons. There is a small badlands area to the northwest. The area has had a history of mining, which explains a number of roads that disappear into the mountainous terrain. Several of the canyons in the area sport flowing springs. Flower displays on the alluvial fans that extend out from many of the canyons are seasonal and very colorful. For best mobility and access, as well as for all-weather safety, a four-wheel-drive vehicle is highly recommended when heading into the Panamint Range on the number of jeep trails. Begin your hike on the north side of the road. At about 1.7 miles you will arrive at Limekiln Spring, followed by Brewery Spring at three miles. Panamint City is located approximately 5.5 miles from Chris Wicht Camp with a 3,480-foot elevation gain—yep, plan on sucking big wind on this one even though the climbing is not steep. Remember that some of the land in Panamint City is privately owned, so please respect landowner rights. Panamint City was once a bustling mining town, but all that remains now are fascinating ruins. All artifacts and cultural sites are federally protected, so look, but don't collect.

---

## 5. TRONA PINNACLES          1.5 mi/1.0 hr

*Reference:* **Located at Searles Lake, east of State Road 178 near Trona; map G6, grid j5.**

*User groups:* Hikers, mountain bikes, horses and dogs. No wheelchair facilities.

*Permits:* No permits are required.

*Directions:* From Highway 395 at Ridgecrest, take the Highway 178 exit heading east. Highway 178 begins as Ridgecrest Road and then turns into Trona Road. Turn right onto Pinnacles Road towards the Trona Pinnacles Recreation Lands. Turn left at the sign indicating Trona Pinnacles. Park in the designated area.

*Maps:* For a topographic map, ask for Searles Lake from the USGS.

*Who to contact:* Bureau of Land Management, Ridgecrest Resource Area, 300 South Richmond Road, Ridgecrest, CA 93555; (619) 384-5400.

*Trail notes:* If you are a *Star Trek* fan, you may recognize the pinnacles as the setting for the movie, *The Final Frontier*. If not, you will still find ultimate pleasure within this maze of monoliths jutting out of a dry lakebed. This is typical Bureau of Land Management land—wander wherever your feet will take you but no further than you are willing to walk back. There is a one-mile trail which begins at the parking area. Trona Pinnacles is a designated National Natural Landmark and on this trail you will see why, as it allows a peek at some of the best examples of tufa spires in the country. Within the next few years, the BLM plans on adding interpretive signs, but for now you are left to wander on your own. Summer temperatures can reach the 100s, making it too hot to enjoy.

## LEAVE NO TRACE TIPS

### Sanitation

If no refuse facility is available:

• Deposit human waste in "cat holes" dug six to eight inches deep. Cover and disguise the cat hole when finished.

• Deposit human waste at least 75 paces (200 feet) from any water source or camp.

• Use toilet paper sparingly. When finished, carefully burn it in the cat hole, then bury it.

• If no appropriate burial locations are available, such as in popular wilderness camps above tree line in hard granite settings— Devil's Punchbowl in the Siskiyou Wilderness is such an example— then all human refuse should be double-bagged and packed out.

• At boat-in campsites, chemical toilets are required. Chemical toilets can also solve the problem of larger groups camping or long stays at one location where no facilities are available.

• To wash dishes or your body, carry water away from the source and use small amounts of biodegradable soap. Scatter dishwater after all food particles have been removed.

• Scour your campsites for even the tiniest piece of trash and any other evidence of your stay. Pack out all the trash you can, even if it's not yours. Finding cigarette butts, for instance, provides special irritation for most campers. Pick them up and discard them properly.

• Never litter. Never. Or you become the enemy of all others.

MAP G7

CEN-CAL MAP ...................... see page 466
adjoining maps
NORTH ............................................ no map
EAST ............................................... no map
5 TRAILS
PAGES 604-609
SOUTH (H7) .......................... see page 654
WEST (G6) ............................... see page 598

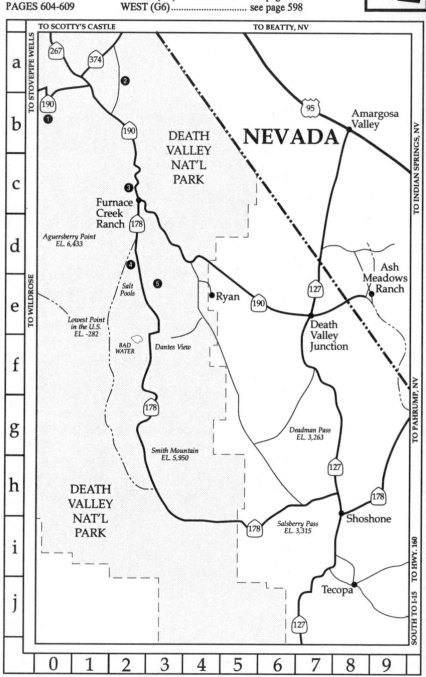

TO SCOTTY'S CASTLE

TO BEATTY, NV

TO STOVEPIPE WELLS

267

374

❷

190

❶

95

Amargosa
Valley

190

DEATH
VALLEY
NAT'L
PARK

NEVADA

TO INDIAN SPRINGS, NV

❸

Furnace
Creek
Ranch

178

Aguersberry Point
EL. 6,433

❹

Salt
Pools

❺

Ryan

190

127

Ash
Meadows
Ranch

Lowest Point
in the U.S.
EL. -282

BAD
WATER

Dantes View

Death
Valley
Junction

TO WILDROSE

TO PAHRUMP, NV

178

178

Deadman Pass
EL. 3,263

Smith Mountain
EL. 5,950

DEATH
VALLEY
NAT'L
PARK

127

178

Salsberry Pass
EL. 3,315

Shoshone

178

SOUTH TO I-15

TO HWY. 160

Tecopa

127

0    1    2    3    4    5    6    7    8    9

## 1. MOSAIC CANYON TRAIL     4.0 mi/2.0 hrs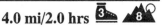

*Reference:* **In Death Valley National Park; map G7, grid b0.**

*User groups:* Hikers. Horses are only allowed away from developed areas. Leashed dogs are allowed on roads, but not on trails. Mountain bikes are allowed on dirt roads, but not on trails or cross-country. No wheelchair facilities.

*Permits:* No permits are required at this time but filling out the backcountry-use register form located at the visitor's center is highly recommended. Camping is allowed anywhere in the park as long as you are at least five miles from a maintained campground, one mile from a major road and a quarter of a mile from the nearest water source. Campfires are not permitted at any time. A $6 day-use fee is charged.

*Directions:* From Highway 395, drive on Highway 190 to Death Valley National Park. Stay on Highway 190 to the Furnace Creek Visitor's Center and check in. From Furnace Creek, retrace your steps toward Stovepipe Wells. Just before Stovepipe Wells, turn left (south) at the signed turnoff for Mosaic Canyon. Although the road is suitable for passenger cars, drive slowly, the going is rough. Park at the signed trailhead.

*Maps:* For topographic maps, ask for Stovepipe Wells and Grotto Canyon from the USGS. One of the best overall maps of the area is published by Trails Illustrated and is titled *Death Valley National Monument.* The cost is $7.95 and may be ordered by calling (800) 962-1643.

*Who to contact:* Death Valley National Park, Death Valley, CA 92328; (619) 786-2331.

*Trail notes:* Yep, there is slick rock outside of Moab, Utah and you'll find a good example of it here, as you scramble your way up this pretty canyon over slickrock and between multi-colored polished walls that look like a giant mosaic. If you keep your eyes peeled, you may be lucky enough to sight bighorn. Hike in as far as you dare and then retrace your steps. Keep an eye out for rattlesnakes when clambering over rocks and dry falls in the canyon. From the parking area, hike into the canyon and along the wash. The canyon narrows quickly, with rock patterns becoming spectacular. After a little more than one-quarter mile, the canyon widens again and bends to the east. You will come to a point where you have a choice of trimming a few feet off the hike by leaving the wash on an informal trail. The choice is yours, but either way, you'll end up in the same place, back along the wash as the canyon heads in a southerly direction and narrows considerably. Hiking becomes more difficult, and there are points where rock-scrambling is the only way to navigate. Further up, dry waterfalls present themselves and the only way to continue is to climb. At approximately 1.5 miles from the start, you will encounter a dry fall that turns most casual hikers around—a 12- to 15-foot-tall rock face that can be negotiated via a ledge, providing you have the courage and requisite clambering skills. Just a few hundred feet beyond, the climbing gets more serious and if you are not a skilled canyoneer, you have no business continuing. Turn around and retrace your steps. The best time to visit Death Valley is between November and April. Please read the safety considerations listed in hike number 2 in chapter G6.

## 2. KEANE WONDER MINE        2.0 mi/2.0 hrs

*Reference:* **In Death Valley National Park; map G7, grid a2.**

*User groups:* Hikers. Horses are only allowed away from developed areas. Leashed dogs are allowed on roads, but not on trails. Mountain bikes are allowed on dirt roads, but not on trails or cross-country. No wheelchair facilities.

*Permits:* No permits are required at this time but filling out the backcountry-use register form located at the visitor's center is highly recommended. Camping is allowed anywhere in the park as long as you are at least five miles from a maintained campground, one mile from a major road and a quarter of a mile from the nearest water source. Campfires are not permitted at any time. A $6 day-use fee is charged.

*Directions:* From Highway 395, drive on Highway 190 to Death Valley National Park. Stay on Highway 190 to the Furnace Creek Visitor's Center and check in. From Furnace Creek, drive north back up Highway 190 to Beatty Junction and turn right onto a paved road. Look for the signed Keane Wonder Mill exit to the right and drive to the parking area.

*Maps:* For a topographic map, ask for Chloride City from the USGS. One of the best overall maps of the area is published by Trails Illustrated and is titled *Death Valley National Monument.* The cost is $7.95 and may be ordered by calling (800) 962-1643.

*Who to contact:* Death Valley National Park, Death Valley, CA 92328; (619) 786-2331.

*Trail notes:* This is a very steep and narrow route up the ridge—no wonder they needed an aerial tram to shuttle workers back and forth from the mine to the mill. If they had to walk this every day, miners would have keeled over for sure. The sweat paid out is worth it, however, as you are afforded stunning views of Death Valley. It's a Kodak moment for sure. While there are a number of mine shafts located around the mountain, do not enter them as it is most dangerous. The best time to visit Death Valley is between November and April. Please read the safety considerations listed in hike number 2 in chapter G6.

---

## 3. HARMONY BORAX WORKS   0.25 mi/0.5 hr

*Reference:* **In Death Valley National Park; map G7, grid c2.**

*User groups:* Hikers and **wheelchairs**. Horses are only allowed away from developed areas. Leashed dogs are allowed on roads, but not on trails. Mountain bikes are allowed on dirt roads, but not on trails or cross-country.

*Permits:* No permits are required at this time but filling out the backcountry-use register form located at the visitor's center is highly recommended. Camping is allowed anywhere in the park as long as you are at least five miles from a maintained campground, one mile from a major road and a quarter of a mile from the nearest water source. Campfires are not permitted at any time. A $6 day-use fee is charged.

*Directions:* From Highway 395, drive on Highway 190 to Death Valley National Park. Stay on Highway 190 to the Harmony Borax parking area located just off Highway 190 and just before the Furnace Creek Visitor's Center.

*Maps:* For topographic maps covering the Furnace Creek Area, ask for Beatty Junction, Nevares Peak, West of Furnace Creek and Furnace Creek from the USGS. One of the best overall maps of the area is published by Trails Illustrated and is titled *Death Valley National Monument*. The cost is $7.95 and may be ordered by calling (800) 962-1643.

*Who to contact:* Death Valley National Park, Death Valley, CA 92328; (619) 786-2331.

*Trail notes:* This is a quick, self-guided trail on asphalt around the historic ruins of a late 1800s borax works. If you have the time, head northwest across the salt flats to some borax piles in the distance. It adds about 2.6 miles to your hike and the trail is not suitable for wheelchairs—it can be very muddy. The best time to visit Death Valley is between November and April. Please read the safety considerations listed in hike number 2 in chapter G6.

---

## 4. GOLDEN CANYON TRAIL    1.5 mi/1.0 hr

*Reference:* In Death Valley National Park; map G7, grid d2.

*User groups:* Hikers. Horses are only allowed away from developed areas. Leashed dogs are allowed on roads, but not on trails. Mountain bikes are allowed on dirt roads, but not on trails or cross-country. No wheelchair facilities.

*Permits:* No permits are required at this time but filling out the backcountry-use register form located at the visitor's center is highly recommended. Camping is allowed anywhere in the park as long as you are at least five miles from a maintained campground, one mile from a major road and a quarter of a mile from the nearest water source. Campfires are not permitted at any time. A $6 day-use fee is charged.

*Directions:* From Highway 395, drive on Highway 190 to Death Valley National Park. Stay on Highway 190 to the Furnace Creek Visitor's Center and check in. From Furnace Creek, drive south on Highway 178 to the signed exit for Badwater on the right. Head south on this paved road for approximately two miles to the Golden Canyon parking area on the left, located several hundred yards off the road.

*Maps:* For a topographic map, ask for Furnace Creek from the USGS. One of the best overall maps of the area is published by Trails Illustrated and is titled *Death Valley National Monument*. The cost is $7.95 and may be ordered by calling (800) 962-1643.

*Who to contact:* Death Valley National Park, Death Valley, CA 92328; (619) 786-2331.

*Trail notes:* The Golden Canyon Trail takes the visitor on a self-guided interpretive walk through a colorful canyon area notable for gypsum crystals and ripplemarks. There are a number of spur options if you wish to extend your hiking trip, the best of which is the Red Cathedral Spur Trail located near the final interpretive marker. The best time to visit Death Valley is between November and April. Please read the safety considerations listed in hike number 2 in chapter G6.

# 5. NATURAL BRIDGE CANYON   0.6 mi/0.5 hr

*Reference:* **In Death Valley National Park; map G7, grid e3.**

*User groups:* Hikers. Horses are only allowed away from developed areas. Leashed dogs are allowed on roads, but not on trails. Mountain bikes are allowed on dirt roads, but not on trails or cross-country. No wheelchair facilities.

*Permits:* No permits are required at this time but filling out the backcountry-use register form located at the visitor's center is highly recommended. Camping is allowed anywhere in the park as long as you are at least five miles from a maintained campground, one mile from a major road and a quarter of a mile from the nearest water source. Campfires are not permitted at any time. A $6 day-use fee is charged.

*Directions:* From Highway 395, drive on Highway 190 to Death Valley National Park. Stay on Highway 190 to the Furnace Creek Visitor's Center and check in. From Furnace Creek, drive south on Highway 178 to the signed Natural Bridges turnoff and the parking area on the left.

*Maps:* For a topographic map, ask for Devil's Golf Course from the USGS. One of the best overall maps of the area is published by Trails Illustrated and is titled *Death Valley National Monument*. The cost is $7.95 and may be ordered by calling (800) 962-1643.

*Who to contact:* Death Valley National Park, Death Valley, CA 92328; (619) 786-2331.

*Trail notes:* If you already happen to be in Death Valley, this is a great area to explore. Take a walk up an easy graded trail into a narrow canyon and to a natural bridge carved by the forces of nature. The trail ends at a dry waterfall—do not attempt to climb it! The best time to visit Death Valley is between November and April. Please read the safety considerations listed in hike number 2 in chapter G6.

## Leave No Trace Tips

### Plan ahead and prepare

- Learn about the regulations and issues that apply to the area you are visiting.

- Avoid heavy-use areas.

- Obtain all maps and permits.

- Bring extra garbage bags to pack out any refuse you come across.

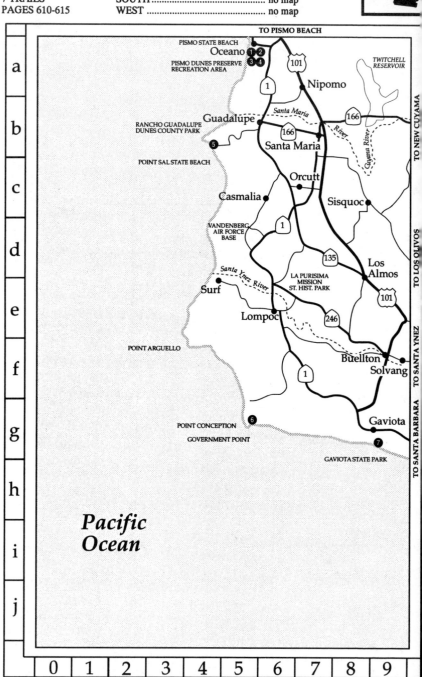

**Map H2 featuring:** Pismo Beach, Gaviota State Park, Jalama County Park, Oso Flaco Lake

## 1. OSO FLACO LAKE          3.0 mi/2.0 hrs

*Reference:* **South of Pismo Beach and west of Highway 1; map H2, grid a5.**

*User groups:* Hikers only. No mountain bikes, horses or dogs are allowed. There are **limited wheelchair facilities.**

*Permits:* No day-use permits are required.

*Directions:* From Pismo Beach, south of San Luis Obispo, drive south on Highway 1 to Oso Flaco Lake Road (three miles north of Highway 166). Turn right and drive 3.6 miles to the end of the road, pick up a free area map at The Nature Conservancy kiosk and then park. Parking is $4.

*Maps:* For a topographic map, ask for Oceano from the USGS.

*Who to contact:* The Nature Conservancy offers guided walks. For information call (805) 546-2910. The Nature Conservancy San Luis Obispo Office, P.O. Box 15810, San Luis Obispo, CA 93406; (805) 546-8378.

*Trail notes:* A 1980 Department of the Interior report described the Nipomo Dunes as "the most unique and fragile ecosystem in the state of California," a slice of sand and wildflowers on the coast south of San Luis Obispo. From the parking area, follow the signed walk to freshwater Oso Flaco Lake and the beginning of a boardwalk. Ruddy ducks, mallards, herons and, in the winter, white pelicans, frequent the lake. Walk down the boardwalk from the lake and then across the dunes to the beach. For dune walking, wear comfortable shoes that won't let sand in. Wear a broad-brimmed hat, sunscreen and sunglasses. Pack along two quarts of water and snacks. Also pack a windbreaker and a warm sweater. Limit your unbridled romping to unvegetated areas—the dunes are fragile.

## 2. MOBIL COASTAL PRESERVE  7.0 mi/7.0 hrs

*Reference:* **South of Pismo Beach and west of Highway 1; map H2, grid a5.**

*User groups:* Hikers only. No mountain bikes, horses or dogs are allowed. No wheelchair facilities.

*Permits:* No day-use permits are required.

*Directions:* From Pismo Beach, south of San Luis Obispo, drive south on Highway 1 to Oso Flaco Lake Road (three miles north of Highway 166). Turn right and drive 3.6 miles to the end of the road, pick up a free area map at The Nature Conservancy kiosk and then park. Parking is $4.

*Maps:* For topographic maps, ask for Oceano and Point Sal from the USGS.

*Who to contact:* The Nature Conservancy offers guided walks. For information call (805) 546-2910. The Nature Conservancy San Luis Obispo Office, P.O. Box 15810, San Luis Obispo, CA 93406; (805) 546-8378.

*Trail notes:* This is "the most unique and fragile ecosystem in the state of California" (see Oso Flaco Lake Trail note). From the parking area, follow the signed walk to Oso Flaco Lake and the beginning of a boardwalk. Walk down the boardwalk from the lake to the boardwalk's end. Continue walking toward the ocean and cross Oso Flaco Creek. After the crossing, head south along the beach to the state boundary sign and turn inland into deep dune hollows. If you can find it (The Nature Conservancy guides walks to this location), seek out Hidden Willow Valley, a secluded and peaceful spot created by willow woodlands tucked between sandy dunes. See hike number 1, this chapter, for more information on dune walking.

## 3. COREOPSIS HILL    5.0 mi/4.0 hrs

*Reference:* **South of Pismo Beach and west of Highway 1; map H2, grid a5.**
*User groups:* Hikers only. No mountain bikes, horses or dogs are allowed. No wheelchair facilities.
*Permits:* No day-use permits are required.
*Directions:* From Pismo Beach, south of San Luis Obispo, drive south on Highway 1 to Oso Flaco Lake Road (three miles north of Highway 166). Turn right and drive 3.6 miles to the end of the road, pick up a free area map at The Nature Conservancy kiosk and then park. Parking is $4.
*Maps:* For a topographic map, ask for Oceano from the USGS.
*Who to contact:* The Nature Conservancy offers guided walks. For information call (805) 546-2910. The Nature Conservancy San Luis Obispo Office, P.O. Box 15810, San Luis Obispo, CA 93406; (805) 546-8378.
*Trail notes:* Nipomo Dunes is a slice of sand and wildflowers on the coast south of San Luis Obispo. From the parking area, follow the signed walk to Oso Flaco Lake and the beginning of a boardwalk. Walk down the boardwalk from the lake to the boardwalk's end. Continue walking toward the ocean and cross Oso Flaco Creek. After crossing, turn inland across the vast dunes to the distant green hill. In the spring, if your timing is right, the green hill turns yellow because it is coated with coreopsis blossoms. See hike number 1, this chapter, for more information on dune walking.

## 4. MUSSEL ROCK DUNES    5.0 mi/5.0 hrs

*Reference:* **South of Pismo Beach and west of Highway 1; map H2, grid a5.**
*User groups:* Hikers only. No mountain bikes, horses or dogs are allowed. No wheelchair facilities.
*Permits:* No day-use permits are required.
*Directions:* From Pismo Beach, south of San Luis Obispo, drive south on Highway 1 to Oso Flaco Lake Road and then three miles more to Highway 166/Main Street. Turn right and drive to the end of the road and the designated free parking area.
*Maps:* For a topographic map, ask for Point Sal from the USGS.
*Who to contact:* The Nature Conservancy offers guided walks. For information call (805) 546-2910. The Nature Conservancy San Luis Obispo Office, P.O. Box 15810, San Luis Obispo, CA 93406; (805) 546-8378.
*Trail notes:* Nipomo Dunes is "the most unique and fragile ecosystem in the state of California" (see Oso Flaco Lake Trail note). This walk takes you to Nipomo's largest dunes and requires more than just casual effort. From the top of the dunes, the views of the wild coastline are stunning. From the parking area, it is an approximate 2.5-mile walk down the beach and dunes to Mussel Rock—the wind will likely be in your face during the return. See hike number 1, this chapter, for more information on dune walking.

## 5. POINT SAL TRAIL     7.0 mi/4.0 hrs

*Reference:* **South of Pismo Beach and west of Highway 1; map H2, grid b4.**

*User groups:* Hikers only. No mountain bikes, horses or dogs are allowed. No wheelchair facilities.

*Permits:* No day-use permits are required.

*Directions:* From Pismo Beach, south of San Luis Obispo, drive south on Highway 1/Brown Road, approximately three miles south of Guadalupe. Turn west on Brown and after a few miles turn right on Point Sal Road. Follow this road five miles to its end at the parking area above Point Sal State Beach.

*Maps:* For a topographic map, ask for Point Sal from the USGS.

*Who to contact:* Bureau of Land Management, Caliente Resource Area, 3801 Pegasus Drive, Bakersfield, CA 93308; (805) 391-6000.

*Trail notes:* Jutting out into the Pacific Ocean, the rocky coastline of Point Sal and the clear waters below offer a haven for seals and sea lions as well as a super point from which to watch the winter migration of whales. The trail can be a little tenuous at points, and it is no place for those afraid of heights. From the parking area, follow the trail down to the bluffs and the beach. Hike up the coast along the beach to several rocky reefs which are challenging to negotiate. Unless it is low tide, head for the narrow trail above the reefs. Several pocket beaches offer seclusion and romance. You will hear Lions Rock before you see it—seals seem to bark here just for the heck of it. The trail will pass near the seals, but don't go near them or do anything to disturb them—watch from a distance and then move on. From here, it is up to the rocky point of Point Sal. You can turn around here or continue onward to Guadalupe Dunes County Park. If you head off to Guadalupe, remember you are now embarking on a 12-mile roundtrip journey—plan accordingly and be careful, the trail is precariously carved into the bluffs and cliffs in places.

## 6. POINT CONCEPTION TRAIL 12.0 mi/6.0 hrs

*Reference:* **South of Pismo Beach and west of Santa Barbara; map H2, grid g5.**

*User groups:* Hikers only. No mountain bikes, horses or dogs are allowed. No wheelchair facilities.

*Permits:* No day-use permits are required.

*Directions:* From Santa Barbara drive 35 miles north on Highway 101. Exit on Highway 1 north towards Lompoc. Drive approximately 14 miles to Jalama Road. Turn left and drive approximately 14 more miles to the county park. Park in the day-use lot. A $4 parking fee is charged.

*Maps:* For a topographic map, ask for Point Conception from the USGS.

*Who to contact:* Jalama County Park; (805) 736-3504 (beach) or (805) 736-6316 (recorded information). For group reservations, call (805) 934-6211.

*Trail notes:* Jalama County Park is the only point of public access to the beach between Jalama and Gaviota State Park to the south. Hikers must stay below high tide line when crossing ranch land. Private land means exactly that around here, and you do not want to be caught off the designated pathway. From the parking area at Jalama, head south over picturesque dunes. The sandy beach soon narrows and then disappears altogether, replaced by rock reefs and sea walls. If the tide is low enough, walk along the top of the sea walls—just watch your footing as the going can be very slick. As you near the lighthouse, the beach will disappear completely and your passage appears to be cut off by surging waves crashing on the rocks ahead. Look for a cut in the cliffs that leads to a badly maintained dirt road heading up to the bluffs above. Once on top, follow the cow paths towards the lighthouse, but don't go near the lighthouse or the Coast Guard boundaries—they don't welcome visitors here. Turn around when ready and return the way you came.

---

## 7. GAVIOTA PEAK TRAIL     6.0 mi/3.0 hrs

*Reference:* **Gaviota State Park south of Pismo Beach and 35 miles west of Santa Barbara; map H2, grid g9.**

*User groups:* Hikers, horses, mountain bikes and leashed dogs. No wheelchair facilities.

*Permits:* No day-use permits are required.

*Directions:* From Santa Barbara, drive north on Highway 101. Take the Highway 1 north exit towards Lompoc. Turn east and travel a very short distance and look for the signs for the park. Then go right for two-tenths of a mile to the parking area. A $2 parking fee is collected. Parking is allowed only from sunrise to sunset—cars left after the gate closes will be cited. There is no overnight camping in the backcountry, except on Forest Service land. For overnight parking, call the California State Department of Parks and Recreation at (805) 968-1711 to make arrangements. Free parking is allowed on the frontage road.

*Maps:* Send $3 to the USDA-Forest Service, 630 Sansome Street, San Francisco, CA 94111 and ask for the Los Padres National Forest map. For a topographic map, ask for Gaviota from the USGS.

*Who to contact:* Gaviota State Park, 10 Refugio Beach, Goleta, CA 93117; (805) 968-1711, or Los Padres National Forest, Santa Barbara Ranger District, Star Route, Santa Barbara, CA 93105; (805) 967-3481.

*Trail notes:* This hike begins in Gaviota State Park and ends up in Los Padres National Forest. Along the way, you will pass by warm mineral pools, suitable for splashing around in, and then continue up to the top of Gaviota Peak, elevation 2,458 feet. There are excellent views of the Santa Barbara County coast from the top. From the parking area, head up the fire road towards the hot springs—it's well traveled since most people go straight to the hot springs and turn around. After passing by Gaviota Hot Springs, continue hiking to the top of the ridge, where you will come to a saddle and a junction, marked by a steel gate. From the steel gate and junction, turn right and climb one-quarter mile up a steep path to the summit. It can be quite windy up on the ridge as you climb to the top of Gaviota Peak—pack along a windbreaker and a warm sweater. Enjoy the view (all the way to Morro Bay on a clear day) and then retrace your steps. A nifty side trek may be enjoyed on either the hike up or down. Keep a sharp lookout for a faint and unmaintained trail, which branches off the main route and leads to a secluded grotto and a small, seasonal waterfall. During extreme fire season months, call ahead at (805) 967-3481 for updates.

## LEAVE NO TRACE TIPS

### Keep the wilderness wild

• Let nature's sound prevail. Avoid loud voices and noises.

• Leave radios and tape players at home.
At drive-in camping sites, never open car doors with music playing.

• Careful guidance is necessary when choosing any games to bring for
|children. Most toys, especially any kind of gun toys with which children
simulate shooting at each other, should not be allowed on a camping trip.

• Control pets at all times, or leave them with a sitter at home.

• Treat natural heritage with respect. Leave plants,
rocks and historical artifacts where you find them.

# MAP H3

CEN-CAL MAP ...................... see page 466
adjoining maps
NORTH (G3) ........................... see page 554
EAST (H4) ............................. see page 628
SOUTH (I3) ........................... see page 666
WEST (H2) ............................. see page 610

14 TRAILS
PAGES 616-627

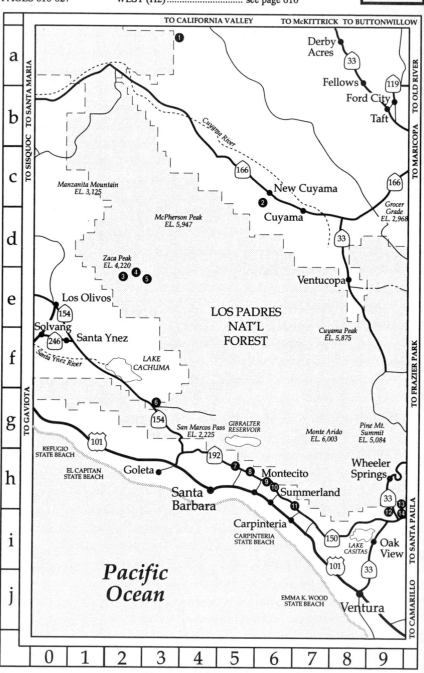

TO CALIFORNIA VALLEY    TO McKITTRICK  TO BUTTONWILLOW

❶

Derby
Acres

**a**

Fellows

Ford City

Taft

**b**

Cuyama River

166

**c**

New Cuyama

Manzanita Mountain
EL. 3,125

McPherson Peak
EL. 5,947

Cuyama

❷

166

Grocer Grade
EL. 2,968

**d**

33

Zaca Peak
EL. 4,220

❸ ❹ ❺

Ventucopa

**e**

Los Olivos

154

LOS PADRES
NAT'L
FOREST

Cuyama Peak
EL. 5,875

Solvang

246

Santa Ynez

**f**

Santa Ynez River

LAKE
CACHUMA

❻

**g**

154

San Marcos Pass
EL. 2,225

GIBRALTER
RESERVOIR

Monte Arido
EL. 6,003

Pine Mt.
Summit
EL. 5,084

101

REFUGIO
STATE BEACH

EL CAPITAN
STATE BEACH

Goleta

192

❼

❽ Montecito

Wheeler
Springs

**h**

Santa
Barbara

❾
❿ Summerland

❶❶

33

❶❸
❶❷ ❶❹

Carpinteria

CARPINTERIA
STATE BEACH

150

LAKE
CASITAS

Oak
View

**i**

101

33

**j**

Pacific
Ocean

EMMA K. WOOD
STATE BEACH

Ventura

TO SANTA MARIA    TO SISQUOC    TO GAVIOTA    TO CAMARILLO    TO SANTA PAULA    TO FRAZIER PARK    TO MARICOPA    TO OLD RIVER

119

33

0  1  2  3  4  5  6  7  8  9

Map **H3 featuring:** San Joaquin Valley, Carrizo Plain Natural Area, San Rafael Wilderness Area, Los Padres National Forest, Ojai Valley, Painted Rock National Monument

## 1. CARRIZO PLAIN NATURAL AREA

1.0 mi/1.0 hr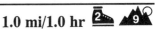

*Reference:* West of the Buttonwillow exit on Interstate 5 and near the towns of Maricopa and Atascadero in the San Joaquin Valley; map H3, grid a4.

*User groups:* Hikers and mountain bikes. No dogs or horses are allowed. No wheelchair facilities.

*Permits:* No day-use permits are required.

*Directions:* From Buttonwillow on Interstate 5, take Highway 58 west for approximately 45 miles to Soda Lake Road. Turn south and drive approximately 14 miles to the signed entrance for the Painted Rock Visitor Center.

*Maps:* Contact the BLM at (805) 861-4236 and ask for the Carrizo Plain Natural Area brochure. For topographic maps, ask for McKittrick Summit, Painted Rock and Panorama Hills from the USGS.

*Who to contact:* Bureau of Land Management, Caliente Resource Area, 3801 Pegasus Drive, Bakersfield, CA 93308-6837; (805) 391-6000. The Nature Conservancy, Carrizo Plain Natural Area, P.O. Box 3098, California Valley, 93453. California Department of Fish and Game, Region 3, P.O. Box 47, Yountville, CA 94599.

*Trail notes:* Carrizo Plain is indeed spectacular, partly because of its enormity—at 60 miles long, it is the largest wildlife preserve in the state. While there is only approximately one mile of level trail around Painted Rock near the visitors center, the eager adventurer can set out on foot in almost any direction and wander to his or her heart's content. Nearly 5,000 sandhill crane are known to winter here, attracted by a 3,000-acre alkali wetland. Surrounding grasslands are home to San Joaquin antelope squirrels, blunt-nosed lizards, San Joaquin kit fox, giant kangaroo rats, western bluebirds, horned larks, tule elk and pronghorn antelope. There are also heavy concentrations of wintering birds of prey including: short-eared owl, ferruginous hawk, northern harrier and bald eagle. Spring wildflower displays are stunning.

## 2. McPHERSON PEAK TRAIL

10.0 mi/5.0 hrs

*Reference:* **North of Ventura and southwest of the town of Gorman on Interstate 5; map H3, grid c6.**

*User groups:* Hikers, dogs and horses. No mountain bikes are allowed. No wheelchair facilities.

*Permits:* No day-use permits are required.

*Directions:* From Ventura and US 101, drive north on Highway 33 for approximately 72 miles to the junction with Highway 166. Head northwest on Highway 166 for 13 miles to the signed turnoff for Aliso Park Campground—approximately 2.5 miles past the town of New Cuyama. Turn south on Aliso Park Road, drive 1.5 miles and bear right at the first fork. Then drive another 4.5 miles to the Aliso Park Camp. The Forest Service Road can be very rough and is only recommended for high-clearance vehicles. From Interstate 5, drive north past Gorman, exit Highway 166 west to Aliso Park Road. Turn left onto Aliso Park Road, bear right at a junction and drive 4.5 miles to Aliso Park Camp.

**Maps:** Send $3 to the USDA-Forest Service, 630 Sansome Street, San Francisco, CA 94111 and ask for the Los Padres National Forest map. For a topographic map of the area, ask for Peak Mountain from the USGS.

**Who to contact:** Los Padres National Forest, Mt. Pinos Ranger District, HC-1, Box 400, Frazier Park, CA 93225; (805) 245-3731.

**Trail notes:** This trail takes the hiker into the heart of what was once California condor country and into the San Rafael Wilderness. From the top of McPherson Peak, you will enjoy a commanding view of both the Dick Smith Wilderness to the south and the barren Cuyama badlands to the north. The hike is tough and not to be attempted in the heat of summer. The best times to enjoy the journey are from late October to early June—early in the morning when the sun is not as intense. Keep your eyes peeled for condors as scientists have been reintroducing zoo-bred birds since 1991. From Aliso Park Campground, hike up the unmarked dirt road for two miles to Hog Pen Spring Camp and then follow Forest Service Trail 27W01 for another two miles up moderate switchbacks to Sierra Madre Road (Forest Service 32S13). Turn right and head up the road to the now visible McPherson Peak ahead. From the summit, look for the Old McPherson Trail to the east and head back. At an indistinct and unsigned junction on the ridge at two miles, head right. Your route continues downhill to Aliso Park two more miles distant.

**Special note:** Follow your map carefully because the trail is overgrown in places, unsigned, and at times, very difficult to follow.

---

## 3. DAVY BROWN TRAIL          7.5 mi/4.0 hrs

**Reference: Just north of Santa Barbara in the San Rafael Wilderness Area; map H3, grid e2.**

**User groups:** Hikers, horses (no pack stock), dogs and mountain bikes. No wheelchair facilities.

**Permits:** No day-use permits are required. Campfire permits are required. Contact the Santa Lucia Ranger District at (805) 925-9538.

**Directions:** From Highway 101 in Santa Barbara, take Highway 154 north over San Marcos Pass to Lake Cachuma. Just past Lake Cachuma, turn right onto Armour Ranch Road and drive approximately 2.5 miles to Happy Canyon Road. Turn right onto Happy Canyon Road and drive for about 16 miles to the turnoff for Davy Brown Campground. Note: Happy Canyon Road becomes Sunset Valley Road after passing through the intersection with Figueroa Mountain Road. Park in the hiking parking area at the campground.

**Maps:** Send $3 to the USDA-Forest Service, 630 Sansome Street, San Francisco, CA 94111 and ask for the Los Padres National Forest map. For a topographic map of the area, ask for Figueroa Mountain from the USGS.

**Who to contact:** Los Padres National Forest, Santa Lucia Ranger District, 1616 North Carlotti Drive, Santa Maria, CA 93454; (805) 925-9538.

**Trail notes:** If it is a spring wildflower display you are after, then this hike usually delivers in spades—the lower slopes of Figueroa Mountain are often a carpet of striking color contrasts. If the seasons are kind and the weather cooperative, you can even experience fall colors when the leaves of the big leaf maple turn—nothing like aspen or the trees back East, but then you can't be too picky. From the mountain's peak, the views are memorable of the San Rafael Wilderness, Santa Ynez Valley and the Channel Islands. From the campground, hike up the Davy Brown Trail for approximately two miles to an unsigned trail branching off to the right just before the Munch Canyon Trail. The trail to this point is quite scenic with little elevation gain or loss. If it is a simple wander or picnic escape you are seeking, then the ruins of an old cabin nearby or a number of other shaded, creekside spots are perfect. You need hike no further. Assuming you want to reach the summit, however, then begin looking hard for an unsigned route heading up towards Figueroa Peak, just upstream from the cabin and a few hundred yards before reaching the signed Munch Canyon Trail to the left. The hike up the trail climbs quickly and at times steeply through chaparral and pines, all the way to a firebreak leading to Figueroa Peak. Turn left and hike for one-half mile on the firebreak to the top. Take your time—the hiking is steep. Return the way you came.

## 4. MANZANA CREEK TRAIL   17.0 mi/2.0 days
## to MANZANA SCHOOL HOUSE CAMP

*Reference:* **Just north of Santa Barbara in the San Rafael Wilderness Area; map H3, grid d3.**

*User groups:* Hikers, horses and dogs. No mountain bikes are allowed. No wheelchair facilities.

*Permits:* No day-use permits are required. Campfire permits are required. Contact the Santa Lucia Ranger District at (805) 925-9538.

*Directions:* From Highway 101 in Santa Barbara, take Highway 154 north over San Marcos Pass to Lake Cachuma. Just past Lake Cachuma, turn right onto Armour Ranch Road and drive approximately 2.5 miles to Happy Canyon Road. Turn right onto Happy Canyon Road and drive about 16 miles to the turnoff for Davy Brown Campground. Note: Happy Canyon Road becomes Sunset Valley Road after passing through the intersection with Figueroa Mountain Road. Just past the turnoff, the road crosses Davy Brown Creek with parking available after the crossing.

*Maps:* Send $3 to the USDA-Forest Service, 630 Sansome Street, San Francisco, CA 94111 and ask for the Los Padres National Forest map. For topographic maps of the area, ask for Bald Mountain, Zaca Lake, Hurricane Deck, Figueroa Mountain and San Rafael Mountain from the USGS.

*Who to contact:* Los Padres National Forest, Santa Lucia Ranger District, 1616 North Carlotti Drive, Santa Maria, CA 93454; (805) 925-9538.

*Trail notes:* This section of the Manzana Creek Trail leads you through a historic section of the San Rafael Wilderness, past stone foundations, chimneys, and scattered bits of glass and barbed wire—all a reminder of those who carved out a rugged homesteading existence for many years. While 17 miles does seem a lot to cover in one day, the route is fairly level and, given an early start and cool temperatures, it is manageable. Still, we recommend spending the night at Manzana School House Camp—a pleasant meadow camp with an outhouse view that has to be experienced to be believed! From the parking area, begin hiking downstream on the Manzana Creek Trail. Upon reaching Potrero Camp, you will have a choice of hiking either the high route or the low route—the low route will probably wet your feet with the many crossings while the high route tends to be hotter and drier. Both are good trails, with perhaps the best alternative being to hike out on one and back on the other. Coldwater Camp, set amid a pine and oak grove, offers a super picnic spot. Cool water seeping up through the bedrock here is pleasant—but don't drink it unless you treat it first. Following Coldwater, you will arrive at Dabney Cabin, which lies locked and unused. Continue on to Manzana School House Camp at the confluence of the Sisquoc River and Manzana Creek. There is an interpretive display with photographs of the area back in the 1890s.

## 5. MANZANA CREEK TRAIL    14.0 mi/7.0 hrs
## to MANZANA NARROWS

*Reference:* **Just north of Santa Barbara in the San Rafael Wilderness Area; map H3, grid e3.**

*User groups:* Hikers, horses and dogs. No mountain bikes are allowed. No wheelchair facilities.

*Permits:* No day-use permits are required. Campfire permits are required. Contact the Santa Lucia Ranger District at (805) 925-9538.

*Directions:* From Highway 101 in Santa Barbara, take Highway 154 north over San Marcos Pass to Lake Cachuma. Just past Lake Cachuma, turn right onto Armour Ranch Road and drive approximately 2.5 miles to Happy Canyon Road. Turn right onto Happy Canyon Road and drive all the way to NIRA Camp. Note: Happy Canyon Road becomes Sunset Valley Road after passing through the intersection with Figueroa Mountain Road. There is a designated parking area for hikers located at the south end of the campground.

*Maps:* Send $3 to the USDA-Forest Service, 630 Sansome Street, San Francisco, CA 94111 and ask for the Los Padres National Forest map. For topographic maps, ask for Bald Mountain, Hurricane Deck, Figueroa Mountain and San Rafael Mountain from the USGS.

*Who to contact:* Los Padres National Forest, Santa Lucia Ranger District, 1616 North Carlotti Drive, Santa Maria, CA 93454; (805) 925-9538.

*Trail notes:* When Michael guided backpacking trips for a company in Los Angeles, this was one of the more popular destinations and for good reason. The trail winds through alder thickets and thick carpets of wildflowers in the spring. There are numerous streamside meadows that practically scream "picnic spot" with a particular favorite area being Manzana Narrows—a narrow part of the canyon where swimming holes abound. From NIRA Camp, hike out on the Manzana Creek Trail, past Lost Valley Camp and Trail (the trail leads to Hurricane Deck and the very center of the San Rafael Wilderness. Horses are not recommended on this trail as it is too brushy). Then cross and recross the creek all the way to the narrows. If you have an inclination to fish, you will like the fact that trout are stocked in this stream every year—providing you get there before the hundreds of other anglers with the same idea. Although it is possible to head out and back in one long day, we would heartily recommend planning on spending the night at any one of the trail camps along the way. Manzana Narrows Camp is one of Michael's favorites.

---

## 6. SANTA YNEZ RIVER TRAIL    6.0 mi/3.0 hrs

*Reference:* **Just north of Santa Barbara; map H3, grid g3.**

*User groups:* Hikers and horses. No mountain bikes or dogs are allowed. No wheelchair facilities.

*Permits:* No day-use permits are required.

*Directions:* From Santa Barbara and Highway 101, exit onto Highway 154 to Lake Cachuma. Head east over San Marcos Pass. Just beyond the pass, turn right onto Paradise Road and drive to the road's end and a dirt parking area next to the trailhead and a locked gate.

*Maps:* Send $3 to the USDA-Forest Service, 630 Sansome Street, San Francisco, CA 94111 and ask for the Los Padres National Forest map. For a topographic map, ask for Little Pine Mountain from the USGS.

*Who to contact:* Los Padres National Forest, Santa Barbara Ranger District, Star Route Paradise Road, Santa Barbara, CA 93105; (805) 967-3481.

*Trail notes:* You've got to love the "No Nudity" sign at the beginning of this trail—it almost begs you to disrobe just to see what would happen. Keep your clothes on and keep hiking because the Santa Ynez River Trail heads up through oak woodlands (watch out for those ticks) and jumps from one side of the river to the other. Swimming is encouraged when the swimming holes look inviting, and they often do. The trail ends at the Gibraltar Dam, just above the Gibraltar Picnic Area. Stay out of the signed and restricted areas. Children will get a kick out of the pond turtles who are often seen basking in the sun along the route. Look but don't touch is the rule—these turtles look better on the river than they would in an aquarium anyway.

---

## 7. INSPIRATION POINT    9.0 mi/4.0 hrs
## via TUNNEL TRAIL

*Reference:* **Just north of Santa Barbara; map H3, grid h5.**

*User groups:* Hikers and horses. No mountain bikes or dogs are allowed. No wheelchair facilities.

*Permits:* No day-use permits are required.

*Directions:* From Santa Barbara and Highway 101, exit onto Mission Street to Laguna Street and then left past the Santa Barbara Mission. From the Mission, head up Mission Canyon Road, your route will take a brief jog right onto Foothill and then back onto Mission. At a split intersection in the road, bear left onto Tunnel Road and keep driving to the road's end. Park alongside the road's shoulder. The trailhead begins at the locked gate.

*Maps:* Send $3 to the USDA-Forest Service, 630 Sansome Street, San Francisco, CA 94111 and ask for the Los Padres National Forest map. For a topographic map of the area, ask for Santa Barbara from the USGS.

*Who to contact:* Los Padres National Forest, Santa Barbara Ranger District, Star Route Paradise Road, Santa Barbara, CA 93105; (805) 967-3481.

*Trail notes:* This is a great hike, but expect lots of company on the weekends—everyone in the area appears to be drawn by the series of small falls along the way. Hike up the road past the gate. It turns to dirt before long and then crosses over the West Fork of Mission Creek. To get to the waterfalls, drop down on the signed Jesuita Trail to Mission Creek—Tunnel Trail keeps heading uphill. Follow the creek along sandstone walls. Watch your step and be very careful when scrambling off trail in the canyon as the rock scrambling up and over boulders and small rock walls can be tricky and dangerous. Jesuita Trail climbs very steeply out of the canyon up to a road and then to nearby Inspiration Point. The views from on top of the 1750-foot sandstone point are expansive.

---

## 8. RATTLESNAKE CANYON     6.5 mi/3.0 hrs

*Reference:* **Just north of Santa Barbara; map H3, grid h5.**
*User groups:* Hikers and horses. No mountain bikes or dogs are allowed. No wheelchair facilities.
*Permits:* No day-use permits are required.
*Directions:* From Santa Barbara and Highway 101, exit onto State Street and drive north to Los Olivos Street. Turn right onto Los Olivos and drive a half mile to Mission Canyon Road. Drive on Mission Canyon to Las Canoas Road, just past Foothill Road. Then drive on Las Canoas to Skofield Park. Parking is available along the road's shoulder before the park entrance. The trailhead is located next to the bridge on Las Canoas over Rattlesnake Creek.
*Maps:* Send $3 to the USDA-Forest Service, 630 Sansome Street, San Francisco, CA 94111 and ask for the Los Padres National Forest map. For a topographic map of the area, ask for Santa Barbara from the USGS.
*Who to contact:* Los Padres National Forest, Santa Barbara Ranger District, Star Route Paradise Road, Santa Barbara, CA 93105; (805) 967-3481.
*Trail notes:* Though the trail and creek carry the name of a poisonous reptile, they are not actually named for the snake, but are more indicative of the winding, serpentine nature of the route. A wander through this parkland makes for an outstanding picnic walk and, if you have the energy, a super climb up to Gibraltar Road. From the highest vantage point, and if the winds and thermals are just right, you can watch hang gliders slicing through the sky above you—there is a popular launching spot nearby. Wildflower displays in the spring are wonderful. From the bridge, and across from Skofield Park, hike up the trail and then up a dirt road alongside Rattlesnake Creek. There are plenty of informal trails leading down to the creek's banks from the road, evidence enough that picnicking and splashing along the creek are popular. The route follows the creek for just over two and a quarter miles to Tin Can Meadow, which is where you will turn around if you want a short hike. Keep hiking another three-quarters of a mile or so, if you have the energy, up the Rattlesnake Canyon Trail to Gibraltar Road and a superb view of the coast.

---

## 9. EAST FORK COLD     3.5 mi/1.5 hrs
## SPRINGS TRAIL

*Reference:* **Just north of Santa Barbara; map H3, grid h6.**
*User groups:* Hikers and horses. No mountain bikes or dogs are allowed. No wheelchair facilities.
*Permits:* No day-use permits are required.
*Directions:* From Santa Barbara, drive south on Highway 101. Exit onto Hot Springs Road and drive toward the mountains for 2.5 miles to Mountain

Drive. Turn left onto Mountain Drive and continue for another mile to the Cold Springs Trailhead. Park off the road.

*Maps:* Send $3 to the USDA-Forest Service, 630 Sansome Street, San Francisco, CA 94111 and ask for the Los Padres National Forest map. For a topographic map of the area, ask for Santa Barbara from the USGS.

*Who to contact:* Los Padres National Forest, Santa Barbara Ranger District, Star Route Paradise Road, Santa Barbara, CA 93105; (805) 967-3481.

*Trail notes:* From the trailhead, hike up the shaded canyon to the junction of the East and West Forks of Cold Spring Creek at three-quarters of a mile. The West Fork Trail is easily missed and branches off to the left, leading one and a half miles to Gilbraltar Road. Continue hiking up the canyon on the East Fork Trail, climbing away from the creek and then rejoining it within a half mile. You will hike past a number of excellent swimming holes, and then the trail switchbacks up and out of the shade and to Montecito Overlook. Spend some time admiring the views of the Channel Islands (assuming they are not fogged in) and the Santa Barbara coast. Return the way you came. Watch out for poison oak along the creek and canyon. If you wish to add a mile or two to your wander, cross the fire road just ahead and continue uphill to the Hot Springs connector trail. Bear right and drop down into Hot Springs Canyon through bamboo, banana and palm trees—remnants of the once magnificent Hot Springs Resort which flourished here from the late 1800s to the early 1960s. Head back the way you came when ready.

---

## 10. WEST FORK COLD SPRINGS TRAIL

4.0 mi/2.0 hr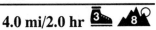

*Reference:* **Just north of Santa Barbara; map H3, grid h6.**

*User groups:* Hikers, horses and mountain bikes. No dogs are allowed. No wheelchair facilities.

*Permits:* No day-use permits are required.

*Directions:* From Santa Barbara drive south on Highway 101. Exit onto Hot Springs Road and drive toward the mountains for 2.5 miles to Mountain Drive. Turn left onto Mountain Drive and continue for another mile to the Cold Springs Trailhead. Park off the road.

*Maps:* Send $3 to the USDA-Forest Service, 630 Sansome Street, San Francisco, CA 94111 and ask for the Los Padres National Forest map. For a topographic map of the area, ask for Santa Barbara from the USGS.

*Who to contact:* Los Padres National Forest, Santa Barbara Ranger District, Star Route Paradise Road, Santa Barbara, CA 93105; (805) 967-3481.

*Trail notes:* This trail is an ancient route up a canyon that is extremely lush. It leads, with a bit of boulder-hopping, to a super waterfall. The waterfall is best in the spring, as is the display of monkeyflowers typically sprinkling color among the rocks around the falls. From the trailhead, hike up the shaded canyon to the junction of the East and West Forks of Cold Spring Creek. The trail leading up the West Fork is unsigned, but fairly obvious and just downstream from the confluence. Once at the falls, turn around and head back the way you came.

# 11. ROMERO CANYON TRAIL   7.5 mi/4.0 hrs

*Reference:* **Just north of Santa Barbara; map H3, grid h7.**

*User groups:* Hikers, horses, dogs and mountain bikes. No wheelchair facilities.

*Permits:* No day-use permits are required.

*Directions:* From Santa Barbara, drive south on Highway 101. Exit onto Sheffield Drive and turn right. Drive approximately 1.5 miles to East Valley Road. Turn left onto East Valley and then make a quick right onto Romero Canyon Road. In approximately a half mile, the road will fork. Bear right and drive approximately one mile to Bella Vista Road. Turn right onto Bella Vista and proceed up the road to a red gated entrance to a fire road on the left side. Park alongside Bella Vista Road. Do not block the fire road and be sure you are well off the main drag so other cars can safely pass.

*Maps:* Send $3 to the USDA-Forest Service, 630 Sansome Street, San Francisco, CA 94111 and ask for the Los Padres National Forest map. For a topographic map of the area, ask for Carpinteria from the USGS.

*Who to contact:* Los Padres National Forest, Santa Barbara Ranger District, Star Route Paradise Road, Santa Barbara, CA 93105; (805) 967-3481.

*Trail notes:* This is a popular canyon for family groups and youngsters, because of the creek in the lower canyon which seems ideal for splashing in. Watch out for that poison oak! At the gate, head up the canyon on the fire road, crossing a bridge and then crossing Romero Creek itself within the first half-mile. Head left on a trail that follows the creek. Enjoy the shade and lush feeling for the next mile before embarking on a one-quarter-mile, steeply switchbacked climb to a trail intersection. Either return the way you came or turn right and hike four scenic miles down the dirt road back to the lower reaches of the Romero Canyon Trail and then back on the trail to Bella Vista and your car.

# 12. MATILIJA TRAIL   14.5 mi/7.0 hrs

*Reference:* **Just north of Ventura near Ojai; map H3, grid h9.**

*User groups:* Hikers and horses. No dogs or mountain bikes are allowed. No wheelchair facilities.

*Permits:* No day-use permits are required. Campfire permits are required. Contact the Ojai Ranger District at (805) 646-4348.

*Directions:* From Highway 101 in Santa Barbara, take Highway 33 north and four miles beyond the town of Ojai to the left turnoff to Matilija Hot Springs. Drive one mile past the springs turnoff and turn left onto Matilija Canyon Road (Forest Service Road 5N13). Drive five miles to a locked gate across the road and park in the established area just before the gate.

*Maps:* Send $3 to the USDA-Forest Service, 630 Sansome Street, San Francisco, CA 94111 and ask for the Los Padres National Forest map. For topographic maps of the area, ask for Wheeler Spring and Old Man Mountain from the USGS.

*Who to contact:* Los Padres National Forest, Ojai Ranger District, 1190 East Ojai Avenue, Ojai, CA 93023; (805) 646-4348.

*Trail notes:* Although the Wheeler Fire in 1985 obliterated much of the upper backcountry, the vegetation has returned nicely and this has once again become a super spot to adventure with the family on a day-hike and picnic or with experienced hikers on an overnight. Early summer should bring the towering Matilija poppy into flower—five-foot-tall blooms on average are guaranteed to draw attention. The lower canyon offers an excellent place to romp with children, as it features pleasant swimming/splashing pools, sunning rocks (with sunscreen of course), and picturesque picnic sites. The first short section of dirt road will take you past Matilija Canyon Ranch and a wildlife reserve—it's all private, so stay on the road. After the fire road crosses Matilija Creek twice, head right on the trail that veers away from the road and follows the creek. Matilija Camp, approximately one mile from the trailhead, is a great place to spend the night with your family—a short, level, one-mile hike in and out, but still offering a sense of wilderness for the little ones. Matilija Trail continues to climb up the canyon, past Middle Matilija Camp just over 2.5 miles further on, and then up to Maple Camp at 3.7 miles and Forest Service Road 6N01, and then the Cherry Creek trailhead for Matilija Trail—three and three-quarter miles beyond Middle Matilija.

---

## 13. GRIDLEY TRAIL          8.6 mi/4.5 hrs

*Reference:* **Just north of Ventura near Ojai; map H3, grid h9.**
*User groups:* Hikers, horses, dogs and mountain bikes. No wheelchair facilities.
*Permits:* No day-use permits are required. Campfire permits are required. Contact the Ojai Ranger District at (805) 646-4348.
*Directions:* From Highway 101 in Santa Barbara, take Highway 33 north to the town of Ojai and the intersection of Highways 150 and 33. Continue on Highway 150 (Ojai Avenue) for two miles to the Ojai Ranger Station on the left. Drive a half mile to Gridley Road and turn left. Drive to the road's end (approximately 1.8 miles). The trailhead is located at the end of the road on the left.
*Maps:* Send $3 to the USDA-Forest Service, 630 Sansome Street, San Francisco, CA 94111 and ask for the Los Padres National Forest map. For a topographic map of the area, ask for Ojai from the USGS.
*Who to contact:* Los Padres National Forest, Ojai Ranger District, 1190 East Ojai Avenue, Ojai, CA 93023; (805) 646-4348.
*Trail notes:* Outstanding views of the surrounding area, including the town of Ojai and the Ojai Valley, can be yours—with a little sweat equity. Shade is minimal so pick a cool day. If the weather cooperates and the air remains clear—especially right after a rain storm—you will be able to see forever from the top of 4,425-foot-high Nordhoff Peak. Climb up the Gridley Trail to Gridley Fire Road (Forest Service Road 5N11) and head right. Keep climbing to Gridley Spring (water runs here but treat it before drinking). From Gridley Spring, hike up to the Nordhoff Fire Road (Forest Service Road 5N05) via a steep trail and turn left. Head up to the peak and enjoy the expansive view. Return the way you came.

---

## 14. FOOTHILL TRAIL          5.5 mi/2.0 hrs

*Reference:* **Just north of Ventura near Ojai; map H3, grid h9.**
*User groups:* Hikers, horses, dogs and mountain bikes. No wheelchair facilities.
*Permits:* No day-use permits are required. Campfire permits are required. Contact the Ojai Ranger District at (805) 646-4348.

*Directions:* From Highway 101 in Santa Barbara, take Highway 33 north to town of Ojai and the intersection of Highways 150 and 33. Continue east on 33 for approximately one mile to North Signal Street. Turn north on North Signal and drive three-quarters of a mile to a junction with an unsigned road on your left. A large water tower and a chain link fence mark the junction. If you run into Shelf Road, you have gone about 100 yards too far. Park at the junction on North Signal Street.

*Maps:* Send $3 to the USDA-Forest Service, 630 Sansome Street, San Francisco, CA 94111 and ask for the Los Padres National Forest map. For a topographic map of the area, ask for Ojai from the USGS.

*Who to contact:* Los Padres National Forest, Ojai Ranger District, 1190 East Ojai Avenue, Ojai, CA 93023; (805) 646-4348.

*Trail notes:* Ojai means "nest" in the language of the Chumash Indian, which is appropriate because Ojai Valley and the town of Ojai are "nested" in a 10-mile long valley that is both lush and somewhat mystical. This trail, leading from the town of Ojai, affords the hiker an excellent view of both the city and the valley beyond. From the North Signal Road parking area, turn west just below Shelf Road, and head up toward the Stewart Canyon Debris Basin. Look for a white pipe fence and a Forest Service sign indicating a trail, and exit onto the trail. The trail you are now on drops into Stewart Canyon and then climbs back out again. Watch out for poison oak. At Foothill Trail head left. It's a dirt road for a short distance before the trail branches off. Stay on Foothill up the slope and over a meadow for outstanding views. Keep hiking on Foothill until it drops down and joins Gridley Road. Turn right, walk to Shelf Road, and then head back to the North Signal and your car on Shelf Road.

# LEAVE NO TRACE TIPS

**Respect other users**

• Horseback riders have priority over hikers. Step to the downhill side of the trail and talk softly when encountering horseback riders.

• Hikers and horseback riders have priority over mountain bikers. When mountain bikers encounter other users, even on wide trails, they should pass at an extremely slow speed. On very narrow trails, they should dismount and get off to the side, so the hiker or horseback rider can pass without having their trip disrupted.

• Mountain bikes are not permitted on most single-track trails and are expressly prohibited on all portions of the Pacific Crest Trail, in designated wilderness areas and on most state park trails. Mountain bikers breaking these rules should be confronted, told to dismount and walk their bikes until they reach a legal area.

• It is illegal for horseback riders to break off branches that may lay in the path of wilderness trails.

• Horseback riders on overnight trips are prohibited from camping in many areas, and are usually required to keep stock animals in specific areas where they can do no damage to the landscape.

## MAP H4

2 PCT SECTIONS
10 TRAILS
PAGES 628-639

CEN-CAL MAP ...................... see page 466
adjoining maps
NORTH (G4) .......................... see page 556
EAST (H5) ............................. see page 640
SOUTH (I4) ........................... see page 672
WEST (H3) ............................. see page 616

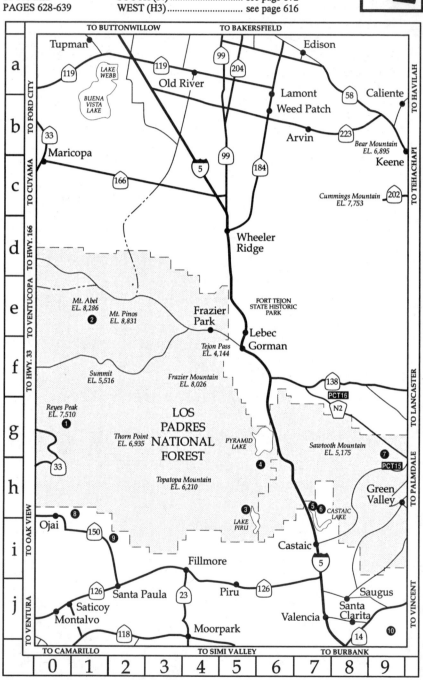

TO BUTTONWILLOW                    TO BAKERSFIELD

TO FORD CITY

**a**

Tupman                                    Edison
119
LAKE
WEBB
119
Old River
99
204
58    Caliente
Lamont
BUENA
VISTA
LAKE
Weed Patch

TO HAVILAH

**b**

33
Maricopa
Arvin
223
Bear Mountain
EL. 6,895
Keene
5
99
184

TO CUYAMA

**c**

166
Cummings Mountain
EL. 7,753
202

TO TEHACHAPI

**d**

Wheeler
Ridge

TO HWY. 166

**e**

TO VENTUCOPA

Mt. Abel
EL. 8,286
② 
Mt. Pinos
EL. 8,831
Frazier
Park
FORT TEJON
STATE HISTORIC
PARK
Lebec

**f**

TO HWY. 33

Summit
EL. 5,516
Gorman
Tejon Pass
EL. 4,144
Frazier Mountain
EL. 8,026
138
PCT16
N2

TO LANCASTER

**g**

Reyes Peak
EL. 7,510
①
LOS
PADRES
NATIONAL
FOREST
Thorn Point
EL. 6,935
PYRAMID
LAKE
④
Sawtooth Mountain
EL. 5,175
⑦
PCT15
33

TO PALMDALE

**h**

Topatopa Mountain
EL. 6,210
③
⑤ ⑥
CASTAIC
LAKE
Green
Valley

**i**

TO OAK VIEW

⑧
Ojai
150
⑨
LAKE
PIRU
Castaic
5

TO VENTURA

**j**

126
Santa Paula
23
Piru
126
Saugus
Fillmore
Saticoy
Montalvo
118
Moorpark
Valencia
Santa
Clarita
14
⑩

TO VINCENT

TO CAMARILLO          TO SIMI VALLEY          TO BURBANK

0   1   2   3   4   5   6   7   8   9

**Map H4 featuring:** Los Padres National Forest, San Fernando Valley, Lake Piru, Castaic Lake, Bouquet Reservoir, Los Padres National Forest, Three Points

## 1. REYES PEAK TRAIL      11.6 mi/6.0 hrs  

*Reference:* **Northeast of Ojai off Highway 33 in Los Padres National Forest; map H4, grid g0.**

*User groups:* Hikers and horses. No mountain bikes or dogs are allowed. No wheelchair facilities.

*Permits:* Day-use permits are not required. Wilderness permits are required if you are planning to stay overnight in the national forest. For more information, contact the Ojai Ranger District at (805) 646-4348.

*Directions:* From Ojai, drive north on Highway 33 for 33 miles to Reyes Peak Road. Turn right (east) on Reyes Peak Road and drive past Reyes Peak Campground for approximately four miles to the end of the road.

*Maps:* Send $3 to the USDA-Forest Service, 630 Sansome Street, San Francisco, CA 94111 and ask for the Los Padres National Forest map. For topographic maps, ask for Reyes Peak, Lion Canyon and San Guillermo from the USGS.

*Who to contact:* Los Padres National Forest, Ojai Ranger District, 1190 East Ojai Avenue, Ojai, CA 93023; (805) 646-4348.

*Trail notes:* This trail is in the Sespe Wilderness Area. No water is available at any of the campgrounds, so bring all that you will need with you. This hike is a dry one along ridgetops. Pack plenty of water, as there is no reliable water source along the route either. From the parking area, begin hiking east on the old road along the ridgeline. In a short distance, take a trail to the left, staying on the north slope until you reach Haddock Peak (7,416 feet). The trail drops steeply to Haddock Camp, located at the headwaters of Piedra Blanca Creek. Along the way, there are outstanding places to camp for the night, providing you have a stove and plenty of water.

## 2. VINCENT TUMAMAIT      6.5 mi/3.0 hrs  

*Reference:* **West of Frazier Park and Interstate 5, north of San Fernando Valley; map H4, grid e1.**

*User groups:* Hikers, horses and dogs. No mountain bikes are allowed. No wheelchair facilities.

*Permits:* Day-use permits are not required. Wilderness permits are required if you are planning to stay overnight in the national forest. For more information, contact the Mt. Pinos Ranger District at (805) 245-3731.

*Directions:* From Interstate 5 north of San Fernando Valley, take the Frazier Park Highway exit (just north of Gorman) and turn left onto Frazier Park Highway. Drive approximately 14 miles to the base of Mt. Pinos and then drive nine more miles to the top. Park here at the Chula Vista Parking Area if you are in a 2WD. If you have a good 4WD, you can drive the next 2.5 miles to the Vincent Tunamait Trailhead (FS 21W03); otherwise, you must walk.

*Maps:* Send $3 to the USDA-Forest Service, 630 Sansome Street, San Francisco, CA 94111 and ask for the Los Padres National Forest map. For a Forest

Service Recreational map showing the Chumash Wilderness, call the Forest Service at (805) 683-6711. For a topographic map, ask for Sawmill Mountain from the USGS.

***Who to contact:*** Los Padres National Forest, Mt. Pinos Ranger District, HC-1, Box 400, Frazier Park, CA 93225; (805) 245-3731 or (805) 245-3462.

***Trail notes:*** Cross-country skiing aficionados recognize Mt. Pinos as one of the better Southern California winter destinations for gliding and sliding. When snow is not covering the ground, Mt. Pinos and the surrounding area offers some superb hiking opportunities as well. This particular hike, one of the best in the area in our opinion, begins at the summit of 8,831-foot Mt. Pinos—the highest peak in both Kern and Ventura countics and in the Los Padres National Forest. The trail was dedicated in the summer of 1994, two years after Vincent Tumamait passed away. He was a storyteller of the Chumash tribe who worked with the Forest Service and the Sierra Club to get this area designated as the Chumash Wilderness. There is an interpretive sign that explains the legend and mythology of the surrounding Mt. Pinos area. This hike is a dry one along ridgetops, so pack plenty of water. There is no reliable source along the route. From the parking area, begin hiking west along the Mt. Pinos ridgeline. Continue following the trail along the slopes of Sawmill Mountain, eventually leading to a fire road heading up to Cerro Noriste (also known as Mt. Abel) with an elevation of 8,283 feet. The last half-mile or so of this hike is a real butt-kicker, gaining 500 feet. Ahh well, you wouldn't appreciate the spectacular view as much if you didn't earn it, now would you? Head back the way you came. Wildflowers bloom from June to August and are quite pretty.

# 3. POTHOLES 11.6 mi/6.5 hrs

***Reference:*** **Northwest of San Fernando Valley near Lake Piru; map H4, grid h5.**

***User groups:*** Hikers and horses. No dogs or mountain bikes are allowed. No wheelchair facilities.

***Permits:*** Day-use permits are required. Wilderness permits are required. For more information, contact the Ojai Ranger District at (805) 646-4348.

***Directions:*** From Interstate 5 driving north from Los Angeles, exit at Castaic Junction and drive west on Highway 126 for approximately 11 miles to the signed turnoff for Lake Piru. Drive north, now on Main Street, to the tiny village of Piru and then on to the entrance kiosk for the Lake Piru Recreation Area. Inform the attendant that you are going to park at the Blue Point Campground and hike into the Pothole, and you will receive a day-use Forest Service permit. You will park at the United Water Swimming Area parking lot. There is a parking fee charged. Call the gatehouse at (805) 521-1500 for parking information.

***Maps:*** Send $3 to the USDA-Forest Service, 630 Sansome Street, San Francisco, CA 94111 and ask for the Los Padres National Forest map. For a topographic map, ask for Cobblestone Mountain from the USGS.

***Who to contact:*** Los Padres National Forest, Ojai Ranger District, 1190 East Ojai Avenue, Ojai, CA 93023; (805) 646-4348.

***Trail notes:*** This trail is in the Sespe Wilderness Area. Water is not reliable along the route, so before heading out, we recommend you top off your water bottles. We also recommend packing along a pair of all-terrain sandals or old tennis shoes if you plan on adventuring through the Devil's Gateway in often waist-deep water. The first three miles of the Pothole Trail are, dare we say, mind-bending in terms of their maniacal elevation gain in a short span of time—almost 1,000 feet per mile. Once over the initial ridge, the trail will drop down into the Sespe Wilderness, past Devil's Potrero. Nearby the Potrero, look for an indistinct trail leading south to the trail's namesake, the Potholes. It's a natural depression caused by an earthquake fault, filled with grass and lined with trees—it's beautiful. Head back up to Pothole Trail and then, dodging poison oak, descend to Aqua Blanca Creek, 5.8 miles from the trailhead. Now comes the Devil's Gateway—a hoot and a thrill for sure. If the water is too high, don't attempt it. If the water in the creek seems manageable, don your water footwear and head downstream through the 20-foot narrow passageway between high rock walls. The water is *coooold!* Join the trail on the other side of the Gateway and then hike upstream to a junction. Bear right on Agua Blanca Trail and head back to the Bluepoint Campground (closed until 1996 due to earthquake damage in the 1994 quake). Hike south on Blue Point Road for one mile to return to your car.

---

## 4. PIRU CREEK        15.0 mi one-way/12.0 hrs

*Reference:* **Northwest of San Fernando Valley near Lake Piru; map H4, grid h6.**

*User groups:* Hikers only. No horses, dogs or mountain bikes are allowed. No wheelchair facilities.

*Permits:* Day-use permits are required. Campfire permits are required. For more information, contact the Ojai Ranger District at (805) 646-4348.

*Directions:* This is a shuttle trip. Park the first vehicle at trail's end, Lake Piru Recreation Area. From Interstate 5 driving north from Los Angeles, exit at Castaic Junction and drive west on Highway 126 for approximately 11 miles to the signed turnoff for Lake Piru. Drive north, now on Main Street, to the tiny village of Piru and then on to the entrance kiosk for the Lake Piru Recreation Area. Park at the United Water Swim area—there is a fee for parking here. Call the gatehouse at (805) 521-1500 for parking information. In the second vehicle, drive back out to Interstate 5 and head north to Templin Highway. Drive west on the frontage road to the Oak Flat Campground entrance and then past it for approximately two more miles to Frenchman's Flat. If it is trout season, you won't be alone, as this is a popular fishing parking area.

*Maps:* Send $3 to the USDA-Forest Service, 630 Sansome Street, San Francisco, CA 94111 and ask for the Los Padres National Forest map. For topographic maps, ask for Cobblestone Mountain and Whitaker Peak from the USGS.

*Who to contact:* Los Padres National Forest, Ojai Ranger District, 1190 East Ojai Avenue, Ojai, CA 93023; (805) 646-4348.

*Trail notes:* Welcome to Los Angeles County's one and only Wild and Scenic River. Fed by runoff from Pyramid Lake, the stream stays cool and green even when everywhere else is getting hot and dry. The canyon walls at times rise as high as 500 feet above the floor. Trees line the canyon, creating shade and also creating some serious negotiating problems as you battle thickets and branches to work your way through a few clogged stream sections. Before heading out, check with the Forest Service regarding water levels. Typically, spring brings the highest water and often makes the stream unhikable. Remember, there is no trail. You are hiking along the stream, most often *in* the stream, for the duration of the hike. You will have wet feet. Neoprene socks, available from many specialty sporting goods stores, make the wet feet ordeal a little more pleasant—and warm. Be sure that your boots have sufficient room to accommodate the thin (but still bulkier than wool) socks. If you are a fisherman, pack along your pole (and your fishing license of course) and enjoy the super trout fishing along the way.

*Special note:* This is a rugged one-way trip that is sure to leave you physically and mentally exhausted (although unbelievably happy). We would recommend turning this trip into an overnight, if you have the time and inclination. There are a number of suitable streamside camping areas along the way. Since Bluepoint Campground closed in January 1995 (and you had to leave your vehicle at the swim area parking), add six more miles to your trek to get back to your car.

---

## 5. FISH CANYON  14.0 mi/10.0 hrs

*Reference:* **North of San Fernando Valley near Castaic Lake; map H4, grid h7.**

*User groups:* Hikers, horses and dogs. No mountain bikes allowed. No wheelchair facilities.

*Permits:* Day-use permits are not required. Campfire permits are required. For more information, contact the Saugus Ranger District at (805) 296-9710.

*Directions:* From the San Fernando Valley, drive north on Interstate 5 to Lake Hughes Road. Exit on Lake Hughes and drive 12 miles to Warm Spring Truck Trail. Turn onto Warm Springs and drive eight miles to Cienaga Campground.

*Maps:* Send $3 to the USDA-Forest Service, 630 Sansome Street, San Francisco, CA 94111 and ask for the Angeles National Forest map. For topographic maps, ask for Liebre Mountain and Whitaker Peak from the USGS.

*Who to contact:* Angeles National Forest, Saugus Ranger District, 30800 Bouquet Canyon Road, Saugus, CA 91350; (805) 296-9710.

*Trail notes:* Fish Canyon Trail has no signs and has not been maintained in over eight years, and it shows. Still, it is a fun jaunt that you can chew on for as long as your sense of adventure holds up. The mileage above covers the length of the canyon hike, all the way to its connection with the Pacific Crest Trail at the top of Sawmill Mountain. Hike upstream along the banks and sometimes on the remains of the dirt road. In a short while, the canyon walls begin to close in and you will be forced into the creek itself, unless you enjoy beating your brains and filleting your skin on bushes and dense underbrush, including that old nemesis of hikers—poison oak. Wear boots you can get wet and that are comfortable to hike in when wet. At the fork in the canyon— Redrock to the right and Cienaga Canyon (Castaic Creek) to the left—leave the trail and head left. The next 2.5 miles or so up the canyon are extremely fun, with a combination of desert wash, gravel and shallow pools. The banks are lined with willow, and rattlesnakes love the environment so watch where you tread and place your hands. Turn around at anytime and retrace your steps. Late September through early June is the best time to visit.

## 6. FISH CANYON NARROWS    4.5 mi/3.0 hrs

*Reference:* **North of San Fernando Valley near Castaic Lake; map H4, grid h7.**

*User groups:* Hikers, dogs and horses (on the trail only). No mountain bikes are allowed. No wheelchair facilities.

*Permits:* Day-use permits are not required. Campfire permits are required. For more information, contact the Saugus Ranger District at (805) 296-9710.

*Directions:* From the San Fernando Valley, drive north on Interstate 5 to Lake Hughes Road. Exit on Lake Hughes and drive 12 miles to Warm Spring Truck Trail. Turn onto Warm Springs and drive eight miles to Cienaga Campground.

*Maps:* Send $3 to the USDA-Forest Service, 630 Sansome Street, San Francisco, CA 94111 and ask for the Angeles National Forest map. For topographic maps, ask for Liebre Mountain and Whitaker Peak from the USGS.

*Who to contact:* Angeles National Forest, Saugus Ranger District, 30800 Bouquet Canyon Road, Saugus, CA 91350; (805) 296-9710.

*Trail notes:* This canyon and its narrows provide a truly magical walk into an area dubbed Rogers Camp (although no sign of it exists today) opposite an old mining tunnel that was bored into the rock walls. The trail in begins at the campground and heads up the main Fish Canyon on an old roadbed. The road soon disappears as the route heads into the narrows, hopscotching from bank to bank along narrow benches on either side of the creek. Rogers Camp is an oak-shaded and grassy bench—watch out for ticks. Turn around here and head back the way you came. Since it rains about six months out of the year, expect there to be water in the riverbed, and that means wet feet.

## 7. SHAKE TRAIL    10.0 mi/5.0 hrs

*Reference:* **North of San Fernando Valley near Castaic Lake; map H4, grid g9.**

*User groups:* Hikers, horses and dogs. No mountain bikes are allowed. No wheelchair facilities.

*Permits:* Day-use permits are not required. Campfire permits are required. For more information, contact the Saugus Ranger District at (805) 296-9710.

*Directions:* From the San Fernando Valley, drive north on Interstate 5 to Lake Hughes Road. Exit on Lake Hughes Road and drive for approximately 23 miles north to Elizabeth Lake Road. Turn left onto Elizabeth Lake Road, which becomes Pine Canyon Road. From this point, where it becomes Pine Canyon, drive seven miles to the Shake Trail Trailhead.

*Maps:* Send $3 to the USDA-Forest Service, 630 Sansome Street, San Francisco, CA 94111 and ask for the Angeles National Forest map. For a topographic map, ask for Burnt Peak from the USGS.

*Who to contact:* Angeles National Forest, Saugus Ranger District, 30800 Bouquet Canyon Road, Saugus, CA 91350; (805) 296-9710.

*Trail notes:* Hike up the canyon along Pine Canyon Road for approximately one-quarter mile. The road will turn into a trail and climbs through oak along Shake Canyon to the canyon's head and an intersection with the Pacific Crest Trail (PCT). Head east on the PCT through what many hikers believe is one of the more scenic sections of the trail in this area. You'll find Douglas firs and oak trees along a flat route, with periodic views out over Antelope Valley. As you hike along, look closely for a trail that veers off the PCT to the left and will lead you back to the parking area.

## 8. HORN CANYON TRAIL          3.4 mi/2.0 hrs

*Reference:* **Just north of Ventura near Ojai; map H4, grid h1.**
*User groups:* Hikers, horses and mountain bikes (on Horn Canyon Parkway only). No dogs allowed. No wheelchair facilities.
*Permits:* Day-use permits are not required. Campfire permits are required. For more information, contact the Ojai Ranger District at (805) 646-4348.
*Directions:* From Highway 101 in Santa Barbara, take Highway 33 north to the town of Ojai and the intersection of Highways 150 and 33. Head east on Highway 150 to a Forest Service ranger station on the left. Continue driving past the station for a short distance to Gridley Road and turn left. Drive approximately a quarter of a mile to McAndrew Road and turn left. Drive on McAndrew Road to Thatcher School and onto the school grounds to the designated visitor parking. The trailhead begins up the paved road heading towards the mountains and at a signed intersection indicating "Gymkana Area and Jameson Field."
*Maps:* Send $3 to the USDA-Forest Service, 630 Sansome Street, San Francisco, CA 94111 and ask for the Los Padres National Forest map. For a topographic map, ask for Ojai from the USGS.
*Who to contact:* Los Padres National Forest, Ojai Ranger District, 1190 East Ojai Avenue, Ojai, CA 93023; (805) 646-4348.
*Trail notes:* This is a wonderful little hike down a shady path, cooled by the nearby waters of a seasonal stream. Although the Horn Canyon Trail (Forest Service 22W32) continues further, the primary destination of this hike is The Pines, a pine tree plantation and the site of a Forest Service trail camp with available water, 1.7 miles from the trailhead. At the sign for Jameson Field at Thatcher School, head right onto a dirt road, through the orchard and to a gated road on the left, with a Forest Service sign indicating the beginning of the Horn Canyon Trail. Hike up to The Pines and then, once rested, return the way you came. If you wish to extend your journey, the trail continues up and along the ridge, ending just east of Chief Peak and west of Topa Topa Bluffs.

## 9. SANTA PAULA CANYON          7.0 mi/3.0 hrs

*Reference:* **Just north of Ventura near Ojai; map H4, grid i2.**
*User groups:* Hikers, horses, dogs and mountain bikes. No wheelchair facilities.
*Permits:* Day-use permits are not required. Campfire permits are required. For more information, contact the Ojai Ranger District at (805) 646-4348.
*Directions:* From Highway 101 in Santa Barbara, take Highway 33 north to the town of Ojai and the intersection of Highways 150 and 33. Head east on Highway 150 for approximately 9.5 miles to the bridge crossing Santa Paula Creek. Although the trailhead is located here, just inside the entrance to St. Thomas Aquinas/Ferndale Ranch College entrance, keep driving a few hundred more yards to a wide turnout on the right (south) side of the highway. Park here and then hike back to the trailhead.
*Maps:* Send $3 to the USDA-Forest Service, 630 Sansome Street, San Fran-

cisco, CA 94111 and ask for the Los Padres National Forest map. For a topographic map, ask for Santa Paula Peak from the USGS.

*Who to contact:* Los Padres National Forest, Ojai Ranger District, 1190 East Ojai Avenue, Ojai, CA 93023; (805) 646-4348.

*Trail notes:* Although this canyon occasionally experiences violent flooding which washes out the trail and serves to cleanse the canyon of debris, the hike will lead you into a peaceful world of waterfalls, swimming holes, tranquil pools, and shaded woodlands. This trail sees heavy use on weekends—we would recommend trying to visit on a weekday. Although you can complete this hike easily in a day, we would recommend bringing along a friend and spending the night at either Cross or Cienega & Bluff camps. The mileage listed above indicates the roundtrip mileage to Big Cone Camp, located near where the trail splits. Add approximately another two miles round trip to visit Cross and six miles round trip to visit Cienega. From the college entrance, pass through the gate onto the grounds and stay on the main road curving past lawns and buildings. Follow the signs indicating the direction "Hikers" should go. After approximately .5 miles of asphalt trekking, you will head through an orchard and a pipe gate to Santa Paula Creek—at last—and begin the scenic portion of the hike. Stay on the trail to Big Cone. The best bet is hiking up to Cross Camp, 3.5 miles from the trailhead, as the swimming holes there can't be beaten.

*Special note:* During the spring runoff and after a heavy rain, use caution as the stream can kick up quite an aggressive side, with currents strong enough to sweep even the hardy and experienced off their feet.

---

# 10. LOS PINETOS WATERFALL TRAIL

**8.0 mi/4.0 hrs**

*Reference:* In Placerita Canyon County Park, north of Van Nuys; map H4, grid j9.

*User groups:* Hikers, horses and dogs. No mountain bikes are allowed. There are some **wheelchair facilities.**

*Permits:* Day-use permits are not required. Campfire permits are required if you are planning to stay overnight in the national forest. For more information, contact the Tujunga Ranger District at (805) 296-9710.

*Directions:* From Interstate 5 north of San Fernando Valley, head east on Highway 14 to Newhall. Exit onto Placerita Canyon Road and turn east (right), driving approximately two miles to the entrance to Placerita Canyon County Park. Park in the large lot near the nature center. There is a $3 parking fee.

*Maps:* Send $3 to the USDA-Forest Service, 630 Sansome Street, San Francisco, CA 94111 and ask for the Angeles National Forest map. For a topographic map, ask for Mint Canyon from the USGS.

*Who to contact:* Placerita Canyon County Park, 19152 Placerita Canyon Road, Newhall, CA 91321; (805) 259-7721, or Angeles National Forest, Tujunga Ranger District, 12371 North Little Tujunga Canyon Road, San Fernando, CA 91342; (818) 899-1900.

*Trail notes:* There are a number of trails worth exploring in scenic Placerita Canyon County Park. By all means, visit the Nature Center before you head out on any of them. Michael's favorite trail in the park is the Los Pinetos

Waterfall Trail which heads up Los Pinetos Canyon for four miles from the Nature Center to a deeply shaded grotto and trickling waterfall—a private Eden that is guaranteed to cleanse the mind of worries if only for a short while. If it is an overnight you seek, the head up the Los Pinetos Trail to the Wilson Canyon Saddle and over into Forest Service land. Spend the night, subject to fire and permit regulations at the time, and head back the way you came.

# PACIFIC CREST TRAIL    65.0 mi. one way/7.0 days
## GENERAL INFORMATION

**Reference:** Trail sections extend from the San Francisquito Canyon Road Trailhead north to the trailhead parking on Tehachapi/Willow Springs Road.

**User groups:** Hikers, horses and dogs (except in national parks). No mountain bikes are allowed. No wheelchair facilities.

**Permits:** A wilderness permit is required for traveling through various wilderness and special-use areas that the trail traverses. Contact the national forest, BLM or national park office at your point of entry for a permit that is good for the length of your trip.

**Maps:** For an overall view of the trail route in this section, send $3 to the USDA-Forest Service, 630 Sansome Street, San Francisco, CA 94111, ask for the Angeles National Forest map. Topographic maps for particular sections of trail are provided under each specific trail section heading listed below.

**Who to contact:** Contact either the national forest, BLM or national park office at your trailhead—see specific trailheads and corresponding agencies listed within each section.

**Trail notes:** Trail elevations within this section range from just under 3,000 feet to over 5,800 feet. Much of this track passes through mountainous and high desert terrain that is both arid and hot—especially in the summer. It is not unusual to encounter over 100 degree temperatures on the trail even in the late spring—begin your hikes early in the day and season to ensure more comfortable traveling temperatures. There are very few water points along the trail, so carry at least one gallon of water per person per day as a reserve. The Mojave Desert is best crossed at night with the light of a head lamp. Much of this route is rather monotonous as it utilizes dirt roads and service routes—some of it alongside the aqueduct. Having explored this section we have one thing to ask—why would anyone want to hike this unless they were PCT thru-hikers on a longer trek?

---

# PCT-15    34.0 mi. one way/4.0 days
## SAN FRANCISQUITO CANYON ROAD to THREE POINTS

**Reference:** From the San Francisquito Canyon Road in map H4, grid h9 northwest to the trailhead parking at Three Points.

**User groups:** Hikers, horses and dogs. No mountain bikes are allowed. No wheelchair facilities.

**Permits:** A wilderness permit is required for traveling through various wilderness and special-use areas that the trail traverses. Contact the Angeles National Forest at (805) 296-9710 for a permit that is good for the length of your trip.

**Directions:** To the San Francisquito Canyon Trailhead—From Palmdale and Highway 14, drive west on County Road N2 (Elizabeth Lake Road) and turn left onto San Francisquito Canyon Road, just before reaching Elizabeth Lake. The trailhead is located near the San Francisquito Ranger Station and the campground.

To the Three Points Trailhead—From Palmdale and Highway 14, drive west on County Road N2 (Elizabeth Lake Road) to the town of Three Points. Turn right (north) onto Three Points Road. The PCT trailhead is located near a small store at the junction of Three Points Road and Pine Canyon Road. The PCT runs adjacent to Three Points Road heading north.

*Maps:* For an overall view of the trail route in this section, send $3 for to the USDA-Forest Service, 630 Sansome Street, San Francisco, CA 94111, ask for the Cleveland National Forest map. For topographic maps, ask for Lake Hughes, Burnt Peak and Liebre Mountain from the USGS. Two BLM surface maps cover the area as well and may be ordered from the BLM office listed below. Send $3.50 for each map ordered and ask for Tehachapi and Lancaster.

*Who to contact:* Angeles National Forest, Saugus Ranger District, 30800 Bouquet Canyon Road, Saugus, CA 91350; (805) 296-9710.

*Trail notes:* Enjoy the shade and oaks at San Francisquito as you are now off through dense chaparral and no water in sight until you reach Three Points. Wear a hat, sunscreen, sunglasses and light, long-sleeved clothing. The route is steep up and down at times—a thankless and hot trudge up and down gullies. The only saving grace are the wildflowers in the spring and the nifty views towards the Tehachapi Mountains. As you near Three Points, you have a hot grind up Liebre Mountain which makes you almost forget the shade you had been briefly enjoying among the coulter pines earlier. Dropping off the front side of Liebre, you reenter the pines and find blessed shade relief. Now it's a matter of hiking along roads and shoulders to Three Points.

---

# PCT-16        31.0 mi. one way/3.0 days
# THREE POINTS to TEHACHAPI/WILLOW SPRINGS RD.

*Reference:* **From the trailhead parking at Three Points, map H4, grid g8 northeast to Tehachapi/Willow Springs Road.**

*User groups:* Hikers, horses and dogs. No mountain bikes are allowed. No wheelchair facilities.

*Permits:* A wilderness permit is required for traveling through various wilderness and special-use areas that the trail traverses. Contact the Angeles National Forest at (805) 296-9710 for a permit that is good for the length of your trip.

*Directions:* To the Three Points Trailhead—From Palmdale and Highway 14, drive west on County Road N2 (Elizabeth Lake Road) to the town of Three Points. Turn right (north) onto Three Points Road. The PCT trailhead is located near a small store at the junction of Three Points Road and Pine Canyon Road. The PCT runs adjacent to Three Points Road heading north. To the Tehachapi/Willow Springs Road Trailhead—From Mojave and Highway 14, head west on Oak Creek Road to the intersection with Tehachapi/Willow Springs Road. The trailhead is located near the intersection.

*Maps:* For an overall view of the trail route in this section, send $3 for to the USDA-Forest Service, 630 Sansome Street, San Francisco, CA 94111, ask for the Cleveland National Forest map. For topographic maps, ask for Burnt Peak, Nenache School, Fairmont Butte, Tylerhorse Canyon, Tehachapi South and Monolith from the USGS. Two BLM surface maps cover the area as well and may be ordered from the BLM office listed below. Send $3.50

for each map ordered and ask for Tehachapi and Lancaster.

*Who to contact:* Angeles National Forest, Saugus Ranger District, 30800 Bouquet Canyon Road, Saugus, CA 91350; (805) 296-9710 or Bureau of Land Management, Caliente Resource Area, 3801 Pegasus Drive, Bakersfield, CA 93308; (805) 391-6000.

*Trail notes:* After tanking up on cold drinks at Three Points, and filling up your canteen with water for the next stretch, you will head out and north toward the aqueduct. It's a hot and boring schlep along the route towards Tehachapi. Up and down and up and down goes the path (read dirt road). It's a grateful moment when you at last reach Tehachapi/Willow Springs Road. If you want cold drinks and are heading on, bear right and hike approximately four miles east to the town of Mojave. Otherwise, onward and upward!

*PCT CONTINUATION:* To continue hiking along the Pacific Crest Trail, see Chapter H5, PCT-17 and PCT-18, pages 648-649.

# MAP H5

CEN-CAL MAP ...................... see page 466
adjoining maps
NORTH (G5) .......................... see page 560
EAST (H6) ............................. see page 650
SOUTH (I5) ........................... see page 696
WEST (H4) ............................ see page 628

4 PCT SECTIONS
9 TRAILS
PAGES 640-649

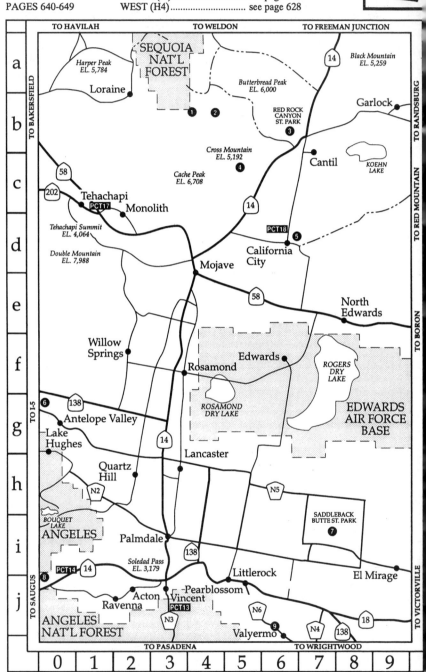

**Map H5 featuring:** Red Rock Canyon State Recreation Area, Antelope Valley California State Poppy Preserve, Butterbredt Canyon, Angeles National Forest, Saddleback Butte State Park

## 1. THE PIUTES 11.5 mi/8.0 hrs

*Reference:* **West of Highway 395 near California City; map H5, grid b4.**
*User groups:* Hikers, dogs and horses. No mountain bikes are allowed. No wheelchair facilities.
*Permits:* Day-use permits are not required. A campfire permit is required for camping. For more information, contact the Greenhorn Ranger District for more information at (805) 871-2223.
*Directions:* From Highway 58/Highway 14 head north on Highway 14, past California City Boulevard and to Jawbone Canyon Road. Turn left onto Jawbone Canyon Road and drive past Kelso Valley Road. Continue driving on Jawbone for approximately eight miles, up a series of switchbacks to the signed Pacific Crest Trail crossing and parking area.
*Maps:* For a topographic map, ask for Claraville from the USGS.
*Who to contact:* Sequoia National Forest, Greenhorn Ranger District, P.O. Box 6129, Bakersfield, CA 93386; (805) 871-2223.
*Trail notes:* This is a pleasant roundtrip hike along the PCT through shaded woodlands that are periodically peppered with wildflowers. A number of streams course through the area and there are a number of historical sites along the way, including an old mine. Stay out of the mine as it is considered hazardous. From the Jawbone Canyon Road trailhead, the trail heads north through a number of meadows and suitable camping areas if you wish to camp. Once you reach Landers Meadow and Piute Mountain Road, turn around and head back the way you came. Water is available at Piute Mountains Road, but treat it before drinking as there are cattle around.
*Special note:* Watch out for ticks and poison oak.

## 2. BUTTERBREDT CANYON 8.0 mi/4.0 hrs

*Reference:* **West of Highway 395 near California City; map H5, grid b5.**
*User groups:* Hikers, horses and dogs. No mountain bikes are allowed. No wheelchair facilities.
*Permits:* Day-use permits are not required.
*Directions:* From Highway 178 east of Lake Isabella turn right (south) on Kelso Valley Road and drive to Butterbredt Canyon Road. Look for the PCT sign crossing and limited parking along the shoulder.
*Maps:* For a topographic map, ask for Pinyon Mountain from the USGS.
*Who to contact:* Bureau of Land Management, Ridgecrest Resource Area, 300 South Richmond Road, Ridgecrest, CA 93555; (619) 384-5400.
*Trail notes:* This is a pleasant high desert hike, best experienced in the early spring or late fall. Summer is too hot! You will be hiking through canyon country with views of the San Gabriel Mountains to the south and the southern Sierra to the north. When you reach the base of Pinyon Pine Mountain, we recommend heading west and up to the summit. There is a jeep

road that contours up the mountain's side from the north. At the summit there is a protected area of rocks and trees where people have obviously camped. Looks like a good spot, but make sure you are at least 300 feet away from the trail.

---

## 3. RED ROCK CANYON 2.0 mi/1.0 hr
## STATE RECREATION AREA NATURE TRAIL

*Reference:* **Red Rock Canyon, north of Mojave; map H5, grid b6.**

*User groups:* Hikers, dogs, horses and limited mountain bikes (only on off-highway-vehicle routes). **Limited wheelchair facilities**—campground and visitor center only.

*Permits:* Day-use permits are not required. A $5 picnic fee is charged if you are using the picnic site. Camping is $7 per vehicle per night.

*Directions:* From Highway 58 in the town of Mojave, turn north on Highway 14 and drive approximately 25 miles to the signed park entrance.

*Maps:* Pick up the Red Rock Canyon State Recreation Area brochure/map. For topographic maps, ask for Cantil and Saltdale NW from the USGS.

*Who to contact:* Red Rock Canyon State Recreation Area, 1051 West Avenue M, Suite 201, Lancaster, CA 93534; (805) 942-0662.

*Trail notes:* We would recommend beginning your exploration of the park with a short trip around the park nature trail. It's a three-quarter mile jaunt that begins to the south of the campground and, with an interpretive brochure in hand, it offers a fascinating peek into the geologic history of the area as well as a look at some common desert plants. The entire park and beyond (into the El Paso Range managed by the Bureau of Land Management) is made up of fascinating rock formations and canyons splashed with colors ranging from vivid red and stark white to chocolate brown and tan. Mountain bikes and vehicles are allowed on the network of roads, but are not allowed into the several designated natural preserves, which were created to protect spectacular and fragile natural features. Redrock provides the best access to the adjacent and popular Dove Springs and Jawbone Canyon regions located on Bureau of Land Management lands. Recently, the park expanded from 10,000 acres to 30,000 acres and with that change came a new visitors center and a plan to include developed trails just for hikers—no sharing with motorized traffic. Plan on visiting between October and May—summer is too hot. Spring is the most popular time to visit because of the desert wildflower blooms.

---

## 4. CHUCKWALLA MOUNTAIN 3.5 mi/2.0 hrs

*Reference:* **West of Highway 395 near California City; map H5, grid c5.**

*User groups:* Hikers only. No horses, dogs or mountain bikes are allowed. No wheelchair facilities.

*Permits:* Day-use permits are not required.

*Directions:* From Highway 58/Highway 14 head north on Highway 14, past California City Boulevard and to Pine Tree Canyon Road. Turn left onto Pine Tree Canyon Road (if you reach Jawbone Canyon Road you have driven too far) and drive approximately 2.2 miles to an aqueduct service road and turn right, up the canyon to a second junction, approximately 3.8 miles from the start. Turn left onto a four-wheel-drive road and drive to a fork, approximately 4.5 miles from Highway 14. Park without blocking the road.

*Maps:* For a topographic map, ask for Cinco from the USGS.

*Who to contact:* Bureau of Land Management, Ridgecrest Resource Area, 300 South Richmond Road, Ridgecrest, CA 93555; (619) 384-5400.

*Trail notes:* Begin hiking on an unsigned motocross path to the very obvious peak to the north. Before long, amid the maze of paths and tracks, you will encounter a trail that is marked by rock cairns periodically, proving that many others have been here before—it is a "peak-baggers" goal. Quite honestly, you really cannot go wrong even if you get off-track, as long as you keep the summit in sight and keep working towards it. When ready, take a bearing and head back the way you came. Views from the summit are quite good—all the way to Telescope Peak in Death Valley to the east and the southern Sierra to the north.

---

# 5. DESERT TORTOISE NATURAL AREA

5.0 mi/2.0 hrs

*Reference:* **East of Highway 395 near California City; map H5, grid d6.**

*User groups:* Hikers only. No horses, dogs or mountain bikes are allowed. No wheelchair facilities.

*Permits:* Day-use permits are not required.

*Directions:* From Highway 58 or Highway 14, take California City exit approximately four miles to California City and California City Boulevard. Drive east for nine miles to 20 Mule Team Parkway and then drive one mile on 20 Mule Team Parkway to Randburg-Mojave Road. Drive three miles to the parking kiosk.

*Maps:* For a topographic map, ask for California City North from the USGS.

*Who to contact:* Bureau of Land Management, Ridgecrest Resource Area, 300 South Richmond Road, Ridgecrest, CA 93555; (619) 384-5400.

*Trail notes:* Although this is a tortoise preserve, you will have to look hard to spot one—they are a bit shy and reclusive. The best time to view the threatened California state reptile is between early March and late May. If you spot one, keep your distance. Tortoises traumatize easily and human contact could lead to their death. Wildflowers are spectacular here during the spring, with over 150 species in bloom. Check with the visitor center for guided tours during the spring. Summer is too hot to visit and viewing is poor anyway. Bring plenty of water, a wide-brimmed hat, lots of sunscreen and your camera and binoculars.

---

# 6. ANTELOPE LOOP TRAIL

2.5 mi/1.0 hr

*Reference:* **In Antelope Valley State Preserve west of Lancaster; map H5, grid g0.**

*User groups:* Hikers only. No horses, dogs or mountain bikes are allowed. No wheelchair facilities.

*Permits:* Day-use permits are not required. An entry fee of $5 is charged. The preserve is open from 9 a.m. to 4 p.m. daily.

*Directions:* From Highway 14 in Lancaster, exit on Avenue I and head west for approximately 15 miles to the entrance for the Antelope Valley State Preserve (Avenue I become Lancaster Road before the Preserve).

*Maps:* For topographic maps, ask for Fairmont Butte, Little Buttes, Del Sur and

Lake Hughes from the USGS.

*Who to contact:* Antelope Valley California State Poppy Preserve, 1051 West Avenue M, Lancaster, CA 93534; (805) 724-1180.

*Trail notes:* Not since Dorothy and the Wizard of Oz has there been such a colorful and massive display of poppies, but don't expect this field of color to lull you to sleep. March through early May is the best time to visit but since you never know when the peak bloom time is, we recommend that you call the Antelope Valley Preserve at the number listed above. For the best intro to the park, head out on the Antelope Loop Trail North which begins to the left of the visitor's center. Hike past the Kitanemuk Vista Point where you will stand amazed at the display of color—flowers at your feet and off into the distance coupled with the spread of the Mojave Desert and the often snow-capped Tehachapi Mountains is an awesome sight. After you have burned a roll of film, continue hiking up to the Antelope Vista Point for more views, although not as stunning as those at Kitanemuk, and then join the Antelope Loop Trail South for a return to the visitor's center.

---

# 7. SADDLEBACK BUTTE TRAIL 4.0 mi/2.0 hrs

*Reference:* **East of Lancaster; map H5, grid i7.**

*User groups:* Hikers only. No horses, dogs or mountain bikes are allowed. No wheelchair facilities.

*Permits:* Day-use permits are $5. Camping is available for $10 per night.

*Directions:* From Highway 14 in Lancaster, take the 20th Street exit and drive north on 20th to Avenue J. Turn right (east) onto Avenue J and drive approximately 17 miles to the signed park entrance for Saddleback Butte State Park. Drive down the dirt road to a campground and parking for the trailhead.

*Maps:* For a topographic map, ask for Hi Vista from the USGS.

*Who to contact:* Saddleback Butte State Park, 1051 West Avenue M, Suite 201, Lancaster, CA 93534; (805) 942-0662.

*Trail notes:* Few people visit this park and fewer still hike the trail to the top of Saddleback Peak. Why this light visitation? Perhaps it is due to the fact that the park sits smack in the middle of practically nothing, but all you have to do is hike to the top of the peak and you see why this is such a great place to visit—it's the view. From the trail sign, follow the yellow posts all the way to the peak. The last half-mile is quite vertical so take your time. The 3,641-foot Saddleback Butte sits nearly 1,000 feet higher than the surrounding Mojave Desert floor, which translates into 360-degree views of a spectacular nature, although construction on the surrounding terrain does detract from the overall aesthetics. We would recommend a sunrise hike to fully appreciate the awakening of a desert as the sun's rays tickle its surface and warm the air. Plan on visiting between October and May—summer is too hot.

---

# 8. VASQUEZ ROCKS COUNTY PARK          3.0 mi/2.0 hrs

*Reference:* **Northeast of Valencia on Highway 14; map H5, grid j0.**

*User groups:* Hikers, horses and dogs. No mountain bikes are allowed. No wheelchair facilities.

*Permits:* Day-use permits are not required. Overnight camping in the park is not permitted.

*Directions:* From San Fernando Valley, drive north on Interstate 5 to the Highway 14 exit. Drive north on Highway 14 to Agua Dulce Canyon Road and exit north. Drive on Agua Dulce Canyon Road to Escondido Canyon Road and the signed park entrance.

*Maps:* Send $3 to the USDA-Forest Service, 630 Sansome Street, San Francisco, CA 94111 and ask for the Angeles National Forest map. For a topographic map, ask for Agua Dulce from the USGS.

*Who to contact:* Vasquez Rocks County Park, 10700 West Escondido Canyon Road, Saugus, CA 91350; (805) 268-0991.

*Trail notes:* You probably know Vasquez Rocks without even realizing it—especially if you are a *Star Trek* fan or a watcher of late night *Bonanza* reruns. The tilted sandstone slabs are a rock scrambler's paradise. There are numerous informal and a few formal (including a section of the Pacific Crest Trail) trails within the park. The rock formations create a playground of mazes and hiding places for children of all ages—have fun, but be careful.

*Special note:* If you get disoriented—easy to do—clamber to a high point and reacquaint yourself with your location.

---

## 9. PUNCHBOWL TRAIL   6.0 mi/3.0 hrs

*Reference:* East of Lancaster; map H5, grid j6.

*User groups:* Hikers only on the Punchbowl Trail. Horses, dogs and mountain bikes are allowed on the Burkhart Trail. No wheelchair facilities.

*Permits:* Day-use permits are not required. A $3 parking fee is collected on weekends.

*Directions:* From Highway 138 in Pearblossom, turn right (south) on Longview Road, then left onto Fort Tejon Road. Drive for three-quarters of a mile and turn left into the parking lot for the park. The trailhead is located at the south end of the parking area.

*Maps:* For a topographic map, ask for Valyermo from the USGS.

*Who to contact:* Devil's Punchbowl County Regional Park, 28000 Devil's Punchbowl Road, Pearblossom, CA 93553; (805) 944-2743.

*Trail notes:* California is well known as Earthquake Central—evidenced in recent years by the massive quakes in both San Francisco and Los Angeles. Devil's Punchbowl sits atop the most active of all the faults, the San Andreas, and nowhere is the power of the earth's sudden upheavals more dramatically evident than in the Punchbowl itself. Huge rocks are tilted this way and that, in such a dramatic and crazed manner that some may feel as if it is the work of the devil himself—hence the name. Views from the trail and the trail's ultimate goal, the Devil's Chair (a monolith of white rock that juts out into the punchbowl), are spectacular and wondrous. There is a protective fence around the Devil's Chair to keep you from taking an inadvertent plunge. No matter what the devil may suggest, stay behind the fence because a trip into the Punchbowl from the chair is a one-way ticket to hell. Begin hiking at the picnic area on the signed Punchbowl Trail and follow it for three-quarters of a mile to a junction. Head left and hike three miles to reach the Devil's Chair. The trail to the right is signed as the Burkhart Trail and continues all the way to Vincent Gap—an ideal 30-mile loop trip for horses and mountain bikes. From the Punchbowl and park headquarters, it is approximately 7.25 miles to Burkhart Saddle, where you will enjoy superb views of Highway 2 and the Antelope Valley below. If you are planning on completing the entire loop, keep on hiking to Buckhorn Campground (12.5 miles from Punchbowl) and then to Vincent Camp. Plan on visiting between October and May—summer is too hot.

## PACIFIC CREST TRAIL      140.0 mi. one way/14.0 days
## GENERAL INFORMATION

*Reference:* **Trail sections include from the Mill Creek Picnic Area to San Francisquito Canyon; and from Tehachapi to Walker Pass.** (San Francisquito Canyon to Tehachapi are covered in Chapter H4, pages 627-629, as their trailheads are located on the map for that chapter.)

*User groups:* Hikers, horses and dogs (except in national parks). No mountain bikes allowed. No wheelchair facilities.

*Permits:* A wilderness permit is required for traveling through various wilderness and special-use areas that the trail traverses. Contact the national forest, BLM or national park office at your point of entry for a permit that is good for the length of your trip.

*Maps:* For an overall view of the trail route in this section, send $3 for each map to the USDA-Forest Service, 630 Sansome Street, San Francisco, CA 94111, ask for the Angeles National Forest, Sequoia National Forest maps. For topographic maps for particular sections of trail are provided under each specific trail section heading listed below. Two BLM surface maps cover the area as well and may be ordered from the Bureau of Land Management, Caliente Resource Area, 3801 Pegasus Drive, Bakersfield, CA 93308; (805) 391-6000. Send $3.50 for each map ordered and ask for Tehachapi and Lancaster.

*Who to contact:* Contact either the national forest, BLM or national park office at your trailhead—see specific trailheads and corresponding agencies listed within each section.

*Trail notes:* Trail elevations within this section range from just under 3,000 feet to over 6,900 feet. Much of this track passes through mountainous and high desert terrain that is both arid and hot—especially in the summer. It is not unusual to encounter over 100 degree temperatures on the trail even in the late spring—begin your hikes early in the day and season to ensure more comfortable traveling temperatures. There are very few water points along the trail so carry at least one gallon of water per person per day as a reserve. The Mojave Desert is best crossed at night with the light of a head lamp. Snow is possible in the higher elevations as you travel through the Angeles National Forest and also in the Sequoia National Forest.

*Special note:* Watch out for ticks in the dry grasses in the Angeles National Forest.

## PCT-13      35.0 mi. one way/4.0 days
## MILL CREEK PICNIC AREA to VASQUEZ ROCKS

*Reference:* **From the Mill Creek Picnic Area, map H5, grid j3 northwest to the trailhead parking at Vasquez Rocks.**

*User groups:* Hikers, horses and dogs. No mountain bikes are allowed. No wheelchair facilities.

**Permits:** A wilderness permit is required for traveling through various wilderness and special-use areas that the trail traverses. Contact the Angeles National Forest at (805) 296-9710 for a permit that is good for the length of your trip.

**Directions:** To the Mill Creek Picnic Area Trailhead—From Highway 14 at Vincent, head south on the Angeles Forest Highway (Road N3) to the Mill Creek Summit and picnic area and the signed PCT trailhead.

To the Vasquez Rocks Trailhead—From San Fernando Valley, drive north on Interstate 5 to the Highway 14 exit. Drive north on Highway 14 to Agua Dulce Canyon Road and exit north. Drive up Agua Dulce Canyon Road to Escondido Canyon Road and the signed park entrance. Part of the PCT runs through the park.

**Maps:** For an overall view of the trail route in this section, send $3 for to the USDA-Forest Service, 630 Sansome Street, San Francisco, CA 94111, ask for the Angeles National Forest map. For topographic maps, ask for Pacifico Mountain, Acton and Agua Dulce from the USGS.

**Who to contact:** Angeles National Forest, Saugus Ranger District, 30800 Bouquet Canyon Road, Saugus, CA 91350; (805) 296-9710.

**Trail notes:** This section of trail is routed through oak, pine, spruce and chaparral woodlands. There are some very pretty campsites along this section. Keep a sharp eye out for ticks as it seems as if they are breeding like rabbits here and clinging to every available surface. The up and down nature of the trail, much like it has been for the entire San Gabriel section, will test your mettle. As you cross over Soledad Canyon Road, you may elect to head left (east) up the road to the town of Acton—six miles distant with services that cater to the PCT hiker. This section ends in the spectacular rocky and jagged terrain of Vasquez Rocks County Park. You can camp here as long as you obtain the ranger's permission, who will tell you where to put your tent.

---

# PCT-14        23.0 mi. one way/2.0 days
# VASQUEZ ROCKS to SAN FRANCISQUITO CANYON

**Reference:** From the trailhead parking at Vasquez Rocks, map H5, grid i0 northwest to San Francisquito Canyon Road.

**User groups:** Hikers, horses and dogs. No mountain bikes are allowed. No wheelchair facilities.

**Permits:** A wilderness permit is required for traveling through various wilderness and special-use areas that the trail traverses. Contact the Angeles National Forest at (805) 296-9710 for a permit that is good for the length of your trip.

**Directions:** To the Vasquez Rocks Trailhead—From San Fernando Valley, drive north on Interstate 5 to the Highway 14 exit. Drive north on Highway 14 to Agua Dulce Canyon Road and exit north. Drive on Agua Dulce Canyon Road to Escondido Canyon Road and the signed park entrance. Part of the PCT runs through the park.

To the San Francisquito Canyon Trailhead—From Palmdale and Highway 14, drive west on County Road N2 (Elizabeth Lake Road) to a left turn onto San Francisquito Canyon Road, just before reaching Elizabeth Lake. The trailhead is located near the San Francisquito Ranger Station and the campground.

*Maps:* For an overall view of the trail route in this section, send $3 for to the USDA-Forest Service, 630 Sansome Street, San Francisco, CA 94111, ask for the Angeles National Forest map. For topographic maps, ask for Agua Dulce, Sleepy Valley, Green Valley and Lake Hughes from the USGS.

*Who to contact:* Angeles National Forest, Saugus Ranger District, 30800 Bouquet Canyon Road, Saugus, CA 91350; (805) 296-9710.

*Trail notes:* From Vasquez to Agua Dulce is a short trek into a town with supplies and a cafe—blessed coffee! From here, the trek begins to toughen as the temperature rises. We are heading into the Mojave, gang. It's up and down often poor track, sometimes torn up by off-road bikers who aren't supposed to be on the PCT. There are some delightful meadows and open grasslands through this stretch, which are especially gorgeous in the spring when wildflowers add a sprinkle of color to the green. At San Francisquito Canyon Road there is a nearby campground and picnic area.

---

For PCT-15 and PCT-16 (San Francisquito Canyon to Tehachapi), see Chapter H4, pages 637-639.

---

# PCT-17        41.0 mi. one way/4.0 days
## TEHACHAPI to JAWBONE CANYON ROAD

*Reference:* **From the trailhead parking at Tehachapi, map H5, grid c1 northeast to Jawbone Canyon Road.**

*User groups:* Hikers, horses and dogs. No mountain bikes are allowed. No wheelchair facilities.

*Permits:* A wilderness permit is required for traveling through various wilderness and special-use areas that the trail traverses. Contact the Sequoia National Forest at (805) 871-2223 for a permit that is good for the length of your trip.

*Directions:* To the Tehachapi/Willow Springs Road Trailhead—From Mojave and Highway 14, head west on Oak Creek Road to the intersection with Tehachapi/Willow Springs Road/Cameron Road. The trailhead is located near the intersection.

To the Jawbone Canyon Road Trailhead—From Highway 58/Highway 14 head north on Highway 14, past California City Boulevard and to Jawbone Canyon Road. Turn left onto Jawbone Canyon Road and drive past Kelso Valley Road. Continue driving on Jawbone for approximately eight miles, up a series of switchbacks to the signed Pacific Crest Trail crossing and parking area.

*Maps:* For an overall view of the trail route in this section, send $3 for to the USDA-Forest Service, 630 Sansome Street, San Francisco, CA 94111, ask for the Sequoia National Forest map. For topographic maps ask for Tehachapi South, Monolith, Tehachapi NE, Cache Peak, Cross Mountain, Pinyon Mountain, Claraville and Emerald Mountain from the USGS. A BLM surface map covers the area as well and may be ordered from the BLM office listed below. Send $3.50 and ask for Tehachapi.

*Who to contact:* Sequoia National Forest, Greenhorn Ranger District, P.O. Box 6129, Bakersfield, CA 93386; (805) 871-2223. Bureau of Land Management, Caliente Resource Area, 3801 Pegasus Drive, Bakersfield, CA 93308; (805) 391-6000.

*Trail notes:* As you leave Tehachapi Road heading north, the route begins to climb into what many argue are the true foothills of the Sierra. Wildflowers often cover the area in the spring, making this a superb wander during April and early May. As you scramble among the rocks and deadfalls, keep a sharp eye out for rattlesnakes which do love to bask in the sun. Be especially cautious of flash floods in the canyons of this section during storms which are brief, but often intense. Little water-fed oases and meadows along the route are fantastic. Views are also good as you work your way up into increasingly higher terrain on the way toward the Sierra.

---

# PCT-18      41.0 mi. one way/4.0 days
# JAWBONE CANYON ROAD to WALKER PASS

*Reference:* From Jawbone Canyon Road, map H5, grid d6 to Walker Pass.

*User groups:* Hikers, horses and dogs. No mountain bikes are allowed. No wheelchair facilities.

*Permits:* A wilderness permit is required for traveling through various wilderness and special-use areas that the trail traverses. Contact the Sequoia National Forest at (805) 871-2223 for a permit that is good for the length of your trip.

*Directions:* To the Jawbone Canyon Road Trailhead—From Highway 58/Highway 14, head north on Highway 14, past California City Boulevard and on to Jawbone Canyon Road. Turn left onto Jawbone Canyon Road and drive past Kelso Valley Road. Continue driving on Jawbone for approximately eight miles, up a series of switchbacks to the signed Pacific Crest Trail crossing and parking area.

    To the Walker Pass Trailhead—From Highway 14, turn west onto Highway 178 and drive to the Walker Pass Trailhead Campground, built especially for Pacific Crest Trail hikers. The trailhead begins at the east end of the campground.

*Maps:* Send $3 to the USDA-Forest Service, 630 Sansome Street, San Francisco, CA 94111 and ask for the Sequoia National Forest map. For topographic maps, ask for Claraville, Pinyon Mountain, Cane Canyon, Horse Canyon and Walker Pass from the USGS.

*Who to contact:* Sequoia National Forest, Cannell Meadow Ranger District, P.O. Box 6, Kernville, CA 93238; (619) 376-3781.

*Trail notes:* We begin climbing in earnest here. Wildflowers are spectacular in the spring. Although water becomes more frequent along the route, you should still tank up at every opportunity to top off your bottles, as there is no telling when the next water source will be and the route can sometimes be hot and dry. Some nifty rock formations and interesting tree groves keep the trip interesting. At Walker Pass there is water and a campground set up exclusively for PCT hikers.

*PCT CONTINUATION:* To continue hiking along the Pacific Crest Trail, see Chapter G5, pages 594-596.

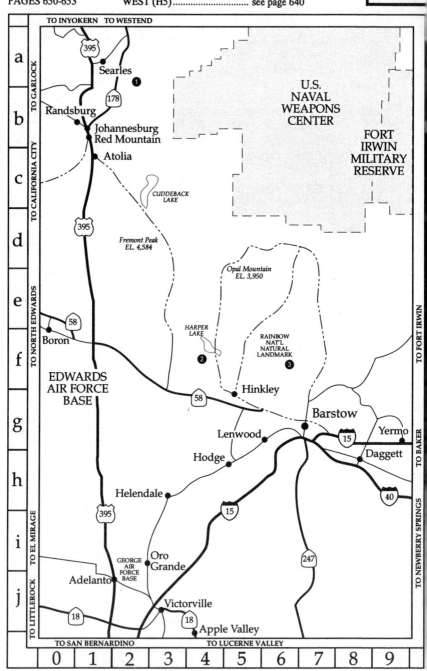

## 1. SPANGLER HILLS   3.0 mi/3.0 hrs

*Reference:* **South of Ridgecrest and east of Highway 395; map H6, grid a2.**
*User groups:* Hikers, horses, dogs and mountain bikes. No wheelchair facilities.
*Permits:* Day-use permits are not required.
*Directions:* From Highway 395 near Ridgecrest, exit onto Highway 178. Turn
   south (right) off Highway 178 on Randsburg Wash Road and then drive to
   Stephens Mine Road and turn right (south) again. Numerous entrances head
   east and west off Stephens Mine Road—take your pick. There are no defined
   trails, it's free-form wandering here.
*Maps:* For topographic maps, ask for Spangler Hills East and Spangler Hills
   West from the USGS.
*Who to contact:* Bureau of Land Management, Ridgecrest Resource Area, 300
   South Richmond Road, Ridgecrest, CA 93555; (619) 384-5400.
*Trail notes:* Although a fair number of off-road vehicles frequent the area, there
   is plenty of room in the 57,000 acres for hikers and mountain bikers to enjoy
   the recreational pleasures of this high desert site. The best time to visit is in
   the spring when the area is sprinkled with color from seasonal wildflowers.
   At other times, the miles of rugged terrain that have been carved up by off-
   roading amid the endless backdrop of creosote bush can get a little, shall we
   say, unappealing?

## 2. HARPER LAKE   1.0 mi/1.0 hr

*Reference:* **Northwest of Barstow; map H6, grid f4.**
*User groups:* Hikers only. No horses, dogs or mountain bikes are allowed. No
   wheelchair facilities.
*Permits:* Day-use permits are not required.
*Directions:* From Barstow, take Highway 58 west for approximately 25 miles
   to Harper Lake Road and turn north. Drive for approximately six miles and
   then turn right (east) onto Lockhart Road. Drive for another two miles (the
   last one-quarter mile is not maintained and can become very rough). There
   is no official parking, and no sign designating the site, but it is obvious when
   you arrive. The road is too narrow for large vehicles to turn around, and way
   too narrow to try with a trailer.
*Maps:* For a topographic map, ask for Lockhart from the USGS.
*Who to contact:* Bureau of Land Management, Barstow Resource Area, 150
   Coolwater Lane, Barstow, CA 92311; (619) 256-3591.
*Trail notes:*  Bring your binoculars. A number of short and informal trails
   network the area, providing excellent access to an oasis of richly vegetated
   lakes and marshland in the middle of the Mojave Desert. Please remember
   that this area is surrounded by private land, so stick to the marshland and lake
   edges. This water attracts a wide variety of wildlife to the area, which is why
   it has officially been declared a Watchable Wildlife Viewing Area, although
   there is no sign designating it as such. Wading and songbirds can be seen
   year-round. You have a very high probability of viewing birds of prey,

waterfowl and shorebirds from fall to spring. Keep a sharp eye out for short-eared owls who live around the marshy area—nearly 300 have been officially reported and counted in one marsh. Wildflowers are super in the spring.

***Special note:*** There are no facilities nearby so bring along plenty of water. Wear a wide-brimmed hat and sunscreen.

---

## 3. RAINBOW BASIN      4.0 mi/2.0 hrs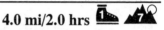

*Reference:* **Northwest of Barstow; map H6, grid f6.**

*User groups:* Hikers, horses, dogs and mountain bikes. No wheelchair facilities.

*Permits:* Day-use permits are not required.

*Directions:* From Barstow, take Irwin Road north for five miles. Then turn west on Fossil Beds Road and drive for five miles. Turn right on the signed road leading to Rainbow Basin.

*Maps:* For topographic maps, ask for Mud Hills and Lane Mountain from the USGS.

*Who to contact:* Bureau of Land Management, Barstow Resource Area, 150 Coolwater Lane, Barstow, CA 92311; (619) 256-3591.

*Trail notes:* Millions of years of geologic history are the primary drawing card here. Take a hike down Owl Canyon Wash or choose to drive or pedal your mountain bike on the short (1.5-mile) loop trail through the basin. Geology enthusiasts will think that they have died and gone to rock heaven when they discover the wealth of rock formations that exist here. Don't forget your camera, either—the spectacular scenery demands to be photographed.

## LEAVE NO TRACE TIPS

### Travel lightly

• Visit the backcountry in small groups.

• Below tree line, always stay on designated trails.

• Do not cut across switchbacks.

• When traveling cross-country where no trails are available, follow animal trails or spread out with your group so no new routes are created.

• Read your map and orient yourself with landmarks, a compass and altimeter. Avoid marking trails with rock cairns, tree scars or ribbons.

## MAP H7

CEN-CAL MAP ..................... see page 466
adjoining maps
NORTH (G7) ........................ see page 604
EAST (H8) ........................... see page 656
SOUTH (I7) .......................... see page 750
WEST (H6) ........................... see page 650

1 TRAIL
PAGES 654-655

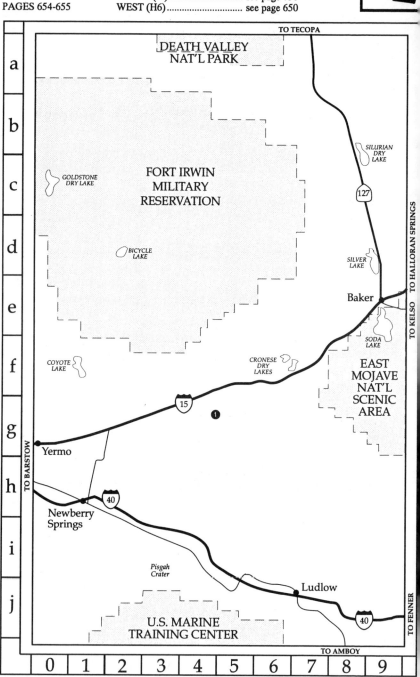

TO TECOPA

DEATH VALLEY NAT'L PARK

SILURIAN DRY LAKE

FORT IRWIN MILITARY RESERVATION

GOLDSTONE DRY LAKE

127

TO HALLORAN SPRINGS

BICYCLE LAKE

SILVER LAKE

Baker

TO KELSO

SODA LAKE

COYOTE LAKE

CRONESE DRY LAKES

EAST MOJAVE NAT'L SCENIC AREA

15

❶

TO BARSTOW

Yermo

40

Newberry Springs

Pisgah Crater

Ludlow

40

TO FENNER

U.S. MARINE TRAINING CENTER

TO AMBOY

# 1. PYRAMID CANYON TRAIL    3.0 mi/1.5 hrs

*Reference:* **Afton Canyon Natural Area, northeast of Barstow; map H6, grid g5.**

*User groups:* Hikers, horses, dogs and mountain bikes. No wheelchair facilities.

*Permits:* Day-use permits are not required. Camping is available for $4 per night per site.

*Directions:* From Barstow, drive 33 miles east on Interstate 15 to the Afton turnoff. Follow the dirt road southwest for three miles to the Afton Campground. Numerous informal trails branch off from the campground.

*Maps:* For topographic maps, ask for Dunn, Manix and Hidden Valley West from the USGS.

*Who to contact:* Bureau of Land Management, Barstow Resource Area, 150 Coolwater Lane, Barstow, CA 92311; (619) 256-3591.

*Trail notes:* The canyons, nooks and crannies here wandered years ago by Native Americans, Spanish missionaries and mountain men practically scream to be explored. Wagon trains once stopped here to rest and water beside the Mojave River, which still flows most of the year. The sheer walls of this multi-colored mini-Grand Canyon tower above the river. There are a number of informal and unmarked trails that will guide you past the multi-colored cliffs and through the nooks and crannies of this magical region— all beginning at the Afton Campground. We would suggest beginning your tour by hiking up Pyramid Canyon for a three-mile roundtrip introduction to the area. This side canyon heads south from across the river and under a set of railroad trestles just across from the campground. You will really enjoy the towering rock walls that begin to close in on you until stopping abruptly at a deadend. It is possible to scramble up the rocks for a nifty view of the area. Retrace your steps to the Mojave River and campground. Mountain bikers will want to stick to the Mojave Road that runs through Afton along the railroad tracks. Any place off the road is too soft and practically impossible to pedal through.

*Special note:* The railway tracks that run through the canyon are a hazard. The train rockets through at a fast clip and is not always easily heard. At no time should children or pets be allowed to run unsupervised. Also, rocks are fragile in the canyon area, so rock climbing is not allowed. Pack along plenty of water, as there is none available!

# MAP H8

CEN-CAL MAP ...................... see page 466
adjoining maps
NORTH ........................................... no map
EAST ............................................... no map
SOUTH ............................................ no map
WEST (H7) ............................... see page 654

6 TRAILS
PAGES 656-660

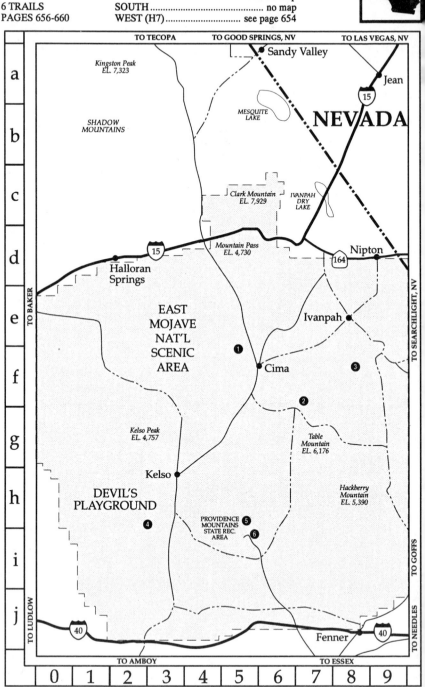

## 1. CIMA DOME/TEUTONIA PEAK TRAIL    4.0 mi/2.0 hrs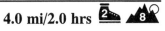

*Reference:* **Mojave National Preserve; map H8, grid f5.**

*User groups:* Hikers and horses. No dogs or mountain bikes are allowed. No wheelchair facilities.

*Permits:* Day-use permits are not required. Camping is available 20 miles away at either Mid-Hills or Hole-In-The-Wall campgrounds, which are currently free although the BLM anticipates fees to be $10 in the near future.

*Directions:* From Barstow, drive 89 miles north on Interstate 15 to Cima Road. Turn right (south) and then drive 11 miles on Cima Road to the signs indicating the trailhead.

*Maps:* For a topographic map of the area, ask for Cima Dome from the USGS.

*Who to contact:* Mojave National Preserve, Cal Desert Information Center, 831 Barstow Road, Barstow, CA 92311; (619) 256-8313.

*Trail notes:* This four-mile roundtrip trek over a primitive trail leads to the top of Teutonia Peak, a rock outcropping near the summit of the 5,500-foot Cima Dome. The 70-square-mile, gently rounded granite dome is reported to be the most symmetrical of its type anywhere in the nation, although the best view of the dome is from Mid-Hills campground nearly 20 miles away. A weird and magical Joshua tree forest carpets the area and provides a home for a variety of desert wildlife. The cinder cones you see off in the distance are part of the Cinder Cones National Natural Landmark, noted for petroglyph-covered basalts and other geologic features.

## 2. MID HILLS to HOLE-IN-THE-WALL TRAIL    16.0 mi/7.0 hrs

*Reference:* **North of Interstate 40 near Essex; map H8, grid f7.**

*User groups:* Hikers and horses. No dogs or mountain bikes area allowed. No wheelchair facilities.

*Permits:* Day-use permits are not required. Camping is available at either Mid-Hills or Hole-In-The-Wall campgrounds, which are currently free although the BLM anticipates fees to be $10 in the near future.

*Directions:* From Interstate 40 near Essex, take the Essex Road exit and drive 16 miles northwest on Essex Road to Black Canyon Road. Turn north on Black Canyon and drive 19 miles, following the signs to the Mid Hills campground.

*Maps:* For topographic maps of the area, ask for Fountain Peak, Van Winkle Spring and Mid Hills from the USGS.

*Who to contact:* Mojave National Preserve, Cal Desert Information Center, 831 Barstow Road, Barstow, CA 92311; (619) 256-8313.

*Trail notes:* This is the Old West at its best. The high desert area, with its dramatic volcanic formations punctuated by twisty stands of juniper, is authentic cowboy country. Pungent sage perfumes this eight-mile point-to-point treadway over rolling hills—perfect for hikers and horses. If you feel someone watching you, it's probably a desert bighorn sheep, wondering about your progress as he stands guard on a far-away ledge. Begin your journey at Mid Hills, hiking mostly downhill over the well-defined tread, spend the night at Hole-in-the-Wall and then retrace your steps (now uphill) the next day. If you wish to make this a one-day affair, then leave one vehicle at Hole-in-the-Wall.

---

## 3. CARUTHERS CANYON     3.5 mi/2.0 hrs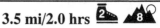

*Reference:* **Mojave National Preserve; map H8, grid f8.**

*User groups:* Hikers, horses, dogs and mountain bikes. No wheelchair facilities.

*Permits:* Permits are not required.

*Directions:* From Barstow, drive approximately 120 miles east on Interstate 40 to Mt. Springs Road and turn north. Drive to the town of Goffs and tank up with gas, water and any other needed supplies—it's your last stop. From Goffs, head north for approximately 25.5 miles on Ivanpah Road to New York Mountains Road. The turnoff is identified by OX Cattle Ranch buildings located at the intersection. Set your odometer to zero at the intersection. Head left (west) on New York Mountains Road and drive 5.6 miles to an unsigned junction with a dirt road heading north to Caruthers Canyon. Drive north for two miles on this dirt road to a wooded area and park. This area has become an informal campground.

*Maps:* For a topographic map of the area, ask for Ivanpah from the USGS.

*Who to contact:* Mojave National Preserve, Cal Desert Information Center, 831 Barstow Road, Barstow, CA 92311; (619) 256-8313.

*Trail notes:* Take a trek into a rock pine island amid a sea of desert. From the parking area, continue hiking up the now abandoned mining road heading into a historic gold mining region. Old shafts still exist in the area. The BLM does not prohibit access to the shafts, but common sense would indicate that to explore these abandoned mines is dangerous and foolhardy—unless you are looking for a knock on the head from a rock fall. The pinyon pine and juniper woodland is a pleasure to hike through. Wander where you will, set up camp if you wish as long as you have brought along plenty of water, and retrace your steps down the road to your car when ready. Fall through spring is the best time to visit. Summer is too hot!

---

## 4. KELSO DUNES     3.0 mi/2.0 hrs

*Reference:* **North of Interstate 40 in the Mojave National Preserve; map H8, grid h2.**

*User groups:* Hikers only. No horses, dogs and mountain bikes are allowed. No wheelchair facilities.

*Permits:* Day-use permits are not required.

*Directions:* From Interstate 40, head north on Kelbaker Road to a signed dirt road indicating Kelso Dunes to the left. Turn left and drive carefully along this sometimes rough road for approximately three miles to a designated BLM parking area for Kelso Dunes. The trailhead begins just up the dirt road from the parking area.

*Maps:* For a topographic map, ask for Kelso Dunes from the USGS.

*Who to contact:* Mojave National Preserve, Cal Desert Information Center, 831 Barstow Road, Barstow, CA 92311; (619) 256-8313.

*Trail notes:* Trek or schlep up to the top of one of America's tallest sand dunes. Due to the shifting nature of sand and dunes, there is no official trail other than the first quarter mile or so to get you heading in the right direction. Head up the dunes on a route of your own choosing—we would recommend not heading straight up unless you have bionic legs and lungs. Wildflowers are super on the way up in the spring, sprinkling the lower dune sands with yellow, white and pink. Once at the top, stand quietly and take in the view and, if you are lucky, the vibrations emanating from the sonorous dunes. What sonorous vibrations? The dunes are not actually singing, but vibrating as sand slides down the steep slopes—it's a deep sound that is almost felt more than heard. The trip down is outstanding, with somersaults optional.

---

## 5. MITCHELL CAVERNS TRAIL 1.5 mi/2.0 hrs 🏔 ⛰8

*Reference:* **North of Interstate 40 near Essex; map H8, grid h5.**

*User groups:* Hikers only. No horses, dogs and mountain bikes are allowed. No wheelchair facilities.

*Permits:* You cannot tour the cavern without a ranger guide. Sign up at the visitor's center upon arriving. A cave tour fee of $4 for adults and $2 for children is charged. No more than 25 people are allowed on each trip, get there early to ensure a spot. The middle tour on weekends fills up early.

*Directions:* From Interstate 40, take the Essex Road exit and drive 17 miles northwest on Essex Road into the park.

*Maps:* For topographic maps, ask for Fountain Peak and Van Winkle Spring from the USGS.

*Who to contact:* Providence Mountains State Recreation Area, P.O. Box 1, Essex, CA 92332; (805) 942-0662.

*Trail notes:* Tours are scheduled at 1:30 p.m. on weekdays and 10 a.m., 1:30 p.m. and 3 p.m. on weekends. Groups of 10 or more require a reservation with 10-day advance notice. No matter what the temperature is outside, it is a constant 65 degrees in the caverns. Along the route you will hear tales from the rangers—some wilder than others, depending on the ranger's storytelling skills. You will also view some wonderful cave features such as stalactites, stalagmites, cave ribbon and flow stone. The hike through the caverns runs approximately two hours, less if no questions are asked. Once you are out of the tour and if it is not too hot outside, we recommend that you also take in the half-mile, self-guided, interpretive Mary Beal Nature Trail. Pick up a trail brochure at the park headquarters. On this trail, you will receive a wonderful introduction to high desert plant life. If you are camping (it's $12 per night per site), and even if you aren't, you might also enjoy the very short Overlook Trail which departs from the campground to an overlook—makes sense. From there you will enjoy expansive views of the nearby desert ranges and basin.

---

## 6. PROVIDENCE MOUNTAINS    1.5 mi/1.0 hr 🏔 ⛰7
## STATE RECREATION AREA

*Reference:* **North of Interstate 40 near Essex; map H8, grid i5.**

*User groups:* Hikers, horses, dogs and mountain bikes. No wheelchair facilities.

*Permits:* Day-use permits are not required.

*Directions:* From Interstate 40, take the Essex Road exit and drive 17 miles northwest on Essex Road into the park.

*Maps:* For topographic maps, ask for Fountain Peak and Van Winkle Spring from the USGS.

*Who to contact:* Bureau of Land Management, California Desert District Office, 6221 Box Springs Boulevard, Riverside, CA 92507; (909) 697-5217. Also, you can contact the California State Parks at (805) 942-0662.

*Trail notes:* The Providence Mountains extend northeast for about 20 miles from Granite Pass, just south of Kelso. Limestone cliffs and caverns add a unique blend of variety to the rhyolite crags and peaks and the broad bajadas. If you are a Zane Grey fan, you may recognize the large flat-topped Wildhorse Mesa as the setting for his book of a like name—*Wildhorse Mesa.* There are plenty of opportunities for hiking away from it all and discovering a peaceful sense of isolation. Within the designated state park boundaries, the primary attraction is the Mitchell Caverns Natural Preserve—see hike number 5.

# SOUTHERN AREA HIKING TRAILS

## OVERALL RATING

🏔1 🏔2 🏔3 🏔4 🏔5 🏔6 🏔7 🏔8 🏔9 🏔10

Poor.................................................Fair.................................................Great

## DIFFICULTY RATING

👢1 👢2 👢3 👢4 👢5

A Stroll ........................................Moderate .................. A Real Butt-Kicker!

## LEAVE NO TRACE TIPS

### Plan ahead and prepare

• Learn about the regulations and issues that apply to the area you are visiting.

• Avoid heavy-use areas.

• Obtain all maps and permits.

• Bring extra garbage bags to pack out any refuse you come across.

# MAP I2

SO-CAL MAP ........................ see page 662
adjoining maps
NORTH (H2) .......................... see page 610
EAST (I3) ............................... see page 666
SOUTH ................................... no map
WEST ..................................... no map

1 TRAIL
PAGES 664-665

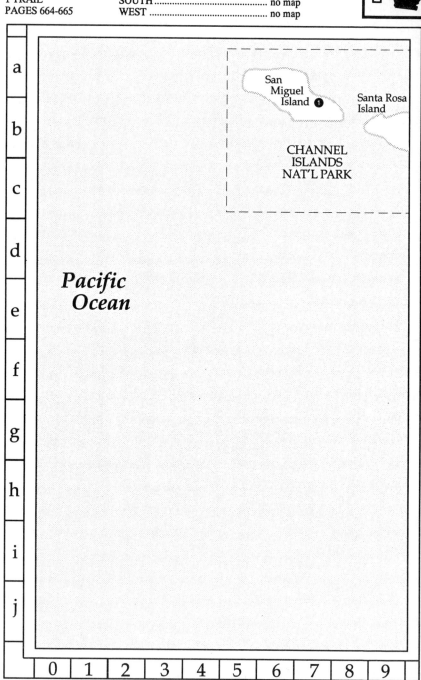

a

San
Miguel
Island ❶

Santa Rosa
Island

b

CHANNEL
ISLANDS
NAT'L PARK

c

d

*Pacific
Ocean*

e

f

g

h

i

j

| 0 | 1 | 2 | 3 | 4 | 5 | 6 | 7 | 8 | 9 |

# Map I2 featuring: San Miguel Island

## 1. POINT BENNETT TRAIL   15.0 mi/2.0 days

*Reference:* On San Miguel Island, part of the Channel Islands, south of Santa Barbara; map I2, grid b7.

*User groups:* Hikers only. Horses, mountain bikes and dogs are not allowed. No wheelchair facilities.

*Permits:* A free camping permit is needed if you wish to stay overnight—stays are limited to two nights, and no more than 30 campers are allowed. Campers are restricted to the campground from 7 p.m. to 7 a.m. Camping is subject to the availability of the ranger. Backcountry permits are also required for those planning to travel inland from the beach. Contact the National Park Service for permits at (805) 658-5711. Island Packers runs the boat to and from the island, call (805) 642-1393. A day-use roundtrip boat ride runs $65 (it's a long boat ride just for the day). If you wish to camp, and we recommend it highly, the boat fee is $90. The boat ride is five hours each way.

*Directions:* The Channel Islands Visitor Center and Island Packers are located adjacent to each other. From Highway 101, north of Los Angeles and south of Santa Barbara, take the Seward Harbor Boulevard exit and head south on Harbor Boulevard (Harbor Boulevard is located off Seward on the ocean side of 101). Take a right on Spinnaker Drive and stay on Spinnaker until it dead ends, parking is on the right. The visitor center and Island Packers are located on the right—look for the signs.

*Maps:* For a free map of the Channel Islands, write to the superintendent at the address listed below. For topographic maps, ask for San Miguel Island East and San Miguel Island West from the USGS.

*Who to contact:* Channel Islands National Park, 1901 Spinnaker Drive, Ventura, CA 93001; (805) 658-5730.

*Trail notes:* This 15-mile roundtrip hike heads out from Cabrillo Monument over San Miguel Hill and across the island to Point Bennett. Even the most seasoned hiker will marvel at the incredible display of scenery and wildlife on this trek. Wind and weather sweep dramatically across this island, the most western of the Channel Islands. The harshness of the environment creates a profoundly beautiful landscape for those hardy and well-prepared enough to enjoy it. In addition to being the only island in the world where six different species of pinniped (seals and sea lions) gather, San Miguel is also noted for its famous caliche forest. Caliche is a mineral sandcasting and its visual effects and sculptures are quite dramatic. San Miguel is also the place where the European discoverer of California, Juan Rodriquez Cabrillo, is thought to have been buried in 1543. Numerous archeological sites exist upon the island from the days of the seafaring Chumash—look but do not touch!

*Special note:* Campers will need to bring a very sturdy tent, all the water they need, a stove, toilet paper, food and warm, waterproof clothing. Although wind shelters have been constructed at each campsite, the wind can roar through in an unnerving fashion.

TO VENTURA

TO OXNARD

Port Hueneme

Santa
Cruz
Island

Santa
Rosa
Island ❶

❷

CHANNEL
ISLANDS
NAT'L PARK

❸

Anacapa
Island

*Pacific
Ocean*

Santa
Barbara
Island ❹

CHANNEL
ISLANDS
NAT'L PARK

San
Nicolas
Island

| 0 | 1 | 2 | 3 | 4 | 5 | 6 | 7 | 8 | 9 |

a b c d e f g h i j

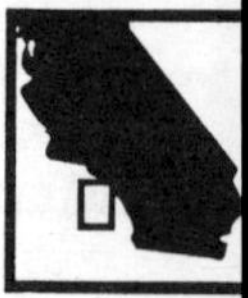

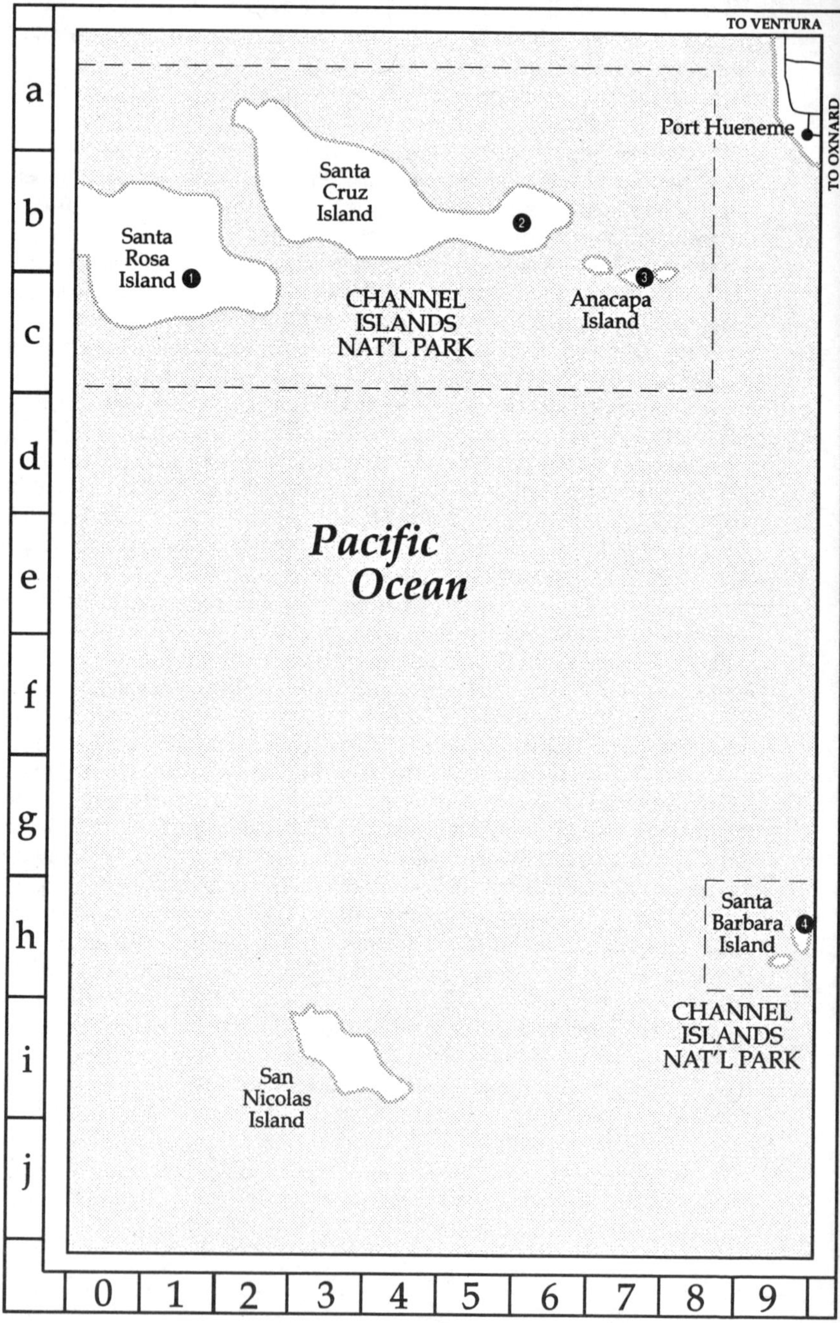

**Map I3 featuring:** Santa Rosa Island, Santa Cruz Island, Anacapa Island, Santa Barbara Island

## 1. SANTA ROSA TRAILS          5.0 mi/1.0 day

*Reference:* **On Santa Rosa Island, part of the Channel Islands, south of Santa Barbara; map I3, grid c1.**

*User groups:* Hikers only. Horses, mountain bikes and dogs are not allowed. No wheelchair facilities.

*Permits:* A free camping permit is needed if you wish to stay overnight. Contact the National Park Service at (805) 658-5711. While no permit is needed for day-use landings on the beach, a backcountry permit is required for any travel inland—also available from the NPS. Island Packers runs the boat to and from the island. Call (805) 642-1393. A day-use roundtrip boat ride runs $52; if you wish to camp, the fee is $80. The boat ride requires three hours each way. Reservations are suggested up to two weeks in advance. Channel Island Adventures Aviation offers Saturday-only flights and tours of Santa Rosa and Santa Cruz Islands for $85 per person. Call (805) 987-1301 for information and reservations.

*Directions:* The Channel Islands Visitor Center and Island Packers are located adjacent to each other. From Highway 101, north of Los Angeles and south of Santa Barbara, take the Seward Harbor Boulevard exit and head south on Harbor Boulevard (Harbor Boulevard is located off Seward on the ocean side of 101). Take a right on Spinnaker Drive and stay on Spinnaker until it dead ends, parking is on the right. The visitor center and Island Packers are located on the right—look for the signs.

*Maps:* For a free map of the Channel Islands, write to the superintendent at the address listed below. For topographic maps, ask for Santa Rosa Island North, Santa Rosa Island South, Santa Rosa Island East and Santa Rosa Island West from the USGS.

*Who to contact:* Channel Islands National Park, 1901 Spinnaker Drive, Ventura, CA 93001; (805) 658-5730.

*Trail notes:* At 10 miles wide by 15 miles long, Santa Rosa Island is the second largest of the Channel Islands. Like all the islands, Santa Rosa may be visited year round, but the best months to visit are from March through July when the expansive grasslands turn emerald green and are sprinkled with the bright colors of numerous wildflowers. A small grove of Torrey pines are located just south of the campground, but they are the only trees around— bring plenty of sunscreen and a good hat. The freshwater marsh located at East Point is the largest freshwater marsh on all of the islands. Bring your binoculars because kelp beds encircle Santa Rosa, attracting everything from seals and sea lions to whales. There are also a number of archeological sites associated with early man's presence in North America. Cherry Canyon Trail is four miles roundtrip and offers views of unique wildlife and sweeping glances into the island's interior. Lobo Canyon Trail is five miles roundtrip and descends a canyon to a Chumash village site, then heads out to an excellent tidepooling area. The East Point Trail is one mile roundtrip and offers a glimpse of a rare stand of Torrey pines as well as the freshwater marsh mentioned above.

## 2. SANTA CRUZ ISLAND    6.0 mi/1.0 day

*Reference:* On Santa Cruz Island, part of the Channel Islands, south of Santa Barbara; map I3, grid b6.

*User groups:* Hikers and mountain bikes. Horses and dogs are not allowed. No wheelchair facilities.

*Permits:* No camping permit is required, but permission must be obtained to stay overnight on the island from The Nature Conservancy—something Island Packers can do when you arrange your boat trip with them. A day-use landing permit is needed for anywhere on the island—available when arranging your trip with an outfitter. Island Packers runs the boat to and from the island. Call (805) 642-1393. A day-use roundtrip boat ride is $47; if you wish to camp, the fee is $55 plus $25 per person, per night. The boat ride requires two hours each way. Channel Island Adventures, an air-taxi service to the island, also offers packaged overnight stays. Call (805) 987-1301 for more information. If you wish to charter your own boat trip to the island, landing permits are required and may be obtained by contacting The Nature Conservancy at (805) 962-9111. Channel Island Adventures Aviation offers Saturday-only flights and tours of Santa Rosa and Santa Cruz Islands for $85 per person. Call (805) 987-1301 for information and reservations.

*Directions:* The Channel Islands Visitor Center and Island Packers are located adjacent to each other. From Highway 101, north of Los Angeles and south of Santa Barbara, take the Seward Harbor Boulevard exit and head south on Harbor Boulevard (Harbor Boulevard is located off Seward on the ocean side of 101). Take a right on Spinnaker Drive and stay on Spinnaker until it dead ends, parking is on the right. The visitor center and Island Packers are located on the right—look for the signs.

*Maps:* For a free map of the Channel Islands, write to the superintendent at the address listed below. For topographic maps, ask for Santa Cruz Island A, Santa Cruz Island B, Santa Cruz Island C and Santa Cruz Island D from the USGS.

*Who to contact:* Channel Islands National Park, 1901 Spinnaker Drive, Ventura, CA 93001; (805) 658-5730.

*Trail notes:* At 96 square miles, Santa Cruz Island is the largest of the Channel Islands. The highest of all the mountains on the Channel Islands is found here—2,450-foot Devil's Peak. Santa Cruz, although rugged, is also one of the more hospitable islands with sheltered canyons and, in places, fresh springs. It is the variety of topography and freshwater that supports a remarkable array of flora and fauna—over 600 plant species, 140 bird species, and a distinctive population of land animals. There are numerous hikes that you can enjoy once on the island—many beginning from the overnight campground at Scorpion Ranch. A recommended hike leads from the ranch to Prisoner's Bay—a six-mile roundtrip walk through old oaks and eucalyptus groves. Another popular excursion begins at Pelican Bay, where a small skiff drops off visitors onto a rocky ledge. From the ledge, it is a somewhat precipitous climb up a cliff face to the picnic spot overlooking the bay. Short loop trails lead along the north shore through two special botanical sites, a bishop pine forest and a small grove of Santa Cruz Island ironwood. Many of the hikes can be enjoyed with the company of a Nature Conservancy naturalist, who will be more than happy to point out the tremendous variety of botanical and historical highlights of the island. Scorpion Ranch also offers bunkhouse style accommodations and—yes—bathrooms and showers for the less primitively inclined. Contact Island Packers for more information and reservations.

---

# 3. ANACAPA ISLAND       2.0 mi/1.0 day

*Reference:* **On Anacapa Island, part of the Channel Islands south of Santa Barbara; map I3, grid b8.**

*User groups:* Hikers only. Horses, mountain bikes and dogs are not allowed. No wheelchair facilities.

*Permits:* A free camping permit is needed if you wish to stay overnight. Contact the National Park Service at (805) 658-5711. Camping is limited to 14 days. No day-use permit is needed. Island Packers runs the boat to and from the island. Call (805) 642-1393. Day use roundtrip boat ride runs $37; if you wish to camp, the fee is $48. The boat ride requires 90 minutes each way.

*Directions:* The Channel Islands Visitor Center and Island Packers are located adjacent to each other. From Highway 101, north of Los Angeles and south of Santa Barbara, take the Seward Harbor Boulevard exit and head south on Harbor Boulevard (Harbor Boulevard is located off Seward on the ocean side of 101). Take a right on Spinnaker Drive and stay on Spinnaker until it dead ends, parking is on the right. The visitor center and Island Packers are located on the right—look for the signs.

*Maps:* For a free map of the Channel Islands, write to the superintendent at the address listed below. For a topographic map, ask for Channel Islands National Park from the USGS.

*Who to contact:* Channel Islands National Park, 1901 Spinnaker Drive, Ventura, CA 93001; (805) 658-5730.

*Trail notes:* Anacapa is the closest island to the mainland and is composed of three small islets inaccessible from each other except by boat. The Loop Trail is located on East Anacapa, along with the camping area, a ranger station and a small museum. There is no fresh water on the island, so bring all that you will need. Landing on the island is a dramatic and exhausting experience, as you are dropped off at the base of a 154-step iron stairway that leads you up the steep cliff to the island's crest and camping area. The trail loops in a figure-eight and gives you a good tour of the island's natural history. Pick up the available pamphlet which describes the most significant features of the island. Views are inspiring and picnic spots abound. Please stay on the trail at all times when hiking—the terrain is fragile and easily damaged. Time your visit to coincide with two significant natural events if you can. In February and March, huge gray whales may be viewed migrating south to their mating and calving sanctuaries near Baja. In the early spring, the giant coreopsis, commonly referred to as the "tree sunflower," bursts into bloom. When you consider that the plants grow as tall as ten feet, this is indeed a stunning spectacle. West Anacapa has been designated a Research Natural Area to protect nesting and endangered brown pelicans, and is closed to public access.

# 4. SANTA BARBARA ISLAND TRAILS

**5.5 mi/1.0 day**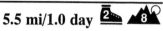

**Reference:** On Santa Barbara Island, part of the Channel Islands, south of Santa Barbara; map I3, grid h9.

**User groups:** Hikers only. Horses, mountain bikes and dogs are not allowed. No wheelchair facilities.

**Permits:** A free camping permit is needed if you wish to stay overnight. Contact the National Park Service at (805) 658-5711. No day-use permit is needed. Island Packers runs the boat to and from the island, call (805) 642-1393. A day-use roundtrip boat ride is $49; if you wish to camp, the fee is $75. The boat ride requires 3.5 hours each way.

**Directions:** The Channel Islands Visitor Center and Island Packers are located adjacent to each other. From Highway 101, north of Los Angeles and south of Santa Barbara, take the Seward Harbor Boulevard exit and head south on Harbor Boulevard (Harbor Boulevard is located off Seward on the ocean side of 101). Take a right on Spinnaker Drive and stay on Spinnaker until it dead ends, parking is on the right. The visitor center and Island Packers are located on the right—look for the signs.

**Maps:** For a free map of the Channel Islands, write to the superintendent at the address listed below. For a topographic map, ask for Channel Islands National Park from the USGS.

**Who to contact:** Channel Islands National Park, 1901 Spinnaker Drive, Ventura, CA 93001; (805) 658-5730.

**Trail notes:** Santa Barbara is the smallest of the Channel Islands with one square mile of land surface. Bird watchers will thrill to the proliferation of seabirds—some quite rare. Webster Point on the island is well known as a favorite beach for sea lions and elephant seals. There are 5.5 miles of trails on the island, all beginning and ending at the campground and visitor center. Canyon View Self-Guided Nature Trail is a great place to begin your exploration. Be sure to pick up a Santa Barbara Island Trail booklet which will highlight most of the island's interesting features. If camping, you will need to bring plenty of water, as there is none on the island. Plan on one gallon per person, per day.

**Special note:** There are no shade trees anywhere, so pack plenty of sunscreen and a good hat.

## Leave No Trace Tips

### Camp with care

- Choose a pre-existing, legal site. Restrict activities to areas where vegetation is compacted or absent.

- Camp at least 75 steps (200 feet) from lakes, streams and trails.

- Always choose sites that will not be damaged by your stay.

- Preserve the feeling of solitude by selecting camps that are out of view when possible.

- Do not construct structures or furniture or dig trenches.

SO-CAL MAP ........................ see page 662
adjoining maps
NORTH (H4) ......................... see page 628
EAST (I5) .............................. see page 696
SOUTH ................................. no map
WEST (I3) ............................ see page 666

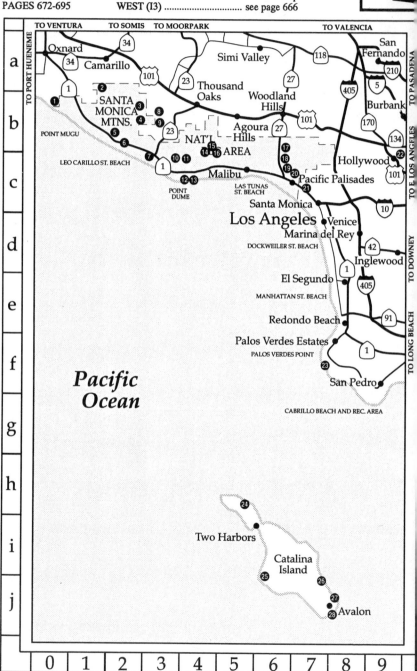

**Map I4 featuring:** Point Mugu State Park, Santa Monica Mountains National Recreation Area, Leo Carrillo State Beach, Solstice Canyon, Malibu Creek State Park, Topanga State Park, Will Rogers State Historic Park, Temescal Canyon, Palos Verdes Peninsula, Catalina Island

## 1. MUGU PEAK LOOP
**11.0 mi/6.0 hrs**

*Reference:* **Point Mugu State Park, east of Oxnard on Highway 1; map I4, grid b0.**

*User groups:* Hikers and horses. Mountain bikes are allowed on fire roads only. No dogs are allowed. No wheelchair facilities.

*Permits:* No permits are needed. If you wish to stay overnight at the La Jolla Valley Walk-in Camp, you don't need reservations, but you do need to self-register at the Ray Miller Trailhead before heading out.

*Directions:* From Santa Monica, drive approximately 30 miles north on Highway 1 (21 miles from where Malibu Canyon Road joins Highway 1 if you are coming from the Ventura Freeway or the San Fernando Valley side) to the turnoff to Ray Miller Trailhead, located opposite Thornhill Broome Beach Campground and approximately 1.5 miles up the coast from the Big Sycamore Canyon and Sycamore Canyon Campground turnoff. Head inland to the parking area. The trailhead is located near an interpretive display and the signed La Jolla Canyon Trail. To the right is the La Jolla Ridge Trail.

*Maps:* For a topographic map, ask for Point Mugu from the USGS. Tom Harrison Cartography publishes an excellent map of the area. Call (415) 456-7940 and ask for the trail map of the Santa Monica Mountains West. The cost is $5.95 plus tax and shipping.

*Who to contact:* California Department of Parks and Recreation, 1925 Las Virgenes Road, Calabasas, CA 91302; (818) 880-0350 or for basic trails and campground information contact Mountain Parks Information, (800) 533-PARK. You can also contact the Santa Monica Mountains National Recreation Area, 30401 Agoura Road, Suite 100, Agoura Hills, CA 91301; (818) 597-9192, extension 201. Ask for the free, quarterly Santa Monica National Recreation Area publication that lists guided hikes and other events being held in the area.

*Trail notes:* This day-hike offers sweeping views of the coastline and, if the weather cooperates, the distant Channel Islands. The best time to attempt the route is from October to June. The wildflowers in the spring are outstanding. Begin hiking up the La Jolla Ridge Trail to the Overlook Trail (2.5 miles). Turn left and hike to the junction with Wood Canyon Trail, leading to Deer Junction to the right and the La Jolla Valley Trail to the left, and descending to La Jolla Valley Walk-in Camp, which is five miles from the trailhead. Head left, past the camps (there are restrooms, picnic tables and potable water here) and towards the distant La Jolla Peak. You will soon find yourself on the Loop Trail which will take you to the Mugu Peak Trail (now seven miles in). Stay on the Mugu Peak Trail around Mugu Peak—ignore the side trails and work on contouring around the peak to the southwest, then south. Views out to the Pacific Ocean here are stunning. Continue contouring around Mugu Peak to the east where the trail will come to a junction with the Loop Trail again. Head right and hike until reaching the La Jolla Canyon Trail at 10 miles. Turn right again and hike down the La Jolla Canyon Trail to the parking area. Wildfires during the fall of 1993 swept through a large section of the Santa Monica National Recreation Area. Vegetation will regrow with time, as fire is a natural part of these mountains. Wildflowers should be especially beautiful as a part of the regrowth process. Keep in mind that trail signs and other developed facilities along many of the trails in the area are being rebuilt and replaced as quickly as money allows, but may not be in place by the time you decide to "hit the trail." Common sense, alert eyes, a good map and good navigational abilities will aid you tremendously in staying on the "right" path.

---

## 2. BONEY MOUNTAIN STATE WILDERNESS LOOP

10.0 mi/5.0 hrs

*Reference:* **Point Mugu State Park west of Malibu, east of Oxnard on Highway 1; map I4, grid a1.**

*User groups:* Hikers and horses. Mountain bikes are allowed on fire roads only. No dogs are allowed. No wheelchair facilities.

*Permits:* No permits are needed.

*Directions:* From Thousand Oaks, head west on Highway 101 and exit onto Wendy Drive in Newbury Park. Drive south on Wendy Drive until it dead ends at Potrero Road. Turn right on Potrero and drive a half mile to Reino Road and bear left, still on Potrero Road, and drive another four-tenths of a mile to Rancho Sierra Vista's entrance, located on the south side of the road. Park inside the entrance in the parking area. From here, pass through the locked vehicle gate walking up the main road. It's a three-mile hike down this service road to the trailhead located at Danielson Multi-Use Area which serves hikers, equestrians, campers and backpackers. There are restrooms, shaded picnic areas, a pay phone and potable water—fill up here because the trail can be hot and dry.

*Maps:* For topographic maps, ask for Newbury Park and Triunfo Pass from the USGS. Tom Harrison Cartography publishes an excellent map of the area. Call (415) 456-7940 and ask for the trail map of the Santa Monica Mountains West. The cost is $5.95 plus tax and shipping.

*Who to contact:* California Department of Parks and Recreation, 1925 Las Virgenes Road, Calabasas, CA 91302; (818) 880-0350 or for basic trails and campground information contact Mountain Parks Information, (800) 533-PARK. You can also contact the Santa Monica Mountains National Recreation Area, 30401 Agoura Road, Suite 100, Agoura Hills, CA 91301; (818) 597-9192, extension 201. Ask for the free, quarterly Santa Monica National Recreation Area publication that lists guided hikes and other events being held in the recreation area.

*Trail notes:* Until the unfinished section of the Backbone Trail within the Old Boney Wilderness is completed, this loop remains the best way to experience the heart of this unique urban wilderness area. From the Danielson Multi-Use Area, head east and sharply uphill on the Blue Canyon Trail under shade until the intersection with the Old Boney Trail. Head left and keep climbing, now in open and hot chaparral onto the ridge. The trail continues to climb up and down with views into Big Sycamore Canyon and, on a clear day, the distant Channel Islands. Once on Boney Mountain's 1820-foot summit, head right on the trail that descends beneath the rock outcrops on Boney's north flank, a favorite playground for climbers. At a beautiful monument to Richard Danielson, a generous park donor, look for a trail that is descending from the mountain and begin hiking down a twisting route to a sharp turn in the trail that contours around upper Big Sycamore Canyon's stream. There is a side trail here which is worth detouring onto if the stream is running well, as there are a number of pretty cascades to be viewed in the ravine. From the sharp turn, still on the Old Boney Trail, keep hiking to a Y-like junction and head right and up a trail that climbs to the top of the ridge with views of Big Sycamore Canyon to the left and open grasslands of Rancho Sierra Vista (where you left your car) on the right. Pick a trail that looks appealing and head back to your car—approximately one mile distant. The summer months can be rather unpleasant and dry—the best months to hike are November through June. Although mountain bikes are allowed on fire roads in the rest of the park, they are not allowed here in keeping with the wilderness designation.

*Special note:* See hike number 1, this chapter, for information on changes to this area from the wildfires of fall 1993.

---

## 3. THE GROTTO                   3.5 mi/2.0 hrs

*Reference:* **Circle X Ranch, east of Oxnard on Highway 1; map I4, grid b2.**
*User groups:* **Hikers and horses. No dogs or mountain bikes are allowed. No wheelchair facilities.**
*Permits:* **No permits are needed. If you wish to camp overnight at the Happy Hollow Campground, you will need reservations; call (818) 597-9192, extension 201; $6 per site, per night.**
*Directions:* **From Santa Monica, drive north on Highway 1 for approximately 28 miles to Yerba Buena Road, just past Mulholland Highway. Turn right on Yerba Buena Road and drive five miles to Circle X Ranch. Park near the entrance and the park headquarters. The trailhead begins at the group camping area near the entrance, off the dirt road leading down towards Happy Hollow Campground.**
*Maps:* **For a topographic map, ask for Triunfo Pass from the USGS. Tom Harrison Cartography publishes an excellent map of the area. Call (415) 456-7940 and ask for the trail map of the Santa Monica Mountains West. The cost is $5.95 plus tax and shipping.**
*Who to contact:* **Santa Monica Mountains National Recreation Area, 30401 Agoura Road, Suite 100, Agoura Hills, CA 91301; (818) 597-9192, extension 201. Ask for the free, quarterly Santa Monica National Recreation Area publication that lists guided hikes and other events being held in the recreation area.**
*Trail notes:* **If you can only visit two trails in the Santa Monica Mountains, make this one of them and the Mishe Mokwa the other (see hike number 4). The Grotto is a natural playground that inspires the imagination with a jumble of huge boulders, rocky ledges, sheer volcanic walls, spooky hollows, and even a dark cave through which the sounds of a subterranean stream can be heard trickling. This place is an absolute hoot! To get here, hike**

down the dirt road leading to Happy Hollow Campground for several hundred yards to a trail branching south from the group camping area. Head down the trail, past a 30-foot trickle that qualifies as a small waterfall in the winter. Keep hiking down towards Happy Hollow Campground. At the campground, head left and then right (south) along a brook which leads up to the Grotto. Return the way you came, remembering it is uphill all the way back.

*Special note:* See hike number 1, this chapter, for information on changes to this area from the wildfires of fall 1993.

---

## 4. MISHE MOKWA TRAIL     7.0 mi/3.0 hrs

*Reference:* **Circle X Ranch, east of Oxnard on Highway 1; map I4, grid b2.**

*User groups:* Hikers and horses. Mountain bikes are allowed on fire roads only. No dogs are allowed. No wheelchair facilities.

*Permits:* No permits are needed. If you wish to camp overnight at the backcountry backpack site, you will need reservations; call (818) 597-9192, extension 201.

*Directions:* From Santa Monica, drive north on Highway 1 for approximately 28 miles to Yerba Buena Road, just past Mulholland Highway. Turn right on Yerba Buena Road and drive five miles to Circle X Ranch. From the entrance and the park headquarters, continue driving another mile to a signed trailhead on your left and a parking lot.

*Maps:* For a topographic map, ask for Triunfo Pass from the USGS. Tom Harrison Cartography publishes an excellent map of the area. Call (415) 456-7940 and ask for the trail map of the Santa Monica Mountains West. The cost is $5.95 plus tax and shipping.

*Who to contact:* Santa Monica Mountains National Recreation Area, 30401 Agoura Road, Suite 100, Agoura Hills, CA 91301; (818) 597-9192, extension 201. Ask for the free, quarterly Santa Monica National Recreation Area publication that lists guided hikes and other events being held in the recreation area.

*Trail notes:* If you can only visit two trails in the Santa Monica Mountains, make this one of them and Grotto Trail the other (see hike number 3). The Mishe Mokwa Trail leads to Sandstone Peak, the destination of choice for "peak baggers" as it is the highest point in the Santa Monica Mountain Range, 3,111 feet. Plan your picnic/day-hike excursion for late fall or early winter when the skies are predictably clearer than any other time of the year. From the signed trailhead, hike up the fire road to a signed junction with the Mishe Mokwa Trail. Hike up the trail and a ridge before descending into Carlisle Canyon—check out the volcanic rock formations including Balanced Rock. The trail will also pass by another unique rock formation, Split Rock. Be sure to hike between the sections of Split Rock—hey, don't mess with tradition! At Split Rock there is a year-round stream, a spring, and a shaded camp. If you are planning a picnic, this is as good a spot as any. From Split Rock continue hiking to the junction with the Backbone Trail. Head east on the trail (actually a fire road), past Boney Peak and up to a spur trail leading to Sandstone Peak. We're not sure where the name Sandstone comes from as the rock is actually volcanic. Sign the summit register, spend some time marveling at the expanse of wild lands and urban sprawl spreading out beneath your feet, then return to the fire road and descend a mile to return.

*Special note:* See hike number 1, this chapter, for information on changes to this area from the wildfires of fall 1993.

## 5. SYCAMORE CANYON LOOP  8.0 mi/4.0 hrs

*Reference:* **In Point Mugu State Park west of Malibu, east of Oxnard on Highway 1; map I4, grid b2.**

*User groups:* Hikers and horses. Mountain bikes are allowed on fire roads only. No dogs are allowed. No wheelchair facilities.

*Permits:* No permits are needed.

*Directions:* From Oxnard, drive 16 miles south on Highway 1, or from Santa Monica drive 32 miles west on Highway 1, to the entrance for Sycamore Canyon Campground. Day-use parking inside the campground is available for a fee. You may park for free at the dirt lot located just outside the entrance, alongside Highway 1.

*Maps:* For a topographic map, ask for Point Mugu from the USGS. Tom Harrison Cartography publishes an excellent map of the area. Call (415) 456-7940 and ask for the trail map of the Santa Monica Mountains West. The cost is $5.95 plus tax and shipping.

*Who to contact:* California Department of Parks and Recreation, 1925 Las Virgenes Road, Calabasas, CA 91302; (818) 880-0350 or for basic trails and campground information contact Mountain Parks Information, (800) 533-PARK. You can also contact the Santa Monica Mountains National Recreation Area, 30401 Agoura Road, Suite 100, Agoura Hills, CA 91301; (818) 597-9192, extension 201. Ask for the free, quarterly Santa Monica National Recreation Area publication that lists guided hikes and other events being held in the recreation area.

*Trail notes:* A park brochure proudly proclaims the sycamores in Sycamore Canyon to be the "finest example of sycamore savanna in the State..." Fair enough. Whether they are or not, there is no disputing the feeling of romance and awe when hiking amid these trees, which reach heights of nearly 80 feet. In early morning, it is possible to see deer, coyote and, if you are very alert and stealthy, bobcat. From the campground, begin hiking up Sycamore Canyon on the Sycamore Canyon Trail. Pass by the Serrano Canyon Trail junction to your right at one mile and keep hiking until you reach the Wood Canyon Junction and the Wood Canyon Trail at three miles. Head left to Deer Camp Junction where you will find picnic tables and potable water—a good spot for a picnic or lengthy rest, about four miles from the trailhead. From Deer Camp, head south and up the ridge on the Wood Canyon Trail towards La Jolla Camp and La Jolla Canyon at five miles. At the junction with Overlook Trail, you will turn south again and head back to Sycamore Canyon and a fire road seven-and-a-half miles from the start that leads you back to the parking area one-half mile away. Mountain bikes use the fire roads, so be alert and courteous.

*Special note:* See hike number 1, this chapter, for information on changes to this area from the wildfires of fall 1993.

## 6. SCENIC TRAIL    2.6 mi/2.0 hrs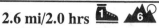

*Reference:* **In Point Mugu State Park west of Malibu, east of Oxnard on Highway 1; map I4, grid b2.**

*User groups:* Hikers and horses. Mountain bikes are allowed on fire roads only. No dogs are allowed. No wheelchair facilities.

*Permits:* No permits are needed.

*Directions:* From Oxnard, drive 16 miles south on Highway 1, or from Santa Monica drive 32 miles west on Highway 1, to the entrance for Sycamore Canyon Campground. Day-use parking inside the campground is available for a $6 per car parking fee. You may park for free at the dirt lot located just outside the entrance, alongside Highway 1.

*Maps:* For a topographic map, ask for Point Mugu from the USGS. Tom Harrison Cartography publishes an excellent map of the area. Call (415) 456-7940 and ask for the trail map of the Santa Monica Mountains West. The cost is $5.95 plus tax and shipping.

*Who to contact:* California Department of Parks and Recreation, 1925 Las Virgenes Road, Calabasas, CA 91302; (818) 880-0350 or for basic trails and campground information contact Mountain Parks Information, (800) 533-PARK. You can also contact the Santa Monica Mountains National Recreation Area, 30401 Agoura Road, Suite 100, Agoura Hills, CA 91301; (818) 597-9192, extension 201. Ask for the free, quarterly Santa Monica National Recreation Area publication that lists guided hikes and other events being held in the recreation area.

*Trail notes:* This is an excellent early morning or late afternoon hike up to an overlook that offers super sunset views as well as a bird's-eye perspective of the churning ocean surf and turquoise blue shallows below. From just north of the campground and just beyond a vehicle gate, begin hiking up the Scenic Trail to the left. The trail will soon lead you to a pretty saddle. The best views are to be found by hiking southeast along the narrow ridge. To return, head down the fire road that leads down the ridge to Big Sycamore Canyon and then to Sycamore Canyon Campground and your car. Mountain bikes use the fire road so be alert and be courteous.

*Special note:* See hike number 1, this chapter, for information on changes to this area from the wildfires of fall 1993.

## 7. NICHOLAS FLAT TRAIL    7.0 mi/3.0 hrs

*Reference:* **Leo Carrillo State Beach, east of Oxnard on Highway 1; map I4, grid c3.**

*User groups:* Hikers and horses. No dogs or mountain bikes are allowed. No wheelchair facilities.

*Permits:* No permits are needed.

*Directions:* From Santa Monica, drive north on Highway 1 for approximately 25 miles to Leo Carrillo State Beach. Free parking is available along the Pacific Coast Highway. Parking is also available for $6 in the park's day-use area. The trailhead for Nicholas Flat is located just a short jaunt beyond the park entry kiosk, opposite the day-use area.

*Maps:* For a topographic map, ask for Triunfo Pass from the USGS. Tom Harrison Cartography publishes an excellent map of the area. Call (415) 456-

7940 and ask for the trail map of the Santa Monica Mountains West. The cost is $5.95 plus tax and shipping.

***Who to contact:*** California Department of Parks and Recreation, 1925 Las Virgenes Road, Calabasas, CA 91302; (818) 880-0350. For basic trails and campground information, contact Mountain Parks Information, (800) 533-PARK. You can also contact the Santa Monica Mountains National Recreation Area, 30401 Agoura Road, Suite 100, Agoura Hills, CA 91301; (818) 597-9192, extension 201. Ask for the free, quarterly Santa Monica National Recreation Area publication that lists guided hikes and other events being held in the recreation area.

***Trail notes:*** Get an early start on the day if you are hiking this trail, as there is little shade—noon sun can bake even the most hardy hiker into a shriveled raisin by day's end. Spring wildflowers are pretty along this trail, although because of the sun's intensity, are short lived. Hike up the Nicholas Flat Trail, staying to the left when it branches. After a few switchbacks and some moderate climbing, the trail will meet the alternate trail that branched off to the right earlier. There is also a spur trail leading to a super viewpoint from which you can watch for migrating whales during the winter—pack along a pair of powerful binoculars or a spotting scope. Keep on hiking up on Nicholas Flat, along the ridgeline to Nicholas Flat and a pleasant picnic spot complete with a pond. Retrace your steps to the parking area.

***Special note:*** See hike number 1, this chapter, for information on changes to this area from the wildfires of fall 1993.

---

# 8. MALIBU SPRINGS     1.0 mi/0.5 hrs

***Reference:*** **East of Oxnard, west of Santa Monica, north of Highway 1 off Mulholland Drive; map I4, grid b3.**

***User groups:*** Hikers and horses. No dogs or mountain bikes are allowed. No wheelchair facilities.

***Permits:*** No permits are needed.

***Directions:*** From Santa Monica, drive north on Highway 1 to Mulholland Highway and turn right. Drive on Mulholland Highway to mile marker 3.7, located on the left at a hairpin turn—if you pass Little Sycamore Canyon Road on your left, you have driven too far. Parking is along the shoulder. There is limited space, room for only two or three vehicles.

***Maps:*** For a topographic map, ask for Triunfo Pass from the USGS. Tom Harrison Cartography publishes an excellent map of the area. Call (415) 456-7940 and ask for the trail map of the Santa Monica Mountains West. The cost is $5.95 plus tax and shipping.

***Who to contact:*** Santa Monica Mountains National Recreation Area, 30401 Agoura Road, Suite 100, Agoura Hills, CA 91301; (818) 597-9192, extension 201. Special note—ask for the free, quarterly Santa Monica National Recreation Area publication that lists guided hikes and other events being held in the recreation area.

***Trail notes:*** This short but very scenic and peaceful dirt road offers those trapped in an urban state of mind a few moments of natural wonder with which to restore themselves—a perfect lunch-break respite. Volcanic rock parapets, a quiet meadow, the gurgle of a brook and the sound of wind whispering through the branches of oak and sycamore should bring a smile to even the most serious frown. From the parking area, jump the fence and head up a dirt road through a gorge. There are remains of a number of cabins along the way. Keep a sharp eye out for poison oak, which abounds. The road disappears and you can stop wandering when you have a mind to. Retrace your steps to the road and your awaiting car.

*Special note:* See hike number 1, this chapter, for information on changes to this area from the wildfires of fall 1993.

## 9. ARROYO SEQUIT PARK  1.2 mi/0.5 hr

*Reference:* **East of Oxnard, west of Santa Monica, north of Highway 1 off Mulholland Drive; map I4, grid b3.**

*User groups:* Hikers, horses, dogs and mountain bikes. No wheelchair facilities.

*Permits:* No permits are needed. The park is open daily 8 a.m. to sunset.

*Directions:* From Santa Monica, drive north on Highway 1 to Mulholland Highway and turn right. Drive on Mulholland Highway to mile marker 5.6 or mailbox number 34138 and the turnoff located to your right—if you pass Little Sycamore Canyon Road on your left, you have driven too far. Parking is along the shoulder or in the driveway access, as long as you do not block the gate.

*Maps:* For a topographic map, ask for Triunfo Pass from the USGS. Tom Harrison Cartography publishes an excellent map of the area. Call (415) 456-7940 and ask for the trail map of the Santa Monica Mountains West. The cost is $5.95 plus tax and shipping.

*Who to contact:* Santa Monica Mountains National Recreation Area, 30401 Agoura Road, Suite 100, Agoura Hills, CA 91301; (818) 597-9192, extension 201. Ask for the free, quarterly Santa Monica National Recreation Area publication that lists guided hikes and other events being held in the recreation area.

*Trail notes:* The trails are mostly unmarked in this quaint park—wander at will. A good trail for an introduction is a marked one that heads off to the right from the shaded picnic area across a meadow and then to the rim of Arroyo Sequit Canyon. If the water is running well, a number of routes lead down into the cool canyon and beside the stream.

*Special note:* See hike number 1, this chapter, for information on changes to this area from the wildfires of fall 1993.

## 10. CHARMLEE NATURAL  3.0 mi/1.5 hrs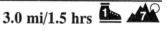
## AREA COUNTY PARK

*Reference:* **East of Oxnard, west of Santa Monica, north of Highway 1 near Malibu; map I4, grid c3.**

*User groups:* Hikers, horses and leashed dogs. No mountain bikes are allowed. No wheelchair facilities.

*Permits:* No permits are needed. A parking fee of $3 is collected on weekends and holidays.

*Directions:* From Santa Monica, drive north on Highway 1 to Malibu and then continue driving approximately another 12 miles to Encinal Canyon Road on the right. Turn right and drive 4.5 miles to the entrance to Charmlee Natural Area County Park. Park in the designated parking area.

*Maps:* For a topographic map, ask for Triunfo Pass from the USGS. Tom

Harrison Cartography publishes an excellent map of the area. Call (415) 456-7940 and ask for the trail map of the Santa Monica Mountains West. The cost is $5.95 plus tax and shipping.

***Who to contact:*** City of Malibu Parks and Recreation Department, 2577 Encinal Road, Malibu, CA 90265; (310) 457-7247.

***Trail notes:*** There are a number of trails worth wandering on in Charmlee. Two noteworthy trails are the Ocean Vista Trail and the Botany Trail. Both trails begin at the picnic area near the Nature Center. (The Nature Center has interpretive displays and small live animals, and is open on weekends.) Be sure to pick up a free brochure that offers interpretive information, which is useful when hiking the Botany Trail. The Ocean Vista Trail leads to an "official" rocky Ocean Overlook with outstanding views of, you guessed it, the ocean. From the picnic area, head out on a dirt road through an oak woodland. At a junction with another fire road, head downhill, beside a meadow and then out to views of the ocean, the best being at the Ocean Overlook. Retrace your steps when ready. Michael loves to picnic and notes that just west of the Overlook are several super picnicking spots tucked in among the oaks, near a small reservoir. In the spring, the wildflowers are truly stunning. This is also a great place to visit with the family on a cool, clear winter's day for ocean viewing and, perhaps, whale watching.

---

# 11. ZUMA CANYON to ZUMA RIDGE TRAIL LOOP

8.3 mi/7.0 hrs

***Reference:*** East of Oxnard, west of Santa Monica, north of Highway 1 near Malibu; map I4, grid c4.

***User groups:*** Hikers only. Horses and mountain bikes are allowed on the Zuma Ridge Trail only. No dogs are allowed. No wheelchair facilities.

***Permits:*** No permits are needed.

***Directions:*** From Santa Monica, drive north on Highway 1 for approximately 26 miles to just past Zuma Beach County Park. Turn right onto Busch Drive and head approximately one mile to the road's end and an informal dirt parking area.

***Maps:*** For a topographic map, ask for Point Dume from the USGS. Tom Harrison Cartography publishes an excellent map of the area. Call (415) 456-7940 and ask for the trail map of the Santa Monica Mountains Central. The cost is $5.95 plus tax and shipping.

***Who to contact:*** Santa Monica Mountains National Recreation Area, 30401 Agoura Road, Suite 100, Agoura Hills, CA 91301; (818) 597-9192, extension 201. Ask for the free, quarterly Santa Monica National Recreation Area publication that lists guided hikes and other events being held in the recreation area.

***Trail notes:*** From the trailhead and the closed gate in front of the fire road, begin hiking up the fire road for about 2.5 miles to Zuma Edison Road. Then head downhill for about 2.5 miles (what goes up must come down) to the trail's lowest point at Zuma Creek. Turn right at this point and begin boulder-hopping in earnest. You are officially off-trail, dealing with poison oak and pushing through underbrush at times. It's not as bad as it sounds, but it is somewhat rugged. Keep a sharp eye out for rattlesnakes. You will follow this boulder-strewn route for about 1.5 miles until you arrive at a man-made dam, built in the early 1900s during ranching days. From here, it is one-eighth of a mile to the Zuma Canyon Trail—there's no sign, but it is clearly a trail. After crossing Zuma Creek about four times, you will arrive at a trail junction with the Zuma Loop Trail and Zuma Canyon Trail—take the Zuma Loop back to the parking area, about 1.5 miles away. The route is best traveled between October and June, although use caution during winter rains as the runoff can be quite heavy and potentially dangerous. If you are seeking a family-oriented option, we would recommend the Zuma Canyon Trail out-and-back from a slightly different trailhead (to make things easier). From Busch Drive, turn right onto Rainsford Drive and then left onto Bonshall Drive. Head to the end of the road, where it becomes dirt, and park at the trailhead. The Zuma Canyon trail is flat and crosses Zuma Creek about seven times. It is a three-mile roundtrip jaunt. Use caution if the stream is running full, as the crossings may be hazardous.

## 12. POINT DUME TRAIL     1.0 mi/0.5 hr

*Reference:* **East of Oxnard, west of Santa Monica, south of Highway 1 near Malibu; map I4, grid c4.**

*User groups:* Hikers and horses. No mountain bikes or dogs are allowed. No wheelchair facilities.

*Permits:* No permits are needed.

*Directions:* From Santa Monica, drive north on Highway 1 for approximately 25 miles to just before Zuma Beach County Park. Turn left, towards the ocean on Westward Beach Road and follow it to the parking area. A $6 entrance fee is charged.

*Maps:* For a topographic map, ask for Point Dume from the USGS. Tom Harrison Cartography publishes an excellent map of the area. Call (415) 456-7940 and ask for the trail map of the Santa Monica Mountains Central. The cost is $5.95 plus tax and shipping.

*Who to contact:* Santa Monica Mountains National Recreation Area, 30401 Agoura Road, Suite 100, Agoura Hills, CA 91301; (818) 597-9192, extension 201. Ask for the free, quarterly Santa Monica National Recreation Area publication that lists guided hikes and other events being held in the recreation area.

*Trail notes:* Plan on hiking this trail at low tide as passage is typically easier—no worries about rogue waves. Zuma Beach is well known to Southern Californians as one of Los Angeles County's finest beaches. During the winter months, Point Dume draws many visitors since the lookout area is a super place from which to spot migrating California gray whales—their migration route passes very close to shore here. From the parking area, hike down the coast along Westward Beach. Before long you will see a distinct and well-traveled path leading through vegetation up towards the point. Once at the lookout, retrace your steps back to the parking area or take a short out-and-back visit down to secluded Paradise Cove, approximately another mile of walking down the coast.

## 13. SOLSTICE CANYON TRAIL   6.0 mi/3.0 hrs

*Reference:* East of Oxnard, west of Santa Monica, north of Highway 1 near
　　Malibu; map I4, grid c4.

*User groups:* Hikers and horses. No mountain bikes or dogs are allowed. No
　　wheelchair facilities.

*Permits:* No permits are needed. A $5 parking fee is charged.

*Directions:* From Santa Monica, drive north on Highway 1 for approximately
　　17 miles to Corral Canyon Road, about 3.5 miles past Malibu Canyon Road.
　　Drive up Corral Canyon Road for two-tenths of a mile, to the entrance to
　　Solstice Canyon Park, located at the first bend. Drive to the Foundation
　　Office and park at the Visitor Center. The trailhead is located up the road near
　　a small house, which is headquarters for the park.

*Maps:* For topographic maps, ask for Point Dume and Malibu Beach from the
　　USGS. Tom Harrison Cartography publishes an excellent map of the area.
　　Call (415) 456-7940 and ask for the trail map of the Santa Monica Mountains
　　Central. The cost is $5.95 plus tax and shipping.

*Who to contact:* Santa Monica Mountains Conservancy, 3800 Solstice Canyon
　　Road, Malibu, CA 90265; (310) 456-5046. Call the Visitor Center direct at
　　(310) 456-7154.

*Trail notes:* Begin hiking on the TRW Trail up past some former TRW
　　buildings, now administrative buildings for the Santa Monica Mountains
　　Conservancy, and into Solstice Canyon. Turn right onto Old Solstice Road
　　and hike past Fern Grotto Picnic Area and then up to Tropical Terrace—a
　　man-made paradise of tropical plants gone wild, an old dam, a waterfall, a
　　fountain, and more. Plan to linger a while. After soaking in the feeling of
　　tranquility, you can either turn around and head back the way you came or
　　hike off onto the Sostomo Trail up to Sostomo Overlook for super views of
　　Point Dume, Solstice Canyon, and the ocean beyond. This spur trail is not
　　maintained and can get quite brushy. Watch your step and stay alert for
　　rattlesnakes. Head back towards the ocean, briefly rejoining Old Solstice
　　Road and then hiking past El Asisar Picnic Area and finally arriving at the
　　trailhead and your car.

*Special note:* See hike number 1, this chapter, for information on changes to this
　　area from the wildfires of fall 1993.

## 14. BACKBONE TRAIL   14.0 mi/6.0 hrs
## from TAPIA COUNTY PARK

*Reference:* East of Oxnard, west of Santa Monica, north of Highway 1 near
　　Malibu; map I4, grid c4.

*User groups:* Hikers, mountain bikes and horses. No dogs are allowed. No
　　wheelchair facilities.

*Permits:* No permits are needed.

*Directions:* From Santa Monica, drive north on Highway 1 for approximately
　　13.5 miles to Malibu Canyon Road. Then drive another five miles up the road
　　to Tapia County Park, situated just south of Malibu Creek State Park. From
　　the parking area, walk back out to Malibu Canyon Road and walk south
　　towards the bridge. Cross the bridge, using extreme caution because of the
　　traffic, and continue to the trailhead a few hundred yards beyond the bridge.

*Maps:* For a topographic map, ask for Malibu Beach from the USGS. Tom Harrison Cartography publishes an excellent map of the area. Call (415) 456-7940 and ask for the trail map of the Santa Monica Mountains Central. The cost is $5.95 plus tax and shipping.

*Who to contact:* California Department of Parks and Recreation, 1925 Las Virgenes Road, Calabasas, CA 91302; (818) 880-0350. For basic trails and campground information, contact Mountain Parks Information, (800) 533-PARK. You can also contact the Santa Monica Mountains National Recreation Area, 30401 Agoura Road, Suite 100, Agoura Hills, CA 91301; (818) 597-9192, extension 201. Ask for the free, quarterly Santa Monica National Recreation Area publication that lists guided hikes and other events being held in the recreation area.

*Trail notes:* This hike offers perhaps the best chance to tour the majority of Malibu Creek State Park in one fell swoop. The upper Backbone Trail offers dramatic views along the ridgeline heading towards Castro Crest while the lower route of the Backbone Trail follows the wandering whims of Malibu Creek and offers a more subtle appeal. Begin hiking on the Mesa Park Motorway fire road over the ridgelines, past outstanding fossil beds and nifty sandstone formations to the paved Castro Motorway or Corral Canyon Road. Continue on the paved route for another mile to an intersection with the Bulldog Motorway. The Backbone Trail itself continues on towards Point Mugu (several sections remain uncompleted but officials hope to link the trail within the next year). Head back via the Bulldog Motorway, descending into Triunfo Canyon. Turn right on Twentieth Century Road—*MASH* TV series fans will recognize the area as that of the set. Hike past Century Lake, now on High Road, then go right on Crags Road through the day use parking area and past the campground. Head off on a dirt road to the Group Camp where you will find the Tapia Spur Trail to guide you over a low ridge to Tapia County Park and your nearby car.

*Special note:* See hike number 1, this chapter, for information on changes to this area from the wildfires of fall 1993.

---

# 15. ALL ACCESS / BRAILLE TRAIL

2.0 mi/1.0 hr

*Reference:* **In Malibu Creek State Park; map I4, grid c5.**

*User groups:* Hikers and wheelchairs. No mountain bikes, dogs or horses are allowed. The trail is **wheelchair-accessible**.

*Permits:* No day-use permits are required. A $5 parking fee is collected.

*Directions:* From Santa Monica, drive north on Highway 1 for approximately 13.5 miles to Malibu Canyon Road. Drive up the road to Tapia County Park and then continue for 3.5 miles to a left turn into the entrance for Malibu Creek State Park. The trailhead is located at the lower parking lot, across the road to the left.

*Maps:* For a topographic map, ask for Malibu Beach from the USGS.

*Who to contact:* California Department of Parks and Recreation, 1925 Las Virgenes Road, Calabasas, CA 91302; (818) 880-0350.

*Trail notes:* This is a brand new trail that will eventually have a more catchy name, but for now, its name says it all. The trail winds on an easy route through oak trees, with a stream nearby. There is a wonderful "geologic bench" that has been constructed using nothing but stones and rocks found within the park. Braille interpretive plaques along the trail provide an educational nature-learning opportunity for the blind.

---

## 16. COLD CREEK CANYON PRESERVE    2.0 mi/1.0 hr

*Reference:* East of Oxnard, west of Santa Monica, north of Highway 1 near Malibu; map I4, grid c5.

*User groups:* Hikers only. No dogs, horses or mountain bikes are allowed. No wheelchair facilities.

*Permits:* This trip requires an individual hiking permit which may be reserved three days or more in advance by calling the Mountains Restoration Trust at (310) 456-5625. Scheduled guided hikes do not require a permit.

*Directions:* From Santa Monica, drive north on Highway 1 for approximately 13.5 miles to Malibu Canyon Road. Turn right on Malibu Canyon Road and drive to the Malibu Canyon/Las Virgenes/Mulholland intersection. Turn right onto Mulholland Highway and drive to the Stunt Road turnoff to the right. Turn onto Stunt Road and drive approximately 3.5 miles up the hill to the signed entrance for the preserve on the left. Park in the turnout and display your permit clearly on the dashboard.

*Maps:* For a topographic map, ask for Malibu Beach from the USGS. Tom Harrison Cartography publishes an excellent map of the area. Call (415) 456-7940 and ask for the trail map of the Santa Monica Mountains Central. The cost is $5.95 plus tax and shipping.

*Who to contact:* Mountains Restoration Trust, 24955 Pacific Coast Highway, Suite C-301, Malibu, CA 90265; (310) 456-5625 or contact the Santa Monica Mountains National Recreation Area, 30401 Agoura Road, Suite 100, Agoura Hills, CA 91301; (818) 597-9192, extension 201. Ask for the free, quarterly Santa Monica National Recreation Area publication that lists guided hikes and other events being held in the recreation area.

*Trail notes:* The trail is an out-and-back proposition that will lead you into a pristine gem of a preserve. The year-round stream tributary serves as life-giving moisture to a rich diversity of plants and wildlife. If you are seeking a slice of heaven to restore your senses, this is it. Trails are beautifully maintained and open dawn to dusk. Interpretive walks are led on the second Saturday of each month (by reservation only). The docent program here is recognized as one of the state's best.

*Special note:* See hike number 1, this chapter, for information on changes to this area from the wildfires of fall 1993.

---

## 17. MUSCH RANCH TRAIL to EAGLE ROCK    6.3 mi/3.0 hrs

*Reference:* East of Malibu, west of Santa Monica, north of Highway 1 in Topanga State Park; map I4, grid b6.

*User groups:* Hikers and horses. Mountain bikes are allowed on the fire road only. No dogs are allowed. No wheelchair facilities.

*Permits:* No permits are needed. A $5 parking fee is charged.

*Directions:* From Santa Monica, drive north on Highway 1 to Topanga Canyon

Boulevard and turn right. Drive on Topanga Canyon Boulevard to Entrada Road and turn right (east). Stay on Entrada Road all the way to Topanga State Park and Trippet Ranch by making a left turn at every opportunity—watch the signs carefully and you will have no problem. The trailhead is located at the end of the parking lot.

**Maps:** For a topographic map, ask for Topanga from the USGS. Tom Harrison Cartography publishes an excellent map of the area. Call (415) 456-7940 and ask for the trail map of the Santa Monica Mountains East. The cost is $5.95 plus tax and shipping.

**Who to contact:** California Department of Parks and Recreation, 1925 Las Virgenes Road, Calabasas, CA 91302; (818) 880-0350. For basic trails and campground information, contact Mountain Parks Information, (800) 533-PARK. You can also contact the Santa Monica Mountains National Recreation Area, 30401 Agoura Road, Suite 100, Agoura Hills, CA 91301; (818) 597-9192, extension 201. Ask for the free, quarterly Santa Monica National Recreation Area publication that lists guided hikes and other events being held in the recreation area.

**Trail notes:** When Michael was guiding map and compass outings for Adventure 16 in West Los Angeles, this was one of his favorite destinations for the classes. Eagle Rock offers a breezy perch overlooking Santa Ynez Canyon and the ocean beyond. Plan your hike for early in the day or during a cool spell, as there is little shade along the entire route. Begin hiking at Trippet Ranch on the Musch Trail. After one mile of contouring a number of ravines, you will arrive at Musch Ranch, a trail campground serving through-hikers and equestrians traveling the Backbone Trail. Keep trekking on the Musch Trail up the ridge to Eagle Junction. Eagle Rock will now be obvious, standing guard over the headwaters of Santa Ynez Canyon. Turn left onto the fire road and hike up to the top of Eagle Rock. From the peak, continue east along the fire road and ridgeline to a four-way junction of fire roads. Head sharply right back on the Backbone Trail which will guide you west and under Eagle Rock again. Once at Eagle Junction, you can either select the longer route by retracing your steps down Musch Trail or turn left on the fire road for a more direct passage back to Trippet Ranch and your car.

**Special note:** See hike number 1, this chapter, for information on changes to this area from the wildfires of fall 1993.

---

# 18. BACKBONE TRAIL 9.5 mi. one way/5.0 hrs  from TRIPPET RANCH to WILL ROGERS

**Reference:** East of Malibu, west of Santa Monica, north of Highway 1; map I4, grid c6.

**User groups:** Hikers and horses. No mountain bikes or dogs are allowed. No wheelchair facilities.

**Permits:** No permits are needed. A $5 parking fee is charged.

**Directions:** This is a one-way trip that requires arranging for a car shuttle or to be dropped off at Trippet Ranch and picked up at Will Rogers State Park. From Santa Monica, drive north on Highway 1 to Topanga Canyon Boulevard and turn right. Drive on Topanga Canyon Boulevard to Entrada Road and turn right (east). Stay on Entrada Road all the way to Topanga State Park and Trippet Ranch by making a left turn at every opportunity—watch the signs carefully and you will have no problem. The trailhead is located at the end of the parking lot. To get to Will Rogers State Historic Park from Santa Monica, drive north on Highway 1 to Sunset Boulevard in Pacific Palisades and turn right. Drive up Sunset Boulevard to the signed entrance to Will Rogers State Historic Park. The park is open daily from 8 a.m. to 5 p.m.

*Maps:* For a topographic map, ask for Topanga from the USGS. Tom Harrison Cartography publishes an excellent map of the area. Call (415) 456-7940 and ask for the trail map of the Santa Monica Mountains East. The cost is $5.95 plus tax and shipping.

*Who to contact:* California Department of Parks and Recreation, 1925 Las Virgenes Road, Calabasas, CA 91302; (818) 880-0350. For basic trails and campground information, contact Mountain Parks Information, (800) 533-PARK. You can also contact the Santa Monica Mountains National Recreation Area, 30401 Agoura Road, Suite 100, Agoura Hills, CA 91301; (818) 597-9192, extension 201. Ask for the free, quarterly Santa Monica National Recreation Area publication that lists guided hikes and other events being held in the recreation area.

*Trail notes:* From the picnic area at Trippet Ranch, head southeast on the fire road heading up the hill towards Santa Ynez Fire Road. Turn left on Eagle Springs Fire Road and head to Eagle Junction, below Eagle Rock. Go right at the junction to Hub Junction. Turn right on Temescal Ridge Trail, past Cathedral Rock to another junction—this time with Backbone Trail. Head left, past Temescal Peak (worth a climb if the weather is good and sky is smog-free) and along the ridgeline to Will Rogers State Historic Park. At Inspiration Point, choose any number of trails back to the big lawn above Will Rogers' home.

*Special note:* See hike number 1, this chapter, for information on changes to this area from the wildfires of fall 1993.

## 19. SANTA YNEZ TRAIL    3.0 mi/1.5 hrs

*Reference:* **East of Malibu, west of Santa Monica, north of Highway 1 in Topanga State Park; map I4, grid c6.**

*User groups:* Hikers and horses. No mountain bikes or dogs are allowed. No wheelchair facilities.

*Permits:* No permits are needed. There is a $6 day-use fee.

*Directions:* From Santa Monica, drive north on Highway 1 to Sunset Boulevard in Pacific Palisades and turn right. Drive on Sunset Boulevard a short distance to Palisades Drive and turn left (north). Drive 2.4 miles and turn left onto Verenda de la Montura. Park at the signed trailhead.

*Maps:* For a topographic map, ask for Topanga from the USGS. Tom Harrison Cartography publishes an excellent map of the area. Call (415) 456-7940 and ask for the trail map of the Santa Monica Mountains East. The cost is $5.95 plus tax and shipping.

*Who to contact:* California Department of Parks and Recreation, 1925 Las Virgenes Road, Calabasas, CA 91302; (818) 880-0350. For basic trails and campground information, contact Mountain Parks Information, (800) 533-PARK. You can also contact the Santa Monica Mountains National Recreation Area, 30401 Agoura Road, Suite 100, Agoura Hills, CA 91301; (818) 597-9192, extension 201. Ask for the free, quarterly Santa Monica National

Recreation Area publication that lists guided hikes and other events being held in the recreation area.

*Trail notes:* We think the trailhead is a bit gauche—designer walls and an artificial waterfall complete with potted trees and silly concrete stepping stones across the stream remind us of an amusement park attempting to look like the outdoors. Still, once past the visual assault of the ridiculous, your senses will be soothed by the pleasant treadway winding along a seasonal creek lined with oak, sycamore and bay trees. Just past a gate, a sign will point the way to the 15-foot Santa Ynez Falls. During the winter and after a good rain, the falls are truly beautiful. Retrace your steps to find the parking area. Trail signs are often vandalized here, so if you don't find signs, don't panic. Just stay on the main trail.

*Special note:* See hike number 1, this chapter, for information on changes to this area from the wildfires of fall 1993.

---

## 20. TEMESCAL CANYON   3.6 mi/2.0 hrs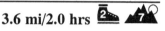
   TRAIL LOOP

*Reference:* **East of Malibu, west of Santa Monica, north of Highway 1 in Topanga State Park; map I4, grid c7.**

*User groups:* Hikers and horses. No dogs or mountain bikes are allowed. No wheelchair facilities.

*Permits:* No permits are needed, but you must sign in at the trailhead register.

*Directions:* From Santa Monica, drive north on Highway 1 to Sunset Boulevard in Pacific Palisades and turn right. Drive on Sunset Boulevard a short distance to Temescal Canyon Road and turn left (north). After a half mile, you will arrive at an open area just before the Presbyterian Conference Grounds. Park here. The trailhead is signed.

*Maps:* For a topographic map, ask for Topanga from the USGS. Tom Harrison Cartography publishes an excellent map of the area. Call (415) 456-7940 and ask for the trail map of the Santa Monica Mountains East. The cost is $5.95 plus tax and shipping.

*Who to contact:* California Department of Parks and Recreation, 1925 Las Virgenes Road, Calabasas, CA 91302; (818) 880-0350. For basic trails and campground information, contact Mountain Parks Information, (800) 533-PARK. You can also contact the Santa Monica Mountains National Recreation Area, 30401 Agoura Road, Suite 100, Agoura Hills, CA 91301; (818) 597-9192, extension 201. Ask for the free, quarterly Santa Monica National Recreation Area publication that lists guided hikes and other events being held in the recreation area.

*Trail notes:* You must sign in at the trailhead gate. The area is a religious retreat—respect the privacy and quiet of the grounds. Follow the trail signs; the route turns to a fire road alongside Temescal Creek. Follow the canyon past a small waterfall, then past a recently rebuilt bridge, and up a steep scramble and series of switchbacks to the ridgetop. The fire road levels atop the ridge and the intersection with the Temescal Ridge Trail. Continue hiking a half mile to the north to view a wind-carved sandstone outcropping named Skull Rock. Retrace your steps, past the intersection with the fire road and head down the ridgeline on the route that heads towards the ocean. The trail descends the ridge in a series of switchbacks and arrives back at the trailhead in the Presbyterian Conference Grounds.

*Special note:* See hike number 1, this chapter, for information on changes to this area from the wildfires of fall 1993.

---

# 21. WILL ROGERS STATE HISTORIC PARK

2.0 mi/1.0 hr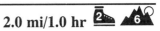

*Reference:* **East of Malibu, west of Santa Monica, north of Highway 1; map I4, grid c7.**

*User groups:* Hikers, horses and leashed dogs. Mountain bikes are allowed on fire roads only. No wheelchair facilities.

*Permits:* No permits are needed, but you must sign in at the trailhead register. A $5 parking fee is charged.

*Directions:* From Santa Monica, drive north on Highway 1 to Sunset Boulevard in Pacific Palisades and turn right. Drive on Sunset Boulevard to the signed entrance to Will Rogers State Historic Park. The park is open daily from 8 a.m. to 5 p.m.

*Maps:* For a topographic map, ask for Topanga from the USGS. Tom Harrison Cartography publishes an excellent map of the area. Call (415) 456-7940 and ask for the trail map of the Santa Monica Mountains East. The cost is $5.95 plus tax and shipping.

*Who to contact:* California Department of Parks and Recreation, 1925 Las Virgenes Road, Calabasas, CA 91302; (818) 880-0350. For basic trails and campground information, contact Mountain Parks Information, (800) 533-PARK. You can also contact the Santa Monica Mountains National Recreation Area, 30401 Agoura Road, Suite 100, Agoura Hills, CA 91301; (818) 597-9192, extension 201. Ask for the free, quarterly Santa Monica National Recreation Area publication that lists guided hikes and other events being held in the recreation area.

*Trail notes:* This two-mile trail makes a wide loop, beginning at the north end of the giant lawn next to Will Rogers' home, passing over the top of Inspiration Point with its outstanding views, and then back again. The benches on top of Inspiration Point create a nice place to rest and wonder at the vistas spreading east and southeast.

*Special note:* See hike number 1, this chapter, for information on changes to this area from the wildfires of fall 1993.

---

# 22. PALOS VERDES PENINSULA from MALAGA COVE

10.0 mi/5.0 hrs

*Reference:* **Palos Verdes Peninsula south of Santa Monica and west of Los Angeles; map I4, grid f7.**

*User groups:* Hikers and dogs. No mountain bikes or horses are allowed. No wheelchair facilities.

*Permits:* No permits are needed.

*Directions:* From Santa Monica, take the Pacific Coast Highway/Highway 1, south to Palos Verdes Turn right onto Palos Verdes Drive. Just before you reach the Malaga Cove Plaza, turn right onto Via Corta, at the stop sign. From Via Corta, turn right onto Via Arroyo and then another right into the parking lot next to Malaga Cove School. The trailhead is located on the ocean side of the parking lot.

*Maps:* For a topographic map, ask for Redondo Beach from the USGS.

*Who to contact:* There is no managing agency for this area. General information may be obtained by contacting the Palos Verdes Estates Shoreline Preserve at (310) 378-0383.

*Trail notes:* Plan on hiking this trail at low tide as passage is typically easier—no worries about rogue waves. From the school, descend the wide pathway to the beach a sign indicating that you are entering a seashore reserve where all living things are protected. Head down the coast along the rocky cliffs and clamber over a beach that resembles so many scattered cannon balls. Tidepools are everywhere and invite lingering and exploration. Just be sure to treat all tidepool residents with respect and care. Also, keep a watchful eye out for waves that can come crashing in on your peaceful bliss at any time besides low tide. The pathway follows the beach around Flat Rock Point, Bluff Cove, Rocky Point, Lunada Bay and Point Vincente. The last mile or so to Point Vincente is rough and rugged—inviting to boulder-hopping fiends, tiring to others. The lighthouse, the designated guardian of these waters since 1926, is open to guided tours by appointment.

---

## 23. MOUNT HOLLYWOOD    5.0 mi/2.0 hrs

*Reference:* **At Griffith Park, near Hollywood; map I4, grid c9.**

*User groups:* Hikers, leashed dogs and horses. Mountain bikes are allowed on fire roads only. There are no wheelchair facilities on the trails.

*Permits:* No permits are needed. The park is open from 5 a.m. to 10:30 p.m.

*Directions:* From Interstate 5 (Golden State Freeway), exit on Los Feliz Boulevard and drive west along the southern boundary of the park. Pass Hillhurst and Vermont avenues, and in about one mile turn left onto Fern Dell Drive. Parking is located on the right side of the road at a sharp turn in the road.

*Who to contact:* Griffith Park, Park Ranger Headquarters, 4730 Crystal Springs Drive, Los Angeles, CA 90027; (213) 665-5188.

*Trail notes:* Griffith Park is the largest municipally owned and operated park in the United States at 4,107 acres. There are places in the park where, with just a short walk from the road or trailhead, you can almost forget that you are surrounded by urban sprawl and pollution—peace in the middle of the frenetic city pace. Within the park boundaries there are over 100 miles of trails, lacing through the urban mountain "wilderness." The best introduction to the area is the Mount Hollywood Trail, leading up to the 1,625-foot summit of Mount Hollywood. From here, you can enjoy wonderful vistas of the Los Angeles Basin (assuming it's not too smoggy) and the nearby San Gabriel Mountains. From the trailhead, the Mount Hollywood Trail climbs and winds its way up through oaks and then onto a chaparral-covered ridgeline to the summit. Retrace your steps when ready.

---

## 24. PARSONS LANDING    14.0 mi/6.0 hrs

*Reference:* **On Catalina Island, 22 miles off the coast, southwest of Los Angeles; map I4, grid h5.**

*User groups:* Hikers, mountain bikes, horses and dogs. No wheelchair facilities.

*Permits:* A free hiking permit is required for traveling into the backcountry outside of the towns of Avalon and Two Harbors and is available in Two Harbors at the Visitor Information Office and in Avalon at the Catalina Camping Reservations Office. For more information on hiking permits, contact Doug Bombard Enterprises, (310) 510-2800. Mountain bikers must pay a $50 fee for a one-year permit (March 1 to March 1) and are restricted to certain trails ($75 per family). Permits may be obtained at Brown's Bike Rental in Avalon and at the Two Harbors Visitor Information Office. Contact the Catalina Island Conservancy at (310) 510-1421 for bike permit information. Camping reservations for Two Harbors, Black Jack, Little Harbor and Parsons Gulch campgrounds are available through Doug Bombard Enterprises at (310) 510-2800. Hermit Gulch Campground, located in Avalon, may be reserved by phoning (310) 510-8368.

*Directions:* Ferries depart for Catalina Island from San Pedro, Long Beach, Newport and, in the summer, San Diego. Air service is also available from Long Beach. Specific schedules and rates vary. Getting around the island can be accomplished via the Safari Shuttle Service which provides connecting service between Two Harbors, Avalon, Black Jack Junction and Little Harbor. Call (310) 510-2800 for reservations and more information.

*Maps:* For a free information brochure with basic trails map entitled *Camping Catalina Island*, contact Catalina Camping Reservations at the address listed below. For the topographic map series for the entire island, ask for Santa Catalina East, Santa Catalina West, Santa Catalina North and Santa Catalina South from the USGS.

*Who to contact:* Catalina Camping Reservations, Doug Bombard Enterprises, P.O. Box 5044, Two Harbors, CA 90704; (310) 510-2800.

*Trail notes:* From Two Harbors, hike along the West End Road, just west of Isthmus Cove. The route follows a serpentine line, hugging the coast much of the way with brief detours inland. We would recommend you spending the night at Parsons Landing Campground and enjoying several side hikes—to Starlight Beach via Parsons Landing Road, and to Silver Peak, via the Boushay and Silver Peak trails. The Silver Peak route is quite strenuous and not suitable during the heat of summer. Sweat equity pays off, however, in the stunning mountaintop views from Silver Peak (providing the weather is clear).

*Special note:* Stove fuel is not permitted at any time on the ferry boats or in the airplane taxi. Stove fuel may be purchased in Two Harbors, or easier yet, complete camping equipment rental is also available in Two Harbors. Call (310) 510-2800.

---

# 25. COTTONWOOD   5.5 mi. one way/3.0 hrs
# BLACK JACK TRAIL

*Reference:* **On Catalina Island, 22 miles off the coast, southwest of Los Angeles; map I4, grid i6.**

*User groups:* Hikers, mountain bikes, horses and dogs. No wheelchair facilities.

*Permits:* A free hiking permit is required for traveling into the backcountry outside of the towns of Avalon and Two Harbors and is available in Two Harbors at the Visitor Information Office and in Avalon at the Catalina Camping Reservations Office. For more information on hiking permits, contact Doug Bombard Enterprises at (310) 510-2800. Mountain bikers must pay a $50 fee for a one-year permit (March 1 to March 1) and are restricted to certain trails ($75 per family). Permits may be obtained at Brown's Bike Rental in Avalon and at the Two Harbors Visitor Information Office. Contact the Catalina Island Conservancy at (310) 510-1421 for bike permit information. Camping reservations for Two Harbors, Black Jack, Little Harbor and Parsons Gulch campgrounds are available through Doug Bombard Enterprises at (310) 510-2800. Hermit Gulch Campground, located in Avalon, may be reserved by phoning (310) 510-8368.

**Directions:** Ferries depart for Catalina Island from San Pedro, Long Beach, Newport and, in the summer, San Diego. Air service is also available from Long Beach. Specific schedules and rates vary. Getting around the island can be accomplished via the Safari Shuttle Service which provides connecting service between Two Harbors, Avalon, Black Jack Junction and Little Harbor. Call (310) 510-2800 for reservations and more information.

**Maps:** For a free information brochure with basic trails map entitled *Camping Catalina Island*, contact Catalina Camping Reservations at the address listed below. For the topographic map series for the entire island, ask for Santa Catalina East, Santa Catalina West, Santa Catalina North and Santa Catalina South from the USGS.

**Who to contact:** Catalina Camping Reservations, Doug Bombard Enterprises, P.O. Box 5044, Two Harbors, CA 90704; (310) 510-2800.

**Trail notes:** For an excellent overnight backpack trip, combine Cottonwood Black Jack Trail with the Little Harbor Trail (see hike number 26). Spend the night in Little Harbor Campground and then hike out to Two Harbors—there is no extra charge for the ferry trip if you plan to depart from Two Harbors, even though you were dropped off in Avalon. Just be sure to inform the company. Black Jack is an excellent trail for sampling the variety of terrain and island wildlife which includes bison, deer, boar, wild goats, and rabbits. Sidetrips to Mt. Orizaba (2,097 feet and the tallest island mountain) and Black Jack Mountain (2,006 feet and the second tallest island mountain) may be enjoyed from this trail. Black Jack Camp, just off the trail, provides tables, water, shade and a great spot to picnic with views of channel and ocean. Bring plenty of sunscreen and a wide-brimmed hat—shade is minimal and the sun intense.

**Special note:** Stove fuel is not permitted at any time on the ferry boats or in the airplane taxi. Stove fuel may be purchased in Two Harbors, or easier yet, complete camping equipment rental is also available in Two Harbors. Call (310) 510-2800.

---

# 26. LITTLE HARBOR TRAIL    7.0 mi. one way/5.0 hrs

**Reference:** On Catalina Island, 22 miles off the coast, southwest of Los Angeles; map I4, grid j7.

**User groups:** Hikers, mountain bikes, horses and dogs. No wheelchair facilities.

**Permits:** A free hiking permit is required for traveling into the backcountry outside of the towns of Avalon and Two Harbors and is available in Two Harbors at the Visitor Information Office and in Avalon at the Catalina Camping Reservations Office. For more information on hiking permits, contact Doug Bombard Enterprises, (310) 510-2800. Mountain bikers must pay a $50 fee for a one-year permit (March 1 to March 1) and are restricted to certain trails ($75 per family). Permits may be obtained at Brown's Bike Rental in Avalon and at the Two Harbors Visitor Information Office. Contact the Catalina Island Conservancy at (310) 510-1421 for bike permit information. Camping reservations for Two Harbors, Black Jack, Little Harbor and Parsons Gulch campgrounds are available through Doug Bombard Enterprises at (310) 510-2800. Hermit Gulch Campground, located in Avalon, may be reserved by phoning (310) 510-8368.

*Directions:* Ferries depart for Catalina Island from San Pedro, Long Beach, Newport and, in the summer, San Diego. Air service is also available from Long Beach. Specific schedules and rates vary. Getting around the island can be accomplished via the Safari Shuttle Service which provides connecting service between Two Harbors, Avalon, Black Jack Junction and Little Harbor. Call (310) 510-2800 for reservations and more information.

*Maps:* For a free information brochure with basic trails map entitled *Camping Catalina Island*, contact Catalina Camping Reservations at the address listed below. For the topographic map series for the entire island, ask for Santa Catalina East, Santa Catalina West, Santa Catalina North and Santa Catalina South from the USGS.

*Who to contact:* Catalina Camping Reservations, Doug Bombard Enterprises, P.O. Box 5044, Two Harbors, CA 90704; (310) 510-2800.

*Trail notes:* For an excellent overnight backpack trip, combine Little Harbor Trail with Cottonwood Black Jack Trail, described also in this section. Begin the backpack at Black Jack Junction and spend the night in Little Harbor Campground. Hike out to Two Harbors —there is no extra charge for the ferry trip if you plan to depart from Two Harbors, even though you were dropped off in Avalon. Just be sure to inform the company. Little Harbor Trail begins at Little Harbor Campground and follows the Little Harbor Road to Rough Banning House Road. The last several hundred yards or so, from the edges of Little Harbor, involve a little creative wandering as you pick your way between private clubs and houses—but this should not be a problem. Little Harbor Road will lead the hiker past herds of buffalo which are wonderful to watch. Buffalo are not native to the island. The current herd of approximately 500 grew from 14 which were brought to the island by Hollywood as "extras" for the filming of a Zane Grey western, *The Vanishing American*—they couldn't recapture the buffalo and the rest is history.

*Special note:* Stove fuel is not permitted at any time on the ferry boats or in the airplane taxi. Stove fuel may be purchased in Two Harbors, or easier yet, complete camping equipment rental is also available in Two Harbors. Call (310) 510-2800.

---

## 27. AVALON BOTANICAL GARDEN LOOP TRAIL

8.5 mi/6.0 hrs

*Reference:* **On Catalina Island, 22 miles off the coast, southwest of Los Angeles; map I4, grid j8.**

*User groups:* Hikers, mountain bikes and dogs. No horses are allowed. **Wheelchair accessible** to the Botanical Gardens.

*Permits:* A free hiking permit is required for traveling into the backcountry outside of the towns of Avalon and Two Harbors and is available in Two Harbors at the Visitor Information Office and in Avalon at the Catalina Camping Reservations Office. For more information on hiking permits, contact Doug Bombard Enterprises, (310) 510-2800. Mountain bikers must pay a $50 fee for a one-year permit (March 1 to March 1) and are restricted to certain trails ($75 per family). Permits may be obtained at Brown's Bike Rental in Avalon and at the Two Harbors Visitor Information Office. Contact the Catalina Island Conservancy at (310) 510-1421 for bike permit information. Camping reservations for Two Harbors, Black Jack, Little Harbor and Parsons Gulch campgrounds are available through Doug Bombard Enterprises at (310) 510-2800. Hermit Gulch Campground, located in Avalon, may be reserved by phoning (310) 510-8368.

**Directions:** Ferries depart for Catalina Island from San Pedro, Long Beach, Newport and, in the summer, San Diego. Air service is also available from Long Beach. Specific schedules and rates vary. Getting around the island can be accomplished via the Safari Shuttle Service which provides connecting service between Two Harbors, Avalon, Black Jack Junction and Little Harbor. Call (310) 510-2800 for reservations and more information.

**Maps:** For a free information brochure with basic trails map entitled *Camping Catalina Island*, contact Catalina Camping Reservations at the address listed below. For the topographic map series for the entire island, ask for Santa Catalina East, Santa Catalina West, Santa Catalina North and Santa Catalina South from the USGS.

**Who to contact:** Catalina Camping Reservations, Doug Bombard Enterprises, P.O. Box 5044, Two Harbors, CA 90704; (310) 510-2800.

**Trail notes:** Any visit to the island probably should include a trip to the Botanical Gardens—an impressive array of plants native to the island, Southern California, and other parts of the world. Hike out of Avalon on the Avalon Canyon Road up to the Botanical Gardens, then up to the Wrigley Memorial. Continue climbing up Memorial Road to Divide East End Road. Turn left toward East Mountain. Turn left again on Renton Mine Road, past the Renton Mine, and down to Wrigley Road. Turn left on Wrigley Road and follow it back to town. Views from the ridges on this hike are spectacular. From East Mountain, you will be able to see north down onto Avalon Bay and south to the distant San Clemente Island.

---

# 28. LONE TREE POINT 5.5 mi/3.0 hrs

*Reference:* **On Catalina Island, 22 miles off the coast, southwest of Los Angeles; map I4, grid j8.**

*User groups:* Hikers, mountain bikes, horses and dogs. No wheelchair facilities.

*Permits:* A free hiking permit is required for traveling into the backcountry outside of the towns of Avalon and Two Harbors and is available in Two Harbors at the Visitor Information Office and in Avalon at the Catalina Camping Reservations Office. For more information on hiking permits, contact Doug Bombard Enterprises, (310) 510-2800. Mountain bikers must pay a $50 fee for a one-year permit (March 1 to March 1) and are restricted to certain trails ($75 per family). Permits may be obtained at Brown's Bike Rental in Avalon and at the Two Harbors Visitor Information Office. Contact the Catalina Island Conservancy at (310) 510-1421 for bike permit information. Camping reservations for Two Harbors, Black Jack, Little Harbor and Parsons Gulch campgrounds are available through Doug Bombard Enterprises at (310) 510-2800. Hermit Gulch Campground, located in Avalon, may be reserved by phoning (310) 510-8368.

**Directions:** Ferries depart for Catalina Island from San Pedro, Long Beach, Newport and, in the summer, San Diego. Air service is also available from Long Beach. Specific schedules and rates vary. Getting around the island can be accomplished via the Safari Shuttle Service which provides connecting service between Two Harbors, Avalon, Black Jack Junction and Little Harbor. Call (310) 510-2800 for reservations and more information.

**Maps:** For a free information brochure with basic trails map entitled *Camping Catalina Island*, contact Catalina Camping Reservations at the address listed below. For the topographic map series for the entire island, ask for Santa Catalina East, Santa Catalina West, Santa Catalina North and Santa Catalina South from the USGS.

**Who to contact:** Catalina Camping Reservations, Doug Bombard Enterprises, P.O. Box 5044, Two Harbors, CA 90704; (310) 510-2800.

**Trail notes:** This is an excellent spring hike which begins at Hermit Gulch Campground in Avalon (located just below Wrigley Memorial and the Botanic Gardens, just off Avalon Canyon Road) and ends at Lone Tree Point—views of the Palisades' sheer drop to the ocean are outstanding from here. The trail leading up from the campground is somewhat narrow and steep in places—wear adequate footgear with good traction. The trail crosses Divide Road, a fire road traversing the eastern spine of Catalina Island. On the return trip, if you wish to divert to Wrigley Memorial and the Botanic Gardens, hang a right on Divide Road and then a left on Memorial Road. Hermit Gulch Campground is a little less than 12 miles below the Botanic Gardens on Avalon Canyon Road.

# MAP I5

2 PCT SECTIONS
32 TRAILS
PAGES 696-719

SO-CAL MAP .......................... see page 662
adjoining maps
NORTH (H5) ........................... see page 640
EAST (I6) ................................ see page 720
SOUTH (J5) ............................ see page 760
WEST (I4) ............................... see page 672

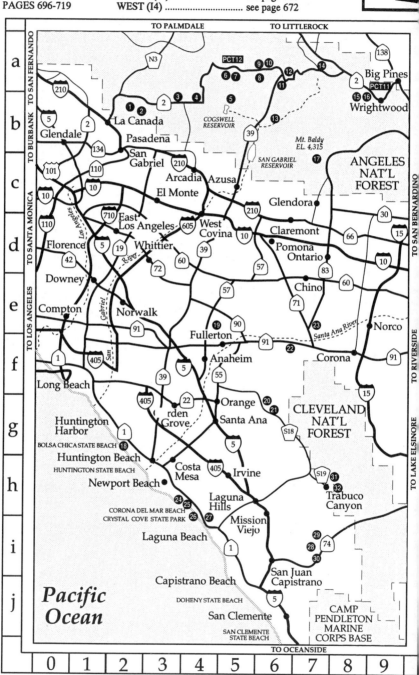

TO PALMDALE
TO LITTLEROCK

138
N3
PCT12
9 10
6 7
14
2
138
Big Pines
PCT11
12
8
210
2
3 4
11
15 16
1 2
5
13
Wrightwood
La Canada
COGSWELL
RESERVOIR
5
2
39
Mt. Baldy
EL. 4,315
Glendale
Pasadena
134
San
Gabriel
SAN GABRIEL
RESERVOIR
17
ANGELES
NAT'L
FOREST
101
110
210
Arcadia
Azusa
10
10
El Monte
Glendora
710
East
210
30
Los Angeles
West
Claremont
66
15
110
605
Covina
10
Florence
5
Whittier
39
Pomona
57
83
10
42
72
60
Ontario
Downey
57
Chino
60
Compton
57
71
91
Norwalk
19
90
23
Norco
Fullerton
91
22
Corona
91
1
405
Anaheim
55
15
Long Beach
39
5
Huntington
405
22
Orange
20
CLEVELAND
Harbor
1
rden
21
NAT'L
BOLSA CHICA STATE BEACH
18
Grove
Santa Ana
S18
FOREST
Huntington Beach
5
HUNTINGTON STATE BEACH
Costa
405
S19
31
Mesa
Irvine
32
Newport Beach
Laguna
Trabuco
24
Hills
Canyon
25
CORONA DEL MAR BEACH
CRYSTAL COVE STATE PARK
26
27
Mission
Viejo
29
Laguna Beach
28
74
1
30
Capistrano Beach
San Juan
Capistrano
*Pacific
Ocean*
DOHENY STATE BEACH
5
CAMP
PENDLETON
MARINE
CORPS BASE
San Clemente
SAN CLEMENTE
STATE BEACH
TO OCEANSIDE

0 1 2 3 4 5 6 7 8 9

**Map I5 featuring:** Angeles National Forest, San Gabriel Mountains, Mt. Baldy, Cucamonga Wilderness, Bolsa Chica Ecological Reserve, Irvine Regional Park, Featherly Regional Park, Santiago Regional Park, Chino Hills State Park, Crystal Cove State Park, Cleveland National Forest, Trabuco Canyon, San Gabriel River

---

## 1. RATTLESNAKE TRAIL to MOUNT WILSON

**9.0 mi/4.0 hrs**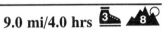

*Reference:* In Angeles National Forest, north of Pasadena; map I5, grid b2.

*User groups:* Hikers, mountain bikes, horses and dogs. No wheelchair facilities.

*Permits:* No day-use permits are required. A campfire permit is required for overnight stays.

*Directions:* From Interstate 210, north of Pasadena, take the Angeles Crest Highway exit (Highway 2). Drive north on Angeles Crest Highway to Red Box. Turn right onto Mt. Wilson Road and drive approximately four miles to just below the summit. The Rattlesnake Trailhead begins a quarter of a mile west of the summit where the road becomes a one-way loop. Park in the clearing just south of the road.

*Maps:* Send $3 to the USDA-Forest Service, 630 Sansome Street, San Francisco, CA 94111 and ask for the Angeles National Forest map. For a topographic map, ask for Mt. Wilson from the USGS. During extreme fire season months, call ahead to (808) 967-3481 for forest status updates. Tom Harrison Cartography also publishes excellent maps of the area. Call (415) 456-7940 and ask for the trail map of the Angeles Front Country, the trail map of the Angeles High Country and the recreation map of the San Gabriel Mountains. The cost for each map is $5.95 plus tax and shipping.

*Who to contact:* Angeles National Forest, 701 North Santa Anita Avenue, Arcadia, CA 91006; (818) 574-5200.

*Trail notes:* From the trailhead, hike the Rattlesnake Trail down to West Fork Campground. Loop back via the Gabrielino Trail to the Valley Forge Trail and the Eaton Saddle on Mt. Wilson Road. You will exit on Mt. Wilson Road and have to hike the final two miles back down to your car—unless you have trained it to come and pick you up. The trail is a mostly forested route with oak, chaparral and manzanita along the lower sections and alder, laurel and big-leaf maple trees above Strains Canyon, leading to excellent views of the Mt. Wilson Observatory and the highest peaks of the San Gabriels, as well as the sprawl of the city down below. Near the top of this trail, approaching Mt. Wilson, Professor Michaelson made the first precise measurement of the speed of light in the 1920s. He did it by placing an instrument just off the trail near the summit and a mirror device on Mt. Baldy, 20 air miles to the east. The foundation for this instrument is still around, but it is not visible in the thick overgrowth.

## 2. SILVER MOCCASIN TRAIL

**53.0 mi. one way/5.0 days**

*Reference:* In Angeles National Forest, north of Pasadena; map I5, grid b3.

*User groups:* Hikers, horses and dogs. Limited access for mountain bikes. No wheelchair facilities.

*Permits:* No day-use permits are required. A campfire permit is required for overnight stays.

*Directions:* A car shuttle is required. To hike the entire trail leave one car at Vincent Gap on the Angeles Crest Highway. From La Canada, drive east on the Angeles Crest Highway for approximately 53 miles to the Vincent Gap Parking Area. To get to Vincent Gap from Interstate 15, take the Wrightwood exit south of El Cajon Pass and drive eight miles west on Highway 138 to the Angeles Crest Highway (2). Turn left and drive approximately 14 miles to the trailhead. There is a clearly signed and designated parking area. Be aware the Vincent Gap may not be accessible in the winter due to snow on the highway. You will begin hiking at Chantry Flats. From the Foothill Freeway (210) in Arcadia, exit onto Santa Anita Avenue and drive approximately six miles north to its end at Chantry Flats. There is a small store that sells maps and refreshments for a last minute soda and candy bar. The trailhead begins across the road from the parking area.

*Maps:* Send $3 to the USDA-Forest Service, 630 Sansome Street, San Francisco, CA 94111 and ask for the Angeles National Forest map. For topographic maps, ask for Mount Wilson, Chilao Flat, Waterman Mountain, Crystal Lake and Mount San Antonio from the USGS. For other maps of the area, see "maps" under hike number 1.

*Who to contact:* Angeles National Forest, 701 North Santa Anita Avenue, Arcadia, CA 91006; (818) 574-5200.

*Trail notes:* The Silver Moccasin Trail has been a rite of passage for young Boy Scouts since 1942. Upon completion of the trek, proud Scouts are bestowed the coveted Silver Moccasin award. You will enjoy walking this route too as it offers some of the best of the San Gabriels in one complete package. The Forest Service outlines the entire route in red on its Angeles National Forest map. Begin at Chantry Flats, climbing Santa Anita Canyon to Newcomb Pass before dropping into the West Fork of the San Gabriel River. Head up Shortcut Canyon, cross the head of Big Tujunga to Charlton Flat, and then up and down to Chilao. From Chilao, parallel the Angeles Highway over Cloudburst Summit, into Cooper Canyon and Little Rock Creek, and then over the shoulder of Mt. Williamson. From there, head through Islip Saddle, past the Boy Scout Monument to its founder, Baden-Powell, (yes it's on Mt. Baden-Powell), and then down to Vincent Gap. Recommended overnight stays are at West Fork Campground, Chilao Campground, Cooper Canyon Trail Camp and Little Jimmy Trail Camp.

---

## 3. CHARLTON FLAT to VETTER MOUNTAIN

**3.0 mi/1.0 hr**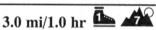

*Reference:* In Angeles National Forest, north of Pasadena; map I5, grid b3.

*User groups:* Hikers, mountain bikes and dogs. No horses are allowed. No wheelchair facilities.

*Permits:* No day-use permits are required. A campfire permit is required for overnight stays.

*Directions:* From Interstate 210 north of Pasadena, take the Angeles Crest Highway (Highway 2) north to Charlton Flat. Turn left into the Charlton Flat Picnic Area, turn right on the first road and drive approximately a half mile to a gate. Park off the road, taking care not to block the gate.

*Maps:* Send $3 to the USDA-Forest Service, 630 Sansome Street, San Francisco, CA 94111 and ask for the Angeles National Forest map. For a topographic map, ask for Chilao Flat from the USGS. For other maps of the area, see "maps" under hike number 1.

*Who to contact:* Angeles National Forest, 701 North Santa Anita Avenue, Arcadia, CA 91006; (818) 574-5200.

*Trail notes:* This is an outstanding family hike that winds its way up the ravine to the site of a former Forest Service fire lookout. You'll encounter a variety of forest trees, birds and flowers along the way that will be enjoyable even for the young hiker. It's uphill all the way from the signed trailhead, as the Vetter Trail winds through coulter pine and oak before leaving the trees behind in favor of chaparral-covered slopes leading to the lookout site, about 1.5 miles from the start. Views in all directions are excellent, once you have gained the peak.

## 4. WOLF CREEK NATURE TRAIL   0.5 mi/0.5 hr

*Reference:* In Angeles National Forest, north of Pasadena; map I5, grid b4.

*User groups:* Hikers and dogs. No mountain bikes or horses are allowed. No wheelchair facilities.

*Permits:* No day-use permits are required. A campfire permit is required for overnight stays.

*Directions:* From Interstate 210 north of Pasadena, take the Angeles Crest Highway (Highway 2) north to Charlton Flat. Turn left into the Charlton Flat Picnic Area, turn right on the first road and drive approximately a half mile to a gate. Park off the road, taking care not to block the gate.

*Maps:* Send $3 to the USDA-Forest Service, 630 Sansome Street, San Francisco, CA 94111 and ask for the Angeles National Forest map. For a topographic map, ask for Chilao Flat from the USGS. For other maps of the area, see "maps" under hike number 1.

*Who to contact:* Angeles National Forest, 701 North Santa Anita Avenue, Arcadia, CA 91006; (818) 574-5200.

*Trail notes:* The trail branches right, just after passing the gate. It's another outstanding family hike that winds along a conifer shaded route, with interpretive signs pointing out clear evidence of a fire in 1878 as well as other information of interest to budding naturalists. Take a peek, though not too close, at the Coulter pine whose cones are the largest and heaviest of all the native conifers—14 inches long and five pounds heavy in some cases. One of those babies falls in the woods and you better believe you are going to hear it. Just hope you're not standing under it—ouch!

## 5. CHARLTON FLAT to DEVIL PEAK

**3.0 mi/1.0 hr**

*Reference:* In Angeles National Forest, north of Pasadena; map I5, grid b5.

*User groups:* Hikers, horses and dogs. No mountain bikes are allowed. No wheelchair facilities.

*Permits:* No day-use permits are required. A campfire permit is required for overnight stays.

*Directions:* From the Foothill Freeway (210) in La Canada, exit onto the Angeles Crest Highway (2) and drive to Charlton Flat. Turn left into the Charlton Flat Picnic Area and park. The trailhead begins across the Angeles Highway on a dirt road leading to Mt. Mooney and Devil Peak.

*Maps:* Send $3 to the USDA-Forest Service, 630 Sansome Street, San Francisco, CA 94111 and ask for the Angeles National Forest map. For topographic maps, ask for Chilao Flat and Waterman Mountain from the USGS. For other maps of the area, see "maps" under hike number 1.

*Who to contact:* Angeles National Forest, 701 North Santa Anita Avenue, Arcadia, CA 91006; (818) 574-5200.

*Trail notes:* Here's a short trek that offers a superb view down into the San Gabriel Wilderness from on top of Devil's Peak. From the parking area, take the right fork heading south, past a small astronomical observatory to a pass on the ridgeline about one mile away. Hike up the ridge to the left, heading southeast for about one-half mile through a forest of coulter pines to the top of Devil's Peak.

## 6. CHILAO to DEVIL'S CANYON

**10.0 mi/8.0 hrs**

*Reference:* In Angeles National Forest, north of Pasadena; map I5, grid a5.

*User groups:* Hikers, horses and dogs. No mountain bikes are allowed. No wheelchair facilities.

*Permits:* A wilderness permit is required. A campfire permit is required for overnight stays.

*Directions:* From the Foothill Freeway (210) in La Canada, exit onto the Angeles Crest Highway (2) and drive to the prominent sign for the Devil's Canyon Trail, located approximately 27 miles from La Canada and 200 yards before the Chilao Visitor's Center. Park in the area on the west side of the road located directly across from the trailhead.

*Maps:* Send $3 to the USDA-Forest Service, 630 Sansome Street, San Francisco, CA 94111 and ask for the Angeles National Forest map. For topographic maps, ask for Chilao Flat and Waterman Mountain from the USGS. For other maps of the area, see "maps" under hike number 1.

*Who to contact:* Angeles National Forest, 701 North Santa Anita Avenue, Arcadia, CA 91006; (818) 574-5200.

*Trail notes:* Although the ideal season to enjoy this hike is short—spring and early summer only because streams dry up later in the year—the trek will guide you into an area where you can enjoy solitude and peace within the rugged San Gabriel Wilderness. Where the trail ends, it is possible to continue downstream by boulder-hopping, wading and bush-thrashing. Be warned, however, that as the canyon walls begin to narrow, the Devil's

Canyon becomes a playground only for experts with climbing experience and skill—and even then it's dangerous! From the Devil's Canyon Trailhead, switchback quickly down for 1.5 miles to the floor of the canyon and a stream that should be running, except during drought years. Keep wandering downstream, crossing from one side of the stream to the other periodically and negotiating some small pools and wet areas. At about five miles, the trail completely disappears and the canyon closes in. DO NOT go any further, unless you have strong canyoneering skills and adequate gear to negotiate the slippery rock faces and small waterfalls you must descend to continue on. Head back the way you came.

---

# 7. THREE POINTS to TWIN PEAKS

**14.0 mi/7.0 hrs**

**Reference:** In Angeles National Forest, north of Pasadena; map I5, grid a5.

**User groups:** Hikers, horses and dogs. No mountain bikes are allowed. No wheelchair facilities.

**Permits:** No day-use permits are required. A campfire permit is required for overnight stays.

**Directions:** From the Foothill Freeway (210) in La Canada, exit onto the Angeles Crest Highway (2) and drive to Three Points Junction, approximately 2.5 miles north of Chilao. The exit to Three Points is marked by a sign indicating Horse Flats. The trailhead for Mt. Waterman Trail is just west of the turnoff and parking area.

**Maps:** Send $3 to the USDA-Forest Service, 630 Sansome Street, San Francisco, CA 94111 and ask for the Angeles National Forest map. For a topographic map ask for Waterman Mountain from the USGS. Tom Harrison Cartography also publishes excellent maps of the area. Call (415) 456-7940 and ask for the trail map of the Angeles Front Country, the trail map of the Angeles High Country and the recreation map of the San Gabriel Mountains. The cost of each map is $5.95 plus tax and shipping.

**Who to contact:** Angeles National Forest, 701 North Santa Anita Avenue, Arcadia, CA 91006; (818) 574-5200.

**Trail notes:** This is a pretty hike along the northern boundary of the San Gabriel Wilderness through some of the finest Angeles National Forest high country. Enjoy the outstanding views, varied landscape and solitude. Keep a sharp lookout and you may be fortunate enough to see bighorn sheep. Much of the trip winds through dense forests of pine, fir, cedar and mahogany. The best time to visit is spring and early summer when the six-mile segment between Three Points and Waterman-Twin Peaks is at its best, with small streams and miniature meadows full of wildflowers. The trail begins across the highway from Horse Flats and soon passes two junctions. Head left at the first junction and then right at the second. Follow the Mt. Waterman signs. The trail switchbacks for about one mile, leveling off and tucking in and out of small ravines across the western slopes of Mt. Waterman for five miles to the Twin Peaks junction. Head right to reach the saddle between Mt. Waterman and Twin Peaks and the site of a wonderful grove of large cedar trees. At the Twin Peaks Saddle, hike south up the informal climber's trail leading to the top of 7761-foot Twin Peak—the eastern peak is the highest. Return the way you came.

## 8. BUCKHORN
## to MT. WATERMAN

6.0 mi/3.0 hrs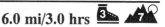

*Reference:* In Angeles National Forest, north of Pasadena; map I5, grid a6.
*User groups:* Hikers, horses, mountain bikes and dogs. No wheelchair facilities.
*Permits:* No day-use permits are required. A campfire permit is required for
   overnight stays.
*Directions:* From the Foothill Freeway (210) in La Canada, exit onto the
   Angeles Crest Highway (2) and drive to the Buckhorn Ranger Station,
   approximately 34 miles from La Canada. Parking is along the wide shoulders. The profusion of fire roads and trails can be confusing, but if you look
   for the Mt. Waterman Trail sign, you won't go wrong.
*Maps:* Send $3 to the USDA-Forest Service, 630 Sansome Street, San Fran-
   cisco, CA 94111 and ask for the Angeles National Forest map. For a
   topographic map, ask for Waterman Mountain from the USGS. For other
   maps of the area, see "maps" under hike number 1.
*Who to contact:* Angeles National Forest, 701 North Santa Anita Avenue,
   Arcadia, CA 91006; (818) 574-5200.
*Trail notes:* Mt. Waterman is perhaps best known to downhill and backcountry
   skiers in the winter, but in the spring and summer it offers an enjoyable
   hiking opportunity through open pine and fir forest. The well-graded trail
   begins on the uphill side of the highway near Buckhorn Ranger Station and
   west of the Buckhorn Campground entrance. The mountain summit is so
   broad and long that there are actually three summits. The highest, and the one
   with the best views of the San Gabriel Range, lies about one-quarter mile off
   the trail to the southwest. Bighorn sheep are often seen in this area, so keep
   a sharp lookout. At the peak, notice the gorgeous sugar pines with their long,
   hanging cones—some as long as 18 inches.

---

## 9. BUCKHORN
## to COOPER CANYON

3.0 mi/1.5 hrs

*Reference:* In Angeles National Forest, north of Pasadena; map I5, grid a6.
*User groups:* Hikers, horses and dogs. No mountain bikes are allowed. No
   wheelchair facilities.
*Permits:* No day-use permits are required. A campfire permit is required for
   overnight stays.
*Directions:* From the Foothill Freeway (210) in La Canada, exit onto the
   Angeles Crest Highway (2) and drive to the Buckhorn Campground,
   approximately 35 miles from La Canada and a half mile beyond the Mt.
   Waterman Ski Area. Turn left and follow the campground road through the
   campground to the hiker's parking area just beyond the camping area. The
   trailhead begins at the sign for the Burkhart Trail.
*Maps:* Send $3 to the USDA-Forest Service, 630 Sansome Street, San Fran-
   cisco, CA 94111 and ask for the Angeles National Forest map. For a
   topographic map ask for Waterman Mountain from the USGS. For other
   maps of the area, see "maps" under hike number 1.
*Who to contact:* Angeles National Forest, 701 North Santa Anita Avenue,
   Arcadia, CA 91006; (818) 574-5200.
*Trail notes:* This trail is considered by many to be one of the most beautiful short

walks in all of the San Gabriels, and they will have no argument from us. The wide variety of trees, ferns, wildflowers and birds—coupled with pictur-esque waterfalls—remind you of a protected mountainous Eden. Hike down the Burkhart Trail for 1.5 miles to a junction with the Pacific Crest Trail. The waterfalls, especially the one nearest the beginning of the trail, are truly spectacular.

## 10. EAGLES ROOST to LITTLE ROCK CREEK

7.0 mi/3.0 hrs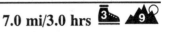

*Reference:* **In Angeles National Forest, north of Pasadena; map I5, grid a6.**
*User groups:* Hikers, horses and dogs. No mountain bikes allowed. No wheelchair facilities.
*Permits:* No day-use permits are required. A campfire permit is required for overnight stays.
*Directions:* From the Foothill Freeway (210) in La Canada, exit onto the Angeles Crest Highway (2) and drive to the Eagles Roost Picnic Area, approximately 39 miles from La Canada. Park in the clearing. The trailhead for Rattlesnake Trail is located across the highway.
*Maps:* Send $3 to the USDA-Forest Service, 630 Sansome Street, San Francisco, CA 94111 and ask for the Angeles National Forest map. For a topographic map ask for Waterman Peak from the USGS. For other maps of the area, see "maps" under hike number 1.
*Who to contact:* Angeles National Forest, 701 North Santa Anita Avenue, Arcadia, CA 91006; (818) 574-5200.
*Trail notes:* This treadway traverses some of the most beautiful forested area of the high country in the Angeles Forest. Lush forests of pine, fir and cedar and a tiny waterfall fill the senses with pleasing sights, smells and sounds. This is an excellent walk to enjoy a few moments of peace and solitude. The unmarked Rattlesnake Trail descends on a fire road which narrows to a trail along the canyon floor. At a junction with the Burkhart Trail, you can return the way you came.

## 11. CRYSTAL LAKE to MT. ISLIP

7.0 mi/4.0 hrs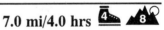

*Reference:* **In Angeles National Forest, north of Pasadena; map I5, grid a6.**
*User groups:* Hikers, horses and dogs. Mountain bikes are allowed but not recommended. No wheelchair facilities.
*Permits:* No day-use permits are required. A campfire permit is required for overnight stays.
*Directions:* From the Foothill Freeway (210) in Azusa, take the Highway 39/ Azusa Avenue exit and drive north on Highway 39 for approximately 24 miles to the turnoff for the Crystal Lake Recreation Area. In one mile, you pass the Forest Service entry station. One more mile will take you to the Crystal Lake Visitor's Center. From the visitor's center, it is another half mile to a dirt parking area and the signed trailhead for Windy Gap Trail.
*Maps:* Send $3 to the USDA-Forest Service, 630 Sansome Street, San Francisco, CA 94111 and ask for the Angeles National Forest map. For a topographic map, ask for Santiago Peak from the USGS. For other maps of

the area, see "maps" under hike number 1.

*Who to contact:* Angeles National Forest, 701 North Santa Anita Avenue, Arcadia, CA 91006; (818) 574-5200.

*Trail notes:* Crystal Lake is the only naturally-occuring lake in the San Gabriel Mountains. The entire hike on Windy Gap Trail wanders through beautiful forest, with good opportunities to enjoy trickling springs and brief glimpses of deer, numerous songbirds and other wildlife. On a clear day, the views over the desert mountains and out to the ocean are stunning. Little Jimmy Trail Camp is a recommended overnight stay if you plan on camping. From the parking area, hike through the middle of three gates and follow the road, looking for a trail that branches off to the right, about one-quarter mile from the campground. Hike three-quarters of a mile up the trail and across a road, then head left and down to Big Cienega, a small clear spring (treat the water before drinking). Keep hiking up the trail to Windy Gap, a low spot on the ridge between Mt. Islip and Mt. Hawkins and 2.5 miles from the start. Turn left at the trail junction and in one-half mile you will arrive at Little Jimmy Spring and then Little Jimmy Campground. Look for the trail heading off to Islip from the upper western edge of the campground. After a mile of climbing, you will reach the top of 8,250-foot Mt. Islip.

---

## 12. CRYSTAL LAKE    10.0 mi/5.0 hrs
## to SOUTH MT. HAWKINS

*Reference:* In Angeles National Forest, north of Pasadena; map I5, grid a6.

*User groups:* Hikers, horses, mountain bikes and dogs. There are no wheelchair facilities.

*Permits:* No day-use permits are required. A campfire permit is required for overnight stays.

*Directions:* From the Foothill Freeway (Highway 210) in Azusa, take the Highway 39/Azusa Avenue exit and drive north on Highway 39 for approximately 24 miles to the turnoff for the Crystal Lake Recreation Area. Drive a short distance past the store, Forest Service Information Station and lake access road to the upper (north) edge of the campground area. Look for the sign indicating the trailhead for the Windy Gap Trail.

*Maps:* Send $3 to the USDA-Forest Service, 630 Sansome Street, San Francisco, CA 94111 and ask for the Angeles National Forest map. For a topographic map, ask for Crystal Lake from the USGS.

*Who to contact:* Angeles National Forest, 701 North Santa Anita Avenue, Arcadia, CA 91006; (818) 574-5200.

*Trail notes:* This is a wonderful hike through open forest, offering nice views of the surrounding mountains. From the trailhead, hike up and north from the road, crossing a dirt fire road in a short distance. In another mile, you will cross this road again as it switchbacks its way to South Mt. Hawkins. Leave the trail and follow the fire road to the right as it winds its way around the side of the mountain. You will be hiking through a forest of fir, pine and cedar all the way, with excellent views overlooking Crystal Lake and the mountains beyond. From the top of South Mt. Hawkins, elevation 7,783 feet, take in the grand views before heading back the way you came.

## 13. EAST FORK TRAIL 14.0 mi/8.0 hrs

*Reference:* In Angeles National Forest, north of Pasadena; map I5, grid b6.

*User groups:* Hikers and dogs. No mountain bikes or horses are allowed. No wheelchair facilities.

*Permits:* A wilderness permit is required for all visitors. Permits can be filled out at the self-service dispenser at the base of East Fork Ranger Station Road. On weekends, you will need to pick up a parking permit en route at the Dalton Ranger Station. A campfire permit is required for overnight stays.

*Directions:* From Interstate 10 (known as the San Bernardino Freeway) exit onto Azusa Avenue (Highway 39) and drive north. Pick up your parking permit at the Dalton Ranger Station on Highway 39, weekends only. Turn right on East Fork Road and drive eight miles to the East Fork Ranger Station where you will self-register for a wilderness permit. Drive up the service road to Heaton Flat Campground and the parking area and trailhead.

*Maps:* Send $3 to the USDA-Forest Service, 630 Sansome Street, San Francisco, CA 94111 and ask for the Angeles National Forest map. For topographic maps, ask for Glendora, Crystal Lake and Mount San Antonio from the USGS. For other maps of the area, see "maps" under hike number 1.

*Who to contact:* Angeles National Forest, 701 North Santa Anita Avenue, Arcadia, CA 91006; (818) 574-5200.

*Trail notes:* Expect to get your feet wet on this hike as there is almost as much wading as hiking. All the boulder-hopping and stream crossings lead to a paradise amid rock walls and tumbling waters. This is one of Michael's favorite hikes in the San Gabriels. You'll also be amazed at the now-dubbed "Bridge to Nowhere" which you will encounter mid-hike. There is no road on either side of the bridge, leading one to believe that a crazed engineer lost his mind and built this wilderness bridge for the heck of it. Not so. In 1938 there was a road that went with the bridge, but it washed out and was never rebuilt. Hike up the canyon floor to the Bridge to Nowhere. The trail drops here into The Narrows where you will squeeze through granite walls and continue up-river to Fish Fork and an outstanding picnic spot. If you are feeling adventurous and don't mind pruned feet, wade up Fish Fork until a waterfall and sheer canyon walls hint that it is time to stop—do not attempt to climb the walls or falls!

## 14. VINCENT GAP 8.0 mi/4.0 hrs
## to MT. BADEN-POWELL

*Reference:* In Angeles National Forest, north of Pasadena; map I5, grid c7.

*User groups:* Hikers, horses and dogs. No mountain bikes are allowed. No wheelchair facilities.

*Permits:* No day-use permits are required. A campfire permit is required for overnight stays.

*Directions:* From La Canada, drive east on the Angeles Crest Highway for approximately 53 miles to the Vincent Gap Parking Area. The trailhead is located at the northwest edge of the parking lot. For access from the east and from Interstate 15, take the Wrightwood exit south of El Cajon Pass and drive eight miles west on Highway 138 to the Angeles Crest Highway (2). Turn left and drive approximately 14 miles to the trailhead.

*Maps:* Send $3 to the USDA-Forest Service, 630 Sansome Street, San Francisco, CA 94111 and ask for the Angeles National Forest map. For a topographic map, ask for Crystal Lake from the USGS. For other maps of the area, see "maps" under hike number 1.

*Who to contact:* Angeles National Forest, 701 North Santa Anita Avenue, Arcadia, CA 91006; (818) 574-5200.

*Trail notes:* The trail to Mt. Baden-Powell is one of the more popular trails in the high country. The excellent treadway winds its way through open forests of pine and cedar and finally to the gnarled 2,000-year-old limber pines near the peak. While this is not a strenuous hike, it is not an easy trip either because of the 2,800-foot elevation gain over just four miles of trail. Hikers have experienced shortness of breath when they are not used to the altitude, so take your time. Across the rugged San Gabriel Canyon looms Mt. Baldy, the highest peak in the San Gabriels. If you have the energy, take the side trail to the Limber Pine Forest on your way to Mt. Baden-Powell or on the way back. The pines twist and sway in the wind like tiny dancers and are one of the few trees hardy enough to exist in this subalpine environment.

---

# 15. VINCENT GAP to PRAIRIE FORK & BEYOND

**8.0 mi/4.0 hrs**

*Reference:* In Angeles National Forest, north of Pasadena; map I5, grid b8.

*User groups:* Hikers, horses and dogs. No mountain bikes are allowed. No wheelchair facilities.

*Permits:* No day-use permits are required. A campfire permit is required for overnight stays.

*Directions:* From La Canada, drive east on the Angeles Crest Highway for approximately 53 miles to the Vincent Gap Parking Area. The trailhead is at the south edge of Vincent Gap.

*Maps:* Send $3 to the USDA-Forest Service, 630 Sansome Street, San Francisco, CA 94111 and ask for the Angeles National Forest map. For a topographic map, ask for Santiago Peak from the USGS. For other maps of the area, see "maps" under hike number 1.

*Who to contact:* Angeles National Forest, 701 North Santa Anita Avenue, Arcadia, CA 91006; (818) 574-5200.

*Trail notes:* If it is solitude that you are seeking, this trail offers it in spades as it guides you into one of the most isolated areas of the Angeles National Forest. If you are lucky, you may get to see bighorn sheep or catch some trout in the clear, snow-fed streams along the way. There are some really great wilderness campsites along the route towards the narrows. From the trailhead, the route descends quickly for three miles, losing 2,000 feet in elevation—easy going down, but a thigh-burner on the way out. Prairie Fork is a major tributary of the East Fork of the San Gabriel River. With permission from the ranger, camping is allowed at the bottom of the trail where Vincent Gulch joins Prairie Fork. A trek down the 11 miles to the East Fork Ranger Station is a super adventure for the prepared, but it involves rock-hopping the entire route with many stream crossings and no trail to speak of—not for the ill-prepared or inexperienced.

## 16. BLUE RIDGE to MT. BALDY

12.0 mi/6.0 hrs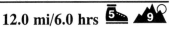

*Reference:* In Angeles National Forest, north of Pasadena; map I5, grid b8.

*User groups:* Hikers, horses and dogs. No mountain bikes are allowed. No wheelchair facilities.

*Permits:* No day-use permits are required. A campfire permit is required for overnight stays.

*Directions:* From Interstate 15 near Cajon at Highway 138 east, turn left (west) onto the Angeles Crest Highway and drive five miles to Wrightwood. Continue for three more miles to Big Pines. Bear left and continue on Angeles Crest Highway for 1.5 miles to Blue Ridge Road (opposite Inspiration Point). Turn left and drive three miles to the Blue Ridge Campground. If the roads are bad, begin your trip at the campground. This will add another three miles to your hike each way. The road is generally good enough for a high-clearance vehicle to make it to Guffy Camp. Begin hiking on the Pacific Crest Trail.

*Maps:* Send $3 to the USDA-Forest Service, 630 Sansome Street, San Francisco, CA 94111 and ask for the Angeles National Forest map. For a topographic map, ask for Santiago Peak from the USGS. For other maps of the area, see "maps" under hike number 1.

*Who to contact:* Angeles National Forest, 701 North Santa Anita Avenue, Arcadia, CA 91006; (818) 574-5200.

*Trail notes:* This particular high country trip is spectacular, reaching the three highest peaks in the San Gabriel Mountains—Pine Mountain at 9,648 feet, Dawson Peak at 9,575 feet, and Mt. Baldy at 10,064 feet. You must be in good physical condition to enjoy the trek, but if you are, and are used to hiking at high elevation, then the rewards are unforgettable. As you are wandering through the gnarled and stunted trees and past the outstanding views, remember that you are treading on true alpine country and the congested Los Angeles basin is less than an hour away. Amazing, isn't it? From Guffy Camp, head east on the Pacific Crest Trail for 2.5 miles to the Pine Mountain Trail heading south. From here, keep hiking south along the spine to the Dawson Peak Trail and then over Dawson Peak and over to Mount San Antonio (Mt. Baldy). Return the way you came.

## 17. ICEHOUSE CANYON TRAIL 7.5 mi/4.0 hrs

*Reference:* In Angeles National Forest, north of Pasadena; map I5, grid c7.

*User groups:* Hikers, horses and dogs. No mountain bikes are allowed. No wheelchair facilities.

*Permits:* Wilderness permits are required for all hikers. A campfire permit is required for overnight stays.

*Directions:* From the San Bernardino Freeway (10) in Upland, exit onto Mountain Avenue. Drive north on Mountain Avenue which joins Mount Baldy Road in the San Antonio Canyon and where it begins to wind its way up to Mount Baldy Village. Drive approximately 1.5 miles past the village to the Icehouse Canyon Resort. Park in the dirt lot. The trailhead is located on the right, just below the resort.

*Maps:* Send $3 to the USDA-Forest Service, 630 Sansome Street, San Francisco, CA 94111 and ask for the Angeles National Forest map. For topographic maps, ask for Mt. Baldy and Cucamonga Peak from the USGS. For other maps of the area, see "maps" under hike number 1.

*Who to contact:* Angeles National Forest, 701 North Santa Anita Avenue, Arcadia, CA 91006; (818) 574-5200.

*Trail notes:* Heading into the Cucamonga Wilderness, which is managed by both the San Bernardino and Angeles national forests, offers the hiker an excellent introduction to the high country and sub-alpine wonders of several 8,000-foot peaks including Timber Mountain, Telegraph Peak and Thunder Mountain. The canyon was originally named for the ice that was cut and shipped from the lower canyon in the mid-1800s. This trail is the best and easiest way to gain access to the wilderness interior. The trail begins to the right, behind the restaurant. The first part of the hike is up a rocky wash that is dry, but soon becomes wet. A forest of pine, oak and fir line the way. About three miles up the canyon you will arrive at Columbine Spring, a cold stream running out of the mountain. At four miles you will arrive at Icehouse Saddle, a forested parklike area. The views from the upper canyon are super. You will also enjoy the shade and sounds of the creek in the canyon bottom as you hike up. Once in the Icehouse Saddle, you can choose to return the way you came, loop back via the Chapman Trail, or head to one of the nearby peaks via a number of side trails and add to your hike.

---

## 18. BOLSA CHICA ECOLOGICAL RESERVE

1.5 mi/1.0 hr

*Reference:* **In Bolsa Chica Ecological Reserve south of Long Beach; map I5, grid g2.**

*User groups:* Hikers only. No dogs, horses or mountain bikes are allowed. No wheelchair facilities.

*Permits:* No permits are required.

*Directions:* From Seal Beach, drive south on the Pacific Coast Highway (Highway 1) to Warner Avenue. Continue driving on Highway 1 for approximately 1.5 miles to a parking area just opposite the main entrance to Bolsa Chica State Beach, a left turn.

*Maps:* For a topographic map, ask for Seal Beach from the USGS.

*Who to contact:* California Department of Fish and Game, 330 Golden Shore, Suite 50, Long Beach, CA 90802; (310) 590-5132 or Amigos de Bolsa Chica, 15545 Computer Lane, Huntington Beach, CA 92649; (714) 897-7003. Amigos de Bolsa Chica is a private nonprofit organization which coordinates activities and walks in Bolsa Chica Reserve.

*Trail notes:* From the parking area, cross over a wooden bridge to a path that runs on top of a levee and then circle around the preserve. Bring along your binoculars so that you may better enjoy and view the numerous sea birds and waterfowl that call the slough home. The nearby traffic and noise from Highway 1 is a distraction to be sure, but a mild one.

---

## 19. CARBON CANYON NATURE TRAIL

2.0 mi/1.0 hr

*Reference:* **East of Anaheim and south of Ontario; map I5, grid f5.**

*User groups:* Hikers only. No horses, mountain bikes or dogs are allowed. No

wheelchair facilities.

*Permits:* No permits are required.

*Directions:* From Anaheim, drive east on the Riverside Freeway (91) to Highway 90 (Imperial Highway). Turn north onto Highway 90 and turn left onto Carbon Canyon Road (Highway 142). Just past the city of Brea, turn right into the signed entrance for Carbon Canyon Regional Park. A fee is charged for parking.

*Maps:* For a topographic map, ask for Yorba Linda from the USGS.

*Who to contact:* Carbon Canyon Regional Park, 4422 Carbon Canyon Road, Brea, CA 92621; (714) 996-5252.

*Trail notes:* Here's a place where you can get a little education as well as a little quiet. It's a self-guided nature trail through pines, trees, water-loving plants and alongside a small stream. It's peaceful and picturesque. Rangers offer guided tours on Saturdays. Call (714) 996-5252.

# 20. IRVINE REGIONAL PARK  2.0 mi/1.0 hr

*Reference:* **In Irvine Regional Park, east of Orange; map I5, grid g6.**

*User groups:* Hikers, horses, leashed dogs and mountain bikes. No wheelchair facilities.

*Permits:* No permits are required. There is a $2 day-use fee.

*Directions:* From Interstate 5, just north of the Interstate 405/Interstate 5 interchange, exit north onto Highway 55 towards Orange. Turn right (east) on Chapman Avenue and drive until Chapman Avenue intersects with Santiago Canyon Road. Cross Santiago, still on Chapman, and drive to the park entrance.

*Maps:* Pick up the Irvine Regional Park map and brochure at the entrance station. For a topographic map, ask for Orange from the USGS.

*Who to contact:* Irvine Regional Park, 1 Irvine Park Road, Orange, CA 92669; (714) 633-8072.

*Trail notes:* Although the park can seem a little crowded—the zoo, concessions and wildlife exhibits draw thousands on peak weekends—you can leave the press of humanity behind by heading out on the trail. The William Harding Nature Trail begins at the nature trail parking area and is a good self-guided opportunity to enjoy a brief educational walk suitable for all ages. From the nature trail loop, a path continues onward, basically completing a larger loop around the perimeter of the park. There is a place, called the Lookout, to spend a few pleasant moments munching a snack and enjoying the scenery. Head down to the picnic area and then back to the parking lot and your car.

# 21. SANTIAGO OAKS REGIONAL PARK  2.0 mi/1.0 hr

*Reference:* **In Santiago Regional Park, east of Orange; map I5, grid g6.**

*User groups:* Hikers, horses, leashed dogs and mountain bikes. No wheelchair facilities.

*Permits:* No permits are required. There is a $2 day-use fee.

*Directions:* From Interstate 5, just north of the Interstate 405/Interstate 5 interchange, exit north on Highway 55 towards Orange. Turn right (east) onto Chapman Avenue and drive until Chapman intersects with Santiago Canyon Road. Turn right onto Santiago Canyon Road and turn right onto

Windes Drive. Look for the signed park entrance on Windes Drive.

*Maps:* Pick up the Santiago Oaks Regional Park map/brochure at the entrance station. For a topographic map, ask for Orange from the USGS.

*Who to contact:* Santiago Oaks Regional Park, 2145 North Windes Drive, Orange, CA 92669; (714) 538-4400.

*Trail notes:* Although only a small system of trails totaling three miles cuts through the park, nearby trails winding through the Anaheim Hills development can also be accessed from here, adding a number of miles to the day if you desire. Michael suggests beginning your visit by wandering along the self-guided Windes Nature Trail and the Pacifica Loop. From the high point on the trail, the views are wonderful, as is the streamside shade on the lower reaches.

## 22. FEATHERLY REGIONAL PARK NATURE TRAIL
0.5 mi/0.5 hr

*Reference:* In Featherly Regional Park, east of Anaheim and west of Riverside; map I5, grid f6.

*User groups:* Hikers only. No horses, mountain bikes or dogs are allowed. No wheelchair facilities.

*Permits:* No permits are required. There is a $5 day-use fee.

*Directions:* From Interstate 5, just north of the Interstate 405/Interstate 5 interchange, exit north onto Highway 55 towards Orange. Turn right (east) onto Highway 91. Look for the signed exit for Featherly Regional Park just beyond the point where Santa Ana Canyon Road joins Highway 91.

*Maps:* For a topographic map, ask for Black Star Canyon from the USGS.

*Who to contact:* Featherly Regional Park, 24001 Santa Ana Canyon Road, Anaheim, CA 92808; (714) 637-0210.

*Trail notes:* You can choose to enjoy the trail here with the company of a naturalist on weekend guided walks, or on your own with permission. Either way, you will enjoy this short walk through a tunnel of reeds and under a canopy of willow and cottonwood. The official trail washed out, leaving you to wander on informal exploration trails. The Boy Scouts have constructed a half-mile trail they use to earn merit badges.

## 23. HILLS-FOR-PEOPLE/ TELEGRAPH CANYON TRAIL
15.0 mi/5.0 hrs

*Reference:* In Chino Hills State Park, east of Anaheim and south of Ontario; map I5, grid e7.

*User groups:* Hikers. Limited access for horses and mountain bikes. No dogs are allowed. No wheelchair facilities.

*Permits:* No permits are required. A $5 parking fee is charged.

*Directions:* From Anaheim, drive east on the Riverside Freeway (91) to Highway 71. Turn north onto Highway 71 and turn left onto Pomona-Rincon Road (just past Los Serrano Road). Drive a half mile on Pomona-Rincon Road to a brickyard and a mailbox labeled "15838 Rolling M Ranch." Turn onto the dirt road next to the brickyard and drive two miles to the park entrance. Stay on the main road past the entrance to the park office and ranger station. The road forks at the ranger station. Take the left fork and drive a half mile to the trailhead parking area.

*Maps:* For topographic maps, ask for Yorba Linda and Prado Dam from the USGS.

*Who to contact:* Chino Hills State Park, 1879 Jackson Street, Riverside, CA 92504; (909) 780-6222.

*Trail notes:* Word has it that this park was a most expensive venture for the California Parks system—$47 million spent before it even opened in 1986 and it still has few facilities developed. Considering that nearly nine million people live all around the park, perhaps it was money well spent for an island of peace and greenbelt sanity amid a frenetic world. Begin hiking on the signed Hills-For-People Trail (mountain bikers and equestrians will have to use the dirt road just below the Hills-For-People Trail). Water is a major feature of this trail, as it passes by a number of livestock ponds—a throwback to the park's earlier life as a cattle range. At McDermont Spring, Hills-For-People Trail will meet up with the Telegraph Canyon Trail, which is in reality a dirt road leading gently down-canyon past the remains of a shepherd's camp and under a canopy of oak and walnut trees. The road dumps out onto Carbon Canyon Road where, if you wish to head to Carbon Canyon Regional Park, you will turn left for a brief jaunt down the shoulder of the road to the parking area. Otherwise, turn around and retrace your steps. While this hike is planned as an out-and-back venture, you could park a vehicle at Carbon Canyon Regional Park (see directions in hike number 19) for a one-way trek of 7.5 miles. Don't even think of visiting here in the summer—smog and heat make it downright unpleasant. Save this trek for a clear and cool winter's day if possible.

## 24. TIDEPOOLING from PELICAN POINT

1.0 mi/ 2.0 hrs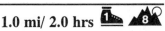

*Reference:* North of Laguna Beach and south of Corona Del Mar; map I5, grid h4.

*User groups:* Hikers only. No dogs, horses or mountain bikes are allowed. No wheelchair facilities.

*Permits:* No permits are required. A $6 parking fee is charged.

*Directions:* From Laguna Beach, drive north on Highway 1 for approximately 4.5 miles to the northernmost parking area in the state park's Pelican Point area, one mile beyond Crystal Cove.

*Maps:* For a topographic map, ask for Laguna Beach from the USGS.

*Who to contact:* Crystal Cove State Park, 8471 North Coast Highway, Laguna Beach, CA 92651; (714) 494-3539.

*Trail notes:* This is tidepooling at its best. Watch your tide charts and pick a time when the tide is at its lowest. Remember that California law mandates that private property extends down to the mean high tide line—stay below this line and public passage is legal. Stray onto private property and you may have a problem. From the Pelican Point parking area, wander down the paved path to the bluff's edge and then descend to the beach and continue hiking up it over boulders and rock formations and into the tidepooling area. It's a wondrous world as you peer into pools filled with crabs, starfish, urchins, sponges, snails, and more. Michael has even found the odd octopus lurking in the deeper pools—keep your eyes peeled!

*Special note:* Remember that all the marine life is protected by law. If you pick something up for a closer look, put it back carefully.

---

## 25. REEF POINT 0.5 mi/1.0 hr

*Reference:* **North of Laguna Beach and south of Corona Del Mar; map I5, grid h4.**

*User groups:* Hikers only. No dogs, horses or mountain bikes. There are no wheelchair facilities.

*Permits:* No permits are required. A parking fee of $6 is charged.

*Directions:* From Laguna Beach, drive north on Highway 1 for approximately 3.5 miles to the parking area at Crystal Cove.

*Maps:* For a topographic map, ask for Laguna Beach from the USGS.

*Who to contact:* Crystal Cove State Park, 8471 North Coast Highway, Laguna Beach, CA 92651; (714) 494-3539.

*Trail notes:* Reef Point provides more tidepools—you can never have enough tidepooling. This is a new area established in Crystal Cove for tidepool and beach-wandering enthusiasts. There is a paved path that leads from the parking area to the tidepools and beach, and approximately one-quarter mile of tidepools to satisfy the most gluttonous tastes.

---

## 26. EMERALD VISTA POINT 2.0 mi/3.0 hrs

*Reference:* **North of Laguna Beach and south of Corona Del Mar; map I5, grid i4.**

*User groups:* Hikers, horses and mountain bikes. No dogs are allowed. There are no wheelchair facilities.

*Permits:* No day-use permits are needed. For backcountry permits, call (714) 494-3539. A $6 parking fee is charged.

*Directions:* From Laguna Beach, drive north on Highway 1 for approximately four miles, then turn right into the signed entrance for Crystal Cove State Park and the visitors center. Park in the El Morro parking lot.

*Maps:* Be sure to pick up the Crystal Cove State Park backcountry trail map, available for 50 cents from the visitors center. For a topographic map, ask for Laguna Beach from the USGS.

*Who to contact:* Crystal Cove State Park, 8471 North Coast Highway, Laguna Beach, CA 92651; (714) 494-3539.

*Trail notes:* From the bottom of the parking area, follow the trail over a knoll and down the El Moro Canyon; then hike steeply up a slope and ridge to the Emerald Vista Point, one mile from the trailhead. If the day is clear (very rare), your views will encompass Emerald Bay, Laguna Beach, the Palos Verdes Peninsula and even the distant and always hazy Santa Monica Mountains.

---

## 27. EL MORO CANYON LOOP 8.4 mi/4.5 hrs

*Reference:* **North of Laguna Beach and south of Corona Del Mar; map I5, grid i4.**

*User groups:* Hikers, horses and mountain bikes. No dogs are allowed. No wheelchair facilities.

*Permits:* No permits are required.

*Directions:* From Laguna Beach, drive north on Highway 1 for approximately four miles and turn right into the signed entrance for Crystal Cove State Park and the visitor's center. Park in the El Moro parking lot.

*Maps:* Be sure to pick up the Crystal Cove State Park backcountry map, available for 10 cents from the visitor's center. For a topographic map, ask for Laguna Beach from the USGS.

*Who to contact:* Crystal Cove State Park, 8471 North Coast Highway, Laguna Beach, CA 92651; (714) 494-3539.

*Trail notes:* While the views from the ridges and overlooks are super, the most outstanding part of this hike is the quiet and peace of shaded El Moro Canyon. From the visitor center parking area, follow the dirt road heading east towards the ridge. Stay right at the road split and climb gently up the ridge. Stay left at the next intersection (if you go right, you will drop down into the canyon below) and keep hiking to West Cut-Across Trail. Turn right and descend to an intersection where you will head left on a dirt road named Red Tail Ridge. Stay on Red Tail Ridge to a gate, barring access to private land. Turn right here, head past another gate and then onto the East Loop Road, which heads steeply up and then down into El Moro Canyon. Stay in El Moro Canyon all the way back to the visitor center.

---

## 28. WEST RIDGE to BELL CANYON LOOP

3.5 mi/2.0 hrs

*Reference:* In Caspers Wilderness Park, east of San Juan Capistrano; map I5, grid i7.

*User groups:* Hikers, dogs and mountain bikes (on dirt roads only). Horses are not recommended. No wheelchair facilities.

*Permits:* Currently, there is a $2 entry fee for vehicles. Wilderness use permits are required for all visitors. No person under the age of 18 is allowed within the park boundaries because of the fear of mountain lion attacks, although that ban may be lifted soon. Camping is available for $10 per night.

*Directions:* From Los Angeles area, head south on the San Diego Freeway (Interstate 5) to the Ortega Highway 74 exit at San Juan Capistrano. Turn east (inland) along the Ortega Highway and proceed 7.5 miles to the park entrance.

*Maps:* For a topographic map, ask for Canada Gobernadora from the USGS. A basic trail map, sketchy at best, is available upon request when entering the park. Send $3 to the USDA-Forest Service, 630 Sansome Street, San Francisco, CA 94111 and ask for the Cleveland National Forest map—it offers a general overview but little detail of the park.

*Who to contact:* Caspers Wilderness Park, P.O. Box 395, San Juan Capistrano, CA 92675; (714) 831-2174.

*Trail notes:* This hike will take you through some fascinating white sandstone rock formations and along a main ridge with outstanding views. Beginning at the windmill, head out on the Nature Trail. Turn left onto Dick Loskorn Trail (formerly and still informally known as Gunsight Pass Trail). Loskorn winds its way up to a knife-edge ridge with an unnerving drop-off. At the West Ridge Trail, turn right (north) to the Star Rise Trail. Right again and down to the Bell Canyon Trail and another right. Head back to the windmill and parking area. We believe this to be the most beautiful and wonderful park in the Orange County park system. It is too bad that youngsters cannot share the visit, but because of liability concerns and all the flames of fear of mountain lion attacks being fanned by public paranoia (even though such attacks are extremely rare), anyone under 18 is prohibited from visiting. Ah well, if you are over 18, you are going to fall in love with this place. October through June is the best time to visit—summer is too darn hot! Unfortunately, the fall fires of 1993 swept through this park too. Vegetation is growing back and the wildflowers this spring should be superb. All trail signs have been replaced.

---

## 29. EAST RIDGE to BELL CANYON LOOP

6.8 mi/3.5 hrs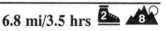

*Reference:* In Caspers Wilderness Park, east of San Juan Capistrano; map I5, grid i7.

*User groups:* Hikers, horses and mountain bikes (on dirt roads only). No dogs are allowed. No wheelchair facilities.

*Permits:* Wilderness permits are required for all visitors. No person under the age of 18 is allowed within the park boundaries because of the fear of mountain lion attacks.

*Directions:* From Los Angeles area, head south on the San Diego Freeway (Interstate 5) to the Ortega Highway 74 exit at San Juan Capistrano. Turn east (inland) along the Ortega Highway and proceed 7.5 miles to the park entrance. Currently, there is a $2 entry fee for vehicles.

*Maps:* For a topographic map, ask for Canada Gobernadora from the USGS. A basic trail map, sketchy at best, is available upon request when entering the park. Send $3 to the USDA-Forest Service, 630 Sansome Street, San Francisco, CA 94111 and ask for the Cleveland National Forest map—it offers a general overview but little detail of the park.

*Who to contact:* Caspers Wilderness Park, P.O. Box 395, San Juan Capistrano, CA 92675; (714) 831-2174.

*Trail notes:* Enjoy the views from the ridges and the quiet and cooling peace of the woodlands lining Bell Canyon on this hike. From the San Juan Meadow picnic area, wander up the East Flats Trail and then head right on the East Ridge Trail. At Pointed Hill, take a break and enjoy the view of the distant Santa Ana Mountains. At Cougar Pass Trail, turn right and then head left on the Oso Trail. At the Bell Canyon Trail, head left and back to the parking area.

*Special note:* For more information on Caspers Wilderness Park and the fire damage of fall 1993, please see hike number 28.

---

## 30. COLD SPRING TRAIL LOOP

4.2 mi/3.0 hrs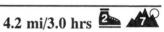

*Reference:* In Caspers Wilderness Park, east of San Juan Capistrano; map I5, grid i7.

*User groups:* Hikers, horses and mountain bikes (on dirt roads only). No dogs are allowed. No wheelchair facilities.

*Permits:* Wilderness permits are required for all visitors. No person under the age of 18 is allowed within the park boundaries because of the fear of mountain lion attacks.

*Directions:* From Los Angeles, head south on the San Diego Freeway (Interstate 5) to the Ortega Highway 74 exit at San Juan Capistrano. Turn east (inland) along the Ortega Highway and proceed 7.5 miles to the park entrance to pick up your wilderness permit. Currently, there is a $2 entry fee for vehicles. After picking up your permit, exit the park and drive approximately five miles east on the Ortega Highway to Ortega High School. The Old San Juan Hot Springs Resort burned in the fire and is fenced in.

*Maps:* For a topographic map, ask for Canada Gobernadora from the USGS. A basic trail map, sketchy at best, is available upon request when entering the park. Send $3 to the USDA-Forest Service, 630 Sansome Street, San Francisco, CA 94111 and ask for the Cleveland National Forest map—it offers a general overview but little detail of the park.

*Who to contact:* Caspers Wilderness Park, P.O. Box 395, San Juan Capistrano, CA 92675; (714) 831-2174.

*Trail notes:* This is considered by many to be the most secluded and scenic canyon in the park and we certainly haven't discovered any evidence to overturn that belief—it is superb. Indeed, the panorama as you are climbing out of the canyon is almost devoid of human clutter—a rarity in these parts. From the fenced in ruins, hike over a hill and onto the Cold Springs Trail. Hike up-canyon to the Oso Trail (in reality a fire road). Head left (west) on the Oso Trail until reaching the Ortega Highway and then turn left onto another trail that parallels the highway. A firebreak leads to a trail that contours over to the alders at the head of Cold Spring Canyon. Return the way you hiked in.

*Special note:* For more information on Caspers Wilderness Park and the fire damage of fall 1993, please see hike number 28.

---

## 31. HOLY JIM TRAIL     2.5 mi/2.0 hrs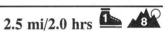
## to HOLY JIM FALLS

*Reference:* East of Laguna Hills; map I5, grid h8.

*User groups:* Hikers, horses and dogs. No mountain bikes are allowed. No wheelchair facilities.

*Permits:* No permits are required.

*Directions:* From Interstate 5 in El Toro, take the El Toro Road exit and head east through Mission Viejo. Turn right onto Live Oak Canyon Road. After passing O'Neill Regional Park, drive approximately one mile to Trabuco Wash and turn left into the wash and up rocky Trabuco Road. This is no place for a low-slung vehicle. Within five miles, you pass a volunteer fire station and arrive at the signed Holy Jim turnoff to the left. Park in the large parking area.

*Maps:* Send $3 to the USDA-Forest Service, 630 Sansome Street, San Francisco, CA 94111 and ask for the Cleveland National Forest map. For a topographic map, ask for Santiago Peak from the USGS.

*Who to contact:* Cleveland National Forest, Trabuco Ranger District, 1147 East 6th Street, Corona, CA 91719; (909) 736-1811.

*Trail notes:* Waterfalls and a cooling rock grotto are a welcome paradise—especially on a hot day. Walk one-half mile up Holy Jim Road to a gate. Pass through the gate and hike up the trail alongside Holy Jim Creek for about a mile. Look for an unsigned but well-used side trail branching off to Holy Jim

Falls. The falls are one-quarter mile from the junction. The trail to the left heads up to Santiago Peak—it's 10 miles away.

## 32. HOLY JIM TRAIL to SANTIAGO PEAK

16.0 mi/8.0 hrs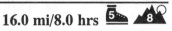

*Reference:* **East of Laguna Hills; map I5, grid h8.**

*User groups:* Hikers, horses and dogs. No mountain bikes are allowed. No wheelchair facilities.

*Permits:* No permits are required.

*Directions:* From Interstate 5 in El Toro, take the El Toro Road exit and head east through Mission Viejo. Turn right onto Live Oak Canyon Road. After passing O'Neill Regional Park, drive approximately one mile to Trabuco Wash and turn left into the wash and up rocky Trabuco Road. This is no place for a low-slung vehicle. Within five miles, you pass a volunteer fire station and arrive at the signed Holy Jim turnoff to the left. Park in the dirt area located near the turnoff.

*Maps:* Send $3 to the USDA-Forest Service, 630 Sansome Street, San Francisco, CA 94111 and ask for the Cleveland National Forest map. For a topographic map, ask for Santiago Peak from the USGS.

*Who to contact:* Cleveland National Forest, Trabuco Ranger District, 1147 East 6th Street, Corona, CA 91719; (909) 736-1811.

*Trail notes:* Santiago Peak is the highest summit in the Santa Ana range and worth the 3,000 feet of climbing effort to trek up it. Wait, if you can, until just after an atmosphere-clearing rain, because then the views will be unbelievably inspiring and clear in almost every direction. Walk up Holy Jim Road for about one-half mile to a gate. Pass through the gate and hike up the trail alongside Holy Jim Creek. Look for an unsigned but obviously well-used side trail branching off to Holy Jim Falls for a one-quarter-mile side journey to a watery paradise. Continue hiking up Holy Jim to Bear Springs and the intersection of Holy Jim Trail and Main Divide Truck Trail. Continue climbing, 1,800 feet in the next three miles, up the Main Divide Truck Trail to Santiago Peak. Catch your breath and feel for your pulse, which should be perceptibly pounding by now. Retrace your steps to your car.

## PACIFIC CREST TRAIL                    48.0 mi. one way/5.0 days
## GENERAL INFORMATION

*Reference:* **Trail sections extend from Angeles Crest Highway to Mill Creek Picnic Area.**

*User groups:* Hikers, horses and dogs (except in national parks). No mountain bikes are allowed. No wheelchair access.

*Permits:* A wilderness permit is required for traveling through various wilderness and special-use areas that the trail traverses. Contact the national forest, BLM or national park office at your point of entry for a permit that is good for the length of your trip. For this section of the Pacific Crest Trail, no day-use permits are required.

*Maps:* For an overall view of the trail route, send $3 for each map ordered to the USDA-Forest Service, 630 Sansome Street, San Francisco, CA 94111, ask for the Angeles National Forest and the San Bernardino National Forest maps. Topographic maps for particular sections of trail are provided under each specific trail section heading listed below.

*Who to contact:* Contact either the national forest, BLM or national park office at your trailhead—see specific trailheads and corresponding agencies listed within each section.

*Trail notes:* Elevations range from 3,000 to over 8,000 feet throughout this section of trail. Views are superb, when the smog hanging over the valley and the LA basin doesn't interfere. Water stops along the route are limited so be sure to stock up whenever you can.

---

## PCT-11                    32.0 mi. one way/3.0 days
## ANGELES CREST HIGHWAY to THREE POINTS

*Reference:* **From the Angeles Crest Highway, map I5, grid a8 to Three Points.**

*User groups:* Hikers, horses and dogs. No mountain bikes are allowed. No wheelchair facilities.

*Permits:* A wilderness permit is required for traveling through various wilderness and special-use areas that the trail traverses. Contact the Angeles National Forest at (805) 296-9710 for a permit that is good for the length of your trip. For this section of the Pacific Crest Trail, no day-use permits are required.

*Directions:* For the Angeles Crest Trailhead—From Interstate 15 near Cajon, take Highway 138 east. Turn left (west) on the Angeles Crest Highway and drive five miles to Wrightwood. Continue for three miles to Big Pines. Bear left and continue on Angeles Crest Highway for 1.5 miles to Inspiration Point, opposite Blue Ridge Road.

For the Three Points Trailhead—From the Foothill Freeway (210) in La Canada, exit onto the Angeles Crest Highway (2) and drive to Three Points Junction, approximately 2.5 miles north of Chilao. The exit to Three Points is marked by a sign indicating Horse Flats.

*Maps:* Send $3 to the USDA-Forest Service, 630 Sansome Street, San Francisco, CA 94111 and ask for the Angeles National Forest map. For topographic maps, ask for Waterman Mountain, Crystal Lake and Mount San Antonio from the USGS.

**Who to contact:** Angeles National Forest, 701 North Santa Anita Avenue, Arcadia, CA 91006; (818) 574-5200.

**Trail notes:** Enjoy the outstanding views, varied landscape and solitude. Keep a sharp lookout and you may be fortunate enough to see bighorn sheep.

---

## PCT-12      16.0 mi. one way/2.0 days
## THREE POINTS to MILL CREEK PICNIC AREA

**Reference:** From Three Points, map I5, grid a4 to Mill Creek.

**User groups:** Hikers, horses and dogs. No mountain bikes are allowed. No wheelchair facilities.

**Permits:** A wilderness permit is required for traveling through various wilderness and special-use areas that the trail traverses. Contact the Angeles National Forest at (805) 296-9710 for a permit that is good for the length of your trip. For this section of the Pacific Crest Trail, no day-use permits are required.

**Directions:** For the Three Points Trailhead—From the Foothill Freeway (210) in La Canada, exit on the Angeles Crest Highway (2) and drive to Three Points Junction—approximately 2.5 miles north of Chilao. The exit to Three Points is marked by a sign indicating Horse Flats.

For the Mill Creek Picnic Area Trailhead—From Highway 14 at Vincent, head south on the Angeles Forest Highway (County Road N3) to the Mill Creek Summit and picnic area and the signed PCT trailhead.

**Maps:** Send $3 to the USDA-Forest Service, 630 Sansome Street, San Francisco, CA 94111 and ask for the Angeles National Forest map. For topographic maps, ask for Waterman Mountain, Chilao Flat and Pacifico Mountain from the USGS.

**Who to contact:** Angeles National Forest, Saugus Ranger District, 30800 Bouquet Canyon Road, Saugus, CA 91350; (805) 296-9710.

**Trail notes:** This is a short and pleasant section of trail through a combination of wooded and badlands terrain. Mixed chaparral, pine and oak are all along the trail. The trek is mostly dry, so carry plenty of water. The views from the high points along this tread are superb! Mill Creek is a good resting spot and important place to tank up on water if you are continuing on—the next reliable water lies nearly 18 miles away.

**PCT CONTINUATION:** To continue hiking along the Pacific Crest Trail, see Chapter H5, pages 646-649.

## Leave No Trace Tips

### Campfires

• Fire use can scar the backcountry. If a fire ring is not available, use a lightweight stove for cooking.

• Where fires are permitted, use exisiting fire rings, away from large rocks or overhangs.

• Do not char rocks by building new rings.

• Gather sticks from the ground that are no larger than the diameter of your wrist.

• Do not snap branches of live, dead or downed trees, which can cause personal injury and also scar the natural setting.

• Put the fire "dead out" and make sure it is cold before departing. Remove all trash from the fire ring.

• Remember that some forest fires can be started by a campfire that appears to be out. Hot embers burning deep in the pit can cause tree roots to catch on fire and burn underground. If you ever see smoke rising from the ground, seemingly from nowhere, dig down and put the fire out.

# MAP I6

4 PCT SECTIONS
36 TRAILS
PAGES 720-749

SO-CAL MAP ......................... see page 662
adjoining maps
NORTH (H6) ........................... see page 650
EAST (I7) ................................. see page 750
SOUTH (J6) ........................... see page 766
WEST (I5) ............................... see page 696

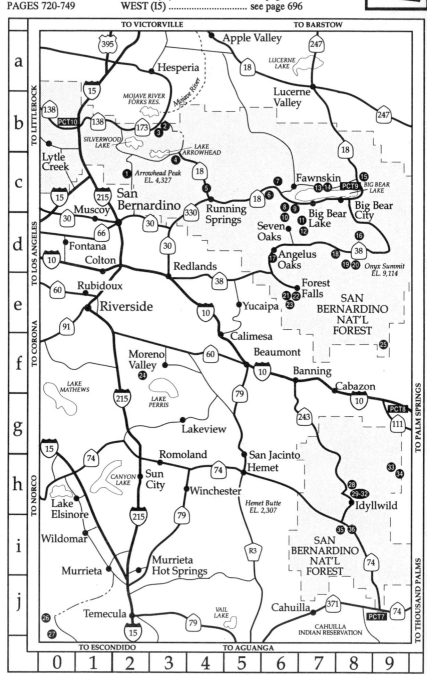

**Map I6 featuring:** San Bernardino National Forest, Lake Arrowhead, Big Bear, San Gorgonio Wilderness, Santa Ana River, Lake Perris State Recreation Area, Lake Elsinor, Cleveland National Forest, Idyllwild, Big Bear Lake

## 1. MONUMENT PEAK TRAIL from BAILEY CANYON

10.0 mi/5.0 hrs

*Reference:* In San Bernardino National Forest; map I6, grid c2.

*User groups:* Hikers, horses, dogs and mountain bikes. No wheelchair facilities.

*Permits:* No day-use permits are required. Camping permits are required. For more information, contact the Lytle Creek Ranger District at (909) 887-2576.

*Directions:* From San Bernardino, drive north on Interstate 215 for 5.5 miles and turn north onto Palm Avenue. Drive approximately 1.5 miles on Palm Avenue to the end of the road and a gate at the entrance to Bailey Canyon and Forest Service 2N49. Park off the road so you do not obstruct the gate.

*Maps:* Send $3 to the USDA-Forest Service, 630 Sansome Street, San Francisco, CA 94111 and ask for the San Bernardino National Forest map. For a topographic map, ask for San Bernardino North from the USGS.

*Who to contact:* San Bernardino National Forest, Arrowhead Ranger District, P.O. Box 350, Skyforest, CA 92385; (909) 337-2444.

*Trail notes:* The vistas from the summit, especially after a valley-cleansing rain, are worth the effort it takes to get there. Hike up Forest Service Road 2N49 to the stone monument on top of Monument Peak. It's a steep scramble over a hot and dusty route, gaining almost 3,000 feet in only five miles. Switchbacks the last three miles or so help, but not much. Take your time and keep thinking of the view. This trail is often closed in the summer, due to fire hazard. But no matter, because the best time to hike is between November and May. No matter when you decide to go, make it a cool day, because you are at the mercy of the sun all the way up. Pack plenty of water.

## 2. DEEP CREEK TRAIL

8.0 mi/4.0 hrs

*Reference:* In San Bernardino National Forest, Lake Arrowhead; map I6, grid b3.

*User groups:* Hikers, horses and dogs. No mountain bikes are allowed. No wheelchair facilities.

*Permits:* No day-use permits are required. This is a day-use area only.

*Directions:* From Interstate 15, take the Highway 138 exit, turn right and drive approximately nine miles to Highway 173. Turn left and drive approximately eight miles to the highway's end. The road is dirt—narrow and windy—so proceed with care. The road is not maintained and signs are posted saying it's closed, but everyone uses it anyway.

*Maps:* Send $3 to the USDA-Forest Service, 630 Sansome Street, San Francisco, CA 94111 and ask for the San Bernardino National Forest map. For a topographic map, ask for Lake Arrowhead from the USGS.

*Who to contact:* San Bernardino National Forest, Arrowhead Ranger District, P.O. Box 350, Skyforest, CA 92385; (909) 337-2444.

*Trail notes:* Hike up a disintegrating old asphalt road into Deep Creek Canyon. Apparently, three-wheel and motocross idiots think this is a perfect place to chew up turf because on Michael's last trek through here, their unregulated access to the area was all too evident. Fortunately, you will soon leave all that behind as you hike up to the top of the Mojave River Forks Flood Control Dam and then cross to where the trail resumes on the other side. Just beyond the spillway, head east at another signed trailhead toward Deep Creek Hot Springs. There are a number of good picnic spots along the way, the best of which is McKinley Creek. Beyond McKinley, you will arrive at the hot springs with a selection of rock-walled pools ranging from tepid to scalding—take your pick. Head back the way you came when ready. Be forewarned that many bathers are nude.

---

## 3. THE PINNACLES        6.0 mi/4.0 hrs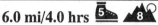

*Reference:* In San Bernardino National Forest; map I6, grid b3.

*User groups:* Hikers and dogs. No horses or mountain bikes are allowed. No wheelchair facilities.

*Permits:* No permits are required. This is a day-use area only.

*Directions:* From Interstate 15, head east on the Angeles Crest Highway (Highway 18) and drive to Highway 173 at Lake Arrowhead. Drive north on Highway 173 to the Rock Camp Ranger Station and then drive approximately a half mile more to Forest Service Trail 3W16 on the left. Park on the shoulder of the highway.

*Maps:* Send $3 to the USDA-Forest Service, 630 Sansome Street, San Francisco, CA 94111 and ask for the San Bernardino National Forest map. For a topographic map, ask for Lake Arrowhead from the USGS.

*Who to contact:* San Bernardino National Forest, Arrowhead Ranger District, P.O. Box 350, Skyforest, CA 92385; (909) 337-2444.

*Trail notes:* Like the Pinnacles that are more famous up north, these pinnacles are quite rocky and invite those who love to scramble among boulders and jagged peaks. Unlike the Pinnacles up north, these pinnacles are not as stunning and not as heavily visited. Still, they are well worth a look. From the trailhead, draw a bead on the rocky ridge ahead of you and then keep heading towards it—the trail tends to vanish at times. At the top of the ridge, the rocky summit will become evident and you can easily and carefully work your way there. Keep a sharp eye on your bearings because it is possible to become disoriented and spend quite a bit of time wandering around aimlessly. There is quite a bit of rock scrambling involved in this trip, so be sure to wear sturdy footwear. Since navigation can get a bit curious, pack along a map and compass, and know how to use them. The Forest Service has worked to mark the trail and the recent placement of rock cairns has helped—we just hope no one removes them.

*Special note:* This trail is often closed in the summer due to fire hazard. The best time to hike anyway is between November and May. Pack plenty of water—you're in sun all the way.

# 4. LITTLE BEAR CREEK TRAIL 5.0 mi/2.5 hrs

*Reference:* In San Bernardino National Forest, Lake Arrowhead; map I6, grid c3.

*User groups:* Hikers, horses and dogs. No mountain bikes are allowed. No wheelchair facilities.

*Permits:* No permits are required. This is a day-use area only.

*Directions:* From Interstate 10 in San Bernardino, turn off at the Waterman Avenue/Highway 18 exit and drive approximately 18 miles north into the mountains. At Highway 173, turn left and drive approximately 4.5 miles to Hospital Road. Turn right and drive just past the hospital to the North Shore Campground entrance. The trailhead is located between campsites 10 and 11. The Forest Service closes the campground in the winter, but if you still wish to use the trail the hospital allows parking in its lower lot. From there it is a short walk to the campground and trailhead.

*Maps:* Send $3 to the USDA-Forest Service, 630 Sansome Street, San Francisco, CA 94111 and ask for the San Bernardino National Forest map. For a topographic map, ask for Lake Arrowhead from the USGS.

*Who to contact:* San Bernardino National Forest, Arrowhead Ranger District, P.O. Box 350, Skyforest, CA 92385; (909) 337-2444.

*Trail notes:* From the trailhead, hike down the hill and straight through a junction to a dirt road and a trail signed Forest Service Trail 3W12. The trail crosses this road, continuing on the other side and then terminates on another dirt road. This is an out-and-back hike into a pretty and peaceful little canyon through which Little Bear Creek runs. The pine trees add a wonderful scent to the air and become even more soothing when the frequent breezes blow through their branches.

---

# 5. HEAPS PEAK ARBORETUM  0.75 mi/1.0 hr
# INTERPRETIVE TRAIL

*Reference:* In San Bernardino National Forest, Lake Arrowhead; map I6, grid c4.

*User groups:* Hikers only. No mountain bikes, dogs or horses are allowed. No wheelchair facilities.

*Permits:* No permits are required.

*Directions:* Take Interstate 10 to Interstate 215. Exit at the Waterman/Highway 18 exit, signed for "Mountain Resorts." Go left towards Lake Arrowhead. After two miles, Highway 18 begins. Drive 10 miles past the Lake Arrowhead turnoff to Santa's Village. One-quarter mile past Santa's Village is Heaps Peak Arboretum on the left.

*Maps:* Send $3 to the USDA-Forest Service, 630 Sansome Street, San Francisco, CA 94111 and ask for the San Bernardino National Forest map. For a topographic map, ask for Lake Arrowhead from the USGS.

*Who to contact:* San Bernardino National Forest, Arrowhead Ranger District, P.O. Box 350, Skyforest, CA 92385; (909) 337-2444.

*Trail notes:* This is the perfect educational leg stretcher if you are driving the Rim of the World Highway either on the way to or from Big Bear or Lake Arrowhead. Be sure to pick up the interpretive pamphlet at the start of the trail—it is as entertaining as it is informative. On this trip you will learn all about the trees and vegetation that are typical in this forest area. Two thumbs up for one of the best interpretive trails we have experienced.

---

# 6. CAMP CREEK NATIONAL RECREATION TRAIL

**7.2 mi/3.0 hrs**

*Reference:* **In San Bernardino National Forest, Big Bear; map I6, grid c6.**

*User groups:* Hikers, horses and dogs. No mountain bikes are allowed. No wheelchair facilities.

*Permits:* No day-use permits are required. Overnight permits are required. For more information, contact the Big Bear Ranger District at (909) 866-3437.

*Directions:* From Interstate 15 at Cajon Junction, turn east onto the Rim of the World Highway (Highway 18) to Snow Valley Ski Area and then drive another half mile to Forest Service Road 2N97. Turn right and drive to the parking area and trailhead for Siberia Creek and Camp Creek National Recreation Trail.

*Maps:* Send $3 to the USDA-Forest Service, 630 Sansome Street, San Francisco, CA 94111 and ask for the San Bernardino National Forest map. For a topographic map, ask for Keller Peak from the USGS.

*Who to contact:* San Bernardino National Forest, Big Bear Ranger District, P.O. Box 290, Fawnskin, CA 92333; (909) 866-3437.

*Trail notes:* The trail offers a quick way to drop down into the cooling depths of Siberia Creek and the Siberia Creek Trail Camp and Bear Creek Canyon. See hike number 8 for more information. The best time to visit is late spring through November.

---

# 7. GLORY RIDGE TRAIL

**2.0 mi/1.5 hrs**

*Reference:* **In San Bernardino National Forest, Big Bear; map I6, grid c6.**

*User groups:* Hikers, horses and dogs. No mountain bikes are allowed. No wheelchair facilities.

*Permits:* No day-use permits are required. Overnight permits are required. For more information, contact the Big Bear Ranger District at (909) 866-3437.

*Directions:* From Interstate 15 at Cajon Junction, head east on the Rim of the World Highway (Highway 18). Turn right onto Forest Service Road 2N15, approximately 1.5 miles before arriving at Big Bear Lake, and drive to the road's end and the parking area.

*Maps:* Send $3 to the USDA-Forest Service, 630 Sansome Street, San Francisco, CA 94111 and ask for the San Bernardino National Forest map. For topographic maps, ask for Keller Peak and Big Bear Lake from the USGS.

*Who to contact:* San Bernardino National Forest, Big Bear Ranger District, P.O. Box 290, Fawnskin, CA 92333; (909) 866-3437.

*Trail notes:* This is a short but enjoyable hike down a steep trail that fishermen once used to access Bear Creek. Once at the bottom, wander up and down the creek or just hang out and enjoy the sounds of the stream. Return the way you came—up the 1,000 or so feet to your car, yowza! The best time to visit is late spring through November.

# 8. SIBERIA CREEK TRAIL    8.0 mi/4.0 hrs

*Reference:* In San Bernardino National Forest, Big Bear; map I6, grid c6.

*User groups:* Hikers, horses and dogs. No mountain bikes are allowed. No wheelchair facilities.

*Permits:* No day-use permits are required. Overnight permits are required. For more information, contact the Big Bear Ranger District at (909) 866-3437.

*Directions:* From Interstate 15 at Cajon Junction, head east on the Rim of the World Highway (Highway 18) to Big Bear Lake. From Highway 18 at the west end of Big Bear Lake, turn right (south) onto Tulip Lane. Turn right onto Forest Service Road 2N11, approximately a half mile from the highway. Watch for the Champion Lodgepole signs that will keep you on track for the next five miles until you reach the signed trailhead. Park alongside the road.

*Maps:* Send $3 to the USDA-Forest Service, 630 Sansome Street, San Francisco, CA 94111 and ask for the San Bernardino National Forest map. For topographic maps, ask for Big Bear Lake and Keller Peak from the USGS.

*Who to contact:* San Bernardino National Forest, Big Bear Ranger District, P.O. Box 290, Fawnskin, CA 92333; (909) 866-3437.

*Trail notes:* The trail terminates at Bear Creek and the Seven Pines Trail, just south of Siberia Creek Trail Camp. The first couple miles of the trek, winding alongside a fern-lined Siberia Creek, are quite easy and most suitable for family groups. From the Gunsight, an interesting rock formation, the trail drops quickly, around 2,500 feet in only two miles. Only the very fit should attempt this trek as a dayhike—even as an overnight it is a challenging climb out. Once the trail intersects with Seven Pines, turn right and hike approximately one-half mile to Siberia Creek Trail Camp. The oak- and alder-shaded camp offers a wonderful place to kick up your feet and rest a while, pitch a tent even. The best time to visit is late spring through November.

# 9. CASTLE ROCK TRAIL    1.6 mi/1.5 hrs

*Reference:* In San Bernardino National Forest, Big Bear; map I6, grid c6.

*User groups:* Hikers, horses and dogs. No mountain bikes are allowed. No wheelchair facilities.

*Permits:* No day-use permits are required. Overnight permits are required. For more information, contact the Big Bear Ranger District at (909) 866-3437.

*Directions:* From Interstate 15 at Cajon Junction, head east on the Rim of the World Highway (Highway 18) to Big Bear Lake. Drive approximately one mile past the dam on Highway 18 to a parking area in a clearing next to the highway.

*Maps:* Send $3 to the USDA-Forest Service, 630 Sansome Street, San Francisco, CA 94111 and ask for the San Bernardino National Forest map. For a topographic map, ask for Big Bear Lake from the USGS.

*Who to contact:* San Bernardino National Forest, Big Bear Ranger District, P.O. Box 290, Fawnskin, CA 92333; (909) 866-3437.

*Trail notes:* Castle Rock, rising sentry-like above the lower reaches of Big Bear Lake, is steeped with legend. A hike to the top of the rock during a spring or summer breeze may bring your imagination to a peak level—is that or isn't it the sound of a saddened Indian princess wailing across the lake for her lost husband? You decide. Breeze or Indian princess, the trip is well worth the short trek and promises to offer a soothing respite. From Highway 18, the trail climbs uphill to Castle Rock. The hike is rich in scenery and is especially enjoyable in the summer and fall when colors are at their best.

## 10. BLUFF MESA TRAIL   0.8 mi/1.0 hr

*Reference:* **In San Bernardino National Forest, Big Bear; map I6, grid d6.**
*User groups:* Hikers, horses and dogs. No mountain bikes are allowed. No wheelchair facilities.
*Permits:* No day-use permits are required. Overnight permits are required. For more information, contact the Big Bear Ranger District at (909) 866-3437.
*Directions:* From Interstate 15 at Cajon Junction, head east on the Rim of the World Highway (Highway 18) to Big Bear Lake. From Highway 18 at the west end of Big Bear Lake, turn right (south) onto Tulip Lane. Turn right onto Forest Service Road 2N11, approximately a half mile from the highway. Watch for the Champion Lodgepole signs that will keep you on track for the next five miles until you reach the signed trailhead. Park alongside the road.
*Maps:* Send $3 to the USDA-Forest Service, 630 Sansome Street, San Francisco, CA 94111 and ask for the San Bernardino National Forest map. For a topographic map, ask for Big Bear Lake from the USGS.
*Who to contact:* San Bernardino National Forest, Big Bear Ranger District, P.O. Box 290, Fawnskin, CA 92333; (909) 866-3437.
*Trail notes:* This trail starts at the Champion Lodgepole Pine and runs north, terminating at Bluff Mesa Group Camp. It is an easy hike through gorgeous stands of large Jeffrey pines and most pleasant for families. Best time to visit is late spring through November.

## 11. LODGEPOLE PINE TRAIL   0.6 mi/1.5 hrs

*Reference:* **In San Bernardino National Forest, Big Bear; map I6, grid d7.**
*User groups:* Hikers, horses and dogs. No mountain bikes are allowed. No wheelchair facilities.
*Permits:* No day-use permits are required. Overnight permits are required. For more information, contact the Big Bear Ranger District at (909) 866-3437.
*Directions:* From Interstate 15 at Cajon Junction, head east on the Rim of the World Highway (Highway 18) to Big Bear Lake. From Highway 18 at the west end of Big Bear Lake, turn right (south) onto Tulip Lane. Turn right onto Forest Service Road 2N11, approximately a half mile from the highway. Watch for the Champion Lodgepole signs that will keep you on track for the next five miles until you reach the signed trailhead. Park alongside the road.
*Maps:* Send $3 to the USDA-Forest Service, 630 Sansome Street, San Francisco, CA 94111 and ask for the San Bernardino National Forest map. For a topographic map, ask for Big Bear Lake from the USGS.
*Who to contact:* San Bernardino National Forest, Big Bear Ranger District, P.O. Box 290, Fawnskin, CA 92333; (909) 866-3437.
*Trail notes:* What more could you want? Here's an easy, quiet hike along a brook lined with ferns and wildflowers to one of the tallest known lodgepole pines in California. Best time to visit is late spring through November.

## 12. PINEKNOT TRAIL     6.0 mi/3.0 hrs

*Reference:* In San Bernardino National Forest, Big Bear; map I6, grid d7.

*User groups:* Hikers, horses and dogs. No mountain bikes are allowed. No wheelchair facilities.

*Permits:* No day-use permits are required. Overnight permits are required. For more information, contact the Big Bear Ranger District at (909) 866-3437.

*Directions:* From Interstate 15 at Cajon Junction, head east on the Rim of the World Highway (Highway 18) to Big Bear Lake. Drive on Highway 18 toward Big Bear Village and turn south (right) onto Mill Creek Road. Drive approximately a half mile to the Aspen Glen Picnic Area on the left. The signed trailhead begins from the east end of the parking area.

*Maps:* Send $3 to the USDA-Forest Service, 630 Sansome Street, San Francisco, CA 94111 and ask for the San Bernardino National Forest map. For a topographic map, ask for Big Bear Lake from the USGS.

*Who to contact:* San Bernardino National Forest, Big Bear Ranger District, P.O. Box 290, Fawnskin, CA 92333; (909) 866-3437.

*Trail notes:* This trail heads up over a lupine-covered ridge with good views down into Big Bear Lake, through a number of meadows dotted with as many boulders as wildflowers, through Deer Group Camp and then up to Grand View Point—the best spot from which to take in the stunning view of San Gorgonio. Best time to visit is late spring through November. If you are inclined to don cross-country skis, we can attest that the view from Grand View in the winter is as stunning if not more so than at any other time of the year—but dress warmly because the wind blows cold up top.

## 13. COUGAR CREST TRAIL     4.0 mi/1.5 hrs

*Reference:* In San Bernardino National Forest, Big Bear; map I6, grid c7.

*User groups:* Hikers, horses and dogs. No mountain bikes are allowed. No wheelchair facilities.

*Permits:* No day-use permits are required. Overnight permits are required. For more information, contact the Big Bear Ranger District at (909) 866-3437.

*Directions:* From Interstate 15 at Cajon Junction, head east on the Rim of the World Highway (Highway 18) to Big Bear Lake. Turn north onto Highway 38 and drive to the signed Cougar Crest Trailhead and parking area located on the north side of the highway, a short distance before the Big Bear Ranger Station.

*Maps:* Send $3 to the USDA-Forest Service, 630 Sansome Street, San Francisco, CA 94111 and ask for the San Bernardino National Forest map. For a topographic map, ask for Fawnskin from the USGS.

*Who to contact:* San Bernardino National Forest, Big Bear Ranger District, P.O. Box 290, Fawnskin, CA 92333; (909) 866-3437.

*Trail notes:* The trail is actually more of a retired dirt road at first, winding its way up and past a number of old mining roads. Before long, Cougar Crest narrows and begins climbing through the forest up to its junction with the Pacific Crest Trail. This is as far as the mileage noted above has taken you, but if you are still fresh, you can add another one mile each way to your hike by heading right on the PCT towards Bertha Peak. Head south at the next junction, leaving the PCT and climbing up to Bertha Peak—nice views may be enjoyed from the summit, although you will share them with a microwave relay station. Best time to visit is late spring through November.

## 14. WOODLAND TRAIL          1.5 mi/1.0 hr

*Reference:* **In San Bernardino National Forest, Big Bear; map I6, grid c7.**

*User groups:* Hikers, horses and dogs. No mountain bikes are allowed. No wheelchair facilities.

*Permits:* No day-use permits are required. Overnight permits are required. For more information, contact the Big Bear Ranger District at (909) 866-3437.

*Directions:* From Interstate 15 at Cajon Junction, head east on the Rim of the World Highway (Highway 18) to Big Bear Lake. Turn north onto Highway 38 and drive to the signed Woodland Trail Trailhead and parking area located on the north side of the highway, an eighth of a mile past the Big Bear Ranger Station and across the highway from the MWD East Launch Boat Ramp.

*Maps:* Send $3 to the USDA-Forest Service, 630 Sansome Street, San Francisco, CA 94111 and ask for the San Bernardino National Forest map. For a topographic map, ask for Fawnskin from the USGS

*Who to contact:* San Bernardino National Forest, Big Bear Ranger District, P.O. Box 290, Fawnskin, CA 92333; (909) 866-3437.

*Trail notes:* This is a beautiful little nature trail with 20 interpretive stops. Be sure to pick up an interpretive brochure at the ranger station before heading out. This is a perfect to opportunity to learn a little about the natural history of the Big Bear area before or after picking up your overnight permit for camping. The trail is right by the ranger station. The best time to visit is late spring through November.

## 15. CHAMPION JOSHUA TREE    2.0 mi/1.0 hr

*Reference:* **In San Bernardino National Forest; map I6, grid c8.**

*User groups:* Hikers, horses, dogs and mountain bikes. No wheelchair facilities.

*Permits:* No day-use permits are required. Camping permits are required. For more information, contact the Big Bear Ranger District (909) 866-3437.

*Directions:* From Interstate 15 at Cajon Junction, head east on the Rim of the World Highway (Highway 18) to Big Bear Lake. Turn north onto Highway 38 and drive past Big Bear Lake to where it rejoins Highway 18. Continue on Highway 18 to Baldwin Lake and then drive approximately 3.5 miles further to Smarts Ranch Road (Forest Service Road 3N03), branching right and southeast. Turn right on Smarts Ranch Road and drive approximately 5.5 miles up the valley to just past a crossing over Arrastre Creek. Look for jeep tracks heading left and park off the road.

*Maps:* Send $3 to the USDA-Forest Service, 630 Sansome Street, San Francisco, CA 94111 and ask for the San Bernardino National Forest map. For topographic maps, ask for Big Bear City and Rattlesnake Canyon from the USGS.

*Who to contact:* San Bernardino National Forest, Big Bear Ranger District, P.O. Box 290, Fawnskin, CA 92333; (909) 866-3437.

*Trail notes:* Joshua Tree to the east has been named a National Monument, but it doesn't have anything over the area this trail heads into when it comes to Joshua trees. In fact, there are those who would argue that the Joshua tree forest in the San Bernardino range is much better—we can't disagree. The granddaddy of the trees is reported to be the largest Joshua tree in the world and has been dubbed, somewhat unoriginally, Champion Joshua Tree. From the jeep tracks, head northeast through a mixed forest of pinyon, juniper and Joshua trees. After approximately half a mile, you will find yourself among giant Joshua trees. Continue hiking and before long, under the shadow of Granite Peak, you will come upon the Champion—no need to bow. The tree stands over 33 feet tall and has a measured girth of over 15 feet. Return the way you came. The best time to hike is between November and May, because you're in sun all the way. Pack plenty of water.

## 16. SUGARLOAF NATIONAL RECREATION TRAIL 10.0 mi/5.0 hrs

*Reference:* In San Bernardino National Forest, Big Bear; map I6, grid d8.

*User groups:* Hikers, horses and dogs. No mountain bikes are allowed. No wheelchair facilities.

*Permits:* No day-use permits are required. Overnight permits are required. For more information, contact the Big Bear Ranger District at (909) 866-3437.

*Directions:* From Interstate 15 at Cajon Junction, head east on the Rim of the World Highway (Highway 18) to Big Bear Lake. Continue driving on Highway 18 to Big Bear City and the junction with Highway 38. Turn east on Highway 38 for approximately three miles and turn right onto Forest Service Road 2N84. (The Forest Service recommends that low-slung passenger cars not drive on this road in poor conditions so be prepared to walk if the road gets too dicey for your vehicle.) When Forest Service Road 2N84 makes a sharp left, drive straight on Forest Service Road 2N93 which climbs up to Green Creek crossing. Cross the creek and then turn right onto an unsigned dirt road which you follow for several hundred yards to a parking area near a locked gate.

*Maps:* Send $3 to the USDA-Forest Service, 630 Sansome Street, San Francisco, CA 94111 and ask for the San Bernardino National Forest map. For a topographic map, ask for Moonridge from the USGS.

*Who to contact:* San Bernardino National Forest, Big Bear Ranger District, P.O. Box 290, Fawnskin, CA 92333; (909) 866-3437.

*Trail notes:* If you are looking for a good view, but don't want to trek into the San Gorgonio Wilderness, then Sugarloaf Peak is your best bet. At 9,952 feet, it is the tallest peak in the San Bernardino Mountains outside of the wilderness boundaries. From the trailhead, hike two miles up the jeep road alongside Green Creek to a trail junction. Nearby lies Wildhorse Camp, a good picnic or short trek overnight spot. At the junction, head right, now climbing on the Sugarloaf Trail all the way to the summit. Retrace your steps when ready. This is a great summer hike when cool breezes chill an otherwise overheated mind. The best time to visit is late spring through November.

## 17. SAN BERNARDINO PEAK 16.0 mi/8.0 hrs

*Reference:* In San Bernardino National Forest, San Gorgonio Wilderness; map I6, grid d6.

*User groups:* Hikers only. No mountain bikes, dogs and horses are allowed. No

wheelchair facilities.

*Permits:* Day-use and camping permits are required to enter the San Gorgonio Wilderness. For more information, contact the San Gorgonio Ranger District at (909) 794-1123.

*Directions:* From Interstate 10 in Redlands, head east and then exit at Highway 30/38. Turn right onto Highway 38 towards Camp Angelus. Drive approximately 20 miles (you will pass by the Mill Creek Ranger Station in Mentone where you can pick up a permit) to Camp Angelus. Turn right at a sign that reads "San Bernardino Peak Trail" and drive for approximately a quarter mile to the parking area for the trailhead.

*Maps:* Send $3 to the USDA-Forest Service, 630 Sansome Street, San Francisco, CA 94111 and ask for the San Bernardino National Forest map. For a topographic map, ask for Big Bear Lake from the USGS. Tom Harrison Cartography publishes an excellent map of the area. Call (415) 456-7940 and ask for the trail map of the San Gorgonio Wilderness. The cost is $5.95 plus tax and shipping.

*Who to contact:* San Bernardino National Forest, San Gorgonio Ranger District, Mill Creek Ranger Station, 34701 Mill Creek Road, Mentone, CA 92359; (909) 794-1123.

*Trail notes:* The trail begins at the north end of the lot. San Bernardino Peak at 10,624 feet sits as the eastern anchor of the San Bernardino Range, a distinction it shares with its sister peak San Gorgonio, the tallest peak in Southern California at 11,499 feet—located five miles to the east. The trail leading to the peak climbs up, and up, and oh-my-goodness up. Views are superb along the way. A number of trail camps present themselves as good overnight resting spots if you choose to turn this trek into a two-day venture. At the summit, be sure to sign the register and then retrace your steps back to the parking area. Visit between late May and early November.

# 18. SOUTH FORK TRAIL       21.0 mi/2.0 days 🛌5 ⛰️8

*Reference:* In San Bernardino National Forest, San Gorgonio Wilderness; map I6, grid d8.

*User groups:* Hikers and horses. No mountain bikes or dogs are allowed. No wheelchair facilities.

*Permits:* Day-use and camping permits are required to enter the San Gorgonio Wilderness. For more information, contact the San Gorgonio Ranger District at (909) 794-1123. Call in advance as there is a quota on permits.

*Directions:* From Interstate 10 in Redlands, head east and then exit at Highway 30/38. Turn right onto Highway 38 towards Camp Angelus. Drive to the Mill Creek Ranger Station in Mentone where you can pick up a permit. From the ranger station, drive approximately another 19 miles to Jenks Lake Road and turn right. Drive approximately three miles to the South Fork Trailhead and the generous parking area.

*Maps:* Send $3 to the USDA-Forest Service, 630 Sansome Street, San Francisco, CA 94111 and ask for the San Bernardino National Forest map. For topographic maps, ask for Moonridge and San Gorgonio Mountain from the USGS. Tom Harrison Cartography publishes an excellent map of the area. Call (415) 456-7940 and ask for the trail map of the San Gorgonio Wilderness. The cost is $5.95 plus tax and shipping.

*Who to contact:* San Bernardino National Forest, San Gorgonio Ranger District, Mill Creek Ranger Station, 34701 Mill Creek Road, Mentone, CA 92359; (909) 794-1123.

*Trail notes:* No mountain in all of Southern California commands such a view as San Gorgonio Peak. North, west, south and east—you can see for hundreds of miles in every direction if the weather cooperates. From the parking area, cross Jenks Road and begin hiking on the trail. In approximately 1.5 miles you will intersect with Poopout Hill Road (near the old trailhead and now closed to vehicular traffic). In another .75 miles you will intersect with the old Poopout Hill Trail and turn right. Hike up to a soggy meadow area known as South Fork Meadows—there are good camps around here and a great spot to picnic if you are dayhiking with the family. If you are continuing on toward the peak, head off on the South Fork Trail all the way to Dollar Lake. If you are seeking a romantic picnic spot to share with someone special, this might just be the spot. Keep in mind that many others share the same sentiment so you won't be alone, but there is plenty of room for everyone to find some peace and quiet. Keep climbing to Dollar Saddle and then on and through a three-way junction, still heading for San Gorgonio Summit. You are above 10,000 feet now so take it slow and easy—altitude sickness can strike the unwary and unwise. Pass Dry Lake View Camp and the junctions with the Sky High Trail and the Vivian Creek Trail. Stay to your left at both junctions and keep heading onward and upward to the heavens. Your breath a little short and your legs quite tired, you will suddenly come up on the bare back of San Gorgonio and a quick trip to the summit itself. Look around and take in the expansive views—the southern Sierra to the north, Mexico to the south, the Pacific Ocean to the west and the Mojave Desert to the east. When you are ready, head down via the Sky High Trail for a little variety. Descend rapidly past an old DC-3 wreck to Mine Shaft Saddle and then down to Dry Lake. From Dry Lake it's down to South Fork Meadows and again on the trail leading back to the South Fork Trailhead and your car. Best time to visit is between June and early October.

---

# 19. SANTA ANA RIVER TRAIL 9.0 mi/4.0 hrs

*Reference:* In San Bernardino National Forest, Santa Ana River; map I6, grid d8.

*User groups:* Hikers, horses and dogs. No mountain bikes are allowed. No wheelchair facilities.

*Permits:* No day-use permits are required. Overnight permits are required if camping. For more information, contact the San Gorgonio Ranger District at (909) 794-1123.

*Directions:* From Interstate 10 in Redlands, head east and then exit at Highway 30/38. Turn right onto Highway 38 and drive approximately 32 miles to South Fork Campground. The signed trailhead and parking area is located opposite the campground, more or less.

*Maps:* Send $3 to the USDA-Forest Service, 630 Sansome Street, San Francisco, CA 94111 and ask for the San Bernardino National Forest map. For a topographic map, ask for Moonridge from the USGS. Tom Harrison Cartography publishes an excellent map of the area. Call (415) 456-7940 and ask for the trail map of the San Gorgonio Wilderness. The cost is $5.95 plus tax and shipping.

*Who to contact:* San Bernardino National Forest, San Gorgonio Ranger District, Mill Creek Ranger Station, 34701 Mill Creek Road, Mentone, CA 92359; (909) 794-1123.

*Trail notes:* We would recommend that you plan your visit here for the early summer, as the meadows along the way are full of color—paintbrush, monkeyflower, lupine and columbine. Early in the morning, wildlife is quite often seen—deer, fox, raccoon and even beaver. Views of the often snow-capped San Gorgonio Peak towering above you and the broad expanse of Big Meadow along the way are picturesque, so pack a camera. From the trailhead, the trail makes a quick winding trip through South Fork Campground to that camp's trailhead, built to accommodate the many horse users staying at the campground. Then the trail takes off, taking you through a woodland of pine, fir and oak. At every intersection, follow the Santa Ana River Trail signs and you cannot go wrong. The trail ends when it intersects with Forest Service Road 1N02. Turn around and retrace your steps.

## 20. ASPEN GROVE TRAIL       5.0 mi/2.5 hrs

*Reference:* In San Bernardino National Forest, San Gorgonio Wilderness; map I6, grid d8.

*User groups:* Hikers and horses. No mountain bikes or dogs are allowed. No wheelchair facilities.

*Permits:* Day-use and camping permits are required to enter the San Gorgonio Wilderness. For more information, contact the San Gorgonio Ranger District at (909) 794-1123.

*Directions:* From Interstate 10 in Redlands, head east and then exit at Highway 30/38. Turn right onto Highway 38 towards Camp Angelus. Drive to the Mill Creek Ranger Station in Mentone where you can pick up a permit. From the ranger station, drive about another 24 miles to the signed turnoff for Heart Bar Campground and turn right onto Forest Service Road 1N02. Drive for approximately one mile to a fork in the road, bear right and drive another 1.5 miles to a small parking area and a sign indicating the Aspen Grove Trail on your right.

*Maps:* Send $3 to the USDA-Forest Service, 630 Sansome Street, San Francisco, CA 94111 and ask for the San Bernardino National Forest map. For a topographic map, ask for Moonridge from the USGS. Tom Harrison Cartography publishes an excellent map of the area. Call (415) 456-7940 and ask for the trail map of the San Gorgonio Wilderness. The cost is $5.95 plus tax and shipping.

*Who to contact:* San Bernardino National Forest, San Gorgonio Ranger District, Mill Creek Ranger Station, 34701 Mill Creek Road, Mentone, CA 92359; (909) 794-1123.

*Trail notes:* There is nothing so romantic and wonderful as watching golden aspen leaves dance in a fall wind, every so often breaking loose to flutter and tumble to the ground. This trail will guide you to one of only two known aspen groves in all of Southern California. If you plan your hike in the fall, after the first frost has nipped the leaves and the first snow frosted the top of San Gorgonio, you are in for a treat. Dress warmly though. From the trailhead, drop down on the signed trail (actually more of a fire road for the first four hundred yards or so). At Fish Creek, you will cross into the

Wilderness Area and also cross the creek—expect wet feet at high water. Just across the creek you will find yourself in the aspen grove. If you are with young children, or just in a casual mood, this is probably as far as you will want to go. Otherwise continue on to Monkey Flower Flat, so named for all the wildflowers (especially monkey flowers) that bloom here in the spring and early summer. Keep going to Fish Creek Meadow and the Fish Creek Trail. Head right and hike to Fish Creek Camp, set in the pines, a super overnight spot or simple picnic spot. Hike back the way you came.

## 21. BIG FALLS TRAIL      1.0 mi/1.0 hr

*Reference:* **In San Bernardino National Forest, San Gorgonio Wilderness; map I6, grid e6.**

*User groups:* Hikers only. No mountain bikes, horses or dogs are allowed. No wheelchair facilities.

*Permits:* Day-use and camping permits are required to enter the San Gorgonio Wilderness. For more information, contact the San Gorgonio Ranger District at (909) 794-1123.

*Directions:* From Interstate 10 in Redlands, head east and then exit at Highway 30/38. Turn right onto Highway 38 towards Camp Angelus. Drive to the Mill Creek Ranger Station in Mentone where you can pick up a permit. From the ranger station, drive approximately another seven miles to the signed turnoff for Forest Home Road. Drive 4.5 miles to Forest Home Road's end and the parking area.

*Maps:* Send $3 to the USDA-Forest Service, 630 Sansome Street, San Francisco, CA 94111 and ask for the San Bernardino National Forest map. For a topographic map, ask for Forest Falls from the USGS. Tom Harrison Cartography publishes an excellent map of the area. Call (415) 456-7940 and ask for the trail map of the San Gorgonio Wilderness. The cost is $5.95 plus tax and shipping.

*Who to contact:* San Bernardino National Forest, San Gorgonio Ranger District, Mill Creek Ranger Station, 34701 Mill Creek Road, Mentone, CA 92359; (909) 794-1123.

*Trail notes:* The best time to visit these falls is in the spring, when the snowmelt swells the water cascading off the edge of Falls Creek into a roaring torrent, which plunges dramatically into Mill Creek below. Under no circumstances should you ever try to climb up the falls—people have died in the attempt. From the parking area, follow the signed trail across Mill Creek wash, up a short distance to the base of the falls. Return the way you came.

## 22. VIVIAN CREEK TRAIL    14.0 mi/2.0 days

*Reference:* **In San Bernardino National Forest, San Gorgonio Wilderness; map I6, grid e6.**

*User groups:* Hikers only. No mountain bikes, horses or dogs are allowed. No wheelchair facilities.

*Permits:* Day-use and camping permits are required to enter the San Gorgonio Wilderness. For more information, contact the San Gorgonio Ranger District at (909) 794-1123.

*Directions:* From Interstate 10 in Redlands, head east and then exit at Highway 30/38. Turn right onto Highway 38 towards Camp Angelus. Drive to the Mill

Creek Ranger Station in Mentone where you can pick up a permit. From the ranger station, drive approximately another seven miles to the signed turnoff for Forest Home Road. Drive 4.5 miles to Forest Home Road's end and the parking area.

*Maps:* Send $3 to the USDA-Forest Service, 630 Sansome Street, San Francisco, CA 94111 and ask for the San Bernardino National Forest map. For topographic maps, ask for Forest Falls and San Gorgonio Mountain from the USGS. Tom Harrison Cartography publishes an excellent map of the area. Call (415) 456-7940 and ask for the trail map of the San Gorgonio Wilderness. The cost is $5.95 plus tax and shipping.

*Who to contact:* San Bernardino National Forest, San Gorgonio Ranger District, Mill Creek Ranger Station, 34701 Mill Creek Road, Mentone, CA 92359; (909) 794-1123.

*Trail notes:* No mountain in all of Southern California commands such a view as San Gorgonio Peak. The Vivian Creek Trail is Michael's favorite way to head up to the peak—it's a bit more intense, but less traveled and offers terrain reminiscent of the Sierra. From the trailhead, hike on an old road through a closed campground and then across the rocky Mill Creek wash. The next bit is very steep, switchbacking up to Vivian Creek Trail Camp—plan on hiking this section in the early morning to beat the midday sun, which can be brutal. Vivian Creek is very pleasant, set amid lush meadows and stands of pine, and a good overnight spot if you are starting out late on Friday to get an early start on the weekend. From Vivian Creek Trail Camp, hike up past Halfway Camp to High Creek Camp. If you are planning a two-day trip, this should be your goal as it is an outstanding trail camp complete with wildflowers and a waterfall. From High Creek Camp, the trail winds its way up the back of San Gorgonio. You are above 10,000 feet now so take it slow and easy—altitude sickness can strike anyone who is not acclimated. At the junction with the trail from Dollar Lake, head right, through a junction with Sky High Trail and to the peak. Your breath a little short and your legs quite tired, you will suddenly come up on the bare back of San Gorgonio and a quick trip to the summit itself. Look around and take in the expansive views—the southern Sierra to the north, Mexico to the south, the Pacific Ocean to the west and the Mojave Desert to the east. When you are ready, head down the way you came up.

---

# 23. GALENA PEAK/ MILL CREEK HEADWALLS TRAIL

7.0 mi/5.0 hrs

*Reference:* **In San Bernardino National Forest, San Gorgonio Wilderness; map I6, grid e6.**

*User groups:* Hikers only. No mountain bikes, horses or dogs are allowed. No wheelchair facilities.

*Permits:* Wilderness permits are required to camp in the San Gorgonio Wilderness. Contact the San Gorgonio Ranger District at (909) 794-1123. Note: This hike enters a private area. Call the Ranger District and they will put you in touch with the landowner to secure permission.

*Directions:* From Interstate 10 in Redlands, head east and then exit at Highway 30/38. Turn right onto Highway 38 towards Camp Angelus. Drive to the Mill Creek Ranger Station in Mentone where you can pick up a permit. From the ranger station, drive approximately another seven miles to the signed turnoff for Forest Home Road. Drive 4.5 miles to Forest Home Road's end and the parking area.

**Maps:** Send $3 to the USDA-Forest Service, 630 Sansome Street, San Francisco, CA 94111 and ask for the San Bernardino National Forest map. For topographic maps, ask for Forest Falls and San Gorgonio Mountain from the USGS. Tom Harrison Cartography publishes an excellent map of the area. Call (415) 456-7940 and ask for the trail map of the San Gorgonio Wilderness. The cost is $5.95 plus tax and shipping.

**Who to contact:** San Bernardino National Forest, San Gorgonio Ranger District, Mill Creek Ranger Station, 34701 Mill Creek Road, Mentone, CA 92359; (909) 794-1123.

**Trail notes:** Don't even think about trying this trip unless your backcountry navigation and traveling skills are in the expert level. If they are, this trek is a gem among gems as it guides you into a part of the San Gorgonio Wilderness that few if any ever travel. From the parking area, head up the Mill Creek wash to the headwall at the eastern end—there is a trail along the northern bank that will take you most of the way there. Once at the headwall, the going is cross-country and hazardous. The best way up the loose rock is via the ridge just left of center and then working your way carefully across the loose rock slope, up the steep ridge to the base of Galena Peak. An old and faint climber's trail leads to the top of the peak for superb views. Continuing into the valley is up to you—there are no trails, but we assure you that it is gorgeous. Return the way you came, carefully descending the rocky slope at the headwall. Serious injury is possible if you are the least bit careless or overestimate your skill. A number of years ago, on a fall trip, Michael encountered literally thousands of lady bugs gathering for the winter. Every fern, blade of grass and leaf was coated in a thick layer of scarlet—like a living coat of enamel paint. Bighorn sheep, deer and bobcat are not uncommon sights. Humans are.

---

# 24. TERRI PEAK TRAIL     3.5 mi/2.0 hrs

**Reference:** In Lake Perris State Recreation Area; map I6, grid f2.

**User groups:** Hikers only. No mountain bikes, dogs or horses are allowed. No wheelchair facilities.

**Permits:** No permits are required. There is a $6 day-use fee.

**Directions:** From Riverside, drive south on Interstate 215 to Highway 60, also known as the Pomona Freeway. Drive east on Highway 60 to Moreno Beach Drive south for four miles to the park. You will have to pay a $5 day-use fee to enter the park at the kiosk. From the kiosk, turn right onto Lake Perris Drive. Park in the Interpretive Center parking lot. The trail is currently unsigned, but begins directly to the left of the campfire area.

**Maps:** For topographic maps, ask for Yorba Linda and Prado Dam from the USGS.

**Who to contact:** Lake Perris State Park, 17801 Lake Perris Drive, Lake Perris, CA 92571; (909) 657-0676.

**Trail notes:** You need not worry about crowds—while the parking lot is bound to be crowded, most are casting their lot upon the water of Lake Perris with lure and line. You are apt to have the backcountry to yourself. A pity for others, because in the spring when the wildflowers are in bloom, or just after a sky-clearing, air-freshening rain, it would be hard to think of a more beautiful spot with a view. Head up the trail from the parking area, climbing west and following an occasional wooden trail marker (post). The trail will cross a small meadow and then climb quickly to the peak above you known as Terri Peak. If the weather and smog cooperate, you should be able to see the San Bernardino Mountains and the Santa Ana Mountains, as well as the lake below. Head back the way you came.

---

## 25. KITCHING CREEK TRAIL  9.5 mi/5.0 hrs
## to KITCHING PEAK

*Reference:* **In San Bernardino National Forest, San Gorgonio Wilderness; map I6, grid f9.**

*User groups:* Hikers only. No mountain bikes, horses or dogs are allowed. No wheelchair facilities.

*Permits:* Wilderness permits are required to camp in the San Gorgonio Wilderness. Contact the San Gorgonio Ranger District at (909) 794-1123.

*Directions:* From Interstate 10 in Banning, drive approximately two miles east and exit on Fields Road. Head north through the Morongo Indian Reservation to Morongo Road. Turn right on Morongo Road toward Millard Canyon. After approximately a half mile turn left onto Forest Service Road 2S05 and drive to the parking area before a creek crossing and the signed trailhead.

*Maps:* Send $3 to the USDA-Forest Service, 630 Sansome Street, San Francisco, CA 94111 and ask for the San Bernardino National Forest map. For topographic maps, ask for Cabazon and San Gorgonio Mountain from the USGS. Tom Harrison Cartography publishes an excellent map of the area. Call (415) 456-7940 and ask for the trail map of the San Gorgonio Wilderness. The cost is $5.95 plus tax and shipping.

*Who to contact:* San Bernardino National Forest, San Gorgonio Ranger District, Mill Creek Ranger Station, 34701 Mill Creek Road, Mentone, CA 92359; (909) 794-1123.

*Trail notes:* This hike is best as a winter's day wander because the air will be cool, but not too chilled, and the views are stunning—snow-capped San Jacinto to the south and San Gorgonio to the north, Joshua Tree National Park to the east and Palm Springs below. If you are lucky, you may glimpse bighorn sheep. Black bear make their home here too, so if you are planning on camping, take adequate bear precautions. This trail is one of the few that cut through this mostly trackless wilderness, newly added to the San Gorgonio Wilderness in 1984. It's wild and very beautiful. From the trailhead, hike up Kitching Creek to a junction with the Kitching Creek Trail at four miles and a trail branching right toward Kitching Summit, 1.5 miles away. Head right, climbing up a dry and brush-choked ridge. Once at the peak (elevation 6,598 feet), retrace your steps.

---

## 26. BLUEWATER TRAIL  12.0 mi/7.0 hrs

*Reference:* **West of Laguna Hills and south of Lake Elsinor; map I6, grid j0.**

*User groups:* Hikers, horses and dogs. No mountain bikes are allowed. No wheelchair facilities.

***Permits:*** No day-use permits are required. Wilderness permits are required for camping. Contact the Trabuco Ranger District at (909) 736-1811.

***Directions:*** From Lake Elsinor, drive south on Interstate 15 for approximately six miles to the Clinton Keith Road exit. Drive seven miles south on Clinton Keith Road to Tenaja Road. Turn right onto Tenaja Road (Forest Service Road 7S01) to the Tenaja Fire Station and adjacent campground. The campground is available on a first-come, first-served basis and it has water and restrooms. To get to the trailhead, drive another three miles on Tenaja Road (7S01) until it intersects with Forest Service Road 7S04. Park in the trailhead parking pullout.

***Maps:*** Send $3 to the USDA-Forest Service, 630 Sansome Street, San Francisco, CA 94111 and ask for the Cleveland National Forest map. For topographic maps, ask for Sitton Peak and Margarita Peak from the USGS.

***Who to contact:*** Cleveland National Forest, Trabuco Ranger District, 1147 East Sixth Street, Corona, CA 91719; (909) 736-1811.

***Trail notes:*** The 62-square mile San Mateo Canyon Wilderness is a rugged slice of heaven. It clings tenuously to a sense of nature and wildness amid the bulging urban boundaries of Orange, Riverside and San Diego counties. California's newest wilderness is a challenge to get to and an equal challenge to explore—and that's the beauty of it. We would recommend that you spend at least one full day wandering and an overnight or two if you have the time—you won't regret it. Poison oak grows prolifically among the canyons and alongside the trails. Long pants and long sleeve shirts are a recommended trail outfit for any adventurer seeking to wander extensively within this wilderness. From the trailhead, hike up the canyon on the San Mateo Canyon Trail to the Bluewater Trail. Turn right and continue climbing and scrambling on the Bluewater Trail for as long as you wish. We recommend you head up to the Oak Flats area and spend the night near either Serrano Spring or Garcia Spring. The live oak woodlands and shaded ravines make this a very pleasant spot to hang out for a while. After camp is set up, a scramble to the top of a nearby peak will reveal views out to the ocean and, if you linger past sunset, the twinkling lights of nearby urban sprawl.

---

# 27. FISHERMAN'S CAMP     14.0 mi/1.0 day

***Reference:*** **West of Laguna Hills and south of Lake Elsinor; map I6, grid j0.**

***User groups:*** Hikers, horses and dogs. No mountain bikes are allowed. No wheelchair facilities.

***Permits:*** No day-use permits are required. Wilderness permits are required for camping. Contact the Trabuco Ranger District at (909) 736-1811.

***Directions:*** From Lake Elsinor, drive south for approximately six miles on Interstate 15 to the Clinton Keith Road exit. Drive seven miles south on Clinton Keith Road to Tenaja Road. Turn right on Tenaja Road (Forest Service Road 7S01) to the Tenaja Fire Station and adjacent campground. The campground is available on a first-come, first-served basis and it has water and restrooms. To get to the trailhead, drive another three miles on Tenaja Road (7S01) until it intersects with Forest Service Road 7S04. Park in the trailhead parking pullout.

***Maps:*** Send $3 to the USDA-Forest Service, 630 Sansome Street, San Francisco, CA 94111 and ask for the Cleveland National Forest map. For topographic maps, ask for Sitton Peak and Margarita Peak from the USGS.

*Who to contact:* Cleveland National Forest, Trabuco Ranger District, 1147 East Sixth Street, Corona, CA 91719; (909) 736-1811.

*Trail notes:* When you visit the San Mateo County Wilderness, we recommend that you spend at least one full day wandering and an overnight or two—you won't regret it. From the trailhead, hike down the fire road known as the San Mateo Canyon Trail. Within 1.5 miles you will arrive at Fisherman's Camp, one of many former camps that attracted anglers seeking the once superb fishing here for steelhead and trout. Leave your rod at home, though, because the steelhead run no more. From the camp the trail descends into the canyon, becoming indistinct in places. As long as you are following the creek, you are okay. Pass by the intersection with the Bluewater Trail and continue down-canyon past increasingly bigger boulders and swimming holes. Loads of picnic spots and swimming hole possibilities abound. Take your pick and turn around when you have a notion to. If you keep walking, you will eventually reach the Clark Trail junction. Keep in mind that if this is a day hike, you will need to leave plenty of daylight and a reserve of energy for your return trek. This hike is super all year except during very high water after heavy rains.

*Special note:* Poison oak grows prolifically among the canyons and alongside the trails. Long pants and long sleeve shirts are a recommended trail outfit for any adventurer seeking to wander extensively within this wilderness.

---

# 28. SEVEN PINES TRAIL          14.0 mi/7.0 hrs

*Reference:* **In San Bernardino National Forest, Idyllwild; map I6, grid h8.**

*User groups:* Hikers only. No mountain bikes, horses or dogs are allowed. No wheelchair facilities.

*Permits:* Day-use and camping permits are required to enter the San Jacinto Wilderness. For more information, contact the Mt. San Jacinto State Park at (909) 659-2607 or the San Jacinto Ranger District at (909) 659-2117.

*Directions:* From Interstate 10 in Banning, exit at 8th Street onto the Banning/ Idyllwild Highway (Highway 243) and drive approximately 20 miles to the turnoff to Forest Service Road 4S02, located just past the Alandale Forest Service Station. Turn left, driving 2.5 miles toward Dark Canyon Campground. Drive through the camp and turn right on a dirt road, traveling 1.5 miles to the Seven Pines Trailhead and parking.

*Maps:* Send $3 to the USDA-Forest Service, 630 Sansome Street, San Francisco, CA 94111 and ask for the San Bernardino National Forest map. For topographic maps, ask for San Jacinto Peak and Idyllwild from the USGS. Tom Harrison Cartography publishes an excellent map of the area. Call (415) 456-7940 and ask for the trail map of the San Jacinto Wilderness. The cost is $5.95 plus tax and shipping.

*Who to contact:* Mt. San Jacinto State Park, 29505 Highway 243, Idyllwild, CA 92549; (909) 659-2607. San Bernardino National Forest, San Jacinto Ranger District, P.O. Box 518, Idyllwild, CA 92549; (909) 659-2117.

*Trail notes:* When most of the crowds are schlepping up the trail from Humber Park in Idyllwild, you will be happily hiking up the Seven Pines Trail in relative solitude—heading to the same place, San Jacinto Peak. Hike up 3.8 miles on the Seven Pines Trail and go right onto Deer Springs Trail. Plan on a good rest break, or long picnic stop, at the old Deer Springs Trail Camp, now abandoned due to overuse. Keep hiking one-half mile up the Deer Springs Trail to a right turn at a junction, now heading towards Little Round Valley, still on Deer Springs Trail. If you wish to turn this into an overnight, Little Round Valley Camp is a good choice. From Little Round Valley Trail Camp, the trail climbs for a mile or so to a junction with the San Jacinto Peak Trail. Head left and hike up to the stone shelter and then onward for another quarter of a mile to the 10,084-foot peak. John Muir called the view from the top here, "the most sublime spectacle to be found anywhere on this earth." We think you will too, assuming the smoggy haze from Los Angeles doesn't intervene in the spectacle. Bask in the glorious views and then return the way you came.

*Special note:* Don't even think of heading up here if the weather looks bad!

## 29. DEER SPRINGS TRAIL 6.6 mi/3.5 hrs
## to SUICIDE ROCK

*Reference:* **In San Bernardino National Forest, Idyllwild; map I6, grid h8.**

*User groups:* Hikers only. No mountain bikes, horses or dogs are allowed. No wheelchair facilities.

*Permits:* Day-use and camping permits are required to enter the San Jacinto Wilderness. For more information, contact the Mt. San Jacinto State Park at (909) 659-2607 or the San Jacinto Ranger District at (909) 659-2117.

*Directions:* From Interstate 10 in Banning, exit at 8th Street onto the Banning/Idyllwild Highway (Highway 243) and drive approximately 25 miles to the Idyllwild County Park Visitor's Center parking area. The trailhead is located across the highway from the visitor's center.

*Maps:* Send $3 to the USDA-Forest Service, 630 Sansome Street, San Francisco, CA 94111 and ask for the San Bernardino National Forest map. For topographic maps, ask for San Jacinto Peak and Idyllwild from the USGS. Tom Harrison Cartography publishes an excellent map of the area. Call (415) 456-7940 and ask for the trail map of the San Jacinto Wilderness. The cost is $5.95 plus tax and shipping.

*Who to contact:* Mt. San Jacinto State Park, 29505 Highway 243, Idyllwild, CA 92549; (909) 659-2607. San Bernardino National Forest, San Jacinto Ranger District, P.O. Box 518, Idyllwild, CA 92549; (909) 659-2117.

*Trail notes:* Suicide Rock is another one of the favorite climbing area for rock-jocks and they frequently use this trail to access the top of the rock or hike back down after a climb. The name of the rock is earned from a legend that has it that an Indian princess and her lover leapt to their deaths from the rock rather than be parted as the tribe's chief had ordered. The trail climbs steeply for 2.3 miles to Suicide Junction, where you will head right and leave the Deer Springs Trail. In a little over a mile you will arrive at the white granite top of Suicide and be able to enjoy the views of Idyllwild below and Tahquitz Peak across the way. Retrace your steps when ready.

## 30. SOUTH RIDGE TRAIL 6.0 mi/3.0 hrs

*Reference:* **In San Bernardino National Forest, Idyllwild; map I6, grid h8.**

*User groups:* Hikers only. No mountain bikes, horses or dogs are allowed. No wheelchair facilities.

*Permits:* Day-use and camping permits are required to enter the San Jacinto

Wilderness. For more information, contact the San Jacinto Ranger District at (909) 659-2117 or Mt. San Jacinto State Park at (909) 659-2607.

*Directions:* From Interstate 10 in Banning, exit at 8th Street onto the Banning/ Idyllwild Highway (Highway 243) and drive approximately 26 miles to Idyllwild. From the south end of town, turn onto Saunders Meadow Road, then left onto Pine Avenue, right on Tahquitz Drive and finally right onto South Ridge Road—got all that? Sometimes the gate at South Ridge is closed which means you park here and add an extra 1.5 miles to your hike each way. Assuming the gate is open, drive slowly on the dirt road to the parking area for the South Ridge Trailhead.

*Maps:* Send $3 to the USDA-Forest Service, 630 Sansome Street, San Francisco, CA 94111 and ask for the San Bernardino National Forest map. For topographic maps, ask for San Jacinto Peak and Idyllwild from the USGS. Tom Harrison Cartography publishes an excellent map of the area. Call (415) 456-7940 and ask for the trail map of the San Jacinto Wilderness. The cost is $5.95 plus tax and shipping.

*Who to contact:* San Bernardino National Forest, San Jacinto Ranger District, P.O. Box 518, Idyllwild, CA 92549; (909) 659-2117.

*Trail notes:* For an outstanding view from a fire lookout atop Tahquitz Peak, this is your trail. It is best to start early in the morning as the trek up can become quite hot and miserable under a noon sun. The trail is well-constructed and easy to follow. From the trailhead, hike up and up to the lookout and spend some time—a picnic is a great idea. Return the way you came.

*Special note:* Don't head up here if the weather is threatening—it's not a good place to be in a thunderstorm!

---

# 31. DEVIL'S SLIDE TRAIL     7.8 mi/4.0 hrs

*Reference:* **In San Bernardino National Forest, Idyllwild; map I6, grid h8.**

*User groups:* Hikers only. No mountain bikes, horses or dogs are allowed. No wheelchair facilities.

*Permits:* Day-use and camping permits are required to enter the San Jacinto Wilderness. For more information, contact the San Jacinto Ranger District at (909) 659-2117 or Mt. San Jacinto State Park at (909) 659-2607.

*Directions:* From Interstate 10 in Banning, exit at 8th Street onto the Banning/ Idyllwild Highway (Highway 243) and drive approximately 26 miles to Idyllwild. From the downtown area, drive on Fern Valley Road following the signs for Humber Park. There is a large parking area, but it pays to arrive early as it often fills up with hikers, climbers, sightseers and more, leaving late arrives to seek parking further down the road.

*Maps:* Send $3 to the USDA-Forest Service, 630 Sansome Street, San Francisco, CA 94111 and ask for the San Bernardino National Forest map. For topographic maps, ask for San Jacinto Peak and Idyllwild from the USGS. Tom Harrison Cartography publishes an excellent map of the area. Call (415) 456-7940 and ask for the trail map of the San Jacinto Wilderness. The cost is $5.95 plus tax and shipping.

*Who to contact:* San Bernardino National Forest, San Jacinto Ranger District, P.O. Box 518, Idyllwild, CA 92549; (909) 659-2117. Mt. San Jacinto State Park, 29505 Highway 243, Idyllwild, CA 92549; (909) 659-2607.

*Trail notes:* From Humber Park, head out on the Devil's Slide Trail up to Saddle Junction at 2.5 miles and then go right on the trail leading to Tahquitz Peak and Chinquapin Flat, 1.4 miles away. At Chinquapin Flat, head left and pick a campsite. If you don't mind packing water up to a dry camp, a superb spot is located off-trail to the south and just below the summit of Red Tahquitz Peak. This will put you in a good position to hike up easily to the peak for a memorable sunrise breakfast, watching the suns rays gently probe their way across the desert floor below and then gradually up the peak until its warming fingers caress you and welcome in a new day. We would recommend that you plan your trip so that your climb up Devil's Slide is completed in the early morning—afternoon sun bakes the trail and its occupants unmercifully.

## 32. ERNIE MAXWELL SCENIC TRAIL  5.2 mi/2.0 hrs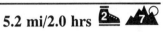

*Reference:* In San Bernardino National Forest, Idyllwild; map I6, grid h8.

*User groups:* Hikers only. No mountain bikes, horses or dogs are allowed. There are no wheelchair facilities.

*Permits:* Day-use and camping permits are required to enter the San Jacinto Wilderness. Contact the San Jacinto Ranger District at (909) 659-2117 or Mt. San Jacinto State Park at (909) 659-2607.

*Directions:* From Interstate 10 in Banning, exit at 8th Street onto the Banning/Idyllwild Highway (Highway 243) and drive approximately 26 miles to Idyllwild. Turn at North Circle and drive to Fern Valley Road. Drive up Fern Valley Road following the signs for Humber Park. There is a large parking area, but it pays to arrive early as it often fills up with hikers, climbers, sightseers and more, leaving late arrives to seek parking further down the road.

*Maps:* Send $3 to the USDA-Forest Service, 630 Sansome Street, San Francisco, CA 94111 and ask for the San Bernardino National Forest map. For topographic maps, ask for San Jacinto Peak and Idyllwild from the USGS. Tom Harrison Cartography publishes an excellent map of the area. Call (415) 456-7940 and ask for the trail map of the San Jacinto Wilderness. The cost is $5.95 plus tax and shipping.

*Who to contact:* San Bernardino National Forest, San Jacinto Ranger District, P.O. Box 518, Idyllwild, CA 92549; (909) 659-2117. Mt. San Jacinto State Park, 29505 Highway 243, Idyllwild, CA 92549; (909) 659-2607.

*Trail notes:* The trail begins just before Humber Park. Head off on the signed trail across wooded slopes for 2.6 miles to Saunders Meadow. Turn around here—to go further dumps you out on a dirt road. As you hike, take the time to peer over your shoulders at Tahquitz Peak, the playground for rock climbers from all over the Southern California area. The trail is level and peaceful, wandering through stands of Coulter pine, Ponderosa, fir and cedar. Even the ground is soft under foot.

## 33. MT. SAN JACINTO TRAIL  12.0 mi/6.0 hrs

*Reference:* In San Bernardino National Forest, Palm Springs; map I6, grid h6.

*User groups:* Hikers only. No mountain bikes, horses or dogs are allowed. No

wheelchair facilities.

*Permits:* Wilderness permits are required to camp in the San Jacinto Wilderness. Contact Mt. San Jacinto State Park at (909) 659-2607 or the San Jacinto Ranger District at (909) 659-2117.

*Directions:* From Interstate 10, take the Palm Springs exit (Highway 111) and drive approximately nine miles to Tramway Road and the turnoff for the Palm Springs Aerial Tramway. Turn right and drive four miles to the parking area at Mountain Station. The tramway operates every half hour from 10 a.m. weekdays and 8 a.m. on weekends. The last car down is at 9:45 p.m. Roundtrip tramway fares are $15.95 for adults and $9.95 for children 5 to 12 years old.

*Maps:* Send $3 to the USDA-Forest Service, 630 Sansome Street, San Francisco, CA 94111 and ask for the San Bernardino National Forest map. For a topographic map, ask for San Jacinto Peak from the USGS. Tom Harrison Cartography publishes an excellent map of the area. Call (415) 456-7940 and ask for the trail map of the San Jacinto Wilderness. The cost is $5.95 plus tax and shipping.

*Who to contact:* Mt. San Jacinto State Park, P.O. Box 308, 29505 Highway 243, Idyllwild, CA 92549; (909) 659-2607. San Bernardino National Forest, San Jacinto Ranger District, P.O. Box 518, Idyllwild, CA 92549; (909) 659-2117. Palm Springs Aerial Tramway (619) 325-1444.

*Trail notes:* From Mountain Station, walk down the concrete walkway, through the Long Valley Picnic Area and to the state park ranger station where you can obtain a permit if you haven't gotten one already. From the ranger station, hike on the trail leading to Round Valley, 1.8 miles away. There is a backcountry camp and a ranger station located here—a great spot to camp if you are introducing someone to backpacking for the first time or camping with children. To keep going to the summit, head towards Wellman Divide Junction at 3.1 miles, where you will enjoy superb views. Head right at the junction towards San Jacinto, to the intersection at 4.5 miles with a trail leading to Little Round Valley and the Summit Trail. Bear right on the Summit Trail and hike up to the stone cabin and then past it for approximately one-third of a mile to the summit. John Muir called the view from the top here, "the most sublime spectacle to be found anywhere on this earth!" We think you will too, assuming the smoggy haze from Los Angeles doesn't intervene in the spectacle. Retrace your steps back to the tramway.

*Special note:* Don't even think of heading up here if the weather looks bad!

---

## 34. DESERT VIEW TRAIL    2.0 mi/1.0 hr

*Reference:* **In San Bernardino National Forest, Palm Springs; map I6, grid h6.**

*User groups:* Hikers only. No mountain bikes, horses or dogs are allowed. No wheelchair facilities.

*Permits:* Wilderness permits are required to camp in the San Jacinto Wilderness. Contact Mt. San Jacinto State Park at (909) 659-2607 or the San Jacinto Ranger District at (909) 659-2117.

*Directions:* From Interstate 10, take the Palm Springs exit (Highway 111) and drive approximately nine miles to Tramway Road and the turnoff for the Palm Springs Aerial Tramway. Turn right and drive four miles to the parking area at Mountain Station. The tramway operates every half hour from 10 a.m. weekdays and 8 a.m. on weekends. The last car down is at 9:45 p.m. Roundtrip tramway fares are $15.95 for adults and $9.95 for children 5 to 12 years old.

*Maps:* Send $3 to the USDA-Forest Service, 630 Sansome Street, San Francisco, CA 94111 and ask for the San Bernardino National Forest map. For a topographic map, ask for San Jacinto Peak from the USGS. Tom Harrison Cartography publishes an excellent map of the area. Call (415) 456-7940 and ask for the trail map of the San Jacinto Wilderness. The cost is $5.95 plus tax and shipping.

*Who to contact:* Mt. San Jacinto State Park, P.O. Box 308, 29505 Highway 243, Idyllwild, CA 92549; (909) 659-2607. San Bernardino National Forest, San Jacinto Ranger District, P.O. Box 518, Idyllwild, CA 92549; (909) 659-2117. Palm Springs Aerial Tramway (619) 325-1444.

*Trail notes:* From Mountain Station, wander down the concrete pathway to the signed beginning of the trail to Desert View. Views on the loop are magnificent overlooking the Coachella Valley, distant desert canyons and Palm Springs below. The trail loops around the valley and junctions with a path leading back to Mountain Station. Wildflowers are super in the spring. If you enjoy cross-country skiing, this loop provides a wonderful slide and glide opportunity and an introduction to the winter climate on top of the mountain. Winter touring up here is super when there is enough snow.

---

## 35. SPITLER PEAK TRAIL   10.0 mi/5.0 hrs 

*Reference:* In San Bernardino National Forest, Hemet; map I6, grid i8.

*User groups:* Hikers, horses and dogs. No mountain bikes are allowed. No wheelchair facilities.

*Permits:* No day-use permits are required. Camping permits are required. For more information, contact the San Jacinto Ranger District at (909) 659-2117.

*Directions:* From the town of Hemet, drive approximately 20 miles to Mountain Center. From the intersection of Highway 74 and Highway 243 in Idyllwild, drive south on Highway 74 for approximately three miles and turn left at the signed junction for Hurkey Creek County Park. Drive past Hurkey Creek County Park and up Apple Canyon Road to the sign for Spitler Peak Trail on the right. Park at a turnout located just south of the trailhead.

*Maps:* Send $3 to the USDA-Forest Service, 630 Sansome Street, San Francisco, CA 94111 and ask for the San Bernardino National Forest map. For a topographic map, ask for Idyllwild from the USGS. Tom Harrison Cartography publishes an excellent map of the area. Call (415) 456-7940 and ask for the trail map of the San Jacinto Wilderness. The cost is $5.95 plus tax and shipping.

*Who to contact:* San Bernardino National Forest, San Jacinto Ranger District, P.O. Box 518, Idyllwild, CA 92549; (909) 659-2117.

*Trail notes:* This trail takes you up through pine and juniper forest to a very windy divide located northwest of Spitler Peak. It does not actually go to the peak itself, as the trail's name implies. Still, the divide is a wonderful spot to head for a dayhike and to hang out or frolic among the rocky outcrops. The vistas from the divide of Palm Springs and desert canyons below are beautiful. From the trailhead, hike up on the well-defined Spitler Peak Trail to the divide and its intersection with the Pacific Crest Trail. It is a steep climb, gaining just over 2,000 feet in only a few miles. Pace yourself! Wander up and down the PCT if you desire, or just stay put and when you are ready, turn around and retrace your steps back to the car.

## 36. RAMONA TRAIL          6.0 mi/3.5 hrs

*Reference:* **In San Bernardino National Forest, Hemet; map I6, grid i8.**

*User groups:* Hikers, horses and dogs. No mountain bikes are allowed. No wheelchair facilities.

*Permits:* No day-use permits are required. Camping permits are required. For more information, contact the San Jacinto Ranger District at (909) 659-2117.

*Directions:* From the town of Hemet, drive approximately 20 miles to Mountain Center. From the intersection of Highway 74 and Highway 243 in Idyllwild, drive south on Highway 74 for approximately eight miles to the signed trailhead alongside the highway. Park along the highway shoulder.

*Maps:* Send $3 to the USDA-Forest Service, 630 Sansome Street, San Francisco, CA 94111 and ask for the San Bernardino National Forest map. For a topographic map, ask for Idyllwild from the USGS. Tom Harrison Cartography publishes an excellent map of the area. Call (415) 456-7940 and ask for the trail map of the San Jacinto Wilderness.

*Who to contact:* San Bernardino National Forest, San Jacinto Ranger District, P.O. Box 518, Idyllwild, CA 92549; (909) 659-2117.

*Trail notes:* Wildflowers often sprinkle the open slopes in the spring. From the highway, hike past a gate, down a dirt road and then bear left onto the Ramona Trail. The trail climbs steadily along a well-graded route which passes through pleasant shade of a Jeffrey pine forest just before arriving at Tool Box Spring and a dirt road. Turn right on the road and hike a short distance for Ramona Camp and a pleasant rest among the pines. Retrace your steps. In the summer, this trail can be quite hot and dry, but in the spring, fall and winter, the trail is most pleasant.

# PACIFIC CREST TRAIL    250.0 mi. one way/25.0 days
## GENERAL INFORMATION

*Reference:* Trail sections extend from the Highway 74 Trailhead north to the Angeles Crest Highway.

*User groups:* Hikers, horses and dogs (except in national parks). No mountain bikes are allowed. No wheelchair facilities.

*Permits:* A wilderness permit is required for traveling through various wilderness and special-use areas that the trail traverses. Contact the national forest, BLM or national park office at your point of entry for a combined permit that is good for the length of your trip.

*Maps:* For an overall view of the trail route in this section, send $3 for each map ordered to the USDA-Forest Service, 630 Sansome Street, San Francisco, CA 94111, ask for the San Bernardino National Forest and the San Gabriel National Forest maps. Topographic maps for particular sections of trail are provided under each specific trail section heading.

*Who to contact:* Contact either the national forest, BLM or national park office at your trailhead—see specific trailheads and corresponding agencies listed within each section.

*Trail notes:* Trail elevations within this section range from 1,200 feet to over 9,000 feet. The high country in this region is typically open and snow-free between May and November but it is important to note that rockslides and rain during this time can make travel difficult. Washed out trails, swollen streams and difficult crossings are commonplace in the spring. Due to the high fire danger in much of the area, a camp stove is required.

---

## PCT-7    60.0 mi. one way/6.0 days
## HIGHWAY 74 to NEAR SAN GORGONIO PASS

*Reference:* From the Highway 74 Trailhead, map I6, grid j9 north to the trailhead parking at Interstate 10 near San Gorgonio.

*User groups:* Hikers, horses and dogs (except in national parks). No mountain bikes are allowed. No wheelchair facilities.

*Permits:* A wilderness permit is required for traveling through various wilderness and special-use areas that the trail traverses. Contact the San Bernardino National Forest at (909) 659-2117 for a permit that is good for the length of your trip.

*Directions:* To the Highway 74 Trailhead—From the town of Hemet, head south on Highway 74 to the junction of Highway 74 and Highway 371 (Cahuilla Road). The trailhead for the PCT lies approximately one mile southeast on Highway 371, just west of the Santa Rosa Summit.

    To the Interstate 10 Trailhead—From Interstate 10 near the Palm Springs exit, take the Verbania Avenue exit and drive north to Tamarack Road. Turn left onto Tamarack and drive approximately a quarter mile to the signed PCT Trailhead, located just past Fremontia Road.

*Maps:* For an overall view of the trail route in this section, send $3 for each map ordered to the USDA-Forest Service, 630 Sansome Street, San Francisco, CA 94111, ask for the San Bernardino National Forest map. For topographic maps, ask for Butterfly Peak, Palm View Play, Idyllwild, San Jacinto Peak and White Water from the USGS.

**Who to contact:** San Bernardino National Forest, San Jacinto Ranger District, P.O. Box 518, Idyllwild, CA 92549; (909) 659-2117.

**Trail notes:** Finally, good-bye for now to the chaparral (oh, it still remains here and there throughout the trek, just not as thick and heavy) as the treadway climbs up a series of ridgelines to the San Jacinto Wilderness and San Jacinto Peak. Pines and oaks begin to dominate. Views to the east from the Desert Divide are spectacular and look over the Anza-Borrego Desert and the Santa Rosa Mountains. Nice views of Tahquitz Peak in the San Jacinto Wilderness may also be enjoyed and help to take your mind off the continually climbing and dry trail. Once into the wilderness, the pines thicken, and pretty, wet meadows offer a lush escape from the desert heat you have been experiencing of late. At the junction with the San Jacinto Peak Trail, drop your pack and head up—the views are spectacular. From the peak, the trail begins to descend in earnest along the Snow Creek drainage, showing evidence of the power of avalanches. San Gorgonio looms to the north, in the direction you are heading. Once down to the valley floor, your screaming knees can relax as you wander from PCT marker to marker heading towards Interstate 10.

---

# PCT-8      64.0 mi. one way/6.0 days
## SAN GORGONIO to VAN DUSEN CANYON ROAD

**Reference:** From the trailhead parking at Interstate 10 near San Gorgonio Pass, map I6, grid g9 north to Van Dusen Canyon Road near Big Bear.

**User groups:** Hikers, horses and dogs (except in national parks). No mountain bikes are allowed. No wheelchair facilities.

**Permits:** A wilderness permit is required for traveling through various wilderness and special-use areas that the trail traverses. Contact the San Bernardino National Forest at (909) 794-1123 for a permit that is good for the length of your trip.

**Directions:** To the Interstate 10 Trailhead—From Interstate 10 near the Palm Springs exit, take the Verbania Avenue exit and drive north to Tamarack Road. Turn left onto Tamarack and drive approximately a quarter mile to the signed PCT Trailhead located just past Fremontia Road.

    To the Van Dusen Road Trailhead—From Highway 18 in Big Bear City, head north on Van Dusen Canyon Road for three miles to the signed PCT Trailhead.

**Maps:** For an overall view of the trail route in this section, send $3 for to the USDA-Forest Service, 630 Sansome Street, San Francisco, CA 94111, ask for the San Bernardino National Forest map. For topographic maps, ask for White Water, Catclaw Flat, Onyx Peak, Moonridge and Big Bear City from the USGS.

**Who to contact:** San Bernardino National Forest, San Gorgonio Ranger District, Mill Creek Ranger Station, 34701 Mill Creek Road, Mentone, CA 92359; (909) 794-1123 or Bureau of Land Management, Palm Springs-South Central Coast Resource Area, P.O. Box 2000, North Palm Springs, CA 92258; (619) 251-0812.

**Trail notes:** Downshift the gears, 'cause from here on it is up and up and oh lord up! Your thighs will get more exercise than Suzanne Sommers does with a Thigh Master. After crossing a dry but interesting section of high desert through BLM jurisdiction, you reenter the San Bernardino National Forest and leave the desert gravel, scrub and heat behind. Pines begin to shade you again. Pack plenty of water and retop at every opportunity. Big Bear City is located about three miles south of the trailhead and is a good place to resupply if you are through hiking or on a lengthy segment hike. Wildflowers in the meadows and high desert sections of this trail are gorgeous.

---

# PCT-9     99.0 mi. one way/10.0 days
# VAN DUSEN CANYON ROAD to CAJON PASS

*Reference:* **From the trailhead parking at Van Dusen Canyon Road near Big Bear, map I6, grid c6 west to the trailhead parking at Interstate 15 near Cajon Pass.**

*User groups:* Hikers, horses and dogs (except in national parks). No mountain bikes are allowed. No wheelchair facilities.

*Permits:* A wilderness permit is required for traveling through various wilderness and special-use areas that the trail traverses. Contact the San Bernardino National Forest at (909) 866-3437 for a permit that is good for the length of your trip.

*Directions:* To the Van Dusen Road Trailhead—From Highway 18 in Big Bear City, head north on Van Dusen Canyon Road for approximately three miles to the signed PCT Trailhead.

    To the Cajon Trailhead—From San Bernardino, take Interstate 15 north to Cajon Junction, where Highway 138 passes over the freeway. Exit here and follow the paved road branching off Highway 138, just east of the exit, to the trailhead.

*Maps:* For an overall view of the trail route in this section, send $3 for each map ordered to USDA-Forest Service, 630 Sansome Street, San Francisco, CA 94111, ask for the San Bernardino National Forest and the San Gabriel National Forest maps. For topographic maps, ask for Big Bear City, Fawnskin, Butler Peak, Lake Arrowhead, Silverwood Lake and Cajon from the USGS.

*Who to contact:* San Bernardino National Forest, Big Bear Ranger District, P.O. Box 290, Fawnskin, CA 92333; (909) 866-3437.

*Trail notes:* The trail from Big Bear onward continues a traverse of the San Bernardino Range's spine contouring up and down slopes and ridges through mixed mahogany, chaparral, pine, cottonwood and oak. As the route passes near Lake Arrowhead the track become hot and dry—wear sunscreen and a good shade hat. As the route descends to Deep Creek Hot Springs, you are invited to soak awhile. There is no camping allowed at the springs as you should know that despite its popularity, amebic meningoencephalitis has struck a few bathers down. Perhaps the water doesn't sound that good after all. Off-roading proximity all the way to the Cajon Pass makes the final trudge from near Silverwood Lake less enjoyable than it might ordinarily be. The presence of periodic water from springs and streams adds some diversion from the heat and exposed nature of the treadway. If you are hungry and thirsty when you reach Cajon Pass, there was a restaurant nearby the Interstate exit when we last checked.

## PCT-10                27.0 mi. one way/3.0 days
## CAJON PASS to ANGELES CREST HIGHWAY

*Reference:* **From Interstate 15 near Cajon Pass, map I6, grid b0 to the Angeles Crest Highway.**

*User groups:* Hikers, horses and dogs. No mountain bikes are allowed. No wheelchair facilities.

*Permits:* A wilderness permit is required for traveling through various wilderness and special-use areas that the trail traverses. Contact the Angeles National Forest at (818) 574-5200 for a permit that is good for the length of your trip. No day-use permits are requires for this section of trail.

*Directions:* For the Cajon Trailhead—From San Bernardino, take Interstate 15 north to Cajon Junction, where Highway 138 passes over the freeway. Exit here and follow a paved road branching off Highway 138, just east of the exit, to the trailhead.

For the Angeles Crest Trailhead—From Interstate 15 near Cajon, take Highway 138 east. Turn left (west) on the Angeles Crest Highway and drive five miles to Wrightwood. Continue for three miles to Big Pines. Bear left and continue on Angeles Crest Highway for 1.5 miles to Inspiration Point, opposite Blue Ridge Road.

*Maps:* Send $3 to the USDA-Forest Service, 630 Sansome Street, San Francisco, CA 94111 and ask for the Angeles National Forest map. For topographic maps, ask for Telegraph Peak and Cajon from the USGS.

*Who to contact:* Angeles National Forest, 701 North Santa Anita Avenue, Arcadia, CA 91006; (818) 574-5200.

*Trail notes:* A hot, dry and generally uninspiring slog up from the Interstate and into the San Gabriel Mountains. The first water you will find is at Guffy Campground. As you near Inspiration Point the views do become memorable as you look into the East Fork San Gabriel River basin.

*PCT CONTINUATION:* To continue hiking along the Pacific Crest Trail, see Chapter I5, pages 717-718.

# Leave No Trace Tips

## Sanitation

If no refuse facility is available:

• Deposit human waste in "cat holes" dug six to eight inches deep. Cover and disguise the cat hole when finished.

• Deposit human waste at least 75 paces (200 feet) from any water source or camp.

• Use toilet paper sparingly. When finished, carefully burn it in the cat hole, then bury it.

• If no appropriate burial locations are available, such as in popular wilderness camps above tree line in hard granite settings— Devil's Punchbowl in the Siskiyou Wilderness is such an example— then all human refuse should be double-bagged and packed out.

• At boat-in campsites, chemical toilets are required. Chemical toilets can also solve the problem of larger groups camping or long stays at one location where no facilities are available.

• To wash dishes or your body, carry water away from the source and use small amounts of biodegradable soap. Scatter dishwater after all food particles have been removed.

• Scour your campsites for even the tiniest piece of trash and any other evidence of your stay. Pack out all the trash you can, even if it's not yours. Finding cigarette butts, for instance, provides special irritation for most campers. Pick them up and discard them properly.

• Never litter. Never. Or you become the enemy of all others.

SO-CAL MAP .......................... see page 662
adjoining maps
NORTH (H7) ........................... see page 654
EAST ........................................ no map
SOUTH (J7) ........................... see page 800
WEST (I6) ............................... see page 720

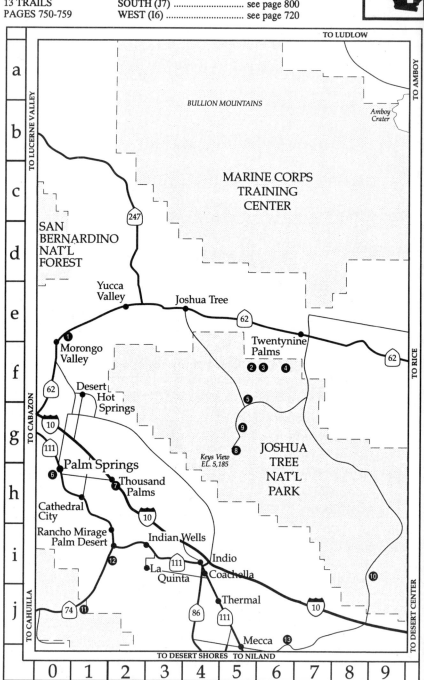

Map I7 featuring: Joshua Tree National Park, Palm Springs, Santa Rosa Mountains, Coachella Valley Preserve, Salton Sea, Morongo Valley

## 1. BIG MORONGO TRAIL     10.0 mi/4.0 hrs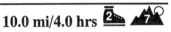

*Reference:* **Palm Springs; map I7, grid e0.**

*User groups:* Hikers and horses. No mountain bikes or dogs are allowed. **Limited wheelchair facilities.**

*Permits:* No permits are required. The preserve is closed on Mondays and Tuesdays.

*Directions:* From northwest of Palm Springs on Interstate 10, drive on Highway 62 north to Morongo Valley. Turn right (east) on Covington Park and follow the road north for a short distance to the signed entrance and parking area.

*Maps:* For a topographic map, ask for Morongo Valley from the USGS.

*Who to contact:* Bureau of Land Management, Palm Springs-South Central Coast Resource Area, 6300 Garnet Avenue, P.O. Box 2000, North Palm Springs, CA 92258; (619) 251-4800, or call Big Morongo Preserve at (619) 363-7190.

*Trail notes:* This region is nationally recognized for its birdwatching opportunities. The desert springs ecosystem and Mojave riparian woodland are exemplary. Cottonwood Trail follows a creek lined by cottonwood and willow, which creates a haven for raccoons, ringtails, great horned owls and numerous songbirds. The rare Peninsular bighorn sheep can be spotted here at dawn or dusk during the summer months—the only time you will want to be out because of the oppressive summer heat. This trail is really several hikes in one, making it suitable for all ages and hiking abilities. There is a **wheelchair-accessible** boardwalk which leads out and over the springs. From the parking area, the Cottonwood Trail follows an easy grade to a man-made dam, which creates a peaceful place to hang out and listen to the sound of birds and water intermingling. It is about a mile to this point and it's a good spot to turn around if time or breath are short. If not, keep on hiking down-canyon for as long as you wish, reaching the preserve's boundary nearly five miles from the start. Turn around and retrace your steps. A number of other trails branching off from the boardwalk (near the beginning of the trail and parking area) offer one-third-mile to one-mile loops if you choose to remain closer to home base.

## 2. INDIAN COVE NATURE     0.74 mi/0.5 hr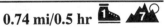

*Reference:* **Joshua Tree National Park; map I7, grid f5.**

*User groups:* Hikers only. No dogs, horses or mountain bikes are allowed. No wheelchair facilities.

*Permits:* A day-use fee of $5 is charged. No permits are required although you do have to sign in and out at the backcountry trail registers.

*Directions:* From Interstate 10, just past the exit for Palm Springs, head north on Highway 62 toward Yucca Valley and Joshua Tree. After passing through the town of Joshua Tree turn right onto Indian Cove Road. Drive approximately 4.3 miles and turn right at the bulletin board/campground junction.

Continue driving to the loop at the road's end and the parking area. The trailhead begins at the end of the road near a cluster of signs.

*Maps:* For a topographic map, ask for Indian Cove from the USGS. Trails Illustrated publishes the best private topographical map available, called *Joshua Tree National Monument.* The map includes detailed backcountry and hiking information. The cost is $7.95 and may be ordered by calling (800) 962-1643. Tom Harrison Cartography also publishes an excellent map of the area. Call (415) 456-7940 and ask for the recreation map of Joshua Tree National Park. The cost is $5.95 plus tax and shipping.

*Who to contact:* Joshua Tree National Park, 74485 National Monument Drive, Twentynine Palms, CA 92277; (619) 367-7511.

*Trail notes:* This is a short interpretive nature trail through relatively flat terrain (it's amazing that the trail is flat, considering the jumble of rocks and boulders scattered all around). It provides a peek at the plants (Joshua tree, yucca and cholla), animals (coyote, rabbit and kangaroo rat) and natural features that make up the park called Joshua Tree. Enjoy watching the rock climbers on nearby outcrops performing their aerial acrobatics. Don't even think about visiting here in the summer unless you enjoy having your brain steamed to mush and your skin cooked to medium rare. The best time to visit is from October to May, with the spring being the most popular time because of the wildflower displays.

---

## 3. RATTLESNAKE CANYON    3.0 mi/1.5 hrs

*Reference:* **Joshua Tree National Park; map I7, grid f6.**

*User groups:* Hikers only. No dogs, horses or mountain bikes are allowed. No wheelchair facilities.

*Permits:* A day-use fee of $5 is charged. No permits are required although you do have to sign in and out at the backcountry trail registers.

*Directions:* From Interstate 10, just past the exit for Palm Springs, head north on Highway 62 toward Yucca Valley and Joshua Tree. After passing through the town of Joshua Tree turn right onto Indian Cove Road. Drive approximately 4.3 miles and turn left at the bulletin board/campground junction. Continue driving to the picnic area at the end of the road and park.

*Maps:* For topographic maps, ask for Indian Cove and Queen Mountain from the USGS. Trails Illustrated publishes the best private topographical map available, called *Joshua Tree National Monument.* The map includes detailed backcountry and hiking information. The cost is $7.95 and may be ordered by calling (800) 962-1643. Tom Harrison Cartography also publishes an excellent map of the area. Call (415) 456-7940 and ask for the recreation map of Joshua Tree National Park. The cost is $5.95 plus tax and shipping.

*Who to contact:* Joshua Tree National Park, 74485 National Monument Drive, Twentynine Palms, CA 92277; (619) 367-7511.

*Trail notes:* If the playful adventurer side of you has been tugging at your soul to explore the rugged Wonderland of Rocks, this is the perfect introduction. There are no trails, no aid station, no signpost and little water. It's rugged, challenging, frustrating, inspiring and intimately magical. From the picnic area, head east into and up the dry streambed of Rattlesnake Canyon. Turn right from the streambed and begin hopping and bopping your way up the boulder-choked canyon. Wander as far as you dare in a day, but remember that you have to hike out what you hiked in and that park regulations require you be out of the Wonderland by dark—this is as much for your safety as for the well-being of the timid bighorn who need uninterrupted access to water. Few who enter into the domain of the Wonderland return without a sense of accomplishment and an intense desire to return again and again. This is no place for a tenderfoot. You must have solid map and compass skills and a level of patience that doesn't easily rattle, even if you have tried for the third time to get out of a canyon and been thwarted by a sea of cactus or an insurmountable wall. See hike number 2 for more information on when to visit Joshua Tree.

## 4. FORTYNINE PALMS TRAIL   3.0 mi/1.5 hrs

*Reference:* **Joshua Tree National Park; map I7, grid f6.**

*User groups:* Hikers only. No dogs, horses or mountain bikes are allowed. No wheelchair facilities.

*Permits:* A day-use fee of $5 is charged. No permits are required although you do have to sign in and out at the backcountry trail registers.

*Directions:* From Interstate 10, just past the exit for Palm Springs, head north on Highway 62 toward Yucca Valley and Joshua Tree. After passing through the town of Joshua Tree and just before reaching Twentynine Palms and the park's visitor's center, turn right onto Canyon Road. Drive to the end of the road and the park service parking area.

*Maps:* For a topographic map, ask for Queen Mountain from the USGS. Trails Illustrated publishes the best private topographical map available, called *Joshua Tree National Monument.* The map includes detailed backcountry and hiking information. The cost is $7.95 and may be ordered by calling (800) 962-1643. Tom Harrison Cartography also publishes an excellent map of the area. Call (415) 456-7940 and ask for the recreation map of Joshua Tree National Park. The cost is $5.95 plus tax and shipping.

*Who to contact:* Joshua Tree National Park, 74485 National Monument Drive, Twentynine Palms, CA 92277; (619) 367-7511.

*Trail notes:* So close to civilization and yet seemingly a world away—that's what hiking into this spring-fed palm oasis is like. Bring a good book, your journal, or just your imagination and pass some quiet time among the wind, water and palms. From the parking area, hike up the trail through cactus and rocks to a ridgetop with nice views of the surrounding area and nearby Twentynine Palms. The trail drops down from the ridge and leads you quickly into the heart of the oasis. Bighorn sheep frolic around here so keep a sharp lookout—they don't like to be seen. Once you have drunk your fill of paradise, retrace your steps to your car and our man-made reality. See hike number 2 for more information on when to visit Joshua Tree.

## 5. BARKER DAM LOOP TRAIL   1.3 mi/1.0 hr

*Reference:* **Joshua Tree National Park; map I7, grid f5.**

*User groups:* Hikers only. No dogs, horses or mountain bikes are allowed. No wheelchair facilities.

*Permits:* A day-use fee of $5 is charged. No permits are required although you do have to sign in and out at the backcountry trail registers.

*Directions:* From Interstate 10, just past the exit for Palm Springs, head north on Highway 62 toward Yucca Valley and Joshua Tree. In Joshua Tree drive to Park Boulevard and turn right. Park Boulevard becomes Quail Springs Road. Pass through the park entrance and drive approximately 10 miles to Hidden Valley Campground. From the campground, there is a signed dirt road that leads approximately two miles east to the Barker Dam Trail parking area.

*Maps:* For a topographic map, ask for Indian Cove from the USGS. Trails Illustrated publishes the best private topographical map available, called *Joshua Tree National Monument.* The map includes detailed backcountry and hiking information. The cost is $7.95 and may be ordered by calling (800) 962-1643. Tom Harrison Cartography also publishes an excellent map of the area. Call (415) 456-7940 and ask for the recreation map of Joshua Tree National Park. The cost is $5.95 plus tax and shipping.

*Who to contact:* Joshua Tree National Park, 74485 National Monument Drive, Twentynine Palms, CA 92277; (619) 367-7511.

*Trail notes:* Follow an interpretive trail on a wonderful walk that offers a brief introduction to the pleasures of exploring the Wonderland of Rocks (see hike number 3). From the parking area, hike on the signed trail into the Wonderland and 1.1 miles from the trailhead, squeeze through a passage and scramble over rocks and boulders to arrive at the edge of Barker Lake, a holdover from the cattle days of earlier years. If you are a birder, you will enjoy peeking through binoculars at the variety of birds that visit the water source. Follow the trail around the man-made dam, past some petroglyphs and back to the parking area. See hike number 2 for more information on when to visit Joshua Tree.

---

## 6. PALM CANYON TRAIL    4.0 mi/2.0 hrs

*Reference:* **Palm Springs, Santa Rosa Mountains; map I7, grid h0.**

*User groups:* Hikers only. No mountain bikes, horses or dogs are allowed. No wheelchair facilities.

*Permits:* No permits are required. An entry fee of $3.50 per person is charged to enter Aqua Caliente Tribal lands.

*Directions:* From Interstate 10, exit onto Highway 111 (Palm Canyon Drive) and drive to downtown Palm Springs. In Palm Springs the highway forks, continue straight, now on South Palm Canyon Drive. Follow the signs indicating "Indian Canyons." At the Agua Caliente Indians tollgate, pay the entrance fee and drive to the parking area just beyond the tollgate at a trading post, located at the head of Palm Canyon. Remember that the reservation is open from 8:30 a.m. to 5:00 p.m. daily. You must be off the reservation at closing.

*Maps:* For a topographic map, ask for Palm View Peak from the USGS.

*Who to contact:* Bureau of Land Management, Palm Springs-South Central Coast Resource Area, 63500 Garnet Avenue, P.O. Box 2000, North Palm Springs, CA 92258; (619) 251-4800.

*Trail notes:* According to the Bureau of Land Management, Palm Springs and the surrounding canyons are home to the largest concentration of palm trees in the United States—Florida, move over. Of the display of palms, Palm Canyon is the crown jewel with thousands of palms dotting a lush canyon, made even more pleasant by the presence of a meandering stream. From the trading post, hike down into Palm Canyon on the Palm Canyon Trail to a small but pretty grotto that is the ideal turnaround point. If you are feeling energetic, the trail does continue climbing from the grotto, following a very steep route for approximately 13 miles until it meets up with Highway 74. Don't even think about trying this "extra" bit unless you are carrying plenty of water, snacks and extra clothing and are in superb shape!

## 7. COACHELLA VALLEY PRESERVE TRAILS

5.0 mi/2.0 hrs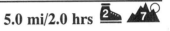

*Reference:* **In Coachella Valley Preserve, Palm Springs; map I7, grid h2.**

*User groups:* Hikers and horses. No mountain bikes or dogs are allowed. No wheelchair facilities.

*Permits:* No permits are required.

*Directions:* From Palm Springs, take Interstate 10 east 10 miles to the Ramon Road exit. Drive east to Thousand Palms Canyon Drive. Turn north and drive two miles to the signed entrance to the Coachella Valley Preserve.

*Maps:* For topographic maps, ask for Cathedral City and Myoma from the USGS.

*Who to contact:* Bureau of Land Management, Palm Springs-South Central Coast Resource Area, 63500 Garnet Avenue, P.O. Box 2000, North Palm Springs, CA 92258; (619) 251-4800.

*Trail notes:* This 1,000-palm oasis is a joint BLM-Nature Conservancy Preserve established to protect the endangered Coachella Valley fringe-toed lizard. Crystal clear springs shaded by greenery attract a wide variety of wildlife and birds. The stunning palm oasis was once used as the backdrop for DeMille's classic movie, *King of Kings.* Start by touring the 1.5-mile self-guided McCallum Nature Trail. The route wanders through a wonderful grove of willow, palm and cottonwood. There is an interpretive brochure available to offer botanical information. For the more ambitious, head out on other signed trails leading past sand dunes, through desert washes, and to overlooks which afford views all the way to the Salton Sea. Stay very alert on the Sand Dune Trail and you may even be lucky enough to see the tiny sand swimmer lizard doing its laps.

## 8. LOST HORSE MINE TRAIL PARK

3.5 mi/1.5 hrs

*Reference:* **Joshua Tree National Park; map I7, grid g5.**

*User groups:* Hikers only. No dogs, horses or mountain bikes are allowed. No wheelchair facilities.

*Permits:* A day-use fee of $5 is charged. No permits are required although you do have to sign in and out at the backcountry trail registers.

*Directions:* From the Joshua Tree National Park Visitor's Center at Twentynine Palms, drive south for three miles on Utah Trail Road to the Pinto Wye Junction. Bear right at the junction and drive approximately 10 miles to Caprock Junction, just past the Ryan Campground turnoff. Turn right onto Keys Road and drive approximately 2.5 miles and turn left onto a dirt road leading to the Lost Horse Mine and a park interpretive display about one of the mine's former owners Johnny Lang.

*Maps:* For topographic maps, ask for Keyes View and Malapai Hill from the USGS. Trails Illustrated publishes the best private topographical map available, called *Joshua Tree National Monument.* The map is printed with detailed backcountry and hiking information. The cost is $7.95 and may be ordered by calling (800) 962-1643. Tom Harrison Cartography also publishes an excellent map of the area. Call (415) 456-7940 and ask for the recreation map of Joshua Tree National Park. The cost is $5.95 plus tax and shipping.

*Who to contact:* Joshua Tree National Park, 74485 National Monument Drive, Twentynine Palms, CA 92277; (619) 367-7511.

*Trail notes:* Begin hiking at the road's end where you left your car, past a road barrier and onto the old mine road. Follow it up the left side of the wash to the Lost Horse Mine. Use caution when poking about as there are a number of open shafts still in existence among the mine ruins. From 1896 to 1899, this mine churned out a rich gold store, but one of the partners, Johnny Lang, was caught stealing and banished. He died from apparent starvation not too far from what is now known as Keys Road—his mummified remains were found in a sleeping bag by passing prospectors. From the mine, take a quick trek to the hill above the mine for a view of the surrounding desert. See hike number 2 for more information on when to visit Joshua Tree.

---

# 9. RYAN MOUNTAIN TRAIL    4.0 mi/2.0 hrs

*Reference:* **Joshua Tree National Park; map I7, grid g5.**

*User groups:* Hikers only. No dogs, horses or mountain bikes are allowed. No wheelchair facilities.

*Permits:* A day-use fee of $5 is charged. No permits are required although you do have to sign in and out at the backcountry trail registers.

*Directions:* From the Joshua Tree National Park Visitor's Center at Twentynine Palms, drive south for three miles on Utah Trail Road to the Pinto Wye Junction. Bear right at the junction and drive approximately eight miles to Sheep Pass Campground. Just beyond the Sheep Pass Campground turnoff is the trailhead parking for the Indian Cave/Ryan Mountain Trail, located on the left.

*Maps:* For a topographic maps, ask for Keyes View from the USGS. Trails Illustrated publishes the best private topographical map available, called *Joshua Tree National Monument.* The map includes detailed backcountry and hiking information. The cost is $7.95 and may be ordered by calling (800) 962-1643. Tom Harrison Cartography also publishes an excellent map of the area. Call (415) 456-7940 and ask for the recreation map of Joshua Tree National Park. The cost is $5.95 plus tax and shipping.

*Who to contact:* Joshua Tree National Park, 74485 National Monument Drive, Twentynine Palms, CA 92277; (619) 367-7511.

*Trail notes:* A climb up to the top of Ryan Mountain (5,470 feet) takes you to the top of one of the best viewpoints in the entire park, rewarding you with a 360-degree view. From the peak, the Wonderland of Rocks (an amazing jumble of boulders and blocks) spreads out before you. The trail cuts through Joshua Tree groves and among jumbles of boulders on the way up to the summit. Although the trail is not difficult to follow, it is moderately steep in places, so pace yourself. Sign the register at the top. If you are so inclined, pack along a thermos of hot chocolate and a light breakfast and head up to the peak for a sunrise you won't forget. As long as you are here, take a brief sidetrip from the parking area to Indian Cave, which will offer you a look at the kind of shelter used by Native Americans who wandered this desert many years ago. See hike number 2 for more information on when to visit Joshua Tree.

## 10. LOST PALM OASIS TRAIL   4.0 mi/2.0 hrs

*Reference:* **Joshua Tree National Park; map I7, grid i9.**

*User groups:* Hikers only. No dogs, horses or mountain bikes are allowed. No wheelchair facilities.

*Permits:* A day-use fee of $5 is charged. No permits are required although you do have to sign in and out at the backcountry trail registers.

*Directions:* From Interstate 10 just east of Indio, exit onto Cottonwood Springs Road and drive north to the Joshua Tree National Park south entrance. From the park entrance, drive approximately eight miles to Cottonwood Springs Campground and park. The trailhead is located at the far end of the campground.

*Maps:* For topographic maps, ask for Cottonwood Spring and Hayfield from the USGS. Trails Illustrated publishes the best private topographical map available, called *Joshua Tree National Monument.* The map includes detailed backcountry and hiking information. The cost is $7.95 and may be ordered by calling (800) 962-1643. Tom Harrison Cartography also publishes an excellent map of the area. Call (415) 456-7940 and ask for the recreation map of Joshua Tree National Park. The cost is $5.95 plus tax and shipping.

*Who to contact:* Joshua Tree National Park, 74485 National Monument Drive, Twentynine Palms, CA 92277; (619) 367-7511.

*Trail notes:* Apparently, a lot of things in the desert either were lost and now found, or get lost and then refound—at least that's what it seems like when you read all the trail names, doesn't it? Actually, this trail was named for a very picturesque oasis of palms that remains hidden from sight in a deep canyon until you are almost upon them. Without the Park Service signs pointing the way, we doubt if many would-be palm seekers would ever find the place—it can get confusing amid the jumble of boulders and washes. From the campground, the trail wanders through a wash and to the Cottonwood Spring Oasis. That buzzing you hear is bees—lots of them. Don't even think about honey because we can assure you, they aren't in the mood. From Cottonwood Spring Oasis, the trail becomes more confusing to follow, but fortunately the park service anticipated the confusion and provided key trail signs along the way to point you in the right direction. Before long, you will find yourself amid palms. Keep a sharp eye on the rocks around the ridges and you may be lucky enough to see desert bighorn sheep. Retrace your steps when ready. See hike number 2 for more information on when to visit Joshua Tree.

## 11. CACTUS SPRING        5.0 mi/2.5 hrs

*Reference:* **Palm Springs, Santa Rosa Mountains; map I7, grid j1.**

*User groups:* Hikers and horses. No mountain bikes or dogs are allowed. No wheelchair facilities.

*Permits:* No permits are required although you do have to sign in and out at the register located at the Santa Rosa Wilderness boundary.

**Directions:** From Highway 111 in Palm Desert, drive approximately 16 miles up Highway 74 to the Pinyon Flat Campground. Opposite the campground entrance is Pinyon Flat Transfer Station Road which you will follow for approximately .75 miles. Directly before the Transfer Station (a rubbish dump) turn left onto a rough jeep trail and follow it for several hundred yards to the road's end and trailhead parking. As of this printing, the Forest Service has begun construction on a staging area with trailhead parking on Highway 74, directly across the road from Pinyon Flat Campground. No word on when this will be completed, but look for it just the same as it will save that last bit of dirt road jockeying.

**Maps:** For topographic maps, ask for Toro Peak and Martinez Mountain from the USGS.

**Who to** contact: San Jacinto Ranger District, P.O. Box 518, Idyllwild, CA 92549; (909) 659-2117.

**Trail notes:** Legend has it that horse thieves used to ply their trade quite actively in these parts, rustling horses from down south, herding them into Horsethief Canyon for a brand change, and then herding them again to San Bernardino to sell. Apparently they had quite a scam going, because then they would steal them again, repeat the rebranding process and sell them to the folks down south. As you drop into the canyon on this trek, perhaps you will feel the ghosts of horse rustlers past stirring up the dust on the canyon floor with renegade hooves. Hike east from the trailhead to Fire Road 7S01, then south for one-quarter mile, and then left on the first road—note a sign indicating Cactus Spring, which means you are on the right track. You will soon pass the ruins of an old dolomite mine. Within one-half mile, you will come to a sign-in register at the wilderness boundary. Beyond the boundary, the trail winds its way down to Horsethief Creek, and just beyond and across the creek, Horsethief Camp. Set up camp here and enjoy the surroundings. Walk up and down Horsethief Canyon among the cottonwoods. If you wish, the trail does continue onward to Cactus Springs and Agualata Springs, 10 miles from the trailhead. Retrace your steps back to your car when ready. The best time to hike in here is between October and early May. This is desert country, so don't even think of heading out on the trail without carrying plenty of water for the trip.

---

# 12. WILDERNESS LOOP TRAIL 5.0 mi/2.0 hrs

**Reference: Palm Springs; map I7, grid i2.**

**User groups:** Hikers only. No mountain bikes, horses or dogs are allowed. There are no wheelchair facilities.

**Permits:** No permits are required. An entry fee of $7 per adult and $3.50 per child is charged.

**Directions:** From Highway 111 in Palm Desert, drive south on Portola Avenue for 1.5 miles to the park entrance. The park is open daily from 9 a.m. to 5 p.m. The park is closed from June 15 to August 31.

**Maps:** For a topographic map, ask for Rancho Mirage from the USGS.

**Who to contact:** The Living Desert, 47900 Portola Avenue, Palm Desert, CA 92260; (619) 346-5694.

**Trail notes:** If you are the least bit curious about what a desert is, then you will want to visit the Living Desert, a nonprofit facility dedicated to desert education, research and conservation, whose gardens represent flora from California's Mojave, Arizona's Sonoran, and Mexico's Chihuahuan deserts. There is a miniature zoo with desert bighorn, Arabian oryx, rare Mexican wolves, mountain lion and coyote as well as a walk-through aviary and a pond with desert pupfish to peek at. There is more to the park than just displays, however, which you will discover as you head out from the exhibit area onto the numbered nature trail—be sure to bring along the visitor guide that is available at the entrance station. If you are with children, cut the hike short by only going on the inner two-thirds-mile loop of the nature trail. Otherwise, keep on hiking on the Middle Loop to the Canyon Leg of the Wilderness Loop Trail and to the base of Eisenhower Mountain and a pleasant picnic area. If you wish, you can hike up to the summit of Eisenhower Mountain. It's a steep climb, however, with a strenuous scramble up several hundred feet of loose shale to earn the view. From the picnic area, hike down on the Eisenhower Leg of the Wilderness Loop Trail, back onto the Middle Jaeger Nature Trail Loop and back to the park.

---

## 13. MECCA HILLS 6.5 mi/4.0 hrs

*Reference:* **North of the Salton Sea, south of Interstate 10; map I7, grid j6.**

*User groups:* Hikers, horses, mountain bikes and dogs. There are no wheelchair facilities.

*Permits:* No day-use permits are currently required, but this is subject to change. Call to confirm.

*Directions:* From Palm Springs, head east on Interstate 10, to Cactus City Rest Area. Drive another five miles or so, still on Interstate 10, to Cottonwood Springs Road/Box Canyon Road exit. Turn south on Box Canyon Road. In approximately 10 miles, you enter the Mecca Hills Recreation Area. Look for a BLM sign indicating the trailhead for Sheephole and Hidden Springs Oasis on the left. Further on down Box Canyon, turn onto Painted Canyon Road (near All-American Canyon) and drive to the end of the road, where you will find another BLM sign indicating Ladder Canyon Trail. Parking is available at each trailhead.

*Maps:* For topographic maps, ask for Thermal Canyon, Mortmar and Cottonwood Basin from the USGS.

*Who to contact:* Bureau of Land Management, Palm Springs-South Central Coast Resource Area, 63500 Garnet Avenue, P.O. Box 2000, North Palm Springs, CA 92258; (619) 251-4800.

*Trail notes:* Picturesque badlands, hidden palm oases, colorful box canyons, ridgetops with views south to the Salton Sea and west to the Santa Rosa Mountains offer excellent opportunities for adventurous exploration, hiking and photography. Sheephole and Hidden Springs Oasis offer 2.5 miles of hiking trail to a palm tree oasis. Ladder Canyon features approximately four miles of trail through narrow-walled canyons and up to scenic vistas. There are numerous other opportunities and informal trails for the willing and skilled adventurer.

SO-CAL MAP ......................... see page 662
adjoining maps
NORTH (I5) ............................ see page 696
EAST (J6) ............................... see page 766
SOUTH ..................................... no map
WEST ........................................ no map

6 TRAILS
PAGES 760-765

TO SAN CLEMENTE

San Onofre

CAMP
PENDLETON
MARINE
CORPS
BASE

5

San Luis Rey R.

San Luis Rey

S21   76   1

Oceanside

Carlsbad

Leucadia

San
Clemente
Island

U.S.
MILITARY
RESERVE

PYRAMID
HEAD

Encinitas

Cardiff by the Sea   2

Solana Beach

Del Mar

S21

TORREY PINES STATE RES.

3

La Jolla

4

Pacific Beach

Mission Beach

San Diego

5

CABRILLO NAT'L MONUMENT   6

TO SAN MARCOS, TO BONSALL

TO CORONADO

*Pacific
Ocean*

| 0 | 1 | 2 | 3 | 4 | 5 | 6 | 7 | 8 | 9 |

**Map J5 featuring:** Torrey Pines State Reserve, San Diego, Del Mar, Cabrillo National Monument, La Jolla

## 1. GUAJOME COUNTY PARK    3.0 mi/1.0 hr

*Reference:* **East of Oceanside; map J5, grid b9.**

*User groups:* Hikers. Limited access to mountain bikes and horses. Dogs on leashes only. No wheelchair facilities.

*Permits:* There is a $1 parking fee. Camping is available for $14 per night.

*Directions:* From Oceanside and Interstate 15, head east on Mission Avenue (Highway 76). Highway 76 becomes San Luis Rey Road, which you follow to Santa Fe Avenue, just before Guajome Lake. Turn right onto Guajome Lake Road, just past Guajome Lake, and then take an immediate right into the main entrance for the park. Parking is located just inside the entrance.

*Maps:* Pick up the free Guajome County Park trail map and brochure. For a topographic map, ask for San Luis Rey from the USGS.

*Who to contact:* Guajome County Park, San Diego County Parks, 5201 Ruffin Road, Suite P, San Diego, CA 92123; (619) 694-3049.

*Trail notes:* Trails lace their way through a scenic little regional park that is definitely worth a trip. Guajome is considered to be one of the best areas in north San Diego County to birdwatch, with over 144 species identified within the park boundaries. The self-guided nature trail beginning at the parking area is a perfect place to start exploring. The lakes are spring-fed, with adjacent marshes and surrounding grasslands and woodlands supporting a variety of wildlife. The park reports that a new trail will be completed by the spring of 1995, winding through the willows.

## 2. SAN ELIJO LAGOON    3.0 mi/1.0 hr

*Reference:* **North of San Diego along the coast; map J5, grid d9.**

*User groups:* Hikers only. No mountain bikes, horses or dogs are allowed. No wheelchair facilities.

*Permits:* No day-use permits are required.

*Directions:* From San Diego, drive north on Interstate 5 to Manchester Avenue and exit. San Elijo Lagoon is bisected by Interstate 5. Park on the north side of Manchester Avenue approximately a quarter of a mile east of Interstate 5. Then carefully cross Manchester Avenue, entering the lagoon through a gate preventing vehicle access.

*Maps:* For a topographic map, ask for Encinitas from the USGS.

*Who to contact:* San Elijo Lagoon, San Diego County Parks, 5201 Ruffin Road, Suite P, San Diego, CA 92123; (619) 634-3026.

*Trail notes:* From the gate, take a trail leading east along a flood-control dike. Road sounds will quickly fade as bird and insect sounds begin to fill the air. Egrets and the great blue heron are common visitors and attractions. To get to the west basin, on the other side of Interstate 5, walk along Manchester Avenue and then head left into the lagoon on a short trail. Bring your binoculars as this is bird sanctuary area.

# 3. TORREY PINES STATE RESERVE

3.0 mi/2.0 hrs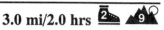

**Reference: North of San Diego and south of Del Mar; map J5, grid e9.**

*User groups:* Hikers only. No mountain bikes, horses or dogs are allowed. No wheelchair facilities although a number of trails are suitable for **wheelchairs**.

*Permits:* A $4 parking fee is charged.

*Directions:* From San Diego, drive north on Interstate 5 to Carmel Valley Road. Turn west onto Carmel Valley Road and drive approximately 1.5 miles to North Torrey Pines Road (also known as Camino Del Mar or Pacific Coast Highway). Turn left and drive approximately one mile to the park sign and entrance for Torrey Pines State Reserve.

*Maps:* A free trail guide (actually a sheet of paper with trail information printed on it) is available at the entrance station—you are asked to return it once you have enjoyed your hike. For a topographic map, ask for Del Mar from the USGS.

*Who to contact:* Torrey Pines State Reserve, c/o San Diego Coast District, 3990 Old Town Avenue, Suite 300C, San Diego, CA 92110; (619) 236-6766, or contact the park ranger station directly at (619) 775-2063.

*Trail notes:* Torrey Pines grow naturally in only two places on earth—in Torrey Pines State Reserve and also on Santa Barbara Island (see chapter I3). The state reserve's capacity on weekends (except during the winter) is strictly controlled and sometimes maxes out, limiting entry. Plan your visit for early in the day on a weekend or any day during the week. If the park is full, you might try the Torrey Pines Extension, a fairly recent acquisition of property, located just north on North Torrey Pines Road. Head left on Carmel Valley Road and then left again onto Del Mar Scenic Parkway and drive to the deadend—trails branch out from here. Perhaps the best trail in the Extension is the Daughters of the Revolution Trail, up onto a ridge with superb views.

In the main reserve itself, head out first on the Beach Trail, which offers excellent views onto the beach lying steeply below, and then follow that trek with a loop journey onto Razor Point Trail. Youngsters and those who are young at heart will enjoy Flat Rock, the ultimate destination of the Beach Trail, as it offers very good tidepooling opportunities. Razor Point offers excellent views and interesting wind caves and cliff formations—fascinating for outdoor photographers. No trip to Torrey Pines would be complete without a half-mile loop trip through several stands of the park's namesake. Head out on the Guy Flemming Trail to South Overlook. If you are lucky while hiking during the winter months, you may catch a glimpse of a migrating California gray whale. If wandering on your own is not your cup of tea, take part in one of the docent-guided tours leaving at 11:30 a.m. and 1:30 p.m., Saturday and Sunday. Trips depart from the Visitor Center and Museum, more affectionately known as "The Lodge."

*Special note:* One word of caution—the cliff edges and tops throughout the park are fragile. Keep a safe distance from the edge.

## 4. LA JOLLA CAVES & COAST  2.0 mi/1.5 hrs

*Reference:* **In La Jolla, just north of San Diego; map J5, grid f9.**

*User groups:* Hikers only. No mountain bikes, horses or dogs are allowed. There are no wheelchair facilities although a number of trails are suitable for **wheelchairs.**

*Permits:* No day-use permits are required.

*Directions:* From San Diego, drive north on Interstate 5 and exit onto Ardath Road (Soledad Freeway exit). Drive north on Ardath to Torrey Pines Road and turn left (east). Park in La Jolla on the street where space is available. Hike down to the bay.

*Maps:* For a topographic map, ask for La Jolla from the USGS.

*Who to contact:* There is no managing agency to contact for information.

*Trail notes:* Wander the cliffs above the blue waters below and gaze at sea life and scuba divers who flock to this area to view the marine life. La Jolla caves may be accessed by a stairway that begins inside the La Jolla Cave Curio Shop. Low tide is the only time to visit if you want maximum access. This is a great place for families and lovers. Blue sky, blue water and frothing waves make this a tourist spot that is not really a tourist spot—it's worth going to.

## 5. SUNSET CLIFFS  0.5 mi/0.5 hr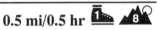

*Reference:* **San Diego Bay; map J5, grid g9.**

*User groups:* Hikers only. No mountain bikes, horses or dogs are allowed. No wheelchair facilities.

*Permits:* No day-use permits are required.

*Directions:* From San Diego and the Interstate 8/Interstate 5 interchange, head east on Interstate 8 to Sunset Cliffs Boulevard. Then turn south (left) onto Sunset Cliffs Boulevard. Drive past Hill Street and then turn left onto Ladera Street. Park on Ladera Street.

*Maps:* For a topographic map, ask for Point Loma from the USGS.

*Who to contact:* City of San Diego Parks and Recreation, Coast Line Parks Division, 2581 Quivira Court, San Diego, CA 92109; (619) 221-8900.

*Trail notes:* As the name implies, this is a great spot to watch the sun slip into the ocean—if you listen really closely, you may even hear the water sizzle. Wander freely on the small network of trails that criss-cross the cliffs above the beach. This is a natural park, so please stay on the trails. Watch your step near the edge of the cliffs, as they are unstable.

## 6. CABRILLO NATIONAL  1.9 mi/1.5 hrs  MONUMENT'S BAYSIDE TRAIL

*Reference:* **On San Diego Bay; map J5, grid g9.**

*User groups:* Hikers only. No mountain bikes, horses or dogs are allowed. There is some **wheelchair access** (with assistance).

*Permits:* No day-use permits are required.

*Directions:* From San Diego and the Interstate 8/Interstate 5 interchange, head east on Interstate 8 to Sunset Cliffs Boulevard. Then turn south (left) onto Sunset Cliffs Boulevard. Drive to Hill Street and turn left. Then turn right onto Catalina Boulevard which then becomes Cabrillo Memorial Drive (Highway 209). The trailhead is at the end of Cabrillo Memorial Drive.

*Maps:* For a topographic map, ask for Point Loma from the USGS.

*Who to contact:* Cabrillo National Monument, P.O. Box 6670, San Diego, CA 92166; (619) 557-5450.

*Trail notes:* From Cabrillo National Monument, you will enjoy nearly unobstructed views of the San Diego coastline, the city skyline, and out to San Clemente Island. If you time your visit just right, when the air is at its wintertime clearest just after a cleansing rain, you can even see all the way to the snow-capped summit of San Jacinto—a marvelous sight to behold. Once you have had your fill of wandering around the monument grounds, hike east of the old lighthouse and descend steeply on the paved road to a barrier and a junction with a gravel road. Head left, hiking past military ruins from World War II, out to an informal observation point where you can watch the ships sailing by. Return the way you came.

*Special note:* Treading off the trail or within restricted areas is not allowed. Stay on the paths at all times and obey all closure and restricted access signs.

## Leave No Trace Tips

**Plan ahead and prepare**

• Learn about the regulations and issues that apply to the area you are visiting.

• Avoid heavy-use areas.

• Obtain all maps and permits.

• Bring extra garbage bags to pack out any refuse you come across.

# MAP J6

**6 PCT SECTIONS**
**47 TRAILS**
**PAGES 766-799**

SO-CAL MAP .......................... see page 662
adjoining maps
NORTH (I6) ........................... see page 720
EAST (J7) ............................ see page 800
SOUTH .................................. no map
WEST (J5) ........................... see page 760

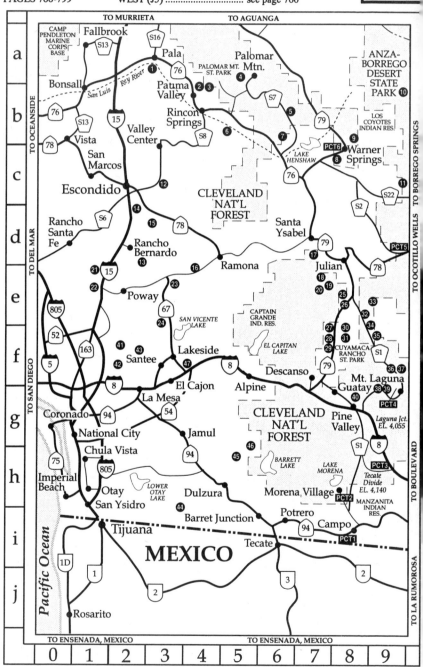

**Map J6 featuring:** Cleveland National Forest, Palomar Mountain State Park, Cuyamaca Rancho State Park, Los Coyotes Indian Reservation, Anza-Borrego Desert State Park, Los Penasquitos Canyon Preserve, Laguna Mountains, Mission Trails Regional Park, Pine Valley, Lake Morena

## 1. WILDERNESS GARDENS COUNTY PRESERVE

5.5 mi/3.0 hrs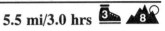

*Reference:* **North of Escondido; map J6, grid a3.**

*User groups:* Hikers only. No mountain bikes, horses or dogs are allowed. **Wheelchair facilities** at the picnic and parking area only.

*Permits:* No day-use permits are required. There is a $2 parking fee.

*Directions:* From Interstate 15 north of Escondido, head east on Highway 76 for approximately 10 miles to a signed right turn just before the bridge over Agua Tibia Creek. Park in the designated lot near the ranger station.

*Maps:* For a topographic map, ask for Pala from the USGS.

*Who to contact:* San Diego County Parks, 5201 Ruffin Road, Suite P, San Diego, CA 92123; (619) 694-3049.

*Trail notes:* Closed until recently for renovation, Wilderness Gardens County Preserve offers the hiker an opportunity to visit a gorgeous riparian environment that, while not really wilderness, is pristine none the less. The park is open from 9:30 a.m. to 4:00 p.m. on Thursday, Friday and Saturday only. Renovation is ongoing while the park is in operation, as the County and Friends of the Wilderness Gardens Preserve redesigns the trails and removes buildings. A number of trails trace pathways through the park. We recommend beginning with the Meadows Trail, which heads up and through wildflower-filled meadows (in the spring) and onto the summit of Pala Mountain.

## 2. DOANE VALLEY NATURE TRAIL

1.0 mi/0.5 hr

*Reference:* **In Cleveland National Forest, Palomar Mountain; map J6, grid b4.**

*User groups:* Hikers only. No dogs, horses or mountain bikes are allowed. No wheelchair facilities.

*Permits:* No day-use permits are required. A day-use fee of $5 is charged.

*Directions:* From Interstate 15, head east on Highway 76 to S7. Turn left (west) onto S7 (East Grade Road) and drive to the park office and entrance. Park at the Doane Pond parking area.

*Maps:* Pick up the Palomar Mountain State Park map/brochure (50 cents) at the entrance. Send $3 to the USDA-Forest Service, 630 Sansome Street, San Francisco, CA 94111 and ask for the Cleveland National Forest map. For a topographic map, ask for Boucher Hill from the USGS.

*Who to contact:* Palomar Mountain State Park, c/o Cuyamaca Rancho State Park, 12551 Highway 79, Descanso, CA 92016; (619) 765-0755.

*Trail notes:* A small stream and numerous interesting trees and plants are the drawing card here. Pick up a free interpretive trail guide at the start of the trail. From the trailhead at Doane Pond, descend along Doane Creek for about one-quarter mile and then climb gently around a hill to meet up with Doane Valley Campground. Along the way, you will pass incense cedar, dogwood, box elder and gooseberry—all identified with signage for your botanical pleasure.

---

## 3. THUNDER SPRINGS TRAIL LOOP

4.2 mi/2.5 hrs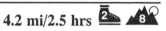

*Reference:* **In Cleveland National Forest, Palomar Mountain; map J6, grid b4.**

*User groups:* Hikers only. No dogs, horses or mountain bikes are allowed. No wheelchair facilities.

*Permits:* No day-use permits are required. A day-use fee of $5 is charged.

*Directions:* From Interstate 15, head east on Highway 76 to S7. Turn left (west) onto S7 (East Grade Road) and drive to the park office and entrance. Park at the Doane Pond parking area.

*Maps:* Pick up the Palomar Mountain State Park map/brochure (50 cents) at the entrance. Send $3 to the USDA-Forest Service, 630 Sansome Street, San Francisco, CA 94111 and ask for the Cleveland National Forest map. For a topographic map, ask for Boucher Hill from the USGS.

*Who to contact:* Palomar Mountain State Park, c/o Cuyamaca Rancho State Park, 12551 Highway 79, Descanso, CA 92016; (619) 765-0755.

*Trail notes:* Enjoy outstanding views as well as some interesting historical sites and a pleasant meadow bounded by a stream. From the Doane Pond parking area, skirt the pond and pick up the Thunder Spring Trail. Hike up it to Chimney Flats and head right onto the Chimney Flats Trail (actually a fire road). Turn left again at a spur and cross East Grade Road to meet up with the Silver Crest Trail. From here, the views are stunning. At the Silver Crest Picnic Area, recross East Grade Road and head back on Scott's Cabin Trail. At the Cedar-Doane Trail, head right and down steeply to the Doane Pond and your car.

*Special note:* Watch our for ticks and be especially vigilant for poison oak, which lurks in the shadows along many of the trails.

---

## 4. OBSERVATORY

2.0 mi. one way/1.0 hr

*Reference:* **In Cleveland National Forest, Palomar Mountain; map J6, grid a5.**

*User groups:* Hikers, horses, dogs and mountain bikes. No wheelchair facilities.

*Permits:* No day-use permits are required.

*Directions:* From Interstate 15, head east on Highway 76 to S7. Turn left onto S7 and drive to the Palomar Observatory. This trip is best enjoyed as a one-way hike, which requires a car shuttle—leave one car at the Observatory Campground on the way up S7.

*Maps:* Send $3 to the USDA-Forest Service, 630 Sansome Street, San Francisco, CA 94111 and ask for the Cleveland National Forest map. For topographic maps, ask for Palomar Observatory and Boucher Hill from the USGS.

**Who to contact:** Cleveland National Forest, Palomar Ranger District, 1634 Black Canyon Road, Ramona, CA 92065; (619) 788-0250.

**Trail notes:** This trail is one of only a few National Recreation Trails in the entire San Diego County area. Begin hiking on the trail just below the entrance gate to the Observatory. The hike takes you on a pleasant little wander through pines, flowery meadows (in the spring) and out to a wooden platform overlooking Mendenhall Valley. The sound of a nearby stream will accompany you much of the way, unless it is during the summer when the heat dries everything up. Watch out for ticks.

---

# 5. BARKER VALLEY          6.0 mi/5.0 hrs

**Reference:** In Cleveland National Forest, Palomar Mountain; map J6, grid b6.

**User groups:** Hikers, horses, mountain bikes and dogs. No wheelchair facilities.

**Permits:** No day-use permits are required. A camping permit is required for overnight stays. No campfires are allowed.

**Directions:** From Interstate 15, head east on Highway 79 through Oak Grove and Holcomb Village and turn right onto unpaved Palomar Divide Road (milepost 41.9, approximately 6.5 miles north of Warner Springs). This road can be difficult in a low-slung car in normal conditions and almost impossible in anything but a four-wheel-drive vehicle if the weather turns wet. Call the Palomar Ranger District for road information. Follow Palomar Divide Road for approximately eight miles to the Barker Valley Spur Trailhead located on the left (west) side of the road. There is plenty of parking off of the road.

**Maps:** Send $3 to the USDA-Forest Service, 630 Sansome Street, San Francisco, CA 94111 and ask for the Cleveland National Forest map. For topographic maps, ask for Palomar Observatory and Boucher Hill from the USGS.

**Who to contact:** Cleveland National Forest, Palomar Ranger District, 1634 Black Canyon Road, Ramona, CA 92065; (619) 788-0250.

**Trail notes:** Barker Valley is a true gem. Even in the summer, when the rest of the mountain is baking, Barker Valley offers a cool escape. From the trailhead, hike down an old roadbed for almost 1.5 miles and then bear left on a trail that follows a slope 1.5 miles down into Barker Valley. We would recommend that you set up a camp in Barker Valley (at least 200 feet away from the water) and then spend a day exploring the falls and romping around in the pools that appear downstream. Wild trout even ply these waterways. Retrace your steps to your car when ready.

---

# 6. SAN LUIS REY RIVER          3.1 mi/3.0 hrs

**Reference:** In Cleveland National Forest, Palomar Mountain; map J6, grid b5.

**User groups:** Hikers, horses and dogs. No mountain bikes are allowed. No wheelchair facilities.

**Permits:** No day-use permits are required. A $5 day-use fee is charged.

**Directions:** From Interstate 15, head east on Highway 76 for approximately 25 miles to the La Jolla Indian Reservation Campground. Park at the campground.

*Maps:* Send $3 to the USDA-Forest Service, 630 Sansome Street, San Francisco, CA 94111 and ask for the Cleveland National Forest map. For topographic maps ask for Palomar Observatory and Boucher Hill from the USGS.

*Who to contact:* La Jolla Indian Reservation, c/o La Jolla Travel Hall, Star Route, P.O. Box 158, Valley Center, CA 92082; (619) 742-1297.

*Trail notes:* Summer is too hot for hiking here—unless you have an inner-tube tucked under one arm and some lazy-day tubing on the river in mind. Assuming it is hiking you are looking for, then plan your trek for either the spring or late fall, when the river is down and the crowds have thinned. The trail you will follow is one worn bare by tubing enthusiasts and other river recreationists and begins at the campground along the northwestern bank of the river. Hike down as far as you desire and then retrace your steps. Once the canyon narrows, you can continue if you have a mind to, but be warned that the going is slow and challenging. Watch out for poison oak along the entire river stretch.

---

# 7. LOVE VALLEY        2.0 mi/1.0 hr

*Reference:* **In Cleveland National Forest, Palomar Mountain; map J6, grid b6.**

*User groups:* Hikers, horses, dogs and mountain bikes. No wheelchair facilities.

*Permits:* No day-use permits are required.

*Directions:* From Interstate 15, head east on Highway 76 to East Grade Road, just before Lake Henshaw, and turn left (north). Drive approximately 3.3 miles to a turnout located on the south side of the road. The trailhead begins at the locked gate.

*Maps:* Send $3 to the USDA-Forest Service, 630 Sansome Street, San Francisco, CA 94111 and ask for the Cleveland National Forest map. For a topographic map, ask for Palomar Observatory from the USGS.

*Who to contact:* Cleveland National Forest, Palomar Ranger District, 1634 Black Canyon Road, Ramona, CA 92065; (619) 788-0250.

*Trail notes:* Bring your picnic basket on this stroll—and someone special to share the hike with. Wildflowers in the spring are superb. The trail descends gently through oak woodland on an easy-to-follow and easy-to-hike dirt track. Once you reach Love Valley, pick your spot either under the spreading oak branches or out in the meadow near a pond. Do watch out for ticks if you linger under the oaks for an extended period. Retrace your steps to your car. Overnight camping is not allowed—you will be cited.

---

# 8. AGUA CALIENTE        8.0 mi/4.5 hrs

*Reference:* **In Cleveland National Forest, Warner Springs; map J6, grid c8.**

*User groups:* Hikers, horses and dogs. No mountain bikes are allowed. No wheelchair facilities.

*Permits:* No day-use permits are required. Camping permits are required. Campfires are not allowed. Contact the Palomar Ranger District at (619) 788-0250.

*Directions:* From Warner Springs, head west on Highway 79 for approximately one mile to mile marker 36.7 and a turnout parking area next to the highway. Hike back to the bridge and mile marker 36.6 for the Pacific Crest Trail trailhead. (This is not an official PCT trailhead and there are no facilities).

***Maps:*** Send $3 to the USDA-Forest Service, 630 Sansome Street, San Francisco, CA 94111 and ask for the Cleveland National Forest map. For topographic maps, ask for Warner Springs and Hot Springs Mountain from the USGS.

***Who to contact:*** Cleveland National Forest, Palomar Ranger District, 1634 Black Canyon Road, Ramona, CA 92065; (619) 788-0250.

***Trail notes:*** When the Pacific Crest Trail was routed through this canyon, it became a favorite stopping point for hikers and for good reason—there's water to be found and a number of picturesque streamside campsites to be enjoyed. From the Agua Caliente Bridge, hike upstream on the PCT, past Warner Ranch (private property and no camping allowed) and into the Cleveland National Forest. From here, the trail follows a hot and streamless trek for several miles before rejoining Aqua Caliente Creek as it heads into a deep canyon with slopes several hundred feet high on either side. Willow and alder line the creek. Plan on spending the night if you have the time and then turn around and retrace your steps back to the highway.

---

# 9. INDIAN FLATS CAMPGROUND 0.5 mi/0.5 hr

***Reference:*** **In Cleveland National Forest, Warner Springs; map J6, grid b8.**

***User groups:*** Hikers only. No horses, dogs and mountain bikes are allowed. No wheelchair facilities.

***Permits:*** No day-use permits are required.

***Directions:*** From Warner Springs, head west on Highway 79 for 1.5 miles to Indian Flats Road and drive north to the Indian Flats Campground. We would recommend spending the night at this first-come, first-served campground, but you had better arrive during the week or early on Friday. Most weekends, late arrivals find only full sites.

***Maps:*** Send $3 to the USDA-Forest Service, 630 Sansome Street, San Francisco, CA 94111 and ask for the Cleveland National Forest map. For a topographic map, ask for Warner Springs from the USGS.

***Who to contact:*** Cleveland National Forest, Palomar Ranger District, 1634 Black Canyon Road, Ramona, CA 92065; (619) 788-0250.

***Trail notes:*** This is a great spot to head with small children or even curious adults out for their first camping adventure. The attraction is the East Fork of the San Luis Rey River—perfect for splashing, wading, crawdad hunting, tadpole chasing, and frog snatching. Be sure to wear protective footwear such as old tennis shoes—bare feet in the water is asking for trouble. The best place to access the river is from the far end of the campground, by hiking down to the river bank. From there, head upstream as far as you desire. Bear in mind that this is not an "official" trail and that the water is seasonal. Youngsters love the stream scramble.

---

# 10. SHEEP CANYON                    4.0 mi/4.0 hrs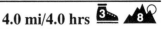

***Reference:*** **In Anza-Borrego Desert; map J6, grid b9.**

***User groups:*** Hikers only. No dogs, horses and mountain bikes are allowed. No wheelchair facilities.

***Permits:*** No permits are required, but they are recommended so the park knows where you are. This area is closed between June 15 and September 15 to protect the watering rights of bighorn sheep.

*Directions:* A four-wheel-drive vehicle is highly recommended for access to the trailhead. From Borrego Springs and Christmas Circle, drive east on Palm Canyon Drive and then north on DiGiorgio Road for approximately five miles to the pavement's end. From here it is another three miles or so to Desert Garden and then on through several wet crossings of Coyote Creek. Non-four-wheel-drive vehicles should park at the water gauging station. (Add eight miles roundtrip to your journey and plan on backpacking overnight at Sheep Canyon Primitive Camp.) If you have a four-wheel-drive vehicle, continue on an increasingly rougher road up and over a pass and then down to the Sheep Canyon Primitive Camp and the trailhead.

*Maps:* For topographic maps, ask for Borrego Palm Canyon and Hot Springs Mountain from the USGS.

*Who to contact:* Anza-Borrego Desert State Park, P.O. Box 299, Borrego Springs, CA 92004; (619) 767-5311 or (619) 767-5312.

*Trail notes:* This hike, along an unofficial "use" trail, will take you into a picturesque bowl suitable for a quiet picnic amid rugged peaks and seasonal springs or a wonderful backpack camp for those inclined to wander further off-trail. From December to March, the water should be flowing well in the streams and springs from winter runoff. Wildflowers are particularly nice in here during March. From the campground, head upstream along the banks of the stream (or dry wash depending on the season) and bear right at the major canyon fork. Keep trekking along the main canyon, at times negotiating carefully around some brushy areas and a few waterfalls, some as high as 30 feet. The trail, such that it is, will disappear completely, but just keep to the canyon and you won't go wrong. Before long, the canyon will widen and you will emerge into the large bowl. Enjoy the scenery and retrace your steps. It is possible to continue exploring up the canyon, but only if you are very experienced at canyoneering and well prepared to spend a night or two out. A caveat—don't jump down into anything that you cannot once again climb out. When Michael worked search and rescue in San Diego many years ago, he heard tales of hikers who had taken the jump thinking they were heading down the canyon, only to find that they had run into a dead end and could not climb out where they had jumped down—stuck till help arrived.

---

# 11. CULP VALLEY WANDERING 1.8 mi/1.0 hr

*Reference:* **In Anza-Borrego Desert; map J6, grid c9.**

*User groups:* Hikers only. No dogs, horses or mountain bikes are allowed. No wheelchair facilities.

*Permits:* No permits are required.

*Directions:* From Borrego Springs, drive west approximately 9.5 miles on Montezuma Highway and turn north onto the entrance road to Culp Valley Primitive Camp—the only camp that remains cool enough to enjoy during the sweltering summer months. Park at the camp.

*Maps:* For topographic maps, ask for Tubb Canyon and Hot Springs Mountain from the USGS.

*Who to contact:* Anza-Borrego Desert State Park, P.O. Box 299, Borrego Springs, CA 92004; (619) 767-5311 or (619) 767-5312.

*Trail notes:* At the far end of the road leading into the primitive campground, begin hiking toward Pena Spring. Note the intersection with the California

Riding and Hiking Trail to the right and drop down a short way past it to the spring—a pleasant little watering hole frequented by animals. Backtrack to the CRHT and head left (east) up to a point where views of Culp Valley come into play. The cactus and wildflower bloom in Culp Valley in the spring is memorable. At a trail branching right, head off and back down to the campground. If you desire, before heading down, walk another several hundred yards further on and clamber up onto the rock outcrops for some truly outstanding views.

## 12. HELLHOLE CANYON    1.6 mi/1.0 hr

*Reference:* **North of Escondido; map J6, grid c3.**

*User groups:* Hikers only. No mountain bikes, horses or dogs are allowed. No wheelchair facilities.

*Permits:* No day-use permits are required. A $1 parking fee is charged.

*Directions:* From Interstate 15 and the city of Escondido, head east on Valley Parkway (S6) which turns into Valley Center Road. Turn right onto Lake Wohlford Road, drive past Lake Wohlford and then turn right onto Paradise Mountain Road. Then turn left onto Kiavo Drive and drive approximately a half mile to the signed park entrance and the parking area for Hellhole Canyon Open Space Preserve.

*Maps:* For a topographic map, ask for Rodriguez Mountain from the USGS.

*Who to contact:* San Diego County Parks, 5201 Ruffin Road, Suite P, San Diego, CA 92123; (619) 694-3049.

*Trail notes:* Acquired a number of years ago from the Bureau of Land Management, this land is now owned by the county, who has been busy building trails where there once were none. We recommend that you explore the trail that heads down the ridgeline and into Hell Creek. The shade provided by live oaks and sycamores coupled with the tumbling creek (in winter and spring—it's more of a trickle in the summer) create an atmosphere that begs to be picnicked in. If you are so inclined, continue exploring downstream to an old canal bed and a picturesque oak forest. Turn around whenever you are ready to head back to the parking area.

## 13. BLUE SKY ECOLOGICAL    3.0 mi/1.0 hr
## RESERVE

*Reference:* **East of Poway; map J6, grid e3.**

*User groups:* Hikers and leashed dogs. No mountain bikes or horses are allowed. No wheelchair facilities.

*Permits:* No day-use permits are required.

*Directions:* From Interstate 15 north of San Diego, exit onto Rancho Bernardo Road and head east for 3.2 miles. Look for the brown Watchable Wildlife viewing signs on the left. The entrance and parking area is just off Espola Road.

*Maps:* For a topographic map, ask for Escondido from the USGS.

*Who to contact:* Blue Sky Ecological Reserve, P.O. Box 724, Poway, CA 92074; (619) 486-7238.

*Trail notes:* If you love wildflowers, then you'll want to visit here between April and June. From the signed entrance, follow a dirt road (called the Green Valley Truck Trail, but don't expect to see any 18-wheelers roaring through) along the creek bank, under a shady canopy of oak and sycamore. Poison oak flourishes in here, so stay on the beaten track. After a mile or so, the road passes through Lake Poway primitive campground and then meanders on a little further to a junction. If you wish to keep hiking, you can continue left and hike 2.5 more miles to Ramona Lake, or go right and head to Lake Poway and the Lake Poway Trail, three miles from the junction. The Lake Poway Trail meets up with the Mt. Woodson Trail for even more hiking possibilities. Docents offer guided tours of the reserve on Saturday and Sunday. Call (619) 486-7238 for more information.

## 14. SAN DIEGUITO RIVER PARK SOUTH TRAIL

6.4 mi/3.0 hrs

*Reference:* **East of Escondido; map J6, grid d2.**

*User groups:* Hikers and leashed dogs. No mountain bikes or horses are allowed. No wheelchair facilities.

*Permits:* No day-use permits are required.

*Directions:* From Interstate 15 and the city of Escondido, head east on Highway 78 to the San Diego Wild Animal Park. Continue past the park and drive for approximately 5.3 miles to a parking area located on the south side of the highway. The first parking area is for the South Trailhead and is approximately 2.2 miles east of Brandy Canyon Road on Highway 78.

*Who to contact:* San Dieguito River Valley Regional Open Space Park, 1500 State Street, Suite 280, MS A-22, San Diego, CA 92101; (619) 235-5445.

*Trail notes:* This park is a model for the protection of our irreplaceable river valleys, having been established through a diligent and combined public and private effort. In all, nearly 60,000 acres of greenway and open space along the San Dieguito River will be preserved. Although only a few trails exist currently, it is important to remember that this truly is a park-in-process and that soon, over 55 miles of trail will exist leading from the ocean to the mountains. Of the two trails, south and north trail, the south trail is the shorter and easiest and for that reason is the best introduction to the area. By hiking it, you will experience the dramatic, steep-sided canyons, lush riparian vegetation, cool, shaded streams and sunny, wildflower-dotted open slopes that make up the Santa Ysabel Creek Canyon area. From the parking area, the trail climbs gently up open slopes to a trail fork at one-half mile. Go right for approximately nine-tenths of a mile, to a 1,550-foot-high knoll where you get rewarded with wonderful views of the San Pasqual Valley. The east branch of the fork drops into a ravine, over a stream, and then climbs steadily, joining a jeep road at 1.4 miles and then meeting up with a side trail at 1.7 miles. Take the opportunity to climb this short spur to enjoy the sweeping views of the valley below. The main trail keeps going, meeting up with another jeep trail at 1.9 miles, where it soon heads north along the west side of the ridge to a summit, elevation 1,635 feet and 2.3 miles from the trailhead. The view from this summit is spectacular, looking down over the San Pasqual Valley, lower Santa Ysabel Creek and Clevenger and Boden canyons. Wildflower displays on the open slopes are stunning in the spring. Watch out for poison oak throughout the park, especially on the spur trails, which are not as well traveled.

## 15. MOUNT WOODSON          8.0 mi/4.0 hrs

*Reference:* **East of Poway; map J6, grid d3.**

*User groups:* Hikers, mountain bikes, horses and dogs. No wheelchair facilities, although **wheelchairs** can manage the paved road without difficulty.

*Permits:* No day-use permits are required. A $4 parking fee is charged. There is a hike-in (eight-tenths of a mile to get there) primitive campsite available by reservation for $10 per night plus a $1.50 processing fee.

*Directions:* From Interstate 15, take the Rancho Bernardo Road exit and head east. Rancho Bernardo Road becomes Espola Road—follow it for about four miles to Lake Poway Road. Turn left into the park.

*Maps:* For a topographic map, ask for San Pasqual from the USGS.

*Who to contact:* Lake Poway Recreation Area, 14644 Lake Poway Road, Poway, CA 92064; (619) 695-1400.

*Trail notes:* Michael used to romp around here a lot when he lived in San Diego—it's a climbing destination for those seeking prime bouldering practice. Certainly, this is no place to come if you desire solitude, because shouts of "on-belay" and "climbing" coupled with the clinking of hardware on rock fill the air most weekends and many weekday evenings. The main reason for most hikers to head up to the top is for the views looking out over the city of Poway and the Pacific Ocean. The most scenic way to the top is from the west side (well away from most of the climbing action), which is where you will begin—at Lake Poway. The trail is very steep, so take your time, and pick a cool time of the day (or year) as it can be a scorcher on this route, with the sun beating down overhead. The trail carves through chaparral and twists its way up to the summit, where you can while away the time, catching your breath and contemplating the return trek, after you have enjoyed the scenery.

## 16. MOUNT GOWER          10.0 mi/2.0 hrs
## OPEN SPACE PRESERVE

*Reference:* **Northeast of El Cajon; map J6, grid e4.**

*User groups:* Hikers, mountain bikes, horses and dogs. No wheelchair facilities.

*Permits:* No day-use permits are required. A $1 parking fee is charged.

*Directions:* From Interstate 8 in El Cajon, take the Highway 67 exit and drive on Highway 67 to Mapleview Street in Lakeside. Turn east onto Mapleview and drive for approximately three-tenths of a mile to Ashwood Street. Turn left (north) onto Ashwood Street, it becomes Wildcat Canyon Road after approximately one mile. Continue driving up Wildcat Canyon Road to San Vicente Road and turn right. Drive on San Vicente Road to Gunn Stage Road and turn left, driving approximately another 1.7 miles to the signed preserve entrance. Drive on the entrance road for a few hundred yards to the designated parking area.

*Maps:* For a topographic map, ask for Ramona from the USGS.

*Who to contact:* San Diego County Parks, 5201 Ruffin Road, Suite P, San Diego, CA 92123; (619) 694-3049.

*Trail notes:* Begin hiking from the trailhead next to the information kiosk and under the shadow of rocky Mt. Gower. Follow a five-mile out-and-back trail heading west and passing by a pleasant little overlook sitting at 2,300 feet, at the top of an open ridge. Views of the surrounding region, even out to the ocean and distant islands, are outstanding. Work on the trail system continues, with the eventual goal being an eight-mile system providing access into the shaded canyon and other overlooks.

## 17. INAJA NATIONAL RECREATION TRAIL

0.5 mi/0.5 hr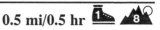

*Reference:* **In Cleveland National Forest, Julian; map J6, grid d7.**

*User groups:* Hikers, horses and dogs. No mountain bikes are allowed. **Wheelchair facilities** are available at the picnic area only.

*Permits:* No day-use permits are required. Campfire permits are required for camping. For more information, contact the Palomar Ranger District at (619) 788-0250.

*Directions:* From Santa Ysabel, located at the Highway 79/Highway 78 intersection, head one mile east on Highway 79/Highway 78 to the Inaja Picnic Area.

*Maps:* Send $3 to the USDA-Forest Service, 630 Sansome Street, San Francisco, CA 94111 and ask for the Cleveland National Forest map. For a topographic map, ask for Santa Ysabel from the USGS.

*Who to contact:* Cleveland National Forest, Palomar Ranger District, 1634 Black Canyon Road, Ramona, CA 92065; (619) 788-0250.

*Trail notes:* Pick up the trail brochure at the trailhead, which will give you a good introduction to the vegetation and ecology of the area. The picnic area was created in memory of the 11 firefighters who lost their lives fighting a massive forest fire here in 1956. From the trailhead, the treadway takes you quickly to a overlook with a nice view down into the San Diego River Canyon. If the weather is cooperating (early winter days are best), the canyon fills with fog, leaving nearby peaks and ridges to peek out from the fluffy layer like islands in a sea of white foam. Over the summer of 1994, work was completed to make the picnic area accessible to wheelchairs—the trail still remains unpaved, however.

## 18. CEDAR CREEK FALLS RIDING AND HIKING TRAIL

5.0 mi/2.5 hrs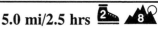

*Reference:* **In Cleveland National Forest, Julian; map J6, grid e7.**

*User groups:* Hikers, horses and dogs. No mountain bikes are allowed. No wheelchair facilities.

*Permits:* No day-use permits are required. Campfire permits are required for camping. For more information, contact the Palomar Ranger District at (619) 788-0250.

*Directions:* Note: Road conditions vary and can become impassable during wet weather. Call the Palomar Ranger District to determine road conditions before heading out. Take Highway 78 east towards Julian. Just before the town of Julian, on the right side of the road, is Pine Hills Road. Turn right onto Pine Hills and continue on Pine Hills until you come to Eagle Peak Road. Turn right onto Eagle Peak Road, which is paved for the first mile, but veers right (watch closely for the road sign) and descends down a dirt road. You will drive on the dirt road for approximately seven miles until you reach

Cedar Creek Falls. It is suggested that you park your vehicle at the eucalyptus grove at Saddleback Junction, since there is an unpassable rock slide one mile further down the road.

**Maps:** Send $3 to the USDA-Forest Service, 630 Sansome Street, San Francisco, CA 94111 and ask for the Cleveland National Forest map. For topographic maps, ask for Santa Ysabel and Tule Springs from the USGS.

**Who to contact:** Cleveland National Forest, Palomar Ranger District, 1634 Black Canyon Road, Ramona, CA 92065; (619) 788-0250.

**Trail notes:** From the trailhead, follow the old roadbed toward the falls. Branch off the main route along another old roadbed over to the Cedar Creek drainage. The route stays along the bank of the creek, heading downstream to a pool at the top of the falls. Footing is extremely slippery here and the Forest Service advises extreme caution. If you work your way along over to a ridge next to the falls, you will have a good view of the nearly 100-foot cascade. (Note that in the late summer it becomes nothing more than an inspired trickle). It is apparent from the informal trails here that numerous people work their way down to the deep pool at the bottom of the falls, no doubt an awesome sight from the bottom up. However, the bottom of the falls is privately owned and you need permission to enter. Also, the traverse down to the bottom is considered dangerous and ill-advised by the Forest Service. In other words, if you choose to venture down, you do so at your own risk and take your life into your own hands—clear enough? When you are ready, retrace your steps.

---

# 19. DESERT VIEW TRAIL     2.5 mi/1.0 hr

**Reference:** In Cleveland National Forest, Julian; map J6, grid e7.

**User groups:** Hikers only. No dogs, mountain bikes or horses are allowed. No wheelchair facilities.

**Permits:** No day-use permits are required. There is a $1 parking fee. Camping is available at 111 sites for $11 per night. Reservations are needed on weekends from Labor Day to Thanksgiving.

**Directions:** From Santa Ysabel, located at the Highway 79 and Highway 78 intersection, head approximately six miles east on Highway 78/79 to Pine Hill Road. Turn right (south) and drive to Frisus Drive. Make a left onto Frisus Drive and head to the William Heise County Park entrance.

**Maps:** Pick up the free William Heise County Park trail map and brochure. Send $3 to the USDA-Forest Service, 630 Sansome Street, San Francisco, CA 94111 and ask for the Cleveland National Forest map. For a topographic map, ask for Julian from the USGS.

**Who to contact:** William Heise County Park, City of San Diego Parks and Recreation Open Space, 1250 Sixth Avenue, San Diego, CA 92101; (619) 685-1350.

**Trail notes:** Find the trailhead three-quarters of a mile past the park entrance, adjacent to campsite #87. Take a hike up to Glen's View, an overlook set on a windy ridge above the vast and rolling terrain of the wooded foothills and mountains of Cuyamaca and Laguna. If you look very carefully, and the air quality is cooperating, you may even see the Salton Sea glimmering in the distance. Perhaps the Pacific Ocean as well—is that a surfer?

## 20. CEDAR TRAIL  1.0 mi/0.5 hour

*Reference:* In Cleveland National Forest, Julian; map J6, grid e7.

*User groups:* Hikers only. No dogs, mountain bikes or horses are allowed. No wheelchair facilities.

*Permits:* No day-use permits are required. There is a $1 parking fee. Camping is available at 111 sites for $11 per night. Reservations are needed on weekends from Labor Day to Thanksgiving.

*Directions:* From Santa Ysabel, located at the Highway 79 and Highway 78 intersection, head approximately six miles east on Highway 78/79 to Pine Hill Road. Turn right (south) and drive to Frisus Drive. Make a left onto Frisus Drive and head to the William Heise County Park entrance.

*Maps:* Pick up the free William Heise County Park trail map and brochure. Send $3 to the USDA-Forest Service, 630 Sansome Street, San Francisco, CA 94111 and ask for the Cleveland National Forest map. For a topographic map, ask for Julian from the USGS.

*Who to contact:* William Heise County Park, City of San Diego Parks and Recreation Open Space, 1250 Sixth Avenue, San Diego, CA 92101; (619) 685-1350.

*Trail notes:* The trailhead for the Cedar Trail begins at the parking area located adjacent to Campsite Area 2. Stay under the shaded canopy of pine and cedar along this pleasant walk—ideal for the entire family. Early in the morning it is not uncommon to see mule deer browsing along the route.

---

## 21. BLACK MOUNTAIN  3.0 mi/1.5 hrs

*Reference:* Rancho Penasquitos north of San Diego; map J6, grid e1.

*User groups:* Hikers, mountain bikes, horses and dogs. No wheelchair facilities.

*Permits:* No day-use permits are required. A $1 parking fee is charged.

*Directions:* From Interstate 15 at Scripps Ranch and Mira Mesa, take the Rancho Penasquitos Boulevard exit and drive west to Black Mountain Road. Turn right onto Black Mountain Road and head north for approximately two miles. The road turns to dirt; drive one more mile to the park entrance.

*Maps:* For a topographic map, ask for Poway from the USGS.

*Who to contact:* Los Penasquitos Canyon Preserve, City of San Diego Parks and Recreation Open Space, 1250 Sixth Avenue, San Diego, CA 92101; (619) 685-1350.

*Trail notes:* OK, we know that there are antennas on the top of this mountain, but it's not the top of the mountain that you are going to be looking at. The attraction of hiking to the peak is the view beyond—rather like climbing to the top of a tall building, except this one is natural. You can see northwest to Dana Point, south to Tijuana and west to Catalina Island. If it is really clear, you can even see snow-capped mountains to the far north. There are a maze of informal trails here and one designated trail—choose the designated one and keep heading uphill on a well-maintained treadway toward the microwave towers and antennas above. Once you have had your fill of the view, head down the way you came.

## 22. LOS PENASQUITOS CANYON PRESERVE

6.5 mi/3.5 hrs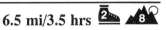

**Reference:** Rancho Penasquitos north of San Diego; map J6, grid e1.

**User groups:** Hikers, mountain bikes, horses and dogs. No wheelchair facilities.

**Permits:** No day-use permits are required. A $1 parking fee is charged.

**Directions:** For the east staging area, exit off Interstate 15 at Mercy Road and drive to Black Mountain Road. Continue through the stoplight and enter the signed trailhead staging area. For the west staging area, take Interstate 5 to Interstate 805 and then exit on Cerrinto Valley Road and drive north to Cerrinto Valley Boulevard. The staging area is located three-quarters of a mile on the right.

**Maps:** For a topographic map, ask for Del Mar from the USGS.

**Who to contact:** Los Penasquitos Canyon Preserve, City of San Diego Parks and Recreation Open Space, 1250 Sixth Avenue, San Diego, CA 92101; (619) 685-1350.

**Trail notes:** Picnic spots abound in the numerous sunny meadows and oak-shaded flats along this creekside pathway. Wildflowers are quite showy along the way in late March and April. Stay on the pathway as poison oak has created a rather dense presence here among the oaks—we really think they must be doing something to encourage its growth. Follow the pathway (actually more of a dirt road) alongside the creek to the canyon's midpoint, where a number of inviting pools, a narrow canyon for scrambling, and a series of waterfalls offer a reason to dally. You could hike on, but the trail heads towards the western entrance and really becomes too hot and dry—nothing like the 3.5 miles you just wandered. Turn around and retrace your steps when ready.

## 23. IRON MOUNTAIN TRAIL

6.4 mi/3.0 hrs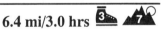

**Reference:** East of Poway; map J6, grid e3.

**User groups:** Hikers, mountain bikes, horses and dogs. No wheelchair facilities.

**Permits:** No day-use permits are required.

**Directions:** From Interstate 15 north of San Diego, take the Poway Road (S4) exit and drive through the city of Poway to Highway 67. Turn right onto Highway 67 and immediately park along the eastern shoulder of the highway—there is limited parking.

**Maps:** For a topographic map, ask for San Vicente Reservoir from the USGS.

**Who to contact:** Lake Poway Recreation Area, P.O. Box 789, Poway, CA 92067; (619) 679-4393.

**Trail notes:** From the trailhead alongside Highway 67, hike up a dirt road, which soon melts down into a trail until the junction with the Iron Mountain Trail, nearly 1.5 miles from the start. Head south and keep hiking on the Iron Mountain Trail for about 1.75 miles to the top of Iron Mountain's 2,696-foot summit. Sign your name on the visitor's register and spend some quiet time gazing out over the ocean beyond—assuming it's not fogged in, of course. You can either retrace your steps (as the listed time and mileage reflect above) or you can head right when the trail forks (left is the way you came) and follow another trail past Ramona Overlook and Table Rock out onto Ellie Lane and an equestrian staging area for the Iron Mountain Trail. If it is just after a rain, you will notice the pungent aroma of sage, a welcome scent to urban-tired olfactory senses. In the spring, you will enjoy the wildflowers. Turn left at the staging area and hike alongside Highway 67 for approximately three-quarters of a mile back to the trailhead and your car. Fall through early spring is the best time to experience this hike.

## 24. SYCAMORE CANYON OPEN SPACE PRESERVE    3.5 mi/1.0 hr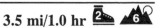

*Reference:* **Southeast of Poway; map J6, grid f3.**

*User groups:* Hikers only. No mountain bikes, horses or dogs are allowed. No wheelchair facilities.

*Permits:* No day-use permits are required.

*Directions:* From Interstate 15 north of San Diego, take the Poway Road (S4) exit and drive through the city of Poway to Garden Road, just before Espola Road. Turn right onto Garden Road and then right again onto Sycamore Canyon Road—this is the back way into the park which we prefer. Park at the end of the road at the staging area.

*Maps:* For a topographic map, ask for San Vicente Reservoir from the USGS.

*Who to contact:* San Diego County Parks, 5201 Ruffin Road, Suite P, San Diego, CA 92123; (619) 694-3049.

*Trail notes:* If you have but an hour to spare and you are looking for a little peace in which to reflect and slow down, head here. From the trailhead, the treadway quickly drops into a ravine and then into Martha Harville Memorial Oak Grove. Benches there provide a nice spot to sit and ponder, but don't wander while you ponder as there is poison oak spread thickly all over the place. Keep on hiking down the trail to a pleasant meadow and an intersection with a dirt road. Turn right, hiking past the model airplane airfield (no, that buzzing you heard was not a giant fly) and right again onto another dirt road, which will take you back to the staging area and your car.

## 25. KELLY DITCH TRAIL    5.7 mi/2.5 hrs

*Reference:* **In Cleveland National Forest, Cuyamaca Rancho State Park; map J6, grid e7.**

*User groups:* Hikers and horses. No dogs or mountain bikes are allowed. No wheelchair facilities.

*Permits:* No day-use permits are required. A $5 day-use fee is collected.

*Directions:* From Interstate 8 east of San Diego, head north on Highway 79 to Rancho Cuyamaca State Park—the highway bisects the park. The park can also be accessed from the north via Highway 79 from Julian. This trail is best hiked one way, from Cuyamaca to William Heise County Park. Leave one car at William Heise County Park. Drive north on Highway 79 to Julian and then drive west on Highway 78/Highway 79 for approximately one mile to Pine Hill Road. Turn left (south) and drive to Frisus Drive. Make a left onto Frisus Drive and head to the park entrance. Begin hiking at the dam for Cuyamaca Reservoir, where Highway 79 crosses the dam near the intersection with Engineer Road, approximately 8.5 miles south of Julian.

*Maps:* Pick up a Cuyamaca Rancho State Park trail map and brochure for 50 cents. Send $3 to the USDA-Forest Service, 630 Sansome Street, San Francisco, CA 94111 and ask for the Cleveland National Forest map. For topographic maps, ask for Julian and Cuyamaca Peak from the USGS. Tom Harrison Cartography also publishes an excellent map of the area. Call (415) 456-7940 and ask for the trail map of Cuyamaca Rancho State Park. The cost is $5.95 plus tax and shipping.

***Who to contact:*** Cuyamaca Rancho State Park, 12551 Highway 79, Descanso, CA 92061; (619) 765-0755.

***Trail notes:*** What a wonderful trail! Scenic, easy, well maintained and fun to hike. We would recommend the fall season when the colors are at their best in this region. Oak leaves are turning gold, the poison oak leaves turn crimson (it's the only time you can actually appreciate the darn plant), and the glades of ferns are sporting a burnished rust color. However pretty the surrounding countryside, we recommend sticking to the trail and not traipsing off—poison oak is everywhere. Midway along the route, you will enter a superb meadow—a great picnic spot. Part of the trail goes alongside or near Cedar Creek and its tributary. From the trailhead all the way to Heise Park, the trail is practically all downhill—what a concept.

---

## 26. MIDDLE PEAK LOOP TRAIL 6.0 mi/3.5 hrs

***Reference:*** In Cleveland National Forest, Cuyamaca Rancho State Park; map J6, grid e8.

***User groups:*** Hikers and horses. No dogs or mountain bikes are allowed. No wheelchair facilities.

***Permits:*** No day-use permits are required. A $5 day-use fee is collected.

***Directions:*** From Interstate 8 east of San Diego, head north on Highway 79 to Rancho Cuyamaca State Park—the highway bisects the park. The park can also be accessed from the north via Highway 79 from Julian. Begin hiking at the parking area located just south of Cuyamaca Reservoir.

***Maps:*** Pick up a Cuyamaca Rancho State Park trail map and brochure for $1. Send $3 to the USDA-Forest Service, 630 Sansome Street, San Francisco, CA 94111 and ask for the Cleveland National Forest map. For a topographic map, ask for Cuyamaca Peak from the USGS. Tom Harrison Cartography also publishes an excellent map of the area. Call (415) 456-7940 and ask for the trail map of Cuyamaca Rancho State Park. The cost is $5.95 plus tax and shipping.

***Who to contact:*** Cuyamaca Rancho State Park, 12551 Highway 79, Descanso, CA 91916; (619) 765-0755.

***Trail notes:*** While this trail is scenic enough to warrant a hike just on its own merit, the side attraction and frankly the main reason most visit this part of the park is to view what are reportedly some of the largest conifers in all of San Diego County with diameters measured over six feet. Begin your hike by crossing Highway 79 and cruising along the Mardy Minshall Trail north. Turn left onto the Sugar Pine Trail at about one mile and then hike up toward Middle Peak. The sugar pines most come to see will be seen along the Sugar Pine Trail—makes sense, doesn't it? When you meet up with the Middle Peak Fire Road, nearly three miles out, head left a short distance and them meet up with the Middle Peak Loop Trail. It doesn't really matter which way you choose to go on the loop because it is, after all, a loop. One way or another, you are going to end up where you began. Once the loop is completed, retrace your steps to the Sugar Pine Trail and then back down to the parking area.

## 27. AZALEA GLEN TRAIL    2.8 mi/1.5 hrs

*Reference:* In Cleveland National Forest, Cuyamaca Rancho State Park; map J6, grid f7.

*User groups:* Hikers only. No dogs, horses or mountain bikes are allowed. No wheelchair facilities.

*Permits:* No day-use permits are required. A $5 day-use fee is charged.

*Directions:* From Interstate 8 east of San Diego, head north on Highway 79 to Rancho Cuyamaca State Park—the highway bisects the park. The park can also be accessed from the north via Highway 79 from Julian. Begin hiking at the parking area located in the Paso Picacho Camp and Picnic Area.

*Maps:* Pick up a Cuyamaca Rancho State Park trail map and brochure for $1. Send $3 to the USDA-Forest Service, 630 Sansome Street, San Francisco, CA 94111 and ask for the Cleveland National Forest map. For a topographic map, ask for Cuyamaca Peak from the USGS. Tom Harrison Cartography also publishes an excellent map of the area. Call (415) 456-7940 and ask for the trail map of Cuyamaca Rancho State Park. The cost is $5.95 plus tax and shipping.

*Who to contact:* Cuyamaca Rancho State Park, 12551 Highway 79, Descanso, CA 91916; (619) 765-0755.

*Trail notes:* You will want to plan on enjoying this hike in either May or June, when the trail's namesake, the azaleas, are in bloom. Other times of the year, you will draw immense pleasure simply from hiking through the dense forest with brief forays into sunny meadows and open areas. A tiny brook along one section adds sensory pleasure. Begin hiking at the Paso Picacho Picnic Area on the signed Azalea Trail. You will soon join the California Riding and Hiking Trail, but you are still officially on the Azalea Trail segment. At Azalea Spring, keep following the Azalea Glen Trail left and now down, generally in the direction of the campground and picnic area.

## 28. PASO SELF-GUIDED NATURE TRAIL    0.5 mi/0.25 hr

*Reference:* In Cleveland National Forest, Cuyamaca Rancho State Park; map J6, grid f7.

*User groups:* Hikers only. No dogs, horses or mountain bikes are allowed. No wheelchair facilities.

*Permits:* No day-use permits are required. A $5 day-use fee is charged.

*Directions:* From Interstate 8 east of San Diego, head north on Highway 79 to Rancho Cuyamaca State Park—the highway bisects the park. The park can also be accessed from the north via Highway 79 from Julian. Begin hiking at the parking area located in the Paso Picacho Camp and Picnic Area.

*Maps:* Pick up a Cuyamaca Rancho State Park trail map and brochure for $1. Send $3 to the USDA-Forest Service, 630 Sansome Street, San Francisco, CA 94111 and ask for the Cleveland National Forest map. For a topographic map, ask for Cuyamaca Peak from the USGS. Tom Harrison Cartography also publishes an excellent map of the area. Call (415) 456-7940 and ask for the trail map of Cuyamaca Rancho State Park. The cost is $5.95 plus tax and shipping.

*Who to contact:* Cuyamaca Rancho State Park, 12551 Highway 79, Descanso,

CA 91916; (619) 765-0755.

*Trail notes:* This is a perfect way to familiarize yourself with the flora of the Cuyamaca Mountains. The trailhead is located at the north end of the picnic grounds and crosses the highway. Also take the time to visit the nearby Interpretive Center, located just across the highway from the Picacho entrance.

---

## 29. CUYAMACA PEAK TRAIL    7.0 mi/3.5 hr

*Reference:* In Cleveland National Forest, Cuyamaca Rancho State Park; map J6, grid f7.

*User groups:* Hikers, mountain bikes and horses. No dogs are allowed. No wheelchair facilities.

*Permits:* No day-use permits are required. A $5 day-use fee is charged.

*Directions:* From Interstate 8 east of San Diego, head north on Highway 79 to Rancho Cuyamaca State Park—the highway bisects the park. The park can also be accessed from the north via Highway 79 from Julian. Park in the parking area located in the Paso Picacho Camp and Picnic Area.

*Maps:* Pick up a Cuyamaca Rancho State Park trail map and brochure for $1. Send $3 to the USDA-Forest Service, 630 Sansome Street, San Francisco, CA 94111 and ask for the Cleveland National Forest map. For topographic maps, ask for Julian and Cuyamaca Peak from the USGS. Tom Harrison Cartography also publishes an excellent map of the area. Call (415) 456-7940 and ask for the trail map of Cuyamaca Rancho State Park. The cost is $5.95 plus tax and shipping.

*Who to contact:* Cuyamaca Rancho State Park, 12551 Highway 79, Descanso, CA 91916; (619) 765-0755.

*Trail notes:* Cuyamaca Peak is San Diego County's second highest peak, but because it sits almost smack dab in the middle of the county and offers 360 degree views (you have to negotiate around a few antennas and the odd tree or two), it is perhaps the best point from which to gaze at the region round about. Begin hiking at the far end of Paso Picacho Campground on the Cuyamaca Peak Fire Road. The route is wide and easy to follow and open to all users with the exception of motorized vehicles. Hike the fire road all the way to the peak and then back down again.

---

## 30. STONEWALL PEAK TRAIL   4.0 mi/2.5 hrs

*Reference:* In Cleveland National Forest, Cuyamaca Rancho State Park; map J6, grid f8.

*User groups:* Hikers only. No dogs, mountain bikes or horses are allowed. No wheelchair facilities.

*Permits:* No day-use permits are required. A $5 day-use fee is charged.

*Directions:* From Interstate 8 east of San Diego, head north on Highway 79 to Rancho Cuyamaca State Park—the highway bisects the park. The park can also be accessed from the north via Highway 79 from Julian. Park in the parking area located in the Paso Picacho Camp and Picnic Area.

*Maps:* Pick up a Cuyamaca Rancho State Park trail map and brochure for $1. Send $3 to the USDA-Forest Service, 630 Sansome Street, San Francisco, CA 94111 and ask for the Cleveland National Forest map. For topographic maps, ask for Julian and Cuyamaca Peak from the USGS. Tom Harrison

Cartography also publishes an excellent map of the area. Call (415) 456-7940 and ask for the trail map of Cuyamaca Rancho State Park. The cost is $5.95 plus tax and shipping.

*Who to contact:* Cuyamaca Rancho State Park, 12551 Highway 79, Descanso, CA 91916; (619) 765-0755.

*Trail notes:* Begin your hike directly across Highway 79 from the entrance to Paso Picacho Camp and Picnic Area. The trail itself is quite pleasant as it wanders through oak woodland much of the way, but it is the view from the peak you are after. From the 5,730-foot summit, you will overlook Cuyamaca Reservoir and broad expanses of forest and meadow spreading out beneath your feet. Climbers often are seen clambering around the short but vertical walls on the west and south side. The last few hundred feet are perhaps the most adventurous, since the trail is nothing more than rough steps cut into the rock, with a handrail provided for stability. Return the way you came.

---

# 31. HARVEY MOORE TRAIL   11.0 mi/6.0 hrs

*Reference:* **In Cleveland National Forest, Cuyamaca Rancho State Park; map J6, grid f8.**

*User groups:* Hikers and horses. No mountain bikes or dogs are allowed. No wheelchair facilities.

*Permits:* No day-use permits are required. An overnight camping permit is required if you wish to camp at Granite Spring. For more information, contact the park ranger at (619) 765-0755. A $5 day-use fee is charged.

*Directions:* From Interstate 8 east of San Diego, head north on Highway 79 to Rancho Cuyamaca State Park—the highway bisects the park. The park can also be accessed from the north via Highway 79 from Julian. Begin hiking at the Sweetwater Bridge parking area, located alongside the road at milepost 4.8 on Highway 79.

*Maps:* Pick up a Cuyamaca Rancho State Park trail map and brochure for $1. Send $3 to the USDA-Forest Service, 630 Sansome Street, San Francisco, CA 94111 and ask for the Cleveland National Forest map. For topographic maps, ask for Julian and Cuyamaca Peak from the USGS. Tom Harrison Cartography also publishes an excellent map of the area. Call (415) 456-7940 and ask for the trail map of Cuyamaca Rancho State Park. The cost is $5.95 plus tax and shipping.

*Who to contact:* Cuyamaca Rancho State Park, 12551 Highway 79, Descanso, CA 91916; (619) 765-0755.

*Trail notes:* This is a great tour of rolling meadows, often frequented by deer; as well as Harper Creek canyon and chaparral, oak and pine woodlands. From the trailhead, follow the Harvey Moore Trail up quickly and then gently along an area of very broad grasslands. Granite Springs Primitive Camp sits about four miles into the hike—perfect for a late weekend or Friday afternoon start. Hike out the next day staying on the Harvey Moore Trail through Harper Creek Canyon. You will enjoy the walk as it is mostly downhill to Harper Creek, winding through the pleasant shade and peace of oak and pine woodlands. After several crossings of Harper Creek, the trail climbs quickly before descending again and meeting up with the East Side Trail and your route back to the trailhead. Head left and hike back about three miles to the Sweetwater Bridge on East Side Trail.

## 32. KWAAYMII POINT  1.0 mi/0.5 hr

*Reference:* In Cleveland National Forest, Laguna Mountains; map J6, grid e8.

*User groups:* Hikers, dogs and horses. No mountain bikes are allowed. No wheelchair facilities.

*Permits:* No day-use permits are required.

*Directions:* From Interstate 8 east of San Diego, head north on County Road S1 (Sunrise Highway). Drive to the Pioneer Mail Picnic Area, milepost 29.3.

*Maps:* Send $3 to the USDA-Forest Service, 630 Sansome Street, San Francisco, CA 94111 and ask for the Cleveland National Forest map. For a topographic map, ask for Monument Peak from the USGS. Tom Harrison Cartography also publishes an excellent map of the area. Call (415) 456-7940 and ask for the recreation map of the San Diego backcountry. The cost is $5.95 plus tax and shipping.

*Who to contact:* Cleveland National Forest, Descanso Ranger District, 3348 Alpine Boulevard, Alpine, CA 91901; (619) 445-6235.

*Trail notes:* Take a brief walk on a short section of the Pacific Crest Trail—a section that had a former life as a road, clinging tenuously to the side of a cliff high above Cottonwood Canyon. Views are spectacular!

## 33. COTTONWOOD CANYON  3.0 mi/6.0 hrs
## BUSHWHACK

*Reference:* In Cleveland National Forest, Laguna Mountains; map J6, grid e9.

*User groups:* Hikers only. No dogs, horses or mountain bikes are allowed. No wheelchair facilities.

*Permits:* No day-use permits are required. A campfire permit is required for camping. For more information, contact the Descanso Ranger District at (619) 445-6235.

*Directions:* From Interstate 8 east of San Diego, head north on County Road S1 (Sunrise Highway). Drive to the Pioneer Mail Picnic Area, approximately 29 miles from Interstate 8.

*Maps:* Send $3 to the USDA-Forest Service, 630 Sansome Street, San Francisco, CA 94111 and ask for the Cleveland National Forest map. For a topographic map, ask for Monument Peak from the USGS. Tom Harrison Cartography also publishes an excellent map of the area. Call (415) 456-7940 and ask for the recreation map of the San Diego backcountry. The cost is $5.95 plus tax and shipping.

*Who to contact:* Cleveland National Forest, Descanso Ranger District, 3348 Alpine Boulevard, Alpine, CA 91901; (619) 445-6235.

*Trail notes:* If you have been gazing down into the Cottonwood Canyon from above—especially from the Kwaaymii Point section described in hike number 32—you will probably feel a tug to explore the depths below. You can, but it's tough going and all off-trail. Begin early in the morning when the sun won't bake you dry. Keep in mind that what you hike down, you must also scramble up. There are a number of rocky sections which require minimal rock climbing skills and where a 30-foot length of 8mm perlon will come in handy to lower your gear. Near the canyon floor, watch out for poison oak and stinging nettle—if you don't know what stinging nettle is, touch one and you soon will. Ouch! Water is nonexistent until the canyon floor. From the Pioneer Mail Picnic Area, begin your descent along a draw heading north and somewhat east. It won't be long until you are scrambling and stumbling in earnest. Watch your footing and take it slow. This is no place for a tenderfoot or beginning hiker. The canyon bottom is extremely pleasant with wonderful smells and cooling breezes.

---

## 34. OASIS SPRING       2.0 mi/1.0 hr

*Reference:* In Cleveland National Forest, Laguna Mountains; map J6, grid f9.

*User groups:* Hikers only. No dogs, horses or mountain bikes are allowed. No wheelchair facilities.

*Permits:* No day-use permits are required. A campfire permit is required for camping. For more information, contact the Descanso Ranger District at (619) 445-6235.

*Directions:* From Interstate 8 east of San Diego, head north on County Road S1 (Sunrise Highway) for approximately 26.5 miles to a turnout on the right (east). The trailhead begins just below the turnout on the Pacific Crest Trail.

*Maps:* Send $3 to the USDA-Forest Service, 630 Sansome Street, San Francisco, CA 94111 and ask for the Cleveland National Forest map. For a topographic map, ask for Monument Peak from the USGS. Tom Harrison Cartography also publishes an excellent map of the area. Call (415) 456-7940 and ask for the recreation map of the San Diego backcountry. The cost is $5.95 plus tax and shipping.

*Who to contact:* Cleveland National Forest, Descanso Ranger District, 3348 Alpine Boulevard, Alpine, CA 91901; (619) 445-6235.

*Trail notes:* This is a trek to a mini Garden of Eden, complete with an out-of-place tree (a maple of all things), a shady canyon, and a stream rushing out of the earth. This is a great spot to curl up with a good book by Edward Abbey or Zane Grey. From the parking area, hike north on the PCT. It will join a dirt road that leads to Oasis Spring. At the road's end, a series of switchbacks on a narrow trail lead down to the spring.

---

## 35. FOSTER POINT       1.5 mi/1.0 hr

*Reference:* In Cleveland National Forest, Laguna Mountains; map J6, grid f9.

*User groups:* Hikers only. No dogs, horses or mountain bikes are allowed. No wheelchair facilities.

*Permits:* No day-use permits are required. A campfire permit is required for camping. For more information, contact the Descanso Ranger District at (619) 445-6235.

*Directions:* From Interstate 8 east of San Diego, head north on County Road S1 (Sunrise Highway) for approximately 25.5 miles to a parking area opposite the Horse Heaven Group Camp.

*Maps:* Send $3 to the USDA-Forest Service, 630 Sansome Street, San Francisco, CA 94111 and ask for the Cleveland National Forest map. For a topographic map, ask for Monument Peak from the USGS. Tom Harrison Cartography also publishes an excellent map of the area. Call (415) 456-7940 and ask for the recreation map of the San Diego backcountry. The cost is $5.95 plus tax and shipping.

*Who to contact:* Cleveland National Forest, Descanso Ranger District, 3348 Alpine Boulevard, Alpine, CA 91901; (619) 445-6235.

*Trail notes:* The Sierra Club built a stone monument at Foster Point, complete with a direction finder that will help you identify 17 major peaks in the southland—peak-baggers unite! From the parking area, follow a rather nebulous treadway to the Pacific Crest Trail and head north. Leave the PCT on a shunt trail to the right, signed "Foster Point." Return the way you came, taking care not to miss the junction off onto the indistinct treadway leading back to the parking area.

---

## 36. SUNSET TRAIL  7.0 mi/4.0 hrs

*Reference:* **In Cleveland National Forest, Laguna Mountains; map J6, grid f9.**

*User groups:* Hikers, dogs, horses and mountain bikes. No wheelchair facilities.

*Permits:* No day-use permits are required. A campfire permit is required for camping. For more information, contact the Descanso Ranger District at (619) 445-6235.

*Directions:* From Interstate 8 east of San Diego, head north on County Road S1 (Sunrise Highway) for approximately 19 miles to the Meadows Information Station and a parking area.

*Maps:* Send $3 to the USDA-Forest Service, 630 Sansome Street, San Francisco, CA 94111 and ask for the Cleveland National Forest map. For topographic maps, ask for Monument Peak and Mount Laguna from the USGS. Tom Harrison Cartography also publishes an excellent map of the area. Call (415) 456-7940 and ask for the recreation map of the San Diego backcountry. The cost is $5.95 plus tax and shipping.

*Who to contact:* Cleveland National Forest, Descanso Ranger District, 3348 Alpine Boulevard, Alpine, CA 91901; (619) 445-6235.

*Trail notes:* This relatively new trail provides access to the entire western rim of the Laguna Mountain plateau and, consequently, offers tremendous views and scenic opportunities. As the name indicates, the trail's exposure faces the sunset, not the sunrise. From the Information Station, walk one-eighth mile north on the Highway to the Sunset Trailhead (mile marker 19.1). Head north for two miles through a meadow area over flat and open terrain rimmed by a pine forest. At the Big Laguna Trail intersection, turn around and retrace your steps, or head south on the Big Laguna Trail and then at Big Laguna Lake continue directly south across the meadow until you intersect the Sunset Trail to the southwest. We prefer to head out on the trail and sit, watch the sunset, and then with head lamps on, hike back on the Sunset Trail after dusk to the parking area and our car.

---

## 37. BIG LAGUNA TRAIL  5.0 mi/3.0 hrs

*Reference:* **In Cleveland National Forest, Laguna Mountains; map J6, grid f9.**

*User groups:* Hikers, horses, dogs and mountain bikes. There are no wheelchair facilities.

*Permits:* No day-use permits are required. A campfire permit is required for camping. Contact the Descanso Ranger District at (619) 445-6235.

*Directions:* From Interstate 8, take the Laguna Mountains/Sunrise Highway (S-1) exit and drive north 13.5 miles to the trailhead, just opposite the Laguna

Campground parking lot near the Amphitheater.

*Maps:* Send $3 to the USDA-Forest Service, 630 Sansome Street, San Francisco, CA 94111 and ask for the Cleveland National Forest map. For topographic maps, ask for Monument Peak, Mount Laguna and Descanso from the USGS. Tom Harrison Cartography also publishes an excellent map of the area. Call (415) 456-7940 and ask for the recreation map of the San Diego backcountry. The cost is $5.95 plus shipping.

*Who to contact:* Cleveland National Forest, Descanso Ranger District, 3348 Alpine Boulevard, Alpine, CA 91901; (619) 445-6235.

*Trail notes:* This is a very scenic trail, best hiked in the early spring because of the proliferation of wildflowers and the likelihood of finding water in Big Laguna Lake—it's typically dry by late spring and early summer, especially during drought years. From the trailhead, hike for one mile through pretty woodlands to a meadow. The trail turns west across this portion of meadow into another wooded section, before bending around another meadow to arrive at Big Laguna Lake. Wildflowers carpet the meadows near the lake in April and early May. If there is water in the lake, you are likely to see numerous ducks and other birds. We enjoy sitting on the rocks above the lake, reading a little Thoreau and basking in a warm afternoon sun—the peace is most relaxing. Head back the way you came, or if you wish to extend your journey, continue north down a ravine to Pine Creek Road and the Noble Canyon Trail—one heck of a great loop back to the campground, but your feet will be tired when you arrive.

---

## 38. KWAAYMII CULTURAL TRAIL  0.5 mi/0.5 hr

*Reference:* In Cleveland National Forest, Laguna Mountains; map J6, grid f9.

*User groups:* Hikers and dogs. No mountain bikes or horses are allowed. No wheelchair facilities.

*Permits:* No day-use permits are required. A campfire permit is required for camping. For more information, contact the Descanso Ranger District at (619) 445-6235.

*Directions:* From Interstate 8 east of San Diego, head north on County Road S1 (Sunrise Highway) for approximately 23.5 miles to the Visitor's Information Office and parking area.

*Maps:* Send $3 to the USDA-Forest Service, 630 Sansome Street, San Francisco, CA 94111 and ask for the Cleveland National Forest map. For a topographic map, ask for Mount Laguna from the USGS. Tom Harrison Cartography also publishes an excellent map of the area. Call (415) 456-7940 and ask for the recreation map of the San Diego backcountry. The cost is $5.95 plus tax and shipping.

*Who to contact:* Cleveland National Forest, Descanso Ranger District, 3348 Alpine Boulevard, Alpine, CA 91901; (619) 445-6235.

*Trail notes:* Kwaaymii Cultural Trail is a short, self-guided interpretive trail wandering through pine and oak, with an accompanying leaflet that describes how the Kwaaymii Native Americans used plants for food, shelter, clothing and medicine. The trail begins near the Visitor Center Information Office and climbs gently to Pinyon Point, a site utilized by Native Americans for grinding pinyon nuts, as evidenced by the mortars found there.

## 39. WOODED HILL NATURE TRAIL

1.5 mi/1.0 hr

*Reference:* In Cleveland National Forest, Laguna Mountains; map J6, grid f9.

*User groups:* Hikers, dogs and horses. No mountain bikes are allowed. No wheelchair facilities.

*Permits:* No day-use permits are required. A campfire permit is required for camping. For more information, contact the Descanso Ranger District at (619) 445-6235.

*Directions:* From Interstate 8 east of San Diego, head north on County Road S1 (Sunrise Highway) for approximately 21.5 miles turn left onto the road leading to Wooded Hill Campground and the Wooded Hill Trailhead.

*Maps:* Send $3 to the USDA-Forest Service, 630 Sansome Street, San Francisco, CA 94111 and ask for the Cleveland National Forest map. For a topographic map, ask for Mount Laguna from the USGS. Tom Harrison Cartography also publishes an excellent map of the area. Call (415) 456-7940 and ask for the recreation map of the San Diego backcountry. The cost is $5.95 plus tax and shipping.

*Who to contact:* Cleveland National Forest, Descanso Ranger District, 3348 Alpine Boulevard, Alpine, CA 91901; (619) 445-6235.

*Trail notes:* A pretty interpretive trail with an accompanying booklet guides the visitor up to Wooded Hill, the highest wooded summit in the Laguna Mountains. Panoramic views are not 360 degree, but the vista offers a look, when the weather cooperates, out past San Diego and over to Catalina Island.

## 40. NOBLE CANYON NATIONAL RECREATION TRAIL

10.0 mi one-way/6.0 hrs

*Reference:* In Cleveland National Forest, Laguna Mountains; map J6, grid g8.

*User groups:* Hikers, dogs, horses and mountain bikes. There are no wheelchair facilities.

*Permits:* No day-use permits are required. A campfire permit is required for camping. For more information, contact the Descanso Ranger District at (619) 445-6235.

*Directions:* This trail is best hiked one-way, requiring a car shuttle. Leave one vehicle at the Laguna Mountain Trailhead and begin your hike from the Pine Creek Trailhead. To reach the Pine Creek Trailhead, take Interstate 8 to the Pine Valley turnoff and turn north, driving one-quarter mile to Old Highway 80. Turn left and drive 1.2 miles to Pine Creek Road. Turn right (just past the bridge) and drive 1.6 miles to the trailhead turnoff—it's signed. Turn right and drive one-quarter mile to the trailhead. Restrooms, tie racks and water for horses is available. To reach the Laguna Mountain Trailhead, take Interstate 8 to the Laguna Mountain / Sunrise Highway turnoff (S-1) and exit, driving north for 14.3 miles to the trailhead located just beyond the cattleguard. The Noble Canyon Trail crosses the Sunrise Highway here and travels to the west, toward the head of Noble Canyon.

*Maps:* Send $3 to the USDA-Forest Service, 630 Sansome Street, San Francisco, CA 94111 and ask for the Cleveland National Forest map. For topographic maps, ask for Mount Laguna, Monument Peak and Descanso from the USGS. Tom Harrison Cartography also publishes an excellent map of the area. Call (415) 456-7940 and ask for the recreation map of the San Diego backcountry. The cost is $5.95 plus tax and shipping.

**Who to contact:** Cleveland National Forest, Descanso Ranger District, 3348 Alpine Boulevard, Alpine, CA 91901; (619) 445-6235.

**Trail notes:** There is no potable water at either trailhead, so come prepared. Water does run year-round along the canyon floor. Springtime blooms along the grassy open area above Noble Canyon are excellent. Campsites are numerous along the entire canyon floor, but be sure to camp at least 200 feet away from a water source. Beginning on Pine Creek Road, the trail travels through chaparral, riparian woodlands and forested areas. The trail's end is near Oasis Spring and the Pacific Crest Trail. Elevations range from 3,740 feet at the Pine Creek Trailhead to 5,420 feet at Oasis Spring. The middle third of the trail is perhaps the most scenic, as it wanders alongside a creek flowing through Noble Canyon. The sound of water coupled with the play of light through the trees and the periodic splashes of color from wildflowers, moss and ferns are very soothing. Along the way, you will pass the ruins of an old mining camp from the gold mining era of the late 1800s—what a wonderful place to live and work!

---

# 41. FORTUNA MOUNTAIN    4.0 mi/2.0 hrs

**Reference:** Mission Trails Regional Park, San Diego; map J6, grid f2.

**User groups:** Hikers, horses and mountain bikes. No dogs are allowed. No wheelchair facilities.

**Permits:** No day-use permits are required. A $1 parking fee is charged.

**Directions:** From Interstate 15 north of San Diego, take the Mission Gorge Road exit, just past Jack Murphy Stadium. Head east on Mission Gorge Road to Father Junipero Serra Trail Road. Turn left onto Father Junipero Serra Trail Road and drive approximately six-tenths of a mile to the Old Mission Dam parking area. Keep in mind that vehicle gates on either end of the Father Junipero Serra Trail Road are locked just after sunset—it's a long walk if you get locked inside.

**Maps:** Pick up a free Mission Trails Regional Park map at the trailhead or at the visitor's center located on Mission Gorge Road near the Father Junipero Serra Trail Road intersection. For a topographic map, ask for La Mesa from the USGS.

**Who to contact:** Mission Trails Regional Park, 5201 Ruffin Road, Suite P, San Diego, CA 92123; (619) 533-4051.

**Trail notes:** Fortuna Mountain is one of four major peaks in the park that show off part of the oldest exposed physical feature in the county—50-million-year-old molten rock formed into a rugged ridge. Fortuna Mountain is actually two summits, North Fortuna (elevation 1,291 feet) and South Fortuna (elevation 1,094 feet). From the parking area, head west, past the old dam and over the San Diego River. Take the time to enjoy the river with its lush riparian habitat of willow, cottonwood and sycamore trees. You'll quickly leave the cool of the river and begin climbing on dusty chaparral hills. Head east a short distance and pick up a path that leads along the floor of Oak Canyon. After about one mile, you will head left (west) along a dirt road leading into the Fortuna Mountain Area. Keep your eyes peeled and, especially in the early morning and late afternoon, you may be rewarded with the sight of deer grazing on grassy slopes. After a very steep climb, bear right at the next intersection and head northwest to the top of North Fortuna Mountain. Retrace your steps.

---

## 42. OAK CANYON          2.7 mi/1.5 hrs

*Reference:* **Mission Trails Regional Park, San Diego; map J6, grid f2.**

*User groups:* Hikers only. No horses, dogs or mountain bikes are allowed. No wheelchair facilities.

*Permits:* No day-use permits are required. A $1 parking fee is charged.

*Directions:* From Interstate 15 north of San Diego, take the Mission Gorge Road exit, just past Jack Murphy Stadium. Head east on Mission Gorge Road to Father Junipero Serra Trail Road. Turn left onto Father Junipero Serra Trail Road and drive approximately six-tenths of a mile to the Old Mission Dam parking area. Keep in mind that vehicle gates on either end of the Father Junipero Serra Trail road are locked just after sunset—it's a long walk if you get locked inside.

*Maps:* Pick up a free Mission Trails Regional Park map at the trailhead or at the visitor's center located on Mission Gorge Road near the Father Junipero Serra Trail Road intersection. For a topographic map, ask for La Mesa from the USGS.

*Who to contact:* Mission Trails Regional Park, 5201 Ruffin Road, Suite P, San Diego, CA 92123; (619) 533-4051.

*Trail notes:* Mission Trails Regional Park at 5,700 acres is one of the largest urban parks in the country. Still, it is possible to get away from most of the humanity that visits here and this trail is one such place. From the parking area, head west, past the old dam and over the San Diego River. Head east a short distance and pick up a path that leads along the floor of Oak Canyon. The next mile or so is a wonderland of rock-hopping. Explore as far as you are willing. Once you reach a small canyon that is seasonally filled with water, creating a narrow pool, the "trail" for all practical purposes ends. Retrace your path to the parking area.

---

## 43. COWLES MOUNTAIN          3.1 mi/1.5 hrs

*Reference:* **Mission Trails Regional Park, San Diego; map J6, grid f2.**

*User groups:* Hikers and horses. No mountain bikes or dogs are allowed. No wheelchair facilities.

*Permits:* No day-use permits are required. A $1 parking fee is charged.

*Directions:* From Interstate 15 north of San Diego, take the Mission Gorge Road exit, just past Jack Murphy Stadium. Head east on Mission Gorge Road, past Father Junipero Serra Trail Road and turn left onto Golfcrest Drive. Cowles Mountain looms on your left as you drive to the staging area at the junction of Navajo Road and Golfcrest Drive.

*Maps:* Pick up a free Mission Trails Regional Park map at the trailhead or at the visitor's center located on Mission Gorge Road near the Father Junipero Serra Trail Road intersection. For a topographic map, ask for La Mesa from the USGS.

*Who to contact:* Mission Trails Regional Park, 5201 Ruffin Road, Suite P, San Diego, CA 92123; (619) 533-4051.

*Trail notes:* This is a trek up to the top of San Diego's highest point. Hike up the trail to a major junction—one branch traverses down and around the mountain slope to the east and the other heads left and up towards the peak. Head left and up via a series of switchbacks to the summit. Views extend in all directions. The number of "informal trails" on the way up lead to more quiet overlooks—inviting to lovers and those seeking more solitude or a quiet picnic-with-a-view. This is one of Michael's favorite places to watch the sunset and enjoy a full moon. We encourage you to do the same, but don't head up without a warm jacket and a head lamp to use on the way down.

## 44. OTAY MOUNTAIN 14.0 mi/8.0 hrs

*Reference:* In Cleveland National Forest, Pine Valley; map J6, grid i3.

*User groups:* Hikers, dogs, horses and mountain bikes. No wheelchair facilities.

*Permits:* No permits are required.

*Directions:* From Interstate 805, south from San Diego, head east on the Otay Freeway which becomes Otay Mesa Road. Stay on Otay Mesa Road to Alta Road and turn left (north). Drive approximately one mile on Alta Road to an unmarked road on the right, just past the entrance to the Donovan State Prison and before some farm buildings. Park off the road.

*Maps:* Send $3 to the USDA-Forest Service, 630 Sansome Street, San Francisco, CA 94111 and ask for the Cleveland National Forest map. For a topographic map, ask for Otay Mountain from the USGS.

*Who to contact:* Bureau of Land Management, Palm Springs-South Central Coast Resource Area, 63500 Garnet Avenue, P.O. Box 2000, North Palm Springs, CA 92258; (619) 251-4800.

*Trail notes:* This hike is not particularly inspiring, except for the walk through a wonderful grove of cypress. The views from the top of Otay Mountain are good, assuming you can overlook the clutter of electronic gear on top. Follow the road up and back to your vehicle. Along the way you will pass remnants of the fortifications erected to repel the predicted Japanese attack in WWII. This area has been designated as a Wilderness Study Area.

## 45. LAWSON PEAK TRAIL 4.5 mi/3.0 hrs

*Reference:* In Cleveland National Forest, Pine Valley; map J6, grid h5.

*User groups:* Hikers only. No dogs, horses or mountain bikes are allowed. No wheelchair facilities.

*Permits:* No day-use permits are required. A campfire permit is required for camping. For more information, contact the Descanso Ranger District at (619) 445-6235.

*Directions:* From Interstate 8 at the Highway 79 exit, head south on Japatul Valley Road and turn left onto Lyons Valley Road. Drive south on Lyons Valley Road to mile marker 13 and park at one of the several small turnouts.

*Maps:* Send $3 to the USDA-Forest Service, 630 Sansome Street, San Francisco, CA 94111 and ask for the Cleveland National Forest map. For a topographic map, ask for Barrett Lake from the USGS. Tom Harrison Cartography also publishes an excellent map of the area. Call (415) 456-7940 and ask for the recreation map of the San Diego backcountry. The cost is $5.95 plus tax and shipping.

*Who to contact:* Cleveland National Forest, Descanso Ranger District, 3348

Alpine Boulevard, Alpine, CA 91901; (619) 445-6235.

*Trail notes:* Begin hiking on the unsigned four-wheel-drive road to an intersection with Wisecarver Road. Look directly ahead and you will see the craggy summit of Lawson Peak. Cross-country your way through the brush toward the peak. At the peak, if you explore around you will find the easiest route up which is via a west-side crack in the rock with near perfect hand and foot holds. Work your way up and into a cave above the crack and then head to the back of the cave—a flashlight is most helpful—to a ledge at an obvious opening. Head up onto the ledge and then up to the peak via an obvious route—the one way that doesn't lead you to a free-fall down. The very top of Lawson Peak has room enough for several people to stand and not much more, although there is plenty more room around the peak just below the top. Take in the windswept views. Sunrises can be very special here, but require climbing experience and a good head lamp.

---

# 46. SECRET CANYON TRAIL    8.0 mi/4.0 hrs

*Reference:* In Cleveland National Forest, Pine Valley; map J6, grid h5.

*User groups:* Hikers, dogs and horses. No mountain bikes are allowed. No wheelchair facilities.

*Permits:* No day-use permits are required. A campfire permit is required for camping. For more information, contact the Descanso Ranger District at (619) 445-6235.

*Directions:* To get to the trailhead, exit Interstate 8 at Pine Valley and drive north on Old Highway 80 to Pine Creek Road. The trailhead parking is located opposite (south) of the intersection with Pine Creek Road, near Pine Creek Stables. If you want to make this a long day and hike approximately 16 miles one-way, you will need to leave a vehicle at the Espinoza Trailhead near Japatul Station. From Interstate 8 and the Highway 79 exit, head south on Lyons Valley Road to the signed trailhead parking.

*Maps:* Send $3 to the USDA-Forest Service, 630 Sansome Street, San Francisco, CA 94111 and ask for the Cleveland National Forest map. For topographic maps, ask for Barrett Lake, Descanso and Viejas Mountain from the USGS. Tom Harrison Cartography also publishes an excellent map of the area. Call (415) 456-7940 and ask for the recreation map of the San Diego backcountry. The cost is $5.95 plus tax and shipping.

*Who to contact:* Cleveland National Forest, Descanso Ranger District, 3348 Alpine Boulevard, Alpine, CA 91901; (619) 445-6235.

*Trail notes:* The Secret Canyon Trail is an amazing trail that follows a rugged route through Pine Valley gorge and alongside Pine Valley Creek before actually encountering its namesake, Secret Canyon, almost 10 miles from the trailhead. What is really amazing is that some of the trail utilizes the engineering efforts of workers who were trying to complete a water flume to shunt water back in the late 1800s. The up and down trail is best hiked in the late fall to early spring. We won't be going all the way to Secret Canyon on this hike, however. Begin trekking up Pine Valley Creek for two miles or so to the Interstate 8 bridge spanning the canyon. The trail climbs out of this scenic gorge to join the flume, which cuts into the slope about 100 yards above the canyon floor. Hike up for as long as you wish, but we would recommend turning around at about four miles before the serious up-and-down hiking begins. If you choose to continue on, the route shunts up and down the slope, reaching Secret Canyon and then joining up with the Espinoza Trail at around 14 miles. Two more miles of strenuous hiking will find you at the Espinoza Trailhead and your awaiting shuttle vehicle—we hope you didn't lock your keys in the car, as one of us did (we're not telling who).

## 47. STELZER COUNTY PARK/ RIPARIAN TRAIL          1.5 mi/1.0 hr

*Reference:* **Northeast of El Cajon; map J6, grid f4.**

*User groups:* Hikers and leashed dogs. No mountain bikes or horses are allowed. **Wheelchair facilities** are available—this park was designed with the physically challenged in mind.

*Permits:* No day-use permits are required. A $1 parking fee is charged.

*Directions:* From Interstate 8 in El Cajon, take the Highway 67 exit and drive on Highway 67 to Mapleview Street in Lakeside. Turn east on Mapleview for approximately three-tenths of a mile and then turn left onto Ashwood Street. Ashwood Street becomes Wildcat Canyon Road after approximately one mile. The well-signed entrance to Stelzer County Park is just off Wildcat Canyon Road on the right.

*Maps:* For a topographic map, ask for San Vicente Reservoir from the USGS.

*Who to contact:* San Diego County Parks, 5201 Ruffin Road, Suite P, San Diego, CA 92123; (619) 694-3049.

*Trail notes:* The primary purpose of this unique park's design was to attract handicapped persons, which it does wonderfully by making sure its trails are wide enough and graded well enough to accommodate **wheelchairs.** The park reports that it is having problems with erosion, which makes it challenging at times for wheelchairs, even though the trails are wide enough to accommodate them. You might want to call ahead for updated information. Two trails are worth a peek. The Riparian Trail does just what it advertises with its name—follow a creek. The trail cuts along the bottom of Wildcat Canyon for about one-half mile to a quiet picnic site with one table. The trail is a one-way-only route and is used as an exercise course for the handicapped, covering 1.4 miles. The Stelzer Ridge Trail, two miles roundtrip, switchbacks up a ridgeline to either the Kumeyaay Promontory or the Stelzer Summit. The park is quite busy weekdays, as school programs set up by the Stelzer Foundation bring school children into the park. Call (619) 694-3049 for information.

# PACIFIC CREST TRAIL          154.0 mi. one way/15.0 days
## GENERAL INFORMATION

***Reference:*** **Trail sections extend from the Campo Border Station Trailhead north to the Highway 74 Trailhead.**

***User groups:*** Hikers, horses and dogs (except in national parks). No mountain bikes are allowed. No wheelchair facilities.

***Permits:*** A wilderness permit is required for traveling through various wilderness and special-use areas that the trail traverses. Contact the national forest, BLM or national park office at your point of entry for a permit that is good for the length of your trip.

***Maps:*** For an overall view of the trail route in this section, send $3 for each map ordered to the USDA-Forest Service, 630 Sansome Street, San Francisco, CA 94111, ask for the Cleveland National Forest and the San Bernardino National Forest maps. Topographic maps for particular sections of the trail are provided under each specific trail section heading listed below.

***Who to contact:*** Contact either the national forest, BLM or national park office at your trailhead—see specific trailheads and corresponding agencies listed within each section.

***Trail notes:*** Trail elevations within this section range from 3,000 feet to over 6,000 feet. Much of this trek passes through mountainous and high desert terrain that is both arid and hot—especially in the summer. It is not unusual to encounter over 100-degree temperatures on the trail in the late spring even—begin your hikes early in the day and season to ensure more comfortable traveling temperatures. Snow may be encountered in the higher elevations at any time during the winter months.

---

# PCT-1          20.0 mi. one way/2.0 days
## CAMPO BORDER PATROL to LAKE MORENA PARK

***Reference:*** **From the Campo Border Patrol in map J6, grid i8 north to the trailhead parking at Lake Morena south of Interstate 8.**

***User groups:*** Hikers, horses and dogs (except in national parks). No mountain bikes are allowed. No wheelchair facilities.

***Permits:*** A wilderness permit is required for traveling through various wilderness and special-use areas that the trail traverses. Contact the Cleveland National Forest at (619) 445-6235 for a permit that is good for the length of your trip.

***Directions:*** To the Campo Trailhead—From Highway 94, east of San Diego and south of Interstate 8, drive south on Forest Gate Road in the town of Campo to the U.S. Border Patrol Station, you are requested to check in here. The trailhead is located approximately 1.5 miles south of the station at the Mexican border. Specific directions will be given at the border patrol station.

To the Lake Morena Trailhead—From San Diego, drive approximately 53 miles east on Interstate 8. Then drive south on County Road S1 (Buckman Springs Road) for five miles to Oak Drive. Turn right and follow the signs to the park. The PCT trailhead is located at the corner of Lake Morena Road and Lakeshore Drive.

***Maps:*** For an overall view of the trail route in this section, send $3 to the USDA-Forest Service, 630 Sansome Street, San Francisco, CA 94111, ask for the

Cleveland National Forest map. For topographic maps, ask for Campo, Potrero and Morena Reservoir from the USGS.

**Who to contact:** Cleveland National Forest, Descanso Ranger District, 3348 Alpine Boulevard, Alpine, CA 91901; (619) 445-6235.

**Trail notes:** This section travels from the Mexican border northward through a series of low ridges, hills and valleys. Periodic shade among cottonwoods and willows near seasonal streams provide some respite from the sun's heat. Views from Mount Hauser are impressive. Just before reaching Lake Morena County Park, the trail passes though a small portion of the Hauser Wilderness. Watch out for poison oak along stream bottoms and valley slopes. Be alert for rattlesnakes.

---

## PCT-2          6.0 mi. one way/1.0 day
## LAKE MORENA PARK to BOULDER OAKS CAMP

**Reference:** From the trailhead parking at Lake Morena south of Interstate 8, map J6, grid h8 north to Boulder Oaks Camp near Interstate 8.

**User groups:** Hikers, horses and dogs (except in national parks). No mountain bikes are allowed. No wheelchair facilities.

**Permits:** A wilderness permit is required for traveling through various wilderness and special-use areas that the trail traverses. Contact the Cleveland National Forest at (619) 445-6235 for a permit that is good for the length of your trip.

**Directions:** To the Lake Morena Trailhead—From San Diego, drive approximately 53 miles east on Interstate 8. Drive south on County Road S1 (Buckman Springs Road) for five miles to Oak Drive. Turn right and follow the signs to the park. The PCT trailhead is located at the corner of Lake Morena Road and Lakeshore Drive.

To the Boulder Campground Trailhead—From San Diego, drive approximately 53 miles east on Interstate 8. Drive south on County Road S1 (Buckman Springs Road) to Boulder Oaks Road and bear left. The Boulder Oaks Campground and the PCT trailhead are located just off Boulder Oaks Road.

**Maps:** For an overall view of the trail route in this section, send $3 to the USDA-Forest Service, 630 Sansome Street, San Francisco, CA 94111, ask for the Cleveland National Forest map. For topographic maps, ask for Morena Reservoir, Cameron Corners and Mount Laguna from the USGS.

**Who to contact:** Cleveland National Forest, Descanso Ranger District, 3348 Alpine Boulevard, Alpine, CA 91901; (619) 445-6235.

**Trail notes:** Still winding through chaparral, this segment travels through oak woodlands and a pretty meadow before arriving at Boulder Campground. There is a store near the campground for basic supplies.

---

## PCT-3          22.0 mi. one way/2.0 days
## BOULDER OAKS CAMP to SUNRISE HIGHWAY TRAIL

**Reference:** From the trailhead parking at Boulder Oaks Campground near Interstate 8, map J6, grid h9 north to the Sunrise Highway Trailhead near Horse Heaven Campground.

**User groups:** Hikers, horses and dogs (except in national parks). No mountain bikes are allowed. No wheelchair facilities.

*Permits:* A wilderness permit is required for traveling through various wilderness and special-use areas that the trail traverses. Contact the Cleveland National Forest at (619) 445-6235 for a permit that is good for the length of your trip.

*Directions:* To the Boulder Campground Trailhead—From San Diego, drive approximately 53 miles east on Interstate 8. Drive south on County Road S1 (Buckman Springs Road) to Boulder Oaks Road and bear left. The Boulder Oaks Campground and the PCT trailhead are located just off Boulder Oaks Road.

To the Sunrise Highway Trailhead—From San Diego, drive approximately 50 miles east on Interstate 8 to the Laguna Junction exit. Drive approximately 11 miles north on the Sunrise Highway to the town of Mt. Laguna. Drive two miles past Mt. Laguna on the Sunrise Highway/Laguna Mountain Road to the campground entrance and PCT trailhead.

*Maps:* For an overall view of the trail route in this section, send $3 to the USDA-Forest Service, 630 Sansome Street, San Francisco, CA 94111, ask for the Cleveland National Forest map. For topographic maps, ask for Monument Peak, Cameron Corners and Mount Laguna from the USGS.

*Who to contact:* Cleveland National Forest, Descanso Ranger District, 3348 Alpine Boulevard, Alpine, CA 91901; (619) 445-6235.

*Trail notes:* After passing under Interstate 8, the trail winds up past Kitchen Creek to a pass with wonderful views. Heading up into the Laguna Mountains you begin to leave the chaparral behind and enter a more predominant pine and oak forest. As you near Laguna Mountain, you will pass along the Desert View Nature Trail for outstanding views of the desert below. The up and down pathway continues to the campground.

---

## PCT-4      32.0 mi. one way/3.0 days
## SUNRISE HIGHWAY TRAIL to HIGHWAY 78 TRAIL

*Reference:* From the trailhead parking near the Sunrise Highway Trailhead and Horse Heaven Campground, map J6, grid g9 to the Highway 78 Trailhead.

*User groups:* Hikers, horses and dogs (except in national parks). No mountain bikes are allowed. No wheelchair facilities.

*Permits:* A wilderness permit is required for traveling through various wilderness and special-use areas that the trail traverses. Contact the Cleveland National Forest at (619) 445-6235 for a permit that is good for the length of your trip.

*Directions:* To the Sunrise Highway Trailhead—From San Diego, drive approximately 50 miles east on Interstate 8 to the Laguna Junction exit. Drive approximately 11 miles north on Sunrise Highway to the town of Mt. Laguna. Then drive two miles past Mt. Laguna on Sunrise Highway/Laguna Mountain Road to the campground entrance and PCT trailhead.

To the Highway 78 Trailhead—From Julian head east on Highway 78 to the Highway 78/County Road S2 (Great Southern Overland Stage Route of 1849) junction. The PCT crosses here near the Butterfield Stage Line commemorative marker.

*Maps:* For an overall view of the trail route in this section, send $3 to the USDA-Forest Service, 630 Sansome Street, San Francisco, CA 94111, ask for the

Cleveland National Forest map. For topographic maps, ask for Monument Peak, Cuyamaca Peak, Julian and Earthquake Valley from the USGS.

***Who to contact:*** Cleveland National Forest, Descanso Ranger District, 3348 Alpine Boulevard, Alpine, CA 91901; (619) 445-6235.

***Trail notes:*** From the campground, the trail traverses around peaks and does its best to maintain elevation into Cuyamaca Rancho State Park. Open air and lots of it leaving you exposed to the sun and elements along the ridge from the park on to Oriflamme Canyon—pack plenty of water as it is a dry walk. From the canyon, you head through a picturesque meadow to Cuyamaca Reservoir. Stock up on water as the next chance for water will not be for many miles. The trail skirts the Anza-Borrego Desert State Park's western boundary up to Highway 78.

---

# PCT-5        33.0 mi. one way/3.0 days
# HIGHWAY 78 TRAILHEAD to WARNER SPRINGS

***Reference:*** From the Highway 78 Trailhead, map J6, grid d9 to the Warner Springs Trailhead.

***User groups:*** Hikers, horses and dogs. No mountain bikes are allowed. No wheelchair facilities.

***Permits:*** A wilderness permit is required for traveling through various wilderness and special-use areas that the trail traverses. Contact the Cleveland National Forest at (619) 445-6235 for a permit that is good for the length of your trip.

***Directions:*** To the Highway 78 Trailhead—From Julian head east on Highway 78 to the Highway 78/County Road S2 (Great Southern Overland Stage Route of 1849) junction. The PCT crosses here near the Butterfield Stage Line commemorative marker.

To the Highway 79 Trailhead—From Warner Springs, head west on Highway 79 for approximately one mile to mile marker 36.7 and a turnout parking area next to the highway. Hike back to the bridge and mile marker 36.6 for the PCT trailhead.

***Maps:*** For an overall view of the trail route in this section, send $3 to the USDA-Forest Service, 630 Sansome Street, San Francisco, CA 94111, ask for the Cleveland National Forest map. For topographic maps, ask for Earthquake Valley, Julian, Ranchita, Hot Springs Mountain and Warner Springs from the USGS.

***Who to contact:*** Cleveland National Forest, Descanso Ranger District, 3348 Alpine Boulevard, Alpine, CA 91901; (619) 445-6235.

***Trail notes:*** It's a long way to Warner Springs—at least it seems that way. This section is a hot and dry walk along exposed ridge lines with little shade for the weary. We are back in the chaparral again. At Barrel Spring you will find a welcome watering hole and camping area under, yes, shade! The last miles of the trek to Warner Springs pass through clusters of oak and cottonwoods for periodic shade relief. Grassy meadow lands for the final mile make for good camping.

# WARNER SPRINGS to HIGHWAY 74

*Reference:* From the Warner Springs Trailhead, map J6, grid c8 to the Highway 74 Trailhead.

*User groups:* Hikers, horses and dogs. No mountain bikes are allowed. No wheelchair facilities.

*Permits:* A wilderness permit is required for traveling through various wilderness and special-use areas that the trail traverses. Contact the Cleveland National Forest at (619) 445-6235 for a permit that is good for the length of your trip.

*Directions:* To the Highway 79 Trailhead—From Warner Springs, head west on Highway 79 for approximately one mile to mile marker 36.7 and a turnout parking area next to the highway. Hike back to the bridge and mile marker 36.6 for the PCT trailhead.

To the Highway 74 Trailhead—From the town of Hemet, head south on Highway 74 to the junction of Highway 74 and Highway 371 (Cahuilla Road). The trailhead for the PCT is approximately one mile southeast on Highway 74 just west of the Santa Rosa Summit.

*Maps:* For an overall view of the trail route in this section, send $3 for each map to the USDA-Forest Service, 630 Sansome Street, San Francisco, CA 94111, ask for the Cleveland National Forest and San Bernardino National Forest maps. For topographic maps, ask for Hot Springs Mountain, Warner Springs, Bucksnort Mountain and Butterfly Peak from the USGS.

*Who to contact:* Cleveland National Forest, Descanso Ranger District, 3348 Alpine Boulevard, Alpine, CA 91901; (619) 445-6235 or San Bernardino National Forest, San Jacinto Ranger District, 54270 Pinecrest, Idyllwild, CA 92549; (714) 659-2117.

*Trail notes:* Wildflowers, streams and pine trees interspersed with scrubland and chaparral are the menu for this section. Watch out for ticks which seem to come out of nowhere to reside on your body—especially when wading through tall grasses. There are a number of very steep climbs and descents as the PCT traverses a checkerboard of public and private lands, doing its best not to trespass on any private holdings. Pack plenty of water and refill at any opportunity—there are some very long and dry sections in here. The views from the slopes of Table and Bucksnort Mountains are super. Ditto the view from the backside of Lookout Mountain as you climb to Highway 74.

*PCT CONTINUATION:* To continue hiking along the Pacific Crest Trail, see Chapter I6, pages 745-748.

# MAP J7

SO-CAL MAP ........................ see page 662
adjoining maps
NORTH (I7) .......................... see page 750
EAST (J8) ............................. see page 810
SOUTH .................................... no map
WEST (J6) ............................. see page 766

16 TRAILS
PAGES 800-809

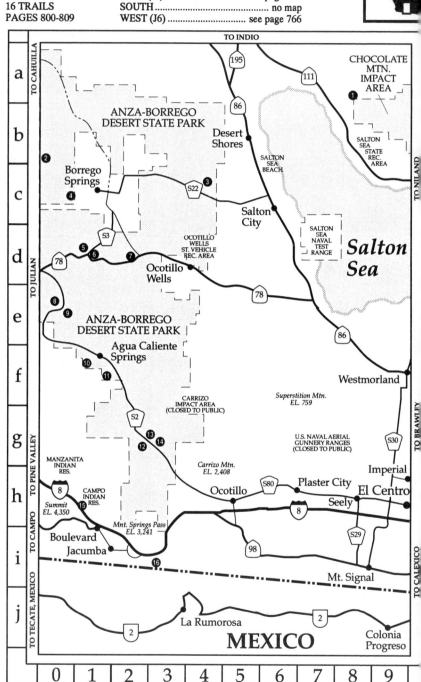

TO INDIO

TO CAHUILLA

CHOCOLATE
MTN.
IMPACT
AREA

❶

a

195

111

86

ANZA-BORREGO
DESERT STATE PARK

Desert
Shores

SALTON
SEA
STATE
REC.
AREA

b

❷

SALTON
SEA
BEACH

TO NILAND

Borrego
Springs

S22

❸

c

❹

Salton
City

SALTON
SEA
NAVAL
TEST
RANGE

Salton
Sea

S3

OCOTILLO
WELLS
ST. VEHICLE
REC. AREA

d

78

❺
❻

❼

Ocotillo
Wells

78

TO JULIAN

❽

86

e

❾

ANZA-BORREGO
DESERT STATE PARK

Agua Caliente
Springs

Westmorland

❿

f

⓫

CARRIZO
IMPACT
AREA
(CLOSED TO PUBLIC)

Superstition Mtn.
EL. 759

TO BRAWLEY

S2

g

⓭

U.S. NAVAL AERIAL
GUNNERY RANGES
(CLOSED TO PUBLIC)

S30

TO PINE VALLEY

⓬ ⓮

Carrizo Mtn.
EL. 2,408

Imperial

MANZANITA
INDIAN
RES.

S80

Plaster City

El Centro

h

8

Ocotillo

Seely

TO CAMPO

Summit
EL. 4,350

⓯

CAMPO
INDIAN
RES.

8

Mnt. Springs Pass
EL. 3,241

S29

Boulevard
Jacumba

98

i

TO TECATE, MEXICO

⓰

Mt. Signal

TO CALEXICO

j

La Rumorosa

2

2

MEXICO

Colonia
Progreso

0 1 2 3 4 5 6 7 8 9

**Map J7 featuring:** Salton Sea, Anza-Borrego Desert State Park, McCain Valley Conservation Area, Ocotillo Wells, Borrego Springs, Agua Caliente Springs

## 1. DAS PALMAS PRESERVE          1.0 mi/1.0 hr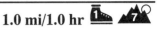

*Reference:* **Just east of the Salton Sea; map J7, grid a8.**

*User groups:* Hikers only. No mountain bikes, horses or dogs are allowed. No wheelchair facilities.

*Permits:* No day-use permits are required.

*Directions:* From the town of Indio, drive south on Highway 111 for approximately 25 miles to Parkside Drive. Turn left onto Parkside Drive and drive one mile and turn right onto Desertaire Drive. The paved road will end but keep driving on the dirt road for three miles to the signed preserve.

*Maps:* For a topographic map of the area, ask for Otocopia Canyon from the USGS.

*Who to contact:* Bureau of Land Management, South Coast Resource Area, 63500 Garnet Avenue, P.O. Box 2000, North Palm Springs, CA 92258; (619) 251-4800.

*Trail notes:* Yet another BLM-Nature Conservancy Preserve—an island of biological diversity protecting the endangered pupfish and Yuma clapper rail. It's hot in the summer, but worth a peek if you are passing through on Interstate 10—it's a mini-oasis.

## 2. COUGAR CANYON          3.0 mi/3.0 hrs

*Reference:* **In Anza-Borrego Desert; map J7, grid b0.**

*User groups:* Hikers only. No dogs, horses or mountain bikes are allowed. No wheelchair facilities.

*Permits:* No permits are required. This area is closed between June 16 and September 15 to protect the watering requirements of bighorn sheep.

*Directions:* A four-wheel-drive vehicle is highly recommended for access to the trailhead. From Borrego Springs and Christmas Circle, drive east on Palm Canyon Drive. Then travel north on DiGiorgio Road for about five miles to the pavement's end. From here it is another three miles or so to Desert Garden. Then there are several wet crossings of Coyote Creek—just before the second crossing is a far as non-four-wheel-drive vehicles should go. If you begin hiking here, add eight miles roundtrip to your journey and plan on backpacking overnight at Sheep Canyon Primitive Camp. If you have a four-wheel-drive vehicle, continue on a rough road up and over a pass and then down to the Sheep Canyon Primitive Camp and the trailhead.

*Maps:* Obtain an Anza-Borrego State Park map for $1 from the park office. For a topographic map of the area, ask for Borrego Palm Canyon from the USGS.

*Who to contact:* Anza-Borrego Desert State Park, P.O. Box 299, Borrego Springs, CA 92004; (619) 767-5311 or (619) 767-5312.

*Trail notes:* From the mouth of Sheep Canyon, head south on a spur trail that crosses and recrosses Cougar Creek. Your route will take you all the way up Cougar Canyon until you cannot go any further without rock climbing expertise and gear. Along the way you will pass a number of rock caves—

probably ceremonial sites of the Cahuilla Indians. Note a huge eye on one of the rocks in the canyon as it narrows. It's actually graffiti—early '70s, we are told. We can only hope the artist was appropriately strung up by the thumbs for defacing the natural character of the area. The path will disappear, but the route becomes obvious—just stay in the canyon, which isn't hard considering the vertical nature of the surrounding canyon walls. Your goal is a deep and secluded pool of water fed by a 15- to 20-foot waterfall. Enjoy the solitude and excellent (though very chilly) swimming hole. Bask in the sun awhile, but don't forget to wear sunscreen. Retrace your steps carefully to the primitive camp and your car. Summer is too darn hot so save your visit for late fall to early spring.

## 3. CALCITE MINE TRAIL    4.0 mi/2.0 hrs

*Reference:* **In Anza-Borrego Desert; map J7, grid c4.**

*User groups:* Hikers only. No dogs, horses or mountain bikes are allowed. No wheelchair facilities.

*Permits:* No permits are required.

*Directions:* From Borrego and the Christmas Circle, take County Road S22 east for approximately 20 miles to Calcite Jeep Road, located just west of a large microwave tower. Park at the roadside turnout just east of Calcite Jeep Road and then hike the short distance back to the trailhead.

*Maps:* Obtain an Anza-Borrego State Park map for $1 from the park office. For a topographic map of the area, ask for Seventeen Palms from the USGS.

*Who to contact:* Anza-Borrego Desert State Park, P.O. Box 299, Borrego Springs, CA 92004; (619) 767-5311 or (619) 767-5312.

*Trail notes:* Weird and wonderful rock formations are the primary draw. Wind and rain have shaped the sandstone here and exposed exquisite calcite crystals. These drew miners interested in extracting the crystals which were used in WWII for the making of bomb sights, among other things. Follow the jeep road to its deadend near the mine. You are still a few hundred yards away—search carefully up the canyon and you will find the mine easily enough. Marvel at the glittering caused by the sun's rays refracting in the calcite fragments. Return by walking down the middle fork of Palm Wash, which can be accessed by retracing your steps about one-half mile to a tributary wash that heads left and steeply down into the main wash. Here, the walls close in on you—in places so narrow it appears as if you can just squeeze through. When you reach the main canyon, follow it for about one-quarter mile to a jeep trail that leads to the Calcite Mine Road. Hike back to the parking area on Calcite Mine Road, retracing your earlier steps. Best time to visit is November through May. Watch out for storm clouds and rain as Palm Canyon Wash is the last place you want to be in a flash flood.

## 4. BORREGO PALM CANYON    3.0 mi/1.5 hrs
## NATURE TRAIL

*Reference:* **In Anza-Borrego Desert; map J7, grid c0.**

*User groups:* Hikers only. No dogs, horses or mountain bikes are allowed. No wheelchair facilities.

*Permits:* No permits are required.

*Directions:* From Borrego and County Road S22, turn north at the intersection of Montezuma Valley Road and Palm Canyon Drive onto the road access for both the visitor center and Borrego Palm Canyon Campground.

*Maps:* Obtain an Anza-Borrego State Park map for $1 from the park office. For a topographic map of the area, ask for Borrego Palm Canyon from the USGS.

*Who to contact:* Anza-Borrego Desert State Park, P.O. Box 299, Borrego Springs, CA 92004; (619) 767-5311 or (619) 767-5312.

*Trail notes:* You will be hiking to one of the largest palm oases in California and the site that served as the foundation for developing the current Anza-Borrego State Park. Pick up an interpretive brochure at the visitor center to use on the hike. On this trail, which begins at the west end of the campground, head up-canyon. You will see many of the plants that exist within the desert region. We guarantee as you trek up an apparently dry trail under the hammering rays of sun that you will be mildly stunned to suddenly come upon a rocky grotto where water cascades over large boulders amid a veritable forest of palm trees. Retrace your steps.

---

## 5. YAQUI WELL NATURE TRAIL

1.5 mi/0.75 hr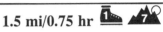

*Reference:* In Anza-Borrego Desert; map J7, grid d1.

*User groups:* Hikers only. No dogs, horses or mountain bikes are allowed. No wheelchair facilities.

*Permits:* No permits are required.

*Directions:* From Borrego Springs, head south on Yaqui Pass Road (County Road S3) to the Tamarisk Grove Campground located near the Yaqui Pass Road/Highway 78 intersection. Park in the campground.

*Maps:* Obtain an Anza-Borrego State Park map for $1 from the park office. For a topographic map of the area, ask for Tubb Canyon from the USGS.

*Who to contact:* Anza-Borrego Desert State Park, P.O. Box 299, Borrego Springs, CA 92004; (619) 767-5311 or (619) 767-5312.

*Trail notes:* This self-guided nature trail begins across the road from the Tamarisk campground. The trail climbs gently before descending an equally gentle grade down to the well. Interpretive signs along the way identify desert wash plants such as cholla and barrel cactus. Yaqui Well is recognized by the Audubon Society as one of the best birding spots in all of San Diego County. You will note that the constant presence of surface moisture keeps the area cooler and more rich in food sources and nutrients than the surrounding desert region—consequently birds and animals flourish here. A fence keeps humans away from the seep, allowing wildlife undisturbed access to water. The trail is best hiked from late October to early May. Wildflowers are usually best in early March.

---

## 6. CACTUS LOOP TRAIL

1.0 mi/0.75 hr

*Reference:* In Anza-Borrego Desert; map J7, grid d1.

*User groups:* Hikers only. No dogs, horses or mountain bikes are allowed. No wheelchair facilities.

*Permits:* No permits are required.

*Directions:* From Borrego Springs, head south on Yaqui Pass Road (County Road S3) to the Tamarisk Grove Campground located near the Yaqui Pass Road/Highway 78 intersection. Park in the campground.

*Maps:* Obtain an Anza-Borrego State Park map for $1 from the park office. For a topographic map of the area, ask for Tubb Canyon from the USGS.

*Who to contact:* Anza-Borrego Desert State Park, P.O. Box 299, Borrego Springs, CA 92004; (619) 767-5311 or (619) 767-5312.

*Trail notes:* From the campground, cross the county road and pick up the Cactus Loop Trail. The trail is fairly easy to hike, following a moderately steep grade over rocky terrain, marked by interpretive signs that identify common desert plants such as barrel cactus and cholla along the way. Most common on this walk is the jumping cholla, so named because even a slight touch can cause a spike to penetrate the skin and a chunk of cholla to leave with the hiker—almost as if the cactus jumped out and grabbed flesh. The wildflowers are usually best in early March.

---

## 7. NARROWS EARTH TRAIL    0.4 mi/0.25 hr

*Reference:* **In Anza-Borrego Desert; map J7, grid d2.**

*User groups:* Hikers only. No dogs, horses or mountain bikes are allowed. No wheelchair facilities.

*Permits:* No permits are required.

*Directions:* From Highway 78, south of Borrego Springs and just east of Yaqui Pass Road (S3) and west of Borrego Springs Road, park off the road at the trailhead for the Narrows Earth Trail.

*Maps:* Obtain an Anza-Borrego State Park map for $1 from the park office. For a topographic map of the area, ask for Borrego Sink from the USGS.

*Who to contact:* Anza-Borrego Desert State Park, P.O. Box 299, Borrego Springs, CA 92004; (619) 767-5311 or (619) 767-5312.

*Trail notes:* Pick up an interpretive brochure at the trailhead which will present the geology lesson being offered by way of the trail. The trail itself loops over some of the oldest kinds of sedimentary rock formations exposed within the Anza-Borrego Desert. Best hiked from late October to early May. Wildflowers are usually best in early March.

---

## 8. ORIFLAMME CANYON    3.0 mi/2.5 hrs

*Reference:* **In Anza-Borrego Desert; map J7, grid e0.**

*User groups:* Hikers and mountain bikes. No dogs or horses are allowed. No wheelchair facilities.

*Permits:* No permits are required.

*Directions:* From Interstate 8 at Ocotillo, east of San Diego, drive north on County Road S2 into Anza-Borrego State Park and to the signed Oriflamme Canyon turnoff on the left—just before Blair Valley. If you have a four-wheel-drive vehicle you can continue driving almost three miles to an old campsite where you will park and hike down to the creek bank and shade. If you don't have a four-wheel-drive vehicle, park just off the road after leaving S2 and then hike in the three miles.

*Maps:* Obtain an Anza-Borrego State Park map for $1 from the park office. For topographic maps of the area, ask for Earthquake Valley and Julian from the USGS.

*Who to contact:* Anza-Borrego Desert State Park, P.O. Box 299, Borrego Springs, CA 92004; (619) 767-5311 or (619) 767-5312.

*Trail notes:* From the old campsite, head up the Oriflamme Canyon on any number of old fire roads that appear to exist—they are all heading the same place, so choose the best one. If you are heading correctly, you will end up on the right bank of the creek, hiking into the narrowing canyon. Before long, the only place you will be able to tread is along the canyon bottom itself, almost right up the creek bed. Your goal is a small waterfall, approximately 1.5 miles from the trailhead, and a pool framed dramatically with sycamore—and of course poison oak. Geeze, can't we ever get away from that stuff? When you have had enough, head back the way you came.

## 9. PICTOGRAPH TRAIL 2.5 mi/1.5 hrs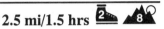

*Reference:* **In Anza-Borrego Desert; map J7, grid e1.**

*User groups:* Hikers only. No dogs, horses or mountain bikes are allowed. No wheelchair facilities.

*Permits:* No permits are required.

*Directions:* From Interstate 8, at Ocotillo, east of San Diego, drive north on County Road S2 into Anza-Borrego State Park and to the signed Blair Valley turnoff on the right. Drive on the dirt road into Blair Valley and turn left onto an unnamed road after 2.7 miles. At 3.6 miles, continue straight ignoring the road that branches right to Little Blair Valley. Drive another 1.5 miles to the road's end and a parking area.

*Maps:* Obtain an Anza-Borrego State Park map for $1 from the park office. For a topographic map of the area, ask for Whale Peak from the USGS.

*Who to contact:* Anza-Borrego Desert State Park, P.O. Box 299, Borrego Springs, CA 92004; (619) 767-5311 or (619) 767-5312.

*Trail notes:* Pick up the trail at the parking area and hike over a pass; then along a sandy wash named Smuggler Canyon. The yellow- and red-colored pictographs can be located on the face of a huge boulder to the right, one mile or so from the parking area. Ponder their meaning as many others before you have—scientists are still at a loss to explain their significance, although a number of theories do exist. Keep on walking about a half-mile to the lip of a dry waterfall—the idea is to stop before falling over the lip. The view is wonderful. Retrace your steps.

## 10. MOONLIGHT CANYON 2.5 mi/1.0 hr

*Reference:* **In Anza-Borrego Desert; map J7, grid f1.**

*User groups:* Hikers only. No dogs, horses or mountain bikes are allowed. No wheelchair facilities.

*Permits:* No permits are required.

*Directions:* From Interstate 8 at Ocotillo, head north on County Road S2 for approximately 27 miles to the signed entrance for Aqua Caliente County Park.

*Maps:* For a topographic map of the area, ask for Agua Caliente Springs from the USGS.

*Who to contact:* Anza-Borrego Desert State Park, P.O. Box 299, Borrego Springs, CA 92004; (619) 767-5311 or (619) 767-5312.

*Trail notes:* From the trailhead at the south end of the campground next to Campsite 63, head up and over a rocky saddle and then down into the trail's namesake, Moonlight Canyon—actually more of a wash than a canyon. There is a pretty willow oasis in the wash. As you are hiking through the saddle, take a quick jaunt up another 250 feet or so to the top of the adjacent peak for a superb view of the nearby Carrizo Valley. Keep hiking the trail around and ending up again in the campground, only this time at Campsite #140. Best time to hike in this area is in the fall to spring.

---

## 11. SQUAW POND TRAIL    1.4 mi/1.0 hr

*Reference:* **In Anza-Borrego Desert; map J7, grid f1.**

*User groups:* Hikers only. No dogs, horses or mountain bikes are allowed. No wheelchair facilities.

*Permits:* No permits are required. A $2 parking fee is charged.

*Directions:* From Interstate 8 at Ocotillo, head north on County Road S2 for approximately 27 miles to the signed entrance for Aqua Caliente County Park.

*Maps:* For a topographic map of the area, ask for Agua Caliente Springs from the USGS.

*Who to contact:* Anza-Borrego Desert State Park, P.O. Box 299, Borrego Springs, CA 92004; (619) 767-5311 or (619) 767-5312.

*Trail notes:* The trailhead for this short hike is located just off the entrance road across the road from a parking area for the trailhead. This is a pretty hike that wanders through thickets of mesquite and a sandy wash before arriving at a green and marshy oasis of sorts—Squaw Pond. There is a single palm tree here and a number of willows. The surrounding slopes are dotted with barrel cactus and cholla. Look closely and you may see tracks of the numerous animals who come here to water throughout the day and night. Head back the way you came when ready.

---

## 12. ROCKHOUSE CANYON    7.0 mi/4.0 hrs

*Reference:* **In Anza-Borrego Desert; map J7, grid g2.**

*User groups:* Hikers only. No dogs, horses or mountain bikes are allowed. No wheelchair facilities.

*Permits:* No permits are required.

*Directions:* From Interstate 8 in Ocotillo, head north on County Road S2 for 16 miles to the signed turnoff for Bow Willow Campground. Drive on the unpaved route for approximately 1.5 miles to the campground and park anywhere but in a usable camping site.

*Maps:* Obtain an Anza-Borrego State Park map for $1 from the park office. For a topographic map of the area, ask for Borrego Palm Canyon from the USGS.

*Who to contact:* Anza-Borrego Desert State Park, P.O. Box 299, Borrego Springs, CA 92004; (619) 767-5311 or (619) 767-5312; or Bureau of Land Management, El Centro Resource Area, 1661 South Fourth Street, El Centro, CA 92243; (619) 353-1060.

*Trail notes:* Although the route is not well marked ( posts and cairns lead the way along a series of poor trails) the attraction of an historic stone cabin is enough to draw crowds during the year. Rumor has it that the cabin is that of gold-miner Nick Swartz who, despite claiming to have removed a small fortune in gold from his mine, died without ever leaving a map—don't they all? Don't expect to find gold, but the trek is rather pleasant and the cabin site interesting. From the campground, head up Bow Willow Canyon on a road signed "closed," and then jaunt cross-country for several hundred yards to a foot trail, which climbs through a desert rock garden of boulders, agave and cholla—don't touch because the needles dislodge amazingly easily into the skin...Yeow! Near Rockhouse Canyon, you will join an old jeep trail which leads west to the abandoned rock house. From the rock house, locate and begin hiking on another trail that drops into Bow Willow Canyon and begin walking down the canyon on the sandy wash to where the canyon widens and then head back to the campground and your car.

---

# 13. ARROYO TAPIADO          8.0 mi/1.0 day

*Reference:* In Anza-Borrego Desert; map J7, grid g3.

*User groups:* Hikers only. No dogs, horses or mountain bikes are allowed. No wheelchair facilities.

*Permits:* No permits are required. No campfires are allowed.

*Directions:* From Interstate 8 at Ocotillo east of San Diego, drive north on County Road S2 past Sweeney Pass to the signed Palm Springs turnoff on the right, located just beyond the Canebrake turnoff and ranger station on the left. Head east and pass the spur road to Palm Springs. A four-wheel-drive vehicle or a high-clearance vehicle is highly recommended for this road. If you have any doubts do not continue driving and drive no further than you are willing to walk out if need be. If you do continue, head down to Vallecito Creek wash and park at the intersection of this road and the road leading left into Arroyo Tapiado, approximately 4.5 miles from County Road S2.

*Maps:* Obtain a Anza-Borrego State Park map for $1 from the park office. For a topographic map, ask for Arroyo Tapiado from the USGS.

*Who to contact:* Anza-Borrego Desert State Park, P.O. Box 299, Borrego Springs, CA 92004; (619) 767-5311 or 5312.

*Trail notes:* Caves, caves and more caves! Bring your sense of adventure, flashlight, hard-hat, plenty of water and an abundant dose of caution. If you wish to camp overnight, the best sites are to be found in the upper reaches of Arroyo Tapiado Canyon. Hiking north in the wash, you will soon reach the beginning of a deep and twisting canyon. Geologists call the rock you are hiking on pseudokarst. The area is full of sinkholes, blind valleys and caves. Subterranean drainage systems pock the region like holes in a block of Swiss cheese. Some of the caves are reported to be over 1,000 feet long, 70 feet high and 30 feet wide. Be warned that this area is potentially unstable and it is possible for the unwary to drop unexpectedly into a sink hole, never to be heard from again. Rumors abound about hikers, illegal aliens and other unfortunate travelers who were last seen heading into the region but never seen heading out. We recommend that you stay on or near the main track and do not wander off into the numerous tributary washes and other valleys. Big Mud Cave is one cave worth peeking into, and it should be relatively safe, although it is not without some danger and the park sign at the entrance indicates that you do enter at your own risk. There are other large and fairly "stable" caves along the canyon and nearby that will pique your curiosity and should be safe to explore, but remember, you explore at your own risk—be smart and be aware at all times. If a small voice hints that this is not safe, listen! When your Indiana Jones alter ego has been satisfied, head back out the way you came.

## 14. CANYON SIN NOMBRE 5.0 mi/3.5 hrs

*Reference:* In Anza-Borrego Desert; map J7, grid g3.

*User groups:* Hikers only. No dogs, horses or mountain bikes are allowed. No wheelchair facilities.

*Permits:* No permits are required.

*Directions:* From Interstate 8 at Ocotillo, east of San Diego, drive north on County Road S2 to a turnout and small parking, just beyond the Carrizo Badlands Overlook. This turnout is just before Sweeney Pass—if you reach it, you have gone too far.

*Maps:* Obtain a Anza-Borrego State Park map for $1 from the park office. For a topographic map, ask for Sweeney Pass from the USGS.

*Who to contact:* Anza-Borrego Desert State Park, P.O. Box 299, Borrego Springs, CA 92004; (619) 767-5311 or (619) 767-5312.

*Trail notes:* The track you will be traveling is a sandy four-wheel-drive route through the canyon to Carrizo Creek, but few vehicles travel this way and even fewer hikers—ahhhh solitude. If you like canyons, this is your ticket. While the main treadway follows the canyon floor, there are numerous tributaries just begging to be explored—just be sure you know how to get out and back from where you came. One tributary in particular is outstanding for its high walls—over 150 feet—and narrow cleft which leaves you squeezing to get through and dumps you out on the canyon rim. If you are an amateur geologist, you will enjoy peering at the sedimentary rock and sandstone that makes up the canyon's walls. Retrace your steps to the canyon floor again. When you are ready, head back the way you came, back to Sweeny Pass and the road.

---

## 15. PEPPERWOOD TRAIL 8.0 mi/4.0 hrs

*Reference:* **McCain Valley Conservation Area, south of Anza-Borrego State Park; map J7, grid h1.**

*User groups:* Hikers, mountain bikes, horses and dogs. No wheelchair facilities.

*Permits:* No day-use permits are required.

*Directions:* From Interstate 8, approximately 70 miles east of San Diego, take the Highway 94 exit and drive south approximately a half mile to Old Highway 80. Turn left (east) and drive two miles to McCain Valley Road (it's a well maintained dirt road) and then drive approximately 12 miles to Cottonwood Campground.

*Maps:* For topographic maps, ask for Sombrero Peak and Agua Caliente Springs from the USGS.

*Who to contact:* Bureau of Land Management, El Centro Resource Area, 1661 South Fourth Street, El Centro, CA 92243; (619) 353-1060.

*Trail notes:* The BLM refers to this site as "an ideal family retreat year-round." That is because it is often uncrowded and tucked into the In-Ko-Pah Mountains, part of the coastal range, forming a rocky garden playground for bighorn sheep and humans alike. Although the BLM promotes year-round access, we feel that the summer months are just too darn hot! The best time to visit, especially if you plan on exploring at all, is October through May. The Pepperwood Trail begins at the Cottonwood Campground and heads north on an old jeep road. Approximately two miles from the campground, you will encounter other routes shunting off right and left along the way. Ignore them and stay on the main tread, which will begin descending quite steeply into Pepperwood Canyon. The spicy aroma of pepperwood trees will begin to waft through the air. If you are lucky, the seasonal waterfall may be flowing. No matter what time of year, the nearby spring (four miles from the trailhead) is always running. The trail peters out after the spring, so retrace your steps back to the campground.

---

## 16. VALLEY OF THE MOON 7.0 mi/4.0 hrs

**Reference:** In Anza-Borrego Desert; map J7, grid i3.

**User groups:** Hikers only. No dogs, horses or mountain bikes are allowed. No wheelchair facilities.

**Permits:** No permits are required.

**Directions:** From Interstate 8 east of San Diego, exit onto In-Ko-Pah Road and drive south approximately two-tenths of a mile along the frontage road (Old Highway 80) and turn left onto an unmarked dirt road. Drive approximately three-quarters of a mile up the road to a large turnout suitable for parking. Unless you are driving a four-wheel-drive vehicle, this is where your hike begins. Four-wheel-drive vehicles can actually head almost all the way to the Valley of the Moon and park near the primitive camping sites along the way.

**Maps:** For the El Centro BLM surface map, contact the El Centro Resource District at the number listed below. Maps cost $3.50. For a topographic map, ask for In-Ko-Pah Gorge from the USGS.

**Who to contact:** Bureau of Land Management, El Centro Resource Area, 1661 South Fourth Street, El Centro, CA 92243; (619) 353-1060.

**Trail notes:** From the parking area, hike up the jeep road, ignoring two intersections with roads branching first left and then right. Descend quickly toward a small mountain peak (the site of a now abandoned amethyst mine) and continue hiking straight, ignoring side trails that lead to campsites among the rocks. Turn left before the main road heads uphill to the mine and skirt the base of the mountain before dropping into the Valley of the Moon. Marvel at the giant granite outcrops laced with numerous cracks and fissures—they almost seem to be begging to be climbed, but don't try it without climbing experience and the correct gear. Late afternoon and sunset are especially beautiful here. Head back the way you came when ready.

# MAP J8

SO-CAL MAP ........................ see page 662
adjoining maps
NORTH ............................................. no map
EAST ................................................. no map
SOUTH .............................................. no map
WEST (J7) ............................... see page 800

1 TRAIL
PAGES 810-811

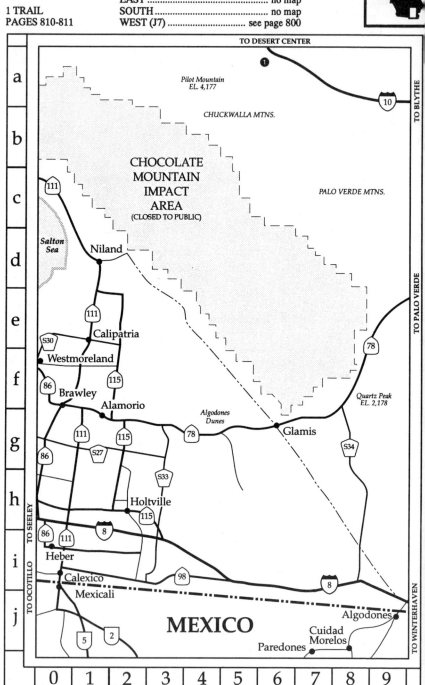

## 1. CORN SPRINGS INTERPRETIVE TRAIL

0.5 mi/0.5 hr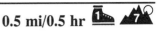

*Reference:* **East of the Salton Sea in the Chuckwalla Mountains; map J8, grid a6.**

*User groups:* Hikers only. No mountain bikes, horses or dogs are allowed. No wheelchair facilities.

*Permits:* A $4 day-use fee is charged.

*Directions:* From Palm Springs, drive east on Interstate 10 to the Desert Center/Highway 177 turnoff. Continue for approximately 12 miles on Interstate 10 to Chuckwalla Road and turn right (south). Drive on Chuckwalla Road to Corn Springs Road and turn right again. Drive approximately eight miles west to Corn Springs Campground, where the trail begins and ends.

*Maps:* For a topographic map of the area, ask for Corn Spring from the USGS.

*Who to contact:* Bureau of Land Management, Palm Springs-South Central Coast Resource Area, P.O. Box 2000, North Palm Springs, CA 92258; (619) 251-0812.

*Trail notes:* Set in a deep canyon among the fabled Chuckwalla Mountains, this site produces a wealth of botanical pleasures from groves of native fan palms to lush clumps of cattail. The water in the canyon attracts an impressive array of wildlife including screech owls, western pipistrelle bats, Gambel's quail and cactus wrens. Tennis shoes will carry you nicely over this quarter-mile, well-maintained, self-guided interpretive trail. Signs along the trail highlight the canyon's ecology, wildlife and Indian art thousands of years old. It's the best winter hike in the area.

# ALL TRAIL LISTINGS ARE IN CAPITAL LETTERS

# INDEX

INDEX

# ALL TRAIL LISTINGS ARE IN CAPITAL LETTERS

# ALL TRAIL LISTINGS ARE IN CAPITAL LETTERS

# BEST HIKES

*Can't decide where to hike this weekend? Here are our picks for the best hikes in California in 25 different categories:*

## WATERFALLS

Bridalveil Falls, Yosemite National Park, E4, pp. 437-439

Chilnualna Falls, Yosemite National Park, E4, p. 444

Middle Falls, Shasta-Trinity National Forest, B2, p. 111

Mist Falls, Kings Canyon National Park, F5, p. 510

Wilderness Falls, Siskiyou Wilderness, A1, p. 33

Waterwheel Falls, Yosemite National Park, E4, p. 426

Feather Falls, Plumas National Forest, C3, p. 180

Rainbow Falls, Devils Postpile National Monument, E5, p. 459

Berry Creek Falls, Big Basin State Park, E1-South Bay, p. 382

Vernal Falls, Yosemite National Park, E4, pp. 441-442, 449

Lower Yosemite Falls, Yosemite National Park, E4, p. 440

Frazier Falls, Bucks Lake Wilderness, C3, p. 186

Brooks Falls (Montara Mountain Trail), San Pedro Valley County Park, E1-SF Pennisula, p. 314

Burney Falls, MacArthur-Burney Falls State Park, B2, p. 122

Pfeiffer Falls, Julia Pfeiffer Burns State Park, F1, p. 472

## LEVEL WALKS/EASY

North & South Valley Floor Trails, Yosemite National Park, E4, pp. 438, 439

Stout Grove Trail, Jedediah Smith Redwood State Park, A0, p. 18

Lower Yosemite Falls, Yosemite National Park, E4, p. 440

Evans Grove Trail, Sequoia National Park, F5, p. 507

South Tufa Trail, Mono Lake Tufa State Reserver, E5, p. 454

Angora Lakes Trail, Lake Tahoe Area, D4, p. 238

7. Bald Mountain Botanical Trail, Dome Lands Wilderness, G5, p. 575

8. Fitzgerald Marine Reserve, Moss Beach, E1-SF Pennisula, p. 316

9. Tallac Historic Site, Lake Tahoe, D4, p. 237

10. Cogswell Marsh Loop, Hayward Regional Shoreline, E1-East Bay, p. 347

## BUTT-KICKERS!!!

1. Whitney Trail, Mt. Whitney, F5, p. 537

2. Muir Pass, John Muir Wilderness, PCT-21, F5, pp. 538-539

3. Half Dome, Yosemite National Park, E4, p. 441

4. Crystal Lake Trail, Sequoia National Park, G5, p. 561

5. Rooster Comb Loop, Henry Coe State Park, E1-South Bay, p. 390

6. Beacroft Trail, Tahoe National Forest, D3, p. 218

7. Peak Trail, White Mountain, E5, p. 463

8. Hartman Bar National Trail, Plumas National Forest, C3, p. 180

9. Devil's Punchbowl, Siskiyou Wilderness, A1, p. 32

10. Vivian Creek Trail, San Gorgonio Mountain, I6, p. 733

## VIEWS/SCENIC OVERLOOK

1. Muir Pass, John Muir Wilderness, PCT-21, F5, pp. 538-539

2. North Dome, Yosemite National Park, E4, p. 428

3. Half Dome, Yosemite National Park, E4, p. 441

4. Moro Rock (Moro Rock Trail), Kings Canyon National Park, F5, p. 522

5. Thousand Island Lake, Ansel Adams Wilderness, B3, p. 458

6. Lassen Summit, Lassen Volcanic National Park, B3, p. 127

7. Rocky Ridge Loop, Garrapata State Park, F1, p. 344

8. Mitchell Peak Trail, Sequoia National Park, F5, p. 516

9. North Ridge/Sunset Trail, Angel Island State Park, E1-Marin, p. 301
10. Mugu Peak, Point Mugu State Park, I4, p. 673

## MEADOWS

1. Panther Meadows, Mount Shasta Wilderness, B2, p. 101
2. Muir Grove Trail, Sequoia National Park, F5, p. 517
3. El Capitan Meadow, Yosemite National Park, E4, p. 438
4. Manter Meadow, Dome Lands Wilderness, G5, pp. 581, 582
5. Vidette Meadow, John Muir Wilderness, PCT-21, F5, pp. 538-539
6. Los Penaquitos Canyon Preserve, J6, p. 779
7. Barker Valley, Cleveland National Forest, G5, p. 769
8. Crescent Meadow, Sequoia National Park, F5, p. 523
9. Tuolumne Meadows, Yosemite National Park, E4, pp. 428-432
10. Bort Meadow, Chabot Regional Park, E1-East Bay, pp. 343, 355

## STREAM WALKS

1. Rush Creek (Silver Lake Trail), Ansel Adams Wilderness, E5, p. 456
2. Pauley Creek Trail, Tahoe National Forest, C3, p. 184
3. Manzana Creek Trail, San Rafael Wilderness, H3, pp. 619, 620
4. McCloud River Trail (Nature Conservancy Section), B2, p. 109
5. Kern River Trail, Sequoia National Forest, G5, p. 575
6. Fern Canyon Trail, Van Damme State Park, CØ, p. 152
7. Woodpecker Meadow, Dome Lands Wilderness, G5, pp. 574, 584
8. Stoney Creek Trail, Smith River National Recreation Area, AØ, p. 17
9. Sunset Rock Trail, Sequoia National Park, F5, p. 521
10. Little Bear Creek Trail, San Bernardino National Forest, I6, p. 723

## SWIMMING HOLES

1. Weaver Lake, Kings Canyon National Park, F5, p. 514
2. Toad Lake, Shasta-Trinity National Forest, B2, p. 104
3. Hospital Rock Swimming Hole Trail, Sequoia National Park, F5, p. 536
4. Big Falls Canyon, San Lucia Wilderness, G2, p. 551
5. Benson Lake, Yosemite National Park, E4, PCT-24, pp. 417, 450

## SELF-GUIDED NATURE WALKS

1. Balancing Rocks Nature Trail, D.L. Bliss State Park, D3, p. 234
2. Methuselah Trail, Inyo National Forest, E5, p. 464
3. Trail of the Gargoyles, Stanislaus National Forest, E4, p. 411
4. McCloud Nature Trail, Shasta-Trinity National Forest, B2, p. 109
5. Forest View Trail, Tahoe National Forest, D3, p. 221

## REDWOODS/SEQUOIA

1. Tall Trees Trail, Redwood National Park, AØ, p. 28
2. Boy Scout Tree Trail, Jedediah Smith State Park, AØ, p. 19
3. Maripsoa Grove Trail, Yosemite National Park, E4, p. 445
4. Redwood Exhibit Trail, Richardson Grove State Park, CØ, p. 146
5. Trail of the Sequoias, Sequoia National Park, F5, p. 524
6. Main Trail, Muir Woods National Monument, E1-Marin, p. 289
7. Redwood Loop, Big Basin State Park, E1-South Bay, p. 381
8. Goat Hill Trail, Butano State Park, E1-South Bay, pp. 372, 373
9. Eagle Creek Trail, Henry Cowell Redwood State Park, E1-South Bay, p. 385
10. Pioneer Tree Trail, Samuel P. Taylor State Park, E1-Marin, p. 273

## DESERT

1. Surprise Canyon, Death Valley, G6, p. 6Ø
2. Afton Canyon Natural Area, H7, p. 6Ø5
3. Mosaic Canyon Trail, G7, p. 605

Sheep Canyon, Anza-Borrego Desert State Park, J6, p. 771

Fossil Falls Trail, G5, p. 590

## WILDFLOWERS

Antelope Loop Trail, Antelope Valley State Reserve, H5, p. 643

Vidette Meadow, John Muir Wilderness, PCT-21, F5, p. 539

Coreopsis Hill, Nipomo Dunes, H4, p. 612

Sheep Canyon, Anza-Borrego Desert State Park, J6, p. 771

Sunol Loop, Sunol Regional Wilderness, E1-East Bay, p. 354

## BEACH/COAST WALKS

Cypress Grove Trail, Point Lobos Preserve, F1, p. 469

Lost Coast Trail, Sinkyone Wilderness State Park, CØ, p. 73

Lost Coast Trail, King Range National Conservation Area, BØ, p. 149

Coast Trail, Point Reyes National Seashore, E1-Marin, p. 268

Beach Trail, Torrey Pines State Reserve, J5, p. 762

Rim Loop, Patrick's Point State Park, BØ, p. 69

Point Dume Trail, Zuma Beach, I4, p. 682

Palos Verdes / Malaga Cove, I4, p. 689

Point Reyes Lighthouse, Point Reyes National Seashore, E1-Marin, pp. 264, 265

. Tidepooling Pelican Point, Crystal Cove State Park, I5, p. 711

*e invited Maria Goodavage, author of*
*"he California Dog Lover's Companion"*
*Foghorn Press, to furnish her secret*
*ots for the following:*

## BEST HIKES WITH DOGS

King Crest Trail, King Range National Conservation Area, BØ, p. 75

Salmon Creek Trail, Dome Lands Wilderness Area, Sequoia National Forest, G5, p. 580

Tahoe/Yosemite Trail, Desolation Wilderness, D4, pp. 232-233

South Kelsey Trail, Smith River National Recreation Area, AØ, p. 23

5. Pine Creek Trail, South Warner Wilderness, Modoc National Forest, B4, pp. 137-138

6. Blue Crag Loop, Inyo National Forest, E5, p. 462

7. Buckhorn to Cooper Canyon, Angeles National Forest, I5, pp. 702-703

8. Fort Funston Sunset Trail, Golden Gate National Recreation Area, E1-San Francisco Bay, p. 310

9. Champion Joshua Tree, San Bernardino National Forest, I6, p. 728

## WITH MOUNTAIN BIKES

1. Spicer Reservoir to Sand Flat, Stanislaus National Forest, E4, pp. 405-406

2. Big Meadow, Dome Lands Wilderness, G5, p. 578

3. American River Parkway, B2, p. 209

4. Zuma Ridge Trail, Santa Monica Mts. National Recreation Area, I4, p. 681

5. Backbone Trail, Santa Monica Mts. National Recreation Area, I4, pp. 683, 686

## WHEELCHAIR

1. Kangaroo Lake, Shasta-Trinity National Forest, B2, p. 95

2. Stelzer County Park, San Diego, J6, p. 794

3. All Access / Braille Trail, Malibu Creek State Park, I4, p. 684

4. Big Morongo Trail, west of Joshua Tree, I7, p. 751

5. Round Meadow Loop Trail, Sequoia National Park, F5, p. 522

6. Taylor Lake, Russian Wilderness, A1, p. 44

7. Abotts Lagoon, Point Reyes National Seashore, E1, p. 261

8. Bear Valley Trail, Point Reyes National Seashore, E1, p. 271

9. Lands End Trail, Golden Gate National Recreation Area, E1-SF Pennisula, p. 306

10. Golden Gate Bridge Trail, Golden Gate National Recreation Area, E1-SF Peninsula, p. 307

## CHILDREN/FAMILY HIKES

1. Año Nuevo Trail, Año Nuevo State Reserve, E1-South Bay, p. 380

2. The Balconies and Bear Gulch Caves Trails, Pinnacles National Monument, F2, pp. 478, 479
3. The Grotto, Santa Monica Mts. National Recreation Area, I4, p. 675
4. Pinecrest Lake, Stanislaus National Forest, E4, p. 413
5. Kelso Dunes, Mojave, H8, p. 658

## SHORT BACKPACK TRIPS WITH CHILDREN
1. Gardisky Lake, Inyo National Forest, E4, p. 421
2. Winnemucca Lake, Eldorado National Forest, D3, p. 246
3. Taylor Lake, Russian Wilderness, A1, p. 44
4. Coast Camp, Coast Trail, Point Reyes National Seashore, E1-Marin, p. 268
5. Ten Lakes Basin, Yosemite National Park, E4, p. 427

## ONE-WAY HIKES WITH SHUTTLE
1. John Muir Trail, F5 to E4, pp. 538, 540
2. Skyline-to-Sea Trail, Big Basin Redwoods State Park, E1-South Bay, p. 376
3. Lost Coast Trail, Sinkyone Wilderness State Park, CØ, p. 149
4. Marble Fork Bridge/Sunset Rock Trail, Sequoia National Park, F5, p. 521
5. Noble Canyon National Recreation Trail, Cleveland National Forest, J6, p. 789

## LOVERS
1. Fern Canyon Loop, Prarie Creek Redwoods State Park, AØ, pp. 26-27
2. Love Valley, Palomar Mountain, J6, p. 770
3. Berry Creek Falls (Skyline-to-Sea Trail), Big Basin National Park, E1-South Bay, p. 382
4. Hearts Desire Beach, Tomales Bay State Park, E1-Marin, p. 263
5. Cowles Mountain, Mission Trails Regional Park, J6, p. 791

## HORSES
1. Rainbow Falls Trail, Devil's Postpile National Monument, E5, p. 459
2. John Muir Trail (horse trail: Happy Isles to Nevada Falls), Yosemite National

Park, E4, pp. 448-449
3. Lover's Camp Trailhead, Marble Mountain Wilderness, A1, pp. 38-40
4. Gold Lake Trailhead, Plumas National Forest, C3, p. 186
5. South Kelsey Trail, Smith River National Recreation Area, AØ, p. 23

## WILDLIFE
*note: seeing wildlife is not guaranteed and is often seasonally influenced.*
1. Tomales Point Trail, Point Reyes National Seashore, E1-Marin, p. 260
2. Año Nuevo State Reserve, E1-South Bay, p. 380
3. Santa Rosa Island, Channel Island, I3, p. 667
4. Prairie Creek Redwood State Park, AØ, p. 26
5. Timber Mountain, Modoc National Forest, A3, pp. 61-62
6. Matterhorn Canyon, Yosemite National Park, E4, PCT-24, pp. 416, 450
7. Spirit Lake Trail, Marble Mountain Wilderness, A1, pp. 42-43
8. Capt. Jacks Stronghold, Lava Beds National Monument, A3, p. 57
9. Summit Lake, Lassen Volcanic National Park, B3, pp. 128-129
10. Darwin Falls, Death Valley, G6, p. 599

## BIRDWATCHING
1. Carrizo Plain, H3, p. 617
2. Big Morongo Trail, west of Joshua Tree, I7, p. 751
3. Bolsa Chica Ecological Reserve, Long Beach, I5, p. 708
4. Tidelands Trail, San Francisco Bay National Wildlife Refuge, E1-East Bay, pp. 352-353
5. Sanctuary Trail, Arcata Marsh and Wildlife Sanctuary, BØ, p. 70
6. Pescadero Marsh, Pescadero State Beach, E1-South Bay, p. 363
7. Harper Lake, Mojave Desert, H6, p. 65
8. 20 Lakes Basin, Hoover Wilderness, E4, p. 419
9. Santa Barbara Island, I3, p. 670
10. Yaqui Well Nature Trail, Anza-Borrego Desert State Park, J7, p. 803

## SUMMITS

Shasta Summit Trail, Mount Shasta, B2, p. 99

Whitney Trail, Mt. Whitney, F5, pp. 537-538

Lassen Peak Trail, Lassen Volcanic National Park, B3, p. 127

Vivian Creek Trail, San Gorgonio Mountain, I6, p. 733

Ubehebe Peak Trail, Death Valley National Park, F6, p. 543

Thompson Peak, Trinity Alps Wilderness, (Hobo Gulch Trail), B1, pp. 86-87

Peak Trail, White Mountain, E5, p. 463

Preston Peak, Siskiyou Wilderness, A1, p. 34

Mt. San Jacinto Trail, Mt. San Jacinto, I6, p. 741

East Peak Trail, Mt. Tamalpais, E1-Marin, p. 285

## FALL COLORS

1. Cold Springs Nature Trail, Sequoia National Park, G5, p. 561
2. Aspen Grove Trail, San Gorgonio Wilderness, I6, p. 732
3. Hooker Trail, Sequoia National Forest, G5, p. 573
4. Spring Lake Trail, Spring Lake Regional Park, D1, p. 204

## ISLAND WALKS

1. Point Bennett Trail, San Miguel Island, I2, p. 665
2. North Ridge/Sunset Trail, Angel Island State Park, E1-Marin, p. 301
3. East Point Trail, Santa Rosa Island, I3, p. 667
4. Agave Trail, Alcatraz, E1-SF Pennisula, p. 308
5. Cottonwood Black Jack Trail, Catalina Island, I4, p. 691

# BACKPACKING PROS AND CONS

## PROS

Body conditioned perfectly.

You won't be bugged by anybody.

You won't be eating any crap.

The views are astounding.

For every up, there's a down.

The wildlife is incredible.

You become an expert with maps.

Meals and diet all figured.

Nothing like the camp life.

Rangers always glad to see you.

Trout for dinner every night.

No dishes to clean.

Pure air at 10,000 feet.

Nothing like sleeping out of doors.

Pack gets lighter as you go.

Visiting nature's temple.

The best of all outdoor gear.

Best tasting water in the world.

Spectacular cumulus clouds.

Wildflowers everywhere.

You become one with nature.

Sense a spiritual force.

## CONS

Is death near?

Damn, I'm homesick.

Pay anything for a cheeseburger.

Climbs have your gut heaving.

Mind-bending pain in your knees.

They all want your food.

Hey, the map is wrong.

God, I'm starving to death.

Mosquitoes will suck you dry.

Only a ranger can write you up.

Need a trout? Guaranteed jinx.

Try scraping the rice pot.

Altitude sickness makes you gag.

I'd pay $500 for my pillow.

Uh-oh, not much food left.

Who said anything about rain?

So much stuff it weighs a ton.

Five miles to the next stream.

Lightning has you trembling.

Step on a beehive and you die.

Coated with weeks of dirt.

There really is a devil.

**USDA-Forest Service,** Office of Information, 630 Sansome Street, San Francisco, CA 94111; (415) 705-2874

**U.S. Geologic Survey,** Western Distribution Branch, P.O. Box 25286, Federal Center, Denver, CO 80225

**U.S. Bureau of Land Management,** California State Office, 2800 Cottage Way, E-2841, Sacramento, CA 95825; (916) 979-2800

**California State Parks,** Office of Information, P.O. Box 942896, Sacramento, CA 94296-0001; (916) 653-6995

### NATIONAL PARKS/ORGANIZATIONS

**Cabrillo National Monument,** P.O. Box 6670, San Diego, CA 92166; (619) 557-5450

**Channel Islands National Park,** 1901 Spinnaker Drive, Ventura, CA 93001; (805) 658-5730

**Death Valley National Park,** Death Valley, CA 92328; (619) 786-2331

**Golden Gate National Recreation Area,** Marin Headlands, Building 1056, Fort Cronkite, Sausalito, CA 94965; (415) 331-1540

**Golden Gate National Recreation Area,** San Francisco Headlands, Building 210, Fort Mason, San Francisco, CA 94123; (415) 556-0560

**Joshua Tree National Park,** 74485 National Monument Drive, Twentynine Palms, CA 92277; (619) 367-7511

**King Range National Conservation Area,** Bureau of Land Management, Arcata Resource Area, 1125 16th Street, Room 219, Arcata, CA 95521; (707) 822-7648

**Kings Canyon National Park,** Grant Grove, CA 93633; (209) 335-2856

**Klamath Basin National Wildlife Refuge,** Route 1, Box 74, Tulelake, CA 96134; (916) 667-2237

**Lassen Volcanic National Park,** P.O. Box 100, Mineral, CA 96063; (916) 595-4444

**Lava Beds National Monument,** P.O. Box 867, Tulelake, CA 96134; (916) 667-2282

**Pinnacles National Monument,** 5000 Highway 146, Paicines, CA 95043; (408) 389-4485

**Point Reyes National Seashore,** Point Reyes, CA 94956; (415) 663-1092

**Redwood Naitonal Park,** 1111 Second Street, Crescent City, CA 95531; (707) 464-6101

**San Francisco Bay National Wildlife Refuge,** P.O. Box 524, Newark, CA 94560; (510) 792-0222

**Santa Monica Mountains National Recreation Area,** 30401 Agoura Road, Suite 100, Agoura Hills, CA 91301; (818) 597-9192

**Sequoia National Park,** Ash Mountain, Three Rivers, CA 93271; (209) 565-3341; Wilderness office, (209) 565-3708

**Smith River National Recreation Area,** P.O. 228, Gasquet, CA 95543; (707) 457-3131

**Whiskeytown Lake National Recreation Are** P.O. Box 188, Whiskeytown, CA 96095; (91 241-6584

**Yosemite National Park,** P.O. Box 577, Yosem National Park, CA 95389; (209) 372-0200 or (209) 372-0265

### REGIONAL/COUNTY PARKS

**Arcata, Environmental Services,** 736 F Stree Arcata, CA 95521; (707) 822-5953

**Blue Sky Ecological Preserve,** P.O. Box 724, Poway, CA 92074; (619) 486-7238

**Carbon Canyon Regional Park,** 4422 Carbon C yon Road, Brea, CA 92621; (714) 996-5252

**Caspers Wilderness Park,** P.O. Box 395, San Juan Capistrano, CA 92675; (714) 831-2174

**Del Norte County Parks,** 840 Ninth Street, Crescent City, CA 95531; (707) 464-7230

**Devil's Punchbowl County Regional Park,** 28000 Devil's Punchbowl Road, Pearblosson CA 93553; (805) 944-2743

**East Bay Regional Parks District,** 2950 Peral Oaks Court, P.O. Box 5381, Oakland, CA 94605-0381; (510) 635-0135, ext. 2200

**Featherly Regional Park,** 24001 Santa Ana C yon Road, Anaheim, CA 92808; (714) 637-0:

**Guajome County Park,** 3000 Guajome Lake Road, Oceanside, CA 92057; (619) 694-304

**Humboldt County Parks,** 1106 Second Street, Eureka, CA 95501; (707) 445-7652

**Irvine Regional Park,** 1 Irvine Park Road, Orange, CA 92669; (714) 633-8072

**Jalama County Park,** (805) 736-3504 (beach) (805) 736-6316 (recorded information)

**Malibu Parks and Recreation Department,** 2577 South Encinal Road, Malibu, CA 9026 (310) 457-7247

**Marin Water District,** 220 Nellen Avenue, Co Madera, CA 94925; (415) 924-4600

**Midpeninsula Regional Open Space District,** 300 Distel Circle, Los Altos, CA 94022; (415 691-1200

**Mountains Restoration Trust,** 24955 Pacific Coast Highway, Suite C-301, Malibu, CA 90265; (310) 456-5625

**Placerita Canyon County Park,** 19152 Placer Canyon Road, Newhall, CA 91321; (805) 259-7721

**Poway, Lake Recreation Area,** 14644 Lake Poway Road, Poway, CA 92064; (619) 695-1400

**San Diego Park and Recreation, Coast Line Parks Division,** 2581 Quivira Court, San Diego, CA 92109; (619) 221-8900

**San Diego Park and Recreation Open Space,** 1250 6th Avenue, San Diego, CA 92101; (619) 685-1350

**San Dieguito River Valley Regional Open Space,** 1500 State Street, Suite 280, San Diego, CA 92101; (619) 235-5440

**San Mateo County Parks and Recreation Department,** County Government Center, 590 Hamilton Street, Redwood City, CA 94063; (415) 363-4020

**Santa Clara County Parks Department,** 298 Garden Hill Drive, Los Gatos, CA 95030; (408) 358-3741

**Santiago Oaks Regional Park,** 2145 North Windes Drive, Orange, CA 92669; (714) 538-4400

**Vasquez Rocks County Park,** 10700 West Escondido Canyon Road, Saugus, CA 91350; (805) 268-0991.

## INFORMATION SERVICES

**Bodega Bay Chamber of Commerce,** P.O. Box 146; Bodega Bay, CA 94923; (707) 875-3422

**California Department of Fish and Game,** 1416 9th Street, Sacramento, CA 95814; (916) 653-6420

**Catalina Camping Reservations,** Doug Bombard Enterprises, P.O. Box 5044, Two Harbors, CA 90704; (310) 510-2800

**Grassland Water District,** 22759 Mercy Springs Road, Los Banos, CA 93635; (209) 826-5188

**Kesterson, San Luis, and Merced National Wildlife Refuges,** National Wildlife Refuge Complex, P.O. Box 2176, Los Banos, CA 93635; (209) 826-3508

**Lake County Visitor Information Center,** 875 Lakeport Boulevard, Lakeport, CA 95453; (800) 525-3743 or (707) 263-9544

**Lassen County Chamber of Commerce,** 36 South Lassen Street, P.O. Box 338, Susanville, CA 96130; (916) 257-4323

**Mammoth Lakes Visitors Bureau,** P.O. Box 48, Mammoth Lakes, CA 93546; (800) 367-6572

**Mendocino Coast Chamber of Commerce,** P.O. Box 1141, Fort Bragg, CA 95437; (707) 961-6300

**Nature Conservancy, The,** 2010 Mission Street, 4th Floor, San Francisco, CA 94105; (415) 777-0487

**Plumas County Chamber of Commerce,** P.O. Box 11018, Quincy, CA 95971; (800) 326-2247 or (916) 283-2045

**Shasta Cascade Wonderland Association,** 14250 Holiday Road, Redding, CA 96003; (800) 326-6944

**Tahoe Rim Trail Organization,** P.O. Box 11551, South Lake Tahoe, CA 96158; (916) 577-0676

**Trinidad Chamber of Commerce,** P.O. Box 356, Trinidad, CA 95570; (707) 677-3448

## MAP COMPANIES

**Earthwalk Press,** 2239 Union Street, Eureka, CA 95501; (800) 828-MAPS

**Map Link,** 25 East Mason Street, Santa Barbara, CA 93101; (805) 965-4402

**Olmsted Brothers,** P.O. Box 5351, Berkeley, CA 94705; (510) 658-6534

**Tom Harrison Cartography,** 333 Bellam Boulevard, San Rafael, CA 94901; (415) 456-7940

**Wilderness Press,** 2440 Bancroft Way, Berkeley, CA 94704; (510) 843-8080

## BOOKS

*Day Hiker's Guide to Southern California* (published by Olympus Press, Santa Barbara)

*Day Hiking Kings Canyon, Day Hiking Sequoia* (published by Manzanita Press)

*Great Outdoor Getaways to the Bay Area and Beyond* by Tom Stienstra, *California Camping: The Complete Guide* by Tom Stienstra, *America's Secret Recreation Areas* by Michael Hodgson (all published by Foghorn Press, San Francisco; 1-800-364-4676)

*Hike Los Angeles Vol. 1 & 2, Hike the Santa Barbara Backcountry* (published by Western Tanager Press)

*The Hiker's Hip Pocket Guide to the Humboldt Coast/Mendocino Coast/Sonoma County* (published by Bored Feet Publications)

*Hiking the Bigfoot Country* (published by Sierra Club Totebook)

*Pacific Crest Trail (California), John Muir Trail, Peninsula Trail, Emigrant Wilderness and Northwestern Yosemite, Yosemite National Park, 50 Best Short Hikes in Yosemite & Sequoia/Kings Canyon, Carson-Iceberg Wilderness, Afoot and Afield in Los Angeles County, Afoot and Afield in Orange County, Afoot and Afield in San Diego County, Trails of the Angeles, Exploring the Southern Sierra: East Side, Desolation Wilderness & the South Lake Tahoe Basin, San Bernardino Mountain Trails, The Anza-Borrego Desert Region* (published by Wilderness Press, Berkeley)

*Tamalpais Trails* (published by Protrero Meadow Publishing Company)

## American Hiking Society...
### promoting hiking and trails in America.

**If you enjoy the wonder** of the natural world on foot,
**If you think trails** are important pathways to America's special places,
**If you want to help** grassroots trail groups build
and save your favorite trails,
**If you believe** hikers need a strong voice in our nation's capital,
**You should join American Hiking Society today!**

Since its founding in 1977, **American Hiking Society** has been the voice for the American hiker. Here is what AHS membership supports:

*American Discovery Trail.* AHS is developing the country's first trans-national trail, from San Francisco to the Atlantic Ocean in Lewes, Delaware. Intersecting with such famed trails as the Appalachian, the Pacific Crest and the Continental Divide, the American Discovery Trail will become a 6,000-mile east-west spine of the national trails system.

*National Trails Day.* Introduced in 1993 by AHS, National Trails Day is America's largest celebration of the outdoors. A day of exciting trail events, it gets businesses, government and trail groups working together for trails.

*America's Voice for Trails.* AHS is the only national group working on many trail issues. That means testifying before Congressional committees, working for funding for trail programs and maintenance, and leading trail coalitions. The result? Federal budgets for trail programs have increased 800 percent since 1984.

*Leading the Volunteer Effort.* The majority of America's 300,000 miles of trail are maintained by volunteers. Each year, AHS sends teams of trail workers into the hills and mountains to build and maintain trails as part of the AHS Volunteer Vacations program.

*Keeping Hikers Informed.* Through *American Hiker* magazine, legislative alerts and special publications, AHS members learn about building trail coalitions, funding new trails, volunteer opportunities and everything needed to enjoy and protect trails.

### Join AHS and receive:

- A full-year subscription to *American Hiker,* the informative, entertaining magazine that brings you the trails, tells you the story about how they got there and introduces you to the people who care about them.

- 20 percent discounts on selected maps (including most Trails Illustrated maps), guide books and outdoor equipment offered through AHS's Hikers Emporium. You can easily save the cost of your membership each year!

- Direct access to more than 100 AHS-affiliated trail clubs, which can provide information and maps to help you plan your next hiking excursion.

- Special legislative alerts on issues facing trails, with details on how you can help.

To join American Hiking Society by phone
or to receive more information, call 703-255-9304.

**American
Hiking
Society**

---

____ **Yes!** I want to help American Hiking Society preserve, protect and improve America's foot trails.

Name _____

Address _____

City, State, Zip _____

### Member Categories

____ $25 Individual          ____ $250 Trailblazer
____ $35 Family              ____ $500 Life
____ $50 Hiker               ____ $15 Student/Senior
____ $100 Pathfinder

Additional Contribution $_____
                Total $_____

____ Charge my visa or mastercard.

No. _____ Exp. date _____

Signature _____

Telephone _____

*Add $15 for outside U.S. Dues and contributions are tax deductible to the extent allowed by law. Please make check payable to American Hiking Society.*

**Please detach and mail to:
American Hiking Society, P.O. Box 20160
Washington, DC 20041-2160**

*We are grateful for the help of many park rangers, recreation officers and fieldscouts wh help make this book as accurate as possible. For their greatly valued input, we thank the following:*

**Tom's Acknowledgments:**

Bill Grummer, Stan Boettcher—California State Parks
Ned MacKay—East Bay Regional Park District
Malcolm Smith—Midpeninsula Open Space District
John Dell-Osso—Point Reyes National Seashore
Ken Lee—Marin State Park District Headquarters
Julie Bondurant—Santa Clara County Parks and Recreation
Ray Richey—Redwood National Park
Matt Mathes—U.S. National Forest headquarters
Charles Simis—Inyo National Forest
Jack Donnell—Klamath National Forest
Dave Reider—Lassen National Forest
Wayne Chandler—Modoc National Forest
Fred Bell—Mendocino National Forest
Tamera Wilton—Plumas National Forest
Bob Ramirez—Shasta-Trinity National Forest
Jim Crossland—Six Rivers National Forest
Larry Raley—Toiyabe National Forest
Fieldscouts Michael Furniss, Jeffrey Patty, James Solomon, Janet Tuttle, Robert Stienstra, Jr., Robert Stienstra, Sr., Eleanor Stienstra, Rosemary O'Neill, Jim & Alma McDaniel, Ed Dunckel, Allan Bruzza, Tom Harrison

**Michael's Acknowledgments:**

Ken Massa, Bob Wetzel, Steve Brougher—Stanislaus National Forest
Rick Murray, John Louth, Leslie Gaunt, Jo Beth—Inyo National Forest
Margaret Wood—Toiyabe National Forest
Fran Coldwell, Audrey Scranton, Jennifer Smith—San Bernardino National Forest
Laura Lolly, Lee Digregorio—Cleveland National Forest
Karen Finlayson—El Dorado National Forest
Paula Martinez, Steven Dean, Leslie Jehnings, Sandy DeBruyn, Bob Stone, Tracie Welton—Los Padres National Forest
Ann Westling, Fran Herbst, Ed Moore—Tahoe National Forest
Dave Harvey, Teresa Fraser, Mike Mendoza—Sequoia National Forest
Jim McGauley, Marilyn Reynold—Angeles National Forest
Martin Schramm—Sierra National Forest
Melanie Casprey—Sequoia and Kings Canyon National Parks
Kris Fister—Yosemite National Park
Bill Lister—Pinnacles National Monument
Glenn Gossard—Death Valley National Park
Bill Faulkner—Channel Islands National Park
Debbie Ohlfs—Joshua Tree National Park
Terry Joyce—Cabrillo National Monument

Meg Pearson—BLM Hollister Resource Area
Jeff Horn—BLM Folsom Resource Area
Pat Foulk—BLM State Office
John Hervey—BLM Caliente Resource Area
Joe Pollini—BLM Bishop Resource Area
Rosemarie Perry, Tim Finger—BLM El Centro Resource Area
Roni Fortun, Dave Wash—BLM California Dese District
Nancy Zepf—BLM Barstow Resource Area
Jim Foot—BLM Needles Resource Area
Mark Conley—BLM Palm Springs South Coast Resource Area
John DeWitt—Guajome County Park
Gina Drury—Caspers Wilderness Park
Neil Underhill—Irvine Regional Park
Ron Nadeau—Featherly Regional Park
Don Monahan—Chino Hills State Park
John Kalko—Crystal Cove State Park
Bob Keimach—Placerita Canyon County Park
Nancy Warner—The Nature Conservancy
Mike Lunsford—Gaviota State Park
Jack Farley—Devils Punchbowl County Regiona Park
Lynda McDowell and Kathie Pedersen—Tahoe Rim Trail Organization
Donna Bertolina—Lake Tahoe Basin Manageme Unit
John Harbison—D.L. Bliss State Park
Elizabeth Featherstone—Sugar Pine Point State Park
John Maggee—Point Lobos State Preserve
JoAnne Allison—Garrapata and Pfeiffer State Parks
Sue Cortese—National Wildlife Refuge Complex
Rene Avant—Montana de Oro State Park
David Welburn—Santa Cruz Island Preserve
Bonnie Clairefield, Jean Bray—Santa Monica Mountains National Recreation Area
Greg Nelson—Topanga State Park
Matt Kouba—Charmlee Natural Area County Par
Rick Campbell—San Jacinto State Park
Joseph Ramos—Lake Perris State Park
Michelle Corbett—San Jacinto Ranger District
Harley Patrick—The Living Desert
Gene Tendler—San Dieguito River Valley Regional Open Space
Ethan Rotman—Blue Sky Ecological Reserve
Bill Lawrence—Los Penasquitos Canyon Preserve
Jack Vargo—William Heise County Park
Chris Bail—Cuyamaca Rancho State Park
Jim Meyer and Chris Smith—Anza Borrego Dese State Park
Larry Beauchamp, Ray Navarette—Lake Poway Recreation Area

# ABOUT THE AUTHORS

*Tom Stienstra (left) and Michael Hodgson (right)*

**Tom Stienstra** is the outdoors writer for the *San Francisco Examiner,* which distributes his columns to 300 newspapers across the country. He was named California Outdoor Writer of the Year in 1990 and 1992, and in 1995 he won Best Outdoor Newspaper Story of the Year, awarded by the Outdoor Writers Association of America. His books *California Camping* and *Great Outdoor Getaways* were honored as Best Outdoor Books in California. His other books with Foghorn Press include *California Fishing, Epic Trips of the West* and *Pacific Northwest Camping,* the latter rated No. 1 on the *Portland Oregonian's* best-seller list.

**Michael Hodgson** is the senior editor for *Adventure West* magazine, contributing editor of *Backpacker Magazine,* a self-syndicated columnist for major western newspapers, and technical editor for *Outdoor Retailer* magazine. He has written eight books, most recently *America's Secret Recreation Areas,* one of the fastest new sellers in the outdoors market. He was named California Outdoor Writer of the Year in 1993, is a multiple first-place award winner with the Outdoor Writers Association of America, and was awarded a Maggie in 1993 for Best Technical Writing for western magazines.

# CHAPTER REFERENCE MAP